W9-BHE-193

To live without a past is worse than to live without a future.

ELIE WIESEL

Die hele lewe leef in ons: om onsself te ken – en om selfs intelligent nederig te wees – moet ons al die gestaltes ken wat in ons
aanwesig is.   N.P. VAN WYK LOUW

Reconsiderations in Southern African History
Richard Elphick and Jeffrey Butler, Editors

THE AFRIKANERS

Biography of a People

HERMANN GILIOMEE

UNIVERSITY OF VIRGINIA PRESS
CHARLOTTESVILLE

Published jointly by
University of Virginia Press
P.O. Box 400318
Charlottesville, VA 22904-4318
USA
Tafelberg Publishers Limited
Heerengracht 40, Cape Town 8001
South Africa
© 2003 Hermann Giliomee

All rights reserved. No part of this book may be reproduced or
transmitted in any form or by any means, electronic or mechanical, including
photocopying, recording or any information storage and retrieval system,
without permission in writing from the publisher.

Jacket design by Willem Jordaan,
based on the painting 'Karoo Landscape' by Stanley Pinker © Stanley Pinker
Book design by Nazli Jacobs
Set in Berkeley

Printed on acid-free paper and bound by Paarl Print, Oosterland Street, Paarl, South Africa
First edition, second impression 2004

ISBN 0-8139-2237-2

Cataloging-in Publication Data is available from the Library of Congress

To Annette

Acknowledgements

A book that covers 350 years and takes ten years to complete is bound to incur huge debts. The first is institutional. I started work on the manuscript as a research fellow in 1992-93 of the Woodrow Wilson Center for International Scholars in Washington, which provided a highly stimulating environment. I was able to complete a chapter as a scholar in residence in the idyllic circumstances of the Rockefeller Foundation's center in Bellagio, Italy. Congenial working conditions were provided by the University of Cape Town, which employed me during the first half of the time that I worked on the manuscript. The University of Stellenbosch, where I subsequently was appointed, gave me much assistance in the final years of working on the manuscript. I have a special debt to Albert Grundlingh in this regard.

Outside the university and foundation environment I received invaluable support from the publishing house Naspers, which enabled me to work full time on the book in the final stage without interfering in any way with my interpretation of a history in which the firm also played a significant role. Het Jan Marais Nationale Fonds, under the chairmanship of the late Mike de Vries, allocated the book and its projected Afrikaans version a generous subsidy to help cover publishing costs.

At the institutions some people deserve a special word of thanks. Ton Vosloo, managing director and later chairman of the board of Naspers, has been a *steunpilaar*, unwavering in his support. The staff of the two universities was unfailingly helpful. I wish to single out the librarians Hannie van den Heever at UCT and Hanna Botha at US and Janet Sandell, secretary of the Politics department at UCT. I was blessed in having two excellent publishers, Hannes van Zyl at Tafelberg Publishers and Richard Holway, at the University Press of Virginia, who tolerated missed deadlines and a long manuscript.

It was a pleasure to have Willem Jordaan design the cover, using the painting 'Karoo Landscape' by Stanley Pinker. I wish to thank the painter and the owners, Sue and the late Basil Robinson, for permission to use it.

A special word of thanks is due to two editors who have helped to turn the manuscript in something much more readable than the original. In the USA there was the incomparable Jeannette Hopkins, with an uncanny ability to banish clutter and improve logical flow. In Cape Town, Jill Martin worked on the manuscript with meticulous care and enormous patience. Erika Oosthuysen and Linette Viljoen, editors at Tafelberg, have been cheerfully efficient.

The comments, criticisms and encouragement of friends and colleagues have played a decisive role in improving the manuscript. My greatest gratitude goes to Richard Elphick, who has believed in the book from the start and has offered crucially important advice and assistance at every stage. Like him, Jeff Butler, Fanie Cilliers, J.M. Coetzee, and Karel Schoeman read the entire manuscript and offered detailed criticism and comments.

The comments of the following people who read one or more chapters also helped to improve the manuscript: Heribert Adam, Neville Alexander, Karen Press, Lawrence Schlemmer, Johannes Grosskopf, Ton Vosloo, Ebbe Dommisse, John Kannemeyer, Rodney Davenport, Christopher Saunders, Albert Grundlingh, Jannie Gagiano, Saul Dubow, Sandra Swart, Mordechai Tamarkin, R.W. Johnson, Stanley Uys, Jonny Steinberg, Pallo Jordan, James Myburgh, Jaap Steyn, Z.B. du Toit, André du Toit, Andrew Nash, Frederik van Zyl Slabbert, David Welsh, Robert Schell, and Hans Heese.

No one in her right mind would hold a single individual mentioned here accountable for my views.

I wish to thank Ernst Stals and the Afrikanerbond for allowing me to cite from the study by Stals on the Afrikaner Broederbond, based on the Broederbond archives. I hope this valuable work will soon be published. I have a great debt to the economist and demographer Jan Sadie for responding to my incessant inquiries. His recent doctoral dissertation on the political demography provides rich socio-economic data for a reinterpretation of apartheid.

I could count on the solidarity of my two daughters, Francine and Adrienne, and earlier of my parents. The latter unfortunately did not live to see the publication of a book that I think would have given them pleasure. My greatest debt is to my wife, Annette, who accompanied me at every step in the adventure of writing the book. She read every word, listened to my arguments, invariably offered a common-sense correction of more wayward and uncharitable interpretations, and encouraged me when my spirits flagged and celebrated when I announced far too early, as it turned out, that the work was done. Without her the book would never have appeared in its present shape. It is to her that I dedicate it with all my love.

Abbreviations used

BOOKS AND PAPERS

AYB Archives Yearbook for South African History
Afrikaner Political Thought André du Toit and Hermann Giliomee, *Afrikaner Political Thought: Documents and Analyses, 1780-1850*
HAD House of Assembly Debates
Hertzog-toesprake F.J. du Toit Spies et al. (eds.), *Hertzog-toesprake, 1900-1942*
Ontwikkeling G.D. Scholtz, *Die ontwikkeling van die politieke denke van die Afrikaner*
RCC G.M. Theal (ed.) *Records of the Cape Colony*
SAPA South African Press Association
Smuts Papers W.K. Hancock and Jean van der Poel (eds.), *Selections from the Smuts Papers*
SSA Collected Seminar Papers on the Societies of Southern Africa, University of London Institute of Commonwealth Studies
SSAS (1) Richard Elphick and Hermann Giliomee (eds.), *The Shaping of South African Society, 1652-1820*
SSAS Richard Elphick and Hermann Giliomee (eds.), *The Shaping of South African Society, 1652-1840*
UG Union Government

OTHER ABBREVIATIONS

ANC: African National Congress
APO: African Political Organization
Company: Dutch East India Company
CPSA: Communist Party of South Africa
DRC: Dutch Reformed Church
FAK: Federasie van Afrikaanse Kultuurvereniginge
LMS: London Missionary Society
NP: National Party
PAC: Pan-Africanist Congress
SABRA: Suid-Afrikaanse Buro vir Rasse-aangeleenthede
SAP: South African Party
SWAPO: South West African People's Organisation
UP: United Party

Contents

Introduction

This book is a biography of the Afrikaner people of South Africa, whose roots in the continent of Africa go back to the seventeenth century. Their often turbulent history obscures the fact that they numbered only 1.2 million in 1936 and 2.6 million in 1980, when they formed close to 60 per cent of the dominant white group but less than 10 per cent of the total South African population. Yet they were, in the twentieth century, often in the world's spotlight. They were the first anti-colonial freedom fighters of the twentieth century to take on the might of the British Empire. In the second half of the twentieth century the Afrikaners, through their system of apartheid, became, in the term of Piet Cillié, editor of *Die Burger*, 'the polecat of the world.' Faced with international condemnation and internal resistance, they did something rare: surrendering power rather than resorting to more extreme forms of suppression and a suicidal last stand.

This book attempts to tell the Afrikaners' story from the beginning with empathy but without partisanship. 'To understand is not necessarily to pardon, but there is no harm in trying to understand.'[1] So wrote a scholar of slavery in ancient Greece. It is also the approach of this book.

It is quite a story. 'What young nation can boast a more romantic history, one of more far-reaching human interest? Color, incident, tragedy and comedy, defeat and victory, joy and sorrow . . . our early history is full of the most gripping human interest. If only we had the pen of Greeks, what a literary contribution should we make to our future treasures! There is gold not only in our earth, but still more in our history.'[2] So Jan Smuts, politician, statesman, philosopher, co-drafter of the UN Declaration of Human Rights, world citizen and Afrikaner, said in 1949 when a monument was unveiled to commemorate the Great Trek of the 1830s when thousands of Afrikaners moved out of the Cape Colony into the deeper interior. There was indeed drama, heroism and magnanimity in Afrikaner history, but also oppression, greed and the dehumanization of others.

Afrikaner history began at the Cape of Good Hope, a settlement founded in 1652 by the Dutch East India Company at the tip of Africa. Most settlers were immigrants from

---

1 H.D.F. Kitto, *The Greeks* (Harmondsworth: Penguin Books, 1951), p. 132.
2 *Smuts Papers* (Cambridge University Press, 1973), vol. 7, p. 327.

Western Europe who had enlisted as soldiers or sailors in the Company's service and became farming free burghers at the Cape. Few ever went back or looked back. They were
among the first colonial peoples to cut most of their family and community ties with
Europe and to develop a distinct sense of self-consciousness; they made the new land
genuinely their own. An exception was a small party of fewer than two hundred Huguenots from France but, by the mid-eighteenth century, they had been assimilated into
the burgher community.

The Afrikaners were both a colonized people and colonizers themselves, both victims
and proponents of European imperialism. They were a colonized people in being obliged
to respect the laws and authority of the Dutch East India Company, even if they were freed
from its service to make a living of their own. If the burghers misbehaved the Company
could take them back into its service as sailors or soldiers, even in some cases tearing
them from their families. But they were also slave-owners and colonizers. In the western
Cape almost every European family of standing owned slaves. Commandos, made up of
burghers and Khoikhoi auxiliaries, formed the fighting force that established European
control over the land and seized or recovered stolen stock. Farmers indentured the
indigenous people's children and destroyed their culture.

The burghers who lived in great isolation in the interior beyond the first mountain
ranges went to great lengths to maintain their link with the established Dutch Reformed
Church with its Calvinist creed, but were largely self-sufficient administratively and politically. Their representatives, the *heemraden* and field cornets, played a key role in the
local administration in the interior. In the absence of a standing police force or army
outside Cape Town, they had to assert their authority as masters. They guarded against
any form of *gelykstelling* or social leveling with their slaves and servants and restricted
their church largely to Europeans. But they admitted their most trusted servants into the
family's regular devotions and developed other paternalistic practices. Together with
their slaves and semi-free servants they turned the Dutch language into Afrikaans, one
of the genuinely multi-racial achievements of the new colony.

The British conquered the Cape in 1795 and, after returning it briefly to the Netherlands, again in 1806. The Afrikaners – the name now more common than in the eighteenth century – became a colonized people in a different sense. They were now British
subjects, enjoying all the rights that went with the status but ruled by a foreign nation.
Their rulers spoke a different tongue and were ready to display the contempt British
imperialists so often showed for what they regarded as lesser cultures and breeds of men.
Afrikaners were 'represented' in the literature by writers of whom many could not speak
their language or pronounce their names, and who considered them backward, lacking
in industry and cruel and unjust in their dealings with the indigenous people.

Between the mid-1820s and mid-1830s the British ushered in a near social revolution,
ending all statutory discrimination and ultimately also slavery. But they did so after first
abolishing all the institutions to which the burghers had become accustomed. The peaceful revolt of Afrikaner frontier farmers that came to be called the Great Trek was partly
a rejection of the gelykstelling these reforms seemed to bring about. In other ways, however, it was a peaceful revolt against the marginalization they experienced, flowing from
their lack of representation and the breakdown of security on large parts of the frontier.

The result of the trek was the dispersal of Afrikaners across the area of the present South Africa, with the exception of the southeastern seaboard. The trek destroyed any chance there was of the Afrikaners establishing themselves in a land that was all their own and in which they were self-sufficient in their labor needs. In many areas the trekkers encroached on the land of indigenous people and soon were embroiled in a variety of disputes when they forced those who lived there to work. However, it was not the trekkers or their children but British armies who defeated indigenous African resistance in the eastern half of South Africa in the 1870s and 1880s.

When gold was discovered on the Witwatersrand in the mid-1880s the scale decisively tilted against the Africans. But it also swung against the trekkers and the republics they had founded in the Transvaal and Orange Free State. To establish its dominance over all of South Africa and also in order to secure a more efficient exploitation of the gold deposits, Britain crushed the Boer republics in the Anglo-Boer War of 1899-1902. Fighting the twentieth century's first anti-colonial war, the northern Afrikaners were one of the first peoples to experience the horror of total war and concentration camps for civilians. One-tenth of the Boer population perished and almost all the farms were devastated.

The first eight chapters that form the first part of the book provide the background for the next eight that deal with the twentieth century and constitute the second part. Apart from the negotiated pact of the 1990s to introduce an inclusive democracy (Chapter 17), three aspects of the history of the Afrikaners during the past hundred years deserve particular attention. The first is their relative economic backwardness. Francis Fukuyama considers 'the failure of the Calvinist Afrikaners to develop a thriving capitalist system until the last quarter of the century' an anomaly that needs explanation.[3] Their relative economic backwardness is analyzed here with reference to the heritage of more than two centuries of subsistence farming, the devastation of the Anglo-Boer War, the Afrikaners' late and often traumatic urbanization (until 1890 more than 90 per cent lived on farms) and their lack of industrial skills. This gave rise to the problem of the poor whites, who formed approximately a quarter of the Afrikaners by the early 1930s. The voters who supported the National Party in the 1920s and 1930s were mainly less successful farmers, semi-skilled or unskilled workers, civil servants on the lower rungs, teachers and clergymen. Lewis Gann was not far off the mark when he wrote: 'The National Party resembled a pre-World War Two peasant party in Eastern Europe – anti-capitalist, anti-urban, ethnocentric and anti-Semite.'[4] Yet, significantly, the Afrikaners made no serious attempt to nationalize any part of the economy despite the fact that foreign capital and local English-speakers totally dominated mining, industry and commerce during the first half of the twentieth century.

The book also highlights the divided nature of the dominant white group, the British-Afrikaner rivalry for status and symbolic power, and the rise of Afrikaner nationalism. Afrikaners dominated politics, but in the economic, social and cultural spheres had to take a back seat to the English-speakers, who were better educated, better skilled and spoke what was virtually the only language in use in industry and commerce. They

---

3 Francis Fukuyama, *Trust: The Social Virtues and the Creation of Prosperity* (New York: Free Press, 1995), p. 44.
4 L.H. Gann, *South Africa: War? Revolution? Peace?* (Cape Town: Tafelberg, 1979), p. 77.

maintained close ties with Britain with its industrial strength and cultural riches. They interpreted South Africa to foreign writers and journalists. But they were also the only sizeable English-speaking community in the world that was without any formal political power of its own.

David Yudelman, a perceptive English-speaking South African historian, criticized South African anglophones for disseminating a distorted picture to the world. The English-speakers were, he remarked, not significantly more liberal than the Afrikaners on race questions, yet they tended to present the Afrikaner as 'the villain, the fanatic, who created or at least perfected institutionalized racial discrimination', while whites of British extraction supposedly only passively accepted segregation and apartheid. The latter were, he added, quite prepared 'to use apartheid as a pretext for indirectly expressing their culturally chauvinistic distaste for the Afrikaners while continuing to enjoy the benefits of white supremacy.'[5]

The Afrikaners themselves are also responsible for the skewed picture. They depicted themselves as the only whites who had become truly indigenous and who were prepared to fight to the end for white supremacy. The Afrikaner-British rivalry should be understood as a typical fight over relative group status and symbols similar to other such struggles around the world.[6]

Previous attempts by historians to analyze Afrikaner nationalism have used various approaches. Liberal historians have tended to focus on the Afrikaners' racial prejudices, their Calvinism and xenophobia, and, more recently on their civil religion,[7] Marxist historians have explained the class interests of the constituent parts of the Afrikaner people,[8] and Afrikaner nationalist historians have recounted the establishment of white supremacy and nationalist struggles against British imperialism.[9] Although this work does not share its perspective on the racial issue, it is indebted to the prodigious research that went into G.D. Scholtz's *Die ontwikkeling van die politieke denke van die Afrikaner* that appeared in eight volumes.[10]

These interpretations have neglected several areas. There is, for example the importance of religion as a social-political force, a factor that historians still greatly underestimate.[11] It receives special attention in Chapter 13 on the making of apartheid ideology. So, too, the role of Afrikaner women, who enjoyed more independence than their counterparts in most other European colonies, has been underplayed. Afrikaner women,

---

5 David Yudelman, *The Emergence of South Africa* (Westport: Greenwood Press, 1983), pp. 13-14.

6 Donald Horowitz, *Ethnic Groups in Conflict* (Berkeley: University of California Press, 1985).

7 T. Dunbar Moodie, *The Rise of Afrikanerdom* (Berkeley: University of California Press, 1975); G.H le May, *The Afrikaners: An Historical Interpretation* (Oxford: Blackwell, 1995).

8 Dan O' Meara, *Volkskapitalisme: Class, Capital and Ideology in the Development of Afrikaner Nationalism, 1934-1948* (Cambridge: Cambridge University Press, 1983) and Dan O'Meara, *Forty Lost Years: The Apartheid State and the Politics of the National Party, 1948-1994* (Athens: Ohio University Press, 1996.)

9 C.M. van den Heever, 'Die Afrikaanse gedagte', C.M. van den Heever and P. de V. Pienaar (eds.), *Die kultuurgeskiedenis van die Afrikaner* (Cape Town: Nasionale Boekhandel, 1950), vol. 3, pp. 1-32; F.A. van Jaarsveld, *Die ontwaking van 'n Afrikaner nasionale bewussyn, 1868-1881* (Johannesburg: Voortrekkerpers, 1959).

10 It was published between 1967 and 1984 by Voortrekkerpers and Perskor.

11 This is highlighted in the forthcoming work of Richard Elphick and in particular his 'Evangelical Missions and Racial Equalization in South Africa' and 'Missions and Afrikaner nationalism', unpublished papers, 1999.

the most determined participants of the Great Trek, urged their menfolk to fight to the bitter end in the war against Britain in 1880-81 and again in 1899-1902. In the aftermath of the war they took the lead in the rehabilitation of the Afrikaner poor and in Johannesburg and neighboring towns they were among the most militant in the white working class. But after the Afrikaner nationalists won power in the mid-1920s, the political militancy of women dwindled and they played almost no role in the agitation for the franchise of women. Female liberation and nationalist liberation did not go hand in hand; the latter in fact undermined the former.

Another neglected area is the interrelationship between language and nationalism.[12] Chapters 11 and 12 tell how the Afrikaners developed Afrikaans into a public language, both as a means of overcoming their feelings of inferiority towards English-speakers and as a unique form of cultural expression. Afrikaans became one of four languages in the world – Hebrew, Hindi and Indonesian are the others – which, in the course of the twentieth century, were standardized and used in all branches of life and learning, including as sole medium of instruction at some universities and in science and technology. Its link with Afrikaner nationalism is best described by the title of a scholarly study: 'Building a Nation from Words.'[13]

A major challenge that faces any historian is to write a dispassionate analysis of apartheid at a time in world history when, as Irish historian Roy Foster phrases it, 'apology is easier than explaining.' Foster urges historians to remind their public that 'the continuums and the inheritances of history are matters of complex descent.'[14] Chapter 9 shows that the attempt to project South Africa as a 'white man's country' dates back to the late nineteenth century; Chapters 10 and 13 point out that an elaborate system of racial segregation was in place by the 1920s. This book rejects the orthodoxy that the appeal to apartheid made it possible for the National Party to capture power in 1948. The decisive turning point was in fact South Africa's entry into the Second World War on a split vote in Parliament and the sharp cleavages that developed during the war between pro-war and anti-war factions in the white community, which largely ran along language lines.

This book rejects the standard view that apartheid policy was mainly the work of populist Afrikaners in the north who were members of the Afrikaner Broederbond and argues that it was, in fact, forged in the more settled western Cape, where politicians, academics and journalists were preoccupied with the removal of the colored vote and the reduction of Africans in the region. Chapter 13 points out that the main ideological influences on apartheid were not Nazi racial dogmas but (i) the established practice of segregated schools (accepted by virtually the entire white community); (ii) the theology of the Dutch Reformed Church – a people's church or *volkskerk* with a mission strategy of working towards self-governing indigenous churches; (iii) racial discrimination in the United States; (iv) imperialist ideas about indirect rule and trusteeship; and (v) the

---

12 Stephen May, *Language and Minority Rights: Ethnicity, Nationalism and the Politics of Language* (London: Longman, 2001), p. 7.

13 Isabel Hofmeyr, 'Building a Nation from Words: Afrikaans Language, Literature and Ethnic Identity, 1902-1924', in Shula Marks and Stanley Trapido (eds.), *The Politics of Race, Class and Nationalism in Twentieth-Century South Africa* (London: Longman, 1987), pp. 95-123.

14 Roy Foster, 'Fashion for apology can invite danger of amnesia', *Sunday Independent*, 25 July 1999.

emerging theories of social conflict in plural societies. As Chapter 14 shows, apartheid went further than pre-1948 segregation in denying blacks all claims to the common area and in systematically treating not only Africans but also coloreds and Asians as people who belonged to subordinate statutory categories.

The Afrikaner nationalists applied apartheid with a mixture of political zeal and ideological bigotry that went beyond their economic interests. The explanation lies not – at least not principally – in their Calvinist beliefs or racial obsessions but in their preoccupation with ethnic survival. Afrikaner nationalist leadership of the mid-twentieth century was obsessed with the idea that the NP's surprising victory of 1948 was a God-given chance to secure finally the future of the Afrikaners as a small white people on the African continent. Fighting to ensure survival was seen as a personal responsibility, a higher calling. In a host of ways the nationalist obsession with survival became intertwined with apartheid projected as a policy aiming at the maintenance of ethnic groups and cultures.

Apartheid failed because the plan was imposed, because whites lacked the numbers to make it work and because the world had changed. By the 1960s the West had renounced colonialism and racism unequivocally and the new member states of the United Nations had come to see South Africa as a tangible symbol of racially based Western colonialism. Universally condemned and facing widespread domestic resistance, apartheid threatened over time to spark a devastating racial conflagration in South Africa. The fight against apartheid was perhaps the single most burning moral cause in the world during the 1970s and 1980s.

Yet apartheid was never a closed ideological system. Particularly important was N.P. van Wyk Louw, the premier Afrikaans man of letters, who warned as early as 1952 against an obsession with survival at all costs. He urged Afrikaners not to choose 'mere survival' over 'survival in justice.'

'I believe that the greatest, almost mystical crisis of the *volk* is that in which it is re-born and re-emerges young and creative, the "dark night of the soul" in which it says: "I would rather go down than to continue to survive in injustice".'[15]

Chapters 15 and 16 relate the Afrikaner retreat from apartheid, culminating in the decision in a referendum, held in 1992 among whites, to abandon exclusive white power.

The term 'survival' often crops up in Afrikaner history, but it needs to be stressed that a *nationalist* concern about survival, as distinct from a more generalized anxiety over white survival, is a twentieth-century phenomenon. In the history of the Cape Colony slave-owners feared that they could not survive without a steady supply of imported slaves. So, too, burghers on the remote pastoral frontier were troubled by the thought that their children would lose their European culture and become 'barbarized.' By the nineteenth century survival fears concerned the assimilation of the Afrikaner elite in the Cape Colony into English culture. Afrikaner fears of being wiped out as a people were particularly acute during the Anglo-Boer War. In the twentieth century widespread white poverty threatened white domination.

The term 'survival' is a loaded one, particularly as used by Afrikaners in the past. How

---

15 N.P. van Wyk Louw, *Versamelde prosa* (Cape Town: Tafelberg, 1986), vol. 1, p. 463.

does the historian know that a concern expressed over the survival of a culture or a people is not in fact a camouflage for concern about a standard of living, a concern about privilege or even sheer racism? It is a difficult call, one that the historian must approach with great circumspection. Still, it would be shortsighted to dismiss the Afrikaner debate over ethnic survival as peripheral compared to an assessment of interests. At the heart of the decision to introduce apartheid shortly after the 1948 election and the 1990 decision to abolish all its pillars was a calculation about the survival prospects of the Afrikaners.

A note on terminology: The term 'Afrikaners' for whites was first used early in the eighteenth century, but it had to vie with designations like burgher, Christian, Dutchmen and Boer. For the period 1652 to approximately 1875 this book mostly uses burgher for a white person who spoke Dutch or Afrikaans; for the history after 1875 it employs the term Afrikaner, although it was not until the mid-twentieth century that the term was reserved only for white Afrikaans-speakers. But the invitation to become Afrikaners was extended to white English-speakers and rarely to colored Afrikaans-speakers. Again from the 1980s the term started to become racially inclusive. I mostly refer to the colonists of British descent and to Jewish South Africans as the English-speakers, although one-fifth of the colored people in Cape Town spoke English at home. I call Bantu-speaking black people either blacks or Africans, while the descendants of whites and slaves or Khoisan are referred to as colored people. People of Asian descent are usually called Indians. I have avoided as much as possible the term 'non-white', seen as offensive, for all black, colored and Indian people.

Stellenbosch
16 December 2002

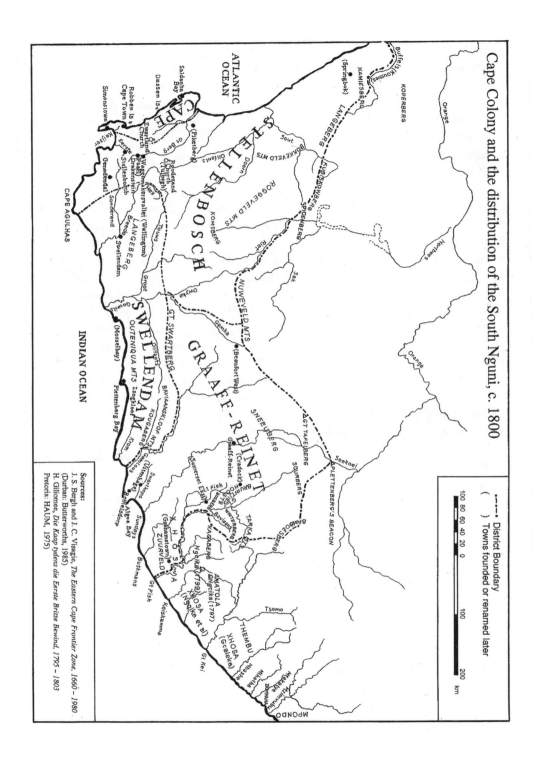

Cape Colony and the distribution of the South Nguni, c. 1800

- – - – District Boundary
( ) Towns founded or renamed later

100 80 60 40 20 0   100   200
km

Sources:
J. S. Bergh and J. C. Visagie, *The Eastern Cape Frontier Zone, 1660–1980*
(Durban: Butterworths, 1985)
H. Giliomee, *Die Kaap tydens die Eerste Britse Bewind, 1795–1803*
Pretoria: HAUM, 1975)

ATLANTIC OCEAN

INDIAN OCEAN

CAPE AGULHAS

CAPE

STELLENBOSCH

SWELLENDAM

GRAAFF-REINET

Cape Town
Robben Is.
Dassen Is.
Simonstown
Saldanha Bay
(Springbok)
KAMIESBERG
KOPERBERG
Buffels(R) (Kousie(R))
Orange
Sout
BOKKEVELD MTS
LANGEBERG
KUIBISKOWBERG
SPIOENBERG
ROGGEVELD MTS
Doorn
Oliphants
Gt Berg
(Piketberg)
Zwartland
Church
Roodezand
Church (Tulbagh)
Wagenmakersvallei (Wellington)
Drakenstein
Stellenbosch
Genadendal
Sonderend
Swellendam
Breede
LANGEBERG
Gouritz
Gouritz
(Mosselbay)
OUTENIQUA MTS
Langkloof
Plettenberg Bay
Krom
Gamtoos
Swartkops
Algoa Bay
Bethelsdorp
Sundays
Bushmans
Gt Fish
Keiskamma
KOMSBERG
Tows
Groot
GT. SWARTBERG
Dwyka
NUWEVELD MTS
Gamka
Sak
Riet
Hartbees
Orange
(Beaufort West)
GT TAFELBERG
SNEEUBERG
SUURBERG
PLETTENBERG'S BEACON
Seekoei
BAVIAANSKLOOF
KOIGABERG
(Uitenhage)
(Somerset East) Lt Fish
BRUINTJIES
HOOGTE
(Graaff-Reinet) (Cradock)
TARKA
BAMBOESBERG
BRUINTJIES
HOOGTE
WINTERBERG
Baviaans
KAGABERG
H O S A (Grahamstown)
ZUURVELD
Ngqika(1799)
XHOSA (Ndlambe)
Ndlambe(1797)
AMATOLA
XHOSA (Gcaleka)
THEMBU
Tsomo
Gt Kei
Mbashe
MPONDO
Mzimvubu
Mngazane
Mngazi
(Ngqika et al)

South Africa 1900

SOUTH WEST AFRICA

BOTSWANA

SOUTPANSBERG
• Sibasa
Schoemansdal
• Tzaneen
WATERBERG • Pietersburg
TRANSVAAL
Andries Ohrigstad
• Pilgrims Rest
Groblersdal • Lydenburg
• Rustenburg
• Mafeking • Pretoria • Middelburg
• Lichtenburg • Johannesburg
Potchefstroom • Vereeniging • Bethel
SWAZI-
LAND
• Heilbron • Piet Retief
• Kuruman
Taung • Kroonstad Vryheid
Welkom New Castle
Harrismith NATAL
• Upington Kimberley • Winburg
Griquatown ORANGE • Ladysmith Eshowe •
Bloemfontein Thaba
Nchu
• Springbok FREE LESOTHO Pieter-
Hopetown STATE maritzburg • Tongaat
Durban

CAPE PROVINCE
• Port Shepstone

• Burgersdorp

• Van Rhynsdorp • Carnarvon • Richmond • Elliot
GLEN GREY
• Queenstown
• Cradock
• Beaufort West • Graaff-Reinet • Cathcart
Bedford • • Adelaide Fort Jackson
Somerset East •
Willowmore King Williams Town
Wellington Oudtshoorn • Grahamstown
Tulbagh • Ceres Uitenhage • Bathurst
Paarl • Worcester George • Knysna Alexandria
Stellenbosch • Paarl Port Elizabeth
Cape Town Genadendal • Swellendam
Bredasdorp

0 50 100   200   300 km

Sources
Monica Wilson and Leonard Thompson, *Oxford History of South Africa*, vol. 2
(Oxford: Clarendon Press, 1971)
Rodney Davenport and Christopher Saunders, *South Africa: A Modern History*,
(London: Macmillan, 2000)

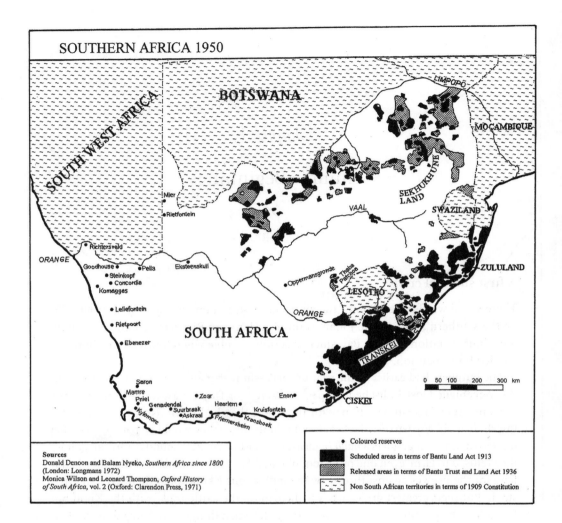

SOUTHERN AFRICA 1950

SOUTH WEST AFRICA

BOTSWANA

MOÇAMBIQUE

LIMPOPO

Mier

Rietfontein

VAAL

SEKHUKHUNE LAND

SWAZILAND

ORANGE

Richtersveld

Goodhouse

Steinkopf

Concordia

Komaggas

Pella

Eksteenskuil

Oppermansgronde

Thaba Patchoa

LESOTHO

ZULULAND

Leliefontein

Rietpoort

Ebenezer

ORANGE

SOUTH AFRICA

TRANSKEI

0 50 100   200   300 km

Saron

Mamre

Pniel

Kylemore

Genadendal

Suurbraak

Askraal

Zoar

Haarlem

Friemersheim

Kruisfontein

Kranshoek

Enon

CISKEI

• Coloured reserves

■ Scheduled areas in terms of Bantu Land Act 1913

▦ Released areas in terms of Bantu Trust and Land Act 1936

⬚ Non South African territories in terms of 1909 Constitution

Sources
Donald Denoon and Balam Nyeko, *Southern Africa since 1800*
(London: Longmans 1972)
Monica Wilson and Leonard Thompson, *Oxford History
of South Africa*, vol. 2 (Oxford: Clarendon Press, 1971)

Chapter 1

Humble Beginnings

A first survival crisis

There was a whiff of sedition in the air at noon on a summer day in December 1658 on the southern tip of Africa. Johan Anthonisz (Jan) van Riebeeck, commander of the refreshment station at Table Bay, smelled serious trouble when fourteen free burghers handed him a petition.

The burghers had earlier in the year unsuccessfully demanded to know the price that the Vereenigde Oost-Indische Compagnie (VOC), or Dutch East India Company as it was known in English, would pay for the wheat they had sown. Now they refused to thresh their already harvested wheat if not told the price they would be paid. Unless they received at least ten guilders a *muid* (a measure of just under 200 pounds or 91 kilograms), they refused to farm 'even one more foot of land.' They also complained that they had to fend for themselves against threats by the indigenous Khoikhoi to their lives and livestock. But their greatest grievance was the ban on the cattle trade with the Khoikhoi. Pervading the petition was a sense of outrage that such things were being done to them while they were 'the defenders of the land', as they described themselves. They wanted to be 'no Company slaves.' Instead of 'being assisted, they were being oppressed.'

On instructions from the Company, Van Riebeeck had founded the settlement that became known as the Cape of Good Hope on 6 April 1652. (The name Cape Town would only come into vogue late in the next century.) In 1657 he released nine Company servants to become full-time farmers on their plots of 13.3 morgen (about 11.4 hectares)[1]. The VOC had not intended to found a colony for European settlement at the Cape. All it wanted was a modest refreshment station to service VOC ships on their way to and from its empire in the East. The burghers' task was to produce fresh food, sowing and planting what the Company prescribed and accepting the low prices it set. The next year Van Riebeeck banned all trade between the burghers and the Khoikhoi and prohibited the burghers from selling cattle to each other or the passing ships without government

---

1 The term 'morgen' is a Dutch land measure used in South Africa until the adoption of the metric system. It roughly represents the amount of land that could be ploughed in a morning. One morgen equalled 0.856 hectares.

permission. There was a reason why Van Riebeeck did not tell the burghers the wheat price. Taking their cue from the price in the Netherlands, his superiors in Amsterdam had instructed him to pay only five guilders a bag, which he knew was far too low. In the smuggling trade that would develop a few years later the burghers, to the horror of the officials, would get twelve guilders from ships that stopped at the Cape.

In the altercation with the burghers in December 1658, Van Riebeeck immediately felt that more than just the price of wheat was at stake. In his diary he wrote that the burghers 'would greatly like to be their own masters and overrule the lawful authorities placed over them, yes, even the Company and their own Lords and Masters.' Accordingly, he admonished them 'to behave as behove obedient servants, and not to compel the Company in any way or to threaten it as has now been done pretty seditiously and rebelliously.' The Company had fed them and had provided them with everything they needed. It had raised the burghers 'from a lowly position and at great expense to itself.' Although not the Company's slaves, they were its subjects. The Company could offer them only six guilders a bag. Van Riebeeck noted how 'the burghers lost heart and became quite despondent', whereupon he offered them wine and they went home 'in good spirits and poking fun at each other.'[2]

Grim times lay ahead. The climate was fickle for the wheat farmers. The rain often stayed away and, during spring and early summer, a vicious southeast wind might come up to destroy a promising harvest. At times the farmers barely recovered their seed wheat.

Van Riebeeck might have berated the burghers for laziness and for drinking too much, but he knew that they had a right to protest about the price. He conceded in a letter, in 1661, that the free burghers could scarcely subsist on what they were paid for cultivating their wheat. Three years later, the government decided to distribute Sunday church collections and some petty fines to poor burghers burdened with 'naked children, and [who] from simple poverty must sleep each night beside the livestock in the stable on a little straw and the naked earth.'[3]

There were some 150 Europeans at the Cape in 1662 when Van Riebeeck left. The settlement's population was made up as follows (technically, women were not burghers and were not enumerated under that category, but they shared many of the rights of their adult male family):

CAPE POPULATION 1662

	Company servants	Burghers
Males	57	36
Family	113	37
Slaves	24	23

Most of these burghers worked in the small town as carpenters, bricklayers, smiths and keepers of taverns and boarding houses. Sixteen were farmers.

The Company did not release its European employees in order to implement some grandiose scheme. Some of the VOC's top officials would have preferred Chinese or

2 H.B. Thom (ed.), *Journal of Van Riebeeck* (Cape Town: VRS, 1954), vol. 2, pp. 390-400.
3 P.J. van der Merwe, *The Migrant Farmer in the History of the Cape Colony, 1657-1842* (Athens: Ohio University Press, 1995), pp. 4-5.

free blacks to European farmers, and in their letters they frequently expressed contempt for the abilities of the free burghers. The burghers' sense of vulnerability and distrust of the government would not subside for more than three centuries.

An unpromising career

During the first half of the seventeenth century the Dutch were the world's leading trading nation. The mighty VOC was established in 1602 in Amsterdam as a chartered company in an amalgamation of rival Dutch companies trading with the East. Like its English counterpart, the English East India Company (established two years before), the Dutch company had an extensive trading network. Amsterdam, its home base, was a huge entrepôt for spices, sugar, tobacco, timber and manufactured articles from across the globe and particularly from its empire in the East.

The VOC had become the world's largest trading enterprise by 1650. It could be called the world's first multi-national corporation. Some four hundred years after the founding of the Dutch and the English East India Companies, *The Economist* wrote that in their impact on the world, both good and bad, perhaps only the companies of Henry Ford and Bill Gates matched them.[4] Between 1602 and 1699 a total of 1,755 Company ships sailed from the Netherlands to Jakarta (renamed Batavia) in Java. During the first decade of the Cape station (1652-1662) 205 ships with 40,200 people on board sailed to the East, while 103 ships with some 13,000 people returned to the Netherlands.[5]

Although the VOC proclaimed free trade, it practiced a monopoly where it could, and, deciding that it could not trade without waging war, evicted most of its Portuguese and English rivals from the East, compelling local rulers to grant it exclusive trading rights. Soon it had seized Bantam, the Moluccas, Java and Amboyna.

In 1619 it introduced a regular government under a governor general, presiding over a Council of India, in Batavia. The city became the capital of the VOC's Eastern empire. When the VOC founded the Cape it placed it under the authority of both the directors of the Company in Amsterdam, called the Lords Seventeen, and the Council of India in Batavia. To compensate for their low pay, many of the Company's staff stole from their employer, embezzling or trading for their own account. Van Riebeeck himself, before coming to the Cape, was fined for private trading and recalled from a post in Japan.

As a colony for European settlement, the Cape had serious drawbacks. It had no great staple products, like rice, sugar, tobacco, wool or timber that could be integrated into the world's trade systems. Beyond its coastal mountains the climate was harsh and the soil poor. Apart from livestock, the prospects for trade with the indigenous Khoikhoi and the Bushmen (or San), who populated a large part of the subcontinent, were limited. They were much less developed culturally and technologically than the peoples the Dutch had encountered in the East.[6]

---

4 *The Economist*, Millennium Special Edition, 1 January 1000-31 December 1999, pp. 82-3.
5 Karel Schoeman, *Armosyn van die Kaap: voorspel tot vestiging, 1415-1651* (Cape Town: Human & Rousseau, 1999), pp. 88-121.
6 Richard Elphick, *Kraal and Castle: Khoikhoi and the Founding of White South Africa* (New Haven: Yale University Press, 1977), pp. xv-xvi.

But some of the Europeans who settled at the Cape quickly fell in love with the climate and natural beauty of the Cape Peninsula and its environment. One of them was Johannes de Grevenbroek, who could be considered the first Cape intellectual. He came to the Cape as secretary of the Council of Policy, and retired to a farm just outside Stellenbosch, the first inland settlement. He wrote in flawless Latin: 'This remote corner into which I have been thrust is more fertile than I had hoped for or believed, and charms me more than the refinements of European civilization. That I should love it will not surprise you.'[7]

When, on 6 April 1652, three Dutch ships arrived in Table Bay some ninety Europeans disembarked – 'weak and ignorant people', as Van Riebeeck described them.[8] For the first three decades most of the immigrants were single Dutch males. In 1688 a party of French Huguenots composed mostly of families arrived (see pp. 10-11). Apart from the French women, the female European immigrants were Dutch. Some of them were girls sent from orphanages in the Netherlands.

Most of the male immigrants were illiterate or semi-literate peasants or laborers employed by the Company as sailors or soldiers. A career on the lower VOC rungs was an unpromising one. Few inhabitants of the free Netherlands would sign up as sailors or soldiers except out of dire necessity. 'Criminals and rascals' who were on the run were among those who came. Those who joined the merchant navy avoided VOC ships, deemed to be a 'disgrace.'[9] A sailor or a soldier's daily wage was five times less than that received by a polder boy or a peat-cutter in the Netherlands. They had to endure bad food, ferocious discipline and disease. Death was frequent on the ships. Some 15 to 20 per cent who set sail perished on the Company's outward voyages every year. A career in the Company was truly for those who could think of no other solution to their problems.

During the eighteenth century most of the European immigrants were single male Germans. A typical German immigrant of the 1730s and 1740s had been driven to Holland in search of employment through 'poverty and through the utter absence of other means of help', as O.F. Mentzel, a German traveler wrote. He arrived there poorly clad, without money, in want of every necessity and desperate for a job. He dared not beg for fear of being sent to a workhouse. If he stole, he could be hanged. He had no money to support himself while waiting to be recruited as a soldier or a sailor by the VOC and usually fell into the hands of agents, who paid for his subsistence until he received his first pay. In some cases it took five years for someone to pay off the agent. At the Cape the man had to live frugally. He received 28 stuivers (one guilder equaled 20 stuivers) a month as *kostgeld* or a cash wage, an additional 28 stuivers subsistence money, and six pounds of bread per week. With the large debt to pay off, he often lived on less than two stuivers a day. Even in the meanest of eating-houses a small portion of meat cost two stuivers.[10]

---

7 J.G. de Grevenbroek, 'An Account of the Hottentots', in I. Schapera and B. Farrington (eds.), *The Early Cape Hottentots* (Cape Town: VRS, 1933), p. 297; A.V. van Stekelenburg, 'Een intellektueel in de vroege Kaapkolonie: de nalatenskap van Jan Willem van Grevenbroek, 1644-1726', *Tydskrif vir Nederlands en Afrikaans*, 8 (2001), pp. 3-14.

8 Anna Böeseken, 'Die koms van die blankes onder Van Riebeeck', C.F.J. Muller (ed.), *Vyfhonderd jaar Suid-Afrikaanse geskiedenis* (Pretoria: Academica, 1980), p. 22.

9 Schoeman, *Armosyn*, p. 96.

10 O.F. Mentzel, *Life at the Cape in the Mid-Eighteenth Century* (Cape Town: VRS, 1919), p. 27.

Yet while most immigrants came from the lower rungs of society, they should not be considered collectively as dregs. They were enterprising enough to take the risk of working in a distant country for the required term of five years. Some of the Germans who came to the Cape were tradesmen whose lives (or whose parents' lives) had been disrupted by the Thirty Years' War, which ended in 1648. It was they who fared best in their new homeland at the tip of Africa.

European heritage

The Netherlands rather than Germany or France influenced the character of the Cape settlement. In continental Europe, people in the Netherlands enjoyed the most individual mobility and the greatest advances towards the idea of equality before the law. In the province of Holland, Roman-Dutch law, the established form of justice, conferred no special privileges on the nobility, but in the words of the great jurist Voetius, it 'preserves equality and binds the citizens equally.' As a French visitor remarked in 1665, Dutch servants enjoyed so many privileges that their masters could not even hit them.[11] It was this law with its egalitarian thrust that would be applied at the Cape.

In the Netherlands the Reformed Church, based on the Calvinist doctrine, was the official and privileged denomination, but it was not the state church and only about half of the population belonged to it. At the Cape the Reformed Church for more than a century would be the only church. This church set itself against the strict hierarchy of the Catholic Church. More than one Dutch minister contrasted the lack of respect of Dutch laymen for their ministers with the humble deference displayed by Spanish and Portuguese Roman Catholics towards their priests.

The state kept a close watch over the church, both at home and at the Cape. It remunerated some church employees and owned the church buildings. In the Netherlands it instructed the church not to criticize the government, and, at the Cape, ministers as paid officials of the Company were expected to be obedient and respectful towards it.

The Dutch had no great deference to secular authorities. The Netherlands in the seventeenth century was less a nation-state than a loose confederation of provinces and cities. Compared to the rest of Europe, the social structure was fluid, unique in the mobility people enjoyed and in the absence of sharp class cleavages. Below the fairly small strata of the aristocracy and the 'high bourgeoisie' was a wide stratum of the 'broad citizenry' and 'middle estate', comprised of skilled artisans, shopkeepers and suppliers of goods. Below them was the proletariat with poorly paid but regular work and, at the bottom, the *grauw*, the underclass. A poor man could aspire to rise up from the proletariat to enter the *middestand*, the middle class. Citizens in the Netherlands had more liberty to pursue their own interests than elsewhere in Europe.[12]

Early capitalism had a near-revolutionary impact on northwestern Europe. Across the social ranks people were beginning to take the concept of individual land-ownership for granted. Capitalism and Calvinism together produced a potent brew. The Reformed

---

11 Schoeman, *Armosyn*, p. 260.
12 Simon Schama, *The Embarrassment of Riches: An Interpretation of Dutch Culture in the Golden Age* (London: Fontana Press, 1987), pp. 4-7.

Church endorsed the pursuit of wealth through productive investment, thrift, industry and competitiveness. Prosperity was considered a visible sign of a godly life, though Dutch Calvinism warned against worshipping the golden calf. It considered banking a far from honorable occupation, and condemned monopolies and other combinations as conspiracies against the consumer.[13]

Most of the immigrants who became free burghers at the Cape were poor, humble and ignorant, but the term 'burgher' was the same as that used for those at the center of the seventeenth-century Dutch world: the prosperous, self-confident burghers of the Dutch cities portrayed in the work of Rembrandt, Steen, Vermeer, Hals and other painters. The Dutch burgher was not a bourgeois defined by economic function and power but 'a citizen first and *homo economicus* second.'[14]

Company rule and burgher aspirations

Van Riebeeck's step to release some servants to farm as 'free burghers' sprang from the VOC's desire to save money, not from any wish to provide an island of liberty for some of its employees. 'Free burghers' were released from their contract with the Company, but continued to be subject to the Company's regulations for the Cape settlement and the decisions of the Cape authorities.

The main governing body was the Council of Policy, made up of the highest Company officials, some of whom also sat on the highest court, the Court of Justice. Three burghers were nominated when it heard cases involving a burgher. These burgher councilors were entitled to present burgher grievances to visiting commissioners. Thus from an early stage they could speak on behalf of the body of freemen. Two burghers sat with the same number of officials on two other important boards. One was the Matrimonial Court, before which couples intending to get married had to appear, and the other was the Orphan Chamber. No widower or widow might remarry before satisfying the board that the rights of their children had been safeguarded. In the eighteenth century all wills and inventories of estates had to be registered with it. Since money often had to be deposited, it also served as a loan bank in a settlement that would have no regular commercial bank for a long time. The following chapter describes the key role of the burghers in the administration of the districts in the interior.

Much ambiguity surrounded the status of the burghers. Free burghers were not prepared to accept a status radically different from that of the burghers in the Netherlands. They were burghers and citizens, not mere subjects or subordinates. The claim may not have been factually correct, but the burghers never abandoned this aspiration. The burghers in the western Cape who were to take part in the Patriot struggle during the 1780s described themselves as 'free citizens of a colony of the free United Netherlands, sharing the same rights and privileges' (see page 54).

The Cape burghers soon embraced their own foundation myth: that they were indispensable to the Cape settlement and that their interests were of key, if not of paramount importance, to maintaining the settlement. The term 'defenders of the land' offered the

---

13 Schama, *Embarrassment of Riches*, pp. 323-43.
14 Schama, *Embarrassment of Riches,* p. 7.

first sign of an emerging political consciousness. It was further stimulated by the important role that burghers played in the administration.

Company officials never ceased to be outraged by what they regarded as the ordinary burghers' preposterous demands. Van Riebeeck obviously thought that the burghers ought to be grateful for the freedom they had received and should therefore subordinate their own interests to those of the Company. The Company, a sovereign power in its own right according to its 1602 charter, could recruit soldiers, wage war, enter into treaties with other powers and maintain order in the settlements it had founded. Dutchmen in its employ swore fealty both to the Company and the States General in the Netherlands. All Europeans were subject both to the laws of the Netherlands and the regulations framed by the Company.

The Company authorities disputed the comparison free burghers made with their counterparts in the Netherlands, since the Company that granted privileges could also withdraw them. It had the power to free burghers from its service, but also to force those who had misbehaved to return to the Company's service or to deport them. But the Company also had to concede that they were not simply serfs, obliged to submit to any order, as Van Riebeeck discovered in his December 1658 altercation with the burghers.[15]

Struggling to put down roots

For the burghers the issue was economic survival; for the Company it was maximization of profits, which meant fixing a price for their products as low as possible. The Company had envisaged a neat, compact settlement that would not extend much beyond the shadow of the coastal fort. As in the Netherlands, Cape farmers were expected to grow crops in rotation (including clover to allow the soil to recover) and provide fodder for a limited number of cattle, with manure collected for fertilizer.[16] Such a system of intensive agriculture required an injection of capital, which the burghers did not have. Their crops had to be transported to the market over poor roads. They were also required to sow and reap, strenuous labor for which the burghers had little enthusiasm. Officials in colonies across the world discovered that, if slaves or indigenous labor could be found, European immigrants refused to work on the land as their kinsmen did in Europe.

When the first shipload of slaves arrived at the Cape in 1658, most of the farming burghers were far too poor and debt-ridden to afford them, but on their own they could cultivate some wheat and also raise cattle by bartering with the Khoikhoi. They grazed the cattle in the open land adjoining their fields. Many sent their cattle deeper and deeper into the interior to find good pasture. Stock farming soon became an independent enterprise that in the next century would outstrip agriculture.

The switch to extensive agriculture and the increasing involvement of burghers in cattle trading and cattle farming threatened the way of life of the approximately 100,000 Khoikhoi living in the area of the present Western Cape. (The number living in the Cape

---

15 Arend Willem Biewenga, *De Kaap de Goede Hoop: een Nederlandse vestigingskolonie, 1680-1730*, doctoral diss., Vrije Universiteit, Amsterdam, 1998, p. 21.

16 Leonard Guelke, 'Freehold Farmers and Frontier Settlers, 1657-1780', *SSAS*, pp. 69-73.

Peninsula and vicinity, called the Kaapmans or Peninsulars, probably ranged between four thousand and eight thousand.) The Khoikhoi were hunters and herders, except when disaster destroyed their cattle herds and compelled them to assume the lifestyle of the hunter-gatherer San or Bushmen. (The term 'Khoisan', coined by historians, reflects the readiness with which the line between these two groups was crossed.)

The Peninsulars, realizing that the Europeans had come to stay, became hostile and acutely concerned when the burghers ploughed their fields for the first time. They attacked farms and sought to prevent occupation of their grazing lands near the Cape. When the burghers, in the 1658 petition, described themselves as defenders of the land, they referred to their manning the two outlying forts and their efforts to protect the settlement from Khoikhoi attacks. They believed that the real threat to the small settlement emanated from its indigenous enemies and not a European army.

Their worst fears soon came true. In 1659 the Peninsulars attacked under Doman, the first indigenous chief who chose to resist colonial expansion. They destroyed most of the farms and carried off the bulk of the livestock. In April 1660 Van Riebeeck reported that peace had been concluded with the Peninsulars, although they had insisted that the Dutch had been appropriating 'more and more of their land, which had been theirs all these centuries.' When Van Riebeeck remarked that there was not enough grazing land for all, the Peninsulars asked: 'Have we then no reason to prevent you from getting cattle, since if you have a large number, you will take up all our grazing grounds for them?' They continued: 'As for your claim that the land is not big enough for both of us, who should rather in justice give way, the rightful owner or the foreign intruder?'[17]

Van Riebeeck, like his successors, had failed to develop a clear, consistent policy towards the Khoikhoi. His instructions were to treat the Khoikhoi with 'great gentleness.' If thefts by the Khoikhoi continued, hostages had to be taken and held at Robben Island, an island seven miles offshore that would be used as a prison for most of the next three centuries. Its most famous prisoner was Nelson Mandela.

As the tug-of-war over land, cattle and, especially, access to water dragged on, Van Riebeeck wrote that living in peace with the Khoikhoi was impossible, but killing them was 'barbarous and unchristian.'[18] As a compromise he considered enslaving the Peninsulars, but slavery would contravene the Company's specific instructions.

Many Khoikhoi retreated before the guns of European men on horseback. Some clans moved off deeper into the interior, deprived of access to rivers or springs. This was one of the main methods the burghers used to squeeze out those Khoikhoi who wished to remain independent. But it was not merely a fight over land and water that could be solved by partition. Many Khoikhoi and burghers had become dependent on each other. The farmers needed labor and the Khoikhoi food and grazing land for their few head of cattle. Some Khoikhoi became addicted to liquor and tobacco, which the Company supplied liberally. Many become part-time herdsmen on burghers' farms. While some Khoikhoi were kept against their will by threats, others remained on farms voluntarily. Van Riebeeck tried to mark out a border with a fence of poles and a bitter-almond hedge in the hope of separating the people of the peninsula from the indigenous people of the

17 Thom (ed.), *Journal of Van Riebeeck*, vol. 3, p. 197.
18 Böeseken, 'Die koms van die blankes', p. 31.

interior. But even by 1660 this attempt was futile. The settlement needed the Khoikhoi to come in to sell their cattle. A complex plural society was taking shape. Within the confines of the settlement there were already slaves, people of mixed racial origins and Khoikhoi who were beginning to embrace a new composite culture.

Growth pains

What set the Cape as a colony on a distinctive course was not the violence unleashed against native peoples – that was common to all European colonies – but that it preferred to get indigenous people to work for them instead of exterminating or expelling them.[19] The Khoikhoi, whose economy was compatible, could be easily incorporated.

Soon the settlement spun out of the Company's control. The Peninsulars had set themselves up as middlemen, forcing or persuading incoming Khoikhoi peoples to sell cattle to them and reselling them to the Company at a profit. Burghers also forced the Khoikhoi to sell their cattle to them, which they too offered to the Company at a much higher price. The price the Company paid for cattle trebled between 1652 and 1658. Although the government intermittently banned the cattle trade, its reach was not nearly far enough to stamp it out. It also could do little if burghers grazed their cattle beyond the limits of their plots. Van Riebeeck left the Cape in 1662 understanding that his original idea of an intensive settlement had failed. A large area he once thought could provide subsistence for thousands of families was considered fully occupied after a mere fifteen farms had been parceled out.

For seventeen years after Van Riebeeck's departure the settlement did not extend beyond the sandy plains skirting the peninsula, principally because of continued Khoikhoi resistance. Another war was waged between 1673 and 1677. When, by the end of the 1670s, the resistance crumbled, the Company decided to extend the settlement across the sandy plain. There were now 142 adult free burghers, half of them farmers.

Simon van der Stel, who arrived in 1679 as commander of the Cape settlement, was entrusted with the task of supervising the expansion. In the year of his arrival he founded the settlement of Stellenbosch some fifty kilometers away from the fort in Table Bay. Shortly afterwards the government built a *drostdy*, the seat of local government, appointed an official as *landdrost*, and four burghers as *heemraden* or councilors. The college of landdrost and heemraden administered the district, kept order and settled minor civil suits.

The land allocated to a farm was much larger than under Van Riebeeck, ranging from 32 to 64 hectares. While the government set no legal limits for the size of the farms in the Stellenbosch settlement, the farm had to be worked within the first three years. Failure to do so meant that the land reverted to the Company.

The same forces militating earlier against intensive agriculture operated here: though capital and labor were scarce, land was abundant. The greater distance from the market made it even more attractive to switch to extensive agriculture. When Van der Stel, by 1687, virtually terminated land allocations he considered the Stellenbosch area fully settled. Land suitable for arable agriculture was mostly used for grazing. Very much the

---

19 Elphick, *Kraal and Castle*, pp. 117-38, 235-9.

same pattern unfolded in Drakenstein (later called Paarl), French Hoek, Tygerberg, Wagenmakersvallei (Wellington), Swartland (Malmesbury) and the Land van Waveren (Tulbagh), all settled by the end of the first decade of the eighteenth century.

The burghers living near the Cape market kept up arable farming, producing mainly wheat, wine and vegetables, operating in a buyers' market that remained tilted in favor of the Company. Wheat had to be offered first to the Company at prices it fixed. The Company also had first claim on vegetables and fruit. It leased the wine trade to contractors, who had to supply wine to the Company at low prices. They had a monopoly to sell wine to the numerous taverns in the port city, which meant that farmers could not retail their own. The sale of meat was leased in a similar way.

With burghers instructed to sell their produce to the ships only three days after they had docked in Table Bay, large-scale smuggling of all kinds of products was the order of the day. The prospects for export were not bright. The quality of the wine generally was too poor to export in large volumes. The Company rejected appeals from the burghers to export their own produce in its own ships.

So limited were the general prospects for the farming burghers that a visiting commissioner said in 1676 that the 'Dutch colonists here bear the name of free men but they are so . . . restrained in everything that the absence of freedom is rendered only too evident.' If all the regulations had been strictly adhered to, the burghers would have been ruined.[20] Simon van der Stel, who did not show much sympathy with the farmers, once wrote that they were hard put to support themselves, 'having, generally speaking, come hither empty-handed, and being obliged to take up on credit from the Company . . . which must press heavily on them before they can get rid of it.'[21]

The free people in the town in Table Bay had somewhat better opportunities than the farmers. Most kept boarding houses, and they frequently circumvented the restrictions on selling Cape merchandise to passing sailors and on buying European goods. More than one top Company official expressed the desire to rid the Cape of the 'scum' and called taverns the 'beginning or mother of all scandalous practices.'[22] Yet farmers continually begged permission to move to the town that was expanding next to the fort and to practice a trade there. The government often refused such requests. It wanted the free people to farm instead and the farmers to produce what it needed and at low prices. Shortly after the first burghers had received their land, a high Company official had instructed them to attend above all to the cultivation of grain, adding that 'we shall never become noblemen here, until we shall first have been good farmers.'[23] Becoming noblemen remained a distant prospect. The farmers struggled to survive.

Keeping the settlement Dutch

In 1688 a party of some 180 French Huguenots arrived, fleeing religious persecution. Some had been more successful in their homeland than either the Dutch or German im-

20 Donald Moodie, *The Record* (Cape Town: Balkema, 1960), vol. 1, p. 340.
21 Moodie, *The Record*, vol. 1, p. 433.
22 Moodie, *The Record*, vol. 1, p. 304.
23 Moodie, *The Record*, vol. 1, p. 97.

migrants. So, for example, Jacques de Savoye had been a prosperous trader; Josua Celliers, Jacques de la Porte and Isaac Taillefert wine farmers; Jean Prieur du Plessis a physician; and Estienne Bruère a wagon-maker. François Guillaumet, who arrived from Berlin
much later, was a tailor who knew the silk industry well. But most were peasant farmers,
artisans or laborers.[24]

At the start of the Cape venture the Company had assumed that there was no question
that its servants would become or remain Dutch. The influx of the Huguenots prompted Van der Stel to stress the Dutch dimension of the burghers' identity. A veteran of the
Dutch-French war of the 1670s, he had no intention of allowing a French enclave to
take root at the Cape. Accordingly he settled most of them in French Hoek and Drakenstein (today's town of Paarl) and gave instructions that the French be interspersed with
the other burghers 'so that they could learn our language and morals, and be integrated
with the Dutch nation.'[25] When the French asked permission to establish a church congregation, he decried their 'impertinence', warning that they would soon want their own
'magistrate, Commander and Prince.'

The authorities in Amsterdam took a more lenient line, however, and permitted them
to form a congregation. In 1691 Drakenstein became the third congregation after the
Cape and Stellenbosch. In the late 1690s Van der Stel's son and successor as governor,
Willem Adriaan van der Stel, allowed the new minister to preach in French every second
week. In 1701 a tougher policy was imposed; the Lords Seventeen instructed Van der
Stel to take the necessary measures 'to ensure that the French language [would] gradually become extinct and disappear.' This policy of forced cultural assimilation was largely successful; by 1750 no one under the age of forty could still speak French.[26]

Of the male free burghers who lived at the Cape in the first fifty years only 8.5 per
cent came from France, compared to 40.4 per cent from the Netherlands, 32.3 per cent
from German-speaking territories, while 6.9 per cent were born at the Cape.[27] The Huguenots, nevertheless, did much to stabilize the free burgher population. Without a
fatherland to return to, they had to take root or disappear. Religious persecution had
made them more determined and more prepared to overcome obstacles. Descendants
of the Huguenots were to establish positions of leadership in Afrikaner society out of all
proportion to the numbers of the original immigrants.

The Huguenots made a difference in another important respect. Previously the shortage of European women prompted many men to take half-caste slaves as brides or mistresses. The Huguenots were generally already married, young as well as fecund. As the
girls in these large families grew up, men's stable liaisons with non-European women
declined and a clearer pattern of endogamy became established.

The German language, too, made its appearance on the Cape scene. But the Germans
were largely single males, spoke diverse dialects, and married either Dutch or French
women. The language of their children was Dutch, or what the German traveler Henry

24 C.G. de Wet, *Die vryliede en vryswartes in die Kaapse nedersetting* (Cape Town: Historiese Publikasie-
Vereniging, 1981), pp. 26, 44.
25 A.J. Böeseken, *Simon van der Stel en sy kinders* (Cape Town: Nasou, 1964), p. 95.
26 C.G. Botha, *Die Kaapse Hugenote* (Cape Town: Nasionale Pers, 1939), pp. 40-49.
27 De Wet, *Die vryliede en vryswartes in die Kaapse nedersetting*, p. 31.

Lichtenstein, early in the nineteenth century, called 'an abbreviated forcible [forceful] Afrikaans Dutch.'[28] The VOC made no effort to accommodate their religious sensibilities. Permission for a Lutheran Church was not granted until 1780, and, by then, the principle of one language and one church for the European community had become well established.

A fateful decision

Within ten years of the founding of the Cape station the fateful decision was made to import slaves. The Cape's first shiploads of slaves were imported from Angola and Dahomey in West Africa in 1658. Subsequently other sources were tapped. The Company sponsored voyages to Madagascar and later to Mozambique on the East African coast to purchase slaves. Slaves were brought from Batavia and Ceylon on the Company's annual return fleets, which sold most of the slaves to burghers. Foreign ships, including foreign slavers *en route* to the Americas, sold slaves that they had bought on the East African coast. An analysis of slave imports between 1680 and 1731 reveals that about half were of Malagasy origin, with Indonesia and India together contributing a third.[29]

Slavery fundamentally changed the course of the Cape's history. Unless a government banned slavery from the outset, as happened in Australia, the introduction of slavery in European colonies in this period was almost automatic if land was abundant and labor scarce. Freemen who owned land sought slaves to work for them.[30] Slavery transformed the social ethos of a society, defining freedom and the status hierarchy. High status belonged to those who were free, kept slaves and did not have to work with their hands. To be a servant doing manual work in the employ of someone else carried the connotation of slave status, which the burghers at the Cape did everything possible to avoid.[31]

When the first slaves arrived the Company instructed that the needs of free burghers were to be met first. Almost unobtrusively the institution of slavery took a grip on social and economic life. Within weeks Van Riebeeck issued a proclamation that revealed how much slavery debased everyone. Large numbers of slaves ran away at harvest time, and burghers were, therefore, allowed 'to put slaves in chains, except for some old men, young boys and women.'[32] A second proclamation said that no slave 'shall be bound to the whipping post and flogged by order of the fiscal upon complaint of his master, without the previous knowledge and consent of the Commander.'[33]

Not until 1716 did serious discussion take place on the question of slave labor. A letter by the Lords Seventeen posed the question whether the Cape should continue to import slaves or whether it should turn to the assisted immigration of free, European laborers, who could go on to become overseers and artisans and, ultimately, even farm-

---

28 Cited by Stanley Trapido, 'Van Riebeeck Day and the New Jerusalem,' unpublished paper, 1993.

29 James Armstrong and Nigel Worden, 'The Slaves, 1652-1834', *SSAS*, pp. 110-21.

30 R.C.-H. Shell, *Children of Bondage: A Social History of the Slave Society at the Cape of Good Hope, 1652-1838* (Johannesburg: Witwatersrand University Press, 1994, pp. 1-3.

31 James Armstrong, 'The Slaves, 1652-1795', *SSAS* (1), p. 98.

32 A.J. Böeseken, 'Die Kompanjie aan die Kaap, 1652-1795', in A.J.H. van der Walt, et al. (eds.), *Geskiedenis van Suid-Afrika* (Cape Town: Nasionale Boekhandel, 1954), vol. 1, p. 156.

33 Moodie, *The Record*, vol. 1, p. 398.

ers. In the debate in the Council of Policy, Councilor D.M. Pasques de Chavonnes raised a lone voice against basing the colony on slave labor. Understanding the disastrous social consequences of slavery, he proposed the sponsored immigration of European wage laborers, who would work on farms until able to set up on their own. As free laborers they would boost the domestic market and colonial prosperity, and, equally important, they would improve the security of the colony since no one would have to keep a watchful eye on the slaves.[34]

The rest of the Council, however, had no stomach for a class of free European laborers who, in the words of the secretary, would 'have little respect for their master and [would] lay down the law for him.' Predicting that more immigrants would simply increase the number of poor burghers, the Council recommended the importation of slaves as the cheapest and most desirable option.[35]

In 1750 the Lords Seventeen again asked the Cape government to investigate the feasibility of assisted European immigration. The government considered it important enough to consult the burgher councilors on the Council of Justice and the burghers who served as heemraden in the interior districts. These spokesmen for the burghers said that it was 'absolutely impossible' to have a flow of immigrants into the colony. If anything, it would 'bring ruin upon the Cape, and merely add to the very serious state of poverty which already exists.'[36]

The die was cast. The colony would not be able to grow out of its economic straitjacket by enlarging the market through a steady increase of cash-earning wage laborers. The burghers also saw little need for European immigrants to supplement their numbers and assist them in building a European colony. Slave labor satisfied most of the labor needs of the western Cape. The burghers were defining their survival not in terms of a large self-sufficient European society but in their ability to ensure that the land and other opportunities were reserved for them and their children.

The rise of a complex society: the influences of Europe

The incorporation of slaves and Khoikhoi as the labor force meant that the Cape from the start was a multi-racial society in which Europeans set the tone. In relation to peoples elsewhere in the world, early modern Europeans considered themselves 'the center of mankind and the measure of humanity.' [37] The great European colonial expansion provided the context in which interaction with Others served to crystallize the Europeans' sense of the Self. At the core of this lay a sense of being heirs to and beneficiaries of a superior civilization and religion. Charles Boxer, a historian with a sound comparative grasp of the European colonial empires, concluded: 'Portuguese, Spaniards, Dutch, English and French were nearly all convinced that a Christian European was *ipso facto*

---

34 Shell, *Children of Bondage*, p. 4.

35 *Reports of De Chavonnes and His Council, and of Van Imhoff on the Cape* (Cape Town: VRS, 1918), vol. 1, p. 105.

36 *Reports of De Chavonnes*, p. 150.

37 Ernst van den Boogaart, 'Colour Prejudice and the Yardstick of Civility: The Initial Dutch Confrontation with Black Christians, 1590-1635', in Robert Ross (ed.), *Racism and Colonialism: Essays in Ideology and Social Structure* (Leiden: Marthinus Nijhoff, 1982), p. 45.

superior to members of another race.'[38] He made another statement that deserves to be quoted: 'One race cannot systematically enslave members of another race without acquiring a conscious or unconscious feeling of racial superiority.'[39]

But race as a biological concept did not appear in South Africa before the late nineteenth century. Before then, the term 'race' was used loosely, and often corresponded with the term 'nation', of which the basic element was considered to be culture. Yet seventeenth-century Europeans made more than a passing note of differences in color that corresponded with differences in culture. To seventeenth-century Dutchmen blackness was the opposite of what they considered normal, beautiful, and attractive. This attitude toward color was reinforced by the cultural superiority Christians felt towards heathens. Yet negative views were not restricted to people of color. In Shakespearean England, stereotypes about blacks as sinful, lustful and murderous abounded, but the same negative imagery was also applied to Jews, 'sodomites' and other groups.

Noah's curse on Canaan, the son of Ham, which would become a central justification for racial slavery and servitude, had an ambiguous history. Writers justifying servitude in medieval and early modern Europe referred to Ham as the progenitor of the unfree. The concept also encompassed the serfs of northern Europe, who were described as 'filthy and beastly.' There was also another image of the generation of Ham – that of powerful seducers brimming with sexuality. During the seventeenth century Europeans attempting to justify African slavery began to associate Ham with blacks and Africans. Eighteenth-century thought tended to fuse the images of Ham as slaves and as seducers lusting for white women.[40]

To the Dutch in the early modern period it was the supposed savagery of Africans that defined them. They were deemed to be godless and licentious heathens: people fundamentally different from Europeans.[41] Noah's curse made its way to the Cape too, but here it was not invariably used negatively. In 1703 the church council of Drakenstein declared that it wished to convert the Khoikhoi so that these 'children of Ham' would no longer remain in their heathen bondage. More hostile was a letter of 1707 from some Stellenbosch burghers, who referred dismissively to free blacks as the 'blood of Ham.'[42]

The rise of a complex society: influences of the East

The Cape burghers did not only experience European influences in making up their minds how to deal with people who were not Europeans. An influence that in many ways ran counter to the European one was the policies and practices that developed in the Dutch East Indies from the beginning of the seventeenth century.[43] Ceylon and Batavia

---

38 Charles Boxer, *The Dutch Seaborne Empire* (London: Hutchinson, 1965), p. 233.

39 Charles Boxer, *Race Relations in the Portuguese Colonial Empire* (Oxford: Oxford University Press, 1963), p. 56.

40 For a survey of recent research, see *William and Mary Quarterly*, vol. 54, no. 1 (1997), particularly the overview by David Brion Davis.

41 Van den Boogaart, 'Colour Prejudice and the Yardstick of Civility', p. 54.

42 C. Spoelstra, *Bouwstoffen voor de geschiedenis van de Nederduitsch Gereformeerde Kerk in Zuid-Afrika* (Amsterdam: HAUM, 1906-07), vol. 1, p. 34, vol. 2, p. 15.

43 Pauline Dublin Milone, '*Indische* Culture and Its Relationship to Urban Life', *Comparative Studies in Society and History*, vol. 9 (1967), pp. 407-26.

were the only two places apart from the Cape where the Company managed to put down some roots. The Company only needed a small free burgher population, operating in the interstices of the economy. There were some sixty-eight married burghers in Ceylon in 1650 and 340 in Batavia (Java) in 1674. Retailers of wine and publicans formed the largest group; most of the rest were artisans. As the historian Charles Boxer remarks, they were in every respect 'less advantageously placed than the Company's officials, not excepting indulgence in smuggling and private trade.'[44]

In view of the shortage of European women in the East it was common for Dutchmen to form relationships with Eurasians or 'Indos.' Free burghers in the East could marry Eastern women, but most liaisons were outside wedlock. The children were brought up as Christians and, legally and socially, they and their mothers were considered part of the European community; and indeed were called Europeans. Simon van der Stel himself was the product of such an intermixture. His mother, Maria Lievens, was born in Batavia, the daughter of a Dutch sea captain and Monica da Costa, an indigenous woman from the East.

The European men in the East devoted serious attention to status and ceremony in an effort to emulate the status of the Indonesian aristocracy. Senior officials were ready to display their status ostentatiously as in a grand mansion, a retinue of servants, a parasol carried by a servant, and festive house parties with dancing on the veranda to music supplied by a slave orchestra. Almost everyone with some pretensions to status keenly aspired to the role of a slave-owner who abstained from manual labor.

The Cape would acquire many of the characteristics of Batavia: the power that the officials wielded, the strict Company etiquette, the impotence of the church as an institution, the defective education, the conspicuous consumption, the dependence on slave labor, the use of Malay and Portuguese as *lingua franca* in the early decades, and the introduction of the office of fiscal to maintain law and order.[45] Also transmitted were the subtler influences, which Pauline Milone described in her study of the composite culture of Batavia as 'the pace-of-life, graces, aristocratic attitudes, and arrogated privileges of Indonesian civilization mixed with some of the material uses, technology, fashions and Christianity of European society.' These were imported by senior Company servants who had earlier served in the East, and by Eastern slaves, who made up an important part of the Cape Town slave population. During the first eighty years of the settlement, when European women were in short supply, many European men married manumitted slaves from the East.

As in the East, the top Company officials at the Cape, followed by the wealthiest burghers, set the tone in the development of a new composite culture. They clung tenaciously to their rank and right of precedence. Rank determined seats in church and at public functions, and places in funeral processions. The sumptuary laws of 1755 prescribed in detail, according to rank, which category of person could, for example, use an open large umbrella, how many horses could pull a carriage, and the uniforms of the coachman and footman.[46] As in Indonesia, rearing European children at the Cape would

---

44 For a general discussion see Schoeman, *Armosyn*, pp. 153-80, the quote is on p. 165.

45 Schoeman, *Armosyn*, p. 176-7.

46 Robert Ross, *Status and Respectability in the Cape Colony, 1750-1870* (Cambridge: Cambridge University Press, 1999), pp. 9-30.

be left almost entirely to female slaves. These slaves contributed greatly to the local culture through their dress, household remedies and food preparation.

Like the upper-rank people in the port city, the wealthier people in Stellenbosch displayed their own position of power and status. Reflecting on life in Stellenbosch at the beginning of the nineteenth century, Borcherds wrote that the large landed and other property-owners were 'tenacious of rank and ambitious to be elected as heemraden, or militia officers or church wardens – offices which then conferred dignity.' In church they had their own pews and the wives were seated according to the rank of the husband. If anyone deviated from this there was 'a sensation . . . and [it] provoked a rebuke.'[47] The further one went into the interior the less significant these differences became, and the more ridiculous the rituals that accompanied them.

The Company's legal administrative structure at the Cape was also taken over from its possessions in the East. This structure was color-free, based on legal status groups: Company servants, burghers, and slaves. (Khoikhoi, considered 'aliens', did not at first fall under the colonial law.) These distinctions, along with the identities of Christian and heathen, exerted the single most important influence on the way in which people in the Company's possessions thought about their status in life.

Besides these legal status groups there was also the important intermediate category of free blacks. They had moved out of the slave category to become free persons through one of two types of manumission processes. The first was *manumission censo* in Roman law, by which the freed slave ended up registered in the census as a free citizen – or a burgher, in Cape parlance. In the second the slave was assigned to another category in Roman law, that of someone regarded as a freed person, but not a full citizen. Most freed slaves at the Cape fell into the second category.[48] The term 'free black' was both a racial and a legal term.

Class and color: flux and friction

Between 1705 and 1707 the Cape was in the grip of a political crisis when the burghers vociferously protested against the farming activities of Governor Willem Adriaan van der Stel and certain other high officials. The events are described in the next chapter and here we note only the color and class tensions it exposed at a time when the colony's population was still small. At this stage the population (excluding Khoikhoi servants, who were not enumerated) was approaching four thousand.[49] It was made up as follows.

CAPE POPULATION 1706

	Company servants	Burghers
Males	542	568
Family	104	1,151
Slaves	404	991

47 P.B. Borcherds, *An Autobiographical Memoir* (1861, repr. Cape Town: African Connoisseurs Press, 1963), p. 205.
48 Shell, *Children of Bondage*, pp. 373-4.
49 Shell, *Children of Bondage*, p. 153.

To be able to control the slaves the Company servants and the burghers, as the two dominant status groups, had to stand together. That the Stellenbosch burghers were at loggerheads with the senior officials did not escape the notice of the slaves. With many burghers under arrest, some of the slaves, according to Landdrost Starrenburg of Stellenbosch, began to behave as if they were 'princes of the blood.'[50]

Both Willem Adriaan van der Stel and his father, Simon, were known to have had good relations with their Khoikhoi servants and their slaves, and with the free blacks, who totaled about sixty, with two-thirds living in the Cape district. They baptized and manumitted more slaves than anyone else. Free blacks in the town who made a living from fishing and vegetable farming supported Willem Adriaan van der Stel in the conflict with the burghers.[51]

As would happen so often later, the burghers were quick to suspect the government of undermining their position in order to protect and win the support of the subordinate population. In response, the burghers expressed their interests as part of a general concern about European survival in the colony. In a letter to the Lords Seventeen Adam Tas and some other leading Stellenbosch farmers voiced the concern that the Khoikhoi might seize upon the divisions between farmers and officials 'to annihilate all Christians, bad as well as good.'[52] The farmers also claimed that Van der Stel was constantly favoring the 'swart volkje' (the black populace) over its 'Christian' subjects, probably enraged by the fact that Van der Stel, in his campaign for signatures for his defense, had entertained free blacks and other colored people, along with Cape Town burghers, with wine, beer, coffee and tobacco. Tas and the Stellenbosch farmers wrote that they feared the

> Kaffirs, Mulattoes, Mestiços and Castiços and all that black brood living among us, who have been bred from marriages and other forms of mingling with European and African Christians. To our amazement they have so grown in power, numbers and arrogance and have been allowed to handle arms and participate with Christians in . . . military exercises, that they now tell us that they could and would trample us . . . For there is no trusting the blood of Ham, especially as the black people are constantly being favored and pushed forward.[53]

The terms used in the letter were all taken from social hierarchies elsewhere. 'Kaffir' (also 'kafir' or 'caffre') was a name Arab Muslims used for pagan Africans, originally meaning 'non-believer' or heathen. Dutch-speakers first widely used the term in Batavia where slaves from Angola or Mozambique served as the personnel of the fiscal, the chief prosecuting officer. At the Cape, slaves from both the East and Africa functioned in the same capacity and were known as kafirs or kaffers. As people who imposed a rough order in the streets and arrested suspects, they were particularly hated and despised. Towards the end of the eighteenth century, both government officials and burghers began using the term for the Xhosa people in the east, the first Bantu-speaking people the Europeans encountered.

---

50 Böeseken, *Simon van der Stel en sy kinders*, p. 197.
51 Personal communication, Robert Shell, 21 October 1996.
52 Böeseken, *Simon van der Stel en sy kinders*, p. 183.
53 Hermann Giliomee and Richard Elphick, 'The Structure of European Domination at the Cape, 1652-1840', in *SSAS*, p. 542.

The terms '*mulatto*', '*mestiço*' and '*castiço*' were Portuguese, widely used in Portuguese colonies in South America by Europeans, unlike their counterparts in North America, to describe people of mixed origin between the dominant white and subordinate black population. These terms denoted both a racial consciousness and the rejection of racial mixture. The term '*mulatto*' is derived from 'mule', implying a cross between different biological species. In the case of human beings it referred to a mixture of a European and an African. *Mestizos* (the Spanish equivalent of *mestiços*) were the products of un-sanctioned unions between Spaniards and Indians and between Indians and Negroes.

Although there was a correspondence between legal status, color and religious iden-tity, there was no rigid racial division, particularly during the first seventy-five years of Company rule. People of mixed racial origins were prominent both as burghers and free blacks and did not appear to suffer any *racial* discrimination.

The frequency of racial mixing was due in the first place to the huge gender imbal-ance in the white population. By 1700 there were in the Cape district twice as many men as women in the adult burgher population, and, in the interior, the ratio was three to one. Marriages between white men and fair-skinned non-white women were common during the first seventy-five years. Many stable mixed liaisons occurred outside wed-lock, and there was also large-scale sex miscegenation in the form of casual sex, especial-ly in the slave lodge frequented by local European men as well as sailors and soldiers.

J.A. Heese, a genealogical researcher, has estimated that seven per cent of Afrikaner families have a non-European *stammoeder* or progenitress.[54] During the early years the situation was fluid enough for some children born from unions of non-Europeans parents to be accepted into the European community. There were two particularly strik-ing cases. The slave Armosyn Claasz was born in 1661 at the Cape. Her mother was pre-sumably a slave from the west coast of Africa, the identity of her father unknown. She gave birth to the children of four different fathers in the Company's slave lodge, some de-scribed as *halfslag* (half-caste), which means that the father was white. Many of these children and their descendants were absorbed in what became prominent Afrikaner fami-lies, like the Volschenk, Coorts, Du Plessis, Pretorius, Horn, Myburgh and Esterhuyzen families.

The other case relates to the liaison between Louis of Bengal and Lysbeth van de Caab, both considered non-European. Three daughters were born out of this liaison, and Lys-beth had two daughters from another relationship with a European. All the children entered into relationships, either marital or extramarital, with Europeans, and most of their descendants were absorbed into the Afrikaner community of today. The families most directly involved were the Brits, Van Deventer, Slabbert, Fischer, and Carstens fami-lies.[55]

Genealogies include a few instances of European women marrying non- Europeans. The most striking case was that of Marguerite de Savoye, the daughter of Huguenot parents, who in 1690 married Christoffel Snyman, who according to oral tradition made

---

54 J.A. Heese, *Die herkoms van die Afrikaner* (Cape Town: Balkema, 1971).
55 H.F. Heese, *Groep sonder grense: die rol en status van die gemengde bevolking aan die Kaap, 1652-1795* (Bell-ville: University of the Western Cape Institute for Historical Research, 1984); J.L. Hattingh, 'Die blanke nageslag van Louis van Bengale en Lijsbeth van de Kaap', *Kronos*, 3 (1980), pp. 5-51.

a living from pruning vineyards. He was the son of Anthony of Bengal and a similarly non-white mother. The well-known Snyman family is descended from them. Another case was that of Maria Roos, who, in 1794 married David Simon Hoon, the son of a slave from Madagascar and his wife, Rachael, of Indian descent. Other 'colored' males entered 'white' society, including the progenitors of the Antonissen, Jonker, Jacobs and Serfontein families.[56]

During his 1685 visit to the Cape, High Commissioner Van Rheede prohibited marriages between Europeans and *heelslag* or full-blooded slave women (that is, of pure Asian or African origin). He did, however, permit marriages with halfslag women with the intention of assimilating such half-castes into the European population. The ban was never enforced.

Whites themselves were far from being consolidated in a dense social bloc. Between 1657 and 1707 a total of 1,613 free adult men lived at the Cape. Of these approximately a third were farmers and a quarter were *knechten*, or foremen. People of wealth and power often saw knechten in an unfavorable light and sometimes even as dangerous. A regulation prohibited anyone from inciting a knecht against his master. On the farms knechten addressed their employers as '*baas*' ('boss') and lived in outbuildings. In a few cases they worked for free blacks and, initially, there were free blacks, too, among the knechten. Slaves on occasion could be found drinking and playing cards with knechten, poor burghers and indigent soldiers or sailors.

A European knecht could become free and advance in the world. Pieter Visagie and Willem Schalk van der Merwe were knechten who later became independent farmers and the progenitors of well-known Afrikaner families. In the final decades of the seventeenth century Henning Hüsing rose from the position of knecht to that of the richest man in the colony.[57]

These cases were exceptional. Towards the end of the century slaves were beginning to squeeze out the knechten in the western Cape, first from the pool of manual labor and then from that of overseers of labor. In the eighteenth century some knechten on leave from the Company became teachers on farms in the deeper interior, their status humble and their pay extremely modest. If a knecht did not have the good fortune to marry a farmer's widow, he was more than likely to join the community of destitute whites, riddled with debt and dependent on the church for alms.[58] In Cape Town some had relations with free black or slave women, on the frontier some with Khoisan women. Children from these liaisons were not normally absorbed into the dominant group.

In dealing with the settlement the Company was largely devoid of idealistic motives. Its primary purpose was to achieve a return for its shareholders. But the Company's obsession with profits did not mean it was indifferent to issues like Dutch culture and the moral welfare of its subjects. In both the church and school the Reformed faith and the Dutch language had to be taught. When the first slaves were imported, it issued firm instructions that only Dutch was to be spoken to them. Slaves could not be manumitted without being able to speak and write Dutch. When an official drew up a glossary of

---

56 Heese, *Groep sonder grense*, pp. 6, 20-21, 41, 45, 53, 54.
57 De Wet, *Die vryliede en vryswartes in die Kaapse nedersetting*, pp. 100-2.
58 Shell, *Children of Bondage*, pp. 18-20.

Khoikhoi words, the Company undertook to publish it, but added that it was more important that the Khoikhoi learn the Dutch language than the other way round.[59]

To care for the spiritual welfare of the burghers, the Company appointed ministers, sick-comforters and teachers. Fearing that the burghers might become dissolute, it supported the ministers in their efforts to improve the poor church attendance that was characteristic of the first hundred or more years. The insistence of the church on people's ability to read and write before they could be confirmed would, in the eighteenth and nineteenth centuries, become an important spur for burghers to obtain some rudimentary education.

A sprawling settlement

The final decade of the seventeenth century was a golden period for the smaller farmers in the western Cape. There was enough unoccupied land for their use and they could employ Khoikhoi cheaply to work the land alongside members of their families. The return on capital of the poorer farmers was considerably higher than that of richer farmers, who could afford slave labor.

In the first two decades of the eighteenth century matters deteriorated for the smaller farmers. They lost much of their labor force when the western Cape Khoikhoi were decimated in the smallpox epidemic of 1713. The poorer farmers could seldom afford more than one slave. The market was also detrimentally affected by the fact that a growing part of the population was made up of slaves, with little or no income of their own. Large estates began to swallow up smaller farms.

By 1710 the government considered most of the coastal plain west of the first mountain range to be fully settled. In 1717, by which time some four hundred farms had been given out in freehold property, the government terminated all such allocations. A small free population had extended itself over a large area. In the denser settled areas of Stellenbosch and Drakenstein there were only two free people for every 2.6 square kilometers, too few people to support a proper road network. The poor roads further weakened the incentive to practice intensive farming.

By the second decade of the eighteenth century the Cape market had begun to overproduce. The shift towards cattle farming, which had begun early, was now well advanced. From the 1680s on the Cape was self-sufficient in grain even though only a third of the farmers still produced it. The section of the farming population that could be considered prosperous by 1710 could be put at about seven per cent of the free population. At the other end of the spectrum were those who were desperately poor. In 1705 about two-fifths of all households reported no assets whatsoever.[60] Farmers were clamoring for licenses to graze their cattle beyond the limits of their farms.[61] Simon van der Stel had a premonition of what this development would mean. If the burghers were

---

59 Elphick, *Kraal and Castle,* pp. 206-11.

60 Leonard Guelke and Robert Shell, 'An Early Colonial Landed Gentry: Land and Wealth in the Cape Colony, 1682-1731', *Journal of Historical Geography,* vol. 9, no. 3 (1983), pp. 270-74.

61 Guelke, 'Freehold Farmers, 1657-1780', pp. 69-73.

given a free hand to pursue cattle farming on an extensive scale, he wrote, 'all of Africa would not be enough to suit and satisfy this class of people.'[62]

Early in the eighteenth century the government abandoned control over the outlying areas. In 1703 the ban on burghers grazing their stock further than a day's journey from their freehold properties was reversed. The government now began to issue grazing permits and extended this in 1714, after which it became known as the loan farm system. As Chapter Three notes, this system of landholding would encourage dispersal and limit the government's ability to control its subjects. As the burghers moved deeper into the interior, they developed a strong sense of self-reliance and independence.

A special kind of burgher

The ultimate fate of roughly one-third of the first 1,613 free burghers who lived at the Cape during the settlement's first fifty years is known. Of the 570, more than half remained free burghers, thirty were banished, thirty-nine were taken back into Company service, seventy stowed away in passing ships, and 103 received legal permission to leave.[63] The burghers' identity was drawn from three sources: their European descent closely linked to their Christian faith, their burgher status and the Dutch language. The farming burgher had become a special kind of burgher, who, unlike his counterpart in the town, worked for something more than his immediate interests. They had become defenders of the land against internal enemies, along with being the indispensable producers of food.

But indispensable as they were, their survival depended on the government respecting their rights and privileges. They would suffer a crushing blow if a small but powerful group of Company servants decided to supply the market themselves. Such a blow came early in the eighteenth century.

---

62 A.J. Böeseken (ed.), *Memoriën en instructiën, 1652-1699* (Cape Town: SA Archives Commission, 1966), vol. 1, p. 230.
63 De Wet, *Die vryliede en vryswartes in die Kaapse nedersetting*, pp. 28, 196.

Chapter 2

Company Burghers

Hendrik Biebouw, the first Afrikaner?

One day in March 1707, the landdrost of the small town Stellenbosch, Johannes Starrenburg, found four young men racing on horseback 'like madmen.' After causing havoc, the four proceeded, in a drunken state, to the Company mill and, with 'many curses', they tossed the scales around. When the landdrost rebuked them, hitting a seventeen-year-old youth with his cane and ordering him to leave, Hendrik Biebouw shouted: 'I shall not leave, I am an Afrikaander, even if the landdrost beats me to death or puts me in jail. I shall not, nor will be silent.' ('. . . *ik wil niet loopen, ik ben een Afrikaander, al slaat die landrost mijn dood, of al setten hij mijn in den tronk, ik sal, nog wil niet swygen.*')[1]

The landdrost did put him and the others in jail, and, in a letter to the government in Cape Town, urged that the four be banished. The Cape could not tolerate those who lived 'a debauched and irregular life.'[2] A government resolution on the books provided that idle, single men might be taken back into the Company's service and be shipped abroad as soldiers. Soldiers publicly thrashed three of the young men a month later. A year later, Biebouw's name was deleted from the Stellenbosch census lists with the annotation 'gone.' One account said that he had been sent to Batavia, but was shipwrecked north of Perth and ended up in Australia.[3]

At the beginning of the eighteenth century 'Afrikaner' was applied to indigenous people or to the offspring of 'natives' and slaves or free blacks. Biebouw's public protest in Stellenbosch is the first recorded occasion of a European using 'Afrikaner' as a name for

---

1 For an account and interpretation, see J.M.L. Franken, 'Hendrik Bibault of die opkoms van 'n volk', *Die Huisgenoot,* 21 September 1928, pp. 9-13. For a critical analysis of this interpretation, see André du Toit, 'Hendrik Bibault of die raaisel van prof. J.M.L. Franken', in H.C. Bredekamp (ed.), *Afrikaanse geskiedskrywing en letterkunde* (Bellville: University of the Western Cape, 1992), pp. 1-20.

2 A.J. Böeseken, *Simon van der Stel en sy kinders* (Cape Town: Nasou, 1964), p. 201.

3 There is a theory that Biebouw was responsible for the transmission of the disease *Porphyria variegata* to some aboriginal families. I am indebted to Karel Schoeman for access, prior to publication, to material which has since appeared in the second volume of his study, *Armosyn van die Kaap: Die wêreld van 'n slavin.* For the porphyria theory, see the discussion by Pieter Bol of Geoffrey Dean's work on the disease in the Dutch paper *NRC Handelsblad,* 10 January 1998.

himself. In 1708 the Reverend E.F. le Boucq spoke of the danger that 'the Africaanders will fall to the level of Hottentotdom.'[4] And in 1712 an official document on the conflict between Van der Stel and the burghers used the term 'Africaan' to distinguish among Europeans according to their place of birth. The document refers to a manhunt for 'three Dutchmen, three French refugees and three Africanen.'[5] For Biebouw to use the name Afrikaander for himself and for the Company to designate whites as Africanen was strange.

There are opposing explanations of Biebouw's defiant shout 'I am an Afrikaander!' F.A. van Jaarsveld, a prolific Afrikaner historian, considered Biebouw's response to the question: 'Who am I?' to be as significant as De Crèvecœur's famous question about identity posed in 1783: 'What, then, is the American, this new man?'[6] Others have dismissed the incident, pointing to the context in which the words were uttered, and to Biebouw's background. His father was a German *chirurgijn* (a post below that of medical doctor), who could only sign his name with a cross and was according to all accounts very poor. A liaison with a black woman had resulted in the birth of a daughter before he married Hendrik's mother, a Dutch orphan who had come to the Cape. Far from being an ethnic nationalist, therefore, Biebouw, with his German father, Dutch mother and black half-sister, was perhaps more confused than anyone else about his identity. He called himself an Afrikaner, but was the term more than merely descriptive? Did he only want to indicate that he was a native of Africa (in contrast with natives of Europe), or did he imply that Afrikaners of European descent had rights and enjoyed a status that Landdrost Starrenburg, an immigrant, ought not to ignore? Historians cannot answer these questions with any degree of precision. What they can agree on was that the rowdy behavior reported from Stellenbosch during the first decade of the century was symptomatic of the increasing strains colonial society was experiencing.

A struggle against officials

In 1657, when the first free burghers began farming, the Company issued firm instructions that officials were not to supply the market with food since the burghers, who depended on food production, would otherwise be unable to survive. If a handful of officials – or a coterie of officials and wealthy burghers – cornered the market, the ordinary burgher's link with Cape Town and the small towns would have been cut, and the burgher-dominated system of local administration and defense might have disintegrated.

There would have been no trouble if the Company had consistently applied its policy that officials could hold only enough land for a vegetable garden. But, in 1685, as an exception, Simon van der Stel received the farm Constantia (later Groot Constantia). A few years later his son Willem Adriaan van der Stel, who succeeded his father as governor, was allocated Vergelegen, at the foot of the Hottentots-Holland mountains. Other land was granted to several high officials and the governor's brother, a free burgher.

---

4 C. Spoelstra, *Bouwstoffen voor de geschiedenis der Nederduitsch Gereformeerde Kerken in Zuid-Afrika* (Amsterdam: HAUM, 1906), vol. 1, p. 166.
5 Franken, 'Hendrik Bibault', p. 9.
6 F.A. van Jaarsveld, *Wie en wat is die Afrikaner?* (Cape Town: Tafelberg, 1981), pp. 6-7.

By 1705 land covering a third of the farming area of the colony was in the hands of twenty Company officials. Vergelegen, Willem Adriaan van der Stel's farm, had been developed in the grand style of European estates. The size of ten ordinary farms, it employed two hundred slaves and sixty white *knechten*, or overseers. Soon burgher society was abuzz with rumors about an opulent lifestyle, and about graft, nepotism, and bribery. A comment captured the burghers' envious disapproval of the clique of officials: '[They were] drunk from luxury, desire and frantic pride.'[7]

The governor had set in motion a plan to give him and his agents a monopoly in the sale of wine, meat, fish and wheat. Willem Adriaan van der Stel himself produced a fifth of the total wheat crop, and, along with members of his family, all the wine needed by the wine lessee, who held a monopoly for the product. In addition he owned some eighteen thousand sheep and a thousand head of cattle, which could supply all the meat needed by arriving ships, the hospital, and the Company. Some officials boasted openly that within three or four years there would be no need for free burghers; four or five officials could supply the Cape 'with all things.'[8]

In the face of this aggrandizement the wealthier farmers felt the most threatened.[9] Their leader, Henning Hüsing, the richest man in the colony, long a holder of government meat contracts, had earned the label of the governor's 'chiefest crony.'[10] One of Hüsing's closest allies, Jacob van der Heyden, also had a meat contract. He financed a bartering expedition with the inland Khoikhoi that degenerated into a cattle raid. The government banned future expeditions and ended the contract. Rumors circulated that it was a ruse to let the governor reserve the cattle trade for himself and steer the meat contract towards his friends.

To a considerable extent, then, this was a feud between two sets of elites who had fallen out in a fight over the spoils. But even Van der Stel recognized that there was a clear difference between the top officials, who rarely stayed long, and his adversaries, 'who knew no other fatherland.'[11] He called his adversaries '*boeren*' (farmers), sometimes spelled with a capital as if it denoted a political rather than a class category. '*Boeren*' would be a common term for rural Afrikaners in particular until the early twentieth century.[12]

On the burgher side, Adam Tas, who had married a wealthy niece of Hüsing's wife, played a key role. While most burghers were of poor origins and either illiterate or barely literate, he had been born into the Dutch middle class and had received a good education in the Netherlands before settling at the Cape. Tas drafted a petition to the authorities in Batavia, accusing the Cape officials of misconduct. Some burghers supported Tas's petition because they thought it was in the interests of all the burghers regardless of national origin. They feared that, as the 71-year-old Huguenot Jacques de Savoye phrased it, 'the Cape was going to ruin.'[13] Another Huguenot who signed the petition, Guillaume du

---

7 Böeseken, *Van der Stel en sy kinders*, p. 182.

8 Leo Fouché (ed.), *The Diary of Adam Tas* (Cape Town: VRS, 1970), p. 365.

9 Leonard Guelke and Robert Shell, 'An Early Colonial Landed Gentry: Land and Wealth in the Cape Colony, 1682-1731', *Journal of Historical Geography*, vol. 9, no. 3 (1983), p. 271.

10 Fouché (ed.), *The Diary of Adam Tas*, p. 245.

11 P.J. van der Merwe, *Trek* (Cape Town: Nasionale Pers, 1945), p. 88.

12 Fouché (ed.), *The Diary of Adam Tas*, p. 391.

13 Böeseken, *Simon van der Stel en sy kinders*, p. 195.

Toit, told the governor that he did so for the 'whole community', motivated by 'love of his people.' In his diary, Tas expressed the hope 'that there were many patriots like him.'[14] Half who signed were burghers from the Huguenot community, who had arrived twenty years earlier and were not yet fully integrated into the burgher community.

From the Batavian authorities Tas' petition went to the Company's headquarters in Amsterdam, then to the Cape with the demand that the officials explain their conduct. The officials were outraged; they tended to consider themselves the Company's 'legitimate children' and the burghers as 'illegitimate bastards' without legal rights.[15] Van der Stel, a member of the privileged class of regents in Holland, remembered how the Amsterdam regents had dealt years before with rioters and rebels: they had hanged them from a window. It was said that this was how Van der Stel intended to take care of his own adversaries. He had several burghers arrested. Tas, and some ringleaders, were locked up in the 'Dark Hole' in the Castle (the seat of government) to be kept there until they had provided satisfactory answers to the court. Tas held out for a month, Van der Heyden for even longer, and another detainee for four and a half months. The governor deported Hüsing and three others to the Netherlands and a court sentenced nine others to be deported to the VOC colony in Mauritius.

To orchestrate some mass support the governor entertained the town burghers and some free blacks at the Castle before asking them to sign a petition that sung his praises. Many, including some free blacks, obliged. But, by now, the colony was in turmoil, while in Amsterdam Hüsing and his associates were hard at work lobbying against the Cape officials. Stellenbosch was the heart of local resistance, yet the Landdrost Starrenburg had collected signatures for Van der Stel, apparently oblivious of the fact that the farm Van der Stel had given him compromised his position. A learned and well-read man from Germany, who read Cicero, Cassius and Grotius, Starrenburg was deeply disturbed by the anarchy and the open contempt the burghers were displaying toward the government and toward him personally. It was from Grotius that he quoted when he wrote in a letter to the governor: 'One must wage war against those who cannot be restrained by laws.' He was most upset by a demonstration in 1706 in the town of Stellenbosch where some burghers danced around him, vowing that they would not abandon the struggle. He took refuge in his house, where he wrote to Van der Stel: '[The] women are as dangerous as the men and do not keep quiet.'[16]

Six months later the Cape received the dramatic news that the Lords Seventeen in Amsterdam were recalling Van der Stel and certain officials, including Starrenburg himself. They forbade all officials to own land or trade on the Cape market and they had to dispose of all their landholdings.

It was a resounding burgher victory. A coalition of burghers had defeated the officials and had entrenched their role as the sole suppliers of food. It was in these circumstances that young Biebouw and his friends, who lived on the periphery of burgher society, staged their drunken celebration on horseback in the hamlet of Stellenbosch. It would

---

14 Fouché (ed.), *The Diary of Adam Tas*, p. 390.
15 Fouché (ed.), *The Diary of Adam Tas*, p. 239.
16 G.D. Scholtz, *Die ontwikkeling van die politieke denke van die Afrikaners* (Johannesburg: Voortrekkerpers, 1967), vol. 1, p. 241.

have gone unnoticed by history but for Biebouw's identification of himself as an Afrikaner, at least eighty years before the burghers began to use the term widely for themselves.

The burghers' victory over the officials helped to calm things down. So did the introduction in 1713 of the loan farm system, which made it possible for burghers to settle beyond the first mountain ranges. A large part of the 'surplus' burgher population, of whom Biebouw had formed part, could now move out to the frontier to become farmers themselves and supplement their income by hunting and raiding or become *bywoners* or tenant farmers. On the remote frontier, farmers for much of the eighteenth century were eager to have a European bywoner on their farms.

In the early years of the frontier a bywoner was often a prospective white farmer who provided company, helped protect the farm against wild beasts and enemies, and went on commando, often in the farmer's place. The position of bywoner was not associated with any dependence or inferiority. 'Here they are not considered knechts but as partners', Mentzel wrote during the 1730s. Bywoners took care of the farmer's herds and flocks in return for half the natural increase, and supplemented their income with the proceeds from hunting the abundant game. The most enterprising soon raised enough capital to become independent farmers. But it was only on the pioneering frontier that the bywoners became independent farmers. Once land was in short supply they struggled to maintain a measure of independence, and many had to pay rent for the land they used.

Bywoners were burghers and as such had a higher status than knechten and free blacks. But, as we have seen, the burghers enjoyed only a second-class citizenship. They had to swear an oath to both the States-General and the Company, but they lived under the Company's authority and laws and paid taxes to it. They were the Company's burghers.[17] The fact that the Company could banish them or force them to return to its service reinforced the low status the burghers had in the eyes of top government officials. Although this kind of punishment occurred infrequently, it was a nightmarish prospect that haunted the burghers.

The crucial question seems not have been one's nominal status, but whether one earned a living from an occupation deemed fit for a burgher, like farming, or performing a burgher duty, like going out on commando service without suffering any discrimination, and paying taxes. People who did these were eligible for appointment to a burgher office (*heemraad* or field cornet), and it was they who enjoyed the most status in burgher society and whose views were taken seriously by the government. Within limits these burgher officers could determine how land was allocated and to whom the indigenous people caught by commandos were distributed. A lowly European could aspire to be fully recognized as a burgher, or even become a burgher officer like a heemraad; an upwardly mobile free black could not.

A colony of settlement

As in the seventeenth century, the Company's own gaze was directed seaward toward the servicing of ships. Between 1726 and 1750 an average of seventy-five ships a year stopped in Table Bay. The Cape was not only a trading post, like most of the Company's Eastern

---

17 Gerrit Schutte, 'Company and Colonists at the Cape', SSAS, pp. 287-8.

possessions, but a steadily expanding settlement. Based on slave labor, it had moved a long way from the original idea of a self-sufficient refreshment post based on intensive agriculture. Yet it was not merely a slave camp watched over by transient officials. It was becoming a European colony of settlement, steadily expanding as the burghers practiced a form of subsistence farming. (See map in front.)

The system of government remained almost unchanged throughout the Company period. In Cape Town the Council of Policy, consisting of the governor and other top Company officials, executed policy, and dispensed justice as a Court of Justice. The administrative system of the interior districts rested on a local board called the *collegie* or college. It consisted of a landdrost, who was a government official, and *heemraden,* who were prominent burghers. The first heemraden were four burghers appointed in Stellenbosch in 1682. A college of landdrost and heemraden was introduced in Swellendam in 1743 and in Graaff-Reinet in 1786.

The college dealt monthly with conflicts over land and applications for land and water rights. It mediated in civil disputes and settled minor criminal cases, like assault, though it could also impose severe punishment, like lashes, on insubordinate slaves. In serious criminal cases, as when a slave died at the hands of the master, the college collected evidence for the Court of Justice to hear the case.

The system relied heavily on burghers filling the office of *veldwachtmeester* (later field cornet), one for each *wyk* (ward or division) of the district. They had to inform the burgers of government proclamations, report on crimes, hold post-mortems into unnatural deaths and call the burghers out on commando.

From the start the burghers played a key role in the defense of the district. All male burghers had to perform military service and take part in annual training. In each division the burghers elected their officers and each district had a *Krygsraad* or Council of War of senior officers, who supervised the militia under the overall control of the landdrost. Soon it was apparent that an unofficial division of labor was taking place. After 1715 the Company largely turned the defense of the interior over to the burghers, now indeed as the 'defenders of the land.'

At the port city the Company maintained a standing garrison of about five hundred soldiers (double that in wartime) to defend the station from attacks from the sea. The public prosecutor (fiscal) had at his command a sort of police force of slaves, the so-called 'kaffirs.' They arrested people (including burghers) and dispensed rough justice to those who were causing disturbances.[18] But policing, especially outside Cape Town, was scant. In the extensive districts the landdrosts had at their disposal only three or four petty officials who doubled up as policemen and messengers.

The area of European occupation grew almost tenfold between 1703 and 1780. In 1798 the government fixed the boundaries of an area covering 110,000 square miles (286,000 square kilometers), running from the Buffels (or Koussie) River in the west to the Nuweveld Mountains in the northeast, and from there down to the sea along the Tarka, Baviaans and Fish rivers.

Driving this expansion was a fast-growing burgher population. The burghers mar-

18 Robert Shell, *Children of Bondage: A Social History of the Slave Society at the Cape of Good Hope, 1652-1838* (Johannesburg: Witwatersrand University Press, 1994), pp. 189-94.

ried early and families tended to be large. The *stamvader*, or progenitor, of the best-known and largest Afrikaner family of today, Van der Merwe, was Willem Schalkzoon, who became a burgher in 1661. He and his wife, Elsje Cloete, had thirteen children. Two of their four sons died early and the third had eight children, but this family line became extinct in the fourth generation. The fourth son, Schalk Willemzoon, and Anna Prevot had seventeen children, of whom ten were sons, who, in turn, fathered ninety children carrying the family name. With the forty-five children of the seven daughters, Schalk and Anna van der Merwe had an astounding 135 grandchildren. (In 1900, President Paul Kruger had 156 children, grandchildren and great-grandchildren.)[19]

The population of the slaves held by the burghers grew even more rapidly, along with the increase in the number of burghers who set themselves up as independent farmers and who required slaves. The number of free blacks remained small due to the simple nature of the economy. The Basters (also spelled Bastaards) were a community found mostly in the frontier regions. Here the term 'Baster' did not designate someone born out of wedlock, but people with one European parent, invariably the father, with a Khoikhoi or a free black as the other parent.

The following figures show the population growth:

CAPE POPULATION IN SELECTED YEARS

	Free burghers	Burgher slaves	Free blacks	Khoikhoi and Basters
1730	2,540	4,037	221	Not Available
1770	7,736	8,200	349	NA
1820	42,975	31,779	1,932	26,975

Economically and socially the colony could be divided into three distinct areas: those living in De Kaap (later called Cape Town), the wine and wheat farming community of the rural western Cape, and the stock farmers of the frontier beyond the first mountain ranges. Cape Town itself was a combination of garrison, market (for a long time the colony's only real market), and port, a multi-racial and multi-lingual city. Between a quarter and a third of all the burghers lived there, engaging in commerce and petty trades. Life revolved around the Castle, which housed the Company's headquarters and garrison, numerous taverns, the Company hospital and the marketplace, and provided hospitality for the crews of visiting ships. With no sharp distinction between government business and private business, a tight oligarchy of government officials and the wealthiest of burgher businessmen arose. They secured most of the government contracts, and controlled the monopolies and *pachts*, like the wine or the meat contract.

Cape Town, a multi-racial and multi-lingual city, was considered to be the center of cultural and intellectual life, but, in actual fact, it was a backwater. Until the end of the Company period there was no high school, no theatre, no public hall of entertainment, no bookshop, and no newspaper. Most people did not read and public amusements were few. Dances in the wealthiest private houses, with slaves providing the music, were very popular. Commissioner J.A. de Mist said in 1802: 'The young folk are indolent, and

---

19 C.P. van der Merwe, *My naam is Van der Merwe* (Johannesburg: privately published, 1952).

seem to possess an intense prejudice against exerting themselves mentally, and indeed avoid doing so on every possible occasion.'[20] They frittered their time away with card games, drinking, smoking and incessant *kuyeren* (visiting each other). They were easily influenced by the fashions of Europe or the East, and the presence of French regiments stationed at the Cape in the first half of the 1780s was thought to be responsible for an ostentatious display of 'pride, pomp, lasciviousness and vanity.'[21]

During the last decade of the eighteenth century people in the port city were considered indifferent to religion. Although prohibited from manual work such as carpentry and building on Sundays, they could attend the numerous taverns, along with soldiers, sailors and workmen. Many families went to church accompanied by a retinue of slaves carrying the psalm book, Bible and *kiepersol* (status umbrella) of the mistress, and sometimes the mistress herself in her sedan chair. Generally slaves were expected to wait outside until the service was over. Worshippers tended to be less concerned about the exclusion of slaves from worship than about their raucous behavior.

While Cape Town was a trading city, the rural Cape, west of the first mountain ranges, was based mainly on wine and wheat production on land given out as freehold farms. Production expanded steadily. Between 1720 and 1790 the number of vines increased more than fourfold, the wheat crop trebled, and the average net value of cultivators' estates grew by nearly three times.[22] Historians have used the term 'gentry' for the very wealthy plantation-owners and the reasonably well-off farmers in the western Cape to distinguish them from the great majority of hard-working yeoman farmers.

By 1731 this gentry, measured by farmers who owned more than sixteen slaves, represented a mere seven per cent of the rural burgher community.[23] But if measured by land holdings, vines planted, by wheat crops and livestock, the gentry made up between 10 and 20 per cent of the rural burgher population. They tended to pass their wealth down from one generation to the next. In 1731 there were fifty-three families in the Stellenbosch and Drakenstein districts who had at least one member owning ten thousand or more vines; in 1782 as many as twenty-two of them still did, and in 1825, eighteen. The names of these families are still common Afrikaner names today: Cloete, De Villiers, De Vos, Du Plessis, Du Preez, Du Toit, Joubert, Le Roux, Malan, Marais, Minnaar, Morkel, Myburgh, Retief, Roux, Theron, Van Brackel and Van der Byl. It is striking that more than half were descendants of Huguenots.[24] The biggest success story in the eighteenth century was the career of the German immigrant Martin Melck (1723-1781), who started out as a knecht or overseer, but who, unlike most Company sailors or soldiers, had received training as a builder before he joined the Company to escape the economic depression after the Thirty Years' War. Fortunate to have a benefactor, he worked as a transport rider and supplier of building materials. Four years after his arrival he became a free burgher with enough money to buy two freehold farms and put down half the amount

20 C. Graham Botha, *Social Life and Customs during the Eighteenth Century* (Cape Town: Struik, 1976), p. 41.

21 Botha, *Social Life and Customs during the Eighteenth Century*, p. 42.

22 Robert Ross, 'The Rise of the Cape Gentry', *Journal of Southern African Studies*, vol. 9, no. 2 (1983), pp. 202-7; Leonard Guelke, 'Freehold Farmers and Frontier Settlers', *SSAS*, p. 82-9.

23 Shell, *Children of Bondage,* p. 153.

24 Ross, 'The Rise of the Cape Gentry', p. 207.

in cash. He started a profitable lime-burning industry and two years later married a rich widow, Anna Margaretha Hop. At his death he was the richest man in the colony, owning several farms and 204 slaves.[25]

By the second half of the eighteenth century, the western Cape gentry had amassed sufficient wealth to engage in some conspicuous consumption. Mansions built in the Cape Dutch style were a splendid example. A visitor wrote in 1783 that on several farms he had observed 'nothing except signs of affluence and prosperity, to the extent that, in addition to splendors and magnificence in clothes and carriages, the houses are filled with elegant furniture and the tables decked with silverware and served by tidily clothed slaves.'[26]

Members of the gentry preferred to intermarry, but the shortage of European women, which lasted until the end of the eighteenth century, made this impossible, and they married instead across the class lines. Burghers of all classes attended the four churches in the rural Western Cape (Stellenbosch, Paarl, Roodezand and Swartland). Both wealthy and poor burghers participated in the same militia exercises and rode out on commando together. So, too, the extension of credit tied the burghers to one another. In the absence of banks, the gentry granted credit on an extensive scale to the middling and poor burghers. Borcherds wrote that the Stellenbosch burghers 'were generous in assisting one another either by becoming sureties or giving credit, especially to young beginners and married couples.'[27]

Beyond the western Cape mountains there lay a third socio-economic region, one particularly suitable for stock farming. During the first seventy years of the eighteenth century stock farmers rapidly extended the geographic area of the settlement. A thin layer of Europeans with a voracious demand for labor spread themselves thinly over a large area. Both push and pull factors drove the expansion. The lack of opportunities in the western Cape for those with insufficient capital was one push factor. Another was the strict partible inheritance rule. According to this, half of the estate went to the surviving spouse, the other half divided in equal shares among the children. Some of the sons moved away and set up on their own.

Acting as pull factors were the seemingly abundant land and the system of grazing permits, which, during the first two decades of the eighteenth century, was transformed into a new system of land holding, the loan farm system. The government in 1714 introduced a fee of 24 rix-dollars (one rix-dollar equaled 2.4 guilders) for a loan farm. The system gave holders exclusive control of a minimum of 2,420 hectares (6,000 acres) of pastureland (calculated by a radius of a half-hour walk in each direction). Formally they could not sell the farm, only the *opstal*, or buildings on it. Although the Company could revoke a loan farm, for example when the annual rent of 24 rix-dollars was not paid, it rarely did so.[28] No statutory restrictions prevented non-Europeans from acquiring farms,

25 Helena Scheffler, 'Die geskiedenis van die historiese landgoed Muratie' (private manuscript, 1991, in the possession of Mrs A Melck, Muratie, Stellenbosch), pp. 27-49.

26 S.D. Naudé, 'Willem Cornelius Boers', *AYB*, 1950, vol. 2, p. 414.

27 P.B. Borcherds, *Autobiographical Memoir* (Cape Town: Robertson, 1861), p. 195; Wayne Dooling, *Law and Community in a Slave Society: Stellenbosch District, South Africa, c. 1760-1820* (Cape Town: UCT, 1992), p. 10.

28 The evolution of the system is described in P.J. van der Merwe (translator Roger Beck), *The Migrant Farmer in the History of the Cape Colony, 1657-1842* (Athens: Ohio University Press, 1995).

but it became customary, in the eighteenth century, for only burghers to receive loan farms.[29]

In the stock-farming interior there was little building (the town of Swellendam had only four houses forty years after it was founded), no mining, no industry, no shops, and no professional military establishment. Almost all the burghers in the interior farmed or lived on farms. The problems of the western Cape burghers were of little concern to the stock-farming burghers beyond the first mountain ranges, for whom the important issues were: finding land, the insecurity of frontier life after 1770, the price of cattle and the excessive profits of the butchers who bought the cattle.

In the course of the eighteenth century stock farming surpassed arable farming as the principal means of livelihood. In 1716 independent stock farmers (not engaged in commercial arable farming and owning at least fifty sheep and twenty head of cattle) made up one-tenth of all agricultural producers. By 1770 stock farmers formed two-thirds of all the farmers in the colony.[30] Subsistence farming predominated, but all the farmers remained tied to the market. They needed, at a minimum, to purchase a gun, ammunition, and a wagon, and most required axes, spades, hammers, crowbars, bolts, lanterns, clothes and essential groceries. To buy such goods stock farmers sold stock to the market, and tried to supplement their income by marketing soap, tallow, butter, wax, dried fruit, hides, skins, horns and seed.

Farmers kept large herds, often too large for their farms, which was the only way they could accumulate wealth since land was not bought and sold for profit, and the Company, at certain times, prohibited the selling of loan farms. Farmers with an acceptable farm tended to stay there and, once the frontier had closed, several generations would live on the same farm.

The expansion of subsistence farmers over a great area, spearheaded by *trekboers* or migrant farmers, was not systematic colonization. Markets, towns and proper roads were extremely slow to emerge. Still, for the trekboers on the frontier, it made good sense to have left the western Cape, particularly in the first phase of frontier expansion, where there was abundant pasture and game. Life might be tough and lonely, but it was much better than the fate of a common laborer or a knecht on a wine or a wheat farm. Despite their difficulties, the frontier burghers desired no other life. They had turned their backs on Europe and were trying to become indigenous without losing their commitment to European culture and civilization – a special kind of African.

The trekboers lived simply on the open or pioneer frontier. To survive, they had to change their material culture drastically. Some camped out in their wagons; those better off built rough houses with clay walls and a thatched roof. Furniture was scarce and many lacked beds.

The more affluent gradually improved their condition of rough comfort. They built better houses and bought cloth to turn into European-style clothes. By the end of the eighteenth century the wealthier Graaff-Reinet burghers were acquiring mirrors, curtains,

---

29 More research is needed on this topic. Van der Merwe, *Trek*, pp. 71-85; J.B. Peires, *The House of Phalo* (Johannesburg: Ravan Press, 1981), p. 120.
30 Guelke, 'Freehold Farmers', p. 85.

table linen, porcelain, copper candlesticks, even four-poster beds. An increasing division of wealth steadily became evident in the frontier districts.[31]

After land had been occupied for a decade or so the farmers noted a change in the veld. They called it the 'aging' of the veld. As a result of overstocking, edible grasses and shrubs disappeared and their place was taken by plants like renosterbos, unpalatable to both cattle and game. Farmers rarely conserved the veld by limiting the numbers of their stock. Some moved on, and the great majority of those who stayed wanted their sons to trek further to take possession of new land.

In 1757 the first warning signals of a major crisis came from burghers in Swellendam, who wrote: 'A cattle farmer can hardly survive, as much because of the great change in the veld, which is becoming unhealthier for our own stock, as because of the low prices at which we must presently sell our stock.'[32] In 1775 the landdrost and heemraden of Swellendam wrote that farmers at the Gamtoos River could not 'properly spread themselves with their daily increasing families.' Without further expansion to the east the trekboers would be forced to 'remain in their present impoverished condition.'[33] In 1776 a traveler visiting the Camdebo division, on the eastern border of the Swellendam district, remarked that although the area had been settled only seven or eight years before, 'the luxuriance of the grass' had already started to deteriorate markedly. If the farmers did not begin to conserve artificially the grazing for their cattle this veld would become 'slowly deteriorated just like that which is nearer the Cape.'[34]

Poorer people had great difficulties acquiring a loan farm. Farmers faced declining resources and decreasing farm values. Between 1730 and 1780 the average value of a stock farm declined from two-fifths of the average value of an arable estate to one-tenth. Frontier farmers sank deeper into debt to merchants and financial institutions. Most trekboers died poor – in the 1780s two-thirds left estates worth less than 2,500 guilders. The 1775 letter from Swellendam cited above described how hard it was for farmers 'to liquidate the heavy debts with which they are now burdened.' The records of an eastern Cape merchant for 1821 showed that virtually every farmer with whom he did business was in debt, some by more than six thousand rix-dollars.[35] Not only ties of family and church but ties of debt connected the frontier to the settled parts of the colony.

Stock farming dominated the minds of each succeeding generation. In 1812 the judges in the first circuit court who visited the interior made the following report: 'All the young people, of which many of the houses are full, have no other prospect other than the breeding of cattle and to obtain places [farms] for that purpose . . . All look for-

31 Suzie Newton-King, 'Commerce and Material Culture on the Eastern Cape Frontier, 1784-1812', paper presented at the University of the Witwatersrand History Workshop, 1987. For an extended discussion see her 'The Enemy Within: The Struggle for Ascendancy on the Cape Eastern Frontier', doctoral diss., University of London, 1992, and a book, published by Cambridge University Press in 1999, with the same title.

32 Newton-King, 'The Enemy Within', p. 52.

33 Donald Moodie (ed.), The Record (repr. Cape Town: Balkema, 1960), vol. 3, p. 47.

34 Hermann Giliomee, 'Processes in the Development of the South African Frontier', in Howard Lamar and Leonard Thompson (eds.), The Frontier in History (New Haven: Yale University Press, 1981), p. 97.

35 Clifton Crais, The Making of the Colonial Order: White Supremacy and Black Resistance in the Eastern Cape, 1770-1865 (Johannesburg: Witwatersrand University Press, 1997), p. 39.

ward to becoming graziers, and no person forms for himself any other plan of livelihood.'[36]

The fear of 'barbarization'

The trekboers living at the limits of the settlement endured great insecurity and displayed a pervasive anxiety about maintaining themselves culturally and materially. For
much of the second half of the eighteenth century the only schools and churches were
far away in the western Cape. Some Graaff-Reinet farmers had to travel eight hundred
kilometers in the 1780s to have their children baptized.

Writing about the sheep-farming northeastern frontier in the early years of the nineteenth century, Lichtenstein found it difficult to comprehend how the first stock farmers
could ever think of establishing themselves in such 'a waste' and to be so cut off from the
'delights and advantages of friendship.' Their only task was to see that a Khoikhoi servant went out with their flock in the morning, and brought it safely back at the end of
the day. Their own hours were spent in 'trivial household employment' and 'frequently
repeated devotional exercises.' 'In an almost unconscious inactivity of mind,' Lichtenstein wrote, 'without any attractions to the great circle of mankind, knowing nothing beyond the little circle which his own family forms around him, the colonist of these parts
passes his solitary days . . .'[37] Mentzel, who lived in the colony in the 1730s and early
1740s, said: 'Some of the Boors [sic] have accustomed themselves to such an extent with
the carefree life, the indifference, the lazy days and the association with slaves and Hottentots that not much difference may be discerned between the former and the latter.'[38]

Some called such a life the *lekker lewe* – the easy life; to others it seemed a life of idleness, simplicity, and sloth.[39] Sparrman reported that, in the 1770s, most houses had only
two rooms: a bedchamber where the farmer and his children slept, and the kitchen
where his Khoikhoi servants and guests slept on the floor. 'We all lay pigging together,'
he wrote.[40] Swellengrebel, who traveled during this period, told of one-room houses with
sleeping arrangements in 'Hottentot fashion', all together on the floor of clay and dung,
and thus 'free and easy.'[41]

The burghers' interaction with the Khoisan led to large-scale cultural borrowing. The
trekboers were more African than their kinsmen in the west. Like the Khoikhoi, they
stored milk in skin sacks, dried strips of game (later called biltong), wore *veldschoenen*
(sandals made from cowhide) and sometimes animal skins. Both Afrikaners and Basters
were forced to develop a pragmatic lifestyle that made survival possible in the African
interior.

Observers expressed shock about a European community that appeared to become
ever more African, or as some phrased it, 'degenerate' or 'wild.' Church ministers warned

---

36 *RCC*, vol. 8, pp. 298-9.
37 H. Lichtenstein, *Travels in South Africa, 1803-1805* (Cape Town: VRS, 1928), vol. 1, pp. 446-8.
38 O.F. Mentzel, *Description of the Cape of Good Hope* (Cape Town: VRS, 1944), vol. 3, p. 115.
39 J.M. Coetzee, 'Idleness in South Africa', *Social Dynamics*, 8, 1 (1982), pp. 1-13.
40 Anders Sparrman, *A Voyage to the Cape of Good Hope, 1772-1776* (1785 reprint: New York: Johnson, 1971) vol. 1, p. 122.
41 Noël Mostert, *Frontiers* (New York: Knopf, 1992), p. 178.

darkly of the threat that the frontier posed to European civilization. In 1776 Hendrik Swellengrebel, a typical figure of the Dutch Enlightenment, declared after a visit to the interior that the majority of frontiersmen lived not much better than the Hottentots. There was a real danger of their 'becoming a completely wild nation.'[42] The more affluent fellow burghers in Stellenbosch and Cape Town expressed the fear that their morals could become 'bastardized', leading to a 'completely degenerate nation.'[43]

Frontier farmers themselves expressed anxiety about the prospects for their cultural survival. Farmers who settled in the remote Camdebo area (the present Graaff-Reinet) in the 1770s lived a journey of a month or more away from the nearest school and church in Stellenbosch. In 1778 they petitioned the government: '[On] account of the great distance of that place [Stellenbosch] . . . many here . . . have already departed from the commands of their God, and, to our great injury become disobedient to Him . . . [We] have been hitherto without teachers and clergy so that many fine young people are growing up like the ignorant cattle.'[44]

The petition of the Camdebo stock farmers and the warning of disobedience to God had much to do with the practical fact that they had settled beyond the border and wanted their land claims ratified. But most of the frontier burghers did not become 'degenerate' despite the stereotypes of Africa as the 'Dark Continent' and the 'land of Ham' where evil was deemed to reign. While some farmers were desperately poor and lived the simplest of lives, they strongly wished to conform to the values and norms of the racially exclusive burgher community of the rural western Cape, although the obstacles were severe.

Lacking schools, the burghers had their children taught by barely literate itinerant knechten, who briefly instructed the neighborhood's children before moving on. Such teachers were commonly paid less than farm knechten and were said to drink to excess. Parents had their children educated only to the point where they could read and write and knew the basic contents of the catechism sufficiently to be confirmed as members of the church.

In some ways a new kind of burgher developed on the frontier. The western Cape's distinctions of rank carried much less weight here, although burghers normally respected the offices of heemraad and field commandant. A traveler remarked: 'Every man is a burgher by rank and a farmer by occupation and there is no one so poor that he would not consider himself degraded by becoming the dependent of another.'[45] Nevertheless there were many poor burghers, and once the pioneer phase of the frontier was over a form of class rule appeared with the more affluent burghers shirking commando duty or paying (or forcing) others to go in their place.

A Boer 'race' and Boer racism

The historian Cornelius de Kiewiet wrote that in 'the long quietude of the eighteenth century the Boer race was formed.' He sketched this compelling collective picture: 'Their

42 Mostert, *Frontiers*, p. 177.
43 *Afrikaner Political Thought, 1780-1850*, pp. 43, 89.
44 Donald Moodie, *The Record* (repr. Cape Town: Balkema, 1960), vol. 3, p. 75.
45 George Thompson, *Travels in Southern Africa* (London: Colburn, 1827), p. 324.

life gave them a tenacity of purpose, a power of silent endurance, and the keenest self-respect. But this isolation sank into their character, causing their imagination to lie fallow and their intellects to become inert. Their tenacity could degenerate into obstinacy, their power of endurance into resistance to innovation, and their self-respect into suspicion of the foreigner and contempt for their inferiors.'[46]

As a description it can hardly be improved on, except by providing some context. It was truer of the stock farmers of the deeper interior than the wheat and wine farmers. Some members of the gentry in the western Cape introduced innovations and expanded on a rational basis, but for the majority of farmers there was not much incentive to take risks to step up production. The settlement lacked an export staple and the domestic market, while not stagnant, was far from buoyant. In the immediate hinterland of Cape Town, the farmers could keep a keen eye on market fluctuations and the possibilities for speculation, but farther away the farmers produced only what was necessary to meet their needs. They lived simply and soberly. Their educational level remained very low until well into the nineteenth century. Apart from the Bible, books did not figure in the burghers' lives. It took both tenacity and a spirit of endurance to stick to the uneventful life that revolved around an isolated farm. Yet no traveler recorded any dissatisfaction with a way of life that looks, from today's perspective, monotonous, even dreary.

The way of life produced narrow horizons and parochial concerns together with a considerable degree of complacency and intellectual insularity. Travelers reported that the burghers could not believe that there was a better land or a place more beautiful: 'They would rather listen to a story told by their slaves or half bred Hottentots', one traveler wrote, 'than to one about the Grand Escurial or the beautiful Versailles.'[47] While in Cape Town people could receive news from passing sailors, spread gossip about the malpractices of the Company servants and occupy themselves with circumventing Company regulations on trade, the farther from the port city, the greater the social and intellectual isolation. During the VOC period no one challenged the farmers to change their set ways. Not until the British took over the Cape in 1795 did people point to obsolete equipment like ploughs and suggest ways to improve animal husbandry. Only then did changing market demands give farmers an incentive to improve the quality of their wine and other products.

Historians have long ascribed to Afrikaners a deeply held belief about the inferiority of the blacks. They attributed this to a degenerate form of primitive Calvinism that developed on the frontier and to a culture clash between whites and blacks. Some believe that racism has been a fundamental organizing principle in the relations between white and black ever since Dutch immigrants settled at the Cape of Good Hope, but in fact history took a different course. It is a tale of processes rather than decrees and social institutions (particularly the family and church) rather than political institutions that shaped the rigid structure of Cape society.[48] We note first the processes and then the institutions.

---

46 C.W. de Kiewiet, *A History of South Africa* (Oxford: Oxford University Press, 1941), p. 17.

47 Karel Schoeman, *Dogter van Sion: Machtelt Smit en die 18de-eeuse samelewing aan die Kaap* (Cape Town: Human & Rousseau, 1997), pp. 48-9.

48 The argument that is presented in the pages that follow is one originally developed with Richard Elphick and written up in the concluding chapter of both *SSAS* (1) and *SSAS*.

From the very beginning the Cape settlement displayed an identity hierarchy with a close correlation, both at the top and the bottom, of descent, legal status, class, color, and culture. On the upper rungs almost all the burghers and all the Company servants were Europeans and were white. They were regarded as 'born Christians', which meant that they were invariably baptized when still very young. At the bottom of the status ladder were slaves and Khoikhoi servants, their low status in the colony correlating with their color: they were all brown or black.

It was on the middle rungs of society that some ambiguity existed. There were the free blacks, who were rarely burghers, but who could marry in the church if confirmed and were obliged to do commando duty along with the burghers. The exact status of free blacks would become a burning issue only by the end of the eighteenth century. There were also the knechten or overseers, whites and Christians but not burghers. In the middle, color was not yet decisive.

It is important to emphasize that a sense of this correlation between descent, legal status and culture was only rarely publicly expressed. In one such case, however, the Council of Policy responded to a complaint from convicted Company servants who were doing hard labor on Robben Island and who felt aggrieved that they had to subsist on slave rations. The officials decided to improve the rations since it was indeed a 'barbaric cruelty' to mete out such a severe punishment to people who were 'Christian and white people and free-born like us.'[49]

Color as a sign of difference, and also a correlation between color and social position, was there at the beginning. The real challenge is to explain why the correlation was maintained over time. To put it more specifically: why did almost all the people in the most important status groups remain white and almost all those at the bottom black? To answer this question it is necessary to examine some key forces and institutions, particularly the tendency towards racial exclusion in the burgher family and church and the working of both the economy and the legal system within a context of widespread slaveholding.

To illuminate this point one could begin by asking: why did the slave-based society in the western Cape not become another Brazil? In certain parts of colonial Brazil, particularly in Pernambuco in the northeast, a black person who climbed the occupational ladder invariably found that his status rose in proportion to his income: he was becoming 'whiter' and a fuller citizen. When, after the Civil War of the United States, a few thousand Confederate exiles settled in Brazil, they noted that free blacks enjoyed 'even more rights than the white foreigner.'[50] In the words of the great Brazilian scholar Gilberto Freyre, the family was enlarged by 'a far greater number of bastards and dependants, gathered around the patriarchs, who were more given to women and possibly a little more loose in their social code than the North Americans were.'[51] Freyre continued: 'No Big House in the days of slavery wanted any effeminate sons or male vir-

---

49 Arend Willem Biewenga, *De Kaap de Goede Hoop: een nederlandse vestigingskolonie, 1680-1730*, doctoral diss., Vrije Universiteit, Amsterdam, 1998, p. 273.
50 C. Vann Woodward, *American Counterpoint: Slavery and Racism in the North-South Dialogue* (Boston: Little Brown and Company, 1971), p. 68.
51 Gilberto Freyre, cited by Woodward, *American Counterpoint*, p. 69.

gins . . . The one always approved was the one who went with the girls as early as possible . . . One who lost no time in taking Negro women that he might increase the herd and the paternal capital.'[52]

At the Cape the burgher family on a farm was the basic unit out of which the Afrikaner people developed. Not every burgher family owned a farm; many lived on the land of a wealthier relative or became a bywoner, or tenant farmer. The farm was a virtually autonomous social domain controlled by the owner, functioning as the patriarch.[53] Travelers remarked on the strong and loving bonds in the burgher family. Children readily accepted the guidance and care of their parents. Lichtenstein wrote in the early nineteenth century: 'The respect of children for their parents, and their submission to them even to their latest years is a very estimable feature in the character of the African colonists, which . . . has a great resemblance to the patriarchal days.'[54] Parents had enormous power over their children by retaining title to the estate to the last moment.[55]

Initially many of the wives were not Europeans. During the first seventy-five years of the Cape settlement there was a considerable degree of racial fluidity due, in the first place, to a lack of European women. By 1690 there were 260 male burghers for every hundred female burghers. But this gender imbalance declined steadily: by 1730 it stood at 150:100 and by 1770 at 140:100. As a result, mixed marriages decreased sharply. European women could now use their relative position of power to employ sanctions against mixed marriages and against legitimizing the racially mixed offspring of their husbands and sons. Taking a free black wife evidently entailed such a loss of status that it was considered better to remain a bachelor.[56] European men unable to find a European wife tended not to marry. A study of the 1731 census showed that 59 per cent of Cape Town's European men and 51 per cent in the rural western Cape never married. It had also become much more difficult for children from mixed extramarital liaisons, especially males, to become absorbed into the European community.

A brief comparative note is needed. In Spain and Portugal, and in their colonies, European women did not enjoy high status. There the law gave women few rights and little protection against their husbands, and the Catholic Church allowed no divorce. In the Netherlands, however, the position of women was recognized as more advanced than anywhere else in Europe. In the early modern period Dutch women were closely involved with their husband's job if he was in business or commerce, often enjoying full recognition for the role that they played there and in the house.[57]

European women at the Cape occupied a relatively high status in the family, and could prevent their sons from marrying outside the European community and their husbands

52 Gilberto Freyre, *The Masters and the Slaves: A Study in the Development of Brazilian Civilization* (New York: Knopf, 1956), p. 349.
53 Pamela Scully, 'Liberating the Family? Gender, Labour and Sexuality in the Rural Western Cape, South Africa, 1823-1853', doctoral diss., University of Wisconsin, 1993, p. 69.
54 Lichtenstein, *Travels*, vol. 2, p. 43.
55 Shell, *Children of Bondage*, p. 155.
56 For the work on the 1731 census, see Leonard Guelke, 'The Anatomy of a Colonial Settler Population, 1657-1750', *The International Journal of African Historical Studies*, 21, 3 (1988), pp. 462-3. See also J.A. Heese, *Die herkoms van die Afrikaner* (Cape Town: Balkema, 1971).
57 Karel Schoeman, *Armosyn van die Kaap: voorspel tot vestiging, 1415-1651* (Cape Town: Human & Rousseau, 1999), pp. 251-4.

from bringing illegitimate half-caste children into the family. While a woman could not hold a burgher office, like that of heemraad, she shared the general status of burghers if married to one, and she could own a farm or become a guest housekeeper or publican in the town. Roman Dutch law, in operation at the Cape, was relatively liberal on the rights of burgher women in marital affairs. They could take their husbands to court for offences against their marital duties, *inter alia* on the grounds of adultery. At the Cape, burgher families intermarried widely, which meant that few women had to fend for themselves alone.

Equally important, both the Reformed and the Lutheran churches allowed divorce. Most marriages at the Cape were concluded in community of property, which meant that upon divorce half of the estate would accrue to a woman. There was the case of Abraham Carel Greyling whose wife left him immediately after his slave, Clara, gave birth to a child his wife believed to be Carel's. Greyling tried to shift the blame to his son, but his wife asked for, and received, an order for the dissolution of her marriage and a property settlement.[58] European women at the Cape had the backing of the law to avoid the fate of their Brazilian counterparts, who had to stand by helplessly when a husband took a slave mistress or insisted on bringing a child born to another woman into the family fold.

Even after her husband's death many women retained their strong position, particularly when left some property. The widow inherited half of the estate; the children shared the other half. The property rights enjoyed by European women at the Cape and in other Dutch colonies were almost totally denied to English women in the North American colonies, where any property the wife brought into the family became that of the husband. At the Cape there was even something of a 'widowarchy.' A widow with property could consider the options for a subsequent marriage as an astute modern investment manager would. Many widowed Cape women remarried several times, accumulating a small fortune. From a material perspective, they were in a position to command the respect of their children. They controlled the domestic arrangements, including managing the house servants. A girl was not pampered but put to work in the house and fields. She 'looked everybody straight in the eye . . . and [was] unabashed.'[59] Despite their lack of political power or public role, European women at the Cape developed a greater degree of social self-confidence than their counterparts in most other colonies. Visitors to the Cape viewed them as more intelligent than the male burghers and better informed.[60]

The legal position with respect to children, specifically children born out of wedlock, also worked against the incorporation of blacks into European society. In contrast to the law in Spanish and Portuguese colonies, the law at the Cape made no specific provision for children born out of wedlock. Basters could not make any claims on their father, except for maintenance. The law decreed that the 'Bastaard heeft geen vader of erfenis' (the Baster has no father or inheritance). Unless the father specifically provided for such a child in his will, the child received no inheritance.

---

58 John E. Masson, '"Fit for Freedom": The Slaves, Slavery and Emancipation in the Cape Colony, South Africa, 1806-1842', doctoral diss., Yale University, 1992, p. 215.

59 Schoeman, *Dogter van Sion*, pp. 51-6.

60 I am indebted for these remarks on marriage to Andreas van Wyk (personal communication, 2 May 1998) and his 'The Power to Dispose of Assets of the Universal Community of Property: A Study in South African Law with Excursions in the Laws of Brazil and the Netherlands', doctoral diss., University of Leiden, 1976.

Marginal people

Cape Town and the pioneer frontier represented escape hatches from the racially rigid rural western Cape. Cape Town remained racially fluid in the lower ranks. The poorer burghers, slaves and free blacks lived interspersed. In the 1732 census burghers described as 'poor, indigent, decrepit' formed a tenth of the Cape district's population and a fifth of that of Stellenbosch.[61] Concerned about possibly corrupting social intercourse, officials expressed alarm that slaves congregated at night at the homes of the poorer burghers to drink and gamble.[62] The slave lodge in Cape Town was used as brothel not only by passing sailors but also by burghers and Company servants.

Adding to the image of racial fluidity in the middle ranks was the considerable number of free blacks in the city. By 1770 free blacks comprised 13 per cent of the free population of the Cape district. Free blacks formally had the same rights as other free people, but they were considered more a freed people than free burghers. Some had a chance of being accepted into the dominant group, particularly if they were 'half-breeds' with a European father who had some influence, or if they were fair-skinned women. Cape Town's racial culture fell halfway between that of North America, where there came to be a rigid distinction between whites and people with a drop of 'black blood', and northeastern Brazil, where many members of the intermediate category of mulattos breached the color line to become part of the dominant group.

Still, the racial fluidity in Cape Town was limited. The key factor determining the power and status of a mixed racial group was the economy, and, more specifically, its ability to generate 'interstitial' or 'intermediate' jobs that members of the dominant group did not want to fill and for which it did not want to use slaves. On this, one could contrast the Cape with a region like Pernambuco in Brazil, where slaves were freed in large numbers to become soldiers, tradesmen, shopkeepers and slave-overseers, with the result that a substantial proportion of society consisted of free people of color. Playing a significant role in the economy and society, these people steadily bridged the divide between black and white, bringing into existence a society based more on class than on race.[63]

This did not happen at the Cape. Here, slaves occupied most trades in the simple economy. Few intermediate jobs were available to free blacks, and they generally remained poor as a result. Despite the considerable slave force, the burghers did not ordinarily use free blacks to control their slaves. The rural western Cape economy also did not use blacks except as slaves. Some free blacks did receive land and, by the end of the seventeenth century, several farmed in the Jonkershoek Valley outside Stellenbosch. But by 1710 a clear pattern had been established. The free blacks of Stellenbosch had moved back to Cape Town after failing to make a success of farming, most likely because of a lack of capital, which, in burgher society, tended to be provided by family members.[64]

---

61 Gerrit Schutte, 'Company and Colonists at the Cape, 1652-1795', in SSAS, p. 300.
62 G.C. de Wet, *Die vryliede en vryswartes in die Kaapse nedersetting, 1657-1707* (Cape Town: Historiese Publikasievereniging, 1981), p. 126.
63 Carl N. Degler, *Neither Black nor White: Slavery and Race Relations in Brazil and the United States* (New York: Macmillan, 1971).
64 Shell, *Children of Bondage*, pp. 206-7.

The rural western Cape thus remained a rigidly stratified society, polarized between burghers and slaves. Few blacks could break down the correlation between status and color.

Some fluidity did exist on the newly settled frontiers. Although the great majority of male burghers who moved there had European wives or married European women there, single European men were numerous enough to become a category labeled *eenlopenden*. An option open to the eenlopenden was one taken by the *praezeros*, the Portuguese frontiersmen who settled on the southeastern coast of Africa and became absorbed into the indigenous population through intermarriage. At the Cape a few frontier Afrikaners crossed the racial and cultural boundaries, but never fully joined African society. (See the story of Coenraad de Buys, a white descendant of Huguenots, page 74.)

Mixing with 'native' women outside wedlock was largely restricted to newly settled areas or beyond the frontier. Those who took a non-European wife or a steady concubine were on the social fringe. One estimate puts the proportion of frontiersmen married to or living with a non-European at less than a tenth.[65] In the districts of Graaff-Reinet and Tulbagh, mixed marriages represented only three and one per cent respectively of the total in the first decade of the nineteenth century.

Mixed groups lived alongside and sometimes among the frontier burghers. They were commonly called 'Baster' or by the Dutch word 'Bastaard', which referred to the offspring of liaisons between Europeans, slaves and Khoikhoi, but also to subordinate blacks who could speak Dutch and ride and shoot. Small Baster communities existed in the fringe areas of the northwest – Namaqualand, Cedarberg, Bokkeveld, Hantam and the Roggeveld – and on the eastern frontier. In the Graaff-Reinet district they constituted between 5 and 10 per cent of the district's farming population, listed separately as 'baptized Bastaards' in the 1798 census of Graaff-Reinet. Members of this community with European names were baptized in the church (although increasingly, apparently, in separate ceremonies). They were called upon to do commando service.

Basters were, nevertheless, increasingly squeezed out from the land they held. On contested claims burghers invariably had the stronger claim and better access to the field cornets who reported on any such claims. Lichtenstein commented: '[The] white children of the colonists did not hesitate to make use of the right of the strongest to drive their half yellow relations out of the places where they had fixed abodes. These bastard Hottentots were then obliged to seek an asylum in more remote parts . . .'[66] Basters and other people of mixed racial origin moved first to the outer limits of the colony and then beyond its borders. Adam Kok, a freed slave who managed to obtain burgher rights in the northwestern part of the Stellenbosch district, founded the most vigorous mixed community. According to one tradition he married the daughter of the chief of a Khoikhoi clan, the Chariguriqua (the root of the name 'Griqua'). Kok attracted a coterie as he moved up from Piketberg to Little Namaqualand. Early in the nineteenth century a son of Adam Kok, Cornelis Kok, moved out of the colony to the Orange River and then eastwards along the bank to what is now known as Griqualand West. He had gathered with him a large number of Basters, also some Khoikhoi and escaped slaves.

---

65 Guelke, 'Freehold Farmers', p. 93; Heese, *Die herkoms van die Afrikaner.*
66 Lichtenstein, *Travels in Southern Africa*, vol. 2, p. 317.

The Kok family, the Barends family (another Baster family), and some small clans formed what by 1820 had become known as the Griqua community (at an earlier stage some of them had referred to themselves as 'swarthy Dutchmen'). Missionaries helped them to centralize their political organization and they rapidly accepted Christianity, spoke Dutch or Afrikaans, hunted and traded with other tribes or peoples and used their commandos to raid. In many ways they were only a slightly rougher version of the Afrikaner frontiersmen.[67] Seldom incorporated into burgher society, most of them married within their own community.

The burghers' religion

To be called a Christian during the seventeenth and eighteenth centuries meant much more than a religious designation. In the American colonies in this period, to be English and to be Christian were interrelated. The American historian Winthrop Jordan remarked vis-à-vis the Negro that 'the concept embedded in the term Christian seems to have conveyed much of the idea and feeling of us against them: to be Christian was to be civilized rather than barbarous, English rather than African, white rather than black.'[68] Such an attitude could be found in other European colonies. Perhaps because the Cape was not colonized by people of a single European nationality, the colonists were even more inclined to use their Christian identity as a political identity. During the eighteenth century it was a widespread practice for burghers to refer to themselves as Christians, and others, too, called them by that name. A frontiersman, seeing two members of this community in the company of a Khoikhoi and an Englishman remarked: 'Here come two Christians, a Hottentot and an Englishman.'[69] Governor Janssens of the Batavian administration, after a visit to the interior, reported that the burghers called themselves 'men and Christians, and the Kafirs and Hottentots heathens, and on the strength of this they considered themselves entitled to anything.'[70] Here was one of the first signs of Christianity functioning as justification for European domination.

The burghers did not initially appear to be particularly religious or close to the church. According to inventories, few owned Bibles and few were confirmed members of the church. In 1726, only in the case of one-fifth of burgher couples in Stellenbosch were both partners confirmed members of the Reformed church. By 1770, 90 per cent of the adult female burghers in the Stellenbosch congregation, but only one-third of the male burghers, were confirmed members of the church.

After touring the colony the Dutch official G.W. van Imhoff wrote in 1743 that 'indifference and ignorance in the frontier districts is such that it has the appearance more of an assembly of blind heathen than a colony of European Christians.'[71] Much of this

---

67 Robert Ross, *Adam Kok's Griquas* (Cambridge: Cambridge University Press, 1976), pp. 14-18.

68 Winthrop Jordan, *White over Black: American Attitudes toward the Negro, 1550-1812* (Baltimore: Penguin Books, 1968), p. 94.

69 Cited by Jonathan Neil Gerstner, *The Thousand Generation Covenant: Dutch Reformed Covenant Theology and Group Identity in Colonial South Africa* (Leiden: E.J. Brill, 1991), p. 252.

70 *Belangrijke Historische Dokumenten over Zuid-Afrika* (Cape Town: Van de Sandt de Villiers, 1911), vol. 3, p. 219.

71 Cited by Proeve (pseudonym), *De Gereformeerde Kerkbode*, 1854, vol. 11, p. 169. See also Botha, *Social Life and Customs during the Eighteenth Century*, p. 42.

appearance was due to neglect by the Company, which established the first congregation at the Cape immediately after founding the settlement, but waited more than thirty years to form the next congregations at Stellenbosch (1686) and Drakenstein (1691). Some fifty years later, and only after Van Imhoff's report, were two more established, Roodezand (now Tulbagh) in 1743 and Swartland (now Malmesbury) in 1745. Another fifty years passed before two more were added: Graaff-Reinet (1792) and Swellendam in 1798.

From the 1790s something of a religious awakening swept over the colony, and the proportion of confirmed members of the church in the burgher population rose steadily.[72] Lichtenstein, whose travels were the most extensive of all the visitors, noted that: '[We] never heard from the mouth of a colonist an unseemly word, an overstrained expression, a curse, or an imprecation of any kind . . . The universal religious turn of the colonists, amounting almost to bigotry, is, perhaps, a principal cause to which this command of themselves is to be ascribed.'[73] In the 1830s one traveler stated: "There are certainly no people in the world who are so truly God-fearing as the Afrikaner.' Another described the burghers as 'a serious and religious people . . . with strong sentiments of genuine piety . . . [They] are consistent members of the Christian church.'[74]

In the course of the eighteenth century the church had become largely a white church. This fact is usually attributed to a lack of resources for missionary work. Equal weight must, however, be given to the organization of religion and education, and to the theological interpretations that prevailed. The Company gave a specific imprint to organized religion at the Cape. In the prayer it prescribed to its Commanders and in its instructions to teachers at church schools, special mention was made of the need to preserve the Reformed faith and the Dutch language at the Cape. The burgher community and its church had come to be defined by a particular kind of Christian faith and a particular language.

The notion developed among the burghers that some kind of covenant existed with God to preserve this community with its cultural characteristics. This covenant theology argued that there was continuity between God's covenant with the Jews and the one He had with Christians. It reinforced the idea that Christianity marked the community of burghers.[75] It was birth rather than personal conversion that determined who the 'real' Christians were. Hence they formed a particular social group rather than a community of the faithful. The historian Jonathan Gerstner observed: 'The continuity, through the covenant, of Christians with the Old Testament people of God provided a ground for group cohesion in the midst of the individualism inherent in the Protestant doctrine.'[76]

The strand of baptism theology finally accepted in the DRC at the Cape argued for internal generation, which deemed the children of Christian parents to be saved in the

---

72 Gerrit Schutte, 'Between Amsterdam and Batavia: Cape Society and the Calvinist Church under the Dutch East India Company', *Kronos*, 25 (1998-9).

73 Lichtenstein, *Travels in Southern Africa*, vol. 1, p. 116.

74 Quoted by Van der Merwe, *Migrant Farmer*, p. 199.

75 Jonathan Gerstner, 'A Christian Monopoly: The Reformed Church and Colonial Society under Dutch Rule', in Richard Elphick and Rodney Davenport (eds.), *Christianity in South Africa* (Cape Town: David Philip, 1997), p. 27.

76 Gerstner, 'A Christian Monopoly', p. 18.

womb, which was symbolized by baptizing the child as an infant. At baptism parents were merely expected to promise to educate the child in the faith. When the child reached adulthood he or she made a formal confession and as a confirmed person was permitted to receive the Lord's Supper. Out of this developed the conviction that God had a covenant with a particular body of people and their descendants.[77]

There is a danger in attaching too much attention to the theology before the exact relationship between theology and the historical reality on the ground is established.[78] Yet there was something in the behavior of the small number of burghers, dispersed over a large area, that leads one to conclude that such a theology met the burghers' need to re-affirm their link with the wider community of Christians and Europeans. During the last decades of the eighteenth century, burghers on the remote frontier were prepared to travel as far as eight hundred kilometers to have their children baptized and confirmed at Roodezand. Parents tended to make consent for marriage contingent on both partners being confirmed. Confirmation came to be seen as the threshold that had to be passed for full incorporation into burgher society.[79]

If for the children of burghers the various steps to become fully part of the church were easy and clearly spelled out, the process was much more complicated for the children of slaves, free blacks or Basters. The Reformed church in the Netherlands and its colonies did not administer baptism unconditionally to those who were not 'born Christians', i.e. people, invariably non-Europeans, not born of Christian parents. The theology of external regeneration applied to them (but not to the children of Christian parents) argued that in baptism God was only promising that He would save the child later in life. The church required adult slaves and Khoikhoi servants wanting to be baptized to show some knowledge of the Reformed doctrines and to prove that their lives had been exemplary.

The meeting at Dordt, in the years 1618 and 1619, of the main decision-making body of the Reformed Church in the Netherlands represented an important milestone. The decisions of this Synod of Dordt had much to do with the fact that so few non-Europeans presented themselves for baptism. The synod insisted that the Gospel had to be taught to everyone, but in an important respect Dordt facilitated a separate treatment for servants and slaves. While the Catholic Church considered itself duty bound to baptize everyone regardless of social distinctions, Dordt put the responsibility for having slaves or servants and their children baptized on the shoulders of the Reformed head of the household. Dordt also did not insist unambiguously that baptized slaves had to be freed. At the Cape the decisions of Dordt were well known, but most masters ignored the injunction to have the servants and slaves baptized or confirmed, although it was a violation of the Calvinist creed.

The burghers had various justifications for taking so little trouble to have their slaves baptized or confirmed. Many chose to interpret Dordt wrongly as meaning that once their slaves had been baptized they could not sell them or that they might even be obliged to free them, thereby losing the money invested in them. But the strongest fac-

---

77 Gerstner, 'A Christian Monopoly', pp. 17-26.

78 G.J. Schutte, *Het Calvinistisch Nederland: mythe en werklikheid* (Hilversum: Verloren 2000), pp. 48-50.

79 Van der Merwe, *The Migrant Farmer in the History of the Cape Colony*, pp. 200-4.

tor was the masters' fear that their control would be jeopardized. To sit with them as equals in a church constituted an act of *gelykstelling* or social leveling which would dilute their sense of exclusivity and superiority. The Cape clergy also made no concerted effort to encourage the baptism of slaves. The clergy had to wait for fathers or heads of households to bring a child to the baptismal font. If they appeared, the clergy would baptize the child. If the child was a slave or a Baster from an extramarital liaison there was little chance of the father or employer turning up. The traveler Thunberg summed the situation up nicely: 'If the child is a bastard and its father does not discover himself, the infant remains unapprised. If the mother is a Black or a Hottentot, but the father a Christian, who requires it to be baptized, it is baptized.'[80] All too often community pressure induced the father to remain 'undiscovered', that is unacknowledged.

Some ministers did not apply this rule and, in such cases, children were baptized with the comment 'father absent' appearing in the records. As a result, few slaves in private hands or Khoikhoi servants were baptized.[81] In the nearly 150 years of Company rule only 319 privately owned slave children and 124 privately owned slave adults (fewer than four per year overall) received the sacrament.

Confirmation was often an even more severe test for a slave to pass. Reformed Church ministers had no objection to accepting non-Europeans, but if they wanted peace in their parish they had to send them on a long and arduous route before they could be baptized and confirmed. Conflicts were likely to erupt if they allowed short cuts or admitted non-Europeans not qualified to Communion services. Those non-Europeans who managed to be baptized and confirmed in the Reformed Church were accepted as ordinary members of the church. But while parishes in the southwestern Cape commonly admitted colored or black people to their ranks, there tended by 1750 to be very few colored or black faces at church services in the deeper interior.

In the second half of the eighteenth century increasing numbers of slaves and Basters understood the Christian message and expressed a desire to be baptized. Some congregations began separating people on the basis of color. In 1761 the Swartland church started a separate section of its baptismal records to list Basters and Khoisan. In some cases non-Europeans were baptized in a separate ceremony.

Yet a general missionary fervor was lacking on the part of either the Company or the burghers. There was no independent religious order that was committed to missionary work, such as the Jesuits, who spearheaded the expansion of Catholicism in the colonial world. As paid Company servants the few ministers in a dispersed settlement had neither the resources nor the inclination to extend their task beyond attending to the spiritual needs of the burghers and others of European descent. They saw no material gain in converting slaves or the Khoisan, and conversion happened only for those who worked for a pious employer.

In 1799 Dutch or Afrikaans-speaking colonists at the Cape founded the first local mis-

---

80 C.P. Thunberg, *Travels in Europe, Africa and Asia, 1770-1779* (London; Richardson, 1793) vol. 1, p. 262.
81 Schutte, 'Between Amsterdam and Batavia'. For different interpretations, see Gerstner's work, which emphasizes the centrality of the 'Thousand Years Covenant', and that of Shell, who believes that baptism (as opposed to confirmation) was of key importance.

sionary society, the Zuid-Afrikaansche Zending Genootschap, which erected places called *gestichten*, or chapels, where colored Christians worshipped. A few DRC congregations followed its example. By then foreign missionary societies had begun to take an active interest in the Cape, and they would spearhead the missionary drive in the interior districts and beyond the colonial borders.

The impact of slavery

In the western Cape the fundamental dividing line in society was between slaves and free people. It was reinforced by the fact that, as a result of the simple Cape economy, few slaves performed anything but the most menial jobs. Baron Van Imhoff remarked in 1743 that having 'imported slaves every common or ordinary European becomes a gentleman and prefers to be served rather than to serve.'[82] Even poorer burghers who could not own slaves enjoyed the spin-offs of being part of the dominant class. Slave-holding classes everywhere were keen to conscript all the members of a racial or ethnic community in the defense of slavery by encouraging solidarity in a common hostility to slaves.[83] A proclamation published at the Cape in 1794 decreed that no slave 'might jostle or otherwise behave in an ill-disposed way towards a European, even if he was of the meanest rank.'[84] To mark their status the dress of slaves was prescribed.

The formal legal status distinctions between burghers and Khoisan servants were considerably vaguer than those between burghers and slaves. Informally, however, Khoisan servants labored under many of the same restrictions as slaves, which played an important role in preserving order in the poorly policed settlement. Burghers, slaves and servants knew exactly what their respective places in society were and what was proper and permissible. Within each status category were informal subdivisions of rank, partly determined by the issue of color. There were, for instance, intermediate categories of white knechten and free blacks. They, too, were expected to act in a manner appropriate to the status allocated to them. There were always burghers determined to ensure that everyone below them behaved according to their assigned status.

One of the most pronounced features of the western Cape as a slave society was the remarkably wide spread of slave-ownership. In 1750 half of the male burghers were slave-owners. In Cape Town, two-thirds of the burghers held slaves by the end of the century and 70 per cent of the farmers in Stellenbosch and Drakenstein owned at least one slave.[85] Small slave-owners predominated; by the mid-eighteenth century 57 per cent had only one to five slaves and a further 22 per cent, six to ten. Less than five per cent of the owners in the colony had more than twenty-six slaves. The only big concentration was at the slave lodge in Cape Town, where more than five hundred Company slaves were held by 1795. A gross gender imbalance in the slave population meant that many male slaves lived without a spouse on the isolated farms – a sad fate.

---

82 *The Reports of De Chavonnes and His Council, and of Van Imhoff on the Cape* (Cape Town: VRS, 1918), p. 137.
83 Orlando Patterson, *Freedom in the Making of Western Culture* (New York: Basic Books, 1991), p. 80.
84 *Kaapse Plakkaatboek*, vol. 4, Proclamation of 20 August 1794, p. 249.
85 James Armstrong and Nigel Worden, 'The Slaves, 1652-1834', *SSAS*, pp. 135-6.

Slaves were part of almost every facet of burghers' lives. They looked after the burghers' children, prepared the meals, bought food for the household at the market and often accompanied their owners when they rode out. They were particularly visible in Cape Town. A visitor in the mid-eighteenth century observed that there seemed to be twenty blacks for every white on the street. By 1767 about 40 per cent of the total slave population of more than eight thousand lived in the port and large numbers appeared in public to trade or purchase goods for their masters. By 1821 the average number in a Cape Town household was eleven, of whom nearly half were enslaved or had been slaves.[86]

The ethnic origins of the slaves were very diverse. During the second half of the eighteenth century most came from Madagascar, but others came from Angola, Dahomey, various Indonesian islands and the East African coast. Slaves brought their own languages, but over time spoke a lingua franca. A creolized Portuguese survived until the end of the Company period, and a form of Dutch evolved into Afrikaans.[87]

While slaves made life easier for the burghers they also made it more insecure. They outnumbered male burghers by three to one in the 1760s – a cause for anxiety, particularly since there were no visible armed forces outside Cape Town. With slave-holding so dispersed, a much greater onus weighed on the individual slave-owner to maintain his authority over his slaves. The daily close contact produced a kind of schizophrenia with, on the one hand, a familiarity of contact, accompanied by the mutual contempt that familiarity is said to breed and, on the other hand, the desperate desire of the slave-holding class to remain exclusive, particularly in the church and family.

Familiarity could easily lead to transgressions by slaves, but one thing was certain: the government would punish a slave who lifted a hand against a master swiftly and mercilessly. The eighteenth century was a time when horrific forms of punishment were meted out in Europe, often to precede executions. The convicts England sent to Australia were sometimes sadistically punished, even for minor crimes. On Norfolk Island near the Australian coast two hundred lashes were not uncommon; by the turn of the century one prisoner had been flogged so often – some two thousand lashes in three years – that his back appeared 'quite bare of flesh and his collar bones were exposed looking very much like two ivory polished horns.'[88] At the Cape the burghers also received tough sentences and in a handful of notable cases were severely punished for murdering slaves or Khoisan.[89] Lower-class whites could not expect to be treated with any great consideration by the authorities except when it was necessary to uphold their status relative to slaves.

Slaves convicted of serious offences were commonly punished harshly: impaled, branded and quartered. The government meted out such brutal punishments not only when a slave attacked his master, but also when a slave set a house on fire or made advances to a European woman. The extreme penalty was death preceded by torture. Convicted slaves were broken alive on the wheel, their flesh was pulled off with red-hot tongs; slaves

---

86 Shell, *Children of Bondage,* pp. 138-44.
87 Armstrong and Worden, 'The Slaves', pp. 129-36.
88 Robert Hughes, *The Fatal Shore: The Epic of Australia's Founding* (New York: Vintage Books, 1986), pp. 114-15.
89 Hans Heese, *Reg en onreg: Kaapse regspraak in die agtiende eeu* (Cape Town: University of the Western Cape, 1994), pp. 122-57.

were mutilated, impaled or slowly strangled. The bodies of the executed were left hanging on gibbets or exposed after mutilation in Cape Town or on farmsteads. By 1727 there were so many disfigured and mutilated living slaves that the government decided to brand escaped slaves on the back in order to spare the feelings of the colonists, particularly pregnant women.[90]

The correct procedure for a master who wished a slave to be given a severe beating was to send him to the judicial authorities. The authorities' assistants would do the job under supervision. To save these authorities work, however, the Company felt that masters and mistresses should have enough scope to control their slaves and decreed that punishment should be of a 'domestic' nature, meaning that it should not exceed the punishment the head of a household would mete out to his children. No one was permitted to put a slave in irons or to torture him.

Such regulations reflect a dominant class concern to curb excesses in punishment. The great fear was that slaves, tormented beyond breaking point, would stage a revolt. Seeing their role as guardians of the public peace, the Stellenbosch college of landdrost and heemraden in 1776 observed that ill treatment of slaves could only lead 'to huge misfortune for the general welfare.'[91] Thus the law was used not only to punish slaves but also to protect them. A study noted: 'The overwhelming significance of Roman law in eighteenth-century Cape society was its apparent universality, that is, it was made applicable to all . . . The slave in Roman law was not only property or *Res* (object of rights), but also persona, by which the Roman lawyers meant human being.'[92] While there was no legal equality of slaves and masters, slaves could complain against their masters and give evidence in court.

Masters could not count on the Company's support if they committed murder or punished their slaves excessively.[93] But it was often not so much the law but the reputation of the slave-owner that decided the issue. The views of the gentry were vital in determining the reputations of masters and in establishing the sanctions. There are also indications that the gentry often brought such cases to court. To an important extent this was a form of class rule. A member of the gentry had little reason to fear that a slave's word against him would be believed, but public opinion could be tough on small-scale slave-owners and knechts, who had earlier stepped outside the bounds of the moral community by 'a recalcitrant lifestyle' or by acquiring a reputation for ill-treating slaves or Khoisan servants.[94] Despite the hideous punishments and the rigid controls, masters continued to fear that their slaves would rise up against them and sought more control. A request of burghers, in a petition of 1779, asked for the right to punish their slaves themselves 'without tyrannizing them.'[95] Fears about insubordinate slaves were credible

90 Armstrong and Worden, 'The Slaves', p. 156; A.J. Böeseken, *Slaves and Free Blacks at the Cape, 1658-1699* (Cape Town: Tafelberg, 1977), p. 3.

91 Dooling, *Law and Community*, p. 50.

92 Dooling, *Law and Community*, p. 72.

93 Robert Shell, 'The Family and Slavery at the Cape, 1680-1808', in Wilmot James and Mary Simons (eds.), *The Angry Divide: Social and Economic History of the Western Cape* (Cape Town: David Philip, 1989), p. 21.

94 Dooling, *Law and Community*, pp. 44-82.

95 Coenraad Beyers, *Die Kaapse Patriotte* (Pretoria: Van Schaik, 1967), p. 51.

enough for burghers to cite as grounds for not complying with government orders that would take them away from their farms for a long period. In 1782, seventy-eight farmers from Drakenstein petitioned the government to be absolved from a month's guard duty, lest in their absence their wives and families would be left 'open to the refractoriness and wantonness of their slaves, from which, by continuation, even greater evils, such as rape, theft, robbery and murder can be feared.'[96]

While this could be interpreted as a case of special pleading, Sparrman's reliable account of the mid-1770s suggests that keeping slaves made masters very uneasy about their security. A knecht told Sparrman of the danger of slaves 'becoming furious at night and committing murder, more particularly on the person of the masters.' The traveler noted: 'Everybody in this country is obliged to bolt the door of his chamber at night, and keep loaded firearms by him, for fear of the revengeful disposition of his slaves.'[97]

Negative views of blacks, although not reflected in documents before about 1780, were part of the identity map of burghers well before they met blacks on the frontier. So was racial apprehension. Burghers were not so much afraid of a general slave uprising as of their own slaves murdering them or setting fire to their houses. The insecurity springing from life on isolated farms produced the phobias that were to mark white society in the centuries to come.

Viewed comparatively, the most striking aspect of Cape slavery was that owners offered so few tangible rewards to reconcile slaves to their fate. Since ancient times slaveholding societies had offered inducements, the prospect of manumission being the most powerful. At the Cape, however, there were few incentives. Outside Cape Town no sophisticated system existed for rewarding slaves (for instance sending some to school) or of making distinctions of rank among them. On average only ten slaves belonging to the Cape burghers were freed per year. One reason for the low rate was that at manumission masters had to post a bond that was forfeited if the freed slave became destitute. With few interstitial jobs in the Cape economy this was a real possibility. The manumission rate in Brazil was six times higher than that at the Cape.

The burgher slave-owners made no great effort to have their slaves baptized. Of the slaves belonging to private people two or three children and one or two adults were baptized per year. Nor did burghers encourage the formation of slave families on any noticeable scale.

The ideology of paternalism had to bear the brunt of the burden in reconciling slaves to their fate. Owners propagated the myth that slaves were members of the household and even part of the extended family, consisting of the patriarch's immediate family, some brothers or sisters and their families, one or more bywoner families, Khoikhoi servants and slaves. The master called the slaves and servants his 'volk' (people). Paternalism was supposed to represent a bargain. At the most elemental level, slaves were expected to display loyalty and respect towards the master or mistress. The master class acted as if they were fathers, rewarding faithful slaves and disciplining those who had erred, as they did

---

96 Robert Ross, *Cape of Torments: Slavery and Resistance in South Africa* (London: Routledge Kegan Paul, 1983), p. 30.

97 Anders Sparrman, *A Voyage to the Cape of Good Hope, 1772-1776* (1785, reprint Cape Town: Van Riebeeck Society, 1975), pp. 73, 102.

in the case of their children. They also cared for them, fed them properly, and nursed them when sick.

The concept of a bonded extended 'family' was emphasized by the common worship of the Lord by both masters and slaves. By the end of the eighteenth century it became common practice for masters to admit their most trusted slaves and servants, usually squatting or standing against a wall, to the family prayers held every day. In the master's mind the action of inviting the slave briefly into the inner sanctum of his family demonstrated his benign and moral intent. This 'benevolence' was a counterpoint to the violence inflicted on erring servants, and it boosted the burghers' belief in themselves as Christian colonizers of the land.[98]

The real purpose of paternalism was to justify slavery not to the slave but to the master and to boost the master's own self-respect. Even in the case of horrific punishments and forms of torture meted out to slaves by the judicial system, masters somehow believed that slaves acquiesced in the basic scheme of things. When the British, after occupying the Cape in 1795, sought to abolish this judicial torture, some leading Cape colonists responded: '[We] would flatter ourselves with the hopes that it is not impossible to inspire the Slaves with affection for their Masters, for it is indisputably true that affection is a reciprocal sentiment, and always increases in proportion to the good actions of him towards whom such sentiments are exerted.'[99]

In some cases paternalism produced a stable relationship. Some masters referred to their slaves as 'a sort of child of the family.'[100] Early in the nineteenth century the traveler Lichtenstein described a farm on the northeast frontier as a place where family harmony reigned among master, mistress, slave and Khoikhoi servants.[101] Invariably, however, the most stable forms of paternalism were not to be found in the relationship between a master and a male slave but between a mistress and a female slave, particularly in the case of female slaves born into the household. Slave women seldom did hard manual labor in the fields as in many other slave societies. They had other duties within the house: wet nurse, nanny, cook, cleaner and confidante of the mistress. Bird's 1822 account depicted African-born female slaves as 'the favorite slaves of the mistress, arranging and keeping everything in order.' They were 'entrusted with all that is valuable – more like companions than slaves; but the mistress rarely, and the slave never, forget their relative situations, and however familiar in private, in the presence of another due form prevails.'[102]

The slave wet nurse was a pivotal figure in the burgher family. While wet nursing was frowned upon in Holland, at the Cape the suckling of European babies by slave women was widespread. It made it possible for the biological mother to ovulate sooner and have children at shorter intervals. Thus wet nurses and nannies shared the burden of the prodigious growth of the burgher population. Wet-nursing, in consequence, also contributed to the failure of the slave population to reproduce itself in the eighteenth and

98 Stanley Trapido, 'Household Prayers, Paternalism and the Fostering of a Settler Identity', paper presented at a conference at the London School of Economics, 8 December 2000.
99 *Afrikaner Political Thought, 1780-1850*, p. 93.
100 Shell, 'Family and Slavery', p. 24.
101 Lichtenstein, *Travels in Southern Africa*, vol. 2, p. 23.
102 [W.W. Bird], *State of the Cape of Good Hope in 1822* (London: John Murray, 1823), p. 74.

early nineteenth century, since suckling a child hampered a wet nurse's fertility. Acting as a nanny to white children limited the time a female slave could spend with her own.

Two words survived as testimony to this intimate relationship: 'minnemoer' or 'mina' (love mother) and 'aiya' or 'aia' (old nursemaid). Some visitors speculated that the intimate relationship European boys had with the wet nurse and nanny could, in later life, find expression in being more at ease with black women and even preferring sex with them than with white women. But this is in the range of speculation and it is striking that when boys became adults they did not manumit their wet nurses, while analyses of the pattern of manumission show a tendency for European women to manumit slave women who had been wet nurses or 'foster mothers.'[103]

No slave system is ever mild and it would be a mistake to consider Cape slavery as anything but brutal. The cruelest part was often the tight and suffocating ties.[104] Slave and burgher children played with each other as friends but when they grew up the master-slave hierarchy came into place. The burgher child became a master; the slave remained a slave. Even in adult life a slave continued to be addressed as *jong* (boy) or *meid* (girl), to be called by his or her first name and to go about barefoot.[105] Slave women, especially, developed bonds of allegiance and trust with their 'family', but remained perpetual minors and, like slave men, almost always had to sacrifice an independent family life of their own for that of their master and mistress. Slave women, moreover, had to endure the sexual advances of the master class. For them the suffering was most acute, having to endure both the intimate and harsh side of Cape slavery. It was they who most often felt betrayed by the paternalistic relationship. When the British tried to ameliorate slavery in the second quarter of the nineteenth century, slave women submitted the vast majority of complaints to the guardian of the slaves.

New identities

For most of the eighteenth century the colonists referred to themselves as burghers or Christians and occasionally as Dutchmen, but two other self-concepts also came to the fore, one of being white people, the other of being Afrikaners.

During the first 150 years of the Cape there was no compelling reason to introduce clear racial distinctions or develop an ideology of racism. In every generation the legal status distinctions, which largely corresponded with racial distinctions, were reproduced. Burghers were white and slaves black. A female burgher's children were born as burghers; a female slave's children under the matrilineal system of slave societies were born slaves.[106] These distinctions were reinforced by the Reformed Church, which baptized few outside the ranks of the Europeans.

Beyond Cape Town the lines became rigid from early in the eighteenth century. Cape Town, however, remained socially fluid, with considerable numbers of free blacks and poorer whites mixing socially and sometimes establishing sexual unions. During the

---

103 Shell, 'Tender Ties: The Women of the Cape Slave Society', *SSA*, 17 (1992), p. 14.
104 Shell, *Children of Bondage*; see also Scully, 'Liberating the Family?'
105 Thunberg, *Travels*, vol. 1, p. 115.
106 Personal communication by Robert Shell, 27 April 1997.

1820s the free blacks, together with other free people of color, formed at least one quarter of the free population of Cape Town (the garrison excluded). Of all marriages in the town, 16 per cent were mixed marriages. In comparison with other slave societies these were high proportions.[107]

The increased visibility of free blacks from the 1770s century triggered regulations by the government to control them and efforts by burghers to ostracize them. The records for the first time report the expression of feelings of racial prejudice. The government and the church began to keep separate lists for certain categories of people. After a drill of the Stellenbosch militia in 1788, when some burghers refused to serve under a Corporal Johannes Hartogh on the grounds that he was black and of 'heathen descent', the Company formed a special unit the next year for 'Basters and mistiches', called the Free Corps, and compelled free blacks to serve in it. In 1793 two commissioners commented on the 'superiority of *whites*' (my emphasis).[108] The term 'white' had begun to appear in growing measure in the records.[109]

As the eighteenth century progressed fewer and fewer people considered black entered burgher families. In 1807 only five per cent of a sample of 1,063 children baptized in that year in the Reformed and Lutheran churches had a grandparent indicated by genealogists as 'Non-European' (usually slaves born abroad or from a slave mother at the Cape).[110]

'Afrikaner' was the other term that had become more prominent. A sense of being Afrikaners rather than being Dutch or French or German had crystallized by the end of the eighteenth century. One of the first visitors to report on the emergence of a new social identity, Admiral Stavorinus, wrote in 1770: 'Although the first colonists here were composed of various nations, they are, by the operation of time, now so thoroughly blended together, that they are not to be distinguished from each other; even most of such as have been born in Europe, and who have resided here for some years, changed their national character, for that of this country.'[111] People from Dutch and German descent dominated the make-up of this community; according to J.A. Heese, 36 per cent of them were Dutch, 35 per cent German, 5 per cent French and 7 per cent non-European.[112] Another calculation, using a different method, calculated the composition by 1807 as follows: Dutch 34 per cent, German 29 per cent, French 25 per cent, and non-European 5 per cent.[113]

---

107 Shell, *Children of Bondage*, p. 142; Richard Elphick and Robert Shell, 'Intergroup Relations' in *SSAS*, p. 219.

108 Cited by P. van Arkel, G.C. Quispel and Robert Ross, *De wijngaard des Heren* (Leiden: Martinus Nijhoff, 1983), p. 34.

109 Elphick and Giliomee, 'European Dominance', in *SSAS*, pp. 544-52.

110 This refers to *heelslag* or 'full' non-European as distinct from *halfslag* or 'half-European' when someone was the child of a European and non-European. The figure cited above does not mean that the other grandparents were full European; many were not. G.F.C. de Bruyn, personal communication, 30 November 1999.

111 J.S. Stavorinus, *Voyages to the East-Indies by the Late John Splinter Stavorinus* (London: Robinson, 1798), vol. 3, p. 435.

112 Heese, *Die herkoms van die Afrikaner,* pp. 14-21.

113 G.F.C. de Bruyn, 'Die samestelling van die Afrikaner', *Tydskrif vir Geesteswetenskappe,* 15 (1976), pp. 39-42; and personal communication, 23 February 1977.

The term 'Afrikaander' or 'Afrikaner', which Biebouw had employed in 1707, surfaced again in the 1730s when an equally enigmatic character, called Estienne Barbier, used it. He was born in France and had arrived at the Cape in the mid-1730s as a sergeant in the VOC service. As in Biebouw's case Barbier was on the periphery of European society and spoke his words in the context of political insubordination. His rebellion had its roots in the cattle trade between burghers and Khoikhoi. The government was always unwilling to allow an open door for bartering activities since they tended to become a thin disguise for theft. When some Namas from near the Orange River arrived in the western Cape to complain about losses, the landdrost of Stellenbosch took them under his protection, and the government summoned the accused to appear in the Court of Justice to answer the Khoikhoi's accusations.

During these events Barbier was in prison, after having been convicted of falsely accusing a high Company official. He managed to escape in 1739 and sought refuge among the farmers of the Drakenstein Valley, where he had little difficulty in persuading the burghers of the high officials' iniquities. In a manifesto he appealed to his 'Afrikanders broederen' ('Afrikaner brothers') to join him in opposing a government that favored 'Hottentots, who knew neither salvation nor damnation ' above white men.'[114] Barbier attracted the active support of only a handful of burghers. They began by ripping the government's proclamation against stock bartering off the church door in Paarl. The Company acted with considerable restraint and granted amnesty to Barbier's handful of followers, possibly because they knew that the rebels enjoyed considerable passive support. Barbier himself, however, was executed at the end of 1739.

During the late 1770s and early 1780s the burghers of the western Cape began to demand an extension of their rights in the movement of the Cape Patriots. On one occasion, in a petition to the government, they referred to themselves as 'Africaners.'[115] After the Patriot struggle the burghers increasingly used the term Afrikaner. During the 1790s a Dutch visitor said of the Cape colonist: 'He is proud of the name Africaan and Cape burgher seems to him like a grand title.'[116] Other observers used the term 'Afrikaners', or 'Afrikaanen', for people in the city, and 'Boeren' for those living in the countryside.[117] Some of the British at the Cape were fond of referring to light-skinned slaves born at the Cape as 'Africanders.' However, the name 'Afrikaner' grew to be more broadly used to refer to Europeans who spoke Dutch or Afrikaans. In 1822 Burchell observed that all those born in the Cape Colony who were not of English but of German, Dutch or French descent, and who spoke Dutch called themselves 'Africaanders.'[118] A few years earlier Fisher had written: '[They] all speak a very bad sort of Dutch language . . . and style themselves as an original nation, Africanes [sic].'[119]

---

114 Gerrit Schutte, 'Company and Colonists at the Cape, 1652-1795', SSAS, p. 309.

115 Beyers, Die Kaapse Patriotte, p. 327.

116 Cornelis de Jong, Reizen naar de Kaap de Goede Hoop, Ierland en Noorwegen in de jaren 1791 tot 1799 (Haarlem: Bohn, 1802), p. 134.

117 Schoeman, Dogter van Sion, pp. 28, 232.

118 W.J. Burchell, Travels in the Interior of South Africa (London: Batchworth Press, 1822), vol. 1, p. 21.

119 R.B. Fisher, The Importance of the Cape of Good Hope as a Colony to Great Britain (London: Cadell and Davies, 1816), pp. 12, 99-100.

The 'bad sort of Dutch language' Fisher referred to would come to be known as Afrikaans. Earlier, in 1685, a senior official considered it necessary to warn against a corruption of Dutch. H.A. van Reede expressed concern that, with Dutch people in the colonies
tending to imitate the 'native' use of Dutch, 'a broken language will be established which
will be impossible to overcome afterwards.'[120] But the government's ability to impose the
official form of Dutch was limited. Schools offered a rudimentary education and were
poorly attended. The government was even less able to compel slaves and Khoikhoi servants to adhere to the formal rules of official Dutch.

Afrikaans was, in its essence, a dialect of Dutch that had over time undergone a limited measure of creolization or deviation from the basic Dutch structure. During the first
fifty to seventy years of the settlement, slaves and Khoikhoi servants had the greatest
hand in the development of the restructured Dutch. In the course of the eighteenth century both burghers and their servants, in interaction with each other, took the restructuring further. Dutch was simplified and a considerable amount of Malayo-Portuguese,
as spoken among the slaves, was injected. (The expression 'baie dankie' – 'thank you' –
reflects both the deviation from Dutch and the borrowing of the Malay banja.) By the
end of the century Cape Dutch had largely become what is now Afrikaans.[121] In the western Cape, especially in its rural towns and farms, the main variety of Afrikaans took root
as the shared cultural creation, in countless small-scale localities, of Europeans and
non-Europeans, of whites and blacks, masters and slaves.

There were limits to the extent of creolization. There were few big plantations where
large groups of slaves or servants could develop a fully-fledged Creole language among
themselves. By the end of the eighteenth century half the speakers of Afrikaans were of
European descent and continued to be influenced by Dutch as both the written and the
main public language.[122] The Dutch Staten Bible was widely read by burghers, and on
the frontier. The church itself tried strenuously to preserve Dutch until the third decade
of the twentieth century. In all these ways Dutch both supported and stemmed the development of Afrikaans. Without the continued use of Dutch, particularly in the church
and as written medium, Afrikaans would in all probability have been swept aside by English in the nineteenth century.

The degree of creolization was, in fact, more limited than was the case with the Carib-
bean Dutch creole language. People from the Netherlands understood Afrikaans fairly
easily. Travelers tended to see it as a dialect, not a distinctive language. Burchell, for instance, advised travelers in the colony to have a knowledge of Dutch 'according to the
Cape dialect, and even according to the corrupt dialect of the Hottentots.'[123]

---

120 For a discussion of this passage, which has triggered great academic controversy, see J. du P.
   Scholtz, *Taalhistoriese opstelle* (Cape Town: Tafelberg, 1981), pp. 257-75.
121 Fritz Ponelis, *The Development of Afrikaans* (Frankfurt: Peter Lang, 1993). For a comparative discussion of Afrikaans with special reference to creolization, see John Holm, *Pidgins and Creole*
   (Cambridge: Cambridge University Press, 1989).
122 See the studies by Stanley Trapido, 'Van Riebeeck Day and the New Jerusalem', and 'The Cape in
   the Atlantic World: Problems of Dutch Colonial Identity', *SSA*, 18 (1993).
123 Burchell, *Travels*, vol. 1, p. 15.

Patriots and a founding myth

A much-enhanced sense of political consciousness was in evidence in the struggle of the Cape Patriots between 1778 and 1787, which in turn drew inspiration from the Patriot movement in the Netherlands during this period. The principal thinker of the Dutch movement was Joan Dirk van der Capelin tot den Poll, who campaigned for the overthrow of the Stadholder of the Netherlands and of the self-appointed regents who thwarted the aspirations of the burghers. English theorists like Price, Hutcheson and Locke, in turn, influenced Van der Poll and other Dutch thinkers. The outbreak of the American Revolution in 1776 was a considerable inspiration to European colonists across the world.[124]

But although they quoted from or circulated documents by Enlightenment thinkers, the Cape Patriots were preoccupied with local concerns. Despite the 1706 ban on private economic activities by officials, conflict over economic opportunities persisted between burghers and Company servants at the Cape. By the 1770s VOC officials had become much shrewder in disguising their trading activities. Officials owned the two main trading firms at the Cape. Other officials, either on their own or in partnership with burgher associates, participated in numerous trading activities, enjoying unfair privileges, so the Patriots said. Resentfully the Patriots called the coterie of wealthy Company servants and burghers who were working hand in glove 'Mamluks', after a samurai-like regime of mercenary slaves-turned-masters, who dominated the Middle East until the beginning of the sixteenth century.

At the heart of the Cape struggle lay a clash over the founding myth. The official Hendrik Boers, who arrived in 1774 to become Fiscal (chief prosecutor), held ideas similar to those of Willem Adriaan van der Stel seventy years earlier. In his view the Cape did not exist for the benefit of the burghers, but for the benefit of the Company. Along with Governor Joachim van Plettenberg, Boers insisted that the Company should use the right to recall recalcitrant burghers to its service and send them wherever it chose. In the first few years of Van Plettenberg's term no fewer than eighteen burghers were forcibly re-enlisted and sent overseas. A spur to the Cape Patriot movement was the banishment in 1778 of the eighteenth burgher, Carel Hendrik Buytendagh. Although Buytendagh was a notorious ruffian who beat up both his family and his servants, the burghers felt it important to contest the use of banishment.

The Cape Patriots used the natural rights philosophy along with their version of the foundation myth. One of their pamphlets claimed that the Company and the first settlers it sent to Africa entered into an 'original social contract.' Implausibly it depicted Van Riebeeck's administration as a golden age, in which the settlers enjoyed 'proper, natural and fitting freedom.' Subsequently the colonists had been exposed to an 'arbitrary despotism.' The Patriots considered Boers' claims 'absurd.' In their view every person released from Company service enjoyed all the rights of citizens who had never been in Company service.[125]

---

124 Simon Schama, *Patriots and Liberators: Revolution in the Netherlands, 1780-1813* (New York: Alfred Knopf, 1977), p. 66.
125 *Afrikaner Political Thought, 1780-1850*, pp. 256-64.

The main spokesmen for the Patriots were fairly wealthy men from in and around Cape Town. In 1784 a body called the 'Commissioned Representatives of the People' elected four new delegates to submit a new petition. In the Netherlands these delegates mixed with the Dutch Patriots and other anti-Orangists. Because the Company directors were firmly Orangist, they also appealed to the States-General and to public opinion.

The Cape Patriots' political demands were ambitious. They asked for seven seats for burghers on the Council of Policy when matters affecting burghers were discussed, and for half the seats on the Court of Justice. Instead of the government's co-opting burghers to serve on government colleges, they had to be 'freely elected' by outgoing burgher members. The Cape Patriots sought a clearer definition of burgher rights, the codification of laws, and the prohibition of the banishment of burghers except by permission of the burgher councilors.

The Patriots' other concern was economic. They complained about the trading activities of officials and the lack of free trade, asked for better prices for products, leave to export cargoes annually to the Netherlands, for free trade with the East Indies and a reduction in farm rents. The Patriot efforts to highlight the curbs on their economic advancement were complicated by the presence of a French fleet at the Cape during the first half of the 1780s that resulted in the western Cape enjoying an economic boom. The officials were quick to point this out to the VOC. They also accused the burghers of laziness and claimed that their own trading activities fell well within the limits of established custom.

Of greater significance were the social tensions reflected in the Patriots' documents. They asked, for example, that white men not be arrested by '*kaffers*' (slaves who served as policemen), and that burghers be allowed to punish their own slaves.

The greatest historical significance lies in the fact that for the first time we have a burgher document addressing the issue of their survival in a way that transcended the immediate self-interest of the authors. Because the western Cape was prospering in the early 1780s, the Patriots, who came exclusively from this part of the Cape, were forced to think 'nationally.' Their principal argument was that the 'constitution' of the colony had become so defective that the survival of burgher society as a whole was imperiled. They were playing on the grave fears of the mother country that burghers living among the Khoikhoi in remote areas would 'go native.' They warned that if there were no structural reform, the burgers' dispersal into the interior would result in a 'complete bastardization of morals' and the rise of a 'completely degenerate nation.' The petitioners asked plaintively: 'If this country cannot even support the people with whom any civilization rests, what will it let happen to those who mix their blood with that of Hottentots and Kaffirs?'[126]

All the petitions and deputations to the Netherlands achieved little. The VOC rejected the key demand, namely burgher representation on the Council of Policy. It permitted six rather than three burghers on the Council of Justice. Burghers would no longer be re-enlisted in the Company's service. They were not allowed to trade in their

---

126 *Afrikaner Political Thought, 1780-1850*, p. 40.

own ships, but the directors did permit free trade with foreign ships – but only after the Company's needs had been met. In the western Cape the activities of the Patriots fizzled out as the burghers waited to see what the momentous developments in Europe held in store for them.

In 1787 the Patriot movement in the Netherlands was crushed after the Stadholder had called in Prussian troops. Large numbers of Patriots emigrated to other countries, particularly to the newly independent United States of America. The French Revolution unleashed new tensions in the Netherlands during the early 1790s. In January 1795 the French cavalry entered Amsterdam and Dutch revolutionaries proclaimed the Batavian republic. The Orangist party was routed and the Stadholder fled to London. On 31 January 1795 the 'Provisional Representatives of the People of Holland' proclaimed the rights of man and burgher. They swept away the councils, corporations and colleges of the old constitution and many of the privileges of the nobility.

Having fled to London, the Prince of Orange had asked the British government to send an armed force to occupy the Cape and all other Dutch possessions abroad, and in September 1795 a British force occupied the Cape. It encountered a deeply divided white population with most of the top Cape officials Orangists, anti-revolutionary and pro-Britain, but the burghers, in general, strongly pro-France, pro-revolution, and anti-Britain. General James Craig wrote after the British conquest of the Cape in September 1795: '[It] is certain that the great body of the people are at the moment infected with the rankest poison of Jacobinism.'[127] In the western Cape the British force soon intimidated aspirant revolutionaries into sullen resignation, but the burghers on the eastern frontier would challenge the political order, with near fatal consequences for the colonial settlement in the east.

The rural western Cape as epicenter

During the eighteenth century there was no intellectual elite that reflected systematically and on a continuing basis on the survival of the Europeans or Afrikaners as a collectivity. Indeed, when white people thought of themselves in collective terms they conceived of themselves either as Company servants or as burghers. One of the exceptions was a 1784 document of the Cape Patriots that blamed the colony's defective 'constitution' and bemoaned 'the sorry lot of descendants of proper European parents' on the frontier who could not be supported by the country.[128] Senior Cape-born VOC officials tended to despise the simple frontiersmen whom Willem Stephanus van Ryneveld referred to as having 'grown up in idleness and in the unrestrained indulgence of the wild passions in nature.'[129] The British would find it easy to enlist this class of well-educated colonists.

It was the rural western Cape that wielded the most important influence on the development of a burgher community with certain distinctive institutions and a specific way of thinking about collective survival. Theirs was a rigid society as far as the op-

---

127 *RCC*, vol. 1, p. 163.
128 *Afrikaner Political Thought, 1780-1850*, p. 43.
129 *RCC*, vol. 4, p. 89.

portunities for black and brown people, and more particularly their access to baptism and manumission, were concerned. No free blacks managed to become successful farmers. It was here that the model of a racially exclusive white burgher community with special political and social privileges crystallized. It was this rural Western Cape community that formed the epicenter of the norms the burghers took with them when they settled in the deeper interior.

Chapter 3

Fractious Frontiersmen

Colonizing the interior

'Not worth a pipeful of tobacco.' So a Swellendam burgher described the Cape Colony's government in the second half of the eighteenth century.[1] In 1815 a sixteen-year-old who took part in a rebellion said: 'I am a young man who does not know yet what a Government is, as I was never near one.'[2] The burghers on the frontier realized that they needed a steady supply of ammunition, but many pretended that they could do without the government, which issued it.

Interested only in the farmers' livestock that walked to the market, the government erected the flimsiest of administrative infrastructure in the interior beyond the first mountain ranges, and with no police or military force the task of colonizing the interior fell on the shoulders of the burghers themselves, with their Khoikhoi auxiliaries. During the eighteenth century only two towns, Swellendam (1745) and Graaff-Reinet (1796), were established between the coastal mountain ranges and the Fish River, which lay some 800 kilometers east of Cape Town. Each had its own drostdy, where the landdrost, the government's representative, had his office. These towns remained mere hamlets for several decades after the first landdrost moved in. They were so far from most farms that the burghers settled their own conflicts with their servants rather than go to court. Educational facilities were extremely limited until the end of the nineteenth century. Most farmers were barely literate, depending on itinerant teachers hired to give their children a smattering of learning.

The social order of the land where the stock farmers settled rested on the loan farm system, the government's provision of ammunition and the burgher commando to crush resistance or recover stolen livestock. The loan farm system provided those who arrived first with the opportunity to spread themselves out, giving rise to an unsystematic form of colonization. In 1812 Governor John Cradock wrote that its consequence 'was to extend and scatter the habitations.' British rule ought 'to take the opposite course, and con-

---

1 Leonard Guelke, 'Freehold Farmers and Frontier Settlers, 1657-1780', *SSAS*, p. 95.
2 H.C.V. Leibbrandt, *The Rebellion of 1815* (Cape Town: Juta, 1902), p. 352.

centrate the population to form villages . . . [where] mutual aid can be given and the seeds of civilization take their root.'[3]

As the sole supplier of ammunition, the government made it known that it would not hesitate to cut off the supply if it was used for unnecessary aggression against the burghers' indigenous enemies. Such a suspension of the supply would leave the burghers defenseless. Many burghers believed, nonetheless, that they did not have to heed the government's warnings. They were opposed by those who feared that both unprovoked aggression and a shortage of ammunition could be disastrous. More than once insubordinate frontiersmen provoked clashes with the native peoples. Counter-attacks led to the large-scale withdrawal of burghers from newly settled regions. Frontier lawlessness and insubordination drove the officials to despair and undermined the cohesion and discipline of the commando.

The commando was the fighting arm of the burghers. It originated when the Company sent out soldiers and burghers on expeditions to recover stolen cattle. In 1715 the first commando, comprised entirely of burgher volunteers, went out on such a mission. After 1739 it was compulsory for every burgher with an interest in the outlying districts to do the same. As a result, the burghers were carrying virtually the sole responsibility for defending the land frontier, and the commando leader had considerable discretion to act. In its instructions to one of the first commandos, the Company decreed that it could 'fire freely and take prisoners and act otherwise as they saw fit since the marauders cannot be considered as any other but enemies of the Hon. Company.'[4]

The landdrost appointed a burgher in every district division as *veldcorporaal* of the commando (a title later changed to *veldwagmeester*, then to *veldkornet* or field cornet). Since it was imperative to respond swiftly to recover stolen cattle, the veldcorporaal did not need the landdrost's permission before ordering his men out into the field. The large extent of the district wards, and the poor communications system, produced a further devolution of responsibility. A burgher could ride out in hot pursuit of stock thieves, provided he informed the local field corporal afterwards. Much of the time the Company closed its eyes to the inevitable abuses since the system cost it virtually nothing.

Although relatively few in numbers, the expanding stock farmers had considerable advantages over hostile clans: horses, guns, and wagons, which enabled them to turn conquest into settlement by transporting their families and their goods.[5] Khoikhoi clans had fought the expansion on the frontier until a smallpox epidemic decimated the western Khoikhoi in 1713. Along the northern and northeastern borders Bushmen, often also called Bushmen-Hottentotten, were the principal enemy, most of them in small bands of hunters and Khoikhoi who had lost their stock.

Towards the east lived the Xhosa, a branch of the Nguni-speakers, who dwelled in well-watered settlements, each of which could supply most of the economic needs of its inhabitants, organized into chiefdoms. Like the farmers, the Xhosa considered pastoralism their main occupation. The Xhosa supplemented this by hunting and agriculture,

---

3 G.E. Cory, *The Rise of South Africa* (New York: Longmans, Green, 1910), vol. 1, p. 256.

4 P.J. van der Merwe, *Die noordwaartse beweging van die Boere voor die Groot Trek, 1770-1842* (Den Haag: Van Stockum, 1937), pp. 25-6.

5 C.W. de Kiewiet, *A History of South Africa* (Oxford: Oxford University Press, 1941), p. 25.

cultivating millet, maize, peas, beans, watermelons, tobacco and *dacha*. Once pastures or soil were exhausted a Xhosa chiefdom moved on.

The settlement pattern of the Xhosa was determined by their crops, which required the high summer rainfall of the eastern regions of South Africa. From the beginning of the eighteenth century the Xhosa had been moving slowly from the Kei River westwards towards the Fish River. Much of the area between the Fish and the Bushman's River to its west was sour veld or Zuurveld, as the area was called. It lay in a zone of uncertain rainfall that changed to winter rainfall further to the west. Needing summer rain, the Xhosa had not moved far west of the Fish when they encountered the burghers. Much more numerous and settled than the Khoisan, the Xhosa proved to be formidable adversaries.

Except in some of the eighteenth century campaigns against the Bushmen, the advance guard of the stock farmers, called the *trekboers*, made no attempt to exterminate the indigenous people they encountered. Not only were there too few frontiersmen to embark on campaigns of extermination, but the farmers coveted indigenous labor. While the Bushman economy was incompatible with their own, the Khoikhoi and the Xhosa kept stock and were willing to work as herdsmen on the farms. Farmers put a much higher premium on 'native hands' than 'native corpses.'

An uneasy relationship: burghers and Khoikhoi

In a comparative overview of 1900, the Dutch scholar, H.J. Nieboer, sketched the kind of labor system that could be expected in the conditions in which the burghers found themselves: 'Slavery will generally occur', he wrote, 'where there is still free land available (through which a livelihood can be found without the help of capital), where there are in other words still "open resources" . . . No one is dependent on another for his earnings, and it is necessary to use force if others are to be made to work for an individual.'[6]

The unsystematic colonization, and the absence of interior markets and a cash economy ruled out wage labor at the Cape. Instead, a system of bonded labor arose. The abundant land resources enabled the burghers to avoid working themselves despite a lack of capital. They forced others to work for them.

Slavery was not really an option. The government prohibited it, but more importantly, slavery required the pretence that the slave did not belong to any legitimate social or moral community and enjoyed no independent social existence.[7] On a frontier that essential pretence was difficult to sustain if clansmen lived close by in a stable community. Yet the demands Afrikaner frontier colonists imposed on the Khoikhoi were most exacting. They wanted the Khoikhoi to yield their land and sometimes their cattle as well. They wanted them to work as herdsmen, where they would be exposed as targets for the Bushman raiders. They eagerly drew on the Khoikhoi's invaluable knowledge about maintaining pastoral production in an arid environment.[8] To cap it all, they required

---

6 See the extract published by Robin Winks, *Slavery* (New York: New York University Press, 1972), pp. 194-217; the quote is on p. 195.

7 Orlando Patterson, *Freedom, Volume One: Freedom in the Making of Western Culture* (New York: Basic Books, 1991), pp. 9-10.

8 Nigel Penn, 'The Northern Cape Frontier Zone, 1700-*c.* 1815', doctoral diss., University of Cape Town, 1995, p. 187.

some of the Khoikhoi male servants to go out on commando carrying guns. This pre-supposed a large measure of trust.

Some burghers on the pioneering frontier with its open resources forced the Khoi-khoi to work for them, beat them and threatened to shoot them, and mercilessly whipped those who had fled and were recaptured. Such Khoikhoi became little more than serfs or slaves. But coercive and cruel control could be counterproductive. The allegiance of the armed Khoikhoi sent out on commandos could not be won by beatings. Many burgh-ers worked out a more stable relationship; one historians have called 'clientship.' In the clientship tradition a poor and insecure Khoikhoi would seek the protection of a burgh-er as patron and work for him. In exchange the patron helped him build up his live-stock on a frontier where beasts of prey roamed freely and Bushmen herders constantly threatened small herding communities.

O.F. Mentzel's account of the 1730s and 1740s refers to the sons of western Cape farmers who traveled about the country 'looking for a decent place to settle, if possible next to a Hottentot kraal.'[9] Gradually, the kraal became part of their farm, with a piece of land set aside for a Khoikhoi clan or family to pasture their own stock. Anders Sparr-man, who traveled into the interior during the 1770s, and who criticized the way fron-tiersmen waged war against the Bushmen, sketched the clientship relationship between burghers and Khoikhoi in benign terms: 'I must confess', he wrote, 'that the Hottentots, who are in some husbandman's service, are treated in the gentlest manner, and, perhaps, even without ever having a harsh word given them, live very well with regard to pro-visions, are well clad relatively to their condition in life and are very comfortably lodged, in comparison of what others are, in their own straw cottages.'[10]

But as the frontier became more settled, competition for labor intensified and in many cases the clientship relationship broke down. To prevent their laborers from leaving, some farmers introduced mechanisms developed in the slave society of the western Cape, particularly passes and indentureship. In the final decades of the eighteenth cen-tury the district authorities in Graaff-Reinet and Swellendam introduced pass regula-tions, with masters issuing passes. If a laborer left a farm without a pass, a commando would hunt him down. Along with passes, indentureship was imported from the Cape. On western Cape farms, where liaisons between slave men and Khoikhoi women were common, owners indentured the children of such liaisons until the age of eighteen or twenty-one or twenty-five as repayment for bearing the cost of rearing the children. This custom was formally introduced in 1775, but there is good reason to believe that it had been practiced earlier. On the frontier the system started in the same way, but it was soon expanded to cases where both parents were Khoikhoi.

Masters used this device to prevent laborers from leaving. Frontier indentureship was justified with the same paternalistic ideology as slavery. It held that in return for food, shelter and protection the indentured servants had to serve their masters faithfully and show gratitude for what they received. Indentured children were taught the master's language and culture, and allocated menial tasks. Children from Europe and Africa ate the same food and played together in the narrow confines of the home and *werf* or yard.

---

9 O.F Mentzel, *Description of the Cape of Good Hope* (Cape Town: VRS, 1944), vol. 3, p. 111.
10 Anders Sparrman, *A Voyage to the Cape of Good Hope, 1772-1776* (Cape Town: VRS, 1975), p. 200.

The commando as a fighting band

Between 1710 and 1770 the commandos swept aside resistance without much effort, but by the early 1770s the Bushmen on the northeastern frontier fiercely resisted the encroachment on their hunting fields. They were distressed also by the large quantity of game killed by the farmers, often simply for sport. Koerikei, the famous chief of the 'Chinese' Bushmen, asked a farmer: 'What are you doing in my land? . . . You have taken all the places where the eland and the other game live. Why did you not stay where the sun goes down, where you first came from?'[11]

The battles of 1770 to 1810 between burghers and Bushmen were as merciless as those fought between pastoralists and herders on any frontier. Bushmen killed and maimed the burghers' cattle and sheep at random, murdered herders and mutilated their corpses. Once a farmer woke up in the morning to find his herders slain and forty cattle and two hundred sheep – all his stock – dead. Describing the situation in the 1790s, the traveler John Barrow gave an account of the pervasive insecurity in which frontiersmen lived:

> An inhabitant of Sneuberg [sic] not only lives under the continual apprehension of losing his property, but also is perpetually exposed to the danger of being put to death. If he has occasion to go to the distance of 500 yards from the house, he is under the necessity of carrying a musket. He can neither plough, nor sow, nor reap without being under arms. If he would gather a few greens in the garden he must take a gun in hand. To endure such a life of dread and anxiety a man must be accustomed to it from his infancy and unaccustomed with one that is better.[12]

The Bushmen refused to be deterred by the commandos and began to attack houses as well as livestock. Many burghers on the northeastern frontier, particularly in the important sheep-farming division of Sneeuwberg, abandoned their farms. Small commandos could no longer cope with the danger, and in 1773, burgher officers on the frontier asked the government to send soldiers or burghers from the western Cape to help. The government rejected the plea, remarking that the frontier burghers had to defend themselves.

But in 1774 the situation had deteriorated to such an extent that the government decided on tougher action. It gave orders for a 'general commando' of three commandos drawn from divisions across the northern frontier to fight under the leadership of a burgher officer, Commandant Godlieb Rudolph Opperman. The commando had to try to resolve the crisis peacefully, but, if that failed, to wage war. The marauders, if necessary, were to be *verdelgen* or 'eradicated', that is, expelled rather than exterminated. The goal was clear: the commando was to help burghers go back to their abandoned farms.[13] The commando returned at the end of 1774, having killed 503 Bushmen and captured 241 across the width of the northern frontier,

Some aspects of Opperman's commando deserve emphasis. It consisted of a hundred

11 Suzie Newton-King, *The Enemy Within: The Struggle for Ascendancy on the Cape Eastern Frontier* (Cambridge: Cambridge University Press, 1999), p. 176.

12 John Barrow, *An Account of Travels into the Interior of Southern Africa* (London: Cadell and Davies, 1806), vol. 1, p. 203.

13 Moodie, *The Record*, vol. 3, p. 20.

'Christians' and 150 'Hottentots', and ammunition and guns were provided for the latter.[14] It demonstrates that the image of the commando as a fighting band of white men united in common purpose is quite wrong. In 1739, when commando service for burghers became compulsory, the government also permitted burghers to bring their Khoikhoi or 'Bastaard-Hottentot' workers along or send them as substitutes. Those burghers whose farms had not been exposed to attacks were extremely loath to leave farm and family for a dangerous and lengthy expedition. 'I get more excuses than men,' complained a burgher officer from Camdebo.[15] So many wealthier burghers sent Khoikhoi to take their place that a burgher officer warned of a day 'when I shall have to do commando with none but Hottentots, which cannot be.' In 1774, on the eve of the general commando against the Bushmen, the burghers were convinced that nothing could be achieved without the help of 'good and faithful Hottentots.'[16]

The Khoikhoi bore much of the brunt of the conflict between the burghers and the Bushmen and also between the burghers and the Xhosa. With farmers fearing for the safety of their children, the Khoikhoi had become the herders on the farms, hence the first to be attacked by bands of Bushmen intent on carrying off stock. So, too, on commandos that went out against the Xhosa they fought in the most exposed places. Honoratus Maynier, landdrost of Graaff-Reinet, who participated in commandos in the last decade of the century, said that the Khoikhoi on commando 'acted with as much zeal as if it had been their own cause.' 'I have always found,' he said, 'that when there was not a considerable number of Hottentots with them [the burghers] to be placed in the front and the first to be exposed to danger, they never succeeded.'[17]

The Khoikhoi who fought with the burghers on commando sometimes did so out a sense of loyalty to their masters, but their objectives were mixed. Some wanted to revenge themselves against the Bushmen who had attacked them while they herded stock, while others saw the commando as a prime opportunity to accumulate stock. Part of the captured stock was always divided among those on commando with the rest handed over to the burghers. A Khoikhoi invariably received less stock than a burgher did, but he did get some.

The other aspect of the Opperman commando that deserves to be emphasized is the capturing of Bushmen women and children. The government provided trinkets for the commando as gifts for the Bushmen and leg-irons and handcuffs for the women and 'defenseless males' to be detained.[18] The intention was to save lives, particularly during massacres where every member of a Bushman band was shot on the spot. The commandos captured women and children left at the scene of the battle, giving some of the women to the Khoikhoi who had fought with the commando. The children were indentured on the farms until the age of eighteen or twenty-five with the government's permission. Soon capturing women and children became an end in itself. In 1780 Dirk Koetse wrote to a militia officer who had called out a commando against some Bush-

---

14 Van der Merwe, *Noordwaartse beweging*, pp. 27-8.
15 Moodie, *The Record*, vol. 3, p. 102.
16 Moodie, *The Record*, vol. 3, p. 20.
17 *RCC*, vol. 4, pp. 286, 328.
18 Moodie, *The Record*, vol. 3, p. 28.

men: 'I have desired my Hottentot to catch a little one for me, and I beg of you that if he gets one, he may be allowed to keep it.'[19] By 1795 there were an estimated thousand war captives in the district of Graaff-Reinet, and some burghers asked that those who did commando duty be allowed to sell their captives. In 1817, Andries Stockenstrom, a widely respected landdrost in the district, reported a continuing widespread traffic in Bushmen children.[20]

The burghers who captured children often sowed dragon's teeth. A maltreated Khoikhoi servant who ran away with a gun or a resentful San captive could become 'the enemy within', to use the historian Suzie Newton-King's phrase, and wreak vengeance. Often closely connected to the robbers themselves, these servants 'knew all the circumstances on their masters' farms,' as one veldwachtmeester put it. Adriaan van Jaarsveld reported that 'his captain' had betrayed him to his mates while he was away from home and had absconded with seventy-eight of his sheep. The burghers meted out the most severe punishment to such servants if they were caught.[21]

'Conciliation rather than terror': Van Jaarsveld and Van der Walt

Opperman's commando failed in its principal mission to establish peace. He reported the next year that in the Sneeuwberg the Bushmen were 'stealing and robbing in a fearful manner.' More and more burghers left the Sneeuwberg division, weary of performing, virtually every second month, their grim commando duty. Adriaan van Jaarsveld now took the lead in confronting the Bushmen challenge. He had grown up near Piketberg in the west but moved east and acquired two loan farms in Sneeuwberg when he was only twenty-seven. In 1773 he asked permission to launch a pre-emptive strike against the Bushmen in the vicinity, writing: '[We] cannot wait until they steal again, because so many people are thus ruined, for we can never recapture anything, because they leave none of the stolen cattle alive.' He would lead three expeditions shortly after the general commando, which killed 181 Bushmen and captured twenty-nine.[22]

Energetic, enterprising, and more literate than most frontier burghers, Van Jaarsveld was also egotistic, hot-tempered, and devious. He tended to arrogate to himself 'a blind authority', as M.H.O. Woeke, the first landdrost of Graaff-Reinet, later put it.[23] In August 1775 he led a commando that shot twelve hippopotamuses in the Zeekoe River, leaving them as bait for a Bushmen band, whereupon, as the Bushmen were feasting, the commando fell on them, killing 122 and capturing 21. Only five escaped.[24]

Van Jaarsveld seems to have doubted that this atrocity would have the intended effect. In November 1775, shortly after the massacre, he and some of his men also abandoned the Sneeuwberg division. Van Jaarsveld now settled in Agter Bruyntjes Hoogte near the present town of Somerset East and one of the focal points of the conflict with

---

19 Moodie, *The Record*, vol. 3, p. 104.
20 Newton-King, *The Enemy Within*, pp. 120-22.
21 Newton-King, *The Enemy Within*, p. 108.
22 Moodie, *The Record*, vol. 3, p. 65.
23 H.J. Rossouw, 'Adriaan van Jaarsveld', master's diss., US, 1935, p. 105.
24 Moodie, *The Record*, vol. 3, pp. 44-5.

the Xhosa. In 1780 he became field commandant of the eastern frontier with instructions to push the Xhosa over the Fish River.

In the northeast the relentless battle between burghers and Bushmen continued. According to official figures, commandos killed 2,480 Bushmen and captured 654 between 1786 and 1795, when Bushmen captured 19,161 cattle and 84,094 sheep and killed 276 herdsmen, making much of the northeastern frontier uninhabitable for the burghers. British officials considered Sneeuwberg in the final years of the century to be in a state of perpetual warfare.

Another leading figure now appeared among the frontier burghers: Field Commandant J.P. van der Walt. He was at the head of several commandos that rode out in the northeastern frontier in the 1770s and 1780s. In 1793 he settled in a division largely abandoned after Bushman attacks. He received a free hand from the government to set himself up and, as the government's letter phrased it, 'with the help of his family to eradicate and extirpate the robbers.'[25] There is no evidence that at this time he questioned the commando campaigns or the capturing of Bushmen children.

Five years later, however, he had changed his views. After repeated commandos had been unable to prevent the Bushmen from staging attacks along a broad swathe on the northern frontier, many burghers abandoned their farms. Van der Walt asked the landdrost to refuse requests for commandos to attack the Bushmen and capture children since, 'the burghers would also give their all if they were robbed of their children.'[26]

Under his leadership the burghers donated 283 sheep and supplies of tobacco and beads to the Bushman clans to induce them to live peacefully on farms of their own. The veldwachtmeesters of Mid-Roggeveld and of Hantam also began to collect sheep and other gifts to hand over to the Khoikhoi periodically to persuade them to stop stealing. Although attacks by the Bushmen on some parts of the northern frontier continued until the beginning of the second decade of the next century, Colonel Collins wrote, in 1809, how satisfactory it was 'to observe the anxiety evinced by the farmers of the northeastern districts to preserve peace with that people rather by conciliation than by terror.' During the 1820s Landdrost Andries Stockenstrom and the missionary James Clarke made similar statements.[27]

The dispossession of the Khoikhoi

By the 1760s the Khoikhoi were still in undisturbed possession of the area between the Gamtoos and Fish rivers. In the 1770s the burghers and the Xhosa began to squeeze them out. Some Khoikhoi joined Bushman bands in the guerilla struggle in the northeast; others, particularly in the Zuurveld area, had to choose whether to entrust their fate to the Xhosa or the burghers.

It was a difficult choice. Joining the Xhosa meant that the Khoikhoi's cattle would become part of the chiefdom's wealth, but after an initial position of subordination they would be fully integrated into the chiefdom and suffer no social discrimination.

25 Van der Merwe, *Noordwaartse beweging*, p. 52.
26 Hermann Giliomee, *Die Kaap tydens die eerste Britse bewind* (Cape Town: HAUM, 1975), pp. 266-7.
27 Van der Merwe, *Noordwaartse beweging*, pp. 78-9.

Indeed, from the beginning, some Xhosa chiefs took Khoikhoi women as wives, to cement the integration of the newcomers. The westernmost Xhosa chiefdoms had absorbed a large Khoikhoi component.

Entering the service of a farmer offered different possibilities. Members of a Khoikhoi clan would always remain servants and be excluded from the burgher family and church. Yet they could stay together, keep their cattle and, if they went on commando, even supplement their own herds. Particularly if the burghers gained the upper hand over the Xhosa, the prospects of Khoikhoi who fought in commandos were good. Many Khoikhoi enjoyed a position on farms considerably better than that of a serf.

In monetary terms, however, the rewards were few. In 1784 a memorandum from the Patriot movement in the western Cape said that the stock farmers coming to Cape Town to sell their produce made only enough from its sale to buy clothing and other domestic requirements. The historian Suzie Newton-King calculated the cash income of frontier burghers as too low to offer the Khoikhoi proper cash wages. The Khoikhoi could be kept content only through the allocation of sufficient land and stock.[28] A Khoikhoi called Platje Swartland related that, until the turn of the nineteenth century, he and his clansmen who lived with the trekboers had little to complain about – 'until that time the Hottentots were boers and kept on their masters' land large flocks of their own.'[29] In 1798, twenty-five years after trekboers had begun to settle in the Camdebo, the Graaff-Reinet census listed between 1,300 and 1,400 Khoikhoi on farms in the district. They owned 140 horses, 7,571 cattle and 30,557 sheep, an average of five cattle and twenty-three sheep per household.[30]

As the frontier closed and land became scarce it was almost inevitable that the relationship between the burghers and the Khoikhoi would deteriorate. Many masters told their clients to reduce their stock, and, instead of offering incentives, compelled them to work. Masters also prevented the Khoikhoi from leaving under the pretence that their children were still 'indentured' and claimed 'damages' because of the workers' negligence. Many Khoikhoi were becoming part of a captive labor force. Not only the Khoikhoi 'serfs', who had been bludgeoned into submission, but also many Khoikhoi clients, began to find their situation intolerable. When they resisted, their masters resorted to violent punishment.

There are indications that, in the final two decades of the century, some Graaff-Reinet farms were the scenes of acts of great cruelty. Honoratus Maynier, secretary of the district from 1789 and landdrost from 1792, encouraged the Khoikhoi to file complaints against masters who maltreated them. The resulting reports contain evidence of severe punishments, and of masters' refusal to let their servants go. There were increasing reports of Khoikhoi seeking refuge among the Xhosa, taking with them both guns and horses, which had given the frontier burghers such a great advantage over their own adversaries. Fugitive Khoikhoi captured or destroyed stock, burned crops and razed homes. When the frontier between 1795 and 1799 became destabilized after burgher uprisings against the government, Khoikhoi servants seized the opportunity to revolt.

---

28 *Afrikaner Political Thought*, p. 42; Newton-King, *The Enemy Within*, Chapter 8.
29 (Cape Archives) Moodie Afschriften, vol. X1. See also Mentzel, *Description of the Cape*, vol. 1. pp. 36, 83.
30 Hermann Giliomee, 'The Eastern Frontier, 1770-1812', *SSAS*, p. 431.

The resistance of the Xhosa

But it was the Xhosa who offered the most formidable resistance to burgher expansion. The Khoikhoi and San challenge had subsided by the early nineteenth century, but the Xhosa would pin down the white colonists until the 1850s along a line that ran from the Fish River mouth in the south to the Kagaberg-Winterberg mountain escarpment in the north. The Xhosa had superior numbers and a denser pattern of settlement than the Khoikhoi and San. In 1752 the number of Xhosa living east of the Fish was estimated at twelve thousand. Further to the east were the Thembu, the Pondo, and other tribes belonging to the southeastern Bantu-speaking people. By the early 1790s, it was estimated that some six thousand Xhosa were living in the eastern and southeastern divisions of Graaff-Reinet. The numbers of burghers remained small; as late as 1798, when the first census was taken in Graaff-Reinet, there was a total white population of only 4,262, thus fewer than a thousand adult male burghers in a district approximately the size of modern Portugal. Of these, fewer than half lived in the area into which the Xhosa had moved.

There were two areas of intensive burgher-Xhosa interaction: the Zuurveld between the Lower Fish and the Bushmans rivers, and the Bosberg-Bruyntjes Hoogte area in the present Somerset East district, lying west of the Upper Fish River. In a 1778 visit to the frontier, Governor Joachim van Plettenberg made an ineffectual attempt to impose a form of separation. He agreed with some minor Gwali chiefs that the upper Fish River and the Bushmans River would serve as a border, and that they would keep on the other side of it. Two years later the Council of Policy proclaimed the Fish River along its entire length as a boundary. This included the Zuurveld area, which even Van Jaarsveld believed had first been settled by Xhosa tribes. In 1794 he said that this land belonged to the Xhosa, and had to be given back for the sake of a lasting peace.[31]

Both the government and the burghers from now on referred to the area west of the Fish River as colonial territory. A much more suitable border would have been the Sundays River that runs north-south for most of its length and enters into Algoa Bay, which offered a quick sea connection, rather than the Fish River which twists and turns before it reaches the sea. But the border was no more than a paper entity. The chiefs with whom Van Plettenberg had come to an agreement were minor chiefs. The Xhosa were no monolithic political entity on whose behalf a single chief or even a paramount chief could enter into binding negotiations. Nor was there an authority to enforce a border settlement. Several farmers in the Bruyntjes Hoogte area continued to pasture their cattle beyond the Fish River, while the chiefs living on 'colonial territory' had no desire to move back. These chiefs also used this land for pasture, and could barter cattle and work on the burghers' farms and wander around begging for handouts.

They also had a political reason for staying: it allowed them to remain independent. The Xhosa nuclear unit had recently split between the Gcaleka and the Rharhabe. Living between the Gcaleka in the east and the chiefs west of the Fish River, the chief of the Rharhabe considered the Zuurveld Xhosa as subjects who had revolted against him. He ordered them to come back, but they refused. When he died in the early 1780s, the regent, Ndlambe, continued, in vain, the efforts to get these chiefs to move back.

31 J.S. Marais, *Maynier and the First Boer Republic* (Cape Town: Maskew Miller, 1944), p. 7.

In the final years of the century the situation would become even more complicated with a power struggle in the Rharhabe chiefdom between Ngqika, the successor, and Ndlambe, the regent. Ndlambe lost and, in the final years of the century, fled to the Zuurveld where he sought to establish control over chiefdoms living there in order to boost his power in the continuing battle against Ngqika. Both Ndlambe and Ngqika were eager to engage the burghers as allies in conflicts with other chiefs. Only in the 1840s, after major losses in land and cattle, did some Xhosa chiefs begin to consider the need to stand together against colonial encroachment.

There was much that tied the burghers and the Xhosa together and much that caused an ongoing conflict between them. Both were cattle-farming societies competing for finite land resources on the frontier.[32] For the burghers, continued expansion into new land was an important social safety valve, for without land the sons of frontier farmers could not achieve the independent lifestyle they coveted. For the Xhosa, new land would enable some of the sons of reigning chiefs to hive off and establish new chiefdoms at a distance from the Great Place where the paramount chief lived. The concepts of land-holding differed: to the burghers their farm was their exclusive property; they resented having a Xhosa clan or chiefdom move onto it; to a Xhosa chiefdom, the land they occupied was communal property, the boundaries of which were seldom sharply defined. They had difficulty in accepting that a single farmer could claim such a large tract of land as his own.

In the early stages of the settlement of the Zuurveld the Xhosa and the burghers sometimes lived peaceably together, or at least, that was how the Xhosa later remembered it. In 1819 Andries Stockenstrom recorded the words of a Xhosa councilor that obviously referred to the 1770s and 1780s: 'When our fathers and the fathers of the amabulu [Boers] first settled in the Zuurveld they dwelt together in peace. Their flocks grazed the same hills, and their herdsmen smoked together out of the same pipes.'[33] The councilor attributed the conflicts that broke out to cattle raiding on the part of the Boers, but obviously conflicts over pasture were almost inevitable once an area had been fully settled.

In this situation no generally accepted authority existed to resolve conflicts. The Xhosa and the burghers were not implacable enemies but neither knew a way to compete for land other than by force. They also settled disputes over cattle and labor 'contracts' by force. The balance of raw power and not any abstract principles nor governmental intervention determined their behavior. When the Xhosa were in the ascendancy (as in the first decade of the nineteenth century) the burghers were fearful and ready to flee; when Colonel Henry Somerset's patrols and commandos had a long leash to harass the Xhosa in the frontier zone, the Xhosa were apprehensive and ready for retreat.

Unable to live with or without the other, the two communities were drawn into a tangled web from which it was difficult to extricate themselves. The ties that bound them also caused conflict. Barter was one such tie. The Company itself banned all trade with the Xhosa, but the burghers nonetheless enthusiastically sought to trade because they

---

32 Martin Legassick, ' The Frontier Tradition in South African Historiography', in Shula Marks and Anthony Atmore (eds.), *Economy and Society in Pre-Industrial South Africa* (London: Longman: 1980), pp. 1-44.

33 T. Pringle, *Narrative of a Residence in South Africa* (1835, repr. Cape Town: Struik, 1966), p. 284.

could acquire cattle cheaply in exchange for tobacco, copper, iron and beads. But when the burghers tried to barter with the Xhosa as they had done with the Khoikhoi, by dragooning them into parting with their cattle, the Xhosa retaliated if duped or dispossessed of their cattle. Colonel Collins wrote in 1809 that the Xhosa, at first, 'gave their cattle and labor without knowing its value, but a little experience having opened their eyes on these points, altercations between them and the farmers were the necessary consequence. These contentions grew into enmities.'[34]

The tie of labor also bound and chafed. Many Xhosa began to work on farms – sometimes for food and other times for beads, buttons and trinkets or a heifer or two. Some burghers beat and humiliated their Xhosa workers as they did the Khoikhoi, but with the Xhosa chiefdoms intact, maltreated workers could draw on their chiefs to avenge themselves. Many years later an old colored man said of the pioneer frontier: 'The Caffres, when not regularly paid or [when they were] flogged, informed their chief and came and stole cattle from the farmers by way of repaying themselves for the injuries they had sustained.'[35] Despite this the frontier farmers continued to employ Xhosa servants. At the same time, however, they remained anxious about the large numbers of Xhosa in their vicinity, especially those who wandered in parties through the district, stopping at houses to beg for 'presents.'

At first, the burghers had put great faith in their ability to subjugate the Xhosa through force. Van Jaarsveld expressed the view that a commando of sixty men would be enough to chase the Xhosa out of the colony.[36] But this was a fatal miscalculation. The Xhosa numbers and the dense Zuurveld bush neutralized the military advantage of the burghers' horses and guns.

The points on which the burghers felt superior – the Christian religion, monogamous marriage, dress and artifacts of Western civilization – had little meaning for the Xhosa. Still, the burghers considered themselves superior. Rather than call the Xhosa by their names, they usually called them 'Kaffers', a derogatory term and one that the Xhosa from early in the nineteenth century resented.

The Xhosa attempted to enmesh the burghers in their networks and eventually integrate them into their society along the pattern of the Xhosa absorption of Khoikhoi clans.[37] Trading, begging, and military alliances all formed part of the Xhosa's initial interaction with another society, followed by marriage and other forms of social incorporation. All hinged on outsiders accepting African leadership and on payment of tribute to a chief, according to Xhosa custom. The Xhosa paramount chief Ngqika, for example, was eager to marry the daughter of the burgher Coenraad de Buys, who had struck up a relationship with the royal kraal.

Yet, despite the friction and mutual misunderstanding, the Xhosa and the burgher society managed to find ways to prevent frequent clashes. The few wars that did break out followed a deliberate act of provocation that outraged the other side. Once war began, both sides made the capturing of cattle a key objective.

---

34 Moodie, *The Record*, vol. 5, p. 10.
35 Giliomee, 'The Eastern Frontier', p. 433.
36 Rossouw, 'Van Jaarsveld', p. 44.
37 J.B. Peires, *The House of Phalo: A History of the Xhosa People in the Days of Their Independence* (Johannesburg: Ravan Press, 1981), pp. 53-4.

The first hostilities, 1770-1793

Early in the 1770s three Prinsloo families, headed by the brothers Willem, Marthinus and Hendrik Frederik, settled northeast of the present town of Somerset East at Bosberg, east of Bruyntjes Hoogte, beyond the border. Also moving into the same area were two Klopper families, and the Nel and Labuschagne families. The first veldwachtmeester, hand in glove with the Prinsloos, turned a blind eye to the illegal trade these families conducted with the Xhosa. Most of these men or their sons would crop up again in the rebellions of 1795, 1799 and 1815 against government authority.

The first hostilities between burghers and Xhosa that gave rise to the First Frontier war of 1779 to1781 were described by the landdrost of Stellenbosch: 'Willem Prinsloo,' he wrote, ' . . . under the pretext that the Xhosa had stolen a sheep from him, shot one of them dead, whereupon the Xhosa rose up and attacked the inhabitants [farmers], resulting in a terrible slaughter of the Xhosa and the ruin of many inhabitants.'[38] The Xhosa sacked several farms and raided 21,000 head of cattle; Willem Prinsloo's house was burnt and his entire herd lost.

When the government called out a commando under Adriaan van Jaarsveld, the landdrost wrote: 'Upon the proceedings of this commando, as it appears to me, will depend the doubtful question whether the Kafirs are to be forcibly dislodged, or the inhabitants obliged to abandon that country.'[39] Van Jaarsveld, determined to resolve the 'doubtful question' quickly, led his commando in seizing some five thousand head of cattle; they drove several Xhosa chiefs over the central sector of the eastern border.

He also perpetrated a massacre. Fearing a surprise attack while he was negotiating with a Xhosa clan, he tossed out some pieces of tobacco to them, and gave the order to fire while they were scrambling to pick them up. This massacre was remembered for many generations among the Xhosa, who gave Van Jaarsveld the nickname of the 'Red Captain.'

Van Jaarsveld's commando, so one source said, concluded peace with several Xhosa chiefs, but the 'doubtful question' of whether the Xhosa could be dislodged was unresolved as far as the Zuurveld was concerned. Some of the chiefs in the region had no intention of leaving, and the battle between the burghers and the Xhosa became a stalemate. The simple military fact was that the burghers lacked the force to deal the Xhosa a blow crushing enough to drive them out permanently.

When the war ended in 1781, Van Jaarsveld tried to carry out the government's policy to forbid contacts between burghers and Xhosa. He also refused the burghers permission to attack Xhosa kraals simply because they suspected them of harboring stolen cattle. The greatest obstacle to enforcing his policy came from the Prinsloo and Klopper families and the first veldwachtmeester, Cornelis Bothma. Van Jaarsveld and Marthinus Prinsloo had clashed over the division of the booty after the war, and thereafter Prinsloo and Bothma both openly ignored the ban on crossing the border to barter cattle or to hunt; they even branded Van Jaarsveld a traitor and 'tenfold scoundrel', and refused to go on any commandos against the Bushmen while there were some of their cattle among the Xhosa.

---

38 P. J. van der Merwe, *The Migrant Farmer in the History of the Cape Colony, 1657-1842* (Athens: Ohio University Press, 1995), p. 220.
39 Moodie, *The Record*, vol. 3, p. 93.

Van Jaarsveld felt that unless this 'rebellious band' was expelled from the border it would again provoke hostilities against the Xhosa. He warned that they might grow in strength and incite others to rise, as Estienne Barbier had done forty years earlier in Drakenstein. Exceeding his authority, he sacked Bothma, but the militia council in Stellenbosch and the Council of Policy in Cape Town did not support him. Tired of being ruled from afar, he became the leading voice in the clamor for the establishment of a drostdy in Graaff-Reinet, and, in 1786, the government agreed to establish a new district in the east with jurisdiction over the entire border with the Xhosa and over the area of the fiercest Bushman resistance. Moritz Hermann Otto Woeke was appointed as landdrost for the new district, with Van Jaarsveld as heemraad and one of the two captains in the Graaff-Reinet militia. Woeke soon grasped the impossibility of attempting to impose laws in the district with only three or four messengers-cum-policemen as his staff, and, in despair, he reported that unless he was supported by fifty or sixty soldiers 'the rot will continue . . . and if not suppressed will increase to such an extent that everyone will act arbitrarily and do everything at his sweet will.'[40]

By the end of the 1780s the Xhosa had lost their sense of awe towards the burghers. A Xhosa chief in the Zuurveld sent word that 'the Christians [whites] should not think that he was afraid to make war.'[41] In 1792 Woeke sent this report to Cape Town: 'On some farms the Xhosa assemble in troops and with their weapons in their hands make enormous demands for everything they want, neither can it be refused them. And they resort to force on farms where the men are not at home, and take what they like, and make themselves master of farm, house and goods.'[42] A farmer in the vicinity expressed his dissatisfaction. 'It is hard to be oppressed by the heathens on our own loan farms.'[43]

Soon the burghers took the law in their own hands to deal with what some called Xhosa *assurantie* (arrogance), and to settle the question of who owned the Zuurveld. An act of burgher lawlessness in 1792 led to the Second Frontier War, when a field cornet, Barend Lindeque, acting without authority, called out a commando to expel the Zuurveld Xhosa. He had struck up an alliance with Ndlambe, the acting paramount chief of the Rharhabe, who, for his own reasons, wanted the Zuurveld Xhosa to be driven back. Only a small number of burghers and Khoikhoi responded, and the Zuurveld Xhosa counter-attacked. According to some estimates they captured more than fifty thousand head of cattle, eleven thousand sheep and two thousand horses, and burned down all but four of the 120 homesteads in the Zuurveld. The farmers abandoned the Zuurveld almost completely thereafter, many of them seeking security by drawing together in a *laager*, or *laer* in modern day Afrikaans. Together with the commando, the defensive *laager* was indispensable for survival on the frontier.[44] As Van Jaarsveld observed, this was really a military camp, with fifty or more heavy wagons in a circle with thorn trees thrust between the openings. In the middle were four wagons in a square, roofed over with planks and raw hides to serve as protection for women, the elderly and children.[45]

40 Giliomee, 'The Eastern Frontier', p. 429.
41 Giliomee, 'The Eastern Frontier', p. 436.
42 Marais, *Maynier*, p. 25.
43 *Afrikaner Political Thought*, pp. 145-6.
44 J.L.M. Franken, *Piet Retief se lewe in die Kolonie* (Pretoria: HAUM. 1949), p. 512.
45 Eric Walker, *The Great Trek* (London: Adam and Charles Black, 1938), pp. 122-3.

In 1793 a commando of Graaff-Reinet and Swellendam burghers captured some eight thousand cattle and forced a considerable number of Xhosa to retreat beyond the Fish River. But large numbers of colonial cattle remained in Xhosa possession; many Xhosa stayed in the Zuurveld, and some who were driven back soon returned. Passions had now become so inflamed that it was no longer possible, as in the previous ten years, to treat the Xhosa as a mere nuisance. Their numbers had built up substantially and they daily captured some cattle. A large number of displaced Zuurveld burghers now joined forces with the Prinsloos, the Kloppers and the other fractious men from Bruintjes Hoogte and Bosberg who had caused trouble as early as the late 1770s.

The replacement of Woeke as landdrost by Honoratus Maynier, the district secretary, compounded the crisis. Maynier, who was fluent in Dutch, French and English, was an exceptionally well-educated man from the circle of the most prominent Company servants and burghers of the western Cape, but he had no military experience. From the start the burgher officers in the militia refused to serve under him in a commando.

Maynier has been depicted as a negrophile, but he was rather a typical Company servant, whose first concern was to avoid trouble with the Xhosa because war would be risky and expensive. The historian J.S. Marais offered a spirited defense of his actions, but the fact is that he was ill suited to his office. He had a curious inability to understand that in the absence of a military force to intimidate he could function only through the sustained support of some influential burghers. He was also reluctant to face the worsening relationship with the Xhosa. Without a grasp of the situation and with no real power at his disposal he took extreme measures, and, over the next decade, repeatedly ordered people who had fled from their farms in the face of real danger to return within a month or lose their farms. A traveler who visited Graaff-Reinet commented that his 'ill-timed severity' had much to do with the disturbances.[46]

The second troublesome factor was the Company's decision to prevent its own imminent financial collapse by a more vigorous collection of taxes. One of the taxes was the annual fee of 24 rix-dollars on a loan farm. The farmers were increasingly reluctant to pay because they often had to travel a long way to do so, and because the Company, as they thought, offered virtually nothing in return for the tax. Why did they have to pay rent on farms they had to defend themselves? But the Company now hit on an ingenious method of collection. It instructed the butchers' servants who traveled into the interior with the sole right to buy stock to collect up to three years' arrears from the farmers with whom they did business. The farmers in Graaff-Reinet were outraged and many refused to sell any stock. Maynier, connected to the Van Reenen brothers who held the meat lease, did not try to intervene with the government, whereupon the frontier burghers branded him a *slagterskneg*, a butcher's servant. He had become the focus of all the burghers' insecurities and resentments.[47]

A burgher rebellion

It was Van Jaarsveld who was at the heart of the turmoil that would soon turn the burghers' entire world upside down. He had made life difficult for the landdrosts. He was among

---

46 Henry Lichtenstein, *Travels in South Africa* (Cape Town: VRS, 1928), vol. 1, p. 458.
47 Newton-King, *The Enemy Within*, p. 147.

those who walked out at the first meeting over which Maynier presided. He had not yet come out in open revolt, however. Since 1785 he had been living on a farm west of the town of Graaff-Reinet, almost at the same distance from the two main factions in the district. They were the Sneeuwberg faction, supported by Maynier, who insisted that the energies of the district be spent on fighting the Bushmen, and the eastern and south-eastern factions (Bruintjes Hoogte and Zuurveld), who wanted the Xhosa driven over the border and their stolen cattle recaptured. Most of the heemraden and burgher officers backed Maynier in deciding not to send a commando against the Xhosa when the danger from the Bushmen was worse than ever.[48]

In 1792 Van Jaarsveld said: 'For myself I have nothing to do in Kafirland and I could not wish that this nation were given cause for enmity, since we have our hands full with the Bushmen.' But Van Jaarsveld had become the victim of his own deviousness and re-calcitrance. In a move that foreshadowed the Great Trek forty years later he asked per-mission to go up as far as the Great [Orange] River and beyond it. He added a postscript: 'Since all the parts in our district are pretty well known with the exception of what lies to the north, we also are curious to know what may be found there.'[49]

Maynier rejected the request to explore the interior, but Van Jaarsveld went anyway, though a lack of men and a severe drought drove him back. On a visit to Cape Town shortly afterwards, he used what the government in Cape Town called some 'unseemly expressions' towards Maynier and the Graaff-Reinet heemraden. The government put him on trial for disobedience to Maynier and for undermining his authority.

He was also summoned by the Court of Justice to appear in Cape Town on a charge of financial fraud. It drove him into the arms of his old enemy, Marthinus Prinsloo of Bruyntjes Hoogte. In February 1795 a party of armed burghers appeared at the drostdy and ordered Maynier to leave the town. Claiming to be acting on behalf of the *volk-stem*, the voice of the people, some of the heemraden and militia officers took over the administration. Wearing the tricolor cockade of the French revolution, they labeled the district government a 'National Convention', and refused to pay taxes to the Company or obey its laws. Van Jaarsveld was obviously one of the leaders, but he kept himself in the background. The rebels were mainly men from the southeastern divisions keen to recapture the land and cattle they had lost to the Xhosa in the 1793 war.

In Swellendam, too, in June 1795, a group of sixty burghers terming themselves 'Na-tionals' deposed the landdrost in Swellendam, who along with Maynier had led the unsuccessful 1793 commando. The rebels appointed their own 'National' landdrost and a new governing body, also called the 'National Convention', protested against the taxes and inflation, and asked for the indentureship system to be extended to Khoikhoi chil-dren, and for the right to hold Bushmen captives as property, which meant that they could buy and sell them like slaves. The Swellendam rebellion fizzled out, however.

The constitutional ideas of the rebels were murky. They did not proclaim republics, as is often assumed, but rather expressed the desire for their districts to fall directly un-der the new republic in the Netherlands. But cut off as they were from the Netherlands, no one could think of a mechanism to establish direct contact with the republican gov-

---

48 Marais, *Maynier*, pp. 36-8.
49 Marais, *Maynier*, p. 37.

ernment in The Hague. All this became immaterial, however, in September 1795 when Britain took occupation of the Cape.

But the rebels enjoyed only the shadow of power. After the 1795 uprising, the Cape government cut off the ammunition supply to the Graaff-Reinet burghers, leaving them exposed to attacks by the indigenous people. At a meeting in August 1796 the northern and western divisions decided to accept British authority. Early in 1797 the rebels capitulated.

A world upside down

The rhetoric of the Graaff-Reinet rebels, of whom the majority were illiterate or barely literate, has been analyzed and interpreted as if they represented the dawn of a new democratic scheme of thought on African soil. However, the significance of the events lies rather in the evidence they offer of the breakdown of orderly government and the rise of anarchic tendencies. Future developments would demonstrate the tenuousness of white control over the frontier zone and the great risk to the colonial order of intra-white divisions. Burghers on the periphery of society would make common cause with blacks, or rather threaten to do so, to promote their own individual prospects rather than any common burgher cause.

Some very rough characters had settled in close proximity to the Xhosa, ready to take the most reckless initiatives and to respond scornfully to those with authority over them. Henry Lichtenstein, a German traveler relatively sympathetic to the colonists, declared early in the nineteenth century that 'unexampled disorder' had been introduced in 'every part of the administration of the district.' He noted the 'bitterness and irreconcilable animosity with which they [the burghers] carry on differences among each other', and the 'harshness with which they treated their slaves and Hottentots', and provided this sketch of their composite character: 'Selfishness, lawlessness, hardiness, intolerance and a thirst for revenge are the reigning vices of their character.' There was, however, also 'their hospitality, a firm adherence to the truth and a great respect for religion.'[50]

In this situation, with the political order already disturbed, the remarkable figure of Coenraad de Buys appeared on the scene, and Adriaan van Jaarsveld played his last desperate card. De Buys, the descendant of a Huguenot, had worked in his youth for a family that withheld his pay until he took them to court. In his twenties and thirties De Buys was described in tones of awe by travelers. Their accounts mentioned that he was an impressive figure, nearly seven feet tall and with enormous self-confidence.[51] His name first appears in the frontier records of 1780s as the holder of a loan farm near the Bushmans River in the Zuurveld. He lived with a Baster woman with whom he had seven children, then married the mother of Ngqika, the Rharhabe chief, and also took a Thembu wife living well beyond the border. In 1788, De Buys appears in the records complaining of the influx of Xhosa into the Zuurveld penetrating his farm. But he was a man who sinned as much as others sinned against him. A member of his family, also living on the social fringes of burgher society, described him as follows: 'He is an in-

---

50 Lichtenstein, *Travels*, vol. 2, pp. 452-64.
51 Lichtenstein, *Travels*, vol. 1, p. 261.

triguer who has not a single friend. He has been no good since his earliest years. He has always been a disturber of the peace and the persecutor of the Christians as well as the blacks.'[52]

Maynier considered De Buys' conduct one of the principal causes of the outbreak of war in 1793. A Baster who lived on De Buys' farm declared that De Buys had been on good terms with the Xhosa until 1791, after which he crossed the Fish River and raided cattle from the Xhosa. When some Xhosa complained, he almost beat them to death, and had five Xhosa killed by his Khoikhoi servants. The Xhosa chief Langa charged that De Buys had seized his wife and used her as a concubine, and two other chiefs said that De Buys had 'withheld' their wives and cattle. An ex-heemraad and a veldwachtmeester warned Maynier about the dangers of De Buys' maltreatment of individual Xhosa.[53]

The Xhosa who raided the Zuurveld farms in 1793 targeted De Buys, burned down his homestead and stole all his cattle. De Buys, reported 'wandering about in poverty', soon became notorious for gunrunning. In 1795 he signed the *Te Samenstemming*, a memorandum containing the rebel grievances against Maynier, and suddenly acquired a new lease of life when he was invited to live at the royal homestead of the Rharhabe chief Ngqika, beyond the Upper Fish border. Ngqika, seventeen or eighteen years old, had just defeated Ndlambe and was acquiring a reputation among the Xhosa as a cruel and avaricious ruler. He was keen to acquire an advisor from the colonial side who could help him to obtain horses and guns. He chose De Buys, with his contacts with the burghers and his fluency in both Dutch and Xhosa, instead of one of the usual Khoikhoi advisors. Having grown up without a father, he regarded De Buys as a father and, as noted, De Buys duly took Ngqika's mother as his own wife.

In the colony Marthinus Prinsloo, the rebel leader, came to believe that there were elements of a good plot in the making. At the heart of it was his desire to call up a commando to raid Xhosa cattle or recapture colonial cattle in the Xhosa's possession. He and his followers knew that Van Jaarsveld could be arrested on fraud charges at any moment. What the rebels needed was a dire threat that could galvanize large numbers of burghers into action. They wrote a letter to De Buys informing him that the burghers were about to rise up against the British, and asked him to use his influence over Ngqika to secure Xhosa help. Early in 1799 Prinsloo and a party of thirty armed men held up the party that was escorting Van Jaarsveld to Cape Town and took him away with them.

Prinsloo and his followers knew that De Buys nourished a burning hatred towards the new rulers, calling the English the 'Bushmen of the sea.' The message they now spread was that De Buys would let loose the Xhosa under his influence on all the burghers who failed to join the rebellion to kill them and hand all their cattle over to the Xhosa. But apart from misjudging the effect of the threat, the rebels had no common purpose. De Buys wanted to kill the landdrost at Graaff-Reinet, others wanted to take him hostage, and still others wanted to seize the Graaff-Reinet district or even the entire colony.

At the behest of Prinsloo, Van Jaarsveld wrote several letters to the burghers informing them that 'all communications with the Xhosa will take place through our fellow-

---

52 Noël Mostert, *Frontiers* (New York: Alfred A. Knopf, 1992), p. 317.

53 Marais, *Maynier*, pp. 30-31.

burgher Coenraad de Buys.'[54] Undoubtedly this was an attempt to intimidate them with the prospect that De Buys could use some of his Xhosa allies against them if they refused to join.

There is a temptation to read too much into the rebels' threat to use the Xhosa against their burgher opponents. Nevertheless, one cannot fail to notice the absence of any racial taboo on the part of either the government or the burghers to use whatever allies they could get. After conquering the Cape in 1795, the British government lost little time in raising a corps of approximately three hundred Khoikhoi, later known as the Cape Regiment. ('Nothing I know would intimidate the Boers more,' the British commander wrote in 1796.[55]) When the news reached Cape Town in 1799 of what became known as the Van Jaarsveld revolt the government included fifty Khoikhoi troops in the force sent to crush it. When the rebels received word of this they warned that De Buys 'with all of Kaffirland would be unleashed if a single *Pandoer* [a Khoikhoi soldier] was included.'

The Batavians, who succeeded the British in 1803, also contemplated using non-Europeans against recalcitrant burghers. In 1805 Governor Janssens of the Batavian Administration wrote in exasperation that if the disorder in Graaff-Reinet did not cease 'he would have to adopt such measures as would exterminate [meaning expel] those who were the cause of the turbulence, even if it were only possible with the assistance of Hottentots and Kafirs.'[56]

As part of their own effort to crush the 1799 revolt the British resorted to extreme measures, whose effects they clearly did not think through. They cut the wagon road link between Graaff-Reinet and Cape Town, and suspended the supply of ammunition to the southeastern part of the district. Under the bumbling General Dundas, the acting British governor, they declared martial law in these areas and instructed the troops to disarm the inhabitants and arrest the rebel leaders.

The force under General T.P. Vandeleur marched to Bruyntjes Hoogte where Prinsloo and a following of 150 men laid down their arms. Van Jaarsveld had been arrested a few days earlier. Vandeleur imposed fines of 9,000 rix-dollars on ninety-three rebels and sent twenty to Cape Town to stand trial. In September 1800 the Court of Justice, composed of colonists, sentenced Van Jaarsveld and Prinsloo to death, and banished ten others from the colony. In passing sentence the Court of Justice termed the forces unleashed by the rebels as 'in a thousand respects dangerous for their colony.'[57]

On the frontier the so-called Van Jaarsveld rebellion did not end with the arrest of the rebels. The arrival there of a force of British and Khoikhoi soldiers, the arrest of the rebel leaders and the disarmament of the burghers created the impression among the Khoikhoi that the tables had been irrevocably turned. Some burghers alleged that as Vandeleur's forces marched to the frontier the soldiers incited their servants to rise against them. It is impossible to say whether this is true, but many Khoikhoi considered the moment propitious to rebel against their masters. A large group of servants did so, going from farm to farm and demanding guns and 'surplus clothes' as payment for wages owed.

54 Giliomee, *Die Kaap tydens die eerste Britse bewind*, p. 75.
55 Giliomee, *Kaap tydens die Britse bewind*, p. 55.
56 Herman Giliomee, 'The Burgher Rebellions on the Eastern Frontier' in *SSAS* (1), pp. 338-56.
57 *RCC*, vol. 3, p. 221.

They then attached themselves to the military force and asked for protection. In a long oration their leader, Klaas Stuurman, recounted their suffering under the burghers, asking the commander to restore Khoikhoi independence before he left the frontier. The Court of Justice said later that the Khoikhoi had either been incited or had acted from 'a notion they also have conceived of liberty and equality.' In Cape Town the specter loomed of something similar to the slaves' uprising in Saint-Domingue (Haiti) five years earlier.

John Barrow, a young British civil servant, soon to write a book that painted the frontier burghers in unflattering terms, was escorting five hundred Khoikhoi back to Algoa Bay and met a party of 150 burghers who had fled their farms. Each side had 'vowed vengeance on the other', but the British had no desire to help either side. Vandeleur's instruction from Dundas was to arrest the rebels. Much more difficult was an order to Vandeleur to embark on 'gently hushing' the Zuurveld Xhosa over the Fish River. The British now discovered how difficult it was to fight an enemy in the dense bush and ravines of the Zuurveld. Dundas declared that it was almost impossible for troops to follow the Xhosa with any effect through their fastnesses over wide and mountainous country. Vandeleur's troops beat a hasty retreat to Algoa Bay. Most of them were sent back by sea to Cape Town. For the assembled Khoikhoi this was an ominous message: the British force was leaving them to the tender mercies of their masters. A few years later a British commander would declare that this military effort was 'certainly not calculated to inspire any of the contending parties with a high opinion of British power.'[58] One night the Khoikhoi all abandoned the British camp, with many joining the Gqunukhwebe, who had been roused by Vandeleur's attack.

For the burghers the darkest moment since the founding of the settlement had arrived. The eastern Khoikhoi rebels were intent on getting back their country between the Gamtoos and Fish rivers – a stretch of more than 300 kilometers. They were organized in a confederacy of clans. In their ranks were many who had fought in burgher commandos and knew all their strengths and weaknesses. They had both horses and guns, backed up by large numbers of Xhosa fighters on foot. (According to one estimate there were at least three thousand Xhosa in the Zuurveld.) In April and May the insurgents began to attack the burghers' farms. What made matters worse for the burghers was that they had an acute shortage of ammunition. There was no supply in either the Graaff-Reinet or Swellendam drostdies, and the government refused to issue any in Cape Town, though Vandeleur had permission to issue ammunition in deserving cases.

Dundas refused to commit British troops, but he could not afford to lose the Graaff-Reinet district, and particularly its livestock, indispensable to Cape Town and the British force. He gave instructions to call out a burgher commando to expel the Xhosa over the Fish River and get the Khoikhoi to return to their masters. But the commando suffered a disastrous defeat when a force of 150 Khoikhoi and Xhosa attacked it in a night action. The insider knowledge that the Khoikhoi had of the ways of the commandos no doubt helped.[59]

---

58 Moodie, *The Record*, vol. 5, p. 13.
59 Peires, *House of Phalo*, p. 140.

'Universal consternation' followed, as an official described it. Without ammunition the frontier burghers had little option but headlong flight. The insurgents raided far and wide, burning farms and carrying away stock. By July, Vandeleur reported that the once flourishing division of Swartkops River had been devastated. With three exceptions all the burgher families between the Swartkops and Fish rivers had fled, huddling together in the laagers or military camps. The entire Fish River was 'lying exposed.'

In June and July the insurgents invaded the Swellendam district with armed Khoikhoi in the forefront. On the farms of the Scheepers and Strydom families they killed fifteen burghers and kept twelve women and children captive for two weeks. In the Langkloof valley panic reigned. B. Lindeque wrote from the most westerly part of the valley that 'if we do not get help we gamble away our land and also our lives.'

Taken by surprise, the British blamed the burghers for their fate. Dundas called the frontier burghers 'timid to an extent beyond example' and a 'troublesome and disaffected race' characterized by the 'strongest compound of cowardice and cruelty, of treachery and cunning.' Vandeleur also poured scorn on the burghers for failing to fight.[60] It is difficult to see the grounds for the charge of cowardice since the burghers were short of ammunition and the British forces had failed in their only battle and subsequently were kept out of the fighting by Vandeleur. The landdrosts in Graaff-Reinet and Swellendam instructed the burghers to stand but made no attempt themselves to leave their own offices and organize a defense. In Cape Town there was a marked lack of resolve. Several ex-Company officials implored the British to use conciliation rather than armed force.

The British had little intention of committing any real resources to restoring the colonial order on the frontier. Conciliating the Xhosa had become the objective. Accompanied by Maynier, Dundas traveled to the frontier and decided that no armed response was necessary: 'I believe that the intention of the Caffres and the Hottentots is merely to possess themselves of as many cattle and destroy as many habitations as possible.'[61] Dundas and Maynier tried to persuade the Xhosa to leave the Zuurveld, now an even more remote possibility. They told the burghers to return to their farms or risk losing them. To get the Khoikhoi to return to their employers they offered the protection of labor contracts with the landdrost rather than with a field cornet as an arbiter. Patrols of young burghers and armed Khoikhoi would follow the spoor of stolen cattle and shoot thieves if necessary. Maynier now took over in Graaff-Reinet as resident commissioner with some twenty-two British soldiers, nineteen Khoikhoi regulars, and eighty other armed Khoikhoi, who aroused burgher suspicions. A breakdown of order was only a matter of time.

The situation was destabilized even further by the arrival in Graaff-Reinet of the Rev. Johannes van der Kemp, a Dutch missionary employed by the London Missionary Society (LMS). In the town he encountered James Read, another LMS missionary, and decided to join him. With nearly a thousand Khoikhoi converging on the town of Graaff-

---

60 Such statements were fairly typical of the first British officials at the Cape. See Michael Streak, *The Afrikaner as Viewed by the English, 1795-1854* (Cape Town: Streak, 1974), see esp. pp. 50-52.

61 Giliomee, *Kaap tydens die Britse bewind*, p. 293. For a different interpretation of the war see Marais, *Maynier* and Suzie Newton-King and V.C. Malherbe, *The Khoikhoi Rebellion in the Eastern Cape, 1799-1803* (Cape Town: UCT, 1981).

Reinet to seek security and food, Maynier provided supplies and allowed the missionaries to use the colonists' church for religious instruction. They also attended the regular services on Sundays. Many colonists were outraged by this act of social leveling, which forced them to worship with servants, some of whom may have committed theft or murder.

The rebels planned to attack the town but, at the last moment, did not. In late 1801 British troops from Cape Town relieved the town and handed Maynier orders for his recall. But the Xhosa did not abandon the Zuurveld and the thefts continued, with rumors that sent the burghers fleeing in panic. By early 1803 observers put the number of farms 'burnt, plundered and abandoned' at 470, a figure equal to almost half of the farms registered in Graaff-Reinet and Swellendam. Stock losses were estimated at fifty thousand cattle and fifty thousand sheep. A wealthy western Cape farmer believed the losses so enormous that the Graaff-Reinet district would not return to prosperity for fifteen years. It was by far the most traumatic setback suffered by the burghers since the founding of the European settlement. With peace briefly restored on the frontier in 1802, the government gave the two missionaries, Van der Kemp and Read, an abandoned farm near Algoa Bay where they established the mission station Bethelsdorp.

'To strike terror into the enemy'

The representatives of the Batavian Republic who administered the Cape from 1803 to 1806 wanted to run the colony on the Enlightenment principles of good government. Like the British before them they deplored the brutality with which some frontiersmen treated their servants, but the farms needed Khoikhoi labor and the Batavians thought there was no alternative but for the Khoikhoi to return to the farms. When some chiefs accepted land offered to them by the government, the Khoikhoi resistance disintegrated. To improve control over the interior the Batavians established two new districts, Tulbagh in the west and Uitenhage, with a drostdy of the same name, near Algoa Bay and close to the Zuurveld. They also built a military post called Fort Frederick in Algoa Bay to rush military reinforcements to the frontier. The Batavians announced severe penalties for any burghers who crossed the colonial border and ill-treated servants.

In 1806 Britain took possession of the Cape again, and in 1809 a balanced report by a British officer, Colonel Richard Collins, noted that the condition of the Khoikhoi farm workers had hardly improved: 'A Hottentot can now seldom get away at the expiration of his term. If he should happen to be in debt to his master . . . he is not allowed to take his children, or he is detained under some frivolous pretense, such as that of cattle having died through his neglect, and he is not permitted to satisfy any demands of this nature otherwise than by personal service.'[62]

Security on the frontier steadily deteriorated. Ngqika had lost his grip on Xhosa society, and, in 1807, he was badly beaten in a battle by his rival, Ndlambe, and fled with his followers to the Amatola mountains, where, it is said, even his own children starved. His relationship with De Buys ended, and De Buys left the eastern frontier region and

---

62 Moodie, *The Record*, vol. 5, p. 22.

settled in the northern part of the present South Africa, where a community of mixed-blood transfrontiermen, the Buys Basters, took root.

Ndlambe and Chungwa, the two most powerful chiefs west of the Fish River, failed to control the lesser Xhosa chiefs. The burghers themselves were disorganized and on the defensive. More Xhosa were raiding cattle or 'visiting' farms along a broad swathe from the seaboard to Bruintjes Hoogte in the central border region, and to the town of Graaff-Reinet in the north. Ex-Company servants persuaded the Earl of Caledon, the first British governor under the second occupation, that some suffering by frontier farmers was preferable to risking a frontier war. To maintain the peace the government prohibited burghers from pursuing or firing on marauders except in self-defense, and, as a result, the Xhosa gained in confidence. A field cornet wrote that all the benevolence the burghers displayed by offering gifts to the Xhosa had produced no result other 'than a general mockery of and contempt for Christians.' A British officer stationed on the frontier warned from Bruintjes Hoogte (near the present Cradock) that, 'unless a sufficient force is immediately sent to the aid of this part of the colony, it must fall, and I shall not be surprised to see the Kaffre Nation extend itself to within a short distance of Cape Town.'[63] The specter of a repetition of the events of 1799 to 1802 loomed again: abandoned farms, slain herdsmen and fearful burgher families congregating in laagers. Again the call went up to expel all the Xhosa west of the Fish River.

What was to be done? At this time two reports were written, each trying to grapple with the intractable frontier situation in different ways. Colonel Collins urged that a community of some six thousand new settlers should be placed in a compact settlement in the Zuurveld to protect the border. Another perspective was offered in August 1810 by the Swede, Anders Stockenström. He had joined the VOC to escape his debtors, and had been appointed as landdrost of Graaff-Reinet. He expressed a gloomy view of the prospects for co-existence by giving a detailed account of the sources of friction. 'The Kaffers', he wrote, 'are naturally insatiable beggars and thieves. All domestic and agricultural labor being performed by the women, and the cattle being herded by the boys, the men have nothing to do but to hunt and to wander among the colonists.' On arriving at a farm, a party begged for victuals while 'watching their opportunity to carry off something for their journey into the bargain.' Once they had reached a nearby kraal with the stolen cattle, their tracks could no longer be followed.

Through such practices, Stockenström continued, some farmers were reduced to poverty. The Xhosa treated the frontier farmers with contempt and alarmed them with indirect messages 'that in the long nights they will attack farmers, and commit robbery and murder.' To Stockenström, the expulsion of the Xhosa from the colonial territory was the only feasible remedy. In the meantime, there was only one prudent course of action: '[We] must hold out no threats, if we do not intend to execute them, for I consider this the great cause of their boldness, as they fancy us afraid or unable to punish them according to their deserts.'[64]

But enforcing strict separation between the Xhosa and the burghers was not as easy

---

63 H.B. Giliomee, 'Die administrasietydperk van Lord Caledon', *AYB*, 1966, 2, p. 329.
64 This was a letter from Anders Stockenström, dated August 1810, published in *Afrikaner Political Thought*, pp. 158-9.

as it sounded, nor was there a general demand for it. Burghers continued to trade with the Xhosa and employ them as workers. It was the British military who insisted on a radical solution. When Sir John Cradock, unlike Caledon a military officer, arrived in 1811 to become governor, he found the frontier situation intolerable: no benefit could 'possibly arise either to the Kaffir tribes or the Dutch settlers from any intercourse and all the present evils proceeded from their intermixture.'[65] A military operation was for him the only solution. The question was how to avoid the blunders of previous commandos against the Xhosa that had failed to set any clear goal or to develop any unity of purpose.

The burgher commandos that had gone out before 1811 lacked numbers and discipline and and their tactics were generally poor. Instead of concentrating on dislodging the Xhosa and making it impossible for a return, they focused on capturing cattle. Hubert Dirk Campagne, an observer sympathetic to the burghers in the Company days, remarked that the early commandos' failure had to be sought in the fact that while it was not possible to subjugate the Xhosa by force of arms, it was easy to capture cattle. Colonel Collins made the same point: 'The wars that were at first waged against the Caffres were carried on exclusively by the settlers, who seem, whenever they have been unsuccessful, to have failed in a large degree from their having considered the recovery of stolen cattle as the principal object of hostility.'[66] To counter the lack of discipline, the bane of so many earlier commandos, the government announced that martial law would begin the moment a military expedition started.

In the final months of 1811 a large force was assembled of 440 British troops, 431 Khoikhoi soldiers, and 450 burghers on commando. An enormous amount of £47,750 was levied as tax on districts that did not supply men for the force. Orders were given to ensure that the men would stay in the field until their task was completed. Leadership was assigned to a British officer, Colonel John Graham. Over the previous forty years the Xhosa, in the eyes of the burghers, had been many things – foes, certainly, but also trading partners, laborers and potential military allies. To Graham the Xhosa were simply 'horrid savages.' He ordered the pursuit of plundering parties of Xhosa to their settlements where 'every man Kaffer' who could be found was to be slain. If possible the chief had to be 'destroyed.' All was designed to inspire the Xhosa with 'a proper degree of terror and respect' to prevent their return.[67]

Any lingering doubts about whether to use the harshest possible methods were removed by an event that occurred just before the colonial force took the field. As head of a party of twenty-four men, landdrost Stockenström had gone in unarmed among a group of a hundred Xhosa to persuade them to retreat peacefully across the Fish River, when a message went out to them that a soldier had shot some Xhosa. Stockenström and seven men were massacred.[68]

In the first three months of 1812 the force expelled some eight thousand Xhosa from

---

65 B. Maclennan, *A Proper Degree of Terror* (Johannesburg: Ravan Press, 1986), p. 79.

66 Giliomee, 'Eastern Frontier', p. 434.

67 Giliomee, 'Eastern Frontier', p. 448.

68 Stockenström's son, Andries, did not give this version in his autobiography. C.L. Stretch probably based it on a Xhosa source. See Basil le Cordeur (ed.), *The Journal of Charles Lennox Stretch* (Cape Town: Maskew Miller, 1988), p. 11.

the Zuurveld and destroyed their crops. A series of forts were built along the border. Two new frontier villages, Grahamstown and Cradock, were marked out. But cattle rustling started again and drought compounded the crisis. At the end of 1813 a British officer, Captain George Fraser, led a large commando, which, in the words of Sir John Cradock, had to 'prove to these savages and unceasing robbers that His Majesty's government can no longer be trifled with.' Fraser's deputy stationed at Cradock was Andries Stockenstrom, a young deputy landdrost from Graaff-Reinet, son of landdrost Stockenström. The purpose of the commando, his son said, was 'To kill, to make an example of, to strike terror into the enemy was a duty, a standing order.'[69]

For the Xhosa the expulsion of 1811-12 and the follow-up operation was a new and shattering experience, nothing less than total war. The number of lives lost, the killing of the chief Chungwa in his bed by soldiers and the destruction of Xhosa chiefdoms in the Zuurveld were incomprehensible to them. They discovered that the colony could draw on more military and other resources than they could ever imagine. Nor did the conquerors deign to incorporate the defeated into their society. As the historian Jeffrey Peires remarks, they were not only expelled, but also rebuffed and in other ways rejected, as if they were unfit to live with. After forty years the cultural differences between Africans and Europeans were for the first time etched out in the starkest possible way.[70]

The rise of Andries Stockenstrom

While the lines between whites and blacks on the frontier became more firmly drawn, those between burghers on the frontier and their new rulers became somewhat more blurred. At first Graham had been almost as scathing in his contempt of the burghers as Dundas and Barrow twelve years earlier, calling them 'the most ignorant of all peasants', but, after the Zuurveld campaign of 1811-12, in which soldiers and burghers fought well together, he sang a different tune. He commended the burghers for their 'cheerfulness and alacrity', adding that the 'African Boer' was 'by no means deficient in point of intellect, and possesses many good qualities.'[71]

Frontier burghers nevertheless remained suspicious of British motives and intentions and ready to believe wild rumors. Stockenstrom woke up one night during the 1813 campaign to find the entire force of five hundred burghers ready to fight to the last man rather than surrender. They believed that the British were ready to impress them as soldiers and march them to Algoa Bay for duty elsewhere. Their fear of British military or naval impressment would not disappear until mid-century.[72]

The British rulers themselves could only scoff at the gullibility of the frontier farmers, and, as Graham did, put it down to the 'almost total want of intercourse with mankind.' The British slowly tried to bring the frontier burghers and the relationship between them and their Khoikhoi servants within the framework of regular government and the rule of law. The government combined a concern over the brutal maltreatment of servants

---

69 Andries Stockenstrom, *Autobiography* (Cape Town: Juta, 1887), vol. 2, p. 138.
70 Peires, *House of Phalo,* p. 66.
71 Mostert, *Frontiers,* p. 296.
72 Stockenstrom, *Autobiography,* vol. 2, p. 138.

with a zeal to ensure that farmers had enough labor. The Hottentot Proclamation of 1809, which gave more protection to servants by requiring written contracts, also formalized the pass system. All Khoikhoi had to carry passes and could obtain a pass only after they had duly served out their time. On the road they could be challenged by 'everyone' to show their passes and those who failed to do so could be delivered to the field cornet. Masters and field cornets ready to tie the Khoikhoi down on the farms had more than enough levers at their disposal.

The principal reform instrument of the government was the introduction of an annual circuit court with the judges from Cape Town touring the interior to hear cases. The second circuit, in 1812, became known as the Black Circuit, because of the many charges of maltreatment of Khoikhoi laborers raised by the missionaries Van der Kemp and Read from their mission station in Bethelsdorp. The demonstration effect of the Black Circuit was immense, and for the first time, frontier burghers appeared before a high court in their districts to answer charges brought against them by their servants. The judges of the Black Circuit found most of the accused not guilty, seeming to vindicate the views of the aggrieved burghers and of later nationalist historians. But only perpetrators of crimes committed after 1806 were prosecuted and, in the trials, the judges almost certainly gave greater weight to the evidence of the burghers than to their servants. Even landdrost Jacob Cuyler of Uitenhage, who clashed with the Bethelsdorp missionaries over his demands for free Khoikhoi labor, observed that in earlier times barbarous cruelties had indeed been committed. The real significance of the Black Circuit was that the missionaries had succeeded in attracting the attention of influential people in London to the issue of the maltreatment of the Khoikhoi. External pressure had built up, which neither the colonial government nor the burghers could ignore.

The government nonetheless initially introduced further restrictions on the Khoikhoi in order to ensure a stable labor supply. In 1812 a regulation provided that colonists who had maintained a Khoikhoi child for the first eight years could apprentice that child for ten years. In 1819 a further proclamation authorized farmers to apprentice orphans and other Khoikhoi children not in their parents' care until the age of eighteen. This could easily be abused when officials imposed this on children who required no protection.[73] These laws were intended also for the Khoikhoi's benefit, but often the effect was to tie down entire families and to keep wages low. Before 1828 it was not unusual to hear of cases where Khoisan worked for long periods on farms for nothing but food and clothing.

The British government in further steps to stabilize the frontier zone stationed Khoikhoi troops at the border posts as a ready resource for the frontier landdrosts should they want to detain someone. Cradock hoped to attack one of the root causes of the lawlessness by announcing the end of the loan farm system. His new system of perpetual quitrent title required that farms be surveyed, and that their borders be marked by beacons. In theory, security of title would push up prices and drive out the most inefficient farmers, while tying successful farmers more firmly to the land. In practice the reform misfired. It tended to make farms smaller and the rent more expensive. The government's inability to process the new land claims speedily only added to the insecurity of the frontier burghers.

---

73 Richard Elphick and V.C. Malherbe, 'The Khoisan to 1828', *SSAS*, p. 41.

The biggest boost to frontier stability came though the appointment of shrewd frontier landdrosts, who could explain to the heemraden and burghers that accepting the new order of the rule of law was in their own best interests. The prime example was Andries Stockenstrom, one of the most remarkable individuals in South Africa history. Because a great-great-grandmother was the daughter of two slaves from Guinea, his enemies denigrated his line of descent, although a touch of 'colored blood' was common among the best of Cape families. His father was from a prominent Swedish family, and his mother the daughter of a German lawyer.

Unlike a predecessor, Maynier, who had also tried to intercede on behalf of the Khoikhoi and who had also faced a rebellion, Stockenstrom had more success in his long career in winning staunch allies among the most respected burghers. Despite Stockenstrom's criticism of the burghers who trekked out of the colony in the 1830s, a Voortrekker leader, Andries Pretorius, called him his 'best friend and father.'[74]

From an early stage Stockenstrom believed that justice fairly dispensed was the key to stability on the frontier. Just before his father's tragic death in December 1811, he was with him in a meeting with the missionary Van der Kemp and Cuyler, landdrost of Uitenhage, accused by Van der Kemp and Read of blatantly favoring burghers over the Khoikhoi. The two missionaries, who had demanded complete equality between the colonists and the Khoikhoi, had run into tough opposition from the burghers. Stockenstrom, then eighteen, who had grown up in the hierarchical social order of the Company, took a similar line to the missionaries on equality before the law and would hold it for the rest of his life. 'Strict and equal justice at all costs was the only safe course,' he said on that occasion.[75] Stockenstrom said this with the Khoisan in mind, but he soon extended these principles to deal with the relationship between burghers and Xhosa.

Stockenstrom was a slave-owner himself, and shared to some extent the paternalistic world-view of the Afrikaners. But with his strong commitment to the rule of law and justice, he supported the need for sweeping reforms. At the same time he was an articulate exponent of the view that the Afrikaner colonists had to be won over to the cause of reform rather than have reforms imposed from without. Unlike most well-educated people born at the Cape during the reign of the Company, he identified himself as an Afrikaner and a Boer. A brave, honest and fiercely independent man with no illusions about human nature, he detested the hypocrisy in abundant supply on all sides of the frontier conflict.[76] In 1816 Stockenstrom observed that 'the greatest majority of the Boer population was not opposed to equal justice to black and white.'[77] The core problem, he believed, was the inadequacy of the legal system. Despite the establishment of some new districts, most farms were still a considerable distance from the towns, making it very difficult for masters to lay complaints before the magistrate.

A rebellion, which historians call the Slagtersnek Rebellion of 1815, was Stockenstrom's first acid test. Only firm action could stamp out the lawlessness that characterized the early stages of the frontier. The rebels' discontent had arisen mostly from

---

74 Stockenstrom, *Autobiography*, vol. 2, p. 296.
75 Stockenstrom, *Autobiography*, vol. 1, p. 83.
76 Stockenstrom, *Autobiography*, vol. 2, pp. 8-12.
77 Stockenstrom, *Autobiography*, vol. 1, p. 93.

two sources. One was the perception that the Khoikhoi were given privileges by the British. As evidence they pointed to the Black Circuit. Equally offensive to the rebels was the fact that the main military force stationed at the frontier was the Cape Regiment, comprised of Khoikhoi and other 'colored' troops under white officers. As Stockenstrom would later remark, 'the people were talking that the "black nation was protected and not the Christians".' Hendrik Prinsloo, son of Marthinus Prinsloo, declared that 'the Hottentots [were] preferred to the burghers.'[78]

A shortage of land was the second source of discontent. The ideal of a farm for every adult burgher was never attainable. By 1798, 39 per cent of the male burghers in Graaff-Reinet owned land; by 1812 the percentage had shrunk to 25. A few burghers were considering radical alternatives, including the strategy adopted most prominently by Coenraad de Buys, of moving beyond the border in small groups and settling among the Xhosa, accepting the overlordship of an African chief and paying tribute to him, but retaining a degree of independence.

Among the Slagtersnek rebels were outlaw types or frontier ruffians, as historians sometimes call them. Several of them lived with Baster women. Rough, uncultivated men, they farmed on unwanted land and owned limited stock. They tended to come from families ruined by the Xhosa incursions of 1793 and 1799. After the 1799 rebellion some fled across the Fish River to live close to Ngqika. The most prominent among them were Jan and Christoffel Botha, Coenraad Bezuidenhout and Cornelis Faber. Also among the rebels were more established farmers in the Baviaans River and Tarka divisions south and east of Winterberg, an area within the colonial borders but wild and inhospitable. They held a host of grievances, particularly over the quitrent system introduced in 1813, the Black Circuit, and the English as 'God-forgotten tyrants and villains.' Behind them was a tradition of fractiousness and revolt. At least one contemporary observer said that Marthinus Prinsloo was 'the principal promoter of the late [Slagtersnek] disturbances.' All his sons participated. Of the thirty-nine who were sentenced afterwards, seven bore the name of Prinsloo and a further five were married to Prinsloo women. Three bore the name of Klopper and two of Bothma, the sons of veldwachtmeester C. Bothma, who had been dismissed by Adriaan van Jaarsveld more than forty years before.

The Slagtersnek Rebellion began early in 1813 when a Khoikhoi laborer, named Booy, came to complain about his master to Stockenstrom, deputy landdrost of Cradock. The master was Freek Bezuidenhout, brother of Coenraad Bezuidenhout, and a notorious frontier ruffian who lived with a Baster woman and whose Baster son called him 'baas' (the term non-whites used for a white master). Booy claimed that his master had withheld his wages and had severely assaulted him. When Stockenstrom summoned Bezuidenhout to appear, he ignored the order, exclaiming 'What does Stockenstrom think? I care for my life just as much as nothing.' Stockenstrom requested help from the military stationed in the frontier, and a company of two British officers and twelve Khoikhoi troops arrived at Bezuidenhout's house. A brief battle ensued and Bezuidenhout was killed. At the funeral his brother Johannes (Hans) Bezuidenhout swore vengeance and Hendrik Prinsloo began to enlist support.

---

78 This section draws mainly on my 'The Burgher Rebellions on the Eastern Frontier, 1795-1815', *SSAS*, (1), pp. 351-4.

The rebels used similar tactics to those in the 1799 rebellion. Cornelis Faber went twice to Ngqika with a proposal. If he would drive away the Cape Regiment, expel all government officials on the frontier, and allow the rebels to occupy the fertile Kat River Valley well east of the border, he could take possession of the Zuurveld, which in any event was largely unoccupied. One of the Bothmas told his fellow-rebels that the Ngqika's people were unanimous in agreeing 'that they would fight for the Zuurveld and we would fight for our land.' As in 1799 there was a threat that burghers who refused to join would be killed and their families and property given over to the Xhosa. One rebel leader proposed a grander scheme that foreshadowed the Great Trek two decades later. His plan was to 'maintain a certain understanding with the Kafirs, which would enable them [the rebels] . . . to cross over the proclaimed boundaries, and settle down in one or other portion of Kafirland to take possession of the territory at the Gonap [Koonap] in the form of an independent Union.'

From the start of the Slagtersnek Rebellion, Stockenstrom saw the issue as involving a clear choice between order and civilization on the one hand, and anarchy on the other. In countering the spread of the rebellion, he showed great courage; at a crucial point riding in alone and unarmed among a group of disaffected burghers, persuading them not to join the rebellion. It was in a large measure because of such actions that the well-to-do farmers sided with the government. The rebellion was crushed without any shots being fired. Five of the leaders were hanged.

In the twentieth century Afrikaner nationalist writers and politicians tried hard to use the unpromising material of Slagtersnek to support a nationalist myth. The rebels were depicted as brave martyrs paying the ultimate penalty for standing up against British autocracy. At the unveiling of the Slagtersnek monument a century later, the nationalist leader Daniël François Malan suggested that De Buys would have held a restraining hand over the invading Xhosa force! What was ignored was the way Slagtersnek-as-nationalist-myth clashed with the nationalist myth of racial purity and with its corollary that whites never made common cause with blacks.[79] Twentieth-century nationalists also ignored the fact that the more settled farmers wanted nothing to do with rebellion.

Slagtersnek was a critical turning point in establishing the government's control of the frontier. By 1825 the landdrost of Grahamstown reported that the field cornets drawn from 'Dutch Boers' on the frontier were always ready to respond to calls for assistance and were much more effective than those appointed from the ranks of the British settlers.[80] Governors began to comment favorably on the human quality of the people who had settled on the frontier. While never truly trusting the British rulers, most burghers had accepted the fact that obeying the government and its laws was in their best interests. In 1833 the governor, Sir Lowry Cole, not overly sympathetic to the burghers, wrote with reference to them: 'Such is their dread of criminal laws that many are afraid to defend their persons and property even in a lawful manner.'[81]

---

79 J.A. Heese, *Slagtersnek en sy mense* (Cape Town: Tafelberg, 1973), Introduction and p. 205; Leonard Thompson, *The Political Mythology of Apartheid* (New Haven: Yale University Press, 1985), pp. 105-43.

80 J.L.M. Franken, *Piet Retief se lewe in die Kolonie* (Pretoria: HAUM, 1949), p. 289.

81 G.D. Scholtz, *Die ontwikkeling van die politieke denke van die Afrikaner* (Johannesburg: Voortrekkerpers, 1970), vol. 2, p. 266.

For much of the eighteenth century the frontier had remained open, and it seemed as if it would be possible to ensure the survival of a certain lifestyle through continuous expansion. The burghers wished to dominate in any new region, but used different means in different circumstances. The grim wars of extermination of the Bushmen in the 1770s and 1780s gave way to attempts to reconcile them through gifts in the 1790s. In the southeast, they tried on their own to drive the Xhosa across the border, but failed. The catastrophic third war of 1799-1802 made the burghers much more inclined to allow the government to direct military operations and to accept its administrative measures. They nevertheless remained convinced that they were better equipped to negotiate an understanding with the Xhosa chiefs than was the government in Cape Town. They would consider other options if the policies of the British government failed to bring about security on the frontier.

Chapter 4

Masters, Slaves and Servants:
The Fear of *Gelykstelling*

'Before the law of equal standing'

In 1797 a dispute arose between the landdrost and heemraden of Stellenbosch when a Khoikhoi sued his employer to appear before the court on the question of a debt. The heemraden objected to this, stating that 'such practices have never before obtained here.' They were 'ignorant of whether or not a Hottentot has a right to summon a burgher before the college, and of whether, once being allowed, it would open a door and give Hottentots the idea that they are on a footing of equality with the burghers.' The landdrost, R.J. van der Riet, on the other hand, maintained that a 'Hottentot should be recognized before the law in the same way as himself, and that this constituted true equality, since before the law all were of equal standing.'[1]

In the days of the Company, slaves and Khoikhoi did have the right to lay complaints before a court, even against their own masters and mistresses. The burghers resented it, particularly if the accused was a person of good social standing. But not until the 1790s did landdrosts like Honoratus Maynier of Graaff-Reinet and, on this occasion, Van der Riet, strongly defend the principle of equality before the law. In opposing *gelykstelling*, or social leveling, the burghers initially did not cast the issue in terms of race or color. The Company's status hierarchy was carried over to the British period: burghers with property enjoyed high status, those without property somewhat less and a white *knecht* or a servant considerably less. Even lower down were free blacks, and Khoikhoi servants lower still, while slaves were at the bottom of the social ladder. The principal objection of the burghers was being put on an equal footing with servants and slaves. When the government indentured white servants brought from Britain with western Cape farmers they refused to take the servants with them to church.[2]

On the frontier the opposition to gelykstelling could even include preventing the Khoikhoi from becoming literate or receiving the Christian sacraments. In mid-1801 the missionaries Johannes van der Kemp and James Read began to give religious instruction to about a thousand Khoikhoi who had converged on the town of Graaff-Reinet at a time of great instability on the frontier (see p. 78). This caused outrage among the burghers

---

1 *Afrikaner Political Thought*, p. 94.
2 C.F.J. Muller, *Die oorsprong van die Groot Trek* (Cape Town: Tafelberg, 1974), p. 207.

who had rebelled against government authority. According to Van der Kemp, the rebels declared that the government 'protected the Hottentots and Caffrees and were instructed by us [the missionaries] in reading, writing and religion, and thereby put upon an equal footing with the Christians especially that they were admitted to the church of Graaff-Reinet.' A group of rebels demanded that the Khoikhoi be barred from the church: 'the seats should be washed, the pavement broken up, and the pulpit be covered with black cloth as a demonstration of mourning.'[3] Van der Kemp was undeterred: 'The Hottentots should be perfectly free, upon an equal footing in every respect with the colonists and by no sort of compulsion brought under a necessity to enter their service, but have a piece of ground given them by Government as their own.'[4]

Over time the opposition to gelykstelling changed in form, with equality before the law becoming more acceptable. The stiffest opposition was now to people not properly confirmed participating in Holy Communion, the prospect of large numbers of blacks getting the vote, and miscegenation. Behind it all was a fear that the loss of control over laborers would have a ripple effect, ultimately causing a collapse of law and order that would pull the master class down into a morass of squalor and licentiousness.

The new British rulers were no social revolutionaries. They abolished burgher status but permitted many of the obligations and privileges associated with it to survive. They were firmer than the VOC in insisting that the Khoikhoi had recourse to the courts and the right to own land, but, in practice, these rights amounted to little since most Khoikhoi were not Christians and as such could not swear an oath. Without an oath their evidence counted for less. So, too, almost no Khoikhoi owned land. Lord Charles Somerset, the third governor of the second British occupation, said that the Khoikhoi could become owners of farms, but he could mention only small grants made to three 'Hottentots' and three 'Bastaard Hottentots.' Even after 1828, when the Khoisan were 'freed' by Ordinance 50, the British granted land only to applicants with sufficient capital, which the Khoikhoi invariably lacked. There was only one successful Khoikhoi applicant for a farm in the eastern districts.[5] For such reasons, the burghers continued to think of themselves as a superior kind of subject with special duties and privileges.

Central to burgher status was voluntary participation in commandos as 'defenders of the land', as the earliest free burghers had expressed it. In Company times the burghers fought under their own officers, who called them up. In the aftermath of the Sixth Frontier War (1834-35), they strongly opposed a government plan to summon them regularly for militia service because, so the officials said, they 'dislike[d being] considered other than as free burghers.'

During the 1847 frontier war the governor, Sir Henry Pottinger, was still using the term 'burghers'.[6] And, as late as 1891, a commission of inquiry by English-speakers in the Cape Colony said that the government's education policy was 'to get the burghers to learn English.'[7]

---

3 *Transactions of the Missionary Society* (London: Bye and Law, 1804), pp. 481-83.

4 *Transactions*, vol. 1, pp. 490-91.

5 The above two paragraphs are largely based on V.C. Malherbe, 'Testing the Burgher Right to the Land', *South African Historical Journal*, 40 (1999), pp. 1-20.

6 Basil le Cordeur and Christopher Saunders (eds.), *The War of the Axe* (Johannesburg: Brenthurst Press, 1981), p. 52.

7 M. du Toit Potgieter, 'Die Nederduits Gereformeerde Kerk en die blanke onderwys in Kaapland', doctoral diss., US, 1961, p. 308.

'A necessary evil'

Slave status, too, remained intact for quite some time. Indeed, the transfer of the colony to British hands in 1795 and again, more permanently, in 1806, had revived the institution of slavery, bringing much-expanded markets, far stronger international linkages, and a voracious demand for slave labor to produce wheat and wine for the market. As a result, the production of both wheat and wine trebled between the mid-1790s and the mid-1820s, with close to 40 per cent of Stellenbosch and Drakenstein farmers using only slave labor in 1806. Slaves boosted production levels. For certain years under British rule a clear correlation between slave numbers and farm output can be established. It was not at all certain that free labor, even if available, would be able to replace slaves without significant losses to the farmers.

With slaves one of the most important forms of property, any attack on the institution would severely damage their owners' financial prospects. On the arable farms slaves represented 13 to 17 per cent of the total value. Slaves provided a greater facility than any other form of property for raising money on mortgage, and, on the eve of emancipation, were the principal mortgageable assets of the colony. Although slavery did not ordinarily adapt well to cities, Cape Town represented an exception and slave artisans there brought a return of 18 per cent in the 1820s.[8]

There had nevertheless long been doubts about the economic rationality of slavery for the colony as a settlement. In the 1717 Council of Policy debate on slavery, Pasques de Chavonnes argued that money spent on slaves was 'dead money.' The poor reproduction rate of Cape slaves meant that much-needed foreign exchange had to be spent on importing slaves. Toward the end of Company rule the government became concerned about the enormous capital locked up in the colony's slaves, and about the use of slaves for 'luxury' purposes rather than for necessary labor. In the final decades of the century, when farmers had acquired more slaves than agricultural prices justified, many farms became overcapitalized and ready capital was so scarce that some farmers were forced to pay their land rent in kind instead of cash.[9]

Nonetheless, slavery as a system was remarkably resilient. With few investment opportunities at the Cape, slavery remained profitable as long as no likelihood existed that the government would abolish it. To virtually all colonists in the western Cape their own survival and that of slavery as an institution had become identical. They could scarcely imagine how the financial, economic and security structure of the Cape could withstand a radical attack on the institution. In the 1717 debate K.J. Slotsboo declared: 'No matter how poor a person is, he will not accustom himself to perform the work of slaves, as he thinks in this way to distinguish himself from slaves.'[10]

By the end of the century the mould had been set. Slavery affected virtually every burgher, and for more than 150 years it penetrated almost all aspects of the burghers' way of life. Slave-ownership was remarkably widespread among the burghers themselves, and even the status of non-owners depended on their membership of a slave-holding com-

---

8 James Armstrong and Nigel Worden, 'The Slaves, 1652-1834', *SSAS*, p. 141.

9 Nigel Worden, *Slavery in Dutch South Africa* (Cambridge: Cambridge University Press, 1985), pp. 34-73, 84-5.

10 *The Reports of Chavonnes and His Council, and of Van Imhoff* (Cape Town: VRS, 1918), pp. 105-6, 121.

munity. Most slaves passed from one generation in a family to the next at the owner's death. Selling slaves out of the family occurred mostly as a result of bankruptcy. The ideology of paternalism remained intact despite the transfer of power to the British. As a Graaff-Reinet slave-owner remarked in 1826: '[Do] not deprive me of my paternal authority, under which both my children and slaves are happy, and which is necessary for their and my peace.'[11] Slave-owners could not conceive of peace in or outside the house were the paternalistic relationship to be disturbed.

But slavery by the second half of the eighteenth century had become a controversial institution in the Western world. Both Roman law and the Christian church accepted slavery but displayed an ambivalence towards it. Powerful voices in the state and the church saw slavery as a necessary compromise to be made in a sinful world. Even with the advent of the Enlightenment, many political leaders considered slavery compatible with progressive thinking. George Washington, Thomas Jefferson and James Madison were all slave-holders and, at the same time, authors of the Declaration of Independence and the liberal American constitution. They were embarrassed by slavery and viewed it even as a dangerous social evil, but they did not propose abolition. Neither did they free their own slaves in their lifetimes. At the Constitutional Convention of 1787 a heated argument arose over the slave trade, but states that wanted to abolish it gave way when the representative of South Carolina said that the state would never accept a constitution that prohibited the slave trade. Slavery as an institution was retained, since the principle of private property, on which the economy and society rested, weighed far more heavily than liberty for all people, including slaves. Between 1792 and 1845 the American political system encouraged and rewarded the expansion of slavery into nine new states.[12]

In Britain by the final decades of the eighteenth century, slavery had become increasingly unacceptable. The campaign against slavery had become, for many, a moral and a religious crusade. Enlightenment philosophers declared slavery irrational. To Adam Smith, whose *The Wealth of Nations* appeared in 1776, it was an intolerable obstacle to human progress. British legal opinion with respect to slavery began to change fundamentally, an early sign the judgment of Lord Mansfield in 1770, holding slavery too odious an institution to exist in England without specific legislation sanctioning it. In 1787 the Society for Effecting the Abolition of the Slave Trade was founded.

The French Revolution with its doctrine of liberty, equality and the inalienable rights of man imparted a severe shock to the slave system on both sides of the Atlantic. In 1793 slavery was abolished in all French colonies. Reports of these momentous events in France had filtered through to the slaves and other servile people at the Cape, and the colony was suddenly in the grip of wild rumors and fears. In 1793 an official reported from Stellenbosch a 'general fear' of slaves and Khoikhoi planning to 'attack the farms of Christians and murder the inhabitants.'[13] In Cape Town rumors circulated that slaves expecting imminent liberation were holding meetings to discuss the fate of their masters.[14]

---

11 *Afrikaner Political Thought,* pp. 36, 67.
12 David Brion Davis, 'At the Heart of Slavery', *The New York Review of Books*, 17 October 1996, p. 54.
13 Armstrong and Worden, 'The Slaves', p. 160.
14 John Barrow, *Travels into the Interior of South Africa* (London: T. Cadell, 1806), vol. 2, pp. 163-4.

However, in September 1795, immediately after taking over the Cape, the British announced that they would not violate property rights. Slaves who had joined the occupying force in the hope of being set free were returned to their masters. The new rulers did, however, make clear their revulsion at some of the practices associated with Cape slavery. The British commander asked the Court of Justice whether it would be possible to impose the death penalty on convicted slaves without the various forms of torture that accompanied these executions (see p. 46). The court's reply was direct: many slaves were 'descended from wild and rude Nations', and would 'hardly consider the privation of life as a punishment unless accompanied by such cruel circumstances as greatly aggravated their bodily suffering.' To do away with judicial torture would, in the members' view, be detrimental because it 'would raise in the minds of many of the Inhabitants great apprehensions for their personal safety.'[15] The British were not persuaded by the argument. They kept capital punishment, but abolished judicial torture.

Pressure for the abolition of the slave trade had built up in Britain sufficiently for the new British government at the Cape to seek an opinion on ending the importing of slaves into the colony. It turned to Willem Stephanus van Ryneveld, an official who was one of the most progressive thinkers born and bred under Company rule, and asked a simple question: could the colony survive without the further importing of slaves? The query reopened the issue addressed by the Council of Policy in 1717: could whites be used instead of slaves as the principal source of labor?

In addressing the question posed by the British authorities, Van Ryneveld, a slave-owner himself, wrote: 'It is true, slavery is hard of itself. I have at the moment that I write . . . a feeling of all its weight.' Slavery held the owners as much as the slaves in a clenched grip. Still, he could not propose ending slave imports. He argued that a ban would be disastrous since the slave population at the Cape, indispensable for the cultivation of wheat and wine, did not reproduce itself. The majority of slave women were not fertile and most of those who were had only one child. He attributed this to 'continual labor', poor living conditions and diet, and the extensive use of slaves as wet nurses. There were few free laborers in and around Cape Town because slavery had depressed wages, and, on the pastoral frontier, the burghers had become accustomed to a steady expansion of land. The sons of burghers refused to become laborers as long as there was some hope that they could become stock farmers.

Van Ryneveld recognized that slavery had made the burghers 'lazy, haughty and brutal', but argued that it had become 'a necessary evil, which cannot be removed without sacrificing the Colony and perhaps the poor slaves that are in it.' Ending slavery would 'render both the country and these poor creatures themselves miserable, not only all tillage would then be at an end, but also the number of freemen, instead of their being (as now) useful members of, would then really become a charge to, society.' He believed that ending slavery would ultimately be the work 'not of years, but as it were of centuries.'[16] The government should start by proclaiming firm borders for the Cape Colony and making it impossible for colonists to settle beyond them. Then the sons of the poorer farmers would seek employment on others' farms. Such borders were announced

---

15 For the document see *Afrikaner Political Thought*, pp. 91-4.
16 The document is published in *Afrikaner Political Thought*, pp. 46-9.

in 1798, but even a government much tougher than the old Company could not prevent burghers from crossing them. Seasonal migrations of pastoral farmers beyond the northeastern boundary had started early in the nineteenth century.

To defend slavery Van Ryneveld proposed his version of the foundation myth: the settlers had acquired slaves as an important investment and they now had the fullest right to resist abolition. Eight years later, when the Batavian administration (1803-1806) asked him the same question about slavery, his reply was even more emphatic. Slavery had taken root along with the settlement and had acquired 'a certain permanence.' Abolition would lead to 'the immediate destruction of the entire Colony, and cause misfortune for both free man and slave together.' Van Ryneveld gave the Batavians two bits of advice, one to 'accept things as they are and not as one might wish them to be', the other, to be firm – 'in no aspect of management in the Colony should government be uncertain.' Tampering with slavery, like introducing an extraordinary tax or abolishing the importation of slaves, would be extremely harmful, he warned.[17] J.W. Janssens, the Governor during the Batavian period, abhorred slavery but did not propagate abolition. To do so, he wrote, would 'destroy all property and plunge the colony into misery – perhaps for good.'[18] Both Van Ryneveld and Janssens implicitly believed that hesitant reforms of slavery, not slavery itself, threatened stability. A half century later, Alexis de Tocqueville, reflecting on the French Revolution, wrote that 'the most perilous moment for a bad government is one when it seeks to mend its ways.'

During the last decade of the eighteenth century and the first decade of the next, the fear of a major slave revolt in the western Cape was greatly compounded by the Khoikhoi revolt on the frontier (see Chapter 3), and the uprising on the French colonial island of Saint-Domingue (later called Haiti), which stirred the worst fears of slaveholders on both sides of the Atlantic. At the time of the French Revolution Saint-Domingue's population included 30,000 whites, 24,000 free blacks, and 452,000 slaves. (In the Cape Colony there were, by 1820, just under 43,000 whites, 1,932 free blacks, 31,779 slaves and approximately 26,000 Khoikhoi and 'Basters.') Slavery was abolished in all French colonies in 1793 and ten years of fighting on Saint-Domingue followed, with gross atrocities. The first strong black leader, Toussaint L'Ouverture, introduced forms of labor oppression that differed little from slavery itself. The threat of French reconquest and the reintroduction of slavery brought the black forces together to crush the power of the slave-owning class. In 1804 the black leaders proclaimed the island's independence and the freedom of all its inhabitants and warned off from the island all those 'blinded so much as to believe themselves the essence of human nature and assert that they are destined by Heaven to be our masters and our tyrants.'[19]

In 1808 and in 1825, slave revolts broke out at the Cape. The first occurred after Britain abolished the slave trade; the second after measures to ameliorate slavery were announced. Two passing Irish sailors, James Hooper and Michael Kelly, and two slaves, Abraham and Louis, instigated the 1808 uprising. They planned to assemble slaves from the farms for a march to Cape Town, to gather up town slaves and establish a new

---

17 *Afrikaner Political Thought*, pp. 52-3.
18 Armstrong and Worden, 'The Slaves', pp. 136-43.
19 John Hope Franklin, *From Slavery to Freedom* (New York: Random House, 1969), p. 346.

government that would decree emancipation. As Abraham told a slave woman: 'Tomorrow the troop [sic] will hoist a red flag and fight itself free, and then the slave women will all be able to say "Jij" ['you' instead of 'thou'] to their mistresses.' The judge in the court case that followed called this form of address so 'disrespectful in the Dutch language' that Abraham in his view could use it only in a context of resistance and revolt.[20] About three hundred slaves and some Khoikhoi servants from Koeberg and Tygerberg farms defied the authority of their masters and joined the march to Cape Town. The revolt was swiftly quashed and the government sent most of the slaves back to their masters. The sailor James Hooper and the slave Abraham and three other slaves were executed.

The phasing out of Cape slavery and its accompanying institutions would take nearly forty-three years. That it did not all go horribly wrong was due primarily to the fact that the most powerful empire in the world controlled the process of reform and abolition.

Reforming slavery

Two waves of reform, of the system of slavery and of Khoisan servitude, washed over the colony between 1795 and 1838. From 1795 to 1825, the Cape was under conservative British governors, who, in the aftermath of the French Revolution, had no taste for radical reform. A second, more radical wave, from 1825 to 1838, brought both the freeing of the Khoisan and the emancipation of the slaves.

The British moved slowly to reform the basic institutions of the Cape Colony, but they were swift to tell the colonists that their history had little to be proud of. During the first British occupation (1795 to 1803), General Francis Dundas, acting governor, and John Barrow, a writer and official at the Cape, delivered a sweeping indictment. Dundas called the frontier colonists cruel, cowardly and cunning. Barrow said that scarcely an instance of cruelty committed against West Indian slaves could find no parallel in the frontier Afrikaners' treatment of their Khoisan servants: 'Beating and cutting with thongs of the hide of a sea-cow or rhinoceros are only gentle punishments, though the sort of whips they call *shambocs* are most horrid instruments being tough, pliant and heavy almost as lead.'[21]

When, in 1801, the British, concerned about reports of the horrendous treatment of Khoisan servants, turned to Van Ryneveld for advice, he called the administrative apparatus 'wholly insufficient to preserve good order in general, and to administer Justice to everyone in particular.' In his view, the interests of the Khoikhoi and the farmers were diametrically opposed. The farmers knew that only 'awe and a superior power' kept the Khoikhoi in a state of submission, while vagrant Khoikhoi would steal the farmers' cattle. In this Hobbesian world the government had the duty to install a proper system of administration and a common framework of criminal law.

Van Ryneveld said that the burghers and the Khoikhoi were now 'equally to be considered as real inhabitants of the country and equally entitled to the protection of the

---

20 Robert Ross, *Cape of Torments: Slavery and Resistance in South Africa* (London: Routledge and Kegan Paul, 1983), p. 103.

21 Cited in G.D. Scholtz, *Die ontwikkeling van die politieke denke van die Afrikaner* (Johannesburg: Voortrekkerpers, 1967), vol. 1, pp. 347-8.

government', yet assigned the Khoikhoi a restricted position. They had to live only on a missionary station, a licensed kraal, or a farm, and could not travel without a certificate. Van Ryneveld proposed additional deputy landdrosts and a commission to be sent annually from Cape Town to keep an eye on the farmers.[22]

Soon after conquering the Cape again in 1806 a partnership developed between the British rulers and the wealthier burghers, with the British commanding military and bureaucratic power and the burghers controlling agriculture. Some four thousand British settlers arrived in 1820, but the valuable strategic post at the tip of Africa could not be maintained cheaply should the burghers unite in opposition to British rule. Hence the British tried to balance reforming the old order with placating the burghers and ensuring a steady labor supply on the farms.

The British soon introduced some measures suggested by Van Ryneveld's report by issuing the Hottentot Proclamation of 1809 to regulate the employment of Khoisan laborers, and introducing circuit courts to stamp out the more brutal forms of maltreatment (see p. 83). But Sir John Cradock, Governor from 1811 to 1814, maintained a firm belief in the 'authority, power and property of the master'[23], and in the first fifteen years of the second British occupation the government did not interfere in the relationship between masters and slaves. Governor Caledon (1807-1811) had believed that the law offered slaves ample provision for redress against ill treatment, and Cradock, his successor, declared that slaves were treated better at the Cape than any place he had seen. His own successor, Lord Charles Somerset, remarked that 'no portion of the [slave] community is better off or happier than the domestic slave in South Africa.'[24] But, as recent studies of slavery had correctly pointed out, the idea of mild slavery was a contradiction in terms.

Some leading burghers thought even the mild British reform exercises fraught with peril, particularly if not accompanied by a firm government commitment to preserve both property and order. Landdrost Van der Riet of Stellenbosch asked: 'What would become of us and of the whole country if the natives were to feel that they should be free, were to know their power, and then to join together to regain their natural freedom as the original possessors of this country? In effect, nothing but a second Saint-Domingue.' Was there not every reason for countering 'the dangerous and idealistic feeling of freedom' or at least keeping it within certain limits?[25]

Senior Cape-born officials tried patiently to persuade their fellow colonists to accept reform, most prominent among them Chief Justices W.S. van Ryneveld and J.A. Truter and landdrost Andries Stockenstrom. All were keenly aware of the perils of reforming a profoundly unjust order. Neither radicals nor hostile critics, they did not contemplate undermining property rights, redistributing land or imposing an all-embracing social equality. Yet these colonial-born officials understood that it was impossible to resist the Enlightenment insistence on the freedom and dignity of all people. For their own sake

---

22 *Afrikaner Political Thought*, pp. 95-8.
23 Timothy Keegan, *Colonial South Africa and the Origins of the Racial Order* (Cape Town: David Philip, 1996), p. 56.
24 For a collection of contemporary statements, see Eric Stockenstrom, *Vrystelling van die slawe* (Stellenbosch: KSV Boekhandel, 1934), pp. 61-5.
25 *Afrikaner Political Thought*, p. 54.

the burghers had to make some fundamental changes in the way they viewed their slaves and servants if their future prospects were not to be seriously jeopardized. The Cape-born officials challenged the burghers' conviction that most of their Khoikhoi servants were too backward and depraved to enjoy the same liberties as the burghers, and that their word had to be given lesser weight in the courts. Stockenstrom argued that the old system of oppression had not been 'productive of one single beneficial effect.' It had 'degraded the moral character of the natives' and had given rise to the view that they 'were too miserable a species' to enjoy any rights.[26] Hence he did not doubt that a new system resting on personal liberty and security of property could only be an improvement. Truter wrote that 'the [Hottentots] are, and remain, people, and free people at that.'[27]

Van Ryneveld had insisted that the Khoikhoi be granted equal protection under a framework of criminal law, but Truter went much further to assign the state the task of promoting the progress of civilization and the reconstruction of society. Binding legal contracts were to reshape all labor and civic relations, with the law a crucial instrument in a civilizing process. Here was the beginning of thinking about a *Rechtstaat* in which the arbitrary authority of the master would be replaced by laws providing the framework for rights and liberties.[28]

A missionary challenge

The challenge issued by missionaries was, in many ways, a more direct assault on the burghers' view of life than were the legal doctrines. By 1800 Cape Town and the towns in the vicinity were not rigidly segregated. Europeans of all classes and baptized non-Europeans attended the same church. People of all colors and classes attended the few schools. In 1779 eight teachers offered classes in Cape Town to 696 pupils, eighty of them slaves. In Stellenbosch, in the final days of the Company, forty to fifty children 'of all colors' attended the public school. At the same time, however, the burghers feared that a form of Christian religion would be preached that would undermine their own authority. As a result, very little formal missionary work was done at the Cape until the end of the eighteenth century.

A spiritual revival, spearheaded by John Wesley and other evangelical preachers in Britain, created a new interest in missionary work that would soon have important repercussions in the colonies. The man who took the lead in organized missionary work among the Khoikhoi and slaves at the Cape was Helperus Ritzema van Lier. He had been born in the Netherlands and became the minister of the DRC congregation in Cape Town in 1786. Van Lier stressed the mission of the church to spread the Word to the heathen. By 1788 some sixty volunteers in Cape Town were instructing slaves, free blacks and Khoikhoi in the Christian faith. A year after Van Lier's death in 1793, Michiel Christiaan Vos, a Cape-born minister, became minister in the parish of Roodezand (later Tulbagh) some hundred miles to the north of Cape Town.

---

26 *Afrikaner Political Thought*, pp. 104-5.
27 *Afrikaner Political Thought*, p. 99.
28 *Afrikaner Political Thought*, pp. 82-9, 118.

Soon after his arrival he told the members that he would bring the Gospel to those ig-norant of it and urged slave-owners to send him their slaves. An uproar ensued, with the owners objecting that they would be unable to control educated slaves. Vos promised that the slaves he instructed would become more obedient and loyal, not less, where-upon the resistance subsided.[29]

In 1795 the London Missionary Society (LMS) was formed and two years later forty Dutchmen, including Johannes van der Kemp, founded the Dutch (or Rotterdam) Mis-sionary Society, which soon became affiliated to the LMS. Van der Kemp and James Read, along with two other LMS missionaries, arrived in Cape Town in 1799. With Van der Kemp and Vos in the lead, a local missionary society, first called Het Zuid Afri-caansch Genootschap and later the Zuid-Afrikaansche Zending Genootschap (ZAZG) was organized as an independent society. By 1804 an imposing structure, named the South African Mission Building, was consecrated.

The ZAZG encountered opposition because it allowed women as contributing or ac-tive members to participate in the formulation of policy. Among these women was the remarkable Machtelt Smit, a class instructor, perhaps the first Cape-born woman to be-come well known in her own right. A 'superior woman' so contemporaries said, one who, in the most emphatic sense of the word, 'minded the things of the Lord.'[30] Smit's prominence, some feared, would undermine the dominance of male members of the Re-formed Church. The truly zealous must be wakeful to guard against gelykstelling in all its forms.

The ZAZG's focus was not exclusively on slaves, but on all backward people, whites and free blacks, without any color discrimination. It established a class for such people. The destitute condition of some whites did not become an object of concern until near the end of the nineteenth century. Similar societies began in Roodezand, Stellenbosch, and Wagenmakersvallei (Wellington), with branches of the ZAZG in Swellendam and Graaff-Reinet. In Graaff-Reinet, where there was opposition, only two individuals joined. A.A. van der Lingen, a Dutch missionary employed by the society, left town in 1803, be-cause, he said, the Christians were filled with 'too much hate against the heathens.'[31]

On the frontier some burghers tried to indoctrinate the Khoisan to accept a permanent position of inferiority based on the grounds that they were neither Christian nor part of the act of creation that put Europeans on earth. Couragie, a Khoikhoi captain, asked Van der Kemp shortly after his arrival 'if it were not true that God had created them as well as the Christians. For you know (said he) that the Dutch farmers teach us that [God] never created us nor take any notice of us.'[32] Even a Graaff-Reinet burgher, whom Van der Kemp described as 'one of the best-intentioned members' of the church, refused to have a female slave baptized, not because he might lose the right to sell her, but because

29 M.C. Vos, Merkwaardig verhaal (Amsterdam: Noveker, 1867), pp. 118-20.

30 Karel Schoeman, Dogter van Sion: Machtelt Smit en die 18de eeuse samelewing aan die Kaap, 1749-1799 (Cape Town: Human & Rousseau, 1997), p. 299.

31 D.P. Botha, Die twee-eeue erfenis van die SA Sendinggestig, 1799-1999 (Cape Town: LUS Uitgewers, 1999), pp. 15-22; Hermann Giliomee, Die Kaap tydens die eerste Britse bewind (Cape Town: HAUM, 1975), pp. 242-51.

32 Susan Newton-King, The Enemy Within: The Struggle for Ascendancy on the Cape Eastern Frontier (Cam-bridge: Cambridge University Press, 1999), p. 221.

of 'his apprehension lest her pride should grow unsupportable by her admission among the Christians.'[33]

In 1792 Moravian missionaries returned to Baviaanskloof (later Genadendal), some hundred miles east of Cape Town, to resume the work that Georg Schmidt, also a Moravian, had done there between 1837 and 1844. Their approach was quietistic with a strong emphasis on discipline in social behavior. Although they refrained from social activism or promotion of gelykstelling, their teachings sometimes led to tragic misunderstandings. An account notes: ' [A] sister, Martha, had become drunk and had boasted that she was at least the equal of the Colonists because of her baptism. She . . . was excluded.'[34]

At the Bethelsdorp missionary station near Algoa Bay (later Port Elizabeth), Johannes van der Kemp and James Read wished to go much further than the Moravians and openly preached the need to put the Khoikhoi on an equal footing on all levels. Both married to Khoikhoi women, they insisted that the new British government protect the Khoikhoi's freedom and equality. But protection for the Khoikhoi beyond a limited refuge on a missionary station was difficult to ensure. The burghers who farmed on the frontier did little manual labor themselves, but declared themselves appalled by the indolence of the Khoikhoi at Bethelsdorp, in sharp contrast to Moravian Genadendal's stress on discipline and cleanliness. John Philip, who arrived from Scotland in 1819 as resident director and superintendent of missions of the London Missionary Society (LMS), lamented that Van der Kemp had 'begun at the wrong end with the Hottentots, that he had spoiled them.' He was even more severe on Read, who would have brought 'disgrace and ruin upon the cause of missions across the world' had he remained in control.[35] Nonetheless, Philip discovered that many of Read's charges against his archenemy, the American-born Jacob Cuyler, landdrost of Uitenhage, were indeed true. He now backed Read and also defended Van der Kemp's accusation of trekboer atrocities against the Khoisan. In consequence the burghers distrusted servants from the LMS and the work they were doing.

Between 1792 and the mid-1830s missionaries also arrived from the Wesleyan Church (1816); the Glasgow Missionary Society (1821); the Rhenish Missionary Society (1829); the Paris Missionary Society (1829); and the Berlin Missionary Society (1834).

Wary of the religious enthusiasms of the missionaries and religious schisms, the Dutch Reformed Church was left behind in this surge of missionary activity. Its approach was influenced by the church order passed by the Batavian Administration (1803-1806), which re-established the virtual monopoly of the DRC and prohibited the extension of missions, except under the auspices of its ministers. In Stellenbosch the formidable Rev. Meent Borcherds continued to insist that he could prohibit services in his parish that conflicted with those of the established church, and that he also had the right to baptize those the missionaries had prepared. The British did not countenance what amounted to a form of licensing of the missionaries and in due course gave them the right to act

---

33 *Transactions of the Missionary Society* vol. 1, p. 491.
34 Bernhard Kruger, *The Pear Tree Blossoms: The History of the Moravian Church in South Africa, 1737-1869* (Genadendal: Moravian Book Depot, 1966), p. 59.
35 Noël Mostert, *Frontiers* (New York: Knopf, 1992), p. 513.

independently and baptize their converts themselves. Those DRC ministers arguing that the church had to play a much more active part in missionary work were hamstrung by the fact that the British only in 1824 allowed the first colonial synod of the Reformed Church, where a new policy could be discussed, to meet.[36]

To the British rulers it seemed strange that the DRC was so little concerned that the vast majority of the slaves and Khoikhoi had not been converted to the Christian faith. It was in conflict with the Christian message and also seemed to clash with the interests of slave-owners themselves. By 1820 slave-owners in the American South tended to believe that Christian slaves were better slaves for becoming Christians.[37]

The policy of the Reformed Church at the Cape was firm: the church was open to all who had been baptized and Communion had to be served to all those who were confirmed, regardless of whether they were free or slaves. Although the church was not hostile to the missionary work, it wanted to bring missionary work done by its members under its own control, particularly since they dominated the ranks of the ZAZG and its affiliated local bodies. But the ZAZG and its associates did not want to be absorbed by the DRC, which would mean sacrificing their autonomy and parting with those members who were Lutherans.

Yet while open, the Reformed Church showed no enthusiasm for bringing large numbers of non-European converts into the congregation. Sometimes its inaction was blatant; at other times it was more subtle. A minister might keep the door closed by failing slave or free black candidates in the test on the Reformed faith required before baptism (in the case of adults) or confirmation (see pp. 42-4). In the early 1820s the church council of Stellenbosch noted that 'while there might be slaves who feared God in their hearts they were too dim to memorize much.'[38]

The effort to spread the Word among the slaves was impeded by interpretations of the Synod of Dordt. Some slave-owners said that their reluctance to baptize slaves stemmed from the fear that they would then be compelled to free them (see pp. 48-9). Efforts to clear up the issue had made matters worse. In 1770 a statement by the Batavian authorities declared it the duty of Christians to instruct their slaves in the Christian religion. It added that confirmed slaves could not be sold, and had to be manumitted when the owner died or left the Cape. As a result, the rates of both baptism and manumission declined even further.

After the British ended the slave trade in 1808, slave prices at the Cape increased fourfold until 1824. If baptism gave a slave the right to claim freedom, the owners now were far less likely to bring their expensive slaves to the baptismal font. In 1812, Fiscal Daniel Denyssen, a Cape-born public prosecutor, reported few slaves confirmed. Although 'a number of slaves are to be found in whom the principles of the Christian faith are imprinted from their childhood still, however, there is scarcely one who has got so far as to be confirmed.'[39] He advised Governor Cradock to abolish the ban on selling Christian

---

36 Robert Ross, 'Social and Political Theology of Western Cape Missions', in Henry Bredekamp and Robert Ross (eds.), *Missions and Christianity in South African History* (Johannesburg: Witwatersrand University Press, 1995), pp. 97-112.

37 Robert Shell, *Children of Bondage* (Johannesburg: Witwatersrand University Press, 1994), p. 343.

38 P.S. de Jongh, 'Sendingwerk in die Landdrosdistrikte Stellenbosch en Tulbagh, 1799-1830', master's diss., US, 1968, pp. 78-9.

39 Shell, *Children of Bondage*, p. 355.

slaves but to grant baptized and confirmed slaves some privileges, such as the right to legal marriage, the right to have their children legalized, and the liberty to attend church services at certain times.

In 1812 the government repealed the ban on the sale of Christian slaves, but between 1808 and 1824 only eighty-six slaves, or an average of six per year, out of a total of more than 35,000 slaves were baptized. Christianity for slaves still represented risks that were too grave for their masters both in terms of the money invested in slaves and a possible loss of control over them.[40] The manumission level dropped to levels as low as that in the US slave South, the slave society with the lowest recorded manumission rate in the Americas.

The question of how baptized slaves could be incorporated into the established churches remained unresolved. The ZAZG instructed large numbers of slaves in the catechism, but it appears that few were confirmed in the Reformed or Lutheran congregations. All over the colony missionary societies were organizing their followers into separate parishes. In 1819 Dr John Philip, superintendent of the LMS stations, advised the ZAZG to organize its converts into a separate parish, as the LMS had decided to do. The directors agreed to accept Philip's offer to assist the society in every way should it decide to adopt such a policy.[41] Many years later, in 1851, two ZAZG directors submitted a document stating that they had supported the 1819 decision with major qualifications. It was unwise, they decided, to found separate congregations; instead 'all illiterates and heathen [should] be instructed and be prepared to become members of established Protestant churches.'[42] But the pattern had been set. By 1824, when the Reformed Church convened its first colonial synod, it passed regulations for its own missionary work and also ordained L. Marquardt as its first missionary. He had strict instructions to administer the sacraments only to heathens he had gathered together in a separate congregation.

It may seem a supreme irony of Afrikaner history that the liberal Philip took the lead in a road that ended in religious segregation (see pp. 122-8). But for Philip himself it had been a purely practical arrangement. In the larger scheme of things he wanted slaves, free blacks, and Khoisan people living among the burghers to be fully integrated in society. He favored equality and what the burghers called gelykstelling as well. He desired, he said, a firm law that gave 'equal civil rights' to all, and he yearned for the day 'when the magical power of caste will be broken and all classes of inhabitants blended into one community.' There were Khoikhoi, he said, who in all respects might be superior to the burghers.[43]

Many slaves had come to see Christianity as the religion of slave-owners, and, with the door to the Christian church virtually closed to them, growing numbers turned to Islam. In 1825, the first year in which records were kept, there were 846 male and 422 female Muslims. Some observers believed that, by the mid-1830s, most Cape Town slaves

---

40 Richard Elphick and Hermann Giliomee, 'The Origins and Entrenchment of European Domination at the Cape, 1652-1840', *SSAS* (1), pp. 366-7.

41 DRC Archives (Cape Town), SA Sendinggestig Documents, File 1/7 Notes of Directors, 14 December 1819, p. 67. I wish to thank D.P. Botha for drawing my attention to this document.

42 Botha, *Die twee-eeue erfenis*, p. 23.

43 W.M. Macmillan, *The Cape Colour Question* (London: Faber and Gwyer, 1927), pp. 170-72.

were Muslims. The authorities were becoming concerned about the rapid spread of Islam.

Islam also provided the first incentive to use the Afrikaans vernacular in written form. In Muslim schools the slaves were taught to read and write in the Arabic script.[44] During the 1840s an observer said: 'All the Malays in Cape Town speak Dutch but the better class understand and write Arabic and Malay.'[45] But the Dutch was, actually, Afrikaans (or a creolized Dutch). The first Afrikaans book, printed around 1856, used Arabic script. By the end of the century at least eleven Arabic-Afrikaans works had been produced. When Arnoldus Pannevis, in the early 1870s, considered translating the Bible into Afrikaans, it was already an established medium of religious instruction in the Cape Muslim community.[46]

The accelerating movement toward the abolition of slavery forced the owners to re-think their views on bringing slaves into the church. In 1824 Chief Justice Johannes Andreas Truter, in an address to the annual meeting of the ZAZG, pointed out that the Christian church and other Christian organizations had been instrumental in the ban-ning of slavery in Europe. He suggested that the Cape church had to play an important role in smoothing the transition to a new labor system. Masters had to be instructed to prepare slaves for the day when they would be free and under no compulsion to serve a master. The evil of slavery, Truter said, did not lie in the punishments meted out but in their masters' failure to love their servants, as Christ commanded, and in the hostility of the slaves, the consequence of this lack of love. Hence the task of the ZAZG and other Christian associations was to work towards a future order in which the ex-slave would serve the master 'out of love for his duty', while the master treated the slave with Christ-ian tolerance 'as someone of the same nature as himself.'[47]

Slave-owners began to devote themselves with greater energy to win slaves for Chris-tianity. They had come to believe that Christianity could help rather than hinder the owners in controlling their slaves. Landdrost Stockenstrom and the Graaff-Reinet heem-raden wrote in a 1826 letter: '[The] more they [the slaves] made religious principles their own, the better they would be as servants and the greater the benefits to their owners.'[48] He wrote in the same year that the burghers had already done much on their own ini-tiative to ameliorate slavery. Some had 'gone to great expense, others have engaged in personal activity in order to make the slaves better members of society.'[49]

But the DRC left the mission field largely to the ZAZG and other missionary societies and to the English churches. Until Emancipation Day the rate of slave baptism and con-firmation in the DRC remained low.

---

44 Frank Bradlow, 'Islam at the Cape of Good Hope', *South African Historical Journal*, no. 15 (1981).

45 G.F. Angas (or Angus), *The Kaffirs Illustrated* (London: J. Hogarth, 1849), p. 19.

46 Achmat Davids, 'The Afrikaans of the Cape Muslims from 1815 to 1915: A Socio-Linguistic Study', mas-ter's diss., University of Natal, 1991, pp. 80-1.

47 Dutch Reformed Church Archives (Cape Town), Annual Meeting of the ZAZG, 1824. I wish to thank David Botha for bringing this document to my attention.

48 *Afrikaner Political Thought*, p. 66.

49 *Afrikaner Political Thought*, p. 66.

Radical reform

With the exception of Andries Stockenstrom, no Cape-born colonist played a leading role in the second, more radical, round of reform that started in 1823 and ended with the emancipation of slaves in 1834. With the exception of Ordinance 50, these measures were conceived in London and imposed on the colonies with little attention to local circumstances.

After his arrival in 1819, the missionary John Philip and the burghers had steadily become alienated from each other. Philip hated slavery and the great majority of the slave-owners were burghers (British settlers were prohibited from owning slaves). Philip opposed any kind of settler capitalism in which the interests of the farmers weighed more heavily than those of native peoples. His early fairly cordial relations with the English-speaking colonists soured once he concluded that they, like the Afrikaners, exploited native labor. But his principal antipathy was toward the Afrikaner farmers. Although British soldiers and British settlers had joined with burghers in military action on the frontier, the burghers, he believed, were guiltier than the others of brutalities. What hurt the burghers the most was Philip's assailing of their Christian morality. And to top it all, Philip knew quite well how to lobby among the humanitarians in London. The burghers had no way to present their side of the story.[50]

In 1828 Philip caused a sensation with the publication of his book *Researches in South Africa*, with its frontal attack on 'the Colonial System.'[51] In his view, colonial expansion spearheaded by the trekboers repeated the same cruel pattern. Commandos took the Khoisan's land and cattle, and then forced them to become laborers, treating them like slaves. Writing at a time when the abolitionist movement was rapidly reaching its culmination, he defined his own objective as that of ending 'the slavery of the Aborigines within the colony of the Cape of Good Hope.'[52]

Philip knew from the start that his book would arouse the Afrikaner colonists. He wrote disparagingly of 'the despot' who preferred 'the obsequiousness of slaves.' He never appealed to the traditions of the colonists or sought their support, but constantly held up to them *British* standards of 'humanity and justice.' His approach represented a new departure in missionary work. He had little interest in a Gospel message that wanted mainly to save souls and he had no patience with missionary stations that were mere places of refuge or of squalor and sloth. For him the stations had to be showcases of the liberal order, demonstrating 'civilization and industry.'[53]

For Philip the new liberal order had to start with a change in the Khoisan's legal status. They had to be freed from all bonds. In words that could have been written by Adam Smith, Philip wrote: '[Make] the colored population in your colony free, permit the natives to choose their own masters . . . allow them to bring their labor to a free market, and the farmers will no longer have an occasion to complain of a want of servants.'[54] The

50 Keegan, *Colonial South Africa*, pp. 88-93.

51 John Philip, *Researches in South Africa* (London: Duncan, 1828), two volumes. See also P.H. Kapp, 'Dr. John Philip: die grondlegger van Liberalisme in Suid-Afrika', *AYB*, 1985.

52 Philip, *Researches in South Africa*, vol. 1, p. xxix.

53 Robert Ross, *Status and Respectability in the Cape Colony, 1750-1870* (Cambridge: Cambridge University Press, 1999), pp. 110-24; the quotation from Cole is on p. 115.

54 Philip, *Researches in South Africa*, vol. 1, p. 329.

humanitarian drive to end slavery only became unstoppable after metropolitan capitalism had undergone profound changes, both in theory and in practice.

Philip was born in Kirkcaldy, Scotland, the small town where Adam Smith had written his great book on the capitalist system, *The Wealth of Nations*. Philip went to South Africa greatly inspired by Smith's vision that free trade and free people would maximize wealth.[55] Most of the British merchants at the Cape found slavery and Khoisan servitude as repugnant as Philip. They, too, wanted laborers to be free to enter into contracts. When Britain ended the imperial preference on Cape wine in 1825, they argued that a new economy had to be built on free labor, free trade, and a steadily expanding consumer market in the interior, including among indigenous peoples. Their chief voice was John Fairbairn, who, in 1824, founded the colony's first newspaper, the *South African Commercial Advertiser*. In 1827, Fairbairn began to move in Philip's circles and soon married his daughter. The classic statement of the new mercantile interests was these words of Fairbairn: 'To stimulate Industry, to encourage Civilization, and to convert the hostile Natives into friendly Customers is a more profitable speculation than to exterminate or reduce them to slavery.'[56]

In 1830 Sir Lowry Cole described Philip as 'more a *politician* [emphasis in the original] than a missionary.' Philip denied this, but it is fair to say that his interventions effectively combined political and economic arguments with moral and religious exhortations. For him the Khoisan were both people with souls and people of reason who could be taught the value of their labor. Their incorporation into the economy as free laborers would be not only an act of justice but also increase the consumption of British-manufactured goods.

A two-person Commission of Inquiry sent to the Cape by the British Parliament between 1823 and 1825 supported the arguments of Philip and Fairbairn. The commission, from the start, appeared to have little sympathy for the burghers and, apart from Stockenstrom, no Afrikaner voluntarily gave evidence before it. Like Philip, the commissioners found the Dutch-speaking colonists the chief obstacles to human progress. They were scathing in their judgment and shocked by the farmers' singular lack of interest in progress. They lamented their 'want of intelligence', their habits of 'severe economy' in their mode of living, and 'their indifference to those comforts that are indispensable to Englishmen.' They proposed freeing the Khoisan and emancipating the slaves. Liberating labor was not only just, but it would also serve to root out the 'indolence and indifference' of the Dutch colonists and infuse them with 'a spirit of active industry and intelligence in their life.'

The commissioners had an equally low opinion of the burghers' institutions. The legal and administrative system, they said, was exposed to the influence of 'local partialities, of hereditary prejudices, and of family connections.' They recommended that lawyers be compelled to receive their qualifications in England. One commissioner observed that color prejudice made it impossible for aspirant lawyers at the Cape to attain judicial impartiality, a quality that 'constitutes the brightest excellence of the English judicial character.'[57]

---

55 Keegan, *Colonial South Africa*, p. 91.
56 Keegan, *Colonial South Africa*, p. 98. See also his 'The Overthrow of Cape Slavery', *Southern African Review of Books*, July/October 1991, pp. 20-1.

This negative impression created by Barrow, Philip, and the commissioners prompted the imperial government to conclude that the existing institutions could not be adapted, but had to be destroyed root and branch. Between 1825 and 1834 the government
did usher in a near-revolution in the system of administration and justice. The Court of
Justice, the Orphan Chamber, the colleges of landdrosts and heemraden in the interior
districts, and the Burgher Senate, which served as a kind of city council for Cape Town,
were all abolished. The senate's functions were transferred to two British officials until
a form of municipal government was introduced in 1837. In place of the colleges of landdrost and heemraden in the country districts two officials were appointed: a resident
magistrate to perform judicial functions and a civil commissioner for administrative matters. The field cornets were retained but lost their petty judicial functions. In a new judicial system headed by a Supreme Court, all judges were to be appointed from the British
bar and all lawyers required to obtain their degrees in England. Criminal law became,
principally, English law. The government also announced the anglicization of the administration (see pp. 197-99).

In addressing the economic framework, the government promoted free enterprise and
free trade by abolishing the monopolies enjoyed by butchers, bakers, wine traders and
vendue masters (auctioneers), and many of the old rents, tithes and taxes. The old merchant class of the Company era was already losing out to English-speaking traders much
better versed in the ways of the free market, and now it lost more.

All of these reforms were imposed from the outside on a hostile people who had virtually no form of representation. The historian Eric Walker wrote that the effect of the
reforms was to give the colony a greater efficiency at the price of almost all proper sharing in the functioning of government.[58] Stockenstrom, undoubtedly the most liberal
Afrikaner, had no problem with the reforms in principle; he favored thoroughgoing
modernization. Still, he considered it of the greatest importance to win broad acceptance
for the far-reaching reforms among the burghers. He would later call it a great mistake
to abolish the colleges of landdrost and heemraden, the means through which government could influence the whole community. From this point on, he wrote: '[All] confidence between the Government and the masses ceased, and many of the evils which
have retarded our advancement and disturbed our peace may be traced to misunderstandings which the executive had not the means nor the channels of clearing up.'[59]

The freeing of the Khoisan

Ordinance 50, passed in 1828, formally put the Khoisan on an equal legal standing with
the burghers. It was a remarkable achievement. The imperial government did not impose
the measure from above. It was largely the work of two individuals, Philip, the Scottish
missionary, and Stockenstrom, the Afrikaner with a Swedish father and a German mother. The two worked separately (and without contact with each other) to achieve the same
result.

---

57 J.B. Peires, 'The British and the Cape, 1814-1834', *SSAS* (1), pp. 497-8.
58 Eric Walker, *A History of Southern Africa* (London: Longman Green, 1957), p. 165.
59 An 1851 speech published in *Afrikaner Political Thought*, pp. 297-8.

Philip lobbied philanthropical circles in London, while Stockenstrom used local channels. He became commissioner-general for the eastern province and was one of two
colonists who sat on the new Council of Advice to the governor, introduced in 1825.
Three years earlier, when Philip was his guest in Graaff-Reinet (see pp. 134-6), Stockenstrom had observed that all decent and respectable 'Boers' agreed that the Khoisan had
been cruelly dispossessed and were suffering harsh legal discrimination. In a memorandum to Acting Governor Richard Bourke he demanded a law 'embracing all free inhabitants without reference to color or name of the tribe.'

Acting independently of the moves initiated by Philip in London, the Council of Advice at the Cape, on 17 July 1828, passed Ordinance 50, a measure Stockenstrom had
recommended.[60] The British Parliament ratified it the following year. Stockenstrom had
outlined the thrust of Ordinance 50 in stating that the law would place 'every free in-
habitant in the Colony on a level, in the eye of the law, as to the enjoyment of personal
liberty and the security of property.'[61] It would remove all disabilities suffered with respect
to marriage and testimony, and abolish the passes the Khoisan were requested to carry,
and also the indenturing of Khoisan children. It prohibited employers from inflicting
corporal punishment on their workers or punishing stock thieves themselves.

Something truly exceptional had happened. Few other societies based on slavery and
other forms of involuntary labor had at that stage introduced free labor and non-racialism. Yet it triggered no revolt. Stockenstrom reported, towards the end of 1828, from
Grahamstown that the new laws for the Khoikhoi and the pending emancipation of the
slaves were 'merely occasionally talked of and commented on.'[62] Yet the absence of resistance to the non-racial principle of the Ordinance was not all that surprising. The freeing of the Khoikhoi put them on the same level as another well-established status group,
the free blacks, non-white people who were free before the law but not holding the status of burghers.

The burghers' criticism focused on the application, not the principle, of the Ordinance. The great distances that many masters lived from the drostdy made it difficult to
bring erring servants or people suspected of theft to court. Then there was the lack of
protection, often referred to as the problem of Khoikhoi 'vagrants.' Spearheading the
philanthropic lobby, Philip succeeded in blocking a vagrancy law in order to protect the
Khoikhoi's new freedom. But other people were also concerned about protection. The
colonists wanted protection against thieves who stole their cattle.[63] In 1829 the Supreme
Court judges pointed out that the law-enforcing agencies were insufficient to combat
crime if people roamed about freely.[64]

Philip denied that abuses resulted from Ordinance 50, but on one occasion he did request 'more prisons, magistrates and constables.'[65] Stockenstrom agreed with those who

---

60 See the account in Noel Mostert, *Frontiers* (New York: Alfred Knopf, 1992), pp. 588-90.

61 *Afrikaner Political Thought*, p. 95.

62 Mostert, *Frontiers*, pp. 590-92.

63 Andrew Nash, 'Dr Philip, the "Spread of Civilization" and Liberalism in South Africa', paper presented
to the Development Studies Conference on 'The History of Opposition in South Africa', University of
the Witwatersrand, Johannesburg, 1978.

64 J.C. Visagie, 'Die Katriviernedersetting, 1829-1839', doctoral diss., University of South Africa, 1978, p. 120.

65 Macmillan, *The Cape Colour Question*, p. 224.

demanded a vagrancy law because they felt that it would be difficult to protect stock without it. He said of the Khoikhoi: 'They should be made to work unless they can prove that they can live without it, and in this respect they should be closely watched, for in a country where property, particularly large flocks of sheep and cattle, are so much exposed, it is easy to live by theft.'[66] He rejected the claim that the clamor of the frontier farmers against the Ordinance sprang from resentment of the new freedom granted to the Khoisan. 'I deny that there was a general feeling against the freedom of the Hottentots,' he said. 'The clamor was about their depredations, which acquired in the eyes of the ignorant (and not unnaturally) the appearance of being warranted by that enactment [Ordinance 50].'[67]

Stockenstrom's view seemed borne out by a 1829 letter signed by Field Cornet P. Aucamp and forty-six co-signatories from the Renosterberg division, who wrote to tell the civil commissioner that they had long wished for the rehabilitation of the Khoisan to help them rise to a higher level of civilization and become more useful members of society. For that reason they welcomed Ordinance 50. Their grievance was 'the sudden change in [the Khoikhoi's] situation, giving rise to licentiousness and joblessness causing the signatories great damage.' In the mid-1830s Stockenstrom observed that the community wished the Khoisan well, but that good feeling was contingent on an effective vagrancy act.[68]

The role of Ordinance 50 as a contributing factor to the Great Trek is discussed in the next chapter (p. 146). Here we only note that while Stockenstrom supported a vagrancy law he had little patience with farmers who wanted a vagrancy law simply to keep the Khoikhoi in a miserable state of subjugation, working for very low wages. This is clear in 1837 from an exchange between him and some Colesberg farmers on the northeastern border. They wrote to Stockenstrom as lieutenant governor in charge of both the eastern and northeastern frontiers: '[Not] only servants but the black population in general have a contempt for all just restraint, are not subject to their superiors, not satisfied with an equality, [but] thirst for and in various instances have exercised unlawful authority. Their conduct may therefore justly be styled a system of licentiousness and insubordination.'[69]

At the same time, Stockenstrom received a letter from N.T. van der Walt, also from Colesberg, whom he called a worthy and respectable man. Van der Walt's request was simple and unsophisticated: he wanted Bushmen in the vicinity to be compelled to work on farms. But what gave this letter a distinct tone was its aggrieved note of a paternalist employer unable to stop servants raised on the farm from leaving. He had always served 'the best interests of every creature.' Van der Walt continued: 'We have been educated in one house; nothing would hurt me so much as to see that peace destroyed . . . I continue daily to provide the living with cattle and provisions.' (This probably referred to Bushmen and other 'creatures' still living on the farm.) He attempted to formulate a

---

66 *Afrikaner Political Thought*, p. 70.

67 Andries Stockenstrom, *Autobiography* (1887, repr. Cape Town: Struik, 1962), vol. 2, p. 8.

68 G.D.J. Duvenage, *Van die Tarka na die Transgariep* (Pretoria: Academica, 1981), pp. 111-12; V.C. Malherbe, 'The Cape Khoisan in the Eastern Districts of the Colony before and after Ordinance 50 of 1828', doctoral diss., 1997, p. 231.

69 *Afrikaner Political Thought*, pp. 116-17.

general rule for the relationship between masters and servants: 'Liberty [for the Bushmen workers] without subordination produces insecurity, but liberty with submission and due respect is necessary for our existence.'

Stockenstrom discovered that the letter from Van der Walt and the Colesberg farmers exaggerated the security threats. A few cattle had been stolen and some kind of vagrancy law was needed. But while a vagrancy law could counter stock theft, it could also severely limit the capacity of work-seekers to move around and to secure better wages. Stockenstrom understood the paternalist relationship that suffused Van der Walt's letter all too well. Some farmers would as little think about paying their servants well as they would consider paying their own children. In an acute shortage of labor, the cloak of paternalism was often used simply as an excuse for forcing workers to stay.

In writing to the governor, Stockenstrom observed that farmers were still paying miserable wages – as few as three to twelve goats and four shillings and sixpence to eighteen shillings annually. He himself had no time for a vagrancy law if the purpose was simply to tie people down and force them to work at extremely poor wages. 'I have never believed', he wrote, that civilization consisted 'in one man being forced to serve another who had deprived him of his country, his game, his all, under a severe lash for four shillings and sixpence per annum.' To Van der Walt he wrote that if wages were paid 'not according to the will of the master but according to the demand of the servant' there would be no reason to force Bushmen workers to stay on the farms. The old status order of restrictions had been irreversibly abandoned. 'Let me tell you this – and you may rely on it, my dear friend,' he wrote , 'we shall never again see the day when under British rule different degrees of rights and privileges will exist for different classes of His Majesty's subjects.'[70] Stockenstrom had developed an idea about survival strikingly different from that of most colonists. He told Van der Walt that an 'oppressive partiality', which the old status order represented, did not guarantee the colonists' safety. Quite the opposite was true: 'We should thereby entail upon us the hatred of the blacks and be in danger every moment that they would avail themselves of the first opportunity to break their bonds and be revenged upon us.'[71]

The Khoisan themselves welcomed Ordinance 50 as liberation from an order that trapped them on the lowest rungs of society. In 1834 a Khoikhoi, Platje Jonker, movingly expressed his view of what Ordinance 50 meant to his people: 'Every nation has its screen, the white men have a screen, the color of their skin is their screen, the 50th Ordinance is our screen.'[72] Ordinance 50 has gone down in history as a great legal turning point in establishing the principle of non-racial equality. Yet the reality on the ground was rather different. Without land a Khoikhoi was destined either to remain a servant or to spend his days in great poverty in a shack on the outskirts of a town or on a mission station. Some Khoikhoi lived on mission stations and went out to work on neighboring farms.

Philip had little success in persuading the government to make more land available for

---

70 *Afrikaner Political Thought*, p. 118.
71 *Afrikaner Political Thought*, pp. 114-18.
72 Clifton Crais, *The Making of the Colonial Order* (Johannesburg: Witwatersrand University Press, 1992), p. 147.

mission stations, and virtually no farmland came into Khoisan hands. The most Stockenstrom himself could achieve was the establishment, in 1829, of the Kat River Settlement on the eastern frontier for small-scale Khoikhoi farms. It is significant that the
motive cited was frontier defense, not social transformation. A total of 2,114 Khoisan
and Basters had moved there by 1833. Gratitude ran high among the recipients of the
land, who received allotments of four to five acres and rights in common pasture. They
dug furrows for irrigation and produced a surplus of barley in the second year. As Andries Stoffels of the Kat River Settlement said: 'The 50 Ordinance came out, then did we
first taste freedom that other men eat so sweet and now that it is mingled with Water &
Ground it is 20 times sweeter than forced labor.' When colonists complained that 'irregularities' arose from the new freedom of the Khoisan, the Kat River residents replied
simply: 'Give us more land.'[73]

But in the government's view it was enough to confer individual liberty and impartial
justice. Its justice did *not* include restitution and social rehabilitation of the previously
subjugated. Even Stockenstrom remarked about the Khoisan: '[No] extraordinary measures towards forcing their advancement can be necessary . . . On the contrary, these can
only retard their real improvement by turning things out of their natural course.'[74]

The Khoisan did not benefit much from the new legal framework. A study of the way
in which Ordinance 50 operated found that it was largely 'inoperable' because of the
large distances from the farms to the towns. The British judges were supposed to be free
of color prejudice, but they did little to give substance to the principle of equality before
the law. It is an illusion that Ordinance 50 in terms of substantial social rehabilitation
actually achieved anything of great magnitude.[75]

Indeed, legislation tended to control workers rather than to open up alternative possibilities. The 1841 Masters and Servants Ordinance, passed after the abolition of slavery, obliterated all the distinctions that had made the Khoisan freer than the slaves
since the founding of the settlement. More than in the eighteenth century, Cape society
was now becoming polarized between whites and an undifferentiated category of people who were very poor and brown or black, and who could do little but work for
whites.

Nor did the government expand its education efforts to rehabilitate the Khoisan. Instead, it assigned to missionary societies the task of educating 'colored' and poor people.
Missionaries not only spread the message of the Gospel, but also taught the 'gospel of
work', the English language, and how to read and write it. Education became segregated
in practice. Lord Charles Somerset introduced free government schools to teach what
he called 'the burghers of the colony' the disciplines of reading, writing, arithmetic and
English.' A future head of the education department explained that the term 'burghers'
meant people of European descent. By 1827 there were 372 colored and slave children
in government schools but, increasingly, colored children and perhaps also white children from poor families had to struggle to gain access to government schools. An 1834

---

73 Richard Elphick and V.C. Malherbe, 'The Khoisan to 1828', *SSAS*, p. 48.
74 Malherbe, 'The Cape Khoisan', p. 133.
75 L.C. Duly, 'A Revisit with the Cape's Hottentot Ordinance of 1828', in M. Kooy (ed.), *Studies in Economics
   and Economic History* (London: Macmillan, 1972), pp. 26-56.

report noted that 'the poorer classes and colored children . . . were not allowed to take advantage of the [government] schools.'[76]

Most slave and colored children went, instead, to schools founded by missionary societies. In 1841 the government decided to pay subsidies to the schools the missionary societies had founded, as well as to the government schools. These missionary schools had no color bar and apparently many poorer white children attended such schools. By the end of the century a third of the white children at school in the Cape Colony were in mission schools.[77]

The missionaries also taught their followers to dress, and otherwise present themselves, as what they considered to be 'respectable people.' Not unreasonably, those Khoisan who met those standards expected to be treated respectfully, even like burghers. Stockenstrom wrote, in 1832, in the Dutch paper *De Zuid-Afrikaan*, that this was indeed the implication of Ordinance 50: 'The Hottentots . . . born to right of citizenship and entitled to hold land . . . stand naturally on a level with the burghers.'[78] Some Khoikhoi boldly asserted their new status under the law. When, in 1831 a Dutch colonist, J. de Villiers, asked some 'whose Hottentots they were', they replied: 'That is nothing to you, we are just as much free burghers as you are.'[79]

But burgher status – even if informal – went hand in hand with meeting burgher obligations, and, in particular, commando service and payment of taxes. Something of a vicious circle had developed. As a result of a lack of land many Khoikhoi continued a wandering life and shirked commando duty or the payment of taxes. In 1834 the civil commissioner reported from Graaff-Reinet that only one out of five hundred Khoikhoi had done commando service. When taxes were collected some Khoikhoi simply moved to another district. A farmer near the Kat River spoke dismissively of the 'wandering free coloreds, so-called yellow and black free burghers.' The burghers began referring to the Khoikhoi as *knapsak burgers* or back-pocket burghers.[80] Both were now colonial subjects but only whites were considered burghers.

Although large numbers of whites lived precariously on farms as overseers, tenants or poor relatives, there was an increasing tendency for whites to define themselves as a community in which a common racial identity transcended the internal class divisions. The traveler George Thompson referred to this when he wrote in 1827 about the lack of any 'gradation' among them: 'Every man is a burgher by rank, and a farmer by occupation.'[81] During the 1840s another traveler observed no distinctions or ranks in Cape society except those indicated by the color of the skin.[82]

Ordinance 50 had removed all status distinctions, but both the government and the white colonists lumped all people of color – whether of slave or Khoisan descent – to-

76 Edna Bradlow, 'Capitalists and Labourers in the Post-Emancipation Rural Cape', *Historia*, 31, 1 (1986), p. 57.

77 H.P. Cruse, *Die geskiedenis van Kleurlingonderwys in die Kaapprovinsie* (Cape Town: Nasionale Pers, no date), pp. 20-21.

78 *De Zuid-Afrikaan*, 23 March 1832.

79 Malherbe, 'The Cape Khoisan', p. 442.

80 Visagie, 'Die Katriviernedersetting', p.117.

81 George Thompson, *Travels and Adventures in Southern Africa* (London: Colburn, 1827), p. 324.

82 W. von Meyer, *Reisen in Süd-Afrika während der Jahren 1840 und 1841* (Hamburg: J. Erie, 1843), p. 82.

gether as members of a separate category, almost as if they were naturally bound together. In the 1830s the government enumerated slave apprentices and Khoikhoi together as the 'Colored population.' *De Zuid-Afrikaan* also began to refer to the same groups as '*gekleurden.*' The term 'coloreds' or 'Cape coloreds' increasingly came into vogue in the western Cape for people of mixed descent.[83]

There was a growing tendency to associate color with poverty. Thus, *The South African Commercial Advertiser* used phrases such as 'the poor or colored population.' No significant section of free colored people with property had emerged that could break down the correlation between race and status and the simultaneous polarization of society between whites and the rest.[84]

The emancipation of the slaves

As late as 1825 all signs pointed to slavery's remaining a permanent feature of Cape society. In the preceding decade wine farmers had experienced a boom with the reduction of the British tariff on Cape wine, and owners had large amounts of capital locked up in slaves, whose price remained high. Then everything changed rapidly and radically. In 1825 Britain lowered the tariffs on continental wines, causing the wine industry and the entire Cape economy to sink into a deep depression. With the value of western Cape slaves dropping sharply, investment in slaves was suddenly much less profitable. Owners who had bought slaves on credit or had put them up as surety for loans faced economic ruin. Their only hope was that the government would bail them out by paying adequate compensation when it set the slaves free.

But slavery was not only an economic issue. The prospect of abolition threatened the collapse of the public order and social status hierarchy. Owners began to experience a sense of pervasive insecurity. They had no form of political representation,[85] and the legal position of the slave at the Cape with regard to his master was stronger than in many other slave colonies. The testimony of a slave against his or her owner was often admitted.[86]

Slave-owners believed that their old paternalist world was on the brink of collapse. They felt degraded by reform measures, like one ordinance that permitted the courts to accept the evidence of slaves without corroboration from a colonist. An 1826 memorandum from Stellenbosch complained that this practice placed the slave-owner in an inferior position to his slave. While the owner had to pay taxes and defend the colony, the slave had to do neither. Did that not mean, the petitioners asked, that masters, 'who are educated in morals and religion', would get less credit than 'an immoral and heathen slave'?[87]

Finally there were the great fears of security surrounding the ending of slavery. So

---

83 John E. Mason, '"Fit for Freedom": The Slaves, Slavery and Emancipation in the Cape Colony, South Africa, 1806-1842', doctoral diss., Yale University, 1992, p. 589.

84 Elphick and Giliomee, 'Origins and Entrenchment of European Domination', pp. 521-67.

85 Andrew Bank, 'Slavery in Cape Town, 1806-1834', master's diss., University of Cape Town, 1991, p. 98.

86 Robert Ross, 'The Rule of Law at the Cape of Good Hope in the Eighteenth Century', *Journal of Imperial and Commonwealth History*, 1 (1980), pp. 5-16.

87 *Afrikaner Political Thought*, p. 103.

grim was the life of a slave that many owners anticipated a terrible retribution at the hands of their slaves, while others feared anarchy. They dreaded the possibility that the time might come when they would be unable to defend the lives of their family and the honor of their wives and daughters.

Political, financial, security and sexual anxieties had all become inextricably linked. Some of the fears were, in fact, not wholly irrational. The sizeable British garrison at the Cape and the dispersal of the slave population across the colony in numerous small-scale holdings made a large-scale uprising unlikely, yet, slave-owners did have reason to fear for their personal safety. By the mid-1830s the rural towns, for all practical purposes, had no regular police force. Cape Town had a force of a mere twenty men for a population of twenty thousand – one policeman per thousand people – in a city that did not even have street lighting.

The memory of a slave uprising in the deep interior in 1825 continued to haunt the owners. It had occurred against the backdrop of a regulation, passed in 1823, limiting the number of lashes given to slaves to twenty-five and the working day to ten hours. The slave Galant, who lived on the farm Houd-den-Bek in the remote Koue Bokkeveld, was aware of the debate over emancipation and the opposition to it by the masters, and had himself been maltreated and punished by his master. He had heard that the masters intended to fight the British if they carried out a plan to emancipate the slaves. In the course of 1825 Galant persuaded other slaves to join him in a rebellion, telling them that he had heard that 'between Christmas Day and New Year's Day the slaves were to be made free – and that if it should not take place at that time then their masters must be killed.' In the small-scale uprising the master and several members of his family were murdered.[88] A commando crushed the revolt, but it had sent shock waves through the colony.[89] In the court case that followed the judges found that 'philanthropists and evil-minded persons' had misinformed the slaves that the powers-that-be were on their side. In the trial the state prosecutor, D. Denyssen, expressed something of the profound shock of the slave-owners. He could not bring himself to see the rebellion as at least partially a quest for freedom. Instead he referred to the Saint-Domingue revolt and suggested that the Bokkeveld uprising could only be interpreted as 'a desire to withdraw from the laws and authority of the Government, as a desire for bloodshed, for war and confusion, for disastrous anarchy.'[90]

An 1826 memorandum to the Cape Town Burgher Senate, signed by F.R.L. Neethling and other Stellenbosch colonists, depicted in apocalyptic terms the political and sexual nightmares of the colonists:

> The flame of devastation will not alone destroy our habitations, but will also cause your houses to fall in ruin! Not only our wives and daughters, but also yours will in libidinous manner be prosecuted by our slaves with rape and defloration, and when, after all this out of the pit of our murdered fellow citizens a Saint Domingo

---

88 *Afrikaner Political Thought*, pp. 82-9, 118.

89 Armstrong and Worden, 'The Slaves', p. 161. André Brink's novel *A Chain of Voices* is based on the events.

90 *Afrikaner Political Thought*, p. 61.

has arisen, then may God grant that we be no more amongst the living, but then you yourselves will be compelled by the slaves who fought themselves free to carry the bones of your wife and your child to make a monument of their freedom obtained by fire and murder.'[91]

In such diverse ways the imminent freedom of the slaves fundamentally challenged the colonists' notions about their own freedom. A 1991 study by Orlando Patterson reminds us that freedom in the West in its historic evolution since antiquity developed three forms: personal freedom (the liberty to do as one pleases in so far as one can), civic freedom (the right to participate in governing one's community of birth) and sovereign freedom (the freedom to exercise power over others, including even the right to enslave people).[92] At the Cape, paternalist slave-owners developed exaggerated ideas about all these forms of freedom for themselves alone. When Britain curtailed their sovereign freedom over slaves, they experienced this as an assault on their own freedom.

De Zuid-Afrikaan, the Dutch-language newspaper that first appeared in 1830, articulated the temper of the Afrikaner slave-owners. It was incensed when the government issued regulations limiting corporal punishment of slaves and when it banned protest meetings against the measure. In 1831 a new measure gave slave-protectors the right to inspect slave quarters and compelled farmers to hand in their punishment record book twice a year. This caused a near-riot in Stellenbosch. *De Zuid-Afrikaan* spoke openly of resistance, warning of 'the rights of Dutch burghers and the length of Boer rifles.'[93]

As the controversy intensified, slave-owners realized that their resistance was futile. By the late 1820s the terms of the debate over slavery had changed substantially. Instead of defending slavery in principle, owners now concentrated on the way in which their authority was being undermined. Some of the government's attempts to ameliorate slavery caused greater agitation than would the act of emancipation later. For masters these interventions turned ownership of slaves into nothing less than a vexatious burden. In 1830 the slave-protector, an official appointed to watch over the treatment of slaves, noted a distinct deterioration in the ethos of paternalism that infused the system of slavery: 'The tie which [had] existed between the Master and the Slave seems . . . completed [sic] severed. The Master does little for his Slave from real regard, and the Slave nothing for his Master from affection.'[94]

But the Afrikaner slave-owners did not only wallow in dire predictions of the consequences of abolishing slavery. Some recognized that slavery as an institution was doomed and that it would be a wise step for the owners to take the initiative in bringing about its demise. In 1826 a meeting of Cape Town slave-owners suggested freeing female slave children after a certain date, and, in the same year, a proposal that slave children be freed was sent from the college of landdrost and heemraden in Graaff-Reinet. Stockenstrom commented that there was 'so liberal a sentiment among the inhabitants

---

91 *Afrikaner Political Thought*, p. 104.

92 Orlando Patterson, *Freedom, Volume One: Freedom in the Making of Western Culture* (New York: Basic Books, 1991).

93 *Afrikaner Political Thought*, pp. 109, 246-8.

94 John Mason, 'Slaveholder Resistance to the Amelioration of Slavery at the Cape', unpublished paper, University of Cape Town Centre of African Studies, 1986, pp. 1-2.

of that district [Graaff-Reinet] in respect of the slave question that they – instead of opposing themselves to the measures which the Government had in mind for bringing
about a gradual but complete emancipation – were prepared to go ahead of the Government and would gladly stipulate a time . . . after which all female children would
be born as free people.'[95]

John Philip, always quick to detect duplicity in the colonists' arguments, took these
proposals seriously. For him the freeing of the Khoisan was a priority. Although they
could not be sold, their position was in many ways worse than that of the slaves, since
employers had made no financial investment in their Khoikhoi laborers.

A recent study concludes that in the course of the 1820s Philip even became reticent
on the issue of the abolition of slavery. He favored gradual emancipation and supported
the proposal some owners adopted in 1826.[96] Stockenstrom, by contrast, come to conclude that the only solution was to abolish slavery. He wrote: '[Nothing] short of the extermination of slavery can save us from the greatest calamities; without a prospect of it
the people and the Government at home [Britain] will never cease plaguing the masters,
and the slaves will torment them to such a pitch that one execution after the other must
be the result . . . The evils connected with too much power in the hands of the master are
inseparable from slavery, and this is the principal reason why I wish to have that state
extinct in the present or at least the following generation.'[97] Slave-owners in the western
Cape had also come to support abolition, provided that the right to property and to what
they regarded as fair compensation was respected. *Zuid-Afrikaan* editorials now began
to talk of a general desire of owners for the abolition of slavery. In 1832 Governor Cole
noted the financial plight of owners as a result of plummeting slave and wine prices, and
wrote that the ruin of the farmers seemed to be actually 'sealed by the necessity of their
keeping up a large establishment of slave labor for which no profitable employment can
be found.'[98]

For a fleeting moment there seemed to be the prospect of an alliance between the
Afrikaner slave-owners and the English-speaking humanitarians at the Cape, like John
Philip and John Fairbairn, to end slavery voluntarily, based on a mutual regard for property rights. In attacking slavery Fairbairn concentrated on arguments such as the greater
productivity of free labor, something that owners took far more seriously than moral
arguments. Humanitarians locally and abroad never advocated abolition without adequate compensation. In their view private property extended to slave-ownership, even
if they found it repugnant that human beings could be owned. They understood that abolition without compensation would plunge masters into bankruptcy, and harm the freed
slaves as well.[99]

Knowing how much the owners desired self-government, Fairbairn, editor of *The
South African Commercial Advertisers*, toyed with the possibility that they might well be

95 *Afrikaner Political Thought*, p. 65.

96 R.L. Watson, *The Slave Question: Liberty and Property in South Africa* (Johannesburg: Witwatersrand University Press, 1991), pp. 177-8.

97 *Afrikaner Political Thought*, p. 67.

98 Mary Rayner, 'Wine and Slaves: The Failure of an Export Economy and the Ending of Slavery in the
Cape Colony, South Africa, 1806-1834', doctoral diss., Duke University, 1986, p. 210.

99 Keegan, *Colonial South Africa*, pp. 110-12.

willing to end slavery if self-rule was introduced. He raised this possibility with Christoffel Brand, a member of the first generation of well-educated Afrikaners, and a legal
adviser to the *Advertiser*. Brand had taken a leading hand in founding the Dutch newspaper *De Zuid-Afrikaan*, which first appeared in 1830, and helped to shape its editorial
policy. He championed representative government, but hesitated to give any firm commitment on the part of Afrikaner slave-owners that they would support abolition after
a grant of self-rule. All he did was to give vague assurances that under a system of representative government the 'owners of slaves [would] pay attention to the interests of
themselves, as well as the interests of the slaves.'[100]

Faced with Brand's prevarication, Fairbairn began to question the idea that representative institutions should precede emancipation. He feared that a legislative assembly
dominated by Afrikaner slave-owners would never abolish slavery. His suspicion was
fed by the outrage of slave-owners, and of *De Zuid-Afrikaan* in particular, over amelioration, especially the regulations limiting the corporal punishment of slaves. Fairbairn began openly to question the commitment of *De Zuid-Afrikaan* to the reform and abolition
of slavery. The shift in his position corresponded with his move into the circles of John
Philip. Fairbairn's report of a visit by him and Philip to the frontier increased the distance between him and Brand, for he set excessive store by the contacts made with the
inhabitants of the mission stations. He even expressed the peculiar belief that he and
Philip had enough influence to ensure that unprovoked attacks by Khoikhoi or Xhosa
on farms would not occur. In the meantime Philip's *Researches of South Africa* had appeared with few good words for the Afrikaner colonists.

De Zuid-Afrikaan was outraged over what it believed to be a haughty and arrogant
attitude. What also rankled was its perception that Fairbairn considered the free press
his own personal property and the *Commercial Advertiser* as the only truly independent
newspaper. *De Zuid-Afrikaan* declared that, in future, it would focus on four important
'humbugs': 'FREE PRESS humbug, INDEPENDENT NEWSPAPER humbug, MISSIONARY
humbug and the most extreme form of all humbugs PHILIPISH humbug.'[101]

The gloves were off. *De Zuid-Afrikaan* and the *Commercial Advertiser* turned their political conflicts into a struggle between Afrikaner and English colonists for the higher
moral ground. The Dutch paper denounced 'English hypocrisy', charging abolitionists
with constantly singling out the inhumanity of slave-owners, but overlooking the huge
profits their own forebears had made from the slave trade.[102] At a meeting of slave-holders
Brand hit out at people who 'accuse us Afrikaners of being vicious oafs.'[103] Fairbairn responded that a legislative assembly for the Cape dominated by Afrikaner slave-owners
would be 'a ridiculous insult to the common sense of mankind.' While he disliked the
autocratic rule at the Cape, the despotism of fifty Koeberg Boers was 'fifty thousand
times worse.' Fairbairn nevertheless found a reason to be optimistic: 'JOHN BULL has
been awakened from his dream of confidence in the Afrikander.' Because of this 'all
danger of Dutch domination' was at an end.[104]

100 *Afrikaner Political Thought*, p. 282.
101 H.C. Botha, *John Fairbairn in South Africa* (Cape Town: Historical Publication Society, 1984), p. 73.
102 Watson, *The Slave Question*, pp. 126-7.
103 *Afrikaner Political Thought*, p. 109.
104 Stanley Trapido, 'From Paternalism to Liberalism: The Cape Colony, 1820-1834', unpublished paper,
     pp. 27-9.

The imperial government took the controversy seriously enough to delay granting self-government for more than two decades, not only because it thought it would leave slaves and Khoisan at the mercy of the colonists, but also because it feared a confrontation between Dutch and English-speaking colonists.[105] Yet all this thunder and lightning subsided. There was more that kept the two white groups together than set them apart. They were, after all, a small minority in a colony with a large slave population and an insecure frontier in the east.

The imperial government never seriously considered the burghers' proposals to free the slaves. It was – with some justification – suspicious of their intentions. It knew also that the anti-slavery agitation in London could not be denied its prize of prompt abolition. Early in the 1830s the imperial government decided on rapid abolition with monetary compensation to owners, and Fairbairn supported this course of action. His *Commercial Advertiser* declared euphorically: 'What no man can have hoped for, time has brought about out of its own accord. The vineyards can attract . . . no more capital and the money sunk in the labor is about to be recovered by the colonist . . . through the justice and generosity of the mother country.'[106] Fairbairn implied that the owners had to show their gratitude to the government for freeing their slaves and rescuing them from their financial plight.

The fact that slavery was abolished abruptly and through outside intervention had some important implications. The squabble between Brand and Fairbairn deflected attention from the efforts of Stockenstrom and others to rid the colony of the system. The Afrikaners received little credit for abandoning the idea, expressed by W.S. van Ryneveld at the end of the eighteenth century, that slavery was essential for survival. Because the owners had no legislative assembly they could not explore issues like freedom and individual liberty in the cut and thrust of debate.

Sidelined, slave-owners accepted the inevitable, but were outraged over the inadequacy of the compensation. (The government paid £34 per slave, far less than the £73 computed by the committee appointed to evaluate the financial value of the colony's slaves.) Another grievance was over the fact that compensation was to be paid out only in London, which few farmers could arrange to reach on their own. Claims therefore had to be handed to agents, who took a hefty slice.

Masters and slaves approached Emancipation Day with starkly different expectations. The slaves had fervently prayed for the day, but had no idea what their new status would bring. The masters dreaded a scenario of slaves embarking on an orgy of revenge leading to a total collapse of the social order. But their fears did not materialize. The stipulation that slaves had to serve four years as apprentices before emancipation did much to ease the transition. In addition, the colony was not quite unprepared for the day. The amelioration measures had already eroded slavery and the masters' sense of control.

Emancipation Day, 1 December 1838, surprised everyone. Instead of the skies falling, they opened in early summer: three days of heavy rain, flooded rivers and snow on the mountaintops compelled all believers to try to fathom the heavenly meaning. For some slaves it symbolized the tears of slaves who had died before liberation, but for slave-owners it signaled some kind of divine intervention to save the colony from all kinds

---

105 Ross, *Status and Respectability in the Cape Colony*, p. 48.
106 Rayner, 'Wine and Slaves', p. 205.

of disasters. The Tulbagh correspondent of *De Zuid-Afrikaan* reported that the ex-apprentices were 'quiet, proper and peaceful', adding: 'We look upon the weather as providentially happening . . . [For] a great part [it] occasioned the avoidance of idle assemblages, and its [sic] consequences; and also prevented improper rejoicing and drunkenness from which nothing but evil must have arisen.'[107] Reports from other parts of the country indicated that the vast majority of the ex-apprentices were sober and orderly and that many went to church. In Stellenbosch they filled the church of the Rhenish Missionary Society on the Braak (the town square), to overflowing for each of the three worship services. Many slaves found it difficult to break off the bonds of paternalism immediately. The ex-slave Katie Jacobs remembered the run-up to the magic day of emancipation as follows: 'My missus wept at the idea of my leaving her. "No, you must stay!" she cried. "Think of my son, whom you have suckled and nursed, and who has now grown fond of you."'[108] Despite the exhortations of her husband to leave the farm, Jacobs stayed on for another three or four years.

The colonists feared a massive labor shortage but, as a level-headed observer, H. Calderwood, remarked in December 1838, 'it is ridiculous to talk of them [the freed slaves] refusing to work when they know very well they must either work or starve.'[109] Many stayed with their masters but as many left them for a day or permanently. Perhaps a thousand or two found makeshift homes on government land on the outskirts of towns and villages, and another thousand may have gone to live at missionary stations. Since the government made no land available for small-scale farmers, the majority had little option but to remain lowly laborers.

Emancipation did produce some subtle changes in labor relations on the farms. The days of complete submission had gone. A.J. Louw, a wealthy farmer from Koeberg, complained in December 1838: 'They come to the field after the sun has risen and if we look sour about it, they go away and abandon work.'[110] Workers tended to shun long-term contracts. A correspondent explained to *De Zuid-Afrikaan*: '[They] have been in many cases so accustomed to harsh treatment, and have seen their race suffer so much from bad masters, that they are unwilling to extend their services, until they ascertain the character of their masters.' The correspondent added that masters had been 'too familiar with the whip, the cat and the samboc.'[111]

Masters had to employ day laborers, a practice they disliked, but cash wages remained very low and workers were paid mostly in food, wine (perpetuating the 'tot' system of slavery in which an abundant supply of liquor was supplied), clothes, housing and stock. While under slavery some had received land for garden plots and pasturage for their cattle, and in the aftermath of emancipation this developed into a system of labor tenancy. Masters continued to clamor for a vagrancy law to secure a cheap and docile labor force, but the government refused.

---

107 Mason, 'Fit for Freedom', p. 538.

108 Shell, *Children of Bondage*, pp. 311-12.

109 Nigel Worden, 'Adjusting to Emancipation: Freed Slaves and Farmers in the Mid-Nineteenth Century South Western Cape', in Wilmot James and Mary Simons (eds.), *The Angry Divide: Social and Economic History of the Western Cape* (Cape Town: David Philip, 1989), p. 37.

110 Mason, 'Fit for Freedom', pp. 558-9.

111 Mason, 'Fit for Freedom', p. 559.

The old fears about economic ruin for the agricultural sector did not materialize. Between 1834 and 1842 wheat and barley production dropped by a third, but then went up to earlier levels. Wine production was little affected. By the mid-1840s arable production was back at its pre-emancipation levels.[112] All the fears that the colony could not survive without slavery proved to be groundless.

A campaign for representative government

With the emancipation of the slaves in 1838 having removed the greatest obstacle to representative government, the burghers stepped up their campaign for it. The imperial government would grant only a non-racial constitution, but to the Afrikaner colonists that did not pose a formidable obstacle since the colony had been shaped by a VOC system that rested, in principle, not on race or color but on non-racial status distinctions. Nor had Afrikaner spokesmen defended slavery on racial grounds; leaders in the Western Cape had paid at least lip service to a non-racial liberal order. *De Zuid-Afrikaan* had called the slave-owners 'anything but illiberal' and, as early as 1832, had declared its confidence in the Supreme Court as guardian of the burghers' rights and liberties.

From the 1830s the Afrikaners in the western Cape attached great importance to their rights and liberties as British citizens. During the 1840s they no longer demanded political rights based on their historic rights as Dutch or Cape burghers, but as the common aspiration of British citizens. The imperial government's colonial secretary, Lord Stanley, nevertheless rejected self-government. He did not want to turn the Cape over to the Afrikaners, whom he considered inferior to English-speakers 'in all respects except in numerical strength.'[113]

The imperial government realized that representative institutions for the Cape could not be delayed indefinitely, and the burghers recognized that Ordinance 50 had firmly established the principle of non-racial rights under the law. Self-rule, not white self-rule, was the only viable constitutional option. Not that the burghers had any less faith in the viability and legitimacy of white domination, but they understood that white domination did not have to be buttressed by explicitly racial legislation. The Afrikaner colonists represented more than three-quarters of the white population, and even under the low voting qualification most of the colored or black people in the rural areas would be denied the right to vote.

The rural Cape Colony itself had long been characterized by its racial rigidity, by the fact that few blacks or colored people had been able to escape from servitude. But, even in Cape Town, emancipation did not enhance racial fluidity. It still had racially mixed residential areas but most whites and coloreds worshipped separately and attended separate schools. The class order that had emerged in many ways resembled the Company's own status hierarchy. Ex-slaves, free blacks and Khoikhoi were much more likely than whites to be suspected of disorder and crime or be accused of 'relapsing into a state of

---

112 Nigel Worden, 'Adjusting to Emancipation', pp. 31-9; D. van Arkel, G. Quispel and R.J. Ross, 'De wijngaard des Heren': een onderzoek naar de wortels van de 'blanke baasskap' in Zuid-Afrika (Leiden: Marthinus Nijhoff, 1983), p. 63.

113 Ross, Status and Respectability in the Cape Colony, pp. 168-71.

savage barbarism', and were also more likely to be severely punished for crimes. Also, racial intermarriage declined.[114]

With slavery gone, the *Commercial Advertiser* lost much of its humanitarian zeal and concern for the underclasses; its editor, Fairbairn, became part of Anglo-Dutch Cape Town bourgeoisie. Most of the foreign missionaries on the frontier no longer sought radical intervention to achieve social equality. On the eastern frontier, James Read, who had married a Khoikhoi woman, had fallen out with his colleagues. He considered them too concerned about 'the danger and difficulty' of 'bring[ing] the [Khoikhoi] to a state of equality.' 'I am not made to act with these white men', Read wrote, 'I am too much of a Hottentot.'[115]

Despite its different racial mix, the Cape's constitutional development took a similar course to that in other British colonies. A Council of Advice made up of high officials was appointed in 1825 to act as a check on the governor with his arbitrary powers. If he ignored their advice he had to explain his action to the secretary of state. In 1827 two unofficial nominees were added to the Council. In 1834 the Cape was granted a decision-making Executive Council. Five to seven nominees of the governor were appointed to the Council, which also served as Legislative Council. But real power lay with the governor and the secretary to the colonial government. In 1837 the government made provision for the election of municipal councils by British subjects of all colors on a low franchise qualification as a first step in democratic government.

The imperial government's introduction of local government institutions opened a door to Afrikaners for entering into politics. Afrikaners who took the lead included F.W. Reitz, a wealthy farmer who had studied and traveled in Europe before settling in the Swellendam district, the lawyer C.J. Brand, and city businessmen, like the brothers J.H. and J.A.H. Wicht. When Cape Town's first council was elected in 1840, Afrikaner businessmen like the two Wichts played a dominant part. Increasingly this council organized itself as a counterweight to the impotent Legislative Council. Afrikaner and English businessmen in Cape Town shared so many common interests that, in 1841, Brand declared that 'party feeling' had died away.

In the course of the 1840s the Cape Town business and professional community, with Brand as its principal spokesman, expressed their discontent about the lack of leverage over the governor and his administration, and were dismayed that so little revenue was spent on 'colonial improvement.' They were eager to invest in the colony's infrastructure, such as harbor improvement, but the Colonial Office itself was not ready to provide the necessary guarantees. As the historian Timothy Keegan puts it: 'Local businessmen became determined to gain access to a new, popular colonial legislature free of Colonial Office control and answerable to local and not metropolitan interests. Only in this way would loans for speculative ventures be guaranteed.'[116]

During the late 1840s the agitation increased under the rule of the autocratic and domineering Harry Smith (1847-1852) as governor, and the conservative colonial secre-

---

114 Elphick and Giliomee, 'Origins and Entrenchment of European Domination', pp. 557-9.

115 Basil le Cordeur and Christopher Saunders, (eds.) *Kitchingman Papers*, (Johannesburg: Brenthurst Press, 1976), p. 248.

116 Keegan, *Colonial South Africa*, pp. 166-8.

tary, John Montagu, who acted for Smith when he was called to the frontier. The increasingly self-confident Cape Town bourgeoisie described this form of rule as unrepresentative and irresponsible. *De Zuid-Afrikaan* warned the government not to try to force unpopular taxes on people, and the commissioners of the Cape Town municipality and the government clashed over new taxes. The popular uprisings of 1848 in Europe aroused even stronger feelings about a government controlled by a narrow autocratic clique. F.S. Watermeyr, a young anglicized Afrikaner, warned that the 'revolutionary genius of the age has reached even unto the Cape.' The people 'choose no longer to have others rule them. They will not that the heel of power shall longer be on their necks.'[117]

When the issue of a parliament came up the colony found itself divided into two main factions. There was a 'conservative party', which was concentrated in the eastern districts of the Cape Colony. Here a vociferous minority group of British settlers, under the leadership of Robert Godlonton, rejected a political system based on universal franchise with low property qualifications. This conservative party called for higher voting qualifications and a nominated chamber. Godlonton declared that the people were not ripe for the liberal institutions proposed for them, and that he had no stomach for giving the vote to the 'untutored aborigines' of the Kat River. Richard Southey, secretary to the governor, to whom Godlonton wrote, responded that they would be 'swamped' by the 'Dutch *and coloreds*' if an excess of democracy were allowed. Both Godlonton and Southey were so averse to the prospect of an 'unprogressive majority' that they preferred to remain under direct imperial rule.[118]

Opposing the conservative party was the 'popular party.' In the west it took the form of a loose coalition of Afrikaner and English business and professional people and Afrikaner farmers. In the east Andries Stockenstrom emerged as a leader of the popular party. Afrikaner farmers supported him, as did the Khoikhoi of Kat River. When yet another war against the Xhosa broke out in 1846, the frontier burghers refused to fight in a commando under British command, and only did so after Stockenstrom was put in charge. The British settler faction on the frontier was as fiercely opposed to him as ever.

The final stage of the campaign for a parliament began in March 1849 when it had already become clear that the British government could not delay much longer the introduction of representative government. The Cape colonists heard that convicts, mostly Irishmen captured in the 'potato-patch rebellion' of 1848, would be sent to the Cape, turning it into a penal colony, like Australia. The popular party strongly opposed the plan and, in 1849, Fairbairn, Stockenstrom and Brand joined hands to force the government to back off. Despite the fact that the Legislative Council had been discredited, the imperial government decided to reconvene it to consider a new constitution for the Cape. As a sop to public opinion, the governor asked the elected municipal and district road boards to suggest individuals who might assist the Council. From all the nominations a list was drawn up. Five members of the popular party, Stockenstrom, Fairbairn, the two Wichts and F.W. Reitz, headed it. The result showed how isolated the conservative party itself had become. To give the eastern province some representation, the gov-

---

117 André du Toit, 'The Cape Afrikaners' Failed Liberal Movement', in Jeffrey Butler et al. (eds.), *Democratic Liberalism in South Africa* (Middletown: Wesleyan University Press, 1987), p. 42.

118 Keegan, *Colonial South Africa*, p. 232 (emphasis in the original).

ernor, Harry Smith, replaced J.H. Wicht with Robert Godlonton, leader of the conservative party, who was listed eleventh. Nonetheless, a draft bill drawn up by the Cape's attorney-general and backed by the popular party later became the framework for the new
constitution. The property franchise of £25 it proposed for voters to both chambers of
the elected parliament would counter the influence of both the very wealthy, who tended to be staunch imperialists, and the working class of all colors.

For a brief time in 1850-51 it looked as if the frontier war, accompanied by a rebellion at Kat River, would scuttle the drive for a constitution. Previously the Kat River people had fought valiantly on the colonial side in frontier wars, but many were now
alienated. At this time the *Grahamstown Journal* was leading a campaign to break up
missionary stations, a campaign strongly backed by land speculators. The Kat River settlers became more and more suspicious of colonial intentions. An attempt by the governor to enact vagrancy legislation alienated them further.

In the 1850-51 war, a group of the Kat River people, plus residents of other missionary stations and some landless farm laborers, aligned themselves with the Xhosa invaders. Projecting themselves as representatives of a 'colored nation' committed to regain
their independence, they announced that their fight was not with the Boers but with
the British. Earlier, Stockenstrom, as the leading patron of Kat River, had warned that
the 'malicious calumny' suffered by the Kat River people could have serious consequences. Governor Smith now believed the rebels might consider taking up arms against
the government in order to promote the views of their patron. When Stockenstrom's
house on the frontier was the only house left standing in an area devastated by the Xhosa
invaders, some British settlers burned it down.[119]

Colored disaffection now spread to colored troops who had fought in the frontier war,
and rumors circulated that the returning colored troops had said that the 'Hottentots
and Caffres are fighting for land formerly theirs and are right in so doing.' Farmers in
the rural western Cape were in the grip of a brief panic lest their servants rebel. A commission found afterwards that these rumors had been spread deliberately to rouse opposition to a non-racial franchise based on a low voting property qualification.

The constitutional debate revealed a welter of racist sentiments. Public meetings of
the conservative party were peppered by expressions of racial hostility. An LMS missionary in the Eastern Cape, Nicholas Smit, who defended the missionaries against a
charge of inciting their followers at Kat River and other stations, explained the situation thus: 'Many of the Hottentots attended the public meetings of the English at which
they hear enough to satisfy their minds about the real state of feeling towards the colored races.'[120]

An 1852 appeal by the conservatives to the imperial government catches the potent
amalgam of racial, ethnic and language fears that pervaded the rhetoric of the conservative party. It said that the 'diversity of race, the extensive influence of the Dutch colonists
and the exercise of a common language by the Dutch, Malay and Hottentot communities was a further fact, the consideration of which, with the evil of the low franchise,

---

119 Keegan, *Colonial South Africa*, pp. 237-40.
120 The quotations in this paragraph are all drawn from Ross, *Status and Respectability in the Cape Colony*,
     pp. 153-6.

placed at once this large majority in the ascendancy, to the imminent peril and jeopardy of the rights and privileges of the English colonists.'[121] Low voter qualifications would give undue power to 'ignorant colored persons.'[122]

The Kat River rebellion and the virulent racism reflected in the debate did not deflect the leadership of the popular party from their own stand for a non-racial franchise with a low property qualification. Thus Brand asked in 1851: '[Why] should [people] of color not have the vote? . . . Shall we withhold from them the same liberties we ourselves enjoy? If we had the slightest idea of such a thing, we would be unworthy of having a free constitution.' F.W. Reitz told a colored audience that he fully subscribed to the view that 'the simplest farmer and the simplest Hottentot' were able to judge who would best represent them. Rank-and-file Afrikaners in some of the country districts held similar sentiments. The members of a delegation from Clanwilliam in the northwestern Cape informed the Governor that they shuddered at the idea of any distinction in political rights 'between rich and poor, white and colored.' The colored man, they declared, was as much entitled to civil rights as a white man.

Stockenstrom, who for so long had stood virtually alone among Afrikaners in pressing the liberal cause, now wrote to the delegation as 'a countryman and as a boer like yourselves', to tell them how proud he was of their 'noble generosity.' In an obvious rebuke to some of his English-speaking opponents, he wrote of his admiration for the way the delegation had upheld the interests of the weaker and colored classes 'in defiance of the machinations and intrigues of those who have always boasted of their superior education, liberality and philanthropy.'[123]

A remarkable change had occurred in the short space of less than two decades: Afrikaner slave-owners had accepted a franchise that was open to former slaves who could meet the property qualifications. Governor George Cathcart noted in 1853 that there were 'many English people who sided with the Dutch on what are commonly styled liberal principles.'[124] In the 1820s it would have been the other way round. The Cape Afrikaners, particularly the modernizing elite, accepted the liberal idea of progress and the English language as public medium. They offered little open resistance to the introduction of secular education in 1863. So, too, an Afrikaner took the lead in elaborating on the liberal principles in the field of jurisprudence; J.H. de Villiers, who was to become chief justice in 1874, broke new liberal ground in taking a stand for the principle that 'no man's fundamental rights should depend on the color of his skin.' As Sachs points out, De Villiers used the court to shape common values and standards of conduct. Jealously guarding civil liberties, he ruled against the government when it imprisoned brown and black political leaders without trial.[125]

Although Afrikaners accepted the new liberal constitution, some of the assumptions of the old hierarchical order were still alive. *De Zuid-Afrikaan*, on one occasion, protest-

---

121 D.J.P. Haasbroek, 'The Origin of Apartheid', *Historia*, vol. xv1, no.1, p. 15.

122 Du Toit, 'The Cape Afrikaners' Failed Liberal Moment', p. 44.

123 The quotations in these paragraphs are all drawn from Du Toit, 'The Cape Afrikaners' Failed Liberal Moment', pp. 42-7.

124 S. Trapido, 'The Origins of the Cape Franchise Qualifications of 1853', *The Journal of African History*, 5, 1 (1964), p. 49.

125 Cited by Albie Sachs, *Justice in South Africa* (London: Heinemann, 1973), p. 45.

ed against schools in which the children of 'Boers', who formed the 'colonial aristocra-cy', had to share the same benches with the children of ex-slaves. (It was probably re-ferring to schools founded by the Cape Town elite for the black and white poor.) Yet Afrikaners mostly employed class, or sometimes nationality (in the nineteenth-century sense), rather than race in defending their interests.

Occasionally objections to irregularities in elections were expressed in what today would be called ethnic or racist terms. In 1854 *De Zuid-Afrikaan* wrote scathingly of elections as a 'demoralizing disease' that pitted the 'people' against the 'rabble', and in 1866 expressed its disgust in explicitly racial terms: 'Malays, Hottentots, and Kaffirs were easily bribed by rich and ambitious aspirants to political power, making a farce of elec-tions and of representative government a mere slogan.'[126] But such protests were directed primarily against the power of money in winning votes, not against the principle of non-racial participation. Afrikaner politicians continued to try to win non-white votes and strongly defended the colored vote in the constitutional debates of 1908 and 1909.

Colored people did not welcome the non-racial franchise as warmly as they had Or-dinance 50. They would have preferred the colony to remain under the Queen and the British Parliament. Their suspicion of the new democratic order was justified in 1856 when the new parliament passed the Masters and Servants Act, providing harsh penal-ties for desertion, absenteeism, and breaches of discipline. Verbal contracts were once again considered legal, as they had been before 1809. The government did nothing dra-matic to break the correspondence between racial and class cleavages. It was firmly on the masters' side.

Segregating the church

The official policy of the Reformed Church (DRC) was always that race or color was not to count in its decision to baptize or confirm. But while most parishes in the south-western Cape admitted colored or black people to their ranks, there tended to be few coloreds or blacks in most of the parishes in the deep interior. During the first decades of the nineteenth century, in several cases whites objected to the presence in church of colored people, or introduced various forms of segregation. But in 1829 the second DRC synod resolved firmly that no form of segregation in the church could be countenanced. Present at this synod was P. J. Truter. He was a leading colonist and also the *Kommis-saris-Politiek*, or political commissioner, who represented the government at a time when the DRC was still an established church. As a government representative he was bound to stress the importance, also to the church, of the new non-racial order that Ordinance 50 of 1828 ushered in. As a colonist he knew how important the Christian religion and a non-racial church would be for stable labor relations in a post-slavery era.

Some burghers in the eastern districts objected to the church's non-racial policy. J.N. Boshoff, a Graaff-Reinet official, explained the exodus of the Afrikaner frontier farm-ers in the second half of the 1830s, later called the Great Trek, as caused in part by the fact that 'blacks' were encouraged to consider themselves 'upon an equal footing with the

---

126 Scholtz, *Die ontwikkeling van die politieke denke van die Afrikaner*, vol. 3, pp. 85, 317.

whites in their religious exercises in church, though the former are heathens and not members of such a church community.'[127] The church leadership was undeterred, and, in 1847, the DRC reiterated its policy that 'it recognizes no distinction of color, but that all classes, whether black or white, are admissible to a participation in all her rites and ordinances.'[128]

Both the Anglican Church and the Roman Catholic Church refused to condone separate churches within the colonial border for the different racial communities. But the dominant pattern in organized Christian religion as a whole was that the racial communities worshipped separately. In Cape Town the Dutch Zuid-Afrikaansche Zending Genootschap (ZAZG), under the direction and discipline of its own directors and minister, served a large colored parish. In some towns a DRC congregation or individual members erected a separate building, called a *gesticht* or chapel, for colored Christians to worship in.

The DRC-sponsored missionary work did not make much progress. At its 1847 synod the church established a special committee for missions, which at the 1852 synod reported that the church's missionary work was hamstrung by a lack of financial support. The church was not prepared to commit any significant resources to missionary work. By the early 1850s it had five ordained missionaries in its service. By mid-century the failure of the DRC in the field of missionary work had become too striking to be ignored. Archbishop Merriman of the Anglican Church, who had just arrived, referred in a book that appeared in 1854 to the 'unaccountable neglect' of the colored people by the DRC, which knew the language most understood and their 'habits and ways.'[129] So upsetting was this charge that the Rev. Abraham Faure had used his address at the 1852 bicentenary celebrations to rebut it, but the defense lacked conviction (see p. 204).

One of the most outstanding young ministers of the Reformed Church, Nicolaas Hofmeyr, member of a wealthy and influential Cape Town family, found this a source of embarrassment. He had studied theology in Utrecht with Jan Neethling and Andrew and John Murray, the sons of Andrew Murray, where they were attracted by the appeal of the Dutch 'Reveil' movement, which opposed liberal doctrinal tendencies and emphasized spiritual experience. He had returned in 1850 full of evangelical fervor and energy for missionary work as an inescapable obligation of the church. When Hofmeyr became minister of the Calvinia congregation on the northwestern frontier in 1851, he was appalled by the intense opposition to missionary work. He heard for the first time the biblical story of the curse of Ham used to justify the exclusion of non-whites from church services. When colored people began attending his church, he tried to accommodate white unease by assigning them to the back pews. An outcry arose nevertheless, as also over his reading of the wedding banns of a Baster in a church service. Hofmeyr urged whites in Calvinia to include their servants in family devotions. 'It was in their own interests,' he said, 'since this would tie their servants to them more firmly than in any other way.'[130] As an idealist he wished that the Reformed Church would become

127 *Afrikaner Political Thought*, p. 120.

128 A.J. Botha, *Die evolusie van 'n volksteologie* (Cape Town: University of the Western Cape, 1984), p.56.

129 Archdeacon Merriman, *The Kafir, the Hottentot and the Frontier Farmer: Passages of Missionary Life . . .* (London: George Bell, 1854), p. 127.

130 J.D. Kestell, *Het leven van prof. N.J. Hofmeyr* (Cape Town: HAUM, 1911), p. 39. See also Schalk du Toit, 'Prof. N.J. Hofmeyr, 1827-1909', doctoral diss., University of Stellenbosch, 1984.

the dominant force in missionary work within the colonial borders, but as a pragmatist he recognized that this was unlikely unless there was an accommodation of the sharp increase in new colored and black members that would follow a greatly expanded missionary effort.

Using the pseudonym IT, Hofmeyr addressed the issue of missionary work in a series of articles in 1853 and 1854 in the official church journal, *De Gereformeerde Kerkbode*. (The use of pseudonyms was customary in the journal.) He wrote from the depth of his evangelical convictions. He did not want to disturb the differences in rank or 'station', as the social hierarchy was called. His priority was to bring the Gospel to souls who otherwise would be lost. Hofmeyr broke with the view of many that missionary work was a minor duty of the church. It was the duty of all Christians, he wrote, to rid themselves of all prejudice toward the heathen. People who did not love the heathen could not call themselves Christians, for all were lost sinners. He praised Johannes van der Kemp as a major figure whose greatness was not properly appreciated. Such views radically challenged the Afrikaner colonists' own traditional interpretation of their history and their place in society.

Hofmeyr investigated three possible options for the Reformed Church's missionary activities. First he rejected a policy of *afscheiding*, which would later be known as 'segregation', the practice of setting up completely separate mission stations or 'congregations' for coloreds. In his view, it tended to destroy the bond between whites and coloreds and also the influence of the church in society. Second, he rejected as unsuitable the 'fusion' of white and colored Christians by identical treatment. Colored people, he said, had a lower level of development; the Gospel must be brought to them in a simpler and concretely intelligible way. It was important that coloreds understood their place in the status hierarchy and did not confuse religious and social privileges. Hofmeyr quoted the experience of a minister who had admitted many coloreds into his own parish and found that they forgot their 'station' or estate in life.

Hofmeyr declared himself in favor of a third or 'middle way' as a means of overcoming the barriers to missionary work and the fear of gelykstelling. Every parish would have a minister and a missionary, and both a church and a separate gesticht or chapel. While separate like a mother and her daughter, they would be intimately bound together. The minister would conduct the service in the church, which colored members would always attend. The missionary would use the gesticht for religious instruction, tailored to the needs of the coloreds. In the gesticht the minister would perform all baptism and confirmation ceremonies and administer Holy Communion.

Hofmeyr quoted no biblical sources or authorities on missions policy in support of his position, but pointed instead to two successful models in Cape Town. One was St Stephens, a colored DRC parish that shared a minister with a white Lutheran parish nearby; the other was the Presbyterian Church, which housed white and colored parish meetings in the same church but at separate times. Hofmeyr was a practical man and wanted a 'serviceable' policy.[131]

No other articles in the *Gereformeerde Kerkbode* during this period favored *afscheiding* or segregation. The debate was essentially one between proponents of fusion and Hof-

---

131 *De Gereformeerde Kerkbode*, 5 March, 28 May and 25 June 1853.

meyr's third way. Leading ministers defended the Church's non-racial policy in no un-certain terms. In 1855, the Rev. J.H. Neethling and the Rev. A.A. Louw, traveled to the Transvaal, where the Rev. Dirk van der Hoff was campaigning for the exclusion of non-whites from the church. The two pointed out that the Cape church recognized the 'existing differences in rank and station', and allowed in 'numerous instances' separate buildings for people who were not white. But there could be no racial exclusion.[132]

The debate came to a head a few years later as a result of two cases. One case involved a request by the white members of the Stockenstrom congregation in the Kat River Valley, 120 kilometers northeast of Grahamstown. It was a largely colored congregation with a colored church council. It also had a minority of white members, who entered the parish after the Kat River Rebellion of 1851, which had led to some rebels losing their land. A group of forty-five white members asked permission from the church coun-cil to have the Holy Communion administered separately to them either before or after the service (but not on a separate day). The church council turned down their request.

In the synod of 1857 there was only a brief reference to the Stockenstrom issue. The main discussion related to a controversy that had arisen in the Reformed Church parish of Ceres in the western Cape. Probably influenced by the articles in the *Kerkbode*, an enthusiastic supporter of missionary work had asked permission from the church coun-cil to erect a building on church grounds where colored people could be instructed 'and enjoy all privileges of their religion.' The church council supported the request and voted a sum for the purpose. The Rev. R. Shand, the minister presiding over the meeting, objected. In his view the decision could be in conflict with the synod's earlier decisions to make no distinction between members. This matter was referred to the 1857 synod.

Significantly, also at this synod, a special commission for mission work reported that the time was not ripe for a co-ordinated effort to extend missionary work. In response, the synod appointed a new committee, composed of Hofmeyr, the Murray brothers, and P.K. Albertyn, and it promptly informed the synod that with the necessary zeal progress would indeed be possible.

In the synod debate on the Ceres issue, several participants urged a strong stand against the racial prejudices that seemed prevalent in some frontier parishes. After they called for a reaffirmation of the church's policy of non-discrimination, Hofmeyr, one of the last two speakers, insisted that there was a more important issue than addressing racial prejudice. That issue was to identify the most effective way for the church to pro-mote the Christianization of the heathen. According to newspaper reports, after he spoke the debate took a new turn. In the end a compromise resolution, proposed by Andrew Murray, senior, of Graaff-Reinet, who was a prominent evangelical and mission enthu-siast, was accepted. The resolution declared that it was 'desirable and according to the Scriptures to absorb members from the heathen population in existing congregations' wherever this was possible. However, in cases where 'the weakness of some' hindered spreading the Gospel, the church would grant permission to people in parishes formed out of the 'heathen' to enjoy their Christian privileges in a separate building.[133]

---

132 Haasbroek, 'The Origin of Apartheid', p. 13.
133 C.J. Kriel, *Die Geskiedenis van die Nederduits Gereformeerde Sendingkerk in Suid-Afrika, 1881-1956* (Paarl: Paarl Drukpers, 1963), pp. 54-9.

This resolution sanctioned separate facilities but not segregated parishes, and it was not in conflict with what other Protestant churches were doing at the time. As David Botha argues, it introduced Hofmeyr's 'middle way.' Yet the resolution was poorly formulated and the inclusion of the phrase 'weakness of some' proved a fatal mistake; it opened the door for prejudiced whites to exclude coloreds.[134]

Only a few ministers realized at the time what a fateful step it was. One who did was the Rev. Huet, a recent immigrant from the Netherlands and a rather eccentric man, based in Natal where he worked among Voortrekkers or their children. He had found it virtually impossible in some parishes to have a black person confirmed and accepted in the church.

Huet analyzed the objections he had encountered to the presence of non-whites in the church. One was the presumed biblical justifications for the exclusion of 'Basters.' Another was a form of biological racism, an argument that brown and black people had to be kept separate because they represented a different human species marked by their color and their hair. It was contended, for example, that brown and black Christians stood on a much lower level of 'civilization' and often understood only the simplest of services.[135] Yet another was the argument that coloreds formed a separate 'nation', which, like the French or the Dutch, should form their own church. (This line of argument surfaced again in the twentieth century in the development of the apartheid ideology.)

Huet himself did not object to separate church buildings or 'gestichten', as they were called, if they could accommodate the special needs of non-whites, but he believed that the synod had erred. It had focused on white prejudice and had elevated the 'weakness of some' almost to the level of principle, thereby extending a blanket permission to 'the powerful and the proud' to exclude the truly weak and vulnerable – the very persons about whom the church ought to be most solicitous. As he put it, the rejection of gelykstelling – 'that terrible, secret word viewed by so many as the greatest of evils' – had been carried into the realm of ecclesiastical organization.[136]

Huet had the conditions in Natal in mind, where conflict between white and black had led to a polarized racial situation. He sensed that the church would have to take a much stronger stand against racial prejudice if it did not want to be overwhelmed by it. Hofmeyr was from the western part of South Africa and was in many ways naïve in his idealism. The poor formulation of the 1857 compromise had paved the way for racist practices. As David Botha argued a century later, the 'pious intentions of honest idealists' were no match for the 'callousness of the sinful.'[137]

In 1859 Hofmeyr and John Murray took up their positions as the first professors of the newly established DRC theological seminary in Stellenbosch. Missionary work now rapidly expanded. Much of the religious fervor and zeal of the Great Revival that gripped the western part of the colony in the early 1860s was channeled into missionary work.

134 Botha, *Evolusie van 'n volksteologie*, pp. 56-61; D.P. Botha 'Historiese agtergrond van die stigting van afsonderlike etniese N.G. Kerkverbande', unpublished paper, pp. 22-33.

135 P. Huet, *Eene kudde en een herder* (Cape Town: N.H. Marais, 1860), pp. 28-53.

136 See a review of Huet's book and his response in *Elpis*, 4 (1860).

137 Botha, 'Historiese agtergrond', p. 37.

Convinced that Christians must take personal responsibility for the millions of heathens around them who lived and died without being saved, Hofmeyr regularly reminded his Stellenbosch students of the church's calling and their own responsibility toward this end. With the younger Andrew Murray and Jan Neethling – the three were referred to as the church's 'triumvirate' – Hofmeyr would direct the church's missions policy for several decades.

Hofmeyr's writings show no sign that he felt that the church had made a wrong turning. Indeed, its direction was not yet settled. During the 1870s the synod seriously considered absorbing several parishes of colored people that had been founded by the Rhenish Missionary Society. Financial considerations, not racial objections, prevented it, but if the plan had gone ahead the church at the level of its synod would have entered the next century as a multi-racial body.

The pattern that actually developed was inconsistent. Some coloreds who worshipped separately in a gesticht were under the direct control of a Reformed congregation; others fell under the authority of the synod's Home Committee for Missions. Many others continued to attend the white church. In 1857 St Stephens, a colored parish in Cape Town, was accepted as a congregation of the Reformed Church.

Between 1878 and 1881 another crucial event occurred, which, like the 1857 synod decision, was not intended to promote segregation. In 1878, the Wellington church council made arrangements to bring into its fold the town's colored parish, which had been built up by the Paris Missionary Society. It proposed the appointment of a board of white directors to supervise the mission parish, a proposal made in typically paternalist fashion. The all-white council assumed that the servants who made up the colored parish would have no objection to being controlled by the masters' parish, which, in any case, would provide some of the future funding.

But as it happened, the minister of the colored parish immediately objected. He was the Rev. Jacobus Cornelis Pauw, a Dutch missionary, who had done excellent work in the colony over the preceding fifteen years. Pauw knew his church law. No parish and minister could be subordinate to another parish and minister. Accepting a board of white directors would fatally undermine the power and status of the church council of his mission parish. The only control he would accept was that of the synod's Home Committee for Missions, which represented a higher authority in the church structure than the local white parish. If there was to be separation it had to be based on the equality of parishes within the church polity.[138]

In 1881 Pauw took the lead when delegates from four mission parishes moved to form the Dutch Reformed Missions Church. Pauw and his colleagues simply sought to solve an organizational problem, which had arisen from the fact that no existing tie bound the four colored Reformed parishes or gestichts together. The impetus for the move did not come from the DRC itself, although its 1880 synod provided the legal basis for the establishment of a missionary church. No alternative to the establishment of a mission church was considered. *De Christen*, at that time the official organ of the DRC, thought the church was not yet 'ripe' enough to absorb colored parishes as regular DRC parishes, but this was the opinion of the editor.

---

138 For these paragraphs I have drawn on Botha, 'Historiese agtergrond', pp. 37-46.

Two dynamics promoted increased segregation; one was the desire of white church councils to get rid of their colored members. Some church councils instructed their colored members to take the sacrament of Communion in the gesticht. Polarization accelerated after the Anglo-Boer War, during which Afrikaners and coloreds backed opposite sides. The other dynamic was generated by the wish of colored people to escape from discrimination. Some colored members of established parishes had requested a separate ministry where colored people could be elected as deacons and elders and become ministers. One of the four founders of the Mission Church in 1881 was the Rev. Ruytenbeek, a Dutch minister of the racially mixed Reformed parish of Wynberg. In an implicit acknowledgement of the marginalized state of the colored members in the white-dominated parish, he later wrote that in the mission parish he had got to know them for the first time in eighteen years and was 'very delighted with the quality of the men that were found to become deacons and elders.'[139]

No opposition and no public outcry arose as a result of the establishment of the Mission Church. It would, in any case, be many years before most of the colored parishes in the DRC fold joined it. The ZAZG did not join until 1937. As a major donor the DRC retained a veto power over changes in the Mission Church's constitution until 1975.

Adapting to equality

The burghers had adapted remarkably well to two major changes in the social order between 1806 and 1853: the freeing of the Khoisan and the emancipation of the slaves. While some frontier farmers may have joined the Great Trek because of labor shortages, most burghers generally found ways to attract and keep labor.

With slavery consigned to history, the Afrikaner elite in the middle third of the century became increasingly attracted to the idea of liberal progress, with its emphasis on the non-racial franchise, representative democracy, separation between church and state, secular education, and the value of scientific inquiry. On issues of color, the burghers continued to search for a way to reconcile their older paternalism with the new non-racial liberalism, accepting the principle of equality before the law and the universal franchise, but rejecting gelykstelling, which was rooted in the old status hierarchy of burghers and slaves. They supported missionary work with much more enthusiasm now than before, but the price was allowing segregated facilities as a concession to 'the weakness of some.'

The principal political representative of this hybrid racial ideology, J.H ('Onze Jan') Hofmeyr, a nephew of N.J. Hofmeyr, became leader of the Afrikaner Bond, the first Afrikaner political organization, during the early 1880s. His biography includes a revealing account of the ambiguities of his ideology. He once picked up a native's hat that had been blown off by the wind. To a friend who had accused him of demeaning himself to a 'dirty nigger', he replied: 'Why, he would have done the same for me.'[140] He nevertheless regarded the indigenous people as children who needed courteous and kind paternalist guidance and education adapted to their needs.

---

139 Botha, 'Historiese Agtergrond', p. 54.
140 J.H. Hofmeyr, *The Life of Jan Hendrik Hofmeyr* (Cape Town: Van de Sandt De Villiers, 1913), p. 308.

To Hofmeyr, colored people who had qualified for the vote should be treated as adults and be granted full human rights. But there were limits. One day a delegation of colored voters inquired whether they could become members of the Afrikaner Bond, the political party he led. Instead of replying, Hofmeyr invited the members to lunch at his home. According to the biographer, Jan Hofmeyr, a nephew who was destined to become the leading liberal politician of the 1930s and 1940s, the members of the delegation immediately understood the message. Just as they knew that it was impossible to accept, they realized that they could not be treated in all respects as the equal of the white man. Hofmeyr had no problem with equality before the law and competing for the colored vote. This was equality and acceptable. By contrast, the idea of lunch in his house with colored people hoping to become members of his political party was unthinkable. It was gelykstelling.

Chapter 5

The Eastern Frontier Cauldron

An uncertain peace

Between approximately 1770 and 1812, whites and blacks lived together in the Zuur-veld area on the frontier, with neither side able to establish ascendancy over the other. It was an unstable order. In 1810 Anders Stockenström, landdrost of Graaff-Reinet, said: 'Neither peace nor friendship can subsist between the inhabitants and the Kaffirs while both inhabit the same country.' The cause, he said, was 'interwoven in the character of the Kaffir, in that of the colonist and in the nature of the country.'[1]

For both whites and blacks the frontier was an area of incomplete conquest, and al-most all the problems flowed from this fact. What can be called the cauldron of the eastern frontier refers to the area between the Fish River and the Bushmans River, which was called the Zuurveld, and the Bosberg and Bruintjes Hoogte area, northeast of this area. The proclamation of the so-called neutral belt in 1819 extended the primary zone of conflict to the land between the Fish and the Keiskamma and Tyhume rivers. Ten years later the large Tarka ward in the Somerset district had also become a turbulent frontier zone (see map in front).

The frontiersmen did not view the Xhosa-speaking Africans as implacable enemies. Many Xhosa worked for them and, although it was illegal, trade took place across the border. On occasion there were even temporary military alliances. But Anders Stocken-ström's son, Andries, realized that relations on the frontier had steadily become more polarized. As the landdrost, or chief government official, in the frontier district of Graaff-Reinet, he advised the government on the eve of what became known as the Fourth Frontier War (1819) not to enlist Xhosa auxiliaries in a government force: 'The general cry is, let us meet any number of Kaffirs, but let us meet them as enemies, for enemies they are all of them.'[2]

The most unstable kind of peace is one which embitters 'the losers without depriving them of the capacity for seeking revenge and without establishing a system able to re-

---

1 *Afrikaner Political Thought*, pp. 158-9.
2 *Afrikaner Political Thought*, p. 161.
3 Donald Kagan on the Punic wars cited by Gordon Craig, 'No More Wars', *New York Review of Books*, 20 April 1995, p. 7.

strain them – and then taking the trouble to make it work.'[3] Such a peace characterized the frontier from the time the Xhosa were expelled from the Zuurveld in 1811-12 (see pp. 80-82) to the late 1850s. Hampered by financial constraints and bewildered by all the complexities of the problem, the British governors struggled to formulate a fixed frontier policy. This inconsistency was exacerbated by the imperial government's interventions. In all, the policy amounted in the words of Andries Stockenstrom to a 'vacillating and contradictory doctrine.'[4]

'We do not do things as you do them': A Xhosa chief's dilemma

After the Third Frontier War (1799-1802), the British sought to bring about peace by separating white and black with the Fish River as the dividing line. The peace was quickly shattered. The expulsion of the Zuurveld Xhosa added to the conflict over land and other resources among the Xhosa in the area east of the Fish River, which led to a major disruption of Xhosa society and the relationships between chiefs. The military force stationed on the Fish River after the 1811-12 expulsion was much too small to deter the Xhosa from cross-border raids. The governor of the colony, Lord Charles Somerset, in a visit to the border in 1817, found that ninety of the 145 burgher families had abandoned their dwellings, while the rest were ready to flee.[5]

Somerset wanted the Xhosa to assume collective responsibility for thefts. He devised a 'spoor' or reprisal system under which a farmer who discovered a loss would report it to the military post. The commander would then send a patrol to follow the tracks to the first kraal and the kraal would hand over the stolen cattle or pay compensation. A chief innocent of the theft could recoup the loss by demanding the equivalent number of cattle from the real thieves. The Xhosa were said to use such a system for dealing with thefts among themselves.

On arriving at the frontier, Somerset summoned Ngqika, whom he considered the supreme Xhosa chief, and also his main rival, Ndlambe. He told Ngqika that the theft of cattle and horses had to stop and that it was Ngqika's responsibility to make sure that it did. A Xhosa eyewitness left a vivid account of the sham negotiations:

> Ngqika said to the governor, '[We] do not do things as you do them, you have but one chief, but with us it is not so, but although I am a great man and king of the other Xhosa, still every chief rules and governs his own people . . . The governor then said, 'No, you must be responsible for all the cattle and horses that are stolen.' The other chiefs then said to Ngqika, 'Say yes, for we see the man is getting angry', for we had the cannon and artillerymen and soldiers and Boers with loaded muskets standing about us. Ngqika then complied. He said he would be responsible for all the cattle and horses stolen from the colony. The governor said moreover that the Xhosa were not to pass the Fish River.[6]

For Ngqika the task was impossible. His avarice and cruelty had alienated many of his followers. He had, as he said, no real power over other chiefs, and if he were to act against

4 Andries Stockenstrom, *Autobiography* (1887, repr. Cape Town: Struik, 1964), vol. 2, p. 37.
5 *RCC*, vol. xi, pp. 303-9.
6 *Report of the Select Committee on Aborigines, 1836*, vol. 1, p. 569.

the thieves among his own followers they would join other chiefs. When the government failed to provide any material assistance, many of Ngqika's followers absconded to join his enemy, Ndlambe.

In 1818 a force of Ndlambe's men inflicted a defeat on Ngqika, who appealed to the government for help, whereupon a force of soldiers, burghers, and Khoikhoi troops rode out and defeated Ndlambe's force. British soldiers backed up by burgher commandos blasted the wooded valleys to capture 23,000 cattle, almost the entire subsistence of Ndlambe's followers. Stockenstrom wrote of 'populous tribes driven to desperation by being deprived of all their cattle.'[7] In the final days of December 1818 and January of 1819 a Xhosa force struck back. It raided farms in the colony in the first phase of the Fourth Frontier War. By February it looked as if the Zuurveld was back in Xhosa hands. A desperate burgher, holed up with his neighbors in a laager, wrote from there: 'God alone will know what will become of us . . . One can have no idea but that the whole of Kaffirland is here. For God's sake please come to our assistance.'[8]

During the second phase of the war, the 'war doctor', Nxele (or Makanda), who had the chief Ndlambe as his patron, attacked the small garrison town of Grahamstown with six thousand men. Assisted by Khoikhoi marksmen, the garrison narrowly averted defeat and possibly also the collapse of the settlement on the southeastern frontier. When another large force of soldiers, Khoikhoi troops and burgher commandos went out, the Xhosa fled towards the Kei River, Nxele gave himself up and the war was ended.

Somerset relied on Stockenstrom's judgement and was influenced by people in Cape Town who urged a neutral and unpopulated belt beyond the boundary. He decided that the colony's border would remain the Fish and the Baviaans rivers, but the border of what the government considered the land of the Xhosa would be moved eastward to the Keiskamma and Tyhumie rivers. The area between the Fish and the Keiskamma rivers was designated a neutral belt. Even Ngqika, the government's chief ally, was told to leave his Great Place and move beyond the Keiskamma. But for Somerset the ban on settlement between the two borders would only apply to the Xhosa. The 'neutral territory' soon became the Ceded or Conquered Territory.

Effectively nearly 7,800 square kilometers had been added to a colony already hard to defend. Jeffrey Peires, a historian of the Xhosa people, argues that it was a turning point in frontier relations.[9] With the loss of the land in the neutral belt, the Xhosa found the land deprivation acute; the western Xhosa who were driven eastward impinged on other peoples already hard-pressed for pastoral land.[10] Somerset had no wish to impose partition. He permitted regular trade fairs on the Fish River, attracting many Xhosa, and allowed Xhosa laborers in the colony to remain. It was a hotchpotch of policy, destined to destabilize the frontier.

To complicate matters further, two new waves of people arrived in the early 1820s. Most of the four thousand or so new British immigrants were settled on Zuurveld farms abandoned by the burghers in the preceding two decades, while a small group was given

---

7 *Afrikaner Political Thought*, p. 160.

8 George Cory, *The Rise of South Africa* (London: Longman Green, 1910), vol. 1, p. 381.

9 Jeffrey Peires, *The House of Phalo* (Johannesburg: Ravan Press, 1981), p. 145.

10 Thomas Pringle, *Narrative of a Residence in South Africa* (1835, repr. Cape Town: Struik, 1966), p. 439.

farms in the western part of the 'neutral territory.' To improve the administration of the frontier, the government established a new district with Grahamstown the seat of the board of landdrost and heemraden. Five years later, in 1825, it created another district, called Somerset, between Grahamstown and Graaff-Reinet to its northwest.

The second influx was of refugees from the bloody upheavals in Natal and on the High-veld called the *Mfecane* (the crushing) in Nguni, *Difaqane* in Sotho, fostered by drought and overcrowding, heightened competition for land and, as recent studies have shown, trade, particularly in ivory.[11] Gun-carrying Griquas attacked the remnants of chiefdoms who had fled from Delagoa Bay into the area between the Vaal and the Orange rivers; some, given the name of Mantatees, became indentured servants on frontier farms.

So, too, between 1818 and 1828, the armies of the Zulu chief Shaka in Natal attacked the tribes who fled to the north, west, and south, disrupting, in turn, the Thembu, Mpondo and Bhaca who were Xhosa-speaking tribes living along the southeast coast. The great explosion of violence ultimately gave rise to states formed by the Swazi, Ndebele, and Sotho. From the early 1820s the eastern frontier experienced the ripple effects of the violence in the deeper interior. Remnants of the Thembu chiefdom fled to settle near the present Queenstown, just inside the border of the Somerset district. Farmers gave the refugees food, but this soon became a burden.[12]

'Strict and equal justice': Stockenstrom on survival

During the period between the Fourth Frontier War (1811-12) and the effective end of Somerset's term of office in 1826, two Afrikaners with sharply divergent views on survival on the frontier began to make their mark on frontier politics. One was Andries Stockenstrom, appointed landdrost of Graaff-Reinet in 1815, the other Piet Retief. Not yet 23 when he assumed office, Stockenstrom had become the most important frontier official with a district that bordered the Xhosa in the east and the Griqua and Bushmen in the north – an extensive district that had hardly known effective government. He had to explain to the burghers major changes in government policy, like the abolition of the loan farm system, the introduction of a perpetual quit rent, and equality before the law.

Stockenstrom seemed to be everywhere. He attended the 1817 Kat River conference and headed a Graaff-Reinet commando that accompanied Colonel Thomas Brereton's force in 1818 to avenge Ngqika's defeat. In 1819 he was in charge of a commando in a force that swept the area between the Fish and Keiskamma rivers. He had serious doubts about the wisdom of intervening in the conflict between Ngqika and Ndlambe and of capturing such a huge number of cattle. 'Revenge, starvation and desperation', he said, drove Ndlambe's men into the colony on reprisal raids. If Nxele's attack on Grahamstown had not been checked, the question of white settlement on the frontier 'would have

---

11 John Omer-Cooper, *The Zulu Aftermath* (Evanston: University of Indiana Press, 1966) and his 'The Mfecane Defended', *Southern African Review of Books*, vols. 4 and 5, July/October 1991, pp. 12-15. A volume under the editorship of Caroline Hamilton was published of the proceedings of a colloquium, held in 1991, on the historiographical controversy over the *Mfecane*, started by Julian Cobbing. For an attempt at a new synthesis of the research on the white and black migrations see Norman Etherington, *The Great Treks* (Harlow: Penguin 2001).

12 C.F.J. Muller, *Die oorsprong van die Groot Trek* (Cape Town: Tafelberg, 1974), p. 94.

remained doubtful until overwhelming reinforcements could have been sent from the mother country [Britain].'[13]

Yet Stockenstrom believed it of overriding importance to leave the Xhosa in no doubt about the government's resolve to defend the colony and to punish stock theft. Even before Nxele's attack, he wrote to Somerset of the 'absolute necessity . . . that a force be employed capable of crushing the Kaffirs most effectively, so as to reduce them to the necessity of praying for mercy.' He ended his letter with the words. 'Believe me, the Kaffirs may be brought to their bearing, but they are no more to be trifled with.'[14] It was essential to 'root out any gang of robbers, murderers and marauders, as soon as they were discovered, before the evil would spread to such an extent as to involve the lives of hundreds.'[15] At the same time, however, he realized that military force must be used sparingly and only when absolutely necessary. Burgher commandos could still track down stolen cattle in the colony, but were not allowed to cross the border. Increasingly, military officers headed patrols made up of British soldiers as well as mixed units of burghers and soldiers.

The reprisal system failed to stamp out stock theft and was open to all kinds of abuse. Since farms were not fenced, stock losses were frequent. When stock went missing farmers went to the nearest military post and applied for a search party with no effort having been made to check whether the stock had actually been stolen. Kraals were seldom given the opportunity to prove their innocence.

The major offenders included marauding bands outside the control of any chief. Chiefs used the system to get back at their enemies. One patrol, led by Colonel Henry Somerset, twice burned the wrong village with loss of life.[16] Stockenstrom said later that he knew of fifty cases where innocent kraals had been plundered. Patrols that crossed the border to seize more stolen cattle or to force innocent kraals to give up cattle of their own simply invited Xhosa counter-raids. The Xhosa frequently told him: 'We don't care how many Xhosa you shoot if they come into your country, and you catch them stealing, but for every cow you take from our country you make a thief.'[17]

The question of survival on the frontier came up in a week-long informal discussion in 1825 at Graaff-Reinet, where Stockenstrom played host to two missionaries, Dr John Philip and Dr William Wright of the London Missionary Society (LMS), and a British settler, Thomas Pringle, with a reputation as someone of a strongly liberal persuasion. Wright had been travelling in and beyond the frontier zone and was, in Stockenstrom's words, 'literally frantic about the injustices and oppression which he had heard of and witnessed.' Philip was already well known as a major critic of the Afrikaner farmers. He distrusted Stockenstrom and said as much to his fellow-Scotsman, the Rev. Andrew Murray of Graaff-Reinet. Stockenstrom was 'a good fellow' but one who remained 'a Dutchman', naturally prejudiced in favor of the old system of oppression of the natives.[18]

---

13 Stockenstrom, *Autobiography,* vol. 1, pp. 12-24, 153-60.
14 *Afrikaner Political Thought,* pp. 160-61.
15 *Afrikaner Political Thought,* pp. 160, 166.
16 W.M. Macmillan, *Bantu, Boer and Briton* (Oxford: Clarendon Press, 1963), p. 89, 99.
17 Noël Mostert, *Frontiers* (New York: Knopf, 1992), p. 468.
18 R.U. Kenney, *Piet Retief: The Dubious Hero* (Cape Town: Human & Rousseau, 1976), p. 76.

Philip was the principal spokesman of the LMS. He saw missionary work as a vehicle for promoting both the liberties and rights of the indigenous population as well as British cultural, social and political interests. If there was clash between the two he did not detect it, and if he did detect it he did not tell.[19] He wrote in 1824: 'I consider it highly impolitic to drive the Caffres to desperation by depriving them of their cattle, by illicit trade, or by encroachment on their land . . . [The Xhosa] inevitably have no resources left and they inevitably betake themselves to the thickets and attempt to live by plunder.'[20] He considered the Xhosa peace-loving, dependable, honest and credible; the colonists full of 'insatiable avarice and rapacity.' 'We must make the interests of the Natives the grand policy of our conduct,' Philip declared.[21] Philip was at this point working on his *Researches in South Africa*, published three years later, in which he denounced the cruel and unjust dispossession of the Khoisan who were now condemned to servitude. Stockenstrom thought that Philip had downplayed Xhosa and Khoisan responsibility for cattle raids and tended to blame the burghers rather than the British military or the British settlers to win his argument in London.

Believing that the policy exacerbated conflict, Stockenstrom constantly struggled to establish an alternative system that would enable diverse groups to co-exist. He confronted a basic question: how could the farmers defend and maintain themselves on the frontier at the cutting edge of colonial expansion? In his writings he never claimed that conquest gave the burghers a moral claim to the land, acknowledging that 'oppressions' by the colonists and their descendants were 'the cause of the degradation of most of the natives and the hostile feeling existing between the Colony and its neighbors.' At the same time, the burghers had rights, especially the right to security and fair treatment from the government and the right to protect their lives and property.

For Stockenstrom the options of the frontier farmers were stark: '[We] must either run away, sit still and have our throats cut or defend what we have.' 'Running away' was not an option; the burghers should not withdraw from the frontier region. (Ten years later he would condemn the outward movement that became known as the Great Trek.) He dismissed with contempt the notion that the burghers did not have the right to defend themselves. To 'defend what we have', and to identify the principles on which that defense should rest, preoccupied Stockenstrom throughout his career.

In the conversation with his guests, Stockenstrom advanced two principles by which to live: truth and justice.[22] In this particular context he saw himself predominantly as a government man whose duty it was to seek the truth impartially and dispassionately. To deny the facts that Philip highlighted about colonial conquest was to Stockenstrom 'ridiculous' and 'dishonest', but he also insisted that the atrocities were something of the past, and that every burgher 'with the slightest decency and respectability' accepted these facts and lamented them. As he wrote on another occasion, 'a thousand times' leading burghers had spoken to him about the injustice of taking the property of the border tribes.

---

19 Andrew Ross, *John Philip, 1775-1851* (Aberdeen: Aberdeen University Press, 1986), pp. 140-41.

20 Macmillan, *Bantu, Boer and Briton*, p. 37.

21 Pieter Kapp, 'Dr. John Philip: die grondlegger van Liberalisme in Suid-Afrika', *AYB*, pp. 154-5.

22 André du Toit, 'Experiments with Truth: Stockenstrom, Gandhi, and the Truth and Reconciliation Commission', paper presented to the philosophical society of Southern Africa, 2002.

But if there was little dispute between Stockenstrom and his guests about the past, there was no agreement about the present. He wrote: '[They] certainly tried my temper by the virulence with which they persisted to denounce the present generation of the colonists and refused to make any allowance for their actual position, which rendered self-defense absolutely necessary for the preservation of both parties.' Deadlocked in their argument, the guests tried to silence Stockenstrom by remarking: 'You [the colonists] have no business here at all.' To this the landdrost replied that no people violated this principle more than the British.[23]

Alongside truth, Stockenstrom proclaimed justice as a principle on which the survival of all the peoples on the frontier had to be based. Burghers and soldiers on the colonial side could not be allowed to act as both judges and avengers, as the reprisal system enabled them to do. Any military operation, including small army patrols or commandos, required above all a firm policy framework, unambiguous orders, and trustworthy people in positions of command. Stockenstrom told his guests: 'My system is to do my best to get the white man hanged who murders a black; but I also do my best to root out the gang of robbers and murderers among the blacks who cannot otherwise be reclaimed.'

As a government man he believed he had no other choice. As he would write on another occasion, his policy was that of 'strict and equal justice at all costs' and 'of courting neither the white nor the black party.' He wrote: 'Injustice to whites, English or Dutch, or to blacks, Kaffir, Hottentot or Bushman, I will still consider injustice and deal with accordingly.'[24] On another occasion he said: 'But I am not called upon to please either party [white colonists or blacks]. I have the cause of truth to serve. I am to call "murder murder" and "plunder plunder", whatever the color of the perpetrator's skin . . .'[25] Philip and his other guests found 'some reason' in this argument, but were skeptical whether the soil existed in which 'justice and moderation could be cultivated.'[26]

'I was not trusted': Piet Retief's grievance

One of the leading burghers, Piet Retief, had at an early stage challenged the view that all military operations, including commandos, had to operate under a strict set of rules. He was an atypical frontiersman. Born in 1782, the son of a wealthy wine farmer in the western Cape, Retief soon lost all his property in speculation, and arrived penniless on the frontier in 1811 as part of the reserve force in the Fourth Frontier War. Three years later a favorable marriage improved his financial situation but reckless speculation soon led to financial disaster. In the early 1820s he received twenty-four summonses for debt. Forced to sell all his possessions, he went back to farming, planting six thousand vines, but the enterprise failed. He obtained a license to sell liquor, but suppliers he had not paid soon brought suit against him.

This was the man who was appointed a field commandant in 1822 on a frontier still in turmoil. A key clause in his instructions was: 'No armed burgher or any part of the

23 Stockenstrom, *Autobiography*, vol. 2, p. 244.
24 Stockenstrom, *Autobiography*, vol. 2, pp. 8-12.
25 *Afrikaner Political Thought*, p. 169.
26 Stockenstrom, *Autobiography*, vol. 1, pp. 244-5.

Cavalry are on any consideration permitted to enter Gaika's [Ngqika's] territory.'[27] In March 1822 Retief lost four hundred sheep in a raid, and in September he was instructed to mobilize a commando to clear the neutral belt. Afterwards he reported that he had followed the tracks of stolen horses and cattle up to the border. Beyond it he saw thousands of cattle. As he put it: 'I was not permitted to cross over the border with my troops, as I was not trusted . . . As long as neither the Landdrost nor the Commandant of the Frontier is empowered to change it [the instruction not to cross the border] no commando will ever be carried out in this district with any success.' It was unacceptable to him to be a mere functionary of a distant government without having the discretion to act as necessary.

Retief believed that he could have retrieved the stolen cattle peacefully and punished the thieves.[28] By November he wrote again, this time directly to Governor Somerset, with a list of murders and thefts committed by Xhosa during the preceding five years in the divisions under his control. He wished to be permitted to cross the border, following the tracks of stolen cattle to Xhosa kraals. In writing to the governor, Retief had bypassed the landdrost as the chief official, clearly signaling that he thought he was in a better position to judge what kind of operation was needed.

Somewhat shocked, the governor wrote in the margin of Retief's letter that it was impossible to make him independent of the landdrost: 'There must be complete co-operation or nothing can be affected.'[29] For Stockenstrom order and peace were only possible if all officials and all burgher officers obeyed orders strictly. On this occasion Retief did not fall under Stockenstrom's authority, but the two would clash sharply in the mid-1830s over a similar issue.. By 1824 Retief's shady business ethics had led to his dismissal as field commandant, despite a strong letter of support from many farmers caught between a government unable to safeguard their property and unwilling to allow them to maintain themselves as they had in the old frontier days.

New curbs were being imposed on burghers defending their farms. Ordinance 9 of 1825 regulated the right of colonists to fire on persons suspected of being vagrants, deserters or escaped convicts. The Commissioners of Inquiry, who visited the colony from 1823-1825, expressed a fear of measures that could conceal the ruthless 'pursuit and capture of vagabond Hottentots, Slaves and Bushmen', and had led to the 'wanton destruction of them by the Boors [sic] and others.' In 1828 Attorney-General A. Oliphant wrote: 'In no case should deadly weapons be used until all other means have proved abortive . . . Patience and forbearance . . . surely ought always to be exercised when the life of a fellow creature is at stake.'[30] Commandos were now rarely allowed to go out on their own to track stolen cattle and, if they did, operated under severe restrictions.

It had become unclear what was permissible. For the burghers it was most unsettling to be kept in the dark, particularly after the abolition of the landdrost and heemraden in 1828. Apart from Stockenstrom, who was appointed in 1828 as commissioner-general

---

27 J.L.M. Franken, *Piet Retief se lewe in die Kolonie* (Pretoria: HAUM, 1949), p. 155.

28 Franken, *Retief*, pp. 141-59.

29 Franken, *Retief*, p. 155.

30 V.C. Malherbe, 'The Cape Khoisan in the Eastern Districts of the Colony before and after Ordinance 50 of 1828', doctoral diss., UCT, 1997, pp. 100, 188.

with vaguely defined functions, no Dutch- or Afrikaans-speaking colonist was in a position to influence frontier policy. Stockenstrom himself expressed concern that government policy had swung from great severity to 'sacrificing the safety of [His Majesty's] subjects' and 'paralyzing their efforts to defend their lives and property.'[31] In 1830 he noted that 'occasional examples of severity are indispensable to render the frontier at all habitable.'[32] He understood the bitterness among frontier farmers toward officials far away in Cape Town who claimed to know best how to handle frontier conflicts.

'Most clamorous against the Kafir nation': British merchants and speculators

The other major voice was that of British military officers on the frontier and, aligned to them, British merchants and speculators based mainly in Grahamstown. Their mouthpiece, the *Grahamstown Journal*, propagated colonial expansion into Xhosa territory and the complete subordination of the Xhosa with a large military presence, as well as increased military expenditure. To the merchants this held up the prospect of much greater profits in a lucrative trade in the smuggling of arms and in land speculation. The expansionist lobby constantly exaggerated the aggressive nature of the Xhosa and their culpability in the frontier unrest. In 1837, Governor Napier referred to the *Grahamstown Journal* and the merchant lobby in the town as those 'most clamorous against the Kafir nation.'[33] Retief's manifesto issued in 1838 to explain his departure from the colony, and the column by Robert Godlonton, editor of the *Grahamstown Journal*, were written in a similar tone.

The principal figure among the British military on the frontier was Colonel Henry Somerset, the governor's son, whose early clash with Stockenstrom, possibly over the 1820 British Settlers, had led to a serious conflict between Stockenstrom and the governor. In 1823, Henry Somerset became commandant of the frontier and the officer in charge of the Khoikhoi-manned Cape Regiment. Both Somerset and Stockenstrom focused their attention on Maqoma, Ngqika's eldest son, who bitterly resented leaving his home in the Kat River Valley in the neutral territory. Maqoma despised his father as a craven and vacillating coward who was all too often drunk. Early in 1821 Stockenstrom had reported that the advance guard of Maqoma's followers was re-occupying the upper Kat River Valley. Stockenstrom noted this development with concern, but the government turned a blind eye to it and gave out farms to burghers and settlers in the northern part of the neutral belt. The military posts were unable to stop raids, particularly by Maqoma, or counter-raids by burghers, sometimes by small, unauthorized commandos.

One of Colonel Somerset's first actions after becoming commandant was to lead a force of Khoikhoi troops and mounted burghers against Maqoma. They shot women and children, along with Maqoma's warriors, carried off seven thousand cattle, and distributed a quarter of them to colonists who had suffered losses. In 1828 two separate British-led forces struck at chiefdoms living far behind the border. In 1828 a force of burghers and soldiers led by a British landdrost, William Dundas, attacked what he de-

---

31 Stockenstrom, *Autobiography*, vol. 1, p. 150.
32 G.D.J. Duvenage, *Van die Tarka na die Transgariep* (Pretoria: Academica, 1981), p. 47.
33 Peires, *The House of Phalo*, p. 156.

scribed as the 'Fetcani' and brought back 25,000 head of cattle and a hundred people, who were then indentured. Later Colonel Somerset led a motley army of more than a thousand burghers, settlers and Khoikhoi mercenaries, backed up by thousands of African auxiliaries. Near the present town of Umtata in the Transkei, the army attacked Matiwane's Ngwane, who had fled from the Highveld. Somerset claimed that he was responding to a threat to the colonies from Shaka's armies. The sleeping enemy camp was hit with 'great guns and small guns, and sabres and assegais.' Howitzer fire killed more than four hundred Ngwane hidden in a forest. Somerset reported that his African auxiliaries slaughtered thousands and captured all their victims' stock. The colonial army returned with about one hundred women and children and indentured them to farms.[34]

Dundas and Somerset escaped censure and there was no recorded response from British missionaries or journalists, in stark contrast to the outcries that followed an atrocity committed by a burgher commando. Referring to these attacks on the 'Fetcani' or 'Ficane', one burgher remarked to Thomas Pringle, a Scottish settler: 'We were living in a state of bitter feud and constant warfare with the natives, and both parties were intent on mutual extermination. But what had your Ficani done when *they* were destroyed by wholesale slaughter by your British commanders? . . . Here we had a massacre in all its horrors . . . But all this, I hear, your English missionaries defend or wink at, because it was done by Englishmen in authority and does not tell against us unfortunate Boors [sic].'[35] The frontier burghers fiercely resented such double standards, and Retief would articulate their sentiments in his manifesto, which set out the causes of the emigration of burghers from the colony in the mid-1830s.

The burghers' overriding concern on the frontier was security; in pursuit of this they used methods considered both brutal and anarchical. Although the government tried to enforce humanitarian notions, it could not ensure security under the law, and allowed British commanders to inflict extensive violence on African peoples.

'A chain of sanguinary wars': Stockenstrom's fear

By the mid-1820s there was still no sign that the paths of Stockenstrom and Retief would cross in such a fateful way. In 1828 Retief was still living near Grahamstown, in the southeastern frontier zone, and by 1832 a farm in the Winterberg division in the central frontier zone had become his main residence. In Grahamstown he moved in the circles of Stockenstrom's enemies, particularly those of Colonel Somerset and the owner and staff of the *Grahamstown Journal*. Stockenstrom had moved from Graaff-Reinet early in 1828 to Grahamstown to assume the office of commissioner-general of the eastern province.

By the end of the 1820s there were three prominent areas in the frontier zone. The southeastern area included the Zuurveld and the town of Grahamstown; a central section lay between the Upper Fish and Koonap rivers and had been carved out of the neutral

---

34 The above paragraphs are based on Timothy J. Stapleton, *Maqoma: Xhosa Resistance to Colonial Advance* (Johannesburg: Jonathan Ball, 1994), pp. 19-63; Mostert, *Frontiers*, pp. 523-687.

35 Pringle, *Narrative of a Residence* (repr. Cape Town: Struik, 1966), p. 227.

territory; and the northeastern area was made up mostly of the large Tarka division that formed part of the Somerset district.

In the central section there was a stew of burgher grievances: uncertainty about land tenure, lack of protection against cattle raids, a prohibition of slave labor, and the presence of Maqoma, Tyhali, and several other Xhosa chiefs. An authoritative study of the origins of the Great Trek states: 'The entire movement of emigrating from the colony in what later became known as the Great Trek originated in the initiative and organizational ability of a small group of Afrikaner farmers in the central sector of the eastern frontier.'[36]

Burghers in the central sector of the frontier felt more insecure than others elsewhere. The government had given out farms to these burghers and settlers on condition that they kept no slaves, but in 1826 the imperial government decided to delay the transfer of land until it had made up its own mind about the future of the zone. The secretary of state for colonies in London did not hide his opinion that it would be better to settle English-speaking colonists there. The government ordered the burghers to leave the neutral territory, but most decided to sit tight. The area was becoming steadily more insecure with the influx of Mfecane refugees.

One of Stockenstrom's first actions in his new post was to impose policy more strictly. After Maqoma had raided cattle from the neighboring Thembu people, Stockenstrom and Somerset in 1829 expelled Maqoma from the neutral belt, to which he had such a strong historic claim. The loss of this land, one of the few well-watered spots in a period of severe droughts, became a slow burning fuse to him and his brother Tyhali.

The lands seized became the Kat River settlement for the Khoikhoi, Stockenstrom's idea. His first objective was to create a defensive barrier against invaders. The settlement would also provide the opportunity for the Khoikhoi to become small-scale farmers. Contrary to the wishes of the government, the residents claimed allegiance to the London Missionary Society and succeeded in getting as their minister James Read, who had long fought for equality for the Khoikhoi. Some five thousand people were living on the Kat River Settlement by the second half of the 1830s.

Rumors of the imminent transfer of burghers' land to Khoikhoi and English farmers were rampant. The Khoikhoi had been set up in one of the choicest spots of the neutral belt. To the burghers it seemed that their enemies were becoming more powerful every day. Some burghers lamented: 'The Englishman is very learned and we are very stupid. They and the Hottentots will squeeze us all out by degrees.'[37]

Stockenstrom also sought to bring stability to the frontier zone by addressing some of the worst excesses of the reprisal system. He gave instructions that farmers were to guard their cattle well, and tried to restrict attempts to recover stolen cattle. But he had lost faith in the patrols and the frequent commandos that kept the Xhosa in a constant state of alarm, marching at night and attacking at dawn, and firing at random. At a homestead they burned the huts, seized cattle and drove off the inhabitants. Most Xhosa living there, innocent or guilty, fled. Tyhali once asked: 'Shall I never have peace in my own country? Am I to be treated in this way, day after day?'[38]

36 Muller, *Oorsprong*, p. 383.
37 Stockenstrom, *Autobiography*, vol. 1, p. 391.
38 Peires, *House of Phalo*, p. 92.

Colonel Somerset considered Stockenstrom a colonial who did not know his proper place. He was determined to drive the Xhosa and other Bantu-speakers out of the neutral territory altogether. Sometimes patrols and commandos went out every week. Stockenstrom began to suspect that it was part of a sinister agenda to drive the Xhosa on the border to a desperate incursion into the colony, which could then be used as a pretext for a further colonial land grab. He wrote of people 'desiring a chain of sanguinary wars' that would cost vast amounts of money but which 'would popularize themselves by bringing enormous fortunes to some dozens of speculators and overwhelm headquarters with patronage.'[39]

Colonel Somerset appealed over Stockenstrom's head to the governor and continued his aggressive patrols. In 1833 Stockenstrom traveled to London to seek more power for his post, and resigned when it was denied. He decided to leave the Cape permanently for Sweden, the country of his father's birth. After his departure the government's frontier policy lost the little credibility it still had in the eyes both of the burghers and the Xhosa. The government did allow a few Xhosa chiefs to return and Maqoma came back, but was expelled yet again in 1833 to land he described as 'without a morsel of grass . . . as bare as a parade.'[40]

The ability of the frontier colonists to maintain themselves was further weakened by a new set of curbs on arms. Since the arrival in 1820 of British merchants, guns and gunpowder had been sold in increasing quantities to the Xhosa. The government attempted to end the supply of guns to the Xhosa and took steps in 1833 and 1834 to limit the supply of ammunition to the burghers in an attempt to curtail the lucrative contraband trade. These measures were also strictly applied to field cornets and field commandants, who were accustomed to buying supplies for the burghers in their divisions. After late 1835, gunpowder was available only in government stores. The burghers gained the impression that the government did not trust them enough to defend themselves.[41]

John Philip thought that the frontier conflict could be readily explained. When Sir Benjamin D'Urban arrived in January 1834 as the new governor, Philip submitted a memorandum putting most of the blame on 'the effect of the commandos and patrols as hitherto practiced' and on 'unscrupulous colonists and bad men [who] were attracted to the frontier by the opportunities of plunder.' Philip also suggested that policies be put in writing so 'that there might be an end to the fluctuations of frontier policy universally complained of.'[42]

The situation was steadily deteriorating. Thefts of colonists' cattle continued and so did the patrols. They harassed even those chiefs who were struggling to maintain peace. An English surveyor on the frontier noted in his journal: 'The year 1834 may be described as one of unremitting plunder. The patrols were constantly making seizures of the cattle belonging to the Caffres, and every month – almost every week – they were injuring and provoking that miserable people . . . [It] seems to be that it was the expressed object

---

39 Cited by Timothy Keegan, *Colonial South Africa and the Origins of the Racial Order* (Cape Town: David Philip, 1996), p. 137.
40 Peires, *House of Phalo,* p. 90.
41 Muller, *Oorsprong,* p. 194.
42 Macmillan, *Bantu, Boer and Briton,* p. 107.

of some persons in the colony about this time to provoke the Caffres to a war.'[43] Ma-qoma had also come to the conclusion that the cattle question was a pretext in a con-spiracy to grab more Xhosa land. Bhotomane, one of the senior chiefs in the neutral belt, expressed his own outrage: 'Our people have stolen your cattle, but you have by the man-ner by which you have refunded your loss punished the innocent, and after having taken our country from us without even a show of justice, and shut us up to starvation, you threaten us with destruction for the thefts of those you left no choice but to steal or die of famine.'[44]

Patrols had even killed Xhosa chiefs. In Xhosa custom the life of a chief was never threatened in war. A travel account published in 1833 reported that Hintsa, the Xhosa paramount chief, was 'greatly unhinged' by the fact that patrols also targeted chiefs. 'The circumstances of a *chief* having been taken *captive* seemed to arouse the ire of the na-tion, and everyone is enraged while speaking about it.'[45] The chiefs believed that their very existence was threatened, and listened to Maqoma's warning that what was hap-pening was but the 'prelude to other measures, which would not only endanger their independence but lead to a complete subjugation of their country.'[46]

The whites, for the most part, were oblivious to the smoldering fire. They did not see that the harassment of all the Xhosa in the neutral belt had forged a common will to resist, and that even the cautious paramount, Hintsa, living beyond the Kei River, had identified with their plight. Even Stockenstrom, so keenly aware of the damage done by the patrols and commandos, said that there was nothing to fear from the Xhosa as a na-tion: 'All danger of a general hostility is out of the question.' A British settler wrote: 'The Caffres are afraid . . . of the English, so that there is but little danger of them.'[47] As a consequence, only 755 men were stationed on the frontier by the mid-1830s, and the supply of ammunition in Grahamstown was at its lowest level ever when the most devastating frontier war of all broke out.

The Sixth Frontier War

In the final days of 1834, Maqoma and Tyhali attacked with a force of twelve to fifteen thousand Xhosa after consulting with Hintsa. After at least five frontier wars the Xhosa had learned to fight the whites effectively. Instead of massing in a single body or two to be decimated by the guns of their enemies (as the Zulu would be in December 1838 when they attacked the Voortrekkers), they attacked in numerous small detachments. A burgher described an attack on his farm: 'Around eight o'clock in the evening the dogs begin to bark. Suddenly the Caffres storm the house. They whistle and shout and from all sides shoot and throw assegais. Stones hit the roof almost like rain. The sheep bleat, the cattle bellow, the enemy . . . storms, trying to get in. A Caffre is shot dead on entry with a broken assegai in his hand. The din is terrible.'[48]

44 Mostert, *Frontiers*, p. 644.
45 Peires, *House of Phalo*, p. 93 (italics in the original).
46 Peires, *House of Phalo*, p. 91.
47 Mostert, *Frontiers*, p. 649.
48 P.P.J. Coetser, *Gebeurtenisse uit de Kaffer-oorloge* (1889, repr. Cape Town: Struik, 1963) p. 7.

Bypassing the soldiers stationed on the frontier, the invaders carried off masses of livestock and inflicted great damage in a broad swath from Algoa Bay to Somerset. It was reported that 'seven thousand of His Majesty's subjects were in one week driven to utter destitution.'[49] From his own Kat River station James Read noted after the first week: 'The Boors to the north and the south have been plundered almost to a beast . . . The Boors will be left in utter destitution and want.'[50] There were several reported instances of Khoikhoi and Xhosa servants helping their masters or their children to safety. An Afrikaans poem 'Amakaia' tells the story of a faithful Xhosa servant killed while trying to protect a white infant entrusted to her by her slain mistress. It is not thought to be based on a real event since the Xhosa did not normally kill women or children in war.[51] Twenty whites and about eighty Khoikhoi were killed, 455 homesteads were burned and many thousands of horses, cattle and sheep were carried off. Colonial losses were set at £300,000. The Xhosa once again occupied the Zuurveld.

The invasion struck English and Afrikaner colonists alike. Military reinforcements and, eventually, Governor D'Urban also arrived. D'Urban listened most sympathetically to the settlers. He believed that Philip and other critics had grievously misrepresented the farmers and that the Xhosa were 'savage and irreclaimable.' He accepted the policy proposed by some British settlers: bold expansion into the lands of the Xhosa and opening up the area to land speculation and white settlement.[52]

In a counter-attack the colonial forces of British soldiers, Khoikhoi troops, British settlers and burgher commandos pushed ahead well beyond the Kei River. Hintsa, believed to be behind the invasion, was captured. As he tried to escape, an English officer killed him, and his body was mutilated. The colonial force also tried to destroy the Xhosa resource base by burning crops, destroying huts and seizing cattle. Many Xhosa were driven over the Kei, but as many remained in the old neutral belt. The war left a bitter harvest. The Xhosa were not defeated, nor did they accept the white man's new border. Indeed, Tyhali, Maqoma's brother, demanded the return of all the land east of the Fish River. The war embittered relations between whites and blacks.

In 1835 Governor D'Urban extended the eastern border of the colony to the Kei River and the source of the Wit Kei in the Stormberg, with the newly acquired territory designated as the Province of Queen Adelaide. This raised strong hopes among the burghers that a large tract of new land would become available. But a select parliamentary committee in London was hearing evidence from Philip and other missionaries on the treatment of indigenous peoples. Philip had become one of the main sources of information to the imperial government, cutting much of the ground from underneath D'Urban's feet.

A key witness was Stockenstrom, who had traveled from Sweden to London to testify. He blamed much of the violence on the reprisal system and on the compensation exacted from the Xhosa for cattle theft. Many of these actions, he said, were based on fraudulent claims and on a desire to grab more land from the Xhosa. He proposed a treaty system to settle conflicts in the place of the old military solutions.

---

49 Eric A. Walker, *A History of Southern Africa* (London: Longman, 1957), pp. 184-8.
50 Basil le Cordeur and Christopher Saunders (eds.), *The Kitchingman Papers* (Johannesburg: Brenthurst Press, 1976), pp. 147-9.
51 Mostert, *Frontiers*, p. 670.
52 Keegan, *Colonial South Africa*, pp. 142-4.

On 26 December 1835 the colonial secretary in the imperial government, Lord Glenelg, reversed D'Urban's decisions. The colonists had expected the Xhosa to be forced to pay for making war, but Glenelg declared that the Xhosa had been driven 'by a long series of acts of injustice and spoliation' and had 'ample justification' for invading the colony. He announced that the Province of Queen Adelaide was to be abandoned and the colonial boundary moved back from the Kei to the Keiskamma, Tyhume and Gaga rivers, with colonial control over the area between the Fish and the Keiskamma (the neutral territory). The chiefs had to abandon all claims to this land, but the government was prepared to 'lend' this region to chiefs and their subjects on condition of good behavior.[53]

Glenelg asked a surprised Stockenstrom to return to the Cape as lieutenant governor. Not long before, Stockenstrom had written a letter about the hostility displayed toward him by Philip, who had accused him of killing Bushmen to dispose of their children. He noted grimly: 'Thank God, I have nothing more to do with these Cape and Kaffir affairs' and referred to his motherland as 'that devoted, that doomed Colony.' Yet now he was being asked to implement the treaty system he had long advocated. He decided to accept the challenge.[54]

When, in early September 1836, Stockenstrom arrived in Grahamstown, he found many burghers already leaving the colony or preparing to leave. A mass emigration of frontier farmers was well under way. For Stockenstrom, this emigration was a huge setback to his plans for a more orderly form of colonization, which he saw as essential for Afrikaner survival.

Causes of a Great Trek

Two streams of white emigrants left the colony in the second quarter of the nineteenth century. The first was an emigration of people called trekboers; the others would later be called Voortrekkers, and their movement out of the colony the Great Trek. While the Voortrekkers emphasized political issues, the trekboers, who had been crossing the colonial boundaries since the mid-1820s, were concerned about the lack of sufficient pastures. The trekboer expansion, like the one of the eighteenth century, occurred on the basis of individual burghers or single families slowly moving beyond the limits of white settlement to improve their material prospects. By contrast, the Voortrekkers were in trek parties, very often groups of families intending to move far away.

The Great Trek was in fact a bold and dramatic response to a survival crisis that had engulfed the eastern and northeastern districts of the Cape Colony from the mid-1820s to the end of the 1830s. It was not so much 'running away', the term Stockenstrom had used in the 1825 debate with Philip, as an abrupt, yet fairly orderly, mass rebellion against a breakdown of security that the participants considered intolerable.

The Great Trek had diverse causes. In brief, they can be summarized as a lack of land, labor and security, coupled with a pervasive sense of being marginalized. A shortage of land had long been acute, and the situation had steadily worsened between 1812 and

---

53 J.S. Bergh and J.C. Visagie, *The Eastern Cape Frontier Zone* (Durban: Butterworths, 1985), pp. 44-7.
54 See his account in Stockenstrom, *Autobiography*, vol. 2, pp. 94-129.

the mid-1830s. The burghers felt increasingly hemmed in. By 1812 only two-fifths of the married burghers in the district of Graaff-Reinet had land of their own, and with the steady growth of the burgher population and with further expansion blocked, the land shortage became ever more acute. In 1813 the British abolished the familiar loan farm system, and introduced a system of perpetual quitrent tenure. All farms had to be properly surveyed and farmers had to pay the cost of this before they could get a title deed. The quitrent varied from farm to farm and was appreciably higher than the *recognitie* paid earlier.

Compounding the problem was the long delay in the issue of title deeds, many still outstanding ten or twenty years after the farmers had had their land surveyed and had paid the survey fees. Hundreds of farms, in 1834, were found to have been wrongly surveyed. A surveyor appointed to investigate the issue located no surveys and no inspection reports, only the receipts for fees the farmers had paid, and concluded that certain surveyors had pocketed the money.[55]

As early as the 1820s the burghers' hope for crown land that could be acquired cheaply had all but vanished. Stockenstrom and other officials in the eastern districts reported that there was no more crown land available, and, in 1832, the door was finally shut. The governor returned land applications with the note that it could no longer issue land.[56] The market price of established farms rose sharply.

Stockenstrom was convinced that as long as the way of life of the farmers on the frontier depended on continuing expansion rather than better usage, they would continue to covet the native peoples' land. The only hope of ending the conflict over land was for the government to stamp out all hope of further expansion, thus forcing the more efficient farmers into more intensive farming by reducing herds, improving yields, making provision for artificial pasture and conserving the land. Inefficient farmers would be forced to enter the service of other farmers or move to the towns in search of work.

Stockenstrom had formulated the problem in this way: 'Every stretch of emigration throws the mass of the borders back in point of improvement . . . [However] unpalatable I know the theory to be to my countrymen, I think it would not be unfortunate for the colony if the present distress of the graziers were to throw numbers out of that line of life into more active ones, which we cannot expect to take place as long as a hope of the extension of the boundary exists.'[57]

But the farmers did not adapt as Stockenstrom wished. Capital for investment was scarce, and investment opportunities did not yield a high return because the markets were too small. Equipment like windmills and wire fences would not become available until the second half of the nineteenth century, and there were no extension officers to teach farmers modern methods. A risk-taking mentality and, before the advent of wool, the incentive to take risks were slow to develop. People considered leaving the colony because they wished to obtain abundant land to practice subsistence farming along tra-

---

55 J.C. Visagie, 'Willem Fredrik Hertzog', *AYB*, 1980, pp. 89-108.

56 Duvenage, *Van die Tarka na die Transgariep*, pp. 92-3.

57 Hermann Giliomee, 'Processes in the Development of the South African Frontier', in Howard Lamar and Leonard Thompson (eds.), *The Frontier in History: North America and South Africa Compared* (New Haven: Yale University Press, 1981), p. 98.

ditional lines. The overriding reason for the unwillingness to adapt was the seemingly abundant free land beyond the colonial borders. By the mid-1820s migrant farmers in the north and northeast were already expanding beyond the border, and severe droughts spurred them on. Initially they made humble requests to cross the border only as a temporary relief measure. The landdrosts issued temporary permits to pasture livestock north of the Orange River in the present Free State province, provided they did not cultivate the soil or put up buildings.

But, by the end of the 1820s, these trekboers were no longer asking permission, and simply informing the authorities in Graaff-Reinet that they were crossing the boundary. By 1830 many trekboers had sold their farms and were on the other side of the border.[58] The policy of preventing permanent expansion beyond the border had been breached. Those who lived in the southeastern part of the frontier undoubtedly took note of this, as well as of the fact that the government lacked the resources to force them to return. The government's abandonment of the Province of Queen Adelaide was the last straw for many land-hungry frontiersmen.

Labor had long been a critical issue. The farms were large and homesteads were six or seven kilometers apart, with neither fences nor a police force to protect them and stave off the many hungry Xhosa or Khoisan people in the vicinity. Yet many farmers did not pay their servants well. Dr John Philip believed that the farmers would attract labor if they were prepared to pay good cash wages, but Afrikaner colonists were much slower than their British counterparts to switch to commercial farming and cash wages. Wealthier Afrikaner farmers hoped to retain laborers by displaying a benign paternalism, particularly by allowing servants to keep some stock, though the growing pressure on the land meant that few farmers could provide them with enough land for their own stock.

Ordinance 50 of 1828 freed the Khoikhoi from all the curbs on their movement, and they began moving away in large numbers from the farms. An observer who described the scene on the frontier, wrote: 'I have myself known farms which had been completely abandoned by the last remaining Hottentots having given up service or retired to the missionary schools, taking with them the flocks or herds which they have earned in their employer's service and rejecting every offer or bribe to continue any longer in such service.'[59] The Khoisan who left settled either on missionary stations or squatted on crown land or on the outskirts of towns. Until the mid-1840s there were numerous complaints about the difficulties of finding herdsmen. In 1842 a senior British officer commented: 'It is idle to say why do the farmers not properly guard their cattle, the thing I say is impossible in this country where servants are not to be had.'[60] Soon afterwards Xhosa people became the principal labor force on farms.

The trek was also very much a case of common people being inspired or swept along by strong, patriarchal leaders with their own reasons for emigrating. Louis Tregardt, often called the first Voortrekker, was a successful farmer and owner of some skilled slaves.

---

58 P. J. van der Merwe, *Die noordwaartse beweging van die Boere voor die Groot Trek, 1770-1842* (The Hague: W.P. van Stockum, 1937), pp. 205-40, 312-50.

59 Henry Cloete, *Five Lectures on the Emigration of the Dutch Farmers* (Pietermaritzburg: Paul Solomon, 1856), pp. 33-4.

60 Peires, *The House of Phalo*, pp. 120-21.

He became disaffected by the government's refusal to grant him tenure of a farm in the neutral territory as long as he remained a slave-owner. Determined to ignore the emancipation proclamation, he took his ten slaves with him into the interior.[61] Gert Maritz, another slave-holding Voortrekker leader, suffered a loss of nearly £1,000 through emancipation.

But the large slave-holders could not have rallied support for the trek simply by denouncing emancipation. Tregardt owned ten slaves but the other twenty-nine families in his trek had only five slaves among them. Only one-fifth of the colony's slaves were in the districts from which the greatest number of Voortrekkers came.[62] Still, the loss of patriarchal authority over slaves or servants had strongly affected the lives of the leaders of the emigrants. Ordinance 50 of 1828 proscribed the punishment of Khoisan laborers by masters. On 1 December 1834 the right to punish slaves, now called apprentices, was also abolished. Laborers, particularly slave apprentices after 1834, felt free to take their masters or mistresses to court. Several Voortrekker leaders had had brushes with the law about punishing their slaves or servants. In 1825 Retief was accused of maltreating two of his slaves (the court found no grounds for action). Just before Hendrik Potgieter left the colony in 1835, he had to appear in court on a charge by one of his slaves that his master made him work at night. Potgieter claimed that the slave could not do his work by day because at night he was 'playing the fiddle and having dancing parties.'[63] The court rejected the slave's complaint.

Another trek leader, Piet Uys, became interested in trekking as a means of bringing the Gospel to Africans in the deep interior. He did not become politically disaffected until after the arrest of his wife on charges he considered malicious, brought by an indentured slave. When he reached the Orange River on his trek, he wrote about the causes of the emigration. The people, he noted, had asked for a vagrancy law but it was refused; they had asked for *huijs reg* [literally 'domestic rights', meaning the right to punish someone in one's household], but this was also refused.[64] By removing themselves from the colony the trekkers could reassert their old paternalist order. Indeed, the Voortrekkers and trekboers were able to persuade many servants or ex-slaves to go with them.

Another central reason for the trek was the insecurity on the frontier itself. In Tarka and other parts of the northeastern border, Bushmen bands had been stealing cattle; by 1832 large numbers of 'Mantatees', fleeing from enemies beyond the border, entered this frontier zone; but their large numbers soon became a nuisance to farmers as they roamed from farm to farm in search of food. In the central and southeastern sectors of the boundary, wandering parties moved across the frontier, stealing or begging for food.

The thefts by the refugees from the turmoil on the Highveld were often committed out of desperation. Thefts by Xhosa living in the neutral territory were a more complex matter. Several Xhosa tribes had been driven back over the Zuurveld in 1811 and 1812 and remained on sufferance in the neutral territory where congestion was becoming acute. Some Xhosa stole cattle because they resented the loss of their land; others were

61 J.C. Visagie, *Die trek uit Oos-Rietrivier* (Stellenbosch: privately published: 1989), pp. 106-32.
62 Muller, *Oorspong*, pp. 311-70.
63 Muller, *Oorsprong*, p. 371.
64 Jan Visagie, 'Die Katriviernedersetting, 1829-1839', doctoral diss., Unisa, 1978, p. 323.

angered by the reprisal system and yet others were driven by the very ease with which the cattle on farms could be stolen.

In 1828 the government introduced Ordinance 49 in an attempt to bring blacks roaming about in the frontier zone under control and transform some into farm laborers. Government agents could issue passes for short periods; those who wished to stay longer to work had to negotiate a contract. In reality the government was unable to control the influx.[65] Most frontier burghers did not know how to cope with vagrancy and constant cattle theft; many had experienced heavy losses of flocks and herds and some were afraid for their lives.

Lack of security had been part of the frontier experience ever since the 1770s, but had become particularly acute by the late 1820s. All the cattle belonging to Gert Maritz' father were stolen during the Third Frontier War (1799-1802). In the Sixth Frontier War (1834-1835) Maritz' brother suffered near-fatal stab wounds, and Maritz rode to Grahamstown to bring him back to Graaff-Reinet. Piet Retief lost all his livestock in the war and his farm was sacked.

The lack of government authority was worst in the Tarka area on the northeastern part of the frontier, from where one-third of the Voortrekkers would come. After the frontier war of 1818 to 1819, the government had concentrated its few resources elsewhere. Virtually nothing was spent on the administration of the northeastern district of Somerset, covering an area of more than 17,000 square miles (44,200 square kilometers). A justice of the peace stationed at the town of Cradock, assisted by a single constable, had to maintain order. With the increase, after 1825, of complaints against masters, the inadequate administrative structure also became a major issue. Most people had to travel two or three days to the drostdy to lay a complaint or appear before a court to give evidence or to answer a summons.

Consequently many burghers preferred not to file complaints, but submitted instead to the most serious grievances and annoyances. A burgher remarked: 'The protection of the Law is known only by name', and Governor D'Urban declared bluntly that the magistracy of Somerset was 'little better than a dead letter.'[66] Responding to Stockenstrom's remark that they intended to leave the colony in order to lead a lawless existence, some of the prospective Voortrekkers in the northeastern divisions replied: 'It is the contrary, we leave the Colony because we know of neither Government nor Law – of the Government we know nothing except when we have money to pay and the law never reaches us except to fine or otherwise punish, often for acts we did not know to be wrong. Our Field Cornets can give us no assistance, as they are as much in the darkness as ourselves. We are like lost sheep.'[67]

The Sixth Frontier War (1834-1835) was a profound shock to all the frontier colonists. They had believed a Xhosa invasion impossible. Their hope that the colony's counterattack would bring stability was soon dashed; a few months after the end of the war, marauding bands were again squatting on land, plundering and stealing cattle. An English-speaker wrote in April 1836 from the Lower Fish River that the Afrikaner farmers had

---

65 Jeffrey Peires, 'The British and the Cape, 1814-1834', in *SSAS*, p. 486.
66 Duvenage, *Tarka na die Transgariep*, pp. 27, 42.
67 *Afrikaner Political Thought*, p. 298.

little hope for the future, adding: 'One said that in his father's life time and his own they had been five times clean swept out by the Kaffirs . . . that for protection the future would be like the past, indeed he thought they were worse off than fifty years ago; in those old times when they were robbed they redressed themselves, but now their hands were tied while the Kaffirs were loose.'[68] In September 1836 a well-educated English farmer reported from Fort Beaufort, some hundred kilometers from the sea: 'The principal grievance of the Farmers in my Neighborhood', he wrote, 'is . . . their having to support such incredible numbers of Hottentots, Bechuanas and Fingoes that daily vagabondize the Country, and I do myself declare that at no period within the past fifteen years have I ever seen them in such numbers as they are at present . . . ten or fifteen idle vagabonds in a day.'[69]

The entire frontier zone had become unsettled. G. Jarvis, a British officer, reported 'an extraordinary feeling of panic.' People were jumpy and preparing to move immediately. After the dispatch of Glenelg they felt that the imperial government would be indifferent to the 'total ruin or annihilation of the white people.' One observer thought the main motivation of the women who wanted to trek was the government's inability to provide protection.[70]

Regarded as 'a subject and inferior race': political marginalization

Lack of land, labor and security were serious sources of discontent. Yet by themselves they are not enough to explain why not only landless people left the colony but also fairly wealthy farmers, who sold their farms cheaply. Many departed before they had received compensation for their freed slaves, or for the stores they had supplied to the armed forces, or for the losses sustained in the war. Stockenstrom noted that the burghers told him that they no longer felt at home in their own country.[71] Another source commenting on the sense of marginalization was Olive Schreiner, an early feminist writer and a person with strong liberal convictions. As a governess in the frontier districts of Colesburg and Cradock between 1874 and 1881, she knew the people and the stories they told well. Referring to the losses the people suffered in being poorly compensated for their slaves, she remarked: 'But that which most embittered the hearts of the colonists was the cold indifference with which they were treated, and the consciousness that they were regarded as a subject and inferior race . . . [The] feeling of bitterness became so intense that about the year 1836 large numbers of individuals determined to leave for ever the Colony and the homes which they had created.'[72]

The frontier burghers had suffered from an extraordinarily bad English press, starting with the accounts of John Barrow at the turn of the century and culminating in the reports and book by John Philip, singling out the burghers for condemnation for the brutalities committed on the frontier. They saw little hope of ever being considered as

68 Muller, *Oorsprong*, p. 193.
69 Muller, *Oorsprong*, p. 190.
70 Muller, *Oorsprong*, p. 195.
71 Mostert, *Frontiers*, p. 592.
72 Olive Schreiner, *Thoughts on South Africa* (Johannesburg: Ad Donker, 1992), p. 205.

anything but the white outcasts of the British Empire. The magazine *The Spectator* wrote on 17 March 1834, some nine months before the outbreak of the war: 'The maltreatment of the aborigines is one of the darkest and bloodiest stains in the pages of history and scarcely any is equal in atrocity to the conduct of the Dutch Boers.' After the war the condemnation was even worse.

The real issue was the burghers' feeling that they had been marginalized and disempowered where they lived. The behavior of Hendrik Potgieter of the northeastern division of Tarka in Somerset district makes the point. With Piet Retief, Andries Pretorius and Gert Maritz, Potgieter was the most important Voortrekker leader, an affluent farmer and slave-owner, with good economic prospects. Apart from the complaint his servant had filed against him he lacked a title deed. He had had his land surveyed shortly after the new land legislation of 1813, but had no title deed now, twenty-two year later. When he left the colony, at the end of 1835, he had not yet been paid compensation for his slaves or for the supplies he and his brother had provided for the burger commando in the frontier war of 1834 to 1835. (Payment for the supplies was issued a full two years after the war ended.)

Potgieter left no extensive explanation for his emigration, but from what he said it is clear that he found it impossible to live any longer under what he regarded as the yoke of an alien and bungling government. 'We left the colony,' he wrote to the governor in December 1838, 'not only because of your Excellency's laws but especially because it was impossible to survive and to provide for our wives and children.' He added: '[We] do not intend to do anything illegal and we consider ourselves as free burghers who can go where we wish without disadvantaging someone else, since all nations are free and can go where they wish.' Three years later he wrote: 'I do not wish to submit myself to any British or any other power in the world, and I am not British, and I hope and trust never to become that.'[73] Andries Pretorius expressed himself in similar terms in 1838 just before he departed to assume the leadership of the trekkers in Natal. He wrote to the Rev. G.W.A. van der Lingen of Paarl, whom he called 'a true Afrikaner', that the trekkers 'presently wandering around will still become a volk and live in His honor.'[74]

Here was a manifestation of the kind of political consciousness that had been absent in the 1820s. This sense of marginalization and disaffection developed within the context of a government that introduced a social revolution at the same time as removing virtually all the local government institutions with which the burghers had identified. There were no longer burghers serving as heemraden to advise landdrosts, and the function of burghers serving as field cornets had been sharply reduced.

The burghers had come to feel like foreigners in their own land. Stockenstrom described their feelings: 'Now we have a Civil Commissioner to receive our money for Government and for Land Surveyors, a Magistrate to punish us, a clerk of Peace to prosecute us and get us in the *Tronk* [prison], but no Heemraad to tell us whether things are right or wrong.'[75] Although the British government had long abolished burgher status, along with the other status distinctions of the Company period, the burghers clung to it

---

73 Muller, *Oorsprong*, pp. 370-77; Duvenage, *Tarka na die Transgariep*, pp. 140-53.
74 M.C. Kitshoff, *G.W.A. van der Lingen, 1804-1869* (Groningen: V.R.B., 1972), p. 63.
75 Stockenstrom, *Autobiography*, vol. 1, p. 93.

as part of their social identity. In their eyes the status of a burgher was distinct from that of a subject. As burghers they produced most of the food, paid a large part of the taxes, served as field cornets without whom local government would collapse, and fought in the commandos that were indispensable to the colony's defense. When they fought under proper command, with clearly defined objectives, they performed well. Stockenström would declare in later years that when it came to war, 'nothing can be better devised than the old system of Field Commandants and Field Cornets to command the Burghers acting under military orders.'[76]

Despite the burghers' importance as food producers, some British officials and officers treated them as mere underlings. The burghers' feelings of violated dignity came to a head in the Sixth Frontier War when commandos under their own officers fought in the colonial force led by Colonel Harry Smith. D'Urban described them as 'the best troops of their kind I have seen.'[77] Yet although the British force was far too weak to operate without their assistance, they were subjected to humiliating conditions. Forced to take only a minimum of wagons along, many spent five months in the open veld. The government did not pay them, nor did they receive part of the cattle booty as in bygone times. They could not even claim their own cattle from the recovered stock (it was sold at an auction and the proceeds used to compensate all those who had suffered losses). Since their horses had been requisitioned, many had to walk long distances to get home. It was a degrading affair that affronted their sense of dignity and civic self-worth.

After the war the government announced plans to enroll burghers as a militia to provide a modernized form of frontier defense. This only worsened their morale. The Boers feared that they would suffer the same humiliating experience as in the war.[78] Fears that dated back to the Company era, of being taken back into government service as sailors or soldiers, were rekindled. An impetuous Colonel Harry Smith contributed to this fear. When he disbanded the commandos after the 1834-35 war he told the burghers that they held their lands in this Colony 'only on condition of serving the Government when called upon.' (This was the condition under Company rule.) Smith suggested that they were indeed 'very lucky' to get away on such 'easy terms', by which he hinted that he considered their military duties fairly light.[79]

Stockenstrom probably had Smith in mind when he expressed anger about the 'designing miscreants' who had revived 'the old stupid suspicion that the British Government intends by degrees to make Soldiers and Sailors of the redundant male population.' A Voortrekker told an observer of their fear that their children would be taken for soldiers and sent to foreign countries. Even as late as 1848 officials ascribed the burghers' opposition to the government's intentions to call them up regularly for service in a burgher militia to a 'dislike to be considered other than as free burghers.'[80]

An often-quoted expression of outrage came from Anna Steenkamp, a niece of Piet Retief. In 1843, several years after she had left the colony, she gave a brief account of the

---

76 J.C. Visagie, 'Verset teen die Burgermilisieplan', *Historia*, 38, 2 (1993), p. 82.
77 Duvenage, *Tarka na die Transgariep*, p. 77.
78 Visagie, 'Verset teen die Burgermilisieplan', pp. 77-85.
79 Visagie, 'Die Katriviernedersetting', p. 285.
80 Visagie, 'Verset teen die Burgermilisieplan', pp. 83-4.

causes of the trek. Her principal objection was that slaves had been 'placed on an equal footing with Christians, contrary to the laws of God, and the natural distinction of race and religion . . . wherefore we rather withdraw in order to preserve our doctrines in purity.' Steenkamp was probably referring to cases of slaves' complaints against their masters and their being permitted to give testimony against them in court.[81]

On the frontier it was not so much a *racial* hierarchy that the burghers wanted to preserve; but rather their fight was against the *gelykstelling* or social leveling of people belonging to different status groups – master and servant; people born into the Christian community and those the missionaries had converted; and finally – and perhaps most important – burghers who farmed and defended the land and non-burghers. J.N. Boshoff, a colonial Afrikaner serving as a government official in Graaff-Reinet, later called gelykstelling in the church a secondary cause of the trek. In the early stages of settlement on the frontier, Communion was administered separately to slaves, free blacks, Basters and Khoikhoi. After the synod of 1829 this practice was prohibited. Boshoff wrote that the trekkers were aggrieved that 'blacks were encouraged to consider themselves on an equal footing with the whites in their religious exercises in the church though the former are heathens and no members of such community.'[82]

The greatest discontent was aroused when burghers were compelled to appear in court after they had taken action against black vagrants or thieves. 'There are no rights for burghers any more, but only for blacks,' a distressed field cornet exclaimed. He had been summoned to court after he had acted against 'insolent' Khoikhoi who had refused to leave a farm. A more specific ethnic identity was only hesitantly articulated, but there were hints: thus Field Cornet Carel Buchner reported in 1837 from the Zuurveld: 'The unbridled conduct of the Blacks around here goes against the marrow of the Africanders and that and nothing else is the cause of the emigration.'[83]

The frontier burghers' distrust and resentment also focused on the missionaries of the London Missionary Society. Philip, for example, had talks with some of the principal Xhosa chiefs in the neutral belt just before the outbreak of the war. He and his son-in-law, John Fairbairn, the liberal editor of the *Commercial Advertiser*, had long criticized frontier policy, with special emphasis on the damage wreaked by the commandos. The burghers knew that it was Philip who almost single-handedly prevented the passing of a Vagrancy Act in 1834. They suspected the LMS missionary James Read, who lived on the Kat River Settlement, of conniving with the invading Xhosa force; an unfounded suspicion, but the attack was so unexpected that a scapegoat had to be found.

Then came Glenelg's reversal of D'Urban's annexation of the Province of Queen Adelaide, for many the final straw. Both D'Urban and Stockenstrom were in London when it happened. Stockenstrom was likely to have been the stronger influence on Glenelg. Yet the burghers, unlike the settlers, did not seem to blame Stockenstrom, their fellow Afrikaner. In their eyes it was Philip and other ill-disposed LMS servants who had blackened their name in the world, who had constantly held up the Xhosa and the Khoikhoi as more deserving than they. Stockenstrom himself thought it unjust of Philip to single

---

81 *Cape Monthly Magazine*, September 1876.
82 Muller, *Oorsprong*, p. 205.
83 Muller, *Oorsprong*, pp. 207-8.

out the burghers for everything that went wrong on the frontier. In his manifesto Piet Retief obviously had Philip and other missioinaries in mind when he wrote of 'dishonest persons who were believed to the exclusion of all evidence in our favor.' As a result of this 'prejudice' he foresaw nothing but 'the total ruin of the country.'[84]

The Great Trek was not an impulsive move; it was preceded by a careful examination of the prospects in the deep interior. During the early 1830s three reconnaissance parties, called 'commission treks', went out to investigate the options for those wishing to emigrate. One went to Damaraland in the present Namibia, another to the present Mafikeng and Gaborone, and the third to Natal. The third commission trek returned with glowing reports of a most fertile land with abundant pastures. As a result of the *Mfecane*, many areas were sparsely populated or seemingly devoid of people. On their return, the members of the commission treks planted or nourished the idea of emigration.

The implications of the *Mfecane* for the Afrikaner trekkers who moved into the deep interior in the late 1830s and the 1840s were profound. It did make the Voortrekkers' task of settling in the deep interior much easier because large areas were temporarily depopulated. Desirable land seemed to be there for the taking. But some of the greatly strengthened African polities, particularly the Zulu and Swazi states, would offer much tougher resistance than they would have done fifty or sixty years earlier.

Survival on the frontier: Stockenstrom versus Retief

The first Voortrekkers departed late in 1835 and early in 1836. In September 1836 a large party under Gert Maritz left from Graaff-Reinet. But by the end of that year no comprehensive justification had yet been offered for the trek. As late as October 1836, Piet Retief was still trying to persuade people in his division not to trek. An account of his final six months in the colony, specifically his relationship with Stockenstrom, provides a glimpse of the critical alternatives for collective survival, as spelled out by these two major figures.

The protagonists were strikingly different. On the one hand, there was Stockenstrom, undiplomatic and prickly when challenged, and cold and aloof to the point of haughtiness. He could go on at great length defending slights to his ego and justifying every step he had taken. At the same time he warmly identified with law-abiding burghers and rushed to their defense when outsiders condemned them too easily. As an administrator he was conscientious, principled, and totally committed to his task. Then there was Retief: warm, affable, and charismatic despite his crippling debts and repeated business failures, extraordinarily popular among townspeople and farmers, burghers, and British settlers alike. During the invasion of the Xhosa force Retief, along with his stepsons, had played a sterling role in defending his division. He drew together a large group of Winterberg people, which included more than two hundred women and children. It was virtually the only place where a stand was made during the invasion. The curbs on the supply of ammunition nearly cost them their lives. Retief believed that if the attacks had continued much longer the laager would have been overrun. A week after

---

84 *Afrikaner Political Thought*, p. 214.

the attacks had begun, he was appointed provisional field-commandant. When the governor later confirmed this, he referred to Retief's 'excellent character', and his 'active and judicious conduct.'[85]

Retief was now again in serious financial trouble. In the year before the war he had spent a short time in the debtors' prison, and went bankrupt. In the war he and his family suffered serious losses. His house was burned down, and the Xhosa carried away forty-eight head of his cattle, four horses and three hundred sheep. He noted that he had 'lost everything.' Retief would receive letters from creditors until his last days in the colony, including one from the owner of the Freemasons' tavern, for 'spirits and other liquors sold . . . and for lodging and other entertainment.'[86]

Stockenstrom assumed office in Grahamstown on 3 September 1836 in an atmosphere of crisis and confusion. On his way there, the Graaff-Reinet and Cradock burghers had received him warmly and had outlined their grievances soberly in a document. Grahamstown itself was hostile; the expansionists among the British settlers had long considered Stockenstrom their main enemy. They presented a disrespectful address, referring to his evidence in London, which he refused to accept. A letter came from Field Commandant S.J. van Wijk, who was greatly respected by the burghers, urging him to stem the emigration. Another, by a British settler, said that Stockenstrom would stop a number of people from trekking if he would address the burghers' grievances. There was also a message that Retief wanted an interview.

Stockenstrom had a clear mind as to what kind of frontier policy could stabilize the frontier. The highest priority was to give people on both sides of the frontier a sense of security and stability. 'To enable the neighboring tribes to leave us in peace our people must positively remain within the limits of the colony and not molest them.' Until reprisals and commandos ceased, no 'civilization' could take root among them. As for the colonial side, he wrote to Lord Glenelg: 'The colonists [have to be] allowed to protect their property and lives against plunders and marauders, even if it be necessary to shoot the assailants. This in the actual state of things cannot be prevented. The vacillating and contradictory doctrine which has been held forth on this point, rushing from one extreme to the other, has been one of the main causes of our misfortunes.'[87]

In a series of letters to Governor D'Urban in the first month, Stockenstrom elaborated on his ideas to restore peace on the frontier. A strong line of military posts was essential, requiring 'a strong force and great expense.' A burgher force had to be formed and used under strict regulations for defense purposes. As dense a population as possible had to be settled in the areas adjoining the colonial boundary. The frontier burghers had real and just grievances. Many lived great distances from a drostdy, often with no access to people in authority. The result was that they were often ignorant of the law. He recommended additional resident magistrates in Cradock, Colesberg, and a place further east. With armed bands of blacks roaming across the country and plundering, and burghers too afraid of criminal prosecution if they reacted firmly, he advised the governor to clarify the situation as to when they could use arms to protect their lives and property. He

85 Franken, *Retief*, pp. 309-23.
86 Kenney, *Retief*, p. 107.
87 Stockenstrom, *Autobiography*, vol. 2, p. 76.

repeated his view, first expressed to Glenelg in London, that the burghers had to be allowed to shoot plunderers. In 1834 the judges of the Cape Supreme Court expressed the
same opinion. Stockenstrom also recommended prompt action to redress other grievances, amongst them payment by the government of what it owed the burghers for provisions in the latest frontier war, and immediately issuing the long-delayed transfer of
land deeds.[88]

There was no real reason why Retief and Stockenstrom could not work together. Stockenstrom had once said of Retief: 'I always found him sensible and conciliatory when argued with.'[89] But Stockenstrom believed – and he was almost certainly correct – that
prior to the trek Retief had been conspiring with his own greatest enemies, expansionist British officers, merchants, speculators and journalists. They were people who, in his
eyes, were hoping to acquire land cheaply by spreading rumors that could spur the trek
movement. They were constantly advocating an aggressive, forward policy against the
Xhosa. He had nothing but contempt for them. Further, ever since the news of Stockenstrom's appointment, Retief had tried to discredit him. He took the lead in drafting a
sarcastic address from the Winterberg burghers to Stockenstrom. Ostensibly the purpose
was to congratulate him on his appointment, but the sting in the address was this passage: 'We do not wish to burden you with an account of the disasters which have befall-
en us, but we would like to request you to be as kind to give us the reasons, which we
cannot fathom, why we were presented to the English government as Monsters of cruelty and barbarism.' The implication was that Stockenstrom had made such allegations
to the Aborigines Committee in London.[90]

This was a preposterous allegation. In fact, Stockenstrom had often protested against
the bad press the Afrikaner frontiersman had to endure. On one occasion he wrote: 'It is
most unjust to charge the colonists en masse as cut throats and as being averse to the
amelioration of and good understanding with the aboriginal tribes.'[91] In his evidence in
London, Stockenstrom had condemned the reprisal system in general terms and had
pointed out that it provided the opportunity for some people on the frontier to commit
injustices and atrocities. He did not deign to rebut Retief's allegation, but simply told
him that he considered him deluded to sign such a 'ridiculous' document as the Winterberg address.[92]

On 20 September Retief and Stockenstrom met at the Kat River settlement. Retief reported that the country was swarming with plundering blacks and that the frontier system afforded no protection. Stockenstrom replied that people knew him as a frontier
administrator and were aware of his political principles. What he had to offer was still
the same as at the beginning of his career: 'strict justice to all parties' and 'equal rights to
all classes without distinction.' If they thought they would be happier in another country, he would advise them to leave.[93]

A month later Retief reported, in a letter, that many were leaving but some were wait-

---

88 Cited by Eily and Jack Gledhill, In the Steps of Piet Retief (Cape Town: Human & Rousseau, 1980),
    p. 135; Franken, Retief, pp. 393-5.
89 Franken, Retief, p. 448.
90 Franken, Retief, p. 402-5.
91 Kenney, Retief, p. 86.
92 Franken, Retief, p. 405-6.
93 Gledhill, Steps of Retief, p. 134.

ing to hear if measures that would improve their security were in the offing. He had written to military officers stationed nearby, expressing dismay that he was not allowed to arrest blacks who had come into the colony legally with passes that government agents had issued under Ordinance 49. Among the burghers there was suspicion about some of the agents who issued passes.

Retief could see no reason why the Xhosa 'who have deprived us of our goods and blood are allowed to come in among us to deprive us of the little we still have to live on, but also to deride us in our impoverished state.' He added: 'Kaffirs with passes . . . in my ward [are] . . . congregating with not the least other purpose than to live solely on plunder . . . Must I not arrest such and send them to [you]?' Defiantly, he stated: 'I must oppose their entry.'

Stockenstrom would have none of this. Nothing could be salvaged if burghers in government offices took the law into their own hands and ignored regulations. Anarchy would be worse than disorder. The greatest misfortunes on the frontier had come as a result of individuals becoming their own law. In the Slagtersnek rebellion of 1815, burghers who took the law in their own hands had ended up on the gallows. He had seen it all before. He told Retief that if he arrested a person with a pass he would have to face the consequences: 'Until the law is altered you must abide by it.' He threatened to dismiss him as field commandant if he continued to 'trample existing regulations under foot.'[94]

By the end of 1836 Retief had resolved to leave. He disappeared from the scene for a while and there is speculation that he visited the trekkers already beyond the borders and that they asked him to assume the leadership. In January 1837 he went to Grahamstown to bid Stockenstrom farewell. Retief referred later to Stockenstrom's 'inappropriate humor' on this occasion. He told Retief that he could not understand how the trekkers could survive as whites in Africa except by remaining under the British government and its system of law and order, however temporarily defective. He noted passionately that the trekkers seemed to prefer the protection of Dingane and Mzilikazi, two major African chiefs in the deep interior, to that of the British government.

On 2 February 1837, Retief published his manifesto in the *Grahamstown Journal,* no doubt with the help of his young friend, Louis Henri Meurant, the editor. The manifesto was no ringing declaration of independence, but a document aimed above all at dispelling the impression that the trekkers were anarchic frontiersmen desperate to escape the restraint of laws. It sought to create the impression that an ordinarily law-abiding people, pushed beyond all limits, had chosen to trek rather than rise up against the government. 'We despair of saving the colony from those evils which threaten it by the turbulent and dishonest conduct of vagrants.' The trekkers had decided 'to quit this colony with a desire to lead a more quiet life than we have heretofore done . . . under the full assurance that the British government had nothing more to require of us, and will allow us to govern ourselves without its interference in future.'

The manifesto dealt with the causes of the trek; the pervasive lack of security and, in particular, the losses sustained in the last frontier war and the 'turbulent and dishonest

---

94 Gledhill, *Steps of Retief*, p. 136.

conduct of vagrants.' It complained about 'vexatious' laws made with respect to slaves and the financial losses sustained in the emancipation process. It deplored the 'unjustifiable odium' that missionary propaganda cast upon the frontier burghers. The manifesto emphasized that the emigrants did not want to enslave anyone, but rather to restore the old paternalistic relationship between masters and servants. They would take no one's property but would defend themselves against attacks on their lives and property. They would make laws to govern themselves and forward copies to the colony for its information. They would make their intention to live in peace clear to the black tribes amongst whom they settled.

The last passage expressed a 'firm reliance on an all-seeing, just and merciful Being whom it will be our endeavor to fear and humbly obey.' This was in all likelihood Retief's report to Stockenstrom, who had said to him: 'Wherever you may wander do not forget and remind your fellows that you are Christians and that as such you have enduring obligations.'[95] Stockenstrom was not impressed; he dismissed Retief as field commandant on the same day that the manifesto appeared in the *Grahamstown Journal*.

In a letter of July 1837 Retief again assured the British government that no enmity was intended towards the 'British nation.' Leaving the colony had occasioned the trekkers 'enormous and incalculable losses.' He even requested British help to prevent hostilities against African tribes who had been enlisted against them. But he also struck a new note: '[We] desire to be considered a free and independent people.'[96]

Stockenstrom's solution: A treaty system

Back in the colony, Stockenstrom set about finally implementing his own solution to the frontier problems. In November 1836 he had written: 'We must have either extermination [meaning expulsion of the Xhosa from the frontier zone] or conciliation and justice: a middle course is ruin.' To settle issues such as cattle thefts, treaties had to be concluded between the colony and the chiefs of the neutral territory. Treaties were not new to frontier politics, but Stockenstrom went further, considering agreements between the chiefs and the colonial government as on a level similar to treaties between independent states.

Stockenstrom knew how strong the resistance would be to this novel idea. As he said in a later letter, people thought it absurd to apply the rules of intercourse between civilized nations to the colony's dealings with 'savages.' He disagreed. 'I believe the principles of truth and justice to be universal, as well as eternal . . . with nations, as with individuals. I believe them to bind the mightiest power as well as the most insignificant community.' To dismiss the whole issue by calling the Xhosa 'a gang of thieves' did not reflect well on the colony. He pointed out: '[We] have been beaten in the field, as well as in the cabinet, by a gang of thieves,' an obvious reference to the reversal of D'Urban's policy.[97]

Stockenstrom had little faith, however, in Philip's vision of imperialist expansion or

---

95 Franken, *Retief*, p. 408.
96 For Retief's documents see *Afrikaner Political Thought*, pp. 213–17.
97 *Afrikaner Political Thought*, p. 180.

with the agenda of culturally assimilating blacks. He did not believe it was wise to inter-fere with the way in which native peoples ordered their lives or disputes. 'I do not see how the introduction of the English laws is at all practicable. The prejudices of a nation however absurd they may appear are not easily removed or disregarded.' There was no sense in undermining the chiefs' authority. '[By] means of these chiefs,' he wrote, the colony would 'soonest succeed to secure peace and promote civilization.'[98] Without the chiefs, he believed, no peace was possible.

Under the system, chiefs were to be allocated specific areas in the neutral territory. They would have to appoint councilors to supervise the frontier at points along the border. If cattle were stolen, farmers could seek them beyond the border only with the help of the councilors. No patrols would exact compensation. Thefts had to be addressed at the root, that is, on the farms. Farmers must guard their cattle and pay servants a prop-er wage. The farmers, he wrote, 'should remember that they got *good* land *cheap*, and they should not complain of having to protect their flocks.' Colonists had to be allowed to protect their property and lives against plunderers, using arms if necessary. If cattle were stolen, the thieves had to be caught and punished, but according to the law; no risk of a bloody war would be taken for every cow that strayed.[99]

There is no consensus among historians on how well the treaty system succeeded in maintaining stability. One well-informed frontier farmer later declared the policy a dis-aster, that murder and plunder were the order of the day.[100] But these impressions were recorded long after the event. There were also signs that some entrusted with carrying out the policy had made a success of it. C.L. Stretch, one of the most active agents ap-pointed to mediate, was able to settle all of his cases amicably with Xhosa chiefs.[101] But there were major problems in the implementation of the policy. The government was not prepared to spend heavily on military posts and a strong military force on the border – expenditure that would have been far less than that which would be incurred in the ruinous wars that followed. Another problem was that not enough dependable herdsmen could be found to guard the farmers' stock.

The principal obstacle, however, was the undermining efforts of the influential lobby of British officers, speculators and settlers that Stockenstrom was unable to counter. There was the allegation, made also by Retief, that he had besmirched the colonists' repu-tation in London. An even more vicious rumor was that in 1813 he had shot a Xhosa in cold blood to avenge his father's death. This eroded his authority to such an extent that he sued Duncan Campbell, civil commissioner of Albany, for libel. But a cruel fate was in store for him as someone who had nailed his colors to the mast of truth and justice. The Supreme Court, with some of his enemies sitting as judges, found that there was in-sufficient evidence against Campbell. Although a subsequent court finding completely vindicated him, Stockenstrom found himself in an impossible situation. His unpopu-larity prompted the new governor, Sir George Napier, to press for his dismissal. Glenelg rejected the recommendation, but his successor removed him from his post in August

---

98 Stockenstrom's letters from London are in his *Autobiography*, vol. 2, p. 34.

99 Macmillan, *Bantu, Boer and Briton*, p. 264 (emphasis in the original).

100 Coetser, *Gebeurtenisse uit de Kaffer-oorloge,* p. 12.

101 G.B. Crankshaw, 'The Diary of C.L. Stretch', masters diss., Rhodes University, 1960.

1839. This ouster was a blow to the Xhosa chiefs who trusted him and who had tried their best to make his system work. Even Maqoma said five years after Stockenstrom's fall: 'I will hold by Stockenstrom's word until I die . . . If the treaties are forced from us, nothing can preserve us from war.'[102]

Without Stockenstrom, and perhaps even with him, the system was doomed. Cattle thefts by Xhosa never completely stopped, and they increased after 1839. Even Napier, who considered himself a champion of black rights, had become exasperated. He told London that he simply had to attend to the 'complaints and grievances under which the border farmers labor, as regards the constant plunder of their flocks and cattle and the slaughter of their armed herdsmen.' J. Hare, new lieutenant-governor of the eastern province, was at his wits' end. In 1842 he wrote to the governor: 'I have talked till I am tired with the chiefs; on every occasion they make me fair promises which are never performed.'[103] The government again allowed farmers to cross the border and look for their cattle in a way that resembled the old reprisal system. The government started to change the treaties unilaterally and soon scrapped them.

Would Stockenstrom's treaty system, if properly applied, have had a chance of providing stability? Stockenstrom had weaknesses, but he was not naïve. The Xhosa were not 'mild, gentle shepherds', he once wrote. 'Vigor is as necessary as justice in your dealings with them, and if you allow them to become masters you must give up the colony.' He recognized that treaties in themselves could not maintain political equilibrium; ultimately the colonial government would have to enforce them through its own 'irresistible power.'[104] The government lacked the vision and the will to do so.

A costly lesson

With the development of wool farming and the corresponding sharp rise of land prices in the 1830s and 1840s, the opportunities for land speculation greatly increased. As a result, British speculators intensified pressure on the government to permit expansion into Xhosa lands. None of the settler voices was more strident than that of John Mitford Bowker, who wrote that just as thousands of springbok on the plains had been swept aside, so the Xhosa must give way to make room 'for millions of civilized men.'[105]

A new governor, Sir Peregrine Maitland (1844-1847), reintroduced the old spoor law which Stockenstrom had so despised when it was first made policy thirty years earlier. In 1846 war broke out, triggered by the killing of a white frontier farmer and the siting of a military fort in Xhosa territory. Even Philip remarked that the frontier colonists had given the Xhosa no reason for making war. He wrote that he could not help describing the spirit of the colonist 'as being of a more Christian character than appeared on any former occasion.'[106] Stockenstrom came out of retirement with the Seventh Frontier War of

---

102 Peires, *House of Phalo*, p. 128.
103 P. Kapp, 'Suid-Afrika se eerste waarheidskommissie', *Tydskrif vir Geesteswetenskappe*, 42, 1 (2002), p. 63.
104 *Afrikaner Political Thought*, pp. 179-81.
105 J.M. Bowker, *Speeches, Letters and Selections from important Papers* (Grahamstown: Godlonton and Richards, 1864), p. 125.
106 Kapp, 'Eerste waarheidskommissie', p. 64.

1846-47 as the only person the burghers would accept as their commander. The burghers' memories of their treatment in the previous war at the hands of British officers were still bitter. When the Xhosa sued for peace, Sir Harry Smith, the new governor, reverted to D'Urban's policy of twelve years earlier, annexing the area between the Keiskamma and Kei rivers and imposing direct rule on the Xhosa living here. The chiefs became mere functionaries, and many Xhosa were pushed out of their grazing lands. The government sold Xhosa land to English-speaking speculators to fill its own coffers.

Pressed for land and constantly harassed, the Xhosa again invaded the colony in December 1850. Some Khoikhoi in the Kat River settlement, where land had also been alienated to English speculators, joined the Xhosa force, as did some farm workers. Once again a colonial force was raised to repel the invaders. The frontier burghers themselves did not want to get involved, and Sir Harry Smith wrote to the Colonial Secretary that the Boers were 'indifferent' and 'apathetic.' A British settler expressed surprise at how 'anti-English' the frontier Afrikaners had become.

This Eighth Frontier War (1850-1852) was, in the words of the historian, Jeffrey Peires, the 'longest, hardest and ugliest war' on the eastern frontier. The British forces tried to destroy the subsistence base of the enemy where it lived; they burned huts, destroyed crops, and captured cattle. Some sixteen thousand Xhosa were killed. Not even Xhosa women and children were spared. It so disrupted and traumatized Xhosa society that a few years later it became receptive to a millenarian message that called on them to destroy their cattle and crops.

Stockenstrom, giving evidence on the war in London, made it very clear that ordinary colonists were not responsible for the war and that the guilt had to be laid squarely upon the aggressive local governor and rapacious speculators. Only a representative government, he said, would act with the necessary restraint to avoid further frontier wars.[107] He asked: 'What single benefit have the colonists derived from any Kaffir war?' Speculators benefited, but what good did it do the colonists?[108] Representative government was introduced in 1853 in the Cape Colony. By now most Afrikaner leaders in the western part of the colony strongly opposed any further conquest of land beyond the border.

For the burghers, the eastern frontier had been a costly learning experience. Some eighty years had elapsed since the first attempts in the 1770s to push the Xhosa over the Fish River. The 1857 speech of an Afrikaner leader, J.H. Wicht, told Parliament that if colonists were to occupy African land, 'they cannot expect to sleep on a bed of roses. If you go near the savages, it is like going near a nest of hornets – they will sting you.'[109] It was a lesson the Prinsloos should have learned in 1779 after attacking the Xhosa and then being raided by them, and it was one Stockenstrom quickly absorbed. It was a truth that the Voortrekkers and their descendants would painfully discover in their wanderings along new frontiers.

---

107 This and the previous paragraph are based on the synthesis of Keegan, *Colonial South Africa*, pp. 232-41.
108 Stockenstrom, *Autobiography*, p. 344.
109 *Afrikaner Political Thought*, p. 187.

Chapter 6

Settling in the Deep Interior

'A strange and moving spectacle': The Great Trek

'History had seldom witnessed a stranger and more moving spectacle than that of well-to-do farmers, some in their first flush of youth and others already bending under the weight of years, forsaking their farms and homesteads, packing their families with all their household goods into the unwieldy ox-wagon, driving their flocks and herds before them, and trekking away to the distant, unknown interior.'[1] This was a description of what became known as the Great Trek in a biography of Andrew Murray, ordained in 1849 in Bloemfontein as the first DRC minister in a parish beyond the Orange River. Between 1835 and 1845, parties of burgher families, later called Voortrekkers, and their servants, moved out of the Cape Colony in considerable numbers and mingled with the trekboers who had left the colony earlier and were sojourning in the Transorange area before many of the former moved on into Natal or the Transvaal. In the first wave of the emigration of the Voortrekkers, which ended in 1840, some six thousand people (20 per cent of the whites in the eastern districts and 10 per cent of the colony's whites) trekked. By 1845 some 2,308 families, or fifteen thousand burghers and their families, accompanied by an estimated five thousand servants, had left the colony.[2]

Officials and church leaders realized immediately that this was an event of major significance. People in positions of power and influence almost unanimously condemned the trek; some were concerned about the impact on indigenous populations, some about the fate of the trekkers. Andries Stockenstrom, then the leading frontier official, said that he feared that the trekkers would reduce blacks to a state like that of the pre-1828 Khoikhoi. He advised the government to reject any land deal made by the trekkers as 'such bargain or right can evidently only be extorted by violence and fraud in most cases.'[3] Gideon Joubert, a prominent frontier colonist, expected the trekkers to be destroyed speedily and the survivors forced to return, or degenerate into a state 'worse than that of

---

1 J. du Plessis, *The Life of Andrew Murray of South Africa* (London: Marshall Bros., 1919), p. 82.
2 J.C. Visagie, *Voortrekkerstamouers* (Pretoria: Unisa, 2000).
3 John Bird, *Annals of Natal* (Cape Town: Maskew Miller, 1920), vol. 1, pp. 389-91.

the heathen.'[4] The Cape synod of 1837 expressed its concern over the 'departure into the desert, without a Moses or Aaron' by people looking for a 'Canaan' without having been given a 'promise or direction.'[5] *De Zuid-Afrikaan*, the only Dutch newspaper, was dismayed that the Voortrekkers had removed themselves from British authority.

Christoffel Brand, the principal force behind *De Zuid-Afrikaan*, sounded a different note in writing to Andries Pretorius in 1839: 'You must never forget that I am an Afrikaner and hence have an interest in my countrymen who have emigrated.'[6] The Rev. G.W.A. van der Lingen of Paarl gave Pretorius advice before he left, but declined to join the trek as its minister.[7]

At the time when the trekkers began to leave the colony in the 1830s, there was intensive contact between Europeans and Africans along a line of approximately two hundred kilometers near the Fish River. Beyond that there were only a few places where Europeans were in contact with people who were not European. In the vicinity of Port Natal (the present Durban) a few English traders and hunters were living among a large indigenous population. But by the early 1840s the picture had changed. A dramatic extension of the frontier of European contact with Africans had occurred.

Among the principal post-*Mfecane* groupings living in the areas to which the emigrants were moving was Mzilikazi's Ndebele kingdom, which had established itself in the Marico Valley, in what would become known as the western Transvaal. Based on the Zulu style of fighting, the Ndebele army had laid waste large parts of what would become known as the Transvaal and northern Free State. Moshweshwe, who had built the Basotho nation out of refugees, occupied land east and west of the Caledon River. In Natal Dingane had Shaka, king of the Zulu nation, assassinated, then succeeded him as king.

The first two parties, those of Louis Tregardt and Janse van Rensburg, left in September 1835. Hendrik Potgieter's trek moved out of the Tarka area across the colonial boundary in late 1835 or early 1836. Gert Maritz and his trek left Graaff-Reinet in September 1836, with more than seven hundred people, some hundred of them white male adults. Maritz took along legal works, including a study by Grotius, and a cannon – a great legal book and an instrument of violence: the two means of asserting white supremacy.

Piet Retief and his own party of a hundred men, women, and children departed from the Albany district in February 1837. An issue of the *Grahamstown Journal* tried to sketch the scope of the trek movement as a whole at this point: '[Near] the sources of the Caledon River there were, a few weeks ago, 230 wagons [and] on the Orange River upwards of eighty more, and numerous small cavalcades.'[8] In April 1837 a party of more than a hundred members of the Uys family under the leadership of Piet Uys moved out of the Uitenhage district. By the spring of 1837 there were five or six large camps between the Orange and the Vaal rivers and a total of two thousand trekkers.

4 P.J. van der Merwe, *Die noordwaartse beweging van die Boere voor die Groot Trek, 1770-1842* (Den Haag: Van Stockum, 1937), p. 370.
5 M.C. Kitshoff, *G.W.A. van der Lingen, 1804-1869* (Groningen: V.R.B., 1972), p. 60.
6 H.C. Botha, 'Die rol van Christoffel J. Brand in Suid-Afrika', master's diss., Unisa, 1973, p. 120.
7 Kitshoff, *Van der Lingen*, pp. 62-4.
8 Rodney Davenport and Christopher Saunders, *South Africa: A Modern History* (London: Macmillan, 2000), pp. 51-3.

Disaster and victory

The emigrants were well aware that their adversaries suspected that they intended to embark on a campaign of African dispossession. They saw Africans as people with whom they had to reach a working relationship. They coveted them as laborers and wanted them as allies against other Africans, and their commandos always included Africans, usually as *agterryers*, people entrusted with tending the horses and preparing the food. The first large commando of armed burghers on horseback, headed by Potgieter and Maritz, had 103 trekkers and forty colored men, with sixty Africans to assist them.

Among the intellectual baggage of the Voortrekkers were policies like the reprisal system, practices such as the indenturing of indigenous children, fighting techniques like the commando and the laager, and the treaty as a model of 'international' relations. The commando had been in existence since 1715; the laager, a circle of wagons with thorn bushes jammed under and between the wheels had probably first been used by frontiersmen in the First Frontier War of 1779-1781. Verbal agreements or formal treaties with African chiefs were part and parcel of the eastern frontier scene. While the trekkers were leaving, Andries Stockenstrom, on behalf of the colony, signed treaties with various African chiefs as partners in maintaining peace and good order.

Disaster soon struck when near the Limpopo Valley hostile tribes wiped out the Van Rensburg trek. Tregardt and his people who had settled in Soutpansberg in the far north moved out to Delagoa Bay, but most on their trek died from fever, including Tregardt himself. Potgieter's trek began with only thirty-three arms-bearing men, along with women and children, and increased to two hundred after the parties of Sarel Cilliers and Casper Kruger joined the trek. Potgieter, an energetic, active man with a taciturn temperament, concluded agreements with African chiefs to live in peace, but, in August 1836, an Ndebele patrol attacked the Liebenberg family, part of Potgieter's trek, and killed six men, two women and six children, the Ndebele's primary aim probably to plunder the large flocks of cattle the trekkers had brought with them.[9]

Then, on 20 October 1836, an Ndebele army of four thousand to six thousand men attacked Potgieter's laager, and, in the Battle of Vegkop, thirty-five trekkers beat off the massive Ndebele attack with the loss of only two lives. The Ndebele did succeed in carrying off almost all the trekkers' cattle, and in January commandos went out to punish Mzilikazi. The first, headed by Potgieter and Maritz, killed four hundred, sacked Mzilikazi's village at Mosega and took seven thousand cattle. In November another commando, headed by Potgieter and Piet Uys, forced Mzilikazi to flee to the present Zimbabwe. There were no serious rivals now to the emigrants on the plateau of the Highveld.

African enemies were not the only challenge. Divisions, schisms, and squabbles among themselves nearly destroyed the trek. Trekker leaders were wealthy men but lacked the economic controls ordinarily available to enforce loyalty and discipline. The trek had a leveling effect on the class hierarchy. In the end the leadership had to rely on the established patriarchal family structure and on military reputation to maintain their control. But even the leaders did not agree on their ultimate destination, apart from wanting to settle near an outlet to the sea. Retief was intent on Natal, Potgieter on the Highveld

---

9 For a full account see P.J. van der Merwe, 'Die Matabeles en die Voortrekkers', *AYB*, 1986, pp. 45-107.

of the Transvaal, and he sought an agreement with the Portuguese in Mozambique over access to the port of Delagoa Bay (Maputo), as far away as possible from British authority, so that he could establish de facto independence. Retief, on the other hand, preferred to negotiate with Britain for independence.

Ecclesiastical and political disputes, too, threatened the trek. In the absence of a Reformed Church minister, Erasmus Smit, brother-in-law of Maritz and a former missionary in the service of the London Missionary Society, tried to step into the breach, but he was old, sickly, not ordained, and rumored to be an alcoholic. Many trekkers found him unacceptable. Arguments over the form of political organization also ruptured the trekker community. Potgieter, a patriarchal figure, concentrated on the welfare of his own trek party, which developed into an autocracy under the Potgieter clan. Maritz, by contrast, viewed the trek as a common enterprise – a *vereenigde maatschappij* (united community) or a volk – and called for the leaders' submission to an elected council.

There were brief moments of unity. In December 1836, while the treks of Potgieter and Maritz were at Thaba Nchu, the trekkers elected a Burgerraad (Burgher Council) of seven burghers with Maritz as civilian president and Potgieter as military commander. The Burgerraad supervised the making and enforcement of laws. But Maritz and Potgieter soon fell out and the Burgerraad was split. When Retief arrived in Thaba Nchu the next April, he was unanimously elected 'governor' of the trekkers and took over the post of military commander from Potgieter. Maritz became 'judge president of the Council of Policy' and 'deputy governor.' Potgieter's exclusion was confirmed two months later when a meeting at Winburg adopted nine articles, setting up the 'Free Province of New Holland in South East Africa' with Retief as 'overseer' of the *Maatschappij*, as the collective Voortrekker society was called. When the Uys party arrived soon afterwards, Piet Uys, its leader, refused to accept resolutions in which his own trek had no part. The exclusion of Potgieter and Uys from the governing body caused major tensions. Maritz, increasingly suspicious of Retief's autocratic tendencies, warned trek parties that Retief had appropriated 'unprecedented power and dominion.'[10]

Retief, favoring a negotiated treaty with Dingane for land to settle in Natal, met the Zulu king in October 1837. Dingane promised the extensive area between the Mzimvubu and Tugela, on condition that Retief recovered cattle stolen from him by Sekonyela, the Tlokwa chief. Although Retief had been warned against Dingane's treacherous nature, he was now under so much pressure that, almost as in his business ventures in the colony, he risked all against impossibly long odds. An English missionary who had known Dingane for two years warned Retief that the deal he was trying to pull off was 'a mad enterprise.' 'It takes a Dutchman,' Retief reportedly replied, 'not an Englishman, to understand a Kafir.'[11]

Other mistakes lengthened the odds even further. Retief told Dingane of the severe punishment the trekkers had inflicted on Mzilikazi, and Dingane's councilors who accompanied Retief and his men to Sekonyela noticed how disrespectfully they treated the chief. 'Would Dingane be treated the same way?' they asked. The answer was: 'We

---

10 *Afrikaner Political Thought*, pp. 242-6, 282-4.
11 Noël Mostert, *Frontiers* (New York: Alfred Knopf, 1992), p. 812.

shall treat Dingane in the same way should we find him to be a rogue.'[12] Even before a final deal, some trekkers had crossed the Drakensberg in considerable numbers, and Dingane was suspicious and insecure.

Retief arrived at Dingane's kraal with seventy white trekkers and thirty servants, expecting the Zulu king to sign a treaty for the cession of land. On 6 February 1838, just before the signing ceremony, Dingane persuaded Retief to instruct his men to leave their arms outside the chief's village, whereupon the Zulu king's men seized all the unarmed trekkers and their servants and clubbed to them to death one by one. Retief was killed at the end after watching all his men being clubbed down.

The massacre ushered in the grimmest of times. Dingane promptly dispatched six thousand to seven thousand Zulu warriors to destroy the unsuspecting trekking parties on the Natal plains. Against this large force the trekkers had only eight hundred men. Zulu impis (warriors) killed some three hundred whites and two hundred servants and carried off between 20,000 and 25,000 head of cattle in a raid that left many trekkers destitute. Uys and Potgieter rushed to assist the Natal trekkers, but a commando that attacked a Zulu force was defeated and Uys and his son were killed. Potgieter and his men left Natal to establish a settlement on the Highveld. The trekkers who remained were in a precarious situation that worsened when Maritz died in September.

Two months later, in November 1838, Andries Pretorius arrived with a party of sixty and a fine bronze cannon. A tall, robust man with an impressive bearing, Pretorius had a degree of self-confidence that shaded into arrogance, but he was, as Stockenstrom observed, 'no fool' and a brilliant military and political strategist besides. He was appointed commandant-general and led his men out on a carefully planned showdown with the Zulu army. He encouraged the idea of a covenant, and on 9 December and over the next few days the commando, led by Sarel Cilliers, made a vow that if God granted the men victory, they and their descendants would commemorate the day of the battle and would build a church.[13]

A few days later Pretorius drew up a laager at a branch of the Buffalo River (later named Blood River). On 16 December, 468 trekkers, three Englishmen, and sixty blacks faced between ten thousand and twelve thousand Zulu. In a battle lasting two hours, three trekkers were slightly wounded and none killed, but three thousand Zulu lay dead. The defeat dealt a crippling blow to Dingane's power. The Zulu nation split; Dingane's half-brother, Mpande, aligning him with the trekkers, sent an army of ten thousand men to assist Pretorius in a follow-up expedition against Dingane. The 'Cattle Commando' returned with 41,000 head of cattle. Dingane was killed soon afterward and Pretorius proclaimed Mpande king of the Zulus and vassal of the Natal republic. Afrikaner nationalists of the next century considered Blood River the battle that 'saved' the trek and secured the victory of Christianity and 'civilization.' But the victory itself at most secured only a temporary beachhead. The fate of the Great Trek was determined on the Highveld, not in Natal.

The trekkers had acquired a sense of mission at an early stage; in 1841 the Natal Volksraad wrote to Governor Napier at the Cape that they saw themselves as an instru-

---

12 W.M. Macmillan, *Bantu, Boer and Briton* (Oxford: Clarendon Press, 1963), pp. 202-4.
13 B.J. Liebenberg, *Andries Pretorius in Natal* (Pretoria: Academica, 1977), pp. 23-30.

ment in God's hand to promote Christian civilization and to protect blacks from inter-necine 'murder, pillage and violence.'[14] The trekkers themselves, however, played no or little part in promoting Christianity among the Zulu. While, in observance of the covenant, a church was built for their use in Pietermaritzburg, Pretorius is not on record as refer-ring to the vow again and, after 1839, public celebration of the vow was discontinued. It was 1880 before the republican leader, Paul Kruger, who had been a teenager in a family on Potgieter's trek, resurrected it.

In 1839 a republic was established in Natal with Pietermaritzburg as the capital of the two towns that were established: Congella near Port Natal and Weenen. The constitu-tion of the fledgling republic provided for a Volksraad, or council of people's represen-tatives, of twenty-four members, and a system of local government consisting of a land-drost or magistrate, assisted by burghers called heemraden, serving as his councilors. In the districts, burghers, called field cornets, acted as the representatives of government authority. All burghers could be called up for commandos under the direction of field cornets and district commandants. At the head was a commandant-general appointed by the Volksraad, with Pretorius, who filled this post, for all practical purposes the head of state. In 1841 the republic was enlarged to include the trekker communities in Winburg, south of the Vaal, and Potchefstroom, north of the Vaal, with a representative for each of the three communities in the Pietermaritzburg Volksraad.

A union of burghers

Was the best option for the leaders of the trek to accept institutional constraints, as most frontiersmen in the Cape Colony did during the 1820s and 1830s, or should they trans-form themselves into autocrats who were a law unto themselves? The trekkers developed various survival strategies. The following can be discerned: the first was a republicanism supported by Pretorius and a 'Volksraad party' in Natal; the second was the semi-autocracy of Potgieter on the Highveld; the third was the 'statelessness' and extreme individualism of the trekkers in the southern part of what became the Orange Free State.

When the trekkers left the Cape Colony their allegiance was to their own trek party. Freedom had meant freedom from constant threat to life and property. They had no developed conception about their right to settle in the interior and the type of system they would establish. But by the early 1840s the trekkers were confident enough to ex-press their right to colonize the interior. In 1842 the Natal Volksraad wrote to Governor Napier in Cape Town: '[We] took possession of uninhabited tracts of country acquired by friendly treaties as well . . . as with our blood and treasure.'[15] Especially among a sec-tion of the Natal trekkers, there was an increasing tendency to see all the emigrants as a *vereenigde burgerlyke maatskappij* – a united society of burghers with a right to make their own laws in the settlements they had founded.

This section, which became known as the Volksraad party, developed strong opposi-tion to unchecked personal power. In 1840 the party abolished the post of commandant-

---

14 F.A. van Jaarsveld, *Lewende verlede* (Johannesburg: Afrikaanse Pers-Boekhandel, 1961), p. 244.
15 *Afrikaner Political Thought*, pp. 213-22.

general for times of peace. It constantly called for the subjugation of leaders to the will of the people as expressed in an elected council. It introduced a radical form of self-rule with annual elections, white male franchise, and frequent memoranda or appeals to the Volksraad.

Henry Cloete, an anglicized Afrikaner, commenting in 1843 on the 'stern republican feeling of the majority of the inhabitants', added that they appeared to have been 'so inflated with their own ideas as to their power of governing the country collectively that they almost unanimously resisted every proposition of becoming subject to any permanent chief or supreme head.'[16] The republicanism of the burghers of the eighteenth and the early nineteenth century had little philosophical depth, the ideas of the American or French republic transported to the frontier as slogans rather than as thoughtful published tracts. Yet one of the core ideas of the ideology of republicanism, a free, independent, propertied class of burghers with rights, duties and privileges, had taken root by the end of the eighteenth century.

The trekker community itself in Natal at its height numbered only six thousand men, women, and children. The arduous task of building a new state in Natal was made difficult by the absence of a strong executive. Without enough revenue, officials could not be regularly paid and there was also, as a result, no police force to speak of. The currency the trekkers had brought with them was soon depleted and ammunition was running low. In 1839 the Natal Volksraad wrote gloomily that the trekkers had been wandering about for three years in unknown regions 'without compass, without guide, without experience, exposed to all obstacles nature put in [their] way, by insurmountable mountains reaching the clouds, exposed to serious wants and disappointments, surrounded and pursued by innumerable beasts of prey . . . and without any government and laws.'[17]

Acquiring African labor was a high priority. The number of Africans within the borders of Natal jumped from an estimated ten thousand in 1838 to forty thousand in 1842, according to one estimate, to a hundred thousand according to another. The easiest way in which to acquire labor was to seize women and children, as had been done with the Bushmen in the Cape Colony on the pioneer frontier. Before the Battle of Blood River, Pretorius had warned the burghers not to catch Zulu children and women *during* the battle, since it would be a distraction, and to seize them only after the battle. In the follow-up expedition against Dingane, the military council authorized every member of the commando to seize four children. The children had to be formally registered and indentured by officials of the republic, with boys released at the age of twenty-five and girls at the age of twenty-one. Pretorius seized eight children, from five to thirteen years old, in the Cattle Commando of 1839. But it took nearly four years before he registered them with the secretary of the Volksraad. The Volksraad, in 1841, expressed dismay over a reported trade in Zulu children but lacked the power to stamp it out.

It was to Pretorius that the Volksraad turned to head a commando after cattle had been stolen. His way of operating seemed very similar to the reprisals by Colonel Henry Somerset's patrols on the eastern frontier of the colony, where the commando acted on sparse evidence, its intention less to punish the guilty than to intimidate all chiefdoms in the

16 Henry Cloete, *The History of the Great Boer Trek* (London: John Murray, 1899), p. 129.
17 *Afrikaner Political Thought*, p. 218.

vicinity to refrain from stealing. Pretorius led a commando to the south that attacked the chief Ncaphayi without warning, killing thirty people, abducting seventeen children for distribution as apprentices, and making off with some three thousand cattle.[18]

The Natal trekkers tried to get adult Zulu to work for them also, but they had few illusions about the difficulties. J. du Plessis said later: 'There are no other means to rule the Kafirs but by fear, and Kafirs will not work for the white men unless they know they will be punished when they refuse.'[19] Zulu people would not accept agricultural labor in the service of another, especially adult males, unless they feared punishment or even death. In 1840 the Volksraad approved Pretorius' request to send out a patrol to seize chiefs with their entire following and distribute them as laborers among the trekkers. It is not known what the outcome was.

The Volksraad discussed passing a law to force roaming blacks to enter into the service of whites. The Zulu were also constantly told that if they did not work for the trekkers they had to move away, but the threat did not seem to have much effect. Pretorius, agitated about the refusal of Zulu to work on his or others' farms, had no qualms about forcing them to work and assaulting them.[20] The trekkers' passionate commitment to freedom and self-government did not include the Africans. They were regarded as less civilized people who could be ordered to work and punished if they refused. Freedom was a right reserved to whites by this rationale.

The British government was prepared to tolerate the trekkers settling beyond the colonial boundaries since it did not have any claim on the distant interior. But that changed when the perception arose that the trekkers were disrupting African communities. Missionaries had been quick to transmit news of the Pretorius commando against Ncaphayi, and the British government, which learned of the seizure of Zulu children for 'apprentices' and the Volksraad intention to transport 'surplus' Zulu to an area south of the republic's borders, feared Zulu resistance and the destabilization of the Cape Colony's borders. If Britain controlled Port Natal it could check the supply of ammunition to trekkers and reduce the potential for violence. In consequence, in 1838 a small British force briefly occupied Port Natal. In 1842 the Cape government sent a force of 250 men to Port Natal with Henry Cloete, the anglicized Cape Afrikaner, sent out as commissioner to the annexed territory. The Volksraad would be allowed to administer the interior until the British government had made a final decision as to its status. In July 1842 the Volksraad invited Cloete to Pietermaritzburg, and, while a hostile crowd gathered outside the building, deliberated with him, eventually deciding to submit to British authority.

Cloete's arrival had exposed the class and gender divisions in trekker society. There were the predominantly poor and illiterate who were most vociferous in rejecting the British demands; they would lose little if they abandoned Natal and sought their fortunes across the Drakensberg. Then there were the wealthy, literate, influential people who had already put down roots, whose land claims the British were most likely to recognize and who would be prepared to pay the quitrent and the survey costs the new government would demand. As J.N. Boshoff phrased it, they would put material interests higher than

---

18 Liebenberg, *Pretorius*, pp. 140-54.
19 Liebenberg, *Pretorius*, p. 117.
20 Liebenberg, *Pretorius*, pp. 120-1, 296-7.

'the point of freedom.' Among these was Pretorius, a progressive farmer with ten farms, who had managed remarkably quickly to settle down; in 1843 Cloete reported that Pretorius' farm, Welverdiend, had extensive fields and gardens under cultivation.

There were also strong divisions along gender lines. Afrikaner women were a driving force behind the trek. A British settler on the frontier wrote while the trek was getting underway: 'They fancy they are under a divine impulse', 'the women seem more bent on it than the men.'[21] The trekker women had not left the colony as mere adjuncts of their husbands; they had helped to make decisions and had enforced discipline over servants. This authority over servants was greatly undermined in the decade before the trek when servants and apprentice slaves began to take their masters and mistresses to court. Trekker women had made their presence felt as early as 1838 when a British force annexed Port Natal. The commander reported that opposition to British rule was particularly strong among Afrikaner women. They had experienced great want and insecurity, but 'they all rejected with scorn the idea of returning to the Colony.' He added: 'If any of the men began to droop or lose courage, they urged them on to fresh exertions and kept alive the spirit of resistance within them.'

At the meeting in Pietermaritzburg, Afrikaner women gave Cloete a baptism of fire, with the redoubtable Susanna Smit playing a leading role. She was the sister of Gert Maritz and Stephanus Maritz, who at the time was chairman of the Volksraad, and the wife of Erasmus Smit, the missionary-cum-teacher. Smit was not an ordained minister and Susanna Smit had to live on a meager pension, in a precarious financial and social position.[22]

Smit headed the delegation of Afrikaner women who confronted Cloete. He reported that they expressed 'their fixed determination never to yield to British authority . . . but [that] they would walk out by the Draaksberg [Drakensberg] barefooted, to die in freedom, as death was dearer to them than the loss of liberty.' They told Cloete that as a result of the battles they had fought alongside the men, the men had promised them 'a voice in all matters concerning the state of this country.' Yet the all-male Volksraad was now submitting to the British despite the women's protests. The women's fury dismayed Cloete; he considered it 'a disgrace on their husbands to allow them such a state of freedom.'[23]

Their protests were in vain, and by 1843 it became clear on what terms the British would administer the people in the territory. Everyone would be equal before the law, aggression against indigenous tribes would be prohibited, and slavery would not be tolerated. Pretorius postponed moving away from Natal for more than four years after Britain had annexed Natal, and left only after it had become clear that there was little hope of a social order in which blacks would be compelled either to work as farm laborers or to live in distant locations.[24] Susanna Smit, despite her announced willingness to walk barefoot over the Drakensberg to escape British control, continued to live under British rule in Natal for more than two decades.

21 E.A. Walker, *A History of Southern Africa* (London: Longmans Green, 1957), p. 200.

22 Anonymous, *Die dagboek van Anna Steenkamp* (Pietermaritzburg: Natalse Pers, 1937), p. 47.

23 This section on the meeting in Pietermaritzburg is based on Karel Schoeman, *Die wêreld van Susanna Smit, 1799-1863* (Cape Town: Human & Rousseau, 1995), pp. 112-59.

24 Liebenberg, *Pretorius*, pp. 96-7, 188-9, 296-9.

Potgieter's semi-autocracy

By the beginning of the 1840s Potgieter had established his personal authority over the trekkers in the Potchefstroom-Winburg area that straddled the Vaal River. An elected council assisted him, but little is known of its way of functioning. After the Pieter-maritzburg Volksraad submitted to British authority, Potgieter informed Cloete that his people did not consider themselves bound by this decision; they wished as freeborn burghers to manage their affairs independently. In 1844 Potgieter's people established a *Burgerraad* (Burgher Council) and accepted a constitution of thirty-three articles with provision for annual elections.[25] The next year Potgieter decided to move his 'capital' from Potchefstroom to the eastern Transvaal bushveld. He founded Andries Ohrigstad in the bushveld in the northeastern Transvaal, two weeks' ride from Delagoa Bay, intending to use it as a port,[26] but the settlement at Ohrigstad was riddled with crises. The lush appearance of the terrain masked the destruction by the tsetse fly. Cattle perished from disease, one farmer alone losing 1,200 sheep, fourteen horses and two hundred head of cattle. Further, the surrounding African chiefdoms became steadily more hostile. Many trekkers abandoned cattle farming and switched to elephant hunting and the ivory trade.

Potgieter claimed supreme authority on the grounds that the land had been ceded to him personally by Sekwati, the Pedi leader, in return for a promise of trekker protection against future Swazi attacks. He claimed full jurisdiction over the districts of Potchef-stroom and Winburg as 'adjunct colonies', and soon after settling at Ohrigstad announced that the Burgerraad would no longer meet at Potchefstroom, but wherever his own immediate following resided.

Between 1845 and 1860 the far northern frontier was virtually a Potgieter fiefdom. He was succeeded after his death in 1852 by his son Piet, followed by Stephanus Schoeman (1854-1860), who married Piet's widow. Even Potgieter's own son admitted that his father had been interested in a system of 'one headed' government. His opponents feared that he sought dictatorial powers with the right to ignore collective decisions altogether. When the trekkers from the ultra-democratic Volksraad party in Natal moved into the area, conflict immediately ensued. Their leader, J.J. (Kootjie) Burger, who had been a member of the Natal Volksraad, did not hesitate to depict Potgieter's followers as unconcerned about following customary laws because they had lived so long without them. A Volksraad began to function in 1845 in Ohrigstad with Burger as secretary.

The Potgieter people and Burger's Volksraad party clashed over the political system, but not only that. Burger's party saw survival as orderly living in permanent cattle-farming settlements, Potgieter in nomadic hunting, with seizing of African women, children, and cattle. Potgieter cultivated links with the African auxiliaries with whom he raided other chiefdoms, and, with the half-caste sons of Coenraad de Buys, exacted an annual tribute from neighboring African chiefdoms. His opponents accused him of being too harsh on black people and of too much 'lusting after their cattle and elephant tusks.' In 1846 he requested the Volksraad's permission to send a commando against Mzilikazi, his flimsy

---

25 Van der Merwe, 'Die Matabeles en die Voortrekkers', p. 300.
26 F.J. Potgieter, 'Die vestiging van die blanke in die Transvaal, 1837-1868', doctoral diss., Potchefstroom University, 1955, pp. 55-80, 117-22.

justification the recovery of some white children missing after the Ndebele attack on a Voortrekker laager ten years earlier. Burger wanted strict instructions to be given to the leaders of the expedition not to attack innocent kraals and to refrain from shedding innocent blood.[27] But when Potgieter's commando failed to find Mzilikazi it attacked another chiefdom. According to the missionary David Livingstone, an enormous number of cattle and some ten thousand sheep were captured, and four hundred people were taken prisoner.[28]

By now the Potgieter people and the Volksraad party had reached the brink of civil war, each party involved in intra-African conflicts, each attempting to use black allies in the battle. With a Zulu attack on Ohrigstad seemingly imminent, Potgieter left on a commando against Mzilikazi in the present Zimbabwe.[29] Failing to find its enemy or capture any booty, the commando on its return journey launched an unprovoked attack on Langa and his Transvaal Ndebele, allies of the Ohrigstad community. Langa had sent out several emissaries but the commando killed them all, then massacred many of the inhabitants, captured a large number of sheep and cattle, and seized many women and children, whom it separated from each other. Each member of the commando received booty of cattle and three or four of the kidnapped children. Some kept the children; others exchanged or sold them for between £7 and £15.

According to a report, some members of the commando were filled with revulsion and left immediately, and Potgieter faced severe criticism back in Ohrigstad. The Potgieter commando, Adriaan de Lange declared, had plunged the land into a crisis from which it would take many years to recover. He demanded action against Potgieter or that he himself be allowed to act against him as he thought fit. Shots were, apparently, exchanged between a Potgieter faction and its opponents. After that the community rapidly disintegrated. In 1849 Potgieter and his followers established the small settlement of Schoemansdal. His opponents trekked to the eastern Transvaal and founded the town of Lydenburg, in conditions as dismal as in Ohrigstad. In 1850 the town of Ohrigstad was described as totally deserted.[30]

The 'stateless' Transorange Afrikaners

On both sides of the upper Orange River, the trekkers encountered the mixed-race Griqua people who enjoyed some degree of autonomy. They had established 'captaincies' that were recognized by the British colonial government. One was at Klaarwater (later renamed Griquatown), west of the Orange River, where Andries Waterboer, a Griqua chief, was elected captain in 1819; the other at Philippolis, just east of the Orange River, where Adam Kok III, another chief, came to power in 1837. By 1838 a *raad* or council had produced a code of laws with field cornets in each division acting as officials of the raad. The result was some measure of stability.

27 Van der Merwe, 'Die Matabeles en die Voortrekkers', p. 313.
28 Van der Merwe, 'Die Matabeles en die Voortrekkers', pp. 313-20.
29 Phil Bonner, *Kings, Commoners and Concessionaires* (Cambridge: Cambridge University Press, 1983), pp. 47-84.
30 Van der Merwe, 'Die Matabeles en die Voortrekkers', pp. 408-11.

The first trekkers who moved into the present Free State were trekboers, who contin-ued to express loyalty to the government in Cape Town. These trekboers did not clash with other peoples. The missionary John Philip feared that the Voortrekkers moving into that area would act quite differently. He was particularly afraid that they would destroy the independence of the Griqua captaincies and of the Basotho under Moshweshwe. He persuaded the governor, Napier, to sign treaties in 1843 with Waterboer and Kok and the Sotho chief, Moshweshwe, in which they agreed to help preserve peace and securi-ty. But treaties could not protect Griqua autonomy or prevent the Griqua captains from yielding more and more land to whites.[31]

Neither the trekboers nor the Voortrekkers immediately challenged the formal Griqua or Sotho authority over them that Napier's treaties implied.[32] They did not object to asking Moshweshwe's permission to settle on his land, nor his overall authority. They were willing, at first, to deal with Kok and Waterboer on a basis of equality, and, in 1844, Potgieter offered a treaty to Kok. 'We are emigrants,' Potgieter wrote, '[who] . . . togeth-er with you dwell in the same strange land and we desire to be regarded as neither more nor less than your fellow-emigrants, inhabiting the country, enjoying the same privi-leges with you.'[33]

But both trekboers and Voortrekkers protested when the Griqua authority arrested whites, and they had far more firepower than Kok and Waterboer, whose support in Cape Town was dwindling; the Cape government had lost faith in the treaties and Philip's po-litical influence was on the wane. When Kok arrested yet another Afrikaner farmer an armed confrontation loomed and he backed off.

By the end of 1847 Pretorius and large numbers of Natal trekkers had given up on liv-ing under the British in a state of insecurity, threatened by Bushmen and blacks. Pre-torius contemplated fighting the British with Zulu allies but decided against it. He and the great majority of trekkers abandoned their farms early in 1848 to seek independ-ence on the Highveld. As they set out to cross the Drakensberg in torrential rain, Sir Har-ry Smith encountered them and wrote: 'I was almost paralyzed to witness the whole of the population with few exceptions "trêking" [sic]. Rains on this side of the mountains are tropical . . . and [these] families were exposed to a state of misery which I never be-fore saw equaled.'[34] When they refused to return to their farms, Smith informed them that Britain intended to annex both the Transorange and Transvaal as British territory. Refusing to be intimidated, Pretorius in February announced that he intended to turn the Transorange and Transvaal into an independent state with arms if necessary. He had become the man of the hour, ready to use a mix of military force, petitions and negotia-tions to win independence. Early in 1848 Governor Harry Smith annexed the area be-tween the Orange and the Vaal rivers as the Orange River Sovereignty and placed a British resident with a small force at the present Bloemfontein. This was a major setback for the Voortrekkers, who had hoped to establish themselves as an autonomous community in this area.

---

31 Andrew Ross, *John Philip* (Aberdeen: Aberdeen Press, 1986), p. 170

32 Timothy Keegan, *Colonial South Africa and the Origins of the Racial Order* (Cape Town: David Philip, 1996), pp. 248-52.

33 *Afrikaner Political Thought*, p. 173.

34 Liebenberg, *Pretorius*, p. 268.

Pretorius, for the first time, asserted that the trek had as its source a desire for independence and freedom. 'For liberty we sacrificed all', he declared. He tried to present the Afrikaners as a people against whom the British discriminated, as a people with even fewer rights than the Griqua. A manifesto signed by nine hundred burghers pointed out that the British allowed the colored population 'self-government and all the privileges of liberty.' Why were such rights to self-government now denied to the trekkers, who had obtained the land through barter? It suggested that the answer was color: '[Had] we perchance been colored, it might perhaps be possible, but now we find it impossible, because we are white African Boers.'[35]

A British sovereignty on the Highveld

Considering Pretorius and his followers a major threat, Governor Smith took eight hundred regulars to the north and, in a brief but sharp battle, defeated the Boer force at Boomplaats. Pretorius fled, and soon built up a new following near the modern Pretoria. Because of rivalry with Potgieter, he organized trekkers outside Potgieter's own sphere of influence, and in 1849 established a Volksraad for the entire Transvaal region. A commandant-general was appointed for each of four main regions: the central and southern regions, Soutpansberg in the north, Lydenburg in the east and Marico in the west. The Volksraad gave Pretorius a mandate to negotiate a political settlement with Britain for trekkers living north of the Vaal.

British control over Transorangia was tenuous. After the victory at Boomplaats only a small administrative apparatus was left behind to control the Sovereignty: a resident (Henry Warden), four magistrates, five clerks, eight constables, one Dutch Reformed minister, four schoolteachers, and 250 troops. Richard Southey, member of a prominent English settler family in the eastern Cape, was entrusted with fixing the Sovereignty's borders.

A considerable number of English settlers arrived after the proclamation of the Sovereignty. Like the settlers on the Cape eastern frontier, a lobby of English-speaking settlers in the southeast of Transorangia clamored for a tough policy against Moshweshwe, and for border adjustments to give whites the fertile Caledon River valley. The settlers insisted that the whites and the Sotho could not live there in peace unless separated from one another.

There were certain striking differences between the English settlers and the Afrikaners in the region. English farmers tended to appeal to the British imperial state to back up their land claims, provide roads, create markets, and subordinate blacks. Many Afrikaners in the southeast saw no priority in creating a state, much less an English state. Many declared that they would refuse to pay taxes to the British Sovereignty. Nor did they want a firm border separating the white and black territories, or a severing of contacts with, or the expulsion of, the Sotho; some indeed made their living exchanging Sotho wheat for lead and gunpowder at shops in the colony. They did not mind asking Chief Moshweshwe for papers ratifying their land claims. Resident Warden admitted that

---

35 See the analysis and documents in *Afrikaner Political Thought*, pp. 203-4, 223-5.

burghers in the contested area along the Caledon River in the east preferred the rule of Moshweshwe to that of the British government.[36] His appeals to racial solidarity in calls 'to put down the common enemy of the white man', were unheeded.[37] Josias Hoffman, who would become the first Free State president, objected to a plan to expel some three thousand Sotho from the Caledon River valley. 'The natives will not consent to remove and will revenge such unjust treatment,' he wrote. 'If Southey thinks that he can bind the Boers to the British government by giving them all the land he is mistaken and knows neither the Boers nor the natives.'[38]

A spate of cattle rustling prompted Warden to launch what became an unsuccessful attempt to enforce the boundary that excluded the Sotho from a large part of the valley. This defeat and the outbreak of the Eighth Frontier War in 1851 on the Cape frontier created a panic of sorts among English-speakers in the territory. *The Friend*, the English-language settler newspaper in Bloemfontein, wrote: 'We see a war of races . . . the declared aim and intention of the black man being to drive the white man into the sea.' It believed an 'extensive conspiracy' of Africans against whites across South Africa existed. How was the white man to respond? 'We answer in one word: UNION. Let the white man in South Africa be united, and at the same time let them be just.'[39]

In 1852 a large force under a new Cape governor, Sir George Cathcart, attacked Moshweshwe in an offensive that soon faltered. Moshweshwe sued prematurely for peace to help the British force to save face, but it was a hollow victory for the British. Cathcart advised the imperial government to set up a permanent garrison of two thousand men to reinforce British authority in the Sovereignty. But British policy-makers in London were unwilling to be sucked into the quagmire of the deeper interior of South Africa, and, by the late 1840s, retrenchment had become the central imperative of imperial policy.

Missionary and other humanitarian influences continued to wane. The liberal John Fairbairn in Cape Town, who in the 1820s and 1830s had fought to free the Khoisan and emancipate the slaves, no longer took a dim view of the trekkers' venture; he and others were now preoccupied with opening up the interior and 'civilizing' the native peoples. Fairbairn wrote: 'It is now clear that the destruction of Matsilikatzi [Mzilikazi] and the overthrow of Dingaan [Dingane] were steps in the Providential Scheme of tranquilizing Southern Africa.'[40] *De Zuid-Afrikaan* now saw the trek as similar to Israel's exodus from Egypt, and as a means of bringing the Gospel and civilization to the 'wild national tribes into the deep interior of South Africa.'[41]

Britain wanted white allies on the Highveld. It had little enthusiasm for supporting expansionist and militaristic English merchants and speculators clamoring for Moshwe-

36 Leonard Thompson, *Survival in Two Worlds: Moshoeshoe of Lesotho* (Oxford: Clarendon, 1975), pp. 142-4; Timothy Keegan, 'The Making of the Orange Free State, 1846-1854', *Journal of Imperial and Commonwealth History*, 17, 1 (1988), p. 36.

37 Keegan, *Colonial South Africa*, pp. 268-70.

38 Keegan, *Colonial South Africa*, p. 264.

39 G.D. Scholtz, *Die ontwikkeling van die politieke denke van die Afrikaner* (Johannesburg: Voortrekkerpers, 1970), vol. 2, p. 505.

40 H.C. Botha, *John Fairbairn in South Africa* (Cape Town: Historical Publication Society, 1984), p. 126.

41 Scholtz, *Ontwikkeling van die politieke denke*, vol. 2, pp. 489, 503.

shwe's land. Instead, it looked to the trekkers to settle border disputes with African chiefdoms, subjugate Africans into a labor force, and establish commercial relations with the British colonies. Therefore, at the Sand River Convention of 1852, Britain gave Transvaal Afrikaners the right to govern themselves and to purchase ammunition from the British colonies; it also promised to disclaim all prior alliances with the 'colored nations' north of the Vaal, and to prohibit the arms trade with native tribes. Britain's main demand was that no slavery be permitted in the republic.

In the Orange River Sovereignty the British were in such a hurry to withdraw that the negotiator shunned the loyalist trekboers and formed a group of burghers, calling them 'representatives.' With them he negotiated what was called the Bloemfontein Convention of 1854. In terms of this, the trekkers between the Vaal and Orange rivers could form their own government and purchase ammunition from the Cape Colony or Natal. Britain still recognized its treaty with Adam Kok, but in the early 1860s he sold his land and trekked across the Drakensberg to found East Griqualand.

Britain had, in effect, abandoned its treaties with non-European chiefs, and had given the trekkers political power and access to ammunition. Without much preparation and with no fanfare, the Zuid-Afrikaansche Republiek (ZAR) was established in 1852, and two years later the Republic of the Orange Free State (OFS). There were now some twenty thousand burghers in the ZAR north of the Vaal and fifteen thousand in the OFS between the Vaal and the Orange rivers. Some OFS burghers kept alive the idea of the incorporation of their state into the Cape Colony until the late 1860s, but the great majority of burghers became staunch republicans. Since it controlled the ports and the supply of ammunition, Britain had little to fear from these financially strapped republics.

The two new republics were states in little more than name. A few months before his death in December 1850, Hendrik Potgieter had written a despairing letter to his fellow Voortrekker leader Andries Pretorius. 'The time of our general deliverance has not yet been born, and that day will only dawn once we, through our own industry, concern and peaceable behavior, as well as through the blessing of God, will have become a nation, substantial in numbers, acting in concord, courageous, with the sword of righteousness in our hands and with available resources in a struggle to defend ourselves.' It was an accurate description of the difficulties of developing a sense of nationhood, and Potgieter could only lament: 'God only knows how long that day has to await us.'[42]

A chosen people?

In drawing up a constitution for their republics, the burghers considered the membership qualifications of their society. One of the trekkers' grievances when they left the Cape Colony was *gelykstelling* or social leveling between whites and blacks, which Retief's niece Anna Steenkamp called the 'natural distinction of race and religion' (see p. 152). The Natal constitution of 1839 limited the suffrage to white adult males. Potgieter's people adopted the 33 Articles in 1844, which excluded Basters (people born of marriages between Europeans and non-Europeans) 'to the tenth degree' from their

---

42 *Transvaalse Argiefstukkke, Staatsekretaris* (Pretoria: Government Printer, 1949), p. 75.

institutions. Whether the trekkers excluded non-whites from public worship is not known, partly because they had no formal church since the Reformed Church failed to send a minister until 1848 when the British established the Sovereignty in Transorangia. Using missionaries instead – first, Erasmus Smit, and then an American, Daniel Lindley – the trekkers formed congregations, elected church councils, had children baptized when an opportunity arose and appointed commissioners to marry people, schoolmasters to provide some rudimentary education, and 'catechism masters' to instruct children in the church's doctrines. The Reformed Church refused to sanction these marriages and considered the children born of these marriages illegitimate.

The trekkers would not easily do anything that directly clashed with established practice in the Cape, the intellectual and spiritual heartland of South Africa. They were bitterly disappointed that the Cape synod disapproved of the trek in 1837 and sent no minister to them. On the other hand, they prized their membership of the church of their fathers and were aware of the fact that the Reformed Church in the Cape by the early 1850s was asserting its own non-racial character without pressure from the government. They also knew that the Cape Afrikaners supported the 1853 constitution with its non-racial franchise based on a low property qualification. By contrast, British settlers in the eastern part of the colony opposed the low property qualification and the non-racial franchise, occasionally in strongly racist language. Robert Godlonton, editor of the *Grahamstown Journal,* who was sympathetic to the trek, called universal franchise 'a great wrong to the European inhabitants.'[43]

Hence there were conflicting influences. The Free State constitution, drawn up by J. Groenendaal, a Dutch teacher, and A. Coqui and J.M. Orpen, members of the English-speaking party in the Free State, accepted as citizens all white people who had lived in the republic for at least six months. The franchise itself was not specifically based on race (it granted it to adult male burghers) but it was racial in practice.[44] As far as the church was concerned, all parishes in the OFS were absorbed into the DRC of the Cape Colony, accepting its policy of non-discrimination against people on the grounds of color or race.

There was much less ambivalence in the case of the ZAR. Its constitution, accepted in 1858, declared: 'The people are not prepared to allow any equality of the non-white with the white inhabitants, either in the Church or State.' Taking the lead in demanding racial exclusivity in the church was a foreigner, the Rev. Dirk van der Hoff, a Dutch minister, who arrived from the Netherlands in 1852, and was for some years the only minister in the republic.

Eager to incorporate parishes in the Transvaal, the Cape church sent a delegation to the Transvaal. The ministers pointed out that the church recognized the 'existing differences in rank and station' and, in 'numerous instances', allowed separate buildings for non-whites. However, it was the church's duty to spread the Word among the heathen; hence, there could be no racial exclusion.[45]

The delegation reported back that racial equality was the great 'bugbear' of the people

---

43 D.J.P. Haasbroek, 'The Origin of Apartheid in South Africa', *Historia,* 16, 1 (1971), p. 15.
44 J.M. Orpen, *Reminiscences of a Life in South Africa* (Durban, 1908), pp. 203-4.
45 Haasbroek, 'Origin of Apartheid', p. 3.

there. Van der Hoff was determined to found his own church in the Transvaal, and hence had his own agenda in advocating racial exclusivity. He soon won the confidence of Marthinus Wessel Pretorius, son of Andries, who had become the most powerful political and military figure after his father's death in 1853. Van der Hoff chaired a church council that decided to form a new church, the Nederduitsch Hervormde Kerk (NHK). It would be the state church and would not join the synod of the Cape DRC. The Lydenburg parish refused to recognize Van der Hoff as their minister, because he wished to sever relations with the Cape DRC. H.T. Bührman, another Dutchman, wrote from Lydenburg that Van der Hoff insisted that the Cape DRC 'was not good for them because of the equality of coloreds and the white population.'[46]

Had the Cape DRC sent ministers steeped in its own traditions at an earlier stage to the Transvaal, Van der Hoff would have found it much more difficult to carry out his racial agenda. The Lydenburgers, in reaction, formed a DRC parish that was absorbed by the Cape synod. In 1859 another group of burghers founded the Gereformeerde Church of South Africa (the 'Dopper' Church), which was in terms of theological and moral principles the most conservative of the three churches.

One of the founders of the Dopper church was Paul Kruger, who would influence the ZAR politically and ideologically more than anyone else. He is more closely associated than any other leader with the concept of the Afrikaners as a Chosen People like the Ancient Hebrews, with a covenant with God to fulfil a divine plan.[47] Kruger was born into a trekboer family in 1825 and had no more than three months of formal education. He never read any book but the Bible. His Dopper community of the northeastern districts of the Cape Colony was considered more pious and socially conservative than any other community in the colony. He himself was deeply religious, and in his later life strongly influenced by Calvinist beliefs. He frequently relied on a literal interpretation of the Bible as a guide, and there is reason to think that he believed the earth was flat until the end of his life.

The principal religious influence on Kruger was an orthodox Calvinism, unlike the neo-Calvinism S.J. du Toit would propagate in the Cape Colony from the 1870s. The orthodox Calvinism from the early days of the Cape Colony preached a gospel of an omnipotent God who intervened directly in the lives of individuals and communities, and the doctrine of predestination and its corollary, of the Elect. It included a specific strand of Calvinism taught at the Cape, which held that the covenant with God extended to the children of the faithful unto a thousandth generation.[48] This was Kruger's belief, one greatly enhanced by the drama and trauma of the Great Trek. He was a boy of ten when he left the colony with his trekboer family, who soon became part of the trek led by Hendrik Potgieter. Kruger was eleven in the laager of Vegkop when Ndebele warriors attacked it, and in the following year he was in Natal when Dingane's army tried to wipe out the Voortrekkers after the massacre of Retief and his men.

---

46 Haasbroek, 'Origin of Apartheid', pp. 17-19.

47 D.H. Akenson, *God's Peoples: Covenant and Land in South Africa, Israel and Ulster* (Ithaca: Cornell University Press, 1992), pp. 69-71.

48 Jonathan Neil Gerstner, *The Thousand Generation Covenant: Dutch Reformed Covenant Theology and Group Identity in Colonial South Africa* (Leiden: E.J. Brill, 1991).

Another influence on Kruger had its roots in religious dissent in the Netherlands. In 1834 a working-class Calvinist revival there had led to the establishment of a separate church: the Separate Christian Reformed Church. It opposed the theological liberalism of the main Reformed church of the Netherlands, the weakening of the traditional confessional standards, the use of hymns in church services (seen as a symbol of the erosion of the true Reformed doctrine), secular education, and state control of the church.[49] Kruger was among the Doppers who expressed a desire to have a minister of their own from the Netherlands. Dirk Postma, a secessionist in the Netherlands, became the first minister of this church in 1859. Kruger took the lead in achieving a complete split from the state church.[50]

It has recently been argued that it is wrong to think that the Afrikaners saw themselves as a Chosen People with a Divine mission before Kruger started to expound this idea in the 1880s. It is also argued that only after the Anglo-Boer War (1899-1902) did a group of intellectuals in Potchefstroom turn the idea of a chosen people into a motivating ideology. This is not, as it may seem, a minor issue, for, as André du Toit pointed out, the idea of a national mission is a nationalist idea.[51] If nationalist ideas did exist among Afrikaners well before the industrialization of South Africa, it was to be expected that this nationalism would be a durable force, able to overcome temporary setbacks.

But there is indeed evidence of some Voortrekkers, specifically the Doppers, seeing themselves as especially chosen, with a divine mission, like the people of Israel. As a Reformed Church minister in Bloemfontein between 1849 and 1860, Andrew Murray noted the tendency among the trekkers (he appeared to have the Doppers in mind), 'not to distinguish clearly between the relations of Israel and their own to the savages with whom they saw themselves surrounded . . . They thought that in going forth to conquer them they were extending Christianity . . .'[52]

W.W. Collins, who had lived in the Orange Free State since the early days of the republic, emphasized the commitment of a divine mission even more clearly. His reminiscences in his account of the year 1858 referred to the Doppers as a 'peculiar sect', evidently obsessed with 'Jehova's wonderful manifestation to his ancient people in . . . the Old Testament.' 'They [the Doppers] seem to be possessed with the idea that they too are a Divinely favored people in the same sense that Israel was, and have been signally endowed by the Almighty with sufficient intuitive knowledge and understanding to undertake any mental or other duties.'[53]

If Collins' reference to the idea of a chosen people had indeed come down 'from father to son', as he phrased it, it means that the Doppers had developed the notion when they

---

49 James Donald Bratt, 'Dutch Calvinism in Modern America: The History of a Conservative Subculture', doctoral diss., Yale University, 1978, Chapter One.

50 D.W. Krüger, *Paul Kruger* (Johannesburg: Dagbreek, 1961), vol. 1, p. 59.

51 See André du Toit's articles published in *American Historical Review*, 88, 4, (1983); *South African Historical Journal*, 16 (1984) and *Comparative Studies in Society and History*, 27 (1985). For a different view, see Donald H. Akenson, *God's Peoples: Covenant and Land in South Africa, Israel and Ulster* (Ithaca: Cornell University Press, 1992).

52 J. du Plessis, *The Life of Andrew Murray* (London: Marshall Brothers, 1919), p. 416.

53 W.W. Collins, *Free Statia: Reminiscences of a Lifetime in the Orange Free State* (Bloemfontein: The Friend, 1907), p. 158.

were in the Cape Colony, and that in Kruger's case it had been strengthened by his trek experience. Not that the sense of mission was widespread or well articulated among the Voortrekkers; even among the Doppers there were differences about the nature of their mission – to conquer the land, or to do missionary work, or live by an almost literal understanding of the Bible? Kruger certainly did not subscribe to the heresy that all black people were inferior and eternally doomed. Apart from Calvinism, Kruger's main guiding principle was a fierce determination to preserve the ZAR's republican freedom. In a very literal way he was convinced that he would be accursed should he sacrifice the independent state in which the burghers lived.

The 'chosen people' theology was by no means a mainstream doctrine or a source of common inspiration. Church schisms racked the Transvaal burgher community, and the three Reformed churches in the ZAR watched each other with suspicion. The Hervormde Kerk, while relatively liberal in its theological views, firmly opposed all missionary work. The Dopper majority accepted missionary work as long as it avoided common worship, seen as an 'abomination.'[54] They preferred German missionaries, most of whom expected their converts to respect the existing social hierarchy. The pro-British DRC ministers tended to be much more liberal in their attitudes towards blacks but, while in principle in favor of missionary work, did very little in practice. In the early 1880s a hasty merger was concluded between the Hervormde and Reformed churches, but some Hervormde parishes soon broke away.

Fragile new democracies

In 1851 the pre-republican Transvaal Volksraad expressed a commitment to egalitarianism in the following terms: '[E]veryone is free, we make no allowance for who is rich or poor and each is the equal to the other as a full human being.'[55] But despite this egalitarianism the trek failed to create an overarching community or a crystallized sense of national identity. Most Voortrekkers and their children knew better what they were not – they were not British subjects – rather than who they were. The submissions that different OFS divisions sent to the constitutional committee in the early 1850s cited 'Afrikaner' as only one of several terms of identification. One such letter stated: 'We call people Afferkaanders [sic] not when they have merely been born in this country, but they must share our belief.' In eight other letters in the same archive collection, these other terms of identification appear: 'Hollandse Afrikanen' (once), 'Hollandse Boeren' (once), 'Emigrants' (twice), 'Boeren' (eight times) and 'Boers' (three times).[56]

The economy of the new ZAR was much too weak to weld Boer society together and to underpin an efficient democratic state. The colonial ports were far away and neither republic had any major export. Without marketable commodities, currency was soon exhausted and both the state and its burghers became indebted to foreign merchants and banks. Burghers were hard put and reluctant to pay taxes, and many ignored the call-ups for commando. The ZAR was almost solely dependent on subsistence farm-

---

54 See the article by John Murray in *The Cape Monthly Magazine*, 1877, p. 376.
55 A.N. Pelzer, *Geskiedenis van die Suid-Afrikaanse Republiek* (Cape Town: Balkema, 1950), p. 50.
56 Internet *www.24.com/LitNet*, Schalk Jacobs, 18 March 2000.

ing, which meant that markets and towns were slow to develop. To an important extent, the commitment to an egalitarian society of burghers also undermined the effort to build a stable republic and a functioning state. Both republics' policies provided free land to burghers. In the OFS, until 1866 every trekker was entitled to two farms, and a position similar to the ZAR's. But two decades after their founding, both states had squandered virtually their only resource, land.

In 1871 the ZAR government temporarily stopped issuing land in order to promote a more systematic form of colonization. But it was too late. Land speculation had become pronounced in both republics. White settlement had occurred in a lopsided way; many farms supported too many people while large areas in the hands of speculators lay unoccupied. The situation was worst in the Transvaal, where white population density remained low with, even by the mid-1880s, no more than one white person per square mile. Absentee landowners and companies accumulated approximately half the land in the Transvaal, and half of the burgher population was landless by the end of the century.

Furthermore, over its first three decades, the ZAR was nearly crippled by political schisms. During the 1850s and early 1860s, three or four republics with their own personal leaderships were always vying for power. The threat of civil war constantly loomed in the 1860s. Paul Kruger, chosen as commandant-general in 1863, made Herculean attempts to defend the authority of whatever state authority existed and to instill a sense of civic virtue among the burghers. He often expressed despair about the future of the state.

State-building was also an extraordinarily difficult task in the OFS. Twelve years after the founding of the Republic, the Bloemfontein journal *De Tijd* spelled out how weak the young state was in an article in its 27 February 1866 edition: 'Simple people find themselves in a vast land, surrounded in all quarters by enemies, without judges, without soldiers, without money, divided through ignorance and derided by a Colony adjacent to it.'

In both republics local strongmen exercised great influence in the districts, often rivaling the power or authority of office bearers in the system of local government that was based on the pre-1828 system in the Cape Colony. While the president appointed the landdrost of a district, the field cornets of each ward and the field commandant of each district were elected by the burghers, and these field cornets and commandants were the chief sources of authority in the districts well into the 1870s. The state's machinery for raising taxes from its own citizens was inadequate. Not until the final quarter of the century did a landdrost, as an official appointed by the central government, begin to replace the field cornets as the government's main agent in the rural areas. The commando remained the main instrument for police and military action in the Transvaal.

The trekkers in the two republics had excluded blacks from their state and church, but not from the vitally important institution, the commando, though the Africans that went along were unarmed and served as mere auxiliaries. Only when Potgieter took an English hunter along was there an outcry.

Egalitarianism among whites was the official ideology, but on the ground it worked out otherwise. Elected field cornets and commandants were invariably drawn from the ranks of, and beholden to, the large landholders; some developed into local strongmen, prompting some landdrosts to exclaim in exasperation that they behaved like 'emperors of the state.' Many large farmers sent their bywoners (tenant farmers) or other poor whites to take their place in the commandos. A correspondent to a Free State paper bluntly declared that it was mainly the poor burghers and their children who fought the war of 1866 to 1868 against the Sotho.[57] During the first two decades mostly local strongmen, either field cornets or commandants, commandeered and distributed African labor. Much of the taxes Africans paid probably ended up as their property.[58] They were strong enough to resist laws aimed at limiting the number of black families on a white farm as part of an effort to distribute black labor more evenly. The poorer burghers were better represented in the Volksraad.

The incorporation of blacks

In 1852 a trekker, Coenraad Scheepers, spoke for the great majority when he said: '[Whites] and blacks cannot live together, unless the black man is in a state of subjection to the white.'[59] Blacks greatly outnumbered whites. The one factor that worked in the whites' favor was the absence among African chiefdoms of a clear sense of racial identity; alliances between African chiefdoms against whites were very rare. The republican burghers rarely fought alone against Africans and, like the burghers on the eastern frontier of the Colony, they formed alliances with certain African chiefdoms or factions of chiefdoms and avoided having to contend with overwhelming numbers. They also tried to foment trouble within the chiefdoms in order to set faction against faction.

Although finding labor was their constant preoccupation, the trekkers did not seek to build compact settlements or to reach self-sufficiency. The Rev. Van der Hoff wrote of the Transvaal burghers in 1858: 'They are not very energetic and prefer everything to be done by the Kaffers.'[60] They turned most agriculture on farms over to the blacks and adapted to their customary agricultural methods rather than imposing their own.

The more peaceful way to get black labor was to settle near an African settlement and conclude an informal arrangement with the chief. This practice had become so extensive by 1853 that Andries Pretorius had prohibited farmers from settling close to such settlements. The burghers made some efforts to get adult contract labor in exchange for hoes, blankets and heifers, but because they had a meager supply of these they increasingly resorted to force. Some burghers compelled chiefs to supply tribute labor and punished them when this labor deserted; in other cases they seized prisoners on a commando. The smaller chiefdoms, instructed to provide labor, were fined if they refused, their cattle were seized, their chief threatened, or their people whipped.

Stronger African chiefs would not tolerate such action. The Free State burghers had a formidable adversary in Moshweshwe with his consummate statecraft and his force of close to ten thousand mounted men, and, during the 1850s, the Basotho held firmly to the

---

57 See the letters in *De Tyd* of 25 March and 15 April 1868.

58 Stanley Trapido, 'Landlord and Tenant in a Colonial Economy: The Transvaal, 1880-1910', *Journal of Southern African Studies*, Vol. 5, No. 1 (1978), pp. 26-50.

59 Liebenberg, *Pretorius*, p. 116.

60 Potgieter, 'Die Vestiging van die Blanke in die Transvaal', p. 301.

land they occupied. But, by the mid-1860s, the balance of power had shifted; Moshwesh-we was now eighty and unable to stem the growing tension between his people and the burghers. There had been a steady increase of whites in the OFS and President Brand had managed to unite them. After war broke out in 1865, a peace concluded the follow-ing year gave the republic the greatest part of Lesotho. Fighting broke out again but, just before Lesotho was completely conquered in 1868, Britain established a protec-torate over what was now virtually only a mountain kingdom. During the 1870s and 1880s Sotho communities in the OFS and Basotholand faced tremendous pressure from burghers who wanted land, cattle and laborers. Later a chief recalled: 'The Boers treated us very badly, killing several of our people and flogging many, including myself.'[61] Many Sotho had left, trekking over the mountains into Natal. The ZAR struggled to control its much larger African population. There was a chronic shortage of ammunition, while many Africans had acquired guns and ammunition by the early 1870s. Particularly on the ZAR's northern frontier, control over blacks was tenuous. The tiny settlement of Schoemansdal, founded by Potgieter in 1849 in the far north, had had a precarious exis-tence from the start. A small community was surrounded by populous African chief-doms. In the trekker economy elephant hunting and ivory first played an exceptionally important part. Voortrekker hunters in the far north, to overcome their weakness in numbers and the tsetse fly hazard, gave guns to blacks, called *swart skuts* (black hunters). Initially the collaboration worked well, but divisions arose over the spoils and the *swart skuts* transferred their allegiance to Venda chiefs who led the most important of the chiefdoms.[62] Soon the trekkers lost their monopoly of guns.

The trekkers' troubles were compounded by the reckless conduct of the people in power. Potgieter had set the tone with his willful refusal to accept any checks on his au-thority and his raiding activities. Ten years after his death, his son's successor, Stephanus Schoeman, appointed João Albisini, a Portuguese trader with an Afrikaner wife, as super-intendent of the African chiefdoms in the north. With some two thousand African fol-lowers, Albisini exacted tribute for the government and booty for himself by raiding the cattle of African chiefdoms. As the local commandant and field cornets followed his example, resistance mounted among the increasingly hostile Venda people, who launched their own raids on white farms.

In 1864, with the ZAR in its weakest state, Kruger was elected commandant-general of the ZAR. Divisions between trekker factions had threatened to degenerate into civil war, nearly paralyzing the state. In the northern part of the republic, the dispersed trekker settlements were on the point of collapse and, in the eastern part, until the mid-1860s the trekkers were locked into a grim fight against the Mabhogo. In 1864 a burgher wrote to the president that because of the failure to establish control over the blacks, 'the name of the Afrikaner nation had been lost and along with that the fear it had inspired among the natives.'[63] When Kruger called the burghers out for commandos half of them would

61 T. Keegan, 'White Settlement and Black Subjugation on the South African Highveld', in W. Beinart, et al., eds., *Putting a Plough to the Ground* (Johannesburg: Ravan, 1986), p. 233.
62 Roger Wagner, 'Zoutpansberg: The Dynamics of a Hunting Frontier', in Shula Marks and Anthony At-more (eds.), *Economy and Society in Pre-industrial South Africa* (London: Longman, 1980), pp. 313-50.
63 D.W. Krüger, *Paul Kruger* (Johannesburg: Dagbreek Boekhandel, 1961), vol. 1, p. 85.

fail to appear, and even those who had turned out returned home as soon as the commando encountered resistance. The burghers blamed Kruger and other officers. In response he urged the state to punish disobedient burghers and the church to censure them. 'If the law is not enforced I foresee a general destruction of church and state.'[64]

In the late 1860s Kruger went with a commando to shore up the white settlement on the northern frontier, but had too little ammunition to attack the Venda. The two northern districts of Soutpansberg and Waterberg, stretching from the Limpopo to the Olifants rivers, were evacuated. Schoemansdal, the main town in the Soutpansberg, was abandoned and burned to the ground by Africans. The next year, in 1868, Kruger reported that the town of Potgietersrust had been invaded by blacks and burned, and that the Waterberg district was on the point of being 'destroyed.'[65] A year later a combined force of trekkers and Swazi attacked the Venda chief Makhado but failed to subjugate him, and the trekkers abandoned most of the northern part of the republic.

In the early 1870s a Pedi challenge to the white settlement in the eastern part of the republic forced the ZAR to turn to the Swazi under Mswati for help.[66] By the mid-1870s the Pedi were raiding farms with impunity.[67] A commando that went out against them in 1876 ended in a stalemate and an ignominious retreat (see p. 229). Some burghers now moved to the central Highveld, for a long time largely unoccupied by whites; by the end of the 1870s more than half the whites were concentrated in the southern half of the state on farms and small villages.[68]

For leading burghers the attempt to establish white authority seemed to face insuperable odds. In 1871 Commandant-General Paul Kruger declared that there were 'easily a thousand blacks to every white in our state.'[69] (Thirty years later the first census found a ratio of ten to one.) Blacks were the 'fervent enemies of the whites' and, given the chance, 'would not let the whites remain in the country for a single day.'[70]

The British occupation of the Transvaal from 1877 to 1881 (see pp. 228-31) introduced a much more modern form of fighting and the organization of resources in eliminating or subjugating the enemy. Yet the British soon adopted some of the Boer tactics. Earlier the imperial government had been critical of the military alliances of the Transvaal burghers with Africans. But when the British finally defeated the Pedi in 1879, they took a full fifteen thousand Swazis along with them in battle.[71]

African resistance continued, but the scale had tilted in favor of the whites. From the early 1880s the trekkers began to win control. Their numbers had grown and the confidence and discipline of the commando had improved after the victories over the British forces in resisting the British occupation. In 1883 a ZAR commando defeated the Nzu-

---

64 Krüger, *Kruger,* vol. 1, p. 92.

65 Krüger, *Kruger,* vol. 1, pp. 114-22; J.C.A. Boeyens, 'Die konflik tussen die Venda en die blankes in Transvaal, 1864-1869, *AYB,* 53, 2 (1990).

66 Peter Delius, *The Land Belongs to Us* (Johannesburg: Ravan, 1983), pp. 82-3.

67 Bonner, *Kings, Commoners and Concessionaires,* pp. 66-7.

68 Potgieter, 'Die vestiging van die blanke in die Transvaal', pp. 167, 304.

69 State Archives (Pretoria), Replies of Paul Kruger to the 'Kaffir Commission', 1871.

70 *Weekly Press,* August 1895, p. 31.

71 See the memorandum by E. Fairfield published as an annexure to D.M. Schreuder, *Gladstone and Kruger* (London: Routledge and Kegan Paul, 1989), p. 518.

nza chiefdom, a section of the southern Ndebele. Some ten thousand African prisoners were dispersed among the burghers and indentured for five years each.

'Black ivory' and 'inboekelinge'

In the Soutpansberg area, commandos frequently abducted African children and women and indentured the children. In some cases they were sold to other burghers. This was called the trade in 'black ivory', which followed the trade in white ivory after the elephant herds had been decimated. In the early days of the ZAR, people in public posts connived in or condoned this practice.[72] One field cornet asked Acting President Marthinus Wessel Pretorius, due to visit the north, not to forget his need for labor. 'If you could obtain a young girl for my wife, I would be very grateful, but you must not pay more than six or seven pounds, because they are nothing more than a handful of flies.'[73]

To avoid being discredited for permitting slavery, the ZAR authorities tried to regulate the practice, and, in 1851, the Transvaal Volksraad issued the Apprentice Act, which permitted burghers to apply to the landdrost or field cornet to indenture African children 'given as gifts or obtained in any other legal or voluntary manner.' After the age of twenty-five they were to be exempt from 'all compulsory labor obligations' and be released.[74] But the act also permitted the transfer of indentured servants called *inboekelinge*, which encouraged a trade in these children. By the mid-1850s the trade had reached such a scale that, in Cape Town, *De Zuid-Afrikaan* reported 'a regular export' of captives to other parts of the ZAR. President Boshoff told the OFS Volksraad that it was well known that some farmers had bought child apprentices from ZAR burghers. Some burghers made no secret of it and did not consider it a crime.

In the 1860s missionaries considered the inboekelinge the main source of labor in the eastern Transvaal. From Makapanspoort in the north, a German missionary reported that wagonloads of children were regularly brought to the town. And in 1871 the explorer Carl Mauch wrote that once the hunting for white ivory was no longer profitable, the trade in black ivory replaced it.[75]

When in 1858 a Free State commando kidnapped 115 children, a chief, Mahura, wrote to Boshoff, the OFS president, telling him that if they were not returned there was no prospect for peace, adding 'you are surely familiar with the tenderness of a parent towards his children.'[76] In 1865 the Rev. Charles Murray, a Dutch Reformed inspector of missions, incensed when he encountered a child trader, told him that this practice was one of the reasons why the Lord had withheld his blessing from the land. The trader,

---

72 Liebenberg, *Pretorius*, p. 118.

73 Jan Boeyens, '"Black Ivory": The Indenture System and Slavery in Zoutpansberg, 1848-1869', in Elizabeth Eldredge and Fred Morton (eds.), *Slavery in South Africa* (Pietermaritzburg: University of Natal Press, 1994), p. 203.

74 Boeyens, '"Black Ivory"', p. 188.

75 E.E. Burke, ed., *Journals of Carl Mauch, 1869-1872* (Salisbury, National Archives, 1969), p. 113. For this section on *inboekelinge* I have drawn on Peter Delius, *The Land Belongs to Us*, pp. 136-47 and J.C.A. Boeyens, 'Die konflik tussen die Venda en die blankes in die Transvaal, 1864-1869', *AYB*, 1990.

76 H.J. Van Aswegen, 'Die verhouding tussen blank en nie-blank in die OVS, 1854-1902', doctoral diss., University of the OFS, 1968, pp. 142-3, 475.

Gert Duvenhage, retorted that the practice was not slavery since 'it was sanctioned by an *inboeksel* [a certificate of indenture].'[77] In 1869 the synod of the Dutch Reformed Church in the republic considered the situation so serious that it adopted a resolution that stated: 'Church discipline will be applied to all members of our denomination found guilty of buying or selling or exchanging or accepting in exchange Kaffir children, contrary to the laws of the state.' Without explanation it decided two years later to rescind the resolution on the grounds that the evil no longer existed.[78]

Many inboekelinge ran away, but enough remained to become a distinct stratum in the Transvaal labor force. They were given new names and were taught Dutch or Afrikaans. Many became detached from their parents and their indigenous culture. A contemporary account described the fortunes of one child, Mozane (renamed Valentyn), who at the age of eight was indentured along with his siblings: 'Eventually they became used to their new masters and their new life and were no longer as distressed as when they were seized. Valentyn was given over to play with and attend to the young Hermanus Steyn . . . The young white Hermanus and the young black Valentyn soon got to know each other and were always together . . . The one learned from the other, bad as well as good.'[79] Anthony Trollope, the English novelist, wrote in 1878: '[With] the white children there are always to be seen black children playing. Nor does there seem to me any feeling of repugnance at such intercourse on the part of anyone concerned.'[80]

Many of the indentured servants grew up to become what the burghers called a *mak* or docile African, sometimes also referred to as an *oorlamse,* one who spoke Afrikaans well and had absorbed much of Boer culture. The relationship of the mak or oorlamse African with his or her Afrikaner master and mistress was hierarchical, but could also be quite informal and warm. Anthony Aylward, an Irishman who settled in the Transvaal, sketched the relationship through the following vignette: When the oorlamse traveled in a wagon with their master, or hunted with him, or sat at some bivouac fire, 'they keep up a continual chatter about their journeys – the fate of this horse, and the conduct of that bullock, the trouble nephew John had, and the good shot Uncle Peter fired forming subjects of never-failing interest. If his wife or his children want medicine the good Boer supplies it; and it is rare indeed for a family of farmers to visit the townships without buying some little present or another to gladden the hearts of their "volk".'[81]

Aylward offered higher wages to this class to live with him, but they refused, saying that 'the Boers had brought them up and they would remain with the Boers.'[82] Because of his bias against the English and sympathy for the Transvaal burghers, Aylward's evidence must be treated with caution. However, a British commissioner wrote in very similar terms during the annexation of 1877 to 1881: '[The] Boers treat that class of servants [Africans brought up as inboekelinge] remarkably well. I mean to say, that they always mix on an equality; they get their clothes and food and everything else, in fact

---

77 Boeyens, '"Black Ivory"', p. 204
78 *The Truth about the Boer and His Church*, (pamphlet issued by the leadership of the Cape DRC, March 1900), pp. 11-12.
79 The missionary Nachtigal cited by Delius, *The Land Belongs to Us*, p. 140.
80 Anthony Trollope, *South Africa* (1878, repr. Cape Town: Balkema, 1973), p. 397.
81 Alfred Aylward, *The Transvaal of Today* (Edinburgh: Blackwood, 1881), p. 153.
82 Aylward, *The Transvaal of Today*, p. 151.

they are too valuable a class for the Boers to ill-treat.'[83] When they became adults, in-boekelinge and other oorlamses usually received cattle and a piece of land. While the women worked in the house, the men served as wagon-drivers, ploughmen, and herders.

The rise of the OFS 'model' republic

By the end of the 1860s Britain began reversing its policy on non-intervention in the Highveld. At the request of the Sotho king, it annexed Basutoland in 1868, just before the Free State could conquer it. In 1871 Britain annexed the rich diamond fields at what would become known as Kimberley, after a British arbitrator had accepted the claims of the Griqua and the Tlhaping over that of the Republic of the Orange Free State. The OFS considered the British grabbing of the diamond fields a grievous injustice, since the arbitrator rejected what seemed to be a strong OFS claim, but losing the diamond fields was a blessing in disguise and a turning point in the republic's history. It brought a large market onto its border without the disadvantage of having to extend the vote to large numbers of immigrants.

Jan Brand, president from 1864 to 1888, handled the issue well from a diplomatic point of view, and succeeded in getting Britain to pay the sum of £90,000 as compensation. Brand was a gifted leader and instilled new political confidence. He spent the money on a state bank that enhanced the state's financial autonomy, and, by the early 1880s, he had established the basic framework of a remarkably stable state. The state was by no means rich or modern, however. Until the late 1870s it had no highways to speak of and no bridge over the Orange River until 1879. Some wool was exported, but wheat had to be imported from Basotuland until the 1890s. Still, Brand had his priorities right. He put special emphasis on establishing a sound legal system in order to attract trade and other forms of business. He stamped out corruption.

The state eagerly used high-quality immigrants to strengthen the administration. A Scot, Dr John Brebner, reformed the educational system; a German, Dr C.L.F. Borcken-hagen, became editor of De Express in 1877, the Dutch newspaper published from 1875 in Bloemfontein. A strong champion of republican independence, Borckenhagen wielded great influence on both sides of the Vaal River.[84]

British cultural influence remained strong. From the start to the final years of the republic, Bloemfontein was largely an English town. English predominated in the private schools of the towns, and even in rural schools established by wealthy farmers. The Volksraad declared, in 1881, that the preference given to English in the leading state school, Grey College, taught 'children to despise and forget their own language and to consider their nation with contempt.'[85] In the mid-1880s two visiting DRC ministers, A.A. Louw and C.F.J. Muller, expressed astonishment at the widespread use of English. As late as 1899 the Bloemfontein paper De Express wrote despairingly: 'Although the

---

83 Peter Delius and Stanley Trapido, 'Inboekselings and Oorlams', in Belinda Bozzoli (ed.), Town and Coun-tryside in the Transvaal (Johannesburg: Ravan Press, 1983), pp. 76-8.
84 S.F. Malan, Politieke Strominge onder die Afrikaners van die Vrystaatse Republiek (Durban: Butterworth, 1982), p. 70.
85 Malan, Politieke Strominge, p. 92.

English praise the Free State as a model republic they are ceaselessly fusing it with the Empire in language, civilization and culture.'[86]

Nevertheless, a republican spirit had developed among the burghers that stood in marked contrast to the 'colonial patriotism' of the Cape Afrikaners (see the next chapter). When Jan (Onze Jan) Hofmeyr visited the republic, he remarked in a speech in Bloemfontein in 1883 that Afrikaners were reluctant to put themselves up for Parliament in the Cape Colony because they did not speak English well enough. If an Afrikaner appeared in court in the colony 'his case is taken in a language he does not understand.' And 'if he is called up to serve on commando, then he must serve under the command of a man who he has not elected, who does not know his language, who does not understand his character, and who despises him.' North of the Orange River, Hofmeyr continued, there was 'a lively feeling, that Government and people are one, but to the South that feeling is either completely absent or very uncertain.'[87] By 1881 the OFS was considered the best administered part of South Africa .

The stability of the state can be attributed to its agrarian character, the relatively homogeneous electorate, and the absence of large concentrations of wealth. English-speakers and the few Germans who dominated commercial and professional life in the towns had a leavening effect. There was no xenophobia, and even in the 1890s the state welcomed foreign settlers. The OFS combined its republicanism with the inclusive sense of nationhood of the Afrikaner Bond in the Cape. Lord Bryce, a British constitutional expert, described it as in many a ways an ideal commonwealth (p. 235).

A failed state in the Transvaal

By 1872 the ZAR had thirty thousand white people, among them eight thousand able-bodied men (6,650 Afrikaner farmers, one thousand townsmen, who were mostly English speakers, and 350 diggers). An estimated twelve thousand Africans were in the service of farmers. Political developments in the ZAR, with its succession of bungling, incompetent leaders, stood in sharp contrast to the OFS. Marthinus Wessel Pretorius, President of the ZAR during the 1860s, spent his time on a futile attempt to unite his republic with the OFS. His amateurish handling of the ZAR claims to the diamond fields ended in absolute disaster when the republic's claims were dismissed; soon after that the Transvaal became indebted to foreign banks.

The Transvaal burghers, determined to get a clever man as president, approached Thomas François Burgers, a liberal minister who had been suspended by the Reformed Church in the Cape for heresy. He became president in 1872. To a relatively backward agrarian community with conservative religious beliefs had come an excommunicated minister with radically liberal religious beliefs. Burgers had a good intellect and considerable oratorical skills but he tended to be tactless, combative, and brash. He was an idealist with grand visions, but lacked the patience to win the trust of this ultra-conser-

---

86 J.C. Steyn, *Tuiste in eie taal* (Cape Town: Tafelberg, 1980), pp. 158-164. See also Karel Schoeman, *Bloemfontein: die ontstaan van 'n stad* (Cape Town: Human & Rousseau, 1980).

87 J.H. Hofmeyr, *The Life of Jan Hendrik (Onze Jan) Hofmeyr* (Cape Town; Van de Sandt de Villiers, 1913), p. 235.

vative community. He sponsored balls and other forms of entertainment in Pretoria. In a republic that was desperately poor he borrowed money on a large scale for grand projects to modernize the republic. To introduce hard currency he borrowed the substantial sum of £66,000 at a high rate of interest from the Cape Commercial Bank. He did achieve some things, however, including an education department with its own education system, a museum, the first permanent Supreme Court, and a small regular army. He urged that national history be taught in schools to counter the imperialist version, and tried to start a public library. He commissioned the anthem *Kent gij dat Volk* and helped to found the first Dutch newspaper, *De Volksstem*. He propagated a composite (white) nationality, not based on a particular ethnic group but on the white community as a whole who had settled in South Africa and had made the country its home. 'We must stop talking of different nationalities,' he told Afrikaner and English diamond diggers. 'We should be only one nation, and know only one nationality – the Afrikaansche.'[88]

Burgers' most ambitious scheme was a railway line to Delagoa Bay, to be an outlet free from British control. In pursuit of it he spent more than a year on a visit to London and other European capitals in search of a foreign loan of £300,000, but the Cape bank, fearing a ZAR default, put all kinds of obstacles in the way. He raised only £90,000 and spent £63,000 of it on railway material in Belgium, some of it sent to Delagoa Bay, where it lay rotting, the rest later sold in Europe at an enormous loss. When he returned, Transvaal politics was in such turmoil that the railway scheme collapsed. The *Transvaal Argus* said that Burgers aspired to erect 'a structure of marble but with only clay in his hands and without any builders.'[89] Kruger made the cruel but apt comment about all of his ambitious schemes: 'Burgers wanted to fly, but his wings were clipped in time. Now he has to crawl along with us.'[90]

But educational reform as much as the disastrous railway scheme eventually led to the collapse of Burgers' authority. He had wanted to ban religious instruction during school hours, on the grounds that the Bible did not belong in school since school was the place where science had to be taught. In the end, bible studies were permitted during school hours. He also proposed that membership of a church should not be required as a qualification for teachers and education officials. All of this greatly shocked the more conservative burghers, especially the members of the Dopper church. Kruger said he feared for 'the fall of Christendom.' When a group of burghers asked him to lead them out of the Transvaal to a new land where they could express their religious and political beliefs without any disturbance, Kruger was sorely tempted, but decided to stay to build up a 'pure' church in the Transvaal. The trek went on without him. It was close to an utter disaster. Between five hundred and six hundred people left from Pretoria and Rustenburg between 1874-1880, travelling across the Bechuana desert to South West Africa and the south of the present Angola on the *Dorsland Trek* (Thirstland Trek). Between 250 and 300 people perished or turned back.

The ZAR was largely a failed state with incredible confusion in the administration

---

88 M.S. Appelgryn, *Thomas François Burgers* (Pretoria: HAUM, 1979), p. 48.
89 F.A. Van Jaarsveld, 'T.F. Burgers', W.J. de Kock (ed.) *Suid-Afrikaanse Biografiese Woordeboek*, vol. 1 (Cape Town: Nasionale Raad vir Sosiale Navorsing, 1968), p. 142.
90 Appelgryn, *Burgers*, p. 183.

when Lord Carnarvon in 1876 instructed Theophilus Shepstone, Native Administrator in Natal, to annex it. The state was so deeply in debt that many civil servants could not be paid. Land, pledged for public and private debt, was virtually unsaleable. The Transvaal burghers were hopelessly divided and could not even challenge the body of twenty-five troops Shepstone had at his disposal. On 12 April 1877 Shepstone proclaimed the Transvaal a British colony.[91] Burgers returned to the Cape Colony, but the rest of the executive, including Kruger, kept their seats. Most civil servants took the oath of loyalty to the new government. Everyone was waiting to see whether Shepstone could make good on his promise of self-rule and the use of Dutch as a second official language.

British administrators reformed the chaotic finances and defective administrative machinery of the Transvaal during the period of occupation. A separate Department of Native Affairs gave centralized direction to local officials on how to collect taxes and labor service from Africans. There was now a uniform hut tax of ten shillings and clear pass regulations.[92]

The impact of the frontier

For much of the first two hundred years of white settlement many Afrikaners lived on a frontier: a region or zone where Afrikaners interacted with non-whites in a situation where government controls were lacking. By the early 1880s the frontier all over South Africa had effectively closed. There was no more 'open land' ready for white settlement. The frontier turbulence and lawlessness had largely come to an end.

Britain acted as the main agent for stimulating the national cohesion that could overcome the fractiousness and anarchic tendencies of the frontier. During the final decade of the century a perceptive English observer gave this description of the republican Afrikaners: 'Their impatience of restraint, their unwillingness to submit to the irksomeness of government is proverbial.' He cited 'a leading statesman' of the two republics – it was probably F.W. Reitz – who declared that it was only 'the constant succession of acts of British interference that increased the spirit of Republicanism.'[93]

A traveler sketched a compelling picture of the personality the frontier in the Transvaal had produced by the 1890s. He first painted the dark side. Shirking the competition of modern life, the frontiersmen had become indolent and devoid of any ambition beyond retaining their independence on their farms. They were 'deficient in honesty and veracity, ignorant, unprogressive and in most respects two centuries behind other European nations.' There was also a brighter side. They were excellent pioneers 'with marvelous powers of endurance', a brave, self-reliant people, peace-loving yet ever ready to defend their independence, 'slow to move but bitter and obstinate when roused', 'genial, hospitable and affectionate in family relationships', a large-hearted people, to their own kind and, as a result of their stern life, 'possessed of a broad common sense.'[94]

The Afrikaners lived on different frontiers and generalizations are hazardous. What

91 Appelgryn, *Burgers,* pp. 246-55.
92 P. Delius, 'Abel Erasmus: Power and Profit in the Eastern Transvaal', in *Putting a Plough to the Ground,* pp. 176-88.
93 Francis Younghusband, *South Africa of Today* (London: Macmillan, 1890), pp. 245-6.
94 Younghusband, *South Africa of Today,* pp. 41-2.

follows is most applicable to the Transvaal frontier of the late-nineteenth century, where the Afrikaner family on the farm formed the center of frontier life. People tended to marry early. Paul Kruger's mother, for instance, married at fifteen and died at twenty-seven after having given birth to seven children. Virtually no one – including spinsters and bachelors of advanced age – lived outside a family relationship. Family obligations and loyalties took precedence over other commitments. Lack of land or the fear of attacks by blacks often compelled several related families to live on the same farm, forming an extended family. The custom developed of people addressing each other in familial terms such as 'Oom', 'Tante', 'Niggie' or 'Neef'(Uncle, Aunt, and Cousin) even if they were not related to each other, but the nuclear family remained the core of frontier life.[95]

Survival in a very basic sense depended on having enough whites on a farm to defend lives and property. Large families made sense. Farmers often had no option but to make their own children work. Almost every person was valuable and played a role. Looking back on the frontier days, the Boer War hero Koos de la Rey put it in vivid terms: 'The most priceless thing in the world was the life of a white man; we were few and could not afford to lose a single one. Why, the Boers would not sacrifice the life of a white man, not even for murder, cowardice or treachery – and there were bad cases of these – but there never was an execution.'[96]

Families took responsibility for their members, though a tight family unit could be hostile to those on adjoining farms. There was a distinct unwillingness to co-operate with others in groups or organizations to improve their own economic fortunes and the social conditions of the region. Individuals tended to trust their families, but trusted few, if any, outside the family circle. In 1885 W.J. Leyds, a young Dutchman trained in law who had just become the ZAR State Attorney, wrote of the Transvaal frontiersmen: 'The volk is not honest, but I must concede that it is clever. No man trusts another and he is quite right not to do so.'[97] He elaborated: 'The national characteristic appears to be cunning dishonesty or dishonest cunning. In my stay here I have been warned, not least by the farmers: "trust no one – lies, duplicity and egotism are practiced by everyone".'[98] Writing ten years later, Bryce also commented on the lack of trust among the Afrikaners on the frontier: They 'were a slow, quiet, well-meaning people, extremely conservative, very sparing because they have little ready money, very suspicious because afraid of being outwitted by English traders.'[99]

Apart from the church, there was limited institutional life outside the capital that could foster political integration. In the Transvaal only 8 per cent of white children of school-going age were at school in 1877; in the OFS, 12 per cent. In politics and in fighting on commandos an extraordinary degree of political factionalism and division often existed, captured by the term *dwarstrekkery*. The isolated Transvaal frontier produced an extreme individualism and lack of discipline, an unwillingness to risk white lives, and a refusal

95 G. Cronjé, 'Die sosiale ordening van die Afrikaner', in P.W. Grobbelaar (ed.), Die Afrikaner en sy kultuur (Cape Town: Tafelberg, 1974), pp. 160-2.

96 J.P. Fitzpatrick, South African Memories (London: Cassell, 1932), pp. 213-14.

97 G.D. Scholtz, Die ontwikkeling van die politieke denke van die Afrikaner (Johannesburg: Perskor,1977), vol. 4, p. 342.

98 L.E. van Niekerk, Kruger se regterhand: 'n biografie van W.J. Leyds (Pretoria: Van Schaik, 1985), pp. 87-9.

99 James Bryce, Impressions of South Africa (London, 1900), p. 394.

to think about the welfare of the state as a whole as distinct from that of the family farm or the district.

Few in numbers, frontier Afrikaners feared blacks, but not all blacks. In her reminiscences of her youth as a young child with the Voortrekkers in Natal, the wife of Commandant-General Piet Joubert told of the trekker community's great fear of blacks after the massacres in Natal in 1838. For months the trekkers slept with their shoes on because they feared a Zulu night attack. Yet she did not think that all blacks were hostile. Almost in the same breath she mentioned a tribe who wished to trade and wanted to work for the trekkers.[100]

The utility of an African counted for much more than the color of the skin.[101] The trekkers almost always made a sharp distinction between Africans they could trust and could negotiate with, and those of whom they had to be wary and might have to fight. The author of the principal Afrikaans biography of Paul Kruger wrote that after his traumatic experiences as a young boy in Natal he 'learnt never to trust Africans.'[102] Yet in his own account he ventured, unannounced and accompanied by only one burgher, into an assembly of African chiefs at a time of hostilities on the far northern frontier. 'Without displaying the least distrust, I dismounted in their town, and they all kept quiet. They greeted me with the words, "When it is peace, it is peace; and when it is war, it is war", which implied that my arrival without an escort showed them that my disposition towards them was friendly, that I expected the same from them, and that therefore they must keep the peace.'[103]

The frontier produced two starkly different sets of relationships between burghers and servants. One type of relationship was forged between successive generations of African servants or apprenticed children who grew up in Voortrekker households and who early in the twentieth century migrated with their masters to a town or city. An account by a Dutch school teacher sketched the paternalistic relationship as seen from the farmers' point of view in the final decades of the century. The farmers believed that they brought civilization to Africans by teaching them to work and by punishing them when they deserved it, as a father would do in the case of his son. Their assumption that the servants were happy was based on the fact that some servants talked of 'our farm, our cattle, sheep and horses and our wagon.'[104]

In the most harmonious relationships the farmer entrusted the servants with a gun. In the Anglo-Boer War of 1899-1902 many of these servants went to the battlefield as their masters' *agterryers,* serving them faithfully throughout the war as auxiliaries, tending the horses and cooking, but only rarely participating in the actual battles. At the end of this war one of them, Dick Moshene, offered a glimpse of this relationship. 'We as agterryers remained with our masters in the field and where they trod we trod. And

100 L. Rompel-Koopman, *Wat mevrouw generaal Joubert vertelt* (Cape Town: HAUM, 1916), pp. 19-31.

101 Martin Legassick, 'The Frontier Tradition in South African Historiography', in S. Marks and A. Atmore (eds.), *Economy in Pre-industrial South Africa* (London: Longman, 1980), pp. 52-68.

102 Kruger, *Kruger*, vol. 1, p. 15.

103 Paul Kruger, *The Memoirs of Paul Kruger* (New York: The Century, 1902), p. 115.

104 B. Spoelstra, *Ons volkslewe* (Pretoria: Van Schaik, 1924), pp. 147-52.

although we never fought, our hearts were in the right place. When peace came our masters laid down their arms and we went home.'[105]

The liberal Alfred Hoernlé, a professor in Johannesburg, wrote during the 1930s on the basis of personal observation about the class of trusted servants: '[They] have become culturally so completely assimilated to their masters that Afrikaans has become, quite literally, their mother tongue, and their habits and ways of life those appropriate to a servant class in a 'white' world . . . [They have] very little say in the ordering of their own lives, from political rights they are excluded; they worship apart in their own churches. But their worship is none the less a Christian worship of the same type as their masters' worship, they belong to white, not to native, society; they are completely detribalized. Divorced from their tribes and the culture of their tribes, they have become black Europeans.'[106]

The other type of relationship was harsh, cruel and inhuman, degrading both parties. At an early stage some Transvaal and Free State frontiersmen sold 'apprenticed' or indentured black children as 'black ivory' during the 1850s and 1860s. It was the most extreme form of the dehumanization of blacks. The Boers feared black numbers and, in particular, those blacks living outside white control on what were first called locations and later, reserves. But blacks were not mere victims. The Boer republics were not strong enough to impose full control over them. Many farmers were compelled to treat the Africans on their farm leniently. Those blacks who were treated badly simply moved away from the landlord or master, producing on the part of the latter an impotent rage and frustration.[107] In parts of the Transvaal full white control over blacks in the countryside was established only in the twentieth century.

105 Fransjohan Pretorius, *Kommandolewe tydens die Anglo-Boereoorlog, 1899-1902* (Cape Town: Human & Rousseau, 1991), p. 322.
106 R.F.A. Hoernlé, *Race and Reason* (Johannesburg: Witwatersrand University Press, 1945), p. 105.
107 Van Aswegen, 'Verhouding tussen blank en nie-blank in die OVS', pp. 508-750.

Chapter 7

The Queen's Afrikaners

The British at the Cape

In 1806 Britain occupied the Cape for the second time, this time with the intention of making the colony, with its strategic location as a halfway house to India, a permanent possession. The small number of British officials, backed up by a garrison, represented the world's greatest industrial power and trading nation and one of its richest cultures, but it lacked the means to transform the character of the colony. The arrival of four thousand British settlers in 1820 improved the chances of the Cape's transformation into an English colony, and the anglicization of an upper stratum of Afrikaners, called 'the loyal Dutch' or the 'Queen's Afrikaners'.[1]

The British settlers were generally poor and in need of financial assistance to emigrate, but with more skills than the colonial Afrikaners. About a third of them were skilled artisans, and a tenth professionals of some sort.[2] Originally the idea was to settle these immigrants in the Zuurveld region on small landholdings, but it soon became obvious that the soil and the climate were not suitable, and that they had insufficient skills and capital. By the end of the decade most had abandoned the agricultural settlement and had taken up occupations in the towns.

The settlers had arrived on the eve of a fundamental restructuring of the economy. The commission of inquiry that visited the Cape from 1823 to 1825 paved the way for the era of free enterprise and free trade by abolishing all the monopolies, *pachts* and special taxes of the Company period, explaining that their goal was 'to create a material framework in which economic prosperity along free enterprise lines might be developed.'[3]

Newspapers were essential for spreading the gospel of capitalist progress and popular participation in politics. No Dutch newspaper or magazine in the modern sense of the word had appeared during the period of rule by the Dutch East India Company, nor for more than two decades of British rule. In 1824 two British settlers, John Fairbairn and Thomas Pringle, published the first newspaper at the Cape, *The South African Commer-*

---

1 I have borrowed the latter term from Mottie Tamarkin.
2 John Stone, *Colonist or Uitlander?* (Oxford: Oxford University Press, 1970), pp. 100-1.
3 Jeffrey Peires, 'The British and the Cape, 1814-1834', *SSAS*, pp. 490-99.

cial Advertiser. It the same year a Dutch magazine, *Het Nederduitsch Zuid-Afrikaansch Tijdschrift (NZAT)*, edited by Abraham Faure, minister of the DRC parish in Cape Town, also appeared. Faure joined Fairbairn and Pringle in fighting an effort by the governor, Lord Charles Somerset, to clamp down on a free press, and, by 1827, the right of the press to debate politics and to report on government action had been won.

It was the British settlers in South Africa who seized most of the new opportunities. In the towns and cities they became the tradesmen and artisans. Along with Jews from the continent they took over trading both with whites in the interior and with Xhosa on the frontier. It was they, rather than the Afrikaners, who first saw the potential of large-scale land speculation. During the 1830s they introduced wool farming in the eastern part of the Cape Colony, and they founded export-import firms in Port Elizabeth and Cape Town that would soon ease out the firms founded by the older colonists. Even in the Boer republics, Afrikaners would be almost completely absent from the trades by the end of the century. In the second half of the century the engineers who built the network of roads, bridges and railways and constructed deep-level mining shafts of extraordinary complexity were overwhelmingly from the ranks of British immigrants. The entrepreneurs who founded sophisticated industrial and financial companies were primarily British and English-speaking Jews.

By the beginning of the 1830s the ideology of free trade and progress was becoming dominant in the British Empire and in the Cape Colony as part of it. Based on the key belief that the application of rationality and scientific examination would free mankind from the shackles of tradition and superstition, it was essentially a secular religion. In the Cape Colony it was the British settlers who embraced the gospel of progress with the greatest fervor. A commitment to free enterprise and free trade, along with proficiency in English, were considered essential for any 'progressive' person. Once the Cape had been granted representative rule in 1853, the idea of British non-racial democracy was presented as an essential part of this secular religion.

The Afrikaners and the British

From the start, an incipient tension marked the relationship between the Afrikaners and the British at the Cape. The spectacular advance of Britain as a world power had bred a conviction among the British that their way of doing things was superior. In 1822 the colonial secretary, W.W. Bird, who was married to a Dutch-speaking woman, wrote of the Englishman's conviction that 'nothing can be right or proper that is not English, and to which he is unaccustomed.'[4] An English nationalism became the dominant ideology in urban life across much of South Africa, expressed in the English language and reinforced by its symbols of dress, emblems, architecture, food and polite conventions. Robert Ross made the valid point that an English nationalism was the 'prime nationalism to which both Afrikaner and African nationalism reacted.'[5]

Comments by English critics annoyed the Afrikaner colonists. Even during the first

---

4 [W.W. Bird], *State of the Cape of Good Hope in 1822* (London: John Murray, 1823).
5 Robert Ross, *Status and Respectability in the Cape Colony, 1750-1870* (Cambridge: Cambridge University Press, 1999), pp. 4-6.

British occupation of the Cape (1795-1803), John Barrow and other English commentators deplored in extreme terms the social distortions and lack of cultural achievements they found at the Cape. A general theme was that the Dutch East India Company was unfit for governing such a place. It had neglected education, stifled trade and enterprise, supported slavery and its pernicious social influences, failed to check trekboer expansion, and allowed the oppression of the indigenous Khoisan.

Afrikaners found the idea of English cultural supremacy difficult to refute. By 1806 the colony could boast of no great economic advances or cultural achievements, apart from the Cape Dutch homesteads. There were no books, paintings or innovations on which Afrikaners could pride themselves. They were a rural, isolated, relatively backward people with only a few who received more than a rudimentary education. The lack of military resistance to the British conquests in 1795 and 1806 contributed to the sense of social impotence. The feelings of inferiority were compounded by what Barrow called 'the reluctance that a vanquished people must feel in mixing with their conquerors.'[6]

During the first two or three decades after 1806 there were few signs of rebellion against this situation. The only uprising was the work of a handful of semi-literate frontiersmen, the so-called Slagtersnek Rebellion of 1815, which ended in disaster. In the western Cape virtually the only challenge came in the form of a doctoral dissertation. Christoffel Brand, who received his degree in 1820 from Leiden University in the Netherlands, argued that colonies should enjoy 'the same rights of citizenship, the same laws, institutions and privileges as the citizens of the mother cities.' Accordingly, a colony should have a legislative assembly, although not necessarily one that 'should make the colony altogether free from the mother country.'[7] It was perhaps only the fact that the dissertation was written in Latin that persuaded the governor to take no action against Brand when he returned to the Cape.

With the arrival of the British settlers in 1820 the Afrikaners found their own difficulties better understood than they had been by travelers or officials. Both groups confronted challenges on the need for labor and security. By the late 1820s some of the English writers were taking exception to the extremely negative public views of Afrikaners. The well-educated British settler Thomas Pringle, for example, while finding his Afrikaner neighbors uncultivated and highly prejudiced against the Khoikhoi, considered them as a people civil, good-natured, and 'exceedingly shrewd' at bargain making.[8] The traveler George Thompson differentiated between some individual Afrikaners, who were savage, indolent and unprincipled, and the group as a whole, which he considered of superior standing to their counterparts in many other colonies, particularly those in the Americas.[9]

The Afrikaner colonists groped for a new definition of themselves as a community. Faure's NZAT proposed a dual identity. The burghers had to be loyal British subjects, but also identify with their particular history and cultural distinctiveness. Through serialized

---

6 Cited by Hermann Giliomee, *Die Kaap tydens die eerste Britse bewind* (Cape Town: HAUM, 1975), p. 79.
7 *Afrikaner Political Thought*, pp. 273-4.
8 Thomas Pringle, *African Sketches* (London: Edward Moxon, 1834), pp. 169-70.
9 George Thompson, *Travels and Adventures in Southern Africa* (London: Colburn, 1827), vol. 2, pp. 113-15; for a general discussion, see Michael Streak, *The Afrikaner as Viewed by the English* (Cape Town: Struik, 1974).

articles and poetry on instances of Dutch heroism, the journal signaled its allegiance to a Dutch rather than a British imperial connection, presenting the founding of the Cape settlement in 1652 as of momentous significance in both historic and religious terms. It published most of the diary Jan van Riebeeck had kept at the Cape, and characterized both Van Riebeeck and the first settlers as filled with piety and concerned with spreading the Gospel.[10]

In its first editorial, published on 9 April 1830, the first Dutch newspaper, *De Zuid-Afrikaan*, declared that it 'wanted to hoist a banner which will serve as a rallying point for all colonists, old and new.' It gave the name 'Afrikaner' to these old and new colonists, defining the name in a way that could include all colonists and settlers who were loyal to South Africa. 'All who inhabit this land and derive nourishment from its bosom are Africans [sic].' In the Dutch text the name 'Afrikaner' was used. Since it addressed itself to 'colonists' it implicitly excluded colored and black people.[11] Later *De Zuid-Afrikaan* also wrote of the Dutch-speaking colonists in a more specific way, frequently urging burghers to assert what it called their 'nationality.' In 1835 it wrote: 'It is an error that we have frequently opposed to suppose that as British subjects we are compelled to adopt a British nationality. A colonist of Dutch descent cannot become an Englishman, nor should he strive to be a Hollander.'[12]

The driving force behind *De Zuid-Afrikaan* in its early years was Christoffel Brand, who clashed bitterly with John Fairbairn over slavery at the Cape (see pp. 112-15). Yet both knew that the two white groups depended on each other to defend what they saw as their common interests. In one of its first editions the *South African Commercial Advertiser* called for an end to 'national distinctions and loyalties' and for the 'cordial and complete amalgamation of the Dutch and English colonists which is so . . . essential to the future interests and well-being of both.'[13]

Although more sympathetic to the Afrikaner colonists than the officials, the English-speaking journalists, like the businessmen, reinforced the image of Afrikaners as unprogressive and parochial. The great majority of Afrikaner colonists were farmers, for whom the benefits of free enterprise and free trade as a prerequisite for colonial progress were far less obvious than they were for merchants. The British merchants deemed unprogressive the demand of Afrikaner farmers and their organs like *De Zuid-Afrikaan* for tariff protection of colonial products from cheap imports. The concern for the survival of the Dutch language was seen as similarly unprogressive. Also, in contrast to the Afrikaners who had made South Africa their home, the settlers tended to retain their emotional ties with Britain. Trying to transplant something of the British Isles to the harsh African soil, they formed literary societies and discussed the latest books they had ordered from 'home.' They went to their own churches, even in remote *dorps*, and they played their own games. They did little to get to know the Afrikaners and their ways, preferring to keep their own company or occasionally that of an anglicized Afrikaner. In their way they themselves were also parochial.

10 Andrew Bank, 'The Great Debate and the Origins of South African Historiography', *Journal of African History*, 38 (1997), pp. 261-81.

11 J.H. Hofmeyr, *The Life of J.H. (Onze Jan) Hofmeyr* (Cape Town: Van de Sandt de Villiers, 1913), p. 42.

12 J. du P. Scholtz, *Die Afrikaner en sy taal* (Cape Town: Nasou, 1964), p. 83. An earlier edition under the same title was published in 1939.

13 Scholtz, *Afrikaner en sy taal*, p. 23.

A policy of anglicization

After formally acquiring the Cape in 1814 in a treaty, Britain had resolved to develop it, extend it, and 'civilize' it. The first big step was a new language policy. In 1821 Henry Ellis, the deputy colonial secretary, argued that the proclamation of English as the language of government had become essential.[14] The next year the government announced that over the next five years English would be phased in as the only language permitted in the courts and government offices.

The government also embarked on an attempt to anglicize the church (see the next section) and schools. Free government schools offered education through the medium of English alone. Eager to have their children learn English, but resisting the displacement of Dutch, parents demanded schools offering bilingual education.[15] In higher education there was a similar pragmatism; language only became an issue when politicians wanted to enforce English or when the Reformed clergy sensed a challenge to their interests. They did not mind that most of the staff of the Athenaeum (later the South African College and yet later the University of Cape Town), which it helped to found in 1829, was English or Scottish, but became upset when the college wanted to offer religious instruction. It feared that students would end up as members of an English church.

The administrative changes of 1828 saw the abolition in the interior districts of the boards of landdrost and heemraden, and the appointment of largely English-speaking resident magistrates and commissioners. In Cape Town, English-speaking trustees replaced the local city council, called the Raad der Gemeente or Burgher Senate. This was a step some prominent Cape Town Afrikaners considered an insult and abrogation of a historic political right. Advocate D.F. Berrangé remarked that the original settlers were being treated as if they were 'minors, wastrels or mentally deficient.'[16]

The changes in the judicial system, too, made a serious dent in the self-esteem of the Afrikaner colonists. From 1828 English was formally the only language of the courts; evidence given in Dutch or Afrikaans had to be translated, sometimes by a colored or black interpreter. The British jury system was introduced to decide on matters of fact, with proficiency in English a principal criterion for selection. After 1834 jurors who failed the language test could be challenged.[17] By the 1830s English had become the main language of the administration and of political and legal argument and debate in the Cape Colony. All the more senior officials wrote their letters in English. Piet Retief published his manifesto explaining the reasons for the trek out of the colony in the *Grahamstown Journal* in English.

The British were careful not to tamper too much with the legal system, however, and much of the South African legal system was still based on that of seventeenth- and eighteenth-century Netherlands. Early in the nineteenth century the Netherlands had replaced this body of law with a new code of law, but in South Africa what became known as Roman-Dutch law would survive until the present time. Leiden-trained lawyers like

---

14 James Sturgis, 'Anglicisation of the Cape of Good Hope in the Early Nineteenth Century', *Journal of Imperial and Commonwealth History*, 11 (1982), pp. 11-12.

15 Ross, *Status and Respectability*, p. 57.

16 J.C. Visagie, 'Willem Frederik Hertzog, 1792-1847', master's diss., Unisa, 1971, p. 125.

17 Ross, *Status and Respectability*, pp. 51-5.

Christoffel Brand played a major role in developing the law in the Cape Colony on the basis of Roman and pre-revolutionary Dutch precedents. As time went on, the legal system increasingly incorporated English commercial and insurance law.

The political submissiveness of the Afrikaners was a consequence of several cultural and economic factors. The urban Afrikaners were largely a trading people who saw language as an instrument rather than a symbol of identity. They were eager to accommodate the new rulers. Most of the old Company elite of officials and ministers had held on to their jobs and generally did well under British rule. The western Cape farmers profited greatly from the expansion of the market, and farmers living beyond the first mountain ranges were too isolated to be more than superficially touched by British cultural imperialism.

There were also some intangible factors. A British settler, Thomas Phillipps, believed that the institution of slavery had exerted a pernicious influence on the Afrikaner colonists: 'As to the Dutch, with very few exceptions, they are so accustomed to obey that they tremble at a shadow . . . One of the very worst effects of the system of slavery is predominant in them, in proportion as they tyrannize over their domestic slaves, in the same ratio they degradingly crouch at the feet of their rulers.'[18] During the 1830s Andries Stockenstrom, the most senior official who identified himself as an Afrikaner, referred to the 'apathetic acquiescence' of the colonial Afrikaners that created the impression that 'with the Cape Colonists any thing may be done because they submit to everything.'[19] He urged his fellow Afrikaner colonists to resist 'every insult or injury.' The 'accidental possession of official power' qualified no one 'to domineer over his fellows as if they belonged to an inferior species created only to tremble at his frown.'[20]

Yet some of the best-educated colonial Afrikaners were in the process of becoming anglicized. By the early 1830s there was already a distinct stratum, called the Cape Dutch or 'Anglomen.' One of their principal representatives, Henry Cloete, declared in 1831: 'The Cape Dutch were essentially English. Their habits, their intermarriage, their general improvements, all exhibit and prove this fact.'[21]

Others sought to promote a Cape Afrikaner identity, and, in 1832, a group formed the *Maatschappy ter Uitbreiding van Beskawing en Letterkunde* and began preparing a history of the settlement. Among Cape Town professionals who refused to accept a denigration of their history and cultural standing were lawyers like Brand, D.F. Berrangé, Daniël Denyssen, J.H. Neethling and Johannes de Wet, the Reverends Van Oosterzee and Van der Lingen, and the surveyor W.F. Hertzog. In 1835 Denyssen called on the colonist Afrikaners to retain their nationality; although their mother country had changed, he said, they had by no means become a new people with different minds or feelings.[22]

But, as the struggle for a constitution gained momentum during the 1830s, the Afrikaner leaders appealed less to the rights burghers enjoyed under Company rule and more to the common rights all British subjects shared. They downplayed cultural differ-

---

18 T. Phillipps, *Phillipps, 1820 Settler* (Pietermaritzburg: University of Natal Press, 1960), p. 154.
19 C.R. Kotze, 'Reaksie van die Afrikaners . . . 1806-1824', *Historia*, 14 (1968), p. 164.
20 J.C. Visagie, 'Willem Frederik Hertzog, 1792-1847', *AYB*, 37 (1974), p. 56.
21 *Afrikaner Political Thought*, p. 279.
22 Scholtz, *Afrikaner en sy taal*, p. 83.

ences to avoid the impression of any rift between the two white groups. In 1837 Brand remarked: 'England has taken from the old colonists of the Cape everything that was dear to them: their country, their laws, their customs, their slaves, yes, even their mother tongue.' The Afrikaner colonists had done everything to prove they were British, but 'their conquerors had continually worked to remind them that they were Hollanders.'[23] For Brand the priority was the amalgamation of the two white sections. In 1841 he wrote: '[We] are two who must become one and by doing so raise the banner of unanimity in public affairs.'[24] English commentators left little doubt that this 'unanimity' would increasingly be expressed in English cultural terms.

The church and anglicization

The British from the start realized that the church was by far the most important institution of the conquered colonists. Aware of the DRC's importance, the British government kept it as an established church, along with the Anglican Church. It paid a large amount in subsidies to defray salaries and part of the expenses for erecting new church buildings, but retaining the right to station, transfer, and depose ministers. As an established church the Reformed Church was also subservient to civil courts.

Lord Charles Somerset, who served as governor between 1814 and 1826, first sought Dutch ministers to fill vacancies in the DRC, but when that failed, recruited Scottish ministers, who first had to become proficient in Dutch. (By 1834, of the twenty-two DRC ministers, twelve would be Scottish.) Somerset was now urging the Cape clergy to use English in the church, pointing out that proficiency in English would benefit colonial youth who desired employment in government.

The DRC clergy found any pressure to anglicize unacceptable. In 1824 Chief Justice J.A. Truter urged the government to exercise caution. Only when everyone was proficient in English could the step be undertaken 'without any humiliating feeling.'[25] The synod that year refused a request by the Scottish ministers to offer some of their services in English. *De Zuid-Afrikaan* warned that English church services would have unintended consequences. In 1834 it wrote: 'Members of the Synod consult ancient history to persuade yourselves that to change the language of your religion you would be taking the first step to betray your belief and religion.'[26]

During the 1830s and 1840s the Rev. G.W.A. van der Lingen of the DRC parish of Paarl was virtually the only person to actively challenge the British gospel of progress and anglicization. In his twelve years of study in the Netherlands, and in his forty years as minister of the Paarl parish, he read widely and accumulated ten thousand books in his library – a quarter of the number of books held by the South African Library at that time. (He also left thirty thousand high-quality cigars.) The *Cape Argus* obituary gave this description of his appearance at synod meetings: '[His] blanched face, grey locks, velvet

23 *The Mediator,* 10 October 1837.
24 H.C. Botha, 'Die rol van Christoffel J. Brand, 1820-1854', master's diss., University of South Africa, 1973, p. 143.
25 *RCC*, vol. 19, pp. 499-500.
26 G.D. Scholtz, *Die ontwikkeling van die politieke denke van die Afrikaner* (Johannesburg: Voortrekkerpers, 1970), vol. 2, p. 133.

skull-cap, and lappet dropping from the shoulders down the back, made one imagine that one of the members of the Synod of Dordt [of 1618] itself had made its reappearance on earth.'[27]

Van der Lingen may have looked like an historic relic, but he could see all too well that for many Afrikaner farmers free trade and progress had brought a state of affairs close to disaster. For example, the abolition in 1825 of the preferential tariff for Cape wines on the British market was a major blow to wine farmers. Also, the huge investments in the expansion of the vineyards and in slaves suddenly turned sour when the abolition of slavery by the British was announced. Then came the bungle in paying out the promised compensation for freed slaves.

To Van der Lingen no British achievement could rival the glories of the seventeenth century Dutch Empire that had spawned the Cape Colony. A restoration of this empire could not occur in the Netherlands because secularization there had proceeded too far. The regeneration of Dutch power and Dutch culture would recur in a magnificent historical cycle, and the most promising place for this to start was in the Cape Colony itself, the New Jerusalem, the Promised Land. Lauding the Afrikaners for refusing to assimilate with the savage 'Africans', he assigned them this historic mission of initiating a grand Dutch restoration in the world.

Along with the imperial idea of progress, Van der Lingen also targeted liberal theology. His main enemies were liberal Dutchmen like Dr A.N.E. Changuion, who had founded his own institute in Cape Town and was filling the columns of *De Zuid-Afrikaan* with his liberal views. The chief external dangers were the democratic spirit, which he strongly attacked when revolutions broke out in Europe in 1848, and British imperialism with all its associated cultural and material values. 'His keenest antipathy', the *Cape Argus* noted in his obituary, 'was towards the English language.' Language, Van der Lingen argued, is the person, adding: 'Therefore he who apes another language will necessarily fall for that person's vices as well.'[28]

Van der Lingen declared war on some key manifestations of progress. During the 1860s he and his conservative Paarl followers would even launch a campaign to stop trains running on Sundays to Paarl. Seeing their effort as a great conservative offensive against unbelief, they formed two omnibus companies to provide the people of Paarl with alternative means of transport. Just to keep the venture afloat some individuals donated sums of up to £500. Van der Lingen would probably have won a partial victory if at a critical point he had not overreached, arguing for a total boycott of trains and urging his followers to act as though the new mode of transport did not exist until there was an unequivocal subjugation of the colony to the value system of the Reformed faith. By now the struggle against progress by Van der Lingen and his Paarl conservatives had become an object of derision.

---

27 Jean du Plessis, 'Colonial Progress and Countryside Conservatism: An Essay on the Legacy of Van der Lingen', master's diss., US, 1988, p. 208.
28 Du Plessis, 'Colonial Progress', p. 199.

Responses to representative government

When representative rule was introduced in 1853 there were about fifty towns in the colony. The colony had undergone considerable development in the preceding half century, improving credit facilities, cutting the colonial debt, and introducing a more modern educational system. The number of children at school rose from four thousand in 1842 to almost twenty thousand in 1860.

Roughly 200,000 Afrikaners lived across South Africa by the mid-1860s, and 136,000, or nearly two-thirds, lived in the Cape Colony. Afrikaners made up three out of four whites in the Cape Colony and nine out of ten in the two Boer republics.[29]

WHITE SOUTH AFRICAN POPULATION, CA. 1860

	WHITES	AFRIKANERS	AFRIKANERS AS %
Cape Colony	181,592	c. 136,000	75%
Orange Free State	35,000	c. 30,000	86%
Transvaal	30,000	c. 27,000	90%
Natal	15,000	c. 2,750	20%

Although the cities and even many towns increasingly took on an English character, the Afrikaner colonists had by no means been squeezed out of the urban economy in Cape Town. The capital that became available as compensation for the emancipation of their slaves raised many Afrikaners to prominence in the colonial bourgeoisie. In Cape Town they invested on a large scale in urban and peri-urban property. Afrikaner property tycoon J.A.H. Wicht, for instance, was reported to own 'hundreds of houses' in Cape Town.[30]

The Afrikaner energy in campaigning for a parliament in the 1840s and early 1850s was soon dissipated. The system of representative rule was a disappointment. Although all decisions had to be formally approved by Parliament, the governor, appointed in Britain, was still the dominant factor in the system. His executive, also nominated in London, operated largely independently of Parliament and was paid out of a civil list over which Parliament had no control. Afrikaners formed only a third of the representatives in the Cape legislature, although they comprised close to three-quarters of the electorate.

Parliament was dominated by the concerns of the English or anglicized section of the community in small towns and in Cape Town and Port Elizabeth. The main issue under discussion was the devolution of power to the eastern districts, of little interest to Afrikaners. A canvasser found in 1869 that in his area nine-tenths of the young farmers under twenty-five had not bothered to register. Many who did register gave all kinds of excuses for not voting: Parliament did not benefit the colony, they had been ploughing, the field cornet had not warned them.[31]

---

29 The figures are mostly those of G.D. Scholtz, *Die ontwikkeling van die politieke denke van die Afrikaner*, vol. 3 (Johannesburg: Perskor, 1974), pp. 22-3.

30 Timothy Keegan, *Colonial South Africa and the Origins of the Racial Order* (Cape Town: David Philip, 1996), p. 165.

31 J.L. McCracken, *The Cape Parliament* (Oxford: Clarendon Press, 1967), p. 35.

It was estimated that at least 70 per cent of Afrikaners in the Cape Colony during the 1860s could not understand English. Despite this, the rise of English as public language was proceeding apace. Candidates for the roughly 4,500 positions in central and local government had to be proficient in English (but not in Dutch). In the courts all the Dutch that was spoken was interpreted in English.

In 1865 the government decided that all future instruction in government schools had to be given in English. The few top schools attended by the children of the white elite became bastions of the English cultural influence, among them the Diocesan College (1849) in Cape Town, St Andrew's in Grahamstown (1856), Grey Institute in Port Elizabeth (1856), and the Stellenbosch Gymnasium (1866). But even in schools in small towns, English and Scottish teachers attempted to teach Afrikaner children English, fined them for speaking Dutch, and instructed them in behaving like British ladies and gentlemen. English domination in the town of Swellendam was described in these words: 'Of all the groups or people the following were English or Scottish: all the shopkeepers except two . . . the most senior shop assistants, the magistrate, the doctor, the postmaster, the attorneys, all the teachers except a few assistants, later also the bank manager and his clerks and the few policemen . . . Barry and Nephews controlled the biggest commercial concern in the town and district. The Anglican and Wesleyan ministers were English, and the DRC minister, in the person of Dr. Robertson, was also British.'[32]

In the judgment of the English-speaking Victorians, the rural Afrikaners, apart from being white, were almost everything they themselves were not: ignorant, superstitious, and conservative – and not interested in 'progress.' They lauded their hospitality, but noted disapprovingly their heavy use of coffee and brandy and the men's incessant chewing of tobacco, and their refusal to 'improve' themselves. They failed to understand how Afrikaners could attach so little value to education.[33] The English writer Olive Schreiner, who spent much of her early life in the 1860s and 1870s among Afrikaners in the Karoo, reflected later on how as a girl she thought that it was 'not quite just of God to make us so much better than all the other nations.' She also remembered that it would have been absolutely impossible for her to eat sugar that had been touched by a Boer child or 'to sleep between sheets a Dutchman had slept between.'[34]

The Afrikaans author M.E. Rothman, who grew up in Swellendam in the last quarter of the nineteenth century, noted with resentment that the English in the town used social etiquette and other ways to demonstrate their superiority as a nation and as a class. British traders and civil servants considered Afrikaner farmers, even those who were quite wealthy, as their inferiors. They called them by their first names; the Afrikaner farmers addressed them as 'Mister.'[35] In many ways Afrikaners, ironically, were being subjected to the same rituals of subjection and degradation as those they employed to keep coloreds and blacks in their inferior place.

---

32 M.E.R[othman] (ed.), *Oorlogsdagboek van 'n Transvaalse burger te velde* (Cape Town: Tafelberg, 1976), pp. 45-6.

33 For an account of English society in the rural areas, see Karel Schoeman, *Olive Schreiner* (Cape Town: Human & Rousseau, 1989).

34 Olive Schreiner, *Thoughts on South Africa* (London: Fisher Unwin, 1923), pp. 16-17.

35 M.E.R., *Oorlogsdagboek*, pp. 42-6.

It would be simplistic to see all this as an irreversible process of anglicization. The great majority of church services in the Reformed church were in Dutch, and, outside Cape Town, in 1871, twenty-four newspapers that usually appeared twice a week had pages in both Dutch and English. Still, the Afrikaner elite increasingly identified with the Empire after representative rule under a liberal constitution had been granted. Brand was elected as the first speaker and was knighted.[36] The Afrikaners dominated the electorate, but the fact was that only English was allowed in Parliament. J.H. (Onze Jan) Hofmeyr, who in the early 1880s would become the leader of the colonial Afrikaners, described the impact of this language policy: 'If it comes to the election of a Parliamentary representative . . . then the influential Oom Piet and Oom Klaas felt that he ought not offer himself as a candidate because he could speak no English. If the Dutch farmer in the Colony is summoned to appear before the Court, then his case is taken in a language which he does not understand, and then he repeatedly has to see acting as interpreter between the magistrate and himself a Kafir, who is far below him in society, but who now looks down on him, because he understands two languages against the farmer's one.'[37]

English newspapers like the *Cape Argus* and *Monitor* expressed a militant form of cultural imperialism, deploring efforts by the governor to 'please all parties', and calling the English 'the dominant race.' They pointed out that the Cape was an English colony, and that the Dutch colonists had no reason to bewail the possible loss of their language and nationality. Dutch had little status among the languages of Europe and was steadily declining in the colony. Afrikaans was, in the words of the *Cape Argus*, a 'miserable, bastard jargon', not worthy of the name of 'language' at all. Nothing would more advance the 'moral and social progress' of the colony than the 'substitution of the English language for the present Cape Dutch.' The future language of the country was English, the *Cape Argus* boldly proclaimed on 19 September 1857, adding: 'Let your language and your nationality go, and you need not fear for your religion.'

In an editorial on 21 May 1857, *De Zuid-Afrikaan* admitted that the Dutch 'nationality' in the colony was bound to disappear completely, though there was the possibility of a composite 'nationality', a fusion of the nationalities of the two white groups. The paper committed itself to resist the eclipse of the Dutch heritage; it denounced those who, in a desire to present themselves as 'civilized', abandoned 'their ancestors' language, morals, outlook, in short, their own nationality and, eventually also, their own religion.'[38] Nonetheless, enormous pressure to anglicize had built up. In 1859 the journal *Elpis* published an article on the widespread wish among parents to have their children educated only in English; it pointed out that even in the border districts 'colonial civilization' went together with the dominance of the English language.[39]

---

36 Botha, 'Die rol van Christoffel Brand', p. 189.
37 Hofmeyr, *Life of Hofmeyr*, p. 235.
38 For the quotes in the two paragraphs above see Scholtz, *Ontwikkeling van die politieke denke*, vol. 3, pp. 241-57; Scholtz, *Die Afrikaner en sy taal*, pp. 90-94.
39 Scholtz, *Die Afrikaner en sy taal*, pp. 120-21.

A modernizing church

Most towns were founded as *kerkplekke,* where the Reformed Church had established a parish and subsequently built a church. Despite an accelerating rush of modernity, the church remained largely locked in its traditional ways, the status distinctions of the Company period reinforced by the Victorian emphasis on rank and class differences. It was usually rich Afrikaners who provided the means to establish the first *kerkplekke,* or to redeem the debts incurred in erecting a church building. While the everyday life of the colonial Afrikaners tended to be egalitarian, the richer Afrikaners exhibited their rank by reserving the front church pews for their family, walking in front in funeral processions and negotiating a prominent position for family graves. An oligarchy of ministers and a few wealthy men controlled the church councils, chosen on a co-optive basis, with members of the outgoing council nominating new members.[40]

Among the Reformed clergy there was an almost instinctive tendency to remain loyal to the government of the day as part of a God-willed social order. A majority of ministers at a synod of 1837 had expressed disapproval of the Great Trek as an insurrection against a God-given dispensation. Abraham Faure proposed a toast to Queen Victoria as the rightful sovereign of the region when he visited the Voortrekkers in Natal, but, as a result, the Voortrekkers in other parts of Natal shunned him.

In many ways the bicentenary of the white settlement in 1852 was a moment of truth for the church and the Afrikaner colonists' attempt to claim a special place. The DRC clergy asked the government to proclaim 6 April, the day Jan van Riebeeck and his party arrived, as a religious holiday to stress the connection between the European settlement and Dutch Reformed Christianity, thus dramatically projecting the church onto center stage of the colony's history, but the government refused the request. Its duty, it said, was to promote all religious denominations, not one at the expense of the others. This symbolic withdrawal of the state's special blessing on an historic occasion constituted a crisis of identity.[41]

The texts of sermons delivered by Faure and Van der Lingen on 6 April 1852 form the only surviving record of the way in which the occasion was marked. Faure's sermon was a learned disquisition drawing on historical records, a somewhat desperate effort to defend his church against the charge that it had neglected its calling to bring the Gospel to slaves and the indigenous people in the colony. While the DRC kept the colonists under its wing, its missionary efforts were so meager that they were hardly worth celebrating.[42]

Van der Lingen's sermon aimed at different targets: one was the 'new colonists' – a reference to the British section – for failing to celebrate the establishment of Christianity at the Cape, another the 'older colonists.' They had forgotten 'the language and customs of their ancestors . . . [and] prefer to speak a foreign tongue no matter how badly and ridiculously; have their children taught in a foreign language, without ever taking the trouble to have them learn thoroughly the language which God had given them.'[43] In

40 See Bun Booyens, 'Kerk en Staat, 1795-1843', *AYB* (1965), p. 2; Du Plessis, 'Colonial Progress'.
41 Du Plessis, 'Colonial Progress', pp. 83-139.
42 Abraham Faure, *Redevoering by het tweede Eeuw-feest . . .* (Cape Town: Van de Sandt de Villiers, 1852).
43 Ross, *Status and Respectability in the Cape Colony,* p. 68.

many ways Van der Lingen's sermon was as much at odds with reality as Faure's. Only the well-educated stratum of Afrikaner colonists still spoke Dutch correctly and fluently; the others spoke the vernacular that became known as Afrikaans. There was also little indication, at least in the western Cape, that the tide of anglicization could be stemmed.

In the course of the 1850s, some clear divisions developed within the church hierarchy. On the one end of the spectrum was a younger generation of ministers who had returned from the Netherlands preaching a liberal theological creed. On the other end were conservatives, united on some issues, divided on others. Van der Lingen was traditional and pro-Dutch and opposed to democracy, progress, and secular education. At considerable personal expense he founded the Gymnasium in the town of Paarl in 1857 as a Dutch-medium private school under church control, the only school in the colony that stood unequivocally for the Dutch culture and language and for the Reformed religion. It was a harbinger of what would later be called Christian-National education.

The younger conservatives were modern men who welcomed democracy and subscribed to many of the progressive ideas. They had no desire to make fools of themselves by opposing all forms of progress and modernity as Van der Lingen did by urging a boycott of trains running on Sundays. They made effective use of newspapers and other modern means of communication to disseminate their views. They reached out to other Christian churches, establishing *Elpis* as a quarterly journal with international ecumenical connections. In 1860 they held the first interdenominational Christian conference in Worcester, where Andrew Murray had just become minister.

The modern conservatives tended to consider the British Empire a basically benign empire that could help to overcome the social backwardness of the colony. They were in many ways the forerunners of J.H. (Onze Jan) Hofmeyr and Jan Christiaan Smuts in promoting a colonial nationalism that stressed the values of loyalty to the Empire, a great respect for the English language and English customs, and admiration for the progressive changes that the Empire promoted, while also insisting that the interests of the colony should not be subservient to those of Britain, and that the scope of colonial self-government should steadily increase. Andrew Murray, junior, a towering figure as moderator of the church between 1862 and 1897, reflected this colonial nationalism in its earliest phase. He always kept in mind that he was 'a Dutch minister', though the son of a Scottish minister and a staunch supporter of the Empire as the foundation of order and liberty in South Africa. (In 1854 he even traveled to London to plead with the imperial government not to withdraw from Transorangia.) At the 1862 DRC synod he was elected moderator. At the same synod permission was first given to hold English services in the Reformed Church. Such services soon became a common occurrence in Cape Town and some country towns.

Van der Lingen took a dim view of such anglophile views, but in certain key areas he could unite with the younger conservatives. One was the need for a local theological seminary. While Dutch universities kept on turning out liberal Afrikaners as church ministers there was little hope of realizing his dream to transform the church into a bastion of theological conservatism. As a student in the Netherlands, Van der Lingen was shocked by the state of the Christian religion. A liberal theology had developed that set great store on rationality and advocated the critical questioning of the Bible, particularly the orthodoxy on original sin and the biblical miracles. Van der Lingen became deeply influenced by the struggle of the conservative Réveil movement in the Netherlands, which was anti-revolutionary and opposed to the rational critique of the church's doctrines. The Dutch revival stressed a return to the pure Reformed faith and Calvinist principles. Van der Lingen had returned to the Cape imbued with an anti-revolutionary and anti-liberal zeal.

Some members of a younger generation who studied in the Netherlands in the late 1840s were as horrified as Van der Lingen by the predominance of liberal theology in the Dutch church, the most prominent among them Andrew and John Murray (sons of Andrew, senior), N.J. Hofmeyr, the leading proponent of missionary work (see p. 123) and J.H. Neethling, who would become minister of the Stellenbosch parish. Having returned to the colony by mid-century, and stimulated as Van der Lingen had been by the Réveil movement, they styled themselves the 'orthodox party', as campaigners against theological liberalism.

In 1857 Hofmeyr, in a key speech at the synod, pleaded for a local seminary to keep young candidates from the Cape from the 'pernicious sphere of influence' of theological schools in the Netherlands, which denied the divine nature of Christ and the Holy Spirit. The liberals immediately recognized the threat this posed to their beliefs, and, at the 1857 synod, Dr A.N.E. Changuion, an advocate of a liberal Reformed Church, campaigned against a local seminary. There was a danger, he wrote, that a local seminary would turn out 'reactionary theologians, semi-enlightened people and semi-civilized members of society.' The movement to establish a seminary had, however, become unstoppable, and the 1857 synod decided to establish one. At its inauguration in 1859, P.E. Faure, moderator of the church, made it clear that it would be expected to teach the 'true Reformed, Christian religion.' (There was no reason for concern, because two prominent members of the orthodox party, John Murray and Hofmeyr, became the first professors.)

Van der Lingen, who wanted it to be sited in the conservative heartland of Paarl, had been offered one of the first chairs, but withdrew when Stellenbosch was chosen as the site after it offered the imposing drostdy building for the purpose. His proposal that the professors be obliged to speak Dutch both in class and at home was narrowly defeated. Still, a new beachhead for Dutch culture had been established; the synod decided that a proper study of the Dutch language and culture was to be an essential part of the syllabus. An outraged *Cape Argus* wrote: 'It was intended only to foster by such means a spirit of spurious nationality, calculated to produce the most mischievous results in the minds of unthinking persons who may be weak enough to be led away by such a delusion.'[44]

The younger and older conservatives united also on the issue of missionary work. Both Van der Lingen and N.J. Hofmeyr admired Johannes van der Kemp, a Dutch pioneer in missionary work in the colony at the beginning of the century. The 1857 synod

---

44 Scholtz, *Die Afrikaner en sy taal*, p. 127.

decision to condone separate worship for whites did not spring from an urge to impose segregation as part of a reactionary movement. Hofmeyr, who had a leading hand, saw it as compromise aimed more at promoting missionary work by the DRC than placating the racially prejudiced (see pp. 124-6).

There is no evidence that the liberals in the church were more tolerant than the conservatives in racial matters. Both groups accepted or accommodated themselves to the *de facto* racial division, but did not try to turn it into a principle. The *Volksvriend*, founded to express the conservative view, declared in 1865 that there was no reason to deny the son of any black man access to any educational institution if the father could pay his son's way.[45] Since few could do so, this was not much more than a refusal to make an issue of race or color.

The defeat of theological liberalism

While the orthodox party was now in control of the theological school, its battle against the liberals was far from won. The fact that the Reformed Church was an established church meant that the courts would become one of the key battlegrounds. In one case the Supreme Court, petitioned by a liberal, decided that representatives from parishes beyond the colony's boundaries had to be excluded from the Cape synod. Since most of these were conservatives, this strengthened the liberals' position in the synod. Another momentous effect of this decision was that the Reformed Church in South Africa would remain territorially split for more than a century.

The liberals sought to wrest control from the orthodox party in church councils, usually tight oligarchic cliques controlled by a few rich people and the minister, despite the fact that it was an established Reformed Church principle that lay members had a say in the election of church councils. The liberals wished to introduce free elections for church councils, and when blocked by church authorities, a church member secured the support of Parliament for the principle of free elections. The government, however, refused to intervene; church councils continued to reflect class divisions in Afrikaner society. In 1864 a commission of the synod suspended two liberal ministers, J.J. Kotzé and Thomas François Burgers, finding them guilty of heresy. Both appealed to the courts and the cases ended up in the Privy Council in London. Burgers and Kotzé were victorious and continued to participate in synod meetings. The liberals won some other victories as well.

The fiercest fight was over the so-called voluntary principle, which sought to end state subsidies to the DRC and the Anglican Church, deployed for salaries for ministers and the erection of churches. Although the orthodox party in the DRC did not wish to relinquish its position as an established church receiving state subsidies, it bitterly resented being taken to court by liberals like Burgers and Kotzé. Burgers, for example, wrote in an open letter to Andrew Murray that never was there 'a more anomalous claim than this demand for state support but without state control . . . You want to serve one Lord, but receive wages from two.' Saul Solomon, a Congregationalist, fought the issue

---

45 J.H. Hofmeyr, *Het leven van Jan Hendrik Hofmeyr* (Cape Town: Van de Sandt de Villiers, 1913), pp. 85-91.

in Parliament and secured victory in 1875.[46] From now on the DRC was financially dependent on its own resources. It meant that its future was threatened by the increasing number of Afrikaners who were unable to make a contribution to the church's coffers on account of their destitute condition.

Initially the liberals had the upper hand in the press in a society where debating theological controversies had become the main public passion. They had in their camp the *Onderzoeker*, a monthly theological journal, and a lively newspaper, the *Volksblad*. *De Zuid-Afrikaan* tried to maintain a neutral stand, but was believed to veer towards the liberal side. Almost in desperation, Hofmeyr and other conservatives in 1862 established the *Volksvriend* as 'a religious and social' paper, but it was deadly dull. It seemed headed for collapse, when, at the end of that year Professor N.J. Hofmeyr appointed a nephew, Jan Hendrik Hofmeyr, then only seventeen years old, as editor. Hofmeyr achieved a notable success. He developed a lively and lucid style, greatly improved the news coverage, championed the orthodox cause, and raised issues like Dutch culture and nationality. He took over *De Zuid-Afrikaan* in 1871 and by 1880 assumed the leadership of the Afrikaner Bond, the first Afrikaner political organization, as a financially secure man. The establishment of a successful journal was an important part of the conservative battle plan.

An important reason for the success of the orthodox cause was the development of an evangelical strand in their religion. Traditionally, the Calvinist doctrine that the church spread emphasized the sovereignty of a God who intervened in all essential matters, and a covenant theology, which gave rise to the common practice of the children of Christian parents being baptized in infancy, not on adult confession (see pp. 42-4). By the midnineteenth century many considered this type of religious practice as unemotional and routine to the point of being frigid. Religion seemed to be a matter of participating in the rituals of baptism, confirmation, and Communion in a way that affirmed membership of an ethnic rather than a confessional group. Those who experienced the absence of any spirit or soul in their religion as a great personal crisis were, to use the words of Thomas Carlyle in the *Westminster Review* in 1838, 'destitute of faith and yet terrified of skepticism.'[47]

A pronounced evangelicalism rose in response.[48] Andrew Murray personified this rise. His father had grown up in Scotland when the French Revolution and the Industrial Revolution dominated public discussion, and when the evangelical movement played a profound role in winning working-class acquiescence of a harsh order by emphasizing the heavenly reward of those who upheld the virtues of orderliness and submission. Apart from religious orthodoxy, evangelicalism stressed a 'vital religion of the heart', of which the central elements were conversion, the Atonement, and the winning of souls for the Kingdom of God. That something was seen as lacking in the religious life of the Afrikaner colonists is apparent in the outpouring of emotion in the Great Revival

---

46 André du Toit, 'The Cape Afrikaners' Failed Liberal Moment', in Jeffrey Butler, et al. (eds.), *Democratic Liberalism in South Africa* (Cape Town: David Philip, 1987), p. 52.

47 J.F.C. Harrison, *The Early Victorians* (St Albans: Panther Books, 1971), p. 161.

48 For a general discussion, see Boyd Hilton, *The Age of Atonement: The Influence of Evangelicalism in Social and Economic Thought, 1785-1865* (Oxford: Clarendon, 1988), pp. 8-35.

that swept the western part of the Cape in the early 1860s. Religious revivals had occurred during the mid-nineteenth century in North America and England, and some DRC ministers were well informed about it, yet the Cape Revival took them by surprise. In its first stage people with marginal status like recently freed slaves or lowly laborers in towns or cities were the most strongly affected.[49]

According to oral tradition, the Cape Revival started in Worcester in the rural western Cape, where some ex-slave women gave expression to outbursts of great emotion. Murray, the DRC minister, first tried to restrain them by saying: 'God is a God of order, but this is disorder',[50] but he soon supported it as a positive development. It quickly spread to other congregations. In Paarl, even Van der Lingen, a much more conventional Calvinist than Murray, fell down in a trance during a celebration of the Pentecost.

Over the next few decades a fervent piety marked the religious life of many Cape Afrikaners. There was a strong emphasis on personal conversion as a highly charged emotional experience, supposed to change utterly an individual's life to avoid eternal doom. Those not yet converted were regularly warned of the wrath of God and the certainty of suffering in Hell. The young Petronella van Heerden gave an account of how she and her friends responded to the sermons by Andrew Murray during periodic revivals in his congregation:

> Everywhere the eye of a wrathful God follows you. He reads your thoughts. He sees everything but He notices only sin and His wrath will be fearsome. An almost tangible feeling of dread spreads through the hall, children cry and cling to each other. The end of the world may come at any moment and you are lost; others become hysterical out of fear that it will happen before you are 'enrolled' with the Lord and everyone who has converted has to stand. Then the old man with the beard and the voice of a Muscovy duck [Murray] says to each individual: 'Sit down brother, sit down sister', until everyone sits. The fear does stay behind in the hall. The place is drenched with it. No one dares to be alone; they clutch each other's hands, sleep in the same bed, and go together to the toilet. Everyone is unnaturally sweet.[51]

The fervor generated by such experiences had manifest results, such as a desperate concern about lost souls, including those souls among the poorer sections of the population. It also generated a newfound enthusiasm for missionary work, which, in the western Cape, would soon give rise to efforts to make the Bible available in a language that was simpler than Dutch. It would be the initial impetus behind the first Afrikaans language movement.

The church leadership seized the opportunity to channel some of the energy of the Revival into organized religion, introducing special services and Sunday schools for children and founding working groups for women and children to raise funds for mission projects. The principal organizational expression was prayer meetings, often attended

49 Robert Ross, 'The Fundamentalisation of Afrikaner Calvinism', in H. Diederiks and C. Quispel (eds.), *Onderscheid en minderheid* (Hilversum: Verloren, 1987), pp. 212-13.
50 Du Plessis, *The Life of Andrew Murray of South Africa*, p. 206.
51 Petronella van Heerden, *Kerssnuitsels* (Cape Town: Tafelberg, 1962), pp. 120-1.

by large numbers of people, who revealed in emotional and personal terms how they had struggled to find salvation. All this was a source of great alarm for the liberals with their emphasis on a rational, essentially unemotional, form of religion.[52]

By the mid-1870s the orthodox party had conclusively won the battle against the liberals. The church retained its confessional character, with a strong recent overlay of evangelicalism. But the defeat of the liberals did not mean that irrational prejudices and parochial concerns had wholly triumphed and that the 'liberal moment' of the democratic constitution of 1853 had 'failed.' There is no single model of modernization. Conservatives can be innovative, and secular liberalism and religious liberalism often do not go hand in hand. In secular affairs Murray and his orthodox party were modernizers and in some respects liberals. They supported the secular school education that the state introduced in 1865. They welcomed progress in the form of the extension of the railways to Stellenbosch and Paarl in the early 1860s. (In the case of Stellenbosch a special train from Cape Town was organized for people wishing to attend the consecration of a new Reformed church building.) The *Volksvriend* regularly exhorted farmers to display a greater spirit of enterprise.

In other ways they were conservative. Evangelicals like Murray tended largely to shy away from political or social activism or from a close alliance with a social movement or party. They spelled out broad Christian principles as they saw them, but rarely made their meaning concrete for political life. They did, however, encourage submission to the existing authorities except in extreme cases. Murray would be outraged when the British crushed the Boer republics in 1899-1902, but the liberal side of British imperialism, generally, could not have wished for a more loyal supporter (see p. 232).

Murray met with little opposition until the end of his very long life. The strength of the evangelical tradition, with its tendency to submit to the earthly powers, helps to account for the extraordinary devotion of even non-anglicized Cape Afrikaners to Queen Victoria and the Empire that began to manifest itself in the 1880s.

'Less care bestowed than upon the beasts'

Murray was one of only a few ministers who realized that the church had to take a special responsibility for the education of its members. While Afrikaners could still derive a living from subsistence farming, education was of no special concern. The church urged parents to get their children to read and write but did not refuse to confirm children if they were illiterate.

By the time of the disestablishment of the DRC in 1875, concern was developing about the woeful level of education of the Afrikaner youth and the relatively backward state of the Afrikaners. Only when the DRC was forced to stand on its own financial feet after being disestablished did most ministers wake up to the economic crisis many of its members were experiencing.

Most colonial Afrikaners were engaged in subsistence farming, which required little education, but many of these farming operations were stagnating because the fields

---

52 Du Toit, 'The Cape Afrikaners', pp. 60-61.

were overgrazed. Economic and social decline went hand in hand. Rural Afrikaners rarely read any books apart from the Bible and a few tracts of a devotional nature. In the Cape Colony's white population the economic winners were the largely urbanized English-speakers with their much better political and economic linkages to the imperial nexus, superior education and skills, and their early urbanization.

By the 1870s there were the first signs of anxiety about poverty and the lack of literacy of a growing part of the white population. These concerns began to focus on the level of child illiteracy. In the 1875 census it was estimated that only 43 per cent of children between the ages of five and fifteen in the Cape Colony could read and write. For Afrikaners the proportion was undoubtedly considerably lower, assuming that Cape English-speakers probably attained the level of their counterparts in Victoria and New Zealand, where it was about 60 per cent. Most did learn to read and write, but the level of these skills was, in most cases, extremely rudimentary.

The concern about the lack of education, particularly among rural Afrikaners, was expressed in a series of anonymous articles in the *Cape Monthly Magazine* in 1873, obviously the work of a well-informed person. The author asked the ministers of religion if they were satisfied with things as they were: Did they realize that

> the children of Dutch-speaking, European parentage [are] growing up with less care bestowed upon them than upon the beasts of the field – without the ability to read or write even their mother tongue, without any instruction in the knowledge of a God that made them, having at their command no language but a limited vocabulary of semi-Dutch, semi-Hottentot words, and those only concerning the wants or doings of themselves and the animals they tend?

The writer went on to deliver a searing indictment of unconcerned 'State-paid ministers' whose only visible activity was a Sunday sermon in the village church. He warned that if no remedy were found a growing criminal class would develop.[53]

But equally responsible for the poor state of education was the government policy on language medium in education. The great majority of Afrikaner children could not understand English, yet the government in 1865 made it the compulsory medium of instruction in all first- and second-class schools. The original intention was to extend it also to third-class schools (rural elementary schools), but this remained a dead letter. Parents complained that their children could hardly write or read after a few years of school, and had only picked up some rudimentary English. In the early 1880s the Rev. Adriaan Moorrees, who was to become a major figure in the church, pointed out the 'absurdity' that while the majority of white children could not speak English most teachers could not speak Dutch or Afrikaans.

The teaching of the Dutch language itself was extremely poor. In 1870 only three first-class schools in the western part of the colony offered it as a subject. By 1880 it was estimated that only four thousand out of sixty thousand Afrikaner children received any instruction in Dutch; in desperation parents founded private schools, so that by 1889 there were 146 such institutions in the western part of the colony. The government

---

53 *Cape Monthly Magazine*, 6, 33 (1873), p. 130.

did not believe that qualified teachers had to have a working knowledge of Dutch, and, in examinations at the Cape teachers' college, Dutch was an optional subject, as were Sotho and Xhosa. In 1875 a church delegation to the education authorities asked for state support for Dutch-medium schools, but the authorities rejected the request.[54]

A large minority of ministers, moreover, remained so convinced that English would become the sole public language that they resisted efforts to exert pressure on the authorities to introduce mother-tongue education. One of these was Andrew Murray, who openly endorsed English in public schools, considering as futile attempts to revive Dutch as a public language. When the church founded several church schools for Afrikaner girls he supported English as the sole medium of instruction. The most prominent of church schools for Afrikaner girls, the Huguenot Seminary in Wellington, founded in 1874, was reported to be 'breathing an English spirit.'[55] The church imported Scottish and American teachers, because they feared that Dutch teachers would disseminate liberal principles.

In a debate at the synod of 1880 this minority advanced arguments similar to those that would be made in a democratic South Africa 110 years later. They argued that it would do Dutch children a disservice to deprive them of full exposure to an English education. Children had no need to learn Dutch at school because they could do so at home. The language of the economy, indeed the very language of progress, was English. A nationalist newspaper commented that there was a faction in the synod that seemed to believe that salvation could only be attained in English. The synod did, however, manage to get the education department to make some minor changes in favor of Dutch. Ten years later little concrete change had taken place. One reform of the 1880s allowed school committees to decide on the school's language policy. Parents tended to favor English, and there was a serious shortage of teachers who could teach Dutch. Teaching through the medium of Dutch remained a distant ideal.[56]

A new brand of politics

The push for Dutch (and later Afrikaans) as a medium in schools and other spheres of public life only gained momentum once politics at the Cape began to involve the masses. The first signs of a new brand of politics were reported during the 1869 election campaign. 'On the hustings and at some of the meetings men of position and ability stated amid the applause of their hearers that they or their candidates were Afrikanders.'[57] During the early 1870s Afrikaner farmers formed several *boereverenigings* (farmers' societies) to push for the protection of colonial products against imports and promote farming interests in other ways. English-speaking farmers, as a rule, did not join these *verenigings* and tended to form their own associations.

The trigger for the new political consciousness was both political and economic. The

---

54 M. du T. Potgieter, 'Die rol van die NG Kerk in blanke onderwys in Kaapland sedert die eerste sinode', doctoral diss., US, pp. 291-304.

55 D.A. Scholtz, 'Ds. S.J. du Toit as kerkman en kultuurleier', unpublished doctoral diss., University of Stellenbosch, 1975, p. 110.

56 Potgieter, 'Die rol van die NGK in blanke onderwys', pp. 274-328.

57 McCracken, *The Cape Parliament*, p. 109.

British annexation of Basutoland, the diamond fields, and later the Transvaal, had caused outpourings of Afrikaner resentment across South Africa, sometimes mistakenly interpreted as signs of the 'awakening' of Afrikaner nationalism. The Cape Afrikaners did not persevere with their protests and saw their interest best served by working within the liberal constitution of the Cape Colony.[58]

Disenchantment with free trade had a more lasting impact. Free trade was never supposed to benefit everyone equally and at the same time. In the Cape Colony during the second half of the nineteenth century it was benefiting bankers, manufacturers, and merchants. In pursuing free trade the imperial government in 1860 had removed all vestiges of preference for Cape wines on the London market and forced Cape wines to compete on equal terms with wine from countries like France. As a result, between 1863 and 1875, Cape wine exports dropped by more than 80 per cent. A huge wine surplus resulted in depressed prices.

Another bone of contention was the free trade in financial transactions. In 1860 the Supreme Court lifted the historic ceiling of 6 per cent interest on all mortgages and financial transactions. Afrikaner farmers, who had previously borrowed from other farmers, now increasingly resorted to merchants who charged higher interest rates. Merchants, in turn, usually got their credit from the 'imperial banks', which had their head offices in London and started to operate in the colony in the 1860s. The most prominent among them was the Standard Bank, which rapidly spread its network across the colony after numerous local banks, often based on Afrikaner capital, had failed. In times of recession the imperial banks called up their credit, causing a chain reaction that bankrupted many farmers. Strong resentment of the 'imperial banks' developed.

Until approximately the 1870s the interests of wine and wheat farmers, who were predominantly Afrikaners, and the merchants, who were either British or European Jews, largely converged, with the latter marketing the farmers' produce both locally and abroad. The relationship began to sour as merchants began to import increasing quantities of foreign wine, spirits and wheat, contributing to the Afrikaner farmers' conclusion that their own interests lay in acting also as Afrikaners rather than only as farmers.

By the early 1870s there were other reasons for becoming active in politics. First, the economy had become more broadly based than two or three decades earlier. As a result of the opening up of the diamond fields the colony's revenue increased sharply. Politics no longer concentrated on retrenchment but on benefits for voters and their constituencies. Also helping to raise the political consciousness of voters was the question of large-scale government expenditure on military expeditions. Sir Bartle Frere, the British High Commissioner, with the support of Gordon Sprigg, who became prime minister of the Cape Colony in February 1878, sent colonial forces to disarm the Sotho in Basutoland, which still fell under the colony, and against the Ngqika and the Gcaleka factions on the eastern frontier. The war in Basutoland cost the Cape nearly £6,000,000. An official in the colonial office wrote of the 1880 military campaign against the Sotho that the Cape colonists 'got nothing for it.'[59] A campaign on the eastern frontier against the Ngqika and Gcaleka cost nearly £1,500,000.[60]

58 F.A. van Jaarsveld, *The Awakening of Afrikaner Nationalism* (Cape Town: Human & Rousseau, 1961).
59 D.M. Schreuder, *Gladstone and Kruger* (London: Routledge and Kegan Paul, 1969), p. 514.
60 Schreuder, *Gladstone and Kruger*, p. 514.

In 1872, the Cape received an advanced form of colonial self-rule, called 'responsible government', with a prime minister heading a cabinet that was accountable to Parliament. With much more power devolved on the colony, voters became increasingly agitated about the excessive government expenditure on military expeditions that had landed the colony in heavy debt. Ever since the mid-century, Cape Afrikaners had opposed wars in territories in which no whites lived. More often than not, these expeditions were the result of failed imperial policies or costly earlier military or political blunders.

The final straw was the actions of the Sprigg cabinet. An avowed imperialist who championed 'British supremacy in South Africa', Gordon Sprigg formed a cabinet of politicians from the east and the Midlands, with not a single Afrikaner nor western Cape politician. To cover the cost of new railways and colonial intervention in the war between two Xhosa factions, the Sprigg cabinet decided to impose a tax on brandy producers, almost all western Cape Afrikaners. The wine farmers, who were experiencing tough times marked by debts and overproduction, were outraged, but, ignoring their protests, the Sprigg cabinet steamrollered the bill through Parliament.

On the day the excise law was published, some of its members met with Jan Hofmeyr, editor of De Zuid-Afrikaan, who recommended parliamentary action. Hofmeyr by the age of twenty-five already had a library of 250 books on religion and mathematics and the greatest treasures of Dutch and English literature, but he lacked the politician's lust for the limelight and was not endowed with an intense personal ego or drive for power. Critics saw him as a Sir John Falstaff, Shakespeare's fat knight of brazen assurance with few scruples; he would be nicknamed 'The Mole' for his refusal to accept a cabinet post except for one brief period, preferring to plot his moves while remaining in the background. Nevertheless, Hofmeyr's political skills were formidable, and Cecil John Rhodes considered him the most capable politician in South Africa.[61] Surveying his career, one is struck by the deftness with which he kept adjusting his footing to find a new political balance.

In October 1878 Hofmeyr formed the Zuid-Afrikaansche Boeren Beschermings Vereeniging (BBV) to oppose the excise law. It was an inclusive organization, although colored Afrikaans-speakers were hardly mentioned. They were welcome to vote for the party but not welcomed as members. Hofmeyr won the Stellenbosch seat in the 1879 parliamentary election. The BBV won nearly half of the upper-house seats and a third of those in the lower house, but enthusiasm soon dwindled and the BBV failed to extend itself much beyond the electoral districts of the Cape, Stellenbosch, Paarl and Malmesbury. At the BBV's first annual meeting in 1879 it was reported that not a single branch had paid its subscriptions as required by the constitution.[62] More was needed to provide a sustained momentum for the entry into politics of the colonial Afrikaners. It took the efforts of a gifted and volatile young minister, Stephanus Jacobus du Toit, to promote the language of Afrikaans as the vehicle of a new political consciousness.

---

61 Robert Rotberg, The Founder: Cecil John Rhodes and the Pursuit of Power (Johannesburg: Southern Books, 1988), p. 132.
62 Rodney Davenport, The Afrikaner Bond, 1880-1911 (Cape Town: Oxford University Press, 1966), pp. 12-18.

The rise of Afrikaans

Stephanus (or 'S.J.', as he was called) du Toit was born in 1847, the thirteenth child, on a Paarl wine farm that had been in the family's possession since the arrival of the Huguenots. He attended school at the Paarl Gymnasium, the Dutch-medium school that Van der Lingen had founded. Du Toit was short in stature and his bold forehead, piercing eyes, and finely carved features gave him a striking appearance. He was an intelligent man whose vaulting ambition was often tripped by an impatience for glory and by a disputatious temperament. In a biography, one of his sons called him a modern Ismael: his hand was against everyone and everyone's hand was against him.[63]

Du Toit had little patience with the revivals, emotional outpourings and demonstrative pietism that had become a feature of the Cape DRC. He was much more interested in Calvin's sterner, more intellectual message. He had developed a great admiration for Abraham Kuyper, the great Dutch neo-Calvinist thinker whom he met on an 1880 visit to the Netherlands; they stayed in close contact until Du Toit fell out with him, too.

Du Toit drew together the different political and theological strands of Cape Afrikaner thinking into a coherent philosophy with strong neo-Calvinist underpinnings. He had finished his theological studies in 1872 at the Theological Seminary in Stellenbosch, three years after Van der Lingen's death. In the struggle that ensued in the Paarl parish with regard to a successor, Du Toit's supporters were pitted against an opposing faction who had had more than enough of Van der Lingen's campaigns against 'progress' and his efforts to maintain Paarl Gymnasium as a private, Dutch-medium school. They wanted a modern *dominee* who would normalize the relationship with the forces of progress.

The acrimonious struggle ended in a deadlock. Eventually, a second congregation was established in Paarl to represent one side; among its members an extraordinary number of poor people, mostly coloreds. It invited Du Toit to become its minister. In such unpropitious circumstances Du Toit became the driving force behind the first Afrikaans language movement that spanned the years 1875-1890.

Because most of the Afrikaner colonists, ex-slaves and servants lacked a proper education, or any education at all, Afrikaans was the common tongue they spoke. In 1825 M.D. Teenstra published a dialogue between a Caledon farmer, his wife and a slave, to show his readers how the Cape vernacular differed from pure Dutch. In the same year a Dutch interpreter who worked at the Cape Town courts referred to Afrikaans as 'a language entirely new to me, namely the form of mongrel Dutch which is spoken in this country by the farmers and slaves and also by the Hottentots and all sorts of free heathen tribes.'[64] By 1875 Afrikaans or some form of simplified Dutch was spoken across most of the present South Africa. Johannes Brill, a Dutch educationist in Bloemfontein, pointed out that while Dutch was the official language of the republic in which he resided, the 'Zuid-Afrikaansche taal [Afrikaans]' was 'the unofficial language that was not written but spoken from Cape Town to deep in the interior of South Africa.'[65] There was no suggestion in these remarks that Afrikaans was unfit as a public language.

---

63 J.D. du Toit, *Ds. S.J. du Toit in weg en werk* (Paarl: Paarl Drukpers, 1917), p. iii.
64 Ross, *Status and Respectability in the Cape Colony*, p. 58.
65 Scholtz, *Die ontwikkeling van die politieke denke van die Afrikaner,* vol. 3, p. 276.

Afrikaans first appeared in print in Arabic prayer books prepared for the Cape Town Muslim community during the 1840s and 1850s. In 1861 the first secular book was published in Afrikaans on the secession of the eastern Cape. The author was a participant in the controversy, Louis Henri Meurant, who realized that the eastern Cape farmers among whom he moved understood Afrikaans much better than Dutch. The previous year *Het Cradocksche Nieuwsblad* had published his *Zamenspraak tussen Klaas Waarzegger en Jan Twyfelaar.* In the 1860s and 1870s Afrikaans was employed by newspapers, often in poems, with the specific intention of achieving a humorous effect.

A section of the English-speaking part of the population considered Afrikaans as a public language beneath contempt. But Afrikaans' greatest enemies were the status-conscious colonial Afrikaners in towns and cities, desperate to win acceptance in a society dominated by English-speakers. To them Afrikaans was an embarrassment; a language welded from different tongues by white, brown and black people that sent the wrong signal in a society obsessed with class and racial distinctions. According to J.H.H. de Waal, these educated Afrikaners considered Afrikaans an impoverished dialect, degenerate Dutch, an incomprehensible Creole tongue, a 'Hotnotstaal' (Hotnot is a derogatory term derived from Hottentot) without any future.[66]

In 1876 a lecture by the Chief Justice, Lord John Henry de Villiers, whose parents in Paarl had once fervently prayed for him to succeed Van der Lingen as minister, dismissed the possibility that Afrikaans could ever become a literary language. He characterized Afrikaans as follows: 'Poor in the number of its words, weak in its inflections, wanting in accuracy of meaning and incapable of expressing ideas connected with the higher spheres of thought, it will have to undergo great modification before it will be able to produce a literature worthy of the name.' For De Villiers the energy of colonial Afrikaners would be better spent in appropriating English, 'that rich and glorious language', which ultimately would become 'the language of South Africa.'[67]

Unlike many other language movements, the attempt, starting in the 1870s, to develop Afrikaans as a public language was not the work of the higher stratum of a group who used it as tool to advance their career chances. Its initial impetus came on a wave of religious enthusiasm that sprang from the Revival of the 1860s and, more particularly, in the desire to disseminate the Christian message to the very poor, both white and colored. A simple medium was required to spread the Christian message widely in print.

During the early 1870s two Dutch immigrants began to champion the use of Afrikaans to serve the poorer Christians. Arnoldus Pannevis proposed in *De Zuid-Afrikaan* that the Bible be translated and printed in Afrikaans. His primary target was the great mass of illiterate or semiliterate colored people. Another Dutch immigrant and teacher, Casper Peter Hoogenhout, who had spent some time in prison in his youth, argued that an Afrikaans Bible would also help a great many whites 'who did not half understand Dutch.' Acknowledging that Dutch was not understood by what it called 'simple Afrikaners', *De Kerkbode,* the voice of the Reformed Church, noted such proposals but argued that better education that made children proficient in Dutch was the solution.

---

66 J.H.H. de Waal, *My herinnerings van ons taalstryd* (Cape Town, Nasionale Pers, 1932), p. 21.
67 Scholtz, *Die ontwikkeling van die politieke denke van die Afrikaner*, vol. 3, p. 278.

In 1874 Du Toit entered the debate in *De Zuid-Afrikaan* under the name 'Ware [True] Afrikaander', and took the debate to a new level of sophistication. A mother tongue, he said, was a person's most precious possession: 'The language of a nation expresses the character of that nation. Deprive a nation of the vehicle of its thoughts and you deprive it of the wisdom of its ancestors.'[68] He deplored the great damage done to Afrikaner colonists by the policy of English as the sole official language. In an obvious dig at Andrew Murray and his allies, he criticized the DRC hierarchy for allowing 'unnecessary' English sermons and for promoting English in the schools it had founded. He refuted the argument that Afrikaans could not be considered a proper language since it supposedly lacked a grammatical structure and was composed of different linguistic elements. He also denied that Afrikaans was the language of the colored people; instead, the 'Hottentots had abandoned their language and had adopted ours.' Afrikaans was a white man's tongue, 'a pure Germanic language', one of purity, simplicity, brevity and vigor. Afrikaners must be taught that Afrikaans was their mother tongue, and that their duty was to develop Afrikaans as a *landstaal* (national language), along with Dutch.[69] In a subsequent exchange of letters in *De Zuid-Afrikaan*, Du Toit formulated one of the main spelling rules of the language: 'We write as we speak.'

On 7 November 1874 Pannevis pointed out to the British and Foreign Bible Society that since the English and the Dutch Bible were both incomprehensible to many, this was contributing to rapidly increasing social degradation , especially of the colored population. In his estimate at least a million people in the colony would benefit from the publication of the Bible in Afrikaans. Pannevis suggested S.J.du Toit as translator of the Bible into Afrikaans in his letter to the British and Foreign Bible Society. When he was approached by an official with that in mind, Du Toit called a meeting in Paarl at the home of Gideon Malherbe, the son-in-law of Van der Lingen. There, on 14 August 1875, three weeks after the establishment of the new congregation, the *Genootskap van Regte Afrikaners* (GRA, the Society of True Afrikaners) was founded. Six of the eight founding members, including Du Toit, were younger than thirty, and except for two, all were members of the Northern Paarl congregation. Du Toit, having just emerged from the battle in Northern Paarl parish with all its class overtones, now assumed leadership of the language movement.

But the time was not ripe for a Bible translation, the meeting concluded, though there was an urgent need to persuade the Dutch and Afrikaans-speaking white people of the importance of Afrikaans in their national life and to see themselves as a distinct community, calling themselves Afrikaners.[70] The term 'Afrikaner' was sometimes used for slaves born in Africa or the offspring of slaves, free blacks and Khoisan, but it was predominantly reserved for burghers and, later, colonists of Dutch, German and French origins. Descent, not language, was the defining characteristic. But the term was elastic. In 1830, when *De Zuid-Afrikaan* was founded, the editor defined the term Afrikaner to

---

68 *De Zuid-Afrikaan*, 22 July 1874.

69 P.H. Zietsman, *Die taal is gans die volk* (Pretoria: University of South Africa, 1992), p. 9; Hermann Giliomee, 'The Beginnings of Afrikaner Ethnic Consciousness', in Leroy Vail (ed.), *The Creation of Tribalism in South Africa* (London: James Currey, 1989), p. 35.

70 J.C. Kannemeyer, *Die Afrikaanse Literatuur, 1652-1987* (Pretoria: Academica, 1988), pp. 27-9.

include white settlers of British descent. It was the fervent hope of middle-class Afrikaners, at whom the paper was directed, that 'Afrikaner' would become the name of the amalgamated two white communities.

When Cecil John Rhodes during the early 1880s began promoting his sub-imperialism with the Cape as the base for British expansion, the term 'Afrikaner' was often used inclusively to attract English-speakers (see p. 196). But the more aggressive imperialists, insisting on the closest ties with London, considered it a dubious honor to have the name Afrikaner bestowed on them. The *Cape Times* spurned it as originally applied to 'the half-bred off-spring of slaves, and even in a word the mark of slavery is detestable.' Twenty years later an imperialist history would dismiss 'Afrikaner' as a name that meant little more than 'a person of Dutch descent who believed in the advancement of the brandy market, protection to the corn farmer, and the repression of the native.'[71]

Du Toit and his colleagues embraced 'Afrikaner' as a term of honor, designating an exclusive group. At the GRA's first meeting they isolated three categories of Afrikaners: those with Afrikaans hearts, those with English hearts, and those with Dutch hearts. It made it clear that its mission was to build a group of Afrikaners with 'Afrikaans hearts.' Its prime target was the large section of Afrikaners who were not particularly affluent and who had received limited education.

To spell out its message, the GRA launched its own newspaper, *Di Afrikaanse Patriot*, its first issue appearing on 15 January 1876. Its circulation began at fifty and rose to 3,700 in the early 1880s. The only Afrikaans paper until the early twentieth century, it had, for a brief spell, the largest circulation of all the Dutch-Afrikaans papers. Its style was clear, crisp and concise, with simple sentences and monosyllabic words – to which Afrikaans easily lends itself. Here is an example: 'Die hoogste wet is di wil van di volk. Wat di volk wil, moet wet wore. En as 'n volk ni eenstemmig is ni, dan gaat dit met meerderheid van stemme. Di meerderheid maak di wet . . . Geen regering kan staan teen di volkswil . . .'[72]

Du Toit almost single-handedly turned a movement for Afrikaans as a religious medium into one with classic nationalist aims. Pannevis had identified the need for an Afrikaans Bible for colored people, but Du Toit omitted this from his own agenda; his *De Zuid-Afrikaan* articles linked Afrikaans as a language to the nationality of the Afrikaners. Even Pannevis soon forgot his initial concern; it was not enough, he wrote, to write and read 'Hottentots' Afrikaans'; the time had come to discover how the 'civilized part of our people' speaks Afrikaans and, having established that, to formulate rules for the language.[73]

The language movement was concentrated in a very small area, Paarl and its immediate surroundings. A single man dominated it as the moving spirit and creative genius. In 1878 an elder brother of S.J. du Toit, D.F. du Toit, known as 'Oom Lokomotief', became editor of *Patriot* and Du Toit's assistant. With limited resources, the GRA depended on Du Toit, who claimed that he had to sell part of his own library to fund it.

71 Hermann Giliomee, 'The Beginnings of Afrikaner Nationalism, 1870-1915', *South African Historical Journal*, 19(1987), pp. 121, 131.
72 Davenport, *The Afrikaner Bond*, p. 337.
73 Scholtz, *Die Afrikaner en sy taal*, pp. 183-201.

Du Toit and his associates would publish much in Dutch as well, but to them Afrikaans was the primary language of white Afrikaners. That Du Toit could entertain such grand ambitions for Afrikaans as a language, which at that stage was virtually without literature, suggests both his boundless intellectual self-confidence and his nationalist zeal. He worked himself almost to a standstill in his constant emphasis that Afrikaners had to do more than champion their language: they had to speak up for 'their nation and their country.'

To cultivate a feeling of nationality, Du Toit tried to counter the great emphasis on British history in schools. In 1877 a team effort with Du Toit as its main author produced a nationalist history entitled *Die Geskiedenis van ons Land in die Taal van ons Volk* (The History of Our Land in the Language of our People), which sketched the history of the colonial Afrikaners in heroic terms. They were oppressed throughout their history, it said, but nevertheless they remained true to their Christian faith and lived honorable lives. It hailed as martyrs the executed Slagtersnek rebels and painted the role of the British government and 'the English' invariably in negative terms. On one page it even stated: 'In this way we can see that the English have been scoundrels from the earliest times.'

The GRA's other publications included *Eerste Beginsels van die Afrikaans Taal* (First Principles of the Afrikaans Language); a history of the Afrikaans language movement; an anthology of Afrikaans poetry; and a picture book for children, particularly close to Du Toit's heart. Also close to his heart was a demand for Christian-National education, strongly propagated by neo-Calvinists in the Netherlands. Du Toit took up this topic in a pamphlet he published in 1876, protesting against the colony's education system, which after 1865 was almost completely secular. He believed that parents had the right to insist that their children receive confessional religious instruction and be taught national history of which they themselves approved.

As editor of *De Zuid-Afrikaan*, J.H. Hofmeyr published the GRA's history of South Africa and arranged for publication of the first issues of *Die Afrikaanse Patriot*, but even he wrote in 1876 that 'the men of the *Patriot* were waging a hopeless battle.'[74] The work of the GRA exposed the class divisions in the Afrikaner community. As the voice of the better-educated and more affluent Afrikaners, *De Zuid-Afrikaan* dismissed the *Patriot* and brandy as 'the common enemies of civilization.' But others recognized that the GRA newspaper, the *Patriot*, had managed to cross the class gulf in Afrikaner ranks. A correspondent in the Free State paper, *The Friend*, wrote from Kroonstad of the *Patriot*: 'It is not only the lowly *bywoners* who read it, but also the civilized people among us.'[75] The *Patriot* from the start had managed to get some of its copies distributed in the two Boer republics. When Theophilus Shepstone annexed the Zuid-Afrikaansche Republiek in 1877, interest in the paper quickened among Afrikaners, most of whom rejected the annexation. Although both the *Zuid-Afrikaan* and the *Patriot* were critical of it, in October 1880 the *Patriot* went one step further by arguing that the time had come for active resistance. Some Transvaal leaders later claimed that this had been a decisive spur for them to take up arms.

---

74 Scholtz, *Die ontwikkeling van die politieke denke van die Afrikaner*, vol. 3, pp. 276-9.
75 *De Zuid-Afrikaan*, 23 April 1879; *The Friend*, 17 February 1881.

The church hierarchy watched the *Patriot* with growing concern. For many, Du Toit had been a thorn in the flesh; he opposed many things for which the Reformed Church stood: revivals, special prayer meetings, English in schools, meek submission to the colonial and imperial government, and, in a pamphlet on the prophecies of the apocalypse, he criticized certain aspects of the church itself. Now he was openly encouraging resistance in the Transvaal to the God-given authorities. The 1880 Cape synod discussed the paper over three days, one speaker after the other denouncing its 'pernicious' influence as casting suspicion on the government, the church, and its office-bearers. Du Toit defended himself and the paper at the synod, but the die was cast. In a vote of 114 to 2 the synod condemned the paper. As could be expected, its circulation promptly rose, helped further by the successful Transvaal revolt against the British annexation that culminated in a stunning victory at Majuba on 27 February 1881 (see p. 230).[76] An Afrikaner movement seemed ready to take off across political boundaries, with burghers in many places expressing solidarity with the Transvaal burghers, viewing the revolt as a struggle that affected everyone 'with a true Afrikaans spirit.' In Hofmeyr's words it filled the Cape Afrikaners, 'otherwise groveling in the mud of materialism, with a national glow of sympathy for their brothers across the Transvaal.'[77] Efforts had already been made to channel this enthusiasm into forming the first modern political party in South Africa.

The rise of the Afrikaner Bond

The advance to modernity in the nineteenth century in the Western world typically brought to the fore socialists, who questioned the profit system; populists, who protested against the concentration of capital; and nationalists, who celebrated a national culture and history. In the case of the Cape Afrikaners, Hofmeyr demanded some respect for the Dutch culture but supported capitalism. Du Toit showed signs of both nationalist and populist responses to modernity.[78] Seizing the initiative, Du Toit, in an editorial on 20 June 1879, proposed the formation of an Afrikaner Bond with the slogan of '*Afrika voor de Afrikaners*' and with branches across South Africa. The first two clauses of his proposal advocated an organization in which 'any Afrikaner can feel at home and work together for the good of a united South Africa.' The next clause made explicit his intention to make his target group much wider than 'Afrikaners with Afrikaner hearts', as the GRA had done. He saw it as a body in which 'no nationality divides us from each other, but in which everyone who recognizes Africa as his Fatherland can live together and work as brother of a single house, be they of English, Dutch, French or German origin.'

The second part of Du Toit's document gave a hint of the nationalist and populist agenda of its founder: it would be the task of the Bond to prevent 'the sacrifice of Africa's interests to England and those of the Farmer to the Merchant.' Trade and industry must

---

76 Scholtz, 'Ds. S.J. du Toit as kerkman en kultuurleier', pp. 96-8.
77 J.H. Hofmeyr, *The Life of J.H. Hofmeyr* (Cape Town: Van de Sandt de Villiers, 1913), p. 164.
78 See the *International Social Science Journal*. Special Issue on Modernity and Identity, 118, November 1988, and particularly the contribution by Alan Touraine.

be developed to benefit the land, 'not to fill the pockets of speculators' and the money market 'must not be dominated by English banks.' It protested against the great sums spent on education for English-speakers, while the largest sector (the Afrikaners) was neglected. It demanded equal recognition for Dutch as a public language.[79]

The *Patriot* elaborated on many of these points, playing on the Afrikaners' common resentment of free trade in goods and money and of merchants, bankers, and other agents of British financial capitalism. A prime target was the Standard Bank, which sent a large part of its dividends to its London head office. The paper accused the bank of conspiring to bring about the collapse of numerous small banks. It proposed forming a national bank by amalgamating local banks and evicting the Standard Bank, as the Republic of the Orange Free State had done in the mid-1860s. In 1882 the *Patriot* called the Standard Bank a 'gigantic devil fish', while in Parliament an Afrikaner politician insinuated that the Standard Bank had the western Cape farmers 'so much under the whip that it could buy up all wine farms.'[80] Even *De Zuid-Afrikaan* admitted that Afrikaners were united in their antipathy against the imperial banks. But when the *Patriot* launched its campaign, money was so tight that the proposal seemed to make little sense. The colonists preferred being exploited by the imperial banks to not being exploited by them.

Du Toit and the *Patriot* also proposed consumer boycotts, calling it the duty of 'every true Afrikaner not to spend a copper at an Englishman's shop if he can avoid it.' The paper suggested that Afrikaner *boerewinkels* (co-operative stores) be founded in every town,[81] a plan that failed to get off the ground. Even if there had been enough capital to start the stores, it would have been almost impossible to circumvent the merchants who imported goods from London.

Hofmeyr had no taste for this type of populist politics. He wanted an organization that would unite Afrikaner and English farmers, and that would benefit both farmers and merchants.[82] He was keen to attract a new generation of well-educated Afrikaners, but it was only in the 1890s that the Bond would attract bright young men like Jan Smuts and F.S. Malan. Hofmeyr was also careful not to alienate the church, which was pro-Empire and opposed to political activism, or the English section, which could easily be stampeded by allegations that the Bond was a radical organization.

Hofmeyr cared about the culture of the colonial Afrikaners but did not want to elevate it to a divisive issue. He identified with the Afrikaners in the Boer republics and would on occasion stress that 'blood was thicker than water', but he also wanted the colonial Afrikaners to be loyal to the Empire and the Colony, though, at the same time, he saw no need to glorify the Empire. He defined the commitment of colonial Afrikaners to the Empire in purely pragmatic and material terms. As he remarked in October 1878, the Cape Afrikaners agreed that Britain provided security in an era of rivalry between the Great Powers but did not believe that Britain had a 'glorious mission' to spread 'Christianity

79 Davenport, *The Afrikaner Bond*, pp. 35-6.
80 Hermann Giliomee, 'Aspects of the Rise of Afrikaner Capital and Afrikaner Nationalism in the Western Cape', in Wilmot James and Mary Simons (eds.), *The Angry Divide: Social and Economic History of the Western Cape* (Cape Town: David Philip, 1989), pp. 63-81.
81 Giliomee, 'Afrikaner Capital', p. 71.
82 Mordechai Tamarkin, *Cecil Rhodes and the Cape Afrikaners* (London: Frank Cass, 1996), pp. 54-5.

and civilization.' Cape Afrikaners were 'as loyal British subjects as any other people' but were not prepared to become Englishmen.[83]

The Transvaal revolt temporarily cut the ground from under Hofmeyr's feet, the humiliating British defeats dismaying the English sector and greatly encouraging Du Toit, who believed that the Afrikaner nation was born in the crushing British defeat at Majuba. The Afrikaner Bond benefited from the upsurge of nationalist emotion. While, by the end of 1880, it had only three branches, after the Transvaal revolt numerous branches were formed, particularly in the eastern Cape, but also in the Orange Free State and Transvaal.

Becoming more radical now, Du Toit pushed the anti-liberal, neo-Calvinist line of his spiritual hero Abraham Kuyper. Early in 1882 Du Toit, who left the Cape in February to become head of the education department in the Zuid-Afrikaansche Republic in the Transvaal, drew up a new program of principles that defined the Bond's mission in more explicit nationalist terms. He now described Afrikaners as all those of predominantly Dutch or Huguenot descent. He also called for self-determination and stated that the 'ultimate object of our national development must be a united South Africa under its own flag.'[84]

Realizing that his own farmers' association (BBV) lacked emotional appeal in its narrow focus on material interests, Hofmeyr himself became a member of the Bond and began to plot to moderate its aims. At a Bond congress at Cradock in late 1882 he told his audience that independence for South Africa could not be attained before a 'sane feeling of nationality had developed.' It was not language that bound members of such a nationality, but mutual respect between the two white groups and their ability to act as a cohesive force.

In 1883 a congress was called at Richmond to amalgamate the Bond and the BBV, a clear shift in course. Hofmeyr's hand can be seen in the inclusive definition of the term 'Afrikaner' in the constitution: 'The Bond knows no nationality at all except that of the Afrikaners and regard as belonging thereto anyone, of whatever origin, who strives for the welfare of South Africa.' It also diluted Du Toit's emphasis on South African unity as a concrete objective. It was now a 'destiny' rather than a goal to be actively pursued. The meeting gave three enthusiastic cheers for the anniversary of their 'Honorable Queen.' Daantjie van der Heever, the heart and soul of the Afrikaner movement in the eastern districts, declared: 'I am, I hope, a patriotic Dutch-Afrikaner but if anyone dares to touch the English flag I shall shoot him point blank.'[85] Hofmeyr soon assumed full control of the Bond.

Hofmeyr constructed a new identity in which the two white 'nationalities' were envisaged as growing into a composite nationality that recognized each other's language, culture, education and religion. In 1882 Hofmeyr won the right for Dutch to be used in Parliament. In 1883, knowledge of Dutch became compulsory for a certain class of civil servant, and in the following year it was permitted in the higher courts. It became a compulsory subject for civil service candidates in 1887. But this was a permissive form

---

83 Hofmeyr, *Leven van Hofmeyr*, p. 93.
84 Tamarkin, *Rhodes and the Cape Afrikaners*, p. 53.
85 Hofmeyr, *Leven van Hofmeyr*, p. 235.

of language rights. Dutch was permitted, but not enforced with any degree of conviction.

Hofmeyr represented the more prosperous wheat and wine farmers and the financial and legal middlemen in the towns. His agenda included protective tariffs; attracting foreign capital for the development of the colony's infrastructure to the benefit of the farmers; control over labor; the opening up of interior markets for Cape wine and brandy; and higher franchise qualifications. He favored secular education but did not counter Christian-National schools directly. Instead he introduced legislation that would allow religious instruction to be given at the discretion of the school committee. He assured Parliament that, in practice, little would change, and this was what happened. At almost every synod over the next three decades members would vainly deplore the inadequate religious instruction at schools and the unwillingness of school committees to improve it. The influence of the secular state and secular education proved to be as extensive as Van der Lingen and Du Toit had feared.

Du Toit failed to make a new career in the Transvaal. At first he was a confidant of Paul Kruger there, but, sent out as Kruger's representative to deal with land disputes on the republic's western border, he rashly annexed the disputed territory to the ZAR, causing great embarrassment to the republic. He became marginalized when Kruger began preferring the advice of Dutch officials, and he neglected his duties as head of the education department. By the end of the 1880s his relationship with Kruger had broken down, and he was personally bankrupt as a result of speculation in gold mining. Having arrived as a hero in the Transvaal in 1882, he returned to the Cape in 1890 embroiled in personal feuds and nourishing a bitter resentment of Kruger. His nationalist views had been discarded. He was now in favor of the unification of the states in Africa under British coastal protection. It is quite likely that Cecil John Rhodes was now supporting him financially and that Du Toit was playing his backer's tune. This led to a break with his brother D.F. (Oom Lokomotief) and Hoogenhout at the *Patriot*. In 1896 he started a Dutch daily newspaper, *Het Dagblad*, in the Cape, but it lasted only two years. He continued to back Rhodes even after Hofmeyr had irrevocably broken with him over the Jameson Raid. Du Toit ended up as a British supporter in the Anglo-Boer War.

A language in eclipse

Du Toit's so-called First Language Movement could boast some achievements, for instance, a print run of 93,650 Dutch and 81,000 Afrikaans books, but by 1890 his movement was all but dead. The secret meetings of the Genootskap vir Regte Afrikaners and Du Toit's emphasis on Kuyper's kind of Calvinism sent the wrong message. The movement was too dependent on one man who had far too many enemies. Du Toit erred when he chose an ultra-phonetic form of spelling, which very often emphasized the western Cape origins of the movement. He wrote, for example, 'oek' and 'o'er' instead of 'ook' and 'oor.'[86] Du Toit also made the mistake of wanting Dutch and Afrikaans to replace English as the *landstaal*. It was a hopeless quest: the real challenge was to eliminate Dutch

---

86 Scholtz, 'Ds. S.J. du Toit as kerkman en kultuurleier', p. 85.

and to develop Afrikaans to a point where it could take its place next to English as an official language. But Afrikaans still carried the stigma of a *bastertaal*, or mongrel language, and as the language of the uneducated. Only when educated people over a broad front started to claim it as their mother tongue and as a medium of instruction at all levels of education would Afrikaners themselves cease to be ashamed to speak it in public and also to write in it.[87]

Hofmeyr's Bond continued to promote Dutch, but it was an uphill battle. The British had given up attempting to murder Dutch as a language and were willing to allow the Afrikaners to commit the foul deed themselves. Nor were they disappointed. Considering English the symbol and measure of success, a growing number of the Afrikaner elite used English, even in the privacy of their homes. It was with some despair that Hofmeyr in 1890 cried: 'Do not ask for rights in Parliament and school which you do not wish to have in your home. The language question is a matter of life and death. Despise your language and you despise your nationality.'[88]

Hofmeyr supported the establishment in 1890 of the Zuidafrikaanse Taalbond, which pledged itself to promote the *volkstaal* and an awakening of a developed feeling of nationality. With a vote of 48 to 37 the Taalbond opted for High Dutch rather than Afrikaans as *volkstaal*. It hoped to revitalize Dutch by simplifying its spelling, but Dutch was itself a dying language in South Africa, with ever fewer people able to speak it properly and displaying any affection for it. Even Kruger, unwavering in his support of Dutch as the ZAR's official language, spoke much better Afrikaans than Dutch. Visiting Rotterdam in the Netherlands in 1884 as part of a Transvaal delegation, he stopped using his broken Dutch for the first time and switched to Afrikaans. A Dutch report noted the great difference: in his own language the speech was 'lively, glowing and spirited.'[89]

Afrikaans was also struggling to exist. As a written language it was considered to be *morsdood* (as dead as a dodo) in the final years of the century.[90] In Cape Town only the Muslims were reported to be still loyal to Afrikaans. Observers believed that within a generation Afrikaans would no longer be spoken in the cities and by the better-educated classes in the rural areas. English, on the other hand, proceeded on its steady advance. In the Groote Kerk, the church building of the oldest DRC parish, the practice continued of offering an English service together with Dutch services. The cessation of the English services at the end of the century did not come about as a result of any increasing cultural awareness but the calculation of material gain. Jan Christoffel Hofmeyr (1826-1897), an eccentric Afrikaner money-lender, had bequeathed £20,000 in his will to the church on condition that the two ministers had to give at least two services in Dutch every Sunday.

In many other walks of life English and the symbols of imperialism had edged out Dutch and local symbols. Stellenbosch Gymnasium, which became the Stellenbosch College in 1881, six years later asked that its name be changed to Victoria College. Its

---

87 Oral tradition suggests that Du Toit suspected that the Freemason movement wanted to crush him. See V.E. d'Assonville, *S.J. du Toit* (Weltevredenpark: Marnix, 1999), p. 119.

88 Hofmeyr, *Life of Hofmeyr*, p. 469.

89 D.W. Krüger, *Paul Kruger* (Johannesburg: Dagbreek Boekhandel, 1961), vol. 2, p. 45.

90 J.H.H. de Waal, *Die lewe van David Christiaan de Waal* (Cape Town: Nasionale Pers, 1928), p. 307; J.C. Steyn, *'n Tuiste in eie taal* (Cape Town: Tafelberg, 1981), pp. 169-72.

medium of instruction was English and the first professors and lecturers were all Englishmen or Scotsmen. In 1882 Paarl Gymnasium felt compelled to accept state subsidies for the first time, and, in doing so, abandoned the attempt to run a Dutch-medium school on the basis of private donations.

The Cape Afrikaners valued the freedoms they enjoyed under the British crown and had no desire to free themselves from a colonial yoke that sat lightly on them. In a revealing 1878 editorial *De Zuid-Afrikaan* declared that the Afrikaners wanted no 'republican freedom, equality and fraternity.' If aggrieved, they said: 'Let us send a petition to the Queen.' If ever they formed a republic it would be along the lines of the white oligarchies in the southern states of the United States of America.[91] It is striking that there is no reference here to the Boer republics. The colonial Afrikaners identified themselves with their kinsmen across the Orange River, but put the Cape's interests first and rarely hid their sense of superiority over the northern Afrikaners.

Although the Bond, from the second half of the 1880s, held half the seats in Parliament, Hofmeyr would never form a government and refused to become Prime Minister. He felt that holding office would cause divisions in his own camp and upset English-speakers. In 1887 the Afrikaner Bond took the occasion of the jubilee year of Queen Victoria to express in an official address to her the following sentiments: 'We assure you humbly and respectfully [of] our true loyalty to your throne, and we feel proud that in the great British Empire there are not more loyal subjects than those we represent.' At the Bond congress in Paarl the following year a toast was drunk to the Queen and, as the *Patriot* reported, 'Professor Jan de Villiers jumped to his harmonium and *God Save the Queen* was sung in such a way that even the world famous Paarl Rock bowed in respect as the cannon fired twenty-one shots.'

In 1890 D.F. du Toit, as leader of the nationalist wing of the Bond, told a London newspaper that the Bond 'was as loyal as it was possible and that in England they spoke more of a republic than in the Cape.' But not all the Afrikaner voices sang in this choir, and the *Patriot* warned that the Bond was becoming too *Engelsgesind*, too well disposed to the English.

Nevertheless, the pull of English culture and language seemed to become ever stronger as Rhodes and other English-speaking politicians lauded the Cape Afrikaners who were loyal. They loved to display their proficiency in English. Miems Rothman, who under the name M.E.R. would become a noted Afrikaans writer in the twentieth century, remembered how as a girl in Swellendam during the early 1890s she and her friends enjoyed speaking English among themselves. When they married they did not speak Dutch or Afrikaans to their own children, and gave their children, particularly their daughters, English names. Lovers, parents, children and siblings corresponded with each other in English.[92]

At a time when the survival-of-the-fittest scheme of thought dominated colonial discourse, there was a widespread assumption that the fitter nations and languages would absorb those less fit. At the Cape few would put their bets on the survival of Afrikaners and Afrikaans.

---

91 *De Zuid-Afrikaan*, 9 October 1878.
92 M.E.R. (Miems Rothman), *My beskeie deel* (Cape Town: Tafelberg, 1972), pp. 35-6.

The creed of progress

The imperialist creed of free trade and progress disguised the interests of Britain and English-speaking people extremely well. Britain only embraced free trade as a policy after it had been strongly protectionist during its own growing age. During the nineteenth century, free trade was to the greatest benefit of British manufacturers and merchants.[93] The policy of anglicization in the name of progress gave a head start to English-speakers in government, the professions, and commerce. After 1828 all those not fluent in English were handicapped by the primacy of English in the courts, and the dominance of English in Parliament led to a disproportionate number of English representatives. English as the only medium of instruction in the schools imposed a great burden on the great majority of Afrikaner and other children who did not know the language.[94]

Yet apart from the Great Trek, which was a peaceful revolt, colonial Afrikaners made no serious attempt to resist British domination or engage in civil disobedience. Indeed, the one widespread act of civil disobedience occurred in response to an intervention in scab disease, where the forces of 'progress' were clearly in the best interests of all, including the Afrikaner farmers. The disease, which had been endemic among sheep in the colony since the seventeenth century, reduced the quality of wool and the mohair clip, and caused the death of thousands of sheep in times of drought. By the 1880s it was costing farmers £500,000 a year. Yet scientists had recently proved that the disease could be controlled by dipping and quarantine. Between 1886 and 1896 the colonial government sought to enforce these methods and eliminate the disease. Fully accepting the ideology of progress and the veracity of scientific methods, English farmers complied, but there was strong resistance in many parts from Afrikaner farmers, often a religious objection. By 1893 inspectors were prosecuting 1,568 farmers a year for non-compliance, and it soon turned into a serious political crisis, nearly causing a major revolt against the Bond leadership and the break-up of the coalition of Hofmeyr and Rhodes. There is evidence that the agitation prompted Hofmeyr to resign his seat in Parliament in 1895.

The justifications of those who objected to the measures to eradicate scab revealed much of the rural Afrikaner political culture. First there was the identification with the traditional against the official insistence on progress and scientific rationality. Some argued that scab was a plague inflicted by God for the sins committed by His people. It had to be coped with and endured like drought, locusts, or other natural disasters. There were also those who refused to comply with the law on the grounds that it diminished their liberty. The Cape farmers had a tradition of two centuries behind them in which cattle farmers were free to do what they liked on their farms without any government intervention. A farmer explained his stand in the classic terminology of frontiersmen: 'The sheep farmer has been a free man and it is unfair to compel him.' Another farmer stated: '[The] government should not attempt to cripple the glorious freedom which they as a colony possessed under the British flag.'[95] This captured the essence of the ambiguous identity of colonial patriotism.

---

93 David Landes, *The Wealth and Poverty of Nations* (London: Abacus Books, 1998), pp. 265-6.
94 Davenport, *The Afrikaner Bond*, pp. 155-9.
95 The quotes are from the forthcoming study by Mordechai Tamarkin, 'Volk and Flock: the Cape Sheep Farmers in the Late 19th Century.' See also Davenport, *The Afrikaner Bond*, pp. 155-59.

The colonial patriotism that the Bond espoused allowed multiple identities and sympathies: patriotism towards the colony; loyalty towards the monarchy and the imperial tie; solidarity with their republican brothers across the Orange River; and pride in their own cultural distinctiveness, giving rise to a demand for formal equal language rights.[96] Afrikaner loyalty to the Empire (later the British Commonwealth) proved to be long lasting. Although there was always a majority of Afrikaners in the Cape electorate, not until 1958, when the first ever all-white election was held in the Cape Province (previously the Cape Colony), did a pro-republic party in the Cape Province receive the most votes.

---

96 Hofmeyr, *Leven van Hofmeyr*, pp. 293-303. The theme is developed in Tamarkin, *Rhodes and the Cape Afrikaners*, pp. 14-73.

Chapter 8

The Crucible of War

'The Word of God gives us the key': Paul Kruger's belief

When Theophilus Shepstone, special commissioner of the Earl of Carnarvon, the British Secretary of State for the Colonies, arrived in Pretoria in January 1877, he wooed the Transvaal burghers to secure their consent for annexing the republic as part of a plan to engineer a South African federation. He wrote later that of the three thousand people he had canvassed before annexing the republic on 12 April 1877, only Paul Kruger was unequivocal in his rejection of such a move. '[He] positively declined to enter into the discussion if that might involve the independence of the state as a republic.'[1]

During the first months of 1877 a presidential campaign was underway with Kruger, Deputy President, and Thomas François Burgers, the incumbent, as candidates. Burgers later said that he had proposed to Kruger that both of them withdraw for the sake of unity, but that Kruger had refused. Known for his athletic prowess and courage, Kruger had a reputation as a skilled military commander and negotiator with African chiefs, but the more progressive elements in the Zuid-Afrikaansche Republiek rejected his candidacy because of his lack of formal education and entrenched conservatism. A *Dopper* or Gereformeerde Church member, he mostly wore the Dopper short-cut black jacket. Invariably a pipe stuck out of his breast pocket, reminding people of his rough frontier background.

De Volksstem, the Dutch newspaper in Pretoria, said that 'it would be a cause of eternal shame' for the Transvaal if Kruger were elected president. The Cape politician John X. Merriman saw him as a mere *takhaar* (backwoodsman) and Joseph Chamberlain, Secretary of State for the Colonies between 1895 and 1903, as nothing but an 'ignorant, dirty and obstinate man who has known how to feather his own nest.'[2] But to others he displayed a 'gnarled magnificence', to use the term of John Buchan, a well-known British writer. In 1895, Lord James Bryce, a constitutional expert and about to become British ambassador to the USA, saw him as 'shrewd, cool, dogged, wary, courageous, typifying

---

1 G.H.L. le May, *The Afrikaners: An Historical Interpretation* (Oxford: Blackwell, 1995), p. 61.
2 John Fisher, *Paul Kruger* (London: Secker and Warburg, 1974), p. 1.

the qualities of his people.' 'Kruger could foil the statesmen of Europe by their own weapons . . . because his training has been wholly of eventful life and not of books.'[3] So, too, the well-educated and refined medical doctor and Afrikaans poet C. Louis Leipoldt described him as a 'rugged, rough-hewn, primitive old gentleman with an innate courtesy, a sonorous and powerful voice, and a rich and forceful vocabulary.'[4]

Kruger had issued a manifesto after the failure of a campaign in 1876 against the Pedi chiefdom that showed his unique blend of politics and religion. It addressed the recent setbacks to the ZAR.

> How, then, is this retrogression to be explained? The Word of God gives us the key to it. Look to the case of Israel; if people have a devout King everything is prosperous; but under an ungodly ruler the land goes backward and all people must suffer thereby. Read Leviticus 26 and see how literally its words have been fulfilled. In the days of the Voortrekkers a handful of people put thousands of Kaffirs to flight . . . but see how when Burgers is president – he knows no Sabbath; he rides through every part of the country on Sundays; of church and religion he knows nothing.[5]

For Kruger the annexation and loss of republican freedom was the result of the people's unfaithfulness to the Word. Victory would be the blessing of the faithful. He saw a close parallel between the people of Israel and his own people in the experiences of the Great Trek and the revolt of 1880-1881. Both were 'God's peoples', specially called. God punished them when they sinned and saved them when they repented. Military victory and survival as an independent people was God's blessing to a faithful volk.[6]

Leading by personal courage, strong convictions and passionate oratory, Paul Kruger spread the message that without republican independence the Transvaal Afrikaners could not survive as a people with their own language, beliefs and livelihood. Not that Kruger was consistent. Sometimes he seemed to say that his 'oud volk' (old people), as he called the original Voortrekkers, were the only people who counted: they were 'God's people.' On other occasions he included all white people in the state, as well as foreigners, among God's people, suggesting loyalty not to the volk but to the state. At still other times he sounded like a twentieth century nationalist in his appeal to all Dutch or Afrikaans-speaking Afrikaners across South Africa.[7] But Transvaal leaders prized the republic's control over its own destiny much more than pan-Afrikaner unity. One progressive opponent of Kruger, Schalk Burger, chairman of the first Volksraad, declared that 'the word Africander should be interpreted as Transvaaler. Everyone from beyond the borders of the Republic must be viewed as a stranger, no matter if he came from the Free State, the colony, England, or Holland.'[8]

Soon after the annexation Kruger took the lead in organizing resistance. With the

3 James Bryce, *Impressions of South Africa* (New York: The Century, 1900), p. 438.
4 C. Louis Leipoldt, *Bushveld Doctor* (London: Jonathan Cape, 1937) p. 141.
5 Fisher, *Kruger*, p. 50.
6 F.A. van Jaarsveld, *Lewende Verlede* (Johannesburg: Afrikaanse Pers Boekhandel, 1961), pp. 201-7.
7 André du Toit, 'Puritans in Africa?', *Comparative Studies in Society and History*, 27, 2 (1985), p. 225.
8 C.T. Gordon, *The Growth of Boer Opposition to Kruger, 1890-1895* (Cape Town: Oxford University Press, 1970), p. 10.

burghers seemingly paralyzed by apathy and indifference, Kruger twice went to London as a member of a three-man delegation to persuade the Secretary of State for the Colonies to permit a referendum on Shepstone's claim that the majority favored annexation. Lord Carnarvon was unwilling to accede to this request and instead offered a £100,000 loan, considerable spending on education, railways, roads and a telegraph system, and a reduction of custom duties. He promised self-rule for the Transvaal like that enjoyed by the Cape government. There were even guarantees for equal status of the Dutch language with English, although Carnarvon hastened to add that this was not an undertaking that could last forever. Kruger and the other delegates listened patiently, but held to their demand for a referendum.

British officials were taken aback by Kruger's refusal to accept the offer of great material progress for the Transvaal, coupled with a liberal form of self-government as a colony within a federation. But Kruger saw self-government under British supervision as a fatal trap.[9] In his reminiscences recorded at the end of his life he gave an account of how he described the offer to his burghers: 'I will try to explain to you what this self-government in my opinion means. They say to you, "First, put your head quietly in the noose, so that I can hang you up: then you may kick your legs about as much as you please!" That is what they call self-government.'[10]

Slowly momentum mounted among the Transvaal burghers to reverse the annexation. Between one half and two-thirds signed petitions of protest. The other South African states offered moral support. The Orange Free State Volksraad spoke up for the restoration of ZAR independence, and influential Afrikaner and English politicians in the Cape, including J.H. ('Onze Jan') Hofmeyr and John X. Merriman, urged Britain to call a convention to establish what the Transvaal burghers really wanted.

Early in December 1880 mass meetings were held at Paardekraal in the ZAR, attended by thousands of burghers. The old Volksraad convened and appointed Kruger, Piet Joubert, and M.W. Pretorius as a triumvirate to take control of the protest movement that seemed headed for open revolt. A mass meeting on 11 December 1880 proclaimed the restoration of the republic. It was the beginning of an armed rebellion. The British had such a low opinion of the Transvaal forces that they were confident the rebels would quickly disperse after the first skirmish. But the burghers were armed with Westley-Richard rifles that could kill at six hundred yards and, as the enemy soon discovered, were excellent shots. They destroyed a British column at Bronkhorstspruit, laid siege to the rest of the garrison in Pretoria and Potchefstroom, and attacked the column of Sir George Pomeroy Colley, who had arrived with reinforcements from Natal. On 27 February 1881 this force was routed at Majuba and Colley was killed.

Able to draw on only 3,500 troops in all South Africa, the new ministry in London under William Gladstone was in no mood to hang on to the Transvaal for the sake of Carnarvon's discredited federation scheme. It feared that the Zulus in Natal, who had recently defeated a British army, would resume hostilities in the wake of the British reverses. The Foreign Secretary was much impressed by the message of the German statesman

---

9 M.C. van Zyl, *Die protesbeweging van die Transvaalse Afrikaners, 1877-1880* (Pretoria: Academica, 1979), pp. 20-44.
10 Paul Kruger, *Memoirs* (London: T. Fisher, 1902), p. 163.

Otto von Bismarck that white men should not fight each other in front of African tribes. In the negotiations that followed, Kruger was unquestionably the leader. He was deadly serious and lost his temper often. When British commanders contemplated a renewal of hostilities, the triumvirate drafted a proclamation pointedly referring to how the Dutch had flooded their country in the struggle against the Spanish and how the Russians had burnt Moscow to thwart Napoleon's army.

To meet the Transvaal's demands yet salvage some honor, Britain seized upon the formula of a 'suzerainty', under which Britain would retain an important say in the Transvaal's foreign and 'native' affairs. Apart from the fact that the British troops would be withdrawn, this did not differ much from the 'self-government' Kruger had earlier rejected.

Kruger understood that such a face-saving device was the price of peace, and accepted the proposal, though he needed all his political acumen to persuade the burghers, whose military achievements had earned the respect of their adversaries and had bred a strong political awareness. The annexation and the successful rebellion had, as Judge J.G. Kotzé put it, 'given birth to a strong national feeling among the Boers; it had united them and all were now for the state.'[11]

'A woman's war': Olive Schreiner's perspective

Women played a prominent and remarkable part in this assertion of national feeling that brought about the end of British rule. Olive Schreiner, who at the end of the 1870 was a woman in her early twenties living in the eastern Cape, stated in an essay, written in the 1890s: 'The Transvaal War of 1881 was largely a woman's war; it was from the armchair beside the coffee-table that the voice went out for conflict and no surrender. Even in the [Cape] Colony at the distance of many hundred miles Boer women urged sons and husbands to go to the aid of their northern kindred, while a martial ardor often far exceeding that of the males seemed to fill them.'[12]

Some of the reasons for the strong position of the Afrikaner woman in her family and community have been discussed earlier (see pp. 37-8, 169). As an early feminist, Schreiner had a clear grasp of the underlying factors. Boer women shared equally with their brothers in the estates of their parents, and as children tended to receive the same primitive education as their brothers. They married as equal partners. As Schreiner formulated it: 'As a rule she not only brings to the common household an equal share of material goods, but, and this is infinitely of more importance, she brings to the common life an equal culture. The fiction of common possession of all material goods . . . is not a fiction but a reality among the Boers, and justly so, seeing that the female as often as the male contributes to the original household stock.'[13]

Married life on an insecure and isolated frontier further strengthened the position of the women. They bred and fed the children, made their clothes, taught them the religion and traditions of the culture in which they were born, and faced death side by

---

11 J.G. Kotzé, *Biographical Memories and Reminiscences* (Cape Town, no date), p. 501.
12 Olive Schreiner, *Thoughts on South Africa* (Johannesburg: Ad Donker, 1992), p. 176.
13 Schreiner, *Thoughts on South Africa*, p. 175.

side with their men when attacked by indigenous people or wild beasts. Women showed even greater hostility to British rule than men. They were outraged when the British government at the Cape, in an effort to ameliorate slavery, made it possible for slaves to take their mistresses to court in the late 1820s and 1830s. When the Great Trek faltered, women vowed never to return to the Cape Colony. Schreiner wrote that it was the Boer woman 'who still today [the 1890s] has a determining influence on peace or war.'[14] As the war that would break out in 1899 proved, it was a remarkably prescient comment.

Imperialists and jingoes

British imperialism had two faces; it maintained its power by a complex and multi-faceted process. Liberal idealism was the face that redeemed the British Empire and saved it from being 'just robbery with violence', as Marlow, in Joseph Conrad's *The Heart of Darkness*, described imperialism. Britain became increasingly interested in 'regenerating' southern Africa with the 'civilizing' values of commerce and Christianity. Many people in the colonies genuinely believed that the imperial mission would bring development, liberty and peace.

In an anguished open letter just before the Anglo-Boer War broke out in 1899, An-

Liberal imperialism stressed the common, non-racial rights of all British citizens, including the right to democratic government. It promoted industrial and social progress and offered the protection of the British fleet to white-dominated colonies, while interfering little in their affairs. The introduction of regular British steamship services increased the capacity and reduced the cost of coastal transport. South Africa was transformed financially by the introduction of modern banking facilities by British banks; most notably the Standard Bank of London which established its first branch in the Cape Colony in 1862. Large-scale commercial and investment firms joined the 'imperial banks' in branching out into the interior. More and more traders, bankers, and imperial statesmen were gripped by the vision of a rapidly expanding economic empire based on modern communications, like the railways and the telegraph, penetrating the entire subcontinent. At the same time, British and local English missionaries sought to advance Christianity, and it spread at a dramatic rate among Africans. A multitude of ties that did not chafe bound South Africa to Britain.[15]

In an anguished open letter just before the Anglo-Boer War broke out in 1899, Andrew Murray, moderator of the Cape Dutch Reformed Church, called Britain the 'noblest, the most Christian nation in the world' in imploring it not to go to war against the republics.[16] For Murray war threatened his fervent belief that the Empire was one of the most benign forces in the world, working for order, liberalization, modernization and the rehabilitation of subject peoples.

But he appealed in vain, for the other face of British imperialism was aggressive, authoritarian and condescending towards other cultures. It emphasized the autocratic values of hierarchy, obedience, and order, and sanctioned ruthless aggression on their

---

14 Schreiner, *Thoughts on South Africa*, p. 176.

15 P.J. Cain and A.G. Hopkins, *British Imperialism: Innovation and Expansion, 1688-1914* (London: Longman, 1993), pp. 351-96.

16 Johannes du Plessis, *The Life of Andrew Murray* (London: Marshall Brothers, 1919), p. 426.

behalf.[17] 'Jingoism' developed out of this strand, the profession of patriotism loudly, excessively and belligerently. In policy towards South Africa the chief exponents of jingoism were Joseph Chamberlain, Colonial Secretary in the Unionist government that came to power in June 1895, and Alfred Milner, High Commissioner for South Africa between 1897 and 1905.

Chamberlain, like Milner, represented an unusual mix of radical enthusiasm, liberalism and jingoism. He would have become leader of the Liberal Party if his clash with William Gladstone had not forced him to join the Unionists. In his view it was Britain's mission to bring its civilization, which he thought the highest the world had ever known, to the 'colored races.'[18] Milner won a top scholarship to Balliol College in Oxford where he and his small circle of friends embraced the idea of British racial superiority, derived from a popularization of Charles Darwin's theories. Not keen to become a don, he unsuccessfully attempted to enter politics. He was bright but aloof, condescending, arrogant, and lacking the common touch – not a mix that makes for a successful politician. It was more suitable for the imperial civil service, the career he finally chose.

To the end of his life Milner would call himself a 'British Race Patriot', tied by 'common blood, a common language, common history and traditions.' To him this bond was 'deeper, stronger, more primordial than material ties.' He defined the 'true jingo' as one who is for 'limited [British] expansion but unlimited tenacity.' He glorified the Empire as the source of British power and greatness. On one occasion he remarked that when he thought of the great service Britain had rendered to humanity he touched his hat 'with confirmed reverence to the Union Jack.'[19] He wanted the British state to follow the British race wherever 'it settled in appreciable numbers as an independent community.'[20] This included South Africa. Milner coupled his imperialism with the belief, inspired by Alfred Toynbee in Oxford, in the need for social reorganization as opposed to *laissez faire*. 'Society left to itself would not right itself,' he wrote.[21] (His phrase 'damn the consequences', coined in a different context, made it into an edition of the *Oxford Dictionary of Quotations* published a century later.)

A special case was Cecil John Rhodes, who by his own confession was an out-and-out jingo when he arrived in South Africa from Britain in 1870 at the age of seventeen. By 1880, at twenty-seven, he had made a great fortune in the diamond fields of Kimberley; at twenty-eight he was elected to the Cape Parliament as a member for Barkly West, a constituency of the newly annexed Griqualand West; at thirty-seven he launched De Beers Consolidated, which soon controlled 90 per cent of South Africa's diamonds and the bulk of the world's diamond output. Slightly more than ten years later he would be the dominant figure in Consolidated Gold Fields, one of the largest gold-mining companies in Johannesburg, and the British South African Company, which received a royal charter for developing the land north of the Limpopo.

---

17 P.J. Marshall, 'Imperial Britain', *The Journal of Imperial and Commonwealth History*, 23, 3, (1995) pp. 370-94.

18 A.J.P. Taylor, *The Troublemakers* (Harmondsworth: Penguin Books, 1987), p. 90.

19 L.M. Thompson, *The Unification of South Africa* (Cape Town: Oxford University Press, 1961), p. 5; John Marlowe, *Milner* (London: Hamish Hamilton, 1976), p. 18.

20 Thompson, *Unification*, p. 5; W.K. Hancock, *Smuts: vol. 1: The Sanguine Years* (Cambridge: Cambridge University Press, 1962), p. 74.

21 Marlowe, *Milner*, p. 7.

Rhodes was a man of the boldest vision, conceiving of a British advance throughout the world and in Africa at least from the Cape to the Zambezi and beyond to Uganda. What made Rhodes special was that he refused to be a mere agent of the imperial government who received his orders from London. He developed a sub-imperialism in which the Cape Colony under its own elected government would play a semi-autonomous role in ruling itself, colonizing new territories and bringing about a federation in southern Africa under the British flag. To build that base he cultivated the Cape Afrikaners, showing none of the metropolitan contempt for colonial cultures that marked the outlook of Milner and Chamberlain. It was Rhodes' audacious achievement to fuse his imperialism with Hofmeyr's colonial patriotism without, initially at least, giving any hint of being on a collision course with Kruger's republicanism.

'The majority is King': Boer republicanism

Paul Kruger believed that only a committed republicanism could act as a counter to British imperialism and Rhodes' sub-imperialism. In developing his republican ideology he stressed the historic links between the heroic acts of the Voortrekkers and the triumphant rebellion of 1880-81. Kruger turned the movement of the frontier farmers into the deeper interior, now called the Great Trek, into a heroic myth emphasizing the trekkers' 'secret passion for freedom.' The Battle of Blood River of 1838 and the vow made before the battle was to him the symbol of the will of the Transvaal burghers to survive as an independent people against overwhelming odds. The commemoration of these events became a grand political and religious occasion. A festival at the end of 1881 at Paardekraal drew a crowd of between twelve and fifteen thousand. Similar festivals were held every five years thereafter, with Kruger playing the leading role. His speeches and those of others were a litany of grievances of the wrongs, injustices, and oppression that the 'Boers' had suffered at the hands of the 'Britons.' The burghers listened with rapt attention to these addresses. For them a close link was established between religious and national identity, and a growing loyalty to the state as the guardian of those identities.[22]

Kruger was elected President in 1883. The time was now opportune to re-negotiate the agreement with Britain. Kruger led a delegation to London, where Abraham Kuyper, the leader of the neo-Calvinist movement in the Netherlands, joined as adviser. They secured considerable concessions. The Transvaal once more became entitled to call its state the Zuid-Afrikaansche Republiek. No longer would a British resident in Pretoria have the final say in 'native' affairs. The reference to British suzerainty was removed, though Kruger had to agree that the ZAR would not enter into treaties with other countries without permission from the British monarch. Thus, the ZAR (as was also true of the OFS) was not free from British control under international law. During the 1890s some British politicians argued that this clause offered grounds for a British claim of supremacy in South Africa, and its right to intervene in the ZAR's internal affairs, despite its republican status.

---

22 F.A. van Jaarsveld, *The Afrikaner's Interpretation of South African History* (Cape Town, Simondium, 1964), pp. 40-42.

By the 1880s both Boer republics had achieved a considerable measure of consolidation. In both, the white male citizens elected the president and all members of the legislative authority, the Volksraad. In the OFS the executive council consisted of the president, the officials, and the Volksraad nominees, and the legislative chamber had considerable power. Indeed, James Bryce, the renowned British constitutional scholar, said that it carried 'the principle of omnipotence of the representative chamber to a maximum.'[23] Using the yardstick of the time that ignored the exclusion of all but white males, he declared: 'In the Orange Free State I discovered, in 1895, the kind of commonwealth which the fond fancy of the philosophers of the last century painted. It is an ideal commonwealth . . .'[24] Its constitution, like that of the ZAR, was 'the pure and original product of African conditions.' It came closest to the philosophical ideal 'of free and independent persons uniting in an absolutely new social compact for mutual help and defense, and thereby creating a government whose authority has had and can have no origin save in the consent of the governed.'[25]

In the ZAR's participatory democracy white male citizens elected not only the president and members of the Volksraad, but also the commandant-general, who held his position in peace and in war and was a member of the president's executive council. Every bill had to be published three months before the legislative session, so that the burghers could communicate their views personally to representatives, or pass resolutions.

Kruger defined a republic as a form of government where 'the majority of the voters is king, and their power sovereign.' The Volksraad 'represents the volk; if the voice of the majority is not heeded, the State becomes impure.' The president could be removed by a vote of censure of the Volksraad, as Marthinus Wessels Pretorius of the ZAR was in 1871. Kruger, President of the ZAR (1883-1900), and Jan Brand, President of the OFS (1864-1888), could prevail over their Volksraad by virtue of their strong personalities and great political acumen.

However, on some vital issues, like lowering the high import duties on Cape goods, even Kruger could not persuade the Volksraad to his view. Volksraad members were expected to vote according to the wishes of their constituents, he believed; the president was required to execute laws even if he disagreed with them. He said in 1889: 'We live in a Republic and even if there is a great advantage [to the Executive] in a certain matter one must subject oneself to the will of the people and bow to it as long as they are against it.'[26]

In theory the courts of law were independent, but Kruger and other politicians occasionally had great difficulty respecting this. The press in both republics was remarkably free, although in the ZAR it was subject to intimidation by Kruger and others.[27]

---

23 James Bryce, *Studies in History and Jurisprudence* (Oxford, 1901), vol. 1, p. 381.

24 James Bryce, *Impressions of South Africa* (London: Macmillan, 1899), p. 314.

25 M.C.E. van Schoor and J.J. van Rooyen, *Republieke en Republikeine* (Cape Town: Nasionale Boekhandel, 1960), p. 109.

26 F.P. Smit, *Die staatsopvattinge van Paul Kruger* (Pretoria: Van Schaik, 1951), pp. 18-21.

27 For analyses from a different perspective see Van Schoor and Van Rooyen, *Republieke en Republikeine*, pp. 76-129; L.M. Thompson, 'Constitutionalism in the South African Republics', *Butterworths S.A. Law Review* 1954, pp. 49-72.

The mixed blessings of gold

Although increasingly respected as a leader after becoming president, Kruger struggled to build up the state in his first three years. The state's finances were in a parlous condition, with the result that the Standard Bank refused to advance it more money. Travelling through the republic, Kruger encouraged the burghers. Help, he said, would surely come, and so it did in 1886 when the rich and abundant goldfields of the Witwatersrand were discovered.[28] Never before in world history had a mineral discovery so suddenly and dramatically, and so utterly, transformed an obscure rural backwater. Gold became the foundation of the monetary system of the industrialized nations and was to dominate the South African economy and its politics for the next sixty years.

Backed by large-scale investment, particularly from Britain, forty-four mines were in operation two years later, with a nominal capital of nearly £7 million and an output worth more than £1 million. By the end of the century the Witwatersrand mines were producing a quarter of the world's gold.[29] In the early 1890s the industry was employing more than 100,000 men. Johannesburg had a white population of 50,000, only 6,000 of them Afrikaners, the great majority of the rest British.

The quiet town of Pretoria, the capital, was completely overshadowed by Johannesburg, which was one of the most dynamic and volatile places in the world. The gold mines drew avaricious moneymen, schemers, and criminals along with miners, white and black. There was a virtual explosion of industrial enterprise. At the top of Johannesburg's social pyramid were the mining house magnates, the so-called Randlords, and at the bottom, the flotsam and jetsam. In the city there were nearly three hundred bars, almost all with back premises that catered to commercial sex. The streets teemed with diggers, prostitutes, gamblers, saloonkeepers, washerwomen and domestic servants.[30] The Afrikaner poor were migrating in a steady stream to the cities to take up jobs as brick makers, cabdrivers and transport riders. Kruger set aside Vrededorp as a suburb for them.

Large foreign companies monopolized the exploitation of diamonds, gold and coal. By the end of the century a third to half of the land in the Transvaal belonged to foreign individuals or companies, who preferred blacks to burghers on their land. After a visit to the Transvaal the young Jan Smuts wrote that the economic revolution was undermining the old farming and burgher community in a more dangerous way than English supremacy itself would ever have been able to do.[31] President Steyn of the OFS remarked that the struggle to survive had become fiercer: 'Capitalism had appeared in South Africa, the enemy of labor had slung its octopus legs over all forms of labor.'[32]

Kruger immediately realized that gold, which had delivered the republic from its financial troubles, threatened its very survival. He only tolerated the *Uitlanders* ('Outlanders' or aliens) who flooded into the ZAR because they were indispensable, but he never trusted them, considering them as a fifth column intent on overthrowing the state

---

28 Kruger, *Memoirs*, p. 203.

29 Russell Ally: *Gold and Empire* (Johannesburg: Witwatersrand University Press, 1994), pp. 1-28.

30 These scenes are vividly described in Charles van Onselen, *Studies in the Social and Economic History of the Witwatersrand, 1886-1914* (London: Longman, 1982), two volumes.

31 *Smuts Papers*, vol. 1, p. 76.

32 G.D. Scholtz, *Die ontwikkeling van die politieke denke van die Afrikaner* (Johannesburg: Perskor, 1977), vol. 4, p. 487.

by any means, fair or foul. The Uitlanders quickly became disaffected, considering themselves ruled by a small body of people they saw in every way as their inferiors.[33]

Determined to develop an economic and cultural counter to British imperialism, Kruger did his best to prevent gold from undermining the republic. Even before gold was discovered he had accepted a plan for industrialization that would increase the state's economic independence. It handed to individuals or companies the exclusive right to produce articles like liquor, soap, bricks, leather and dynamite, all buttressed by heavy protective tariffs. His policy made good sense for a predominantly agrarian society developing its own manufacturing sector, but not for the rapidly expanding gold industry.

Kruger soon acquired strong enemies and aroused dismay in the Cape Colony, which he shut off from the booming market. The mining industry, intent on holding down costs, complained vociferously about the high railway rates, the price of dynamite, corruption, and the scarcity of African labor, all of which were estimated to cost the mining industry more than £2 million a year. Kruger's proclivity for giving concessions and posts to incompetent family, friends and supporters made matters worse.

Few states, particularly a predominantly rural and backward one like the ZAR, would have coped easily with the mushrooming of a city like Johannesburg and the great influx of immigrants. Yet the ZAR had succeeded remarkably well in devising a proper local administration for Johannesburg and other towns, appointing mostly competent officials to run them. It had allowed foreign capital into the colony without restrictions, imposed a low tax of only 5 per cent on declared profits, and enacted an efficient mining code. Within two years 44 mines produced a gold output worth £1300,000 and after ten years the industry produced gold valued at more than £32 million; with this revenue the ZAR built railways linking Johannesburg to ports, and improved the road system.[34] Enough food reached Johannesburg to feed the rapidly expanding population. After 1895 Kruger made impressive progress with administrative reform.

The ZAR introduced a conservative education policy based on religion. For Kruger the Bible was 'the foundation for educating children at school . . . it [was] the foundation for everything.'[35] And he insisted on Dutch as the medium of instruction. In 1892 the state stopped grants to schools in which Dutch was not the medium of instruction, and in 1895 it opposed attempts to increase the amount of English taught in state schools. 'Every attempt to expand education in English will help towards the destruction of the *landstaal* [the ZAR's official language],' Kruger declared.[36]

From the start of his term as president, Kruger tried to attract Dutch immigrants. After the triumvirate delegation's journey to London in 1884 Kruger addressed a crowd in Amsterdam an observer estimated to be 100,000. 'We have kept our own language,' he said, 'the language of the Netherlands people, who have fought eighty years for faith and freedom. Our people in the wilderness have kept their language and their faith through

33 Iain Smith, *The Origins of the South African War, 1899-1902* (London: Longman, 1996), pp. 83-4.

34 J.H. Hofmeyr, 'The Problem of Co-operation, 1886-1895', in A.P. Newton, et al. (eds.), *Cambridge History of the British Empire* (Cambridge: Cambridge University Press, 1936). For a similar view expressed by two Marxist scholars see H.J. and R.E. Simons, *Class and Colour in South Africa* (Harmondsworth: Penguin Books, 1969), p. 61.

35 M.S. Appelgryn, *Thomas François Burgers* (Pretoria: HAUM, 1979), p. 59.

36 Gordon, *The Growth of Boer Opposition*, p. 9.

every storm. Our whole struggle is bound up with this.'[37] The implied appeal was effective and between five thousand and six thousand Dutch immigrants came into the ZAR in the next fifteen years. Dutch civil servants and teachers strengthened the ZAR's administrative capacity. Willem Leyds, a highly competent young attorney, became Kruger's closest administrative assistant, while Nicolaas Mansvelt as superintendent of education vigorously pursued a policy that required state schools to use Dutch as the sole medium of instruction. By 1897, out of a total of 1958 ZAR civil servants, 306 were Hollanders compared to 682 from the Transvaal itself and 478 from the Cape.[38]

The Dutch were generally very anti-British and also highly critical of the anglicized Afrikaner elite of the Cape Colony. Within two generations they became fully assimilated into the Afrikaner community, and, like the German missionaries who entered Afrikaner society in the second half of the century, they greatly enriched Afrikaner life. Still, the first generation of Dutch immigrants was not exactly loved. Some were arrogant, and many won posts to which educated Transvaal burghers aspired. The newspaper *Land en Volk* persistently attacked undue Dutch influence on the administration.[39]

Kruger's principal Afrikaner opposition was a faction called the Progressives, who urged the more rapid modernization of the republic. They operated under the leadership of Piet Joubert, the commandant-general, and, during the 1890s, included bright, enterprising men like Louis Botha, J.H. (Koos) de la Rey, Carl Jeppe, Ewald Esselen and Schalk Burger. They attacked maladministration, corruption, the conservative educational system, and the parochial ways of Kruger's government.

Kruger also differed on other issues from the modernizers. Piet Joubert, his main opponent, supported a much diluted form of republicanism and, according to one source, actually favored a South African confederacy under English protection, with self-rule for the constituent colonies.[40] The Progressives commanded the support of about a third of the elected representatives in both houses of the legislature. In the 1893 presidential election Kruger defeated Joubert only narrowly.

To prevent the Uitlanders from winning power through the ballot box, Kruger's government in 1890 extended the franchise qualification period from one year to fourteen years and created a second Volksraad to represent Uitlander interests. It was a wrong move since it became the focus of all the wrath of the immigrant population.

The Progressives also demanded substantial lowering of the franchise qualifications, convinced that the Uitlander demand for the franchise was only a bluff. Ludwig Krause, who had a Cambridge law degree, believed that only those 'who really meant to join the Republic and to stand by it would have availed themselves of the privilege [to take up republican citizenship]; no loyal Englishman would have renounced his Queen and country [in order to vote].'[41] But some British officials were ready to reject such a demand.

Prepared as Kruger was to modernize the state, he drew the line at franchise reform. He believed there were 30,000 enfranchised burghers against 60,000 to 70,000 'new-

---

37 Fisher, *Kruger*, p. 130.
38 L.E. van Niekerk, *Kruger se regterhand: 'n biografie van W.J. Leyds* (Pretoria: Van Schaik, 1985), p. 70.
39 Scholtz, *Ontwikkeling van die Politieke Denke*, vol. 4, p. 344.
40 J.A. Coetzee, *Politieke groepering in die wording van die Afrikanernasie* (Johannesburg: Voortrekkerpers, 1941), p. 317.
41 Jerold Taitz, *The War Memoirs of Commandant Ludwig Krause* (Cape Town: VRS, 1995), p. 3.

comers' that could vote if all requirements were waived. Immigrants from the Cape and Natal were included in the latter figure. In the end Kruger's perception was what counted. Bold reform of both the severe franchise qualification and a concession on the price of dynamite would have eased much of the agitation against the ZAR. But Kruger obstinately refused to change his position until it was too late. Jan Smuts noted at Kruger's death that 'he typified the Boer character both in its brighter and darker aspects.'[42]

Kruger's reluctance to reform the franchise became the pretext for British aggression, led by Chamberlain and Milner. But they wanted war not so much because Kruger was obstinate and blocked rapid development, but because he was flexible and pragmatic on most issues and was succeeding in modernizing the ZAR. Left alone, the ZAR would soon dominate South Africa. This was a prospect that Milner had to prevent even if it meant war.[43]

'John Bull Afrikaner': Rhodes, the suitor

Cape Afrikaners had for some time affected a condescending attitude towards the Transvaal, which they considered backward and in need of sound Cape advice. They responded to the discovery of gold with a mixture of envy and awe, hoping that their conservative kinsmen would survive the tumultuous outbreak of modernity, but few considered Kruger able to guide the republic to become a stable state. The *Zuid-Afrikaan* made no secret of its view that the Transvaal needed a more competent man at the helm.

There was, to be sure, some solidarity across political boundaries. Hofmeyr wrote to Gladstone, saying that the Cape Afrikaners were 'connected to the Boers of the Transvaal by the ties of descent, language, religion and – for many of us – of inter-marriage and friendship; we feel that their wrongs are our wrongs and services rendered to them are services rendered to us.'[44] Nevertheless, the tensions between Afrikaners in the south and north became steadily more acute. The Afrikaner Bond saw Afrikaner survival almost purely in Cape-centric terms. In this perception the Dutch language or republican freedom did not count for much. The Bond leadership believed that the interests of Afrikaners across South Africa would be best served through free trade and the integration of the Boer republics into the British imperial system of trade and finance.

This outlook ideally suited Cecil John Rhodes in pursuing his grand vision of a unified South Africa under the British flag, and with the Cape as the senior member. Rhodes was a towering figure and one of the most complex figures in South African history. Close friends spoke of the 'sheer natural power of his mind', his magnetic powers of persuasion, his love of nature and art and his sense of mission. There was a dark side, too, captured by the jibe that he was a man with a first-rate mind and second-rate principles. Devious in pursuit of his grand visions, he believed that every man had his price and did not hesitate to try this out in practice.

---

42 Trewhella Cameron, *Jan Smuts* (Cape Town: Human & Rousseau, 1994), p. 49.
43 I am drawing on Charles van Onselen, *Studies in the Social and Economic History of the Witwatersrand: New Babylon* (Harlow: Longman, 1982), pp. 1-42 and unpublished papers by him.
44 Mordechai Tamarkin, *Cecil Rhodes and the Cape Afrikaners* (London: Frank Cass, 1996), p. 48.

In late 1881 Rhodes, having made a fortune in the Kimberley diamond mines, moved to Cape Town and into politics, representing Barkly-West in the House of Assembly. The seat with its mix of diggers and Afrikaner farmers re-elected him until his death in the House of Assembly. In the placid atmosphere of Cape Town Rhodes set out to woo Hofmeyr and the Afrikaner Bond with all the skill of a confident suitor, with an almost irresistible mix of dynamism, power, humility and charisma. At that point English-speaking politicians tended to speak in negative terms about the Afrikaner population in general. Sir John Gordon Sprigg, a leading Cape politician, spoke openly of the 'demon of ignorance and prejudice' of the Afrikaners. Rhodes, financially vastly more successful than any of the Cape English, respected Cape Dutch culture and the Cape Afrikaners as a people. While affluent Cape Englishmen constructed houses in British styles, Rhodes commissioned the design for a fine Cape Dutch house (to which he gave a Dutch name, *Groote Schuur*) and spoke openly of his admiration for Cape-Dutch architecture and furniture. The Cape Afrikaners were won over. They became what a twentieth-century imperial historian has called the 'ideal prefabricated collaborators.'[45]

Rhodes began calling himself an Afrikaner, in line with the inclusive Bond definition. Soon the pro-Rhodes editor of the *Cape Times*, the brilliant Edmund Garrett, used the term 'John Bull Afrikander' in asserting that Britain and Rhodes in particular were acting in the interests of South Africa as a whole.[46] Jan Smuts later described the spell that Rhodes wove over the colonial Afrikaners between the mid-1880s and mid-1890s: 'He had become the national idol of the Dutch Afrikanders. The Dutch are perhaps a suspicious people, but when they do come to put their trust in a man . . . then the trust becomes almost absolute and religious; such was their faith in Rhodes.'[47]

The policies of Hofmeyr and Rhodes quickly converged, with Rhodes backing the Bond's demand for the official recognition of Dutch, its opposition to Sunday trains, and its insistence on the introduction of religious instruction in state schools. He helped to get a tax on local brandy repealed, supported protection for Cape wheat and wine from cheap foreign imports, a limit on the compulsory dipping of sheep to control the scab pest, and the exclusion of traditional Africans from the franchise, the 'blanket vote' as it was called.

While prepared to allow the Boer republics some scope, Britain was determined to prevent them challenging its hegemony. It was shocked when Kruger showed signs of wishing to expand the Transvaal borders and secure its own seaport. In 1882, white frontiersmen proclaimed two republics, Stellaland and Goshen, on the Transvaal's western border after fighting between African chiefs, each with their own European supporters. This expansion would block the Great Road to the North through Bechuanaland (the present Botswana) along which the Cape's trade with the central parts of Africa passed. In 1883, Germany annexed the land north of the Orange River, and in the following year proclaimed a German protectorate over South West Africa. The possibility that the ZAR and the German protectorate could link up was no longer far-fetched.

---

45 R. Robinson, 'Non-European Foundations of European Imperialism', in R. Owen and B. Sutcliffe (eds.), *Studies in the Theory of Imperialism* (London, 1972), p. 124.

46 E.T. Cook, *Edmund Garrett* (London, 1909), p. 109.

47 Tamarkin, *Rhodes and the Afrikaners*, p. 218.

Rhodes and Hofmeyr were united in the view that Britain must remain the paramount power in South Africa, and that any efforts by Germany to extend its own influence must be thwarted. Rhodes had already made up his mind to use the Cape Colony as a base to extend British control over the larger area of Bechuanaland, and over Mashonaland and Matabeleland further to the northeast, the prime areas on the subcontinent not yet under white control. He was determined to prevent the ZAR from acquiring territory that blocked the so-called Great Road to the North, skirting the ZAR and penetrating the area beyond it. The British government achieved this objective when it established a crown colony over the area south of the Molopo River, and a loose protectorate over the whites living to the north of it. In this way Britain began acquiring control over Bechuanaland, a vast, arid area of 275,000 square miles west of the ZAR.

Kruger had provisionally annexed the republics of Stellaland and Goshen, but had backed down when the imperial government labeled it a violation of the London Convention. Primarily concerned with establishing order on the ZAR's western border, he was prepared to abandon any territorial expansion to the west. But he confidently hoped that in return for retreating he would be allowed to expand through Swaziland in the east and open up a land route to the sea.

The conflict between the ZAR and the Cape government, including the Afrikaner Bond on whose support it depended, came to a head with the clash over a customs union. In the early 1880s, the Cape had rejected the request of the ZAR and OFS to form a customs union. Kruger was then a mere supplicant, but with the opening up of the rich gold fields he had trumps in his hand. The political and economic center of gravity had shifted to the Witwatersrand. The Cape was now very eager to form a customs union that would join the republics and colonies in a common market. Behind this lay a barely disguised political agenda. A customs union would be the vital first step for a united South Africa under the British flag with the Cape as senior member.

Sensing this, Kruger rejected a customs union and imposed heavy duties on Cape goods. He also blocked the extension of railway lines into the Transvaal before the completion of a ZAR line to Delagoa Bay. If ever there was to be a union of the republics and colonies of South Africa, Kruger wanted it to be under a republican flag and free from British interference. Kruger's highest priority was to strengthen the ZAR as the foundation of such a state. He demanded that the Cape Afrikaners support the ZAR as the representative of a pure Afrikaner spirit.

The attempt to encircle the ZAR

To Hofmeyr, Kruger's rejection of a customs union was a bitter disappointment, driving him into the arms of Rhodes. In 1887 he and three other Cape Bondsmen told Kruger that their own attachment 'to the cause of our Transvaal brothers' had cooled, and warned that once 'a division arises between kinsfolk, one cannot foresee where it will end, and the Africander cause is far from being strong enough to be able to face division between the Transvaal and Colonial sons of the soil.' When Hofmeyr traveled to Pretoria three years later to tell Kruger that he could not claim Swaziland before he had entered into a customs union, Kruger thundered at him: 'You are a traitor, a traitor to the Africander cause.'[48] When a free trade area was eventually formed, the ZAR stayed out.

In 1889 Rhodes founded the British South African Company (BSA) as the vehicle for expansion in the far north. He had Hofmeyr's active support for his hope that the Cape Colony would become the launching pad. In 1890 Rhodes became prime minister of the Cape Colony with the help of the Bond, and was now well positioned to advance his aims. Succumbing to Rhodes's blandishments that expansion was an Afrikaner as well as a British imperial project, *De Zuid-Afrikaan* wrote in 1890: 'Under the British flag and with the help of British capital we are marching to the north.'[49] By the end of 1890 a BSA force had occupied Mashonaland, and by the end of 1893 the conquest of Matabeleland was all but completed.

The Bond also supported Rhodes in his drive to retain the diamond monopoly of De Beers Consolidated, and allowed him to serve as both prime minister and chairman of the BSA. In doing so the Bond leadership soon became embroiled in allegations of graft and corruption. It could hardly be coincidental that the Bond leaders had just then acquired considerable numbers of shares in De Beers and BSA. John X. Merriman, a leading liberal, expressed horror at what appeared to him like an abandonment of all principles.

Rhodes' hopes that Mashonaland and Matabeleland would be as rich as the Witwatersrand were soon dashed. In economic terms the ZAR outstripped the Cape. By 1895 the value of the Cape Colony's exports was less than those of the ZAR and looked set to fall ever further behind. The Cape was condemned to be an economic backwater and Britain to lose its claim as the paramount power on the subcontinent. To curb the growing ZAR power, Britain attempted to encircle the republic by blocking any further expansion. The ZAR nevertheless refused to join a railways and customs union. Despite all the obstacles thrown in its way, in 1894 it completed a railway link to Delagoa Bay, an outlet to the sea in Portuguese territory. It now diverted most of its foreign trade away from the Cape. To add to British chagrin, Germany backed Kruger's rejection of a customs union.

Rhodes had become increasingly frustrated by the ZAR's thwarting of his plans for unifying South Africa under a British flag. On the Witwatersrand other magnates overshadowed him. A taker of high risks, he now embarked on a wild gamble to overthrow the ZAR, with co-conspirators including Joseph Chamberlain, Colonial Secretary in the new British cabinet of Lord Salisbury, and Sir Graham Bower, the Imperial Secretary in Cape Town, both aware 'unofficially' of Rhodes' plan. Sir Hercules Robinson, the High Commissioner in Cape Town, while never admitting complicity, was also informed.

On 29 December 1895, Leander Starr Jameson, at the head of some five hundred men drawn from the private army of the BSA and armed with a few Maxim guns, invaded the Transvaal with the intent of triggering a rebellion of the Witwatersrand Uitlanders, thus providing a pretext for the British High Commissioner in Cape Town to intervene and proclaim British sovereignty over the Transvaal. The plan went horribly wrong. The raiders were quickly captured and Rhodes was compelled to resign as prime minister. The Raid cost him his friendship with Hofmeyr, who all along had made it clear that he

---

48 J.H. Hofmeyr, *Het leven van J.H. Hofmeyr* (Cape Town: Van de Sandt de Villiers, 1913), pp. 366-7, 448-9.
49 Tamarkin, *Rhodes and the Afrikaners*, pp. 111, 119.

would countenance no aggression against the republics. The Jameson Raid revealed that Rhodes, the man Hofmeyr had promoted as a genuine ally of Afrikaners, had, and in a cold and calculating way, deceived them. Even the conservative establishment in Britain was embarrassed. Openly contemptuous of it, Rudyard Kipling, bard of the jingoes, wrote his famous poem 'If' to defend Chamberlain, widely suspected of complicity in the Jameson Raid.

Hofmeyr did not publicly express his outrage of Rhodes' type of imperialism, leaving that role to F.S. Malan, a member of the younger generation of Afrikaners who was to become one of the leading Cape liberals of the next century. In 1895 Malan became editor of *Ons Land*, by then the most influential Dutch paper in Cape Town. He wrote that the Jameson Raid had electrified all Afrikaners: 'Once again one writes our history with blood. The monster of jingoism has again shown its abhorrent face. The affairs of South Africa are again arranged from Downing Street.'[50]

What made matters worse was Rhodes' refusal to apologize for the Raid. He re-entered politics in 1898 on an unabashedly jingoist ticket as a supporter of the Progressive government headed by Sir Gordon Sprigg. The Bond found new allies in unexpected quarters among Cape liberals. Repelled by the jingoism of so many English speakers, the liberals Merriman and Sauer, who had opposed the Afrikaner Bond earlier for its 'native' policy, now helped the Bond to win the 1898 election by narrowly defeating the party of Rhodes. The new prime minister was William Schreiner, whose main charge against the Sprigg government was that it had not shown 'any sympathy or conciliatory approach' to 'the sister republic [the ZAR].'[51]

The arrival of new men: Smuts and Steyn

In 1895 Paul Kruger turned seventy, but the Jameson Raid revitalized him. Certain that Britain would soon embark on other acts of aggression, he embarked on arming the state. He expanded the small regular army, and reformed the administration of Johannesburg. For these tasks he brought in or promoted bright, well-educated young Afrikaners.

During the mid-1890s Jan Christiaan Smuts and Marthinus Theunis Steyn, two remarkable men, appeared on the scene to back Kruger. Smuts, born in 1870 on a farm near Riebeek Kasteel in the western Cape, had studied at the Victoria College in Stellenbosch before going to Cambridge University to take up law. The famous Cambridge legal scholar, Frederick William Maitland, called him the most outstanding student he had taught, coming 'not only first but brilliantly first' in both parts of the Law tripos. Smuts came from a Bond-supporting home, and defended Rhodes in 1895 in his first political speech.

Giving up his British nationality, Smuts moved to the Transvaal and in 1898 became State Attorney (Minister of Justice) of the ZAR. He struck up a filial relationship with the old president, who saw him as a 'man of iron will', destined to play a great role in South Africa's future.[52] Merriman, who got to know Smuts well, said that he

---

50 *Ons Land*, 12 March 1896.
51 Marlowe, *Milner*, pp. 51-5.
52 J.S. Marais, *The Fall of Kruger's Republic* (Oxford: Clarendon, 1961), p. 218.

was 'an exceedingly able' politician and a philosopher, a cultured man 'with great intellectual gifts', adding somewhat wryly: 'He has a reputation for shiftiness which is, I
think, in some measure undeserved.'[53] Among Afrikaners the nickname *Slim Jannie*
stuck. The name meant a mixture of being clever, smart, cunning, devious and persuasive. He was undoubtedly the shrewdest white South African politician of the twentieth
century.

Marthinus Theunis Steyn had quite different qualities. Born in 1857, he was the first
Free State-born burgher to become president of the OFS. He grew up on a farm near
Bloemfontein, and from his early years moved in the circles of the sophisticated Bloemfontein elite, that had at its core professional, commercial and political families like the
Brands, the Frasers, the Fichardts and the Fischers, mostly speaking English to each other
before the Jameson Raid. (Steyn married Tibbie Fraser, an English-speaking woman,
and corresponded with her in English.) On a judge's recommendation, Steyn went to the
Netherlands to study law, but because his Dutch was too poor, moved to London to complete his training in the Inner Temple. He became a judge in Bloemfontein in 1889. He
was a tall and vigorous man with considerable charm, described by the son of his predecessor as 'not brilliant, but possessed of a dogged courage.' He won the presidential
election in the Republic of the Orange Free State in 1895 at the age of thirty-eight. *South
Africa*, a London weekly, assessed the young president as: '[A] man of high culture and
sterling character, possessed of a balanced judgement and dignified personal appearance.'[54]

Under Steyn, the OFS balanced itself between the republican Transvaal and the colonial Cape. It was aligned politically to the ZAR and its insistence on a self-sufficient republicanism, but culturally was more in tune with the Cape. The OFS' middle-of-the-
road posture attracted moderate English-speaking South Africans, like Merriman, who
strongly opposed the jingo tendency to assert British interests at the expense of the
colonies. In 1899 a leading Free Stater, Abraham Fischer, wrote to Merriman: 'We do not
trust the motives or policy of those who are just now responsible for safeguarding
British *Imperial* as distinguished from the Colonial or South African interests of this part
of the world'. He declared in the Volksraad: 'One could be a good Afrikaner and sincere
Republican regardless of the language he spoke.'[55]

Steyn's cabinet included several English-speakers. In his inaugural address as president, delivered three months after the Jameson Raid, he urged foreigners to become part
of a great republican nation in the OFS. He urged Kruger to be lenient towards the con-
spirators in the Jameson Raid.[56] He saw the growing tensions more in class terms than
in national terms; the struggle, he said, was between capitalism and individuality, between imperialism and, on the other side, republicanism and colonialism.

Steyn tried to build up his state as a republic of farmers. He proposed a more direct
form of democracy with the use of referenda. He began to take the issue of language and

53 Phyllis Lewsen, *John X. Merriman* (New Haven: Yale University, 1982), p. 370.
54 Karel Schoeman, *In liefde en trou: die lewe van pres. en mev. M.T. Steyn* (Cape Town: Human & Rousseau,
  1983), pp. 25-7.
55 S.F. Malan, *Politieke strominge van die Afrikaners onder die Vrystaatse Republiek* (Durban: Butterworth,
  n.d.), p. 191; Stephen Clingman, *Bram Fischer* (Cape Town: David Philip, 1998), p. 13.
56 N.J. van der Merwe, *Marthinus Theunis Steyn* (Cape Town: Nasionale Pers, 1921), vol. 1, p. 128.

culture more seriously, as an embodiment of nationhood. If the Dutch language languished, he declared, the Free State nation would decline. He instructed his officials to switch to Dutch in corresponding with the Natal and Cape governments, and give Dutch-speakers preference in appointments to the civil service. Departments were told that Dutch was the official language, and pressure was put on the schools which predominantly used English to introduce Dutch as the language medium.[57]

Steyn pressed for franchise reform in the ZAR until, by 1898, he became convinced that British franchise demands on the ZAR were a pretext. He wrote later that even Chamberlain, realizing this, had dredged up the issue of suzerainty to seize control of the ZAR. To Steyn, suzerainty was 'a vague word with an even vaguer meaning' employed by the British to justify demands on the ZAR.[58]

Steyn knew under what conditions he would fight. He told Kruger that he would not go to war over the dynamite concession, or over the ZAR's fourteen-year qualification for the franchise, which he considered 'in conflict with republican and democratic principles', but he would if Britain proved to be using the franchise as an excuse for destroying the independence of both republics. In 1897 the ZAR and OFS concluded a treaty pledging mutual assistance in case of war.[59]

Preparing for war

When he returned to Cape Town early in 1898 after leave in England, Milner's mind was made up. He knew that time was on the Boers' side. Any delay in forcing the ZAR into a humiliating retreat on the franchise would mean the inexorable decline of British hegemony in South Africa. If necessary, Britain had to go to war. Milner wanted a super federal state consisting of Britain, Australia, Canada and a new South Africa, sending delegates to an Imperial Parliament in London. It was not a federation of whites that he had in mind, but the superior Anglo-Saxon race. In this scheme of things the Afrikaners were a mere adjunct of the superior race; the millions of coloreds and Africans would be no more than justly governed servants. In later years a noted British journalist remarked: 'As a racist politician Milner is the only important British leader who deserves some comparison with Hitler. Both looked forward to world domination by their own tribe of the white race; both engineered and provoked war to bring that vision nearer.'[60]

Milner found Chamberlain unwilling to force the issue so soon after the fiasco of the Jameson Raid. To step up the pressure on London, Milner mobilized the Uitlanders to press their demands and soon struck up an alliance with some of the gold magnates. He painted a picture of a seditious Cape Afrikaner community ready to undermine British authority in order to help Kruger. Milner believed that a recalcitrant Transvaal could become the focus of disaffection in all the British colonies. Re-establishing British paramountcy on the subcontinent would bolster its position among other great powers and would have great strategic value.

57 Malan, *Politieke strominge*, pp. 265-7.
58 Van der Merwe, *Steyn*, vol. 1, p. 118.
59 Van der Merwe, *Steyn*, vol. 1, pp. 157-8.
60 Neal Ascherson, 'The War That Made South Africa', *New York Review of Books*, 6 December 1979, p. 12.

The Afrikaner Bond leadership in the Cape Colony did its best to persuade Milner that no pan-Afrikaner conspiracy existed against British interests. But as J.T. Molteno, son of a previous prime minister, remarked, Milner was 'constantly insulting the Dutch and, with his superior Oxford manner, was sneering at their loyalty.'[61] When the Graaff-Reinet branch of the Bond in 1898 presented him with a petition affirming its loyalty, he replied: 'Of course you are loyal. It would be monstrous if you were not.' If they wanted peace, he said, they had to press Kruger to reform. In the bluntest possible manner he told them to take sides. The English press in South Africa 'went wild with delight', he wrote to Chamberlain.[62]

Britain would have thought twice about war if there were a real prospect that the Cape Afrikaners would rise massively in revolt. But the Cape Afrikaners were immobilized by their own multiple identities. Above all, they were colonial patriots with a loyalty both to the Crown and to their own colony. If they had a preference for republicanism, it was, as the liberal politician James Rose Innes called it, 'academic', and an aspiration to be realized 'in a dim and distant future.' Another of their identities was as core of a future white South African nation. They feared that any military contact between Britain and the republics would set the realization of this ideal back for many years. Against these two principal identities was a weaker sense of a common Afrikaner *ethnic* identity, prepared to stand shoulder to shoulder with the republican Afrikaners.[63]

Milner soon realized that the Cape Afrikaner leadership was petrified of war. All its efforts would go towards getting Kruger to make concessions. He also entered into an informal secret alliance with the biggest gold magnates, Alfred Beit and Julius Wernher, Germans who had become naturalized British citizens, and persuaded them that firm action could remove or weaken Kruger, making for a more efficient gold industry. These moves, of which no documentary evidence exists, have led some historians to argue that the issue of gold was a major cause of the war. Put most boldly, they assert that at the heart of Milner and Chamberlain's strategy lay the belief that control over the gold mines and trade with South Africa was a necessity in Britain's struggle for power with other European states and the United States. What gave a special impetus to their actions – so their argument runs – was the switch to gold in the monetary system of the industrialized nations, which made a steady and constant supply of gold from the Witwatersrand mines to the Bank of England crucial. However, the argument does not stand up. There is no substantial evidence that Britain went to war to control the Transvaal's gold supply.[64] The Bank of England was primarily interested in a steady flow of gold to London, and the ZAR had no intention of forcing the mining magnates to sell the gold elsewhere. War would create uncertainty and instability in the markets, which banks abhor.

It would be quite strange if the war in South Africa had nothing to do at all with gold. But then the spotlight has to fall not on the bankers in London, but on some of the gold

---

61 J.T. Molteno, *The Dominion of Afrikanerdom* (London: Methuen, 1923), p. 163.

62 Marais, *Fall of Kruger's Republic*, p. 207.

63 Tamarkin, *Rhodes and the Afrikaners*, pp. 296-301.

64 J.J.Van Helten and P. Richardson, 'The Development of the South African Gold-mining Industry', *Economic History Review,* 37 (1984), pp. 319-40.

magnates in Johannesburg, in particular on Beit, described as someone who 'bestrode the world's gold market like a gnome', his partner, Wernher, their young associate, Percy Fitzpatrick, and the fatally ill colossus in the background, Cecil John Rhodes, kept at arm's length by Milner.

Relations between Kruger and some mining magnates, and between the ZAR and Britain, took a turn for the worse in the final years of the century. Deep-level mining, entailing large investments to cover huge production costs, now predominated on the Rand, and these interests had little patience with Kruger's industrial policy. Even smaller companies were critical of the government's failure to implement the recommendations of its own Industrial Commission to abolish many monopolies whose profits, as a source puts it, 'went less to swell state revenue than to fill private pockets.'[65]

One turning point was the Jameson Raid, where some of the magnates showed their hand. Alfred Beit admitted that he had financed the Raid. Another turning point was Kruger's decisive election victory of 1898, followed by a reiteration of his stand on the franchise. Wernher now said that the magnates 'were quite prepared for war', and 'the situation must be terminated now.'[66] He had lost faith in the ability of Kruger's government to introduce the necessary reforms to ensure efficient gold production. They worked closely with Milner. Together they created the impression in government circles in London that Kruger would buckle under diplomatic and military pressure and concede all the franchise demands. Although they knew that the republics would fight, the message they sent out was one that Rhodes also spread: 'Kruger will bluff up to the cannon's mouth.'[67]

In May 1899 Steyn hosted a Bloemfontein meeting of Kruger and Milner to try to stave off war. Steyn and Smuts, who accompanied Kruger, decided that Milner was not negotiating in good faith and hence not interested in the substantial concessions Kruger had come to propose. When Kruger, for example, offered the vote on a seven-year residence qualification subject to certain conditions instead of the fourteen-year bar, Milner insisted on a five-year retroactive franchise. He also demanded that the Transvaal Volksraad surrender its legislative sovereignty, making Transvaal laws subject to British approval. He insisted, further, that Uitlander members in the Volksraad be allowed to speak English. With tears running down his cheeks, Kruger exclaimed: 'It is our country you want.' John Buchan, part of Milner's entourage and soon to become a well-known writer, described the encounter: 'There was a gnarled magnificence in the old Transvaal President, but [Milner] saw only a snuffy, mendacious savage.'[68]

Hofmeyr and other moderates frantically tried to avert the disaster of war, but their desire to remain loyal British subjects prevailed. The republics had invited Hofmeyr and Prime Minister W. P. Schreiner to attend the Bloemfontein conference, but both succumbed to pressure from Milner to decline. Subsequently the Schreiner cabinet considered dispatching a letter to the imperial government informing them that under no circumstances would it condone British intervention in the affairs of the Transvaal. But this

65 Smith, *Origins of the South African War*, p. 401.
66 Thomas Pakenham, *The Boer War* (Weidenfeld and Nicolson, 1979), pp. 80-89.
67 Pakenham, *The Boer War*, p. 92.
68 John Buchan, *Memory-hold-the-door* (London: Hodder and Stoughton, 1940), p. 102.

idea was dropped for fear that Milner would invite the Progressives, who staunchly supported him, to form a new government.

In Britain, Lord Salisbury's Unionist government found itself in a quandary. Its members had come to power as super patriots and jingoes, and keenly wanted to be seen as
the best defenders of British honor and prestige. At the same time financial constraints
made the prospect of war in a distant corner of the world particularly unpalatable. But
The Times and other jingoist newspapers continued to taunt the cabinet about its unwillingness to put its money where its mouth was. Even Henry Campbell-Bannerman, liberal
leader of the opposition, was not prepared to rule out war as a means of addressing the
denial of the vote to British Uitlanders.

But outweighing everything else was the fact that the world saw British resolve being
tested by the 'Boers', described by George Bernard Shaw as 'a small community of frontiersmen totally unfitted to control the mineral assets of South Africa.'[69] Ultimately the
desire to secure the British geo-political position in South Africa and elsewhere, and with
it British honor, made Britain go to war. Chamberlain summed up what was at stake: 'the
position of Great Britain in South Africa and with it the estimate formed of our power
and influence in our colonies and throughout the world.'[70] '[We], not the Dutch, are Boss',
was the way in which Salisbury phrased it.[71]

This was the reason why early in September the cabinet agreed to a request, engineered by Milner, from the colony of Natal to send ten thousand imperial troops to defend it against an invasion by republican forces. Milner, along with Beit, Werner and the
Uitlanders, had outmaneuvered Salisbury. He was only willing to hold a political pistol
to Kruger's head, but Chamberlain and Milner had forced him to pull the trigger. He
remarked 'We have to act upon a moral field prepared for us by Milner and his Jingo
supporters.' Britain had to engage in 'considerable military effort – all for people whom
we despise and for territory that will bring no profit or power to England.'[72]

The ultimatum was not issued by Britain, but by the Boers, realizing that its only hope
lay in spectacular victories before the British troops arrived, and in the process triggering an uprising by Cape Afrikaners. The republican forces numbered about 54,000,
while, at the time the war broke out there were only 27,000 British troops stationed in
South Africa, the great majority of whom were in the Cape Peninsula. The British, on the
other hand, calculated on a Boer collapse after the first battles. According to a British
Military Intelligence forecast, after one serious defeat the Boers 'would be too deficient
in discipline and organization to make any further real stand.'[73] On another issue, however, Military Intelligence was correct: the Free State would throw its weight behind
the ZAR, which surprised many politicians. Unwittingly the British cabinet made sure
that the OFS would indeed fight. Early in September it warned the OFS to observe strict

---

69 Lawrence James, *The Rise and Fall of the British Empire* (London: Abacus, 1998), p. 266.

70 Pakenham, *The Boer War*, p. 92; Iain Smith, *Origins of the SA War*, pp. 404-7. For an opposite view, see
   S. Marks and S. Trapido, 'Lord Milner and the South African State', *History Workshop*, 8, 1979, pp. 50-80.

71 Andrew Porter, *The Origins of the South African War* (Manchester: Manchester University Press, 1980),
   p. 247. For an extended interpretation, see Smith, *Origins*. See also Andrew Porter, 'The South African
   War: Context and Motive Reconsidered', *Journal of African History*, 31 (1990), pp. 43-57.

72 A.J.P. Taylor, *Essays in English History* (Harmondsworth: Penguin, 1976), p. 183.

73 Pakenham, *The Boer War*, pp. 76-77.

neutrality if war broke out.[74] For the OFS this would mean a shameful passivity that would turn its independence into a hollow shell. Just before the war broke out, Steyn told his Volksraad that he would rather lose the independence of the Free State 'with honor than do so in dishonor or disloyalty.'[75]

Smuts launched a diplomatic offensive, probably supplying most of the ideas for a brilliant propaganda tract, *Een Eeuw van Onrecht (A Century of Wrong)*, written mainly by a lawyer friend, J. de Villiers Roos. It recounted the injustices Afrikaners had suffered at British hands over the preceding century, but the strongest point was a charge against capitalists for fomenting war in South Africa and abroad. In liberal circles in Britain there was a strong revulsion against a rapacious capitalism, and, in consequence, a sizeable pro-Boer lobby arose in Britain.

But the lobby offered no substantial help, nor would any European country. The two small republics faced war against the world's greatest industrial power. In his reminiscences Kruger told a folksy tale to explain why he took the step. A man who suddenly found himself in the presence of a lion would not think of attacking it if armed with only a pocketknife. However, if the lion attacked him he would be a coward not to defend himself. On the eve of war Kruger said simply: 'The *riem* (strap) is around my neck, I have to fight.'[76]

Well aware of the insuperable odds the republics were facing, Jan Smuts thought South Africa 'was on the eve of a horrific blood bath.' Out of the ordeal of war the Afrikaner people would emerge 'either as relics, hewers of wood and drawers of water for a hated race, or as victors, founders of a United South Africa, of one of the great empires of the world.'[77] He pinned his hopes on large-scale assistance from the Cape. In the end some six thousand Cape rebels would join the Boer forces, but no general Cape uprising occurred; had it occurred in the first phase of the war, Britain would have been under severe pressure.

Smuts, like J.B.M. Hertzog, a young judge in Bloemfontein, advocated bold surprise action to ensure quick and dramatic victories. Hertzog wanted the Boer forces to penetrate deep into the Cape Colony and occupy strategic posts. Smuts' idea was that ZAR forces had to push swiftly into Natal and occupy the port of Durban to prevent more British troops from landing. He wanted military experts to be attracted from Germany, and to solicit help from Russia to incite war in India that would tie Britain down. If this program were executed, there could be 'within a few years, perhaps within a year, an Afrikaner republic in South Africa stretching from Table Bay to the Zambezi.'[78]

Nothing came of these bold plans. Bound by treaty to assist the ZAR in war, the OFS under Steyn first exhausted all diplomatic options before sending off an ultimatum. After a delay of nearly a month, Steyn concluded that no honorable alternative to war existed, and that Milner's harping on Uitlander grievances was a mere pretext to deprive the republics of their independence. It was a noble attempt to avert war, short of national

---

74 Keith Surridge, *Managing the South African War* (Woodbridge: Boydell Press, 1998), p. 51.

75 Van der Merwe, *Steyn,* vol. 1, p. 255.

76 Fisher, *Kruger,* pp. 224-35.

77 *Smuts Papers,* vol. 1, pp. 321-2.

78 Martin van Meurs, *J.C. Smuts* (Amsterdam: Suid-Afrikaanse Instituut, 1990), pp. 54-6.

humiliation, but a precious opportunity had been lost. When the inevitability of war stared all in the face there was only a vague, general plan for the republican armies to move to the Natal and the Cape borders, take some towns and await the British armies marching up from Durban and Cape Town.

The first phase of the war

On 9 October 1899, the two republics dispatched an ultimatum to Britain; on 12 October the first shots were fired. Britain had the resources to inflict a humiliating defeat. Against a maximum of 50,000 republican troops, it would have 250,000 men in the field at the height of the war, and would spend £230 million in crushing the republics.

In the first stage of the war Boer forces moved into northern Natal; the northeastern part of the Cape Colony, where some colonists joined them, and the Cape north of the Orange River. The main theatre was northern Natal, where there were a few quick victories before the Boer forces became bogged down in a protracted siege of Ladysmith. Commandant general Piet Joubert refused to use dynamite to force the British garrison out of its entrenchments, considering such an act un-Christian. With similar sieges tying up Boer forces at Kimberley and Mafeking in the colony, the first months, when the Boer forces were at an advantage, were largely wasted. During the siege of Ladysmith the younger generation of Boer officers, like the 37-year-old field cornet Louis Botha, implored their aging commandant general, the 68-year-old Joubert, to allow them to seize the port of Durban to prevent British reinforcements from landing. But Joubert, having fought too many battles in the past, had come to hate war and refused.

In December 1899 Boer forces defeated British armies on all three fronts, with Louis Botha rapidly establishing a distinguished reputation as a result of victories at Colenso and Spioenkop against a British force greatly outnumbering his own. By March 1900 Boer forces had captured several smaller towns along the northern border of the Cape Colony, but no important strategic positions. Commandos of two thousand men strong, under Generals J.B.M. Hertzog and P.H. Kritzinger, penetrated far to the west in the remote northern districts of the colony, but with numbers too small to attract mass support from Cape Afrikaners.

There were other defects. Smuts would comment later on the 'gross prejudice and conservative stupidity' of the older generation of generals, who ensured that the 'golden chance of victory had slipped away.'[79] The Boer forces lacked mobility, as some Boers joined the commandos with their families on wagons or Cape carts carrying many of their possessions.[80] There was a pervasive lack of discipline and commitment. When one commandant arrived at the battle with only three men, he explained what had happened to the rest: 'The one was sick, the other one tired, but the real cause was that most did not want to get up so early.'[81] Denys Reitz reported that the Free State com-

---

79 Jan Smuts, *Memoirs of the Boer War* (Johannesburg: Jonathan Ball, 1994), p. 69.
80 See Fransjohan Pretorius, *Kommandolewe tydens die Anglo-Boereoorlog, 1899-1902* (Cape Town: Human & Rousseau, 1991).
81 F. Seiner cited by Helen Bradford, 'Gendering Africander Nationalism, 1899-1902', unpublished paper, 1998.
82 Denys Reitz, *Commando* (London: Faber and Faber, 1929), p. 93.

mandant-general begged off from one attack because he and some of his men wanted to attend a cattle sale.[82]

In March 1900 Botha succeeded Joubert as commandant-general of the ZAR forces, but by the time Botha and Koos de la Rey in the western Transvaal, and Christiaan de Wet in the Free State, assumed command, the military position was beyond retrieving. British troops were now pouring into the country, decisively tilting the scale. Fighting under the overall command of Lord Roberts, with Field-Marshal Kitchener as his chief of staff, they relieved the besieged towns, captured four thousand men under Piet Cronjé at Paardeberg, and took Bloemfontein on 13 March, Johannesburg on 5 May, and Pretoria on 6 June. From March to July 1900 between twelve thousand and fourteen thousand burghers surrendered.

The bait Lord Roberts used to persuade the burghers to surrender in large numbers was the option of taking an oath of neutrality that allowed a combatant to return to his farm, a tactic later described by General Christiaan de Wet as 'worse than the murderous lyddite bombs in shattering Afrikanerdom.'[83] Those who swore the oath became known as *Hendsoppers* (Handsuppers); those who refused to sign were sent away to prisoner-of-war camps. Others, called Joiners or National Scouts, joined the British forces as scouts or spies in countering the Boer guerrilla fighters in the final eighteen months of the war. They also played a leading part in the peace committees that aimed at getting the Boers in the field to abandon the struggle. According to British estimates, by April 1902 nearly five thousand republican burghers were serving in the British army. The brothers of two senior Boer generals, Piet Cronjé and Christiaan de Wet, played leading roles in setting up committees that advocated peace on the grounds that the Boer cause had become so hopeless that surrender was the only option for survival.[84]

Prominent among those who deserted the republican cause were the wealthy and the very poor. In the years before the war, many of the wealthy, particularly in the Transvaal, had paid the poorer burghers to go in their place on commando and were, therefore, personally quite unprepared to fight. Their disinclination to fight was greatly reinforced when the British forces began to destroy Boer homesteads. By surrendering and returning to their farms and their families they could avoid great material disaster and personal grief. A German fighting on the Boer side noted in June 1900: 'It is especially the richer burghers who sit quietly at home since they have something to lose.'[85] In the case of the very poor a different dynamic was at work. The majority of the Joiners were *bywoners* or tenant farmers before the war. There is evidence of serious discontent at their having had to go on commando in the frontier wars against Africans, without proper recompense, to defend the property of landholders while their own families were destitute. They clearly hoped that the British would offer them a better dispensation. Their treason was often a rebellion against exploitation.[86]

On 21 October 1900, just before the British could take him prisoner, Kruger left for Europe where he died in exile three and a half years later. Lord Roberts proclaimed British

83 A.M. Grundlingh, *Die 'Hendsoppers' en 'Joiners'* (Pretoria: HAUM, 1979), p. 17.
84 Grundlingh, *Hendsoppers en Joiners*, p. 167.
85 J.J. Oberholster (ed.), "Dagboek van Oskar Hintrager", *Christiaan de Wet-annale*, 1973, p. 31.
86 Grundlingh, *Die 'Hendsoppers' en 'Joiners'*, pp. 232-6.

sovereignty over the Orange River Colony (the OFS) and the Transvaal Colony (the ZAR) on 24 May and 1 September 1900 respectively. Britain now controlled the entire railway network of southern Africa, including the line to Delagoa Bay, severing all Boer links with the outside world.

The Bittereinders

By mid-1900 the Boer forces were close to disintegration and the war all but over. On 30 May 1900 Milner jubilantly wrote to a friend, declaring that the battle between republicanism and imperialism was over: 'I have saved the British position in South Africa, and I have knocked the bottom out of "the great Afrikaander nation" forever and ever.'[87] If the fighting had ended in June 1900 the war would have been a rather insignificant event, unlikely to haunt memories and inflame passions for many years to come. But the heights of heroism, the depths of suffering, and the full horrors of the war were yet to unfold.

In June 1900, after the fall of Pretoria, a meeting of Transvaal military leaders, which included Smuts, Botha and De la Rey, recommended immediate surrender to avoid disaster. Kruger cabled Steyn in similarly despairing terms. Steyn now became the rallying point of the republican resistance. Furiously he replied that the Transvaal had got the Free State and the Cape rebels involved in a ruinous war in which the Free State had been laid waste. Did the ZAR now want to conclude 'a selfish and disgraceful peace' the moment the war had reached its borders? He gave notice that whatever the Transvaal might do, the Free State would fight on to the bitter end. As Smuts later confessed, Steyn had practically accused the Transvalers of cowardice, and had become, in Smuts' words, 'the most heroic figure' of the war.[88] Chastened, the Transvaal burghers decided to continue fighting to the 'bitter end' – until they were utterly crushed in defeat or had won the battle and restored the republics' independence. The last stage of the war continued until May 1902.

Among the Transvaal Bittereinders a leading figure was De la Rey of the western Transvaal, prominent in Kruger's progressive opposition. When Kruger questioned the Progressive Party's patriotism in 1899, just before issuing the ultimatum, he delivered a stinging rebuke: if alive, he would be fighting for independence and the country 'long after he [Kruger] has gone away and left us.'[89] Apart from Kruger, those most opposed to any major concessions to avert war were the old and incompetent generals, sometimes called *takhare* or rednecks, Kruger's favorites, or hangers-on. Most of them fought badly and had dropped out of the war by mid-1900. The Bittereinders were mostly commercial farmers and educated professional men. A.H. Malan, an aide to Louis Botha, stressed the paradox of the war. The Bittereinders, he wrote, 'belonged to the party [in the ZAR] that opposed the war most strenuously and also everything that could lead to it.' General P. Pienaar, who fought in both the OFS and Transvaal, stated in September 1900: 'Almost everyone who is still fighting is Progressive and [was] as strongly

87 Donald Denoon, *A Grand Illusion* (London: Longman, 1973), p. 59.
88 Smuts, *Memoirs*, pp. 42-3.
89 J. Percy Fitzpatrick, *South African Memories* (London: Cassell, 1932), p. 201.

opposed to Kruger's political policy as the English themselves. Why are they still fighting? For their independence.'[90] In Cape Town, Merriman gave the same judgement. The prominent leaders were in his words 'either progressive farmers, like Koos de la Rey, Christian de Wet, Louis Botha, Jan Kemp, or educated men from the towns like Steyn, Hertzog, Smuts and others.' He added: 'The soul of the fighting force consisted of young men and progressive farmers, many of them well-to-do, in some cases rich men.'[91]

Adopting guerrilla tactics and operating in small, mobile commandos, the Bittereinders sabotaged railway links, harassed British forces and seized supplies in an unexpected prolongation of the war by elusive enemies. One option open to the British forces was to be more methodical without exceeding the limits of brutality. They could systematically secure each district, extending the existing policy of restricting the guerrillas through blockhouses and barbed wire. But that would take money – and the war was already more costly than any Britain had fought since 1815. It also would take time, and Kitchener was in a great hurry to end the war in order to take up the post he coveted, Commander-in-Chief in India. While Milner was against the rash methods that would soon be employed, this sentiment was overridden by his determination to crush the Boers utterly and force them into unconditional surrender.

But the Bittereinders had developed a steely resolve to fight as long as was humanly possible. They were, in Smuts' terms, 'the men of invincible hope in the future and child-like faith in God.'[92] Their belief was in a very personal God who took a direct hand in shaping the destiny of nations, punishing those who sinned and rewarding the faithful. Contemporary accounts spoke of their fierce conviction that the British cause was so palpably unjust – indeed so sinful – that God would never grant Britain victory. Faith in the country's cause and faith in God had become synonymous. Voluntary surrender would not only be betrayal of the Boer cause, but, as a Free State fighter was reported as saying, an act of *ongeloof* – an absence of faith.[93]

Scorched earth and concentration camps

The war the British fought was not total war without scruples or limitations. They took prisoners and discriminated between taking the lives of soldiers and civilians. Although some Boer women protested about what they delicately called 'being molested', instances of rape were rare. But, as in the case of General William Sherman's army in its march from Atlanta to the sea in the last phase of the American Civil War, the British now fought a 'hard war', characterized by a military policy of 'directed severity.' To compare Roberts and Kitchener to Sherman would be a difficult task, but at first glance it looks as if Sherman struck a better balance than the British commanders between severity and restraint and in taking actions proportional to legitimate needs.[94]

---

90 Grundlingh, *Hendsoppers en Joiners*, p. 86.
91 P. Lewsen, (ed.), *Selections from the Correspondence of John X. Merriman, 1899-1905*, (Cape Town: VRS, 1966), p. 352.
92 *Smuts Papers*, vol. 1, p. 469.
93 Margaret Marquard, *Letters from a Boer Parsonage* (Cape Town: Purnell, 1967), p. 114.
94 Mark Grimsley, *The Hard Hand of War: Union Military Policy Towards Southern Civilians, 1861-1865* (Cambridge: Cambridge University Press, 1995).

Lord Roberts destroyed only the surrounding farms if the railway line had been sabotaged, but Kitchener soon escalated the scorched earth policy of razing houses and destroying livestock and crops to a general policy to terrify the Boer guerrillas and deprive them of all supplies. The British armies wreaked havoc and destruction in a broad swathe covering the greatest part of the Free State and Transvaal. In September 1900 Smuts reported from the northern Transvaal: '[Wherever] the enemy appeared, he carries out indescribable destruction. All houses are burned down, all fields and gardens are utterly destroyed, all cattle and foodstuffs are carried off and all males taken prisoner.'[95] Riding through the Free State a year later, he noted that the veld was covered with slaughtered livestock and the dams were full of rotting animals. 'The horror passes description . . . Surely such outrages on man and nature will lead to certain doom.'[96]

In a similar way the British blundered into setting up concentration camps for Boer civilians on the farms and for Africans displaced by the war. General Valeriano Weyler, commander of the Spanish forces in Cuba, was the first to use concentration camps for civilians. Between 1896 and 1898 he had thousands of civilians thrown into camps to deprive independence fighters of food, shelter and support. Some 200,000 of the *reconcentrados* may have died. In South Africa the camps were initially intended to provide a refuge for the families of burghers who had joined the British forces and faced the wrath of the Boers. At the end of 1900 the British command began destroying Boer homesteads and putting the families of the Boer guerrilla fighters into camps to deprive the fighters of shelter and support. Africans displaced in the war were settled in segregated camps. The camps were situated in poor locations and the inmates put on reduced rations. While there was no question of the British practicing genocide, the inadequate food rations in some camps contributed to the high death toll.

Almost all the concentration camps in the twentieth century had one thing in common: people were put in camps not for what they did, but for who they were. Invariably the inmates were people who were members of an 'enemy' group, or at any rate a category of people who, for reasons of their race or their presumed politics, were judged to be dangerous or extraneous to society.[97] The British anti-Boer propaganda that preceded the war created the conditioning that was necessary for treating harmless civilians callously. A British writer wrote: 'We have conjured up for ourselves a fantastic and outrageous image which we call *a Boer*. This savage being was hideous in form, unkempt, and unwashed, violent, hypocritical, a persecutor and an assassin of the English.'[98] Once the Boers had been defined in derogatory terms, it was not too difficult to put Boer women and children in camps in shocking conditions.

Kitchener thought that the camps needed no defense; what mattered was that the camps would shorten the war. As the historian Thomas Pakenham remarked: '[The plan for concentration camps] had all the hallmarks of Kitchener's famous shortcuts. It was big, ambitious and simple – and extraordinarily cheap.'[99] For the military, under

---

95 Rodney Davenport, *South Africa: A Modern History* (Johannesburg: Macmillan, 1987), p. 214.
96 Pakenham, *The Boer War*, p. 256.
97 Anne Applebaum, 'A History of Horror', *New York Review of Books*, 18 October 2001, pp. 40-43.
98 A.M.S. Methuen, *Peace or War in South Africa* (London, 1901), pp. 130-31.
99 Pakenham, *The Boer War*, p. 494.

whose control the total of 154,000 Boer and African civilians in the camps fell, the well-being of the inmates was a low priority.

A Boer woman, Maria Fischer, kept a diary that gives a glimpse of the trauma from the point that the British soldiers arrived on a Boer farm with a view to wreak as much destruction as possible and carry off the women and children. It seemed that 'many devils were set loose' as they destroyed the farm buildings, felled trees and killed even chickens. The Boer women and children were allowed to take along only the bare necessities. When the Fischer family arrived at the Standerton camp in the middle of winter, they were dumped at a heap of sand. Subsequently they found themselves in a group of thirty-seven that were crammed into a tent.[100] Complaints of the quality of the tents were rife. After visiting the camp at Bloemfontein, a senior British official wrote that the tents were second-hand and virtually worn out. 'The families in there have little privacy or guard against the elements.'[101]

A Boer woman left this description of the extremes of suffering: 'Then there was a Mrs. Coetzee. She had eight children and four were already dead. One day I passed her tent and saw three little boys on khaki blankets on the ground and they were covered in ants. The mother suffered from milk fever, and her newborn son was already dead. The mother lay on a small bed and a girl of seven lay behind her, also ill. To add to her misery, the tent was full of khaki lice.'[102]

Without any proper sanitary conditions, the condition of the underfed inmates quickly deteriorated. Many died, mainly of typhoid and measles, partly because the Boers as a rural people had not built up immunity to diseases and partly because of their weakened condition. Milner wrote to Chamberlain that the high mortality was 'a very dark spot', but neither British politicians nor the general public had any idea that an atrocity was occurring in South Africa. That changed when Emily Hobhouse, a British woman who had organized protest meetings against the war, received permission to visit South Africa to inspect the camps. She left for South Africa in December 1900 and was aghast at what she found. On her return to England in May 1901 she put the matter before the British public, shocking particularly the pro-Boer opposition party. On 14 June 1901 its leader, Sir Henry Campbell-Bannerman, told a Liberal dinner party that he was sickened by a policy of sweeping women and children into camps. He asked: 'When is a war not a war? When it is carried on by methods of barbarism in South Africa.' The situation in the camps was becoming a catastrophe. By October the death rate soared to 344 per thousand; children under five had virtually no chance of surviving.

In the final months of 1901 a commission of British women who supported the war also visited the camps. In the typically race-bound approach of the time they did not inspect the African camps. Shocked almost as much as Hobhouse was, this Fawcett commission recommended that rations be improved with vegetables added, that facilities be provided to boil all drinking water, and that more nurses be sent out from England immediately. These and other improvements were introduced and the death rate fell sharply.

---

100 Maria Fischer, *Kampdagboek* (Cape Town: Tafelberg, 1964), pp. 10-24.
101 Elria Wessels, 'A cage without bars' in Fransjohan Pretorius (ed.), *Scorched Earth* (Cape Town: Human & Rousseau, 2001), p. 67.
102 E. Neethling, *Mag ons vergeet?* (Cape Town: Nasionale Pers, 1938), p. 34.

Nevertheless, a total of 4,177 Boer women and 22,074 Boer children died in the camps. For many women and children the camp was a searing experience that stayed with them for the rest of their lives. When an English woman exhorted Boer children at Maria Fischer's camp to develop a spirit of forgiveness and love for one's enemy, she made the grim comment: 'To my mind it is not only impossible but also undesirable.'[103]

The indomitable resistance of the Boer women was the decisive factor in the war, as Olive Schreiner had predicted (see pp. 231-2). The great suffering and privation that they were prepared to endure baffled men, both Boer and British. They hid in mountains, forests or reed-overgrown rivers, or wandered across the land in so-called *vrouwen laagers*, all to avoid capture and being sent to concentration camps. They were also with few exceptions determined that their husbands and sons had to continue fighting, even to the death. Setting their houses on fire did not cow them. Some candidly declared that they preferred their houses to burn down than to see their husbands surrender. A British officer noted after two months of farm burning that the women without exception said that they would not give in.

Women scorned men who gave up the fight. After the British had overrun the Free State in mid-1900, a Boer woman noted: '[We] think the men should be on commando instead of meekly giving up their arms to, and getting passes from, the English.'[104] In one camp the British authorities considered separating Hendsoppers (Boers who had surrendered) and women, because of the bitter reproaches of the women. In another camp a Hendsopper wrote of being 'unmercifully persecuted by the anti-British sex.'[105] In Cape Town the historian G.M. Theal issued this warning: 'The women are the fiercest advocates of war to the bitter end . . . For independence the Boer women will send husbands and son after son to fight to the last.'[106] J.R. MacDonald, a British visitor, concluded after the war: 'It was the *vrouw* who kept the war going on so long. It was in her heart that patriotism flamed into an all-consuming heat, forgiving nothing and forgetting nothing.'[107]

Defeat in war also made women cling to their culture. Indignation about British war methods prompted a Bloemfontein woman to wonder aloud whether she should continue letting her children speak English. Reflecting on what separated her from the English, another Free State woman came up with an answer: republicanism, history, the *taal* (language) and 'hatred of the [British] race.'[108]

The Cape Afrikaners' anguish

The war and, in particular, the camps and the destruction of the homesteads, presented the Cape Afrikaners with the most painful of dilemmas. During the 1880s and 1890s they had prided themselves on being the most loyal of British subjects, but the war had turned most against the British imperialism that had precipitated the war. Milner reported

---

103 Fischer, *Kampdagboek*, p. 32.
104 Marquard, *Letters,* p. 78.
105 Grundlingh, *Hendsoppers en Joiners*, p. 142.
106 Cited by Helen Bradford, 'Gendering Africander Nationalism', p. 9.
107 J.R. MacDonald, *What I Saw in South Africa* (London: The Echo, 1902), p. 24.
108 Bradford, 'Gendering Africander Nationalism', p. 10; Marquard, *Letters,* p. 39.

that DRC ministers were now preaching a crusade against the Empire, and that Afrikaner Bond members were committing 'outspoken treason.' The governor of the Cape Colony, Sir Walter Hely-Hutchinson, believed that 50 per cent of the white population was more or less pro-Boer, and that the greater part of the colony was in a 'half suppressed state of rebellion.'[109]

The war put the Bond-backed Schreiner government in the Cape in an impossible position. Milner and the cabinet continuously clashed over Milner's demands to declare martial law in affected districts. Schreiner's efforts to walk the tightrope finally failed in June 1900 when the cabinet split over the imperial government's demand that rebels be disenfranchised. Merriman, Sauer and Dr Thomas te Water headed the revolt. In the wake of Schreiner's resignation, Milner appointed Sprigg in his place and suspended Parliament for the rest of the year. It was not to meet again for nearly two years. With his own health impaired by the overheated political atmosphere, Hofmeyr retreated to a spa in Germany.

In October 1900 the desperate top command of both the ZAR and OFS forces decided on massive Boer incursions into Natal and the Cape Colony. The blight of any attempt at Afrikaner collective action, namely internal division, soon reared its head.[110] De Wet had to co-operate with Botha, but did not trust him, and opted for two ineffectual incursions into the colony on his own. In August 1901 a column under Smuts with 250 men left the Transvaal on an epic final effort to instigate an uprising in the Cape. The column penetrated deep into the Cape Colony, reaching the west coast near the northern border and coming within a hundred kilometers of Cape Town. Smuts and his small troop controlled a large area between the Olifant and Orange rivers in the northwestern Cape, but they did not pose any military threat and failed to attract significant numbers of Cape rebels.

The invasion helped to transform the war from a white man's war into a truly South African war that affected virtually all communities deeply. On the Boer side in the OFS and Transvaal were some ten thousand *agterryers* – blacks, usually unarmed, who drove the wagons, tended to the horses and prepared the food. Black farm servants were removed to concentration camps for blacks where an official death toll of more than fourteen thousand was recorded. On the British side between ten thousand and thirty thousand blacks served as scouts, watchmen in the blockhouses, guards and drivers.

In the Cape Colony the British army recruited between two thousand and three thousand colored people for the Border Scouts, and many colored people joined the town guards.[111] The Boers viewed the use of people who were not white against them with the gravest of misgivings. In an open letter to a British journalist Smuts expressed his shock at the enlistment of armed blacks and coloreds to fight whites. Britain was violating 'a special code of morality' on which depended the continued existence of whites as the ruling class in South Africa. One aspect of this code prohibited 'interbreeding' between

---

109 Hancock, *Smuts*, vol. 1, p. 134.
110 The somewhat implausible argument is made that the Boers could have won the war if the invasion had been a success. See Leopold Scholtz, *Waarom die Boere die oorlog verloor het* (Menlo Park: Protea Boekhuis, 1999), p. 14.
111 Peter Warwick, *Black People and the South African War, 1899-1902* (Cambridge: Cambridge University Press, 1983).

whites and non-whites; another forbade the two white groups from appealing 'for assistance to the colored races in their mutual disputes.'[112]

Colored participation in the British defense angered the colonial Afrikaners and Boer
forces. Commandos operating in the northern Cape imposed a harsh regime on the colored population, with imposition of taxes and labor service and even a prohibition on
the speaking of English in public. In 1901 a well-publicized atrocity occurred in Calvinia when a Boer commando in cold blood shot Abraham Esau, a colored man who
led the resistance to occupation by the Boer forces of the region.[113] The colored people's
support for the British side brought them no political gain, but the gulf between the
politically conscious colored people and Afrikaners was now much deeper.

In response to the invasion, the Sprigg ministry early in 1901 placed virtually the entire Cape Colony under martial law.[114] Martial law and military courts seriously alienated
the Cape Afrikaners. Although many of the sentences were fair, the proceedings were
conducted entirely in English, of which most of rural Afrikaners had no or a poor command. Incompetent interpreters and military officers, knowing little about testing evidence, made a mockery of the proceedings in some of the cases. After C.J. Langenhoven,
a young anglophile attorney in the little Karoo town of Oudtshoorn, defended forty
people, of whom all except one woman were convicted, he was so revolted by the defects
of the judicial system, especially by the language barrier, that he withdrew from the military courts altogether, although he badly needed the money. A decade later he would
become the premier writer in Afrikaans.[115]

Between six thousand and seven thousand Cape burghers joined the Boer forces during the war, but tough British action deterred others. Military courts sentenced 360 rebels
to death and more than a thousand to jail. Many more were disenfranchised. Thirty-four
were executed, inspiring Louis Leipoldt to write his moving Afrikaans protest poem, *Oom
Gert Vertel* (Uncle Gert tells a story).[116] Adding to the trauma of the Cape Afrikaners was
the fact that the families were compelled to attend the executions.

The jingo element in the English population constantly accused Bond politicians of
disloyalty. The administration itself largely ignored the fact that Dutch was an official
language and went as far as abolishing the regulation that required entrants to the Cape
civil service to know Dutch. Across the colony English civil servants communicated only
in English with a population whose understanding of that language was limited or non-
existent. Almost as if to prove their loyalty, many of the latter chose to speak their broken English in public rather than Dutch. In Paarl, described by a newspaper as the 'Mec-
ca of Afrikanerdom', the supporters of the republic were too weak to wrest control of the
local trust company from English-speakers and loyalist Afrikaners.

---

112 *Smuts Papers*, vol. 1, p. 484.

113 W. Nasson, 'Abraham Esau: A Calvinia Martyr in the Boer War', *Social Dynamics*, vol. 11, no. 1 (1985),
    pp. 65-73.

114 E. van Heyningen, 'The Relations between Sir Alfred Milner and W.P. Schreiner's Ministry, 1898-1900',
    AYB, 1976, pp. 197-287.

115 Kay de Villiers, 'Die Anglo-Boereoorlog en die mense van Kaapland', paper presented at the Klein Karoo
    National Arts Festival, Oudtshoorn, April 2001, p. 15.

116 Translation by C.D.J. Harvey in A.P. Grové and C.D.J. Harvey, *Afrikaans Poems with English Translations*
    (Cape Town: Oxford University Press, 1962), p. 42.

Slowly, however, a section within the Cape Afrikaner community decided to fight back. The way in which Milner had provoked war, the callousness of the British commanders, the atrocious conditions of the concentration camps, and the injustices perpetrated under martial law in the colony – all this bit deeply into the soul of the colonial Afrikaners and bred a grim resolve to oppose British political and economic hegemony in all its forms. In May 1900 some fifteen hundred Afrikaners in Graaff-Reinet decided 'to act independently in all levels of business and to support Afrikaner enterprises . . . in the interest of the Afrikaner people.' In the western Cape towns of Paarl and Malmesbury the pro-Republic Afrikaners formed their own trust companies.[117] Soon boycotts were launched against loyalist businesses, which caused them serious economic trouble. In Stellenbosch people associated with the District Bank became the core of a proto-nationalist movement.

The final year of the war

In the final year of the war Kitchener continued with his sweep-and-scour strategy, while the Boer commandos launched lightning strikes in a fight-and-flee strategy. De Wet and his men eluded thirty thousand troops in the Free State, and in March 1902 De la Rey, despite being greatly outnumbered, inflicted heavy casualties on the British forces. Botha and his men also scored some victories before being forced out to the mountains of Vryheid, southeast of the Transvaal border, but they lacked food, fresh horses and fodder for further combat.

Botha had won a considerable reputation for his military skills and personal courage, but the Free State leaders, Steyn, De Wet and Hertzog resented the fact that he had met on his own with Kitchener in Middelburg in February 1901 to explore the possibility of peace. (A few days later posters all over London announced that Botha had surrendered to Kitchener.) In this way Botha sowed the seeds of the distrust that would plague him until his death in 1919.

The Bittereinders had come to the point where it was ever more difficult to continue. Hopes of victory had shrunk, ammunition was in short supply, and mental and physical exhaustion had set in. By the end of 1901 Kitchener decided to send no more Boer women and children to the camps; all those wanting to leave the camps would be turned over to the commandos. Food was now so scarce that the Boer women and children would put a great additional burden on the Boer commandos. In the Transvaal alone there were 2,540 families who now had to be cared for by the commandos. By March 1902 the approaching winter increased the anxiety about the women and children in the veld. Even more ominously, there was trouble with Africans occupying large tracts of farmland in the Transvaal. In the southeastern Transvaal a Zulu force retaliated against the theft of their cattle by attacking a Boer laager and killing fifty-six burghers. At the same time the military side looked bleak.

By the beginning of 1902 the republican forces were reduced to a Transvaal force of ten thousand, a Free State force of six thousand, and three thousand Cape rebels, a total

---

117 Anton Ehlers, 'Die geskiedenis van die Trustmaatskappye en Eksekuteurskamers van Boland Bank Beperk tot 1971', doctoral diss., US, 2002, pp. 24-5.

force of less than twenty thousand. Some five thousand Afrikaners – more than a quarter of the Afrikaners in the field at the end of the war – were fighting on the British side. In the last five months of the war the number of 'Joiners', republican burghers who fought with the British, had more than trebled.

Although in a state of almost complete physical collapse after constantly moving about with the commandos, Steyn urged the Free State Bittereinders to prolong the war. 'Independence struggles last a long time', he cried. 'It was true that the women and children were suffering, but that was preferable to the fate of ourselves, our children and grandchildren becoming serfs of the enemy.' Early in 1902, when the British high command allowed delegates of the republics to meet to deliberate over the war, Steyn still stressed the necessity of the burghers not losing self-respect by suing for peace. On this occasion Kitchener remarked of him: 'He is head and shoulders over the rest and has great influence.'[118]

An end 'more bitter than we thought it would be'

In the second half of May 1902 sixty Boer leaders met under British auspices in Vereeniging to debate the issue of peace. It was decided that a two-thirds majority for any decision was required of the sixty delegates (thirty from the Transvaal and thirty from the OFS), and that each delegate would vote as a plenipotentiary, that is, in accordance with his own opinion after the debate was concluded, and without consulting with his men in the field. The Free State delegates continued to resist the idea of surrender, but their resolve was weakened when Steyn's rapidly declining health forced him to withdraw from the meeting. Hertzog was quick to realize that the die had already been cast: once the Boer leaders had agreed to meet at Vereeniging to discuss peace, all their divisions surfaced.[119]

Vereeniging gave the delegates of the Boers still in the field the chance to reflect on what the republican Afrikaners could discard in order to retain some form of independence. ZAR State Secretary F.W. Reitz, backed up by Botha, made some proposals: they could cede Swaziland and dispense with the idea of having a state that maintained its own foreign relations or undertook its own external defense. He even suggested giving up the Witwatersrand and all its gold, which would enable them to be rid of the money that soiled the Boer character and all the *drankjode* (Jews engaged in the liquor trade). The British abruptly rejected the idea of a state within a British protectorate.[120]

Only two options now remained: to surrender or return to the battle with an even weaker force. Smuts no longer believed an independent Afrikaner republic that included the Cape Colony was possible, and he now had the vision of a united South Africa as part of the British Empire.[121] To persuade the Boer delegates, Smuts told them of a conversation he had had with Kitchener, who expressed the view that a Liberal govern-

---

118 Schoeman, *In liefde en trou*, pp. 52-3.
119 For an analysis of the debate see André du Toit, 'Confrontation, Accommodation and the Future of Afrikanerdom', *South African Outlook*, October 1977, pp. 147-52.
120 Kestell and Van Velden, *Die vredesonderhandelinge*, p. 73.
121 Scholtz, *Waarom die Boere die oorlog verloor het*, pp. 126-70.

ment might soon come to power in Britain, making self-rule for South Africa a distinct possibility.[122] It is possible that Smuts, trying to get a vote in favor of peace, may have hinted that he and some other leaders would join a military struggle in the future when Britain found itself in trouble. Steyn alleged after the war that he had received a letter from Smuts along these lines.[123] The Free State leaders were softer on Smuts than on Botha, but in the family of David van Coller, a Free State Bittereinder who was a delegate to the Vereeniging assembly, there is an oral tradition that the suspicion of the Free Staters was aroused by the private talks on this occasion between Kitchener and Smuts.

The British made some concessions. They offered not to punish the Cape Afrikaner rebels too severely (they would be disenfranchised for five years). It was an offer that might well not be repeated if the fighting continued. There was the grim prospect of the war effort degenerating to the point where more Afrikaners were fighting against the republican forces than for them. There was the danger that Milner would succeed in imposing a humiliating peace that would destroy the credibility of the Boer leaders. Privately he proposed banishing the Bittereinder leaders and confiscating their property. But the military had had more than enough of Milner's intransigence; Kitchener told the British government that Britain would have to build South Africa on the whites and the Afrikaners in particular. For him the best future British allies were not the Afrikaner 'loyalists' Milner wanted to use as collaborators, but the Boers who fought and their supporters.

For the sake of peace the British made another major concession. On the eve of the war Milner and Chamberlain had declared that the claims of the black and colored communities for political rights would be considered sympathetically. After the war civilization, not color, would be the test for civil rights. Chamberlain promised the British parliament in London that victory over the Boer republics would bring equal rights and equal liberty to all on the subcontinent. Britain would not purchase 'a shameful peace.' But Britain was always half-hearted in its commitment to avoid a 'shameful peace.' Privately Milner noted that post-war reconciliation of the two white groups would be a priority. 'You only have to sacrifice "the nigger" absolutely and the game is easy', he wrote.[124]

The question of the black franchise in the Transvaal and OFS came up in talks held at Middelburg, Transvaal, in February 1901 between Kitchener and Botha. They agreed that it had to be resolved when self-rule was granted to the territories some time in the future. Commenting on it, the British government a few weeks later indicated that the blacks 'would be so restricted as to safeguard the fair preponderance of whites.'[125] This meant that some Africans would indeed be enfranchised, a policy to which the Boer leaders were bitterly opposed. Now, in the final phase of the war, the British backed down on its stand.

At Vereeniging, in May 1902, Smuts was given the opportunity to draft a proposal. This was what he said: 'The question of granting the Franchise to the Natives will not be decided until after the introduction of self-government.' The little word 'after' made

---

122 J.C. Smuts, *Jan Christiaan Smuts* (Cape Town: Cassell and Co., 1952), p. 83.
123 Van der Merwe, *Steyn*, vol. 1, p. iv.
124 G.H. le May, *British Supremacy in South Africa, 1899-1907* (Oxford: Clarendon Press, 1965), p. 11.
125 F.V. Engelenburg, *General Botha* (George Harrap, 1929), p. 67.

all the difference. It left it to the Boers to decide on the African vote after power had
reverted to them. Having decided to build on a white-ruled South Africa, the British
accepted this without a murmur. 'Surrender was not all on the Boer side', Smuts' biographer, Hancock, aptly remarked.[126]

The burden of persuading the Boer delegates to surrender fell predominantly on the
shoulders of Botha. His opponents, particularly General Christiaan de Wet and General Jan Kemp, had expressed the view that the republics were the very foundation of
Afrikaner power and cultural existence in the northern part of South Africa. If they
were to disappear would Afrikanerdom itself not be shattered?[127] Botha argued the case
for a pre-emptive surrender, in other words for Boer forces to submit before their struggle became self-destructive, or, as he put it, 'while we are still a nation, and before we
have quite vanished as such.' He personally could carry on, and he knew that his family
was well looked after, but, he said, the Boer position was steadily deteriorating. Britain
was redoubling its efforts, the Cape was no longer a factor, there was an ever-increasing
danger from blacks, and the enemy refused any longer to look after the women and
children in the camps. He threw down the gauntlet: 'It has been said that we should fight
to the bitter end, but nobody can tell me where the bitter end is. Is it where every man is
either buried or banished? Do not let us regard a period of universal burial as the bitter
end. If we do we shall be to blame for national suicide.'[128]

De la Rey backed him up in graphic terms. If there were salvation for the *volk* in continuing to fight, he would go along, and if a grave were being dug for the volk he would
get into it. But there was a real chance that the nation would be driven into surrendering
en masse, causing the war to end in dishonor and disgrace.[129] In the final debate, held on
30 May, Smuts, in a moving speech, re-emphasized many of Botha's and De la Rey's
points: The Bittereinders had fought bravely and were prepared to sacrifice everything
for the independence of the Afrikaner *volk,* but there no longer was a reasonable chance
of success. He continued:

> We have moved to stand fast to the bitter end; but let us be men and acknowledge
> that the end has now come and it was more bitter than we thought it would be. For
> death itself would be sweeter than the step we must now take . . . No one shall ever
> convince me that this unparalleled sacrifice that the African [sic] nation has laid
> upon the altar of freedom will be in vain . . . It has been a war for freedom – not
> only for freedom of all the Boers but for the freedom of all the nations in South
> Africa.[130]

Independence, Smuts said, was not the highest value in the struggle for survival. '[We]
must not sacrifice the *Afrikaansche volk* on the altar of independence.' Once the chance

---

126 W.K. Hancock, *Smuts Vol. 1: The Sanguine Years, 1870-1919* (Cambridge: CUP, 1962), p. 159.
127 Engelenburg, *Botha*, p. 85.
128 Engelenburg, *Botha*, p. 91.
129 Except where otherwise indicated these are my translations from the Afrikaans text published in
J.D. Kestell and D.E. van Velden, *Die vredesonderhandelinge* (Cape Town: Human & Rousseau, 1982); for
an English version see C.R. de Wet, *Three Years' War* (New York: Scribner, 1902).
130 De Wet, *Three Years' War*, p. 498. In the original Dutch version the terms 'Afrikaansche volk' for 'African
nation' and 'het gansch volk van Zuid-Afrika' for 'all the nations in South Africa' were used.

of maintaining independence had gone, it was their duty to stop. Smuts warned: 'We must not run the risk of sacrificing our nation and its future to a mere idea which can no longer be realized.'[131]

But if independence was lost, on what other issue could the Afrikaners unite to remain a people? Only one of the delegates of the Bittereinders at the Vereeniging assembly of May 1902 suggested the maintenance of Dutch as a language as the basis of future survival. He was Jozua François Naudé, a 29-year-old Transvaal teacher, later a co-founder of the Afrikaner Broederbond. Naudé reminded delegates that one of the conditions set by the Bittereinders in the field was to have the rights of the Dutch language guaranteed. Dutch 'was of great significance to the volk, forming a channel through which the volk could again become volk.'[132] He refused to sign the peace treaty.

The terms of peace were unconditional surrender and recognition of the British sovereign; the repatriation of all prisoners of war provided they became British subjects; a guarantee to the Boers of their personal freedom and property; a pledge to end military rule promptly; deferral of the issue of the franchise of blacks until after the granting of self-rule; and the allocation of a sum of £3 million as financial help to the vanquished Boers. When the Free State delegates went to tell Steyn the final terms he cried: 'You have sold out the *volk* for £3 million.'[133]

Just after two o'clock on the afternoon of 31 May 1902 a vote was taken. Of the delegates, fifty-four agreed to surrender and six voted 'no.' Stressing Afrikaner unity as the essential prerequisite for future political action, Acting President S.W. Burger of the ZAR urged delegates 'to forgive and forget when we meet our brother: the part that was disloyal must not be shunned.' Representatives of the governments of both sides met late in the evening in Pretoria to sign the peace treaty. Kitchener shook the hands of everyone, declaring 'We are good friends now.' A seriously ill Steyn was absent. He had earlier said. 'I shall never put hand on a piece of paper in which I sacrifice my people's independence.'[134]

Despite the shattering defeat, the Bittereinder stage of the war had changed the course of South African history. At stake were the political character and reputation of the Boer people, their republican commitment, and their willingness to pay the highest price for their freedom. In the early stages of the war Milner had remarked that the Boers loved their property more than they hated the British and would never fight for a political system. It was the valor of the Bittereinders and the courage during the grim but ultimately glorious final phase of the war that won the Boers universal respect as freedom fighters. Smuts, and also the British commander, General Kitchener, observed that this stand had made a vital difference. It meant, as Smuts pointed out, that 'every child to be born in South Africa was to have a proud self-respect and a more erect carriage before the nations of the world.'[135]

---

131 Leaders like Smuts and Hertzog did not always use the term 'volk' in an ethnic or nationalist sense. In this particular case Smuts appeared to be using it in an ethnic sense, referring to white Afrikaans-speakers.

132 Kestell and Van Velden, *Vredesonderhandelinge*, p. 146.

133 Schoeman, *In liefde en trou*, p. 59.

134 Kestell and Van Velden, *Vredesonderhandelinge*, pp. 174-5.

135 G.D. Scholtz, *Die ontwikkeling van die politieke denke van die Afrikaner* (Johannesburg : Perskor, 1978), vol. 5, p. 101.

Milner had been proven wrong, but the losses suffered in lives and possessions were devastating. Some 5,000 Boers died in the fighting or on commando, and nearly 27,000 Boer women and children lost their lives in the camps. This meant that 10 per cent of the Boer people in the republics had perished. The destruction of farms and livestock is discussed in Chapter 10. Speaking in a British parliamentary debate, Campbell-Bannerman described the country outside the towns as a 'howling wilderness', while Milner described it as 'virtually a desert, almost the whole population living in refugee camps along the railway line.'[136]

The immediate post-war years saw the Boer leadership in disarray. Paul Kruger died in exile in 1904. Steyn was so ill that he could no longer pursue an active political career. Botha, De Wet and De la Rey returned to their farms, Hertzog and Smuts resumed legal careers, one in Bloemfontein, the other in Pretoria. Smuts, suffering, like the others, from deep depression in confronting the shattering defeat, wrote to Abraham Fischer, the Free State leader, about new threats to the Afrikaner people: ['There] are years of great danger before us – partly because people have fallen so deep, so fathomlessly deep, into poverty and misery, partly because everything will be done by the other side, through their education system and otherwise, to anglicize the generation now growing up. It is our duty to guard against this and that is why I am so strongly in favor of ourselves, if necessary, providing for the education of our children.'[137]

Milner's British South Africa

Milner and Chamberlain wanted to build a British South Africa closely tied to London in a one-to-one subordinate relationship. It was a time for 'great Empires and not for little States', Chamberlain wrote.[138] The liberal idealism of the early Victorians had fallen by the wayside; the late Victorians were cautious and circumspect, putting security at the center of their concerns. Ideally Chamberlain and Milner would have liked London to retain the right for as long as possible to appoint imperial officials in South Africa, issue instructions to them and dismiss them. Their great prize was to unite all four colonies under British auspices and direction, with Milner at the helm.

Milner was now not only High Commissioner of the Cape Colony, but also Governor of the Transvaal Colony and the Orange River Colony. Partly as a result of the extensive disfranchisement of Cape rebels, the Progressives won the 1904 election under the leadership of L.S. Jameson, who in less than a decade had lived down his 1895 raid. Governments in all four colonies were ready to pledge Milner their support. He commanded the loyalty of a contingent of bright Oxford graduates, called Milner's Kindergarten, brought from England to oversee reconstruction and promote imperialist goals.

Milner wished to construct this new union on the pillars of a capitalist system and an efficient, professional bureaucracy. The blacks had to be governed well and justly, but ruled by the white man since he was elevated 'many, many steps above the black man' which the latter would take 'centuries to climb.' Immediately after the war the British

136 J.L. Sadie, 'The Fall and Rise of the Afrikaner in the South African Economy' (Stellenbosch: US Annale, 2002), p. 16.
137 *Smuts Papers*, vol. 2, p. 38.
138 Taylor, *Essays in English History*, p. 189.

administration followed a much tougher policy. The pass laws controlling the movements of Africans were policed more strictly, and employers called the police to stop any strike action by blacks. The magnates could ignore complaints about the black compounds. In the rural areas Anglo-Afrikaner collaboration began immediately after the war. Some Bittereinders were allowed to take up arms for the protection of whites in areas where there was a high concentration of Africans. Afrikaners were recruited to a rural constabulary under Major-General Robert Baden-Powell, which disarmed rural Africans. Louis Botha expressed satisfaction in giving evidence to the Transvaal Labour Commission in 1903: 'Well, the Kaffirs are gradually beginning to see that the Boers are just as much masters as the other white men. And that the two races [Boer and British] are standing together.'[139] To develop a policy entrenching white supremacy in South Africa, Milner appointed a South African Native Affairs Commission in 1903 to investigate a common policy towards Africans (see pp. 299-300).

Milner also set in place the foundation for a political union of the four colonies. In 1903 he established Central South Africa Railways to unite the railways system. In the same year an experimental South African Customs Union was formed . The civil service of the new colonies was overhauled and municipal councils were set up in the towns. Irrigation and forestry schemes were started. Scientific farming was encouraged through the establishment of a Department of Agriculture, the Onderstepoort veterinary center and a Land Bank, all in the Transvaal. Education for whites was greatly expanded. To reconcile the Boers, some £16 million was spent on getting the defeated Boers back onto their land and ready to farm again.

But Milner did not have a blank slate to work on. The white community in South Africa had long been accustomed to the exercise of power. Sooner or later a form of self-rule for the ex-republics had to be introduced. A majority of English-speakers in the electorate of a future united South Africa could only be achieved through large-scale immigration from Britain, ensuring a compliant, loyalist white electorate.[140] In Milner's eyes such a loyalist British majority was vital. Were there to be 'three of Dutch to two of British, we shall have perpetual difficulty', he wrote.[141]

Milner's plan to attract large-scale British immigration failed spectacularly, with only 1,400 British heads of families arriving in the ex-republics. As a result he pinned his hopes on anglicizing the Transvaal and Free State. The peace treaty stipulated that Dutch would be taught in schools where parents desired it, and allowed in courts, but Milner frankly told the Boer leaders that he wanted only one public language in South Africa, English.[142]

He proclaimed English the sole official language and the sole medium of instruction in schools. Three hours per week were set aside for children to study the Bible in Dutch and the Dutch language, but only if their parents had requested it. He gave firm instructions to spread the imperialist creed in schools by appointing suitable teachers and re-

---

139 Donald Denoon: *A Grand Illusion* (London: Longman, 1973), p. 100.

140 Denoon, *Grand Illusion,* pp. 246-52; Ronald Robinson et al., *Africa and the Victorians* (London: Macmillan, 1976), pp. 410-72.

141 Marlowe, *Milner,* p. 132.

142 Cecil Headlam (ed.) *The Milner Papers* (London: Cassell and Co.1933), vol. 2, pp. 35-6, 467; Kestell and Van Velden, *Die vredesonderhandelinge,* p. 126.

designing the curriculum. In a classic statement Milner observed: 'Language is important but the tone and spirit is even more important. Not half enough attention has been paid to school reading books. To get this right would be the greatest political achievement conceivable.' He continued: 'A good world-history would be worth anything . . . Everything that cramps and confines their [South African children's] views to South Africa only . . . makes for Afrikanerdom and further discord.'[143]

E.B. Sargent, Acting Director for Education for the new colonies, made no secret of his intention of infusing Afrikaner children with what he called the 'the greatness of the English Imperial idea' and on another occasion 'our language and ideals.' Soon it was reported that six hundred young teachers were on their way from Britain and other parts of the Empire to participate in this grand imperial venture. Sargent told his teaching staff that their function was to indoctrinate children as comprehensively as possible: 'You ought to have a political aim in all your school work and that aim should be to make political parties unnecessary.'[144]

Milner scoffed at the possibility that Afrikaner nationalists could thwart his imperialist project. It was a complete illusion, he wrote, that the Afrikaners cared much about 'the great Afrikaner nation.' What he could not see was that his policies and utterances provided the very stuff from which nationalist movements were made. Looking on from the sidelines, Smuts wryly commented: '[Milner] has dreamed a dream of a British South Africa – loyal with broken English and happy with a broken heart.'[145]

The reversal of Milner's hopes

To secure the objective of continued British domination, Milner had to do three things: unite the English element in South Africa, split the Afrikaners by attracting an important section as a collaborating elite, and promote rapid economic growth. His plans became unstuck in pursuing the third objective. He was determined to bring about full production of the gold mines, which provided nine-tenths of the Transvaal revenue and formed the economic engine of South African reconstruction. Milner was confronted with the fact that the war had caused a huge labor shortage at the mines. The British army had raised expectations by offering Africans much higher wages than before the war. But mines were now working cheaper reefs with most of the richer ones exhausted; dividends were lower except where companies reduced production costs by lowering wages. The Chamber of Mines, in December 1900, reduced black mineworkers' wages by nearly a quarter, and, with the full backing of Milner, introduced the Witwatersrand Native Labour Association as a central recruiting agency with employers co-operating in order to impose uniformly low wages for blacks, now only a little higher than some farm wages.

Competitive wages were important because mine work was so dangerous. In 1903 the average death rate per thousand workers per month was 70, with a high of 113 in July.

---

143 *Milner Papers,* vol. 2, pp. 242-3.
144 Irving Hexham, *The Irony of Apartheid: The Struggle for National Independence of Afrikaner Calvinism against British Imperialism* (New York: Edwin Mellen Press, 1981), pp. 19-20.
145 G.H.L. le May, *British Supremacy in South Africa* (Oxford: Oxford University Press, 1965), p. 156.

More than two-thirds of them died from meningitis caused by crowded and damp conditions in the horrible compounds and another tenth from bad food.[146] Migrants from Mozambique, from where most mineworkers came, were not prepared to endure all this at the lower wage.

In a hurry to consolidate British power in South Africa by high economic growth, Milner did not hesitate to intervene on the employers' side in industrial disputes; he had a duty 'to the employer, and to the whole white population, whose well-being is in a hundred ways so deeply affected by the prosperity of the mines.' To remedy the shortage of labor Milner agreed to a proposal from some mining directors to import Chinese workers on short-term contracts ending in compulsory repatriation. More than 63,000 Chinese laborers were imported; they formed a third of the mine labor force by the end of 1905. They worked for dismally low wages and in abysmal conditions. The mining companies could ignore criticism of the compounds where the labor was housed. Soon the accusation was leveled against Milner's administration that Chinese 'slave labor' was being used.

The importation of Chinese laborers realized Milner's worst political nightmare: It brought about a groundswell of revolt against what was described as a rapacious capitalism that had brought on the war.[147] Now the magnates were seen as destroying the hope for post-war reconciliation. The Liberal opposition in Britain, which had been aghast at the burning of farms and the concentration camps, used the South African issue to help it win the election in December 1905.[148] The Boer leaders in the Transvaal employed Chinese labor as one of its main lines of attack on Milner's administration. Even worse from Milner's point of view was that Chinese labor split the Transvaal English-speaking community. After visiting South Africa in the aftermath of the war Chamberlain wrote of the British population of Johannesburg as 'impatient and critical but still at the bottom intensely loyal and Imperialist.'[149] But this was an incorrect assessment: British loyalty was not unconditional. The English-speakers on the Witwatersrand soon split in three: white labor fearing low-wage Chinese labor and disliking the mining industry's concentration of economic power founded a workers' party. A faction called the Responsibles favored a prompt introduction of self-rule, while the progressive faction, which included some mining magnates, supported Milner.

Milner also failed to keep the Cape English-speakers in line. He wrote: 'From what I have seen of the working of "responsible government" in South Africa makes it wholly impossible to labor for its extension with any sort of zeal.'[150] He had hoped that the constitution of the Cape Colony could be suspended while working on unification, arguing that it would simplify matters to have all the colonies in a similar constitutional status. But very few of the Cape voters would have countenanced this. Merriman attacked the suspension plan as 'a raid upon the liberties of this country', and was joined by Sir Gordon Sprigg, who broke with his party on the issue. Leaders of other British Domin-

---

146 L. Callinicos, *A People's History of South Africa* (Johannesburg: Ravan Press, 1982), vol. 1, p. 49.

147 J.A. Hobson, *The War in South Africa* (London: Nisbet, 1900), pp. 230-2, 240.

148 Leonard Thompson, *The Unification of South Africa* (Oxford: Clarendon Press, 1960), pp. 21-2.

149 Taylor, *Essays*, p. 188.

150 Taylor, *Essays*, p. 188.

ions also expressed concern about the implications for their own autonomy. The result was a new resolve among politicians in the two white communities to work towards reconciliation and unification on their, and not Milner's, terms.[151]

To English-speakers in South Africa the Boer leaders sent out the message that they were now loyal British citizens keen to work for the reconciliation of the two groups. 'Forgive and forget' became almost a refrain in their letters. Smuts wrote to his wife the day after the signing of the peace treaty. 'The curtain falls over the Boers as British sub-jects and the plucky little republics are no more . . . Let us do our best to bind up the old wounds, to forgive and forget . . .'[152] The desire for reconciliation made a great impression on moderate English-speakers.

Post-war political recovery

The Afrikaner Bond survived the war relatively unscathed. Only three Bond parliamen-tarians had lost their seats because of their association with the republican forces. The Bond took the lead in forming the South African Party, which linked the Bond as an extra-parliamentary movement and its parliamentary wing, the South African Party. The SAP's aim was the 'development of a feeling of unity among the different nationalities of British South Africa, and the unification of the British South African colonies in a Fed-eral Union, with consideration for the mutual interests of the colonies and of the supe-rior authority of the British Crown.'[153] This approach enabled liberals like Merriman and Sauer to throw their weight behind the SAP.

The first priority of the Boer leaders in the ex-republics was to heal the division be-tween the National Scouts (the Boers who had supported Britain in the war) and the Bittereinders. In 1903 Louis Botha told a secret session of the Dutch Reformed Church synod that the National Scouts should be chastised but accepted back in the congrega-tions. In some towns the efforts failed, leading to the establishment of separate National Scouts churches, but, generally, Afrikaner church schisms were prevented.

The Boer leadership also scrupulously avoided collaboration. Botha, Smuts and De la Rey promptly refused Milner's offer of seats on a nominated legislature and rejected an initial British constitutional offer that granted only limited self-rule and withheld the vote from landless Afrikaners. In 1903 Botha held the first post-war public meeting. Soon afterwards the first farmers' associations were formed. In January 1905 Botha an-nounced the formation of a political party, Het Volk, in the Transvaal, and in May 1906 the Boer leaders in the Orange River Colony (Free State) formed the *Orangia Unie*.

Milner's education policy was so extreme that it lent itself to agitation. He antagonized the Afrikaners with a policy that yielded no worthwhile dividend for his cause. Most Afrikaners still attached little value to education and many children had only a year's schooling, many of the rest leaving school before they were ten.[154] Church leaders never-

---

151 Saul Dubow, 'Colonial Nationalism, the Milner Kindergarten and the Rise of "South Africanism"', 1902-1910, *History Workshop Journal*, 43 (1997), pp. 53-85.

152 J. Cameron, *Jan Smuts*, p. 43.

153 T.R.H. Davenport, *The Afrikaner Bond, 1880-1911* (Cape Town: Oxford University Press, 1966), p. 245.

154 S.E. Katzenellenbogen, 'Reconstruction in the Transvaal', in Peter Warwick (ed.) *The South African War* (London: Longman, 1980), p. 351.

theless feared that over the longer term the policy would fatally erode their own institution. That indeed was the keen anticipation of the English press. The *Pretoria News* wrote confidently in 1905: '[T]his church is dying out . . . and the language of this church will in a short time wholly disappear.' The synod of the Transvaal DRC (Nederduits Hervormde of Gereformeerde Kerk) remarked: 'The education question concerns the very existence of our church. If our children are to grow up ignorant of the official language of the church the result will be that they drift into other churches.'[155]

Milner's policy had turned most teachers who had served the ZAR into fierce enemies. Many, dismissed after the war, were still looking for work. Some now poured all their energy into the establishment of Christian-National private schools, an idea originally developed by the Dutch neo-Calvinist, Groen van Prinsterer, and later by Abraham Kuyper, who between 1902 and 1905 headed the Dutch government. The Reformed (Dopper) ministers and teachers who studied at the theological school in the town of Potchefstroom in the western Transvaal were among the strongest supporters of Christian-National schools. The key figures were Willem Postma, later a Reformed Church minister and political columnist in Bloemfontein; Ferdinand, his brother, who became professor and later rector, and the theology professor J.D. du Toit (the son of S.J. du Toit of Paarl) and writer of Afrikaans poetry under the name of Totius.

The Doppers' influence was out of all proportion to their small numbers. Taking 'In isolation lies our strength' as a motto, the Doppers wove the strands of religion, language and nationhood into a nationalist cloth. Willem Postma urged Afrikaners to protect their identity from being destroyed by English-speakers and their culture. 'Our people are Christian Afrikaners. This is our tradition. The whole development of our people comes from and is the fruit of Christian principles.' To adopt the mother tongue as a badge of identity and to give it a central place in the school and the church was a way of building a strong, separate nation and religious community. 'Take away our language and we will become Englishmen and accept their religion.' He extended the principle of separation between the two white groups to separation between whites and blacks. He envisaged a piece of land for the black nations with their own schools, churches, parliaments and universities; however if 'they came here they must work and not play tennis.'[156] Ferdinand Postma urged the teaching of Afrikaner history to counter the imperialist history taught in schools.[157]

By 1904 the opposition to Milner was stretching beyond the ministers and teachers to the Afrikaner intelligentsia in general. Almost all who belonged to this stratum were Calvinists. More than Catholicism or Lutheranism, Calvinism insisted on remaking this world according to distinct principles derived from or read into the Bible.[158] An activist Calvinism aligned to a political nationalism represented a potent force. In 1905 Milner wrote: '[The] Afrikaner doctrine emanates essentially from the towns and the agricul-

155 The quotes in this paragraph are from J.J. Pienaar, *Die inspirerende opvoedings- en opheffingsaksie van die Ned. Herv. of Gereformeerde Kerke in die Transvaal gedurende 1902 tot 1910* (Pretoria: N.G. Boekhandel, 1970) pp. 34-6, 46-7.

156 Hexham, *Irony of Apartheid*, p. 180.

157 Hexham, *Irony of Apartheid*, pp. 134, 160.

158 G.J. Schutte, 'Abraham Kuyper: vormer van een volksdeel', in C. Augustijn (ed.) *Abraham Kuyper* (Delft: Meinema, 1987), pp. 9-33.

tural middle class and is pumped into the country Boers . . . It is quite certain that, but for the influence of parsons, doctors, attorneys, law agents, journalists, and the more educated and town-frequenting of their own class, the country Boers would not be irreconcilable.'[159]

Botha and Smuts realized that Christian-National private schools provided an excellent way to build a political constituency without directly challenging the imperial authorities. Smuts teamed up with church leaders to establish the Commission for Christian National Education (CNE) in the Transvaal and, with help from the Netherlands, CNE schools rapidly sprang up in the ex-republics.[160] Schools introduced the main principles of CNE education: responsibility to parents for their children's education and a Protestant-Christian spirit in schools, or, to use the words of one of the proponents, 'God's hand in the history of our people . . . and our ancestors' history, language and traditions.'[161] By 1905 there were 228 such schools in the Transvaal with 419 teachers and 9,335 pupils compared to approximately 33,000 children in state schools. CNE schools used mother-tongue instruction in the early school years, but gradually introduced English as a second medium, with the goal of reaching parity between the languages in the fifth school year.

In January 1906 Smuts went to London where the Liberals under Sir Henry Campbell-Bannerman had just come into power. In his memorandum to the government Smuts presented the political conflict in the Transvaal as a battle between the mining industry and the 'permanent population of the land, English as well as Dutch.' After Smuts had met with Campbell-Bannerman, the cabinet decided to grant self-government to the defeated republics. For the rest of his life Smuts believed that the positive response was a 'magnanimous gesture' almost without parallel. But the Liberal decision was not driven by magnanimity alone. The Liberals were eager to extricate themselves from the mess of Milner's Chinese labor policy and happy to have Britain's vital interests in South Africa secured without Britain having to dominate the region.

Victory for Het Volk in the first election scheduled for 1907 in the Transvaal was by no means assured. The electoral arithmetic in the colony argued against paying undue attention to language and culture.[162] Afrikaners, according to some calculations, formed only half of the all-white electorate (according to others even less than half). No rival Afrikaner organization existed that could discredit Het Volk's effort to reach out to English voters. Hence, Het Volk, like the SAP in the Cape, cast its net wide enough to attract moderate English-speakers, while retaining Afrikaner unity.

In wooing English voters Het Volk was careful to downplay the issue of language. It knew that English-speakers almost to a man would be up in arms if their children had to learn Dutch, not to speak of being taught through the Dutch medium. F.V. Engelenburg, who was editor of De Volksstem, remarked: 'The English-speaking section . . . was so irritable on the subject of its children being taught Dutch that the slightest com-

---

159 N.G. Garson, 'Het Volk', Historical Journal, 9,1 (1966), p. 128.
160 P. H. Zietsman, Die taal is gans die volk (Pretoria: Unisa, 1992), p. 127.
161 Scholtz, Ontwikkeling van die politieke denke, vol. 5, pp. 429-40; Hexham, The Irony of Apartheid, p. 115.
162 Thompson, Unification, p. 129.

pulsion caused red-hot indignation, reacting powerfully on the ordinary citizen's politics . . .[It] is hard to understand today how English-speaking South Africans could regard it as a humiliation that their offspring should be obliged to learn the other language.'[163] As the historian P.H. Zietsman noted, one doubts whether under the circumstances Smuts could have approached the matter very differently. 'One could hardly imagine the storm that would have been unleashed, if he [Smuts] had enforced equal language rights in education consistently.'[164]

The small number of children in Christian-National schools in the Orange River Colony prompted Botha to criticize Hertzog for his lack of commitment to the national cause, while the Transvaal Afrikaans press commented scathingly on some leaders who risked 'the suicide of a language, volk and religion.'[165] But there now occurred one of those sudden shifts of course that characterize Afrikaner politics. The proponents of CNE schools had hoped that under self-rule a policy of 'free schools with state subsidies' would enable them to persevere with CNE schools in which the place of Dutch would be secure. But Smuts decided that there was no need to continue with the CNE schools.

Lack of money made it difficult to sustain the CNE schools through voluntary contributions. By 1906 the number of CNE schools in the Transvaal had dropped by a third. In the Orange River Colony the CNE movement was much weaker and by 1907 there were only seven hundred children in CNE schools. For Smuts the priority was to use the state schools to foster reconciliation between the two white communities.

Announcing Het Volk's withdrawal of support for CNE schools, Botha remarked: 'We have to make concessions in education. But it is for no other reason than to realize one of our greater ideals, namely to bring about in this country a single nation of whites.'[166] Also influencing policy was the desperate state of the Afrikaners' education; in 1909 only twenty-six Afrikaners out of a total of three hundred whites passed the examination for the highest school standard in the Transvaal. Smuts felt strongly that education had to prepare Afrikaner children for the job market and that proficiency in English was a priority.

The language issue was the weak spot of the Het Volk leaders. Botha had received only a smattering of formal education and only late in his career was he able to make a speech in English. He never seemed to understand the political potency of the language issue. The puzzle is why Smuts failed to complement his shortcomings, as he did in so many other cases. As a student in the early 1890s Smuts wrote positively about the potential of Afrikaans. It was, he said, not yet a literary medium, but for 'expressing wit or humor as well as the primary emotions of the human heart – and in this it reveals the character of the people – it is scarcely second to any language with which we are acquainted.'[167]

But soon after the Anglo-Boer war doubts arose within his own constituency about his

163 F.V. Engelenburg, *General Louis Botha* (Pretoria: Van Schaik, 1929), p. 222.

164 Zietsman, *Die taal*, p. 185.

165 Zietsman, *Die taal*, pp. 179-89.

166 E. Liversage, 'Die premierskap van Generaal Louis Botha tot en met die uitbreek van die Eerste Wêreldoorlog', doctoral diss., UOFS, 1985, p. 21.

167 W.K. Hancock, *Smuts: The Sanguine Years, 1870-1919* (Cambridge: Cambridge University Press, 1962), p. 359.

sentiments. Gustav Preller asked Smuts' wife why the General 'never spoke about the language question in connection with our nationality.'[168] In 1905 Smuts privately told Richard Jebb, an Australian proponent of colonial nationalism, that English should be the official language of the future South Africa, but with Dutch usage permitted.[169]

Instead of language, Botha and Smuts seized on anti-capitalism to unlock English-speaking support and win the first election held in 1907. It is doubtful whether Smuts himself ever nourished a profound anti-capitalist attitude, although, like other Afri-kaners, he had been deeply angered by the brazen complicity of Cecil John Rhodes in the Jameson Raid and the role some magnates played in encouraging Britain to go to war against Kruger. His anti-capitalism was exhibited principally in propaganda and lobbying. He echoed the views of Hobson whom he had met in the Transvaal in 1899. *A Century of Wrong*, which Smuts co-authored, depicted capitalism as 'a new factor' in the Transvaal, Britain, and the world at large, that endeavored 'to gain political power and to make all other forms of government and influence subservient to its own ends.'[170]

Milner's decision to import Chinese labor for the mines after Africans withheld their labor in pursuit of higher wages was a godsend to Het Volk. It deflected attention from the Boer leaders' determination not to extend the vote to blacks. Projecting itself as a moderate party, eager to curb the excesses of the capitalists, Het Volk was able to attract a decisive measure of support from the Transvaal English. J.B. Robinson, a gold magnate and active supporter, correctly saw the party's anti-capitalism as an electoral gambit. Anti-capitalism helped the Boer leaders in their appeals to the Liberal opposition in England, who combined pro-Boer sentiments with support for social reform and for the welfare of the African and Asian subjects of the Crown. Anti-capitalism also strength-ened the ties with South African liberals, especially with the highly esteemed Merriman.

In the 1907 election Het Volk triumphed in thirty-seven of the sixty-nine seats, with seven victorious English-speaking candidates. Botha formed a six-man government of four Afrikaners and two English-speakers. He took care not to replace too many Eng-lish-speaking civil servants with Afrikaners. What had begun as a tactical shift for Botha and Smuts to win the 1907 election turned into a firm commitment to retain white uni-ty as the core plank of their party. Smuts would remain loyal to this principle until his death in 1950.

The education legislation that Smuts piloted through in 1907 fell far short of the ex-pectations of the CNE camp. Children would receive mother-tongue education in the early school years. English had to be progressively introduced and had to become the medium of instruction in the sixth school year, with the exception of two subjects that could be taken in Dutch. In contrast to the CNE syllabus that made provision for bilin-gual education, and used both Dutch and English as mediums of instruction, the Smuts legislation did not require English schools to use Dutch as a medium.

The legislation also made no mention of the teaching of history in a way that would inculcate national or patriotic sentiments. It was clear that the imperialist interpreta-

---

168 Hancock, *Smuts: The Sanguine Years*, p. 360.

169 Deryck Schreuder, 'South Africa', in John Eddy and Deryck Schreuder (eds.), *The Rise of Colonial Nation-alism* (Sydney: Allen and Unwin, 1988), p. 198.

170 F.W. Reitz (ed.), *A Century of Wrong* (London, 1901), pp. 41-3.

tion of history would continue to be taught. Het Volk's moves had their costs. In 1908 Botha complained to the British High Commissioner: 'Hollanders, Krugerites and a large section of the *predikanten* [ministers] were engaged in a desperate intrigue against his policy of closer union and conciliation.'[171] *De Vereeniging*, journal of the Transvaal DRC, wrote: 'We must seek our political, national, religious and educational salvation along authentic Afrikaans lines.'[172]

Het Volk came to power in auspicious circumstances for establishing white supremacy. Chinese labor had not only sunk Milner's plans but had also undercut the African effort to withhold labor after the war to force up wages. A much better recruiting system saw sufficient cheap labor being offered to the mines from southern African sources. Assisted as well by technological innovations, the gold mines entered a period of rapid growth. Once in power the Het Volk leaders dropped their anti-capitalist rhetoric and quickly convinced the mining magnates that they would have a stable and efficient environment in which to operate.[173] Botha and Smuts were both in a hurry to build a new state. The mines were crucial for producing revenue for improved infrastructure, a proper educational system for whites and modernized agriculture, all of which were vital for the material prospects of the Afrikaners, who were now rapidly becoming urbanized, since the farms were no longer able to provide subsistence for large numbers.

Language struggles in the Orange River Colony

In the Orange River Colony, the white population composition and Milner's reconstruction policy produced a political response quite different from that in the Transvaal. According to Milner's information, Afrikaners made up close to 90 per cent of the white population. He accepted that most Afrikaners were intractable in their opposition to imperialism, but did not rule out 'attempting to leaven' through settling some British immigrants in the colony. He spent substantial funds on expropriating farms on which to settle immigrants. His policy disappointed almost everyone. First to express acute disappointment were the Afrikaners who had sided with the British in the war. When Hertzog, backed by Steyn, in 1906 founded his party, the Orangia Unie, he attracted all classes and factions – the poor and the rich, the collaborator and the Bittereinder, the *takhare* and the well educated – into a single movement.[174]

In the first election for the legislature of the Orange River Colony, in 1907, the party won thirty-one of the thirty-eight seats. Abraham Fischer became the first prime minister, but Hertzog wielded the most influence in the cabinet. Together with Steyn, who played an active role behind the scenes, Hertzog elevated the issue of language policy to a central position in the political recovery of the Boer people. Steyn's determination to fight the Anglo-Boer War to the bitter end was driven by the conviction that the British would look down on the defeated Boers. Lord Kitchener tried to assure him that the valor

171 N.G. Garson, '"Het Volk": The Botha-Smuts Party in the Transvaal, 1904-1911', *Historical Journal*, IX, I (1966), pp. 101-132.

172 Pienaar, *Die inspirerende opvoedings- en opheffingsaksie*, pp. 215).

173 Iain Smith, 'Capitalism and the South African War', in A. Thompson, (ed.), *The Impact of the South African War* (forthcoming).

174 J. Bottomley, 'The OFS and the Rebellion of 1914' Robert Morrell (ed.), *White but Poor* (Pretoria: Unisa, 1992), pp. 29-40.

of the Bittereinders would ensure that this would never happen, but Steyn was not convinced. Steyn and Hertzog now declared that the respect the British displayed towards Dutch as a public language would be the yardstick of the respect the British had for their community. Hertzog stated: 'It is impossible to co-operate with someone who displays contempt for the language. Someone who is lacking in respect for the language in which I was educated is lacking in his respect for me.'[175]

In drawing up education legislation, Hertzog, unlike Smuts, had no need to go out of his way to placate English voters. The legislation established parity between Dutch and English as mediums of instruction in state schools. Every child had to receive instruction in his or her mother tongue, whether it be English or Dutch, up to the sixth school year (called Standard Four). The other language was to be introduced gradually as a subsidiary medium. After the sixth year at least three subjects would have to be taught in Dutch and at least three in English.

W.K. Hancock, an Australian historian, who wrote the best biography of Smuts, called it an imaginative and constructive policy that sought a partnership between the two white communities. Yet it triggered a howl of protest from English-speakers across the country who saw no reason why their children had to learn another language. Hancock called it unjust for the English press to call Hertzog a 'racialist' for pursuing such a policy. If there were racialists, he observed, it was Hertzog's English tormentors who thought it proper for other people's children to speak English, but improper for their own children to speak Dutch.[176]

Differences soon manifested themselves among the Afrikaners in the two defeated republics. Initially these remained restricted to the leaders, and particularly between Botha and Smuts, on the one hand, and Steyn and Hertzog on the other. The Free State leaders remembered that Botha had explored peace terms with the British without consulting them. Matters hardly improved when he sent money to the Free State leaders after the war to buy a newspaper company, pretending that it was a personal gift rather than a sum acquired from an old ZAR government fund.[177] When Botha's Het Volk government in 1907 presented the spectacular newly discovered Cullinan diamond to Britain's King Edward VII as a sign of the Transvaal people's 'loyalty and affection', Steyn remarked: 'It would be better if Botha did not lay the loyalty butter on so very thick.'[178]

The move towards union

Milner left South Africa in April 1905, washing his hands of everything. Referring to the Liberal government's decision to introduce self-rule he wrote: 'In the face of a *volte face* so complete, obviously it would not have made the slightest difference what one did. It was evidently hopeless from the first to try and make a good job of South Africa for the British people.'[179]

---

175 *Hertzog-toesprake*, vol. 1, p. 87.
176 Hancock, *Smuts*, p. 243.
177 D.W. Krüger, *Die Kruger-miljoene* (Johannesburg: Perskor, 1979).
178 Karel Schoeman, *In liefde en trou* (Cape Town: Human & Rousseau, 1983), p. 123.
179 *Milner Papers*, vol. 2, p. 534.

Without large-scale immigration from Britain there was no competing British South African national spirit behind which English-speakers could rally. With the type of imperialism proposed by Milner and Chamberlain thoroughly discredited, Afrikaners began to unite around the idea of a *South African* South Africa.[180] As early as 1904 the Cape Afrikaner leader, F.S. Malan, had made the first plea for unification in terms significantly different from those of Milner. During the war he had fallen foul of the British military authorities. The newspaper *Ons Land*, which he edited, published a letter from two Boer women alleging that General French had allowed his soldiers to train a gun upon a Boer residence in which there were only Boer children and women. Although Malan had instructed his staff to delete all names, he was jailed for a year.

Overcoming great bitterness, he decided to work for national unity. In a major speech in September 1904, he rejected the influence of Downing Street that kept South Africa in a state of dependence and he also abandoned the republican ideal of a federated South Africa under its own flag. For the sake of white unity he was prepared to accept a 'free, united South Africa under the Union Jack.' But white unity could only be achieved on the basis of the equality of the two white sections of the population. They had to share the same privileges and obligations. 'Of course,' he added, that meant 'the maintenance of our language, church, morals and habits.'[181]

The leading role in crafting a political union of the four colonies was played by Smuts in Pretoria and Merriman in Cape Town. In May 1904 Smuts wrote to Merriman, pointing out that a united South Africa had always been a deeply felt political aspiration.[182] They sought the support of Steyn on his farm just outside Bloemfontein. He had emerged after the war as the Afrikaner leader with the greatest prestige (Merriman continued to address him as 'President'). The principles of a union acceptable to white South Africans were taking shape: minimum interference from London and maximum powers short of independence. They also decided to oppose any closer union movement until self-government had been granted to all four colonies. The inter-colonial conflicts over customs and the railways system had become much too acute for Milner's Kindergarten to solve. These divisions prompted the Afrikaner leaders to decide that a union rather than a federation was the best form of government for a future South African state.

In February 1908 the SAP under Merriman won the election in the Cape Colony with a landslide. In Pretoria and Bloemfontein there were also parties in power that favored a union on white South African terms. In Cape Town, Henry Burton, an English-speaking Bondsman and cabinet minister, wrote to Steyn in Dutch: 'Thank God, there are now *Afrikaansche regerings* [Afrikaner governments] from here to the Limpopo.'[183] The term 'Afrikaner' as an inclusive concept was once again popular. From now on Milner's Kindergarten had to take a back seat. In May 1908, at an intercolonial conference, a proposal by Smuts that unification was in the best interests of all South Africans and that all the parliaments of the colonies would send delegates to a national convention to draft

180 Thompson, *Unification*, p. 481.
181 F.S. Malan, *The True Ideal of South African Politics*, pamphlet issued in 1904; Bettie Cloete, *Die lewe van F.S. Malan* (Johannesburg: APB, 1946), pp. 180-83.
182 Davenport, *Afrikaner Bond*, p. 257.
183 Schoeman, *In liefde en trou*, p. 119.

a constitution was unanimously accepted. From the start the British High Commissioner was excluded from the process. At meetings of the national convention, held in different cities between October 1908 and May 1909, Sir Henry de Villiers, Chief Justice of the Cape, presided. Only white delegates attended, which made the continuing political exclusion of blacks outside the Cape Colony a *fait accompli*.

The delegates faced three critical issues. The first was the black and colored vote (see p. 305), the second was the issue of official languages, and the third a choice between a unitary and a federal system and a flexible and inflexible constitution. On the system of governance, delegates opted for a unitary, largely flexible, constitution modeled on the British Westminster system, ignoring the fact that it would take a different system to accommodate a society so diverse, so torn, and so color conscious as South Africa.

Hertzog concentrated on the language issue. He proposed 'equal freedom, rights and privileges' for English and Dutch. Every appointment in the new government had to be made 'with due regard to the equality of the two languages, and the right of every citizen of the Union to claim either language as the medium of communication between himself and any officer or servant in the Union.' According to one account of the convention debates, the English-speakers were so appalled by the proposal that the debate had to be postponed.[184]

The most dramatic moment of the convention was Steyn's subsequent intervention. Referring to the Boers and the British as different races, as was the custom at the time, he asked delegates to expunge 'the devil of race hatred' that had plagued the country for so long. The way to do that was to place the two languages on a footing of 'absolute equality in Parliament, in the Courts, in the schools and the public service – everywhere.' F.S. Malan, who at first opposed a comprehensive equality between English and Dutch, was moved to tears. Smuts kept silent. Steyn's plea was accepted and effective equality of treatment was secured in Article 137 of the Union Constitution. Hertzog was convinced that if necessary, the government would have to use compulsion to achieve it.[185] The article decreed:

> Both the English and Dutch languages shall be official languages of the Union and shall be treated on a footing of equality and possess and enjoy equal freedom, rights and privileges; all records, journals and proceedings of Parliament shall be kept in both languages, and all Bills, Acts and notices of general public importance or interest issued by the Government of the Union of South Africa shall be in both languages.[186]

Writing in *The State*, Preller called the Union's promise to place the two official languages on a footing of 'most perfect equality' as essential to Afrikaner support for the Union.[187]

After a draft constitution had been approved by the four colonies, the imperial cabinet introduced the South African Bill in the British parliament, where it passed without

---

184 Thompson, *Unification*, p. 135.

185 N.J. van der Merwe, *Marthinus Theunis Steyn* (Cape Town, 1921), pp. 227-79; F.S. Malan, *Die konvensie-dagboek* (Cape Town: VRS, 1951), p. 41; Leonard Thompson, *The Unification of South Africa* (Oxford: Clarendon Press, 1960), p. 192-8.

186 Henry John May, *The South African Constitution* (Cape Town: Juta, 1955), p. 623.

187 Gustav Preller, 'The Union and the Boer', *The State*, 1, 6 (1909), p. 638.

alteration. On 31 May 1910, eight years after the Peace of Vereeniging, the four colonies became the constituent provinces of the Union of South Africa. The British government asked Louis Botha to form a government prior to the first election. The Afrikaners inherited the political kingdom a mere eight years after the Boer leaders had signed the Peace of Vereeniging.

Colonialism and republicanism

'There are three competing influences at work in South Africa. They are Colonialism, Republicanism and Imperialism.'[188] So Sir Hercules Robinson, Governor of the Cape Colony and High Commissioner of South Africa, described politics in 1889. Onze Jan Hofmeyr in the Cape personified colonialism, or what historians call colonial nationalism; Alfred Milner and Joseph Chamberlain, an aggressive imperialism or Downing Street autocracy; and Paul Kruger, republicanism.

Between 1899 and 1905, Milner seemed to be the nemesis of the Afrikaner nation, with his emphasis on the aggressive and authoritarian side of British imperialism. But the tide of history was against him. Olive Schreiner astutely observed in 1900 that while Britain might succeed in crushing the republics, the fact that 'she has committed suicide in South Africa is a matter for no doubt.'[189] The ideology that would prevail was not Milner's style of imperialism but what Hercules Robinson termed colonialism, and Richard Jebb, an Australian writer, 'colonial nationalism.' Jebb published his comparative work, *Studies in Colonial Nationalism*, in 1905, after visiting the Transvaal and talking to Smuts. He said that what characterized colonies with a substantial white population, like Australia, Canada and South Africa, was their insistence on the removal of British dominance, or what Smuts called the 'disturbing influence of Downing Street.'[190] Such colonies wanted to develop their own separate sense of nationhood and protect their own liberties. They wanted a dominion status in which they could consider themselves free and could willingly tie themselves to Britain through trade and defense treaties.

Smuts was the one Afrikaner leader who enthusiastically embraced the transformation of the Empire into a family of dominions, soon to be called the Commonwealth. He saw South Africa's British connection as an essential condition for reconciliation between the two white groups and for prosperity for South Africa. He was exceptional in this regard. Pressure for a republic mounted from 1917, putting Botha's ruling South African Party on the defensive. Afrikaner leaders of the party and all its Dutch or Afrikaans newspapers paid at least lip service to republicanism. For Smuts such an idea was 'nonsense', and he said that those who wanted a republic would have to fight for it since the British Empire would not disband voluntarily.[191] But Smuts could not wish republicanism away. It increasingly became entangled with the defeat of the republics and the trauma of the Anglo-Boer War.

---

188 D.M. Schreuder, *Gladstone and Kruger: Liberal Government and Colonial 'Home Rule'* (Routledge and Kegan Paul, 1969), p. 473.

189 Schreiner, *Thoughts*, p. 348.

190 Hancock, *Smuts: The Sanguine Years*, p. 199.

191 D.F. Malan, *Die onafhanklikheid van Suid-Afrika* (Cape Town: Nasionale Pers, 1918); C.F.J. Muller, *Sonop in die Suide: geboorte en groei van die Nasionale Pers* (Cape Town: Nasionale Boekhandel, 1990), pp. 311-13.

Behind the issue of republicanism loomed a much larger issue. During the 1890s Olive Schreiner formulated what she saw as the real challenge for South Africa: *'How, from our political states and our discordant races, can a great, a healthy, a united and an organized nation be formed?'*[192] She pointed out that the 'race question', by which she meant the relationship between the two white communities, 'was complicated by a question of color, which presented itself to us in a form more virulent and intense than that in which it has met any modern people.'[193] For her the way in which the South African races had mixed with each other was the real bond that united them. The challenge was to build on that unity 'so that if in years to come a foreign foe should land upon her shores, and but six men were left to defend her, two English, two Dutch and two of native extraction . . . would stand shoulder to shoulder fighting for a land that was their own, in which each felt . . . that it had a stake.'[194]

But such a war never came. The Anglo-Boer War had etched white-black and white-colored divisions starkly. The British had raised false hopes among blacks and colored people that their political rights and status would be improved. After the war the British forgot about its promises and aided the Boers in restoring the ownership of farms that Africans had occupied. This produced a bitter harvest of racial distrust. The Union of South Africa confirmed black fears that whites did not want to share the land but would fight to keep it in their hands. In 1909 the British government turned down the demand of a multi-racial delegation headed by W.P. Schreiner, brother of Olive and Afrikaner Bond-backed prime minister of the Cape Colony, to override the constitution on the question of the political exclusion of blacks in the new Union. Black and colored people were on their own in their fight to prevent South Africa from becoming a 'white man's land.'

---

192 Schreiner: *Thoughts*, p. 57 (italics in the original).
193 Schreiner, *Thoughts*, p. 59.
194 Schreiner, *Thoughts*, p. 58.

Chapter 9

The Quest for a 'White Man's Country'

A unique society

Between the 1870s and 1913, the idea took root that South Africa, with the exception of areas of dense African settlement, was a white man's land, although the white community was only 340,000 strong in the late 1870s in a population of 2.2 million, and just over 1.25 million in a population of 6.4 million in 1915. During the twentieth century white politicians could glibly refer to South Africa, as Hendrik Verwoerd did in 1948, as 'a white man's country where he must remain the master.'[1] During the 1850s, however, South Africa was a mere territorial expression. In the eastern half of the land, the whites controlled large parts only precariously.

The society that began to take shape at this point was unique in the world of European colonization. It was neither a self-sufficient, essentially white society, like Australia, nor was it an India, where Europeans played a limited role as rulers, traders and missionaries. South Africa was something in between: where whites settled in considerable numbers they dominated but remained dependent on blacks as laborers or sharecroppers. South Africa was unique in another way as well. It was one of the very few European colonial settlements where the dominant racial minority was ethnically divided. The division was between the Dutch and English 'races', as the communities were called at the time. They were prepared to suspend their political rivalry only at the point where it jeopardized white supremacy itself. This was particularly the case in the Cape Colony, where Afrikaners had a majority of almost three to one over the English.

In the Republic of the Orange Free State (OFS), founded in 1854, the burghers experienced stiff Sotho opposition in attempting to acquire control of the fertile Caledon River valley. They later gained the upper hand, but in 1869, when they were on the point of conquering the mountain kingdom of Basutoland, Britain, at the request of the Sotho king, annexed it to prevent its dismemberment. After a brief spell under the control of the Cape Colony, Basutoland reverted to British rule in 1884 and would become independent eighty years later. In the ZAR the burghers had effective control over only the

---

1 A.N. Pelzer (ed.), *Verwoerd aan die woord* (Johannesburg: Afrikaanse Boekhandel, 1963), p. 13.

southern half until the 1880s. In Natal the settlers formed a small minority among the
great majority of Africans. During the 1840s and 1850s there were several unsuccessful
attempts to dump the 'surplus' Africans beyond the southern border. White control over
all of Natal was only established towards the end of the nineteenth century.

In the Cape Colony there was little enthusiasm for annexing the large semi-desert area
north of the Orange River, which became the German colony of South West Africa to the
north and the British protectorate of Bechuanaland to the northeast. The eastern border
of the colony long remained disputed. Between the Fish River, which became the border
in 1812, and the Natal western border was a zone approximately 250 miles wide. It was
excellent land densely populated by Xhosa-speakers. By 1850 the Xhosa had been driv-
en from the Fish River to over the Keiskamma River. Some wondered whether Cape control should also be extended to the Kei River and beyond that to the western border of
Natal (see map in front).

The pressure for such a move came from imperial proconsuls and British merchants
and land speculators in the eastern districts. Among the Cape Afrikaners there was no
strong demand for bringing all Xhosa land under colonial control. *De Zuid-Afrikaan*, the
main Dutch newspaper, wrote that the frontier wars had been the result of the injudicious treatment of the Xhosa. While 'our inferiors in the arts of civilized life, they [the
Xhosa] are perfectly competent to distinguish between power and imbecility, justice
and its contrary.'[2]

In 1855 J. de Wet, a leading Afrikaner in educational and political circles in Cape Town,
pointed to the implications of further land grabs and the fact that a much reduced Xhosa-
land was increasingly unable to support its population. De Wet said that he did not know
'what means remain to a people if you take away their country, more especially if they
depend for support, as the Kaffirs do, on their flocks, unless perhaps if you allow them
to steal.'[3] But F.W. Reitz, another leading western Cape Afrikaner, believed that the issue
could be resolved on the basis of superior white power: if another war against Africans
broke out sufficient colonists had to be called out 'to crush our barbarous neighbors from
one ocean to the other, and thus prevent them for many years from disturbing the safety
of the colony, and then will be the time for a Christian people to tame and civilize them.'[4]

Sir George Grey arrived in 1854 as the new governor after a spell in New Zealand where
he had had considerable success in promoting the integration of the indigenous population into the dominant economic and social order. The Empire at this point was preoccupied with the Victorian mission of extending the benefits of imperial citizenship
and culture to all, regardless of color or creed. After arriving in Cape Town, Grey decided
to apply a similar policy to the Xhosa in the area between the Kei and Keiskamma rivers
just beyond the white settlement. It was first known as British Kaffraria and from the
mid-1860s as the Ciskei.

Grey called his policy 'civilization through mingling', with the aim of transforming the
Xhosa in the east from 'unconquered and apparently unconquerable foes into friends
who may have a common interest with ourselves.' Some success had been achieved be-

---

2 *Afrikaner Political Thought*, p. 187.
3 *Afrikaner Political Thought*, p. 185.
4 *Afrikaner Political Thought*, p. 186.

fore Grey's arrival. The prime example was Lovedale, a racially mixed school in British Kaffraria, offering industrial and agricultural training. In 1878 it was described as an institution that was 'non-sectarian and non-denominational . . . All colors, white and black, and brown and yellow are to be found among the pupils.'[5]

Grey believed that traditional African society stood in the way of the kind of civilization he wished to advance. He curtailed the power of the chiefs and persuaded them to take salaries, which made them little more than functionaries. He also appointed salaried headmen to act as a police force. Over the longer run he wanted to replace chiefs with colonial magistrates, who would teach Africans the colonial laws and expedite modernization by improved educational and health facilities. He also planned to settle progressive white farmers among the blacks in order to stimulate the rise of a class of progressive African farmers, owning land on an individual basis. This class of small farmers had to spearhead the transition of Africans to 'civilization and Christianity.' Yet for all the fine phrases Grey had a subordinate place for most Africans in mind. They were to become 'useful servants, consumers of our goods and contributors to our revenue.'[6]

While the English press strongly supported Grey's initial plans calling for the breaking up of the African 'tribes' and 'nationalities', the Cape Afrikaners viewed them with considerable skepticism. They doubted that the Xhosa could be assimilated without a decisive defeat. They also questioned whether the colonists would embrace Grey's vision of amalgamation. For different reasons the Ciskei Xhosa also had serious reservations. They were already living in such a congested area that the introduction of white commercial farmers would seriously exacerbate the shortage of land. The chiefs feared Grey's plans as a major threat to their own status and role in traditional society.

Traumatized by successive frontier wars, the Ciskei Xhosa in the mid-1850s fell under the spell of a millenarian message of a young girl, Nongqawuse. At her behest they killed their cattle and destroyed their crops, expecting the ancestors to rise and food to fall from heaven. The population of just over 100,000 was decimated and fewer than 40,000 people remained in the Ciskei. Large numbers of Africans settled permanently on colonial farms. The government charged some of the chiefs and headmen who had promoted the slaughter and cleared land on both sides of the Kei for white settlement. Xhosa traditional society in British Kaffraria/Ciskei received a blow from which it would never recover.

When the proposal was mooted to incorporate the Ciskei Africans into the colony it split the colonists. The principal supporters were the English-speaking politicians of the eastern Cape, who sought separation of the eastern from the western Cape. The Afrikaner in general and the English politicians in the western Cape opposed both the incorporation of additional numbers of Africans and eastern separatism.

Despite this opposition, Grey's autocratic successor, Sir Philip Wodehouse, incorporated the Ciskei into the Cape Colony in 1865. The 1865 census taken afterwards recorded about 181,000 colonists and a total of 314,000 people. In 1878, just before a new wave of British annexations of African territories, a census showed 'coloreds' (that

5 Cited by Monica Wilson, 'Co-operation and Conflict: The Eastern Cape Frontier', in Monica Wilson and Leonard Thompson (eds.), Oxford History of South Africa (Oxford: Clarendon Press, 1969), p. 261.
6 Jeffrey Peires, The Dead Shall Arise (Johannesburg: Ravan Press, 1989), p. 317.

is, all people not considered white) making up about two-thirds of the Cape population and more than 80 per cent of South Africa as a whole.[7] Using modern methods, the demographer Jan Sadie puts the 1878 total figure for Africans in all of present day South Africa (excluding the colored people and Indians) at 2.2 million. There were in the late 1870s approximately 340,000 whites, of whom 220,000 were Afrikaners and 120,000 English-speakers.

POPULATION IN SOUTH AFRICAN TERRITORIES, 1878

	WHITES	'COLOREDS'	TOTAL
Cape	235,000	485,000	720,000
Ciskei	–	335,000	335,000
Transkei	–	501,000	501,000
Diamond Fields	15,000	30,000	45,000
Natal	20,000	320,000	340,000
OFS	30,000	15,000	45,000
Transvaal	40,000	250,000	290,000
TOTAL	340,000	1,936,000	2,276,000

Source: Anthony Trollope, *South Africa* (London: Chapman and Hall, 1878), vol. 1, p. 52.

A new wave of annexations

White supremacy depended on will rather than the substance of power. The pattern was set by British control in India, where, even after the dreadful 1857 mutiny, only 65,000 white soldiers controlled 300 million people in a huge area that now encompasses India, Pakistan and Bangladesh. In South Africa the official at the key juncture, Sir Bartle Frere, Governor of the Cape Colony and High Commissioner in South Africa from 1877 to 1880, had had experience in India. In South Africa, too, British military power rested to a large degree on bluff. At one stage in the 1880s, fewer than three thousand British troops were stationed in all of South Africa when the population approached four million.

By the mid-1870s the power balance in the deeper interior of South Africa was precarious, with people thinly scattered over a vast territory and divided into different polities. There were the two white republics and the two white colonies of the Cape and Natal, several semi-autonomous African societies with substantial power, including the Zulu in Natal, the Xhosa beyond the Kei, the Sotho east of the Caledon River, and the Tswana, Pedi and Venda in the Transvaal, and two recent British acquisitions, Basotoland and the diamond fields of Griqualand West, annexed in 1868 and 1871 respectively. Africans now formed a much more formidable opposition than two or three decades earlier after the disruption of the *Difaqane*. They had managed to acquire large supplies of guns on the Diamond Fields and were resisting white land grabs and excessive labor demands.

From far away in London it seemed to make sense to bring this patchwork of quarrelsome states under a single umbrella, which would enable Britain to reduce its ex-

---

7 Anthony Trollope, *South Africa* (London: Chapman and Hall, 1878), vol. 1, p. 52.

pensive military and financial commitments. While whites formed only a small minority, Britain proposed to build a new confederal or federal state around them. But there was a problem that Britain had to confront. It knew that the whites would only agree to accept responsibility for their own defense after British armies had crushed the strongest African societies. If, however, Britain succeeded too well in eliminating all threats to the white settlement, many of the whites would be happy to rid themselves of the British connection.

Despite these difficulties Britain pushed ahead. The Cape Colony received 'responsible government' in 1872, which made the cabinet responsible to Parliament. In return Britain expected it to accept the burden of expansion into native territories east of the Cape Colony's borders on the Cape. In 1873 the Cape cabinet appointed magistrates in the area beyond the Kei River as a first step in assuming administrative responsibility. Britain put both Griqualand West and Basutoland under the control of the Cape Colony.

Britain wished the Cape to become the foundation of a single state in South Africa. Lord Carnarvon, Secretary of State for the Colonies between 1874 and 1878, began pushing strongly for a federation of all the territories in southern Africa. Imperial officials considered the Transvaal burghers and the Zulu as the major obstacles to their plan. Carnarvon sent Theophilus Shepstone, the Natal Secretary for Native Affairs, to annex the Transvaal, which he did in April 1877. Sir Bartle Frere, who arrived in Cape Town in the same year, immediately concluded that a decisive defeat or a public humiliation of the Zulu, the strongest African polity in the deeper interior, would go a long way towards securing the support of the republican Afrikaners.

In 1879 Frere sent an insulting ultimatum to Cetshwayo, the Zulu king, to disband his army within a month. The king refused and defeated a British army, but a second British attack was successful and he was sent into exile to Cape Town. The kingdom was divided into thirteen chieftaincies, and many anti-Cetshwayo chiefs were appointed in order to neutralize the Zulu as a fighting force. In the same year British troops, assisted by a large Swazi contingent, defeated the Pedi under Sekhukhune. There was also violence in Griqualand West in 1877 and 1878, and in the latter year a conflict erupted among the Xhosa across the Kei River. This was put down by a combination of British and colonial troops and African allies. In 1879 the Cape Colony annexed Fingoland and Griqualand East, which formed approximately two-thirds of the territory between the Cape and Natal. When the Cape government tried to disarm the Sotho of Basutoland there was strong resistance, which spilled over into the Transkei. So determined and extensive was the resistance of the late 1870s that G.M. Theal, an early colonial historian, called it 'the most determined attempt ever made by the natives of South Africa to throw off European supremacy.'[8]

In all this tumult the plan for a South African confederation perished. Carnarvon had alienated too many white South Africans with his approach, and the Transvaal burghers had risen up in revolt. In Cape Town, popular enthusiasm for expansion had dwindled by the early 1880s. The humanitarian lobby in Cape Town pushed for direct British rule over the Xhosa beyond the Kei River, and in 1883 the Scanlen government, which de-

8 Cited by D.M. Schreuder, *The Scramble for Africa, 1877-1895* (Cambridge: Cambridge University Press, 1980), p. 62.

pended on Afrikaner support, also expressed itself in favor of the idea. But the Scanlen government soon fell, and with it went the idea.[9]

It is tempting to speculate what would have happened if the Transkei had gone the way of Basutoland, Bechuanaland and Swaziland, which had become British 'protectorates', and yet later High Commission territories. The Transkei would serve as the centerpiece in the ideology of segregation and apartheid. Had Britain also taken over the Transkei, the idea of a white South Africa existing side by side with some African 'reserves' would have lacked any credibility.

The new Cape cabinet favored expansion, and incorporated Gcalekaland and Thembuland in 1885 and Pondoland in 1894. As a result of the incorporation of all the territories beyond the Kei territories, the Cape Colony's population composition altered dramatically. The 181,000 whites of 1865 had doubled to 376,000 by 1891, while blacks in the colonial boundaries had increased fivefold from 314,000 to 1,480,000. Black voters increased fourfold.

Hand in hand with the annexation of the entire area between the Cape Colony and Natal went a change in the ideology of white supremacy. In both imperial circles and among Cape politicians and administrators the conviction had grown that subjected peoples had to be ruled through their own customs rather than be assimilated into Western culture. In India the British emphasis was now on preserving native customs in the personal sphere (marriage, inheritance and family succession). In Africa it would be extended to land, which would be owned by the community and held in trust by the chief.[10]

Cape Colony colonial administrators also abandoned the view that indigenous cultures had to be rooted out. They began to see value in the preservation of traditional African culture, recognizing the potential of using traditional authorities to bolster the colonial administration. John X. Merriman, a liberal Cape politician, seen by many as the most influential Englishman among the Afrikaners, encouraged this shift, and along with others succeeded in getting a Native Laws and Customs Commission appointed. In 1883 the Cape government accepted the commission's recommendation that Africans in the recently annexed territories be allowed to retain much of their own social and legal system. In the colony of Natal, Sir Theophilus Shepstone, Secretary for Native Affairs from 1848 to 1875, had introduced a similar policy. He had persuaded the colonial government in Natal to set aside reserves and to recognize the chiefs and the validity of customary law.

Yet despite these developments, the idea of South Africa as a white man's country was still a tenuous one. Merriman remarked that South Africa could never be a white man's country. Instead, the 'European race' had to see itself as 'the garrison', holding the country 'in the interests of civilization and good government and general enlightenment in South Africa.'[11]

---

9 Christopher Saunders, 'The Annexation of the Transkei', in Christopher Saunders and Robin Derricourt (eds.), *Beyond the Cape Frontier* (Cape Town: Longman, 1974), pp. 185-212.

10 Mahmood Mamdani, *Citizen and Subject: Contemporary Africa and the Legacy of Late Colonialism* (Princeton: Princeton University Press, 1996), pp. 49-50.

11 Cape Colony, *Debates in the House of Assembly*, 1894, col. 346; Phyllis Lewsen, *John X. Merriman*, (New Haven: Yale University Press, 1982), pp. 80-87, 297-8.

An English-Afrikaner clash over black people

In Cape politics the competition between the two white 'races' became superimposed on the white-black conflict. Afrikaners and the British in South Africa were set apart by their respective cultures, but their differences went much further. Within the Empire the British had become accustomed to dominating the political and economic system where they settled in sizeable numbers. In South Africa they were an urban people who, along with Jewish South Africans, were better educated than the Afrikaners, and had better access to capital and the trading network of the empire. They soon completely dominated the urban economy, and from this commanding position fervently advocated free trade. More than 90 per cent a farming people, the Afrikaners were mainly concerned about control over black and colored labor. They opposed free trade if it meant flooding the Cape market with imports at prices with which they could not compete. Instead they demanded protection for their products in a country that tested the ingenuity and endurance of farmers.

British South Africans and Afrikaners also occupied different niches in the industrial workforce. The gold and diamond mines attracted highly skilled white artisans from Britain; the Afrikaners, slow to acquire industrial skills, became supervisors of the black workers who performed the hard labor at the rock face. In the twentieth century the English-speaking workers protected their position through unions of artisans, which controlled access to skills; the Afrikaners formed general unions, much more inclined to seek state protection for white workers. But all white workers had a common interest in white political supremacy.

The Afrikaner-British clash over power and group status was played out predominantly in the field of politics. For some English-speaking politicians in the Cape Colony, power for the numerically superior Afrikaner group was almost as dreadful a prospect as black power. On the eve of the Cape's responsible rule in 1872, Merriman, then still a fervent imperialist, wrote: 'The difficulty in the way of self-government here is the mixed population; there is a great danger that we should become a Dutch republic under such a regime.'[12] The *Port Elizabeth Telegraph* put it even more forcefully: 'If the Afrikaner Bond [the party of the Afrikaners] is to be well beaten it will have to be done with the assistance of the black vote. The Dutch in the colony are to the English as two to one and if they combine . . . they can outvote us and inflict upon us all the absurdities of their national and economic prejudices.'

Both Afrikaner and English-speaking candidates competed hard for the favor of the colored people who had the vote under the Cape's liberal constitution. J.H. Hofmeyr, who in 1883 became leader of the Afrikaner Bond, claimed success in his Stellenbosch constituency where more than half the voters were colored. He warned his Bond followers not to attack the colored vote to avoid its being driven into the hands of the 'jingoes', their code word for extreme imperialists. With the exception of the liberal Afrikaner, Jacobus Wilhelm Sauer, Afrikaner candidates did not capture many African votes in the constituencies in the eastern part of the colony.

The issue of the African vote caused serious political tensions between Afrikaners

---

12 P. Laurence, *The Life of John X. Merriman* (London: Constable, 1930), p. 13.

and English-speaking politicians. Some of the latter saw attempts to limit the African vote not so much as an attack on liberal values but as an Afrikaner effort to weaken their support base. The result was that much more heat was generated in white ranks by infringements of black liberties than would have been the case if the dominant group had been culturally homogeneous. When the Cape Parliament, in 1887, limited the black franchise, the mining tycoon Cecil John Rhodes declared: 'If there had been none but English in that House [Parliament] the native question would have been settled long ago, but there was some peculiar stumbling block in the way of a settlement at present because there appeared to be a race feeling [between whites] in the colony, which gave rise to jealousies and suspicions, perhaps groundless.'[13] Rhodes pointed out that Indians had no vote in India and that Maoris in New Zealand could elect only four representatives. In Natal, where there were 40,000 whites and 500,000 Africans, the qualifications were drawn up in such a rigid way that virtually no non-white was qualified to vote. In all these British-dominated colonies very few had protested against this, but it was a big issue in the Cape Colony because of the rivalry between the two white groups.

With the Western world experiencing an upsurge of racism in the 1880s, the Afrikaner and English-speaking whites tended to justify white supremacy in different ways. English South African politicians and journalists drew particularly on the concept of a biological hierarchy of races and on the (social) Darwinian theory of the survival of the fittest. By contrast, Afrikaans or Dutch publications seldom considered the biological concept of race. They focused on an idealized picture of paternalism, depicting the white master as caring for faithful servants, and punishing them when they erred. The more modern among them sketched a world of competing organic nations, each with its own distinctive cultural heritage and needs, co-existing under the aegis of white supremacy.[14] Later both English and Dutch/Afrikaans publications fostered the idea of white 'trusteeship', under which blacks could gradually progress upwards to the levels Europeans had already reached.

Two issues confronted Cape politicians by the early 1880s after large numbers of Africans had been newly incorporated. One issue was preserving the vote for Westernized black or colored people as a safety valve; another was excluding the mass of traditional Africans. At that stage there were 50,000 white adult males in the colony compared to 200,000 African males of voting age largely confined to six eastern constituencies. Hofmeyr consistently rejected withdrawing the vote from anyone who already had it. He found the idea of exclusion on the basis of race distasteful, but also rejected the idea of adding 'blanket' voters (i.e. traditional African voters living on communal lands). The Bond backed Prime Minister Gordon Sprigg's Parliamentary Voters Registration Bill of 1887 that excluded everyone who met the property qualification only because of holding communal property. It ruled out large numbers of black voters in constituencies in the Transkeian territories. A Dutch newspaper described the bill as originating in a 'righteous and honest instinct of self-preservation.'[15]

---

13 Cape Colony, *Debates in the House of Assembly, 1887*, p. 103.

14 Andrew Walker, 'Boer and Boesman: Folk and Fyand: Attitudes to Race in *Ons Klyntji* and *Cape Monthly Magazine,* 1896-1906', honours diss., University of Cape Town, 1991.

15 For a study of newspaper comments see D.J.P. Haasbroek, 'Die ontstaan van die nie-blanke stemreg en die verskansing daarvan in die Suid-Afrika Wet van 1909', doctoral diss., US, 1958, pp. 99-128; this quote is on p. 111.

The Cape's non-racial franchise was never designed to go beyond the vote as a safety valve and open the door to black majority rule. But what would be the justification for the exclusion of large numbers of blacks? A *Zuid-Afrikaan* editorial formulated the issue bluntly: 'The key political question in all the states of South Africa was "who will be *baas*, Colonists or Natives?"'[16] Charles Darwin's theories of a hierarchy of races attracted some, but there were obstacles to applying them to the system of white supremacy in South Africa. Some British imperialists tended to see the struggle for survival in South Africa not only as one between the white and black races, but also as one in which the British or Anglo-Saxon race had demonstrated its superiority to the Afrikaners as an indolent, inert, and unenlightened people for the most part.

An Afrikaner styling himself 'Kolonist' raised the issue in the *Volksbode* of 14 March 1889. 'Does the white man have the right, merely because he is white and more civilized and stronger, summarily to "move" a Kaffir tribe if he needs their land or if the barbarian acts like a barbarian?' He pointed out that most of the English considered themselves 'just as much superior to the Afrikaners as we consider ourselves to be above the Kaffirs.' What, 'Kolonist' asked, would one say if the English declared that 'the higher race' was entitled in the interests of civilization in general 'to clear up the Afrikaners and expropriate what belongs to them?'

Blacks naturally saw the proposed legislation as an attempt to squash their political voice. The founding of the Afrikaner Bond in 1880 had spurred the founding of the *Imbumba Yama Nyama* in Port Elizabeth, a black political organization that claimed to be 'the true Afrikaner Bond.' Hofmeyr's organization, it said, was only a 'Boeren Bond.' It achieved considerable success in black voter registration. When the agitation for franchise reform built up in white ranks, a Mfengu ex-teacher, John Tengu Jabavu, established the first independent Xhosa-language newspaper, *Imvo Zabantsundu*. It campaigned vigorously for liberal candidates in the east. Jabavu wrote that the black vote had been used in the best interests of the country, and added that it had been steadily and consistently 'employed to strengthen the English, or the party of right and justice in the country.'[17]

But which was 'the party of right and justice'? It was the politicians, mostly English-speaking merchants and professionals, but including J.W. Sauer, who won the African vote and styled themselves the 'Friends of the Natives', or Cape liberals. They were an informal grouping holding the balance of power between the Afrikaner and English-speaking blocs in Parliament. The 'Friends of the Natives' addressed African grievances, such as pass laws and 'location' regulations, which segregated blacks residentially, liquor laws that restricted their access to alcohol, the misadministration of justice, and an increasing anti-black tendency in Parliament.[18] They rejected Sprigg's 1887 bill limiting the 'blanket' African vote. Merriman considered it likely to 'stir up bitter feelings among the natives', while Sauer argued that whites need not fear being outvoted in Parliament because the black voters who were affected lived in only a few constituencies. James Rose Innes and C.W. Hutton, son-in-law of Andries Stockenstrom, said that the bill would commit a grievous wrong against Africans.[19]

16 Rodney Davenport, *The Afrikaner Bond* (Cape Town: Oxford University Press, 1966), p. 101.
17 Davenport, *Afrikaner Bond*, p. 121.
18 André Odendaal, *Vukani Bantu: The Beginnings of Black Protest Politics in South Africa to 1912* (Cape Town: David Philip, 1984), pp. 1-29.
19 Cape Colony, *Debates of the House of Assembly, 1887*, pp. 73-107.

Certain politicians, however, formulated the issue explicitly in terms of the struggle between the two white 'races' for political dominance. In 1887 an outcry erupted when P. Solomon, a member of Parliament, stated frankly: 'We English in this country depend for a large degree upon the native vote.' If the bill were to be carried, he said, Bond candidates would prevail over the English in some eastern constituencies, 'a serious thing for those districts.'[20]

The English press was divided. Calling Solomon's speech unwise, the *Cape Times* denied that the English-speaking colonists used the 'native vote' to 'counteract the Dutch', but the *Cape Argus* said Solomon displayed a rare quality in politics: honesty. In the eastern part of the colony *The Barkly East Reporter* deplored Solomon's stand, but said that he was right to warn that 'the native vote is our only protection from a dominant Dutch majority.' The *East London Advertiser* made it clear that it preferred the Afrikaner colonists to the natives as political allies; it asked its own readers how many members of Parliament could swear that their opposition to the bill was from 'pure love or justice to the native races.' It posed this question: 'Will any other member go through the same pantomime and pledge his honor that his wish is not to overcome Dutch influences by a preponderance of native voters?' Any attempt by an English sector to swamp Afrikaner voters with black support would create a 'Frankenstein monster', who 'learning his strength, turns around in turn upon his master.'[21]

On the Afrikaner side *Di Patriot,* the populist Dutch newspaper, put the issue in the bluntest possible terms: some politicians wanted to keep the Boers in check through 'black troops and black votes.'[22] But Hofmeyr and *De Zuid-Afrikaan* knew that it was dangerous to mobilize the Afrikaners against the English. Any escalation of Afrikaner-English rivalry would be most undesirable as long as the enfranchisement of blacks in the territories beyond the Kei remained unresolved. On 14 April 1885 *De Zuid-Afrikaan* wrote: 'The great majority [of whites] must realize that they must toe one line in the struggle for existence against the natives.' The struggle for supremacy was still unresolved and it was 'not absolutely certain that the colonists rather than the natives would prevail in the great struggle.' On 14 July 1886 *De Zuid-Afrikaan* wrote: 'It is supremely important that the Dutch do not separate themselves, like the Irish, but instead ally themselves with the English who share their views.'

To Hofmeyr, the franchise reform of 1887 still left far too many black voters on the roll. He warned that the white population would be 'utterly swamped' if no further measures at all were enacted, and urged the House to act immediately while 'the natives' were not yet organized, but 'only feeling their way.' Hofmeyr now proposed a franchise and ballot bill, which became law in 1892, raising the franchise qualifications, which were quite low. The law provided for a rudimentary educational test for prospective voters, and increased the existing occupational qualification from £25 to £75. The law did not target voters on the basis of race as such, but fixed a higher standard of Western 'civilization.' It was legislation that liberals could live with more easily. In a speech to Parliament, Sauer praised the 'moderation' of the Dutch in assuring that there would be no legislation de-

---

20 Haasbroek, 'Die ontstaan van die nie-blanke stemreg', p. 108.
21 Haasbroek, 'Die onstaan van die nie-blanke stemreg', p. 126.
22 *Di Afrikaanse Patriot,* 22 and 29 April 1887 and 3 June 1887.

signed purely on color lines. Merriman said that he was eager to minimize the weight of the 'Coolie and barbarian.'[23]

English-speaking liberals and Bond politicians had rivaling views, on the whole, on how whites could best secure their position. Liberals favored *laissez faire* economic policies over protectionism. They defended the right of blacks to hire and purchase land anywhere in the Cape Colony, but proposed no grants of land or other form of remedial action for the poorer classes. They urged Parliament to educate blacks to become a productive labor force, warning that failure would lead to the 'triumph of barbarism.'[24] While maintaining a higher level of subsidy for white schools, the colonial state did give grants-in-aid to mission schools and founded schools for Africans. Many whites also attended mission schools. In 1883 6,000 whites were attending mission schools with 32,000 colored or black pupils, and by 1891 one out of three whites attended these schools.[25]

Liberals advocated the absorption of an educated African elite into the society of the 'civilized'. As James Rose Innes, one the most consistent liberals, remarked: the colony should make its objective to 'draw the natives into the circle of our political, social and national life, as they deserved it and became qualified for it.'[26] Liberals supported the vote as a safety valve, but not as opening the door to mass-based African participation. They did not believe that political parties would be able to shed their racial identity, or would make decisions with the general interest of the population at large in mind.

The Afrikaner Bond shared some liberal values, including the separation of church and state, secular education and the freedom of the press. It supported an independent judiciary to protect common rights and the Cape's progressive administration. Endorsing the principle of political equality for the 'civilized' in 1892, Hofmeyr did not object to a Malay in Parliament. 'His objection to color was not so strong,' he said, 'that he would object to see a well-educated man like [Ahmed] Effendi sitting in the House.'[27]

But Hofmeyr's Bond, as an Afrikaner party, stressed communal ties in a way that excluded non-whites. As a farmers' party, it backed the employer over the employees, and as a party representing the less educated part of the white electorate it protested against the limited funds spent on white education, particularly on rural schools.[28] Hofmeyr believed that blacks had to be kept powerless for the sake of stable economic development. Whites had to civilize blacks under their control, but the goal was to turn them into 'useful assistants of the civilized and civilizing race.'[29]

Although Hofmeyr used culture rather than color or race as a measure, sometimes he used the terms or their euphemisms interchangeably, as when he remarked that the line of demarcation was between 'barbarism and civilization, as existed in India, Natal, and

23 Cape of Good Hope, *Debates in the House of Assembly, 1892*, pp. 157-203.

24 *De Zuid-Afrikaan,* 12 August 1879.

25 The above paragraphs are based on Phyllis Lewsen, 'The Cape Liberal Tradition: Myth or Reality?' *Race,* 13 (1971), pp. 65-80; Stanley Trapido, '"The Friends of the Natives ..."' in S. Marks and A. Atmore (eds.), *Economy and Society in Pre-industrial South Africa* (London: Longman, 1980), pp. 247-74.

26 Cape Colony, *Hansard of the House of Assembly,* 1887, p. 107.

27 Cape Colony. *Hansard of the House of Assembly,* 1893, pp. 205-07.

28 Davenport, *Afrikaner Bond,* p. 118.

29 G.D. Scholtz, *Die ontwikkeling van die politieke denke van die Afrikaner* (Johannesburg: Perskor, 1974), vol. 3, pp. 315-17.

other countries, where the distinction was between the colored barbarian and the civilized European.'[30] Some mainstream English politicians like Sprigg, C.T. Scanlen and Rhodes were eager to align themselves to or work closely with the Bond. In the 1898 election even Merriman and Sauer, the two most prominent liberals, threw their weight behind it.

The Glen Grey Act of 1894

During the 1890s labor had become the most crucial issue confronting South African legislators. How could the large numbers of Africans living in the reserves and locations be channeled to white farms and into the mines, to meet the acute shortages of labor? R.P. Botha, a prominent farmer and member of the Cape Parliament, told the 1893 Labour Commission bluntly: 'A man only works either through the pressure of fear or of hunger.' The Cape's constitution ruled out compulsion or intimidation. Hunger was left. Most blacks lived in the African reserves where they could still find subsistence. However, pressure was building up in white politics to allow whites to buy up land in the African territories. If this were allowed blacks would be compelled to seek work or go hungry.

Afrikaners across South Africa showed little interest in using the reserves to preserve traditional African culture. The Bond criticized African traditions like polygamy, which helped blacks to 'outbreed' whites. *De Zuid-Afrikaan* warned that blacks counted on the 'tribal or quasi-tribal system of property . . . to ensure eventual victory over the colonists for Kaffirdom in South Africa.' The strongest statement against the reserves came from President Reitz of the OFS, writing in a Cape journal in 1891. Reitz urged the eradication of the tribal system altogether, as well as breaking up all urban locations for black residence, thus compelling all blacks living there to become laborers. 'Self-preservation is the first law of nature and if the "Caucasian" must either remain the dominant race or perish, then of the two evils let us choose the least.'[31]

Segregation developed in South Africa by marrying an economic system based primarily on migrant labor and a political system that ruled out black competition. Shepstone's reserves in Natal and the Cape's indirect rule of the Transkei were important formative influences, but so were the precedents established in the mining town of Kimberley that sprung up in the late 1860s. Many local Englishmen and Afrikaners, as well as blacks, colored people and foreigners had sought their fortune there. In response to pressure by white miners in 1872, all 'servants' were denied licenses to search for or to trade in diamonds. All but a few licensed non-white diggers were shut out. Initially, both the white and black labor force was to be housed in compounds, but the white workers refused. They used their rights as full citizens as a means of refusing also to submit to pass laws or beatings. Blacks had no such rights and no similar power; increasingly a white-black labor division came about, which would be reproduced in most other towns and cities.

Cecil John Rhodes, who became prime minister in 1890, looked at the issue of the African labor supply from his position as a mining magnate and large employer in

30 Cape Colony, *Hansard of the House of Assembly,* 1892, pp. 198-203.
31 F.W. Reitz. 'The Native Question', *Cape Illustrated Magazine,* November 1891.

Kimberley. Here his De Beers Consolidated Mines controlled its African migrant labor force tightly through passes, contracts and closed compounds where the workers lived. Migrants were paid the wages of single men on the grounds that their plot in a reserve ensured a livelihood for their families. The idea took root that the small, scattered African reserves provided a home base for the African labor force and for their exclusion from political rights. That these territories were quite insufficient to provide subsistence in the longer term, or a political outlet for all, seemed to trouble few whites. On 7 August 1894 the Bloemfontein *Express* reported a speech by Rhodes on the reserves, stating 'that certain parts of the country must be the home of the natives. Not everyone must have a piece of land, but it must be a place where people could go back to after working.' The economic function of the reserves always predominated.

The idea of developing the reserves as an integral part of both the economic and the political system gained momentum as Rhodes embarked on his grand expansion schemes. In 1894 the Rhodes cabinet annexed Pondoland, the last remaining territory between the Cape and Natal that was not under white control. It brought an additional 400,000 Africans into the colony's bounds. Rhodes dreamed of a South African state under the British flag that would add the Transkeian territories, the vast area of Bechuanaland, and the lands beyond the Zambezi to the two British colonies (the Cape and Natal) and the republics (the OFS and the Transvaal). Since Africans might then outnumber whites by six to one or even more in such a state there was little chance that this could be projected as a white man's country.

Rhodes knew that his chances of winning Bond support for this vision were remote in the absence of a policy towards blacks it could endorse. After consultation with Hofmeyr he worked for what he would later call a 'Natives' Bill for Africa', with principles that could be applied throughout South Africa and the rest of the subcontinent. Such a bill would entrench white supremacy through restricting the advance of a black bourgeoisie and by excluding from the vote those who lived on land held in communal property. Whites should be prohibited from acquiring this land, which should be given on individual tenure to blacks. The 'gentle stimulant' of a labor tax would force blacks living on these lands to work for part of the year in the colony. Behind the scenes Hofmeyr worked for such a law, which he hoped would satisfy both liberals and white supremacists.[32]

The laboratory for the ideas of Rhodes and Hofmeyr was a small, overcrowded but coveted area of some 250,000 morgen north of Queenstown, called Glen Grey. Forty years earlier Glen Grey had been assigned to the Tambookie branch of the Thembu people and was now a reserve, housing about eight thousand Thembu families. A number of men used it as a base, going out from there for short-term employment on white farms. A few white farmers also lived there and, along with the Thembu, they clamored for the land to be opened up to individual tenure. In 1892 Rhodes, with Bond support, appointed a commission to look into the problems there. Its report proposed a shift from communal to individual title, with the land divided up equally into 55-morgen plots among the African families. Hofmeyr insisted that whites be prohibited from buying land in the area, but he and Rhodes also rejected the grant of 55 morgen for each African family,

---

32 This and the following paragraphs are based on Robert Rotberg, *The Founder: Cecil Rhodes and the Pursuit of Power* (Johannesburg: Southern Books, 1988), pp. 468-74.

fearing that large numbers would then congregate on a single plot, and discourage their going out to work in the colony. The new law provided instead for farms of four morgen, each granted on the basis of ownership or freehold. The right of the eldest son to inherit the plot was enforced, with the intention of compelling other sons to learn 'the dignity of labor' and to seek work in the colony. A tax of ten shillings a head was imposed to press all the younger sons to find work to pay the tax. These men were expected to return to the reserve after they had stopped working in the colony, with communal grazing rights preserved to meet their needs. Ownership of the new plots would not be a qualification for the vote.

In presenting this bill in Parliament, Rhodes spoke in terms the Afrikaner Bond welcomed. Africans were 'lazy', he said, at best 'children' and at worst 'barbarians.' 'It had to be brought home to them that in future nine-tenths of them would have to spend their lives in manual labor. African workers needed a special education towards that end. Schools were now overproducing 'a certain class of human being – "the Kafir parson", admirable as individuals but as a class dangerous, inciting other blacks by informing them that they were oppressed.'

It was hoped that the act would deflect black political attention away from Parliament to new institutions in the reserves. There were Location Boards, elected by registered plot holders, and District Councils, for which the Location Boards elected six members, while the government appointed another six to advise on local issues like the allocation of local levies for public works, schools and clinics. The Glen Grey plan was formulated to provide for productive African peasants to influence politics where they lived, but it did not work out this way. Chiefs dominated the councils, edging out the christianized Africans who had been the focus of previous policy. The extension of the act to the rest of the reserves excluded the majority of traditional Africans from the political system and relegated them to a special category 'in a sense citizens but not altogether citizens.'[33]

The notion of South Africa as a white man's country was not compatible with the growing numbers of blacks on the voters' roll. The aim of the Glen Grey Act was not only an attempt to channel sufficient black labor to the colony. It had as much to do with the need of white supremacists to use the existence of black reserves as a justification for the idea of a 'white South Africa.' Liberals also saw some merit in the idea of black reserves, and particularly in legal bars to prevent whites from buying land in the reserves. Innes, Sauer and Merriman supported the Glen Grey Act, which was enacted in 1894.[34]

A much greater number of African migrants began to oscillate between the reserves, but there were also growing numbers living on a permanent basis in shacks on the periphery of towns and cities. In 1899, the prime minister of the Cape, W.P. Schreiner, said that it would be best to get such clusters of Africans 'compounded', while they worked for wages, then 'at the end of their term . . . go back to the place whence they came – to the native territories, where they should really make their home.'[35] Officials seized on

---

33 Richard Parry, '"In a Sense Citizens, but Not Altogether Citizens": Rhodes, Race and the Ideology of Segregation in the Late Nineteenth Century', *Canadian Journal of African Studies*, 17, 3 (1983), pp. 337-91

34 Davenport, *The Afrikaner Bond*, p. 155.

35 Maynard W. Swanson, 'The Sanitation Syndrome: Bubonic Plague and Urban Native Policy in the Cape Colony, 1909-1909', *Journal of African History*, 18, 3 (1971), pp. 387-410.

an outbreak of bubonic plague in the largest cities to insist that the destruction of slums would prevent another plague. Africans had to be housed some distance away in compounds or locations outside of towns. Between 1902 and 1904 cities across South Africa passed legislation compelling Africans to live in such segregated locations. The idea of sealing off the white city from black locations began to take root.

Early segregation

White supremacy in the last quarter of the nineteenth century was not an internally consistent creed. In the Cape Colony political parties were happy to support the black and colored vote provided it was not viewed as something more than a safety valve for the white middle class. Between 1895 and 1897 the number of colored and black voters on the electoral roll went up from approximately 5,000 to 13,900. Most were colored people, who were never seen as a political threat. By the beginning of the next century a census showed that their total population was 445,000. Most shared language, culture and religion with the Afrikaners. Colored people seized the opportunities offered to them for education and industrial training, and, by the end of the century, they dominated at least half of the trades in Cape Town and the major western Cape towns.[36]

From the outset the two Boer republics had ruled out the franchise for any non-white. Merriman had declared in 1876 that the northern Afrikaners practiced what he called 'the Dutch republican mode of dealing with the Natives, which means absolute subjection.'[37] But the policy of oppression was not uniquely Dutch or republican. The English colony of Natal exposed Africans and Indians alike to wide-ranging discrimination and exclusion on the basis of race.

Basutoland served as a pseudo-reserve for the Free State, which used its African labor without assuming any financial or political responsibility for the territory where they lived. Within the Free State's borders the republic carved out three tiny, isolated reserves for Africans, a total of 74,000 morgen, less than one per cent of the land. It made no allowance for African customs and refused to recognize African tribal law or traditional marriages. All civil and criminal disputes were under the jurisdiction of Roman-Dutch law, whatever the race or status of the litigants themselves.

Yet there were limits to the oppression in the Free State. Blacks had access to the courts, although they seldom made use of it, and, in 1894, a labor commission said that blacks were free to refuse to work and rejected legislation to compel them to work for farmers. Its report implied that farmers needed to treat their servants better in order to attract workers. It drafted a bill that aimed at protecting servants against masters withholding wages and establishing a greater measure of equality between masters and servants before the law. But, after a heated debate, the Volksraad rejected the bill by a close vote of 24 to 22.[38]

36 See the essays in Nigel Worden and Clifton Crais (eds.), *Breaking the Chains: Slavery and its Legacy in the Nineteenth Century Cape Colony* (Johannesburg: Witwatersrand University Press, 1994).

37 P. Lewsen (ed.), *Selections from the Correspondence of John X. Merriman* (Cape Town: VRS, 1960), pp. 23-5.

38 H.J. van Aswegen, 'Die Verhouding tussen blank en nie-blank in die Oranje Vrystaat, 1854-1902', doctoral diss., University of the OFS, 1968, pp. 581-6.

During the 1870s President Burgers of the Transvaal sought to pursue a new kind of racial policy. With a penchant for bold schemes regardless of resources or political obstacles, he attempted to introduce Sir George Grey's policy of amalgamation. He sought, he said, to eradicate the 'barbaric' idleness and primitive customs of Africans by breaking up concentrations of them, abolishing chieftainships, and allowing individual Africans to acquire private property. Black demand for Western goods, such as clothes, was to be stimulated to encourage people to work. Industrious blacks would have voting rights and also equal rights with employers. But a Volksraad commission promptly rejected President Burgers' proposals for property rights and the franchise for blacks.[39]

The ZAR appointed the president as paramount chief over all the native tribes. He was to uphold African traditional law in all the tribal areas but appoint white officials as Native Commissioners in each. The ZAR's goal was to subjugate all African chiefdoms within its boundaries. It succeeded in neutralizing the power of the Pedi in the 1880s and the Venda in the 1890s. Swaziland, to the east, became a ZAR dependency, with two-thirds of the land now in white hands. The London Convention required the ZAR to introduce a 'Locations Commission' to demarcate reserves for each tribe. But little additional land for locations was set aside and for some tribes no provision at all was made.

Rank and file Transvaal burghers had strongly opposed reserves, or locations as they were called there, but Paul Kruger argued, in 1893, that small African groups especially needed some land set aside for them so that they did not feel oppressed. He asked: 'Was it fair or Christian to drive them off the land?'[40] The progressive Boer leadership concluded that the locations represented an important safety valve for African unrest. Testifying before the Transvaal Labour Commission of 1903, Koos de la Rey, a Boer general, and Piet Cronjé, Superintendent of Native Affairs prior to the war, warned that breaking up the locations could spur African resistance.[41] Between a fifth and a quarter of blacks in the Transvaal now lived in such areas. Africans could buy land elsewhere but only through third parties, like missionaries, who registered the land for them in a trust that they administered.

The ZAR hoped that Africans would become a source of revenue and labor for whites, but it was too inefficient to impose its will on the countryside.[42] In 1895 the Kruger government replaced the inefficient hut tax with a £2 yearly tax to be paid by every African adult male, in addition to ten shillings for every wife he had. The Volksraad welcomed the new plan, as did the relatively progressive *Weekly Press,* terming the measure 'fair and equitable.' Otherwise, the paper said, only 'a very small proportion [of Africans] can be induced to come out and work.'

The Volksraad, greatly frustrated by the shortage of African labor, urged the government to compel Africans to work and 'know their place' in society. The ZAR political leadership, on the other hand, advised moderation. Kruger publicly disagreed with a

---

39 M.S. Appelgryn, *Thomas François Burgers: Staatspresident 1872-1877* (Cape Town: HAUM, 1979), pp. 105-6.

40 *De Volksstem,* 6 September 1893.

41 *Report of the Transvaal Labour Commission, 1903,* pp. 274-7, 501.

42 C.T. Gordon, 'Aspects of Colour Attitudes and Public Policy in Kruger's Republic', in K. Kirkwood (ed.) *St Antony's Papers* (Oxford: Oxford University Press, 1969), p. 100. Except where otherwise indicated, all the material on race relations in the ZAR that follows is drawn from this article.

burgher who said that Africans should have fewer rights than white men and refused to bar them from access to the highest judicial and executive bodies. He told the Volksraad in 1890 that 'where right and justice were concerned, the highest authority in the land always had to be accessible to hear and consider requests and complaints from whomsoever.' He added that many blacks who were becoming civilized could not be placed on the same tray as the 'raw heathens.'[43] General Piet Joubert, Superintendent of the Natives, and P.J. Potgieter, Native Commissioner of Waterberg in the north of the Transvaal, struck a similar note, with Potgieter writing in 1892: 'These Kaffirs of ours, who are now our friends and who can become a source of strength in our country, may become our enemies if we proceed in an injudicious way.'[44]

A strong lobby in the Volksraad resisted amelioration of the crude and harsh system. When, in 1897, the government proposed exempting educated and more 'civilized' Africans from the necessity to wear a badge – the most humiliating feature of the pass laws – Jan de Beer countered that 'a kafir was a kafir, whether he was educated or not.' Louis Botha, a future prime minister of the Union of South Africa, opposed the exemption, especially because it would also exempt some colored people, already, he said, 'proud, vain, ignorant, impertinent and obstinate.'

There was an outcry also at the idea of providing land where Africans working on the Witwatersrand could live in a community without supervision. A government commission turned it down on the grounds that such places 'do not improve the kaffirs in any way, but only tend to their deterioration.' Carl Jeppe, a spokesman for the mines, defended the mines' own compound system as 'the only method of keeping natives under supervision and preventing them from falling into the temptation of stealing.' Transvaal newspapers, particularly the conservative *Volksstem*, defended racial oppression in all its multiple forms. It even approved the flogging of Africans who dared to walk on Johannesburg's sidewalks as a way of reminding them that the city was part of the ZAR in which 'the descendants of Ham can learn to know their place.' Like Africans, coloreds and Indians, too, could not trade in their own name or own immovable property. Sentiment against both groups was as strong in some respects as against Africans. Any 'colored' man – and by that was meant all non-white men – who had sexual intercourse with a white women could face punishment of six years of hard labor and sixty lashes.

A small minority of ZAR burghers objected to the pervasive ideology of white supremacy. One such was Jan Celliers, who was to become a prominent Afrikaans poet. In a debate among members of a commando during the Anglo-Boer War, Celliers had asked: 'Is the Kaffer treated justly and must he get more or fewer privileges?' Celliers said that the ZAR legislation intended to squeeze the black man out of the political and social system to preserve the entire country for the whites and their descendants. He protested that there was still space for everyone and blacks were not bothering whites. He challenged his audience to mention a single law that had the interests of blacks rather than whites in mind. 'Gentlemen,' he concluded, 'let us be honest, call our action prudence, call it self-preservation, call it a calculated risk in attempting to maintain the upper hand for us and our descendants, call it exercising the right of the strongest, call it business,

---

43 *De Volksstem*, 8 March 1892, ZAR Eerste Volksraad, *Notulen*, 1897, Debate of 11 August 1897.
44 *De Volksstem*, 31 July 1890.

but do not give it the name of *inschikklijkheid, menschlievenheid, billijkheid* (complaisance, brotherly love, fairness).[45] Only six burghers out of the throng, including J.F. Naudé, later a founder of the Afrikaner Broederbond, supported his perspective.

A suggestion that the racial tables might one day be turned appears in a 1911 poem, 'Kafferlied' (Song of a Caffre) written in the variant of Afrikaans many black farm laborers spoke. The poet was Totius (the pen name of J.D. du Toit, son of S.J. du Toit), a leading figure in the first generation of Afrikaner nationalist poets.

> *The caffre first comes; the white man he comes later*
> *The white man seizes the land; the black man seizes later . . .*
> *The white man he lives now, the caffre he lives later*
> *The white man he laughs now, the caffre he laughs later.*[46]

The aggressive policy of imperialism carried out by Joseph Chamberlain and Alfred Milner in South Africa after 1895 caused a sharp intra-white division in Cape politics, which also affected the racial issue. The Progressive Party, now under the leadership of Rhodes, strongly supported the British assault on the republics. Under pressure from the Kimberley branch, Rhodes changed his slogan from 'equal rights for all white men' south of the Zambezi to 'equal rights for all civilized men', in an attempt to attract colored voters, since Rhodes had no intention of politically embracing Africans. To attract the colored votes the Progressives, in association with the pro-British South African League in 1896, established branches for colored voters.

As a counter to the Progressives, the Bond struck up an alliance with liberals like Merriman and Sauer, who strongly opposed the Anglo-Boer War. John Tengo Jabavu, Xhosa editor of the newspaper *Imvo Zabantsundu,* agreed to support that alliance in the 1898 election. Hofmeyr campaigned on a claim that he had never taken the vote away from a single African. The Bond-led alliance narrowly won the election.[47] In the first post-election parliamentary session Rhodes attacked the alliance with great gusto; he could not believe, he said, that a senior Bondsman, I.J. van der Walt of Colesberg, had said he was eager to see Jabavu sit in the house. 'What he has said,' Van der Walt replied, 'was that he would rather sit beside an honest native than a dishonest white man.'[48]

Challenges to the idea of a white land

In his post-war reconstruction of South Africa Milner, now the imperial proconsul for all of South Africa, called the quest for a white man's country 'a root principle' and argued that South Africa could not turn itself into a white man's country if it was 'full of poor whites.' The next chapter deals with the crisis of Afrikaner poor whites posing a threat to South Africa as a white man's country, as defined here by Milner. In this chapter the focus is on the agrarian crisis where Afrikaner bywoners, or tenants-at-will, found themselves challenged by black labor-tenants or sharecroppers.

45 Fransjohan Pretorius, *Kommandolewe tydens die Anglo-Boereoorlog* (Cape Town: Human & Rousseau, 1991), pp. 284-5.
46 *Totius. Versamelde gedigte* (Cape Town: Tafelberg, 1988), p. 42.
47 Rotberg, *The Founder,* pp. 607-16.
48 I wish to thank Mordechai Tamarkin for this quote.

In the final decades of the nineteenth century and in the first decade of the twentieth century, it seemed possible that a substantial section of blacks would be incorporated in a way that would militate against the idea of a white man's land and white solidarity. Black peasants and black voters seemed set to become a new class enjoying greater standing than white bywoners or tenant farmers and other poor whites.

As cultivators, black peasant farmers were well ahead of the republican burghers, who were mostly stock farmers. In 1904 a well-informed observer wrote with reference to the eastern half of the country: 'The archaic Kaffir is the best all-round cultivator of South Africa so far.'[49] Africans in Basutoland and the OFS keenly responded to the large market for wheat, maize and vegetables that had sprung up on the Diamond Fields. During the 1890s a group of farmers from the eastern Free State demanded that the Volksraad prohibit large-scale growing of grain by blacks, because white farmers could not compete.

Lacking capital and experience, the Afrikaners struggled to switch to arable farming. The wheat market was a particularly difficult one since it was often flooded with cheap Australian and American imports. Farmers struck up an arrangement with black sharecroppers, who bore half the risk with them. Land shortage was not yet a problem, with only a small part of the large farms in the republics under cultivation. Replies given to the Transvaal Labour Commission of 1903 revealed that it was rare for more than a hundred acres to be cultivated by a single owner.

Africans were in a position to move around to explore the best offers from farmers. They rarely were attracted to poorer farmers lacking land and offering poor terms. These farmers complained vociferously that they had to work themselves and had to 'use their children as Kaffirs in order to hold their own.' A field-cornet commented: 'It is known throughout the world that the poor rarely want to serve the poor.' As some Afrikaners acknowledged, there was no shortage of black labor in the case of farmers prepared to pay and treat people well.[50]

African participation in farming on white-held land assumed different forms. One was 'Kaffir' farming, in which Africans paid a fixed rental to absentee landowners or companies. This took up between a third and a half of the Transvaal by the end of the century. Secondly, African labor tenants worked for farmers in return for ploughing a piece of land and grazing a limited number of stock. Thirdly, sharecroppers provided ploughs, oxen and seed as inputs and then plowed, sowed and reaped a farmer's land. They then turned over a share of the yield to the farmer. It was usually a third of the yield, but in the northern Free State the share was as much as half in the early twentieth century.[51]

In its optimal form sharecropping involved a co-operative project that approximated a genuine racial partnership. Blacks preferred it to wage labor since it gave them considerable freedom and an opportunity for acquiring large cattle herds, which they called

49 Cited by Donald Denoon, *Settler Capitalism* (Oxford: Clarendon Press, 1983), p. 118.

50 B.J. Krüger, 'Diskussies en wetgewing rondom die landelike arbeidsvraagstuk in die Suid-Afrikaanse Republiek, 1885-1899, master's diss., Unisa, 1965, p. 202; B.J. Krüger, *Diskussies en wetgewing . . .* Communications of the University of South Africa, C62, 1966, p. 30.

51 Dunbar Moodie, 'Class Struggle in the Development of Agrarian Capitalism in South Africa', paper presented at the UCT Centre for African Studies, 1982.

their banks. The entire black household worked on the fields and extended families often pooled their resources.[52]

Before the war both the Free State and the Transvaal legislatures had tried to curb squatters through legislation that limited black families on a farm to five. The idea was that some blacks would move towards poorer farmers and would force prosperous farmers to take on more bywoners. A representative, I.S. Ferreira, warned the Volksraad in 1897 that without tough action the needy burghers would be 'oppressed', as the landowners would simply fill their land with black squatters. But the laws could not be enforced. For the more substantial farmers the economic benefits palpably outweighed the political misgivings. The Bloemfontein paper *The Friend* asked pointedly: 'If the native squatter is so great an evil how comes it that nine farmers out of ten are willing to put their land at his disposal?'[53]

The advance of black sharecroppers spelled great danger to the Afrikaner bywoners. Farmers increasingly needed people with capital and the ability to work hard in the lands. Bywoners had no capital, were reluctant to obey orders and were unwilling to do manual work side by side with blacks. They also liked having some space on the farm for their own use. Farmers hiring out land on a share-cropping basis found that six black families could making a living on two hundred acres, while a single white family insisted that it needed at least a hundred acres on which to subsist.

In frontier conditions bywoners had been the landholder's social equal, but now other white people looked down on them. Black sharecroppers no longer saw them as a 'baas' or master.[54] Mining companies also preferred to lease land to blacks, whom they regarded as more skilled and productive. The South African War exacerbated the deteriorating landowner-bywoner relations. Bywoners formed the majority of the approximately five thousand 'Joiners' who fought on the side of the British in the Anglo-Boer War. After the war many outraged farmers told such bywoners to leave their land.[55]

A proposal for a white land

One of the priorities of the post-war British administration was to provide for an efficient system of urban labor recruitment and regulation. During the war Milner professed to be appalled by the pre-war labor order in the Transvaal; writing to Chamberlain in London, he said he could not 'exaggerate the evils of the old system . . . which formerly made the condition of native labor . . . a crying scandal and a constant source of complaint.' Still, he said that he found some merit in the system of pass laws, for without such control there would be 'pandemonium.'[56]

The British in fact brought a much tougher approach than the ZAR. The latter's labor

---

52 Timothy Keegan, 'Crisis and Catharsis in the Development of Capitalism in South African Agriculture, *African Affairs*, 84, 336 (1985), p. 373.

53 Timothy Keegan, 'The Dynamics of Rural Accumulation in South Africa', *Comparative Studies in Society and History*, 1986, p. 640.

54 Donald Denoon, *The Grand Illusion* (London: Longman, 1973), p. 62.

55 A.M. Grundlingh, *Die 'Hendsoppers' en 'Joiners'* (Pretoria: HAUM, 1979), pp. 232-6.

56 D.B. Burton, 'The South African Native Affairs Commission, SANAC, (1903-1905)', master's diss., Unisa, 1985, p. 31.

system was oppressive, but the state was relatively inefficient and Africans could find loopholes and avoid unpleasant work with a large degree of impunity. And there were some escape hatches. Piet Cronjé, ZAR Commissioner for Native Affairs, told the Volksraad in 1899 that Africans must be allowed to squat on the crown lands because their own segregated locations were too small.[57]

In 1903 Milner appointed the South African Native Affairs Commission (SANAC) to provide a more systematic and co-ordinated native policy for a future federal South Africa. As chairman Milner appointed a British colonial servant, Sir Godfrey Lagden. He had been Administrator of Native Affairs in the Transvaal (1879-1881), in West Africa (1881) and in Basutoland (1884-1901). Two Afrikaners sat on the commission, Johan de la Harpe, a Free State farmer, and J.C. Krogh, who served the ZAR administration in various capacities, including commissioner for Swaziland, but English-speaking administrators dominated the commission.

By 1905 in South Africa the African population was distributed as follows. In the Cape 1,057,610 Africans were living in the reserves of the Transkei and Ciskei, while some 25,000 were working on farms. In Natal, 228,000 Africans lived in reserves, 421,000 on private farms, mostly as labor tenants, and more on crown lands. In the Transvaal, 123,000 Africans were in reserves, some 438,000 squatting on former tribal lands, 180,000 on crown lands, and 130,000 on farms they had combined to buy. In the Free State only 27,000 Africans lived on reserves, but more than a quarter of a million squatted on farms as sharecroppers or labor tenants.

The other major concern of the time was the black labor supply. According to the report, the Transvaal alone needed a black labor force of about 403,000, but had no more than 181,000 black workers. Of the shortage of 221,000 workers, 52,000 were needed on farms and 129,000 in the mines. In seeking to ensure a steady supply of cheap black labor, Lagden as chairman kept conditions in Basutoland in mind. A steady flow of migrant labor had been going from there to the mines and the farms, stimulated by a shortage of land and an efficient tax collection. He also took note of the republican laws and Shepstone's earlier practice of friendly and respectful relationships with chiefs and the lessons learnt in other parts of the British Empire.[58] In British West Africa, where effective colonization had started in the 1890s, working with chiefs and strengthening traditional African culture was found to be an effective way of securing African labor.[59] In private correspondence Lagden tied his thoughts about labor recruitment to the need for a consistent system of white supremacy throughout South Africa. He opposed the Cape's non-racial franchise and advised against granting privileges to an educated minority of Africans. The objective should be the development 'of the whole mass . . . even though the process may be disappointing to the few.'[60]

The term 'segregation' was not heard in the nineteenth century. It was first recorded in South Africa in a 1903 document by R.W. Rose Innes, brother of the liberal politician James Rose Innes. He envisaged more territories like Glen Grey as 'reservoirs of labor', ultimately growing into 'great native states' enjoying large powers of self-government

---

57 Burton, 'SANAC', pp. 119-22.
58 Burton, 'SANAC', pp. 27-8.
59 Anne Phillips, British Policy in West Africa (London: James Currey, 1989).
60 Burton, 'SANAC', p. 156.

and representation in a federal parliament.[61] The SANAC report used the term 'segregation' only once, but the context is significant. It deplored the practice of Africans purchasing pockets of land among white-owned farms and recommended that Africans be denied access to 'white' land through purchase, lease or sharecropping. The state had to reserve for Africans the present 'locations' or other areas of concentrated African settlement.[62] It proposed segregated townships and education for blacks appropriate to lower level jobs. The Cape's non-racial franchise was to be rejected. In a future federal parliament Africans must be put on a separate voters' roll to elect a limited number of representatives, all white, as in the case of the Maoris in New Zealand.

Acting on the SANAC report, the British post-war administration of the Transvaal, under Sir Arthur Lawley, defined the African 'locations' in the Transvaal Colony. In the end only a million morgen, or about three per cent of the Transvaal, was set aside for Africans, compared to, say, the holdings of three major land companies, which comprised eight per cent of the Transvaal. After the introduction of self-rule in 1907 the Botha government accepted these recommendations. In the 1913 Natives Land Act the same areas demarcated in 1907 for Africans in the Transvaal were set aside. In the meantime, the number of Africans living in these locations had considerably increased and land shortages had forced out growing numbers to work elsewhere. An African chief expressed the sentiment: 'It is the same as if a hen were hatching eggs in a pigeon's nest, and the eggs keep rolling out.'[63]

Afrikaner politicians often displayed a wounded innocence when English-speaking members of the opposition challenged segregation as a threat to peace. They were quick to remind them that it was under British Crown Colony rule that the SANAC proposals were issued, and the reserves in the Transvaal formally demarcated. In heated exchanges on segregation in a parliamentary debate in 1917, Louis Botha, by then prime minister, exclaimed 'that the principles contained in the Bill were originally passed by British citizens. I refer to the commission of 1903-1905. And what did that Commission recommend? I say that the whole principle of territorial separation came out of the head of [these] people.' He claimed – it was incorrect – that 'not a single Dutch-speaking South African had served on [SANAC].'[64]

But while SANAC recommended a much more rigid, systematic and internally consistent policy of white supremacy, it would be wrong to see it as the font of the segregation policy of the twentieth century. Much of the report rested on already existing legislation and on the Glen Grey Act in particular. SANAC dealt with the labor demands of large employers, particularly the mine companies, which, unlike the farmers, heavily depended on migrant labor drawn from beyond the country's borders.

Unlike the mining magnates and labor recruiters, Afrikaner farmers and politicians did not think in terms of atomized labor units, as the SANAC report tended to do, but in terms of the paternalistic relationship between masters and servants. They professed

61 Marian Lacey, *Working for Boroko* (Johannesburg: Ravan Press, 1981), p. 16.
62 F. Wilson, 'Farming', in Monica Wilson and Leonard Thompson (eds.), *Oxford History of South Africa* (Oxford: Clarendon Press, 1971), vol. 2, p. 129.
63 Burton, 'SANAC', pp. 169-179.
64 *Debates of the House of Assembly, 1917 (Cape Times reports)*, vol. 2, p. 175.

to be shocked by the atrocious conditions under which blacks worked and died on the mines. In writing to Merriman in 1906, Smuts distanced himself from the 'mine-owner and exploiter', 'the real slave driver in South Africa.'[65] Steyn wrote to Merriman: 'The question of native rights is to my mind a vital question for all of South Africa unless we hold with the Magnates that the natives have no other rights than to work for such wages as will increase their already bloated dividends.'[66] But while Smuts propagated the idea that whites had a duty as the trustees of blacks, he never envisaged any real rights for them.

The common point of departure for Afrikaner politicians was the elimination of the black sharecropper and the potential black voter. Both these categories of blacks posed a direct threat to the rapidly growing class of Afrikaners who were poor, lacked skills, and had only the vote to rely on. Without a formula to exclude them, pressure for the qualified franchise would become steadily stronger. This would spell the political demise of the poorer whites and possibly of Afrikaner political domination as well. The reserves offered a justification for black exclusion from both the land and the vote.

The rise of segregation: tales of some Afrikaner politicians

James Barry Munnik Hertzog, Jan Smuts and Jacobus Wilhelm Sauer personify the foremost Afrikaner approaches to the racial issue. Hertzog, who was the politician mainly responsible for the segregation policy, described himself as anti-capitalist, but it is more appropriate to call him a populist. Like Tom Watson, a counterpart in the American South, he was primarily opposed to big business and monopolies. Both could adapt their racial convictions to circumstances.

Hertzog was born in 1866 near Wellington in the Cape, the son of a struggling farmer, and for much of his childhood lived in the turbulent mining town of Kimberley. His father, through speculation, paid for a proper education, and Hertzog received his high school and undergraduate education at Stellenbosch and a doctorate in Law from the University of Amsterdam. By the time of the outbreak of the war he was a judge in Bloemfontein, and rose to become a general in the Free State forces. He was one of the *Bittereinder* leaders who argued for prolonging the war. Refusing a law chair at the University of Leiden, he decided to concentrate on helping Afrikaners in the devastated Free State. A large inheritance from a Cape family member made him a prosperous farmer. He was a widely read, cultured and incorruptible man with a good legal mind and debating skills. Smuts thought he was lacking 'in the savingest [sic] of Christian graces', a sense of humor. 'A nobler and straighter man I have not met', ex-President Steyn said of him.[67]

Hertzog sought to ensure the security and solidarity of his own group. He made a study of racial problems elsewhere, particularly in the United States, which he believed proved that racial integration did not work. He cited black American authors, like William H. Thomas, who, in his *The American Negro*, argued that integration was 'fatal'

---

65 Cited by Haasbroek, 'Die onstaan van die nie-blanke stemreg', p. 154.
66 Karel Schoeman, *In liefde en trou* (Cape Town: Human & Rousseau, 1983), p. 124.
67 Schoeman, *In liefde en trou*, p. 130.

for both whites and blacks, and that the place of developed blacks was with their own people.[68] For Hertzog, the USA also provided a warning against waiting too long to settle the issue.

He believed that Africans entering into sharecropping arrangements and buying or renting farmland posed a threat to white survival. Instead of his ideal of a tightly knit white community a quite different, partly integrated society would emerge. It would have large landholders, progressive farmers, clerks and professionals, almost all white, at the top; black peasants in the middle, and white (largely Afrikaner) and black menial laborers at the bottom. The poorer and less skilled Afrikaners could not compete with Africans on the farms or with migrants from the reserves in the cities. Hertzog was also convinced that white security would be jeopardized if the vote were granted to growing numbers of blacks.

Hertzog was, in some ways, a conventional white supremacist and in others not. He lauded the racial laws of the Republic of the OFS because he thought such laws led to blacks respecting whites. He used the derogatory word 'kaffer' in Parliament after it had become quite unacceptable. Smuts believed the process of economic development would mitigate racial tensions, but Hertzog thought that it would intensify them. At the same time he did not hold with the concept of innate black inferiority and often expressed his belief in their capacity to advance. 'No one will stop the native from eventually obtaining the franchise', he declared in 1922. 'One cannot deny a people political rights.' He had no doubt that Africans could quickly catch up with ordinary whites in education and in earning respectable wages so that ultimately only skin color would remain as a difference. There was, moreover, a moral imperative to heed black aspirations. The continued denial of the vote in the northern provinces could not occur 'without violating the conscience of the white man.'[69]

It was, however, impossible to grant blacks 'absolute equality.' That would only happen 'if whites pick up all their goods and leave the country.' Abstractly Hertzog saw a solution in blacks developing 'along their own lines' in the reserves. In practical terms, however, far too little land was set aside to sustain viable communities. The reason behind this land allocation was that the reserves had to be kept small enough to force enough Africans to work on the farms and mines. Hertzog thought in group, not individual terms, and, as the theologian Reinhold Niebuhr observed, in human groups there is 'less reason to guide and check impulses, less capacity for self-transcendency, less ability to comprehend the need of others and therefore more unrestrained egotism than the individuals, who compose the group, reveal in their personal relationships.'[70]

Of the leading Afrikaner politicians of the time J.W. Sauer embodied both the potential and the limits of Cape liberalism. Born in 1850 in Burgersdorp, he had been educated at the South African College in Cape Town, where he learned, a contemporary said, to speak better English than the English. He served in the Cape cabinet as Secre-

---

68 C.M. van den Heever, *Generaal J.B.M. Hertzog* (Johannesburg: APB, 1943), p. 335; *Hertzog-toesprake, 1900-1942* (Johannesburg: Perskor, 1977), vol. 3, p. 32.

69 M.D.C. de Wet Nel, 'Generaal Hertzog: beslaggewer van die Bantoebeleid', *Hertzog-annale*, 9 (1962), p. 7; *Hertzog-toesprake*, vol. 5, p. 205.

70 Reinhold Niebuhr, *Moral Man in Immoral Society* (New York: Charles Scribner's Sons, 1932), pp. xi-xxiii.

tary for Native Affairs, among several portfolios. With Hofmeyr's health beginning to wane in the 1890s, he was the Afrikaner best placed to persuade his kinsmen to come to terms on a more liberal basis with the African majority. His friend James Rose Innes said of him: 'By birth a Dutch-speaking Afrikaner, his intellectual qualities, his militant spirit, his debating power marked him out as parliamentary leader of the Afrikaner Nationalist Party. The prize was in his grasp had he stooped to take it. But that would have involved the sacrifice of his views on the Native question, and he put it aside.'[71]

As a liberal Sauer was appalled by some forms of urban segregation then being considered, for example the legislation Rhodes introduced in 1895 for the city of East London to set aside and regulate urban locations for Africans and Asians, impose curfews on them and determine where they might walk. But Sauer also believed in reducing contacts between the races in order to preserve what he saw as a superior white culture. He differed from other Afrikaner leaders in his refusal to agree that 'reserving' land for blacks in 'their areas' justified discrimination against them in the common area.[72]

Yet he did not favor integration. He did not want whites to settle in the Transkei and for this reason supported the Glen Grey Act. He was convinced that if whites lived side by side with 'a race largely in a state of barbarism', 'the more intelligent race' would go down, with 'damnation' for the Europeans. He decided that it might be best if Africans developed as a separate people. In the 1892 franchise debate, Sauer had taken the position that political, but not social, rights must be shared with Africans.[73]

Testifying before the South African Native Affairs Commission in 1904, Sauer withstood pressure from the commissioners to support discrimination. Africans, he said, had progressed in the same ways as a backward European community had, with a steady reduction of the number of 'barbarians.' In the Cape blacks worked the land and as voters they were 'extremely shrewd' and keenly aware of their rights and responsibilities. A policy of justice was more likely to avert trouble than any other. He advocated, for a future Union, extension of the Cape's non-racial franchise on a low qualification level to the rest of South Africa: '[If] we have so little faith in our superiority and our civilization that we think we can only maintain it by keeping the franchise from the Native, I feel assured that we will fail . . . [If] he is going to be a danger in the future, he is more likely to be so if we withhold reasonable rights.'[74]

Sauer, like Hertzog, drew on the American South for a precedent to cope with South Africa's native problems. In introducing that cornerstone of segregation, the Natives Land Act of 1913, he cited the work of the influential Henry Grady, editor of the *Atlanta Constitution* and author of the widely read 1890 study *The New South*. The post-Civil War American South in the final decades of the nineteenth century, when Grady wrote, was at the same historical juncture as South Africa in the two decades after 1902. The North had withdrawn its armies and capital and entrepreneurial talents stood poised to be unleashed. While fully committed to white supremacy, Grady proposed the formula

71 Patricia Grattan Dickson, 'The Natives Land Act of 1913', master's diss., UCT, 1970, p. 99.

72 Cape Colony, *Hansard of the House of Assembly, 1894*, pp. 382-3; Dickson, 'The Natives Land Act', pp. 46, 131-7.

73 Cape of Good Hope, *House of Assembly Debates, 1892*, pp. 158-9.

74 *Report of the South African Native Affairs Commission, 1903-1905*, vol. 4, pp. 914-41; the quote is on p. 920. See also Dickson, 'Natives Land Act', pp. 45, 62, 104-5.

of 'separate but equal' for regulating the relationships of whites and blacks as the only salvation for either race. He advocated a form of segregation with genuinely equal opportunities for both whites and blacks.

Grady wrote before whites of his class engaged in the violent racist practices that followed the undermining of Reconstruction. Well-read white leaders in South Africa like Sauer and Hertzog sought a similar formula to avoid such violence.[75] Standing somewhere between Hertzog and Sauer, but closer to Hertzog, was Jan Smuts, who personified white South African racial ambiguities. A friend and future cabinet colleague, F.S. Malan, revealed that in the early 1890s, while they were both studying at Cambridge, Smuts had spelled out a private vision of bringing civilization, education and religion to Africans, enabling whites and blacks to become one people and one nationality united by common ideals and hopes for the future. But in view of the prejudice among his own people he could see no way to realize his ideal.[76]

Smuts' first political speech, in 1895 in Kimberley, gave little sign of his private views. He noted that about half a million civilized people lived at the tip of a continent inhabited by 100 million 'barbarians' whom whites had to civilize. He urged the avoidance of 'drastic measures', so that each generation could build 'warily' on the experience of a previous generation. But whites also had the obligation to carry out their task as 'trustees for the colored races', bound by the principles of 'honor and justice.' To this concept of white trusteeship Smuts would hold almost to the end of his life.

When he looked back in 1929 on the shaping of racial policy Smuts did not single out the SANAC report as a watershed, but the Glen Grey Act. For him it was a turning point for white domination, away from the perilous course of a non-racial democracy on which the Cape's liberal tradition had put it. What worked in civilized Europe was inapplicable to South Africa where Africans could not, in a day, 'cover the distance which it took the most highly endowed white races hundreds of years to travel.'[77] The Glen Grey Act, on the one hand, provided a 'steel framework' for the white settlement necessary to develop an 'enduring civilization,' and, on the other hand, provided 'indigenous native institutions' to express the specifically African character in their future development.'[78]

Between 1906 and 1908 Smuts and Merriman prepared the ground for a South African constitution through extensive correspondence. They were focused on the imbalance of numbers between whites and Africans. The Union's first census, conducted in 1910, enumerated a population of 5,878 000, with 3,956,000 Africans, 517,000 coloreds, 148,000 Asians and 1,257,000 whites, of whom slightly more than 700,000 were Afrikaners. There was a ratio of roughly 1:4 between whites and Africans. (There would be a ratio of roughly 1:5 between the 1920s and early 1960s and 1:7 in the 1990s when the whites relinquished power.)

The small size of the white population was one of the main themes in the correspondence between Merriman and Smuts. Merriman wrote to Smuts: 'Above all we must

---

75 C. Vann Woodward, *Tom Watson: Agrarian Rebel* (Oxford: Oxford University Press, 1961), pp. 165-6.
76 Bettie Cloete, *Die lewe van F.S. Malan* (Johannesburg: APB, 1946), p. 44.
77 J.C. Smuts, *Africa and Some World Problems* (Oxford: Clarendon Press, 1929), pp. 77-9.
78 Smuts, *Africa*, p. 78.

constantly keep in mind that as Europeans we are but a handful in the face of an over-whelming mass of an inferior race.'[79] Both Smuts and Merriman were acutely conscious of the still fragile white unity in the wake of the recent bitter and devastating war. In the English community there was a widespread fear that the Afrikaners would use their nu-merical majority to win what their republics had lost on the battlefield. The granting of political rights to non-whites would introduce great uncertainties in the Afrikaner-English rivalry, as had happened in the Cape Colony during the 1880s. A qualified fran-chise as an option was particularly problematic in view of the large-scale white poverty and illiteracy, particularly among the Afrikaners. When Merriman proposed a qualified franchise, Smuts rejected it. The way to uplift the poor white, he wrote back, was not to 'ostracize him politically.'[80]

Merriman had proposed a qualified franchise because he saw a vote for blacks as a necessary safety outlet. 'These people,' he wrote, referring to the Africans, 'are numerous and increasing in both wealth and numbers . . . They are the workers and history tells us the future is to the workers.' Smuts responded: 'I don't believe in politics for them . . . [It] will only have an unsettling influence.' He preferred to shift 'the intolerable burden of solving that sphinx problem to the ampler shoulders and stronger brains of the fu-ture.' He would help blacks in every legitimate way, but this did not include the vote. The franchise was 'the last argument, more powerful than the sword or the rifle.' The next generation could consider extending the vote, but now it was 'one of the most dan-gerous things' for the white race to do.[81]

Virtually the only Afrikaner leader who proposed a qualified vote for the entire coun-try was F.S. Malan, parliamentary leader of the Afrikaner Bond and editor of *Ons Land*. At the National Convention (1908-1909) he pointed out that it had taken whites a hun-dred years of strife and tears to achieve unification. If the country did not settle the issue of black political rights it would once again head 'for a struggle and tears and suffering.' A union based on black exclusion was not a genuine union [and] the germs of discord would continue to exist.' In 1909 Hofmeyr, too, warned of the dangers of black exclu-sion: 'It would be a bad day if in addition to protecting our northern borders against the teeming millions of Darkest Africa, we had to be continually on our guard against a malcontent colored and native population in our midst, outnumbering us by five or six to one.'[82] The Bond leaders took pride in the fact that people in the Cape were not barred from voting purely on the grounds of color. While they tended to fear the African vote, they did not forget the support John Tengo Jabavu had given them in the elections of 1898 and 1904.

Replying to Malan, Louis Botha, on behalf of the Transvaal, rejected the plea. If the Cape Colony's system was to be applied to all the territories he might as well go home for he had no mandate for that. But he did not completely slam the door; when the time came he would 'be found willing to consider a non-white franchise, safeguarded by

79 Cited by Haasbroek, 'Die ontstaan van die nie-blanke stemreg', p. 156.
80 W.K. Hancock, *Smuts: The Sanguine Years, 1870-1919* (Cambridge: Cambridge University Press 1962), vol. 1, p. 221
81 Hancock, *Smuts*, p. 319; *Smuts Papers*, vol. 1, pp. 240-43.
82 J.H. Hofmeyr, *The Life of Jan Hendrik Hofmeyr* (Cape Town: Van de Sandt de Villiers, 1913), p. 629.

proper qualifications.' But the people of South Africa, he added, were conservative and progress was bound to be slow.[83] The draft constitution of 1909 retained a non-racial franchise in the Cape Colony but debarred blacks from voting in the other three provinces. Only whites would be allowed to sit in Parliament. White unity was sealed on the back of black exclusion.

For a brief period great euphoria reigned among whites about the potential of the new unified state. The liberal W.P. Schreiner led a delegation of white and black South Africans to the imperial government in London to protest against the constitution, but even fellow-liberals, like Merriman, advised that any intervention would 'wreck all the good achieved in the National Convention by the friends of the natives.'[84] There was little chance that Britain would intervene. During the decade after the war British states-men had gone out of their way to defuse issues that could delay the progress towards unification. When, for instance, Dr A. Abdurahman, president of the African Political Organization, asked for political rights for the colored people in the Transvaal on the grounds that it was 'natives' who were excluded from the vote, Winston Churchill, then deputy minister in the Liberal cabinet, replied: 'I believe the precise meaning attached to the word "native" is native from any country other than a European country.'[85]

The African elite, stung into action by the growing conservative trend in white socie-ty, began to take steps to organize themselves effectively. They demanded a qualified non-racial vote and the right to own and purchase land, and in January 1912 they formed the South African Native National Congress. It elected as national president Dr J.L. Dube with Dr W. Rubusana as honorary president. Vice-presidents were also elected for Ba-sutoland, Mafikeng, Pretoria, Johannesburg, Natal, Bloemfontein and Cape Town. Sol Plaatje became the corresponding secretary. In 1923 the organization became the African National Congress.

Segregating the land, 1908-1923

The move to segregate the land emanated from different sources in the aftermath of the Anglo-Boer War. Leaders of the English-speaking working class insisted that it was un-fair to whites to have to compete against blacks willing to work for much lower wages than they. In 1907 an English-speaking labor leader asked for blacks to be 'located on territories set apart according to their different races' and in 1910 the newly founded Labour Party proposed the 'development of Natives in suitable Native reserves.'[86]

The drive to exclude blacks from 'white land' received an impetus when, in the after-math of the war, Africans, acting on behalf of chiefdoms, acquired twenty-three farms in the Transvaal. Here some 130,000 Africans lived. Although by 1915 less than one per cent of the 'white' land in the Transvaal was owned by blacks, the purchases were as-sumed to be a phenomenon of great symbolic significance.[87] A traveler made this com-

83 State Archives, Cape Town, A. 583. F.S. Malan Papers, 'Autobiography of F.S. Malan', circa 1938; Johan Preller (ed.), Konvensie-dagboek van F.S. Malan (Cape Town: VRS, 1951), pp. 54-9.
84 Lewsen, Merriman, p. 326.
85 G.H. le May, British Supremacy in South Africa, 1899-1907 (Oxford Clarendon Press, 1965), p. 205.
86 Elaine Katz, A Trade Union Aristocracy: A History of White Workers in the Transvaal (Johannesburg: Uni-versity of the Witwatersrand, 1976), pp. 64-5.
87 U.G. 22 of 1916, Report of the Native Land Commission (Pretoria: Government Printer, 1916), p. 4.

ment: 'The bugbear of the Africander is the question of political rights. Allow a native to own land in his own individual right, and how can you refuse him the vote? they say.'[88] Another development that disturbed Afrikaner leaders was the buying up of large tracts of land by foreigners and outsiders, who turned them over to blacks to farm. By 1905 about a quarter of the Transvaal farms were held by companies favoring blacks to work their farms on a sharecropping basis.

But political and economic changes steadily undermined the sharecroppers. By 1910 there was a larger and more stable market for food, and transport costs had been reduced. Increasingly the more progressive farmers forced the Africans on their farms to reduce their cattle herds and to work for wages alone. Earlier, sharecroppers and labor tenants provided cheap labor for having their land worked; now, however, farmers discovered that they were expensive.

But the main adversaries of the sharecroppers were the whites who believed they posed a threat to white supremacy in white land. The first moves to legislate against sharecropping occurred in the Free State, where it existed in an advanced form. When a Free State court found against an African sharecropper in a dispute with his master, the judge declared that the African's status was that of a 'partner pure and simple.' He added: 'The question in mind is who is master on this farm – the Native or the European?'[89] Petitions began circulating in the Free State asking for legislation against squatting, and the politicians were quick to respond. In a 1908 debate in the Legislative Assembly J.J. Bruwer warned: 'We are getting into partnership with natives if you allowed that [farming on shares].' M.J. Beukes stated that 'natives must only be allowed on a farm as servants of the white man in order that this may remain a white man's country.'[90]

Politicians sought a justification for banning sharecropping or any other practices that gave blacks some stake in farmland. If blacks could be deemed to have their own land they could be prevented from acquiring rights in the 'white' land. In 1908 Abraham Fischer mooted the possibility in the Orange River Colony legislature of political rights for natives in 'separate kraals', while C.L. Botha, representing Bloemfontein City in the Orange River Colony legislature, advocated a system in which every race could exercise its rights in its own territory.[91]

But those wishing to ban blacks from farming for their own account did not have it all their own way. There were farmers who still found sharecroppers profitable. It was reported that a scuffle broke out at a meeting which Louis Botha, the first prime minister, addressed in the Vereeniging district shortly after Union. A number of people expressed outrage that some black squatters lived in comparative ease while hundreds of white bywoners had to endure poverty. Fanie Cronjé, a farmer, took issue with them: 'Well, gentlemen, I have seven bywoners on the farm and seven black families and I get from one of those black families what I cannot get from the seven bywoners together. And so you are going to ask me to take food out of my mouth?' Enraged, some members of the audience nearly assaulted him.[92]

88 Archibald R. Colquhoun, *The Africander Land* (London: John Murray, 1906), pp. 94-101.
89 *Report of the Select Committee on Native Affairs, 1917*, cols. 2847-2849.
90 *Debates of the Orange River Legislative Assembly, 1908*, pp. 475-6.
91 *Debates of the Orange River Colony Legislative Assembly, 1909*, pp. 14, 49; Haasbroek, 'Die ontstaan van die nie-blanke stemreg', p. 211.
92 Keegan, 'Crisis', p. 485.

Hertzog became the first minister for Native Affairs in the first Union cabinet. Shortly after assuming office, he traveled through the western Transvaal to investigate squatting, and on his return said: 'We must choose whether we keep the land or the native.' He told his audiences that ancient Greece and Rome fell because agricultural work was left to freed slaves; precisely the same would happen there if white farmers lived in the town nearby and left their farms for blacks to work. [93] He began playing with the idea of 'dividing' South Africa between white man's land and black man's land and justifying the division with the 'separate but equal' formula.

But how were the lines to be drawn? A 'settlement' assigning only six or seven per cent to blacks would obviously lack credibility. Some South African Party speakers considered doubling the existing acreage of the reserves.[94] They also saw merit in the idea that a settlement, even if not equitable to blacks, would at least prevent further white encroachment in the reserves. In 1915 the Secretary for Native Affairs referred to a district where fewer than half of the farms formerly owned by 'natives' were still in their possession.[95] As the liberal historian W.M. Macmillan pointed out at the time: '[Open] competition in land is fatal to the weaker race . . . Given free right of entry of whites into native lands, the natives will presently be landless indeed.'[96]

What made the promise of a land 'settlement' easier to make was the fact that the territorial limits of the future South African state were not yet fixed. For quite some time after unification white political leaders hoped that not only the British High Commission Territories of Basutoland, Swaziland and Bechuanaland, making up a land mass 60 per cent of that of South Africa, but also southern Mozambique, Rhodesia and South West Africa would be incorporated into South Africa. The British government made transferring the High Commission Territories conditional on an acceptable South African racial policy, but at the time of Union it was by no means clear whether only a non-racial franchise would be acceptable to London. Some scholars argue that at this point the British government believed that well-developed black local government and councils were more significant than the franchise.[97]

In 1912 Hertzog began giving flesh to his plan for bringing about a white man's country. He indicated that he wanted big reserves for blacks where self-government for them would have some meaning. He was unlikely to get African support unless an attractive offer was made. When he met with an African delegation that included Sol Plaatje, secretary of the South African Native National Congress, he held up a large map and drew circles to indicate 'a vast dependency of the Union.' (It is likely that he included Bechuanaland, Basutoland and Swaziland as part of this 'vast dependency'.) Here the 'energies and aspirations of black professionals could find their outlet with no danger of competition with Europeans.' Plaatje thought this 'a fair ground for discussion.'[98]

93 *Hertzog-toesprake*, vol. 1, p. 134; vol. 2, p. 249.

94 Lewsen, *Merriman*, p. 359.

95 Sol Plaatje, *Native Life in South Africa* (London: King, 1916), pp. 115-16.

96 Cited by Martin Legassick, 'The Rise of Modern South African Liberalism', seminar paper, Institute of Commonwealth Studies, London University, 1973, p. 12.

97 Martin Legassick, 'The Making of South African "Native Policy", 1903-1923', seminar Paper, Institute of Commonwealth Studies, University of London, 1973, pp. 2-3.

98 Plaatje, *Native Life in South Africa*, pp. 371-2.

Hertzog drafted a bill to demarcate black territories, but a clash with a colleague over another issue led to his dismissal as minister for Native Affairs in December 1912. In a speech a month later his ideas on division were still vague – the land between white and black could not be divided immediately, he said, and he was unsure how much land blacks required. For now the priority was to set aside 'reserve native camps' where whites could no longer purchase any land.[99]

The Natives Land Bill introduced in this parliamentary session defined areas of black ownership (referred to as 'scheduled areas'), outside of which blacks could neither purchase nor rent land, and within which no one but blacks could buy or lease land. A commission was to be appointed to report on setting aside additional land as scheduled areas. In the debate the issues of land and labor became hopelessly entangled. The most vociferous lobby was the Free State one, which was clamoring for labor and offering no additional land to Africans. Farmers had already driven off large numbers of African labor tenants and sharecroppers who refused to dispose of their stock. Some threatened to do so but because other farmers were continuing with sharecropping, they had to follow suit in the competition for cheap African labor.[100] A blanket ban would strengthen their hand in compelling Africans to dispose of their stock or leave.[101]

The bill's provisions for the OFS were much more stringent than for the other provinces. It confirmed republican laws limiting to five the number of heads of African households on a farm and prohibiting sharecropping and labor tenancy. In the Transvaal and Natal, sharecropping arrangements were left undisturbed because the power of absentee landlords and land companies was a much greater factor than in the OFS. In the Cape Colony the situation would remain largely unaltered because changes could violate the Constitution. In national terms the most severe setback for Africans was the ban on purchasing land outside the scheduled areas in the three northern provinces.

The bill encountered a mixed reaction. Some proponents, like Edward Dower, Secretary for Native Affairs, considered it as only a 'first step in the direction of the territorial separation of blacks and white.'[102] Others wanted a redistribution of black labor to help the poorer white farmers, but for this the bill was what one study called 'a singularly inept instrument.'[103] And some simply wanted to counter *gelykstelling,* or social leveling. They did not mind large numbers of blacks living on farms as long as the whites and blacks were not partners in farming. One of the bill's main proponents, J.G. Keyter of the OFS, spelled out this objective in the bluntest way: the OFS told blacks 'that the OFS was a white man's country and that they intended to keep it so . . . They [Blacks] were not going to be allowed to buy or hire land and they were not going to tolerate an equality between whites and blacks for if they did tolerate it they would soon find that they would be a bastard nation.'[104]

---

99 *Hertzog-toesprake*, vol. 2, pp. 308-9.

100 Dunbar Moodie, 'Class Struggle in the Development of Agrarian Capitalism in South Africa', paper presented at the UCT Centre for African Studies, 1982.

101 Tim Keegan, 'The Sharecropping Economy . . .', in Shula Marks and Richard Rathbone (eds.), *Industrialisation and Social Change in South Africa* (London: Longman, 1982), pp. 205-11.

102 Plaatje, *Native Life*, p. 115.

103 P. L. Wickens, 'The Natives Land Act of 1913', *South African Journal of Economics*, 49, 1 (1981), p. 128.

104 *House of Assembly Debates*, 19 May 1913, col. 2540.

But the Afrikaner nationalist leaders had not yet brought the rank and file round to their point of view. A commission of inquiry into the Rebellion, which broke out in the northern part of the Free State in the following year, found that the rebels made a 'great deal of capital out of the Natives Land Act.' It was asserted that the farmers could no longer 'make their own agreements with the native laborers, and were in short no longer masters on their farms.'[105]

The Bill caused much turmoil in the House. Hertzog, who a year earlier had set the process in train, was no longer a minister. He had become the symbol of division for the ruling South African Party and also of rivalry for resources among the four provinces. The leader of the Free State party, he had specifically asked that there not be numerous small reserves spread across the country. However, his position was undercut by the fact that in his province only 27,000 Africans lived in three tiny reserves. Since he proposed no additional land for blacks in the Free State, some accused him of trying to solve the 'native problem' at the expense of other provinces. In the debate Prime Minister Louis Botha warned against deceiving whites and blacks alike: 'It is all very nice,' he told the House, 'to talk and take a map and draw lines on it . . . On the map you may be able to beacon off parts and say: "This is for the Natives", but then when you put your schemes into effect you may find that the ground of many individuals has been taken away without any inquiries or investigations having been made.' Hansard noted that this was met with 'laughter and hear hear.'[106]

Sauer, who had taken over as minister for Native Affairs, was known as one of the 'friends of the Natives' in the Cape Parliament, and it was thought unlikely that he would steer a bill through that seriously infringed African rights. But W.P. Schreiner, the most consistent liberal, observed that this was indeed what was happening 'To the bulk of the people we are saying there is no home for you except in a tiny portion of the country . . . It is going to carry us further than we dream to a destiny that is terrible to contemplate.'[107]

Merriman sensed that the bill was both far-reaching and dangerous, and that whites, by undermining black rights, could ultimately undermine their own survival. He warned in Parliament: 'The existence of the white race in Africa is by no means assured, and unless we mend our ways we may go the same way in the south that the Roman and the Greek, the Carthaginian and the Vandal did in the north.' If the intention was 'to bottle the Natives up body and soul', whites might as well pack up their 'portmanteau' for the 'European race would perish.'[108] But in 1908 Merriman had confessed privately that the African franchise, except as a safety valve, was 'repellent' to him, suggesting as an alternative to cut off 'the Native territories and govern them as provinces, allowing large privileges in local government as we do in the Transkei.'[109]

Supporters of the bill argued that it would be better to provide openings for blacks in the reserves since they had little prospect of acquiring common rights in the parliamentary system. Hertzog asked if Merriman would still support the equality of blacks and

105 UG 42-1916, *Judicial Inquiry into the Recent Rebellion*, p. 298.
106 *HAD*, 28 February 1913, p. 579.
107 E.A. Walker, *W.P. Schreiner* (Oxford: Oxford University Press, 1937), p. 349.
108 Lewsen, *Merriman*, p. 359.
109 Haasbroek, 'Die ontstaan van die nie-blanke stemreg', p. 156.

whites if there were enough blacks on the roll of qualified voters to give blacks the majority. He predicted that hardly five members of Parliament would do so.[110]

Botha, as prime minister and leader of the SAP, favored appointing a commission with
a mandate to reach a compromise acceptable to both whites and blacks. But the priority
was to prevent an SAP split. Some legislation had become imperative to reduce tensions.
As in the case of the constitution, white unity was sealed on the backs of blacks.

In June 1913 Sauer, without consulting black leaders, piloted the bill through its final
stages. SAP speakers struggled to find a justification. Botha said that if the need for white
self-preservation was their first principle, the second was to treat Africans as 'a great
people.' Hertzog wanted the policy to operate 'fair and justly' through arranging for reserves as separate territories where Africans could become 'stronger and stronger.' Drawing on the American South, Sauer approvingly quoted Grady's statement that the South
carried within her body two separate races for which it had to ensure 'equal justice.'
The law must become 'the natives' charter.' Merriman commented scathingly in his
diary on the 'nauseous hypocrisy of caring for native interests masking a desire to get
cheap servants.'[111]

Sauer declared in the Senate that the present bill had been 'present in his mind' since
the passage of the Glen Grey Act. But W.P. Schreiner thought the two pieces of legislation had nothing to do with each other; segregation was the main 'way back behind this
measure', and behind that, 'the worst of human motives: apprehension, fear.' Why were
people acting in this manner? 'They know they were doing wrong . . .Why do they do it?
Self-preservation.'[112]

Despite his misgivings, Merriman called Sauer 'the staunchest defender' of the 'weak
and oppressed' when he died shortly afterwards. In 1936, F.S. Malan, Sauer's fellow-
liberal, would write that 'had he [Sauer] been able to foresee the use that was later to be
made of the segregation principle, he would never have consented to sponsor the Bill.'[113]
Yet Sauer did have a premonition. Before his death he confessed that he had never been
so much troubled by an act of law. A member of a delegation of the South African
Native National Congress who saw him just before his death to plead the cause of the
'squatting natives', reported later: '[The] minister never denied the possible hardship
that would follow such a law, but he seemed to be driven by a mysterious force in the
face of which the native interest did not count.'

The Land Act of 1913 restricted Africans to just over 10 million morgen, mainly in
the Cape and Natal. The Beaumont Commission, set up to find additional land, three
years later recommended setting aside an extra 8,365,700 morgen as scheduled areas.
But it added that it was 'too late in the day to define large compact Native areas or
draw bold lines of demarcation.' With few exceptions African land was 'hopelessly in-
termixed with lands owned and occupied by Europeans whose vested interests have to
be considered.' Sol Plaatje now called the land allocation a travesty of the plan that Hertzog had proposed.[114]

---

110 *Hertzog-toesprake* , vol. 3, p. 31.
111 *Correspondence of J.X. Merriman* (Cape Town: VRS, 1969), p. 232.
112 *Senate Debates,* 13 June 1913, col. 538-9. For a recent analysis see Harvey Feinberg, 'The Natives Land
    Act in South Africa', *International Journal of African Historical Studies,* 26, 1 (1993), pp. 65-111.
113 F.S. Malan, 'Autobiography', in Malan Papers; *Correspondence of Merriman*, p. 236.
114 Plaatje, *Native Life,* pp. 172-3.

In the aftermath of the act many enterprising sharecroppers in the Free State moved north into the Transvaal. By the mid-1920s more than 90 per cent of arable farming in the western Transvaal still depended on sharecropping. Here a few enterprising share-croppers like Kas Maine, whose life has been wonderfully reconstructed by the historian Charles van Onselen, managed through great ingenuity and heroic perseverance to con-tinue their sharecropping activities for several decades.[115]

Although a principal objective of the Natives Land Act was the replacement of black sharecroppers with whites, particularly poor whites, this goal was thwarted by a sharp rise in land and stock prices. Farmers decided that it was not in their interest to allow white subordinates on their land. In the early 1920s, Free State magistrates reported that blacks were displacing white bywoners and workers, because, as one report noted: 'The farmer cannot and will not pay a decent living wage to a white man.' The black man worked for less than whites, was more efficient and accepted lower standards for hous-ing and food. Unwittingly the act accelerated the displacement of the poorer whites not related to the farm owner. By the 1950s and 1960 there were serious concerns about *beswarting van die platteland* – the blackening of the countryside.[116]

A legitimating formula for segregation

By the 1920s and 1930s the policy of segregation had come to entail not only political and territorial segregation, but also large state subsidization of white commercial farm-ing, the protection of white urban workers, and the rehabilitation of the poor whites (see Chapter 10). The idea of a white man's country was largely an illusion: the common area had been defined as white, but blacks formed a growing presence. By 1912 there were already 420,000 Africans in the towns and cities in the common or white area, a third of South Africa's urban population and 13 per cent of the total African population.

Shantytowns were springing up rapidly on the outskirts of the cities. The white mu-nicipalities ran these shantytowns in an unplanned way, usually making a profit; the residents themselves got little in return for their rent and taxes. Serious diseases like tu-berculosis found an ideal breeding ground in the unsanitary and overcrowded hovels. Smuts, who became prime minister in 1919 after Botha's death, could not square this with his idea of whites acting as the trustees of blacks: 'The natives have come to our towns unprovided for. They have picked up our diseases, and have found our white civi-lization a curse to them . . . The Native question is so large. We know so little about it.' He believed that proper housing and proper control of Africans in the urban areas was an obligation of the state. If it accepted this obligation, South Africa would remove 'one of the biggest blots resting on our civilization.'[117]

Fitting urban blacks into the ideological framework of the Natives Land Act could not be avoided for long. In 1922 a Transvaal Local Government Commission, headed

115 Charles van Onselen, *The Seed is Mine: The Life of Kas Maine – A South African Share-cropper, 1894-1985* (Cape Town: David Philip, 1996).
116 R.A. Lewis, 'A Study of Some Aspects of the Poor White Problem in South Africa,' master's diss., Rhodes University, 1973, pp. 31-4.
117 Hancock, *Smuts*, vol. 2, p. 123.

by Colonel C.F. Stallard, one of the most prominent English-speaking segregationists, proposed that Africans were only required in the urban areas to 'minister to the needs of whites' and must depart from there when they 'ceased so to minister.'

Smuts depended on the judgment of his friend and leading Cape liberal, F.S. Malan, Minister of Mines, who probably had a major hand in the bills dealing with urban blacks drafted between 1917 and 1923. He did not assume that collectively blacks constituted a threat. He had a vision of native 'villages' where Africans who were 'civilized could feel at home and develop.' Because of their stake in the status quo they could become a bulwark against labor unrest and political agitation. Meeting an African delegation in 1920, he promised a better deal for regular and reliable black workers, better housing, and exemptions from the pass laws.[118]

Smuts allowed Malan to speak in these terms because he himself believed in 'class legislation' that distinguished between the 'ordinary native', who had not yet emerged from 'barbarism', and the more 'advanced' Africans, who could take control of their own social problems in villages of their own. The Native Urban Areas Bill the Smuts government submitted to a consultative Native Conference in 1923 envisaged that settled Africans could acquire freehold property. It aimed to improve the administration of black residential areas.

But white politics had reached the stage where any such improvement would be held up as undermining the claim to a white man's land. Hertzog spelled out the claim in 1922: 'The [native] gets his own territory where all rights would be granted to him. He can live in our land, but can demand no rights here. The opposite is also true.'[119] If Africans could get freehold property, acquiring 'white man's land', they would soon demand 'the white man's vote.' And that would be 'a matter of life and death for white civilization.'[120] White civil servants also maintained that Africans did not value individual title as a superior form of tenure. Smuts caved in and the provision to grant property rights was withdrawn from this bill, which was passed and promulgated as the Native Urban Areas Act. Confronted by an angry delegation from the South African Native National Congress, he pointed to the Bloemfontein location, where no freehold existed, but which was 'one of the most orderly and best run in the country.'[121] Black townships remained a neglected stepchild of urban administration; to add insult to injury the act accepted the formula first developed by the municipality of Durban for funding the townships, its main source of revenue the proceeds from the sale of 'kaffir' or sorghum beer to the captive market. The more the Africans drank the more funds there would be for housing and other necessities.

The Union constitution of 1909, the Natives Land Act of 1913, and the Native Urban Areas Act of 1923 formed the basis of policy towards blacks for the rest of the century. The Natives Land Act was of paramount importance; because it made little new land available, the reserves quickly became congested and the limited opportunities for in-

---

118 Peter Kallaway, 'F.S. Malan, the Cape Liberal Tradition and South African Politics', *Journal of African History*, 15, 1, (1974), pp. 126-7.

119 *Hertzog-toesprake*, 1V, p. 236.

120 Hancock, *Smuts*, p. 127.

121 Rodney Davenport, *The Beginnings of Urban Segregation in South Africa* (Institute of Social and Economic Research, 1971), pp. 1-23.

dividual tenure were further restricted by the strong support for communal tenure in the traditional African system. From 1920 the government increasingly stressed the development of African tribal life.[122] Smuts began speaking of Africans as 'a distinct human type which the world would be poorer without' and who needed to be 'preserved and developed.' By 1924, when Hertzog replaced Smuts as prime minister, Hertzog was ready to concede that too little land had been set aside for blacks for a policy now single-mindedly focusing on segregated institutions. Out of power, Smuts wrote to a friend in England: 'I sometimes despair of the Native question . . . The best possible approach was a Fabian one, but it was almost demanding too much of human nature to ask black and white to be just and fair and generous to each other.'[123]

Among the more liberal whites the belief persisted that with more land blacks would accept the policy. This belief was put to the test at a conference in 1923, organized by the Dutch Reformed Church, and attended by white and black church leaders, delegates from welfare societies, the ANC and chiefs. On behalf of the blacks Selby Msimang of the African National Congress said that they would be happy with territorial segregation if the Natives Land Act granted half of the land in the country for black occupation. But by now every white leader knew that giving half or even a quarter of the land to blacks would have severe political costs. Whites had come to believe that some 90 per cent of South Africa was white man's land, and they were less and less inclined to sacrifice any part of it.

---

122 Saul Dubow, *Racial Segregation and the Origins of Apartheid in South Africa*, 1989.
123 Jean van der Poel (ed.), *Smuts Papers*, vol. 5, p. 389; T. Cameron, *Smuts: An Illustrated Biography* (Cape Town: Human & Rousseau, 1994), pp. 113-15.

Chapter 10

—

'Wretched folk, ready for any mischief':
Poor Whites and Militant Workers

Discovering the poor as a problem

The so-called poor-white problem became the most pressing social issue in Afrikaner politics early in the twentieth century and retained that status until the early 1940s, when the search for a new approach to the racial problem replaced it. For a ruling class to regard poverty as a political problem, it first had to 'discover' the poor. When this happened poverty had not become worse, but the perceptions of the ruling class towards it had changed. In South Africa this development occurred when the proponents of white supremacy concluded that a consolidated white group was needed to dominate the black majority. The main obstacle to such a consolidation was the presence of growing numbers of very poor white people on the land and in the towns and cities. Some were destitute and unemployable; others were unskilled or barely skilled.

The term 'poor white' originated in the American South during the 1870s, when several million whites were almost as wretchedly poor as the emancipated slaves. Some thought that a lack of 'ambition' prevented poor whites from practicing diversified or scientific agriculture. The enduring effects of the Civil War, and particularly the devastation by the earlier invading armies, were not given due weight.[1] In Britain, which strongly influenced the thinking of Cape politicians, poverty was 'discovered' in the 1880s, giving rise to a flood of publications on the subject. Earlier the ruling class had attributed the existence of poverty to the poor's own inability to overcome their lack of enterprise and other moral deficiencies. Now, however, they concluded that the poor deserved assistance because they faced problems that were not of their own making.[2]

In European colonies across the world concern about white poverty intensified during the 1880s and 1890s. It was connected to a more modern sense among Europeans of racial exclusivity. To prevent the white poor from losing caste and to facilitate their rehabilitation, administrators and politicians delineated the criteria for membership of

1 C. Vann Woodward, *Origins of the New South, 1877-1913* (Baton Rouge Louisiana State University Press, 1951), pp. 109-110, 176-7.
2 Gertrude Himmelfarb, *Poverty and Compassion: The Moral Imagination of the Late Victorians* (New York: Vintage Books, 1991), pp. 14, 391-2.

the dominant white community more sharply.[3] Among South African whites in general there was no consensus in the 1860s or 1870s about dealing with white poverty. The dominant view was that the poor were themselves responsible for their sad condition. They wanted the church to deal with the problem as part of its pastoral obligations. The matter only became urgent when the rapid increase in poor whites seemed to threaten white supremacy.

Singling out the white poor

During the late 1880s the Rev. B.P.J. Marchand, minister of the Knysna parish of the Dutch Reformed Church (DRC), was traveling in the Karoo. A storm forced him to take shelter in the miserable one-room dwelling of a desperately poor *bywoner* or tenant farmer. Dismayed to find that numerous children were not attending school and probably never would, he struggled to think of how to save them from a life of poverty.[4] Marchand's own parish had founded schools for children of white woodcutters, whose poverty had been recognized since the 1850s. But not until the 1890s did the Cape synod of the DRC identify poverty among some of its members as a looming crisis.

During the same decade Transvaal newspapers and government reports also began to discuss the incidence of poverty among the burghers of the Zuid-Afrikaansche Republiek (ZAR). They mainly regarded it as an urban phenomenon and made special mention of the poor congregating in Velschoendorp in Pretoria and in the Johannesburg suburbs of Fordsburg, Braamfontein and Vrededorp. A 'Rand Relief Committee' said of the Vrededorp people that 'most of them seem starved, they live from blood and guts discarded at the slaughtering-places, they exchange their clothes for food, children go naked.'[5] Yet the mining commissioner told the government that he saw no reason for the state to intervene since the churches and charity organizations themselves were doing nothing. His view represented the conventional wisdom of the time, which attributed the state of the poor to idleness, and left it to private institutions to aid the most miserable among them.

In the two Boer republics, where citizenship and racial identity were identical, there was no need to justify concentrating relief efforts on only a section of the population. The ZAR spent a third of its budget on poor relief; in relative terms it surpassed that of European countries until deep into the twentieth century.[6] President Steyn of the Republic of the Orange Free State, along with President Kruger of the ZAR, believed that the mining capitalists and the absentee landlords had no sympathy for the Afrikaner poor and would be happy to use black labor at extremely low rates to undercut them. As a result they would become a destitute proletariat in the cities. Steyn declared, in 1898,

---

3 See the articles by Ann Stoler in *Comparative Studies in Society and History*, 1989, pp. 134-6; 1992, pp. 514-51.

4 R.A. Lewis, 'A Study of Some Aspects of the Poor White Problem', master's diss., Rhodes University, 1973, p. 61.

5 A.N. Pelzer, 'Die "arm-blanke" in die Suid-Afrikaanse Republiek tussen die jare 1882 en 1899', *Historiese Studies*, 2, 4 (1941), p. 192.

6 John Bottomley, 'Public Policy and White Rural Poverty in South Africa, 1881-1924', doctoral diss., Queen's University, 1990, p. 127.

that the struggle to survive had become fiercer since 'capital, the enemy of [white] labor, had made its appearance.' He opened an industrial school in Bloemfontein, where, as in other towns, Free State sons had to learn the 'gospel of labor' and help the republic to become self-sufficient in its labor needs.[7]

In the Cape Colony providing superior social services to whites and assisting only the white poor militated against the liberal constitution and the non-racial membership of the DRC. As early as 1861 several leading Cape clergy asked for compulsory education without mentioning race, nearly twenty years before compulsory education was introduced in Great Britain. In 1870 its synod called on government 'to take the necessary measures for the teaching of those poor who had a claim on the care of the Reformed Church, whites as well as colored.'[8] But the church itself was now rapidly becoming segregated and soon the 'mother church', or predominantly white church, focused only on Afrikaner poverty.

The term 'poor white' was probably first used in the Cape Colony during the early 1880s. In 1883 'D.V.', a correspondent based in a western Cape town, wrote in the DRC journal, *De Gereformeerde Kerkbode* (also called *De Christen* then), that the problem was not so much 'poor whites' as 'heathen who live in our midst and who were of our color.' Subsequently a correspondent in the Karoo town of Aberdeen proposed that missionaries hold separate services for 'our poor whites' living out of town.[9] Soon white poverty was seen as a social danger. In 1892 a school inspector in the Karoo wrote that it led to increasing social decline, racial degeneration and crime.[10]

Government officials had already begun to define social reform and social maladies in explicitly racial terms. In 1889 Sir Langham Dale, Cape Superintendent of Education, declared that whites 'should have at least such an education as their peers in Europe enjoy with such local modifications as will fit them to maintain their unquestioned superiority and supremacy in the land.'[11]

But there was no ready-made justification for white privilege in the state's provision of social services. The chairman of an 1894 Select Committee on a bill for relief to destitute children asked the crucial question.

> *M.C. Neethling (Chairman)*: Taking it now as a question of common justice between man and man, why should the Europeans be preferred?
> *Dr T. te Water (witness)*: I, for my part, would like to see the country in the hands of Europeans; that is why when I find that a section of the European population is falling back in the race, I say let us come to their help.[12]

---

7 Timothy Keegan, *Rural Transformations in Industrializing South Africa* (Johannesburg: Ravan Press, 1986), p. 43; *De Express*, 1 March 1898.

8 M. du T. Potgieter, 'Die NG Kerk en die blanke onderwys in Kaapland', doctoral diss., US, 1961, p. 354.

9 Bunyan Booyens, 'De Gereformeerde Kerkbode, 1849-1923', doctoral diss., University of Stellenbosch, 1992, p. 180; *De Christen*, 28 September and 26 October 1883, pp. 452, 498.

10 E.G. Malherbe, *Education and the Poor White: Report of the Carnegie Commission* (Stellenbosch: Pro: Ecclesia, 1932), vol. 3, p. 471.

11 Vivian Bickford-Smith, *Ethnic Pride and Racial Prejudice in Victorian Cape Town* (Johannesburg: Witwatersrand University Press, 1995), p. 121.

12 *Cape of Good Hope Parliament: Select Committee on the Destitute Children's Relief Bill, 1894*, p. 45.

Others rationalized that per capita wealth was too low to afford a modernized system of education for the entire population, yet others that it was best to concentrate resources first on whites, to turn them into a 'healthy group', and then later they could help to rehabilitate the rest of society. John X. Merriman declared: 'The white population was a minority . . . and if their brethren were to sink in the slough, as they saw them doing, it would be impossible to maintain their dominance.' Whites were the 'garrison.' They held 'the country in the interests of civilization and in the interests of good government and general enlightenment of South Africa.' Here were two justifications almost in the same breath: whites deserved to dominate, and a healthy white group would ultimately be in the interest of all South Africans.[13]

There were several reasons why white poverty was predominantly an Afrikaner problem. The first related to large-scale immigration from Europe. Between 1875 and 1904 some 400,000 whites entered South Africa, more than the entire white population of 1875. Increasingly the Afrikaners, who began moving to the towns and cities in the 1890s, found that skilled and semi-skilled work, the professions and civil service positions were already filled by local or immigrant English-speakers.[14] The British section had the advantage of better education, better skills and their command of English, the language of trade and industry. Invariably they had a longer experience of the cash economy and saving money. Although there was always approximately one-fifth of the white poor who were English-speaking, they were never as visible as the Afrikaner poor and some even assumed an Afrikaner identity. In the early 1930s a DRC minister remarked that 95 per cent of the poor whites in his parish were 'Dutch' and that the English-speaking poor tended to become 'Dutch' in outlook and language.[15]

In a racially homogeneous society the Afrikaner poor would have become the urban proletariat and worked their way up from that position. But there already was a proletariat of between 200,000 and 300,000 male Africans who had moved from the reserves to the towns and cities as migrant workers. Employers paid them as single men, arguing that the reserves provided for their family's subsistence. Africans did the unskilled work at a rate far below that for which whites were prepared to work. The term 'poor white' developed in this context. The white elite did not define poverty in terms of physical or economic data, but relationally – how a white person by virtue of being white *ought* to live in comparison to non-whites. The idea of a proper white wage was defined accordingly.

Commissions that studied white poverty over a period of close to sixty years were nearly united in the view that a willingness to do manual labor, together with a superior white education, was essential for alleviating white poverty. However, after nearly 250 years in which almost all the Afrikaners farmed, there was a strong prejudice against doing work that could be done by servants. A young OFS farmer who watched a Dutch immigrant ploughing his own land said: 'No, doctor, that I have never done yet, to hold the plough myself; what did onze lieve Heer (our good Lord) give us the natives for?'

---

13 *Debates of the House of Assembly*, 1894, cols. 345-6.
14 Cecil Headlam (ed.), *Milner Papers* (London: Cassell, 1933), vol. 2, p. 459.
15 Roberta Millar, 'Social Science, Philanthropy and Politics: The Carnegie Corporation in South Africa', unpublished paper, 1992.

The Rev. A.J.L. Hofmeyr explained: 'The young of Afrikaners of our time consider it a scandal to work.' Poor white boys given jobs on the railways quickly left because they found the discipline of regular work in the employ of others intolerable. They wanted to oversee the work of blacks or colored people instead.[16]

Most farmers saw no need for a proper education for their children and were even more reluctant for their children to receive training in skills. An investigation showed that between 1890 and 1905 there was an 'enormous increase' in the number of colored and black school pupils with a 'by no means proportionate increase in the attendance of European children.' More black and colored children than whites attended school in the Cape Colony. J.W. Sauer observed in 1896 that 79 per cent of the white children in Carnarvon and 52 per cent of those in Prieska (both Karoo towns) were not at school.[17] The Rev. Andrew Murray told a commission that many white parents wished to be paid for sending their children to school.[18] In remote areas, like Namaqualand, teachers considered it imprudent to give mid-morning breaks since the children ran away. In 1891, it was found that the average white child in the Transvaal spent only two years in school.

The Cape government established industrial schools for colored and black people in 1854, but not until the 1890s for whites. Afrikaners were reluctant to attend such institutions, not the least because existing legislation projected them also as places for the rehabilitation of criminals and the mentally deficient. Colored people, who entered manufacturing and commercial occupations long before the Afrikaners, dominated half the trades by the end of the century. By the 1890s Afrikaners seeking work in the towns were untrained and in many cases unemployable.

In 1892, a Cape school inspector said it was 'sad to see a class who were once land-owners, endowed by nature with greater possibilities than the natives, allowing their heritage to slip from their hands, and sinking into the class of unskilled laborers.'[19] In the following year J.H. ('Onze Jan') Hofmeyr, leader of the Afrikaner Bond, introduced a motion in Parliament. It was, he said, 'the most important issue ever to be submitted to the House.' Indigenous people were making sacrifices so their children could be educated: 'If the white race desired to maintain its supremacy in the country they would have to submit to sacrifices in order to provide that the next generation would be a thoroughly well-educated one and not a lazy, useless class of the community.' He urged the introduction of measures like compulsory education and the founding of industrial schools, especially for children of poor whites, to teach them habits of industry, order-liness, obedience, and discipline.[20]

In 1893 the Rev. Marchand was among a group of Cape DRC ministers who issued a manifesto warning that those with only the traditional rudimentary education were doomed to becoming 'hewers of wood and drawers of water', serving the steady stream of incoming European immigrants.[21] Shortly afterwards Marchand and the Rev. A. Moorrees

16 G.D. Scholtz, *Die ontwikkeling van die politieke denke van die Afrikaner* (Johannesburg: Perskor, 1977), vol. 4, pp. 68-71.

17 T.R.H. Davenport, *The Afrikaner Bond* (Cape Town: Oxford University Press, 1966), p. 389.

18 T.G. 13-08, *Report of the Transvaal Indigency Commission, 1908* (further references to *TIC*), p. 55.

19 Malherbe, *Education and the Poor White*, p. 46.

20 J.H. Hofmeyr, *The Life of Jan Hendrik (Onze Jan) Hofmeyr* (Cape Town: Vandesandt De Villiers, 1913), pp. 495-7.

21 Scholtz, *Ontwikkeling van die politieke denke*, vol. 4, pp. 70-72.

published a prospectus for a school in Cape Town to offer poor white children the chance to learn trades. When the school opened a year later Merriman called the DRC the most appropriate institution to teach 'poor whites the great and indispensable truth that there was no shame attached to labor.'[22]

The DRC felt compelled to expand its activities. Its synod appointed Marchand to chair a committee; in 1897 it recommended the founding of a labor colony for poor whites at Kakamas on the Orange River in the northeastern limits of the Colony. At Kakamas and three other rural settlements for the Afrikaner poor the church trained eight hundred families. Between 1894 and 1922 it also established and maintained several industrial and agricultural schools that taught fifteen hundred children, and founded 160 state-subsidized boarding houses, which, between 1917 and 1932, made it possible for more than seven thousand indigent children in remote rural areas to attend school. Already in the 1890s W.P. Schreiner's Cape cabinet was so concerned about the problem of poor whites that it proposed compulsory education, with state subsidies, for indigent children of European parents only.

The matter was taken further after the election victory of the Progressive Party under L.S. Jameson in 1904. By now the children of a third of the white community in the Cape Colony were getting no schooling at all. In 1905 the Jameson government passed legislation to enforce compulsory education up to the sixth school year (Standard 4), but only for children of European parentage and descent. A court later ruled that the Act meant 'pure' white, thus ruling out colored children. The African Political Organization, established in 1902 to promote primarily the interest of colored people, protested vigorously against colored exclusion, but to no avail.[23] By the early 1920s white and colored children at schools in the Cape Province were fully segregated, and white schools were invariably better.

A poor country

Agriculture provided a livelihood for the overwhelming majority of Afrikaners. Farming in the western and southeastern Cape was relatively prosperous. Since the final decades of the nineteenth century there had been a steady increase in the demand for wheat and dairy products from the western Cape, with fruit exports a promising option. Wine farming, hit hard by phylloxera in the 1880s, and stagnating until 1910, started to pick up in the first two decades after Union. In the eastern Cape and Karoo midlands the more successful Afrikaner and English wool farmers shared in the steady expansion of wool exports, up from £4 million in 1904 to £20 million in 1919.

But less than one-fifth of South Africa consists of arable land that can be used to plant crops. Large parts are semi-desert with frequent droughts, and other parts get enough rain but have extremely rugged terrain. Some two-thirds of all of South Africa is today used for grazing. Stock farming developed as a way of life and means of subsistence and only in the twentieth century as a commercial enterprise. A wasteful exploitation of agri-

---

22 Potgieter, 'Die NGK en die blanke onderwys, 1961', pp. 342-4.
23 Gavin Lewis, *Between the Wire and the Wall: A History of South African 'Coloured' Politics* (Cape Town: David Philip, 1987), pp. 30-33.

cultural resources contributed to a crisis in pastoral farming. Overstocking, together with grass burning, destroyed the natural vegetation, and thunderstorms swept the top-soil away. Farmers had been accustomed to move on to new grass and fresh land when pastures were exhausted, but, by the 1880s, the frontier of expansion had closed. Spread thinly over the great landmass of South Africa, farmers had accumulated little capital and most were deeply in debt to traders. In 1886 a Bloemfontein paper reported: 'Formerly nearly everyone owned his farm of 2,000 or 3,000 morgen of land and most of it was unencumbered; now the great mass of the country people lack land and those who own it have many mortgage bonds on it.'[24]

The problem of white poverty in South Africa was initially predominantly a rural problem that manifested itself after two centuries of subsistence farming. It was, as a prominent Afrikaans author and social worker writing under the name MER, remarked, 'a natural and inevitable process' that had occurred among the Afrikaner community. In a folksy way she described the process: 'A handful of whites saw the chance of farming the gigantic South Africa . . . We never took into account the way in which the *veld* would react, and the effects on us of the great space, the loneliness, the solitude, the isolation.'[25]

Many farmers were unable to make the transition to a cash economy and market-oriented farming. Some did begin applying scientific methods of stock breeding, and diversified their farming by breaking in land, planting crops, and marketing their produce effectively, but the majority were not prepared for such a major venture and carried on the tradition of largely subsistence farming. J.W. Gunning, a Dutch physician in the southern Free State, observed: 'The idea of breeding better sheep than one's father has done, to feed them differently, to till more soil, to work and manure the soil differently and more carefully than one's ancestors have done occurs alas! to very few as yet.'[26] The switch to risk-taking commercial farming in a country with poor soil and a fickle climate was extremely difficult without a government determined to stabilize prices, to provide specialized training in new agricultural methods, and to extend credit at low rates. Not until the end of the 1930s did the South African government have sufficient revenue to provide such support.

The crisis was exacerbated by the Roman-Dutch Law of inheritance that compelled the division of a farmer's property among his children. In operation in the Cape Colony until 1874 and in the Boer republics until their demise, the law left children on farms subdivided into parts too small to farm efficiently. The Carnegie Commission report of 1932 documented several case studies, of which the following case was fairly typical: one farmer divided his farm of 11,000 morgen equally among his ten children. None could make a living from farming such small lots and some of the children became poor whites.[27] The availability of a large reservoir of native labor, cheaper and also more docile, kept the poorer sons of farmers and the *bywoners* from becoming a class of wage-earning

---

24 Scholtz, *Ontwikkeling, van die politieke denke*, vol. 4, p. 70.

25 A letter by her published in Erika Theron, *Sonder hoed of handskoen* (Cape Town: Tafelberg, 1983), p. 21.

26 *The Friend*, 30 November 1894.

27 J.R. Albertyn, *Verslag van die Carnegie-Kommissie: Sociologiese Verslag* (Stellenbosch: Pro Ecclesia, 1932), p. 7.

farm laborers. An entire Afrikaner underclass formed on the farms, increasingly unable to feed their large families properly, many stunted in mental and physical development.

During the 1890s a natural as well as a man-made disaster greatly intensified the problem. The natural disaster was the devastating rinderpest, an acute, usually fatal infectious disease affecting cattle that broke out in the mid-1890s. It wiped out herds in large parts of South Africa. In the Transvaal alone it destroyed half of the farmers' cattle herds. Then came the Anglo-Boer War, in which the British used scorched earth tactics to break the spirit of the Bittereinders. Some 90 per cent of all the farmhouses in the Orange Free State were damaged, and in the Transvaal homesteads were also destroyed on a large scale. Most of the herds in the republics were decimated, with crops and implements destroyed. In the Transvaal, 80 per cent of the cattle, 75 per cent of the horses and 73 per cent of the sheep were destroyed; in the OFS the figures were 59 per cent of the cattle and 55 per cent of the sheep. Some fifteen thousand Boer fighters, unable to be resettled on their farms, became part of the reservoir of urban unskilled labor.

Alfred Milner, British High Commissioner for all four colonies after the Anglo-Boer War, stressed that South Africa could not turn itself in a white man's country if it was 'full of poor whites.' South Africa needed high economic growth and a secure white population living 'far above of that of the poorest section of the population of a purely white country.' The goal was 'a largely increased white population [who] can live in decency and comfort.'[28] Milner's priorities were in conflict with each other and left a huge problem unresolved. Rapid economic growth in Milner's terms required 'a large amount of rough labor.' Whites were much too expensive for that kind of labor. There was, in fact, no place for the Afrikaners in Milner's scheme. Blacks did the unskilled work at rates far below those for which whites were prepared to work, and recent immigrants filled most of the skilled and semi-skilled positions. Increasingly, Afrikaners found themselves squeezed out from both skilled and unskilled work in the cities.

C.W. de Kiewiet, one of South Africa's most gifted historians, writing in the 1930s, identified three major factors that acted as constraints on economic growth during the first three or four decades of the century: 'its low-grade ore, its low-grade land, and also its low-grade human beings.'[29] Much of South Africa's low-grade gold ore, sold at a low, fixed price, could only be mined by very cheap labor. Low-grade land was responsible for much of agriculture's problems, with low-grade human beings the product of low spending on education and the large distance many rural children had to travel to school. By 1917 one-fifth of white children were not in school.

De Kiewiet highlighted an important social aspect of a stagnant economy and small domestic market: 'It was not the natives alone who were depressed in their power to earn. The country could not afford a high standard of living for the entire population with the result that, in addition to the native population, a very large proportion of the white population was also depressed to a low level of income and livelihood.'[30] White artisans, in fact, received better pay than their counterparts in any country of Europe. Real artisan wages were higher only in the USA, Canada and Australia.[31] Ralph Bunche,

---

28 Headlam, *Milner Papers*, vol. 2, p. 459.
29 C.W. de Kiewiet, *A History of South Africa* (Oxford: Oxford University Press, 1941), p. 212.
30 De Kiewiet, *History*, p. 214.

a distinguished black American on a visit in 1937-38, observed that the standard of living for whites was 'much too high for the poor-white group to live under.'[32]

At the bottom of the labor market was a mass of migrant black workers without rights and with little choice but to sell their labor cheaply. The goldmines of the Witwatersrand, the dynamo of the economy, were based largely on black migrant labor. By 1911 more than 90 per cent of the black population of Johannesburg was male, working for very low wages; if they were paid more they would work less, so the justification went. Intending to return to the reserves, many blacks lived temporarily in wretched shacks or labor compounds. As a source of ultra-cheap labor they were a constant threat to unskilled and even semi-skilled Afrikaner workers.[33]

A traumatic early urbanization

The first three decades of the twentieth century saw the problem of poor Afrikaners at its worst. Urbanization was a rapid, chaotic, and almost always traumatic process. By 1890 fewer than 10,000 Afrikaners (two or three per cent) were urbanized; thirty-six years later, in 1926, 391,000 (41 per cent) lived in towns and cities, in 1936, 535,000 (50 per cent). In the urban environment the employers and their managers invariably spoke English, a language many Afrikaners did not understand at all or, if they did, only poorly.

The Afrikaners who came in the first and second waves of urbanization suffered most. Artisans had organized themselves into trade unions in mining, commerce and industry, hence it was difficult for employers to reduce their wages. This meant that there was very little left for the semi-skilled white workers and unskilled blacks.[34] The first Afrikaners in the cities could not get entry into the trades because they lacked the necessary educational qualifications. They did not have relatives who could help them to find work and had no experience of trade union organization. Unions operating on the closed-shop principle often admitted only people who had been proposed by family members. Until 1907, English-speaking mineworkers on the Witwatersrand excluded Afrikaners from all of the most desirable positions.

Those Afrikaners excluded from the formal job market tended to become the urban poor whites. A 1926 commission referred to urban white workers who 'have no alternative but to swell the ranks of unskilled industrial labor; in other words to put themselves in competition with the native.'[35] An early 1930s survey found that of 462 poor white families, half had attended only primary school, two-fifths more could hardly read or write, and one-tenth were totally illiterate. They could not sell their labor at the lowest levels because Africans were preferred.[36]

Some of the urban white poor managed to find unskilled work. Throughout the first

31 Eric Walker, *A History of Southern Africa* (London: Longmans, Green, 1957), p. 577.
32 Robert Edgar, *The Travel Notes of Ralph J. Bunche* (Athens; Ohio State University, 1992), pp. 160-62.
33 William Beinart, *Twentieth-Century South Africa* (Cape Town: Oxford University Press, 1994), pp. 59-67.
34 David Yudelman, *The Emergence of Modern South Africa* (Westport: Greenwood Press, 1983), pp. 53-4.
35 *Report of the Economic and Wages Commission, 1926*, para. 144.
36 Albertyn, *Sociologiese verslag*, pp. 19-21,169.

four decades of the 1900s, white unskilled workers demanded three shillings and six pence a day, and sometimes five shillings, for the same work for which the unmarried black migrant received two shillings.[37] Between 1902 and 1908, a white mineworker with a family received about ten shillings per shift; a black migrant got between two and three shillings a day.[38]

The urbanizing Afrikaners were expected by their fellow whites to live like whites. A witness commented on their grim struggle to the Transvaal Indigency Commission (TIC, 1906-1908): 'Every white man was undersold. The white man had got his rent to pay and had to wear a shirt of some sort and had far more expenses . . . and had to keep a family and consequently was undersold.'[39] Many white workers preferred unemployment to degrading work or menial wages. Decent jobs paying a living wage were few. In the immediate aftermath of the war, most Afrikaner men in Johannesburg worked as cab or trolley drivers; some became brick makers; others offloaded the wagons that delivered farm produce. Girls found work at hand-laundries and boys as messengers or newspaper sellers. Prostitution and crime were common alternative ways of earning a living. Most young white criminals and street thugs were Afrikaners for many years to come.

Johannesburg and other Witwatersrand towns had some of the worst slums in the world. There were no government housing schemes initially, and many of the urbanizing Afrikaners had to find accommodation in slums. A white woman testified to the TIC about poor whites squatting on government or town lands in and around Pretoria just after the war: 'There are no sanitary arrangements. They are most miserable, huddled together in little tin shanties – married couples, young children and grown-up young people, all living together, sometimes in one little room or tent.' The Rev. D. Theron observed to the same commission: 'I feel very strongly that it does not help to keep a child five hours under the influence of a school and then send it back for the rest of the day to the same hovel from which it comes.'[40]

The traumatic urbanization of Afrikaners had cultural and political dimensions as well. A study depicted the scene: '[Urban Afrikaners] were working like black people, taking orders like black people, living in shabby residential streets adjacent to black shanty towns, and having to speak a foreign language – English – like a conquered race.' Their better-off fellow-Afrikaners did not know whether to avert their eyes or rush to their help, but, whatever they did, the poor represented an acute embarrassment. In the view of English-speakers the Afrikaner usually appeared as 'the poor, uneducated railway worker, the ignorant policeman . . . vacant low class beings. A stigma of poverty and ignorance was attached to the whole group.'[41]

Yet the Afrikaners who began to settle on the Witwatersrand during the 1890s as a poor and downtrodden people were not crushed by the experience. The studies of Charles van Onselen, J.J. Fourie, and Ernst Stals paint a vivid picture of how the more enterprising

---

37 Report on the National Conference on the Poor White Problem, 1934, pp. 163-5.
38 Robert Davies, Capital, State and White Labour in South Africa (Brighton: The Harvester Press, 1979), p. 59.
39 TIC, p. 12.
40 TIC, p. 45.
41 L. Salomon, 'Socio-Economic Aspects of South African History, 1870-1962', doctoral diss., Boston University, 1962, pp. 106, 117.

of them managed to adapt to the Johannesburg environment.[42] People who had been bywoners became self-employed as transport riders, cab drivers and small-scale brick manufacturers. Many of these opportunities disappeared as trains and trams made their appearance. By 1907, with the introduction of self-government for the Transvaal and the rise of Het Volk to power, a crowd of Afrikaner and English unemployed marched from Johannesburg to Pretoria to put pressure on the new colonial secretary, Jan Smuts, to 'employ white labor at fair wages.' The poor were shocked when Smuts told a delegation that there was work for them on the Pietersburg railway line for three shillings and four pence a day and a bag of mealie (maize) meal. Haas Das, editor of *De Transvaler*, told an Afrikaner audience in the poor-white suburb of Vrededorp that such an offer 'was most insulting to the Afrikaner nation.' The sting of the whole thing lay in the offer of mealie meal. 'It was placing them on a level with Kaffirs.'[43]

The loyalties of the Afrikaner poor were still up for grabs. Most supported Het Volk, but some considered the Labour Party as a political home. They entered trade unions despite the opposition of the church. In 1914 the Johannesburg Town Council grudgingly acknowledged the mobilized power of the predominantly Afrikaner community of Vrededorp. 'Every political party truckled to this mass of voters and endeavored to find employment for them. The mass had overturned every political party, and would overturn any political party which might be in power unless a remedy was provided to remove their appalling poverty and degradation.'[44]

From an early stage the Afrikaans church played a vital role in offering spiritual succor. By 1909, in Johannesburg's Afrikaner suburbs of Vrededorp and Fordsburg the church services were reported filled to overflowing.[45] Afrikaner poverty remained a feature of the urban landscape until the early 1940s, but this should not lead to the conclusion that the poor failed to improve their situation. In fact they moved up the ladder and their place was taken by a new wave of poor Afrikaners. By the 1920s urban Afrikaners in general were still poor, but they formed a vibrant community that had moved beyond the depths of despair. They had settled down by organizing their community around Afrikaans schools and churches. The incidence of social evils, like prostitution, gambling and alcohol abuse, was much lower than in the period between 1900 and 1920. They were overcoming illiteracy or semi-literacy, were putting their faith in education and training, and were expressing their power at the ballot booth in a way no politician dared to ignore.

Disputes over a solution

Providing superior education for whites to equip them for the most desirable jobs was an issue on which white political leaders across the political spectrum agreed. But Gen-

---

42 Charles van Onselen, *Studies in the Social and Economic History of the Witwatersrand, 1886 – 1914*: vol. 1: *New Babylon*, vol. 2: *New Nineveh* (London: Longman, 1982); J.J. Fourie, *Afrikaners in die Goudstad, 1924-1961* (Pretoria: HAUM, 1986).
43 Van Onselen, *New Nineveh*, p. 147.
44 Van Onselen, *New Nineveh*, p. 158.
45 Fourie, *Afrikaners in die Goudstad*, p. 148.

erals Smuts and Hertzog, and Dr D.F. Malan, along with Botha, the main Afrikaner leaders of the first four decades of Union, had major disagreements about other issues relating to the poor-white question.

The work of the Cambridge economist, Alfred Marshall, author of *Principles of Economics* (1890), strongly influenced the government commissions of inquiry on poverty
that sat in South Africa. Marshall's work laid the foundation for neo-classical economics,
the dominant economic creed in Britain and its empire over the next four decades. It
argued that government intervention to solve poverty, particularly by artificially creating jobs, made a bad situation worse; governments had to accept that an economy had
its own equilibrium and that they had to allow it to adjust itself. They could assist this
process by providing for a free market, low trade barriers and a balanced budget. Through
introducing compulsory education the state gave the new generation the chance to break
free from the proletariat.

Smuts arrived in Cambridge just after Marshall's work appeared and made some of the
insights his own. A comment he made at the end of the Boer War captured his basic inclination: South Africa's problems could not be solved by 'some master stroke of diplomacy or statesmanship' but by time 'and the free play of the social and economic forces.'[46]
While firmly insisting on the rehabilitation of the poor whites, he placed his emphasis
on education and training. He would offer the whites the first choice of jobs, but the
government should not, like Paul Kruger's republic, succumb to excessive demands for
assistance. The priority of the new Transvaal government was to assist mining, promote
export industries, introduce lower tariffs, and encourage an efficient agriculture to lower the cost of food. The poor would benefit in the rising tide of growth and prosperity.

The Transvaal Indigency Commission, dominated by members of Milner's Kindergarten, expressed similar views. Its report, tabled in 1908, stated that the demand for
state intervention was extensive, farmers expecting government 'to remove all difficulties.'[47] It concluded that it was futile to try to solve poverty by keeping on the land
whites lacking in enterprise, capital and modern farming skills. The rural poor would
have to become manual laborers in the towns and cities. The commission urged government to refrain from protecting the white poor from reasonable competition from black
and colored people.[48]

In 1923, Smuts, now prime minister, met a DRC delegation at a time of high white unemployment and high inflation. He told them that 'the present dismal situation', was
only temporary. It was inevitable that some whites would be pushed out 'and lie there as
wounded on the battlefield.' Attention had to be focused on the next generation, ensuring that it received proper industrial education to face the future. The response of the
ministers is not recorded, but the defeat of the ruling South African Party a year later was
widely attributed to its lack of sensitivity with respect to the poor-white issue.

Hertzog had a quite different approach. A biographer, C.M. van den Heever, sees him
as 'continental' in rejecting the neo-classicist *laissez faire* policy. While studying in the
Netherlands in the 1890s, he was almost certainly influenced by the work of Abra-

---

46 *Smuts Papers* (Cambridge: Cambridge University Press, 1966), vol. 1, pp. 484-90
47 *TIC*, p. 181.
48 *TIC*, p. 197.

ham Kuyper, the prominent Dutch theologian and politician, who urged employers to pay their workers proper wages. Concern for the poor was not a question of charity but an affirmation of the Calvinist principle that man had the right to a decent living.[49] Each church had to assume responsibility for its own poor.[50]

Hertzog, who had become a wealthy man after the war as the result of an inheritance, was one of a small class of *Heere-boeren* or 'landlords.' According to a socialist writer, this class had little influence among the conservative, traditional Boers, who rejected the views of 'towns people and capitalists.'[51] 'These rich farmers,' one small farmer wrote in a Transvaal paper, 'these selfish, self-righteous bloodsuckers! . . . Even our great generals who make such nice speeches, oppress the poor in private and enrich themselves from the impoverished.'[52] In the 1914 election for the Transvaal provincial council the Labour Party attracted strong Afrikaner support in both urban and rural constituencies. Its message was that the 'money capitalist' used farmers to suppress the workers, while the 'land capitalist' employed workers to suppress the burghers on the land.[53] Hertzog was one of those 'land capitalists', but he soon distanced himself from the pro-capital and pro-Empire sympathies of most of the *Heeren-boeren*. The platform of the National Party he had founded in 1914 presented Louis Botha as the 'Prime Minister of Imperialism and Capital.' Hertzog broke with the SAP, he said, because of its capitalist policies.

For Daniël François Malan it was not so much a Calvinist principle that was at stake but the pastoral obligation of the church to care for its poor fellow-Afrikaners. Malan grew up on a farm in the western Cape, and studied first at the Victoria College and then the University of Utrecht in the Netherlands, where he received his doctoral degree in 1904. His theology was shaped by the Cape's evangelical tradition with its emphasis on prayer, mission, education and a puritanical lifestyle, and by the thoughts of the Irish philosopher George Berkeley, the subject of his Utrecht doctoral dissertation. He turned away from the orthodox principle of 'from doctrine to life', meaning that one had to start with the Bible in the search for revelation. Instead he accepted Berkeley's 'ethical strand' of theology, 'through life to doctrine.' Ethical religion had a strong bias towards social activism and modernization.[54]

At the center of Malan's interpretation of 'life' stood the Afrikaners' survival struggle. He believed that the DRC as the church of the Afrikaner people had to assist Afrikaners in overcoming their poverty and maintaining their cultural and national character – this was called the *volkskerk* position. Malan's most crucial social concern was reinte-

---

49 Abraham Kuyper, *The Problem of Poverty* (Grand Rapids: Baker Book House, 1991).

50 G.J. Schutte, 'Arbeid, die geen brood geeft . . .' in G.J. Schutte (ed.), *Een arbeider is zijn loon waardig* (The Hague, Meinema, 1991), pp. 10-23.

51 Joh. Visscher, *De ondergang van een wereld* (Amsterdam: A.B Soep, 1903), pp. 32-3; John Bottomley, 'The Orange Free State and the Rebellion of 1914', in Robert Morrell (ed.), *White But Poor: Essays in the History of the Poor White in South Africa, 1880-1940* (Pretoria: Unisa, 1992), pp. 29-40.

52 Isabel Hofmeyr, 'Building a Nation from Words: Afrikaans Language, Literature and Ethnic Identity', in Shula Marks and Stanley Trapido (eds.), *The Politics of Race, Class and Nationalism in Twentieth-Century South Africa* (London: Longman, 1987), p. 101.

53 Labour Party, *Die nuwe politiek* (Johannesburg, 1915); D. Ticktin, 'The War Issue and the Collapse of the South African Labour Party, 1914-15', *The South African Historical Journal*, 1, (1969), pp. 60-69.

54 George William Brink, 'Daniël François Malan, 1874-1959: An ecclesiological study of the influence of his theology', doctoral diss., US, 1997, pp. 119-26.

grating the poor in the Afrikaner community. His son, Daniël, wrote: 'My father could be literally moved to tears when he thought of the poor whites who in the trek to the cities went under.'[55]

On Malan's return to South Africa in 1905, he spent six months in the Transvaal, where he encountered the acute poverty of the Afrikaners in the wake of the Anglo-Boer War. For three years he was minister of the Montagu parish in the western Cape, where he urged the rehabilitation of the poor whites. In this wine-producing district he also took a brave stand against farmers who deliberately tied their colored laborers to the farm through an abundant supply of liquor. He moved to the parish of Graaff-Reinet, but in 1915 he resigned from the ministry to edit the newly founded daily, *De Burger,* in Cape Town. He was prompted by his grave concern over intra-Afrikaner political divisions and the abject poverty in which many Afrikaners lived. In his farewell sermon Malan posed the question: 'Do we Afrikaners have the right to exist or would it perhaps not be better to commit collective suicide?'[56]

In Malan's view, the 'native question' lay at the very heart of the poor-white issue. Blacks were arduously improving their education and beginning to compete directly with whites for the better-paid jobs. If the 'progressive' blacks were allowed to continue on this course, there was no hope of South Africa's remaining a 'white man's country.' He believed that industrial segregation had become essential to avoid direct competition for work between whites and blacks. Blacks had to be trained to subsist in the reserves.[57] How much the government would have to spend to make the reserves viable and whether they could be made viable at all, Malan did not say.

A turbulent mining town

The mining industry, concentrated in Johannesburg and some other Witwatersrand towns, created the mirage that South Africa was wealthy. Shortly after becoming a member of the Het Volk government in 1907, Smuts expressed his dismay about the large numbers of urban Afrikaners who were unemployed or working at very low wages: 'The situation is rotten to the core . . . That a town of 75,000 whites exporting £26,000,000 in gold per annum should have a threatening unemployment question is a sufficient proof of that.' He noted with an air of desperation: 'We are so wretchedly poor.' A policy for agricultural development and irrigation schemes to provide work would be 'enormously difficult to carry out.'[58]

For most of the twentieth century the gold mining industry towered over the South African economy; a 1932 estimate said half of the state's finances were derived from the mines and that half the population's livelihood came directly or indirectly from the mines. In 1907, there were 18,600 white miners and only 18 per cent were locally born. By 1918 local white miners were in the majority and by 1930 they made up two-thirds

---

55 US University Library (Malan Collection), 1/1/3268, Life Sketch of D.F. Malan by his son, ca 1965, pp. 5, 48.
56 H.B. Thom, *D.F. Malan* (Cape Town: Nasionale Boekhandel, 1980), p. 13.
57 C.F.J. Muller, *Sonop in die Suide: geboorte en groei van die Nasionale Pers* (Cape Town: Nasionale Boekhandel, 1990), p. 649.
58 *Smuts Papers*, vol. 2, p. 336.

of the white miners. At this point there were some 200,000 black mine workers, all migrants drawn from Mozambique, Basutoland, and the Transkei and Ciskei.

Impoverished Afrikaners roamed the streets of Johannesburg and other towns, nourishing a bitter grievance about the Anglo-Boer War and a fierce desire to return to the
land. Afrikaner workers wanted a republic, but not the sort of socialist republic advocated by the communist activists. They were also deeply suspicious of the capitalist class,
with good reason. *The Star*, representing the opinion of the mining magnates, wrote just
after Union that 'South Africa would never become a white man's land like Canada or
Australia, and the best future course was to spur growth by drawing on black labor freely
and in the process create more opportunities for skilled white labor.'[59]

To aggravate the Afrikaners' position, white trade union leaders, like the employers,
were almost all English-speaking. Both capital and organized white labor were staunch
imperialists with little sympathy for Afrikaner aspirations. *Ons Vaderland* wrote in 1917
that 'the contempt with which Afrikaners are treated on the Rand is deeply etched on
the consciousness of the Afrikaners and it is hard for sensitive Afrikaners to collaborate
with this class of people.'[60]

Mineworkers were the most militant section of the Afrikaner working class. They did
work that was very dangerous and carried serious health risks. A study of Cornish miners on the Witwatersrand mines found an average life expectancy of only thirty-six years.
Of the eighteen leaders of a 1907 strike committee, fourteen died of phthisis, a wasting
disease of the lungs, before the next big strike of 1913.[61]

Both the government and the mining industry attempted to provide some assistance
to whites. In 1893 the Transvaal Volksraad established the first legal color bar in the
economy, restricting the job of blasting to whites. After the Anglo-Boer War, Milner tried
to satisfy the white artisans before he imported Chinese workers to solve a labor shortage caused by blacks withholding their labor (see p. 267). A list of jobs restricted to
whites was drawn up, but the measure was intended to be temporary. After 1907, when
blacks began to replace the Chinese, white miners insisted on the retention of the
protected jobs.

Employers accepted the color bar only reluctantly, but the mining companies were
willing to use Afrikaners instead of the assertive immigrant miners they thoroughly disliked.[62] At the end of April 1907 the latter struck against management's plans to put
blacks in higher-level jobs and reduce the ratio of black to white miners. The strike soon
turned ugly. When the Het Volk government called up British troops, large numbers of
Afrikaners volunteered as strikebreakers. Mining circles thought Afrikaners would make
ideal miners, more docile than foreign miners and 'quick of resource, dexterous, highly
intelligent and capable.'[63]

After the strike the Afrikaner scabs kept their jobs and even more Afrikaners entered
the mines. They soon became a militant labor force, thoroughly radicalized by the fear

59 Scholtz, *Ontwikkeling van die politieke denke*, vol. 4, p. 303.

60 Fourie, *Afrikaners in die Goudstad*, pp. 88-9.

61 Yudelman, *Emergence*, p. 93.

62 Yudelman, *Emergence,* pp. 59-65.

63 Fourie, *Afrikaners in die Goudstad*, p. 84.

that the employers would undercut them with cheaper black labor or using even larger teams of blacks under their supervision.[64] In 1911 the Union government passed the Mines and Works Act that protected whites in some categories of work, and Smuts used the Act to write regulations that limited a range of jobs to whites only.

In 1913 another strike by whites on the gold mines occurred over union recognition, with riots, arson, looting and near anarchy across the Rand. The police and the army were unable to contain the disturbances and the new Active Citizen Force (ACF) was still too poorly organized to be effective. The stability of the state itself would be at risk if strike leaders linked up with disaffected rural Afrikaners.[65]

Soldiers shot and killed a hundred strikers and bystanders before the strike ended. The government had to sign a humiliating accord with the strike leaders, only to be challenged again six months later. A 1914 strike on the coal mines spread to the railways and harbors and culminated in a general strike. This time the government was ready. It declared martial law and sent in units of the newly formed Permanent Force and ACF commandos. The English-speaking leaders of the trade union federation were arrested; Smuts deported nine of them summarily and illegally. To break the strike, Smuts relied on the support of men with whom he had fought the Anglo-Boer War. Rural Afrikaners called up for commando duty enthusiastically took up their weapons 'to shoot Englishmen' in Johannesburg.[66]

The combination of a militant white workforce and the urban white poor had become a major source of instability. Soon the white poor as a political danger manifested itself in the countryside. In the rebellion of 1914-15 the rebel leader, General Christiaan de Wet, enlisted the inhabitants of a poor-white settlement near his farm, and many bywoners also participated in the rebellion. He acknowledged that his supporters were not 'gentlemen' but 'slum dwellers.' Albertus Brand, son of President Brand and magistrate of Lindley, commented that people in the northern Free State who rebelled 'were on the "loot". . . they were not people of standing and responsibility.' Most of them were bywoners. Their target was merchants to whom they were in debt, or richer farmers who cared little about their troubles.[67] (For a discussion of the Rebellion, see pp. 379-84.)

The rebellion was suppressed, but the SAP as the ruling party was deeply concerned about the combination of white poverty, anti-imperialism and anti-capitalism. John X. Merriman wrote to Jan Smuts at the end of 1915 about the implications of the rebellion. He referred to the rebels as these 'wretched folk . . . ready for any mischief.' They threatened 'the very foundation of our national existence.' There were two dire possibilities: the 'insidious teachings of the international Socialists' and a 'not impossible alliance with the Natives.' He did not share the thinking that the white poor found themselves in a hopeless situation. 'No cause is hopeless if one only hits on the right plan.'[68]

---

64 Yudelman, *Emergence,* p. 133.

65 Yudelman, *Emergence,* pp. 93-108.

66 Fourie, *Afrikaners in die Goudstad,* p. 86.

67 UG 42-1916, *Judicial Commission of Inquiry into the Rebellion,* p. 323, see also p. 127; Sandra Swart, 'Desperate Men: The 1914 Rebellion and the Politics of Poverty', *South African Historical Journal,* 42 (2000), p. 175.

68 This is drawn from two letters that Merriman wrote on 20 December 1915 to Smuts. See Bottomley, 'The OFS and the Rebellion of 1914', in R. Morrel (ed.) *White But Poor,* pp. 29-40; *Smuts Papers,* vol. 3, p. 329.

The Rand Strike of 1922

The suppression of the rebellion threw the SAP back onto a shrinking support base of mostly richer and older Afrikaners. Hertzog's National Party, founded in 1914, captured half the Afrikaner vote in 1915. Except in the western Cape, it drew predominantly the vote of the rural poor and the smaller farmers. It was generally accepted that landless bywoners had attached themselves to the NP cause.[69]

To break through to the urban Afrikaners, NP supporters in 1915 established two newspapers, *Ons Vaderland* in Pretoria, and the much more substantial paper *De Burger* (from 1922 *Die Burger*) in Cape Town. From the start *De Burger* combined the themes of anti-imperialism and anti-big capital, powerfully assisted by D.C. Boonzaier, one of the most brilliant cartoonists South Africa has had. Boonzaier moved from a farm in the Karoo to cosmopolitan circles in Cape Town (he wrote his diary in English). His cartoons were inspired by a fierce hatred of the greed of mining magnates and the sycophantic admiration he believed Botha and Smuts displayed towards them and the Empire. He depicted the bewildered urban poor whites as scorned and exploited by the unscrupulous capitalists, portrayed by a repulsive Hoggenheimer figure, who regularly got Botha and Smuts to dance to his tune. Although Boonzaier denied it, Hoggenheimer was unmistakably Jewish, and the cartoons stimulated the populist opposition to big capital, Jews in business and the culture of materialism.[70]

The NP tried to win the vote of the white working class voters, but many Afrikaners supported the Labour Party. With its defense of worker rights the Labour Party won 21 seats out of 134 in the 1920 election, the NP won 44, the Unionist Party 25, and the South African Party, which Smuts headed, 41. Labour's appeal, however, was diminished by its strong insistence on the retention of ties to the British Empire, and by its almost wholly English-speaking leadership, of whom a large proportion were immigrants. It had no Afrikaners among its parliamentary representatives.

Trying to capture the labor vote, Hertzog startled South Africa by declaring in 1919 that the attempt by Western powers to crush the Bolshevik Revolution had been inspired by their thirst for economic exploitation. The Communist revolutionaries in Russia, he said, combined worker and national aspirations. Bolshevism as an idea – that a people had a right to be free, to govern themselves, and to resist an alien conqueror – was 'excellent.' 'If we say that we have the right to govern ourselves and we say that it is our duty to see that this right is expressed, we are in fact also Bolshevists.'[71]

In response, *The International*, journal of the International Socialist League – it was the forerunner of the South African Communist Party – said Hertzog was simply using any whip to beat the 'top capitalist class' (a reference to the mining magnates). 'The National Party', it wrote, 'is not a working class party, though it has workers in its ranks. Its mission is not to make the workers the ruling class, but to institute the political regime

---

69 For a case study see Robert Morrell, 'The poor whites of Middelburg, Transvaal', in R. Morrell (ed.) *White but Poor* (Pretoria: Unisa, 1992), pp. 1-28

70 Muller, *Sonop,* pp. 348-70; Milton Shain, *The Roots of Anti-Semitism in South Africa* (University of Virginia Press, 1994), pp. 60-63, 90-99.

71 *Hertzog-toesprake*, IV, p. 141; C.M. van den Heever, *Generaal J.B.M. Hertzog* (Johannesburg: APB, 1943), p. 212.

of the small farmers.' *Labour World* also claimed that the NP's support for farmers would push up food prices. The strife it was fomenting within the white group would delay a solution to the poor-white problem. Only a socialist order could solve it.[72]

In the aftermath of the First World War the young South African state entered its most perilous phase. The economy was stagnating. Between 1920 and 1932 the gross domestic product declined in monetary terms, with almost no increase in industrial output. The industrial sector and the railways shed jobs. At the same time, largely as a result of the post-Anglo-Boer War baby boom, the number of white youths entering the job market jumped by 50 per cent between 1921 and 1926, compared to the first two decades of the century. White unemployment rose sharply. In Johannesburg alone an estimated three thousand families lived on the point of starvation. To compound matters, rampant inflation prices pushed prices up by 50 per cent between 1917 and 1920.

The mines were the flashpoint. Large numbers of immigrant miners had left to return to Europe to fight in the First World War, removing an ageing, more conservative element from the labor force. By 1918 Afrikaners formed the majority of white miners in the dangerous underground jobs. They would soon prove to be the most radical force the mines had ever employed. The distance between the workers and the government of the day widened after 1920 when the SAP absorbed the Unionist Party with its strong support of the mining houses. Smuts, prime minister since 1919, struggled to find his feet after a prolonged absence abroad fighting in the First World War. His government soon resorted to tough methods. In 1921 security forces shot down 163 Israelites, a black religious sect, near Queenstown in the eastern Cape. In South West Africa, which South Africa governed under a League of Nations mandate, a government force in 1922 killed more than a hundred of the Bondelswarts tribe who were resisting taxes. Airplanes that bombed the tribe's flocks also killed women and children. When Smuts used similar methods in the 1922 strike on the Witwatersrand, Hertzog said that his footsteps 'dripped with blood.'

This 1922 showdown took place in a context in which both black and white miners were disaffected. Black miners, who had willingly agreed to refrain from industrial action during the war, found that inflation had depressed their wages, and struck against poor pay and the color bar. In 1920 police and troops put down a strike of 71,000 black workers. Then the gold price began to fall from 130 shillings per fine ounce at the beginning of 1920 to 95 shillings at the end of 1921, while production costs rose by one-third over the 1915 figure.

The Chamber of Mines acted abruptly and recklessly, afraid that many mines would have to close. In 1918 it had concluded an agreement with the white unions that fixed the ratio of white to black workers at 7.4:1, but it now announced its intention to abandon the 1918 agreement and scrap the color bar for semi-skilled work. It expected that no more than two thousand white workers would have to be dismissed, but it was clear that many more ran the risk of losing their jobs over the longer term. The employers' organizations and the mining houses threw caution to the wind by openly suggesting a thorough revision of the position of the white workers. The Chamber called job cuts

72 Wessel Visser, 'Die geskiedenis en rol van die persorgane in die politieke en ekonomiese mobilisasie van die georganiseerde arbeidersbeweging in Suid-Afrika, 1908-1924', doctoral diss., US, 2001, pp. 352, 494.

part of the struggle to ensure the survival of the industry, and the color bar an immoral practice.

South Africa's antiquated system of industrial relations was an accident waiting to happen. In Australia, with a history of militant labor action, the government had realized the importance of compulsory arbitration and other conflict-solving mechanisms. In South Africa worker action was legally curtailed, leaving mine workers with no real alternative to a militant strike. A strike started on 2 January 1922 when the coal miners came out, followed about a week later by the gold miners, engineers, and power-workers. Denys Reitz, a cabinet minister, thought that 90 per cent of the militant strikers were Afrikaners; a government commission said it was 75 per cent, of whom most were nationalists. Most of the two thousand police reinforcements sent from the rural areas to the Witwatersrand were also Afrikaners, and the burgher commandos, a major part of the force that crushed the strike, were Afrikaners too.[73]

Two main tendencies could be discerned among the revolutionary strikers. A commission of inquiry concluded that 'the majority of the revolutionary forces' had as its aim 'the destruction of the existing order and the formation of an independent Republic.' There were also the Communists, hoping to get underway their revolution by leading the 'general uprising of the people against all forms of capitalism.' The commission noted that the 'divergent aims were accountable for the haphazard, spasmodic, and irresponsible features of the outbreak.'[74]

The republican strikers presented the conflict in atavistic terms as a re-enactment of the frontier struggle between white and black. Speakers told a huge outdoor meeting that they had to be 'unanimous in standing by the victory of the Voortrekkers over [the Zulu leader] Dingaan [Dingane] in 1838. It was nothing short of cheek for the Chamber of Mines to reverse this position.' Bernard Sachs wrote that a mineworkers' strike had degenerated into a rebellion against British imperial authority.[75] In court cases evidence was offered that strike leaders referred to the Union Jack as 'nothing but a dirty cloth', and formed commandos as in the days of the ZAR. They promised that the *Vierkleur*, the Transvaal republican flag, would soon fly over the province again, and approved of violent methods to achieve the objective.[76] But many strikers were opposed to an Afrikaner republic.

The Communist revolutionaries, who were all English-speakers, attempted to take over the leadership of the strike and use it to promote a proletarian revolution. Red rosettes and ribbons appeared in many processions and some participants sang 'The Red Flag.' Communist and racial appeals became intertwined. An issue of the *International*, the Communist newspaper, appealed in Dutch to the policemen and armed civilians on the government side: 'Are you prepared to serve idiotic capitalists as their stupid underlings and accomplices in suppressing your fellow Afrikaners? It is their intention to replace

---

73 Yudelman, *Emergence*, p. 184.

74 *Report of the Martial Law Inquiry Judicial Commission* (Pretoria: Wallachs, 1922), p. 32.

75 Bernard Sachs, cited by A.G. Oberholster, *Die Mynwerkerstaking: Witwatersrand, 1922* (Pretoria: HSRC, 1982), p. 3.

76 Jeremy Krikler, 'White Working Class Identity and the Rand Revolt', paper presented to the History Workshop, University of the Witwatersrand, 5-8 July 2001.

us and also you with cheap black laborers.'[77] The white miners' union warned Afrikaner farmers that the workers' defeat would mean that 'the Kafir in future will take up the place of the white man and then we are doomed to national annihilation.'[78]

All the radical non-Afrikaner workers were by no means dogmatic Communists. They tended to see the strike as a fight between free white labor and black slave labor. They believed that victory alone could prevent white 'race suicide.'[79] One of the best-remembered symbols of the strike was the banner declaring: 'Workers of the world unite and fight for a white South Africa.' But vague calls for a white South Africa were not popular among large sections of the strikers – the capitalists, after all, were also white. They wanted a South Africa in which the interests of white workers dominated. Semi-skilled white workers demanded 'civilized wages' for 'civilized labor.' That meant white labor, but the color line was not yet firmly drawn. The term 'civilized labor' originated with the Labour Party, which used it in the 1924 election to attract colored voters. The NP toned down the call for a republic and made 'civilized labor' its main plank.

A striking feature of the strike was the radicalization of Afrikaner women, reported to be 'out in force' in the commandos. Women in Germiston headed a parade of hundreds of strikers on horseback. The Governor General reported to London that 'in the attacks on scabs, women have played a prominent part on several occasions.' In trying to rally Afrikaner farmers to their cause, the strikers played on sexual and as well as racial fears; one Afrikaans pamphlet read: 'As the Kaffirs will get higher wages when they start to do the work of white people they will also take up a certain position in society, with the result that many white girls will enter into marriage with colored people.'[80]

Smuts' greatest fear was that white strikers might provoke an uncontrollable outbreak of violence among black miners. Strike leaders had been spreading rumors of an imminent black uprising. As a study notes, 'even the most reluctant striker was prepared to defend his family against such a threat.' Extremists among the strike leaders tried to use the 'black peril' argument to radicalize the strikers, and some strikers assaulted individual blacks. Fights between whites and blacks broke out in several places in and around Johannesburg, ending in several deaths.[81]

In the end no party or faction controlled the strike. On 10 March 1922, more than two months after it had started, a force of workers, estimated at ten thousand men, attacked Johannesburg, concentrating on police stations, mines and railway lines. It was a small-scale civil war in one of the richest spots in the world. Smuts feared a 'red revolution' and the establishment of a Soviet republic.[82] He declared martial law and rushed in government forces, supplemented by air support, bombs and artillery, machine guns and tanks. The Benoni strikers' position was machine-gunned from the air and the miners'

---

77 H.J. and R.E. Simons, *Class and Colour in South Africa, 1850-1950* (Harmondsworth: Penguin Books, 1969), p. 299

78 Simons and Simons, *Class and Colour*, pp. 285-6.

79 *Rand Daily Mail*, 11 January 1922; Francis Wilson, *Labour in the South African Gold Mines* (Cambridge: Cambridge University Press, 1972), p. 11.

80 Jeremy Krikler, 'Women, violence and the Rand Revolt of 1922', *Journal of Southern African Studies*, 22,3 (1996), pp. 350-55.

81 Oberholster, *Mynwerkerstaking 1922*, p. 156.

82 *House of Assembly Debates*, 21 March 1922.

hall in the town bombed. The strikers were forced to surrender after heavy artillery shells fell on their strongholds; 214 people were killed in five days of fighting.

Although the government was badly shaken by the strike, it decided against extending the color bar on the mines. It saw improved training for whites as a better option. Minister of Mines and Industry F.S. Malan explained to Parliament in 1923 that he did not wish to extend the color bar. 'It was degrading to the white man to say that [he] should be artificially protected against the native and colored man . . . The reason why a number [of white miners] were in danger today was that so many were not efficient miners.' The white workers had not availed themselves of the opportunities at the mining schools to become trained workers. They went into the mines as learners, Malan said, 'and learners they remained.'[83]

After the 1922 strike Tielman Roos, Transvaal NP leader, said: 'The country would always be on the edge of a volcano as they had large numbers of unemployed. If they did not help to absorb the unemployed they would have recurrences on the Rand on a bigger scale than they yet had.'[84] Hertzog also identified the position of the poorer whites as an issue that was of prime importance. In the 1924 election campaign he said that the position of the white laborers merited the most serious attention since it was 'the most important issue for the survival and welfare of the country.'[85]

While Smuts was prepared to accommodate white labor, he felt that they must not 'tyrannize everything.' A legal color bar was an admission by whites that they could not compete against blacks, and had to take recourse to laws that violated right and fairness. He did not contemplate giving blacks the vote, but he also believed that 'no statutory barrier should be placed on the native who wishes to raise himself in the scale of civilization.'[86] Government, he said in a private letter, ought to be seen as fair towards all population groups.[87] It was an 'impossible scheme' to suggest, as the NP did, that blacks should be allowed to perform only unskilled work. He had no objection to helping 'our poor whites', but it was necessary to see that 'no injustice was done to any other section of the community.'[88]

The Smuts government nevertheless embarked on a major shift in the system of industrial bargaining that legalized a superior bargaining position for white workers. Under the old system unions were barely tolerated, and destructive strikes erupted over the color bar. The Industrial Conciliation Act, passed by the Smuts government in 1924, provided for legally binding agreements in industrial councils consisting of employer associations and white or largely white trade unions. Employers could not lock out striking workers and workers could not strike before the council had tried to resolve a conflict. But unionized workers had to sacrifice the lightning strike, their major weapon. On the other hand the industrial conciliation machinery favored white and colored workers by excluding 'pass bearers' (meaning Africans) from trade union membership,

83 Peter Kallaway, 'F.S. Malan, the Cape Liberal Tradition and South African Politics, 1908-1924', *Journal of African History*, 15, 1 (1974), pp. 121-3.

84 *Cape Times*, 13 April 1922.

85 J.H. le Roux, et al., *Generaal J.B.M. Hertzog* (Johannesburg: Perskor, 1987), vol. 1, p. 272.

86 *Debates of the Joint Sitting in Parliament*, 1926, cols. 9, 33-34; J.C. Smuts, *Africa and Some World Problems* (Oxford: Clarendon Press, 1930), p. 94.

87 Bottomley, 'Public policy and white rural poverty', p. 279.

88 Scholtz, *Ontwikkeling van die politieke denke van die Afrikaners*, vol. 7, p. 305.

giving white-led unions a commanding role in determining occupational structures, and access to training and wages.

The Pact government that came to power in 1924 added a weapon that the state could use against employers who wished to undercut white labor, the Wage Act of 1925. It empowered the responsible minister 'to set the same minimum wages for whites and blacks.' The assumption was that if black and white wages were set at the same level employers would prefer whites.

The government and its successors used these weapons sparingly. The priority was to enable the economy, particularly the mining industry, to grow and to provide jobs.[89] Various trade-offs were made between the government and the mining industry. It was not expected that the latter would help solve the poor-white problem by employing them, or even to pay white miners particularly well. (White miners' wages only began rising towards the end of the 1930s, but those of black miners did not increase in real terms before the early 1970s.) But the government would not tolerate unilateral decisions by the industry to reduce its white labor force sharply. An amendment to the Mines and Works Act was added, which protected white mineworkers from displacement. In 1932 the Chamber of Mines told a commission that the mines could manage with 'a materially smaller number' of whites, but such a policy was no longer an option. White miners rose in number from 22,099 in 1922 to about 28,000 in 1930.[90]

These measures enabled the government to buy off the white workers. As Yudelman remarked, the white unions continued to growl, but like a lion without teeth there was no bite. Both employers and the white working class no longer considered the state as a mere watchdog but as an active player, shaping the fortunes of everyone from the mining magnate to the most menial laborer. Both began to see their salvation not in independent organization as a class or in aggressively expressing their interests, but in developing a symbiotic relationship with the state. Both made it their business to get behind the government of the day as soon as possible.

From now on the state increasingly defined the relationship between white prosperity and white supremacy. From the state's point of view the crisis of white unemployment was acute. In 1922 the Unemployment Commission estimated the number of unemployed poor whites at 120,000 in an economically active white population of 540,000. Hence it would do nothing to seriously harm profits or threaten jobs. However, it also insisted that employers and the trade unions had to play their part in uplifting the poorer section of the whites and incorporating them fully into the dominant white group. Margaret Ballinger, a prominent liberal, wrote in her memoirs: 'It is difficult now to remember or to appreciate the dark shadow which poor whiteism cast over this country in the 1920s and 30s of this century. Yet it was the formative force in standardizing the relationship of black and white in this country.'[91] A remark by Hertzog highlighted this observation: 'It was in order to deal with [poor whiteism]', that he advocated his so-called segregation policy.[92]

89 Yudelman, *Emergence*, pp. 223-5.
90 Merle Lipton, *Capitalism and Apartheid* (Aldershot: Wildwood House, 1986), pp. 112-16.
91 John Bottomley, '"Almost bled to death": the effects of the Anglo Boer War on social transformation in the Orange River Colony', *Historia*, 44, 1 (1999), p. 191.
92 Thelma Shifrin, 'New Deal for the Coloured People: A Study of NP Policies towards the Coloured People, 1924-1929', B.A. Hons diss., UCT, 1962, p. 10.

The Pact government and 'civilized labor'

Before the 1924 election Hertzog's NP entered into an alliance called the Pact with the Labour Party not to oppose each other. Both parties expressed some sympathy for the very low wages of blacks at the bottom of the labor ladder. Keen to attract Cape African voters, the NP approached Clements Kadalie, a charismatic black leader who had grown up in Malawi. Shortly after moving to South Africa he founded a black trade union, the Industrial and Commercial Workers Union (ICU). Africans enthusiastically embraced the ICU's call for 'Africa for the Africans'; it had enlisted 100,000 members by the end of the 1920s, but then fell apart.

Hertzog professed sympathy for Kadalie and his organization, and even sent a donation to the ICU. He told Kadalie that their task was to establish 'between white and black Afrikander that faith in and sympathy with one another which is so essential for the prosperity of a nation.' D.F. Malan, the Cape NP leader, went even further. Before the election he sent this message to a meeting of African voters in Queenstown: 'No race has shown a greater love for South Africa than the native and in that respect he is certainly an example of true patriotism. He should therefore take his place alongside the nationalist in the same area.'[93]

The Pact alliance drew a level of support that exceeded its wildest dreams. In the early 1920s the NP was still a party that, in Hertzog's words, represented the 'non-industrial' section of the population, that is, the farmers. The SAP government's brutal suppression of the 1922 strike cost it much of its labor support and even some black and colored votes. Segments of black opinion opposed the Pact, but the black leadership also had little stomach for the SAP, which lacked a clear racial policy. 'No policy, no vote' was the call that went out from the Cape African National Congress. The national leadership of the African National Congress sent a telegram to leaders of the black and colored voters to cast their ballot against the SAP. *Die Burger* remarked that most coloreds voted for the Pact.

Within the white community there was also some unexpected support. *The Star* reported that some Communists had decided to back the Pact. These developments prompted Smuts to declare that 'the Red Flag has come to South Africa', which was being given a foretaste of what the country would be reduced to under a Pact government.[94] Some white English-speakers also looked sympathetically at the NP's policy on segregation. Edgar Brookes, later a prominent liberal, thought that Hertzog's policy rightly aimed at uplifting not a few individuals but 'the Bantu as a whole.'[95] As late as 1927 he considered the reserves 'a useful subsidiary measure to facilitate administration.'[96] In the 1924 election the NP won 63 out of 135 seats against the SAP's 52 and Labour's 18. Smuts was defeated in his own seat.

---

93 Edward Roux, *Time Longer Than Rope: A History of the Black Man's Struggle for Freedom in South Africa* (Madison: University of Wisconsin Press, 1966), pp. 184, 199; *HAD, Joint Sitting*, 1936, col. 325.

94 C.M. O'Dowd, 'The General Election of 1924', *South African Historical Journal*, 2 (1970), pp. 54-76; C. Marais, 'Toenadering en Samewerking', O. Geyser and A.H. Marais (eds.), *Die Nasionale Party* (Bloemfontein: INEG, 1975), vol. 1, pp. 559-76.

95 Cynthia Kros, 'Economic, political and intellectual origins of Bantu education', doctoral diss., Witwatersrand University, 1996, pp. 93-7.

96 Tom Karis, et al. (eds.), *From Protest to Challenge* (Stanford: Hoover Institute Press, 1972), vol. 1, p. 122.

Soon after coming to power, the Pact government began preaching a harsh message of segregation. Hertzog said that Africans were two thousand years behind whites in development, but also maintained that their progress in education represented a threat to white society. F.W. Beyers, Minister of Mines and Industries, in 1926 called a color bar an essential defense mechanism to protect 'civilization from ruin.'[97]

The Pact had toyed briefly with recognizing the ICU, but decided that the time was not ripe. In 1928 Kadalie pleaded for a South Africa with no doctrine of supremacy of one race over another, one 'where Kadalie's children and General Hertzog's children were equal.'[98] But by now Kadalie was largely a spent force and some of Hertzog's ministers attacked his ICU fiercely. Tielman Roos, leader of the Transvaal NP, referred to a 'native menace' in South Africa. 'We will rule the natives,' he exclaimed. 'Every white man in South Africa is an aristocrat and people who are rulers and governors cannot be proletarians.'[99]

During the 1920s and early 1930s, when the country was still backward and the economy struggling to take off, various alternatives to a policy of protecting the small white population through an industrial color bar were discussed. One was large-scale white immigration. Under the Smuts government the director of the census warned that if the white growth rate did not increase white South Africans would be unable to maintain themselves in the face of an 'increasing, and at last, an overwhelming [black] majority.'[100] Smuts argued for stepped-up white immigration. The larger markets that would ensue would solve the problem of poor whites, he said. 'We suffer for our very smallness.'[101]

But immigrants hardly ever voted for the NP. Besides, the NP leadership did not accept the liberal economic creed that skilled immigrants would create new jobs in a stagnant economy and would benefit all by expanding the domestic market. Instead the NP believed that immigrants would jeopardize the effort to rehabilitate the white poor and unemployed. Hertzog referred to state-assisted immigration as 'this insane longing for a big census'; benefiting only the capitalist class with its demand for cheap labor; it would impoverish the Afrikaner people.[102]

Another option was to free up the labor market and allow the very low wages of migrant blacks to rise by forcing employers to pay the same rate for anyone on a similar job. A liberal historian, W.M. Macmillan, argued that the existing policy created a vicious spiral. By restricting blacks to remote reserves and imposing pass laws on them they were forced to work for very low wages. It was not their blackness but their cheapness that threatened white workers. If the curbs on blacks were removed the domestic market would grow and the wages of whites as well as blacks would rise.[103] The Labour Party leader, Colonel Frederic Creswell, in 1924 Minister of Labour in Hertzog's Pact government, had long argued that paying the same rate for all would lead employers to replace

---

97 Kros, 'Origins of Bantu education', pp. 91-3.
98 Helen Bradford, *A Taste of Freedom: The ICU in Rural South Africa, 1924-1930* (Johannesburg: Ravan Press, 1987), p. 174.
99 Edward Roux, *Time Longer than Rope* (Madison: University of Wisconsin Press, 1964) p. 203.
100 U.G. 37-24, *Third Census, 1921*, pp. 27-9.
101 *Cape Times*, 20 February 1920.
102 L.E. Neame, *General Hertzog* (London: Hurst and Blackett, 1930), p. 108.
103 W.M. Macmillan, *Complex South Africa* (London: Faber and Faber, 1930), p. 16.

blacks on the lower levels with whites. But artisans rejected the proposal of a common rate for the job as detrimental to their interests, while the Chamber of Mines opposed it because it did not want a large body of white miners that was certain to organize themselves. In the 1920s the NP rejected it because they wanted to do two things at the same time: save the poor whites and ensure white survival by keeping most blacks in the reserves.

The most radical option was that proposed by the communists, who wanted a socialist system that aimed at eliminating both migrant labor and unemployment. Once socialism was established everyone, white and black, would be paid a proper wage. The most gifted Afrikaner to take up this cause was Bram Fischer, the grandson of Abraham Fischer, the Free State prime minister and Union cabinet minister. As a student in Bloemfontein during the 1920s he was a convinced nationalist, but personal contact with Africans persuaded him of the irrationality of color prejudice and the injustice of segregation. Either in Bloemfontein or in Oxford, where he went as a Rhodes scholar in 1932, he became attracted to the Communist Party, which, as he remarked, 'always refused to accept any color bar and always stood firm on the belief, itself two thousand years old, of the eventual brotherhood of all men.' The Great Depression of these years convinced him that the capitalist system had come to the end of its road.[104] Speaking at a Dingaan's Day ceremony in London in 1933, he pointed out that the need was of an 'integrating' kind, the 'drawing together of not only the two different European races, but [to] see to it that these two advance together with our vast black population.'[105] But while many Afrikaner workers were radical, they were not interested in socialism. They wanted a white supremacist state that protected white workers.

None of these alternative options won favor among mainstream politicians who considered state intervention essential for addressing white poverty, the most critical socioeconomic problem. The more concerned the state became with alleviating white poverty, the more 'racialized' it became. The NP did exploit the issue for political purposes, but the problem of poor whites went far beyond narrow Afrikaner nationalist concerns. As Leader of the Opposition, Smuts probed for a system that would safeguard white domination but would enable some blacks to advance so that the 'iron of oppression' did not enter the 'native soul.' In 1928 he and Hertzog privately exchanged views on the franchise. Smuts proposed a Union-wide non-racial franchise with a qualification of £75 income a year and an occupation qualification of £100, enabling a 'decent' white unskilled worker earning the standard minimum of 5 shillings a day to qualify. Coloreds and blacks who met this requirement could pass an additional civilization test for 'non-Europeans.' Hertzog rejected the proposal because it would exclude unskilled and unemployed whites as voters.

Twenty years earlier Smuts had supported Hertzog's position in an exchange with Merriman, and in the 1928 exchange he did not put up much of a fight. But even the liberal *Cape Times* realized how difficult the issue of de-racializing the Constitution was in a country where there was not only an increasingly bitter white-black conflict but also

---

104 Bram Fischer, '*What I did was right: Statement from the Dock, 28 March 1966*' (London: Mayibuye, n.d.), p. 10.
105 Stephen Clingman, *Bram Fischer: Afrikaner Revolutionary* (Cape Town: David Philip, 1998), p. 99.

a sharp cleavage between the two communities in the dominant white group. The news-paper wrote that expanding the African vote would eventually mean 'either a Parliament dominated by black voters or the break-up of Union, possibly by way of a bloody civil war.'[106] With a qualified franchise ruled out as an option to bring in more Africans, the reserves became the centerpiece of the solution to the racial question.

Protecting industry and white labor

South Africa remained a poor country until the mid-1930s. S.P. Viljoen, a leading econo-mist, makes this observation: 'It is seldom appreciated today how poor a mining and agricultural country South Africa was until [the 1930s].' By 1925 South Africa had a gross domestic product (GDP) of only R537 million, agriculture contributing 21 per cent, mining 16.2 per cent, and secondary industry only 7.8 per cent. Viljoen remarked: 'Since industry tends invariably to act as the growth sector in a newly developing country, South Africa's economic structure was then as undeveloped as those of most African countries [during the early 1980s].'[107] Industry was starved of capital; more than half the profits of the mines sent abroad as dividends. The government levied a tax of only 5 per cent on the value added by the gold mines. Under the next government, based on a fusion of the parties of Hertzog and Smuts, the tax on the mining industry rose sharply, to 15 per cent by 1936.

The protectionist policy introduced by the Pact government did not represent a sud-den change of course. The mines offered only limited opportunities for whites. This made it essential for government to stimulate the development of secondary industry to help provide employment for a turbulent white labor force. The Smuts government had made a half-hearted start to support local industry through tariffs, and it provided sheltered employment for whites on state projects, like the railway lines and irrigation works. In the early 1920s the mining houses began investing a greater share of their profits in the local manufacturing sector.[108]

The Pact's 1924 victory accelerated the trend towards economic nationalism and in-dustrial protection. For the first time since Union the government took a stand against the mining industry. Very sensitive to costs, the industry tried to keep expenses on stores, wages and food prices as low as possible. But that road led to what a minority report of a commission called a South Africa reduced to 'a plantation and raw materials econo-my.'[109] It meant that local industry and agriculture would never become viable. An ex-port-driven economy was not an option for South Africa with its small market, lack of skills and distance from European markets.

Protection gave local industry a major boost. Raw materials were in abundance for an iron and steel industry as the core around which a manufacturing sector would de-

---

106 Die Burger, 16 May 1929, citing the Cape Times, 14 November 1925.
107 S.P. Viljoen, 'The Industrial Achievement of South Africa', South African Journal of Economics, 51, 1 (1983), p. 31.
108 Jill Nattrass, The South African Economy (Cape Town: Oxford University Press, 1981), pp. 138-150; Yudelman, Emergence, pp. 235-43.
109 D.E. Kaplan, 'The Politics of Industrial Protection', Journal of South African Studies, 3, 1 (1977), p. 78.
110 De Kiewiet, History, p. 266.

velop. De Kiewiet notes: 'Few other South African industries enjoy such natural advantages as the industry which was established in 1929 by the Iron and Steel Industry Act.'[110] Soon after the founding of the Iron and Steel Corporation (Iscor), state plans for a national electricity corporation (Escom) were also completed.[111] Iscor and Escom spearheaded the steady expansion of a state sector in secondary industry. Iscor began production in 1933 with an all-white complement. Although the policy of protection was not designed in the first place with a view to white jobs, it did boost white employment. A commission reported in 1932 that the policy of import-substitution provided work for thousands of the white poor and called it 'one of the most potent means of bringing about their economic rehabilitation.'[112]

As a result of the Pact's policy of protection, agricultural prices were maintained at a considerably higher level than world prices. The country built up its manufacturing industry and agricultural enterprises behind high tariff walls. South Africa would establish a large degree of industrial self-sufficiency, but the policy also had drawbacks. Little effort went into becoming efficient enough to widen the export base significantly. By 1990 South Africa's manufacturing exports per capita were lower than any upper-income country except Brazil.

The Pact government had to choose between two priorities: creating new jobs for whites, especially the large numbers of poor whites forming, according to some estimates, nearly half the number of economically active whites, and making it possible for every white man to maintain a 'civilized standard' of living. It soon chose the former. Despite the fact that the Labour Party, the NP's coalition partner, represented mainly unionized, skilled labor, Hertzog wanted to put unskilled or semi-skilled whites in jobs, even if it meant that other white workers would have to pay part of the price. Under Pact rule white wages would fall in real terms, suggesting that skilled white workers paid part of the price of the employment of less skilled white workers.[113]

The government drew a distinction between two types of labor. Those who performed 'civilized labor' had to be remunerated in such a way that they could maintain 'the standard generally recognized as tolerable from the European standpoint.' Those employed as 'uncivilized labor', invariably workers who were not white, required wages to afford only the bare necessities of 'barbarous and underdeveloped peoples.' But these were abstract definitions. What mattered in practice was to provide jobs for whites at wages higher than those for blacks. Smuts soon criticized the government for employing whites in the railways at wages below the level deemed fit for a white.

The newly created Department of Labour had interpreted the concept of civilized labor as applying to all workers, blacks as well as whites, but some employers protested – they would be crippled, they argued, if 'civilized' subsistence wages were applied to blacks, since whites had higher living standards than Africans.[114] Other employers resisted hiring whites at artificially high rates. In 1925 a journal for employers in the manufacturing and commercial sectors proposed that wages be set down for each occupation:

111 J.H. le Roux and P. W. Coetzer, *Die Nasionale Party, 1924-1934* (Bloemfontein: INEG, 1980) pp. 74-87.
112 Verslag van die Carnegie-Kommissie, *Die armblanke-vraagstuk in Suid-Afrika* (Stellenbosch: Pro Ecclesia, 1932), para. 81.
113 Yudelman, *Emergence*, pp. 236-8.
114 Marion Lacey, *Working for Boroko* (Johannesburg: Ravan Press, 1981), p. 224.

'Should a native prove physically and mentally capable of doing a certain kind of work, he will receive the wages laid down for such work.'[115]

The government used sticks and carrots in the attempt to achieve its objective of expanded white employment. Employers who hired only whites received preference for state contracts. Protected industries under the policy of import substitution were informed that customs on imports would be relaxed unless they employed a certain percentage of whites. A Wage Board permitted the state to enforce minimum wages, which could be used to replace large numbers of cheap black labor with semi-skilled whites. As a result the manufacturing sector replaced many unskilled blacks with poor whites. The proportion of blacks employed for each white in this sector declined from 2.11 to 1.49 during the 1920s, which meant that fourteen thousand fewer blacks were employed than would have been the case if the 1920 ratio had remained constant. With the state providing some industrial training to unskilled white workers, industry could absorb them more readily.[116]

The biggest impact of the policy was on the state sector. The government instructed state departments to replace 'uncivilized' labor with the 'civilized type', particularly in the railways, harbors, post office and local government. Many whites received some training in the public sector and then left to find better jobs in the private sector. The railways made the greatest effort to absorb poor whites at 'civilized' wages. Between 1924 and 1933 unskilled white workers rose from 9.5 per cent to 39.3 per cent of the labor force, while unskilled blacks fell from 75 to 49 per cent. By the early 1950s more than 100,000 mainly unskilled and semi-skilled whites worked for the railways, the biggest employer of white labor.

Blacks had to carry the burden of the policy. The argument that they could be paid less than a civilized wage because their needs were less was a spurious one since they faced the same high living costs as whites. In addition, the trades were closed to blacks as a result of the Apprentice Act and the controls the unions exercised through the closed shop and specified wage rates. The Riotous Assemblies Act of 1930 made it possible to crush protests by banning meetings and banishing the recalcitrant. In an emergency assembly in 1932 the African National Congress denounced the government for 'the increasing burdens and disabilities inflicted on the race by retrograde and medieval laws.'[117]

Colored people had good reason to expect to be beneficiaries of the civilized labor policy, since the NP in the 1924 election had promised to treat whites and coloreds as people who politically and economically belonged together. However, the policy did not change matters materially for the colored working class. Although coloreds as well as whites were to be given preference, government circulars urged departments to employ white youths as much as possible in order to solve the poor-white problem. Nor did the civilized labor policy change the policy of paying coloreds wages of half or less than half of those of their white counterparts. In 1926 C.W. Malan, Minister of Railways and Harbours, announced that the civilized labor policy had never intended to pay coloreds

---

115 Lipton, *Capitalism and Apartheid*, pp. 114, 140.
116 I. Abedian and B. Standish, 'Poor Whites and the Role of the State', paper presented to the Carnegie inquiry into black poverty, UCT, 1986, p. 5.
117 Lacey, *Working for Boroko*, p. 248.

equal wages: 'The Colored man is different from the white man in his standard of civilization . . . and must be treated accordingly.' Ten years later the mayor of Johannesburg declared that he interpreted the civilized labor policy to mean the employment of whites.[118] White trade unions, too, used their power on industrial councils to edge out coloreds. Only thirty-six coloreds were among the 641 apprentices entering into contracts in Cape Town between 1932 and 1935.[119]

Confronted with the charge that it was legislating for white privilege, the NP cited white survival as its reason. Many lesser skilled whites could not otherwise compete with cheaper black labor. Any collapse of white civilization would injure all groups, including blacks and colored people, spokesmen for the party argued. S.P. le Roux, who would become a cabinet minister in 1948, said that the civilization level of those not white could be raised only if the survival of white civilization was guaranteed.[120]

In stark contrast the government did little to intervene in the exploitative relationship between many farm owners and their bywoners or other poor whites still on the land. Unlike the advanced regulation of the urban labor market, there were no regulations for farm wages and working hours, or for the provision of housing and other work conditions. 'The man without land, the bywoner, whose condition is becoming ever more desperate, has never been the subject of specific legislation,' a researcher observed in the early 1930s.[121] No body existed to which a bywoner could appeal if he was wronged. Parliament never heard an appeal related to unprotected poor whites on the land.

White poverty and white purity

By 1930 white poverty was predominantly perceived as an urban problem, and as such was much more visible. Afrikaner women's welfare organizations increasingly made the plight of the urban white poor an issue of public concern. These women's organizations were established in the wake of widespread poverty and suffering in the aftermath of the Anglo-Boer War: the Afrikaanse Christelike Vrouevereniging (ACVV) in the Cape, the Oranje Vrouevereniging (OVV) in the OFS, and the Suid-Afrikaanse Vrouefederasie (SAVF) in the Transvaal. Some redoubtable women, of whom Miems Rothman, who wrote under the name MER, was the most outstanding, led the ACVV, the largest and best organized. The organization was as much concerned about white poverty as racial mixing and the exploitation and oppression of women.

Fearing that the white poor in the mixed slums would be lost to the volk, the ACVV sought to persuade Afrikaner families to move out. Rothman described the situation in 1925 in these words: 'Receiving inadequate wages and forced to rent the cheapest rooms or houses, poor [white] people often have to live with coloreds . . . they sometimes chat like neighbors, they help each other when there is illness (it is especially the coloreds

---

118 Lewis, *Between the Wire and the Wall*, p. 162.
119 Sheila Van der Horst, *Native Labour in South Africa* (Cape Town: Oxford University Press, 1942), pp. 244-5.
120 *House of Assembly Debates,* 1924 (Dutch edition), pp. 87-91, 302-4, 319-20; *Debates of Joint Sitting,* 1926, pp. 33-4, 114-15.
121 Albertyn, *Sociologiese verslag,* p. 124.

that help the whites), their children play together in the streets.' The ACVV tried to 'rescue' the children by placing them in institutions or as domestic workers with middle-class Afrikaner families. For Rothman the survival of the Afrikaner volk depended on its working class becoming consciously white and consciously Afrikaner.[122]

The rapid urbanization of the Afrikaner poor had given rise to widespread fears of sexual mixing across racial lines. The gender imbalance on the Witwatersrand compounded these fears. In 1921 there were only 28,735 African women but between 200,000 and 300,000 migrant African men. The 111,708 white women (in 1921), many of them working for very low wages, outnumbered white men. They often could not afford to live anywhere but in the mixed slums. There were widespread fears among Afrikaners that Indian shopkeepers hired Afrikaner women in order to exploit them sexually. The committee of a hostel for white women warned that young women could become 'spiritually lost in the city and become a burden and curse to the volk instead of a blessing.' In 1936 J.G. Strijdom, the NP Transvaal leader, told the provincial congress that his party's responsibility was to keep the white race white. This could only be done by compulsory residential segregation and putting a stop to mixed marriages.[123]

In 1928, the government passed a law prohibiting marriages between whites and blacks (though not between whites and colored people). The widespread fears of miscegenation were greatly exaggerated. During the 1930s, marriages across the racial line fluctuated between a low of 72 in 1934 and a high of 101 in 1937, the vast majority between white men and colored women.[124] In 1936 a bill to ban marriages between a white and a colored person was introduced by the NP member for Vrededorp, a Johannesburg constituency with a large proportion of poor whites, but a commission of inquiry into the colored population recommended against it.

Poor whites and the Carnegie report

Before 1924 Hertzog often expressed outrage at the government's lack of sympathy for the plight of the poor whites. After becoming prime minister he was soon exasperated by their incessant demands. His government had found work for thirteen thousand whites on the railways, he reported in 1928; the only ones still unemployed were those 'who did not want to work – the weaker section.' He thought that the poor-white question had been solved.[125] Now it was Smuts who complained that the wages of white railway workers were too low to support a decent life.

The government was tackling white education with vigor as the main means of rehabilitating whites. Between 1912 and 1926 spending on education as a proportion of the budget and the number of white pupils had doubled.

---

122 Marijke du Toit, 'A Social History of the Afrikaanse Christelike Vrouevereniging', doctoral diss., UCT, 1992, pp. 242, 356.
123 Jonathan Hyslop, 'White working-class women . . .', *Journal of African History* 36 (1995), pp. 67.
124 Hyslop, 'White working-class women . . .', p. 65.
125 *Hertzog-toesprake*, vol. 5, p. 171; Le Roux, et al., *Hertzog*, vol. 1, p. 278.

EDUCATION: EXPENDITURE AND COVERAGE

	1912-13	1925-26
Education as % of budget	14%	26%
Total white pupils	179,000	384,000
% of post-primary white pupils	6%	13%

Source: Malherbe, *Education and the Poor White*, p. 43.

By 1931 vocational and industrial schools were functioning all over the country.[126] Boarding schools for indigent children helped ensure that virtually no white child was out of school. State spending was heavily in favor of whites. In 1943 one estimate said that the state would have to multiply its current spending on black education thirty-six times to bring it to the level of white education; 60 per cent of black children were not in school at all.[127]

White privilege was boosted by coupling education to access to the trades. The Apprenticeship Act of 1922 was a watershed; it stipulated a pass in the eighth school year (Standard 6) as a minimum qualification for entry as an apprentice in forty-one trades. This entry qualification fell within the minimum level set for white pupils, but very few colored schools went as far as the eighth year. Colored artisans in the western Cape, who had dominated over half the skilled trades in the 1890s, were down to dominating only one-thirteenth of the trades by 1961.

The question of white poverty became a national issue in the late 1920s for two reasons. The first was the global economic crisis that began in 1929 and the prolonged drought that destroyed crops and livestock in the early 1930s. Desperate to avoid a huge wave of impoverished farmers leaving the land, the Hertzog government made loans available to farmers. At the same time it boosted unemployment relief and subsidies for temporary employment on public works.[128] Relief measures, 2.6 per cent of the budget in 1930, rose to an astounding 15.8 per cent in 1933. These schemes provided some training for unskilled laborers, educated and trained their children so they might escape the poverty cycle, and provided free housing and medical services for those working on public projects. Many schemes contributed significantly to strengthening the infrastructure of the country, e.g., forestry settlements, irrigation works, and road and rail construction.[129] By 1939 the crisis was largely over and the sum allocated to relief measures was down to 4.1 per cent of the budget.

The other reason why white poverty was given more attention was related to developments in the academic world. Scholars across the world were becoming more scientific and activist in their approach to the study of social ills. In the USA attempts to address social questions through scientific enquiry and management were heralded as 'social engineering.' Afrikaner social scientists began to do the same. During a visit to South Africa in the mid-1930s, Lord Hailey observed that 'South Africa regards itself as USA in the making.'[130]

---

126 Malherbe, *Education and the Poor White*, p. 43.
127 Roux, *Time Longer than Rope*, p. 343.
128 *Official Yearbook*, 1932-3, no. 15, p. 180.
129 The figures and analysis in this section are largely based on Abedian and Standish, 'Poor Whites and the Role of the State'.

During the second half of the 1920s the Carnegie Corporation of New York became interested in the problem of white poverty in South Africa. Many commissions and select committees in South Africa had earlier studied white poverty, but they only heard evidence and did not commission research or do field work. The South African who brought the issue of white poverty in South Africa to the attention of the Carnegie Corporation's staff was E.G. Malherbe, the son of a DRC minister and postgraduate student in education at Columbia University's Teachers College in New York.

Malherbe was one of the first Afrikaners who was well trained as a social scientist, but while his contemporary, H.F. Verwoerd, at an early stage identified with the nationalist struggle, Malherbe remained a strong supporter of Smuts. His views can be read as an indication of the degree to which white poverty became the concern of most whites in South Africa, and even of funding agencies abroad. Malherbe formulated the general white thinking as follows: the poor whites were 'a menace to the self-preservation and prestige of the white people, living as we do in the midst of the native population, which outnumbers us 5 to 1.'[131] They were a 'skeleton in our cupboard, raising questions about the capacity of the ruling white race to maintain its dominance.'[132]

In 1927, when the president and secretary of the corporation visited South Africa, several bodies requested them to investigate white poverty. Since more than four-fifths of the poor whites were Afrikaners, the DRC played a leading role. In 1929 it formally requested the Carnegie Corporation to fund a study on poor whites. When the request was granted it became the main body represented on the board of control supervising the Carnegie Commission on the Poor White Problem in South Africa. In 1932 the commission published five comprehensive reports. In 1934 the DRC organized a *volkskongres* or national conference and subsequently published a report, called *Verslag van die Volkskongres*, in which the findings were discussed and ways suggested to make white poverty one of the top priorities on the national agenda.

The commission recognized that the problem of black poverty was as acute as that of white poverty. To justify a focus only on whites, it was suggested that solving the poverty of whites would ultimately also benefit other communities. W. Nicol, a prominent Dutch Reformed Church minister in Johannesburg, told the 1934 conference: '[We] can do little about a solution for the native question before making progress with the poor-white question . . . Once whites stand firmly on their own feet they would have a better chance to help the native in his turn.'[133] Malherbe, who wrote the report on white education, warned against using white poverty as an excuse for intensifying segregation. At the 1934 conference he remarked: 'To maintain our superiority by pushing the Kaffer lower down would not only be unfair but the height of folly, even seen from our point of view.'[134] But both the commission and the 1934 meeting made recommendations for alleviating white poverty that would widen the gulf between whites and blacks.

---

130 Roberta Millar, 'Science and Society in the Early Career of H.F. Verwoerd', *Journal of Southern African Studies*, 19, 4 (1993), p. 646.
131 E.G. Malherbe, *Never a Dull Moment* (Cape Town: Timmins Publishers, 1981), p. 119.
132 *Cape Times*, 24 July 1929.
133 *Verslag van die Volkskongres oor die Armblankevraagstuk gehou te Kimberley, 2-3 Oktober, 1934* (Cape Town: Nasionale Pers, 1934), p. 13.
134 *Verslag van die Volkskongres oor die Armblankevraagstuk, 1934*, pp. 216, 222.

The Carnegie Commission and the follow-up activities brought much greater clarity about the scope of the problem. Earlier commissions tended to define poor whites simply as very poor people unable to raise themselves and their families without outside assistance.[135] Now there was an effort to define the poor white and white poverty in more exact terms. J.R. Albertyn, author of a report on their social condition, presented a compelling picture: they were generally law-abiding, showing respect for religion and the religious authorities, keeping the family together as a close unit, honoring their traditions and forebears, but also lacking in ambition, thrift and prudence, and inclined to be gullible, dishonest, deceitful, irresponsible, lazy and listless.[136] In his education report Malherbe defined a poor white as a person 'who has a mental attitude towards life, owing for example to lack of intelligence, lack of education, temperamental defects or to physiological conditions, which prevents him rising to or maintaining a decent standard of living when exposed to the economic forces around him.'[137] But he also defined white poverty in relative terms. 'A very appreciable portion of our white population,' Malherbe wrote, 'is sinking below the economic standard of living which we consider that a white man should maintain by virtue of his white skin over the native.'[138]

Before the Carnegie Commission started its work there were only informed guesses about the numbers of South African poor whites. In 1916 the number was thought to be 106,000 (7.5 per cent of the white population), and in the early 1920s General Hertzog spoke of 150,000. A 1924 government report classified 200,000 people as poor whites. The Carnegie Commission made the first proper attempt to research the issue before concluding that there were 300,000 poor whites (17 per cent of whites). H.F. Verwoerd first gained national prominence through his analysis of the Carnegie report for the 1934 conference. He stated that the poor whites were 'for a very large part of Afrikaans-speaking descent' and put the figure at 250,000, or a fourth of the Afrikaner population.[139] Malherbe, who did not share Verwoerd's nationalist sentiments, also thought that the problem of Afrikaner poverty was huge. He referred to a 'flood of poor white-ism that threatened to overwhelm *ons ou volkie.*' He found that if those in the categories 'very poor' and 'poor' were added together, 56 per cent of white pupils were recruited from homes not in a position to provide them with proper food and clothing.[140]

But the commission's greatest contribution was debunking the mythology surrounding the issue of white poverty.[141] There was the conventional myth, also found in other countries, that the very poor formed a natural sediment immune to social intervention. There was the myth of geographical determinism, popular as a result of the work of Ellsworth Huntington, an American scholar, who maintained that so many people were poor in South Africa because the climate was too pleasant. Most hurtful to Afrikaners was the

---

135 Report of a 1906 Cape Select Committee cited by Lewis, 'Aspects of the poor white problem', p. 1.
136 J.R. Albertyn, *Die armblanke en die maatskappy* (Stellenbosch: Pro Ecclesia, 1932), V, pp. 17-21.
137 E.G. Malherbe, *Never a Dull Moment* (Cape Town: Timmins, 1981), p. 128.
138 E.G. Malherbe, *Education and the Poor White*, p. 22.
139 *Verslag van die Volkskongres*, p. 30.
140 *Verslag van die Volkskongres*, p. 221.
141 See the essays of N.P. van Wyk Louw on the Carnegie Commission report in *Die Huisgenoot*, 19 May 1933 and 15 September 1933.

myth that there was something genetically wrong with their poor. As a newspaper reporter, M.E. Rothman heard Sir Carruthers Beattie, Vice Chancellor of the University of Cape Town, blithely tell a public meeting that poor whites were 'intellectually backward and that there was something inherent in the Afrikaners that resulted in the phenomenon [of poor whiteism] assuming such alarming proportions in their case.'[142]

The Afrikaner researchers undertook their task with great empathy. The commission's report heralded a new understanding of the crisis of large-scale poverty. It was not a problem for which the poor themselves were responsible, but the result of social and economic processes over which they had little control. Intelligence tests undertaken by the commission found that the poor whites compared well with the rest of the population. N.P. van Wyk Louw, who reviewed the report in *Die Huisgenoot,* called the rejection of this 'scornful reproach' the commission's most important contribution.[143]

The report's general message was that retaining the rural poor on the land was not a solution. The poor-white problem had to be solved in the towns and the cities through more appropriate education for the poor. About a quarter of whites were leaving the schools inadequately educated or trained with few or no marketable skills. Nearly half of the young white males leaving school (and a far higher proportion of Afrikaners) were going into farming at a time when possibilities for small and medium scale farmers were rapidly contracting. Another survey at the time found that only 18.6 per cent of Afrikaners were receiving training to become artisans compared to 33.1 per cent of non-Afrikaner whites.[144]

For the commission the remedy lay in better education, the acquisition of skills and work opportunities in the towns and cities. It called for improved conditions of employment and for the development of local industry through tariff protection. It proposed the establishment of a department at a university to train professional social workers, and a bureau of social welfare in the central government. Although educational authorities welcomed the report, they did not extend the period of compulsory white education. More emphasis was now put on vocational guidance and a strong message undoubtedly went out that farming was an option for only a steadily shrinking number.[145]

The commission did not really produce findings that the NP in introducing apartheid incorporated, as a study claimed.[146] It concluded that increased self-sufficiency for whites was vital for the resolution of the problem. It saw the danger of a dependency syndrome with whites dependent on the state for free education, cheap housing and medical service, and job protection through 'civilized labor' and a color bar. Much of this dependence was rooted in the political system that granted universal franchise to whites but denied it to the majority. Among the white poor, a sense of collective power had developed. A researcher, R.W. Wilcocks, typified the underlying attitude of the poor as one that saw the government and the rich as having a duty to aid the white poor. He

---

142 M.E.R., *My beskeie deel* (Cape Town: Tafelberg, 1972), p. 236.
143 It appeared in two installments in *Die Huisgenoot,* 19 May 1933 and 15 September 1933.
144 David Welsh, 'The Political Economy of Afrikaner Nationalism' in Adrian Leftwich (ed.), *South Africa: Economic Growth and Political Change* (London: Allison and Bushby, 1974), p. 251.
145 E.G. Malherbe, *Education in South Africa* (Cape Town: Juta, 1977), vol. 2, p. 165.
146 Francis Wilson and Mamphela Rhampele, *Uprooting Poverty: The South African Challenge* (Cape Town: David Philip, 1989), p. x.

quoted some who said that 'charity was the right of the poor [white] man', and others who declared: 'Government is the father of us all – it must help us.'[147]

Other researchers confirmed this. J.R. Albertyn, a DRC minister in Kimberly and author of the report on social work, said he often heard this view: 'The state cannot afford to make the poor work too hard because they have a vote.' He concurred with the view of a visiting American sociologist that, with the possible exception of Russia, in no other society did a greater dependence on government exist. 'A spirit of dependency on the state on the part of the [white] poor and even those better-off had assumed such proportions that it can almost be called a national pathology.' He proposed that the right to vote be withdrawn if a person became wholly dependent on state support.[148] Malherbe told how the poor abused the special care bestowed on them on a government road-building project designed to provide work for poor whites at five shillings a day. 'What many of the poor did was to hire Coloreds at two shillings and six pence a day to do the work, while they sat around supervising.'[149]

Wilcocks felt that it would be fatal if state protection prevented whites from being able to compete with black and colored workers, and hoped that the day would soon come when whites and blacks received the same minimum wages so that they could compete on the basis of performance.[150] The commission did recommend reserving certain jobs on the basis of race as a temporary expedient, but unfortunately did not mention a specific period. J.F.W. Grosskopf, author of one of the Carnegie studies, insisted on the application of the principle of pay according to results. 'It is entirely wrong to talk as if it were the higher rate of pay for white men that constituted "civilized labor" (a favorite catchword). All signs are there that we should be justified in striving to make "civilized labor" mean better organized labor, producing work of a superior quality, and thereby meriting a higher pay.'[151] It was on this point that the ways of Grosskopf and D.F. Malan, soon to become National Party leader, parted. During the 1938 commemoration of the Great Trek Malan said: 'South Africa expects of its poor whites that they remain white and live white', but in the labor market the competition for the white man was 'killing.'[152] The NP was committed to use both formal and informal means to enable poor whites 'to live white.'

The visions of Verwoerd and Malan

South Africa's decision to leave the gold standard at the end of 1932 soon led to a fusion of the parties of Hertzog and Smuts (the NP and SAP), and to the election of Hertzog as leader of the United Party as the new ruling party. A sharp rise in the gold price triggered a period of high economic growth at an average rate of five per cent over the next forty years. The official opposition was now the Purified National Party (NP). Under the leadership of Daniel François (D.F.) Malan the party spearheaded a broad nationalist

---

148 Albertyn, *Sociologiese verslag*, pp. 83-8, 121, 156.

149 Malherbe, *Never a Dull Moment*, p. 126.

150 Wilcocks, *Die armblanke*, p. 93.

151 J.F.W. Grosskopf, *Rural Impoverishment and Rural Exodus* (Stellenbosch, Pro Ecclesia, 1932), p. 240.

152 For this and a similar speech see D.F Malan, *Glo in u volk: D.F. Malan as redenaar* (Cape Town: Tafelberg, 1964), pp. 117, 121-130. See also *House of Assembly Debates*, 1939, col. 5524.

movement, consisting of an array of Afrikaner nationalist organizations (see pp. 405-10). The NP soon tried to outflank the UP on the issue of the poor whites. Smuts had brought into the UP the support of the mining houses, long insensitive to the deplorable working conditions and wages of unskilled or semi-skilled labor.

The NP attacked the government for allowing mining companies to keep a large part of the 'gold premium' – the 60 per cent increase in post-tax corporate profit from 1932-1934. It called for the premium to be redistributed in South Africa.[153] The UP government was already greatly stepping up its efforts to provide relief and assistance, but Malan's NP argued that the state could do even more. By the mid-1930s the Afrikaners had come to speak generally of 'our poor.' One of the few to express doubts about this was the writer M.E.R. In her column in Die Burger MER asked pointedly: 'Are we not going astray if we think of the welfare of the Afrikaner or of the white population as our only task?'[154]

The changed tone of the debate on the poor whites could be heard at the national conference on the topic, which was held in 1934 to discuss the Carnegie report and develop additional recommendations. The Carnegie Commission did not favor expanded statutory protection for white workers, which the apartheid system later would, and the chairman of the 1934 conference, the Rev. W.M. Nicol, stressed that attempts to rehabilitate the white poor had also to be seen as 'fair and healthy' towards blacks.[155] But some speakers offered a justification for concentrating on whites that was intertwined with the ideology of apartheid that was at this point being formulated.

One of them was Hendrik Verwoerd, who helped to organize the congress and became one of the principal authorities on the poor-white issue. His Dutch parents had emigrated from the Netherlands when he was two. He was a brilliant student at the University of Stellenbosch, then spent 1926 in Germany and part of 1927 in the US before returning for an academic career. There is no evidence that he had been infected by the racial ideology of the National Socialists in Germany. He was in fact more impressed by some strands in American sociology. His lecture notes and memoranda at Stellenbosch stressed that there were no biological differences between the big racial groups (or for that matter between Europeans and Africans), and since there were no differences 'this was not really a factor in the development of a higher social civilization by the Caucasian race.'[156]

Unlike the historian W.M. Macmillan, who recommended integrating the reserves into the economic and social system to resolve poverty, Verwoerd paid virtually no attention to structural factors in the impoverishment of blacks. His focus was on individuals, and how, despite adverse conditions, each could be rehabilitated. Verwoerd was energetic, hugely ambitious, exceptionally well organized and methodical in anything he undertook. He had an unshakeable confidence in the right of the state to make decisions not only for whites, but for the rest of the population as well. All that was required to solve the problem of white poverty, he believed, was a leadership with the necessary drive,

153 Yudelman, Emergence, pp. 250-55.
154 Judith Taylor, '"Our Poor": The politicisation of the poor white problem', Kleio, 15 (1992), pp. 42-9.
155 Verslag van die Volkskongres oor die Armblankevraagstuk, 1934, p. 13.
156 Millar, 'Early career of H.F. Verwoerd', p. 650.

vigor and commitment. He had a great ability to marshal arguments for white privilege so as to make it appear that it was not actually the intention for whites to be the sole or even the principal beneficiaries. In his speech to the 1934 Volkskongres Verwoerd advanced the most contentious arguments with great intellectual composure. He started with the generally acknowledged premise that one could not solve white poverty in a way that made the colored and the native problem worse. Yet, he went on, discrimination in favor of the white poor was in the interests of the country: 'If someone has to be unemployed, a white man or a native, it is best in the current circumstances and with the existing differences in living standards more economical for the nation that the native should be unemployed.' He left the matter there, as if the idea was self-evident and not at all controversial.

Verwoerd's analysis of the reasons for the parlous state of things was, however, both contentious and erroneous. He claimed that blacks pushing into the labor market had edged out colored people who, in turn, had squeezed out whites. It was in the country's interests to restore whites and coloreds to their old jobs. He conceded that it might 'superficially' look like 'having the appearance of privilege', but assured his audience that no privilege was at stake because the difficulties could be surmounted by employing South African blacks on the mines in the place of foreign blacks, or by stepping up the development of the reserves.

A resolution for the 1934 conference, which Verwoerd helped to edit, took an even more extreme view: if there was any unfairness in the situation it lay in the competition whites, colored people and 'detribalized natives' faced from 'the tribal native from the Native reserves.'[157] While Grosskopf and Wilcocks, his colleagues, opposed excessive state intervention on behalf of whites, Verwoerd took the position at the 1934 conference that 'the only organization in the country with the power to address the problem properly was the state.'[158] He pleaded for the re-organization of welfare work and the provision of greatly extended state assistance to the white poor. It was vital to get proper administrative structures in place and to achieve optimal co-ordination between private and public bodies. Social workers had to be trained to become professionals, with one stationed in every constituency of the country. He made many other proposals, among them for employment centers, a permanent unemployment fund, the establishment of public works, the provision of vocational guidance, health services and housing, the establishment of social clubs for the unemployed and settlements for the poorly paid, the introduction of pensions for poor mothers, the imposition of minimum ratios of 'civilized' to 'non-civilized' work in industry, an efficacious regulation of 'tenant and bywoner systems' and improved employment opportunities for women. The establishment of a national department of welfare was singled out as of prime importance. There was virtually nothing he left out.

Verwoerd scarcely referred to the fact that the state was already providing extensive assistance to the white poor. Under the new social welfare measures nearly half of the whites now received old age pensions or sick or disability grants. One Carnegie report noted: 'Nearly all state departments, and specifically Labour, Lands, Home Affairs, Edu-

157 *Verslag van die Volkskongres*, p. 301.
158 *Verslag van die Volkskongres*, pp. 30-8; *Die Burger*, 15 February 1935.
159 Albertyn, *Sociologiese verslag*, p. 86.

cation, Health, Agriculture, Railways and Irrigation spend a large part of their time and funds on social rehabilitation.'[159] In 1937 an examination of social welfare provisions concluded: 'Today the provision for [the] European population . . . is scarcely less complete than that of Great Britain.'[160]

Verwoerd, who served as secretary of the Continuation Committee of the Volkskongres, considered the government's response to the crisis of the poor white most disappointing. When the government failed to respond to his request for a separate Department of Welfare he exploded in a speech to students: despite 'resources for research and the ready spirit of reform in the volk, the state with all its financial resources had done virtually nothing for the rehabilitation of our social need.'[161] In 1937 Verwoerd became editor of *Die Transvaler*, a nationalist newspaper in Johannesburg, and focused on the regulation of the labor market. He even proposed the introduction of quotas for the Afrikaners to help them advance in commerce and the professions (see p. 417).[162]

D.F. Malan saw the problem from the point of view of a pastor, caring for his entire flock. The report of the Carnegie Commission concluded that ending the social isolation of the poor was a requisite for rehabilitating them. Speaking at the 1934 Volkskongres, Malan stressed the Carnegie report's recommendation that the poor had to be rescued from their isolation. 'They must not be merely objects of study and even less objects of charity . . . We must consider them and treat them as part of our volk.'[163] It was intolerable, he said, that, despite the wealth of the land, the poor-white question remained unresolved.

During the centenary celebrations of the Great Trek in 1938 the Rev. J.D. ('Father') Kestell of Bloemfontein, called for a mighty *reddingsdaad* or 'rescue action' to save the descendants of the Voortrekkers 'living in hopeless poverty, sunken materially, morally and spiritually.' No government charity or outside help would solve the problem; the answer lay in ethnic solidarity: 'A people is an integrated whole – the poor and rich. There is no unbridgeable gap between them. If pauperism is not curtailed it will mean the ruination of the entire nation. *'n Volk red himself*.'[164] This call that the Afrikaner people had to 'rescue itself' became a leading theme in the ideology of the nationalist movement. But while it was true that the social integration of the poor into the Afrikaner community played an important role, the slogan overlooked the major contribution made by the state.

On 16 December 1938, the culminating day of the emotion-charged commemoration of the Great Trek, D.F. Malan spoke in vivid historical images at the scene of the Blood River battle a century before. He singled out the plight of the poor urban Afrikaners as the greatest challenge to Afrikaner survival. Whites were outnumbered in the towns and cities, in schools and in the industrial labor force, and many worked for the same

---

160 J.L. Gray, 'The comparative sociology of South Africa', *South African Journal of Economics*, 5 (1937), p. 270.

161 *Die Burger*, 30 June 1936.

162 Henry Kenny, *Architect of Apartheid: H.F. Verwoerd – An Appraisal* (Johannesburg: Jonathan Ball, 1980), p. 31.

163 *Verslag van die Volkskongres*, p. 124; *Hertzog-toesprake*, vol. 5, p. 171.

164 FAK, 'Ekonomiese Volkskongres', pamphlet. For a discussion see J.L. Sadie, *The Fall and Rise of the Afrikaner in the South African Economy*' (Stellenbosch: University of Stellenbosch Annale, 2002/1).

wages as people who were not white, often in the same trade union. There was no reason to be confident that Afrikaners with low incomes and few skills could hold their own. 'The odds in the struggle are changing, but to the detriment of whites,' Malan cried out. The Afrikaners of the new Great Trek to the cities 'were meeting the non-white at his Blood River, partly or totally unarmed, without a ditch or even a river to separate them, defenseless on the open plains of economic leveling.'[165]

The question whether enough was being done to address white poverty remained a vexed one. When Malan spoke, the condition of the white poor had not yet dramatically improved. The extent to which the government could substitute white 'civilized labor' for blacks was limited, and the private sector did not allow the government to push it too far. Black labor was much cheaper, and white women and child laborers could be taken on at much lower rates than white men. Between 1930 and 1940 the number of whites in the manufacturing sector rose from 91,024 to 115,292, while that of blacks increased much faster from 90,517 to 147,399. Despite the high economic growth, white wages did not appreciate materially. In 1939 it was found that there were still 298,000 white people living in 'terrible poverty', all with a monthly income below £12 – an amount considered to be the minimum for the preservation of health.[166]

It was true that the position of the most desperate – those at the bottom of the white labor ladder – was improving. They could get work in land and forestry settlements or on public projects, like dams and railways. The Department of Labour reported, in 1939, that it could offer work to every able-bodied white male willing to accept unskilled labor on specific projects designed to relieve unemployment. During the war years the demand for labor was so high that the government could stop supplying jobs specifically for unskilled whites.

A consolidated white group

Between 1890 and 1939 the most burning political issue was the existence of a large white underclass consisting mainly of Afrikaners. On the farms most of the bywoners and tenants had outlived their usefulness and now represented a rural proletariat, passively rotting away. In the cities and towns the poor lived on the periphery of white society. They were barely literate, had few skills, and were often unemployed or unemployable. The challenges from white labor and the white underclass in the strikes of 1913, 1914 and 1922 and in the rebellion of 1914-15, in which the poor also played an important role, nearly brought the fledgling South African state to its knees. The legislation passed in the mid-1920s introduced stability in the system of industrial relations and brought greater security to white workers. Without a militant labor force embarking on violent lightning strikes, the white poor at the bottom of the white labor market ceased to be the 'dangerous classes', as Smuts called them in 1922.

The desperate conditions of the Depression and the drought that ravaged South Africa between 1929 and 1933 prompted the government to intervene on an unprecedented

---

165 Pienaar, *Glo in u volk*, p. 127.
166 Lawrence Solomon, 'The Economic Background to Afrikaner Nationalism', in J. Butler (ed.), *Boston University Papers in African History* (Boston: Boston University, 1964), pp. 234-5.

scale. While the 'civilized labor' policy, education and training all helped to incorporate whites in the dominant group, the intensification of residential segregation probably did more than any other measure to bring about a consolidated white group. By the early 1930s racially integrated slums were a dominant feature of all the major towns. Over the next two decades the white elite across party divisions began to unscramble this omelet. It was not the NP but the United Party that took the initiative through the Slums Act of 1934, which made it possible to expropriate whole areas. Using the law, the Johannesburg City Council and other local authorities began removing all slum dwellers.[167] They re-housed whites, but settled blacks in new townships at a distance from the city. In Cape Town new colored townships were established. But there was still no legislation prohibiting coloreds or blacks in the Cape Province from living where they wanted.

Between 1939 and 1945 the war economy mopped up most of the remaining white unemployment and brought the poor-white problem to an end.[168] By the 1950s economists found that whites were no longer competing with black people for the same jobs; blacks were taking the formerly white jobs as better-trained whites moved up to better jobs.[169] The poor whites had disappeared before the arrival of the apartheid program, which nevertheless promised yet again to rescue them.

167 Susan Parnell, 'Slums, Segregation and the Poor White in Johannesburg, 1920-1934', *White but Poor*, pp. 115-26.
168 For an analysis, see Hermina Forgey, 'Die politiek van armoede: 'n Vergelyking van die 1932 en 1989 Carnegie-verslag', master's diss., RAU, 1994, pp. 129-43.
169 David Berger, 'White Poverty and Government Policy in South Africa, 1890-1934', doctoral diss., Temple University, 1982, pp. 443-67.

Chapter 11

'To stop being *agterryers*':
The Assertion of a New Afrikaner Identity

New quarrels and old battles

'Now that we no longer have to fight the Kaffers or English we are bound to quarrel among ourselves.'[1] This was the response of General Koos de la Rey, *Bittereinder* leader in the Anglo-Boer War and now a Member of Parliament representing the ruling South African Party (SAP), after General J.B.M. Hertzog had broken away to found the National Party (NP) early in 1914. A measured statement about the quarrel in Afrikaner ranks would come many years later from Piet Cillié, the leading Afrikaans newspaper editor of the twentieth century. For him the alternatives open to the Afrikaners were the same in the decades to come: 'It was the difference between Afrikaners turning inward and directing themselves outward, between concentrating on the self, on becoming a *volk*, on fulfilling themselves as Afrikaners, on the one hand, and, on the other, on closer contact, firmer co-operation and at a minimum *political* unification with non-Afrikaners: purity as opposed to association and fusion, exclusive Afrikaner unity as opposed to a more enveloping white unity – even a broader non-black unity that in time could include colored people as well.'[2]

Much of the energy of politicians, civil servants and church ministers from the 1890s to the 1940s was consumed by the battle to incorporate the white poor and a militant working class into a consolidated white ruling group. But in the white community there was also an intense rivalry over power, status and economic opportunity. One side was led by Generals Louis Botha and Jan Smuts, the leading figures in the ruling SAP. It was mainly an Afrikaner party, but there was a not insignificant English component in both the leadership and its grassroots support. Its leaders strongly believed that white supremacy was best served by a close relationship with the Empire, and the merging of the two white cultures. On one flank it was challenged by the staunchly pro-Empire Unionist Party, which vociferously attacked any weakening of the links with the Empire, and which wanted English-speaking civil servants to be under no compunction to speak

---

1 Johannes Meintjes, *General Louis Botha* (London: Cassell, 1970), p. 238.
2 P.J. Cillié, *Hertzog en Malan: die jare van skeuring, 1934-1939* (Potchefstroom: Hertzog-gedenklesing, 1980), p. 8.

Afrikaans. On its other flank was the NP, led by General Hertzog. It was a typical ethno-
nationalist party in both its leadership and its rank and file support. The party insisted
that South African interests had to be put first, and that a sound sense of white nationhood would have to be based on the recognition of both the Afrikaans and English
cultures. The relative economic, cultural and social backwardness of the Afrikaner community could only be overcome by their developing their own identity (the term 'nationality' was then used) as a community, and by establishing separate social institutions. As General Hertzog remarked, the Afrikaners had to wage a language struggle
'to stop considering themselves as *agterryers.*' This was a term from the commando days
that referred to attendants, usually unarmed Khoikhoi or Africans, who provided assistance to fighters.[3]

The outcome of these political battles would shape a more exclusive Afrikaner identity.
This included a strong identification with Afrikaans as a public symbol of its 'nationality', with South Africa as its only national home and with indigenous or local forms of cultural or artistic expression – new attachments that were manifested alongside older ones
such as an adherence to the Reformed faith, an insistence on racial exclusivity, and a rejection of *gelykstelling* or social leveling. Other identities, particularly that of 'Boer', used
predominantly in the republics, faded away in an increasingly urban environment. The
battle between the two main parties, waged mainly along language lines, resulted in the
term 'Afrikaner', previously often used in an inclusive sense, increasingly being defined
exclusively in terms of both race and culture.

Union: 'The Great Adventure'

When the Union of South Africa was founded in 1910, it established a centralized state
with Cape Town as the legislative capital and Pretoria as the executive capital. It had a
population of six million people, of whom 3,956,000 were Africans, 1,278,000 whites,
517,000 colored people and 148,000 Asians. The great wave of immigration that washed
over South Africa had stopped by 1904, and large numbers of English-speakers, fearing
Afrikaner political domination, had gone back to Britain. Afrikaners formed a slight
majority in the white population; they would rise to close to 60 per cent by 1960 as a
result of a high birth rate and only a trickle of white immigration. The 1910 figures for
the white population were:

WHITE POPULATION, 1910

	TOTAL	AFRIKANER TOTAL
Cape	583,177	339,585
Free State	175,435	137,955
Transvaal	420,881	204,058
Natal	98,582	12,300
Total	1,278,075	693,898

3 *Die Burger,* 27 July 1929. For a discussion see D.J. Kriek, 'Genl. J.B.M. Hertzog se opvattinge van die verhouding tussen die Afrikaans- en Engelssprekendes na Uniewording', doctoral diss., University of Pretoria,
1971, pp. 79-87.

For most whites the Union was a tangible symbol of South Africa's progress toward modernity and development. 'South Africa' was no longer a mere territorial expression, but the name of a modern state underpinned by an increasingly sophisticated economy, a rapidly improving communications system and a steadily urbanizing population. It could take its place with pride, along with Australia and Canada, as a self-governing, autonomous British dominion.

To Jan Smuts, Minister of Justice in the new government, Union was the answer to his anguished prayer in the final year of the Anglo-Boer War: 'Cannot the blood-stained races reason together and cannot their leaders in a spirit of mutual forgiveness try to write the word reconciliation over all our feuds and differences?'[4] Earl Buxton, the second governor general, wrote that Union was the 'Great Adventure', undertaken under a stress of deep natural emotion. '[A] wave of racial optimism passed over the country. The slate had been wiped clean and the new Constitution, written clear and broad and based on absolute equality, was to obliterate the dread past with its misunderstandings, and its bitter memories, and to bring about a spirit of partnership and goodwill.'[5]

The man who symbolized the drive to reconciliation was Louis Botha, the Transvaal Afrikaner leader, chosen by the British government to form the first Union cabinet. He was a powerfully built man with a face that seemed to come straight from a painting by Frans Hals or Hans Holbein. He was a successful commercial farmer, who, together with Koos de la Rey and Christiaan de Wet, had emerged from the war with great stature as a military leader. To Jan Smuts, his closest politically ally in the government, Botha was a 'colossal figure', a leader of great personal magnetism with 'a power over men much greater than any other form of superiority could possibly have given.'[6] Tending to be aloof and cerebral, Smuts played a supportive role, unfailingly backing up and complementing Botha, and saving the SAP in difficult situations. Opponents considered him clever and cunning; they saw Botha as honest and forthright, if politically naïve.

Botha's choice as prime minister was popular among moderate English-speakers. With Smuts, he had gone out of his way to attract English support in the 1907 election in the Transvaal Colony. To contest the first election for the new South African state, Botha formed a loose coalition, mainly of the South African Party in the Cape, Het Volk in the Transvaal, and Orangia Unie in the Free State, all Afrikaner-based parties. The alliance secured victory by winning sixty-six seats against the main opposition, the staunchly imperialist Unionist Party under Leander Starr Jameson, with thirty-six seats. Botha's coalition was transformed into the South African Party (SAP) at a congress in 1911, at which Botha was elected party leader. At its founding congress more than a quarter of the delegates were English-speakers.

Botha and Smuts were moved by powerful considerations in reaching out to English-speaking South Africans. In the world of big power rivalry the British imperial system offered the best security umbrella and Britain was, by far, South Africa's most important trading partner. British capital accounted for two-fifths of net investment in the South African economy during the 1910s and 1920s.[7] Rapid economic growth would only be

---

4 *Smuts Papers*, vol. 1, p. 488.

5 Earl Buxton, *General Louis Botha* (London: John Murray, 1924), p. 34.

6 J.C. Smuts, 'Introduction' to F.V. Engelenburg, *Louis Botha* (London: George Harrap, 1929), pp. 15-17.

7 P.J. Cain and A.G. Hopkins, *British Imperialism: Crisis and Deconstruction, 1914-1990* (London; Longman, 1991), pp. 126-9.

possible if the new government maintained the confidence and trust of the English-speakers of British and Jewish descent. Smuts wrote to Steyn that the Afrikaners needed English support to govern.[8]

The ruling party could only retain its unity through inspiring leadership, holding up a bold vision and reconciling internal differences. For Smuts the challenge was much greater than joining together different colonial states: 'The great task was to build up a South African nation . . . In a South African nation alone was a solution . . . Two such peoples as the Boers and the English must either unite or they must exterminate each other.'[9] He made many similar statements.[10] Speaking in Johannesburg in 1912, Botha observed that the city represented the coming together of all people. 'Here all nationalities live on a friendly footing with each other. Here there is no specially chosen band of a single part of the population.'[11]

Coming so soon after a bitter war that traumatized the population of the Boer republics, such talk caused dismay among many Afrikaners. The Anglo-BoerWar was not only a military battle but also a propaganda contest in which a large amount of British resources went into denigrating the Boer population. Such propaganda continued in the war's aftermath, even in juvenile literature. Many of these books reached South Africa and influenced public opinion. G.A. Henty, one of the most popular writers of children's novels, in *Good Change* sketched the situation of the British population in the Transvaal before the war in the following terms: 'Never before had a large body of intelligent men been kept in a state of abject subjugation by an inferior race, a race almost without the elements of civilization, ignorant and brutal, beyond any existing white community.'[12]

The initial tone of public debate outside Parliament was largely that of a jingoist imperialism, espoused by *The Star, Pretoria News, Cape Times, Cape Argus* and other newspapers. Determined to drive a wedge between the English and Afrikaner SAP supporters, they seemed to delight in provoking the Afrikaners. *The Star* even defended the concentration camps, describing a lecture by the Rev. H.P. Schoon on 'The Suffering of Women and Children in the Anglo-Boer War' as 'a disgraceful performance.' 'If a history of humanity in warfare were to be written', *The Star* said, 'the way the British took care of the women and children of the enemy would deserve a marked place of honor.'[13]

For J.B.M. Hertzog, Free State leader and a member of Botha's cabinet, Botha's euphoric talk of Union and reconciliation between the two white groups came much too soon. Formally the Afrikaners and the English-speaking section were on an equal footing, sharing the same political rights, but economically, socially and culturally there was a gulf between them. In 1917 Daniël François (D.F.). Malan, a Cape Afrikaner nationalist, expressed the feeling in these terms: 'From year to year, and from one generation to another the Afrikaner is treated and has been treated as an inferior – it is preached in the civil service, by

8 E. Liversage, 'Die premierskap van generaal Louis Botha', doctoral diss., University of the OFS, 1985, p. 56.
9 *The Star*, 18 April 1907.
10 W.K. Hancock, *Smuts: Vol. 2: The Fields of Force* (Cambridge: Cambridge University Press, 1968), p. 36.
11 C.M. van den Heever, *Generaal J.B.M. Hertzog* (Johannesburg: APB Boekhandel, 1943), p. 312.
12 Gilles Teulié, 'A Portrait of the Boer as an Enemy in British Juvenile Literature in the Anglo-Boer War', *South African Journal of Cultural History*, 18,2 (2001), p. 83.
13 *The Star*, 5 July and 12 October 1911; *Pretoria News*, 28 November 1910.

the school, in every small public notice alongside a road, and through the entire institutional expression and tone of public life. And where others regard and treat him [the
Afrikaner] as inferior he himself begins to regard himself as such.'[14]

At the heart of the Afrikaner nationalist struggle was the attempt to imagine a new
national community with its language enjoying parity of esteem with English in the
public sphere. Only then would the sense of being marginalized be overcome. This
meant that Afrikaans had to be heard in Parliament, the civil service, schools, colleges
and universities, and in the world of business and finance; it had to be the medium of
newspapers, novels, and poems, giving expression to what was truly South African. Instead
of English-speakers portraying Afrikaners in reports, novels or histories as everything
they were not: unrefined, semi-literate, racist, dogmatic, and unprogressive, the Afrikaners had to define and represent themselves as the true South Africans. This cultural
revolution had to pave the way for the establishment of political, economic, and cultural
institutions and ultimately the Union of South Africa had to make way for a Republic of
South Africa that was free and independent.

For the Afrikaner nationalists to build a constituency along such ideological lines
was much more difficult than Hertzog initially thought. He himself said: '[The] circumstances of this country are such that we have largely assimilated English customs, culture and ideals. Our difference is simply that of language and a want of sympathy between the newcomers and the old inhabitants.'[15] The name 'Afrikaner' was being used in
a bewildering confusion of ways. In 1905 John Meiring Beck, a Cape Afrikaner (he also
described himself as a Boer) and cabinet minister, spoke up for 'Afrikanderism – English, Dutch or otherwise descended.' Of 'our Native population,' he said: 'Let us never
forget that they are Africanders; that they are the oldest Africanders in the land, and
that we have great duties towards them.'[16] Both Hertzog and D.F. Malan, who became
leader of the NP in the Cape Province in 1915, used the term 'Afrikaner' to refer both
to a white South African patriot and also to a Dutch Afrikaans-speaking white alone.
Hertzog said at a language festival in 1911 that Dutch-speakers were not the only Afrikaners, that there were also Afrikaners whose mother tongue was English, though Dutch-
speakers were in 'the first row.'[17]

The polarization of politics

The social system on which the Union was built was one that generated conflict rather
than consensus. The free-market system generated great tensions in a society in which
a small minority, the English-speaking section, owned and managed virtually every sizeable company and dominated the professions and the upper ranks of the civil service.
Most Afrikaners in the urban economy were in semi-skilled and unskilled occupations.

Also fostering discord was the Westminster political system of Britain, which the
framers of the constitution almost unthinkingly adopted. So powerful was the influence

---

14 Quoted by J.L. Sadie, *The Fall and Rise of the Afrikaner* (US Annale, 2002), p. 12.
15 *Hertzog-toesprake*, vol. 1, p. 101.
16 J.H. Meiring Beck, *J.H. Meiring Beck* (Cape Town: Maskew Miller, 1921), pp. 36, 63.
17 *Hertzog-toesprake*, vol. 2, p. 166-7.

of this model that, despite its lack of success in racially or ethnically divided societies, scholars only towards the end of the twentieth century began to question its appropriateness as an export product. It concentrates power at the center, making Parliament rather than the constitution sovereign; it gives the majority the right to change all but the most fundamental rules of government. It breeds a winner-takes-all attitude, which in heterogeneous societies invariably produces divisions along racial or ethnic lines.[18]

Perhaps realizing that South Africa should have chosen a different system, John X. Merriman, the last Cape prime minister, in a letter to ex-President Steyn of the Orange Free State, deplored the fact that they had not pressed their views for the Swiss system 'against the stereotyped one' adopted.[19] Based on a proportional vote, the Swiss system encouraged coalition-building and consensus-seeking and facilitated the protection of minorities.

The underlying tensions soon surfaced. Nationalists felt that the Afrikaners' inferior socio-economic status in the white community was replicated in the subordinate status South Africa had in the British Empire, particularly with regard to declaring war. The government was struggling with a considerable budget deficit, but agreed to the imperial government's request to build its own navy. This decision prompted Hertzog to remark that 'imperialism was only important to me when it was useful for South Africa.'[20] The fact that South Africa could not decide if it wanted to stay out of any of the wars Britain might declare also chafed. Hertzog asked: 'What is the point of self-government at all if it failed to grant the right of neutrality, the right of decision in the final test of self-government?'[21] Botha was often criticized about his lack of principles, but on one principle he was quite clear: there was no such thing as optional neutrality for South Africa if Britain was at war.[22] To English-speaking South Africans the fact that the Afrikaners were the dominant political force did not matter much as long as the country was firmly locked into the hierarchical imperial relationship.

The SAP was a catchall party. Botha's first cabinet included in its ranks Hertzog, who did not disguise his nationalist convictions, and a staunch imperialist, Colonel G. Leuchars, who declared 'I am an Englishman and an Imperialist.'[23] To Botha's calls for unity Smuts added an emphasis on large entities. In 1908 Lionel Phillips, an English industrialist, pointed out in a private conversation that rapid industrial development would lead to a large increase in the English-speaking population through immigration. Smuts agreed and gave permission to Phillips to make public his reply: 'We want the big thing. We would welcome any number of newcomers, and are quite ready to let the future take care of itself.'[24]

But for his own ill health, Steyn, called by Botha 'the greatest contemporary Afrikan-

18 Graham Watson, 'The Westminster model in comparative perspective', in I. Budge and D. Mackay (eds.), *Developing Democracy* (London: Sage, 1994), pp. 189-201.

19 Liversage, 'Premierskap van Botha', p. 31.

20 Harold Spender, *General Louis Botha* (London: Constable and Co., 1916), p. 246,

21 G.H. Calpin, *There Are No South Africans* (London: Thomas Nelson, 1940), p. 105.

22 Hancock, *Smuts*, vol. 1, pp. 353-4; Johannes Meintjes; *General Louis Botha* (London: Cassell, 1970), p. 183.

23 A.H. Marais, 'Die Afrikanerdom een en verdeeld', in O. Geyser and A.H. Marais (eds.), *Die Nasionale Party* (Pretoria: Academica, 1975), vol. 1, p. 99.

24 *The Transvaal Leader*, 12 October 1908.

der', would have been prime minister.[25] He and General Hertzog preferred John X. Merriman, prime minister of the Cape Colony and prominent liberal. After the National
Convention, Merriman wrote: 'I have no respect for Botha's political knowledge.'[26] Botha
was unable to ignore insults and rebuffs; he became morose when accused of being too
weak to stand up to British imperialism and called a *papbroek*, a coward. No one mocked
him more cruelly than Boonzaier, the cartoonist of the Cape Town daily *De Burger* that
first appeared in 1915. He often depicted the burly figure of Botha in kilts or courtesan
clothes to make him and his reconciliation efforts appear ridiculous.

There was in public life still no South Africanism that could establish space for itself
between an advancing Afrikaner nationalism and a retreating British imperialism. Some
SAP politicians sought to transcend the differences of the past in 'a spirit of non-racialism',
as it was called, but they lacked broad-based support in the first two decades of Union.
The five Dutch newspapers backed the SAP's policy of reconciliation, but only three of
the twenty-three English dailies did so. The idea of Afrikaner-English reconciliation
based on mutual respect for the different cultures had little backing from English scholars or writers. An exception was Percy Fitzpatrick, author of a best seller about a dog,
Jock of the Bushveld. He became so inspired by the idea of Union that he professed to
identify as much with the Voortrekkers as the British settlers, and learned to speak Dutch
well. The short-lived journal *The State,* founded in 1909 by senior members of Milner's
bureaucracy, published a Dutch edition; it appeared for seven issues only, then ceased
publication. Contributors tended to be condescending or indifferent to South African art,
literature, and culture.[27] *The Star* expressed openly what many of the English-speaking
intellectuals believed: 'There is one and only one Imperial nation under the British crown
. . . A colony is not a nation except for the purpose of minor politicians and minor poets.'[28]

The political system soon became polarized. Hertzog worked for the political consolidation of the 'national minded' Afrikaners and was responsive to the appeals of the
younger generation, such as the Pretoria-based movement *Jong Suid-Afrika,* which declared that there could be no peace until Afrikaners had all their rights. When the first
issue of the Afrikaans magazine *Die Brandwag* appeared in 1910, Hertzog lauded it as an
effort to escape from 'an alien literary hegemony.' He called for a literature in which
issues 'are seen from an Afrikaans point of view, animated by an Afrikaans spirit and
expressed in the language of South Africa.'[29]

From the very first days of the Union of South Africa the language issue surfaced as the
key issue that divided the two white groups and could split the ruling SAP. Accused of
politicizing the language issue, Hertzog pointed out that the British imperialists themselves did not consider language as a neutral instrument. He quoted a letter of Alfred
Milner's Director of Education in the post-war reconstruction, E.B. Sargant. It instructed English teachers to complete the work of the military in teaching 'the children of burgh-

---

25 F.V. Engelenburg, *Botha*, p. 214.

26 Liversage, 'Premierskap van Louis Botha', p. 37.

27 Saul Dubow, 'Colonial Nationalism, the Milner Kindergarten and the Rise of South Africanism, 1902-
1910', *History Workshop Journal*, 43 (1997), pp. 53-85; Peter Merrington, 'Heritage, Genealogy and the
Inventing of Union', paper presented to the UCT African Studies Seminar, 1997.

28 *The Star*, 15 November 1910.

29 E.C. Pienaar, *Die triomf van Afrikaans* (Cape Town: Nasionale Pers, 1943), p. 323.

ers our language and our ideals . . . and eventually our great Imperial ideals.'[30] Language had become embroiled in the issues of war, reconstruction, social identity, and the relative status of the two white communities.

To most English-speakers the English language seemed destined to prevail over both Dutch and Afrikaans. Violet Markham, a British journalist, said that after Union the Afrikaners found themselves 'hopelessly menaced by the great on-coming compelling wave of Anglo-Saxon civilization.' She predicted that in the long run there could be only one outcome: 'English methods and the English language are bound increasingly to win their way and permeate the whole structure of society.'[31] G. Heaton Nicholls, a pro-segregation politician from Natal, said: 'We had gone about talking of a South African nation which would consist of English and Dutch, but at the back of our minds we had supposed that they would talk English. We aimed at Anglicization.'[32] F. V. Engelenburg, editor of the Pretoria *Volksstem* and Louis Botha's biographer and staunch supporter, remarked: 'It should not be forgotten that whereas the fathers of the Constitution accepted the absolute equality of both languages in all good faith, English-speaking South Africa never took the matter seriously. Bilingualism was regarded as nothing more than a polite gesture towards the other section – neither more nor less. The average English-speaking South African was inclined to regard every political recognition of the Dutch language as a menace to the interests of his own race.'[33]

Trying to defuse the issue, Botha and Smuts declared that they took pride in the Afrikaners' cultural heritage.[34] In the first debate in the Union Parliament Botha stated that he loved his language and wished to put both languages on an equal footing. 'The politics of South Africa is one of co-operation and not of compulsion.'[35] But Botha, who knew little about the process of language displacement, was far from being sensitive enough. At the end of 1910 he told a meeting that the language issue would resolve itself naturally, and that 'the fittest language will survive.'[36] His government allowed civil servants to ignore the language clause of the constitution.

Government policy was that no civil servant employed at the time of Union would be forced to learn the other language. New appointees had to be bilingual to be considered for promotion.[37] Under pressure from the Unionist Party, Smuts watered down this requirement, prompting an SAP parliamentarian to warn that the policy would cause the Dutch language to disappear in South Africa in ten years' time. But the SAP leaders were in a difficult situation. Many English-speakers were resentful, suddenly finding themselves in a political minority despite winning the war. The Afrikaner community was well behind them in terms of education, and produced far fewer suitable candidates for the civil service. In 1915 only 15 per cent of Afrikaner children proceeded beyond the seventh school year (Standard 5), and only 4 per cent progressed far enough to become profi-

---

30 *House of Assembly Debates, 1910-1911*, cols. 296-97.

31 Violet Markham, *The South African Scene* (London: Smith, Elder and Co., 1913), p. 187.

32 G. Heaton Nicholls, *South Africa in My Time* (London: George Allen and Unwin, 1961) p. 283.

33 Engelenburg, *Botha*, p. 230.

34 *Volksraad Debatten 1910*, col. 334; Liversage, 'Premierskap van Botha', p. 117.

35 *Volksraad Debatten*, 25 November 1910, col. 330.

36 *Cape Argus,* 5 November 1910.

37 Liversage, 'Premierskap van Louis Botha', p. 132.

ABOVE Andries Stockenstrom,
frontier official committed to 'truth
and justice'.
(National Library of South Africa)

RIGHT Paul Kruger, President of the
Zuid-Afrikaanse Republiek from
1883 to 1900.
*(Manuscripts Division, University Library,
Stellenbosch)*

ABOVE President Marthinus Theunis Steyn, President of the Republic of the OFS, Bittereinder and post-1902 Afrikaner leader.
(Manuscripts Division, University Library, Stellenbosch)

RIGHT General Jan Smuts, politician and philosopher.
(Manuscripts Division, University Library, Stellenbosch)

OPPOSITE Generals Christiaan de Wet, Koos de la Rey and Louis Botha, Bittereinder leaders, as members of a Boer delegation to Europe in 1902.
(Manuscripts Division, University Library, Stellenbosch)

ABOVE General J.B.M. Hertzog, politician and champion of language rights.
(Manuscripts Division, University Library, Stellenbosch)

LEFT N.P. van Wyk Louw in the mid-1930s when he wrote *Lojale verset*.
(Louw family)

OPPOSITE M.E. Rothman, who wrote as M.E.R., a leading figure in the Afrikaner women's movement to rehabilitate the Afrikaner poor.
(Hennie Aucamp collection, Documentation Centre, University Library, Stellenbosch)

ABOVE Nelson Mandela in the 1950s, with a
'softgoods salesman' by the name of Charles
Bikitsha who accompanied Mandela to Johannesburg from the Transkei.
(Private collection)

RIGHT Schalk Pienaar, verligte National Party
editor in the heyday of apartheid.
(Pienaar collection)

OPPOSITE ABOVE Rykie van Reenen, the
most outstanding Afrikaans reporter, who
interviewed both Hendrik Verwoerd and
Steve Biko.
(Die Burger)

OPPOSITE BELOW Thabo Mbeki, Frederik van
Zyl Slabbert and Breyten Breytenbach at the
Dakar meeting in 1987.
(Die Suid-Afrikaan)

LEFT Nobel Peace Prize winner and last white president F.W. de Klerk.
(*Roger Sedres, Die Burger*)

BELOW Anton Rupert, Afrikaner entrepreneur, receiving the highest state award from President Nelson Mandela.
(*Beeld*)

cient in English. As a result, progress in bringing Afrikaners into the civil service was slow, with Afrikaners making up only a quarter of those newly appointed in the first five years of Union. The dominance of unilingual English-speakers of the higher ranks of the civil service was to remain a burning issue until the 1950s.

Another field in which controversy erupted was education. A few months after unification a member of the Unionist Party attacked the Free State policy that made both Dutch and English compulsory as mediums of instruction in every state school. According to him, it was a violation of the spirit of the National Convention. To avoid a split in SAP ranks, F.S. Malan, Minister for Education, appointed a select committee, and, in a major compromise, Hertzog withdrew the provision compelling teaching in both languages. Through some shrewd maneuvering he was locked into a majority report in which the central government recommended to the provinces the use of the mother tongue up to the sixth school year (Standard 4), with the second language taught as a subject. For the upper grades parents could choose one or both languages as the medium of instruction. Three of the four provinces made mother-tongue instruction compulsory, but Natal allowed parents to choose. Hertzog continued to nourish a fierce resentment of the abandonment of his policy of dual-medium education.

A language struggle developed, too, in higher education. With the exception of the college at Potchefstroom, which developed out of a theological seminary, all university colleges in South Africa used English as the medium of instruction. At the time of Union an idea of Cecil John Rhodes to establish a single teaching university using English as the medium of instruction was revived. It was proposed that this university should be built at the Groote Schuur estate in Cape Town, near the prime minister's residence. The intent was to bring students from the two language groups together and, thereby, to strengthen imperial ties. Two mining magnates, Julius Wernher and Otto Beit, offered a substantial grant. They insisted on English as the medium of instruction as a means of attracting the best academic talent from Britain. The cabinet agreed. F.S. Malan, the Minister of Education, said that the 'reasonable wants' of both white communities had to be met, but that his party's effort to promote reconciliation overrode everything else. The immediate need was the 'fusion of the two races into one nation' rather than introducing separate educational institutions on a tertiary level, 'whatever advantages academically or otherwise may be claimed for it.'[38]

At Stellenbosch, stiff opposition built up against the proposal, under which Victoria College would be subordinate to the new university. It would have spelled the end of Dutch as a language of instruction above primary level. Early in 1913 a committee of three, including D.F. Malan, in a memorandum described the proposed university at Groote Schuur as 'an institution artificially called into being for political and other reasons.' By contrast, Victoria College had for many years been 'intimately connected with the spiritual, moral and national life of the Dutch-speaking section of the people.' Victoria College had become the emblem of an 'own, vigorous, growing national life for the Afrikaners seeking to express itself . . . It stands for an idea.'[39]

---

38 F.S. Malan, *The University South Africa Needs* (Cape Town, no publisher, 1912), pp. 7-8.
39 P.S. du Toit and F. Smuts, 'Kollege en universiteit', *Stellenbosch drie eeue* (Stellenbosch: Stellenbosch City Council, 1979), p. 336.

After meeting with a Victoria College delegation, the cabinet withdrew its support for a single teaching university. The plan for a university in Cape Town would go ahead, but the government insisted that Victoria College had to raise £100,000 publicly before it would agree to a university in Stellenbosch. Just before his death in 1915, J.H. Marais, who would also make possible the establishment of Nasionale Pers, left £100,000 to Victoria College. He set the condition that Dutch or Afrikaans must take 'no lesser place' in the institution than English. Part of the fund was used to endow some chairs and the incumbents were expected to give at least half of their lectures in Dutch or Afrikaans.[40] By 1930 virtually no lectures were given in English.

Afrikaans as badge of a social identity

There was no consensus about which language would serve best to rally Dutch- and Afrikaans-speakers. In 1890, when the Zuid-Afrikaansche Taalbond was founded in Cape Town, delegates identified four possibilities: old Dutch, modern Dutch, Dutch with a simplified spelling and Afrikaans. Of the delegates, forty-seven chose the option of using any of the four; another thirty-seven opted for Afrikaans and fifteen for Dutch. The executive interpreted the result as support for Dutch with a simplified spelling. Hertzog, then a law student in Amsterdam, wrote that it was 'total arrogance' to try to maintain such a complex and 'synthetic' language as Dutch. 'We can just as well expect that the stream of a river would run backwards.' He predicted that Afrikaans would become the *volkstaal*, though he did not use Afrikaans himself in public speeches until 1922.[41]

In the Transvaal, one of the first champions of Afrikaans as a written language was Eugène Marais. Born in Pretoria in 1871, he was fluent in English, using it for his first poems and for serious debates. Appointed editor of *Land en Volk* in Pretoria at the age of nineteen in 1890, he turned it into a newspaper strongly opposed to the corrupt practices in Kruger's government and the appointment of large numbers of Dutch immigrants as civil servants. Like Kruger, he saw Britain as 'enemy and persecutor.' In contrast to Transvaal patriotism, he stressed the 'ties of blood' of all Afrikaners across South Africa. To attract subscribers he used Afrikaans along with Dutch in the paper, and, in an editorial branded 'Jingo-Afrikaners despising their mother tongue' as the biggest enemies of Afrikaans.[42] Here was a new type of person identifying with Afrikaans: modern, brash, secular and sophisticated, though also addicted to morphine. It was hardly a mix designed to give Afrikaans a good name among the conservative Boer people.

After the war Marais' path crossed with Gustav Preller's on the Pretoria-based *De Volksstem*, a newspaper started by the Boer generals. Preller, a greater admirer of Louis Botha, continued to support the SAP until 1924, but he had a passion for Afrikaans. He collected oral traditions from first-generation Voortrekkers, and, noticing children playing 'foreign games' at Dingaan's Day festivals, he launched a campaign to invent Afrikaans

---

40 Copy of will of J.H. Marais, University of Stellenbosch, Corporate Affairs.
41 Van den Heever, *Hertzog*, p. 47.
42 Leon Rousseau, *Die groot verlange: Die verhaal van Eugène Marais* (Cape Town: Human & Rousseau, 1974), pp. 52, 85.
43 Isabel Hofmeyr, 'Popularising History: The Case of Gustav Preller', *Journal of African History*, 29,3 (1988), pp. 521-35.

games and songs. Observing that a poor command of Dutch caused people to switch to English, Preller began advocating the use of Afrikaans as a written language.[43] To him it was the only possible bridge between what he called an 'ignorant, uncaring proletariat' and another part 'leaning towards English.'[44] The fact that he was a journalist seeking to build the circulation of his paper gave his efforts a material purpose. But turning Afrikaans into a written language was also a way of developing a distinctive nationality. To produce a national literature was, in his view, not so much the task of the church, the school, and the learned people, as of all Afrikaners.[45]

While the Cape Colony had a stratum of Afrikaners proficient in modern Dutch, many of them considered the language, at best, a necessary evil. Miems Rothman, who wrote under the name MER, said: 'We never really knew the Dutch language; it was never really our language.' It was 'an awkward tool . . . a foreign language, for me, my mother and my grandmother.'[46]

The effort to promote Dutch with a simplified spelling was largely an elite project driven by a few Stellenbosch professors with the support of teachers' organizations. The largest of these teachers' groups was the Zuid-Afrikaansche Onderwysunie (ZAOU), founded in 1905 in the western Cape as a breakaway from the staunchly imperialist South African Teachers' Association, which had adopted English as its sole language of communication. Gawie Cillié, professor of education at Victoria College and a leading figure in the ZAOU, opposed the promotion of Afrikaans on the grounds that it was a dialect not spoken by learned people.[47]

Sharing the preference for Dutch, in a simplified form, were two senior Cape Afrikaner politicians, Onze Jan Hofmeyr and F.S. Malan. In 1905 Hofmeyr gave an important speech, *Is 't ons ernst?* (Are we serious about it?), noting that instruction in Dutch in Cape schools was so defective that no pupil could compose a letter in the language. He asked those who were 'Hollands Afrikaans' whether they seriously intended to maintain Dutch as a language.

But a new generation of Afrikaners had concluded that only Afrikaans could develop as a public language and as the main symbol of their social identity. Responding to Hofmeyr's call, Gustav Preller declared that Afrikaners were, indeed, not serious about Dutch, which they could not speak without stammering. The written language of a people had to evolve out of its spoken language, and that language was Afrikaans. The real question was whether Afrikaners were serious about their mother tongue, Afrikaans.

Willem Postma, writing a column under a pseudonym for a newspaper in Bloemfontein, stated that Afrikaans had already developed into an independent language. D.F. Malherbe, just back from studying linguistics in Germany, in a public lecture maintained that Afrikaans, with its regular and simple structure, was no dialect, but a language in its own right. A key figure was D.F. Malan. As a student first at Stellenbosch and later at Utrecht University in the Netherlands, he was influenced by the work of Immanuel Kant, Johann Gottlieb Fichte and Arthur Schopenhauer. German romantic nationalism attract-

---

44 E.C. Pienaar, *Die triomf van Afrikaans* (Cape Town: Nasionale Pers, 1973), p. 274.

45 *De Volksstem*, 6 September 1905. For a discussion see L.H. Claassen, 'Die ontstaansgeskiedenis van die Suid-Afrikaanse Akademie vir Taal, Lettere en Kuns', master's diss., RAU, 1977, pp. 75-122.

46 M.E.R., *My beskeie deel* (Cape Town: Tafelberg, 1972), p. 83.

47 Claassen, 'Ontstaansgeskiedenis van die Akademie', p. 187.

ed him because it gave such a central place to language in human development and because it equated language, state and nation. In 1904, while at Utrecht, he remarked that the Afrikaners would become strong only if united. The best defense against anglicization was the realization that they had their own heritage, based on their nationality, language, religion and character.[48]

Malan, like Smuts, had grown up in the Afrikaner Bond tradition in the same district in the western Cape, but Smuts was fascinated by the unity and interconnectedness of the universe, Malan by the smaller unit, the volk or ethnic nation, with its own special calling and destiny. Malan took the first step in his public career in 1908 when he issued a ringing call: 'Raise the Afrikaans language to a written language, let it become the vehicle for our culture, our history, our national ideals and you will also raise the people who speak it.'[49]

The language battle would not be won by debates or calls. This was well understood by Jan Celliers, who in 1906 published a poem 'Die Vlakte' about the South African plain, modeled on Shelley's 'The Cloud.' He firmly believed that only a literature 'steeped in the Afrikaner spirit and intelligible to Afrikaners . . . would hit the mark.' He urged writers and poets to come forward. 'We have a people to serve, we have a nation to educate, we cannot wait.'[50] Soon C. Louis Leipoldt, who was widely read in Dutch, English and German, began writing poems on the recent war and on the South African *veld* in a language of spoken idiom and rhythm. Totius (J.D. du Toit) offered simple but striking poetry. One poem, 'Vergewe en Vergeet' (Forgive and Forget), offered an ironic echo of the motto of the SAP's reconciliation policy, using as a metaphor for the vanquished republics a small thorn tree crushed by an ox wagon. While the tree had recovered, its scar had grown ever larger.

But the work regarded as the first significant demonstration of the creative potential of Afrikaans appeared in 1905. This was Eugène Marais' poem, 'Winternag' (A Winter's Night). Capturing the bleakness of a cold Highveld night, it can also be read as a metaphor for the post-war desolation and mood of bitter resignation. Translated by Guy Butler, it reads:[51]

> *O Cold is the slight wind*
> *And sere*
> *And gleaming in the dim light and bare*
> *As vast as the mercy of God*
> *Lie the planes in starlight and shade*
> *And high on the ridges*
> *among the burnt patches*
> *the seed grass is stirring*
> *like beckoning fingers*

48 Bun Booyens, *Die lewe van D.F. Malan* (Cape Town: Tafelberg, 1969), p. 101.

49 S.W. Pienaar (ed.), *Glo in u volk: dr. D.F. Malan as redenaar* (Cape Town: Tafelberg, 1964), p. 175.

50 L.M. Thompson, *The Unification of South Africa* (Cape Town: Oxford University Press, 1960), p. 20.

51 The translation is by Guy Butler. See A.P. Grové and C.D.J. Harvey, *Afrikaans Poems with English Translations* (Cape Town: Oxford University Press, 1962), p. 7.

O tune grief-laden
On the east wind's pulse
Like the song of a maiden
Whose lover proves false
In each grass blade's fold
A dew drop gleams bold
But quickly it bleaches
To frost in the cold

Preller predicted that if only a few lines of Afrikaans survived a hundred or more years this poem might be among them.

Preller used Afrikaans for a series of articles in his newspaper on the Voortrekker leader Piet Retief, which were turned into a book. This demonstrated the strong demand for an Afrikaner nationalist history. By 1930 ten editions had been printed.[52]

By 1907 language associations to promote Afrikaans had been established in Pretoria, Cape Town and Bloemfontein. Initially this move was resisted by proponents of simplified Dutch as interfering with the struggle to prevent the predominance of English. A year later, a truce was declared. The simplified Dutch lobby realized that it was not in its power to expel Afrikaans from the public terrain; the advocates of Afrikaans that it had to be standardized and a more extensive body of literature published before it could take the place of Dutch. Both groups welcomed the legislation on parallel language instruction (English and Dutch) that Hertzog had just introduced in the Free State. Both participated, in 1909, in establishing the Zuid-Afrikaansche Akademie voor Taal, Letterkunde en Kunst, to promote both Dutch and Afrikaans.

The jingoist section in the English press opposed Afrikaans in strident terms. *The Star* inquired, with reference to calls on English-speakers to become bilingual, which language was meant, the written one (Dutch) or the spoken one (Afrikaans). 'Any man who knows the real Dutch language is painfully aware of what a truly stupid patois this South African "taal" is, and it must be a source of surprise and astonishment to the serious inquirer why such a degenerated branch of an originally sound language is so stubbornly maintained in its provoking ugliness.'[53] The *Cape Times* continued its long tradition of publishing letters from readers that denounced Afrikaans as 'a mongrel', 'kitchen', 'hotchpotch', 'degenerate' and 'decaying' language, fit only for 'peasants and up-country kraals.'[54]

The man who did most to win the argument that the Afrikaners should use Afrikaans for all purposes was Cornelis Jacob Langenhoven. As a student at Victoria College in the 1890s he had seen Afrikaans as unsuited for academic work: 'For intellectual training Africander Dutch offers no scope, for it has no literature, and a very poor vocabulary. For internal intercourse and as a trade medium, English is superior to it and as for foreign trade it stands nowhere.'[55] Yet he believed that the simple grammatical structure of Afrikaans offered a better alternative to English than the complex language of Dutch, and that the fight to maintain the latter was futile.

---

52 F.A. van Jaarsveld, *Lewende verlede* (Johannesburg: APB, 1961), pp. 81-6.
53 *The Star*, 30 September 1910.
54 *Cape Times*, 4 May 1901; P.H. Zietsman, *Die taal is gans die volk* (Pretoria: Unisa, 1992), pp. 106-10.
55 J.C. Kannemeyer, *Langenhoven: 'n Lewe* (Cape Town: Tafelberg, 1995), pp. 134-5.

Langenhoven was an obscure attorney in the town of Oudtshoorn when he contributed a remarkable article in 1910 to *The State*. He questioned the value of translating state documents into Dutch, or using it in courts or teaching it in schools. South Africans mastering Dutch would be acquiring 'laboriously and inadequately a language whose literature we shall never read.' Afrikaans, he said, like English, was a simple, 'degraded' language, but retained the expressiveness of High Dutch and 'a luxuriant wealth of additional phrases and idioms of local growth.' He said: '[Afrikaans] is the language of the farm and the home, breathing the spirit of the inexorable expanse of the sunburnt veld, charged with the memories of primitive appliances and crude self-help . . . It is the medium of social intercourse, the channel of expression for the deepest and tenderest feelings of the South African Dutch. It is interwoven with the fiber of their national character, the language they have learnt at their mother's knee, the language of the last farewells of their dying lips.'[56]

He demanded no special rights for Afrikaans and conceded that it had not yet developed a literature, but pointed out that neither had many other languages at a similar stage. He was quite pragmatic about the issue. If a literature was produced in Afrikaans it would be 'our very own – the growth of our national genius.' If the project failed, the language would quietly disappear 'without heartbreaking suddenness.' But he was increasingly confident that Afrikaans would serve all the needs of Afrikaners. 'It is the only tie that binds us together as a people; it is our only national characteristic.'[57]

In 1912 Langenhoven was appointed editor of the local Oudtshoorn paper *Het Westen*, and, when the Dutch newspaper *De Burger* appeared in Cape Town three years later, he became one of its regular and most respected contributors. His vigorous articles in newspapers, journals and books were written in a supple and lucid Afrikaans. He reduced the language issue to a concise and lucid question: 'If Dutch is our language we must speak it; if Afrikaans is our language we must write it.'[58]

In a powerful speech in July 1914 to the ZA Akademie voor Taal, Kunst en Letterkunde in Bloemfontein, he demolished the argument of gradualists that the introduction of Afrikaans in schools and universities had to be postponed until it was a cultivated language. He pointed out that this would leave English in a dominant position for a considerable period. In the meantime Afrikaans children would continue to be taught that they and their language were not only 'uncivilized' but also incapable of becoming 'civilized.' Most Afrikaners did not read at all because the few available tracts in Dutch had no appeal. Literature in Afrikaans was so sparse that avid readers could read everything available in three months. Afrikaners increasingly read English literature and newspapers and corresponded in English because they could not write Dutch correctly, or thought Dutch artificial. For Langenhoven the only hope was to teach Afrikaans in the schools, and create a situation where educated adults would soon be ashamed if they could not write it. By making the choice for Afrikaans the door would be opened to writers and poets, who stood ready to embark on the first serious production of literature in the Afrikaners' history.

56 It was republished in C.J. Langenhoven, *Versamelde werke* (Cape Town: Nasionale Boekhandel, 1958), vol. 16, pp. 126-7.
57 Kannemeyer, *Langenhoven*, p. 268; Langenhoven, *Versamelde werke*, vol. 16, p. 133.
58 Kannemeyer, *Langenhoven*, p. 274.

Langenhoven constantly spread the language gospel: 'Afrikaans is our own, adapted to our own conditions. Having grown up as part and parcel of our national character, it is the only tie that binds us together as a distinct people.'[59] He challenged those, in particular the ministers of the DRC, who professed to be embarrassed by it: 'Embarrassed! Shame on that embarrassment!' he cried. 'It is our highest honor, our greatest possession, the one and only white man's language which was made in South Africa and which had not come ready made from overseas . . . [It is] the one bond which joins us as a nation together, the expressed soul of our *volk*.'[60] In calling Afrikaans a 'white man's language' instead of recognizing its multiracial origins, Langenhoven erred as much as S.J. du Toit had forty years earlier. Both men did so in the context of middle-class Afrikaner and English snobbery, which depicted Afrikaans as a low-class tongue and the language of 'Hotnots', a term of abuse for colored people.

In 1914 Langenhoven, as an SAP member of the Cape Province Provincial Council, successfully proposed Afrikaans as an alternative to Dutch for instruction in primary schools. The same soon occurred in the Free State and Transvaal.

Forming an ethnic party

At the time of Union the hope was that parties would be based either on values (the South African Party) or interests (the Labour Party), transcending ethnic divisions. But the Unionist Party was in essence an ethnic party, uniting English-speakers who made the retention of the tie with Britain their highest priority. Botha's attempts to placate the English-speaking sections quickly led to a decline of Afrikaner support for him personally and for the SAP. In a private letter of 1913 Botha wrote gloomily: 'Today I find that a section of my own people call me, and look on me practically as, a traitor to my race', but he added, that in most districts 'all the men of real importance are with me.'[61] Hertzog depicted Botha as weak, indecisive and unprincipled.

Yet it would be wrong to see the final split between them as fundamentally one of principles. Both Hertzog and Botha saw the English and the Afrikaners as distinct cultural entities. To Botha they existed together in a single stream, but to Hertzog they had to flow in two streams side by side until both were ready to merge. Both believed in South Africa first, but Botha expressed the conviction in diplomatic terms. Hertzog, by contrast, threw down the gauntlet. In 1912 he said that in South Africa the '*Afrikaner is die baas en sal baas speel*' (The Afrikaner is the boss and will continue to dominate). He was using the term 'Afrikaner' in an inclusive sense, portraying a struggle between pro-South African Dutch- and English-speaking whites, who were both Afrikaners in the inclusive sense of the word, and 'foreign fortune seekers.' Had he used the term 'South African' rather than 'Afrikaner' there might well not have been an outcry.

Hertzog's speeches soon became incompatible with cabinet membership. For example, he described as 'criminal' a call Botha made in London for state-assisted British immigration. He declared at another time that 'loyalty' and 'reconciliation' – the shibboleth

---

59 Kannemeyer, *Langenhoven*, p. 268.
60 For an account of the debates and this lecture see Kannemeyer, *Langenhoven*, pp. 245-333.
61 Irving Hexham, *The Irony of Apartheid* (New York: Edwin Mellen Press, 1981), p. 177.

phrases of the SAP – were idle words that fooled nobody.[62] Convinced that Hertzog was gravely damaging reconciliation, Botha dropped him from his cabinet in December 1912.

While still a member of the SAP caucus, Hertzog sometimes held back on the issue of language. He did so in 1912 when the ruling party forced Stellenbosch students to cancel a festival to celebrate the constitutional recognition of language equality. For the SAP leaders such a festival was 'too political.' When the festival was held in 1913, Hertzog had already been dismissed from the cabinet and he considered himself no longer subject to party discipline. He read a telegram from Steyn, which, translated from Dutch, read: 'The language of the conqueror in the mouth of the conquered is the language of slaves.' The words, originally uttered by Cicero two millennia before, caused a sensation, 'and spread like a veld fire', according to one account. Some people promptly stopped speaking English in public.[63]

In January 1914 Hertzog founded the National Party in Bloemfontein, hoping that nationalists in other provinces would do the same. He attracted some support from younger ministers in the Afrikaans church, still the most important institution in Afrikaner life. The most enthusiastic support came from Dopper ministers. They never forgave Botha and Smuts for scuttling the Christian-National schools in the aftermath of the Anglo-Boer War. Their creed of 'in isolation lies our strength' clashed directly with the ruling party's attempts to integrate and fuse the two white communities.

The Doppers and Hertzog formed an unlikely alliance, since Hertzog rarely attended church and, on occasion, deplored what he called the use of God as an 'election agent.' Among Hertzog's staunchest supporters was Willem Postma, who introduced the Doppers' 'principled' line of thinking into the party. The party program referred, for example, to the need to order people's lives along Christian-National lines and the right of parents to choose the direction of their children's education. But neo-Calvinism, with its emphasis on the 'separate spheres of life', never won majority support in the Afrikaner nationalist movement.

In the Transvaal many of the Afrikaner workers were initially attracted to the Labour Party. A policy pamphlet, issued in Afrikaans under the title *Die Nuwe Politiek*, stressed the 'mutual interests of the small land-owner and white worker as against those of the capitalists.'[64] In the 1914 provincial election in the Transvaal the Labour Party made strong gains. It captured large numbers of Afrikaner workers after the government's crushing of the strikes of 1913 and 1914.

In response, some Afrikaner nationalists founded the Transvaal NP and elected Tielman Roos, a Pretoria advocate, as leader. But by mid-1914 there was still no party in Natal or the Cape, and the party showed no signs of real growth. It made Hertzog so despondent that he nearly abandoned the effort to build a party.

---

62 Liversage, 'Die premierskap van Botha', pp. 185-217.
63 E.C. Pienaar, *Triomf van Afrikaans*, pp. 327-332; M.E.R., *My beskeie deel*, p. 264.
64 Labour Party, *Die nuwe politiek*, pamphlet cited by D. Ticktin, 'The War Issue and the Collapse of the South African Labour Party, 1914-15', *The South African Historical Journal*, 1, (1969), p. 60.

'A Nationalist's Confession of Faith'

In 1913 and 1914 Tobie Muller, a man with exceptional promise – he died at the age of thirty-three in 1918 – made the first substantial intellectual pleas for an Afrikaner nationalism in Stellenbosch while working as a DRC minister. One was a speech entitled 'A Nationalist's Confession of Faith'. He received his first degree from Stellenbosch and subsequently refused a Rhodes scholarship, preferring instead to complete his studies in Utrecht in the Netherlands and Edinburgh in Scotland. The speech was widely discussed and later published. It made a nationalist appeal, but also warned against the pitfalls of nationalism. The Afrikaners, he wrote, had developed their nationalism in the 'school of misery', and the line of distinction between them and the English-speakers was 'drawn in blood.' But, he continued, the Afrikaners must not allow their nationalism to degenerate into a hatred of other nations. It was also not good enough simply to aim at being different from the English-speakers.

Muller argued that to be legitimate, nationalism had to have a moral purpose and universal value. Nationalism was the best counter to a 'jingo-imperialism' in South Africa that aimed at dissolving different peoples into an insipid, bland English-speaking 'uniformity' that drew on Britain as a source of strength. He would welcome it if the English-speakers also developed a distinctive South African character. The black peoples in South Africa had to cultivate their own national self-respect instead of imitating one of the two white communities. Even the British Empire would benefit if there were several power centers sustained by a vigorous nationalism instead of Britain providing inspiration for everyone. Ultimately the best world citizens were nationalists. Muller wanted the Afrikaners to become proper Union citizens, but this could only happen if they overcame their sense of marginality and inferiority. This started with education. Most Afrikaner children in the rural areas spent only four or five years in school, and left without learning how to write an English or a Dutch letter properly. Then there was the economy. Large numbers of poor whites created the impression that the Afrikaners were a nation of penurious bunglers. Among the rest there was 'a lack of commercial spirit.' In numerous towns where Afrikaners formed 90 per cent of the white population, all the commercial enterprises were in the hands of English-speakers, who also dominated educational and civic institutions. There was little effort to make the bilingual character of Union a reality. He said how glad he was when he first saw bilingual signs on the trains. They said to him that he was 'not a mere *bywoner* [tenant farmer] but a son of the soil.'[65]

For Muller the cultivation of nationalism was a practical matter rather than an ideological exercise. The issue of language, Muller continued, was intimately connected to the search for social identity. Afrikaners must maintain their language as the 'most intimate expression of our whole national being.'[66] If Afrikaans or Dutch continued to occupy an inferior place in public life, Afrikaners would nourish bitter feelings of injustice. He propagated mother-tongue education and the teaching of national history because it was pedagogically sound and necessary for the development of the individual.

As a politician struggling to build his constituency, Hertzog also invested the task

---

65 Tobie Muller, *'n Inspirasie vir Jong Suid-Afrika* (Cape Town: Nasionale Pers, 1925), pp. 128-53.
66 Muller, *Inspirasie*, pp. 146-7.

of *taalhandhawing* – maintaining the language – with both a moral and a practical purpose. For him Afrikaners who did not honor it nor spoke it in public had no self-respect or respect for their parents. Those who sent their children to English schools did not know that mother-tongue education was the best form of education. Middle-class Afrikaners who failed to speak their language in public deprived the rest of their people of a livelihood. Hertzog explained this as follows:

> Afrikaners are digging their own grave by using English in public. Through speaking Afrikaans to civil servants and through standing on your language rights you make room for an Afrikaner in the civil service, through insisting on your child being educated in Afrikaans you make room for an Afrikaans teacher, through addressing a business man in Afrikaans you make room for an Afrikaans assistant in his shop. There is no single state department or enterprise where you are not in a position to help one of your own sons of the soil to a job. You can do that simply by speaking your own language.[67]

The other part of the language struggle was an elite project for the language activists: Afrikaans for middle class use – *algemeen beskaafde Afrikaans* (general civilized Afrikaans). 'We must make a distinction', Preller wrote, 'between civilized Afrikaans and the language of the street, playground and servants.'[68] A new identity for Afrikaners as a modern, increasingly urbanized people with an expanding intellectual horizon had to be forged on the basis of 'civilized' Afrikaans. The aim was nothing less than 'to build a nation from words.'[69]

'A child of sorrows but also of hope': The story of a newspaper

Since 1902 the encapsulation of Afrikaners in ethnic institutions had steadily increased. In the aftermath of the Anglo-Boer War, Afrikaner teachers had broken away from the staunchly pro-Empire English teachers' organizations to form their own associations. Afrikaner women established welfare organizations to address widespread Afrikaner poverty. There were also attempts to establish Afrikaner financial institutions. From the mid-nineteenth century two banks with headquarters in England, usually called imperial banks, the Standard Bank and Barclays DCO, dominated South Africa's financial system. In the second half of the nineteenth century, Cape Afrikaners had founded some thirty district banks, but over-speculation, incautious lending, and primitive bookkeeping methods had caused the collapse of almost all. By 1900 only one bank remained, the District Bank of Stellenbosch. Predominantly Afrikaner trust companies established in 1900 in Paarl and Malmesbury managed to survive and flourish. During and immediately after the Rebellion, Afrikaner capital began to flow to Afrikaner institutions, just as it had

---

67 *Hertzog-toesprake*, vol. 3, p. 265.

68 E.C. Pienaar, *Taal en poësie van die Tweede Afrikaanse Taalbeweging* (Cape Town: Nasionale Boekhandel, 1926), p. 44.

69 Isabel Hofmeyr, 'Building a Nation from Words: Afrikaans Language, Literature and Ethnic Identity', in Shula Marks and Stanley Trapido (eds.) *The Politics of Race, Class and Nationalism in Twentieth-Century South Africa* (London: Longman, 1987), p. 95-123.

during the Anglo-Boer War. Between 1914 and 1922 no fewer than twenty-six Afrikaans trust companies and boards of executors were established.[70]

No one realized better than the Cape Town lawyer W.A. (Willie) Hofmeyr that Dutch or Afrikaans had no future if it did not become the language of successful businesses. In 1905, when a new Afrikaans language movement was getting under way, his uncle, Professor N. J. Hofmeyr of the Theological Seminary in Stellenbosch, remarked to him: 'Do you know what, Willie? Afrikaans will only come into its own when it acquires commercial value. Only then will Afrikaans be able to hold its own against languages like English and Dutch.'[71] Hofmeyr resigned in 1915 as a partner in a flourishing law firm to become organizing secretary of the Cape NP, which was founded in 1915. He would be instrumental in persuading D.F. Malan to leave the pulpit to take up the dual role of editor and political leader.

The World War that broke out in 1914 galvanized Stellenbosch students. A Dutch journal, *Ons Moedertaal* (Our Mother Tongue), that had been founded in Stellenbosch earlier that year with a pledge to avoid party politics, now found this posture increasingly untenable. The press was overwhelmingly pro-war. *Ons Land,* the leading Dutch newspaper in Cape Town, staunchly supported the cabinet's decision to invade South West Africa and refused to publish dissident views. In Bloemfontein, *The Friend/Vriend des Volks* had fallen into the ruling party's hands. The entire English press was vociferously pro-war.

During the final months of 1914 the idea surfaced in Stellenbosch of starting a pro-Hertzog Dutch daily in Cape Town. Its prospects seemed doubtful. With relatively low education levels, Afrikaners were notoriously reluctant buyers of newspapers and books. *Ons Land* complained that the Afrikaners had the 'ugly trait' of failing to support bookshops. The ACVV, the Afrikaner women's organization, attributed the Afrikaners' ignorance of their history to their parents' neglect of the duty to encourage their children to read.[72]

The other problem was attracting revenue from advertising. Almost all the larger enterprises in Cape Town and the main western Cape towns were in the hands of English-speakers. Any newspaper that failed to support the war effort could expect few advertisers. At the same time, a new paper could be expected to encounter enormous pressure from the younger generation of Afrikaners to take a militant line.

Undeterred, Hendrik Bergh, manager of the Stellenbosch District Bank, and Bruckner de Villiers, businessman and private secretary to his brother-in-law Jannie Marais, decided to start a Dutch newspaper in Cape Town. The District Bank of Stellenbosch was at the center of a proto-nationalist establishment in the western Cape. It included among its members some affluent farmers, who were shareholders or directors of local financial institutions, professional men, and professors at Victoria College. A key figure was Jannie Marais, who had made a fortune on the diamond mines before settling on his farm just outside Stellenbosch. He became the largest shareholder of the District Bank, and was elected to Parliament in 1910 as an SAP candidate. A certain symbiosis of material

70 A. Ehlers, 'The Anglo-Boer War: Stimulus for the Formation of Afrikaans Rural Trust Companies and Boards of Executors', unpublished paper, 1998.

71 N.J. le Roux, *W.A. Hofmeyr* (Cape Town: Nasionale Boekhandel, 1953), p. 38.

72 Scholtz, *Ontwikkeling*, vol. 5, p. 342.

and ethnic interests had begun to develop. The imperial banks, interested primarily in the upper end of the market, did not hesitate to call in credit in times of recession, and sent most of their dividends abroad. As a local institution, the District Bank pitched its service at the community at large; it offered better rates and advanced loans to farmers who had difficulty getting credit from the imperial banks after their harvest had failed.[73]

Bergh and De Villiers issued invitations to a select few to attend a meeting in December 1914 in Bergh's Stellenbosch home; the eighteen people who came included a few farmers, four academics, two lawyers, and two businessmen. Jannie de Waal, the only nationalist with newspaper experience, thought that a Dutch newspaper in Cape Town competing against *Ons Land* would be sure to fail. But ignoring negative predictions, the meeting decided to found a publishing house, to be called *De Nationale Pers*. Jannie Marais was persuaded to buy a quarter of the first twenty thousand £1 shares, which made it possible to proceed with the venture.

F.S. Malan saw the threat to both the SAP and to *Ons Land,* with which he had close ties. He tried to get Marais to withdraw his support, but received a stinging rebuke. *Ons Land,* Marais replied, in all but language resembled the pro-Empire, anti-Afrikaner *Cape Times.* He wanted a newspaper that would 'in the first place inquire about the wishes and rights of our own land and volk and not the wishes and instructions of Johannesburg and elsewhere.' This was unmistakably a reference to the mining magnates perceived to be calling the tune.[74] The support of Marais, who died shortly afterwards, was crucial.[75]

On 26 July 1915 Nationale Pers published the first issue of *De Burger.* D.F. Malan wrote his first editorial under the cloud of a failed rebellion, Afrikaner divisions, and the unresolved poor white question. It read: 'To our own people these are the darkest hours . . . Our hearts are broken and the life of our people has become bitter. We are drinking the waters of Mara.' But *De Burger* was not only 'the child of sorrows'; it was also 'the child of hope.' Without hope the paper would never have been born. There was a new 'stream of Afrikaner consciousness' that would survive if people committed 'both their hearts and heads' to the service of the Afrikaner people.[76]

De Burger from the start carried by far the most weight of the Afrikaans or Dutch newspapers and journals. D.F. Malan as editor was respected in intellectual circles as someone who wrote almost as a theologian-philosopher on the political agenda. He attacked all forms of imperialism, advocated national independence achieved peacefully, promoted the rehabilitation of the Afrikaner poor, and set an economic agenda: 'The Afrikaner desires to be economically free . . . he wants a share in commerce and he insists on standing as an equal with other parts of the [white] community.'[77] Although ponderous at times, *Die Burger* did much to give Afrikaans intellectual and social respectability. When it changed its title in 1922 from the Dutch *De Burger* to the Afrikaans *Die Burger*, it signaled the final transition to Afrikaans.

---

73 Hermann Giliomee, 'Aspects of the Rise of Afrikaner Capital and Afrikaner Nationalism in the Western Cape, 1870-1915', in Wilmot James and Mary Simons (eds.), *The Angry Divide: Social and Economic History of the Western Cape* (Cape Town: David Philip, 1989), pp. 63-79.

74 C.F.J. Muller, *Sonop in die Suide: geboorte en groei van die Nasionale Pers, 1915-1948* (Cape Town: Nasionale Boekhandel, 1990),

75 Gert Pretorius, *Bruckner de Villiers* (Cape Town: HAUM, 1959), p. 62.

76 S.W. Pienaar (ed.), *Glo in u volk – D.F Malan as redenaar* (Cape Town: Tafelberg, 1964), pp. 250-52.

77 *De Burger,* 10 November 1919, p. 3.

De Nationale Pers appointed an outstanding scholar and renowned linguist, J.J. Smith, as editor of its family magazine, *De* (later *Die*) *Huisgenoot*, which first appeared in 1916. (Smith continued to serve as professor of German and French, and later of Afrikaans also, at the University of Stellenbosch.) He countered the phonetic excesses of *Di Patriot* thirty years earlier. The committee of the Suid-Afrikaanse Akademie, of which Smith was a member, published the first list of suggested standardized spelling in 1917. 'It cannot be denied', Smith wrote in 1918, that 'a civilized standard Afrikaans exists. It is in the interest of every Afrikaner concerned about the future of his child to teach him the civilised pronunciation and syntax.' He provided a list of pronunciations that could not be tolerated: *djy* for *jy*, *sjeld* for *geld*, *genog* for *genoeg*, *pegenne* for *begin*.[78]

Die Huisgenoot became known as 'the people's university', reaching one-fifth of Afrikaner families by the early 1930s. Smith believed that the magazine would fail if it concerned itself only with the political and a language struggle. It must help its readers become well-informed and proper citizens who could hold their own in all walks of life, including commerce. It published poems and short stories in Afrikaans and its book review section became a major forum for debate among literary scholars. Smith insisted on quality in all contributions.[79]

Smith's successor as editor, H.G. Viljoen (1923-1931), followed the model. The issue of 26 June 1925 is typical: it included articles on Impressionism and Cape architecture, on natural physics, a section for women, and another section on motorcars, plus a short story and an installment of a novel. In Viljoen's editorial in this issue he said that he yearned for the welling up of a 'mighty spirit' that could create immortal works of art, and it lauded superiority of the white race as the 'core principle of our civilization.'

In their efforts to develop the Afrikaner 'personality' (the term then often used for identity), editors paid much attention to Afrikaner history, to the heroism and martyrdom of the Voortrekkers and the Boer commandos in wars against the British. It even published scholarly treatments of history. By the 1930s *Die Huisgenoot's* subscriptions had risen to forty thousand; it had become a pillar of strength of Nasionale Pers. Its success in stimulating a consciousness of history almost certainly prepared the ground for the hugely successful 1938 centenary celebrations of the Great Trek.[80]

In 1919 the first Afrikaans magazine for women, *Die Boerevrou*, appeared in Pretoria with Mabel Malherbe, a remarkable woman, as editor-in-chief. She had married into a staunchly republican family, but rarely spoke Afrikaans, seldom went to church, and her own family became anglicized. As a young woman she had often visited rural areas in the Transvaal where Afrikaner women asked her advice about childcare, housekeeping, and health. She started *Die Boerevrou* in part because she wanted to address the daily problems of such women in the language they understood and, in part, because she had decided to identify herself as an Afrikaner.[81] The journal addressed Afrikaner women in their new social position: as mothers and as bearers of the Afrikaners' cul-

---

78 *Die Huisgenoot*, June 1918.

79 Muller, *Sonop*, pp. 244-75, 559-76.

80 J.M.H. Viljoen, *'n Joernalis vertel* (Cape Town: Nasionale Boekhandel, 1953); J.J. Joubert, "die geskiedskrywing in *Die Huisgenoot*, 1923-1949', master's diss., Unisa, 1983; Muller, *Sonop*, pp. 559-87.

81 Lou-Marie Kruger, 'Gender, Community and Identity: Women and Afrikaner Nationalism in the *Volksmoeder* Discourse of *Die Boerevrou*, 1919-1931, master's diss., UCT, 1991, pp. 9-15.

tural and nationalist aspirations. Materially their task was to manage the family house-hold with knowledge of hygiene and domestic science. Their reward would be success-ful sons and daughters who achieved much for the country and for the Afrikaner peo-ple.[82]

The social position of Afrikaner women had indeed undergone a major change. Afri-kaner women were remarkably independent, with a strong position in the pre-industrial burgher family and agrarian household. In the Great Trek, the Transvaal rebellion of 1880-81 and the Anglo-Boer War, women had rallied their husbands and sons to resist British domination. In the first phase of Afrikaner settlement in the towns and cities many women in the towns were wage-earners and often were the sole providers. At the time of the unification of South African in 1910, the nationalist leader, J.B.M. (Barry) Hertzog, noticed the large number of Afrikaner women in his audiences. They stood firm in 'maintaining language, life, morals and traditions.' 'They feel more than the men,' he remarked. After the Afrikaner Rebellion of 1914-15 he exclaimed: 'Perhaps they were the greatest rebels!' He concluded with a warning: 'If one ignores the voice of Afrikaner women, one will land this country in a political hell.'[83]

Afrikaner women were prominent in the violent 1922 strike, but two years later the NP came to power and the women, except for some fiery trade unionists, abandoned all political activism. Increasingly Afrikaner women became full-time wives and mothers, staying at home and employing a servant. They abandoned many of the tasks that had once occupied their time: cooking, slaughtering, making clothes and educating their children. They became politically conservative and took little part in the public agitation for the franchise for women. They resigned themselves to the judgment of men, who deemed competition for positions on public bodies (except in women's organizations) not suitable roles for women, although Malherbe later did become mayor of Pretoria and a Member of Parliament.

Women occupied no offices in the Dutch Reformed Church, which increasingly in-fluenced Afrikaner community life in the towns and cities. The church encouraged women to see their main role as the anchor of their family whose place was at home. Many middle-class women became involved in Afrikaner welfare organizations, which concentrated on the Afrikaner poor, incorporating them socially into the ranks of 're-spectable' white society and politically into the Afrikaner nationalist movement. Between 1910 and 1974 only three Afrikaner women went to Parliament.

The 'gamble of Afrikaans'

In 1924 the Pact alliance of the National Party and Labour Party came to power, and in the following year Malan, Minister for the Interior, introduced a bill that added Afri-kaans to Dutch and English as an official language. He noted that in the previous decade more literary works had appeared in Afrikaans than works in English that originated in South Africa. Afrikaans was already being taught in all primary schools. At Dutch uni-versities theses written in Afrikaans were accepted, and renowned Dutch literary critics

---

82 Kruger, 'Gender', p. 170.
83 *Hertzog-toesprake*, vol. 3, pp. 232, 246, 257.

reviewed Afrikaans writing. Malan described the elevation of Afrikaans to the status of an official language in the following terms: 'For the first time the Afrikaners felt that they were fully recognized and fully free and at home in their own country.'[84] Jan Smuts' attitude in the debate was ambivalent; Afrikaans had become 'a mighty flood', he said, but teased Malan for speaking 'Dutch without grammar.'[85]

Afrikaans almost immediately replaced Dutch as a medium of instruction, and as the language in which laws and official documents were published. But there was a question whether a mass demand for Afrikaans existed. With a background of farm life and a relatively poor education, Afrikaans-speakers were notoriously bad readers of books, particularly in their own language. In 1927 libraries reported that in Pretoria only one per cent of the books taken out from the public library were in Afrikaans or Dutch, in Bloemfontein the figure was even less, and in the rural towns of Kroonstad and Lydenburg it was three per cent and five per cent.[86]

Thirteen years after the elevation of Afrikaans to an official language, N.P. van Wyk Louw, the most outstanding of a new generation of Afrikaans poets and essayists, said that in their history the Afrikaners had taken three great gambles in which the future of the Afrikaner people was at stake. The Great Trek brought about the dispersal of Afrikaners into the deep interior, which might have lessened their ability to withstand English influences. The second gamble was the Anglo-Boer War, which might have destroyed the republics and the 'young [Afrikaner] nationalism' of the Cape. In 1925 the great gamble was to replace Dutch with Afrikaans at a point when no body of serious literature yet existed, and when Afrikaans was still not properly formed. The elite could easily have become anglicized before any original work of high quality appeared in Afrikaans.[87]

The Afrikaans literary harvest was indeed still meager in the mid-1920s. Eugène Marais had failed to realize the great potential of his poem 'Winternag', and the nationalist poems of Totius, expressing the grief of the Afrikaner people after the war, lacked grace and subtlety. A.D. Keet, A.G. Visser and T. Wassenaar formed the next generation of indifferent poets. No novel of any great literary quality appeared in the first four decades of the century. The best work, Jochem van Bruggen's *Ampie* trilogy, could hardly be called great literature. The first novel of real merit, J. van Melle's *Bart Nel*, the story of a participant in the rebellion of 1914-15, appeared in 1942 in Afrikaans.

When Afrikaans became an official language in 1925, J.J. Smith, who had now become professor of Afrikaans at Stellenbosch, thought Afrikaans was still not in a position to make do without Dutch. The gamble could easily backfire. 'We may within a hundred or two hundred years still exist as an interesting *boerevolkie* with their own body of poetry, but there would be no question of us being considered a *kultuurvolk* (a cultured people) with a *kultuurtaal* (a high culture language).'[88]

Leipoldt, who wrote the dramatic Afrikaans war poem *Oom Gert Vertel* and other Afrikaans poetry, referred scathingly to the Afrikaans 'language jingoes' – a reference to Lang-

84 *HAD*, (Joint Sitting, 1925); Pienaar, *Malan aan die woord*, pp. 181-5.

85 *HAD*, 1925, col. 72 (author's translation).

86 P.J. du Plessis, 'Die lewe van Gustav Preller, 1815-1943', doctoral diss., University of Pretoria, 1988, p. 376.

87 N.P. van Wyk Louw, *Versamelde prosa* (Cape Town: Tafelberg, 1986) vol. 1, pp. 94-102.

88 Scholtz, *Ontwikkeling van die politieke denke*, vol. 7, p. 61.

enhoven, considered the strongest proponent of Afrikaans as the other official language. Deploring the 'garbage' published in Afrikaans, Leipoldt called the withdrawal of Dutch 'as a literary source of nourishment' premature. The early standardization of Afrikaans had made it a fragile hothouse plant. Yet some Afrikaner nationalists spoke as if Afrikaans was already on a par with Dutch or English. For Leipoldt, Afrikaans without Dutch was a 'monstrosity' that would lead to the demise of Afrikaans.[89] *Die Burger* strongly supported official status for Afrikaans, but complained: 'Out of a hundred there are eighty who do not read, who are scared of a book, for whom reading a book is a burden.'[90]

The strongest resistance to Afrikaans was in the church, where some of the older ministers sought to bar Afrikaans from the pulpit. In 1915 the oldest Dutch Reformed Church congregation, the Cape Town *Moedergemeente*, asked the Cape synod to express official disapproval of Afrikaans. But four years later the DRC's Federal Council decided to give Afrikaans co-equal status with Dutch, a sequel to a 1916 decision to commission a translation of the Bible into Afrikaans. One of the strongest critics of the first draft of the translation was Langenhoven, who called the Afrikaans 'clumsy, defective and awkward.'[91]

The battle to establish Afrikaans as a public medium was largely won in the schools. The swelling numbers of Afrikaner poor added urgency to the switch in schools from Dutch to Afrikaans. In 1919 the Transvaal DRC concluded that the fundamental cause of the Afrikaners' poverty lay in their children's struggle to master Dutch and English.[92] The Afrikaans poet N.P. van Wyk Louw later said that to make Afrikaans a language of instruction in this period was a *broodsaak*. (A rough translation would be 'a bread-and-butter necessity.') Without Afrikaans, the Afrikaner people were 'powerless, of no consequence, doomed to poverty and disadvantage – doomed, one may say, to be forsaken.' Only Afrikaans as a public language could save many Afrikaners from the fate of becoming a 'people with no language.'[93]

Afrikaans also stepped into the breach on the other side of the Afrikaner class spectrum, where many were becoming anglicized. The battle to resist this trend was particularly fierce in Johannesburg and other Witwatersrand towns. Several primary schools for Afrikaner children were established, but they struggled to exist; all the secondary schools used English as the only language medium. In Johannesburg the first Afrikaans-medium secondary school was founded in 1921, when the Helpmekaar High School came into existence. *The Star* bitterly complained about the 'malcontents' behind this 'retrogressive' step. One of the founders was the Rev. Joshua Naude, who, in the Bittereinder deliberations in 1902, spoke up about the language issue. Another was the Rev. W. Nicol, who felt that the predominance of English language schools during the first two decades of the century amounted to 'theft'. It took 'an entire generation out of our national exis-

89 J.C. Kannemeyer, *Leipoldt* (Cape Town: Tafelberg, 1999), p. 474.

90 E.G. Malherbe, *Onderwys en die armblanke* (Stellenbosch: Pro Ecclesia, 1932), p. 109; G.D. Scholtz, *Die ontwikkeling van die politieke denke van die Afrikaners* (Johannesburg: Perskor, 1977), vol. VII, pp. 29-32.

91 Pienaar, *Triomf*, p. 393.

92 Bunyan Booyens, 'De Gereformeerde Kerkbode (1849-1923) as bron vir die Afrikaanse kultuurgeskiedenis', doctoral diss., 1993, p. 122.

93 I have drawn these phrases from Elize Botha's inaugural address as chancellor of the University of Stellenbosch in 1998, published in the *Cape Times*, 25 June 1998.

tence.' He stated emphatically: '[Our] children can only be preserved for our people through Afrikaans schools.'[94]

From the 1920s, schools in a growing measure became single-medium schools. The better-educated Afrikaners in large numbers became teachers. Many of them were both inspiring educators and powerful agents in promoting an Afrikaner nationalist version of history and a love of Afrikaans. Gawie Cillié, a Stellenbosch educator, told Hertzog after he became prime minister in 1924: 'General, without the work of the Afrikaner teacher you and your people would not be in power today. Not that we teach children party politics; we teach them their language and their history. Now they have voted for you.'[95] But while the schoolchildren were made aware of their culture, they were often poorly prepared for the urban labor market. School education remained far too academic, and there was an almost complete absence of vocational guidance.

Afrikaans also became a medium used in tertiary education. Using both Dutch (or Afrikaans) and English were the University of Cape Town, the University of Stellenbosch, the Transvaal University College (later the University of Pretoria), Grey University College (later the University of the Orange Free State) in Bloemfontein, and the Huguenot University College in Wellington. Stellenbosch and the university colleges in Pretoria and Bloemfontein eventually became Afrikaans. Cape Town became unilingual English during the 1930s, while Potchefstroom had used Dutch and Afrikaans from the beginning.

The Rebellion of 1914-15

In August 1914 politics in South Africa changed irrevocably, as it did in Europe, where the nations entered into war. By the beginning of 1914 the high economic expectations of unification had been dashed. Three to four years of drought had devastated farms in large parts of the Free State, and, by 1912, as many as three-quarters of the farms in some districts were bonded. With the establishment of the Land Bank the hope briefly flickered that credit would become more easily available, but the bank decided against granting loans to non-landowners. It had become virtually impossible for a poor man to acquire land. A report on Hoopstad, a rebel district, said that trade in wool, hides, mohair and livestock had been disastrously affected. Bills were falling due, cattle were dying, and food prices were rising.[96]

Commercial farmers told their bywoners to reduce their stock or leave the farms. Many bywoners in the northern Free State moved to the western Transvaal region where farmers were still prepared to accept them. They injected a spirit of political militancy. On the Witwatersrand the government's brutal suppression of the 1913 and 1914 strikes alienated Afrikaner workers. Some hoped to forge a radical alliance between workers and farmers. This caused nervousness in the money market, with bonds recalled by both banks and shopkeepers.

Some rebel leaders were driven by the unfinished business of the Anglo-Boer War,

---

94 W. Nicol, *Met toga en troffel* (Cape Town: NGK Uitgewers, 1958), pp. 93, 203.
95 P.J. Cillié, *Tydgenote* (Cape Town: Tafelberg, 1980), p. 13.
96 John Bottomley, 'The Orange Free State and the Rebellion of 1914', in Robert Morrell (ed.) *White but Poor* (Pretoria: Unisa, 1992), pp. 35-7.

and perhaps by a secret war pact among some Boer leaders to resume the independence struggle when Britain was in trouble.[97] Poor farmers wished for a government like that of Paul Kruger, ready to hand out cash and cattle to help them remain on the land; they did not want to become what economic necessity advised, wage laborers in the city. Sandra Swart noted: '[Men] went into rebellion to preserve their life-style, to avoid having to sell up and migrate to the cities and become laborers. They rebelled to remain Boers.'[98]

The Union was still young and many of its institutions had not yet assumed an image of stability and permanence. Just before the outbreak of the rebellion of 1914-15, General Koos de la Rey, the famous Bittereinder leader of the Anglo-Boer War still living in the western Transvaal, observed: 'Union was never intended to deprive people of their rights and liberty. They will not be content to be shut up in a kraal and be deprived of their liberty and rights.'[99] His words captured the sense of being walled in that had gripped many Afrikaners outside SAP ranks. They found themselves in a system in which 'God Save the King' was the anthem, the Union Jack the national flag, and the King's likeness on every stamp. They found it difficult to identify with many of the new state's institutions, for example, the military. Although the government did its best to draw staff officers on an equal basis from the two groups, a conflict existed between the egalitarian and voluntarist tradition of the Boer commando and the British army ethos with its emphasis on hierarchy and strict discipline. The Permanent Force uniform was of a khaki shade reminiscent of the British uniform in the Anglo-Boer War.

The trigger to the rebellion was Britain's declaration of war in 1914 (the First World War), which also put South Africa in a state of war. In August 1914, Britain asked the South African cabinet to seize part of the German colony of South West Africa, lying to the north of the Cape Province. While South Africa was automatically at war once Britain declared war, its government could decide for itself what the extent of its active involvement would be. South West Africa had no real inherent or strategic value for either Britain or South Africa. With his cabinet deadlocked, Botha would have been better advised to ask Britain to use other troops for the purpose. Smuts, who supported Botha, privately commented on the people's 'genuine dislike' of the South West campaign. F.S. Malan, a cabinet member who reluctantly supported the war, wrote that the party 'risks losing its own people through its pretty politics.'[100]

Botha persisted, presenting the issue as one of 'duty' and 'honor' to meet South Africa's obligations to Britain, which, he asserted, echoing British propaganda, was defending the independence of small nations. In Stellenbosch, Tobie Muller responded that South African burghers were now expected to assist the imperial power that had crushed two small nations little more than ten years before. Britain requested South Africa to fight against 'barbarism', but Britain itself had used 'methods of barbarism' (the words of Henry Campbell-Bannerman, a British politician) against the republican population.[101] Ex-President

---

97 Sandra Swart, '"You were men in the war time" – The Manipulation of Gender Identity in War and Peace', *Scientia Militaria*, vol. 28, 2 (1998).

98 Sandra Swart, 'Desperate Men: The 1914 Rebellion and the Politics of Poverty', *South African Historical Journal*, 42 (2000), p. 175.

99 J. Percy Fitzpatrick, *South African Memories* (London: Cassell, 1932), pp. 212-24.

100 S.B. Spies, 'The First World War and the Botha Goverenment', *SAHJ*, 1 (1969), pp. 50-52.

101 Muller, *Inspirasie vir jong Suid-Afrika*, p. 124.

Steyn remarked that South African forces were being mobilized for action against Germany, which had shown sympathy for the Boer republics. 'Never did I think that any government, and least of all an Afrikaner government, would use the children of concentration camps against the [German] nation.'[102]

Early signals of a storm ahead came in the conduct of De la Rey. He was under the influence of Nicolaas ('Siener') van Rensburg, a religious mystic from Lichtenburg. De la Rey summoned armed burghers to a meeting, apparently to discuss Siener van Rensburg's vision of a call from God for 'the release of the Boer people.' Botha and Smuts persuaded him to meet with them before taking any action. Both leaders held him in high regard, with Smuts calling him 'one of the whitest and noblest souls that ever lived.'[103]

Although De la Rey's son no longer considered him accountable for all his actions, his reputation was so great that thousands of burghers in the Transvaal would rally to his call, particularly if it was cast as an attempt to regain the independence of the republics. One account says that he told General De Wet that if Parliament approved the invasion he would raise the Transvaal republican flag in the 'manner of the Boer.'[104] At his meeting with Smuts and Botha, he undoubtedly reminded them of the agreement among some bittereinder leaders in the final days of the Anglo-Boer war to restore the Boer Republics. Botha is recorded as saying: 'Oom Koos, it may be the will of God that this nation shall be free and independent. But nothing will ever convince me that it is the will of God that this shall be brought about by treachery and dishonor.'[105]

The first congress of Hertzog's NP, held on 26 August 1914, unanimously condemned the planned expedition into South West Africa, and one of the speakers declared that Botha and Smuts would rebel as soon as the moment was 'propitious.'[106] But in a parliamentary session between 9 and 14 September, Botha received a large majority, which included De la Rey's vote, for an invasion of German South West Africa. A military force under the leadership of Lieutenant-Colonel Manie Maritz was sent to launch the invasion from the town of Upington in the northern Cape.

The government's plans suddenly became unstuck. On 15 September De la Rey was shot dead accidentally at a police road blockade. There were widespread rumors that he had been killed on government orders, but a judicial inquest later found that it was an accident. Also on 15 September, General C.F. Beyers resigned his commission as commandant-general of the Active Citizen Force (ACF) in protest against Parliament's decision. There was talk that many other Afrikaner officers would follow suit. On 21 September General Beyers, along with General Christiaan de Wet, the famous Bittereinder leader of the Anglo-Boer War, still living in the northern Free State, and General Jan Kemp, senior ACF officer in the western Transvaal, published a document. It demanded that no South African forces participate in the war. They were guided by the belief that Germany and other Central powers would quickly win the war in Europe and that any action on the side of Britain would be to South Africa's detriment.

---

102 N.J. van der Merwe, *Marthinus Theunis Steyn* (Cape Town: Nasionale Pers, 1921), p. 212.
103 Meintjes, *Botha*, p. 217.
104 Meintjies, *Botha*, p. 220.
105 Engelenburg, *Botha*, p. 19.
106 Engelenburg, *Botha*, p. 283.

Early in October Manie Maritz resigned his commission, crossed the border and joined the German forces with many of his men. In the northern Free State and western Transvaal large numbers of men took up arms against the government. Botha sent a message to Steyn: 'A word from you will go far.' Steyn responded that the 'consternation among many of our people' was such that he preferred to use his influence 'the quiet way.'[107] But Botha and Steyn were already in two Afrikaner camps, grimly hostile to each other.

The cleavage between the two white groups had widened even further, as the breakdown of the relationship between Merriman and Steyn testified. In asking Steyn to use his influence to avert a rebellion, Merriman stressed the peaceful nature of British diplomatic and political initiatives in the present and in previous international conflicts. He thought fit to add: 'The Boer War would never have taken place but for an ultimatum and . . . an aggressive movement that did not come from the side of England.' This flew in the face of Merriman's position in the fateful year of 1899. He then felt that the Boer republics had blundered by issuing an ultimatum, but he also thought that Britain's actions were 'criminal', while the Boer struggle was one 'for independence, not conquest or aggression.'[108] Steyn was obviously deeply offended, but replied in a dignified way: 'If you and I cannot agree on the cause of the South African War when we know all that had passed before and behind the scenes, how can any of us pretend to be able to decide on the right or the wrong of the Great War which is raging in Europe?' Steyn terminated the correspondence and all efforts to restore the relationship failed.[109]

To stem the growing disaffection, Botha announced that the government would use only volunteers for the South West campaign and that he himself would take command. But the government was in desperate trouble. Most of the imperial troops had been sent away to fight the war in Europe, leaving the defense of the young state to an understaffed, poorly equipped and badly organized Permanent Force. There was also the ACF, but it was generally recognized that it would be sheer political folly to use the predominantly English-speaking units against Afrikaner rebels. The government was forced to use the rural (Afrikaner) part of the ACF to stamp out the rebellion. Younger Afrikaners were drawn to Beyers and others who resisted government orders; the older men remembered Botha's heroism in the Anglo-Boer war and volunteered for Botha's force. As Annette Seegers remarks: 'It was a close thing. Loyalty to Botha – and the Union state – consisted of groups of less than a hundred men.'[110]

The rebel leaders in the northern Free State and western Transvaal were fairly wealthy farmers who had made their names in the Anglo-Boer War. In the northern Free State the leader of the rebellion of 1914 was De Wet, who ran a poor-white settlement close to his farm in Heilbron. He offered financial rewards to those who would help him. 'I wish it to be known that my intention is that if we are to attain our ideals, these burghers who support our endeavor to attain independence are to receive a reward. The money for this must come out of an assessment levied upon the burghers who remained at home, the unfaithful who fought us, and from the mines.' In parts of the Transvaal the

---

107 Engelenburg, *Botha*, pp. 215-7.
108 Phyllis Lewsen, *Selections from the Correspondence of John X. Merriman* (Cape Town: VRS, 1966), p. 216.
109 *Correspondence of Merriman*, pp. 266-7.
110 Annette Seegers, *The Military in the Making of Modern South Africa* (London: Tauris, 1996), p. 29.

frontier was still a fresh memory and political rebellion was a deep-seated tradition. At an informal gathering, De la Rey made the following remark to an English-speaker about the split between Botha and Hertzog: 'You talk about Union of all the States, of one government, of one flag, of one King. What does that signify to the Boer? Why, I can remember the time when we had five governments in the up-country – all our own too! . . . No sooner did we start a new Government than there were two parties again and each would want its own Government and Parliament.'[112]

Poorly organized, with little ammunition and food, the rebels widely commandeered livestock to feed themselves. In parts of the Free State the rebellion soon degenerated into a looting expedition. Some of the plundered shops were almost certainly owned by the creditors of the rebels. *The Star* described the events in the town of Lindley as typical: 'The merchants were at once ordered to open their stores, and the crowds streamed in. Each one helped himself not only with what he required for food, but everything that came in his way . . . The merchants lost over £8,000 in value. Further, all horses, forage, and many carts were taken from the inhabitants.'[113] In Winburg, De Wet's men looted so much that their wagons could not carry the booty away. After they left, the veld was littered with dolls, lingerie, expensive hats and rolls of velvet.

The rebellion was confined to six or seven districts in the northern Free State, a few districts in the northwestern Transvaal and one or two districts in the northern Cape. It was almost exclusively a fight between Afrikaners. Some 11, 472 Afrikaners were estimated to have rebelled, of whom 7,123 came from the OFS, 2,998 from the Transvaal and 1,252 from the Cape. Of the rebels, 190 were killed and 132 government troops died. Knowing how unpopular the invasion of South West Africa and the declaration of martial law were, the government treated the rebels leniently. The exception was Jopie Fourie, an ACF officer, who, without resigning his commission, led a band of rebels that inflicted casualties on government troops. Fourie was sentenced to death. An Afrikaner delegation that included D.F. Malan failed to persuade Smuts to extend leniency. Fourie was executed on a Sunday without a blindfold. Kemp was sentenced to six years imprisonment and a £1,000 fine, and De Wet to five years and a £1,000 fine. Beyers drowned while trying to escape. Between four thousand and five thousand rebels received fines and jail sentences, but the government released the rank and file by the end of 1915 and the leaders by the end of the following year.

Malan's active role as editor of *De Burger* and his advocacy of Dutch and Afrikaans had established him as a national political figure. When the National Party was formed in 1915 he was elected as its leader. He kept his post as editor. Party and newspaper maintained a symbiotic relationship, with neither establishing an ascendancy over the other.

The parliamentary election of October 1915 was fought in the shadow of the rebellion. A deeply upset Merriman remarked: 'I will not say that every follower of Hertzog is seditious, but every seditious person claims to be a follower of Hertzog.'[114] The NP won sixteen of the seventeen Free State seats, four out of twenty-two Transvaal seats and seven

---

111 John Bottomley, 'The Rebellion of 1914', paper presented to the African Studies Seminar, University of the Witwatersrand, 1982.

112 *Round Table,* June 1916.

113 Anton Ehlers, 'Die Helpmekaarbeweging in Suid-Afrika', master's diss., US, 1986, p. 10.

114 *Smuts Papers,* vol. 3, p. 210.

of the fifty-one Cape seats. Countrywide it attracted 76,000 votes against 92,000 for the SAP, 49,000 for the Unionists, and 25,000 for Labour. The course of future political alignments had been set. The NP had won the most Afrikaner support, putting itself within reach of power.

Church and ethnic politics

The rebellion triggered another major development that helped shape the emerging Afrikaner nationalist movement: a much more concrete stand by the DRC on some issues. The DRC by the beginning of the twentieth century harbored two quite different social tendencies. In the older one, dating back to the founding of the settlement, the issues of language and religion were intertwined in a way that promoted a specific communal identity. The official prayers the Dutch East India Company prescribed to its officials and the instructions it issued to teachers in the first schools made special mention of the duty to preserve the Reformed religion and the Dutch language. When Britain, in the nineteenth century, tried to anglicize the Cape, *De Zuid-Afrikaan* warned that the loss of the Dutch language would cause the demise of the Reformed faith. The founding of the first Afrikaans language movement, in the 1870s, was spurred by the need to create a written language in which the poorer, semi-literate whites and coloreds could read the Bible. Thus faith and language were ready to be incorporated in imagining a new national community.

But the dominant tradition in the Cape DRC in the late nineteenth century was evangelical, which stressed the need for the church to remain loyal to the secular authority and to eschew everyday politics. The first challenge to it came with the Anglo-Boer War, when the church leadership was revolted by the uncompromising stand of Joseph Chamberlain and Alfred Milner prior to the war, and by British propaganda that painted the history of Kruger's republic in the blackest terms. On 1 March 1900 the DRC leadership in response published a manifesto which declared British demands 'immoral', and refuted accusations against the 'Barbarian Boer.' According to S.J. du Toit, who was pro-British during the war, DRC ministers virtually without exception supported the Boers. So, too, the 1903 Cape synod condemned injustices that had been committed against members of the church and the destruction of church buildings by British troops. The forging of a federal relationship in 1905 between the DRC churches in the four provinces can be seen as the first attempt to unite Afrikaners throughout South Africa.[115]

At the time of unification in 1910, politicians regarded the church as by far the most important institution in the Afrikaner community, and treated it with a mixture of respect and trepidation. Merriman once wrote, after attending a church service: 'I am more sure than ever that in their democratic church lies the salt of the Afrikaner character. Many things they lack – imagination, education, energy – but faith they certainly have and that keeps them strong and sound.'[116]

---

115 *De Ned. Ger. Kerk en die Boeren*, pamphlet, c. 1900; G. van H. Rauch, 'Die optrede en verantwoording van die NGK in SA met betrekking tot die Tweede Vryheidsoorlog', master's diss., US, 1979, pp. 56-70, 121-4.

116 G.D. Scholtz, *Die ontwikkeling van die politieke denke van die Afrikaner*, vol. 5 (Johannesburg: Perskor, 1978), pp. 282-83.

Shortly after the rebellion of 1914-15, Botha asked the Transvaal DRC to censure the rebels. Twenty years earlier the church would in all probability have complied, but now such a demand could only produce dissension. In the OFS the outbreak of the rebellion led to a schism in some congregations and a similar schism seemed possible in the Cape, where eleven Cape DRC leaders warned against the attempt to free South Africa from the Empire, describing the rebellion as an 'exceptionally dangerous undertaking, a faithless violation of the Treaty of Vereeniging, and a definite transgression before God.'[117]

D.F. Malan, a DRC minister at the Karoo town of Graaff-Reinet when the rebellion broke out, traveled to Bloemfontein in January 1915 for a conference of DRC ministers called to prevent a church schism. Some leading voices called for the rebels to be censured. Knowing that this would cause a deep split in Afrikaner society, Malan made a proposal that united the meeting. It declared that the DRC, apart from its general calling as a Christian church, also had a special calling to the Afrikaner people. It was the duty of the church 'to be national in character and to watch over our particular national interests, to teach the people to see in their history and origin the hand of God, and furthermore to cultivate among the Afrikaner people the awareness of a national calling and destiny, in which the spiritual, moral and material progress and strength of a people is laid up.' The editor of *De Kerkbode* summed up the spirit of the resolution with the words 'God is in our history – *ons kerk is nasionaal*' (our church is a church of the people).[118]

Andrew Murray, remaining firmly in the evangelical tradition, agreed with the approach of promoting reconciliation and depoliticizing ethnic tensions. He went along with the Bloemfontein resolution as an attempt to heal Afrikaner divisions, but drew a line at the arguments offered when Malan became editor of *De Burger* and leader of the Cape NP in mid-1915. Malan declared that he had entered politics to prevent Afrikaner political divisions from spilling over into a church schism. Murray responded that the church was not threatened by political differences but by a lack of brotherly love and by a failure to give other loyalties and obligations, including those to the Afrikaner people, their proper place.[119] He expressed his abhorrence of the very thought of the church taking a political stand and declaring its ethnic character. He exhorted Malan to remain true to the classic evangelical view of life: the Christian was to render to God 'domination over His Church', and to 'the King, to the Government, to national feeling, to politics' the things that were theirs.[120] But the church, like so many other institutions, was increasingly acquiring a specific ethnic character.

The newspaper *De Burger*, which became the most important intellectual influence over Afrikaner nationalists, gave Malan the pulpit to develop his ideas. He realized that for a national movement to succeed its members had to believe their community unique. For over 250 years in South Africa, he said, the church had held the colonists together as a social unit on that basis: 'The church was the means by which God guided and forged

---

117 Bun Booyens, *Die lewe van D.F. Malan; die eerste 40 jaar* (Cape Town: Tafelberg, 1969), p. 275 (emphasis added).

118 *De Kerkbode*, 11 February 1915.

119 See in the University of Stellenbosch Library, the D.F. Malan collection, in particular the farewell sermon of Malan published as *Doet het al ter ere Gods*, and Murray's reply published by the SAP under the title *Godsdiens en Politiek: Oordeel van die Oude Kerkvader, Dr. Andrew Murray*.

120 J. du Plessis, *The Life of Andrew Murray of South Africa* (London: Marshall Bros, 1919), p. 432.

our people and our church is still the guarantee of our nationality.'[121] The SAP's policy of Afrikaner-English reconciliation had erred by undermining the sense of Afrikaner uniqueness and insisting on separating politics and religion.[122] Malan saw his duty as building up the NP as a party to preserve both language and community, which was also the call of the church.

'Born out of the volk to serve the volk': mutual aid and insurance

After the 1914-15 rebellion was suppressed *De Burger* turned its attention to the plight of the rebels facing financial ruin as a result of civil claims instituted against them by people who had suffered losses. By the beginning of 1916 the Free State rebels had to settle claims totaling £300,000, of which more than two-thirds were demanded from farmers in the northern Free State. In the Transvaal the claims amounted to £35,000.

The Helpmekaar Vereniging (Mutual Aid Association) was set up with branches in all provinces to seek sufficient funds to pay all the rebels' fines and the civil claims for damages. Contributions were coming in only slowly, when *De Burger* stepped in. With his immediate past as church leader Malan could marry appeals to nationalist sentiment ('No one who calls himself an Afrikaner can stay behind') with calls to Christian duty ('Christians had to give to those in need'). His ringing appeals drew wealthy Afrikaners into the effort. J.E. de Villiers of Paarl pledged £500 if five hundred other individuals contributed £100 each. This turned out to be a rousing success. Many people of modest means also contributed.[123] Women organized fetes, bazaars, concerts and dinners in numerous towns. *De Burger's* Middelburg correspondent wrote that she knew of no more formidable means than bazaars for uniting the Afrikaner people: 'Between those who help and those who are helped a bond is established that will not be broken lightly. That is the great significance of our Helpmekaar bazaars.'[124]

The effort was ostensibly above party politics, but the NP dominated the Helpmekaar movement. While their leaders appeared at fund-raising events, the SAP refused to become officially involved. In 1917 it became clear that the various Helpmekaar associations would be able to pay all the fines and settle all the civil claims related to the rebellion. More than £250,000 was paid out with respect to the northern Free State alone, and approximately £50,000 for claims in other parts of the country, leaving a balance of £92,000.[125]

As important as the funds collected was the enormous sense of self-empowerment and achievement that resulted. The date 10 November 1917, set aside as the day by which the target sum had to be raised, became the occasion for great celebrations. The Stellenbosch correspondent of *De Burger* wrote of people coming out on the streets that day to congratulate one another. 'Can anyone understand fifty or a hundred years from now

121 *Ons Land*, 6 July 1915.
122 J.S.J. Swart, 'Die kerklike begeleiding van die Afrikanervolk soos wat *"De Burger"* dit in sy aanvangsjare stel', master's diss., University of Stellenbosch, 1990, pp. 127-57; Muller, *Sonop in die Suide*, pp. 186-88.
123 Ehlers, Helpmekaar, p. 159.
124 Ehlers, Helpmekaar, p. 191.
125 E.P. du Plessis, *'n Volk staan op* (Cape Town; Human & Rousseau, 1964), p. 48.

how our hearts were lifted? Such a day we have never experienced. We have become different people.'[126] It turned the near fiasco of the rebellion into a great achievement for the nascent social movement, greatly boosting the fortunes of the NP across the country.

It also enhanced the status of *De Burger* and Nasionale Pers. In the second half of 1916 several advertisers had withdrawn their support after an editorial critical of British war policy, and after letters to the *Cape Times* had encouraged advertisers to boycott *De Burger*. (The Nasionale Pers management wisely decided not to retaliate and, by the end of 1916, the editor of the *Cape Times* repudiated the boycott.) On several occasions mobs of soldiers threatened to sack the Nasionale Pers building.

The publishing house survived the turbulent early years. It was an ethnic rather than a commercial enterprise. Volunteers sold shares and recruited advertisers, but during the first ten years the company was kept afloat by large loans from individual nationalists, the Cape NP, and banks. No dividend was paid out until 1928. *Die Burger* on its own was not financially profitable for forty years. Unexpectedly, its family magazine, *De Huisgenoot*, became a money-spinner, and is so still. In 1917 Nasionale Pers started a newspaper in Bloemfontein, called *Het Volksblad*, and brought out a journal for farmers, *Landbouw-Weekblad*. A book publishing firm, Burger (later Nasionale) Boekhandel, was established in 1917; by 1940 it had produced 1,100 books and sold 3,274,581 copies.[128]

The time was ripe to start an insurance company. In Cape Town a Scottish accountant, Alfred MacDowall, told his Afrikaner friends that the Helpmekaar success had revealed the great potential for Afrikaners starting a major business. A similar proposal was made by Fred Dormehl, who had some experience with insurance and trust business and was at that time manager of Nasionale Pers.[129] In 1918 Hofmeyr became chairman of the Suid-Afrikaanse Nasionale Trust en Assuransie Maatskappy (Santam), whose offer of 200,000 £1 shares was quickly taken up. In the same year the company founded the Suid-Afrikaanse Nasionale Lewens Assuransie Maatskappy (Sanlam) with issued share capital of £25,000 pounds. An effort to get some South African Party-aligned directors failed and Sanlam and Santam almost from the start became associated with the NP. The two companies tried to shed some of their exclusively Cape image by appointing directors from other provinces. All their documents were in both official languages, but the companies marketed themselves as 'genuine Afrikaner people's institutions.' The Sanlam motto became 'Born out of the volk to serve the volk.' After major setbacks in their early years, Sanlam and Santam steadily expanded.[130] In 1925 a journal covering the insurance industry called the rise of Sanlam 'extraordinarily rapid.'[131]

The success of Sanlam and Santam was a reflection of growing prosperity on the part of better-established farmers. Wheat and wine farmers in the western Cape fared well after Union, and progressive Free State and Transvaal farmers gradually also became more

---

126 Ehlers, Helpmekaar, p. 143.
127 Muller, *Sonop,* pp. 720-60.
128 Muller, *Sonop,* pp. 498-525.
129 For a discussion of the competing claims see W.P.G. Koen, 'Sanlam tussen twee wêreldoorloë', doctoral diss., Unisa, 1986, pp. 30-59.
130 Koen, 'Sanlam' pp. 141-73.
131 *Insurance, Banking and Finance*, February 1925, p. 20.

prosperous. A movement gathered pace to stabilize the prices of farm produce, the first step towards the establishment by farmers of a wine co-operative, the Ko-operatiewe Wijnbouwers Vereeniging (KWV). In 1924 this was backed up by a law, the Wine and Spirits Act. A co-operative movement in agriculture gained momentum with the passing of the Co-operatives Act of 1922. Farmers steadily rallied behind the NP, except in the Transvaal, where the SAP government concluded favorable marketing agreements between maize farmers and the mining industry.

The management of the public corporations (electricity supply and the iron and steel plant) in the north soon became largely an Afrikaner preserve. But the Afrikaners' economic advance in private business was slow and unspectacular. The enterprises of the few Afrikaner entrepreneurs were modest undertakings. Driving them was not profit alone, but the determination to prove that Afrikaners could succeed in the world of business, which was considered the domain of English or Jewish South Africans. Albert Wessels, a successful future entrepreneur, wrote about his early years in Johannesburg: 'We remained aware of the fact that our parents had been defeated, and deep in our consciousness there was a craving for rehabilitation and the urge to prove that we were at least the equals of the conquerors and their descendants.'[132]

Colored and white Afrikaners

One of the first acts of Sanlam, the insurance company founded in 1918, was to appoint a few colored agents to attract clients from the predominantly Afrikaans-speaking colored community of the western Cape. The company recognized that this community represented a market segment set to grow, yet it was considered different enough to require a special approach and special agents.

Defining the colored people had always proved to be an impossible task. For Abdullah Abdurahman, an outstanding colored leader, the term 'colored' meant 'everyone who was a British subject in South Africa and who was not a European.'[133] The definition of lawmakers in the apartheid period was also a negative one, but even more restrictive: a colored was a person obviously neither white nor African. Yet there were large numbers of colored people who in physical appearance did not differ at all from one of these two groups. Colored people were formed by their exclusion from the white dominant group, particularly in the church and schools, and by the identification of most with Western culture and Christian faith.

The colored community was 445,000 strong in 1904 and 682,000 in 1930. A small minority lived in the Free State and Transvaal where, in the first decades of the century, they were still subjected to the pass laws. More than four-fifths lived in the Cape Province. A large majority of the colored people were very poor, employed as unskilled laborers on farms or as domestic workers. Most of the trade unions refused to accept coloreds as members, and skilled workers earned less than half as much as their white counterparts. There were virtually no colored people in senior administrative positions in the civil service and few in the professions. Colored teachers, nurses, and policemen serving

132 Albert Wessels, *Albert Wessels* (Johannesburg: Perskor, 1987), p. 12.
133 Gavin Lewis, *Between the Wire and the Wall* (Cape Town: David Philip, 1987), p. 50.

the colored population suffered discrimination with respect to their salaries and pensions. But colored people could own property anywhere in the Cape Province, and virtually all the towns in the western part of the province had a mixed area where colored and the poorer whites lived together.

Although there was no statutory segregation, there were no integrated schools or hospitals. Most public facilities and restaurants were segregated or off-limits to coloreds, but in Cape Town the City Hall and some cinemas admitted coloreds, particularly those who were light-skinned. There was virtually no racially integrated sport on an organized basis. In Cape Town a substantial minority spoke English as a first language and there was also a sizable Muslim community, but more than 80 per cent of the colored people were Afrikaans-speaking and the Dutch Reformed Mission Church was the largest church denomination among them.

During the entire twentieth century activists for Afrikaans were confronted with a key issue that was never confronted squarely. Was the Afrikaner community a racial community whose language struggle was subordinate to the entrenchment of white supremacy? Or was it predominantly a language community whose social identity was shaped by the struggle for the acceptance of Afrikaans as a public language co-equal with English? If the latter was the case, the salience of race had to diminish and the creed '*die taal is gans die volk*' (the language constitutes the entire people), which activists often cited, had to be made a reality across racial boundaries.

Language had become increasingly embroiled in the political and status struggles of the different communities. The disdain expressed in public debates by so many English-speakers towards Afrikaans and, to a lesser extent, Dutch, was not simply a question of language imperialism. Both the SAP and white English-speakers, who were greatly over-represented in the civil service, in the professions and the managerial levels of the economy, had an interest in preventing Afrikaans from being used as a mobilizing device by Afrikaners. Langenhoven's description of Afrikaans as the 'only white man's language made in South Africa' hardly attracted half a million colored Afrikaans-speakers. It was brought home forcefully when he attended a function at a colored school where, with one exception, only English poems were recited. Dismayed, he declared: 'There are a million potential readers of *Die Huisgenoot* . . . and what are we doing to ensure that they cling to their mother tongue and are not alienated?'[134]

An activist who favored a racially inclusive Afrikaans-speaking community was J.H.H. de Waal, author of the first Afrikaans novel and Nationalist Member of Parliament. He saw the political struggle as between British imperialists, mining magnates and 'selfish fortune seekers', on the one hand, and, on the other, the 'permanent population' with the colored people an indispensable part of that. He took a stand against those wanting to set 'the Colored population against their fellow-Afrikaners, who speak the same language, have the same love for South Africa, have mostly the same history and interests and are hoodwinked by the same friends.' Their common enemy was the 'imperialists', who wished to encourage immigration to take the bread out of the 'sorely tried sons of the soil', both white and colored.[135]

---

134 Kannemeyer, *Langenhoven*, p. 623.
135 *The Clarion*, 3 May 1919.

One of the strongest opponents of the attempt to align colored people to the NP was the man who dominated colored politics for the first forty years of the century. Dr. Abdullah Abdurahman was a British-trained physician from a prominent Muslim family in Cape Town. In 1905 he became leader of the first major colored political movement, the African Political Organization (APO). The movement was founded in 1902 to seek equal rights with whites for all people of color.

Abdurahman called the attempt by Dutch- or Afrikaans-speaking whites to cling to their language as springing from 'the narrowness and bitterness' of the fight between the two white groups, which 'moved the Boer so deeply.' He urged his colored followers, instead, to become fluent in English, 'the most universal of all languages' and to 'drop the habit of expressing themselves in the barbarous Cape Dutch.'[136] Yet the APO, his organization's newspaper, used Afrikaans and Dutch in the back pages because it was the common language of colored people in Cape Town. The name 'Afrikaner' had not yet acquired a definite racial stamp, and the APO in 1912 accepted a proposal that 'Cape Afrikaners' was a more appropriate term for the community than 'coloreds.'[137]

Abdurahman was almost certainly the author of a column, 'Straatpraatjes' (Street Talk), which appeared in APO between 1909 and 1922, its model the column 'Parlementse Praatjes' (Parliamentary Talk) in the Dutch paper De Zuid-Afrikaan. In spelling and in syntax 'Parlementse Praatjes', largely written by De Waal, used the middle-class version of Afrikaans. By contrast, 'Straatpraatjes' reflected the vernacular spoken Afrikaans of the working class and petty bourgeoisie, both white and colored, in Cape Town. The column freely used English words, as well as slang and colloquial expressions, in mocking the uncouthness and hypocrisy of white, and particularly Afrikaner, politicians.[138]

With the colored people posing no threat to white supremacy, white political parties invariably acted opportunistically towards them. In the Cape Colony the Progressives under Leander Starr Jameson inflicted on them the most lethal blow, when in 1905 they made school education compulsory for whites alone. Yet the party's successor, the Unionist Party, drew substantial support through its platform of 'civilized rights for all civilized people.' The Labour Party was the only party that ever in a pamphlet acknowledged that, despite being commonly regarded as 'whites', there were colored persons 'in some of the highest positions in the land.'[139] It was nevertheless Labour's ally, the trade union movement, that barred colored progress in industry by limiting membership to whites. The South African Party was formally in favor of the advancement of the colored people, but in the first five years of its rule removed all white children from missionary schools, where considerable numbers of whites along with coloreds and blacks had been educated. State spending itself was highly discriminatory. Despairing of attaining equality, a body of colored teachers in 1922 asked for a subsidy of at least half the sum white children received. The SAP government rejected the appeal, stating that it first had to attend to whites and that colored people would have to wait their turn.[140]

---

136 Mohamed Adhikari (ed.), Straatpraatjes: Language, Politics and Popular Culture in Cape Town, 1909-1922 (Pretoria: Van Schaik, 1996), p. 8.

137 Lewis, Between the Wire and the Wall, p. 72.

138 Adhikari, Straatpraatjes, pp. 129-75.

139 R.E. van der Ross, The Rise and Decline of Apartheid (Cape Town: Tafelberg, 1986), p. 72.

140 F.G. Backman, 'The Development of Coloured Education . . .' doctoral diss., University of Stellenbosch, 1991, pp. 37-80.

Abdurahman's APO called the SAP the party of the *dop* and *strop* (the wine tot and the lash), beholden to wine farmers, interested only in cheap colored labor, but it reserved its special condemnation for Hertzog's National Party. It considered his demand for the segregation of Africans disastrous and barbarous. Their fear, prescient as it turned out to be, was that the NP would adopt the approach of northern whites on the issue of color. The north, in other words, would not become like the south, as the cautious liberals of the Cape were hoping, but the Cape would become like the north in segregating the coloreds as comprehensively as Africans. Abdurahman held up the specter of the NP cutting South Africa adrift from the British Empire, leaving the colored people defenseless.

Yet for nearly two decades after its establishment in 1914 the NP remained remarkably ambiguous about the colored people. It was in this period predominantly a party for lower income Afrikaners. Initially the leadership toyed with the idea of building a racially inclusive party based on the common threat white and colored workers faced from ultra-cheap black migrant labor. In a pamphlet called *Die Groot Vlug* (The Great Flight), D.F. Malan, Cape NP leader and editor of *De Burger*, depicted widespread poverty among whites and colored people as identical problems to which the segregation of blacks was the answer.[141] In 1915 Bruckner de Villiers, son-in-law of Jannie Marais, promised, if elected as NP candidate for the Paarl seat in the general election, to resign if he supported any measure detrimental to colored interests.[142] Colored branches of the APO backed him until Abdurahman reminded them that Hertzog was a leader from the Free State where colored people still had to carry passes.

Hertzog saw coloreds as born and educated in the midst of the white civilization, particularly among the Dutch-speaking Afrikaners with whom they shared a language and interests.[143] Coloreds belonged with whites politically and economically. Socially, however, they had to accept segregation. As he phrased it: 'The place of the educated Colored is under his own people . . . He must serve his own people.'

The NP wooed colored voters with increased urgency. It was in all likelihood instrumental in the founding in 1919 of the United Afrikaner League by opponents of the APO, upset by the APO's decision to support the Unionist Party with its British image. The UAL pledged to support the NP and its principle of *Afrika vir die Afrikaner*. It published a newspaper, *The Clarion*, committed to fight for a colored nationalism that strived to win 'respect for our race, the education of our children, the rehabilitation of our people and our economic advancement.' *The Clarion's* ghost writers, in all probability NP politicians or *De Burger* journalists, depicted coloreds as a separate people or community who shared interests with the Afrikaners, but some articles proclaimed: 'The Coloreds are Afrikaners, who speak Afrikaans and nothing else.'

The UAL failed to deliver colored votes in the 1921 election and *The Clarion* ceased publication. In 1924 the NP founded the Afrikaanse Nasionale Bond (ANB) to replace the UAL. Malan drew up the constitution himself. He distinguished among three races in

---

141 D.F. Malan, *Die groot vlug* (Cape Town: Nasionale Pers, 1916). See also Muller, *Sonop*, pp. 632-7.

142 Lewis, *Between the Wire and the Wall*, p. 83.

143 This section is an abridged version of the author's article, 'The Non-Racial Franchise and Afrikaner and Coloured Identities, 1910-1994', *African Affairs*, 94, (1995), pp. 199-225. Fuller references are given there.

South Africa: whites, coloreds and African people. He committed the ANB to protecting white and colored people with a 'civilized' standard of living against competition from 'natives.' The ANB exhorted coloreds not to try to pass for white but also not to despise their Afrikaans heritage. Yet the organization did not embrace Afrikaans. Its journal *Die Bond* declared that only 5 per cent of coloreds understood Dutch and mostly used English. The ANB was not comfortable with the term 'colored', but 'Afrikaner' did not seem to be an option. It wished to be called 'Eurafrican' in its endeavor to build up 'a race that the Europeans could be proud of.' The ANB attracted a surprisingly high membership of several thousand.

The 1924 election presented the nationalists with a bridgehead in the colored community. *Die Burger* judged that most of the 'developed' coloreds voted for the Pact alliance of NP and Labour. Assuming power, the Pact tried to consolidate its colored support. It increased spending on colored education by 60 per cent, which caused the number of colored children in school to grow by 30 per cent. Formally the Pact's 'civilized labor' policy had to give coloreds as well as whites preference in public works and on the railways, but invariably whites were favored over coloreds (see p. 342). The Pact also refused to remove the disparity in pay between whites and colored people. Despite the increased spending on colored education, the differential in spending for whites remained the same. It introduced an old-age pension for coloreds, but the maximum for coloreds was only 70 per cent of that of whites.

The NP entered the 1929 election campaign confident that the patronage it had bestowed would be rewarded. But the NP fared poorly among colored voters. The discrimination against coloreds under the civilized labor policy counted heavily against it, but there was an even more important reason for its loss of colored support. It was connected to the changes Hertzog wished to make in the franchise provisions. Within the NP the plan to enfranchise white women and to remove Africans in the Cape Province from the common voters roll was not contentious. But there were serious divisions over the extension of the vote to colored women and to the coloreds in the northern provinces. Hertzog never renounced his view that the colored people belonged with whites, but he was worried about mixing between coloreds and Africans. Oswald Pirow, one of his closest associates, reported that the perception had taken root that there was 'a vast addition to the Colored population by the assimilation of huge numbers of urban natives.'[144]

Hertzog opposed a blanket grant of the vote to colored people, believing that many designated as such were not superior to blacks and not entitled to equal rights. He intended a narrower target, the colored elite, in his mind genuinely 'colored.' But who was genuinely colored if the group was above all characterized by the absence of clear boundaries? Undaunted, Hertzog declared: 'We can only give rights to colored people if we know who a colored person is . . . [The] necessary stipulations . . . as to who is a colored person and who is a native have not been put on the statute book.' Arthur Barlow, on the basis of private conversations with him, wrote that Hertzog contemplated some kind of 'stud book': he wished to build up 'a sort of *herrenvolk* among them.'

The Pact government decided that the colored vote would not be expanded beyond

---

144 Oswald Pirow, *James Barry Munnik Hertzog* (Cape Town: Howard Timmins, 1957), pp. 194-5.

men in the Cape Province until the colored group had been defined and demarcated. In February 1929, with the election campaign already underway, the government proposed two interconnected bills, one to disfranchise Cape Africans, and the other to extend the vote to coloreds in the north and to introduce revision boards. These boards had to provide a list of colored voters in the four provinces from which Africans had been removed. In the parliamentary debate it became clear that coloreds in the Cape Province would also be required to appear before a board in order to be certified as eligible voters.

The SAP had a field day criticizing the boards, pointing out that the definition of a colored was vague and full of loopholes, making it possible in a single family for one brother to be defined as colored and another as African. Smuts declared that the bill drew distinctions that were 'absurd and arbitrary.' In his judgement coloreds were unanimous in preferring the status quo to the risk of the 'dangers and doubts' of the policy embodied in the bill.

In the 1929 election the NP for the first time won power on its own. It had mobilized the great majority of Afrikaners, but had not succeeded in attracting any significant colored support. *Die Burger* estimated that less than 10 per cent of the coloreds in the urban seats of the Cape Province voted for the NP. At the NP's Cape congress, three months after the election, Malan said that the attempt to define and classify coloreds had 'scared them away.' He backed off from his idea that the coloreds represented one of three races, stating that he did not favor a policy that created 'a definite racial group' out of the coloreds, who were then supposed to vote according to their own racial interests. Coloreds, he declared, should go to the polls as citizens of South Africa.

During the next five years Malan made a complete turn around on the colored vote by propagating their removal from the voters' roll. What happened? The short answer is 'fusion', coupled with the white female vote. In 1933-34 the parties of Hertzog and Smuts first entered a coalition and then merged into the United Party. D.F. Malan became leader of the *Gesuiwerde* or Purified National Party, the official opposition. The middle-of-the-road UP stood poised to draw all the colored support that Malan's party could hope to attract. At the same time the proportion of colored voters had drastically declined as a result of the enfranchisement of white women; in the Cape Province electorate it had dropped from 11 per cent to 6 per cent. The actual cost to a party that ignored the colored vote was much reduced. The NP now sought to outflank the UP by proposing an all-white voters' roll.

Malan and his followers argued that race relations would improve once electoral competition was restricted to whites. The same argument was heard during the 1890s in the American South when African American voters were removed from the roll. The very opposite happened in both cases. Racial discrimination and exclusion flourished once the victimized group had been shut out. As long as colored people were part of the political system in the Cape Province, the definition of the Afrikaner people in the Cape Province tended to be fluid and open-ended. It became rigid once the system had become racially exclusive. The emphasis was now on the historic exclusivity of the Afrikaners and their culture.

In the novels of the 1930s, and specifically *Toiings* by Mikro and *Somer* and *Op die Plaas* by C.M. van den Heever, the central theme is the lack of a common humanity between the Afrikaner master and the colored servant, the latter depicted as an irresponsible child incapable of inventing his own culture and utterly dependent on his benevolent master and what he could get or borrow from him, materially and spiritually.[145]

In Cape Town many colored people switched to English. In 1934 *Die Burger* found that the teaching medium in colored schools in the city was predominantly English. The pressure that Malan's NP began exerting for segregation in residential areas and social intercourse further widened the gulf between educated white and colored Afrikaans-speakers. The NP's concentration on their 'own' poor whites and the folly of trying to classify colored people would mean that after 1930 none or very few of the latter would call themselves Afrikaners.

SAP Afrikaners

Between 1910 and 1933 the leaders of the South African Party were always Afrikaners, while the rank and file membership increasingly became English-speaking. Jan Smuts, who became leader and prime minister in 1919 after the death of Louis Botha, was a brilliant politician but lacked Botha's patience, tact and generosity. Along with Hertzog, he towered over the political scene in the 1920s and 1930s. Unofficially Hertzog represented the Afrikaners and Smuts the English-speakers. The two white communities were locked into an intense and often bitter struggle on the issues of a republic, a national flag, and the official status of Afrikaans. Behind this animosity lay the English-speakers' fear of a republic and the Afrikaners' fear of economic and cultural marginalization. When they did not fight, the two communities formed two 'solitudes', as Hugh MacLennan described English and French Canadians. They were concentrated in different areas of the country, and in those cities where the white population consisted of both communities (Johannesburg, Cape Town, Bloemfontein and Port Elizabeth) they increasingly lived in separate suburbs and sent their children to separate schools.

Smuts captivated English-speaking South Africa. Here was an Afrikaner who had fought bravely on the Boer side in the Anglo-Boer War and had also served in the British war cabinet. He was unmistakably Afrikaans in the accent and idiom in which he spoke, with a private life free of any affectation, yet politicians, newspaper editors, and renowned scholars in Britain, Europe and the United States considered him one of the great intellects of his time. He wrote an internationally respected philosophical treatise on holism in nature, *Holism and Evolution*.

'In this universe we are all members of another' – this was the concise definition Smuts gave of his philosophy of holism. The lower forms give birth to higher wholes, and become incorporated in them. The whole is both 'the source and principle of explanation of all our highest ideals.'[146] Many English-speakers preferred to understand this abstract philosophy as a ringing endorsement of the British Empire and of the SAP as a party welcoming members of both white communities.

---

145 G.J. Gerwel, *Literatuur en apartheid* (Kasselsvlei: Kampen, 1983).
146 Sarah Gertrude Millin, *General Smuts* (London: Faber and Faber, 1936), pp. 44, 402-3. For an analysis of the impact of holism on Smuts as politician see Martin van Meurs, *J.C. Smuts* (Amsterdam: Suid-Afrikaanse Instituut, 1997).

Smuts' mission became to reconcile South Africa's status as a British Dominion with loyalty to South Africa. He had spelled out his vision in 1917: 'We are not one nation, or state, or empire, but we are a whole world by ourselves, consisting of many nations and states and all sorts of communications under one flag.' The Empire was a community of co-equal states and nations, which did not stand for 'standardization or denationalization, but for the fuller, richer and more various life of all the nations that are comprised in it.' It was a dynamic and not a static system, one 'evolving all the time toward new destinies.'[147]

In 1919 Smuts joined leaders of other nations to establish the League of Nations as an international forum to preserve peace. Only a herculean figure like Smuts, who seemed to straddle continents, could keep the disparate elements of the SAP together. Hertzog said of him that South Africa was too small for him: 'He wants to stand on a mountain instead of an ant heap and to have his feet in two continents.' Smuts countered that Hertzog always attacked 'ghosts of his own creation.'[148]

In the 1920 election both Smuts' SAP and the Unionist Party suffered setbacks, the NP emerging as the party with the most seats. Smuts had come to the crossroads: should he align his party with the NP or with the staunchly pro-Empire Unionists? Talks with the NP broke down when that party insisted that members of the new party be allowed to make propaganda for a republic. So desperate were the Unionist leaders to prevent the NP from coming to power that they dissolved their party and urged the members to join the SAP. The new SAP committed itself to recognize the priority of South African interests as a condition for the maintenance of the bond with Empire. The party would also respect the equality of the two white groups. All differences had to be resolved under the Union Jack, as symbol of the Empire.

The SAP was victorious in the 1921 election, but would lose the 1924 and the 1929 elections. In the 1929 election the NP won an outright majority after exploiting a badly worded plea by Smuts for a 'British confederation of African states . . . a great African Dominion stretching unbroken throughout Africa.' Smuts later explained that he had simply meant a confederation of British African territories under white leadership, but the NP charged him with propagating a 'black Kaffir state' that would swallow South Africa.[149] The NP had, for the first time, made race a bone of contention between the parties in an election. A tough stand on segregation had become imperative for any party wishing to succeed at the polls.

English-speakers in general had little difficulty with this, but they fought hard against any symbolic changes that affected the relationship between the two white communities. Few English-speakers in the party were prepared to concede that South Africa had the right to secede from the Empire. They saw themselves, as Patrick Duncan, a senior politician in the SAP, said, as 'a portion of that British stock which has spread its influence over so large a part of the earth.' They firmly believed in the excellence of British institutions. English children learned to sing 'Land of Hope and Glory' rather than South African songs, like 'Sarie Marais.' Although the Boy Scout movement did its best to draw

---

147 Hancock, *Smuts*, vol. 1, p. 431.
148 Oswald Pirow, *Hertzog*, p. 81.
149 Hancock, *Smuts*, vol. 2, pp. 218-9.

children from both language groups, loyalty to the King and the Union Jack occupied center stage in scouting ritual. English-speakers dominated the sports white South Africans played so passionately, except rugby. While English newspapers to a large extent remained dependent on Britain for their senior staff and on British sources for the interpretation of world news, they tended to discourage the jingoist sentiments of earlier times and encourage co-operation between the two white communities.[150]

Afrikaners who followed Smuts in the SAP and later in the UP tended to be anglophile, but were repelled by the jingoist sentiments of the Natal English-speakers in particular in the party. They were united in the conviction that South Africa had to seek the economic kingdom before the political kingdom. Smuts' approach towards the Afrikaans language and Afrikaner history was detached, almost Olympian, in the way in which it transcended bitter memories. He and his wife lost a baby boy during the Anglo-Boer War but it took nearly a year before the news reached him in the field. In a moving speech in 1913 at the unveiling of the monument in Bloemfontein to 26,000 Afrikaner women and children who had died in the camps, Smuts spoke of the 'terrible, overwhelming meaning' of these figures; 'great self-control and austerity' were required to rid oneself of all feelings of bitterness. But, he went on, one could not create a future South Africa on the bloodshed of its past. What mattered was that both the two white communities were still there and that it was their Christian duty to walk the path of love and peace.[151] When *Commando,* a vivid account of the Anglo-Boer War written by his fellow-Afrikaner, Deneys Reitz, appeared in 1929, Smuts wrote in the preface of the 'great vision of a united South African people to whom the memories of the Boer War would mean no longer bitterness, but only the richness and inspiration of a spiritual experience.'[152]

Most SAP Afrikaners loved Afrikaans as a language, although they tended to feel that, as F.S. Malan remarked, the nationalists made a fetish of it. In 1923 the Smuts government took an important step in issuing the Civil Service Act in terms of which the appointment and promotion of civil servants depended on candidates passing a bilingual examination. But the SAP, now relying mostly on English-speaking support, did not apply the law strictly. After the NP came into power in 1924, the government issued a regulation requiring civil servants to alternate the two official languages on a weekly basis. In opposition, the SAP accused government of abusing the language clause as a cloak behind which Afrikaners were favored (the same would happen after the 1948 election). Something more than language as a medium was at stake here. In his book *There Are No South Africans,* G.H. Calpin aptly commented: 'The British in fact, did not want to learn Afrikaans – and for reasons which have little to do with the oft-repeated assertions that Afrikaans was no language at all, and much to do with the fear of an Afrikaner advance.'[153]

---

150 This paragraph is drawn from John Lambert, 'South African British? Or Dominion South Africans?', *South African Historical Journal,* 43 (2000), pp. 197-222. On the press see Gerald Shaw, *The Cape Times: An Informal History* (Cape Town: David Philip 1999).

151 Hancock, *Smuts,* vol. 1, pp. 362-3.

152 Deneys Reitz, *Commando* (London: Faber and Faber, 1929), p. x.

153 G.H. Calpin, *There Are No South Africans* (London: Thomas Nelson, 1941) p. 133; J.H. le Roux and P.W. Coetzer, *Die Nasionale Party, 1924-1934* (Bloemfontein: INEG, 1980), pp. 435-55.

Smuts continued to use Dutch, and later Afrikaans, at home and in speeches, but increasingly employed English in the 23,000 letters he wrote during his lifetime. He quite simply did not see the need for government to be rigorous in enforcing the constitutional requirement for equality between the two official languages. Just before his defeat in the 1948 election Smuts exclaimed: 'They asked what I did for the Afrikaans language, but, good heavens, how much other work did I have to do!'[154] W.K. Hancock, the Australian biographer of Smuts, believed that he wasted opportunities to show his interest in the development of the Afrikaans language.

Afrikaners attracted by Smuts were mostly wealthy and well educated. An English-speaker described them as follows: 'A minority of more intelligent Dutch, who saw that, though South Africa might be the Afrikaner's home, it was not therefore the hub of the universe, *ex officio*.'[155] Smuts indeed was equally at home in London and in his modest house outside Pretoria. He once referred to South Africa in a letter to his British publisher as a 'far-off corner of the world.' N.P. van Wyk Louw, a leading figure in the Afrikaans language movement, seized upon this (perhaps unfairly) as a reflection of a *colonial* cultural consciousness. Louw wanted South Africans to regard themselves as culturally autonomous, and Cape Town or Johannesburg as their metropolis.[156]

Among the followers of Smuts were Afrikaners of outstanding quality, including E.G. Malherbe and Leo Marquard, both educators, C. Louis Leipoldt and Gustav Preller, journalists and writers, and the politicians F.S. Malan, Denys Reitz and Jan Hofmeyr. Smuts' greatest coup was to attract the brilliant young Hofmeyr, the nephew of J.H. 'Onze Jan' Hofmeyr. In 1921 Hofmeyr was still writing sympathetically about the republican movement, and its origins in past 'oppression and suffering.' But by the beginning of the 1930s he had come to believe that the Afrikaner youth had become tired of nationalist appeals and that elections fought on Afrikaner-English lines held the seeds of 'great evil.' The future depended on co-operation between the two communities.[157]

Hofmeyr was wrong in thinking that the NP was losing its appeal. It was increasingly claiming ownership of the Afrikaans language movement and succeeded in drawing the majority of Afrikaners educated in Afrikaans-language institutions. Soon the SAP Afrikaners realized that they had been outflanked. When Leipoldt, as an SAP candidate in the 1924 election, was challenged about his commitment to Afrikaans, he replied that he had perhaps done more for the language than Hertzog.[158] Yet, on another occasion, he said bluntly of his party: 'We did not apply our principles in such a way that they promoted the authentic nationalism on which every people ought be proud. That and that alone is the cause of our defeat . . . While in the saddle we did nothing or next to nothing to promote Afrikaans.'[159]

---

154 H.B. Thom, *Dr. D.F. Malan en koalisie* (Cape Town: Tafelberg, 1988), p. 74; G.D. Scholtz, *Hertzog en Smuts en die Britse Ryk* (Cape Town: Tafelberg, 1975).

155 Leonard Barnes, *Caliban in Africa* (London: Victor Gollancz, 1930), p. 41.

156 N.P. van Wyk Louw, *Versamelde prosa* (Cape Town: Tafelberg, 1986), vol. 1, pp. 411-14.

157 Alan Paton, *Hofmeyr* (Cape Town: Oxford University Press, 1965), pp. 110-135.

158 J.C. Steyn, *Trouwe Afrikaners* (Cape Town: Tafelberg, 1987), p. 102.

159 Steyn, *Trouwe Afrikaners*, pp. 188-9.

The quest for white unity: a bottle half full or half empty?

For those Afrikaners wishing to judge whether South Africa was making progress towards full autonomy the bottle could either be half full or half empty. After coming to power in 1924 Hertzog moved to resolve the question of South Africa's constitutional status in the British Empire. Smuts never wanted an independent South Africa outside the Commonwealth, but he did agree with Hertzog that South Africa should have equal status with Britain and with the other members of the Commonwealth, each with its own flag, each conducting its own foreign relations. At an Imperial Conference in London Hertzog, with the co-operation of the Canadian prime minister, Mackenzie King, secured an unambiguous statement, issued as the Balfour Declaration of 1926, that Britain and the Dominions were equal in status and in no way subordinate one to another.

The issue of adopting a national flag briefly threatened to polarize the two white communities in South Africa. Under the Balfour Declaration South Africa was entitled to have its own flag. In 1925 Dr. D.F. Malan had proposed a 'clean flag', that is, with no Union Jack or any other reminder of a painful past. The flag, D.F. Malan said, had to do 'with the nation itself . . . with the very existence as a separate entity.'[160] Smuts initially supported a clean flag, but it soon became clear that many of his English-speaking supporters would be satisfied with nothing less than the Union Jack displayed prominently on the new flag. Smuts now performed the perfect balancing act: he said that he was so fond of the *Vierkleur* flag, under which he fought the Anglo-Boer War, that he understood why the English themselves were determined to keep the Union Jack. A compromise ensued in which the country chose two flags, a South African flag incorporating both the Union Jack and the flags of the ex-republics, and the traditional Union Jack, to be displayed at certain places to symbolize the country's Empire membership.

The Balfour Declaration was confirmed by the Statute of Westminster (1931), and by the Status Act, a law the South African Parliament passed in 1934, which affirmed the position of the Union as a sovereign independent state along with Australia, Canada, and the other Dominions, tied by a common allegiance to the British crown. For Hertzog and many other Afrikaner nationalists the feelings of subordination and inferiority with respect to Britain had been removed.[161] Much better than almost all other Empires, the British Empire appeared to have evolved from a hierarchical structure to one based on co-equality and consent. As long as no war broke out in which Britain was involved the Afrikaners fully accepted South African membership of the Empire, or the Commonwealth as it was now called.

This did not mean that the Afrikaners now felt themselves more British or experienced a sense of dual loyalty. The Afrikaners' source of strength was their identification with South Africa as their only fatherland. Their name and the language they spoke derived from the name of the continent on which they had taken root. An English journalist wrote that the English-speaker regarded himself as 'a proliferation from an European stem' and had a strong emotional attachment to the 'British national home.' The Afrikaner, by contrast, saw himself as 'a transplant to the African soil. For him the thought of having roots in both Europe and Africa was 'as bad as having a wife in every port.'

---

160 *HAD*, 25 May 1926, cols. 4026-433; D.F. Malan, *Afrikanervolkseenheid* (Kaapstad: Nasionale Boekhandel, 1959), pp. 102-40.
161 Calpin, *There are no South Africans*, p. 139.

Addressing the Briton he would say: 'The Afrikaners' ancestry is Dutch, French and German. But has the Briton ever heard him proclaim his faith in the culture of these countries? Thus the Afrikaner is driven to making a boast of his own insulation.' This observation captures the dialogue – or rather the lack of it – between the two white communities well.[162]

The Afrikaner nationalists claimed that only they were truly South Africans. Hertzog called them the 'pioneers of South African civilization.'[163] During the 1920s and 1930s novelists and essayists celebrated the Afrikaner farmer, the Boer, as a unique type that had been shaped by the country. For Olive Schreiner they were 'a new human modification' and 'one of the most intellectually virile and dominant races the world has ever seen.' In a series of Afrikaans novels, the so-called *plaasromans*, C.M. van der Heever depicted how the farmer was tied to the land, indeed was almost part of the land, refusing to leave despite the constant struggle against drought and other forces of nature.[164]

But the Boer on the farm was a dying breed and the real challenge for the Afrikaners lay in the cities.[165] For the first two decades of Union the British element shaped the character of the cities and most of the towns. English morals, customs and ways of thinking were pervasive, and the English language dominated on the sports fields, and in the shops, offices and courts of law. A.J. van Rhijn, editor of *Die Volksblad*, acknowledged in 1930 that English morals, customs and ways of thinking had so comprehensively influenced the Afrikaners that it would require a major struggle to develop a different, self-sufficient culture. A visiting Dutch scholar remarked four year later that almost everything the Afrikaners did and thought bore the trademark "Made in England".[166]

Much of the Afrikaans literary output was parochial, mediocre and fit only for local consumption. Poetry and non-fiction writing would make a major leap forward in the course of the 1930s (see pp. 428-31), but the standard of novels remained poor. During the early 1950s a nationalist editor remarked: 'Whatever is not intended to titillate is usually so syrupy-sentimental in character that it has nothing in common with real life . . . The Afrikaner people would be spiritually no poorer if 90 per cent of the novels of the last decade would be destroyed.'[167]

The Afrikaners nevertheless were trying to do their own thing. Hertzog frequently cited the words with which the Roman Cicero made his stand against Greek influences: 'Nothing becomes a man so much as that which is his own.' The nationalist intelligentsia did not tire of exhorting people to read and try to write, to play their own games, to perform Afrikaans folk dances and above all to resist merely aping a foreign culture. Politically Hertzog constantly labored to establish an autonomous white South African nation. It was he more than Smuts who defined the idea of 'South Africa First', and who promoted the building up of South Africa's own industries.

The English-speakers' attempt to reshape South Africa in many ways represented the direct opposite: loyalty to the Empire/Commonwealth rather than to South Africa alone, individual rights rather than community rights, middle-class values rather than pop-

---

162 Barnes, *Caliban in Africa*, pp. 52-3.
163 Van den Heever, *Hertzog*, pp. 301-11.
164 J.M. Coetzee, *White Writing* (New Haven: Yale University, 1988), pp. 83-7.
165 Scholtz, *Ontwikkeling van die politieke denke*, vol. 7, pp. 56-8.
166 Scholtz, *Ontwikkeling*, vol. 7, pp. 56-8.
167 Cited by Sheila Patterson, *The Last Trek* (London: Routledge and Kegan Paul, 1957), p. 48.

ulism, and at the center of it all English as a universal language and the basis for a more fruitful unity between the two white groups.

By the early 1930s the attempt to unite whites upon the basis of English culture and values had largely failed. The primacy of local interests was now an established fact; Afrikaans was making headway as a public language. The Afrikaners had managed to win an election on their own. They were using the British Westminster system to impose the will of the electoral majority on the rest of society. An English writer observed of South Africa: 'In essence it is a foreign country [to Britons]. Wherever British forms – constitutional, legal, cultural – persist, they are for the most part mere forms . . . The peculiarity of the Dutch outlook set the dominant tone of South African society . . . Culturally South Africa had for all practical purposes "seceded".'[168] In 1935 the usually staunchly pro-Empire *Cape Times* remarked that English-speaking South Africans had become lazy, content to rest on the great literary heritage of all English-speaking countries. Afrikaners were in the process of producing a national literature, in spirit and achievement truly Afrikaans.[169]

People in both white communities had become receptive to Hertzog's approach towards white unity. The answer lay not in assimilation but in ethnically separate institutions in the white community that were committed to 'South Africa First.' The paradigm of this process was the establishment of the Voortrekker youth movement for Afrikaners, which was officially launched in 1931, following an effort by Hertzog to draw white boys into a single youth organization with a South African ethos. Talks with the Boy Scout movement broke down when its leadership refused to abandon the oath to God and the King, and flying the Union Jack. By now white education had adopted single-medium mother-tongue schools, and the concept of a separate Afrikaner youth movement had become respectable. The Governor General, Chief Justice, Prime Minister (Hertzog) and leader of the Opposition (Smuts), all agreed to serve as patrons of the Voortrekkers. The main parties now officially sanctioned such a form of nation-building.[170]

Organization Afrikaners

It was in Johannesburg, the place where Afrikaners felt most marginalized, that a few Afrikaners in 1918 founded the Afrikaner-Broederbond after a hostile crowd had broken up a meeting addressed by D.F. Malan. The first Bond president, the Rev. Jozua Naudé, was one of the six bittereinders who had refused to sign the peace treaty in the Anglo-Boer War.[171] Large numbers of semi-skilled and unskilled Afrikaners were living in the city. The Afrikaner professional stratum was much smaller in relative terms than in Cape Town or Pretoria. In the first two decades of the century large numbers of Afrikaners had become anglicized due to the absence of Afrikaans-medium high schools.

Restricting membership to Afrikaans-speaking Protestant white males who were financially independent, the Broederbond at first was not a secret organization. Its aims were: 'the promotion of a healthy and progressive spirit of unity among all Afrikaners aimed at the welfare of the Afrikaner nation; the cultivation of a national self-conscious-

---

168 C.M. van den Heever, *Generaal J.B.M. Hertzog* (Johannesburg: APB, 1943), p. 538; Barnes, *Caliban in Africa*, pp. 37-63.

169 J.C. Steyn, *Van Wyk Louw* (Cape Town: Tafelberg, 1998), p. 146.

170 S.F. Zaaiman, *Die Volksblad, 1925-1934*, unpublished manuscript 1983, pp. 614-17.

171 A.N. Pelzer, *Die Afrikaner-Broederbond: eerste vyftig jaar* (Cape Town: Tafelberg, 1979), p. 182.

ness in the Afrikaner and love for his language, religion, traditions, land and people, and the advancement of all the interests of the Afrikaner people.'[172] With its head office in Johannesburg, the Broederbond sent out monthly circulars to its branches, which had to transmit responses back to Johannesburg. As of 1928 there were thirteen branches with 263 members, almost all of them in the Transvaal.[173] In 1929 the Bond made a major breakthrough when it initiated a conference in Bloemfontein, attended by nearly four hundred delegates from cultural associations across the country. Here it was decided to found a federal organization, the Federasie van Afrikaanse Kultuurvereniginge (Federation of Afrikaans Cultural Associations), or FAK as it was generally known, to promote Afrikaans in a co-ordinated way. Almost all Afrikaner cultural associations eventually affiliated with the FAK. A new type of Afrikaner was born; the 'organization Afrikaner', prepared to wage the language 'struggle' on an organized and sometimes secret basis.

The struggle image was not inappropriate. In some quarters the resistance to Afrikaans as a public language was still strong. The Johannesburg newspaper *The Star* called Afrikaans a purely local language. 'At best it has to be regarded as a national disability and at worst a national misfortune.' It wrote dismissively that university lecturers were artificially creating Afrikaans despite the fact that it was a language without a grammar or a vocabulary. When F.W. Beyers rendered the first judgment in Afrikaans in the Appeal Court in 1931, the paper identified him as an ex-politician who pursued 'an extreme form of nationalism, particularly on the language question.'[174]

The Afrikaans language struggle had many facets. The most prominent one was the enforcement of the constitutional provision for language equality, which became government policy after the Pact government came to power in 1924. All things being equal, preference in promotions would now be given to bilingual candidates. Progress was slow. On the railways the regulations enforcing full bilingualism were soon relaxed, to the dismay of Afrikaans-speaking workers. As late as 1936, 60 per cent of the senior civil servants could communicate only in English with the public or the cabinet minister who served as the political head of the department. Morris Kentridge, an English-speaking Member of Parliament, called the situation on the railways 'startling'; the percentage of senior Afrikaner civil servants was 'almost infinitesimal.'[175] The task of building up a distinct culture seemed daunting. In 1931 Jan Jordaan, principal of Jan van Riebeeck, the first Afrikaans high school in Cape Town, confided to his diary: 'How small and puny and insignificant is our volk in actual fact! Not yet a million Afrikaners and virtually all unskilled agriculturalists; we have a language that is not standardized, a literature that is still in its infancy. We are poor, materially and spiritually. Who are we to stand up to the entire world?'[176]

Against this background the activists for Afrikaans saw for themselves a huge task. There was firstly the task of *taalhandhawing*, or maintaining the language. In 1931 the executive of the FAK issued written guidelines for using Afrikaans in commerce and in dealing with civil servants. The activists and their organizations strengthened the trend

---

172 Pelzer, *Broederbond*, p. 10.
173 E.L.P. Stals, 'Die geskiedenis van die Afrikaner-Broederbond, 1918-1994', unpublished ms., 1998.
174 *The Star*, 30 September 1930.
175 Steyn, *Trouwe Afrikaners*, pp. 93-4.
176 Jan J. Jordaan, Dagboek, published in J.G. Meiring, *Wees uself: die verhaal van die Hoërskool Jan van Riebeeck*, 1926-1973 (Cape Town: no publisher given, 1976), p. 11.

towards enforcing the middle-class variant of Afrikaans as the only proper form. This invariably meant cutting public Afrikaans off from its working-class roots. The activists also modernized and elaborated the language to serve all contemporary needs. The FAK published glossaries on motorcars, sports and trades. Even more ambitious was the goal of what the FAK executive in 1934 called 'cultural self-sufficiency.' It declared: 'It is not only a matter of building and expanding our literature, stimulating our desire to read and developing an ability to appreciate, create and sing our own songs and make our own music. We must express an authentic Afrikaans spirit in the houses in which we live, the furniture we use, the paintings on our walls, the books on our shelves, the naming of our places – in short our outlook, frame of mind and spiritual inclination. Our nationhood must be our highest national pride.[177]

To get Afrikaners to sing in their own language, the FAK brought out a volume of folk songs (FAK *Volksangbundel*) consisting of a large number of German songs with Afrikaans translations and some local songs. A few had Malay origins. (The volume was still widely in use in Afrikaans schools in the 1950s and 1960s.) The FAK also organized Afrikaans book weeks and annual celebrations of 'Culture Day.' It sponsored a competition for a national anthem, to be sung along with 'God Save the King.' (In 1938 the government chose a composition by M.L. de Villiers of Langenhoven's 'Die Stem van Suid-Afrika', or 'The Call of South Africa' in English). The FAK and the Bond agitated for an Afrikaans radio service, introduced in 1938 after the government had acquired state control over radio. It conceived of the idea of a monument to commemorate the Voortrekkers and managed to get government support for it.

The Afrikaanse Taal- en Kultuurvereniging was formed in Cape Town in 1930 in response to Afrikaner railway workers' request for a special organization. By 1936, the organization had more than eleven thousand members and forty-six branches. With enthusiasm it embarked on a campaign for Afrikaans as a medium of communication on the railways. It was the ATKV that would organize the highly successful ox wagon trek as part of the 1938 centenary celebrations of the Great Trek.[178]

In 1935 N.P. van Wyk Louw, a young Afrikaans poet and essayist, said of the achievements of Afrikaans in the first twenty-five years of Union that 'a small of amount of literature had been produced; a whole people had developed a sense of personal worth; and the mother-tongue education they received was more valuable than any other form of education.'[179] The real challenge was to articulate universal values in Afrikaans from an Afrikaans viewpoint.

Afrikaans had indeed made some remarkable strides, but language activity was marked by energy and enthusiasm rather than by creativity or intellectual depth. The movement was still only narrowly based, spurning any possible contribution from colored Afrikaans-speakers. Afrikaners were predominantly working class and had very few wealthy businessmen that could fund or participate in cultural initiatives. Much of the Afrikaner advance depended on Afrikaner political power being concentrated in a single party. Politically divided, many things were at risk, including the use of Afrikaans on an equal basis with English in public life and the career opportunities that went with it.

---

177 Pienaar, *Triomf*, pp. 380-81.
178 ATKV, *Monumentaal die bouwerke: ATKV: 1930-1980* (ATKV, 1980).
179 Louw, *Versamelde prosa*, vol. 1, pp. 3-11.

Chapter 12

Fusion and War

'Ultimately numbers will tell'

In 1931 J.H. Hofmeyr and a few prominent academics published a book entitled *Coming of Age*, to commemorate the Union of South Africa's reaching 'adulthood.' Hofmeyr, the most illustrious of a handful of exceptional Cape Afrikaner liberals, was a child prodigy who became a professor at twenty-two, principal of the university college in Johannesburg at twenty-four, and administrator of the Transvaal in 1924 at thirty. Never one to bestow praise liberally, Jan Smuts spoke after Hofmeyr's death of 'the incomparable gifts of the mind . . . that golden heart, that high integrity of character, that noble spirit.'[1]

The contributors to *Coming of Age* addressed the serious structural crises the Union was facing. Hofmeyr identified three causes of the 'present discontents.' First was the lack of national unity between the two white groups. He wrote against the background of the recent squabble over a national flag, which had reinforced the old stereotypes that the English-speaking section cared more for Britain than South Africa and that the Afrikaner nationalists were interested only in the benefits of the imperial ties and none of the obligations.

Secondly, there were major defects in the economic structure. It was an illusion, Hofmeyr wrote, that South Africa was a rich country with vast mineral resources and boundless agricultural possibilities. The gold mines, the only reliable source of foreign exchange, were a wasting asset, the manufacturing sector was sluggish, and agriculture 'no easy oyster for man's opening.' The country was in a race against time to provide food and work for a rapidly growing population. Others besides Hofmeyr also warned that the future of the 'white civilization' was at risk if the country failed to develop speedily a modern manufacturing sector.[2]

Thirdly there was the factor of racial demography, giving rise to the white fear that ultimately black 'numbers will tell' in the struggle for power. Hofmeyr, referring to a related

---

1 *Smuts Papers*, vol. 7, p. 271.
2 G.D. Scholtz, *Die ontwikkeling van die politieke denke van die Afrikaner* (Johannesburg: Perskor, 1984) vol. 8, p. 27. See also David Yudelman, *The Emergence of Modern South Africa* (Westport: Greenwood Press, 1983.)

fear of miscegenation, wrote of the anxiety that 'native development will lead to social equality, to race-mixture and to the drowning of the white man in a black ocean', and to the prospect that some day 'little brown children will play among the ruins of the Union Buildings', the seat of the executive in Pretoria. Would not black vengeance then take over? 'The native – the savage, cruel, wily foe of the past whom he, the white man, has crushed into submission – will he not do him some evil yet?' Hofmeyr concluded that 'from the shadow that these things bring . . . South Africa in our day does not find it easy to escape.'[3]

Hofmeyr wrote against the background of the worldwide Depression, triggered by the 1929 crash of the New York stock market. It had produced a pervasive sense of despondency among the white South African leadership. In a despairing mood General Jan Smuts, leader of the South African Party, wrote: 'There has never been such a test to our economic civilization, and it is still a question whether we can pull through without serious challenge to our spiritual heritage.'[4] Exacerbating the crisis was the attempt by the National Party government under General J.B.M. Hertzog to remain on the gold standard to demonstrate South Africa's independence. Capital flowed in a torrent out of the country in the expectation that South Africa would be forced to devalue.

Plummeting exports and a general crisis in economic confidence were compounded by a prolonged drought. By 1933 the output of manufacturing had dropped by one-fifth since 1929, and 22 per cent of all colored and white males were registered as unemployed. Workers resisted wage cuts and employers tried to smash unions. Agricultural income dropped by half; wool farmers now had to export four times as much wool as five years before to earn the same amount of foreign exchange. By the mid-1930s the Depression and drought had reduced sheep flocks by fifteen million head. The price of maize, the major agricultural product, dropped by half between 1929 and 1933. Rising operating costs as a result of South Africa's overvalued currency and lower prices drove numerous farmers into debt. Some were threatening to repudiate their debts. There was a real danger that some of the commercial banks might be forced to close.

To assist farmers, the government paid huge amounts in subsidies and premiums on agricultural exports and also raised tariffs. Hertzog and Klaas Havenga, his Minister of Finance and close associate from the Free State, found the pressure from farmers for assistance almost unbearable. 'The clamor for state assistance could mean the ruin of Afrikaners,' Hertzog said in 1930. Two years later he warned that the way things were going 'not only points towards [communism], it is the way to that.'[5] Hertzog had developed major doubts about democracy, which he saw as a system that 'slowly and systematically organizes the entire people on the political plane for the systematic furtherance of private interests.'[6]

From the end of the 1920s there was increasing talk of a coalition between the South

3 J.H. Hofmeyr, 'Introduction', in Edgar Brookes, et al., *Coming of Age: Studies in South African Citizenship and Politics* (Cape Town: Maskew Millar, 1930). pp. 6-9. For Hofmeyr's views in the early 1930s, see Alan Paton, *Hofmeyr* (Cape Town: Oxford University Press, 1971), pp. 110-35.

4 Jon Lewis, 'The Germiston By-Election of 1932', in P. Bonner (ed.), *Working Papers in Southern African Studies* (Johannesburg: Ravan Press, 1981), pp. 97-120.

5 *Hertzog-toesprake,* vol. 5, pp. 249-50; vol. 6, p. 19.

6 Dunbar Moodie, *The Rise of Afrikanerdom* (Berkeley: University of California Press, 1975), p. 124.

African Party of Smuts and the ruling National Party. Both white communities experienced a sense of insecurity. In his essay Hofmeyr remarked that increasingly it was English-speakers who worried about cultural survival. They felt apprehensive on account of 'the waning influence of the English language and of men of English speech, and the waxing of Afrikaans and of men of Afrikaans speech.'[7]

'Despised and treated as an inferior': Afrikaners in the cities

Afrikaner nationalists had their own fears. Eric Louw, one of the first Afrikaner diplomats, wrote to D.F. Malan, leader of the NP in the Cape Province, to warn him against any coalition. His motivation is revealing:

> We must admit the fact that the English section is stronger than the Afrikaner one. In the field of language they are stronger because they have a world language. In the economic field they are much stronger because all the enterprises are in their hands. The average English-speaker is better educated than the average Afrikaans-speaker . . . From their connection with Great Britain the local English-speakers derive a measure of political and moral strength. And in the final analysis there is the unpleasant fact that so many of Afrikaners are Anglophiles (*Engelsgesind*) and want to curry favor with the English . . . An authentic republican party is the only means of reviving a national spirit [among Afrikaners].[8]

Louw put his finger on an important spot. A brief exploration of the Afrikaners' social position in the 1930s will bear this out. Afrikaners were rapidly becoming urbanized, from 29 per cent in 1910, 50 per cent 1936, to 75 per cent in 1960. In 1936 they constituted a quarter of the white population of both Cape Town and Johannesburg, and half of that of Pretoria and Bloemfontein.[9]

Afrikaners still dominated farming, with the output of Afrikaner farmers estimated to represent more than 80 per cent of agricultural production. But until the Second World War the position of most farmers was far from secure. Contending with poor soil and a fickle climate in most regions, farmers were, to an extraordinary degree, dependent on a sympathetic government willing to stabilize prices and boost their control over labor.

People from British or Jewish descent virtually monopolized the non-agricultural sectors of the economy. The entrepreneurial activities of the Afrikaners were extremely modest. In 1936, when the future Afrikaner business leader Albert Wessels arrived in Johannesburg, he found only three Afrikaner businesses of any significance: the publishing company Afrikaanse Pers, with its struggling pro-United Party daily, *Die Vaderland*; the bank Volkskas, on the second floor of an old building; and a shop for men's clothes, soon to fold. In 1937 the Johannesburg newspaper, *Die Transvaler*, estimated that there were in total only twenty Afrikaner enterprises in the city.[10]

The educational standards of Afrikaners were still low. A 1933 study reported that out of a hundred who started school together forty-four left without passing the eighth

---

7 Hofmeyr, 'Introduction', p. 7.
8 US Library, D.F. Malan Collection, Correspondence, 1/1/1014, Eric Louw-Malan, 7 June 1933.
9 D. Prinsloo, 'Die Johannesburg-periode in dr. H.F. Verwoerd se loopbaan', doctoral diss., RAU, 1979, p. 27.
10 *Die Transvaler*, 19 April 1945.

year (Standard Six), seventeen passed the tenth year (Standard Eight), and only eight completed the twelfth or final year, called Matric. Fewer than three went on to university. In 1939 less than a third of all white students at universities were Afrikaners, at a time when they comprised 56 per cent of the white population. The principal reason for the low educational level was the continuing popularity of farming as a career among Afrikaner boys, at a time when the steady commercialization of farming was squeezing many farmers out.

Afrikaners were poorly represented in many of the white-collar occupations; in 1939 only three per cent of people in the professional category with the most prestige (owners of companies, directors and self-employed manufacturers) were Afrikaners. Of the white population Afrikaners made up three per cent of the engineers, four per cent of accountants, 11 per cent of lawyers, 15 per cent of the medical doctors, and 21 per cent of the journalists. Less than a quarter of senior civil servants spoke Afrikaans as a first language.[11] The gap between Afrikaners and English-speakers was still large. A study estimated that Afrikaner income was only 60 per cent of that of English-speaking whites in 1935.[12]

A sociologist's report of 1932, published by the Carnegie Commission, concluded that in the cities there had not yet formed any 'solid, civic middle class' between the Afrikaners who were employed in the 'learned professions' and the Afrikaner working class. Concentrated in the lowest levels of the white labor market, Afrikaner workers had low levels of self-esteem. A study commissioned by the Dutch Reformed Church presents a portrait: 'His poverty, servitude and desperate search for work feeds a sense of dependency and inferiority . . . Feeling himself unwelcome, he presents himself poorly, he is timid, walks hat in hand and lacks the greater self-confidence of the English work-seeker. He wields no influence and no one intercedes on his behalf; his *volk* is small and subordinate to a world power that backs up the English work-seeker. He is despised and treated as an inferior by other nations.'[13]

Some artisan unions excluded Afrikaner workers from certain occupational categories, fearing them as a source of potential undercutting. Only a quarter of apprentices in skilled trades were Afrikaners.[14] In 1939 almost 40 per cent of adult male Afrikaners in Johannesburg were clustered in four job categories: unskilled laborer, mineworker, railway worker and bricklayer, compared to 10 per cent of non-Afrikaner males in these occupations. While 69 per cent of the white mine labor force were Afrikaners, approximately 90 per cent of them worked underground in the more dangerous jobs that also paid less. Railway workers earned five shillings a day or less, compared to the widely quoted 'civilized' minimum of eight shillings a day.[15]

---

11 Samuel Pauw, *Die beroepslewe van die Afrikaner in die stad* (Stellenbosch: Pro Ecclesia, 1945), p. 235-43.

12 For a recent discussion of the Afrikaners' economic position see T.J. Steenekamp, "'n Ekonomiese ontleding van sosio-politieke groepvorming met spesiale verwysing na die Afrikaner', doctoral diss., Unisa, 1989; Tjaart Steenekamp, 'Discrimination and the Economic Position of the Afrikaner', *SA Journal of Economic History*, 5,1 (1990), pp. 49-66.

13 J.R. Albertyn, P. du Toit and H.S. Theron, *Kerk en stad* (Stellenbosch: Pro Ecclesia, 1947), p. 46.

14 Dan O' Meara, *Volkskapitalisme: Class, Capital and Ideology in the Development of Afrikaner Nationalism, 1934-1948* (Cambridge: Cambridge University Press, 1983), pp. 240-41.

15 Robert Davies, *Capital, State and White Labour in South Africa, 1900-1960* (Brighton: Harvester Press, 1979), p. 226.

Coalition and Fusion

The idea of a coalition between the NP and SAP attracted some young Afrikaners who were idealistic and had the prospect of entering a profession. Many members of the older generation, however, had bitter memories of the struggle for Afrikaans and national symbols. The future editor of *Die Burger,* Piet Cillié, a schoolboy in Stellenbosch at the time, remembered telling his father, the educationist G.G. Cillié, that it was time 'Afrikaners co-operated with the English.' The curt answer he received was that it was time 'the English co-operated with the Afrikaners.'[16] Alan Paton, later a famous novelist and leading liberal, assessed the English view as follows: 'I believe that we are more inclined to believe in co-operation than we are in "*samewerking*" (co-operation). I believe we are inclined to co-operate in English.'[17]

During the course of 1932 the pressure from the mining industry and the farmers to devalue steadily mounted. A delegation of both NP and SAP farmers urged Hertzog to form a coalition to deal with the crisis. When Hertzog asked how he could be expected to work with a party that had always opposed him, a farmer exclaimed: 'In God's name, General, forget the language and give us bread.'[18] In the final days of that year the government stepped off the gold standard, but by then the entire party system was ready for a major realignment.

By the early 1930s Hertzog had become exasperated with Afrikaner lobbies, particularly the farmers. Smuts was weary of languishing on the opposition benches. Both were eager to build a broader political base to resist the pressure from lobbies and embark on structural reforms to strengthen white supremacy. Hertzog told the NP caucus that their party would lose the next election, risking all the gains it had made for the Afrikaners. 'We shall be defeated and Afrikanerdom will be finished.' Shortly after deciding to form a coalition with the SAP under Smuts, Hertzog used the term Afrikaner in its inclusive sense. White political survival, he said, could only be ensured through the coming together of the 'Afrikanerdom of South Africa.' By that he meant: 'the English-speaker and the Dutch-speaker, the Nationalist and the SAP.'[19] Hertzog continued to hope that the English-speakers would call themselves Afrikaners.

The guiding principle for the coalition government on which Hertzog and Smuts agreed early in 1933 was the development of a predominant sense of national unity, based on the equality of the two white communities and a mutual recognition of their distinctive cultural inheritance.[20] In the general election of May 1933 the coalition won 136 of the 150 seats. The scene was set for a fusion of the two main parties.

Initially Hertzog, as leader of both the Free State NP and the federal NP, encountered little resistance to fusion. The NP of the Transvaal, OFS and Natal accepted fusion with

---

16 P. J. Cillié, *Hertzog en Malan: Die jare van skeuring,* 1934-1939 (Published lecture, Potchefstroom University, 1980), p. 8.

17 G.D. Scholtz, *Die ontwikkeling van die politieke denke van die Afrikaner* (Johannesburg: Perskor, 1970), vol. 7, p. 97.

18 At van Wyk, *Die Keeromstraatkliek* (Cape Town: Tafelberg, 1983), p. 42.

19 *Hertzog-toesprake,* vol. 6, p. 17; H.B. Thom, *Dr. D.F. Malan en Koalisie* (Cape Town: Tafelberg, 1988), pp. 101, 127-31.

20 Hancock, *Smuts,* vol. 2, p. 256.

large majorities. The only serious resistance was in the Cape NP under the leadership of Malan. Some of the parliamentary representatives in the Cape party had no stomach for absorption in a big catchall party in which Smuts and Hofmeyr and, through them, the mining industry, would have a major say. The publishing house Nasionale Pers strongly opposed fusion. Senator W.A. Hofmeyr and three members of the House of Assembly (J.H.H. de Waal, Bruckner de Villiers and D.F. Malan) were directors of the publishing house. Other Cape nationalists who opposed fusion included Paul Sauer (son of J.W.) and Eric Louw. Supporting them in the Free State were C.R. Swart and N.J. van der Merwe. J.G. Strijdom was the sole Transvaal Member of Parliament willing to reject fusion.[21]

Die Burger, by far the most influential Afrikaans newspaper, initially almost all on its own rejected the idea of the NP and SAP coming together. It recognized the fact that the struggle for Afrikaans, opposition to Hoggenheimer and the 'civilized labor' policy, had held the NP together. The merging of the SAP and NP would put all these pillars under pressure. For Albert Geyer (nicknamed *Ysterman* or Iron Man), the redoubtable editor of the newspaper, the time was hardly ripe for Hertzog to join up with Smuts, a presumed agent of Hoggenheimer, a synonym for and caricature of big capital. Geyer was a determined man with a doctorate in history from a German university, who scorned easy compromises and shallow political thinking. He became editor in 1924 and soon clashed with Hertzog, who was over-sensitive to criticism from fellow-nationalists. In 1933 he wrote in a private memorandum that an alliance of the conservative landowners and the mining and financial sectors had long wanted a coalition to come about to control the white working class. The Afrikaners still needed a party based on issues like culture and nationality.[22]

Die Burger was soon conducting a relentless campaign against fusion. One of several anti-fusion Boonzaier cartoons depicted Hamlet asking the ghost of fusion:

> *'Be thy intents wicked, or charitable?*
> *Thou com'st in such questionable shape . . .'*

After an initial hesitation Malan joined the opponents of fusion. 'We had to drag Malan out by the seat of his pants,' Sauer would later say.[23] Malan now returned to his role of 1914-15 in the founding years of the NP, insisting that the Afrikaners still needed a party of their own to preserve their language, faith and traditions. He opposed the UP's call for *vereniging,* or unification of all white people, and proposed instead the *hereniging* of all whites who accepted an independent South Africa and effective bilingualism. 'Bring together all who belong together through inner conviction,' became Malan's rallying cry.[24]

When the NP Federal Council met in mid-1934 to endorse the fusion of the NP under

---

21 J.H. le Roux and P. W. Coetzer, *Die Nasionale Party* (Bloemfontein: INEG, 1982), vol. 3, pp. 209-618.

22 There is a class analysis in O' Meara, *Volkskapitalisme,* pp. 39-48. For an approach stressing the decisive influence of culture and community, see Le Roux and Coetzer, *Die Nasionale Party,* vol. 4, ch. 8; J.P. Brits, *Tielman Roos* (Pretoria: University of South Africa, 1987).

23 Interview with Piet Cillié, 8 December 1998.

24 For D.F. Malan on the National Party as the 'mother' of the nationalist movement see his collection of speeches edited by Schalk Pienaar, *Glo in u volk* (Cape Town: Tafelberg, 1964), pp. 37-42.

Hertzog and the SAP under Smuts, Malan rejected it, depicting the new United Party as a bulwark of 'imperialism and capitalism.' He and eighteen members of Parliament, fourteen elected in Cape seats, four in the OFS and one in the Transvaal, founded the *Gesuiwerde* (Purified) National Party (NP), which became the official opposition in 1934. It retained the old federal structure of Hertzog's NP, with the provinces acting almost as autonomous entities, but the Cape NP, which Malan and his closest followers controlled, dominated the new NP as a parliamentary party until 1954.

Fusion: 'The great experiment'

For Smuts the fusion of the NP and SAP was 'the great experiment', representing a triumph for the principles of universality steadily progressing in the world. 'The driving force in this human world should not be morbid fears or other sickly obsessions, but . . . [an] inner urge towards wholesome integration and co-operation.'[25] Other Afrikaners in the UP leadership suggested that Afrikaners take to heart the different lessons of their history. At the height of the commemoration of the Great Trek, Hofmeyr asked why battles against the British a century ago were kept alive, but innovations like the introduction of wool sheep forgotten.[26] He and Smuts frequently warned against a spirit of isolation. To counter the new Fascist states in Germany and Italy, South Africa needed the Commonwealth bonds more than ever.

But the UP's lofty ideals had to do battle with demography and electoral laws. There was a rough ratio of 55:45 between Afrikaner and English voters and the electoral laws favored the predominantly Afrikaner rural constituencies over urban constituencies. Non-nationalist parties needed at least 25 per cent of the Afrikaner vote to keep the nationalists from power. Demographic trends also favored the Afrikaners. Adults were still rather evenly matched, but in the age group seven to twenty-one Afrikaner numbers were nearly double those of English-speakers.

Afrikaner educational institutions were now turning out a steady stream of young people educated through the medium of Afrikaans. In 1936, 55 per cent of white children were receiving instruction in Afrikaans alone, 37 per cent in English alone, and only 8 per cent in both languages.[27] School-leavers could hardly fail to recognize that if the state enforced the official status of Afrikaans in public life, growing career opportunities would open up for them.

It was not impossible for the UP to placate English fears at the same time as advancing Afrikaner interests. The overwhelming majority of English-speakers flocked to the UP and soon accepted Hertzog as leader.[28] He was convinced that the right of Afrikaans as an official language was now entrenched. South Africa enjoyed national sovereignty with the right to secede from the Crown and to stay neutral in any war which Britain itself had entered. Hertzog knew that Smuts disputed this interpretation, but he, not Smuts, was the leader. The challenge now was to build a safe, white South Africa on the foundation of white unity.

---

25 *The Star,* 13 November 1934.
26 *Die Volksblad,* Special Supplement, 9 December 1938.
27 *HAD,* 1943, col. 2900.
28 *Smuts Papers,* vol. 7, pp. 229-45.

Hertzog brought with him into the UP several leading Afrikaners with nationalist credentials, the most outstanding being Henry Allan Fagan, as a young man an activist for the Afrikaans language movement. Like his cabinet colleagues Oswald Pirow, Attie Fourie and General Jan Kemp, Fagan supported the idea of a republic, but only as a long-term goal. Fourie as Minister of Labour spearheaded the efforts to rehabilitate the poor whites, and Kemp headed the agriculture ministry at a time when the state spent massively to make farming viable. The Marketing Act of 1937, which established marketing councils to undertake single-channel marketing and fix prices, greatly helped to stabilize farming.

The social transformation of urban South Africa

After South Africa stepped off the gold standard in 1932, the price of gold jumped from £4.25 to £6.23 per ounce and in 1939 to £7.70. The ruling United Party, with its broad base, instilled confidence among investors. The mining houses made great profits, and the state's receipts from gold mining more than trebled. The state expanded the infrastructure and stimulated the manufacturing sector through a policy of import substitution. The manufacturing sector's contribution to the national income rose steadily from 15 per cent in 1935 to 24 per cent in 1970. With its own manufacturing sector, South Africa escaped the neo-colonial dependency that hobbled so many other mineral-rich colonies.

South Africa's economic take-off drew people of all communities to the towns and cities. Between the mid-1930s and mid-1940s the number of urban Africans increased from one million to close to two million. Of the two million people who lived in the nine largest urban areas in 1936, 813,000 were Africans, of whom more than half a million had settled in the Witwatersrand area. Only a quarter of blacks in South Africa were urbanized by 1946, but urban blacks already outnumbered urban whites. The rest of the blacks were divided about equally between those living on the farms and in the reserves.

Blacks working in the manufacturing sector spearheaded a transformation of the urban labor force. In 1930 the numbers of white and black workers in this sector had been on a par, but in the next two decades the black workers trebled while the white labor force only doubled. Like the mines, many industries preferred migrant labor to stabilized labor because of its cheapness and docility. However, the manufacturing sector employed a small but growing number of black workers living with their families on a stable basis in the towns or the cities. Between 1936 and 1946 the number of urbanized African women nearly doubled. But among many employers the fiction was perpetuated that Africans had their own land and that the migrant laborer's family did not have to be provided for in the common area. Local authorities preferred to build hostels rather than family houses.

SELECTED POPULATION FIGURES

	1930	1950/51	1970
White population	1,801,000	2,641,689	3,835,000
Black population	5,585 000	8,556,390	15,918,000
Whites in manufacturing	91,024	191,093	276,900
Blacks in manufacturing	90,517	267,070	617,200

Living and working conditions for urban Africans were dismal. About one-third lived in informal houses. Because few Africans could get freehold tenure, there was little incentive for those who lived in formal houses to improve them. Africans in any event received such low wages that it was impossible for most to do so. Neither could they pay sufficient rent or taxes to enable the white municipalities to upgrade the locations under their control. Africans suffered a wide-ranging job color bar. Apprenticeship committees excluded them from skilled jobs. Some white trade unions had African members, but most Africans were members of African trade unions, which could not take part in wage negotiations. The job color bar and deficient education and training formed major obstacles to advancement.

In a multitude of ways African urban life was demeaning. Family income on average was half the living wage and diet was often disgracefully deficient. Africans were subjected to numerous laws that applied only to them. The great majority of those convicted of criminal offences were guilty of contravening the pass laws and the possession of 'native' liquor, giving rise to what a government report called 'a burning sense of grievance and injustice.'

On the white farms, where about a third of Africans lived, servants were largely subject to the whims of their employer. Housing remained very poor and real wages, like those in the mines, did not improve until the early 1970s. In the reserves, which formed seven per cent of the landmass of South Africa, the migrant labor system dominated social and economic life. According to the 1936 census, 54 per cent of the male population of the reserves were absent, working as migrant laborers.

A crisis was building up as result of the congestion in the reserves. The Native Economic Commission of 1932 warned that pressure on land in the reserves was too severe to provide a home subsistence base for most migrant workers. The permanent residents of the reserves became ever more dependent on migrant remittances to buy not only manufactured goods, but also food produced outside the reserves. The migrant labor system not only eroded the subsistence farming in the reserves, but also weakened the ability of migrant laborers in the city to organize. It impacted very negatively on African family life and the prospects for a settled African urban society. In 1947, Donald Molteno, one of the leading liberals, made this comment: 'Our whole African population has been uprooted. They have been proletarianized, pauperized and demoralized. Those – as yet comparatively few – that have acquired some measure of education are denied occupational opportunities and effective civil and political rights. Their consequent bitterness bodes ill for the future of the relations between white and black. Our whole society and economy are being poisoned by our failure to respond to the challenges that these conditions present.'[29]

The 1920s witnessed the first signs of an incipient challenge to white supremacy. Between 1924 and 1930 a radical trade union, the Industrial and Commercial Workers Union of Africa (ICU), swept through the South African countryside, recruiting farm workers as well. Fearing a general upheaval, angry farmers demanded state action, but the ICU collapsed in the early 1930s.

---

29 This paragraph is drawn from documents published in Phyllis Lewsen, *Voices of Protest: From Segregation to Apartheid,* (Johannesburg: Ad Donker, 1988), pp. 42, 51-2, 234, 255, 266.

Segments of the subordinate population expressed their political frustrations in the church. Since the 1880s there had been a rise of Zionism or Ethiopianism among Africans, and several independent or separatist African churches had been established. An expression of African resistance to colonialism, these separatist churches denounced missionaries who frustrated African ambitions by closing off opportunities for African leadership in the church and rejected African culture and customs. Land hunger and labor demands prompted Africans during the 1920s and 1930s to take to Zionism or Ethiopianism in great numbers. In 1921 there were some fifty thousand adherents of Zionist or Ethiopian bodies, out of a total of 1.3 million African Christian converts. By 1936 their numbers had jumped to over a million, of whom the vast majority were in the countryside.

Soon after becoming prime minister in 1924, General J.B.M. Hertzog announced plans to remove African voters from the voters' roll in the Cape Province. This was the catalyst for conferences among delegates from black and colored organizations held between 1935 and 1937. In the latter year the All-African Convention (AAC) was formed for the purpose of 'co-ordinating the activities and struggles of all African organizations in their fight against oppression and as a mouthpiece of the African people.' Dr Abdullah Abdurahman and his mainly colored African Political Organization took part in the AAC conferences in the mid-1930s, but the APO was now a conservative organization and the leadership increasingly under attack from a new generation of colored teachers and other professional people, inspired by the theoretical teachings of Leo Trotsky.

In the English mainstream churches some opposition to segregation had built up. During the mid-1920s the DRC participated in the multi-racial church conferences, but then withdrew from the debate. English liberals and blacks discussed race relations at meetings of the Joint Councils of Europeans and Africans, out of which the South African Institute of Race Relations, founded in 1929, grew. By the early 1930s the leadership of the Anglican Church, Catholic Church and most of the other churches had become critical of segregation and was making racial justice a central demand without, however, spelling out an alternative political order. In 1930 the Anglican bishops asked for full citizenship for all, regardless of color. They challenged the DRC to offer a Christian alternative to the liberal stand of the other churches. The DRC embarked on its apartheid program as a response (see pp. 454-64).[30]

Curbing the native franchise: fair, just, Christian?

There was still enough liberal resistance to prevent Hertzog from getting the necessary two-thirds majority in Parliament when, in the second half of the 1920s, he put the removal of the Cape Africans from the voters' roll on the agenda. But the rapid urbanization of blacks and the growth of black numbers had brought about the steady erosion of political liberalism. Ironically, it was a liberal move, the extension of the vote to white women, that opened the door to curbing the Cape African vote. Before the granting of the vote to white women in 1930 the proportion of Cape African voters in the voting

---

30 John de Gruchy, *The Church Struggle in South Africa* (London: Collins, 1986), pp. 32-8.

population as a whole had been 7.5 per cent of all South African voters; after the inclusion of white women had doubled the number of white voters the African proportion of voters was a mere 3 per cent.

The number of African voters was now so small that this form of representation could no longer serve as justification for the denial of African rights. But although emasculated, the Cape African vote remained symbolically important. Not without reason Hertzog believed that Africans across South Africa would hope that the vote would be extended to them while representatives of Cape Africans sat in Parliament.

Hertzog now conceived the idea of exchanging land for votes. He would remove Cape Africans from the voters' roll and double the size of the reserves. In 1936 he secured the necessary two-thirds parliamentary majority to implement the idea. Cape Africans would have to vote on a separate roll, and could elect three whites to represent them in the House of Assembly; four white senators, elected by electoral colleges, would represent other blacks in South Africa. There would be a Natives Representative Council to discuss issues touching on Africans in both the reserves and the common area. An additional 7.25 million morgen of land would be bought up for the reserves; now 13 per cent of the country's land.

Almost all the principal speakers in the 1936 debate asked the question whether all this was fair, just, and Christian. Jan Smuts, Deputy Prime Minister, thought that the legislation had sufficient elements of 'justice and fair play and fruitfulness for the future.' Instead of risking the abolition of all forms of African representation, he was prepared to work for separate representation, although he disliked it. Hertzog invoked the principles of self-preservation and self-defense as Christian principles. They were the only principles 'by which humanity itself and Christianity itself will ever be able to protect itself.' Those who spoke of injustice had to prove the white fear of black numbers unfounded.

Jan Hofmeyr, the leading liberal in Parliament, strongly differed from them. He opposed any law based on fear; it would fail to secure self-preservation. No nation, 'save at the cost of honor and ultimate security, could take away [franchise] rights without adequate compensation.' The Bill emphasized 'the differences [between whites and blacks], it stimulates hostility, and it pays no regard to the ultimate community of interests.' It said that 'even the most educated Native would never have equality with even the least educated and least cultured White or Colored man.' White civilization could be preserved only with the consent and goodwill of the non-European people within a nation's borders. The Bill reduced black people to an inferior, qualified citizenship. 'The puny breastworks that we put up must be swept away, but I do believe that the mere putting up of those breastworks is going to accelerate the day that the tide will turn . . .' He believed that there was an opposing current, 'a rising tide of liberalism', among young whites in South Africa.[31]

Hofmeyr's statement of high idealism has been praised as one of the great parliamentary interventions, but there was no evidence of the rising tide he detected. A mere five years before he himself had proposed that the qualification for voters be altered

---

31 Paton, *Hofmeyr*, pp. 174-8.

periodically to ensure that Africans never made up more than 10 per cent of the electorate.[32] In terms of *realpolitik*, the exchange between two other Afrikaner politicians,
the two Malans of the western Cape, was more pointed. The liberal F.S. Malan appealed
to the Afrikaner Bond tradition, expressed by its leader J.H. (Onze Jan) Hofmeyr, who,
as far back as 1887, had laid down the broad principle: 'Have one principle for your
voter, make the test as high as you like, but when a man comes up to that test do not
differentiate, let him be treated as a full citizen of the country.'[33] He continued: 'You
cannot divide the interests of a people, whether a man is black or brown or white.' He
proposed extending the Cape Province's qualified franchise to the other provinces.

D.F. Malan, Leader of the Opposition, differed strongly. To him the qualified franchise
for Cape blacks was a bluff, an arrangement that 'was not seriously intended that it
actually was seriously intended.' The overriding principle was white security. Even in the
supposedly liberal Cape Colony, politicians altered the franchise qualifications in 1887
and 1892 in the belief that it was a risk to have too many Africans who had qualified. If
one made the qualification for the franchise too low one got a black man's country in
which 'white civilization' could not survive. Raising it ever higher would produce 'a
small restricted coterie' of white people governing the country. Less affluent whites denied the vote, on that account, would have no protection against exploitation. 'The poor
[white] man's vote is the bulwark against exploitation.'[34]

D.F. Malan was correct in challenging F.S. Malan's assumption that setting the franchise qualifications at a certain level was somehow a neutral act, and that lifting or lowering it was unlikely to disturb the social order. South Africa was a deeply divided society with a dominant white group itself divided along ethnic lines. Growing numbers
of black voters would polarize the relations between Afrikaners and English-speakers
as each competed for the black vote. As more and more blacks qualified, tension between whites and blacks would grow. Once blacks approached parity with whites, it was
unrealistic to expect that blacks would settle for anything less than universal franchise.
Far from stabilizing politics, the qualified vote would almost inevitably be a source of
pervasive instability.

While Hertzog and Smuts did agree to put Africans on a separate roll, which would
count for very little, they accepted them as citizens. Hertzog's plan was to encourage long-
standing racial conventions but 'in a manner that will avoid causing ill-feeling or a sense
of grievance, and will involve no greater discrimination than the necessities of the case
require.'[35] Although this greatly underplays the suffering of blacks as a result of the 'necessities' of segregation, it does illuminate an essential difference between Hertzog and
the future architects of apartheid, who denied blacks rights in the common area on the
grounds that they enjoyed rights in the reserves.

There was no nationalist blueprint for the future development of African rights among
either Hertzog's or Malan's supporters. As late as 1950 A.L. Geyer, the most influential

---

32 Rodney Davenport and Christopher Saunders, *South Africa: A Modern History* (London: Macmillan,
    2000), p. 325.
33 *HAD*, Special Session, *1936*, cols. 117-19.
34 *HAD*, Special Session, *1936*, col. 161.
35 Cited by H.A. Fagan, *Our Responsibility* (Stellenbosch: Universiteitsuitgewers, 1960), p. 43.

nationalist editor of his time (he was the first editor to use the term 'apartheid') and now High Commissioner in London, publicly proposed a 'central council' of Africans drawn from the various 'councils' in the reserves, and 'machinery for close contact and consultation between the Government and reserve Councils and eventually the Central Council.' Two years later in another public speech he said: 'Either the Bantu areas become an independent state, or there will have to be some federal union.'[36] Hendrik Verwoerd, Minister for Native Affairs, firmly closed that door.

From the mid-1930s the NP under D.F. Malan pushed for the removal of colored voters from the roll. This would require a form of racial classification, but a commission that sat in the mid-1930s considered such classification too impractical to apply in the absence of a clear definition of a colored person. Apartheid differed from segregation in its claim that such an obstacle could be overcome.

The new nationalist intelligentsia

Albert Geyer, editor of *Die Burger*, thought that the best opposition to fusion would come from a coalition of 'the [Afrikaner] working class . . . the republican Afrikaners and the Afrikaner intelligentsia.'[37] By the intelligentsia he meant teachers, lecturers, journalists, ministers, politicians and lawyers. The rapid expansion of the white educational system in the first twenty-five years of Union produced an Afrikaner intelligentsia that was much larger and more self-assured than the one that joined Malan and Hertzog in 1914-15. Geyer's coalition of working class and intelligentsia would provide the base of the apartheid order that would be introduced in the early 1950s. But such was the respect in which Hertzog was held that half the teaching staff at Stellenbosch supported the UP until South Africa's disputed entry into the Second World War in 1939. Afterwards their support of the UP all but collapsed.[38]

Heading the NP was Malan, a leader not to be underestimated. He was widely considered an outstanding parliamentarian – a senior English journalist said that he was the 'best fighting force' the Pact government had in Parliament.[39] In public he came across as implacable, ponderous and humorless, but he was a great orator, developing a clear and logical argument and able to hold his Afrikaner audiences spellbound for two hours or more. He combined a passionate belief in Afrikaner unity with a grasp of the need for strategic action to achieve it. On racial issues he was initially flexible. His son wrote in an unpublished memoir that his father grew up with the view that 'the differences between whites and non-whites would be eradicated by education and that all that would remain was skin color.'[40]

Theologically Malan was a liberal and he supported Johannes du Plessis, Professor of

---

36 J.P. Heiberg, 'Dr. A.L. Geyer as Suid-Afrika se hoë kommissaris in die Verenigde Koninkryk, 1950-54', doctoral diss., University of Stellenbosch, 2001, pp. 208-18, 250.

37 Van Wyk, *Keeromstraatkliek*, p. 117.

38 J.J. Broodryk, 'Stellenbosse akademici en die politieke problematiek in Suid-Afrika, 1934-1948', master's diss., US, 1991; C.F. J Muller, *Sonop in die Suide: geboorte en groei van die Nasionale Pers, 1915-1948* (Cape Town: Nasionale Boekhandel, 1990), pp. 409-32.

39 L.E. Neame, *Some South African Politicians* (Cape Town: Maskew Miller, 1929), p. 25.

40 US Library, D.F. Malan documents collection, memoir of D.F. Malan, Jr.

Theology at Stellenbosch, when conservatives in 1928 charged him with heresy. Du Plessis had gained a reputation throughout the country as editor of the journal *Het Zoeklicht* (The Searchlight), which published articles on evolution and the 'higher criticism' in theology, and warned against a doctrinaire approach to the racial problem. In 1930 Du Plessis was removed from his post in the theological seminary and with that a major moderating influence disappeared.[41] There were only a few critical voices with authority in the church when the apartheid ideology began making headway in the late 1930s. By championing apartheid the church leadership would seek to regain some of the influence it had lost in its campaign against Du Plessis.

Apart from Albert Geyer, the other important figure in Malan's circle was Paul Sauer, his main confidant in the NP's parliamentary caucus. Sauer was one of the main opponents of the colored vote. He believed that he had been defeated by the colored vote in the Stellenbosch constituency in 1924. Afterwards he often said that as long as the colored vote held the balance of power in elections, there would be constant friction between whites and coloreds and between Afrikaners and English-speakers. There was, however, no colored homeland to use as a justification for colored political exclusion. All the NP could offer was to rehabilitate colored people more comprehensively than the system of segregation was doing.

Among the main nationalist intellectuals in the north there were Nico Diederichs and Piet Meyer. Both had studied in Germany in the 1930s before returning to South Africa, where Diederichs became a professor at the University of the OFS and Meyer a full-time organizer, based in Johannesburg, of the FAK, the federation of Afrikaans cultural organizations and the public face of the Afrikaner Broederbond. Diederichs pushed the nationalist ideology to its limits by arguing that an individual's life attained spiritual meaning only in the service of the nation, which was service to God. Sympathetic to Nazi ideology, he rejected the democratic system in favor of a totalitarian approach.[42] Another strand of nationalist thinking was the neo-Calvinism of Potchefstroom; for H.G Stoker, for example, there were different social spheres, each grounded in the ordinances of God's creation. One such sphere was the *volk*.[43] Most of the nationalist intelligentsia in the north were members of the Broederbond: in Johannesburg Hendrik Verwoerd, Meyer and Albert Hertzog, the son of the prime minister, were prominent figures. In Potchefstroom there were L.J. du Plessis, a legal scholar who was the leading influence on Broederbond thinking, and J.C. van Rooy, who served as chairman of the Bond's executive council between 1932 and 1938 and from 1946 to 1951.

Hendrik Verwoerd, who in 1937 became the editor of *Die Transvaler* in Johannesburg, soon formed a strong partnership with J.G. Strijdom, Transvaal NP leader. Ideologically he subscribed to neither neo-Calvinism, Nazism or racism (see p. 350). He was above all a social engineer with a mission, ready to call for state intervention if the society developed in what he thought was the wrong direction.[44] Along with a few other Stellenbosch professors he had staged a public protest in 1936 in Cape Town against the arrival of Jew-

41 Andrew Nash, 'The Dialectical Tradition in South Africa', doctoral diss., UCT, 2000, pp. 106-13.
42 Nico Diederichs, *Nasionalisme as lewensbeskouing* (Bloemfontein: Nasionale Pers, 1936), pp. 17-18, 63.
43 J.H. van Wyk, *Etiek en eksistensie* (Potchefstroom, 2001), pp. 188-213.
44 Prinsloo, 'Verwoerd', pp. 392-8.

ish immigrants, escaping from Nazi Germany, on the ship the *Stuttgart*. Their argument was that an influx of Jews would make it even more difficult for Afrikaners to make headway in business and the professions.

The northern nationalist intelligentsia lacked ties with the wealthier Transvaal Afrikaner farmers, almost without exception supporters of the UP. Nationalist leaders in the south subsidized Voortrekkerpers, a company established in 1937 to publish *Die Transvaler*, the only nationalist paper in the Transvaal. Verwoerd left his Stellenbosch chair to become editor. In the first issue he published a four thousand-word article under his name entitled 'The Jewish Question as seen from an NP viewpoint.' It claimed that a conflict of interests existed between the 'disadvantaged Afrikaner majority and a privileged Jewish minority', which had entered the towns and cities long before the Afrikaners and now dominated commerce and industry along with people of British descent. Jewish owners and employers filled the most important positions in their firms with ethnic compatriots. 'The Afrikaner was compelled to become a *handlanger* or subordinate often at a meager wage. Jewish dominance of the economy enabled the younger generation of Jews to crowd out Afrikaners in the professions. They used the English press and political parties to exert a disproportionate influence on government.' Afrikaners were beginning to feel 'that Jews have a chokehold on their continued existence.'

Verwoerd wrote that Afrikaner nationalists admired the way in which Jews stood by their own and that the NP did not take their religion or race into account in developing a policy. The problem was of an economic kind, namely Jewish over-representation in key economic sectors. Yet he failed to identify a reason why Jewish dominance was more dangerous than that of any other ethnic group. Neither did he attempt to make a case that there was a common Jewish agenda in South Africa.

His solution was somewhat unusual. 'Legislation must gradually ensure that each white section [Afrikaners, English-speakers of British descent and Jewish South Africans] enjoy a share of the major occupations according to its share of the white population.' Since Jews held a disproportionate share of the wholesale and retail trade, a future NP government would refuse further trading licenses until the Jewish share was brought back to their share of the white population (it was popularly estimated at four per cent) and English-speakers and Afrikaners 'have gained a proportion that as far as practicable corresponds to their percentage of the white population.' Verwoerd described this as *ewewigtige verspreiding*, or balanced distribution, but added that 'this has also been called a quota system.' He added: 'Any discrimination had to disappear once the right balance has been achieved.'[45]

Verwoerd was not a lone voice. A month before his article appeared, the Cape NP had unanimously accepted a resolution at its congress asking the government to stop all Jewish immigration. It added the following: 'As regards the present Jewish population, congress expresses the view that trading and other licenses have to be granted on a proportional basis to Jews and that all businesses have to operate in the birth name of the owner.'[46]

It has sometimes been suggested that the anti-Semitism of Malan's party in the late

---

45 *Die Transvaler*, 1 September 1937.
46 *Die Burger*, 19 August 1937.

1930s was more vicious than before, that Malan's views represented a volte-face compared to his earlier Jewish-friendly sentiments, and that these developments could be attributed to Nazi influences.[47] This interpretation is difficult to sustain. There is no evidence that the Nazi's anti-Semitic literature that entered South Africa actually influenced more than fringe groups and some individuals in the NP. Verwoerd's article and the Cape NP's resolution reflected the traditional Afrikaner economic anti-Semitism that had developed in the rural areas. Its sources were not German anti-Semitism but local stereotypes of the Jew outsmarting everyone and profiting at their expense. *Die Burger's* cartoonist, Boonzaier, with his Hoggenheimer character had reinforced the image of a cunning and callous Jewish capitalist who had Botha, Smuts and Hertzog in his pocket and who was unconcerned about the suffering of white workers.[48] Anti-Semitic sentiments were fuelled by Afrikaner frustration over their lack of economic progress in the city. But only Eric Louw among future NP leaders spoke of a world Jewry exerting a malignant political influence, the language of Hitler.[49] Once the NP gained power in 1948 Louw quickly shed any vestiges of anti-Semitism. The NP's anti-Semitism was opportunistic rather than deep-rooted. There never was any talk of Jewish expulsion or confiscation of their property.

Although the northern and southern intelligentsia were committed to the same nationalist cause, there was little love lost between them. Provincialism, most frequently taking the form of hostility between the Transvaal and the western Cape, was rife in Afrikaner nationalist ranks throughout the twentieth century. By the end of the 1930s the chief cause of Transvaal resentment was the Cape domination of nationalist politics. Until 1954, when Strijdom became NP leader and Prime Minister, Malan and a small coterie of western Cape people around him called the shots. Nasionale Pers, publisher of *Die Burger* in Cape Town, towered over the Afrikaans press companies and enjoyed such close personal ties with Malan that its editor was allowed to attend the meetings of the NP's parliamentary caucus. To compound matters, a growing proportion of Afrikaner savings was attracted by Sanlam, the Cape Town-based insurance company, leaving little for aspiring Afrikaner entrepreneurs in the north. With a considerable financial stake in the company that published *Die Transvaler*, the Cape NP leadership tried to curb Verwoerd when he advocated a republic too strenuously, a step that the northern intelligentsia strongly resented.

During the 1930s, Afrikaner nationalists in both the north and the south rejected liberalism, but this was a decade in which even Winston Churchill publicly expressed the belief that unfettered universal suffrage was ill advised.[50] However, beyond this anti-liberalism and their common nationalist commitment there were profound differences between the two. The north was influenced by its defeat in the Anglo-Boer War, and the contempt of northern English-language papers for the Afrikaners and their language

47 P. Furlong, *Between Crown and Swastika: The Impact of the Radical Right on the Afrikaner Nationalist Movement in the Fascist Era* (Johannesburg: Witwatersrand University Press, 1991), pp. 102, 224-6.
48 Milton Shain, *The Roots of Anti-Semitism in South Africa* (Johannesburg: Witwatersrand University Press, 1994), pp. 55-63, 90-94.
49 A. van Deventer, 'Afrikaner Nationalist Politics and Anti-Communism, 1937 to 1945', doctoral diss., US, 1991, pp. 256-87.
50 David Cannadine, 'Winston Antagonistes', *New York Review of Books*, 15 June 1989, p. 38.

struggle. They experienced unbridled mining capitalism, whose ugly face was often displayed. The Afrikaner intelligentsia was above all concerned with the competition of poorly qualified whites against swelling numbers of blacks. After taking up the position of editor of *Die Transvaler*, Verwoerd wrote to a friend: 'The Afrikaners of the cities, particularly the workers, have to be retained for Afrikanerdom, religiously, socially and politically . . . [The] future of our *volk* will be won or lost there. It makes me feel that the post offered to me is more of a vocation than a job.'[51] He also wrote: 'The threat to the Afrikaner is not Anglicization, but that in urbanizing he would undergo a process of proletarianization in which he would lose all interest in the Afrikaner culture and would become merely an international worker.'[52]

The Afrikaners in the south, by contrast, had been in contact for more than a century with English financial and commercial capitalism. Unlike the north, the south had a respected newspaper in *Die Burger,* whose influence rivaled that of the political leadership. Together party and paper developed what Schalk Pienaar, a brilliant colleague of Cillié, would later call an 'independence in common commitment' to the nationalist cause.[53] There was no large, impoverished Afrikaner working class and the two white communities had developed a tradition of a mutual tolerance.

Until the 1930s colored people lived next to whites in a section of every western Cape town without any major white opposition. But the Cape Afrikaner intelligentsia were as prepared as their counterparts in the north to prevent mixing or sexual intercourse across racial lines. The understanding of even the reformists of the 'native problem' tended to be abstract, coupled with what a British writer in the 1950s would call 'a rather frigid goodwill' towards Africans.[54]

As nationalists, the intelligentsia in the south and north also differed. Members of the Dopper or Gereformeerde Kerk had long emphasized their identity as 'a divinely favored people in the same sense that Israel was', as an observer remarked in 1858. The Transvaal nationalist intelligentsia tended to see the Afrikaners in metaphysical terms, emphasizing a *volksiel* or a national soul and invariably defined the term Afrikaners exclusively.[55] D.F. Malan, the Cape leader, did not like the neo-Calvinist obsession of the Doppers with 'pure' doctrine and abstract 'points of departure.'[56] He did speak of a God-given Afrikaner identity and of the hand of God in the Afrikaner history, but he added: 'That he claims this as his exclusive right and that he raises his people above others as God's special favorite is a false and slanderous allegation.'[57] In his secular mode he thought of the Afrikaners as people who had evolved as a distinct people, with their own religion, church, language and nationality, as a result of a particular historical process. Hence he used the term 'Afrikaner' inclusively along with an exclusive, ethnic definition.

---

51 Prinsloo, 'Verwoerd', p. 42.

52 *Die Volksblad*, 30 June 1936; G.D. Scholtz, *Hendrik Verwoerd* (Johannesburg: Perskor, 1974), vol. 1, p. 90.

53 Schalk Pienaar, 'Die Afrikaner en sy koerant', *Standpunte*, 108 (1973), pp. 1-5.

54 James Morris, *South African Winter* (London: Faber and Faber, 1957), p. 141.

55 W.M. Collins, *Free Statia* (Bloemfontein: The Friend, 1907), p. 158.

56 The influence of neo-Calvinism on Afrikaner nationalism is exaggerated in Hexham, *Irony of Apartheid*. For Malan's views, see his son's memoir in the D.F. Malan collection at the University of Stellenbosch library.

57 US Library, D.F. Malan Collection, Manuscript 'Op die wagtoring', not dated.

J.G. Strijdom, the leader of the republican north, yearned for the day that Afrikaans would be the only official language, and English-speakers would become Afrikaners. The Cape Afrikaner tradition was quite different: they had nearly a century of parliamentary democracy behind them in which competition between the two white communities never got out of hand. Malan strongly supported the co-equality of the two official languages and the equal status of the two white groups. He was not keen on the establishment of a republic as a priority and agreed to make it a party plank only after pressure from northern nationalists. He continued to insist that a republic could only be proclaimed with the support of a significant section of English-speakers.

On the racial issue the north tended to be dogmatic, rigid and uncompromising, with a strong overlay of racism. The south was much more ambiguous and very often hypocritical. Theoretically the colored people could become part of the dominant group but in practice they were held at arm's length. The southern nationalists were racial pragmatists skeptical of utopian solutions or biblical justifications of racial discrimination. They wanted to defend white supremacy by keeping different options open. Hard-core racism was a red herring that complicated the task of choosing between strategic alternatives.

Except during the early 1960s, when Hendrik Verwoerd dominated the nationalist movement, it was the southern tradition that prevailed. Within the Cape Town-Stellenbosch-Paarl triangle a true ethnic establishment of politicians, academics, journalists, church leaders and businessmen that would form the main opposition to the UP had evolved, and would shape the apartheid ideology. In the north there was no such establishment, and little financial support for the academics and professional men who organized themselves into the Afrikaner Broederbond.

'The Afrikaner Broederbond shall rule South Africa'

When Malan rejected fusion, Hertzog focused his wrath on the institutions with which he was associated. One was the Nasionale Pers and its newspaper, *Die Burger,* for which Malan was writing a column. Hertzog took on the Nasionale Pers by getting allies to buy up shares and proxies, believing that a majority holding would rid him of 'the Keerom Street clique' (the premises of the Nasionale Pers, and the offices of both *Die Burger* and the Cape National Party were in Keerom Street, a short street in Cape Town). While still financially insecure, and passing up a dividend in 1932, the company managed to rebuff Hertzog's attack.[58]

Hertzog's next target was the Afrikaner Broederbond. In 1933 the Bond had 1,003 members in fifty-three cells, or divisions, as they were called, of which only four were in the Cape, the rest in the Transvaal and OFS. Hertzog was not a member of the Broederbond, and it is not known if he was ever asked to become one. Until 1935 he did not object in principle to the Bond, but he did worry that so few of his men were in leading positions. (Henry Fagan remained a member until the late 1940s.)

Historians, journalists and political opponents of the Broederbond have attributed an

---

58 Van Wyk, *Die Keeromstraatkliek*; Muller, *Sonop in die Suide,* pp. 411-31.

importance to the organization that is out of all proportion. A military intelligence report of 1944 asserted that it could 'manufacture' public opinion at will 'in spite of government victories at the polls.'[59] Two journalistic accounts, both published in 1990, have the same thrust. One states that it was the 'central policymaking organ', co-ordinating the entire 'mechanism' of the nationalist movement and forming its 'front-line shock troops'[60], another declares somewhat breathlessly, and without providing evidence, that the organization 'fashioned' apartheid into a radical program and that it was 'unequalled in the world for its pervasive back-room power wielded over nearly every aspect of national life.'[61] Instead of analyzing the nationalist movement as a complex organization with diverse sources of influence, these authors deploy the Broederbond as a *deus ex machina* to explain its every move.

A much-needed reinterpretation is under way. A respected historian, who is a Bond member, recently completed a manuscript on the organization, based on unrestricted access to its archives. This unpublished work reveals a very different picture of a small organization slowly building itself up, struggling to make its influence felt and mostly serving as a debating forum for a small band of activists often far removed from the real political action. The Bond did not make any final decisions or give firm guidance. Much more often it reflected the divisions in Afrikaner nationalist ranks and encouraged debate until a consensus was reached.[62]

During the 1930s and 1940s the Broederbond, as a predominantly northern organization, did not remotely match the influence of the Cape NP and *Die Burger* in the Afrikaner nationalist movement. Because most of the Afrikaner political leaders after 1948 were also Broederbond members, the assumption in the literature is that the organization influenced or even controlled the NP leadership. But this is to turn the power relationship on its head. The NP leaders used the Bond as a sounding board, and the organization invariably submitted to cabinet decisions. Only in the 1960s, in the heyday of apartheid, would the Bond act as an ideological policeman. But even with respect to the 1960s, it is a misconception to rate the Bond's influence as being on a par with that of the NP. It is one of the features of South African historiography that only the Bond's most unreflective members and most biased opponents swallowed the myths about the organization.

During the early 1930s the Bond exercised its greatest influence in the spheres of education and culture. It orchestrated some of the pressures that helped to transform the bilingual university colleges in Pretoria and Bloemfontein into Afrikaans language institutions. It had a hand in the breakaway of the Afrikaans language universities and colleges from the National Union of South African Students (Nusas), seen as a 'denationalizing' influence. The Afrikaner students founded the Afrikaanse Nasionale Studentebond with a radical nationalist program.[63]

59 W.H. Vatcher, *White Laager: The Rise of Afrikaner Nationalism* (New York: Praeger, 1965), p. 257.
60 Charles Bloomberg, *Christian-Nationalism and the Rise of the Afrikaner Broederbond* (London: Macmillan, 1990), p. 36.
61 Allister Sparks, *The Mind of South Africa* (London: Heinemann, 1990), p. 175.
62 E.L.P. Stals, 'Die geskiedenis van die Afrikaner-Broederbond, 1918-1994', unpublished manuscript, 1998. For an earlier study by a Bond member with little attempt at objectivity and perspective, see A.N. Pelzer, *Die Afrikaner-Broederbond* (Cape Town: Tafelberg, 1979).
63 Stals, 'Geskiedenis van die AB', pp. 72-3; Scholtz, *Ontwikkeling van die politieke denke*, vol. 7, p. 114.

The most prominent academics in the Bond propagated a republic with a pronounced Afrikaans character, which was a preoccupation of Afrikaner nationalists in the north, not of those in the western Cape. L.J. du Plessis argued for an authentic Afrikaner political system that would accommodate non-Afrikaners as long as they 'make South Africa their Fatherland, use the Afrikaners' language, and make the South African view of life their own . . . Even Jews can be incorporated.' J.C. van Rooy felt that English-speakers had to be 'implanted', that is grafted, on the Afrikaner stem.[64]

The views of the two Potchefstroom academics provided the background for a Broederbond circular of April 1934. Co-signed by Van Rooy as chairman, it read: 'Afrikanerdom shall reach its ultimate destiny of domination in South Africa . . . Brothers, our solution for South Africa's troubles is not that this or that party shall gain the upper hand, but that the Afrikaner Broederbond shall rule South Africa.' This certainly was a much more ambitious target than the Bond set in any of its other circulars of the time. Undoubtedly some of the northern nationalists endorsed this call, but in the western Cape, where the Bond had only recently established divisions, it would certainly have raised eyebrows. Nonetheless it was only a view expressed by the Executive Council, to which the divisions were expected to send their comments.

Hertzog waited eighteen months before he seized on the circular. He accused the Bond of spreading a 'Potchefstroom fanaticism' intent on excluding the English as true citizens of the country. The Bond also fatally divided Afrikaners by arrogating to itself the right to accept only Afrikaners who met its particular criteria. He attributed to the Bond enormous influence, but without demonstrating how an organization of one thousand members, of whom a quarter were farmers and one-third teachers and lecturers, could carry so much weight.[65]

Hertzog's main aim was to discredit Malan as a political foe, implying that it was due to the influence of the secret body that he rejected fusion. Malan had indeed become a Bond member in August 1933, but moved in the circles of the Cape NP and Nasionale Pers and the principal influences on him were Willie Hofmeyr, Paul Sauer, Albert Geyer and Frans Erasmus (secretary of the Cape NP), none of whom belonged to the Bond. It is quite implausible that Malan, in making up his mind about fusion, would suddenly embrace the view of an organization based mainly in Johannesburg and Potchefstroom, of which he had just become a member, and of academics steeped in neo-Calvinism, a dogma which he specifically rejected.

After a meeting between Hertzog and members of the Bond's Executive, the prime minister accepted the Bond's assurances. The Executive now defined its purpose more modestly than in in the 1934 circular. Its aim was to raise 'the self-consciousness of the Afrikaners by cultivating a love for their own language, religion, traditions, country and people.'[66]

---

64 Moodie, *Rise of Afrikanerdom*, p. 162.
65 E.L.P. Stals, *Generaal J.B.M. Hertzog en die Afrikaner-Broederbond* (Pretoria: Hertzog Memorial Lecture, 1995).
66 Stals, *Hertzog en die AB*, p. 13.

Afrikaner workers: Nationalists or Communists?

Workers made up the bulk of the Afrikaner people in the 1930s. Albert Hertzog cal-culated that 80 per cent of the members of white unions were Afrikaners. With family members included, 500,000 Afrikaners, or one half of the Afrikaner people, were part of the organized white working class.[67]

Despite this Afrikaner preponderance, people from British and Jewish descent domi-nated organized labor. Afrikaners occupied only 10 per cent of the leadership positions, according to Albert Hertzog; another source counted 118 trade union organizations of which about only eighteen had Afrikaners as elected secretaries. E.S. (Solly) Sachs, a prominent trade unionist, was scathing in his condemnation of the way in which trade unions slighted Afrikaners and their culture: 'The workers' organizations looked on the Afrikaner people with an air of disdain.' They 'failed almost entirely to appreciate fully the development, tradition, sentiments and aspirations of the masses of Afrikaners . . . as a people who suffered cultural, economic and political oppression.'[68]

Many of the Afrikaner workers had deep reservations about the capitalist system with its apparently rampant individualism and greed. Afrikaner nationalists deplored the class divisions the system fostered and the exploitation suffered by unskilled and semi-skilled Afrikaner workers. Their feelings were most intense in Johannesburg, a city built, as they saw it, on crude materialism, exploitation, corruption, vice, and almost all other forms of human degradation. While wages stagnated, the mining companies were making prof-its 'beyond the dreams of avarice', as a company history phrased it[69] – the ideal soil for nurturing a communist movement.

A culture clash reinforced this class conflict. A DRC study observed: 'A very great dis-advantage of the South African capitalist system is that those who represent it, and wield power in it, do not belong to the [Afrikaner] people and feel nothing for our ideals, lan-guage and religion. In their mighty press and other sources of influence there is dis-crimination specifically against the Afrikaner. In all possible ways the Afrikaner is held in an inferior, subordinate position. He is welcome as a worker, but not allowed to occu-py any position of power.'[70]

While detesting a capitalism interested only in private gain, the Broederbond and the church had an even greater antipathy towards leftist trade unions. In 1940 the synod of the Cape DRC charged that Communists had drawn Africans into trade unions in a bid for revolution, atheism, equality and the abolition of private property. With their mix of middle-class values and nationalist fervor, the Broederbond tried to organize Afri-kaner workers on the Witwatersrand by inspiring them with a creed of 'Christian-Na-tional trade unionism' that would convey a sense of identity as workers who were also members of a volk and a church.[71]

Nationalists on the Witwatersrand watched the struggles on the labor front with grow-

67 E.P. du Plessis, 'n Volk staan op (Cape Town: Human & Rousseau, 1964), p. 125.

68 Forward, 15 July 1938; for a general discussion see Pauw, Beroepslewe.

69 C. Potts, 'A History of Union Corporation', unpublished, cited by David Yudelman, The Emergence of Mod-ern South Africa (Westport: Greenwood Press, 1983), p. 254.

70 J.R. Albertyn, et al., Kerk en stad (Stellenbosch: Pro Ecclesia, 1947), pp. 290-91.

71 Albertyn, et al., Kerk en stad, pp. 334-7; Bloomberg, Christian-Nationalism, p. 37.

ing concern. Despite its passionate concern about Afrikaner unity, the Broederbond did not want workers as members. It insisted that prospective members had to be persons of social standing, dependable and principled – and 'financially strong enough.'[72] Albert Hertzog bewailed the fact that only 5 per cent of Bond members came from the working class. He told his fellow-nationalists: 'If you want to save the Afrikaner people, you have to save [the Afrikaner workers].' Diederichs put the crisis melodramatically: 'If the worker is drawn away from our nation we may as well write Ichabod on the door of our temple.' (Ichabod became the source of a convivial joke in the family of the advocate Bram Fischer, an Afrikaner active in the Communist Party of South Africa [CPSA].)[73]

In 1936 the Bond and its associated organizations founded the Nasionale Raad van Trustees (National Council of Trustees), or NRT, under the leadership of Albert Hertzog. The immediate aim of these self-styled 'reformers' was to vote their own members into the leadership of trade unions or to establish rival unions, but the larger purpose was 'the welding together of Afrikaner workers and the Afrikaner nation into a mighty unity that would remain faithful to the Afrikaner's cultural and religious tradition.'[74] They proposed a comprehensive color bar to exclude or to disadvantage black and colored workers. The government had to reserve the better-paid jobs for whites and compel employers to employ white workers.[75] Their real enemies were trade unionism, socialism and communism.

The reformers, or for that matter the Broederbond, had no or very few trade unionists in their ranks. Albert Hertzog, trained as a lawyer, had no trade union experience; other members of the NRT council included academics (Van Rooy and Diederichs), ministers of the church and a director of a bank. They were also all male, of course. A series of articles by a trade unionist in *Die Huisgenoot* showed how heavy-handed their approach was; they told women in industry that they 'worshipped' them, but, as the articles noted, young girls in the slums of the big cities wanted assistance in finding work and protection against exploitation, not worship. Secretly, the Executive Council of the Broederbond decided to write to the editor of *Die Huisgenoot* to protest against the articles.[76]

Communist activists indeed targeted Afrikaner workers. As one communist leader exclaimed: 'We must win Afrikanerdom for our side . . . It must be taught to choose between Communism and poor white-ism.'[77] Among the leading Afrikaner communists was Daan du Plessis, who was elected as secretary of the Johannesburg branch of the Building Workers Industrial Union. (His brother, called Sand, would become a prominent nationalist politician in the apartheid years.) In a pamphlet written in Afrikaans, Du Plessis stated that real power was vested in the capitalists, not Parliament nor the cabinet. The capitalist system fomented racial hatred among workers as part of its relentless pursuit

72 E.L.P. Stals, 'Geskiedenis van die AB', p. 79.

73 Stephen Clingman, *Bram Fischer: Afrikaner Revolutionary* (Cape Town: David Philip, 1998), p. 134.

74 Bloomberg, *Christian-Nationalism*, p. 114; See also H.J. and R.E. Simons, *Class and Colour in South Africa, 1850-1950* (Harmondsworth: Penguin Books, 1969), pp. 520-26.

75 Stanley Greenberg, *Race and State in Capitalist Development* (New Haven: Yale University Press, 1980), pp. 273-6.

76 *Die Huisgenoot*, 14 January; 14, 21, 28 July and 4 August 1944.

77 Albertyn, et al., *Kerk en stad*, p. 301.

of profits. The low wages it paid to blacks suppressed the wage levels of all workers. Du Plessis called on workers to unite to overthrow the existing system and turn it over to communism.[78]

But the nationalist bogeyman was Solly Sachs, a Jewish South African, who was a most effective trade unionist. He joined the Communist Youth League in 1922, and soon climbed the ladder of the Communist Party of South Africa. He and most members believed that the first priority was uniting workers across color lines before moving on to achieve the liberation of the oppressed people and the elimination of racial discrimination. In 1928, however, Moscow ordered the CPSA to accept the slogan of a 'Native Republic' in South Africa and to emphasize the African nationalist struggle. Soon Sachs and many others were purged, leaving the party with only 150 members by 1933.

As General Secretary of the Garment Workers Union between 1928 and 1952, Sachs believed that the white workers could be educated to stop thinking in racial or ethnic categories and to rebuff the 'reactionary fascist politicians.' But to do so the union had to respect the different cultural backgrounds of the workers and unite them across the racial and cultural divisions in the struggle for proper working conditions and a decent standard of living. Only once workers had been educated to demand social democracy could socialism be put on the agenda. Underlying it all was the assumption that unionized Afrikaner workers would support a social democratic rather than a nationalist party.[79]

Sachs successfully built up the Garment Workers Union (GWU) as a union primarily of Afrikaner and colored women in the textile and clothing industries on the Witwatersrand. By the mid-1930s the industry employed nearly seventeen thousand white women, the overwhelming majority of them Afrikaners, and some three thousand colored women. Conditions were poor, with the wages of a white woman lower than a white man's living wage. In 1931, Anna Swanepoel, a worker, testified that three-quarters of the young girls supported their families and had a hard time making ends meet. A girl, aged eighteen, who supported a family of eight on a wage of £1 2s 6d a week, told a researcher: 'We have to struggle very hard to keep the home going . . . Often when I come home I feel as if I am too tired even to lift anything.'[80] The industry's rules for sick leave and pregnancy were particularly harsh. Sachs thought that the living conditions of some of the young Afrikaner women were among the worst in the world.

A crisis in gender relations formed part of the crisis in urban Afrikaner society. Married Afrikaner women typically contributed 20 to 40 per cent of the household income of urban Afrikaner families.[81] In many households a woman was the sole breadwinner, challenging the authority of fathers and husbands. There also was a challenge to forms of exploitation within white society. The GWU leadership invoked a host of images: the

---

78 Daan du Plessis, 'n Afrikaner vertel: waarom ek 'n Kommunis is (Cape Town: Communist Party [circa 1940].)

79 Leslie Witz, 'The Rise and Fall of the Independent Labour Party', in B. Bozzoli (ed.), Class, Community and Conflict: South African Perspectives (Johannesburg: Ravan Press, 1987), pp. 261-91.

80 'Elsabé Brink, '"Maar net 'n klomp factory meide": Afrikaner family and Community on the Witwatersrand', in Belinda Bozzoli (ed.), Class, Community and Conflict: South African Perspectives (Johannesburg: Ravan Press, 1987), p. 188.

81 Brink, 'Factory meide', pp. 185-7.

struggling bywoner on a farm, the tenant farmer in debt to the landlord, the backward woodcutter, the impoverished Afrikaner girl in a racially mixed slum, and the mother trying to hold a family together on starvation wages.

With the economy improving after 1933 and Sachs providing shrewd leadership, the GWU made rapid strides in improving working conditions and wages. Afrikaner women were effective trade unionists. Anna Scheepers was elected president of the union in 1938, Johanna Cornelius became national organizer and her sister, Hester, secretary of the Germiston branch. The latter also wrote a play, *Die Offerhande*, extolling the virtues of the Soviet Union and urging workers in South Africa to overthrow the capitalist system. Other Afrikaner women were elected to offices in the union. After a strike in 1931 a researcher wrote as follows about the women in the union: 'They displayed singular solidarity, tenacity, endurance, courage and fortitude in meeting such strikes and have always stood loyally by their leaders.'

Many indeed saw Sachs as a savior, particularly since destitute garment workers received very little help from the church and welfare organizations. In 1948, when the NP came to power, an Afrikaner trade unionist asked a meeting in a working class Johannesburg suburb: 'Has there ever been an Afrikaner or even a minister of the DRC who has come forward to try and better the conditions of the garment workers as Solly Sachs has done?' During the 1980s a researcher asked an ex-garment worker if she had been helped by the Afrikaans church or welfare organizations. 'Which churches? Which women's organizations?' she asked. 'No one cared about us, except the union.'[82]

Nationalist opponents depicted the organized Afrikaner garment workers as Afrikaner daughters 'who went to Johannesburg to dance with Kaffirs.'[83] When Sachs proposed to send members of his union to the celebrations of the Great Trek centenary, nationalists told him 'We Afrikaners acknowledge no classes as you and your satellites are trying to introduce – therefore we do not want the garment workers as a "class" to participate in the celebrations, but all together with us as Boers – the factory girl with the professor's wife. You and Johanna Cornelius, who all day organize and address kaffirs – will you dare to bring them also along to the celebrations? They are your fellow workers and Comrades.'[84] Johanna Cornelius, unruffled, described nationalist efforts to organize a white union in the industry as a capitalist plot: it kept workers in a backward state by fomenting race hatred.[85]

The few Afrikaner employers in industry could not offer their fellow Afrikaners better conditions than their English-speaking counterparts. Albert Wessels, owner of a shirt and clothing factory, gave a revealing account of his uneasy relationship with the Afrikaner women in the GWU: 'In the midst of protracted and unpleasant negotiations one of them suddenly said to me: "Who are you Mr Wessels to say to us what is unreasonable to you manufacturers? Why don't you talk about what is reasonable to us? You are one of us, even if you are a bloody capitalist."'[86] Albert Hertzog's reformers suffered a defeat

---

82 This and the previous paragraphs are based on Brink, 'Factory meide', pp. 185-91.
83 Jonathan Hyslop, 'White Working Class Women', *Journal of African History*, 36 (1995), p. 67.
84 E.S. Sachs, *Rebels' Daughters* (London: McGibbon and Kee, 1957), p. 138.
85 Simons and Simons, *Class and Colour*, p. 522.
86 Albert Wessels, *Albert Wessels: plaasseun en nyweraar* (Johannesburg: Perskor, 1987), p. 60.

when they tried to capture Sachs' control of the GWU. They appealed to racial pride, culture and history, but Sachs could point to improved wages and working conditions.

The reformers' biggest success was on the railways, where large numbers of Afrikaners were employed. There they founded Spoorbond, in the niche between craft unions, which protected their mainly English-speaking white members by keeping skills scarce, and general unions that admitted non-whites as members.[87] Spoorbond offered the symbolic rewards of white supremacy by supporting the color bar. Describing itself as 'more than a trade union, but a popular movement', it also gave workers membership of a resurgent nationalist movement. The English-speaking leader of a rival union soon observed that 'the Afrikaners had thrown off their former feeling of inferiority and were now the dominant force in the service.'[88]

The most publicized reformer struggle was their organization of mineworkers. More than 90 per cent of the fourteen thousand white miners who did not qualify for membership of a craft union were Afrikaners. Most belonged to a general union, the Mineworkers Union (MWU), under the leadership of Charles Harris. The reformers saw the Afrikaner mineworkers as an ideal target since few had the garment workers' sense of class solidarity. Supervising gangs of black miners, they were, as a reformer history puts it, 'not only workers – they are also bosses.'[89] As the MWU leader, Harris was corrupt, autocratic, and patently in the pocket of the Chamber of Mines, which, in 1937, concluded a closed-shop agreement with the union to discipline anyone causing unrest. The MWU was the symbol of all that the nationalists hated. In 1939 a reformer assassinated Harris.

With the real wages of MWU members falling during the war, the reformers redoubled their efforts, but the union leadership had the support of the employers, the Labour Party, the Trades and Labour Council, and, ultimately, also the government, all allies in the war against Fascism. The government suspended elections until after the end of the war.[90] The reformers captured the MWU five months after the NP won the 1948 election.[91]

The Broederbond provided limited financial assistance, but was unwilling to become embroiled. Competition between nationalist organizations for worker support hampered the struggle. In an effort to overcome divisions, a Blanke Werkers Beskermingsbond (White Workers Protection League) was established in 1944; on its executive were seven people who later sat in Parliament. One of them one would be a prime minister (Verwoerd) and four would hold cabinet rank.

But the Beskermingsbond found it difficult to speak in the idiom of unionists. Its journal, *Die Blanke Werker* (The White Worker), was more concerned with spreading the nationalist ideology than with a typical working class agenda; it engaged in myth-making about idyllic early times when there were no class divisions in the Afrikaner community, when the humble sharecropper ate at the table of the farmer. It blamed the capitalist and the trade unionist for antagonism in Afrikaner ranks.[92]

---

87 Cited by Simons and Simons, *Class and Colour*, p. 519.

88 O'Meara, *Volkskapitalisme,* pp. 78-95; Simons and Simons, *Class and Colour*, pp. 508-26.

89 L. Naude (pseud.), *Dr. A. Hertzog, die Nasionale Party en die mynwerker* (Pretoria: Nasionale Raad van Trustees, 1969), p. 19.

90 O'Meara. *Volkskapitalisme*, pp. 91-4; Davies, *Capital, State and White Labour*, pp. 301-5.

91 O'Meara, *Volkskapitalisme*, pp. 238-40; Davies, *Capital, State and White Labour*, pp. 310-11.

92 Simons and Simons, *Class and Colour*, p. 563.

Organized Afrikaner labor tended to treat such stories with justified skepticism. But Solly Sachs also erred in thinking that Afrikaner workers would follow the union leadership in choosing their political party. Large numbers of Afrikaner workers condemned South Africa's entry into the Second World War as evidence of the country's continuing subservience to British imperial interests. A gulf soon opened up between the Afrikaner workers and the Labour Party and United Party, which were both staunchly pro-war. In the hope of attracting the votes of garment workers and other branches of organized labor, Sachs founded the Independent Labour Party to contest the 1943 election. He, Anna Scheepers and Johanna Cornelius stood as candidates in working-class constituencies, but all suffered crushing defeats.[93] When the UP alienated the white working class during the war, the NP was ready to capitalize on its discontent.

Imperial culture and cultural nationalism

When he entered into fusion, Hertzog believed that the Afrikaner and English streams were ready to merge. But in two areas Malan's nationalists identified a need for collective Afrikaner action: developing a cultural nationalism and capturing a greater corporate share of the urban economy.

There were two main obstacles to the development of a cultural nationalism. One was the attraction of the Empire as a cultural and spiritual enterprise, which was continually celebrated by leading English-speaking academics. Cornelius de Kiewiet, the most outstanding historian of the 1930s and 1940s, wrote: 'The empire is a spiritual achievement, with the enduring qualities of spiritual achievements, whether in literature, art, science, or in the relations of human beings on the face of the earth.'[94]

Another obstacle was the undeveloped state of Afrikaans literature and culture. When Afrikaans replaced Dutch as an official language in 1925, C. Louis Leipoldt, who published in both Afrikaans and English, strongly criticized this step. In an essay published ten years later he expressed major reservations about forcing the language on children in schools and on people in general. 'No language can permanently exist on official recognition alone if it lacks the strength and capacity to survive on its own merits. Afrikaans had to develop alongside a world language of proven permanence and adaptability.' Leipoldt added that because Afrikaans had become enmeshed with the Afrikaners' political struggle and was the 'expression of the Afrikaans-national ideas of half the white population of South Africa' there was the serious danger of 'dystrophic development.' As a language it had been recognized too soon. There was the danger that 'it would be nourished upon a national sentiment that is more appreciative of political advantage than of aesthetic and cultural distinction.'[95]

For better or for worse, the struggle to develop Afrikaans as a public language went hand in hand with the political energy unleashed by the Afrikaner nationalist effort to

---

93 Witz, 'Rise and Fall of the ILP', pp. 265-9.
94 C.W. de Kiewiet, *A History of South Africa* (Oxford: Oxford University Press, 1941), p. vi.
95 C. Louis Leipoldt, 'Cultural Development', in A.P. Newton and E.A. Benians (eds.), *Cambridge History of the British Empire* (Cambridge: Cambridge University Press, 1936), vol. 8, pp. 860-61; J.C. Kannemeyer, *Leipoldt* (Cape Town: Tafelberg, 1999), pp. 57-79.

claim for Afrikaans the same rights as English, and to seek to give expression to an authentic local identity. For poets, novelists and the writers of non-fiction the challenge was to build up a national literature with an own character. Leipoldt might warn that Afrikaners would content themselves with 'cultural mediocrity as ineffective as it is dangerous', but he offered no alternative strategy.

By the beginning of the 1930s the syntax and vocabulary of Afrikaans had, to a large extent, assumed its present form. The translation of the Afrikaans Bible appeared in 1933 and was widely acclaimed, in contrast to the first draft, which was considered written in a *stompstert Hollands*, or broken Dutch, that was 'neither fish nor fowl.' Dr. D.F. Malan welcomed the new translation as the greatest event in the life of the Afrikaner people in the field of culture and religion. 'There was a false idea that the *volkstaal*, the language of the volk, would diminish the Bible, but we have experienced the opposite: the Bible has enhanced the volkstaal.' Orders for the Afrikaans Bible poured in in such numbers that it took some time before they could be executed. Some parishes ordered a copy for every child, and crowds streamed to the railway station when the bulk order arrived. At one of several festivals a copy was presented to the prime minister.[96]

Afrikaans made rapid headway in other spheres. The first academically trained Afrikaner historians returned from Europe by the end of the 1920s. They would almost all publish their work in Afrikaans.[97] In 1932 the five-volume study of the Carnegie Commission of Inquiry into the poor-white problem was published in Afrikaans and English. In a review, N.P. van Wyk Louw commented that the report was written in 'a flowing and gripping style.'[98]

Between 1934 and 1937 W.E.G. Louw, N.P. van Wyk Louw, Elisabeth Eybers and Uys Krige published their first volumes of poetry, a flowering of poetic talents. These poets, called the *Dertigers* or Generation of the Thirties, broke radically with their predecessors' romantic tradition. The Dertigers did not concentrate on the local and typical of the Afrikaner experience, but addressed universal themes in poetry of a far higher quality than the work of the previous three decades.[99]

The leading figure was N.P. van Wyk Louw, a lecturer in education at the University of Cape Town, poet, playwright and essayist. He wrote poetry with a wide range of references to world literature, and also contributed articles on world politics to an Afrikaans youth magazine, *Die Jongspan*. Louw joined the Broederbond in 1934, as would his only peer as poet, Dirk Opperman. Louw was initially attracted to National Socialism, but by the end of the thirties had abandoned it. He strongly opposed, perhaps even hated, Jan Smuts, seen by him as someone only committed to a *colonial* nationalism.

Louw's essays of the late 1930s, published in two volumes under the titles *Lojale Verset* (Rebellious Loyalty) and *Berigte te Velde* (Reports from the Field), would have a ma-

---

96 E.C. Pienaar, *Die triomf van Afrikaans* (Cape Town: Nasionale Pers, 1933), pp. 404-9.

97 The first academic history in Afrikaans was written by Coenraad Beyers, *Die Kaapse Patriotte, 1779-1791* (Cape Town: Juta, 1929).

98 *Die Huisgenoot*, 19 May 1933, p. 19.

99 J.C. Kannemeyer, *Die Afrikaanse literatuur, 1652-1987* (Pretoria: Academica, 1988), pp. 129-70. For translations of their work see A.P. Grové and C.J.D. Harvey, *Afrikaans Poems with English Translations* (Cape Town: Oxford University Press, 1962).

jor impact on the Afrikaner intellectual debate.[100] For Louw, the new Afrikaans literary movement had to free itself from a colonial mentality, always receiving cultural direction from Europe or Britain as the nucleus of the Commonwealth.

But Louw also wanted the movement to break with the existing pleasant local realism and idealization of rural life. Half of the Afrikaners had become urbanized, and sharp class divisions had appeared within the community. Life had become 'grimmer, harsher and more naked.' Writers and poets were now grappling with the same issues as their counterparts in Europe, but Louw wanted them to seek their own solutions, their own version of an intellectual and cultural life. 'Everything, indeed all that moves modern man, his joys and sorrows, must find expression in our literature . . . The Afrikaner is nothing more or less than a modern man in an Afrikaans environment.' In such a literature colored and black people could not be mere stereotypes but full human beings. Books must go beyond 'simple liberal solutions' and 'grapple with the entire burden of our nation's fate.'[101]

At times Louw stressed the spiritual and almost mystical character of nationhood, but he also spelled out a message contrary to the uncritical celebration of the work of other Afrikaner nationalists. In his perspective there was no metaphysical volk or people waiting to be 'awakened.' The right of a people to exist was neither a natural right, nor could the Great Powers guarantee it (a reference to the Munich agreement guaranteeing the status of Czechoslovakia). A people 'had to be created anew on a daily basis through the will and the act.'[102] Success was not predetermined and indeed, in the case of the Afrikaners as a small group of people, the challenge was huge. It had to compete daily with English, a great, universal language.[103]

Louw embraced both a political and cultural nationalism, but recognized that nationalism seldom accepted limits – in his early years he wrote that it set 'the same absolute demands as a religion.' As an intellectual he did not shy away from this demand, but set a condition: the right of everyone, including the writer, to be *ten volle mens* – literally, to be fully human – in one's own culture, able to write and work without constraints. For him it was language that distinguished a nation and held its people together. This meant that the best talents among Afrikaans-speakers must choose Afrikaans as the language in which to publish. On the pressure on them to switch to a universal language, he commented: 'It is as if the aspiring young writer were told: "If you have something to say, my boy, then write in English. And if you do not know English well enough, then learn it like Joseph Conrad, but write in English and save your soul."'[104] Some of the most talented Afrikaner academics, in particular the historian P.J. van der Merwe

---

100 For analyses of Louw's ideas, see in particular J.J. Degenaar, *Moraliteit en politiek* (Cape Town: Tafelberg, 1976), pp. 55-91; Gerrit Olivier, *N.P. van Wyk Louw* (Cape Town: Human & Rousseau, 1992); Mark Sanders, 'Complicities: On the Intellectual', doctoral diss., Columbia University, 1998, and J.C. Steyn: *Van Wyk Louw,* (Cape Town: Tafelberg, 1998). For an effective response to Olivier's jaundiced view see J.C. Kannemeyer, *Ontsyferde stene* (Stellenbosch: Inset, 1996), pp. 62-76 and the Steyn biography.

101 These passages come from a speech given in 1936; see N.P. van Wyk Louw, *Versamelde prosa* (Cape Town: Tafelberg, 1986), vol. 1, pp. 5-12.

102 Louw, *Versamelde prosa,* vol. 1, p. 101.

103 Steyn, *Louw,* 1, p. 140.

104 Cited by André Brink, *Mapmakers* (London: Faber and Faber, 1983), p. 96.

and the legal scholar J.C. de Wet, were publishing work of outstanding quality in Afrikaans by the end of the 1930s.

Louw understood that Afrikaans could not survive without serving needs that went beyond nationalism: '[Our] entire striving to remain separate through our language can only be justified through the wealth of irreplaceable values that we bring forth in that language.'[105] Later he moved beyond this. Afrikaans was not a white man's language but the first South African language to be rooted both in Europe and in Africa, a medium that could give expression to the best thoughts of both continents.[106]

Louw introduced two important concepts to combat abuse of the nationalist idea, the first, the *oop gesprek* – literally an open-ended conversation – to prevent the debate from bogging down in dogma. Afrikaner identity was not something fixed but fluid, and nationalist ideas about survival had to be weighed against Christian moral precepts and the ideals of liberty and justice. The second concept was *lojale verset* – loyal resistance or rebellious loyalty, in contrast to loyalty that was a call to the blood, to a narrow, uncritical nationalism. Criticism to him, was, indeed, another form of loyalty; it served as the 'conscience of a nation.' Without criticism a people was lost; there was a need for fearless critics who assailed complacency and pettiness and who were prepared, if the imperative of national renewal required it, to break structures down to their foundations. He recommended 'a never-sleeping suspicion' against 'all systems and intellectual constructions that wanted to argue away or solve the tensions and tragedy in the universe.'[107]

He recognized that the development and promotion of Afrikaans as a language had to a large extent been taken over by the organization men – the FAK, the Broederbond, and other nationalist organizations. Forming organizations was a successful way of resisting the pull of the English and African cultures while an authentic culture was being built, he said, but he was well aware of the threat that the culture would be considered a 'finished' product with 'cultural leaders without culture' setting themselves up as guardians of an ossified culture, driving out all that was daring and innovative. The biggest danger was complacency.

Louw knew that politicians wanting to justify an oppressive order would abuse his loyalty to the nationalist cause, but he had made a conscious choice. A 'loyal resister' voluntarily accepts the limits and obligations of identifying with a people. In order to be heard, he needs to be connected to his people, 'inextricably linked in love, fate and guilt to the people that he dares to castigate: he does not speak of "they", but of "us".' He does not love the people for what they are but for what they can become. 'He must be prepared to go down with them if there is no alternative.'[108]

Louw's 1938 invitation to Afrikaners to remain cultural nationalists, even if they found political nationalism repugnant, would retain its appeal for the rest of the century.

---

105 Louw *Versamelde prosa*, vol. 1, p. 164
106 *Insig*, November 1998, book section, p. 16.
107 Louw, *Versamelde prosa*, vol. 1, pp. 171-2. Louw belongs among the kind of intellectuals discussed in Michael Walzer, *The Company of Critics: Social Criticism and Political Commitment in the Twentieth Century* (New York: Basic Books, 1988).
108 Louw, *Versamelde prosa*, vol. 1, pp. 166-8.

The return of history: the politicization of the Great Trek and Anglo-Boer War

The 1930s saw an upsurge in the interest in Afrikaner history that would ultimately lead to the development of a distinctive Afrikaner nationalist school of South African history. One of the most remarkable features of the public debate between 1902 and 1934 was the public silence about the Anglo-Boer War. Participants found their personal memories of the war too painful to want to talk publicly about them. Between 1906 and 1931 only nine books about the war were published in Dutch or Afrikaans. *Die Burger* wrote that a veil had been thrown over the British concentration camps because Afrikaners were 'ashamed of the way in which women and children of a brave nation had been treated.' Because it was taught so poorly in schools, the younger generation was ignorant about 'these traumatic events.'[109]

During the 1930s a new generation of Afrikaners sought to rediscover themselves through acknowledging both the heroism and the suffering of the war.[110] A spate of popular books on the war suddenly appeared, along with numerous articles in popular magazines and newspapers, almost all glorifying the Boer fighters, particularly the heroic resistance of the Bittereinders, and almost all attacking the deplorable conditions in the concentration camps, largely responsible for the death of 26,000 Boer women and children.

The Great Trek also received much attention from both popular and academic historians, especially as the commemoration of the event in 1938 approached. Van Wyk Louw's choral play *Die Dieper Reg* (The Higher Justice) portrayed the Voortrekkers as heroes and heroines who followed the 'call of their blood.' The celebrations gave Malan and his party a unique opportunity to spread the message that the Afrikaners as a people had had to fight their own battles for survival and could still rely only on themselves.

By the second half of 1938 the celebrations, organized by the Afrikaanse Taal- en Kultuurvereniging, were attracting mass enthusiasm among Afrikaners. Nine ox wagons staged a trek from Cape Town. One route went to Pretoria, where the cornerstone of a massive new monument in honor of the Voortrekkers was to be laid on 16 December, the date of the Battle of Blood River. The other route led to the scene of the battle in northern Natal.

The re-enactment of the Trek turned out to be an electrifying event, sparking mass Afrikaner enthusiasm as the wagons wound their way through hamlets, villages and cities across the land. Men and women, often clad in Voortrekker dress with the men sporting Voortrekker beards, met the wagons. At solemn ceremonies wreaths were laid on the graves of Afrikaner heroes, and streets were re-named for Voortrekker leaders. 'Die Stem van Suid-Afrika' (The Call of South Africa) for all practical purposes was elevated to the Afrikaners' national anthem, while the *volksliedjies* – folk songs from the FAK volume – became part of popular culture. From that time *braaivleis* (barbecue), a re-enactment of how the Voortrekkers cooked their meals on the veld, became fashionable among city people.[111]

---

109 J.C. Steyn, *Trouwe Afrikaners* (Cape Town: Tafelberg, 1987), pp. 191-206.
110 For a general discussion see Ian Burema, 'The Joys and Perils of Victimhood', *The New York Review of Books,* 8 April 1999, pp. 4-9.
111 See the description by Moodie, *The Rise of Afrikanerdom*, pp. 180-81.

The culminating event in Pretoria on 16 December was attended by a crowd of over 100,000. Writing thirty years after the event, a journalist, Schalk Pienaar, who accompanied the wagons from Cape Town, remarked: 'It brought about positively the same result as that which occurs negatively when war breaks out or is being waged, when the volk feels its very existence being threatened. The peaceful wagons made the volk mightily aware of its own existence.'[112]

The celebrations were meant to be above party politics, but the NP was the major beneficiary. At the mass meeting on 16 December at Blood River, Malan spoke in vivid historical images in singling out the plight of the urban poor Afrikaners as the greatest challenge to Afrikaner survival. Smuts attended the celebration in Pretoria, but did not speak. Hertzog did not participate in the ceremony to lay the Voortrekker Monument's cornerstone in Pretoria; he was invited but made his acceptance conditional on the organizers inviting the governor general since the state would contribute most of the funding for the monument. The implication was that 'God Save the King', the British anthem, had to be sung, which caused an outcry. Hertzog withdrew and spent 16 December quietly on his farm, dismissing the event as the work of a small band of people bent on causing discontent. A bitter enemy of everything Malan and his party supported, he warned against 'soiling the youthful innocence' of Afrikaner culture and dragging 'the holy things' of Afrikanerdom into politics.[113]

Z.K. Matthews, a black intellectual and leading figure in the African National Congress, tried to strike a positive note. The centenary, he wrote, could demonstrate a 'large-heartedness and a generous attitude towards former foes.' He pointed to a statement made at a recent DRC conference that the Voortrekkers had advocated social separation without implying that Africans, in consequence, were to 'be oppressed or hindered in their development.' For Matthews, the best Voortrekker monument, apart from an improvement in African health services and education, would be training Africans 'for work among their own people in services *for their benefit*' (his emphasis).[114] The architects of apartheid would soon take up this challenge in a way that Matthews in all probability did not anticipate (Chapter 13).

Entrepreneurial capitalism and ''n Volk red homself' (A volk saves itself)

A remarkable feature of the South African economy is that no nationalization occurred in the first two or three decades of the twentieth century when it was dominated by foreign capital. The fact that English-speakers in South Africa acquired control of a large part of the British-controlled companies between the outbreak of the First World War and the end of the Second World War helped to avert a crisis. Although politically dominant, the Afrikaners had only a very small share of the non-agricultural private sector of the economy. By 1939 Afrikaners controlled or managed no large industrial undertaking, no finance house, no building society, no regular commercial bank, no consumer asso-

---

112 Schalk Pienaar, *Getuie van groot tye* (Cape Town: Tafelberg, 1979), pp. 8-9.
113 *Hertzog-toesprake,* vol. 6, pp. 113, 151-57; *Die Burger*, 30 January 1939.
114 Z.K Matthews, 'Future Race Relations in South Africa', *Race Relations,* vol. V, no. 4 (1938), pp. 84-6. I wish to thank Albert Grundlingh for the reference to this remarkable article.

ciation, and no company listed on the Johannesburg Stock Exchange. The Afrikaner share in the private sector in the entrepreneurial function is calculated as follows: one per cent in mining, three per cent in manufacturing and construction, eight per cent in trade and commerce, and five per cent in finance.[115]

The fact that nationalist politicians did not embark on nationalization must firstly be attributed to South Africa's membership of the Empire. Nationalization would have incurred heavy diplomatic and economic costs and inflamed relations between the two white communities. Much of the steam generated by the lack of Afrikaner economic power was taken out of the system by the establishment of parastatal corporations, in particular the Iron and Steel Corporation (Iscor). Managed largely by Afrikaners, these corporations played an important part in carrying out the policy of Hertzog's Pact government of promoting secondary industrialization and protecting local industry. Michael O'Dowd, in later years a director of the Anglo American Corporation, wrote: 'The primary credit [for the policy] belongs to the Afrikaners, and it was in effect opposed by many, if not all, English-speaking South Africans.'[116]

Some mouthpieces of English-speaking opinion reacted in a hostile way when suggestions were made to mobilize Afrikaner capital to capture for the Afrikaners a part of the urban economy. The Johannesburg *Rand Daily Mail* wrote that 'the sponsors of economic segregation in trade and industry cannot ultimately avoid the charge they are fanning the flames of racial bitterness in South Africa.'[117] W.H. Hutt, perhaps the most prominent economist of his time in South Africa, called it a 'war' against the British section of the community and part of 'the half century-old fight against the *Uitlanders*.'[118] By contrast, J.L. Gray, an academic of the University of Witwatersrand, observed that nothing could be more damaging to an understanding of the conflicts in the white community 'than the complacent belief that the Afrikaans-speaking population have no legitimate and serious economic grievances.'[119]

A strong case has recently been made in abstract terms that an economic minority, like the Afrikaners, suffers more than it would gain in collective action against an economic majority (the white English-speakers, in the South African case).[120] A.C. Cilliers, a prominent Stellenbosch academic and polemicist of the 1930s and 1940s, anticipated this in issuing the warning that 'economic segregation' could easily boomerang.[121] Accordingly, Afrikaners active in promoting economic mobilization went out of their way to give assurances to the business world. T.E. Dönges, later a cabinet minister, said that the Afrikaners were intent on increasing their economic share fairly and peacefully. He added that they had no right to expect others to help them and were too proud to ask others for

---

115 The estimate of Jan Sadie, cited in Heribert Adam and Hermann Giliomee, *Ethnic Power Mobilized: Can South Africa Change?* (New Haven: Yale University Press, 1979), p. 170.

116 Michael O'Dowd, 'An Assessment of English-speaking South Africa's Contribution to the Economy', in André de Villiers (ed.), *English-speaking South Africa Today* (Cape Town: Oxford University Press, 1976), p. 149.

117 *The Star,* 14 July 1941.

118 *The Cape Argus*, 15 August 1946.

119 Scholtz, *Ontwikkeling van die politieke denke*, vol. 8, pp. 61-5.

120 G.S. Becker, *The Economics of Discrimination* (Chicago: Chicago University Press, 1971); for an application to South Africa see Steenekamp, 'Discrimination', pp. 49-66.

121 A.C. Cilliers, *Hertzogisme en die handel* (Stellenbosch: Pro Ecclesia, 1941).

help to work out their economic salvation. They did not intend to embark on a boycott of English firms, but they implored English-speakers to maintain a 'benign neutrality' while the Afrikaners were finding their economic feet.[122]

A stumbling block to overcome was anti-capitalist sentiments in Afrikaner ranks. None of the few larger Afrikaner enterprises was started in the classic capitalist mould of entrepreneurs taking risks in order to reap profits for themselves.[123] The Nasionale Pers published newspapers at a loss because they spread the nationalist message. The insurance companies Sanlam and Santam were mutual corporations, investing primarily in low-risk bonds and property. The farmers' co-operatives, founded between 1920 and 1940, were not geared towards making profits.[124] The NP periodically proposed to nationalize the mines and banks.

The anti-capitalist tendency was exacerbated by the collapse of a number of Afrikaner firms because of corruption and fraud. Afrikaners became deeply suspicious of business people. A Dutch visitor was told that people engaged in trade were dishonest.[125] Very little risk capital was available by the 1930s. An excessive 'familism' had developed in the Afrikaner community – people entrusted their capital only to their own immediate family, rarely to those outside and certainly not to strangers or a company. Building an enterprise of some size required a willingness to trust people beyond the family circle with capital, a willingness absent on the frontier and slow to develop in the cities among Afrikaners. In 1939 Hendrik Verwoerd remarked that Afrikaners were 'almost over-organized on the cultural terrain and unorganized for economic purposes.'[126]

When, in the 1920s, L.J. du Plessis, a prominent Broederbond member, first put forward the idea of a bank, convinced that Afrikaners were economically too weak to advance through the capitalist system, he advocated the establishment of co-operatives to build up a bank and a shopping chain.[127] In 1933 the Executive Council of the Bond decided to start a savings bank to mobilize Afrikaner capital to finance Afrikaner enterprises and employ the Afrikaner poor, but the state refused permission for the registration of a commercial bank. Instead a co-operative was established by the Bond's treasurer, J.J. Bosman, and some sixty Broeders. Called the Volkskas (People's Bank), it started up in Pretoria with paid-up capital of £5,000, and with Bosman as the first manager.[128] Bond and FAK secretary, I.M. Lombard, traveled the country to raise funds 'for all FAK bodies and Volkskas.'[129] Cultural and economic mobilization had become entangled.

Without Bosman and his nationalist zeal the bank would probably not have survived; U. Jooste, its first chief accountant, declared that it would have crashed at an early stage

---

122 *HAD*, 15 April 1941, col. 6367-68.

123 Cited by Du Plessis, *'n Volk staan op*, p. 29: Scholtz, *Ontwikkeling van die politieke denke*, vol. 8, p. 322.

124 For an overview of Afrikaner economic history, see J.L. Sadie, 'Die ekonomiese faktor in die Afrikaner-gemeenskap', in H.W. van der Merwe (ed.), *Identiteit en verandering* (Cape Town: Tafelberg, 1974), pp. 84-101 and his *The Fall and Rise of Afrikaner Capitalism* (Stellenbosch: US Annale, 2002); E.P. du Plessis: *'n Volk staan op* (Cape Town: Human & Rousseau, 1964).

125 Scholtz, *Ontwikkeling van die politieke denke*, vol. 8, p. 57; C.C. Nepgen, *Die sosiale gewete van die Afrikaanssprekendes* (Stellenbosch: CSV, 1938), pp. 224-5.

126 Du Plessis, *'n Volk staan op*, p. 121.

127 Stals, 'Geskiedenis van die AB', p. 125.

128 O'Meara, *Volkskapitalisme*, pp. 102-3.

129 Pelzer, *Afrikaner-Broederbond*, p. 122; *Volkshandel*, June 1947.

'if honor and selfish motive were the driving forces', rather than the need to capture a stake for the Afrikaner people in the banking sector.[130] During the 1940s, Volkskas shed its co-operative character to become a regular commercial bank. It operates today as ABSA, the banking group in the country with the highest gross income of South African banks.

The high rate of economic growth that the country experienced from 1933 boosted the standard of living for whites and virtually eliminated white urban unemployment. By the late 1930s Afrikaner farmers had recovered from the Depression and drought. They were aided by farming co-operatives, which had grown rapidly since the 1920s, offering a service without the profit motive and a low-interest advance on the coming crop. The government stabilized the prices of the principal products through new control boards. A considerable part of the risk of farming was removed by the guarantee of a minimum price. By 1939, when the Second World War broke out, the most enterprising farmers were ready for the boom period that followed. It was also possible for the government to provide much better education and training for whites. As they rose up the job ladder they had less and less cause to fear competition from people of color.

The financial resources of the Afrikaners had dramatically increased. One estimate of 1939 said Afrikaner savings were about £100 million and the Afrikaner purchasing power about the same. Yet little risk capital was made available. Farmers tended to re-invest their profits in their farms, and most of the other Afrikaners put their savings in safe investment havens like banks, building societies and trust companies. T.E. Dönges observed that Afrikaner capital was mainly in bonds, 'absolutely useless' for mobilizing capital to support new Afrikaner businesses.[131]

The 1938 centenary celebrations of the Great Trek provided a spur for the raising of capital, with D.F. Malan and the Free State church leader J.D. ('Father') Kestell suggesting that the best tribute to the Voortrekkers would be to save poor Afrikaners through a *reddingsdaad*, a rescue act. They stressed that only limited help could be expected from the state or the corporate world. *'n Volk help homself* (A people rescues itself), a call that Kestell made, soon captured the imagination. The Afrikaner Broederbond decided to assign the FAK the task of organizing a congress to discuss setting up a large *volksfonds* (people's fund) for the rehabilitation of the Afrikaner poor.[132] Early in 1939 the Broederbond's Executive Council had made up its mind against a 'charity plan.' It preferred deploying Afrikaner savings and capital in enterprises that could 'save' the Afrikaner poor by employing them. Along this route the Afrikaners could also become 'autonomous economically.'[133]

Senior executives at the Cape Town-based insurance company Sanlam came to a similar conclusion. Sanlam was eager to escape from the narrow limits of insurance and agricultural credit to which it was subjected, and to establish its own finance house to centralize efforts to attract Afrikaner savings for investment in promising enterprises.[134]

---

130 Anonymous, *Die bank van oom Bossie,* issued by Volkskas, 1978, p. 128.
131 Du Plessis, *'n Volk staan op*, pp. 112-13.
132 Stals, 'Geskiedenis van die AB', p. 131.
133 Du Plessis, *'n Volk staan op*, p. 95.
134 Grietjie Verhoef, 'Nationalism and Free Enterprise in Mining: The Case of Federale Mynbou, 1952-1965', *South African Journal of Economic History,* 10, 1 (1995), pp. 93-4.

The driving force of the South African economy was the mining houses obtaining investment funds through their financial corporations, which, as listed companies on the Johannesburg Stock Exchange, attracted funds from investors worldwide. The Afrikaner nationalists took this as their model, but they wanted their finance house to marry three quite different objectives: make profit for its shareholders, promote the collective advancement of the Afrikaners and help Afrikaners to escape from poverty by Afrikaner employers offering them respectable jobs.

Tienie Louw's proposal for a finance house to the Sanlam board captured the spirit of Afrikaner entrepreneurship at that time: It was self-evident that an Afrikaner finance house would have to observe sound business principles, and that the profit motive would not be excluded. 'But while management would try to make the greatest possible profits for its shareholders, the main purpose will always be to enhance the Afrikaner position in trade and industry.'[135]

The initiatives of Sanlam and the Bond would not make much impact as separate enterprises. The Bond leadership had little business experience and, acting on its own, Sanlam would be seen as furthering its own interests. The Bond-Sanlam alliance that came about provided the credibility vital in a campaign to attract Afrikaner savings for investment. It can hardly be a coincidence that several Sanlam senior executives, at this point, accepted invitations to become members of the Bond.[136]

The alliance's first step was to hold an economic congress, called the Eerste Ekonomiese Volkskongres (The First Economic Congress of the People). It met in October 1939 in Bloemfontein, and was attended by politicians, businessmen and academics. The poorwhite issue as such received little attention. *Dominees* or church ministers and populist politicians were conspicuous by their absence. The speakers read like a 'Who's Who' of future Afrikaner entrepreneurs.

C.G.W. Schumann, economics professor of Stellenbosch, one of the leading speakers, suggested a formula for making the poor whites part of a project, based on private initiative, to get the Afrikaans people to 'rescue themselves.' He urged delegates not to think of the poor-white question in isolation, and suggested that too much attention was being devoted to this 'unhealthy part' of the people. The task was rather one of 'strengthening the healthier elements in the Afrikaner community and in doing so enhance the position of the weaker elements.' A single 'rescue deed' could not rehabilitate a people. The road that he suggested was, in fact, nothing but a long march through the institutions of private enterprise. The Afrikaner poor would not be saved by charity or public works but by getting Afrikaners to support the fledgling Afrikaner enterprises, which would, in turn, employ Afrikaners. Entrepreneurs creating employment for the poor and hard-working employees were all engaged in a common nationalist enterprise.[137] Schumann sketched a picture of employers and workers united in a shared Afrikaner project in which the question of profits or exploitation was pushed to the back burner.

A considerable effort was made to break down the prevailing opposition among Afrikaners to a form of capitalism in which individuals were enriched without the commu-

---

135 J.P. Scanell, *Uit die volk gebore: Sanlam se eerste 50 jaar* (Cape Town: Nasionale Boekhandel, 1968), p. 46.
136 Du Plessis, *'n Volk staan op*, p. 112.
137 Du Plessis, *'n Volk staan op*, p. 106-12.

nity benefiting. In his opening address L.J. du Plessis defined the goal as mobilizing 'the volk to conquer the capitalist system and to transform it so that it fits our ethnic nature.'[138] This adapted capitalist philosophy was later called *volkskapitalisme*, or capitalism of the people. It meant that free enterprise was not intended primarily to create wealth for individuals for their own sake, or for a handful of individuals. It had to help the Afrikaners escape from their economic thralldom and gain for the people their legitimate share of the economy.

The Volkskongres created three institutions: a finance house, a chamber of commerce and an organization to assist in a 'rescue action.' The most important was the finance house, Federale Volksbeleggings (FVB), controlled by Sanlam. Afrikaners were asked to engage in conventional investment in shares in sound Afrikaans enterprises. By 1943 more than £2,000,000 of new investment had gone to buy shares in Afrikaner companies, mostly of FVB. By the end of the Second World War, FVB had major investments in fishing, wood, steel, chemicals and agricultural implements. Bonuskor, an investment corporation in the Sanlam group, was the first Afrikaner company listed on the Johannesburg Stock Exchange, posted on 26 May 1948, coincidentally also the day when the NP captured power.

One of FVB's first loans to a small Afrikaner enterprise was to a company belonging to a young entrepreneur, Anton Rupert. Within two decades, Rupert would build up the Rembrandt group of companies as a world-scale conglomerate with interests in tobacco manufacturing, wine production and luxury goods. The first shareholders were primarily Afrikaner tobacco and wine farmers. Rupert expressed himself in the classic idiom of the *volksbeweging*. He defined the purpose: 'to further our nation's progress and to help Afrikaners to gain their rightful place in industry and their future as employers and employees.' Dirk Hertzog, his partner in building up the Rembrandt organization, stated: 'Our overriding concern was to prove that, by standing together, we [the Afrikaners] could take our place in the business world with dignity and honor.'[139]

FVB investment in mining in the early 1950s led to its acquiring control over a mining house. In 2001 this mining house had the controlling interest in the Billiton Corporation, which in that year merged with Broken Hill Proprietary, an Australian corporation, to become the world's top mining and minerals business with a market value of almost £25 billion. Within fifteen years of the Volkskongres the strong anti-capitalist sentiment in Afrikaner ranks had been dissipated and, along with that, the reluctance of Afrikaners to invest in Afrikaner-run private enterprises.

The 1939 economic congress also established the Reddingsdaadbond (RDB) or Rescue Act Society. The RDB, by 1947, had 67,131 members in 381 branches, with Nico Diederichs as full-time organizer. Its divisions or chapters included culture, the economy, farmers, women and white labor. Even school children were asked to contribute sixpence each month. The original idea was for the RDB to collect £500,000 in a fund for capital investment in Afrikaner enterprises and various cultural projects. Less than one-

---

138 Du Plessis, *'n Volk staan op*, p. 104.
139 W.P. Esterhuyse, *Anton Rupert* (Cape Town: Tafelberg), 1986, pp. 24-5.
140 Gwendolen Carter, *The Politics of Inequality: South Africa since 1948* (London: Thames and Hudson, 1958), p. 259.

third of this was raised; some invested in FVB shares, some going to Afrikaner organizations and the rest used for study loans. The RDB's most important contribution was encouraging Afrikaners to patronize Afrikaner enterprises. When war broke out almost all the enterprises in rural towns were in the hands of South Africans of British, Jewish or Indian descent. By the end of the war the Afrikaners had taken over many of these.[141]

The Broederbond, too, constantly encouraged its members to support Afrikaner enterprises. In 1941 it issued a circular to its divisions listing ten economic duties for all 'proper' Afrikaners, among them these: 'Every Afrikaner must be a policyholder of an Afrikaans insurance company . . . [and] must save and invest his savings in an Afrikaans institution.'

The Afrikaanse Handelsinstituut (AHI), founded in the wake of the 1939 congress, established Afrikaner business chambers across the country and published a journal, *Volkshandel*, influential with Afrikaner businessmen. In the war economy the emerging Afrikaner businessmen gravitated towards the National Party. The small-scale Afrikaner traders and manufacturers were up against established, large-scale English companies that received governmental preference in the system of war rationing. Their business problems became ethnic grievances. The AHI and Afrikaner farmers resisted attempts by government and large-scale enterprises to drive down agricultural prices. The AHI's president told farmers that 'they must invest their capital in the right places: part of their capital must be invested in Afrikaner investment and business undertakings.' Afrikaner business supported the apartheid program that was being developed during the 1940s, particularly the demand that African urban labor be kept without rights.[142]

In 1951 yet another economic *volkskongres* was held, this time in a mood of self-congratulation. L.J. du Plessis noted that the poor-white question had been solved and that the Afrikaners had entered into key points of the urban economy. For Afrikaans businessmen the channeling of capital to Afrikaner enterprises had replaced the rescue action. Anton Rupert felt that after so much success the Afrikaners had to widen their horizons. First, it was necessary to encourage immigration since there already was a lack of skills, and, second, Afrikaner businessmen had to found a 'Bantu Development Corporation' without private gain that had to help blacks to start enterprises in the reserves. It would show the Afrikaners' good intentions and sincerity towards blacks.[143]

The watershed of war

South Africa inevitably became embroiled in the war that broke out in Europe in September 1939. The right of South Africa not to participate in Britain's wars was one of the most burning issues among Afrikaner nationalists during the first three decades of Union. After the Statute of Westminster of 1934 was passed, General Hertzog, for one, believed that South Africa's autonomy was assured, and in September 1938 he cemented this by tying the cabinet to a position of firm neutrality if Britain joined the war. Smuts seemed to have gone along with this, but with the German invasion of Czechoslovakia he changed his mind. He believed that South Africa, regardless of the political costs, was

---

141 Broederbond Circular 8/40/41 issued in the course of 1941.
142 O'Meara, *Volkskapitalisme*, p. 157.
143 Du Plessis, *'n Volk staan op*, pp. 182-8.

obliged to help stop Germany under Adolf Hitler. For him South Africa's freedom and
the future of Western civilization, even of the human race, was at stake. Yet it was inconceivable by mid-1939 that he would take the country into a war on a very small majority in Parliament, and with most of the electorate in all probability opposed to it.

When, just before a session of Parliament on 4 September 1939, Hertzog proposed
that South Africa remain neutral, Smuts and half the cabinet favored intervention. In the
parliamentary debate Hertzog blundered by ignoring any malevolent and aggrandizing
purpose in Nazi foreign policy. To him Britain and France had brought the war on themselves by imposing the humiliating peace treaty of Versailles on the Germans in 1919,
much as had been the case with the republican Afrikaners at Vereeniging in 1902.

But the other part of his speech carried great force: Entry into the war on a split vote
would severely damage the trust between the two white communities. 'The Afrikaner
people twice tried to bring together the Afrikaans-speakers and the English-speakers
into one nation,' he said, referring to the formation of the South African Party at the time
of Union and Fusion, which brought about the establishment of the UP. He warned that
if the second attempt also failed the shock to the Afrikaner people would be so severe
that it would take years for it to recover. 'But if it comes as a result of a war with which
we have nothing to do it will affect or national life for fifty or even a hundred years.'

Malan formulated his support for Hertzog in telling terms. If South Africa had no ties
with Britain it certainly would not have entered into a war caused by a conflict in distant
Eastern Europe. If South Africa were to be sucked into every war into which Britain entered, he would say out loud: 'You can talk as much as you wish about freedom, but we
are a country of slaves.' Smuts was also blunt. Hertzog's speech sounded like a justification for 'Herr Hitler's actions.' He had no doubt that what was at stake was the same as
that at the time war broke out in 1914: the quality of the system of government, 'the fate
of humanity and the future of our civilization.'[144]

Hertzog's motion was defeated by a vote of 80-67 that went largely along the ethnic
division in the white community. The governor general refused his request to dissolve
Parliament and to call a general election. *Round Table*, an authoritative journal, considered it likely that the anti-war faction would have won such an election at that time.
Instead the governor general asked Smuts to form a government, and he took South
Africa into the war. It was a watershed event in white politics, also destroying the middle ground with respect to the issues of race and color well before the NP announced
its apartheid program.[145] Without the political polarization brought about by the war,
which from the war vote in 1939 was increasingly drawn on language lines, Malan's NP
would have been unlikely to come to power in 1948. The premier Afrikaans man of letters, N.P. van Wyk Louw, typified the radicalization the vote produced among the nationalist intelligentsia; he thought it despicable to fight 'for those who have conquered
your own people.' The only option now was to construct an 'uncompromising spiritual
Afrikanerdom.'[146] Smuts told an Irish journalist after the war that, in view of the trials

---

144 *HAD*, 1939 Special Session, cols. 20-22, 26-30, 50 (author's translation of the Afrikaans Hansard).
145 Newell Stultz, *Afrikaner Politics in South Africa, 1934-48* (Berkeley: University of California Press,
    1974), pp. 146-59.
146 Steyn, *Louw*, pp. 278-9.

and tribulations South Africa had suffered by participating in the war, it was quite clear that Ireland 'had to do what it did' by remaining neutral.[147]

The English-speaking whites, in general, considered it their duty to assist the Allied forces, including acting against those in South Africa who opposed the war. Afrikaners did not boycott the war as a group, as was sometimes alleged. About half the fighting troops were Afrikaners. Most did not participate in the war out of idealism but for 'rather more prosaic pecuniary considerations.'[148] The war offered an opportunity for large numbers of white males with few skills. According to some estimates, one-third of whites between the ages of twenty and sixty were incorporated in a full-time capacity in the domestic and overseas war effort at its height. Smuts proudly declared that this record surpassed that of many of the Allied nations.

Hertzog's break with the United Party did not immediately unite nationalist Afrikaners; instead came a bitter deepening of divisions in nationalist ranks. In January 1940 Malan's NP party and Hertzog's supporters merged in a party called the Herenigde (Reconstituted) National Party under Hertzog's leadership. But while Malan supported Hertzog with enthusiasm, the more radical nationalists in the north constantly undermined him. Hertzog was cool towards the idea of a republic and rejected the plan of some of the northern nationalists to consign the English language, and perhaps even English-speakers, to a subordinate place. After a showdown at a party congress Hertzog withdrew from the party and Malan became leader.[149]

Thirteen of Hertzog's followers in Parliament went on to found the Afrikaner Party under the leadership of N.C. Havenga, Hertzog's most loyal ally. Hertzog himself was now a disillusioned and embittered man, and before his death in 1942 he said that National Socialism's 'true character' was closely attuned to the 'spiritual and religious outlook of the Afrikaner nation.' He opposed a form of democracy that made it possible to declare war against the people's will. But he had not given up his commitment to a form of democracy that was modeled, not on the Westminster system, but on that of the old Boer republics. He also discouraged militant action against the war effort. To Anton Rupert, a future entrepreneur, and some other Afrikaner students who privately asked his advice about militant resistance, he suggested that they return to their studies. The Afrikaners would take over after the war by way of the ballot booth, he assured them.[150]

Hertzog's views revealed the crisis for democracy, but also the initial appeal of the Nazi model. In 1933 Louis Weichardt had founded the South African Christian National Socialist Movement, popularly known as the Greyshirts. It was inspired by the outbreak of violent anti-Semitism and Brownshirt thuggery in Germany under Adolf Hitler. Although membership apparently never rose to more than two thousand, it put pressure on the right flank of Malan's party. The party nevertheless was not in any significant way influenced by the far right in racial policy.

During the early war years two more organizations that were openly pro-German and

---

147 Louis Louw (ed.), *Dawie, 1946-1964* (Cape Town: Tafelberg, 1965), p. 10.

148 Albert Grundlingh, 'The King's Afrikaners: Enlistment and Ethnic Identity in the Union of South Africa's Defence Force in the Second World War', *Journal of African History*, 44, 3 (1999), p. 360.

149 Michael Roberts and A.E.G. Trollope, *The South African Opposition*, (London: Longmans, 1947), pp. 50-51.

150 Roberts and Trollope, *The South African Opposition*, pp. 129-32; C.M. van den Heever, *Generaal J.B.M. Hertzog* (Johannesburg: A.P. B., 1943, p. 754); Interview with A. Rupert, 30 May 1998.

pro-dictatorship operated; one was *Nuwe Orde* or New Order (NO) formed in September 1940 under the leadership of Oswald Pirow, a member of Hertzog's cabinet before the 1939 split. In 1942 it had seventeen parliamentary representatives, all elected in 1938 on a UP ticket, advocating an Afrikaner variant of National Socialism. But the most important anti-war movement was the paramilitary Ossewabrandwag (OB), founded to perpetuate the 'ox wagon' spirit of the 1938 celebrations. In January 1941 the OB came under the leadership of J.F.J. (Hans) van Rensburg, who had served as administrator of the Orange Free State. He was a strong admirer of Nazi Germany and considered himself a man of action rather than a 'cultural fire-eater' (a reference to the NP). He campaigned for 'a free Afrikaner republic based on nationalist-Socialist foundations.' Explicitly rejecting parliamentary politics, the OB insisted that as the only mass movement it represented all Afrikaners. It pinned its hopes on a victory for the Axis powers and German help in establishing an Afrikaner republic. The OB had its own division of storm troopers, called the *Stormjaers*, who actively resisted the war by acts of sabotage and a handful of assassinations.

As a quasi-military organization, the OB, riding on the wave of Afrikaner disillusionment with 'British-Jewish' democracy, acquired a mass membership, estimated by some to be as high as 100,000. It was soon widely ridiculed for its efforts to inspire enthusiasm by uniformed military drills and the introduction of military distinctions of rank. In the Transvaal several prominent members of the nationalist intelligentsia were not only OB members, but even prominent Nazi supporters. Albert Geyer dismissed Nico Diederichs, chairman of the Broederbond's Executive Council from 1938 to 1944, as a 'Nazi through-and-through.'[151] L.J. du Plessis, perhaps the most influential of all Broeders, H.G. Stoker, the leading Calvinist thinker, and Piet Meyer, deputy secretary of the Bond, all published books and articles that represented thinking close to Nazi ideology.[152]

Malan's NP continued to support parliamentary politics and rejected all violent resistance to the war effort. But, on almost every occasion, Malan declared that South Africa should pull out of the war. The government, operating on the assumption that most Afrikaners were anti-war, took the necessary security precautions, including internment on a large scale. One war measure that outraged the anti-war camp was the order that civilians, including farmers, had to surrender their arms and ammunition. Malan protested: 'The Afrikaner is turned into an alien in his own land and is disarmed.'[153] The government also instructed civil servants and teachers to resign from the OB and, at the end of 1944, from the Broederbond as well. But the most hated measure was internment without any prior trial, which was used on a large scale. John Vorster, a young lawyer who would become prime minister, was among the internees. In 1944 J.G. Strijdom, also a future prime minister, expressed his outrage. English-speakers and their Afrikaner supporters were using internment against Afrikaner nationalists despite the fact that the

---

151 Patrick Furlong, *Between Crown and Swastika: The Impact of the Radical Right on the Afrikaner Nationalist Movement in the Fascist Era* (Johannesburg: Witwatersrand University Press, 1991), p. 211.

152 See *Die OB*, particularly the columns for which Meyer was responsible; Moodie, *The Rise of Afrikanerdom*, pp. 225-31.

153 Malan, *Glo in u volk*, p. 46. For a comprehensive discussion of the war measures see P. W. Coetzer (ed.), *Die Nasionale Party* (Bloemfontein, INEG, 1994), vol. 5, pp. 272-453. See also Annette Seegers, *The Military in the Making of Modern South Africa* (London: Tauris, 1996), pp. 60-61.

country's security was not at stake. It had also happened in 1914-18 and in the Anglo-Boer War. 'What right have[they] to call for racial peace and co-operation if every time England is at war the Afrikaans-speakers are humiliated and crushed?'[154]

Many Afrikaners felt victimized by the way in which the government issued its wide array of special permits, especially for rationed petrol, regardless of whether or not they opposed the war. The Smuts government in effect had suspended the non-partisan civil service; it turned the security forces and civil service into instruments of war policy, blurring all distinctions between the ruling party and the civil service. It gave the assurance that no one would be commandeered to fight overseas or beyond the equator, but those who volunteered for service there wore a highly visible orange tab on their shoulders. It was a political distinction; one section of the white population considered the tabbed soldier loyal, the other section saw him as disloyal. Within the armed forces the lives of those who refused to fight were made miserable, and scores were compelled to resign, finding it difficult to get jobs afterwards in any branch of the civil service. One practice that inflamed relations between political parties was the Department of Military Intelligence's transmission on a regular basis of intelligence reports to Louis Esselen, Secretary of the United Party, who used them not only for the war effort but also against the NP.

Other controversial war measures also politicized the civil service. Because large numbers of civil servants had joined the army, the government had to relax the bilingual requirements for new recruits; it promoted to graded posts a number of people who could speak only English. 'Security requirements' also led to denial of promotion to a large number of Afrikaners suspected of anti-war sympathies, often on the word of an informer. So widespread were complaints from Afrikaners on the railways that the NP government, in 1948, appointed a Grievances Commission to investigate. Some 2,875 railway employees testified then that, although innocent of anti-war activities, they had been denied promotion for posts ranging from clerical posts to that of general manager.[155]

A key question in the early war years was whether the NP would be outflanked by the OB and NO, or whether it would become a pro-Nazi party. A recent study by Patrick Furlong argues that Malan's NP, the OB and NO formed an 'interconnecting web', and that the nationalists in the Transvaal, in particular, were a 'hybrid variant' of 'authoritarian and populist ingredients, reminiscent, although never an exact facsimile, of European fascism.'[156] There were, indeed, some NP leaders whose speeches in the early war years were thinly veiled attacks on democracy and the rights of English-speakers, and Malan himself at one stage accepted as a party discussion document a draft constitution for South Africa, drawn up by Verwoerd. It proposed a Christian-National republic in which Afrikaans would be the first official language and English a second or supplementary official language.

But Furlong's attempt to depict the nationalist leaders as proto-Fascists lacks conviction. It represents a poor understanding of both the Nazi and the Afrikaner nationalist movement. The Fascist and other radical right-wing movements were driven by a

---

154 *HAD*, 1944, cols. 911-12 (author's translation of the Afrikaans Hansard).
155 Davies, *Capital, State and White Labour*, p. 298.
156 Furlong, *Between Crown and Swastika*, pp. 102, 224-26.

singular commitment and blind obedience to a leader, a belief in the redemptive power of violence, excessive nationalism and an operational ideology prescribing action. It is far-fetched to describe the NP as Fascist or proto-Fascist in this sense. Malan, and J.G. Strijdom in the Transvaal, were elected as leaders and could be outvoted. Their party was divided over a key issue like the republic, and apartheid had not yet become one of the pillars of party unity. Followers were free to express their views, and join or leave the party, and even to denounce it or the leaders without fear of retaliation. Almost without exception the NP leaders found distasteful the efforts to imitate the paramilitary style of the Fascist movements and rejected violence for all practical purposes. Furlong offers no convincing evidence that radical right-wing movements like the Ossewa Brandwag or the Greyshirts had anything but a fleeting impact on the Afrikaner nationalist movement or on apartheid as an ideology.

From early in 1942 Malan and other NP leaders, including Verwoerd and Strijdom, were unequivocally rejecting National Socialism as an alien import into South Africa, and endorsing parliamentary democracy. They condemned sabotage by the Stormjaers, the OB's paramilitary wing. The major Afrikaner churches expressed a similar view. The influential *Kerkbode,* official journal of the DRC, declared in March 1941: 'The Church could never associate itself with any form of state domination or intervention as is found in the European totalitarian system, which undermines the Church in its freedom.'[157] In 1945, a day after Germany capitulated, the pro-war and pro-government daily *The Star* declared: 'We do not suppose Dr Malan and his disciples were ever Nazis at heart, or that they had any real affection for the Hitler regime.'[158] The HNP was pro-German and anti-Britain. What it wanted was not so much a German victory, as denial of a decisive victory for Britain.

Between 1941 and 1948 Malan displayed shrewd strategic abilities in, first, out-maneuvering and, ultimately, in crushing the NP's opponents on its right. The party, he often said, was the 'mother', and the 'ballot box' the only proper political course.[159] In 1941 NP members were instructed to resign from the OB. Support for the OB and New Order steadily dwindled, and in the 1943 election the NP felt confident enough to reject an electoral pact with these organizations.

The 1943 election was fought on the war issue. Smuts asked his followers for a mandate to see the war through and to make the world safe for democracy. The NP, for its part, asked voters to reject UP 'imperialism' and to express themselves in favor of democracy for South African whites. The UP won eighty-nine, the HNP forty-three seats. Many Afrikaner voters had abstained, but Malan could claim that the opposition was once again one consolidated whole. *Die Burger*, the party's most influential supporter, summed up the significance of the election in a sentence: 'There is no other model than the ballot booth for [our] aspirations.'[160]

Thus one of the most important political battles of the early war years was that won in the Afrikaner nationalist movement by those who favored a democratic system over those who preferred or would accept a dictatorship. After the 1943 election the NP was

157 Scholtz, *Ontwikkeling,* vol. 8, p. 158.
158 Scholtz, *Ontwikkeling,* vol. 8, p. 252.
159 Malan, *Glo in u volk,* pp. 37-43.
160 *Die Burger,* 30 July 1943, editorial.

no longer a small party, but had achieved the status of an alternative government. In the 1938 election 40 per cent of Afrikaners were estimated to have voted for the United Party; approximately 30 per cent did so in 1943. Another drop of ten percentage points for the UP would bring the NP within reach of victory. Malan now began to assuage the fears of English-speakers by stressing that both white sections would have equal language and cultural rights. 'We have to live together in this land, also after the war,' he observed early in 1942.[161] A republic would be declared only after a mutually acceptable test of opinion, such as a referendum.

The consolidation of nationalist unity

The Afrikaner Broederbond tried its best to rebuild Afrikaner nationalist unity, and refused to choose between the NP and OB in the early war years. It also contributed relatively little to the making of the apartheid plan. In 1934 a Bond sub-committee recommended 'comprehensive mass segregation' for blacks, but this did not differ significantly from mainstream segregation. The Bond established a sub-committee on the racial issue, but this committee could not report significant progress. Leading Bond members attended meetings of an 'Afrikaanse Bond vir Rassestudie', founded in 1935, but this foundered a few years later. The 1938 Broederbond general conference (called the *Bondsraad*), felt that since a white consensus on policy towards blacks had already been formulated in the legislation, their attention had to focus on policy towards coloreds. The Bond's Executive Council asked a sub-committee to identify an organization to study the racial problem 'on behalf of Afrikanerdom.' Stals noted that this request 'landed in the doldrums.'[162] In 1940 L.J. du Plessis, one of the most prominent Broederbond academics, did not use the word 'apartheid' in an article on the 'native question.' He called segregation 'the national policy' that had not yet been fully implemented 'because Afrikanerdom had not yet had the chance to carry it out.'[163] Where the Broederbond, with its large contingent of teachers, lecturers and church ministers, did play a prominent role was in promoting Christian-National education (see pp. 468-9).

In 1945 Afrikaner support for the UP and OB had dwindled to such an extent that the Broederbond's Executive Council decided to single out the NP as the sole party that could help the Afrikaners attain their political aspirations. Such a decision would have been inconceivable before the outbreak of the war.[164] In 1944 the Bond initiated a conference on the racial question, but while some broad policy guidelines were suggested, no practical policy was formulated. Two years later a plan had still not crystallized, and the Broederbond intelligentsia in the north were largely dispirited. Albert Hertzog, a Broederbond stalwart, despondently told the Executive Council of the Bond in August 1946: '[The] Afrikaner people is without inspiration . . . and without that no power can emanate from it.' A year later he wrote in his diary that the NP was divided between a conservative Cape group and a northern group, among whom were Hendrik Verwoerd

---

161 Malan, *Glo in u volk,* pp. 60-62.
162 Stals, 'Geskiedenis van die AB', pp. 133-41.
163 L.J. du Plessis, 'Die Naturellevraagstuk', *Koers*, 8, 1 (1940), pp. 5-9.
164 Stals, 'Geskiedenis van die AB', pp. 178-81.

and J.G. Strijdom, who were idealists. He added: 'Unfortunately they are half-baked idealists who, except for a few vague principles, do not propose a major new direction.'[165]

At a 1947 Broederbond conference basic disagreements about key aspects of the racial
policy surfaced. Speakers resigned themselves to the fact that Africans would remain part
of the white socio-economic system for a long time. After the meeting Bond secretary
Ivan Lombard called the proceedings 'depressing', because no solutions had been suggested for the numerous problems that were identified. The Bond as a body agreed with,
and supported, apartheid, but it did not develop and formulate it.[166] A survival plan
grafted as an operational ideology onto Afrikaner nationalism would produce much
greater unity. But by 1948 the Broeders had no such plan.

The orthodoxy among historians is still that the NP victory in 1948 was the outcome
of the Broederbond's manipulative abilities, the upsurge of mass nationalist sentiments
in the 1938 commemoration of the Great Trek and, above all, the formulation of apartheid as an ideology in the early 1940s. However, these factors, separately or jointly, were
not decisive. The crucial turning point was the Afrikaner nationalists' outrage over the
country being taken into the World War on a split vote, confirming in their eyes South
Africa's continuing subordination to British interests, and the disruption brought about
by the war effort.[167] This was the catalyst that enabled the NP to draw together diverse
people in a powerful alliance: cultural nationalists seeking cultural autonomy, farmers
seeking labor, businessmen seeking investment capital and clients, and workers seeking
racial protection and opportunities for training; and all of them seeking to secure Afrikaner political survival and a changed relationship between South Africa and Britain.
This nationalist alliance formed the basis of the NP victory in 1948; apartheid would
soon become the operational ideology of the alliance, and would form part of the NP's
1948 platform, conceived primarily by people in the DRC concerned with strategy towards missions and by the nationalist intelligentsia in the western Cape. Their ideas
had started to take shape in the 1930s and were fleshed out in the five years between
the 1943 and 1948 elections.

---

165 B.M. Schoeman, *Die Broederbond en die Afrikaner-politiek* (Pretoria: Aktuele Publikasies, 1982), pp. 27-30.
166 Stals, 'Geskiedenis van die AB', pp. 203-8.
167 For a discussion see also Newell Stultz, *The Nationalists in Opposition, 1934-1948* (Cape Town: Human
    & Rousseau, 1974); Brits, *Op die vooraand van apartheid*, pp. 8-38, 44-75; Dan O'Meara, *Volkskapita-
    lisme: Class, Capital and Ideology in the Development of Afrikaner Nationalism* (Cambridge: Cambridge
    University Press, 1983), pp. 181-221; P. W. Coetzer (ed.), *Die Nasionale Party, vol. 5: 1940-1948*
    (Bloemfontein: INEG, 1994), pp. 394-441.

Chapter 13

The Making of a Radical Survival Plan

'Go forward in faith': The liberal vision

In 1936, J.H. Hofmeyr, the chief exponent of liberalism in the ruling United Party (UP), stated: 'Certainly the approach I have been adumbrating calls for vision and imagination and faith in no small degree.' The liberal approach could give no guarantees as to where it would lead politically. 'Whether, in fact it will ensure the white man's position in South Africa, will make South Africa safe for European civilization, who shall say?'[1]

Although small in numbers, liberals in some areas had changed the terms of the debate. Crude racist thinking had lost respectability, first among English-speaking liberal scholars and then also among many of the first generation of Afrikaner academics staffing the new Afrikaans universities. Very few white social scientists still held to the old idea of the 'repression' of blacks on account of their supposed racial inferiority. As Saul Dubow has shown, the new theme in the segregation ideology of the 1930s was that of 'cultural adaptation', drawn from the discipline of anthropology. Each culture was deemed to be worthy in its own right and capable of progressive development along its own separate lines. This new ideology was 'able to feed upon a wide range of racist assumptions without being pinned down to a patently untenable theory of biological racism.'[2]

By the early 1940s liberals had taken a further step. They rejected the notion of separate cultures developing along their own lines. They proposed an open or common society and implicitly accepted racial integration, starting with economic integration, as an inexorable process to which the state had to adapt. Liberal intellectuals advocated cultivating a shared political identity, a common loyalty, a lingua franca – English – and, in broad terms, a common Christian faith.[3]

---

1 *The Star,* 14 August 1936.

2 Saul Dubow, 'Race, Civilization and Culture: The Elaboration of Segregationist Discourse in the Inter-War Years', in Shula Marks and Stanley Trapido (eds.), *The Politics of Race, Class and Nationalism in Twentieth Century South Africa* (London: Longman, 1987), p. 89.

3 John D. Shingler, 'Education and Political Order in South Africa, 1902-1961', doctoral diss., Yale University, 1973, p. 223.

For these liberals the foundation of a liberal order was a new education policy. In a tone that was 'aggressively optimistic, modern, efficient and empiricist'[4] Jean van der Poel, an historian with an Afrikaans background who taught at the University of Cape Town, wrote that 'if Western culture should eventually prevail over the Bantu, as it seems now to be doing, where is the cause for sentimental repine? . . . It is not the task of native education to prevent the Europeanization of the Bantu . . . [but] to give him knowledge which is neither black nor white but the public possession of mankind.' A liberal of an older generation, J.D. Rheinallt Jones, said that to drive blacks back into Bantu culture was to set 'the Native's face in the wrong direction, not towards liberty but into thralldom.'[5]

These liberals were swimming against a rough segregationist tide. During the 1980s, when the battle for the South African state reached its final stages, opponents of apartheid propagated the myth of a mild racial order prior to the late 1940s. Piet Cillié, editor of Die Burger, parodied the myth as follows: 'After a period of relatively good and easy race relations before 1948, South Africa, after a change in government, was suddenly plunged into nearly four decades of increasing racial tension and racial hatred. An evil ethnic ideology was imposed on a largely unsuspecting country . . . preventing it from developing the system of friendly relationships towards which it was heading.'[6]

The myth shows no signs of dying out, but Alfred Hoernlé, the most outstanding English-speaking liberal intellectual in the 1930s and early 1940s, would have found it astonishing that people in the final decades of the century could think that race relations were relatively benign before the 1948 election. In an address given in 1936, he said that a visitor from Mars would immediately be struck by the pervasiveness of racial exclusion and discrimination. The visitor, he wrote, would come to only one conclusion: '[There] was a dominant urge towards segregation, which has molded the structure of South African society and made it what it now is.'[7]

Rejection of racial mixing was not restricted to the segregationists. Hoernlé himself opposed racial mixing between whites and blacks, not on biological but on social and political grounds. He considered 'race purity' essential to 'racial respect and racial pride'; it was the view of 'the best public opinion, the most enlightened racial self-consciousness, of natives no less than of whites.'[8] The Forum, a journal founded to support the liberalism of Jan Hofmeyr, was 'revolted' by miscegenation and advocated residential and social segregation.[9]

Hoernlé noted that there existed two kinds of segregationists: the single-minded type, who looked upon blacks as a danger and cared only for the white group; and the 'double-minded' segregationist, who aimed at the 'parallel development' of white and black interests under white control. The double-minded segregationists found that 'whilst they

---

4 Shingler, 'Education and Political Order', p. 228.

5 Jean van der Poel, 'The Education of the Native in South Africa', The Bluestocking, 1, 3 (1931), p. 13; Shingler, 'Education and Political Order', p. 230.

6 Piet Cillié, Baanbrekers vir vryheid (Cape Town: Tafelberg, 1990), p. 65.

7 R.F. Alfred Hoernlé, Race and Reason (Johannesburg: University of the Witwatersrand Press, 1945), pp. 96-7.

8 The Star, 25 September 1931; Die Vaderland, 18 June 1935.

9 Alan Paton, Hofmeyr (Cape Town: Oxford University Press, 1971), p. 232.

have to satisfy single-minded segregationists at all costs, they find it very difficult to extract from the latter any genuine concession to the pro-Native humanitarian other side
of their own policy.'[10] A.L. Geyer, who as editor of *Die Burger* from the mid-1920s to the
mid-1940s was one of the most influential figures in the Afrikaner nationalist movement, would later explain the development of apartheid as a trade-off. If one uses
Hoernlé's terms it was between single-minded and double-minded segregationists.

> Common people are interested in and understand small and everyday things. Large
> concepts like black nation-states are on the periphery of their consciousness. They
> look distant in time and occasionally also in space. But they understand mixed resi-
> dential areas, trains and beaches. They understand separate post office counters
> and toilets. Give them the things that are small but also important to them, and they
> also buy the large things in theory.[11]

For Geyer and other members of the nationalist intelligentsia the development of the
reserves into African homelands represented 'the large things, worth working for.'

In view of the weak bargaining position of the double-minded segregationists, not to
speak of the liberals, Hoernlé challenged the latter to consider afresh the meaning of liberal principles in application to a multi-racial situation. 'Clearly we liberals have not
made up our minds whither we are going, or whither we want to go. We owe it to ourselves to answer the question: what is our long-range goal?'[12] He was pessimistic about
the prospects for a political solution; while he was certain that white supremacy would
one day crumble, he saw no prospect that whites over the short to medium term would
allow Africans to advance socially, let alone to be enfranchised.[13]

In Parliament Hofmeyr was the main torchbearer of liberalism. In his contribution to
the momentous 1936 debate on the Cape African franchise, he did not embrace common citizenship as 'an absolute thing.' His point was that it was unjust and politically unwise to take away someone's vote. But the Second World War prompted him to assert
his liberalism more forcefully. In a 1945 address, 'Christian Principles and Race Problems', he identified 'faith against fear' as the central issue. He admitted that there was
ground for fear, particularly the 'hard central fact of the numerical preponderance of the
Bantu.' The right approach nevertheless was to 'stand firm on principle' and 'to go forward in faith.' The outcome might be unpredictable, but had a reasonable chance of
success.[14] In 1946 he attacked the *Herrenvolk* mentality of many South African whites
and finally clarified his position: 'I take my stand for the ultimate removal of the color bar
from our constitution.' The nationalists directed special criticism at Hofmeyr, acting as
prime minister when Jan Smuts was abroad, and his most likely successor. They identified him as the government's Achilles heel.[15]

---

10 Hoernlé, *Race and Reason*, pp. 97-8.

11 Cillié, *Baanbrekers vir vryheid*, p. 70.

12 R.F.A. Hoernlé, *South African Native Policy and the Liberal Spirit* (Johannesburg: University of Witwatersrand
Press, 1939), p. 180.

13 Phyllis Lewsen, *Voices of Protest* (Johannesburg: Ad Donker, 1988), pp. 97-9.

14 Jan Hofmeyr, *Christian Principles and Race Problems* (Johannesburg: SA Institute of Race Relations, 1945),
pp. 16-17; N.P. van Wyk Louw, *Versamelde prosa* (Cape Town: Tafelberg, 1986), vol. 1, p. 503 (the essay was
first published in 1946).

15 Paton, *Hofmeyr*, pp. 176-8, 328-9.

'Segregation has fallen on evil days': The UP's ambivalence

From its base of white supremacy and segregation, the UP government (1939-1948) followed a two-track policy. While one track elaborated the structures of segregation, the other track accepted the imperatives of the booming war economy and the strong demand for labor. It moved cautiously away from the policy of economic segregation and the exclusion of blacks from social services.

In 1943 the government established a Coloured Affairs Department (CAD) in the Ministry of the Interior. It also set up a Coloured Advisory Council (CAC) to serve as a consultative body. In taking these steps the UP gave colored leaders the assurance that the intent was not to treat them as a separate group or impose residential segregation, but simply to improve administrative efficiency.[16] Yet these segregated institutions developed their own momentum. The CAC soon insisted that colored workers be protected from being undercut by African migrant workers. The Cape Town City Council began to restrict the issuing of work passes to Africans.

The government followed a similar approach in dealing with the small Asian community. In 1936, Asians, who lived predominantly in Natal, numbered approximately 220,000. They faced continuing opposition from sections of the white population, who insisted on their repatriation, or failing that, compulsory segregation. Although the majority remained poor, there was progress among the elite. There were Asian shops in the business districts of numerous Natal and Transvaal towns. By 1950, 19 per cent of all retail enterprises in the country belonged to Asians, although they formed only three per cent of the population. In the city of Durban, Asians had managed to acquire property on a considerable scale in the so-called white town. The Smuts government froze all property transactions between whites and Asians, and in 1946 introduced a Bill that created white areas and Asian areas. No Asian could buy property in a 'white' area.

The Bill gave the Asians representation (but only through white representatives) in Parliament and in the Natal and Transvaal Provincial Councils. Hofmeyr was appalled by the introduction of a color bar in Asian representation. He wrote to Smuts: 'It is the last straw breaking the camel's back and I cannot be party to it.' He suggested 'a loaded franchise on a common roll.'[17]

It could hardly escape the NP's attention that the UP, in a piecemeal manner, was producing parts from which the apartheid machine could be assembled, in particular the basic element of classifying people into racial groups. Pressure had been building up in the provincial councils and local authorities for a 'national register.' Early in 1948 the provinces sent a memorandum to the central government requesting such a register on the grounds that it existed in other countries.[18]

For the NP it was easy to argue that, if only for bureaucratic reasons, such a register had to differentiate between the different population groups. How could some measures be implemented if officials did not know who was an African, an Asian or a colored person? Only Africans were subjected to pass laws and could vote for the Natives Represen-

---

16 *HAD, 1944*, col. 6825-6876 (Afrikaans edition).
17 Paton, *Hofmeyr*, p. 315.
18 L.E. Neame, *The History of Apartheid* (London: Pall Mall Press, 1962), p. 89.

tative Council (NRC), Asians voted for their special representatives and, in the western Cape, colored workers, at the behest of the CAC, were being protected from competition with Africans. The segregation of colored people had intensified: a government commission recommended residential segregation. New suburbs were being built specifically for colored people, and a 1941 law required employers to segregate work, recreation and eating areas. In the Cape Peninsula the beaches were being segregated. An amendment to the electoral law provided for the compulsory registration of white voters only.[19]

Parallel structures had not yet been discredited. The African National Congress, at this stage a conservative and nearly defunct organization, decided to participate in the elections of the NRC, set up in terms of the 1936 legislation, but the more radical All African Convention (AAC) decided to boycott them. Among the colored people in Cape Town the introduction of the CAC and CAD triggered a groundswell of militancy. More radical opponents of white supremacy urged a boycott of parallel structures.

At the same time, however, government social policy was moving in a reformist direction. It gave the moderate African leadership some cause for cautious optimism. Smuts declared that the policy of trying to prevent black urbanization, and to keep black and white apart, had failed. 'Isolation has gone and segregation has fallen on evil days,' he said in 1942.[20] Midway through the war the government put the provision of old-age pensions, grants for invalids and unemployment insurance on a firmer footing, and established the principle that Africans had to be included in any social security scheme and in any legislation conferring such benefits. Africans could be trained as medical doctors, dentists and social scientists and for some other professions at some of the existing white universities. (They normally first went to Fort Hare College, the only tertiary institution for blacks.)

The government also no longer limited government spending on African education to the revenue from direct taxes collected from Africans. It provided free education, free books and free school meals in primary schools and increased its spending on secondary education. By the end of the war spending for African education was three times higher than ten years before. Despite the increased spending, however, most African children were not in school by 1948.

Nevertheless, all the changes under the Smuts government indicated an enhanced sense of government responsibility towards Africans and a more concrete recognition of their citizenship. Blacks experienced greater freedom during the war years than they had known before. Real black wages in the manufacturing sector were rising sharply.

Challenges to white supremacy

The 1940s saw new challenges to white supremacy by broadly based African organizations. The most militant movement was the Non-European Unity Movement (NEUM), founded in 1943 in response to a call from an AAC conference. It was supported by only a small number of people in the colored and black population, but in terms of intellectual and ideological sophistication it was far ahead of any other organization. It declared

19 Gavin Lewis, *Between the Wire and the Wall: A History of South African 'Coloured' Politics* (Cape Town: David Philip, 1987) , pp. 205-6.
20 Bernard Friedman, *Smuts: A Reappraisal* (Johannesburg: Hugh Keartland, 1975), pp. 164-6.

that whites were deliberately oppressing the subordinate population and exploiting all structures for their own benefit. NEUM called for universal franchise, compulsory education and full equality. In a section that became a major source of division, a new division of the land was suggested, which some interpreted as a call for a radical redistribution of land, favoring farm workers. Another source of division was over the capitalist system, which was inextricably linked with white supremacy.[21] Some Africans thought it 'stupid' to associate capitalism with white supremacy.

During the war years Dr A.B. Xuma began to revitalize the ANC by attracting a number of talented young men. Anton Lembede, Nelson Mandela, Oliver Tambo and Walter Sisulu were among the young professional men who entered the Congress Youth League (CYL), formally founded in 1944. It would soon call for the mobilization of Africans to reject their subordination. It did not envisage much white help, but did not rule out some compromise with them once the balance of power had changed. On three conditions whites could share 'the fruits of Africa': the abandonment of white supremacy, the acceptance of a proportional distribution of the land, and 'a free people's democracy.'[22]

For quite some time there were differences in the ANC over whether the struggle had to be waged primarily as a racial one, in which Africans stressing racial pride took the leading role, or a class struggle with workers as the dominant force. The ANC Youth League took a militant, Africanist line in propagating a creed that sought to develop African self-confidence through mass protests.

Xuma rejected white trusteeship and began insisting on common citizenship. The ANC's fight was 'not a fight against the government, but a fight for justice for all.' R.H. Godlo, another leading member, demanded for Africans the right to participate in 'the making of laws for the good government of people of all colors.' They wanted 'equality of opportunity in every sphere' and to be treated as 'co-partners in the country.' Blacks did not want to press their demands for political rights before the war ended, but Z.K. Matthews, the leading ANC intellectual, reminded white South Africans that the best way of 'defending freedom and democracy is to extend them during peace time to all sections of the community in the fullest measure.'[23] In 1943 an ANC conference in response to the Atlantic Charter, issued by the leaders of the USA and Great Britain, issued a pamphlet, 'The Atlantic Charter and African Claims', asking 'for full citizenship rights and direct representation in all the councils of state.'[24]

With the war's end the government clamped down again, restoring the pass laws and, now, for the first time, applied them in the western Cape as well. In 1946 some fifty thousand black miners came out on strike in thirty-two of the forty-five mines over low wages. Hundreds suffered injuries in clashes with the police. The NRC condemned the refusal of government to recognize African unions and the shooting of workers. Xuma and his executive were beginning to accept the need for a liberation movement.

---

21 Richard van der Ross, *The Rise and Decline of Apartheid* (Cape Town: Tafelberg, 1986), pp. 102-4, 200-11; Lewis, *Between the Wire and the Wall*, pp. 220-21, 241-53; F.G. Backman, 'The Development of Coloured Education,' doctoral diss., University of Stellenbosch, 1991, pp. 47-57.

22 Peter Walshe, *The Rise of African Nationalism in South Africa* (Berkeley: University of California Press, 1971), pp. 349-61.

23 *Common Sense*, 2, 12 (1941), p. 7.

24 Thomas Karis and Gwendolen Carter, *From Protest to Challenge* (Stanford: Hoover Institution Press, 1973), vol. 2, p. 215.

In 1947 the Natives Representative Council demanded the removal of all discriminatory laws. For liberals the moment of truth had arrived. Hofmeyr, acting prime minister,
told Z.K. Matthews that this put him in a difficult situation. The council also had to consider the matter from the perspective of the UP government, which could do nothing
that 'would be interpreted as a surrender.'[25] He wrote to Smuts at the United Nations,
where South Africa was facing an increasingly hostile world, about the NRC demands:
'Hitherto moderate [black] intellectuals are now committed to an extremist line against
color discrimination and have carried the chiefs with them. We can't afford to allow them
to be swept into the extremist camp, but I don't see what we can do to satisfy them which
would be tolerated by the European public.'[26]

The government ignored the NRC's resolutions on the removal of discrimination in
the labor market, the repeal of the pass laws and the extension of political rights to blacks.
It prompted the council to describe itself as a 'toy telephone.' It now demanded direct
representation, from the municipal council level up to Parliament. 'The Natives want
rights, not improvements,' Smuts noted in a private letter, but for him effective political
power for Africans was unthinkable. He told the liberal Edgar Brookes that 'our native
policy has to be liberalized at a modest pace, but public opinion has to be carried with
us.' The government's approach was 'practical social policy away from politics', carried
out 'more and more as finance permits.'[27]

The UP accepted that there would have to be less separation of the races. On the eve
of the 1948 election the NP claimed that the UP policy of 'integration' would lead to 'national suicide on the part of whites.' UP policy, by the mid-1950s, was a far cry from this.
It proposed to supplement the existing system of white native representatives in Parliament with a national body of African representatives of both the traditional and non-
traditional communities so that Africans could identify with the 'national interests' of the
country. It accepted the economic integration of all races as a dynamic process, if one
the government had to guide and control. Socially it considered Africans part of the South
Africa community and it pledged to give them 'a more definite and secure place in our
Western way of life.'[28]

But the UP's policy was full of fatal contradictions. This is clear from an account of
an exchange in Parliament between Harry Lawrence, a liberal UP parliamentarian and
a consummate politician, and NP members.

> [Lawrence] was attacking the Nats [nationalists] on their apartheid policy . . .
> but on this occasion interjections from the government benches forced him on
> the defensive.
> 'What is your policy?' they asked. 'Is it integration or segregation?'
> He tried to disregard the question and continue his attack but they repeated it,
> and he hesitated before replying.
> 'Our policy is one of partiality', he said, 'yes, partiality – partiality with justice!'
> It was an unfortunate answer and the Nats roared with laughter.[29]

25 Paton, *Hofmeyr*, p. 338.
26 W.K. Hancock, *Smuts: Fields of Force* (Cambridge: Cambridge University Press, 1968), vol. 2, p. 229.
27 Rodney Davenport, *South Africa: A Modern History* (Johannesburg: Macmillan, 1987), pp. 343-4.
28 Gwendolen Carter, *The Politics of Inequality* (London: Thames and Hudson, 1958), pp. 282-301.
29 Ray Swart, *Progressive Odyssey* (Cape Town: Human & Rousseau, 1991), p. 25.

'The spirit of apartheid': The DRC's faith

The first printed record of the term 'apartheid', used in its modern sense, dates back to 1929. In addressing a conference of the Free State DRC on missionary work, held in the town of Kroonstad, the Rev. Jan Christoffel du Plessis said: 'In the fundamental idea of our missionary work and not in racial prejudice one must seek an explanation for the spirit of apartheid that has always characterized our [the DRC's] conduct.' He rejected a missions policy that offered blacks no 'independent national future.'[30]

By 'apartheid' Du Plessis meant that the Gospel had to be taught in a way that strengthened the African 'character, nature and nationality' – in other words, the *volkseie* (the people's own). Africans had to be uplifted 'on their own terrain, separate and apart.' Blacks and whites had to worship separately to 'ensure the survival of a handful of [Afrikaner] people cut off from their national ties in Europe.' For Du Plessis it was not so much a matter of protecting privilege or exclusivity than finding a policy that concentrated on the *eie*, or that which was one's own, and which promoted what he called the *selfsyn*, or being oneself.[31] Implicit in this was the view that only identification with one's own ethnic community was authentic. Du Plessis envisaged the development of autonomous, self-governing black churches as a counter to English missionaries, who tried to produce converts by copying 'Western civilization and religion.'

The idea of an *eie* (or a *volkseie*) can be traced back to the early days of the Cape settlement. The Dutch East India Company emphasized the importance of the Dutch language and the Reformed religion in institutional life. Out of this developed the idea of a *volkskerk*, a people's church. In its most non-contentious formulation it meant that the church should take the linguistic, cultural and social character of its members into account.

The strongest influence on this line of thinking were the missionary societies in Germany, the Rhenish and the Berlin Mission Society in particular, which accentuated the need to give Asian and African people in the colonies the opportunity to become Christians within their own cultural framework. Between 1892 and 1902, Gustav Warneck, the most important German mission theorist, had published his magnum opus in three volumes. This work stressed the importance of converting the community at large to Christianity, and to establishing national churches that preserved both the mother tongue and traditional customs. These churches had to be self-supportive, self-governing and self-propagating.

This approach reflected the influence of German romantic nationalism, but there was also support for it in circles unaffected by it. At the first general Missions Conferences in South Africa, held in 1904 and 1906, several English-speakers spoke of giving Africans the scope and self-development they needed. There was, as a contemporary account noted, 'a sincere [interdenominational] regard for each other and each other's methods of work'.[32]

---

30 An earlier, eccentric use of the word 'apartheid' is recorded by Irving Hexham, *The Irony of Apartheid* (Toronto: Edward Mellen Press, 1981), p. 188.

31 J.C. du Plessis, 'Die ideale van ons kerk in sendingwerk', *Die NG Kerk in die OVS en die Naturellevraagstuk* (Bloemfontein; Nasionale Pers), pp. 22-5. I wish to thank Richard Elphick for pointing me to this pamphlet. See also Louis Louw (ed.), *Dawie: 1946-1964* (Cape Town: Tafelberg, 1964), p. 49.

32 J. du Plessis, *A History of Christian Missions in South Africa* (New York: Longmans, 1911), p. 465.

In 1912, W.C. Willoughby of the LMS in South Africa published a book in which he called for a 'self-supporting, self-propagating and self-governing indigenous church.'[33] Related to this was support for special education for Africans. A report to a meeting held in 1910 in Edinburgh, Scotland, which had brought together for the first time all the major missionary organizations in the world, criticized the tendency 'to reproduce (without sufficient regard to conditions of native life) methods of educational organization which were in force at the time in the home countries.' It stressed the importance of industrial and agricultural education 'adapted to the needs of the native races', and referred to the possible emulation of Hampton and Tuskegee.[34]

But from the 1920s the English churches, both local or foreign, steadily moved towards the ideal of a common society and promoted it by providing mission education that stressed Westernization and the central importance of a good command of the English language. By contrast, German missionaries and the DRC continued to stress the importance of indigenous customs and languages. The first DRC 'daughter church' was one formed by the Cape DRC out of several colored congregations in 1881. It grew rapidly, but remained dependent on the 'mother church' for clergy and financial support, and had to accept the overall authority of the white synod. By 1950 some 30 per cent of the colored population were members of the DRC mission church.

As regards Africans, the DRC in South Africa established a broad record of missionary activity in places like Rhodesia, Kenya and Nigeria. However, its missionary efforts among Africans in South Africa had lagged. The exception was the black DRC in the Orange Free State. Here the white DRC, which formed an independent synod in 1864, continued to be influenced by the DRC in the Cape. The Free State ministers received their training at the theological seminary at Stellenbosch, where N.J. Hofmeyr, a strong proponent of missionary work, remained professor until 1907. It was very likely as a result of his influence that the Free State church declared it to be the duty of every church council to accept responsibility for missionary work within the boundaries of the parish. Ministers must initiate such work and assist in it. Instruction and services took place in separate buildings and African catechists were appointed as assistants. Africans never attended meetings in the white church itself. Cultural and language differences were partly responsible, but the main factor was racial prejudice. DRC members had no intention of worshipping with anyone who was not white.

By 1910 the DRC in the OFS had fourteen missionaries working for it and had established forty mission congregations with a total of 6,839 members. In that year the white church founded a separate DRC for its black members, using the Mission Church for colored people as its model. The white synod held up a black 'daughter church' as an institution able to regulate itself in a way that suited the customs and 'direction' of black people. The 'mother' or white synod retained a veto over the decisions of its 'daughter', which remained financially dependent on it.[35] The DRC began to project the DRC 'fami-

---

33 W.C. Willoughby, *Tigerkloof* (London: Missionary Society, 1912), p. 25.

34 John D. Shingler, 'Education and Political Order in South Africa, 1902-1961', doctoral diss., Yale University, 1973, p. 177.

35 A.A. Odendaal, 'Die Nederduitse Gereformeerde Sending in die Oranje Vrystaat (1842-1910)', doctoral diss., US, 1970, pp. 546-61.

ly' of white, colored and black churches as an association of co-equal churches, each representing different peoples, but all equal before God as peoples.

In the Transvaal there were three Reformed Churches and the efforts to promote missions ran up against stronger resistance than elsewhere. The Hervormde Church did no mission work in principle, the Gereformeerde (Dopper) Church did very little, and the efforts of the DRC were undermined by personal disputes and a lack of resources. A church for DRC African converts was only established in 1932 when the Dutch Reformed Bantu Church of South Africa was formed.[36]

There were two areas in particular where the DRC was far behind the other churches. One was in ordaining black ministers. By 1911 English South African churches had 341 missionaries in the country and 171 ordained blacks; the DRC had 225 missionaries and only one ordained black.

The other area was in the provision of education to black and colored children. By 1920 education in South Africa was fully segregated. With the help of state subsidies, church or missions schools provided almost all the education for black and colored children. Most black education was in the hands of the Roman Catholic and the Anglican churches, with the state paying its subsidies on teachers' salaries over to them and other churches or missionary societies. The church bodies owned the school buildings, determined the syllabi and decided how much of the state subsidy would be paid over to the teachers. In the higher standards English was virtually the only medium of instruction, and the syllabi were largely based on the British model. Among nationalist educators in the Transvaal the exclusion of Afrikaans from the syllabi rankled. In 1936 Werner Eiselen, Chief Inspector of Native Education in the Transvaal, would condemn 'native education' for its one-sided nature, and asserted that 'efficient training should include a knowledge of both official languages.'[37]

DRC missions provided primary education for both colored and black children, but no secondary education for blacks. By contrast, English South African missions were educating nearly nine secondary school pupils per missionary. A major reason why the DRC lagged behind was political. There was a strong perception among Afrikaners that relatively well-educated blacks would demand to be put on an equal social and political footing with whites, and that English missionaries supported this demand.[38]

In the decade after the end of the First World War there was a surge in the African demands for education. It was not surprising that the white DRC in the Orange Free State took the lead among the DRC churches in developing a response, which was reflected in J.C. du Plessis' 1929 speech. The church was much more aware of the challenges facing the white church. Since the 1890s the Ethiopian movements had formed independent churches which attracted large numbers of Africans frustrated with the fact that all the main Christian churches were loath to advance Africans quickly in church offices. As early

---

36 J.T. Jordaan, 'Die ontwikkeling van die sendingwerk van die NGK in die Transvaal', doctoral diss., University of Pretoria, 1962, pp. 452-3.

37 Cynthia Kros, 'Economic, Political and Intellectual Origins of Bantu Education, 1926-1951', doctoral diss., University of the Witwatersrand, 1995, p. 189. See also pp. 158-88.

38 Richard Elphick, 'Evangelical Missions and Racial Equalization in South Africa, 1890-1914', unpublished paper, 1999.

as 1905 a DRC missionary in the Free State had published a pamphlet in which he observed that the Ethiopians want to make them entirely independent from whites. It is
an attempt to dig 'a gulf of hatred' between whites and blacks.[39] Another challenge
that manifested itself during the 1920s was that of the Industrial and Commercial
Workers Union of Africa, which for the first time rallied masses of Africans to fight under a trade-union banner. It mainly concentrated on urban constituencies, but in some
Free State districts it tried to recruit farm workers. A study noted that by the end of the
1920s 'the [Kroonstad] district was seething with rumors of pending unrest.'[40] The
town of Kroonstad was where the conference was held at which Du Plessis spoke in
1929. For DRC mission strategists, like Du Plessis and J.G. (Valie) Strydom, missions
secretary of the DRC in the Free State (no relation to the later prime minister), missions and politics had become intertwined. In his preface to the volume in which the
proceedings were published Strydom stated: 'By providing the native with the right
kind of Evangelization and the right kind of learning the danger of assimilation will be
removed.'[41] This was the kernel of the apartheid idea.

'Differential development' without 'complete segregation'

By the 1920s there was still no prominent figure in the DRC who advocated extending
the practice of segregated schools, parishes and churches to political rights and representation. Indeed Johannes du Plessis (no relation to J.C. du Plessis), a towering figure in
the DRC in the missions field, rejected any attempt to use the DRC approach as a justification for political or economic discrimination. A very influential figure, Du Plessis
defies labeling. Unlike D.F. Malan, he was unaffected by German romantic nationalism.
In an article published in 1910, Du Plessis, who was now a professor at the theological school in Stellenbosch, urged Afrikaners to govern Africans in a Christian manner.
In 1921 Du Plessis edited a volume with contributions from ten leading figures in the
DRC missionary circles who tried to defend the DRC against the charge of D.D.T.
Jabavu, an influential black academic, that it was 'an anti-native church.' The book
admitted that the record of the church with respect to black South Africans was not
bright, but pointed out that the DRC was the only large church in the country that had
to rely exclusively on local funding for missionary work. While the writers regarded
segregation as a 'most excellent theory', they were, as Richard Elphick pointed out,
'more aware of the ambiguities, contradictions and pitfalls of segregation than many
English-speaking theorists.'[42]

In the book the mission leaders did not restrict themselves to vague expressions of
goodwill towards blacks, but made striking concrete demands. Educated blacks had to
be exempted from the pass laws, black workers had to have the right to strike and the
contributors could see no reason why 'Bantu tradesmen' could not compete against

---

39 H.A. Roux, *De Ethiopische Kerk* (no publisher, 1905).
40 Helen Bradford, *A Taste of Freedom: The ICU in Rural South Africa, 1924-1930* (Johannesburg: Ravan
    Press, 1987), p. 4.
41 Preface to *Die NGK in die OVS*, p. x.
42 Richard Elphick, 'Missions and Afrikaner Nationalism', unpublished paper, 1999.

whites. They insisted on expanded secondary education for blacks.[43] In 1921 Du Plessis took the lead in bringing together some fifty leaders, both white and black, in a conference under the auspices of the DRC's Federal Council, a body of the DRC set up to deal with church issues across provincial boundaries. In Elphick's words, this meeting marked 'the highest level of consensus that Africans, English-speaking whites, and Afrikaners would ever attain on segregation.' It called for 'differential development of the Bantu', but rejected 'complete segregation.'[44] A plea for political segregation is strikingly absent.[45]

As Elphick remarks, Du Plessis developed the intellectual framework for the idea that the DRC was fundamentally a missionary church with a broad social responsibility, and that the church should help shape the social policies of South Africa. While Du Plessis was still a dominant figure there was little chance that the church would embrace a form of political segregation with discrimination and exclusion its main thrust. But he was soon to become bogged down in trying to defend himself against a heresy charge, which related to his modern Scriptural interpretation and only marginally to his views on politics and missions.

Within the church a conservative reaction had made itself felt by the end of the 1920s. It was expressed by Valie Strydom, who would become one of the leading exponents of what he called 'apartheid as the DRC's missions policy.' At a 1927 meeting organized by the DRC Federal Council, and attended by Afrikaans, English and black church leaders, it was suggested that the aspirations of the small Westernized African elite be accommodated. Strydom replied as follows: 'All natives were not as calm and intelligent as those present were. If they were, he would say, "Give them a chance." But the ICU and Ethiopian movement had most support, and he felt the few intelligent natives could never keep them down.'[46]

The new mood did not manifest itself in a rejection of Professor Du Plessis' work. Indeed many of his formulations would find expression and even be repeated verbally in future DRC missions policies.[47] In his major study, Wie sal gaan? Sending in Teorie en Praktyk (Who will go? Missions in Theory and Practice) that appeared in 1932, Du Plessis propagated the founding of Christian churches among non-Christian indigenous people that over time would support and govern themselves. Following some German studies of missionary work, he stressed the need for missions to strengthen the volksgees or national spirit.

'On their own terrain, separate and apart': missions and apartheid

The 1929 speech of the Rev. J.C. du Plessis, which represents the first recorded use of the term 'apartheid', was made against the background of growing concern within the DRC over recent developments. He expressed alarm over the spread of Ethiopianism, which

43 J. du Plessis, et al., The Dutch Reformed Church and the Native Problem (no publisher, no date, ca. 1921), pp. 6-29.

44 Elphick, 'Missions and Afrikaner nationalism'.

45 European and Bantu ... (Cape Town: DRC Federal Council of Churches, 1924).

46 Saul Dubow, 'Afrikaner Nationalism, Apartheid and the Conceptualisation of "Race"', Journal of African History, 33 (1992), pp. 218-9.

47 Richard Elphick, 'Missions and Afrikaner Nationalism'; D. Bosch, 'Johannes du Plessis'; J. du Preez, (ed.), Sendinggenade (Bloemfontein: NG Uitgewers, 1986).

was shared by other speakers. One asked: 'Who is today the best friend of the white man in the land? The native who got his education from the DRC. He is the greatest opponent of political agitators.'[48] In 1906 Lord Selborne, British High Commissioner in South Africa, had said something similar: missions were invaluable and saved the country thousands of pounds in policing expenses.[49]

The Kroonstad conference decided to draft a mission policy and submit it to the synod of the Free State DRC in 1931. At this synod meeting the church policy rejected *gelykstelling,* or racial leveling, and, with it, race degeneration and 'bastardization' as 'an abomination to every right-minded white and native.' Yet the DRC policy also affirmed that the 'native' possessed a soul of equal value in the eyes of God, and on a certain level was the equal of whites. But equality in the hereafter certainly did not mean any social equality in this world. To justify its rejection of gelykstelling, the church proposed that blacks develop 'on their own terrain, separate and apart.'[50]

This raised the question of the type of education that the church had to provide in the schools it now began to establish for blacks. DRC ministers had strong doubts about the emphasis most of the other churches and the missionary societies put on English as language medium to the detriment of African languages, and on the preparation of the child for participation in a common society with whites.

At a meeting in 1935 of the Federal Council of the DRC a common missions policy was formulated. The church was firm that 'education must not be denationalized', but must be based on the group's national culture, giving a prominent place to its language, history and customs. It called for Africans and colored people to be assisted in developing 'into self-respecting Christian nations.' Two aspects were new. For the first time coloreds were brought into the scheme as a separate nation. And the church put the stress on the equal worth of all 'self-respecting nations', while before 1935 it had emphasized the equal worth of all *individuals* before God.[51]

Thus DRC ministers and missionary strategists were first in the field to formulate an apartheid ideology.[52] Church ministers and theologians were much less inclined than secular academics or politicians to condone blatant racial discrimination on account of racial inferiority. For most of them there could be no question of a hierarchy of souls, churches or cultures. Grateful for the opening the church had given them, nationalist politicians and academics were careful not to offend the church's sensitivities.

A similar debate took place in the small *Gereformeerde* (Dopper) Church. The journal *Koers,* based in Potchefstroom, carried several articles in which African culture was portrayed as different from, but not inferior to, that of the whites.[53] God had ordained all

---

48 *Die NG Kerk in die OVS,* pp. 34-5.

49 W. Nicol, ''n Grootse Roeping', G. Cronjé, et al., *Regverdige rasse-apartheid* (Stellenbosch: CSV, 1947), p. 22.

50 This is reproduced as Appendix 2 in J.A. Lombard, 'Die sendingbeleid van die NGK van die OVS', doctoral diss., University of the North, 1985, pp. 308-13.

51 Theological School Library, US, 'NG Sendingraadnotules', unpublished minutes, p. 98. For a discussion see Johann Kinghorn, 'Die groei van 'n teologie',in J. Kinghorn (ed.) *Die NG Kerk en apartheid* (Johannesburg: Macmillan, 1986), pp. 86-9.

52 A different interpretation of the making of the apartheid plan is given by Saul Dubow, *Illicit Union: Scientific Racism in Modern South Africa* (Cambridge: Cambridge University Press, 1995), pp. 246-83.

53 For a recent discussion see J.H. van Wyk, 'Homo Dei', *In die Skriflig,* 27, 1 (1993) Supplement 1, pp. 39-60; and 'Geloof, etnisiteit en kontekstualteit', *In die Skriflig,* 35, 3 (2001), pp. 347-71.

these cultures and it was the Christian duty of whites to help Africans preserve their racial and cultural identity, their own, God-given *volkseie*.

Missions as models for social segregation

By the 1930s people concerned with formulating the DRC missions policy were extending their ideas to areas beyond religious organization. Again it was Free State ministers who took the lead. J.G. (Valie) Strydom, as missions secretary in the DRC of the OFS, strongly propagated Christian-National education, in order to imbue the black child with respect for the history, customs and culture of the ethnic community in which he or she was born. The idea that blacks primarily formed separate nations rather than constituting a single black race or nation had not yet crystallized. In territorial terms the apartheid scheme had in fact not yet moved much beyond segregated suburbs. Strydom was influenced by segregation in the USA and the idea of black separatism expounded by some black leaders in South Africa. In 1937 he addressed a North Carolina audience and after his return wrote of 'the policy of apartheid here in our land and the United States of America.' He held up the example of the American South with its segregated schools, churches and suburbs, as a model to be emulated for both colored people and blacks in South Africa.[54]

NP leaders began to claim that the apartheid system was built on the precedent set by the major churches in South Africa by willingly providing segregated education for black and colored people. In 1947 D.F. Malan, leader of the NP, remarked: 'It was not the state but the church who took the lead with apartheid. The state followed the principle laid down by the church in the field of education for the native, the colored and the Asian. The result? Friction was eliminated. The Boer church surpasses the other churches in missionary activity. It is the result of apartheid.'[55]

The DRC concern with mission and education policy soon became intertwined with another concern: the fate of its poorer members living in racially mixed suburbs and the attendant possibility of miscegenation. A Stellenbosch professor of theology wrote: 'The policy of segregation that is promoted by the Afrikaner and his church is in the best interests of both the white and the non-white.' He referred to 'the holy calling of the church with respect to thousands of the poor whites struggling to survive in the current economic world.'[56] A church commission stressed the sense of inferiority from which less skilled Afrikaners in these mixed suburbs suffered, and the need to help them to regain their sense of dignity.[57] DRC ministers believed that separate white suburbs were essential for stemming the growing class cleavages within the Afrikaner community, and for giving the poorer members a sense of dignity.

From the second half of the 1930s the government was moving towards segregated

---

54 J.G. Strydom. 'Die rasse-vraagstuk in Suid-Afrika', Federasie van Calvinistiese Studenteverenigings (compiler), *Koers in die krisis* (Stellenbosch: Pro Eccelesia, 1941), vol. 3, p. 245.
55 US Library, D.F. Malan Collection, Account of D.F. Malan's reply to the Transvaal delegation, 5 February 1947.
56 D. Lategan, 'Die krisis in die sendingkerk', *Gereformeerde Vaandel*, April 1939, p. 107.
57 For a succinct statement see *Die Kerkbode,* 19 June 1946; for an extended study see J.R. Albertyn et al., *Kerk en stad* (Stellenbosch: Pro Ecclesia, 1947).

suburbs for people who were not white, but some church ministers also wanted the state to go further and proclaim whites-only suburbs. A leading role was taken by G.B.A. Gerdener, Professor of Missiology at the University of Stellenbosch, whose father and father-in-law were both Rhenish missionaries, while he himself was one of the founders of the DRC mission church in the Transvaal.[58] In 1939 he endorsed segregated residential areas for colored people as well as blacks. In 1942 he became chairman of the Federal Mission Council (FMC) of the DRC. Policy towards missions and pseudo-scientific race theory soon became intertwined. In 1942, when the FMC petitioned the government to introduce segregation, it included in its submission a memorandum by a biologist, H.B. Fantham. He maintained that the colored offspring of white-black intermixtures displayed negative social and mental characteristics. In a 1943 meeting between an FMC delegation and Prime Minister Smuts, the delegation requested a ban on racially mixed marriages. Smuts rejected this, declaring that 'the line between white and colored people in many instances could not be drawn.'

The government was more sympathetic to the demand for residential segregation. Gerdener supported this, but differed from most other nationalists in urging that colored people must not be compelled to move to these townships. He seemed to think that residential segregation could be implemented fairly. At a 1945 conference of the DRC Sendingkerk (for coloreds) he demanded that colored townships had to be 'one hundred per cent with respect to privileges and facilities.'[59]

'A Christian and generous political approach'

The peculiar feature of apartheid as an ideology was its attempt to reconcile the demands for white survival and justice. But for those nationalists who were 'double-minded segregationists', to use Hoernlé's term, it was difficult to believe that the bleak, segregated townships could justify the denial of rights to black and colored people. They groped for a bigger idea that could motivate people. In 1940 the Rev. William Nicol of Johannesburg delivered a much-discussed sermon in which he stated that while he labored for the separate survival of the Afrikaner people, he would rather see the Afrikaners swamped by other peoples if they tried to survive without God and His justice. But how was the demand for justice to be met? Nicol proposed that 'self-determination had to be granted to the non-white races on every terrain of life.' Since no limits could be put on the development of blacks, there had to be a 'complete *afskeiding*', or segregation, as a solution that combined the Christian demand for justice with 'the need to give to our posterity a future as a European race.' This was not a plea for partition but for the development of the existing reserves, an idea that Gerdener also propounded.[60]

In 1944 Gerdener, through the FMC, joined with the Federasie van Afrikaanse Kultuurvereniginge (FAK) to organize a *volkskongres*, or peoples' congress, on racial policy, at which other Reformed churches and the full array of nationalist organizations participated. Several principles were adopted for a racial policy. In Nicol's terms, these princi-

---

58 G. van der Watt, 'G.B.A. Gerdener: koersaanwyser . . .', doctoral diss., UOFS, 1990, p. 292.

59 G.B.A. Gerdener, *Reguit koers gehou* (Cape Town: NG Kerk Uitgewers, 1951), p. 102.

60 *Die Transvaler,* 12 June 1940; Steyn, *Louw,* p. 293; W. Nicol, ''n Grootse roeping', pp. 21-2, 39.

ples combined the demand for political survival (full control by whites over the common area) with the plea that black 'nations' be provided with the opportunity to develop in their own areas, administer themselves, and cultivate a feeling of worth and pride in their own group, tribe, or *volk*.[61]

At this congress J.D. du Toit, a Potchefstroom neo-Calvinist and professor of theology, presented the first published theological defense of apartheid. He argued that God had intervened to disperse the builders of the Tower of Babel, who wished to create a single nation by causing them to speak in mutually incomprehensible languages. The lesson was twofold. Those whom God had joined together had to remain united; those whom God had separated had to remain apart, and there could be no *gelykstelling* or *verbastering* – no social leveling or bastardization.[62]

Du Toit drew on Abraham Kuyper, who at the turn of the century said that the ordering of different nations and states could be traced back to the Tower of Babel, where God introduced the confusion of tongues to counteract the Devil's attempt to establish a world empire. But Kuyper was not the original author of the interpretation. It formed part of the main body of Western segregationist thought. In his work on racial views in early America, Winthrop Jordan mentions two books, one published in 1778 in Edinburgh and the other in 1812 in Philadelphia, both of which linked the Tower of Babel to God's plan to settle different nations in different regions. Although theologically a liberal, D.F. Malan clung to this outdated interpretation of the Tower of Babel.[63]

There was among Afrikaner nationalists no agreement that the colored people constituted a volk, which made the Cape DRC initially reluctant to use this justification. Increasingly, however, the policy towards colored people was formulated in virtually the same terms as those used for blacks. A memorandum submitted in 1947 by a church commission declared that God had ordained separate *volke* and races, giving each a *nasiegevoel* or feeling of nationality and *volksiel* or national soul. It recognized the coloreds as a race that had to develop separately and on its own terrain, while whites had to help them to become useful citizens.[64]

Gerdener combined several strands in the church's thinking about apartheid. Apartheid, he wrote in his journal, *Op die Horison*, 'required a Christian and generous political approach.' It was based not on race or color alone but on color 'paired . . . with language, tradition and lifestyle.' It did not imply a social hierarchy but a 'relationship of equals on separate terrains.' He did not go along with biblical justifications of apartheid, and would soon deplore the use of the word, but to him *eiesoortige ontwikkeling* (autochthonous development) was a policy that had merit and promised to be of value to all parties. It met the demands of Christian trusteeship and served Afrikaner interests while bringing to others the message of Christ. 'Autochthonous development', he wrote, 'serves not only our survival as a white nation, but in particular also our missions policy.'[65]

---

61 *Inspan*, October 1944, pp. 15-25.
62 *Inspan*, December 1944, pp. 7-17.
63 Winthrop Jordan, *White over Black: American Attitudes towards the Negro, 1550-1812* (Penguin, 1976), pp. 245-538; US Library, D.F. Malan Collection, biographical notes by his son.
64 Kinghorn, 'Die groei van 'n teologie', p. 92.
65 *Op die Horison*, 9, 1 (1947), pp. 1-2; Van der Watt, 'Gerdener', p. 292.

In 1948 the synod of the Transvaal DRC accepted a report that took as its starting point the 1935 missions policy and used the Tower of Babel and the Old Testament history of Israel as justifications for apartheid. Even Hendrik Verwoerd, editor of *Die Transvaler,* was enthralled, although he rarely used anything but secular arguments. He wrote that the Afrikaners' survival struggle against millions of non-whites would become more difficult. Afrikaners would prevail if they clung to a single idea: 'It was in accordance with God's will that different races and *volke* exist.'[66]

In 1949 the Cape DRC synod gave a slightly more circumspect endorsement of apartheid than the Transvaal synod. As justification it used a few texts from the Bible, including one that would become the mainstay of the apologists (Acts 17:26: 'From one man he made every nation of men . . . and he determined the times set for them and the exact places where they should live.') However, its main argument was based on historical precedents. It referred to the 1857 synod decision to condone segregated worship, to the segregation of schools, and to the church's mission policy laid down in 1935. Apartheid, the synod declared, did not mean oppression or black inferiority but a 'vertical separation' in which each population group could become independent.

Ben Marais and Bennie Keet, professors of theology in Pretoria and Stellenbosch respectively, now began their lonely battle against the church's legitimatization of apartheid. Keet protested against the arbitrary use of biblical texts taken out of context, and pointed out that segregation in the church since 1857 had happened voluntarily and with mutual consent. No 'flight of fancy' could apply this church policy to the present apartheid proposals. At the Transvaal synod of 1948 Marais warned that the church had embarked on a road leading to increasing isolation. He rejected the synod's hermeneutics. The history of Israel was unique and nowhere did one read of separation on account of racial or national origins. As a result of the mixture of peoples, new nations were constantly formed. (After his speech at the 1948 synod, delivered after the NP's victory in the election of that year, a distraught elder said to him: 'You have just spoiled the entire election for me by kicking the biblical grounds for apartheid from underneath us.')

Looking back on these debates many years later, a leading figure in the DRC stated that the church had been faced with the following question: 'How can the church maintain our own people's identity without doing damage to the cause of spreading the Gospel among non-whites?' His reply was: 'The answer came out of our missions policy.'[68] As the historian Richard Elphick remarks, the church leaders were enthralled by their utopian vision of separate peoples, each with their own mission, and would continue to justify the unjustifiable, thus paving the way for the politicians.[69]

The church leaders were fooling themselves. It was an illusion that any government would have the resources to build colored townships that were 'a hundred per cent', to use Gerdener's words. Neither was it able to provide 'the best social, welfare and community services for natives in the reserves', as the Sauer Commission report of 1947 recommended (Gerdener was a member).[70] In the same year Ben Marais warned that 'true

---

66 *Die Transvaler*, 16 February 1947; Kinghorn, 'Groei van 'n teologie', pp. 102-3.

67 Kinghorn, 'Groei van 'n teologie', pp. 110-11.

68 F.E. O'Brien Geldenhuys, *In die stroomversnellings* (Cape Town: Tafelberg, 1982), p. 34.

69 Elphick , 'Missions and Afrikaner nationalism'.

70 'Verslag van die Kleurvraagstuk-kommissie van die HNP (1947), p. 9. (Further references will be to the Sauer Report.)

apartheid would come at an enormously high price.' It would face opposition from 'ninety per cent of those who today are supporters of segregation or apartheid.'[71] Like Bennie
Keet, Marais did not condemn apartheid out of hand in 1948, but gave it qualified support, since very few whites were prepared to concede racial equality. The proviso was,
as Marais phrased it, that the policy would be upheld 'with Christian responsibility and
not naked selfishness.'[72]

There were only a few other dissenting voices in the church. In 1947 James Oglethorpe,
a Stellenbosch student training to become a DRC missionary, wrote that even if apartheid
was the last weapon in Afrikaner hands to ensure its survival, the DRC had no right to
sacrifice 'its most precious possession, its faith.'[73] But it was these survival fears that made
it difficult for the church to listen to the warnings of Oglethorpe, Keet and Marais, and
for white South Africans in general to heed their conscience. Alan Paton, a devout Christian, leading liberal and author of the internationally acclaimed novel *Cry, the Beloved
Country*, told the *New York Times* in 1949: 'We in South Africa also have a conscience.
But our fears are so great that our conscience is not so clearly apparent.'[74] Although Paton did not share these fears, he knew his white countrymen, of whom he was indu-
bitably one.

'An idea that one can bow down before': Apartheid as secular doctrine

The National Party that was formed in 1934 under D.F. Malan's leadership, after the bulk
of the party under General Hertzog had merged with Jan Smuts' South African Party,
was destined to remain a fringe party without clear issues on which it could outflank the
ruling United Party. A reactionary racial policy would not serve the purpose; the NP supporters, who were almost as closely tied to the church as the party, had to perceive it as
just.

Although the word was not yet used, the first secular formulations of what would become apartheid took place during the mid-1930s. An opportunity arose when the government appointed a commission of inquiry into the colored population, which was to
be headed by Professor Johannes du Plessis. When he died early in 1935, he was replaced
R.W. Wilcocks, a professor at Stellenbosch and a member of the Carnegie commission
on poor whites. The commission found acute poverty among the overwhelming majority of colored people due to wide-ranging discrimination by government, employers and
trade unions. Segregation against colored people had intensified and had failed to deliver
opportunities for them above the level of manual labor. The 'civilized labor' policy, which
was supposed to benefit them as well, had aggravated their position. It had accelerated
the trend among colored people 'to pass for white.'

In the inputs of the three Afrikaner members of the commission and the three Stellenbosch professors who gave testimony, a common thread could be discerned. They posited

71 Ben Marais, "n Kritiese beoordeling . . .' *Op die Horison*, 9.1 (1947), pp. 76-9.
72 Ben Marais, *Die Kerkbode*, 14 July 1948, p. 159.
73 James Oglethorpe, 'Segregasie in die kerk', *Die Stellenbossche Student*, November 1947, pp. 34-5. For an
    analysis of the Stellenbosch intellectual tradition in these years see Andrew Nash, 'The Dialectical Tradi-
    tion in South Africa', doctoral diss., UCT, 2000, pp. 97-164.
74 Harvey Breit, *The Writer Observed* (Cleveland: The World Publishing Company, 1956), p. 91.

the existence of a colored race, urged a demarcation in housing schemes between white, colored and 'native' areas, and recommended special sections in government departments to look after colored interests. While the other commissioners, among them Dr Abdullah Abdurahman, advocated common political rights and equal pay for equal work, the Afrikaners propagated the extension of civilized labor to colored people. The testimony of Professor Hendrik Verwoerd provided the outlines of the emerging apartheid ideology. He used colored poverty as a justification for increased discrimination against blacks in the western Cape. He argued that they posed a threat to colored people and poor whites alike in the competition for work opportunities. The place of blacks was in the reserves.[75]

Anther key moment was the 1936 debate on the Cape African franchise. Here D.F. Malan, NP leader, declared that segregated schools and churches eliminated the friction and humiliation suffered by colored people who had to sit on the back benches in the few churches or schools that were integrated. He asked for the principle of segregated schools and churches to be extended to political representation. Both colored and African people had to be put on separate rolls and given segregated institutions.

In the 1936 debate Malan and his party opposed the purchase of more land for the African reserves, as proposed in the bill. Funds should go instead to buying land for white tenants, sharecroppers and bywoners. The acquisition of land by blacks had to happen 'on their own initiative and according to their own real needs.'[76] Such attitudes confirmed the liberal belief that, as Jan Hofmeyr observed in 1937, 'constructive segregation' was not practical, in view of white obduracy.[77] With the doubling of the reserves a *fait accompli*, Malan and his followers had to reconsider their views. They soon proceeded to make a virtue of necessity.

Stellenbosch academics, *Die Burger* journalists and a small circle of western Cape NP politicians who moved in D.F. Malan's orbit conceived the apartheid political plan that took shape between the 1943 and the 1948 elections. They sought a formula for excluding blacks from the political system without having to rely on the principle of race alone. Hard-core racism had become discredited, and in western Cape circles there was no prominent person who denied the basic humanity of blacks or colored people. Academics in the north, forming virtually a separate group, were engaged in their own effort along largely similar lines. There is no evidence of much cross-fertilization, except in the Broederbond with its limited membership. The nationalist intelligentsia in the north tended to stress a hierarchy of races and divine sanction for racial segregation more strongly than their counterparts in the south, who were often embarrassed by the ideological excesses of the north.

Both in the south and the north it was scholars in the fields of anthropology, African administration and law, sociology and history who figured prominently in the construction of the apartheid policy. Three different approaches can be discerned: the first was

---

75 UG 54/1937 *Verslag van die Kommissie van Ondersoek insake die Kaapse Kleurling*, vol. 3, pp. 3163-3171; Lewis, *Between the Wire and the Wall*, pp. 159-69.

76 P.W. Coetzer and J.H. le Roux, *Die Nasionale Party, IV: 1934-1940* (Bloemfontein: INEG, 1986), p. 57.

77 Saul Dubow, *Racial Segregation and the Origins of Apartheid in South Africa* (London: Macmillan, 1989), p. 170.

based on historical claims, the second on ethnic differences and the third on racial differences.

The historical argument consisted of two parts. First it was contended that whites and blacks had arrived simultaneously in the territorial boundaries of the South African state and that in a sense both were colonists. The second argument was that territorial segregation had been the accepted policy of South Africa since the earliest times. Albert Geyer, editor of *Die Burger*, playing a pivotal role in the early formulations of apartheid, presented the first argument: 'The Bantu are no more indigenous to what now is the Union of South Africa than the whites are. Both are colonists from outside . . . Within South Africa two immigration streams clashed. The two races have in every respect an equal right to regard South Africa as their home.' He added: 'The native reserves must be regarded as the home of the Bantu.'[78]

The historical argument for a white South Africa was not as preposterous as it sounds today. Not until the late 1950s was a large measure of consensus established among liberal academics that Africans had crossed the Limpopo fifteen to twenty centuries earlier and soon spread across eastern South Africa. However, it was well known that the San hunters and gatherers and Khoikhoi herders in the western half of the present South Africa had been dispossessed by white colonists, and it was difficult to deny that large parts of the eastern half of South Africa had been settled before the Great Trek, which occurred while the Highveld was temporarily depopulated as a result of the *Mfecane*. Liberal historians took issue with the Tomlinson Commission, which in 1954 reasserted the view that blacks had no strong claim on land outside their reserves.[79]

Liberal historians easily shot down the report's interpretation that the Voortrekkers had followed a policy of 'isolation' and territorial separation with respect to the Khoikhoi and Africans. In numerous places the frontier was marked by 'deep prongs of European settlement into the Bantu area', with or without permission.[80] Territorial segregation failed because Afrikaner farmers ignored it in seeking labor. It was only the 'superfluous' Africans who were shunted off into some remote corner. By 1910 a third of Africans lived on white farms.[81] But Afrikaner historians continued to insist that there was a unique Afrikaner approach to racial issues in their history. They believed that they had found it in an abhorrence of gelykstelling or social leveling between whites and blacks and the endorsement of racial separation and 'differentiation.' As editor of *Die Transvaler*, Verwoerd frequently referred to the Voortrekker principle of rejecting any social leveling of the races.[82]

In many ways these views flew in the face of the facts. During the first seventy-five

78 Cape Archives, A.L. Geyer Collection, Folder 7, speech given at the Cosmos Society, Oxford University, 19 October 1950.

79 US Library, Manuscripts Collection, 'Verslag van die sosio-ekonomiese ontwikkeling van die bantoegebiede binne die Unie van Suid-Afrika' (Tomlinson Commission), vol. 1, chapter 2. For the importance of a certain interpretation of history in the Tomlinson scheme see Adam Ashforth. *The Politics of Discourse of Twentieth-Century South Africa* (Oxford: Clarendon Press, 1990), pp. 161-4.

80 A.K. Fryer, 'The Historical Survey', *Forum*, 5, 2 (1956), p. 13.

81 Leonard Thompson, 'The Political Implications of the Tomlinson Report, *Race Relations Journal*, 23 (1956), pp. 9-12.

82 D. Prinsloo, 'Die Johannesburg-periode in dr. H.F. Verwoerd se loopbaan', doctoral diss., RAU, 1979, pp. 92, 149-166.

years of the Cape settlement there were numerous marriages across racial lines. The driving impulse of the frontier farmers was to incorporate indigenous labor. They wanted control over black labor, not racial separation. However, it is true that resistance to *gelyk-stelling*, originating in the status distinctions of the Dutch East India Company, remained a central theme in Afrikaner political thinking about survival.

One of the first Afrikaner scholars who stressed ethnic differences as a basis for policy was the anthropologist Werner Eiselen. For him the real task in South Africa was not the solution of a *race* problem but 'the creation of effective arrangements for the peaceful existence of different ethnic groups.'[83] As early as 1934 he urged co-ordinated action by the state in 'helping the Bantu in the building up of peoples and cultures.'[84] In 1941, P.J. Schoeman, another Stellenbosch anthropologist, propagated the establishment of three or four large African reserves, which could promote black 'tribal pride' and ultimately could develop into 'statelets.' He stressed the link between Afrikaner nationalism and the proposed racial policy. 'The Afrikaners were called not only to ensure the development and survival of an *eie volk* but also to help backward and less developed people to help themselves and rehabilitate themselves.'[85]

The first book (it was more an extended pamphlet) propagating a policy called apartheid in social science language was written by three other Stellenbosch academics, P.J. Coertze (a lecturer in anthropology), F.J. Language ('native administration') and B.I.C. van Eeden (Bantu languages). The acknowledgement in the preface of Gerdener's influence highlights the marriage of the ideas of mission strategists and secular nationalists. The study's point of departure was the 'extensive dislocation' of the indigenous native social structures under the impact of urbanization. It led to 'egotistic individualism, a lack of social responsibility, and a lack of discipline and moral decay.' They advocated a 'radical and total apartheid' to bring about 'absolute finality' and a lasting, long-term solution. The problems facing blacks in the cities could only be resolved by re-establishing the 'original social order of the natives.'

Blacks had to be steadily withdrawn from the white economy, and transferred to the territories where they 'belonged', with white labor taking their place. Only those 'absolutely necessary' were to be permitted to remain. Coertze, Language and Van Eeden pleaded for the regeneration of traditional institutions in the reserves where Africans could administer themselves, preserve their customs and restore discipline and all 'that was healthy in the *volkseie*.' 'A progressive policy with respect to the reserves would gradually bring about a whole range of national self-supporting economic units – self-supporting as far as it is possible.' What was probably central to the thinking of the three scholars was only mentioned as an aside. The withdrawal of black labor from the common area was indispensable for the 'sound national evolution of the Afrikaner people.'[86]

---

83 Werner Eiselen, 'Die aandeel van die blanke . . . in afsonderlike ontwikkeling' *Journal of Racial Affairs*, 16, 1 (1965), p. 9; T. Dunbar Moodie, *The Rise of Afrikanerdom* (Berkeley: University of California Press, 1974), p. 275.

84 See his two publications, *Die Naturellevraagstuk* (Cape Town: Nasionale Pers, 1929), and 'Christianity in the Religious Life of the Bantu', in I. Schapera (ed.) *Western Civilization and the Natives of South Africa* (London: Routledge, 1934).

85 P. J. Schoeman, 'Territoriale Segregasie', *Wapenskou*, 2,1 (1941), pp. 20-31.

86 P.J. Coertze, F.J. Language and B.I.C. van Eeden, *Die oplossing van die Naturellevraagstuk in Suid-Afrika* (Johannesburg: Publicité, 1943).

L.J. du Plessis, a Potchefstroom legal scholar, offered a Calvinist critique of liberalism and capitalism that reinforced some of these points. The only people really free under unbridled capitalism were employers with the freedom to exploit, a freedom the liberals extolled. Liberals wanted to grant blacks the freedom to assimilate into European civilization, but ignored the fact that detribalized blacks enjoying this freedom represented a danger to white society because they had insufficiently assimilated European sanctions and living standards. A sound social policy depended on 'the acceptance of differences in the nature, quality and level of development' of groups. 'Higher standing groups must not assimilate or destroy lower standing groups . . . but develop them to a higher level on the foundation of their own structure and culture.'[87]

The novelist Joseph Conrad remarked that in order to dominate people one has to have an idea – something one can 'set up, and bow down before and offer a sacrifice to.'[88] What redeemed apartheid in the eyes of the nationalist intelligentsia was the idea that the Afrikaners were prepared to grant (the Afrikaans word 'gun' is much stronger) everything to blacks that they demanded for themselves.[89] Like the Afrikaners, Africans would have their own schools, churches, residential areas, homelands and governments on which they could put their own cultural imprint. Nationalists persuaded themselves that apartheid would be implemented much more 'positively' than segregation, particularly because the Afrikaner nationalists had waged a long and bitter struggle against attempts to assimilate them.[90]

It was within the context of an emphasis on culture that the ideology of Christian-National education developed. Here the Broederbond, with its large contingent of teachers, lecturers and church ministers, did play a prominent role. Christian-Nationalism, spelled with or without the hyphen, was a stock phrase in the vocabulary of Afrikaner nationalism, used more as a shibboleth than as a comprehensive ideology. The Program of Principles of the NP that Hertzog founded in 1914 and the one that Malan established twenty years later both stated that the party had a Christian-National character. But its meaning as a political creed remained vague.

The educational philosophy, called Christian-National Education (CNE), was much more concrete. It proposed schools that accepted the Holy Scriptures as their foundation, used the mother tongue as the medium of instruction, and promoted the 'national principle', which meant 'love for everything that is our own, with special reference to our country, our language, our history and our culture.' When the FAK in 1948 established an Institute for Christian-National education, the founding document declared that the 'natives should be led to an acceptance of the Christian and National principles in education' as set out for whites.[91]

CNE was always controversial. Stals' study of the Broederbond notes that most Afrikaners at the grass-roots level did not 'readily comprehend' it.[92] Many preferred a sec-

---

87 L.J. du Plessis, 'Liberalistiese en Calvinistiese Naturelle-politiek', in Federasie van die Calvinistiese Studentenverenigings van SA (comp.), *Koers in die krisis* (Stellenbosch: Pro Ecclesia, 1940) vol. 2, pp. 226-7.
88 Joseph Conrad, *Heart of Darkness* (Cologne: Könemann, 1999), p. 52
89 Kinghorn, 'Die groei van 'n teologie', pp. 92-6.
90 L.J. du Plessis, 'Die Naturellevraagstuk in Suid-Afrika', *Koers*, 8, 1 (1940), p. 5.
91 A translation of the FAK 1948 pamphlet, *Christelike Nasionale onderwysbeleid* is published in William Henry Vatcher, *White Laager* (New York: Frederick A Praeger, 1943), pp. 288-301.
92 E.L.P. Stals, 'Die geskiedenis van die Afrikaner-Broederbond', unpublished ms., 1998, p. 143.

ular education for their children and, given the choice, would prefer education through the medium of both official languages. Broederbond members propagated the idea of CNE, particularly at synods, but the organization as such could not do much more than wait for the day that the NP captured power. After 1948 it became common to describe an Afrikaner school as one that was Christian and national, but except for the great value attached to the teaching of history in Afrikaner schools, not much changed after 1948. After an outcry among English-speakers the government promised not to impose CNE in English schools.[93]

CNE did find its way into black schools. On the eve of the 1948 election, some church leaders and educationists had begun to wonder whether the DRC was wise to expend such large amounts of resources on missionary efforts outside the country. The Broederbond initiated a discussion of this. At this point 175 church ministers were members, forming the second biggest professional group in the organization. In their ranks were Gerdener and other church leaders. At a special meeting held in 1947, consensus was reached that the Afrikaners' mission effort had to concentrate on domestic missionary work, particularly in the cities. White missionaries had to be replaced by black office bearers and black churches had to be helped to develop into autonomous churches. Werner Eiselen proposed that the state take over black schools, on which it spent £4,000,000 every year, mainly as contributions to the salaries for the church schools. The Sauer report of 1947, commissioned by the NP, recommended a strict Christian-National education for blacks according to their ethnic nature, aptitude and background that would make it possible 'to cultivate Bantu-worthy [sic] citizens.' Eiselen would soon be put in charge of administering such a policy.[94]

A racist policy without racists?

While Eiselen and others stressed culture as the foundation of CNE and the political program, a section of the nationalist intelligentsia emphasized race. Invariably their point of departure was 'racial purity' as the foundation of white supremacy. It is sometimes suggested that such ideas were derived from the Nazi ideology that swept through Germany in the 1920s and 1930s. However, National Socialism had few adherents among the intelligentsia. As we have seen, there was broad support in South Africa for 'race purity', even among liberals.

Many Afrikaner nationalist academics, including Verwoerd (see p. 350), rejected the idea that blacks were biologically inferior to whites or that race had anything to do with intelligence or abilities. A leading Afrikaner educationist wrote: 'I maintain that nothing has been proven about the backwardness of the native mind.'[95] NP leaders increasingly purged racist expressions from their speeches.

But the fact is that the sanitized vocabulary of apartheid made little difference to the reality that the policy resulted in the pervasive stigmatization of all people who were not

---

93 Charles Bloomberg, *Christian-Nationalism and the Rise of the Afrikaner Broederbond* (London: Macmillan, 1990), pp. 208-12.
94 Stals, 'Geskiedenis van die AB', pp. 234-6; Sauer Report, p. 13.
95 J. Chris Coetzee, 'Opvoeding en onderwys van die SA naturel', *Wapenskou*, November 1943.

white. It started from the premise that black and colored people were different, not because they were mostly abjectly poor but because they were racially different. The message that apartheid as a system conveyed, offensively and obscenely, was that black and colored people were socially inferior, morally inadequate, intellectually underdeveloped and sexually unfit for intimate relationships.

How does one square the absence of a racist ideology with a racist program? In some cases it was simply a case of packaging a racist product in inoffensive terms, hoping that this trick would make it less objectionable. But there was also another dimension. Afrikaner nationalists argued that that their survival as a volk was inseparable from maintaining racial exclusivity, and that apartheid was the only policy that systematically pursued that end. But apartheid with its racist outcomes was not a goal in itself; political survival was.

Afrikaner editors emphasized this theme. In his book *Het die Afrikaanse volk 'n toekoms?* (Do the Afrikaner people have a future?), G.D. Scholtz, historian and editor of *Die Transvaler*, stressed the small numbers of Afrikaners as the dominant political factor in their demand for apartheid. The Afrikaners, Scholtz pointed out, had never experienced the luxury of 'safety in numbers.'[96] He cited as a model the Lithuanians and Estonians whose freedom had been subverted by the Soviet Union.

Piet Cillié, together with Hendrik Verwoerd the most articulate apartheid apologist, wrote in 1952 that 'South Africa was remarkably free from racial mythologies.' For him the Afrikaners' desire to survive was a far stronger and more indestructible feeling than race prejudice. 'Like the Jews in Palestine and the Muslims in Pakistan, the Afrikaners had not fought themselves free from British domination only to be overwhelmed by a majority of a different kind. Eventually we shall give that majority its freedom, but never power over *us* . . . They will not get more rights if that means rights over and in *our* lives.'[97]

These can be seen as self-serving statements, but L.E. Neame, liberal editor of *The Cape Argus* and author of a book on apartheid, made the same point. Writing from a comparative perspective, he took issue with the argument that apartheid was based solely on the claim that the white race was inherently superior to all others. An unreasoning prejudice against color was not the root of the matter. The problem is 'national rather than pigmental. Differentiation is not enforced as a brand of inferiority but as a bulwark against the infiltration of people of another civilization. The motive is not detraction but defense.'[98]

Where the argument seems to break down is the apartheid system's discrimination against colored people, who represented neither a threat nor a different civilization. The colored people were, in fact, victims of the white-black struggle. For a long time even the more moderate nationalists were prepared to sanction discrimination against col-

---

96 G.D. Scholtz, *Het die Afrikaanse volk 'n toekoms?* (Johannesburg: Voortrekkerpers, 1954), p. 163.

97 J.C. Steyn, *Penvegter: Piet Cillié van Die Burger* (Cape Town: Tafelberg, 2002) pp. 68-72. See also the views of Cillié's predecessor: P. A. Weber, 'Die Burger – sy stryd, invloed en tradisie', J.P. Scanell (ed.), *Keeromstraat 30* (Cape Town: Nasionale Boekhandel, 1965), pp. 18-38.

98 The article was re-published by the *Journal of Racial Affairs*, 1, 6 (1954), pp. 45-47. See also Heribert Adam and Hermann Giliomee, *Ethnic Power Mobilized: Can South African Change?* (New Haven: Yale University Press, 1979), pp. 61-82.

ored people because their incorporation into a common system would have sent the message to blacks that the same was possible for them. In thinking about a racial policy towards South West Africa, which South Africa administered, Hendrik Verwoerd agreed that there was no logical reason – and as an apartheid ideologue he always prided himself on his logic – to treat colored people as a population group who had to be separated from whites. But Verwoerd was thinking about SWA, not South Africa.[99]

The nationalist academic with the most explicitly racist thesis, both in terminology and the practical suggestions he offered, was Geoff Cronjé, a Pretoria sociologist. Perhaps because his books appeared just before the 1948 election, analysts have mistakenly thought that he was an influential figure. But he had stronger ties to the extra-parliamentary pro-Nazi Ossewa Brandwag movement than to the NP during the war years, and had no standing in D.F. Malan's inner circle. (He was one of the few nationalist academics who declined to send a submission to the committee that drew up the so-called Sauer report.) He went much further in the expression of his racial obsessions than almost any other nationalist academic – John Coetzee calls him 'crazy'[100] – but there is no doubt that his ideas resonated on a grass-roots level.

One of Cronjé's main obsessions was with the colored people. He viewed them as a living example of the disastrous effects of miscegenation. In his terms the 'Colored person' was a *sluwe insluiper,* a 'sly intruder', who had entered the white community almost unnoticed, contaminating its blood. He spoke almost obsessively of his fears about interracial slums where whites would lose their ethnic ties, develop feelings of equality (*gelykvoeling*) with those not white and become conditioned to blood mixing.[101] Whereas thinkers like Hoernlé felt that social sanctions were sufficient to prevent sex across racial lines, Cronjé insisted on a legal ban.

Cronjé opposed mixing between whites and blacks because it would lead to detribalization and the loss of a specific cultural identity. For black people who retained their own culture and avoided mixing with whites he proposed a *gelykwaardigheid*, an 'equality of value', with whites, but expressed strictly in group or ethnic terms. Concerning Africans he wrote that 'the direction of every non-white community in this country is to become equal in value with the white community . . . each community in its own fatherland with its own socio-economic system and political structure.'[102]

In the aftermath of the 1948 election the Rev. Z.R. Mahabane, President of the Interdenominational African Ministers Federation, made the perceptive remark that apartheid sprang from twin psychological sources – 'a fear complex and a superiority complex.' The fear complex revealed itself in the persistent anxiety about survival; the superiority complex in the constant racist references on the level of grass-roots politics during the 1950s to the 'Kafirs', 'Hotnots' or 'Coolies' as subhuman or as members of a childlike race. Cronjé's writings provide a vivid illustration of Mahabane's observation.[103]

99 Brand Fourie, 'Buitelandse Sake onder dr. Verwoerd', in W.J. Verwoerd (ed.), *Verwoerd: só onthou ons hom* (Pretoria: Protea, 2001), p. 132.
100 J.M. Coetzee, 'The Mind of Apartheid', *Social Dynamics*, 17, 1 (1991), p. 30.
101 G. Cronjé, *'n Tuiste vir die nageslag* (Johannesburg: Publicité, 1945), pp. 58-77; Coetzee, *Giving Offence*, pp. 1-30.
102 G. Cronjé, 'Werklikheid en ideaal' in G. Cronjé et al., *Regverdige rasse-apartheid*, p. 155.
103 Neame, *History of Apartheid*, p. 84.

A liberal and a 'liberal nationalist': Hoernlé and Van Wyk Louw

The more reformist Afrikaner nationalists did not take the UP with its vacillating racial policy seriously. The ideas of influential liberals, in particular those of Jan Hofmeyr and Alfred Hoernlé, represented the stiffest challenge. But no debate was really possible because the points of departure were so different. For liberals it was the freedom, rights and sanctity of the individual; for the nationalists it was nationalism and white survival. Yet on a purely rhetorical level and dealing with goals or 'ideals' they had something in common. Anthony Delius, a liberal journalist reporting from the parliamentary gallery in the 1950s, commented on the nationalists' 'hunger' for justification, which they sought through adapting liberalism to their needs. He argued that by appropriating liberal concepts such as freedom the nationalists assuaged the moderate section of their constituency and made it very difficult for authentic liberals to attack the policy.[104]

N.P. van Wyk Louw, the leading intellectual in the nationalist movement, had little time for Hofmeyr's vision of 'going forward in faith' and thought that it bordered on irresponsibility. The single example Hofmeyr had offered in support of a plea for the steady expansion of the franchise was Britain's incorporation of the working class. But, Van Wyk Louw pointed out, Britain was a racially homogeneous society. He accused liberals of failing to come to terms with the preponderance of black numbers and an unwillingness to deal with South Africa as a heterogeneous society. He expressed his frustration in the following terms: abstractly formulated, the demands for 'freedom, equal rights and equal opportunities' were 'almost self-evidently fair.' However, applied to South Africa, these demands would mean that 'a small, relatively highly developed Afrikaner people and the English section would be reduced to an impotent minority in a black mass.' Hence 'to be liberal in South Africa looks to the Afrikaner – who unlike the English-speakers does not have another country to flee to – like national suicide and individual destruction.' He insisted that the Afrikaners were not a small colonial group of 'officials and merchants', like the whites in British and Dutch India, but a volk rooted in the land. In a statement that went well beyond the conventional fears of black rule he wrote that if the Afrikaners became a minority 'they would be as helpless as the Jew was in Germany.'[105]

In articulating his 'liberal nationalism' Louw's point of departure was the political impasse in South Africa that he identified as follows: 'It was the typical tragic situation of history: two "rights" [the white and the black right to self-determination] which confronted each other implacably.' There was a 'balance of power': blacks had their numbers; whites, particularly the Afrikaners, held the upper hand, politically, economically and militarily. The 'stale-mate' could be resolved either by the 'ploughing under' of the less numerous group or by the 'separate development' of each, which he claimed represented a peaceful solution.

He was stimulated by a 1939 lecture by Alfred Hoernlé, which was subsequently widely discussed among nationalist academics. Hoernlé discerned three future political possibilities for South Africa. They were: *parallelism*, in which different races would be

---

104 Anthony Delius, 'The Missing Liberal Policy', *Forum*, 1952, pp. 40-41; Cynthia Kros, 'Bantu Education, 1926-1951', p. 392.
105 N.P. van Wyk Louw, *Versamelde prosa* (Cape Town: Tafelberg, 1986) vol. 1, p. 505.

subjugated to a 'master group', *assimilation*, in which all racial differences would be obliterated, and *separation*. He described the latter as 'a sundering or dissociation so complete as to destroy the very possibility of effective domination' by another group. The third option was ethically sound, but Hoernlé, like Hofmeyr, thought that whites would refuse the enormous sacrifices that would be required to make it a reality.[106]

Van Wyk Louw projected Hoernlé's option of 'separation' as a possible solution to South Africa's racial problem. In 1946 he wrote: 'For nationalism to be based on a true political principle it has to be true for everyone.' Accordingly, the recognition of the nationalist principle for the Afrikaners logically had to be extended to all other national groups in South Africa. Hence, 'we [the Afrikaners] should not speak of ourselves as the volk [nation] of South Africa, but as one of the volke of South Africa.'[107] By 1948 he was envisaging four white and four black separate states in southern Africa. But he left the whole question of the actual division of land obscure, and it was only in the 1960s that he made a brief reference to the 'two halves of this large country of ours' to which whites and blacks had claims.[108]

Louw's words were double-edged. In the 1960s and the early 1970s apartheid apologists used formulations and imagery very similar to those that he had first used in the mid-1940s. But at the same time his conception of Afrikaners forming only one of several co-equal volke over the longer run undermined the ideology of white supremacy.

Yet the real reason why Van Wyk Louw's political ideas outlived him was the ethical dimension he introduced into the debate about Afrikaner survival. He did this by introducing the evocative phrase *voortbestaan in geregtigheid* – survival in justice – and by insisting that national death might be preferable to ethnic survival based on injustice.

His most important essay, 'Kultuur en Krisis', first published in August 1952 in the popular magazine *Die Huisgenoot*, was triggered by the policy of the new NP government towards the colored people that drove a deep wedge between the two communities. He refused to believe that legislation directed against the colored community was necessary for the survival of the Afrikaner people, but did not voice any public criticism, particularly since he was teaching in Amsterdam in the Netherlands at that time. It was in this context that he wrote the haunting passages that would constantly echo in the Afrikaner debate on survival over the next four decades.[109]

He identified three kinds of *volkskrisisse*, or national crises – situations in which the very existence of the ethno-national group was at stake.

- When the Afrikaners were overwhelmed by external military might or 'ploughed under' by mass immigration, as propagated by some pro-British politicians. Louw was referring to the defeat of the Boer republics at the hands of the British in the Anglo-Boer War of 1899-1902, and the subsequent attempt by Lord Alfred Milner to establish an English-speaking majority in the white population by way of state-sponsored mass immigration.

---

106 Hoernlé, *South African Native Policy*, pp. 149-68.
107 Van Wyk Louw, *Versamelde prosa*, vol. 1 pp. 502-6.
108 N.P. van Wyk Louw, 'Inleiding' in D.P. Botha, *Die opkoms van ons derde stand* (Cape Town: Human & Rousseau, 1960), p. viii. I elaborate on this in 'Apartheid, Verligtheid and Liberalism', in Jeffrey Butler et al. (eds.), *Democratic Liberalism in South Africa* (Cape Town: David Philip, 1987) pp. 363-83.
109 Van Wyk Louw, *Versamelde prosa*, vol. 1, pp. 460-63.

- When a great number of the Afrikaner people doubted in themselves 'whether we ought to survive as a volk.' Afrikaners might still survive individually and some might even prosper, but they would no longer constitute a distinctive volk: they 'would be absorbed in either an Anglo-Saxon or Bantu-speaking nation.'

- 'When some time in the future a great number of our people would come to believe that we need not live together *in justice* [Louw's emphasis] with other ethnic groups; when they come to believe that mere survival is the chief issue, not a just existence.'

Particularly in the third crisis, the response of a few intellectuals was critically important. He did not believe that the Afrikaner volk had some metaphysical or inherent right to continue to exist. The Afrikaners formed a small group of people and their survival was at risk if a mere thousand among them, people who 'were intelligent enough to *think*', gave up on the volk. This could happen when the spiritual and cultural life of Afrikaners was too barren. It could also happen if the Afrikaners maintained themselves through unacceptable means.

In a vivid passage he posed this question: 'Can a small volk survive for long, if it becomes something hateful, something evil, in the eyes of the best in – or outside – its fold?' The volk, he warned, ran the risk of the withdrawal of allegiance by a critical number of intellectuals if it yielded to the 'final temptation' of abandoning the quest for 'survival in justice' and preferred 'mere survival.' In the case of a small nation like the Afrikaners this could have a fatal effect. But he did not despair that ultimately Afrikaner survival would come to be based on moral values. As he phrased it: 'I believe that the greatest, almost mystical crisis of a volk is that in which it is reborn and re-emerges young and creative; the "dark night of the soul" in which it says: "I would rather go down than survive in injustice".'

Because Van Wyk Louw remained a staunch member of the Afrikaner Broederbond and supporter of apartheid he has been judged negatively. Ultimately, however, his status as a critic revolves around the question of whether he could envisage a point where the volk deserved to go under. In this essay Louw refuses to go down the route of ethnic survival at all costs. His argument about survival in justice was a moral argument. Put differently, the Afrikaner people were not entitled to use extreme measures to maintain their hold on power. Ultimately there was no justification for a policy aimed at ensuring survival that constantly and consistently flaunted liberal values. Van Wyk Louw died too early, in 1970, for judgment to be passed on whether he would have denounced nationalism and apartheid. During the 1980s a new generation of Afrikaner academics urging the abandonment of apartheid could draw on Louw's work to do so.[110] In the end the seemingly parallel lines of liberalism and liberal nationalism did meet.[111]

---

110 André du Toit, *Sondes van die vaders* (Cape Town: Rubicon, 1982).
111 There is a voluminous literature on Louw. I discuss some of the studies and issues in my 'Critical Afrikaner Intellectuals and Apartheid,' *South African Journal of Philosophy*, 19, 4 (2000), p. 307-20; for criticism see Andrew Nash, 'The Dialectical Tradition in South Africa', doctoral diss., UCT, 2000, pp. 15-22.

Conflicting recommendations: Sauer and Fagan

In the aftermath of the Second World War the government was confronted by major decisions regarding the urbanization of blacks. The war economy had sucked in large numbers of blacks to the cities, and a large proportion had settled illegally. The Native Affairs Department was split between those favoring stricter control and those arguing for a relaxation, while the Minister thought that the problem would resolve itself once the economy returned to normal. City administrators, however, insisted on stronger curbs.[112]

By 1943 the idea of apartheid was becoming crystallized. *Die Burger* first used the term 'apartheid' in that year when it referred to the 'accepted Afrikaner viewpoint of apartheid.'[113] In January 1944, D.F. Malan, speaking as Leader of the Opposition, became the first person in Parliament to employ it. A few months later he elaborated: 'I do not use the term "segregation", because it has been interpreted as a fencing off (*afhok*), but rather "apartheid", which will give the various races the opportunity of uplifting themselves on the basis of what is their own.'[114]

The speeches in this debate by Malan and Paul Sauer, his closest confidant, reveal the framework in which the idea of apartheid developed. Their ideas were far removed from the racial ideology and xenophobia propounded at this time on the continent of Europe. Instead they were firmly rooted in the Cape Afrikaner experience of slavery, with its ideology of paternalism, and British colonialism, with its stress on indirect rule and trusteeship. Paternalism in Cape slavery did not rule out benign feelings towards the slave. Malan told his son how 'civilized and pleasant' two ex-slaves were who lived on his father's farm eighty kilometers north of Cape Town, and how for many years he did not think that racial differences were more than skin deep.[115] In the eyes of their masters, slaves could be deprived of their liberty because they could only improve their physical and spiritual well being under their masters' benevolent care.[116]

The other notion was trusteeship. In his first mention of the term 'apartheid', Malan called for a republic based on the policy of 'apartheid and trusteeship, made safe for the white race and the development of the non-white race, according their own aptitude and abilities.'[117] As the historian Kenneth Robinson points out, the British notions of trusteeship were influenced by the thoughts of a seminal liberal thinker, John Stuart Mill. He argued in 1859 that rule by a dominant country or 'by persons delegated for that purpose' was as legitimate as any other, if it facilitated the transition of a subject people to a higher state of improvement. In 1921, Lord Lugard, the most famous of British African governors, expressed the trusteeship idea in his *Dual Mandate* as follows: Europe was in Africa for 'the mutual benefit of her own classes, and of the native races in their progress to a higher plane.' He believed the benefits could be made reciprocal. This was the 'dual mandate', the title of Lugard's book.[118]

---

112 Deborah Posel, *The Making of Apartheid, 1948-1961* (Oxford: Clarendon Press, 1991), pp. 39-47.

113 Louw, *Dawie*, p. 49.

114 *HAD*, 1944, col. 75; *Die Burger*, 8 May 1944; Louw, *Dawie*, p. 48.

115 US Library, Malan Collection, 'Herinneringe aan my vader' by D. Malan, 1965, p. 9.

116 See the letters of slave-owners in *Afrikaner Political Thought*, pp. 50-71, 103-10.

117 Louw, *Dawie*, p. 48.

118 The quotes are from Kenneth Robinson, *The Dilemmas of Trusteeship* (London: Oxford University Press, 1965), pp. 22, 65.

But trusteeship vitally depended on a perceived reciprocity of benefits. By the early 1940s the balance in South Africa had heavily tipped in favor of the whites, particularly since the introduction of the 'civilized labor' policy. Jan Smuts, who had long been inspired by trusteeship, had abandoned it, but Malan in his 1944 speech did not refer to that shift. He pointed at the failure of ostensibly liberal systems to deal fairly with subordinate people. Eighty years after the victory of the North in the American civil war, blacks in the South could still not vote and were subject to the lynch law. In Australia the government took aboriginal children away from their parents and brought them up as Europeans in special hostels. When the aborigines retrogressed the Australian government reverted to a policy of allowing them to elevate themselves 'on the basis of what is their own.'

Malan's solution was couched in classic terms of paternalism and trusteeship. Subordinate people had to be helped to develop that which was their own, and to climb up the ladder of civilization according to their own aptitude and capacity. At present they were unhappy because they had nothing that was their own. They could only be made happy if opportunities were created that enabled them to rehabilitate themselves. That meant establishing segregated townships with colored doctors, nurses, clerks and policemen. White and colored communities could live alongside each other in 'friendship and cooperation with each other.'[119]

In the same debate Paul Sauer poured scorn on the idea that the western Cape had become more integrated. Forty years earlier it was still possible for coloreds to complete their education in a white school. 'Today such a thing is inconceivable. I cannot image that there is a single high school that would permit this today.' He called for a 'realistic policy' that would prevent blacks or colored people from encroaching on areas where whites lived, worked or cast their vote. Only once racial competition had been ruled out would whites be willing to assume a sympathetic position to colored aspirations.[120]

In 1945 a party commission appointed by Malan recommended a policy of social, industrial and political apartheid with respect to colored people, but argued at the same time that this would have to bring about an improvement in their conditions. The policy had to foster colored community pride and incline them towards the whites rather than the blacks.[121] As a quid pro quo for removing the colored vote, the coloreds would be 'given their own schools, their own well-planned towns, their own civil servants, their own places of entertainment.' Self-government for colored townships would be introduced, and they would be better protected from competition by Africans in the western Cape.[122]

In 1945 the NP accepted apartheid as its official racial policy. From 1946 *Die Burger* acted as the 'mass ventilator' of apartheid.[123] In 1947 Malan appointed Sauer to head a party commission to turn apartheid into a comprehensive racial policy. Also on the commission were three NP parliamentarians (one from each northern province) and the ubiquitous G.B.A. Gerdener as the only non-politician. His presence symbolized apartheid's fusion of racial and mission policy.

---

119 *HAD,* 1944, cols. 6697-6699. See also *Joint Sitting,* 1936, vol. 59 (Afrikaans edition).
120 *HAD,* 1944, col. 6713.
121 J.J. Joubert, 'Die Burger se rol in die Suid-Afrikaanse politiek, 1934-1948', doctoral diss., Unisa, 1990, pp. 230-57.
122 E.J.G. Janson, '*Die Burger* en die Kleurlingstem, 1943-1948', master's diss., Unisa, 1987, pp. 77-8.
123 Nic Rhoodie, *Apartheid and Racial Partnership in Southern Africa* (Pretoria: Academica, 1968), p. 53.

The way in which the Sauer Commission went about its task illuminates the NP's grass-roots character. It did not invite representations from corporate bodies, like the agricultural unions or Afrikaner business. It thought that the need to secure Afrikaner survival outweighed accommodating Afrikaner interest groups. Secondly, the Afrikaners of the 1940s and 1950s attached great importance to culture and learning.[124] They did not look to businessmen or wealthy farmers to justify apartheid but to ministers, academics, professional men and senior journalists. The academics had to incorporate insights from their respective fields, and representatives of the party had to report back what the people wanted.

Accordingly, the commission sent out a circular, inviting opinions, to all elected representatives of the party, all chairmen and secretaries of the party's district councils, all 'well-disposed' Afrikaner lecturers at universities and to other 'knowledgeable experts and interested persons.' The latter were mostly farmers, church ministers and missionaries. Some five thousand circulars were sent out and about five hundred replies were received. Some of the academics who responded were appointed to subcommittees. The commission's report, published late in 1947, was incorporated into the NP platform for the 1948 election.[125]

The report combined the dual nature of NP thinking: both racist and 'ethnicist', both religious and secular. It formulated an antinomy that formed the bedrock of apartheid thinking: 'There are two policy directions towards non-whites: on the one hand there is the apartheid policy; on the other hand there is the policy of gelykstelling (social leveling)', propagated by Communists and others who favor race-mixing.' To justify the rejection of 'equal rights and opportunities', the report used terminology very similar to that first employed in DRC mission and church circles: 'It was decreed by God that diverse races and volke should survive and grow naturally as part of a Divine plan.' The report even incorporated a section on mission policy, which clearly was drafted by Gerdener: 'The Gospel has to be taught to all volke and population groups as part of the calling of the Christian church', and the aim of mission work was 'self-governing, self-supporting and self-propagating churches.'

But while the Sauer report found it easy to make ideological statements about black 'fatherlands', it was much more difficult to deal with the economy in the common area in which close to half of the black population were involved by 1948.[126] The report's call for 'total apartheid between whites and Natives' as 'the eventual ideal and goal' was quite unrealistic. Carrying out such a policy would wreck the economy, which constituted as dire a threat to survival as universal franchise. Qualifying its call for total apartheid, the report stated that the economy would depend on blacks for 'many years.' It did not categorically reject trade unions for blacks, but remarked that they could not be allowed 'at this stage.' Labor bureaus had to ensure that 'supply and demand of [black] labor' functioned in a 'smooth and mobile [sic] way.' The whole thrust of the report is the elimination of 'surplus' black labor, not black labor, and the channeling of sufficient la-

---

124 Sheila Patterson, *The Last Trek* (London: Routledge and Keegan Paul, 1957), p. 253.

125 J.P. Brits, '"The Voice of the People": Memoranda presented in 1947 to the Sauer Commission', *Kleio*, 32 (2000), pp. 61-83; J.P. Brits, *Op die vooraand van apartheid* (Pretoria: Unisa, 1994), pp. 80-108.

126 *Round Table*, December 1948, pp. 815-16.

bor to the mines, farms and industry.[127] The report clearly hoped that temporary or migrant labor would provide the bulk of the new labor demand. However, this clashed with the demand of organized Afrikaner business and agriculture for workers who had settled with their families. The report did not try to resolve this clash. In this sense, then, the report did not constitute a blueprint for apartheid to which all Afrikaner nationalists subscribed, but rather reflects the contradictory tendencies in the nationalist movement.[128]

In the aftermath of the war, the ruling United Party also sought to develop a new approach towards racial policy. Prime Minister Jan Smuts knew that the electorate was far from ready for major changes. Challenged by Malan to spell out his 1942 speech when he said that segregation had fallen on 'evil days', he became vague and cautious. He now resorted to the stock response of ruling parties confronting a thorny issue. In 1946 he appointed Henry Fagan, a former UP cabinet minister and now a judge, to head a commission to investigate the issue of African urbanization.

The Fagan report directly challenged NP assumptions, and in particular the idea of developing a policy towards blacks solely based on the African reserves. It made the obvious point that even if the British protectorates were transferred to South Africa (the black-white division of land would then be roughly equal) the problem would not be solved. A stream of black labor was 'flowing into the Union . . . as the most industrialized of all the countries in Southern and Central Africa.' This flow could be 'guided and regulated, and may be perhaps also limited . . . but cannot be stopped or turned in the opposite direction.' Any policy based on the proposition that the Africans in the towns were all temporary migrants 'would be a false policy.' The reserves were so overcrowded and over-stocked that it was unrealistic to believe that they could accommodate urban blacks as well.

The commission outlined three theoretical options for South Africa: total segregation (partition), which it called 'utterly impracticable', equality (no racial discrimination), which it also rejected, and an 'in-between' one, which it endorsed. It was a policy that recognized that whites and blacks 'will continue to exist side by side, economically intertwined . . . and part of the same big machine.' The report was ambiguous about influx control. Ideally it wanted a voluntary system in which the labor bureau would channel black labor into the common area, and in which African workers were encouraged to settle with their families in the towns and cities. In other passages, however, it propagated compulsory control with the state taking measures 'to ensure that everybody has some fit place to which he is entitled to go.' It favored admitting only those blacks to the towns and cities that industry required. Its proposal that segregated black municipalities must administer the black townships indicated that it did not think the time was ripe to suggest common political institutions.

As a prescription for white survival, Fagan and the other commissioners represented an approach that differed strikingly from apartheid. Instead of advocating a final and definite solution they held that the best approach was an evolutionary one. 'The relation-

---

127 Sauer Report, 1947.
128 Posel, *The Making of Apartheid,* p. 60.

ship [between whites and blacks] will always be fluctuating and changing for life is dynamic and never stands still – and a cut-and-dried solution is therefore something that cannot be.' What was needed was 'the constant adaptation to changing conditions, constant regulation of contacts and smoothing out of difficulties between the races so that all may make their contribution and combine their energies for the progress of South Africa.' The post-war UP embodied the ambiguities inherent in the Fagan report.[129]

The publication of the Fagan report shortly before the 1948 election caused an upsurge of interest in racial policy among Stellenbosch academics. Fagan, after all, had once been a Stellenbosch and a *Die Burger* man, and was still a member of the Broederbond, though *buitelid* or non-active. Some Stellenbosch academics had given oral evidence to the Fagan commission; others made written submissions. But when it was published some leading Stellenbosch academics went on the attack against Fagan's preferred option – the 'in-between' option of parallelism. A statement, mainly drafted by Nic Olivier, a 27-year-old lecturer in Native Administration at Stellenbosch, argued that if the Fagan report used race as the rationale for parallel structures for the white and black communities, it condemned blacks to a permanent status of inferiority since it mentioned nothing about the franchise. If, however, it rejected race as a legitimate criterion, white survival itself was in dire peril and racial leveling would be the result. Olivier and his colleagues argued for a fourth option as the only one that would secure group survival. Any intermingling of the races had to cease and the 'free and untrammeled development and existence of each race' had to be promoted in its place.[130]

Significantly, the declaration referred to a white and a black group, each having its own territory. The idea of ten black ethnic groups each with its own homeland was a later elaboration. In 1950 Albert Geyer, ex-editor of *Die Burger* and now High Commissioner in London, mooted the idea of the black authorities forming a Central Council to discuss matters common to all reserves and the introduction of machinery for 'close contact and consultation' between such a council and the government. Hendrik Verwoerd, Minister for Native Affairs, rejected the idea because he felt that competition would develop between such a council and Parliament.[131]

A momentous election

When the 1948 election campaign started, the UP's machinery failed to see that it was in trouble. Afrikaners had been seriously alienated from the UP by the split decision in 1939 to enter the war and the perceived victimization of Afrikaners during the war. Everyone was affected by war fatigue and growing irritation with the wartime restrictions still in place. The Smuts cabinet was comprised mostly of English-speakers, few of whom had shown much sympathy with the Afrikaans culture. Afrikaners feared that Smuts' call for 'millions' of immigrants would upset the delicate electoral balance between the two white communities. The government's enthusiastic reception of the British royal family in 1947 did not help.

---

129 UG 28-48 *Report of the Native Laws Commission*, see esp. pp. 4, 13, 18-29, 45-50.

130 US Library, A.C. Cilliers Collection, Document 166, p. 6.

131 J.P. Heiberg, 'Dr. A.L. Geyer as Suid-Afrika se hoë kommissaris in die Verenigde Koninkryk', doctoral diss., US, 2001, pp. 211-13.

Living costs had increased sharply, rising in an index (1938=100) from 133 in 1945 to 146 early in 1948. The real wages of white workers had fallen during the war, while the wages of blacks, from a much lower base, had risen considerably. The influx of large numbers of blacks into industry in the 1930s and 1940s, together with mechanization, frightened white workers, particularly those whose skills were not scarce. The UP government assured them that programs would be introduced to train them as artisans and for other better paid positions, but the messages lacked conviction. By 1948, 139,000 white adult males were unemployed, compared to 76,000 in 1945. When the government announced that it intended to bring out fifty thousand immigrants every year to alleviate the shortage of skilled labor, the NP immediately complained that this would undercut local people waiting to be trained.

The UP thought, on the agricultural front, that it had done more than enough to meet farmers' demands, particularly by stabilizing product prices, but farmers were still struggling to make ends meet, with the prices of supplies and equipment rising faster than those of produce. Even more serious was the crisis in labor relationships; at the beginning of the war the liberal South African Institute of Race Relations noted a general deterioration of the racial situation in the rural areas, with farmers complaining that Africans 'had lost their respect for them', and that a 'strained relationship' had come to replace the old forms of co-existence.[132] The average cash farm wage on a farm, including the cash value of food supplied in lieu of cash, was only a quarter of that in manufacturing. The outward-bound stream accelerated during the war years when the Smuts government relaxed the system of influx control that had kept many Africans out of the urban areas. In the mid-1950s a commission found that nearly half of the newly urbanized Africans had come from the farms.

The Smuts government refused to agree to any drastic intervention, the Secretary for Native Affairs publicly declaring that the key reason for labor shortages was that farmers paid their workers too little.[133] The NP indicated that it was prepared to do better than the UP in meeting farmers' demands. As early as 1943 it had declared itself in favor of marketing boards appointed from the ranks of producers. It also supported demands for intensified control over African farm laborers through pass laws. The NP elected in 1948 would prove to be largely a farmers' party, with Afrikaner farmers or people connected to farming making up half of its Members of Parliament, and three-quarters of its rural seats. Some 90 per cent of the UP seats were in the major urban areas.

After the election Malan claimed that the electorate had given the new government a mandate to implement apartheid.[134] In fact apartheid as a policy plank had played a relatively minor part in the campaign. In his final appeal to the electorate, NP leader D.F. Malan referred specifically to apartheid only in a single, ambiguous sentence when he said that the question was 'whether there could be apartheid at the same time as justice, peace and co-operation between white and non-whites.'[135] An analysis of the letter columns in

---

132 M.L. Morris, 'The Development of Capitalism in South African Agriculture', *Economy and Society*, vol. 5, no. 3 (1976), p. 294.

133 Morris, 'Development', p. 335.

134 *Smuts Papers*, vol. 7, p. 277.

135 *Die Burger*, 20 and 24 May 1948.

the most prominent Afrikaans papers, *Die Burger* and *Die Transvaler,* in the six months before the election, showed that there was something more important than race in the writers' minds. It was the perception that the UP government had discriminated against Afrikaners in the previous eight years; next of issue were food shortages and rationing and the treatment of ex-servicemen. Editorials themselves did reiterate the racial issue, but only about one in ten of the letters expressed a similar concern.[136]

English-speakers shared the NP's determination to maintain white domination. On the eve of the election, Arthur Keppel-Jones, a liberal academic whose 1947 book *When Smuts Goes* painted a dark picture of South Africa should the NP ever come to power, wrote that the main concern of whites in general was 'not to be submerged in the oncoming tide of black race. If they were to remain a separate people then they must retain their dominant position.'[137]

The kind of segregation that most English-speakers supported was less aggressive and blatant than that of the NP. They did not agree with crude manifestations, like segregated suburbs and the racial sex laws. As the wealthier white community they could buy their apartheid and, unlike the Afrikaners, did not have to worry about a large section in their community that had just escaped from acute poverty.

Apartheid indeed had a 'dogmatic intensity', as Saul Dubow points out, but its suppleness is underrated.[138] Nelson Mandela maintains that the NP fought the election on the twin slogans of: 'The kaffir in his place' and 'The coolies out of the country.'[139] But there never were any such slogans.[140] The NP leadership had no desire to upset ministers and other apartheid theorists who believed in the capacity of apartheid to uplift people. What it did was to promise that South Africa would remain a 'white man's country.' Unlike the UP, with its liberal wing led by Hofmeyr, the NP spoke in one voice in promising to keep South Africa white.'

The UP under the leadership of Smuts, nearing the age of eighty, fought a poor campaign. De Villiers Graaff, who would become UP leader in 1956, felt that the party's organizers misled Smuts. Hofmeyr conceded two weeks before the election date that the UP, kept on the defensive by the NP on a range of issues, had to fight a 'negative' campaign.[141] Some followers had urged Smuts to change the electoral rules. If the UP had registered more colored voters in key seats it might well have won, but there was a risk that such a step could have boomeranged. A less risky move would have been to change the electoral system in which rural votes counted for more than urban votes so that, at the extremes, 85 rural votes were equivalent to 115 urban votes. If each vote – rural and urban – in the 1948 election had counted the same the UP would have won eighty seats against sixty for the NP-led alliance. Smuts rejected the proposal, explaining his rejec-

---

136 Brits, *Vooraand van apartheid*, pp. 119-20.

137 A.M. Keppel-Jones, 'The Political Situation in South Africa', paper presented to the Royal Institute for International Affairs, 27 March 1947.

138 Dubow, *Racial Segregation*, p. 178.

139 Nelson Mandela, *Long Walk to Freedom* (London: Little Brown, 1994), p. 104.

140 J.P. Brits in communication with Willem Kleynhans, the largest private collector of election material, 23 March 2002. See also Brits – Letter to the Editor, *Beeld*, 8 July 1999.

141 De Villiers Graaff, *Div Looks Back* (Cape Town: Human & Rousseau, 1993), pp. 123-7; *Die Burger*, 15 May 1948.

tion by noting that the roots of the policy lay in the Union Constitution of 1909 that had been accepted in good faith by all parties. Furthermore, he had confidence in his rural followers: 'They are good people. They will never let me down.'[142]

In the May 1948 election the NP, in alliance with the Afrikaner Party under the leadership of Klaas Havenga, an ex-minister of finance, won a majority of five seats, even though it captured only 40 per cent of the vote. Smuts was defeated in his own rural seat of Standerton. When a shattered Smuts mourned that his people had deserted him, an adviser offered the slight consolation that his people had not deserted him; they probably were all dead. The new generation of Afrikaners was overwhelmingly NP.

Good friends told Hofmeyr that he was being blamed for the fall of Smuts, and when the UP secretary came to see him he was utterly depressed. 'There is no hope for this country,' he said, but, after some hesitation, he added, 'unless they [the nationalists] fight among themselves,' and after another pause, 'they always do, don't they?'[143] But it would be twenty years before there was any splintering in the NP, and another twelve years before a serious split occurred.

Fleshing out apartheid

Apartheid was a flexible operational ideology for Afrikaner nationalism, attracting both those wanting to keep down all those who were not white and those who wanted to rehabilitate them and recognize their human dignity – single-minded and double-minded segregationists. The latter – in the literature they are called the apartheid visionaries or idealists, but here they are called the apartheid theorists – took the initiative. They had no argument with the apartheid hard-liners that the racial omelet in the common area had to be unscrambled through extending the ban on sex between whites and blacks to whites and colored people, classifying everyone according to race and forcing everyone into his or her own racial 'group area' or suburb. They also went along with the hard-liners in rejecting political rights for colored people and blacks in a common system. But in two vital areas they differed: whites had to reduce their dependence on black labor, and a dramatic development program had to be launched for the reserves to justify the denial of black rights in the common area.

The apartheid theorists soon began talking of 'total segregation' or 'total apartheid', by which they meant the co-existence of a white state with several black states, each with its own political system and viable economy with a labor force drawn predominantly from its own citizens. This was such a radical idea that the liberals did not know whether to take it seriously, mock it or throw up their hands in horror. Just after the election *Forum*, a liberal journal, wrote: 'Apartheid means sending people away from the mines and industrial areas to some home or reserve which does not exist; it means that the Native not only does not contribute his labor, which is his wealth, to the country, but he also cannot buy the country's products; it means stagnation, poverty, disease and misery for White and Black.'[144]

---

142 Friedman, *Smuts*, p. 211.
143 Paton, *Hofmeyr*, p. 379.
144 Cited by W.M. Eiselen, 'Is Separation Possible?', *Journal of Racial Affairs*, 1, 2 (1950), p. 13.

One liberal decided to take it seriously enough to issue a challenge. He was Rheinallt Jones, ex-director of the SA Institute of Race Relations, the most important liberal organization in civil society. In a speech delivered on 14 July 1949 he said that in principle he could find nothing wrong with apartheid. He would support total apartheid provided the following conditions were met: sufficient land for 'natives' to secure proper economic development for them; enough capital invested in the reserves to bring about such development; the introduction of a 'free government' and a free market in the reserves, and the expenditure of a fixed proportion of the whites' national income on the development of the reserves. However, like Hofmeyr and Hoernlé, he thought that the voters would reject such a plan.[145]

The NP was in fact still struggling to finalize its apartheid plan. Against this background five Stellenbosch academics in 1948 proposed the founding of an institute to make a comprehensive study of the racial issue. The leading figures were Nic Olivier and Barney van Eeden, who were outspoken supporters of the idea to commit large financial resources to what they called a policy of 'territorial separation' or total apartheid. In response to the *Cape Times*' questioning whether the government had a mandate to spend enormous sums to implement such a policy, they replied that in 1939 'neither the *Cape Times* nor South Africa as a whole asked what it would cost to take part in the Second World War.'[146] But Olivier was soon forced to admit that it would take three generations to accomplish territorial segregation.

There were others who also proposed the idea of an institute. The Transvaal nationalist MP, M.D.C. de Wet Nel, who later became Minister for Native Affairs, was an active proponent, and so was the Missions Commission of the Transvaal DRC. The Broederbond first mooted the idea in August 1946, but it took a year before the Broederbond leaders met with the Stellenbosch academics and decided to support the idea of an institute in Stellenbosch. On 23 September 1948 the Suid-Afrikaanse Buro vir Rasse-aangeleenthede (SABRA) was founded in the town. It was a modest operation with only a full-time organizer and a typist on the staff. H.B. Thom, Professor of History, and from 1954 both Vice Chancellor of the university and Chairman of the Executive Council of the Bond, held a protecting hand over the SABRA men of Stellenbosch. Olivier, soon to be a Bond member and Professor of Bantu Law and Administration, acted as the main link between SABRA and the Bond. The Bond was its largest (secret) donor, although SABRA did its best to solicit other funds.[147]

The tie between the Bond and SABRA was much looser than that between the Bond and the FAK. The Bond in typical fashion used it as a front for public statements or to make representations to government. Initially Hendrik Verwoerd, who in 1950 became Minister for Native Affairs, welcomed these initiatives, but soon he began to resent any encroachment on the terrain of his department.

Apart from the establishment of SABRA, the other major move of the proponents of 'total apartheid' took place in 1950. The driving force was G.B.A. Gerdener, still a pro-

---

145 Cited in the editorial notes of *Journal of Racial Affairs*, 1, 1 (1949), p. 11.
146 John Lazar, 'Conformity and Conflict: Afrikaner Nationalist Politics in South Africa, 1948-1961', doctoral diss., Oxford University, 1987, pp. 164-216.
147 Stals, 'Geskiedenis van die AB', pp. 210-11.

fessor at the theological school at Stellenbosch and now also Chairman of SABRA. He organized a church conference on the racial issue which was attended by representatives of all the 'mother' and 'sister' (black and colored) churches in the DRC family, as well as of the Gereformeerde and Hervormde churches. Just before the conference, Gerdener published an article that conveyed a sense of his own unease over apartheid. He confessed that he had never liked the word, which had become 'a shibboleth of sinister intentions, misunderstanding and irresponsible talk.' It suggested a static situation while something dynamic was required. He formulated the Reformed Church's position as follows: 'If the contribution of every racial group in this, our common fatherland, is to be guaranteed, the way of separation and not of integration is the correct one.'[148]

At the conference the Afrikaner church leaders called for 'total separation' and the elimination of Africans from 'white industrial life.' The conference did not specify a territorial base for the plan, but both the church leaders and SABRA academics urged Africans to accept the policy of different homelands for the major African ethnic groups. Whites would rebuff black demands for equality in the common area. Africans were told that they would do better to use their abilities to build institutions in their own autonomous states.

But D.F. Malan, now Prime Minister, rejected the church leaders' call for 'total apartheid.' He remarked: 'If one could attain total territorial apartheid, if it were practicable, everybody would admit that it would be an ideal state of affairs . . . but that is not the policy of our party . . . and it is nowhere to be found in our official declaration of policy.' The next year he repeated his position in even blunter terms: 'The Afrikaans churches' policy of total separation is not the policy of the Nationalist Party.'[149] The government's negative response to total separation came as a great disappointment to the apartheid theorists, though they took heart from the fact that the government, in 1950, had appointed a commission to investigate ways of increasing the human carrying capacity of the reserves. It was to be headed by Professor F.R. Tomlinson, an acknowledged expert in agricultural economics.

By the early 1950s, the theologians who had questioned the biblical defense of apartheid also expressed doubts about it as a practical policy. In 1952, Ben Marais published *Colour: Unsolved Problem of the West* after a period of study leave in the USA. It was an incisive comparative study of Brazilian and American race relations, with lessons drawn for South Africa. Marais considered 'total territorial segregation' as the only real solution, but by that he meant 'a radical policy of huge dimensions, one embracing economic and territorial segregation.' He questioned whether the whites had the will to implement it and were prepared to pay the price. He warned that any stopgap measure would be of very little significance and would leave 'several millions of non-whites' living permanently among whites. If that indeed happened, Marais remarked, the implication was clear: 'There was no honorable manner in which we as Christians and democrats will in the long run be able to deny them political and other rights.'[150]

148 G.B.A. Gerdener, 'The DRC and the Racial Situation in South Africa', *Race Relations,* vol. 17, 1-2 (1950), pp. 1-5.
149 *HAD,* 1950, cols. 4141-4142.
150 Ben Marais, *Colour: Unsolved Problem of the West* (Cape Town: Howard Timmins, 1952), p. 322.

In 1956 Bennie Keet published his *Suid-Afrika – Waarheen?* (*Whither South Africa?* in the English edition) in which he also challenged the talk of 'total apartheid.' It appeared to him as mere wishful thinking, or even worse since the easiest way of solving an intractable problem was to suggest an impossible solution. Keet pointed out that it was whites who desired apartheid, but the people who would suffer and would have to make the sacrifices would not be whites, but people who were not white. Keet's study also questioned social and economic apartheid. Apartheid represented a blatant and explicit form of discrimination and ostracism. It turned into untouchables all non-whites, offending their basic personal dignity even if they were civilized people. By basing the economy to such a large extent on migrant labor, whites were depriving blacks of the indispensable condition for a sound community: tight family connections.

Keet concluded that the basic dichotomy formulated in Afrikaner political debates was a false one. It was not a question of apartheid or racial fusion, but apartheid or racial cooperation. Total apartheid as a solution was a century too late, because the trend among Africans to embrace the Western culture was irreversible. The clock stood at five minutes to twelve and action was urgently needed. In proposing a solution Keet went much further than the NP-aligned intelligentsia. He mooted the idea of multi-party talks between whites and the broadest representation of non-whites to formulate a plan for coexistence that would enjoy general support in the population as a whole.

Keet's contribution was essentially a moral plea. He provided no analysis of white party politics and the electoral pressures to which the parties were subjected. He also did not discuss whether there was sufficient common ground between whites and blacks to reach a stable compromise solution at multi-party talks. It seems as if Keet hoped that the solution to several centuries of conflict between whites and Africans lay in the parties no longer treating it as a political power struggle. Instead of pursuing their own respective interests, he wanted them to work only for the common interest. It was as if Keet in his religious idealism thought that the struggle was the result of a lack of brotherly love and that power could come from the pulpit rather than from the outcome of the political struggle.[151]

The NP leadership tried to avoid the challenges offered by Keet and Marais by asking for time to unravel the racial omelet and for the developmental aspect of apartheid to show fruit. But there was a contrast between what senior ministers said in public and in private. Privately Eben Dönges, who as Minister for the Interior introduced most of the apartheid laws, told a foreign journalist that for him and his colleagues the policy of apartheid was there to protect the present and next two generations against the dangers posed by the growing black and colored population.[152] In public meetings, however, he talked of the system lasting a long time. 'The efforts that are made to combat the immediate situation have to continue, but at the same time we must begin to think of a broader and more thoroughgoing approach. We must look a hundred years ahead and not only five years. The danger exists that we shall win all the battles and still lose the war.'[153]

As the Fagan report pointed out, the chances of the urbanization of blacks being re-

151 Bennie Keet, *Whither South Africa?* (Stellenbosch: CSV Publishers, 1956).
152 John Hatch, *The Dilemma of South Africa* (London: Dennis Dobson, 1953), p. 93.
153 *Die Transvaler*, 17 December 1952.

versed over the longer run were remote. The policy that the NP government implemented after winning the 1948 election could only be enforced by means of repression
and the erosion of civil rights. This raised the specter of a civil war with blacks. A charge
that some nationalists leveled against the English section in general was that, unlike the
Afrikaner nationalists, they could not be trusted to stand firm when the chips one day
were down. Professor A.I. Malan, a nationalist MP and father of a son, Magnus, who
would become head of the Defence Force and Minister for Defence in the last phase of
apartheid, spelled out this view in brutally frank terms. He declared that the English section would also try to preserve its European blood. But if this entailed too much effort and
too much sacrifice, it would under certain circumstances be prepared to capitulate. After
all, there would be at least forty million of the Englishman's 'race' in Britain who would
continue with his way of life.

The Afrikaners' case was quite different, Malan said. 'He belongs to a small nation . . .
If he should vanish from the stage, who remains to perpetuate his way of life, his culture? . . . Can it thus be wondered at that, for the Afrikaner, the matter of survival has
become an irresistible life force, a veritable obsession.' If necessary, the nationalists would
establish their 'hegemony' to make survival possible in the face of the preponderance of
black and colored numbers.[154] He probably meant a dictatorship.

In the aftermath of his defeat in 1948 Smuts also pondered the future. Echoeing the
thesis that Reinhold Niebuhr expressed sixteen years before (see p. 302), he foresaw the
essential paradox of the apartheid system. It allowed for kindness and compassion in the
way in which Afrikaners individually dealt with colored people and blacks. But the same
people were cruel and callous when they acted collectively to secure Afrikaner survival.

> I do not think people mean evil, but they thoughtlessly do evil. In public life they
> do things they would be incapable of in private life. So I heard yesterday from a
> friend who had been in a hot argument with a Nat over taking away the colored and
> native franchise. They were in the car of the Nat and and when along the road
> they met an old colored person wearily marching along the Nat stopped the car and
> picked up the old fellow and drove him on for the next ten or twelve miles. When
> he had been put down at the end of this journey my friend said to the kind Nat:
> 'How do you square it with your policy of apartheid?' To which he replied: 'But
> how could you pass the old fellow without giving him a lift?'[155]

---

154 René de Villiers, 'Political Parties and Trends', in G.H. Calpin (ed.), *The South African Way of Life* (Mel-
    bourne: William Heineman, 1953), p. 137.
155 *Smuts Papers*, vol. 7, p. 251.

Chapter 14

Apartheid

Victory after 'years of pain'

D.F. Malan's National Party, in alliance with N.C. Havenga's Afrikaner Party, had come to power in May 1948 with a razor-thin majority of five, and only 40 per cent of the overall electoral vote. Immediately after the election Malan said: 'Today South Africa belongs to us once more. South Africa is our own for the first time since Union, and may God grant that it will always remain our own.'[1]

D.J. Opperman, a leading Afrikaans poet, celebrated the victory in his epic poem, *Joernaal van Jorik,* which, in translation, reads:

> *How unexpected, after years of pain*
> *Our victory when it came*
> *What sounding hour!*
> *It was that early morning as though rain*
> *Had made a desert burst out in flower*
> *And yet, no bomb or human blood fell ever,*
> *But the oppressèd ones with steel and steam*
> *In lowly work, by their humble endeavor,*
> *With steel and steam a great Republic dreamed.*[2]

South Africa was not only about white domination, but also about which whites would dominate. Potential Afrikaner voters outnumbered potential English-speaking voters by only 135,000 in 1948 and 207,000 in 1958. When Malan said that South Africa 'belonged' to the Afrikaners he did not have the white-black struggle in mind but the rivalry between the Afrikaner and the English community (led politically by Jan Smuts and other Afrikaners). After the 1939 United Party (UP) schism the balance in the party had tilted in the English-speakers' favor. For the first time since Union the cabinet and the ruling party caucus spoke only English. Many Afrikaners felt victimized by the way in which the wartime measures were applied. (A judge told the story of a witness in a court case

---

1 J. Robertson, *Liberalism in South Africa, 1948-1963* (Oxford: Oxford University Press, 1971), p. 3.

2 Dirk Opperman, *Joernaal van Jorik* (Cape Town: Nasionale Pers, 1949), p. 42. This translation is by C.D. Harvey.

who was asked to define the term 'Afrikaner.' 'Someone who is against the war', was the quick answer.)[3] Rumors were rife of Afrikaners who had been refused promotion merely on the say so of informers.

In the final years of the UP government under Jan Smuts, Afrikaner nationalists feared that immigration would tip the delicate political balance between the two white groups, making it impossible for the NP to win. The great majority of approximately seventy thousand British immigrants who had come to South Africa after the war were likely to support the UP once they became naturalized. Soon after the 1948 election the new government announced that it would select future immigrants in a 'more discriminating process.'[4] While Australia was attracting 200,000 immigrants per year, immigrants to South Africa stood at only thirteen thousand in 1950 and remained at that level for quite some time. The UP soon charged that the government's discouragement of immigration was sabotaging the future of whites. If so, it was equally sabotaging the prospects of the English-speakers, voting almost en bloc for the UP, to regain power in coalition with an Afrikaner minority.

Yet despite these differences Smuts, who turned seventy-eight just before the 1948 election, and Malan, who was four years younger, retained their friendly relations with each other, preventing the Afrikaner-English cleavage from deepening even further. At the inauguration of the Voortrekker Monument in Pretoria in December 1949, attended by the largest crowd that the country had ever seen, the speeches of these aging leaders provided a stark contrast. Although devastated by the UP defeat in the previous year, Smuts was upbeat and forward looking in addressing the crowd in what was to be his last great speech. Few young nations, he said, could boast such 'a romantic history . . . and one of more gripping human interest.' But, he warned, 'let us not be fanatical about our past and romanticize it.' Only on the basis of taking from the past what was beautiful could 'fruitful co-operation and brotherhood' between the two white communities be built. And only on this basis could a solution be found for the greatest problem which we have inherited from our ancestors, the problem of our native relations.'[5] This was, he said, 'the most difficult and the final test of our civilization.' Smuts died less than a year later; Hofmeyr had preceded him by nearly two years.

Malan's speech was backward looking and full of grave warnings. Global influences were undermining the Voortrekker spirit and ideals. A 'godless communism' threatened everything they had built up. There was a real danger of blood mixing and the disintegration of the white race. The only way of avoiding the specter of a descent into 'semi-barbarism' was a return to the Voortrekker spirit and a return to the *volk,* church and God.[6]

A people on the move

Malan's speech, with its emphasis on dire poverty among whites, showed that in many ways he was still living in the first three or four decades of the century when he saw

3 O.D. Schreiner, *The Nettle* (Johannesburg: SA Institute of Race Relations, 1964), p. 1.
4 Eric Walker, *A History of South Africa* (London: Longmans, Green and Co., 1957), p. 779.
5 *Smuts Papers*, vol. 7, pp. 332-3.
6 D.F. Malan, *Glo in u volk* (Cape Town: Tafelberg, 1964), pp. 135-7.

himself engaged in a desperate struggle to save Afrikanerdom. But the Afrikaners had put acute poverty behind them. The nationalist movement had a new vision of establishing a firm foothold for Afrikaners in the towns and cities and catching up economically with the English section. At the second economic *Volkskongres* in 1950 Malan gave a keynote address that was much more in touch with reality. The Afrikaners, he said, had to 'get a place in the economic sun not by pushing others out or being carried on the shoulders of others but in their own right and relying on their own strength.'[7] This meant that the Afrikaners could not depend too strongly on the state to advance economically. It would bestow privilege and protection on all whites, but as far as the competition within white society was concerned, the Afrikaners in the private sector had to rely on their own efforts.[8] The state did not directly interfere with the English dominance of the private sector. It is often alleged that the state showed favoritism towards Afrikaner firms and that such assistance might even account for the advance of Afrikaner capital. These stories rest mostly on the kind of unfounded rumors typical of ethnic rivalries.[9]

When the NP gained power the Afrikaners, forming 57 per cent of the white population, had a 29 per cent share of total personal income, compared to 46 per cent for English-speakers and only 20 per cent for the Africans who formed 68 per cent of the population. Approximately a third of the economically active Afrikaners still worked on farms (this proportion would drop by nearly a half in the next fourteen years). Slightly more than a million Afrikaners of a total of 1.5 million people now lived in towns and cities, where they bunched together in the lower income categories of the white population. There were now very few Afrikaners considered to be poor whites or who were unskilled, but the profile of urban Afrikaners was predominantly working class. Some 40 per cent of all Afrikaners were in blue-collar and other manual occupations, only 27 per cent had white-collar jobs and the rest were in farming. It was this profile of the Afrikaners that the NP had in mind when it introduced the apartheid system.[10]

The nationalist mobilizers of the Afrikaner vote had some factors in their favor. The first was demographic. *Die Burger* remarked on 29 December 1948: '[The] future of the *Boerenasie* is assured politically by the sheer weight of their numbers.' Between 1948 and 1994, Afrikaners were responsible for at least 63 per cent of the annual white births, and the margin between potential Afrikaner and English voters steadily widened. In terms of the electoral system, which benefited rural over urban constituencies, the Afrikaners were much better positioned than the English-speakers, who were concentrated in a few cities and large towns. In 1958 the NP could win 103 seats out of 156 Parliamentary seats on the basis of drawing 80 per cent of Afrikaner votes and only 1 per cent of English votes.[11]

---

7 D.F. Malan, 'Toespraak by die tweede ekonomiese volkskongres, 1950', pamphlet.

8 I deal with this in a forthcoming study 'The Afrikaners' Economic Advance'.

9 The most notable case of favoritism is the patronage bestowed during the 1960s on the Afrikaner press companies in the north. See J.L. Sadie, *The Fall and Rise of the Afrikaner in the South African Economy*, pp. 36-8. The pages cited are based partly on an extended unpublished study by the author of this book.

10 The figures in the above two paragraphs were drawn from the research of Jan Sadie and Sampie Terreblanche and were originally published in Heribert Adam and Hermann Giliomee, *Ethnic Power Mobilized: Can South Africa Change?* (New Haven: Yale University Press, 1979), pp. 169-73.

11 Jan Sadie, 'Politiek en taal: 'n ontleding', *Die Burger,* 29 August 1958; Jan Sadie, 'Die demografie van die blanke Afrikanergemeenskap', *Journal for the Study of Economy and Econometrics,* 1998, 22 (3), pp. 17-24.

Overwhelmingly the Afrikaners attended Afrikaans schools and universities where they could be socialized into the nationalist movement. After coming to power in 1948 the NP government accelerated the trend to compulsory use of the home language as the sole medium in schools in all provinces except Natal. The trend towards single-medium instruction is illustrated in the table below:

SHIFT IN MEDIUM USED AT SECONDARY LEVEL

YEAR	ONLY ENGLISH %	ONLY AFRIKAANS %	ENGLISH AND AFRIKAANS%
1932	51.2	28.2	20.6
1958	34.8	62.4	2.8

Source: E.G. Malherbe, *Education in South Africa, Vol. 2: 1923-1975* (Cape Town: Juta, 1977), p. 110.

Yet another source of strength for the nationalists was the social homogeneity of the Afrikaner group as regards both culture and income. According to the 1946 census, some 89 per cent of Afrikaners were concentrated in the income group R0-6,000, with 9 per cent in the class of R6,000-R12,000. Only 1 per cent earned an income of more than R12,000 (in 1980 prices).

The NP government took care not to bestow too much advantage on either rich or poor Afrikaners. Between 1946 and 1980 the income disparity between the top 20 per cent of Afrikaners and the lowest 40 per cent, which in comparative terms was not wide, slightly improved. By 1960 a broad Afrikaner middle class had appeared. Some 60 per cent were still in the income class of R0-R6,000, but nearly a third were now in the category R6,000- R12,000.[12] Only in the 1970s did a class of visibly rich Afrikaners appear who were indifferent to the ideology that the Afrikaner economic advance was a collective activity.

The Afrikaners' educational qualifications steadily improved as fewer and fewer saw a future in farming. In 1955 only 16 per cent of Afrikaner children in the eighth school year in the province of Transvaal went on to complete their high school education; by 1965 the figure had risen to 38 per cent (for English-speakers the figures were 25 per cent and 43 per cent).[13] Political power, together with the Afrikaner youth's encapsulation in separate schools and universities, steadily enhanced their social self-confidence. Rembrandt, Sanlam, Volkskas and other Afrikaner enterprises were beginning to earn the respect of their rivals.

The nationalist alliance that came to power in 1948 consummated the alliance of the Afrikaner intelligentsia and the workers, which Albert Geyer fifteen years earlier had seen as the only possible basis for a NP victory (see p. 415). Apartheid as the racial policy of the alliance was a trade-off between the intelligentsia and the workers. The workers tolerated the intelligentsia's vision of black homelands and a public discourse purged of racial rhetoric. The intelligentsia indulged the workers by accepting them as full members of the nationalist movement (but not in leadership positions), bestowing on them public deference and protecting them from competition from black or colored workers.

---

12 T.J. Steenekamp, "n Ekonomiese ontleding van sosio-politieke groepvorming met spesiale verwysing na die Afrikaners', doctoral diss., Unisa, 1989, p. 193.

13 Stephanus van Wyk, 'Die huidige beroepsposisie van die Afrikaner in die stad', doctoral diss., UP, 1967, pp. 533-5.

The inauguration of the Voortrekker Monument provided the forum for the expression of the heightened cultural awareness. Piet Cillié, a young journalist later known for his cynicism, wrote that the occasion was a revelation to English journalists: 'They did not realize that young Afrikaners could sing so well, that Afrikaner women could dress so well, that Afrikaners could perform such folk dances, and that Afrikaner history could be presented so irresistibly because it was such a living reality to the presenters.' To a friend he wrote: 'The Afrikaners were at their most attractive. It was impossible not to love them.' He added: 'You cannot co-operate with other groups, you cannot be friendly without the self-respect and power you generate from own separate institutions. Our people have become strong and great by growing separately . . . [At the Monument] there was no bitterness, neither towards the English, nor towards the non-whites.'[14]

For Cillié the festival celebrated the Afrikaners' 'refusal to be absorbed in other groups'; it was the Afrikaners' isolation, their 'separate development and growth that had blossomed so spectacularly and movingly at the festival.'[15] Cillié and other Afrikaner nationalists became attracted to the idea of imposing the Afrikaner model of ethnic self-encapsulation on the subordinate groups. Few recognized the fact that the model worked in the Afrikaner case because there was a large degree of voluntary identification of the group, and because the Afrikaners' cultural and political struggle reinforced each other.

Most Afrikaners were inspired not by apartheid but the nationalism that Cillié described above. Malan's autobiography published in 1959 contains hardly a word of racial policy, but deals extensively with his role in achieving Afrikaner unity and in building a white nation that did not look to Britain for guidance and support.[16] During the 1950s the Afrikaners in growing numbers saw themselves as part of a *volksbeweging*, a people on the move, putting their imprint on the state, defining its symbols, making bilingualism a reality, adapting to an urban environment and giving their schools and universities a pronounced Afrikaans character. Teachers made conscious efforts to increase the sense of distinctiveness through encouraging the singing of folk songs at schools and organizing *volkspele* or folk dances as an extra-curricular activity. The Afrikaans radio service played seven hours of *boeremusiek* or Afrikaans folk music every week. Proudly a postgraduate student wrote: 'Virtually everything which the Afrikaner can call his or her own, originated in South African soil – his language, traditions, history, ideals, sense of calling and culture are rooted in South Africa. The English-speaker on the other hand can call very little his own creation. He has not yet been spawned from Mother England and is compelled to be nourished spiritually from England.'[17] What this writer forgot was that rugby football, an import from Britain, was now at the center of the Afrikaners' popular culture. Afrikaners soon dominated the world of rugby in South Africa. International rugby matches were replacing solemn commemorations of holy days of history as the *volksfeeste* where Afrikaners gathered to celebrate.[18]

---

14 J.C. Steyn, *Penvegter: Piet Cillié van Die Burger* (Cape Town: Tafelberg, 2002), pp. 65-6.

15 *Die Burger,* 20 and 24 December 1949; US library ms. collection, Piet Cillié Manuscripts, Cillié-Johan Louw, 6 February 1950.

16 D.F. Malan, *Afrikaner volkseenheid* (Cape Town: Nasionale Boekhandel, 1959).

17 L.S. Erasmus, 'Die nasionale idee in die onderwys', master's diss., US, 1954, p. 47.

18 Albert Grundlingh, et al., *Beyond the Tryline: Rugby and South African Society* (Johannesburg: Ravan, 1995), pp. 90-135.

The NP as a party stood mobilized and ready for action. An English editor described the style of the movement of the 1950s: 'Activity is ceaseless; the contact continuous. There is rarely a weekend without a party or public meeting somewhere in each province. Not a week goes by without one or other Minister speaking to the people and participating in their group activities, easily and spontaneously.'[19]

The march to the republic

When the parties of Malan and Klaas Havenga merged in 1951 under the name of the National Party, any hope among its opponents that the Afrikaner nationalist movement would soon split faded. Retaining their economic dominance, English-speakers were the key to future domestic fixed investment and to overseas investment, with Afrikaner entrepreneurs having just entered the corporate world. The per capita income of English-speakers, by 1948, was more than double that of Afrikaners. Their level of education was much higher and they identified with a British culture that was vastly richer and more diverse than the Afrikaans culture. They tended to find little that was attractive in the Afrikaners' culture and very few read Afrikaans books or newspapers. Yet the English community in South Africa found itself in the political wilderness – one of the largest English-speaking communities in the world without any political power. A British sociologist who visited South Africa during the 1950s remarked on 'a revival of jingoist attitudes as result of the growing feeling of impotent resentment amongst English-speaking South Africans over nationalist aggressiveness.'[20] It would hardly be surprising if the elite of this community conveyed unsympathetic views of the Afrikaners to foreign diplomats, journalists and businessmen, who rarely could speak or read Afrikaans.

While there was very little difference between Afrikaners and English-speakers in their support for white supremacy, residential segregation and migrant labor, English opinion-formers constantly tried to distance themselves as much as possible from the racial policies of Afrikaner parties. They found the crude expression of racism distasteful and resented being shut out from power. A few months before the 1948 election Arthur Keppel-Jones, a history lecturer at the University of Witwatersrand, expressed the anxieties of English-speakers in his study entitled *When Smuts Goes*. He predicted that an NP victory would lead to massive English emigration and large-scale black uprisings.[21] Patrick Duncan was only slightly less despondent when he wrote a few years later: 'English South Africans are today in the power of their adversaries. They are the only English group of any size in the world today that is, and will remain for some time, a ruled, subordinated minority. They are beginning to know what the great majority of all South Africans have always known – what it is to be second-class citizens in the land of one's birth.'[22] It was all a matter of relative deprivation. For Duncan the blow that relegated the English-speakers to a position of seemingly permanent opposition in Parliament seemed almost as harsh as the NP's rigid exclusion of Africans from the privileges of citizenship.

---

19 Morris Broughton, *Press and Politics of South Africa* (Cape Town: Purnell, 1961), p. 170.
20 Sheila Patterson, *The Last Trek* (London: Routledge and Kegan Paul, 1957), p. 284.
21 Arthur Keppel-Jones, *When Smuts Goes* (Cape Town: African Bookman, 1947).
22 Patrick Duncan, *The Road through the Wilderness* (Johannesburg, no publisher given, 1953). See also G.D. Scholtz, *Het die Afrikaanse volk 'n toekoms?* (Johannesburg: Voortrekkerpers, 1955), pp. 126-31.

For a short spell after 1948 serious strife existed in the armed forces between those who had refused to fight in the Second World War (almost all of them Afrikaners) and those whites who had fought (about 50-50 Afrikaners and English). Some senior members of the military command were openly contemptuous of the new government, whose members had to a man opposed the war effort. F.C. Erasmus, the new Minister of Defence, was a republican hard-liner. He was unwilling to forget the injustices he believed Afrikaners had suffered as a result of the war. The co-operation between the UP as a party and some military units still rankled. Erasmus sidelined Major-General Evered Poole, first in line to become Chief of General Staff. Several other members of the top command who were pro-war, including Afrikaans-speakers, were demoted or sidelined.

Erasmus also embarked on a massive effort to South Africanize the defence force, which imitated Britain in its uniforms, the names of the officer ranks, and its medals and colors. Correspondence and instructions were conducted virtually only in English. After the NP victory the policy changed abruptly. Some traditional Afrikaner ranks like commandant were introduced, the uniforms were changed and new medals of honor were created. Erasmus instructed the Permanent Force to alternate between Afrikaans and English every month in its communications. Members of the force would no longer be promoted without first passing a strict bilingual test. Especially in the Air Force a spate of resignations occurred as a result of this. By 1956 three-quarters of the recruits in both the Army and the Air Force were Afrikaners. The Defence Force was becoming an Afrikaner preserve.[23]

The strict application of the bilingual requirement upset many English-speaking civil servants, but there was no massive purge of English civil servants after May 1948, as is often claimed.[24] The most controversial of those purged was W. Marshall Clark, who, during the war, had been appointed General Manager of the SA Railways and Harbours over the heads of two Afrikaner civil servants. After being ousted in 1949 he was offered another civil service job and, when he refused, was paid £80,000 as a pension, which was a small fortune in those years. English-speakers also protested against the appointment of Werner Eiselen, brought in from the outside as Secretary for Native Affairs in 1948.

The predominance of English-speakers in the higher ranks of the civil service continued for a decade, and it was only by 1960 that the people in these ranks reflected the white population composition.[25] New recruits were predominantly Afrikaans-speakers and, in the first twenty years of NP rule, the number of Afrikaners in the civil service doubled. Initially there was an outflow of UP supporters from the service, but the situation soon stabilized. Leo Marquard wrote: 'Appointment, and particularly promotion, of public servants goes on without regard to party-political affiliation until a fundamental difference of policy manifests itself, when it breaks down.'[26]

Although whites were united in their commitment to white supremacy, the two white communities remained deeply divided about how a white nation was to be built and about links with the outside world, particularly the Commonwealth. The divisions were manifested in the debate on the South African Citizenship Bill of 1949. Previously the

---

23 Louisa Jooste, 'F.C. Erasmus as minister van verdediging, 1948-1959', master's diss., Unisa, 1995, pp. 1-99.
24 See the unfounded comments of Peter Wilhelm in *Financial Mail*, 2 October 1998, p. 44.
25 Van Wyk, 'Beroepsposisie', p. 307.
26 Cited by Patterson, *Last Trek*, p. 86.

citizens of Commonwealth countries had enjoyed a common status because of a common British nationality, but this bill moved the basis of citizenship primarily to South Africa and imposed more stringent conditions on immigrants from other Commonwealth countries to become citizens.

Australia had passed similar legislation, but English-speakers in South Africa saw the bill as yet another attempt to reduce the links to Britain, and to force them to turn their back on it. They believed that it was in the best interests of the white minority to cultivate dual or multiple ties and loyalties. South Africa had to strengthen the ties with the older Commonwealth countries, share their values and do everything to attract immigrants and investment. The nationalists, by contrast, believed that white unity, as the bedrock of white supremacy, could only be built through the development of a single and, indeed, a single-minded loyalty to South Africa.[27] Writing in *Koers*, L.J. du Plessis of Potchefstroom called for the absorption of what he called 'English-speaking Afrikaners' along with their cultural heritage. Such 'an inner union or unification was necessary for the maintenance of our civilization in Southern Africa.'[28]

In such debates Afrikaners stressed that they considered South Africa their only home and the Afrikaners as the core of the white nation. Even Havenga, Minister of Finance and a moderate nationalist, emphasized the Afrikaners' uniqueness in a situation in which the survival of the small white community was in doubt. 'As far as the Afrikaners are concerned we cannot get out. We dare not adopt a policy that would make it possible for us to be driven out, because we – the Afrikaners – have no other home in which we can take refuge.'[29] English-speakers resented the charge that as people with a bond to Britain they were less loyal to South Africa or would leave if things came to a head.

Immediately after the 1948 election the government began removing the remaining symbols of the historic British ascendancy, abolishing British citizenship and the right of appeal to the Privy Council (1950); scrapping *God Save the Queen* as one of the national anthems and the Union Jack as one of the national flags (1957); taking over the naval base in Simonstown from the Royal Navy (1957); replacing the British currency (1961), holding a referendum on a republic (1960); and, after winning that whites-only referendum, establishing a republic (1961).

Because apartheid had become unacceptable to other members, South Africa withdrew from the Commonwealth in 1961. The historic tie with Britain was finally severed. The constitution of the republic differed remarkably little from the Union constitution. The object of the exercise was to bring about a single political loyalty for all white South Africans, not a new system. Nationalists hoped that the English-speakers would abandon their dual loyalty once they could no longer look to Britain as a fatherland. This was what happened as Britain embarked on decolonization in Africa. When the South African government introduced conscription for white males at the end of the 1960 there was very little resistance from English-speakers.

---

27 Gwendolen Carter, *The Politics of Inequality* (London: Thames and Hudson, 1958), pp. 51-9.
28 Cited by Patterson, *Last Trek,* p. 287.
29 Patterson, *The Last Trek*, p. 280.

Western and South African racism

The 1948 election and the introduction of the NP's apartheid program dismayed Britain, South Africa's principal foreign investor and trading partner. But, with the shadow of the Cold War falling over the world, the priority for Western governments was to prevent South Africa, with its minerals and strategic location, from falling under communist influence. Soon the British Labour government under Clement Attlee concluded that this was more important than its revulsion of apartheid. In October 1949 Attlee wrote to D.F. Malan about the 'growing and world-wide Communist threat', suggesting that South Africa receive Sir Percy Sillitoe, Director-General of British Security Services, to discuss security co-operation. South Africa was to be offered access to the intelligence secrets of the Anglo-American alliance in exchange for a disciplined anti-communism. Sillitoe admitted in a confidential memorandum that such co-operation could open him up to criticism 'that he had assisted the Boer nationalists in implementing their extremist program by actively helping in the creation of a Gestapo.' But he considered the risk outweighed by the need to make South Africa part of the British and American intelligence community.[30]

The West did not insist on a non-racial democracy in South Africa, arguing that such a system was impossible for the time being. Apartheid was not based on the failed racial ideology of Nazi Germany, but on mainstream Western racism, ranging from a superficial color preference to a pathological abhorrence of race mixing, which was still widespread in both Europe and the USA. In European colonies, for instance French Algeria, the overwhelming majority of the indigenous population was excluded politically and only a small proportion of that population was integrated socially. In the USA, particularly in the South, there was little support for what was called desegregation (or 'integration' in the terms of the table below). Not until toward the end of the 1950s, when apartheid had already been firmly established in South Africa, did white South African racial views begin to diverge markedly from those in Europe. At this point Europe was divesting itself of its colonies, and in the USA the processes of school and social integration had gathered pace.[31]

PERCENTAGE OF USA WHITES APPROVING INTEGRATION

ISSUE	1942	1956	1963
Public school integration			
Southern whites	2	14	30
National whites	40	61	75
Public Transport			
Southern whites	4	27	51
National whites	44	60	78
Residential areas			
Southern whites	12	38	51
National whites	35	51	64

30 The paragraph is based on a report in *Noseweek*, 33, July 2001, based on recently declassified Public Record Office documents.

31 Herbert Hyman and Paul Sheatsley, 'Attitudes towards Desegregation', *Scientific American*, vol. 211 (1964), pp. 18-19; Mildred A. Schwartz, *Trends in White Attitudes towards Negroes* (Chicago: University of Chicago Opinion Research Center, 1967), p. 131. See also E.J. Dionne, *Why Americans Hate Politics* (New York: Simon and Schuster, 1991), pp. 80-81.

In 1946, 21 per cent of Southern whites assessed the intelligence of blacks as equal to that of whites, against 42 per cent for whites on a nationwide basis, but ten years later 57 per cent of Southern whites and 77 per cent of whites nationwide considered black intelligence as equal to that of whites. In 1949, when Eben Dönges, Minister for the Interior in South Africa, introduced a law banning all marriages between whites and non-whites he justified that act by pointing to what he said was the practice in the US (e.g., thirty American states with similar laws; fifteen with a marriage officer to administer them).[32]

During the 1950s it was not uncommon for Western leaders to express racist views. In 1951 Herbert Morrison, Foreign Secretary in the British Labour government, regarded independence for African colonies as comparable to 'giving a child of ten a latch-key, a bank account and a shotgun.'[33] As late as 1957, Dwight Eisenhower, at a presidential news conference, could speak with sympathy about the fears of Southern whites who, he said, 'see a picture of the mongrelization of the race.'[34] Apartheid was marked by the same white paternalism and revulsion of blood-mixing.

The new regime

The Afrikaner-ruled state, which excluded a large and fast-growing majority from the vote in a rapidly democratizing world, faced profound security dilemmas. It was an under-policed state that rested on the assumption that blacks would continue to submit passively to pervasive white domination. But such submissiveness could no longer be taken for granted. Some of the controls on blacks had been lifted during the war. Further, the moral authority of whites throughout the world was declining sharply as a result of their shrinking demographic proportion worldwide and the collapse of European colonialism. The defeat of Nazi Germany and the horror of the Holocaust discredited racial ideologies and speeded up pressure for racial integration, particularly in the United States. The granting of independence to India in 1947 was a major turning point in world history that intensified the pressure to allow black and brown people to rule themselves. The General Assembly of the United Nations became an effective platform for the nations of the Third World to vent their anger over centuries of Western domination. Afrikaner rule and apartheid became the focus of their wrath.

When the NP gained power in 1948 there was a black population of 8.5 million. Of them approximately 2 million lived in towns and cities, compared to 1.6 million urban whites. During the war and its aftermath much black urbanization had occurred unplanned, in squatter camps ringing Johannesburg and in racially mixed slums in every major city. The racial borders had become much more porous. Fears of inter-ethnic violence had mounted. In a 1940 race riot in Stellenbosch, white students and colored people of the town clashed; for two days students sacked the houses of colored people in the center of the town.[35] Riots also broke out in the western suburbs of Johannesburg in November 1944, prompting Verwoerd to write an editorial in *Die Transvaler* that living in racially mixed

---

32 Carter, *The Politics of Inequality*, p. 78.
33 Cited by Tony Judt, 'The Story of Everything', *New York Review of Books*, 21 September 2000, p. 67.
34 William L. O'Neill, *American High: The Years of Confidence, 1945-1960* (New York: The Free Press, 1986), p. 253.

areas had become dangerous and that the government should act.[36] A major shock was the clash between Zulus and Indians in Durban in 1949, ending in 147 deaths, the destruction of 300 buildings, and damage to an additional 1,700.

In 1948 Hendrik Verwoerd, in his first speech in Parliament, referred to 'Europeans and non-Europeans scattered and mingled about the whole of South Africa.' 'Europeans and non-Europeans have been working up to a crisis,' he said, 'with more and more trouble blowing up, clashes in the towns, the creation of all sorts of hamlets on the borders of the towns full of poverty and misery, clashes on the trains, assaults on women.' The Witwatersrand region had become 'one vast breeding place of injustice and crime.' For Verwoerd, increasing white-black competition in the urban labor market would produce 'the most terrific clash of interests imaginable.'[37]

D.F. Malan always believed that the lesser skilled whites could not survive this competition, but Verwoerd turned it around: whites would hold the stronger position for a long time and blacks would be 'defeated in every phase of the struggle.' This was sure to give rise among them to an increasing sense of 'resentment and revenge.' He told the Natives Representative Council after the 1948 election that the only possible way out of this was 'to adopt a development divorced from each other.' To avoid what he called 'an unpleasant and dangerous future' for both whites and blacks, the system of apartheid would 'give to others precisely what it demands for [the white man].' Separation had to be imposed wherever practicable with as its principal object 'the removal of friction.'[38]

From the start the NP's opponents locally and abroad attacked the policy because they thought it sprang predominantly from racist convictions or antiquated religious doctrines. South African liberals appealed to the common values and beliefs that bound all South Africans. For leading thinkers in the NP such arguments almost completely missed the point because the security of the Afrikaners as a dominant minority, and not race per se, was what concerned them. The Cape Town-Stellenbosch axis of the nationalist intelligentsia, which was the most influential lobby in Malan's NP, almost without exception defended apartheid not as an expression of white superiority but on the grounds of its assumed capacity to reduce conflict by curtailing the points of interracial contact.

More than anyone else Piet Cillié spelled out this line of thinking. He served as editor of the Cape Town Afrikaans daily *Die Burger* between 1954 and 1977, writing not only editorials but also most of the influential 'Dawie' column in which new ideas were floated. Cillié had a razor-sharp mind, a zest for intellectual debate, and a sardonic sense of humor, drawing on an inexhaustible supply of one-liners and quips. Along with Verwoerd, he was the most influential thinker in the Afrikaner nationalist movement between 1948 and 1976.

At a 1954 Commonwealth Relations conference in Lahore, Pakistan, Philip Mason, an acknowledged British authority on race relations, argued that the true destiny of South African whites was to serve as a 'creative minority' in a black-dominated society. The im-

---

35 Schalk Pienaar, *Getuie van groot tye* (Cape Town: Tafelberg, 1979), pp. 24-8.

36 *Die Transvaler*, 7 November 1944.

37 This point is also made by L.J. du Plessis, 'Liberalistiese en Calvinistiese Naturelle-politiek', in Federasie van Calvinistiese Studenteverenigings (compiler), *Koers in die krisis* (Stellenbosch: Pro Ecclesia, 1940), vol. 2, p. 229.

38 *Senate Debates*, 1948, col. 227; A.N. Pelzer (ed.), *Verwoerd Speaks* (Johannesburg: APB, 1966), pp. 14-24.

plication was that the Afrikaners had to give up power and put their trust in a democracy. Cillié replied that the Pakistanis themselves had sought a solution in borders between separate countries. 'Instead of clear borders and boundaries we [in South Africa] have a system of internal borders that have multiplied as our society became more mixed. This aspect of apartheid, namely the introduction of internal borders through separate residential areas, has triggered the condemnation of the world. In principle I do not like this, but without these statutory borders and boundaries one would have lynch law in South Africa.'[39]

Cillié's own central commitment was to the Afrikaner nationalist cause, not apartheid, which to him was only an instrument of that cause. He was a Machiavellian who believed that the purpose of politics was not to make men virtuous but the state safer and stronger. One could try to pursue a just racial policy and save one's soul, or one could try to serve a progressively modernizing but still repressive multi-racial state, but not always both at once.[40] For Cillié the latter option, for all its flaws and injustices, was the only available platform for stability, economic growth and incremental progress for all communities. This process of emancipation had started, he argued, with Afrikaner liberation from British imperialism, which, in turn, could lead to a form of decolonization with whites shedding their direct control over colored, Asian, and African communities in a controlled experiment. This internal decolonization and de-radicalization would, however, be allowed only to the extent that it did not threaten the Afrikaner and the larger white community.

Just after the 1948 election Henry Fagan, whose recommendation that the urbanization of Africans should be accepted had been savaged by the nationalists, remarked publicly that the will of the whites to survive would ensure their continuing political leadership.[41] Privately he wrote that the NP now had a mandate to test its policy of 'total territorial segregation.' 'If the attempt succeeds,' he continued, 'well and good. If not, it will nevertheless be a preparatory step . . . to bring the mentality of the public to maturity and to get people to acquiesce in a policy which concedes the impossibility of territorial segregation and . . . to find the best way of adapting ourselves to what is possible.'[42]

A loyal and a radical opposition

Revitalized by the founding in 1949 of a Youth League by Nelson Mandela, Oliver Tambo and Walter Sisulu, the African National Congress leadership attacked the NP government soon after it came to power. In 1952 the ANC leadership wrote to the Malan government to say that apartheid had less to do with the preservation of white identity than 'with the systematic exploitation of African people.' Calling the apartheid laws an insult to the African people, the ANC demanded direct representation for Africans in Parliament and all other legislative bodies. Malan replied that his government refused to give Africans or other 'non-white' groups any administrative or executive or legislative powers over

39 US Library, Piet Cillié documents collection, Cillié-Phil Weber, 26 March 1954.
40 Isaiah Berlin, *Against the Current* (New York: Viking Press, 1979).
41 *Die Transvaler*, 14 June 1948.
42 H.A. Fagan, *Our Responsibility* (Stellenbosch: Universiteitsuitgewers, 1959), p. 24.

whites. In another letter, to an American clergyman, Malan defended his stand. There were, he said, 'two irreconcilable ways of life: between barbarism and civilization, between over-whelming numerical odds on the one hand and insignificant numbers on the other.'[43] In this reply two quite different considerations were joined: white supremacy theory and an admission of white numerical weakness. White supremacy offered no future accom-modation of African demands; the reference to numerical weakness betrayed a white vul-nerability that could, over the longer term, seek a compromise.

The NP government was well prepared to crush radical opposition. Its main target was communists, both white and black; since the late 1930s it had frequently, in its propa-ganda, fused the themes of 'Red Menace' (the communist threat) and 'Black Peril' (the danger of an African uprising). Communist trade unionists appeared to be making some headway among the African labor force.[44] In 1950 Parliament passed the Suppression of Communism Act, banning the Communist Party of South Africa, and giving the govern-ment the power to ban publications that promoted the objectives of communism, and the power to 'name' people who could be barred from holding office, practicing as lawyers or even attending meetings. The Act, which was in 1976 extended in the Internal Security Act, defined communism as any doctrine that aimed at bringing about 'any political, in-dustrial, social or economic change in the Union by the promotion of disturbances or dis-order, by unlawful acts or omissions or by the threat of such acts and omissions.' This definition of communism was so broad and crude that its liberal opponents suspected it was seeking to trap liberals, as well, in its net.

English-speaking businessmen and the new NP government warily regarded each other in the first ten years of NP rule. Initially English big business contributed substantially to the United South African Trust Fund which funded the opposition United Party in an effort to unseat the NP. Ernest Oppenheimer, the magnate controlling the giant conglom-erate Anglo American Corporation, was the main donor. But business was hardly liberal. It refused to back the Liberal Party that Alan Paton helped to form after the 1953 elec-tion with a program of a multi-racial democracy based on universal franchise.

Business was reluctant to invest while there was so much uncertainty, politically and economically. The NP had not yet sworn off its plan to nationalize the mines and Ver-woerd, an upcoming strongman, had once propagated a plan for Afrikaner quotas in the economy (see p. 417). During the mid-1950s some speakers at a secret conference of the Afrikaner Broederbond proposed that cabinet ministers be lobbied to assist Afrikaner enterprises 'to a larger or smaller extent through the allocation of quotas.' Anton Rupert and Andreas Wassenaar, two Afrikaner business leaders, rejected this and the idea was discarded.[45] By the mid-1950s nationalization as a policy option had disappeared from the government's agenda. Business began to look with new eyes at NP rule. Its policy of promoting growth and boosting import substitution through protection received the en-thusiastic support of business, as did the conservative fiscal and monetary policy. If the government could show that it could suppress any black challenge, business would be prepared to embark on large-scale fixed investment.

---

43 These letters are published in Leo Kuper, *Passive Resistance in South Africa* (New Haven: Yale University Press, 1957), pp. 217-41.

44 A. van Deventer, 'Afrikaner Nationalist Politics and Anti-Communism, 1937-1945', doctoral diss., US, 1991, p. 225.

45 E.L.P. Stals, 'Geskiedenis van die Afrikaner-Broederbond, 1918-1994', unpublished ms., 1998, pp. 578-90.

Political apartheid

Although the NP won the 1948 election with the smallest of margins on a platform in which apartheid was only one of several planks, Malan insisted that the party had a mandate to transform society along apartheid lines.[46] There indeed was an obsession among nationalists to try out apartheid. Only when they found it could not ensure Afrikaner political survival would they choose an alternative.

Apartheid rested on several bases: political apartheid restricting all power to whites, the enforced separation of existing communities, segregated education, protection for whites in the labor market, and influx control that restricted African movement into cities. The sixth base, which was the ideological cornerstone, was the setting aside of special land areas called reserves for African residency, later renamed black or Bantu homelands, or Bantustans for short. Four months after the 1948 election Werner Eiselen, one of the leading exponents of apartheid, gave this definition of the new ideology: 'The separating of the heterogeneous groups . . . into separate socio-economic units inhabiting separate parts of the country, each enjoying in its own area full citizenship rights.'[47]

At the core of the NP's rejection of the liberal's common society model was the insistence that people voted in terms of a group identity – Afrikaners voted NP, the English voted UP, and, after 1924, those coloreds and blacks who qualified to vote almost to a man voted against whatever party most Afrikaners supported. The NP argument was that to bring growing numbers of blacks and colored people into the electorate would embitter the relationships between the white groups and between whites and blacks or coloreds.[48]

This argument suited the Afrikaners with its majority in the white electorate, but the Westminster system that was used in South Africa did not lend itself to political moderation. After 1948 the most immediate political challenge facing the NP with its slender majority of five was the coloreds holding the balance of power in several constituencies. Malan's NP, along with *Die Burger*, had abandoned the colored vote during the mid-1930s. After the 1943 election *Die Burger* observed that in thirty-one of the fifty-six Cape seats there were more than four hundred colored voters; it saw the colored vote as having secured a victory for the UP in at least five seats, concluding that the colored vote could become very significant since colored children were steadily becoming better educated and increasing at a faster rate than white pupils.[49] The NP maintained that it was unacceptable for the colored people to hold the political balance of power between the two white groups. *Die Burger* cited the case of a UP candidate who warned colored voters that the NP could do to them what Hitler had done to the Jews.[50]

In 1948 there were approximately forty thousand colored voters on the voting rolls. Of these the great majority opposed the NP. Before the election, George Golding, chairman of a statutory body, the Coloured Advisory Council, warned that an NP government would seriously threaten the colored 'race.' As leader of the moderate Coloured People's National Union, an organization with 85,000 members, he soon abandoned attempts to

46 *Smuts Papers*, vol. 7, p. 279.
47 J. Hatch, *The Dilemma of South Africa* (London: Denis Dobson, 1953), p. 32.
48 *Die Burger*, 6, 9 and 20 August 1956.
49 *Die Burger*, 3 July 1943, editorial.
50 Louis Louw (compiler), *Dawie, 1946-1964* (Cape Town: Tafelberg, 1965), p. 96.

co-operate with the new government.[51] Most of the colored leadership regarded the NP victory with dismay. They scornfully rejected any apartheid effort to foster a separate 'colored culture.' Since no distinct culture could be cited, any effort to disfranchise them had to be based squarely on race.

The NP government's plan to remove the colored vote led to the establishment by war veterans of a Torch Commando under a highly decorated soldier, A.G. ('Sailor') Malan. By 1952 it boasted 125,000 paid-up members. It organized some of the largest demonstrations the country had ever seen, but it failed to agree on the admission of colored ex-servicemen as members and got itself entangled with a Natal separatist movement.

In 1951, Parliament passed the Separate Representation of Voters Act, which relegated colored voters to a separate roll. Because this act violated the entrenched clauses in the constitution, which required a two-thirds majority for any change, a prolonged constitutional struggle ensued. By 1953, when the next election was held, some doubt had entered Cape nationalist ranks about the wisdom of removing the colored vote. An NP electoral defeat seemed increasingly remote, and the UP was making no effort to register large numbers of new colored voters. Colored voters themselves had become apathetic in the face of their circumscribed political rights; from a high of 54,000 in 1945 the registered colored voters dropped to 38,000 in 1954. In 1953 Phil Weber, *Die Burger's* editor, wrote to Albert Geyer, a former editor and then High Commissioner in London, that high qualifications for all new colored voters on a common roll would be a wiser alternative. He had discussed this with two senior Cape NP leaders, Eben Dönges and P.W. Botha, and he took their silence to mean that they agreed.[52]

But by 1953 the NP's center of gravity had shifted to the north. After the 1953 election there were twice as many Transvaal and Free State members in the NP caucus than Cape members. In 1954, J.G. Strijdom, the Transvaal NP leader, succeeded D.F. Malan as NP leader and prime minister, and he was strongly backed by Verwoerd. Weber resigned himself to the new reality and wrote to Geyer: 'We shall have to make the best of it, although I do not know if we shall be consulted much. For the sake of [party] unity we shall have to be prepared to accept a lot.'[53]

After Piet Cillié had replaced Weber as editor of *Die Burger* in 1954, the paper became more radical in defending the Afrikaner nationalist 'revolution' that was ushered in by the 1948 election victory. Cillié relished politics as a blood sport, and derived an almost perverse satisfaction during election times in casting party competition in the most extreme terms. He rarely defended apartheid on its own terms, but superimposed the Afrikaner-English struggle on the white-black or white-colored struggle. In 1952 the liberal journal *Forum* asked him to predict the NP's tactics in the next election. The article was quintessential Cillié. He poured scorn on the pretension of liberals that there was no ulterior motive in their promotion of equal rights. 'English political liberalism has always seemed to the nationalists to be more English than liberal and more concerned with power for the English-speaking section than for the non-Europeans.' The Afrikaner

---

51 D.M. Scher, 'The Disenfranchisement of the Coloured Voters, 1948-1956', unpublished doctoral diss., Unisa, 1983, pp. 71-9.
52 US Library, Weber Collection, Weber-Geyer, 8 November 1953.
53 US Library, Weber Collection, Weber-Geyer, 17 October 1954.

nationalists would approach the election as 'a fight for survival.' Should the nationalists lose, 'either immigration or the extension of non-European voting rights will ensure that they never get another chance.' A UP victory 'will usher in a semi-revolutionary epoch in which internal and external pressures will compel a weak and divided regime to grant one concession after another.'[54]

As editor he continued to warn that the UP, in a future election, could launch a *blitzkrieg* by registering large numbers of colored voters. It could lead to a civil war. *Die Burger* also condemned the 'rotten electoral system' and opposition parties only interested in colored voters at election time. But coloreds no longer represented an electoral threat. Cillié's real concern was that any attempt to reverse the removal of colored voters would split the Afrikaner nationalist movement along provincial lines.

In 1956 the government enlarged the Senate by appointing sufficient members from its own party ranks to get the necessary two-thirds majority to remove the colored vote, violating not the letter but the spirit of the constitution. When Strijdom died in 1958 Cillié lauded him as a hero whose name would be indelibly associated with some 'constitutional beacons', among them 'the regulation of the colored vote.'[55] For the sake of Afrikaner unity Cillié and *Die Burger* were evidently prepared to swallow much.

Four whites now represented the coloreds in Parliament, wielding no power at all. The government itself had shelved the colored issue. A sense of urgency returned only in the late 1970s when black resistance to the regime began to mount. The government allocated only a marginal place to the Asian community. Not until 1963 did the government recognize Asians as citizens of the republic, and it took even longer before they were given a very limited form of 'self-administration'.

Ultimately apartheid hinged on whether it could find a solution for black aspirations. The so-called black moderate urban leadership had been alienated by the time the Second World War ended, and the UP government was unable to strike out in a new, more liberal direction (see p. 453). The NP government abandoned the attempt to woo the urban African elite, who made up most of the membership of the Natives Representative Council. Instead it embarked on a crucial shift in the policy towards Africans. Under Hertzog as prime minister the accent was on 'civilized labor', while the reserves were referred to as places where black groups in an unspecified future could govern themselves. As Albert Geyer, ex-editor of *Die Burger* and now South African High Commissioner in London, pointed out, apartheid differed from pre-1948 segregation in using the reserves as justification for the comprehensive denial of any rights to blacks in the common area.[56]

Apartheid also gave much greater institutional expression to the ethnic differences among Africans. An early manifestation was NP criticism of the election of members of the Natives Representative Council. Blacks nationwide elected twelve of the twenty-two members of this body through four immense constituencies. In the NP's view it 'consolidated the native nation' and violated the 'supreme principle of the protection of the white man.'[57] By 1948 the idea had taken root that each African ethnic group had to be located in its own territory with its own form of government and national identity. In the

---

54 P. J. Cillié, The National Party's Possible Line of Attack', *Forum*, 1,7 (1952), pp. 13-14.

55 Piet Cillié, *Tydgenote* (Cape Town: Tafelberg, 1980), p. 49.

56 US Library ms. Collection, Phil Weber Papers, A.L. Geyer-Weber, 16-18 March 1952.

57 D.F. Malan in *Joint Sitting of Parliament*, 1936, cols. 591-5.

common area Africans were 'visitors', which restated the doctrine of 1921 (see p. 313), despite the extensive urbanization that had taken place in the subsequent twenty-five years.

The apartheid system of ethnic African representation would be built upon the reserves and the chiefs. Verwoerd, appointed Minister for Native Affairs in 1950, remarked that if Africans had 'ambitions in the direction of full citizenship, then they have to go back to the areas that are theirs.'[58] In 1952 the government abolished the Natives Representative Council, which had effectively ceased to function. In 1951 Verwoerd piloted through Parliament the Bantu Authorities Act of 1951, providing for three tiers of authority in the reserves, all under his control as head of the Department of Native Affairs. In opting for tribal authority with power reinforced through revived customary law, the South African government was following the example of certain colonial rulers in Africa.[59] When, for example, a black uprising, the Mau-Mau rebellion, occurred in Kenya in the mid-1950s it seemed to vindicate its choice to use the chiefs, not the urban black elite, to prop up its rule. Verwoerd observed that 'tribal authority' is 'the natural ally of government against such rebellious movements.'[60]

The system of traditional rule in South Africa by now was in an advanced state of decay. Many of the chiefs were already seen as the stooges of white magistrates, but the government favored subservient chiefs who were prepared to enforce government policy even at the cost of their own popularity. Between 1957 and 1962 the apartheid state had to move in to suppress rural resistance in areas of Sekhukhuneland, the Hurutshe reserve in the western Transvaal, and Pondoland and Thembuland in the eastern Cape.

Communal apartheid

The second part of apartheid was communal apartheid, which accorded each state-defined group a different status and different privileges. In terms of the Population Registration Act of 1950, the government classified every citizen in each identified community – whites, coloreds, and Africans – and subdivided ethnological groups of coloreds and Africans. The law transformed apartheid from a loose body of segregation measures into a system, imposing a tight racial grid.

Putting colored people in a rigid statutory pigeonhole was particularly difficult. No one could think of a positive definition of the colored people (as distinct from a definition of who they were not). They shared a Western cultural identity and strongly aspired to be incorporated into the dominant group. Jan Smuts thought of them when he responded to the Population Registration Bill. 'Don't let us trifle with this thing', he pleaded. '[We] are touching on things which go pretty deep in this land.' He called it an attempt to 'classify the unclassifiable' and reminded the government that fifteen years earlier a commission had found racial registration impractical.[61] Undeterred, the NP government pushed ahead.

---

58 Pelzer, *Verwoerd Speaks*, pp. 10-11.

59 Mahmood Mamdani, *Citizen and Subject* (Cape Town: David Philip, 1998).

60 *HAD*, 1956, col. 6617; John Lazar, 'Conformity and Conflict: Afrikaner Nationalist Politics in South Africa, 1948-1961', doctoral diss., Oxford University, 1987, p. 213.

61 *HAD*, 1950, col. 2534. For a description of the absurdities of classification see F. Van Zyl Slabbert, *The Last White Parliament* (Johannesburg: Jonathan Ball, 1985), pp. 43-52; for a brief account of a particularly tragic case see an article by Stanley Uys reprinted in John Western, *Outcast Cape Town* (Cape Town: Human & Rousseau, 1981), pp. vi-vii.

Its main criteria for classifying coloreds were where one belonged in terms of social standing and white public opinion. Whites hired as classifiers passed judgment on a person's race, using common-sense 'conventions' of racial difference.[62]

To specify the elusive identity, people were questioned about their descent and, in extreme cases, their fingernails were examined and combs pulled through their hair (if the combing encountered tough curls a person was identified as colored or not white). A third party could object to a neighbor's or other's classification, opening the door to snooping, as Smuts had warned. In later years descent took precedence over appearance and social acceptability in cases where the natural parents were known and already classified.

Classification had momentous implications. Assigned membership in a legally defined community would determine almost every important daily activity – the area where one lived, one's partner for marriage and for casual sex, the schools, colleges and universities one could attend, the people with and against whom one played any sport, the kind of job for which one qualified, and the place where one would be buried. It determined one's political rights and which bodies one could vote for. Judge L. van Winsen summed it up well. '[A] person's classification is . . . of cardinal importance to him since it affects his status in practically all fields of his life, social, economic and political. An incorrect classification can . . . have a devastating effect upon the life of the person concerned.'[63]

Eben Dönges, the minister who introduced the Bill, had originally thought that fewer than ten thousand problem cases would arise in the registration process. He asked rhetorically in Parliament: 'Is it a stigma to call a colored man a colored man?' *Die Burger* backed him up, asking: 'Why would it be a tragedy and humiliation for those who pass for coloreds to be classified as coloreds? Surely that is what they are.'[64] By 1956 nearly 100,000 borderline cases had been encountered. People were trapped in a Kafka-esque racial maze. Classification caused human tragedies of the cruelest kind. Some lovers classified in different categories, on finding they could not marry legally, committed suicide. Despite such consequences, *Die Burger*'s columnist 'Dawie' made the startling remark in 1958: 'I am still waiting for anyone to give a single example of someone who was unreasonably classified.'[65] Yet every year Parliament experienced the absurdity of government announcements of how many whites had been re-classified as coloreds (or the other way round), and how many coloreds were now deemed to be Africans.

A system of race classification had as a corollary a ban on sex between whites and people who were not white. Between 1943 and 1946 only a hundred marriages took place per year between people who were white and 'non-white', compared to thirty thousand intra-white marriages per year. The Prohibition of Mixed Marriages Act of 1949 extended the 1927 ban on marriages between whites and blacks to cover all marriages between white people and those not deemed white. The Immorality Amendment Act of 1950 outlawed carnal intercourse between a white and a non-white.

Die Burger said that the Immorality Act applied to 'weaklings', but deterred 'others

---

62 Deborah Posel, 'What's in a Name? Racial Categorisation under Apartheid', paper presented to the History workshop, Witwatersrand University, 2001.

63 Cited by John Dugard, *Human Rights and the South African Legal Order* (Princeton: Princeton University Press, 1978), p. 62.

64 *Die Burger,* 8, 17 and 20 March 1950.

65 Louis Louw (ed.), *Dawie, 1946-1964* (Cape Town: Tafelberg, 1965), p. 141.

who might also fall.' Nearly ten years later it had reconsidered its view; it now saw the Immorality Act as a harsh law, 'harsher in impact than we have imagined, causing nameless misery.'[66] To prosecute under the Immorality Act the police used binoculars, tape recorders and cameras, burst into bedrooms, and instructed district surgeons to examine the genitals of suspects. The offenders caught included not only ordinary people but also church ministers, schoolteachers, and even a private secretary to a prime minister. By 1985 some 11,500 people had been convicted and many more had been charged. Facing widespread ostracism, some white offenders committed suicide or emigrated. Not until 1985 was the Immorality Act erased from the books.

The enforced segregation of people into residential or 'group' areas reinforced the apartheid grid. Government policy for two decades had been to build separate colored townships, but by 1950 almost a third of colored people in Cape Town still lived in mixed areas, often called 'onderdorpe.' In the Cape Province no law restricted colored people or Africans from living where they wished or buying property in the Cape Colony. The Group Areas Act of 1950 changed this by establishing different urban living spaces for whites, blacks, colored people and Indians. It restricted ownership and the occupation of land to a specific statutory group. The Reservation of Separate Amenities Act mandated the segregation of public facilities; non-whites and whites were required to use separate entrances, separate buses or separate seats in buses, separate train coaches, separate parks and separate public toilets. Non-whites could only be served over a counter and not at a table in restaurants in the so-called white business areas and were excluded from white theatres and cinemas, hotels (except segregated bars) and swimming pools. Separate beaches were allocated.

In adopting such a policy of residential segregation the government, as earlier, had greatly underestimated the scale of the undertaking. When the Act was introduced, Dönges stated that persons of a single group occupied 80 to 90 per cent of the different residential areas in South African towns and cities. Separation should not be difficult, therefore. But the law had a far more drastic impact. When the government announced its detailed proposals for Cape Town, the UP-controlled City Council was so shocked that it boycotted the public hearings. Eventually one out of every four colored people and one out of six Asian people (against only one in 666 whites) across the country had to move. The most controversial action occurred in the second half of the 1960s, with the removal of 65,000 coloreds from District Six, a vibrant but crime-infested inner city ward of Cape Town, where whites, many of them slumlords, owned 56 per cent of the property. Against their will District Six residents were moved out to the sandy townships of the Cape Flats or the distant township of Mitchells Plain to the east and Atlantis to the north. Colored families across the Cape Province were pushed out from the onderdorpe to townships a mile 'or two outside the main town.[67]

It has been remarked in a different context that it is not only what is bad but what is good in a people that can turn them into unfeeling oppressors. In theory the application

---

66 M.J. Mittner, 'Die Burger en die Kleurling-stem', master's diss., UCT, 1986, pp. 101-33. ; J.J.F.C. Heydenrych, 'Die maatskaplike implikasies by die toepassing van Artikel 16 van Wet 23 van 1957', master's diss., US, 1968, p. 142.

67 Connie Laubscher, 'Die geskiedenis van grondbesit in Distrik Ses tot 1984', doctoral diss, US, 2001.

of the stated liberal principle of freedom and the nationalist principles of brotherhood and community could offer a dignified and satisfactory life. But in the hands of people single-mindedly seeking group dominance these principles can be turned into a horrific cold-blooded system.[68]

Anthony Delius, an outstanding liberal journalist, pointed out in the early 1950s that the nationalist intelligentsia appropriated the good things in Afrikaner history and in particular the quest for cultural pride, group autonomy and freedom.[69] They presented apartheid as a policy that would take away no rights without 'putting something good or something better in its place.' The rationale offered for segregated suburbs was that it would end a situation where black or colored people living as 'appendages' in mixed areas had developed 'a sense of inferiority.' Living in their 'own' townships would provide them with a greater sense of dignity and self-worth. They could start their own businesses in their own place and participate in local government, once their township had developed sufficiently. In this way they could become a real community.

Those on the receiving end of the policy saw the policy very differently. During the late 1980s Allan Hendrickse, leader of the colored Labour Party, asked President Botha to return District Six in Cape Town to the colored people. Botha, who in 1966 was the minister in charge of the District Six removals, responded that 'You must thank me for what I have done, because now you are living in dignity.'[70] By this he meant that people presumably once exploited by slumlords in District Six were now homeowners.

This perspective completely ignored the powerless humiliation of people forced out of beloved homes and neighborhoods and the shortcomings of the alternative the state offered. The new residential areas for blacks, coloreds and Indians failed to develop any economic or social dynamism. Many neighborhoods and even families had been broken up in the removals and people were dumped in new areas that lacked infrastructure. A number had better housing and many coloreds and Indians, previously renters of rooms or houses, had become homeowners, but some property owners had suffered crippling losses, with white speculators realizing enormous returns when a property had to be sold on eviction. The group areas removals put the poor at a considerable distance from their places of work, often without adequate public transport. The absence of established social norms gave rise to high crime rates.

In African townships security considerations were of paramount importance to the government. Just after the 1948 election, Dönges, Minister for the Interior, told a British journalist that the mining compound was the new government's model of social control of urbanized Africans. They were to be closely supervised and could visit the white town only with a permit. 'He believed,' the journalist noted, 'that it was only by this method that Non-Europeans could be completely separate and under control of Europeans.'[71] Verwoerd, appointed Minister for Native Affairs in 1954, and keenly interested in urban security, ordered that every African township be clearly demarcated, with a *cordon sanitaire* separating it from both the white residential areas and the group areas of coloreds

---

68 These remarks were made in the context of Northern Ireland. See Joseph O' Neill, *Blood-Dark Tracks* (London: Granta, 2001).

69 Anthony Delius, 'The Missing Liberal Policy', *Forum,* 1952, pp. 40-41.

70 *Sunday Tribune,* 2 October 1988; Paul Bell, 'Our only sin', *Leadership,* vol. 7, no. 3 (1988), p. 57.

71 Hatch, *The Dilemma of South Africa,* p. 93.

and Indians. Entrances by road were limited to two or three; township streets were purposely wide so police could control movement more easily.

A pattern of residential segregation for Africans had been in place before 1948, but Africans also lived in mixed residential areas, like Sophiatown, where many were homeowners. With the Natives Resettlement Act of 1954 the government removed them all to a vast new township southwest of Johannesburg, called Soweto. Sophiatown was rezoned for whites only and renamed Triomf (Triumph).

Verwoerd had assumed that the discontent of urban blacks could be bought off by providing more orderly living conditions. Thus, in the first fifteen years of apartheid there was large-scale construction of dwellings for black groups. By 1958 many former slums in and around the major cities had been cleared and some hundred thousand houses for Africans had been built under the supervision of Verwoerd's department. As in most township developments, the abodes were small and the township architecturally monotonous with few public amenities.

Apartheid education

By 1948 the education of black people was still for more than 90 per cent an extension of the missionary enterprise. Illiteracy was widespread. Although some mission schools provided good education, the overall state of black education was extremely poor: only three per cent of blacks had received post-primary school education by 1952 and only 8,488 blacks had a Matric qualification, one-fifth of the number of whites passing this standard every year. In 1947 there were only four colored high schools and 182 candidates who qualified for the final examination of the last school year.

White supremacy was clearly incompatible with a steadily rising, better educated, urbanized black population moving up to strategic levels of the economy. Recognizing this, J.G. Strijdom, Transvaal NP leader, warned D.F Malan in 1946 that it would be impossible to maintain racial discrimination if the quality of education of the subordinate people was steadily improved. 'Our church ministers,' he added, 'were far too eager to compete with other church societies in trying to provide on annual basis the most education to *klein kaffertjies* (small black children).' If the state in the future tried to withhold equal rights from educated people it would lead to 'bloody clashes and revolutions.'[72] To put it in non-racist terms, by modernizing the provision of education to the subordinates, however incompletely, the apartheid state was sowing the seeds of its own destruction. Yet for the Afrikaner nationalists to deny the subordinates a proper education would undermine their conception that they were serious in their commitment to rehabilitate the subordinate population. Verwoerd's compromise was to expand black education greatly, with the provision that it be closely linked to and confined to service to the community.

The issue of the reform of black education had already been put on the agenda by the Smuts government, which, in 1945, moved financial control of black education from the provinces to central government. In 1949 the new government established a commission of inquiry into native education, under the chairmanship of Werner Eiselen, which pro-

---

72 H.B. Thom, *D.F Malan* (Cape Town: Tafelberg, 1980), p. 279.

posed a new state-controlled system. Its report ignored theories of racial inferiority and worried mostly about the lack of a *groepsgevoel* (group feeling) among blacks. It pointed out that African cultures were dynamic and could provide the context for the modernization of entire peoples. Instead of imitating English culture, the system had to inculcate pride in the *volkseie* – the history, customs, habits, character and mentality of a people. The report also evinced a strong belief in the superiority of mother-tongue education. As a result of the report, the ethnic language was made compulsory during the entire primary school and, subsequently, in secondary school as well.

The government accepted the report's recommendation that the state take control of black education. The system of education provided by churches and missions was close to collapse. The black labor force in the cities was unsettled, lacking housing, transport and proper wages, and the youth was seen to be uncontrollable. As Jonathan Hyslop notes in his analysis, the new system succeeded in imposing the state's hegemony, drawing the youth into a mass education system and providing a better quality labor force. It was, to be sure, 'grossly inegalitarian and racist, but the fact was that parents supported it and that the attempts to boycott it failed for nearly two decades.'[73]

In announcing the new system in 1945 Verwoerd used words that in subsequent decades doomed the policy in the eyes of many blacks. He said that the black child had been subjected to a school system 'which drew him away from his own community and practically misled him by showing him the green pastures of the European, but still did not allow him to pasture there.' In the future there would be 'no place for him above the level of certain forms of labor.' Within his own community, however, 'all doors are open.'[74] By this Verwoerd meant that black children had to be prepared for serving their own community, firstly in the envisaged black states, where there would be no ceiling on their aspirations, and secondly in the common area as teachers, nurses and policemen serving the black community. The formulation in fact affirmed what was the situation on the ground in the common area where blacks always had been excluded from skilled or other advanced jobs and the central state bureaucracy. As Hyslop remarks, 'what was new was Verwoerd's aim of opening new structures of black incorporation through the homelands.'[75] As with almost all nationalist politicians, Verwoerd's first concern was his own constituency, who, like Strijdom, Verwoerd's close associate, might worry about the political consequences of the dramatic extension of black education.

Verwoerd also provoked hostility by saying that it did not serve any purpose to teach a black child mathematics if he or she could not use it. In fact many schools continued to offer mathematics. In general the syllabuses were very much the same as in the white schools and an improvement on those used previously in the black schools.[76]

The medium of instruction also became a bone of contention. To implement the poli-

---

73 Jonathan Hyslop, '"A Destruction Coming in": Bantu Education as a Response to Social Crisis', in P. Bonner et al. (eds.), *Apartheid's Genesis, 1935-1962* (Johannesburg: Ravan, 1993), pp. 393-410.
74 Pelzer, *Verwoerd Speaks*, p. 83; for an analysis see Jonathan Hyslop, *The Classroom Struggle* (Pietermaritzburg: University of Natal Press, 1999), pp. 57-9.
75 Hyslop, *The Classroom Struggle*, p. 56.
76 Ken Hartshorne, *Crisis and Challenge: Black Education, 1910-1990* (Cape Town: Oxford University Press, 1992), pp. 86-7.

cy of mother-tongue instruction from the first to the eighth years of school the department had the mammoth task of preparing material in the different African languages. To establish what language medium had to be used in secondary education (after the eighth year) the department canvassed the opinion of the boards of control of schools throughout the country. Two-thirds preferred Afrikaans and English; one-third English alone and only one per cent wanted the mother tongue.[77] The department used both languages, but was flexible enough initially not to insist on Afrikaans in the Transkei, Natal and parts of the Witwatersrand where the teachers were not proficient in Afrikaans.

The greatest defect of 'Bantu education', as it came to be called, was the inadequate funding. For nearly two decades the government pegged its own statutory spending on black education through the general budget at the same level. Although the expenditure on black education grew, the sharp increase in the number of children absorbed by the system resulted in per capita spending on black children falling by a third in this period. The system paid very little attention to the need for secondary education until the early 1970s. The number of Africans who passed the highest standard with what was called a school-leaving certificate remained stagnant between the final years of the old system and 1961 (ranging between 279 and 338 between 1954 and 1961 compared to an increase of 12,166 for whites in 1954 to 22,341 during the same period). The government put obstacles in the way of urban black children by locating most of the new schools offering the highest school standards in the reserves. As late as 1966 there were only 1,615 black children in the final school year and only 14,183 in the tenth year (Standard Eight).[78]

Despite its obvious defects, the new black education system did represent a major expansion that saw numbers of blacks in primary education double by 1959. In 1948 only 24 per cent of blacks of school-going age were enrolled in schools; by 1994 the proportion had risen to 84 per cent, a steady increase in black pupils of an average of 5.8 per cent per year.[79] The following figures show the doubling of numbers in black schools in the 1950s.[80]

GROWTH OF AFRICAN EDUCATION

YEAR	NUMBER OF PUPILS	EXPENDITURE
1950	746,324	R 10,144,088
1955	1,013,358	R 15,769,550
1961	1,608,668	R 20,077,245

Westernized Africans continued to refer to the system as 'gutter education', designed to prepare blacks for a marginal place in life.[81] The elite wanted education in the English

---

77 Joubert Rousseau, 'Iets oor Bantoe-onderwys', in W.J. Verwoerd (ed.), *Verwoerd* (Pretoria: Protea Boekhuis, 2001), p. 174.

78 Cynthia Kros, 'Economic, Political and Intellectual Origins of Bantu Education, 1926-1951', doctoral diss., University of the Witwatersrand, 1996, pp. 391-6; Hartshorne, *Crisis and Challenge*, pp. 57-70; Hyslop, *The Classroom Struggle*, pp. 56-60.

79 Personal communication, 9 July 2001.

80 A.J.B. van der Mescht, 'Bantoe-onderwys sedert die wet op Bantoe-onderwys', master's diss., University of Stellenbosch, 1965, p. 375.

81 Ken Hartshorne, *The Making of Education Policy in South Africa* (Cape Town: Oxford University Press, 1999), pp. 19-25.

language because it knew that black career chances depended on it. It wanted jobs in the common economy, not restricted to serving African society. It saw the emphasis on distinct Bantu cultures as an attempt at divide-and-rule rather than as based on any genuine concern for these cultures. During the 1970s these campaigns began to be successful.

The government did not go to the same lengths to restructure education in colored and Indian schools, but there was a pronounced shift in the policy towards the medium of instruction in colored schools. In 1936 some 42,000 colored children were taught in Afrikaans, 16,500 in English and 20,000 in both languages more or less equally. By the 1970s almost all were taught in Afrikaans only; very little instruction was in English and virtually none in both languages.[82] State spending on colored education grew steadily from 1930 as the government accepted increasing responsibility for it. By 1948 the nominal amount spent was nearly ten times higher than twelve years earlier. Under the NP government the improvement in colored education accelerated. Between 1946 and 1953 the number of colored high schools rose from five to eighteen. The total number of colored children in school rose by nearly a quarter and the total number of teachers by nearly half.[83] The number of colored pupils qualifying for the final year (Matric) examination rose from 182 in 1947 to 387 in 1953. The same trends were at work in Asian education.[84]

In 1959 the government introduced legislation to segregate universities by race. 'White' universities could accept no black or colored students for any course also offered at their designated black or colored universities. One of the main objectives of the new policy was to remove black students from the influence of liberal academics and the city environment. Students at the 'bush colleges' did not become the leaders of their respective ethnic communities, as the apartheid system envisaged, but the most disaffected elements in the subordinate population. The system failed to produce the 'apartheid man' among the subordinates, without which it could not survive.

Curbs on blacks

The apartheid system strongly opposed any unionization of black workers. In 1953 blacks were barred from belonging to registered unions, and representatives of black workers were forbidden to attend meetings of industrial councils. Employers were pressured to ignore black unions. Those who tried to organize black workers despite the ban were 'listed' as communists and banned or detained. By 1960 most black unions had been smashed. Coloreds and Asians could remain members of registered unions, but the government sought to get unions to segregate their branches.

The Industrial Conciliation Act of 1956 made it possible to reserve jobs for members of racial communities. For some time, only whites served as lift operators, ambulance men and traffic police. Such determinations, while symbolically important, did not affect more than two per cent of jobs. More important was an informal color bar. The government put strong pressure on employers not to replace white workers with blacks, put blacks in a position of authority over whites or rely too much on black labor.

---

82 E.G. Malherbe, *Education in South Africa* (Cape Town: Juta, 1977), vol. 2, p. 111.

83 N.J. Marais, 'Die voorsiening en administrasie van Kleurlingonderwys in Kaapland veral sedert 1910', Masters diss., US, 1955, pp. 130-38.

84 For figures on black, colored and Asian education see Malherbe, *Education in South Africa*, pp. 721-6.

To reduce the numbers of blacks permanently resident in the common area, the government tried to extend the migrant labor system of the mines to secondary industry and to establish border industries. This made it possible to provide housing for blacks in the reserves. Verwoerd proposed such industries as an important part of the solution. He extolled the value of a society where black workers returned every evening, even if they had to travel long distances, to their home in the reserves. He envisaged the government's increasingly providing new public service infrastructure such as hospitals, schools and housing in the reserves. These measures negatively affected productivity and the acquisition of skills. However, apartheid was introduced when the South African manufacturing sector was still small and unsophisticated, contributing only 17 per cent to the national economy (against a combined contribution of 30 per cent for agriculture and mining). Until the early 1970s employers could adapt to apartheid and still be very profitable.

The most severe curb on black labor was influx control, which underpinned the migrant labor system. Laws passed before 1948 had compelled blacks to carry passes but had exempted women, church ministers and teachers. From the moment he became Minister for Native Affairs in 1950 Verwoerd set as a priority the limiting of permanently urbanized blacks to a minimum by means of stiffer influx control. Passed in 1952, the Natives Laws Amendment Act imposed much harsher influx controls and abolished the exemption for professional blacks. Africans who had not established a claim to be in the urban areas were given only 72 hours in the towns and cities to find work and were compelled to register at a government labor bureau for this purpose. From 1957 on women, too, had to carry passes. Prosecutions for pass law offences rose from an average of 318,700 per year in the 1950s to 541,500 per year in the early 1970s.

The permanently urbanized Africans were considered the apartheid system's elite. They, too, had to carry passes, but they did not have to register at a labor bureau and they were first in line for government housing. At the bottom of the pile were black migrants and farm workers with extremely limited chances. Black farm workers could leave only if a labor bureau certified that the labor supply in the district was already adequate. Black migrant workers had to accept whatever contract they were offered by a labor bureau. They could not go out and search for work on their own. Separated from their families for the greatest part of the year, such workers lived in degrading conditions in single-sex hostels. And, because of the absence of the adult men from the reserves, the agricultural land there could not be worked properly, in turn forcing even more men to become migrants. By 1960 perhaps two out five black workers legally employed were migrants. In no other country of the world did migrant labor last for so long and on such an extensive scale.

The government's tough influx control measures failed in their goal of stemming the tide of black urbanization. Secondary industry, for example, preferred docile and cheap migrant laborers to the settled urban blacks, whom they regarded as choosy, ill disciplined and too expensive. Employers generally called the tune, and, as a result, the urban black population grew from 2.4 million in 1951 to 3.5 million in 1960 – an increase of nearly 45 per cent. The number of blacks employed in the commercial and manufacturing sector increased by half in the same period. The number of migrant laborers rose sharply.

On census day in 1960 there were 65 per cent fewer migrant workers present in the rural areas than there had been on the day the 1946 census was taken.

Apartheid was one of the most extreme systems of state intervention in the lives of its subordinate population ever designed. It turned Africans into foreigners in their own country, who could not own land except in the 13 per cent designated to them, could not move without their passes, could not resettle in another district in the common area without a permit and could not do skilled work. They could be arrested at any moment and there was always some law under which they could be charged and found guilty. The black prison population in relation to the black population was among the highest in the world.

Apartheid was slightly less onerous for coloreds and Asians since they did not have to carry passes and had more labor mobility, but they, too, could only live in their 'group areas', were denied access to all white schools, prohibited from using most public facilities, could not join the Defence Force, were excluded from white competitive sport, also on international level, and were likely to be punished as severely as their white partner if they transgressed the racial sex laws. When a referendum on a republic was held they could not vote and when it was proclaimed Hendrik Verwoerd, Prime Minister, declared: 'When I talk about the nation, I talk of the white people of South Africa.' It meant, Richard van der Ross, a colored leader responded, that 'in future no non-white South African need regard "Die Stem" as his national anthem or the South African national flag as his flag.'[85]

Initial responses to apartheid

From the very first stages of apartheid the ANC spearheaded the opposition to the apartheid laws. The organization, together with the South African Indian Congress, staged largely peaceful protests. The two movements singled out the acts suppressing people deemed communists, the introduction of 'Bantu authorities' in the reserves, the removal of colored voters, residential segregation and the segregation of public amenities, and the pass laws. Volunteers courted arrest by defying apartheid laws, but although the state punished the offenders harshly, ANC membership mushroomed, for a period, from 10,000 to 100,000. Very few whites supported the campaign. After the government restricted the leaders, its financing and volunteers dwindled. In 1956 the police arrested 156 people, including leading ANC activists, and put them on trial for high treason. All were given bail, pending trial, and the charges against most of the accused were later withdrawn, suggesting that the primary purpose was to suppress agitation.

In this the state was largely successful. By the end of the 1950s ANC-led mass resistance had fizzled out, its organizational structures and linkages between leaders and masses weak. Relentless government oppression led to the loss of old members and the failure to recruit new blood. The ANC leadership had become 'realist', calling for multiracial alliances and negotiations to bring about a black-ruled democracy. A new organization, the Pan Africanist Congress, was founded in 1959 as a radical offshoot of the ANC. It stressed the value of Africans organizing on their own and thought that a decisive challenge to the system would come from an escalation of spontaneous mass action.

---

85 R.E. van der Ross, *Coloured Viewpoint* (Cape Town: University of the Western Cape, 1984), pp. 102, 181. The article was originally published on 6 October 1960.

Under apartheid almost all the white classes did well. During the first ten years of NP rule real white wages in manufacturing and construction rose steadily. White farmers had prospered since the outbreak of the Second World War, with the price index of agricultural produce quadrupling between 1939 and 1955 while consumer prices only doubled. At the same time, however, the real wages of farm workers and black miners remained stagnant until the early 1970s.[86] The fact that the system made it almost impossible for a farm worker to move directly from a farm to a town served the interests of the white farmers, who needed a stable labor force. They became one of the strongest bases of NP support.

Afrikaners advanced more rapidly than other groups during the 1950s, particularly as a result of employment in the public sector. Between 1946 and 1960 the per capita income of English-speaking whites, blacks, colored people and Asians doubled (from a very low base in the latter three cases), but that of Afrikaners trebled. Most whites were oblivious of the hardship and misery among African and colored people. According to one estimate made in the early 1950s, not even half of the colored people in Cape Town lived at a minimum level of subsistence, while in the rural areas 'terrible poverty . . . even starvation' existed.[87] The position of Africans was worse. For most black and colored people life was a question of physical survival.

Control of the state and the implementation of the project to Afrikanerize the state rather than apartheid attracted growing Afrikaner numbers to the NP. With regard to apartheid itself, the Afrikaner nationalist movement provided a home to two quite different kinds of supporters. One group, crude apartheid racists, saw the policy as the ideal instrument to keep blacks and coloreds down. Blacks seemed to experience the coming to power of the NP as a much harsher form of white domination. Oliver Tambo, leader of the ANC in exile during the 1970s and 1980s, kept a handkerchief he used to wipe his face after a white man had spat on him while walking down the street on the day the NP victory in the 1953 election was announced.[88] Press reports and court cases suggest that particularly during the first fifteen years of NP rule many blacks experienced violence and insults from policemen, warders and farmers. Practices like the rounding up of 'idle blacks' in towns and forcing them to work on farms were condoned or even permitted by high officials.[89]

Apartheid created a strong momentum of its own. NP supporters, in general, demanded that whites get the better jobs and that ever more services and facilities be segregated: blood transfusions, graveyards, public toilets, parks, benches and the best beaches. Employers wanted an abundant supply of cheap and docile black labor. 'The sober truth', a SABRA booklet observed, is that 'a comparatively large part of the European population wants and makes use of Natives as laborers, but pays little attention to their welfare and future.'[90]

---

86 Heribert Adam and Hermann Giliomee, *Ethnic Power Mobilized: Can South African Change?* (New Haven: Yale University Press, 1979), pp. 160-76; Dan O'Meara, *Forty Lost Years* (Johannesburg: Ravan Press, 1996), pp. 74-82.

87 Scher, 'Disenfranchisement', p. 345.

88 Report of Clive Mennell, member of the business delegation to the ANC leadership in exile, undated.

89 Patrick Duncan, *South Africa's Rule of Violence* (London: Methuen, 1964).

90 SABRA, *Integration or Separate Development* (Stellenbosch, 1952), p. 14..

The other group, apartheid theorists (some scholars call them apartheid idealists), believed that apartheid offered more opportunities for the subordinates than they would get in a common system where they would suffer pervasive discrimination. Apartheid, the theorists believed, would provide a steadily expanding field of jobs serving the subordinate communities.

Until 1960 SABRA was the most prominent organization of the apartheid theorists. They found it difficult to criticize apartheid aloud since the nationalists commonly denounced any such criticism as deserting the Afrikaner cause to curry favor with the English community. There were, nevertheless, some voices that pointed out disturbing political tendencies. Willem van Heerden, editor of the Johannesburg newspaper *Dagbreek*, warned that neither the NP nor the UP was spelling out policy implications and suggested that the color problem could be solved only by 'whites making sacrifices and yielding privileges.'[91]

During the first decade of apartheid rule it was not at all clear that the homelands policy would become the hub of the attempt to justify apartheid. The Afrikaner Broederbond, which had no significant role in shaping the 1948 apartheid platform, hardly mentioned the reserves in its own internal documents and, in a 1954 circular on the racial issue, referred to it along with five other policy objectives.[92] Malan himself was unenthusiastic. Privately he rejected the idea that was being mooted by SABRA of self-governing African homelands as an essential part of apartheid. He was, he said, quite happy to stick to 'group areas apartheid.'[93]

In the cabinet there were serious tensions about the direction of future policy. The pragmatists, with Ben Schoeman, Minister of Transport, leading the fight, emphasized economic growth, even if that would mean increased black numbers in the 'white' area. Opposing him was Verwoerd, who took the line that economic considerations could not be paramount; he suggested legislation to prohibit all new African work-seekers from entering the Witwatersrand area, particularly Johannesburg. Schoeman objected to this: the economic effects, he said, would be disastrous. When Verwoerd later wanted to bar Africans from the western Cape, Schoeman called it a stupid policy; as Minister of Transport he would continue to use black labor on the railways there.[94] He regarded Verwoerd's talk of border industries a 'mirage.'[95]

In *Die Burger* circles there was mounting concern about the disarray over policy, particularly evident in the correspondence between Albert Geyer, at that point the High Commissioner in London, and Phil Weber, the editor, who regularly attended the NP caucus in an ex-officio capacity. 'What really is the conception that old Doctor [Malan] has of apartheid?' Geyer asked Weber in January 1953. 'It seems as if it consists of nothing more than adopting a series of laws with a negative character . . . Do we really want to

---

91 *Dagbreek*, 5 October 1947.

92 E.L.P. Stals, 'Die geskiedenis van die Afrikaner-Broederbond, 1918-1994' unpublished ms., 1998, p. 307.

93 US Library, D.F. Malan Collection 1/1/3268, 'Herinneringe aan my vader' by Daniël Malan, 1965, p. 48; Lombard, 'Ontwikkeling', p. 264.

94 Ben Schoeman, *My lewe in die politiek* (Johannesburg: Perskor, 1978), pp. 41, 241.

95 The vacillation of the first NP cabinets in the eyes of well-placed observers come through strongly in the correspondence between Albert Geyer and Phil Weber, held in the University of Stellenbosch library manuscript collection.

have apartheid as something that is more than making our current position temporarily more secure?' Weber replied: 'We have to make haste with the implementation of the positive aspects of apartheid in order to win over the more conservative blacks, otherwise we are doomed. We cannot over the longer run govern black masses who are actively hostile to us.'[96]

Weber and Geyer were not only unhappy with the emphasis on 'negative apartheid', but also with the fact that African urbanization continued despite the tougher influx control measures. In 1953 Weber wrote to a colleague: 'We say that economic integration will lead to the granting of political rights and our downfall, but in the meantime we are integrating faster than ever over the past ten years. It cannot go on this way. We must realize that apartheid is not separate entrances and counters. Our intelligentsia will probably force us to look facts in the eyes, if *Die Burger* does not do so.' To Geyer he wrote: 'I sometimes think that we shall get apartheid but after horrendous riots, as in India and Pakistan.'[97]

The rejection of the Tomlinson vision

The moment of truth for the apartheid theorists came when the Tomlinson report was tabled in Parliament. During the first half of the 1950s, Professor F.R. Tomlinson, assisted by a research team, of whom most were SABRA members, investigated the condition of the reserves. Apart from Tomlinson, two Stellenbosch academics, Nic Olivier and Jan Sadie, made the most important contributions. Most of the demographic assumptions of both the Tomlinson Commission and Verwoerd and the other apartheid planners were based on Sadie's work. By the beginning of the 1950s, when demography as a science was still unable to provide reasonably accurate projections of African population growth, Sadie estimated that the African population would grow from 7.8 million in 1946 to 18.9 million in 2000, with whites expected to increase from 2.3 million to 5.7 million. In a 1989 article Sadie revisited these projections. The African population was growing by three per cent in the 1980s, compared to two per cent in the decade just before the introduction of apartheid. He now expected African numbers not to stand at nineteen million but to rise to thirty-one million by 2000. Because of the much faster population growth rate of blacks many of the key assumptions of both Tomlinson and Verwoerd proved to be unsound.[98]

In drafting the political report Olivier articulated the basic position of the apartheid theorists. Although twenty years younger, Olivier was one of the very few in the Afrikaner nationalist movement to match Verwoerd's own formidable intellectual ability and force of personality. But from the start the relationship between the two was strained. Shortly after Verwoerd had become Minister of Native Affairs, a SABRA delegation met him to discuss a memorandum Olivier had drawn up. Verwoerd, who could explain the logical consistency of apartheid better than anyone else – even if his premise was flawed –

96 US Library, Weber Collection, Geyer-Weber, 31 January 1953; Weber-Geyer, 6 February 1953.
97 US Library, Weber Collection, Weber-Geyer, 6 February 1953.
98 J.L. Sadie, 'The Political Arithmetic of Apartheid', in P. Hugo (ed.), *South African Perspectives* (Cape Town: Die Suid-Afrikaan), 1989.

declared at the outset: 'I have read the document. Let me state what you wanted to tell me, and then say what you actually should have told me and then I shall give you my reply.' Understandably, Olivier was furious.[99]

Olivier's argument in the Tomlinson report was that there was no middle road, only a choice between total integration or a way that ultimately would lead to total apartheid. One part of the argument built on a political prognosis. The government's policy would lead inescapably towards integration, setting in train inexorable pressures for African industrial and political rights. This development was bound to cause major conflicts since whites would never 'be willing to sacrifice its character as a national entity or as an European racial group.'

The other part of the Olivier's argument was a moral one. For apartheid to be considered just, whites would have to make enormous sacrifices in giving up land and providing funds for the socio-economic development of the reserves. It would be a farce to give Africans political rights in the reserves without sufficient land and without a greatly increased capacity to provide subsistence. Only large-scale homeland development would guarantee the white population its survival free of anxiety.[100]

For the homelands to be considered a solution, even of very limited kind, a gargantuan effort was needed. The reserves had no industries, factories, towns of any significance, services or proven mineral deposits. Most of the residents were women, children and the elderly, all dependent on the earnings of males between the ages of sixteen and sixty working in the common area. Research revealed that not even one-tenth of the permanent population enjoyed an economic existence. Only massive expenditure would push up the capacity of the reserves so that they could become a real home for more than half their population. Even if the proposals for agricultural and industrial development in the reserves were implemented, there would still be large-scale migrant labor, causing a major disruption of African family life.

The Tomlinson Commission report was presented to Verwoerd in October 1954. In Tomlinson's own words, his massive report of seventeen volumes consisting of 3,755 pages and 598 tables was an attempt to give substance to the apartheid slogan. The report argued that the 'homelands' could become economically self-sufficient on the basis of their development and the perpetuation of the migrant labor system. Small-scale labor-intensive farms, held either individually or communally, could ensure 'a minimum standard of decency' for about half the reserves' population and keep the head of the family on the land.[101]

To sustain the rest of the population the report proposed industrial development based on both white private capital and state investment. The government should spend £104 million (R10 billion in 1998 values) over the next ten years to develop the reserves. The Commission calculated that if these steps were taken, fifty thousand new jobs would be created per annum in the reserves, and if this could be sustained until the end of the century the reserves would carry an African population of ten million. (Included in this

---

99 Fanie Botha, 'Leier en Vriend', in W.J. Verwoerd, *Verwoerd*, p. 107.

100 SABRA, *Die Naturellevraagstuk* (Stellenbosch, 1950), pp. 66-81; Lazar, 'Conformity and Conflict', pp. 164-216.

101 F.R. Tomlinson, 'Rejoinders', *Social Dynamics*, 6.1 (1980), pp. 49-52.

figure were the dependants of migrants.) The number of Africans in the white areas, then, would not be larger than the number of whites.

The report couched the apartheid ideology in more scientific terms. It presented the contentious historical argument that blacks had no prior claim to a very large part of South Africa and as a result could not obtain rights in the 'white' areas. It also rejected more strongly than any previous document the homogeneity of the African population. Africans – the report preferred to call them Bantus – were projected as consisting of distinct ethnic groups, each with its own territory as a 'homeland.' It proposed the consolidation of the 'Bantu areas' into 'seven historiological nuclei or heartlands, based on the linguistic and territorial divisions of the country.'[102]

Van Wyk Louw, now a professor at the Gemeentelijke Universiteit in Amsterdam, in two talks on the Dutch radio welcomed the Tomlinson Commission report. 'A small ray of light has come: what is ethically right is perhaps – if the good will is there – not economically impossible.'[103] In his lectures he proposed as a solution for the racial question the idea of a number of black states that would become independent or be federated with a white state. Invariably this triggered the question: 'Will your government do that?' To this Louw could only answer: 'That is what Afrikaner intellectuals think, but whether the government will have the courage is a question you should ask the government.'[104]

Verwoerd had no intention of allowing people like Tomlinson, Olivier and Van Wyk Louw to set the apartheid agenda. He had become Minister of Native Affairs after the commission had been appointed. He disliked both Tomlinson and Olivier, and thought that the commission encroached on his department's turf. And he was under fire from hard-core racists in his support group for 'doing too much for the Bantu.'[105] His government was extremely reluctant to make any sacrifices that would hurt its electoral support. Fearful of alienating farmers, the government had not even bought one-tenth of the additional amount of land for the reserves in terms of the 1936 legislation. There was not much evidence at subsequent NP congresses that either the leadership or the rank and file had much enthusiasm for the visions of SABRA and Tomlinson. Not only Verwoerd, but other senior ministers as well, displayed irritation with their 'unrealistic' proposals that had leaked out. The irony was that Verwoerd, always presented as a politician blinded by ideological obsession, resented the commission because he wanted to deal pragmatically with the demand for black labor.

Verwoerd was one of the strongest contenders for the position of prime minister that the ailing Strijdom was likely to vacate soon. To win support, he could not present himself simply as a Transvaal hard-liner. He now proceeded to formulate a policy that ripped all the economic substance out of the development plans of SABRA and the Tomlinson Commission, but used all their political proposals and ideological arguments to justify his plan. In debating the report in Parliament, Verwoerd employed the commission's demographic projections to demonstrate that whites in white areas would be swamped by

102 US Library, Tomlinson Collection, Verslag van die sosio-ekonomiese ontwikkeling van die Bantoegebiede . . .' (Tomlinson Commission), 17 volumes. See the analysis of it by Adam Ashforth, *The Politics of Official Discourse in Twentieth-Century South Africa* (Oxford: Clarendon Press, 1990), pp. 173-7.

103 N.P. van Wyk Louw, *Versamelde prosa* (Cape Town: Human & Rousseau, 1986), vol. 2, pp. 593-4.

104 J.C. Steyn, *Van Wyk Louw: 'n Lewensverhaal* (Cape Town: Tafelberg, 1998), p. 644.

105 Fred Barnard, *Dertien jaar in die skadu van Verwoerd* (Johannesburg: Voortrekkerpers, 1967), p. 49.

2000 if most of the expected black increase of ten to eleven million lived in the white areas, particularly in the cities. The solution, he said, lay in stopping the urbanization of blacks once and for all and accommodating the black increase in the reserves. Playing the demographic card was a triumph for Verwoerd. Hailing him as 'a man of vision', the 'Dawie' column in *Die Burger* stated: 'If we continue as present, we shall have so many natives in the white territories that the process of integration will overwhelm whites . . . The next fifteen years will be decisive. By then we must already be far along the road of development of the Bantu territories so that they can carry the black population growth.'[106]

But Verwoerd had rejected all the key Tomlinson proposals. The commission had proposed development expenditure of £104 million while Verwoerd refused to commit the government to any sum; the commission recommended a progressive system of land tenure and economic land units while the government opted to continue the outmoded plan of 'one man, one lot.' The commission favored admitting white private capital to facilitate the dynamic industrial development of the reserves to enable them to carry the much increased population by the year 2000; Verwoerd insisted that industries in the reserves would have to depend mainly on 'self-aid and the mobilization of African capital.' To him white private enterprise could make no contribution 'towards keeping the Native Areas truly Bantu.' But without the involvement of private capital the little hope that there had been for a dynamic development of the reserves was extinguished. Tomlinson and the SABRA scholars, who had argued for the rapid economic development of the reserves, were left hanging, twisting in the wind.

The urban African elite rejected Tomlinson's vision. The Interdenominational African Ministers' Conference that met in 1956 in Bloemfontein expressed its grave misgivings. Holding up the condensed version of the report, Dr Alfred Xuma, former President of the ANC, said: 'Here I hold the Bible and your future in my hand. At the SABRA congress it was said that it was a matter of life and death. That is quite correct. It was a matter of life for the whites and of death for the natives.' The conference unanimously rejected the plan's concept 'of national homes for Africans in certain arbitrarily defined areas.' Africans, it declared, 'are the indigenous inhabitants of the country with an indisputable claim to the whole of South Africa as their home.'[107] Z.K. Matthews, the leading intellectual in the ANC, noted that the Smuts government in 1944 had also announced elaborate plans for the development of the reserves. But the Tomlinson Commission had introduced 'an entirely new factor.' The development of the reserves was no longer to be regarded 'as part of the general economic development of the country but as part of a plan to circumscribe and confine the African people as far as their economic rights and political aspirations are concerned to a small portion of the country.'[108] Hence the more the homelands developed an economic and political infrastructure the less could blacks expect to receive political rights in the common area.

When SABRA sent out a fact-finding mission to both traditional and urban African

---

106 Louw, *Dawie*, p. 115.

107 Unpublished report of the meeting by J.J. Ross in the possession of SABRA member, Gerd Schüler. See also the discussion in *Africa South*, 1-2, 1957.

108 Z.K. Matthews and D.G.S. M'Timkulu, 'The Future in the Light of the Tomlinson Report', *Race Relations Journal*, 24, 1-2 (1957), p. 17.

leaders it found little enthusiasm for homeland development and widespread discontent about influx control, lack of job opportunities and the government's failure to consult with them. Robert Sobukwe, leader of the PAC, warned that if whites continued to pursue such policies they would all risk 'being driven into the sea.' A heated exchange followed between him and Olivier, who warned that whites lacked neither the will nor the resources to resist such a challenge.[109]

In the years to come nationalist reformists bewailed Verwoerd's failure to heed the Tomlinson report and embark on the rapid development of the reserves. Some even thought that the political history of South Africa would have taken quite a different course had he done so. But as the next chapter points out, the crucial factor in South African politics was a much more rapid black population growth than anyone had anticipated, which led to a steadily accelerated flow of labor to the cities. It was a delusion to believe that large-scale private capital could be attracted to the reserves or that, in the unlikely event that such capital had been invested, it would have reversed the labor flows to major centers of economic growth. If the Tomlinson proposals had formed part of an overarching scheme of federal government and integrated regional development they may have had a modest chance of attracting black support. However, apart from the minute proportion of Progressive Party supporters very few whites were attracted to such a policy while white domination appeared so stable.

G.B.A. Gerdener, who had influenced NP policy from a missiological perspective and played a leading role in SABRA, was critical of the way the implementation of apartheid steadily deviated from the original conception he and other apartheid theorists had had. Yet in a book published in 1959 he still stressed the fundamental importance of missionary work in the struggle to win the hearts and minds of the black majority. He was pleased to quote the response of M.C. de Wet Nel, Minister of Native of Affairs in the Verwoerd cabinet, to the question of what one's greatest contribution to the welfare of South Africa could be. 'Become a missionary,' was Nel's reply.[110] But even if some Africans were responsive to the DRC's message, its resources were far too limited to make much of an impact. By 1950s the DRC's black 'sister' church had attracted a mere 3.2 per cent of Africans.[111]

Verwoerd takes charge

Verwoerd became prime minister in 1958 when Strijdom died in office. He was bold and decisive, driven by an iron will, and drawing on extraordinary intellectual power and endless energy. He coupled his grasp of policy with the values of *kragdadigheid* and *konsekwentheid* – uncompromising toughness and consistency. Behind his mask of reasonableness lay a simple calculation: a subordinate group would not try to extract concessions if they knew at the outset there was no chance of a compromise. 'I don't believe in a policy of conciliation,' he said. 'I believe in a policy of conviction.'[112]

109 Pierre Hugo, 'A Journey away from Apartheid', *SA Perspectives,* pp. 23-4.

110 G.B.A. Gerdener, *Die Afrikaner en die sendingwerk* (Cape Town: N.G. Kerk Uitgewers, 1959), p. 127.

111 C.H. Badenhorst, 'Die ontwikkeling van die Bantoe op godsdienstige gebied . . .', *Volkskongres oor die toekoms van die Bantoe* (Stellenbosch: Pro Ecclesia, 1956), p. 89.

112 Deon Geldenhuys, *The Diplomacy of Isolation* (Johannesburg: Macmillan, 1984), p. 224.

Piet Cillié described Verwoerd in these terms: 'Dr. Verwoerd's spiritual make-up was overwhelmingly intellectual: ordered thoughts, clear doctrines, fixed future patterns. What was justified and correct in principle, had to be capable of implementation. Obstacles in human nature, must give way to regulation and systematization. The ideal must be imposed on the society.'[113] What counted for him was not the growing numbers of blacks but whether a color bar was in place in politics, the economy, cultural affairs and even in religious life. To ensure white survival he wished the state to bureaucratize racial domination.[114] He lacked an element of personal doubt. Rykie van Reenen, a perceptive journalist from *Die Burger*, was struck by 'his immense charm', and 'razor-sharp brain power' when she interviewed him. But the lasting impression was his response to her question as to whether he could sleep at night, given the awesome responsibility in executing his policy. 'Oh, yes,' he replied, he slept very well, and added: 'You see, one does not have the problem of worrying whether one perhaps could be wrong.'[115]

Verwoerd revolutionized the racial rhetoric of apartheid. Although the policy's application constantly reinforced racial inequality, racist rhetoric itself was all but taboo. In 1960 his Minister of Native Affairs challenged a meeting to name a single instance where a white South African leader had recently said that the black man was doomed to permanent racial inferiority or morally was a lesser creature in the eyes of God.[116] The apartheid system spawned its own black politicians and civil servants, whose courteous treatment was ensured because they did not compete with or challenge their white counterparts.

Verwoerd's conception of self-governing homelands was a political revolution that was conservative in its conception. In May 1959 his government passed a law that abolished the system of African political representatives in Parliament. To Verwoerd these four white representatives kept alive the black hope that they would be represented in the common political system. But this step made it necessary to offer some alternative form of political representation at a time when more and more colonial peoples worldwide were receiving their freedom. Ghana, for example, had become independent in 1957, followed by one African colony after the other.

Four months before the bill abolishing African parliamentary representation was tabled, Verwoerd, almost as an aside, stated that 'when the white man is given full authority only in his own areas . . . the Bantu will acquire full authority elsewhere in the course of time.'[117] Independence for some of the reserves was what Olivier and other SABRA men, encouraged by Cillié in *Die Burger*, had been lobbying for. Spotting the significance of Verwoerd's words, Cillié proclaimed his statement as a 'new vision' in a bold front-page headline in *Die Burger*, causing some unhappiness in NP leadership ranks.

---

113 Cited by David Welsh, 'The Executive and the African Population', in Robert Schrire (ed.), *Leadership in the Apartheid State* (Cape Town: Oxford University Press, 1994), p. 159.
114 Heribert Adam, *Modernizing Racial Domination* (Berkeley: University of California Press, 1971); Deborah Posel, 'Whiteness and Power in the South African Civil Service: Paradoxes of the Apartheid State', *Journal of Southern African Studies*, 25, 1 (1999), pp. 99-119.
115 *Die Burger*, Byvoegsel, 14 June 1957.
116 M.D.C. de Wet Nel, 'Waarom die beleid van apartheid?', *Tydskrif vir Rasse-aangeleenthede*, 11, 4 (1960), p. 174.
117 Pelzer, *Verwoerd Speaks*, p. 241.

The idea of independent homelands had immediate repercussions. Itself conservative, the UP tried to outflank the NP on its right by rejecting the purchase of additional land, as envisaged in the 1936 legislation, as long as the NP proposed to grant independence to the reserves. De Villiers Graaff, UP leader, accepted that Verwoerd's new policy shifted 'the onus on us to come up with a clear alternative.'[118] But the UP would not manage to find this until its demise in 1977. From the outset this had been clear to eleven of its parliamentary representatives, who broke away late in 1959 to form the liberal Progressive Party. Only one of the new Progressives, Helen Suzman, survived the next election on the party's platform of a multi-racial common roll with high voter qualifications.

On 3 February 1960 Harold Macmillan, the British Prime Minister, addressed Parliament in Cape Town at the tail end of a visit to several African states. Macmillan warned that the 'winds of change', the storm of African nationalism, was blowing across the continent as the process of European decolonization gathered pace. It meant that Britain, acting in terms of both moral commitments and material interests, was now siding with the forces of African nationalism against apartheid.

By now Verwoerd had acquired the enormous ideological conviction and intellectual confidence that marked his term in office. Instead of backing down, he seized the moment, and in replying to Macmillan presented apartheid as a form of decolonization, extending increasing rights and responsibilities to blacks in the reserves. His government's policy 'was not in variance with the new direction in Africa, but [was] in the fullest accord with it.' Whites themselves were in South Africa to stay and would uphold their own rights, values and interests as a nation. They saw themselves as the link between the white nations of the world and the nations of the new African states.[119] On other occasions he painted a stark contrast between South Africa under NP rule and the rest of the continent. Abandoning apartheid, he said, would, as in the rest of Africa, lead to the white and other minorities being 'expelled or absorbed.' Experiments with socialism or state capitalism would follow, which would wreck the economy.[120]

Verwoerd's ideological framework skillfully blended the traditional Afrikaner point of view with the new. He reaffirmed the traditional view that the greatest part of South Africa was a white state. He told an illustrious audience in London a year later that three hundred years ago whites and blacks had converged on what was 'practically empty country.' The part whites had developed was theirs, and they were prepared to fight to the death for their survival in this state. The novel part of this ideology was that the whites were not only seeking their own survival, but granted 'survival and full development, politically and economically, to each of the other racial groups as well.'[121] He even envisaged the heads of the white and the homeland governments meeting, as at a Prime Ministers' Conference, 'on a basis of absolute equality', to discuss matters of common interest and eliminate points of friction. 'I foresee that the eventual outcome will be no discrimination and no domination.'[122]

---

118 De Villiers Graaff, *Div Looks Back* (Cape Town: Human & Rousseau, 1993), pp. 160-66.
119 Pelzer, *Verwoerd Speaks*, p. 337.
120 See particularly A.N. Pelzer (ed.), *Verwoerd aan die woord* (Johannesburg: APB, 1963), pp. 403, 620.
121 Pelzer, *Verwoerd Speaks*, pp. 507-09.
122 Pelzer, *Verwoerd Speaks*, p. 583.

Verwoerd was, in fact, engaging in a sleight of hand: Thus, discrimination in 'white South Africa' against a black Xhosa-speaker would no longer be considered racial discrimination but discrimination against a citizen of the Transkei. In these and other ways Verwoerd had a baffling capacity to give the policy moral credibility among almost all NP supporters. He demanded no material sacrifices or territorial concessions on the part of whites, but he nevertheless declared that this new policy was 'one of the most colossal reforms ever tackled by any nation.' He held up the apartheid solution as morally superior to the option of integration, which, he said, offered the present generation of whites comfort, money and prosperity, but cared little about their descendants' security and survival.[123]

Sharpeville and its aftermath

Early in 1960 the PAC announced a campaign to defy the pass laws. The campaign was relatively well organized in Sharpeville, an eastern Witwatersrand township where Africans resented the sharply increased rentals. On 21 March a PAC demonstration there turned into a major tragedy when the police panicked and shot and killed sixty-nine Africans. On 30 March a young man, Philip Kgosana, PAC regional secretary for the western Cape, led a march of thirty thousand protesting blacks from Cape Town's townships to Parliament. Albert Luthuli, leader of the ANC, burned his pass and asked people to stay away from work. The stay-away was nearly total, and brought the many businesses dependent on African labor to a standstill. Many whites were terrified; the Stock Exchange plummeted, followed by a massive capital outflow. With worldwide condemnation of the killings and the harshness of the apartheid policy itself, international isolation seemed a real possibility. On 30 March the government called a state of emergency and detained more than eighteen thousand people over the next few weeks. On 8 April it banned the ANC and PAC. The next day a mentally deranged white man shot Verwoerd in the head and seriously wounded him.

Sharpeville and its aftermath brought to a head the doubts among leaders in the nationalist movement about aspects of its apartheid policy. Anton Rupert, an Afrikaner entrepreneur, met Philip Kgosana on the evening after the mass march on Parliament and was shocked that a young man without laces in his shoes could bring out such a multitude. He told Verwoerd this the next day and suggested that the best guarantee for stability was to grant property rights to urban Africans and to enable them to buy their houses, and at a discount. Verwoerd strongly disagreed. In his view property rights and even a leasehold system would make blacks feel that they had a permanent stake in the common area, which was the last thing he wanted.[124]

A few months later all business associations, including the Afrikaanse Handelsinstituut (AHI), urged reform of the pass laws and other forms of influx control to reduce friction between Africans and the police. It also asked that 'unnecessary interference in Bantu family life' should stop. Verwoerd rebuffed all such appeals and condemned as 'traitors' those business leaders who thought more of profits than the white man's survival.

Concerns like those Rupert had expressed also existed in the circles of *Die Burger.* The

123 G.D. Scholtz, *Dr Hendrik Frensch Verwoerd* (Johannesburg: Perskor, (1974), vol. 2, pp. 155-6.
124 Interview by author with Anton Rupert, 25 May 1999.

influential Albert Geyer wrote, shortly after Verwoerd came to power: 'I have no confidence at all in Verwoerd.'[125] Sharpeville persuaded him that South African whites had only a brief time to produce a viable solution before the country was engulfed by racial unrest. He told a SABRA conference in April 1960 that the situation was extremely grave and that South Africa was becoming an outcast in the eyes of the world. From Black Africa a tidal wave of nationalism was threatening to sweep all whites out of Africa. In the outside world there was an explosion of 'mud slinging, condemnation, even hatred that very few countries had ever experienced in peacetime.' Unless white South Africans were prepared to make 'stupendous sacrifices' to make the policy of separate development work 'the policy itself and the survival of a white nation would become an idle dream.'[126]

Cillié immediately recognized Sharpeville and the ensuing African protests in other cities as a watershed event. In *Die Burger* he stated that the future of white South Africa would depend on whether the position of urban blacks could be resolved over the following weeks and months. For two weeks the paper continued its campaign. It wrote that 'the word "apartheid" has hopelessly failed', having become associated both externally and internally with 'negative action.' If this was not turned around, South Africa risked acquiring permanently 'the status of the world's polecat.'[127]

While Verwoerd was recovering in the hospital, L.J. du Plessis, who as a Potchefstroom academic had long exerted great influence on the Broederbond, proposed, in a letter to Mrs Verwoerd, 'intensive modernization' and 'planned democratization' of the reserves and the incorporation as 'full republican citizens' of those blacks who could not be accommodated in the reserves.[128] It is not known whether Verwoerd, who disliked him, ever replied. Du Plessis resigned that same year from the Bond and joined the liberal Progressive Party. His impatience with the leadership in power reached a culminating point in his warning of the 'deadly dangers of Verwoerdism.'[129]

In the cabinet the principal voices of opposition were Paul Sauer, who considered Verwoerd a *harde kop* – headstrong; Eben Dönges, who voiced the theory that the assassination attempt had exacerbated Verwoerd's despotic tendencies; and Ben Schoeman, who was always dismissive of his grand ideas. Early in April, before Verwoerd was shot, the three had failed to persuade Verwoerd to abolish the passbook system. While Verwoerd was in the hospital, Sauer called for a totally new approach to race relations. In his words, the 'old book of South Africa' had been closed at Sharpeville. Among his specific suggestions were: contacts between whites and 'peace-loving' urban black leaders, changes in the pass laws, and higher wages for Africans. Backing Sauer and his 'conciliatory approach', *Die Burger* mentioned the possibility of a political realignment to address the needs and aspirations of urban blacks.

The *Rand Daily Mail*'s Laurence Gandar, the most consistently liberal editor of the 1950s and 1960s, felt sufficiently encouraged to sound out Nic Olivier to set up a meet-

---

125 US Library, Weber Collection, Geyer-Weber, 13 October 1958.
126 A.L. Geyer, 'Voorsitterrede', *Tydskrif vir Rasse-aangeleenthede,* 11, 4 (1960), pp. 187-93.
127 B.M. Schoeman, *Van Malan tot Verwoerd* (Cape Town: Human & Rousseau, 1973), p. 199.
128 Copy of a letter from L.J. du Plessis to Mrs Verwoerd, 8 May 1960, supplied by Prof. Lourens du Plessis.
129 P. J.J.S. Potgieter, 'L.J. du Plessis as denker oor staat en politiek', doctoral diss., Potchefstroom University, 1976, p. 222.

ing with Cillié. In a private letter to Olivier he suggested the outline for a common platform between the two main political parties. The country, he wrote, was wavering between segregation and integration, while what it needed was to make 'a great leap forward.' Gandar saw no reason why *Die Burger* and the *Rand Daily Mail* could not agree on a program. He proposed a seven-year action plan that entailed spending £10 million a year on the economic development of the reserves; permitting white skills and capital to participate in the economic development of these areas; extending political rights to Africans in the reserves to enable them to govern themselves as soon as possible; introducing the right of self-administration to Africans who continued to live in the townships in the urban areas, and retaining the Native Representatives in Parliament for a seven-year period. The representatives of these developing African municipalities and the Native Representatives in Parliament could act as channels of consultation with urban blacks. Cillié intimated to Olivier that he would be interested in meeting with Gandar, but nothing seems to have come of the initiative.[130]

Recovering remarkably quickly, Verwoerd sent messages to his cabinet from the hospital within the first week. Sauer's privately expressed hope that the bullets would soften his *harde kop* was in vain. Verwoerd rebuked him and announced that there would be no policy shift. He asked that no special tributes or thanksgiving gatherings be held on account of his survival – he was simply 'one of Afrikanerdom's martyrs.' He brought from his narrow escape from death an even firmer belief in the credibility of his policy and in his own political destiny. His recovery soon came to embody the will of the white minority to prevail over all opposition. The quick revival of the economy from the depths into which it had been plunged seemed to confirm this. By the mid-1960s African protest had ebbed and the arrests of pass offenders, which had been temporarily suspended, resumed.

The new frigid peace between whites and blacks did not change the harsh realities of the system the Afrikaners had imposed. When South Africa, on 31 May 1960, celebrated a half-century of the founding of the Union of South Africa, Cillié asked D.J. Opperman, a leading poet, to write an article on 'A Glance into the Future.' Opperman wrote bluntly that the Afrikaner 'had built his own world and had made himself strong, and in the process had alienated the Englishman, colored and Bantu from him.' People in a heterogeneous society needed the power to attract others in order to survive, he said. Apartheid had had the opposite effect. 'Afrikaners developed a strong power to repel . . . we from each other, others from us.' It had become imperative for the Afrikaners to become 'less focused on themselves, less self-protective, more open to criticism, more attuned to the worlds of their fellow countrymen.' That, he added, 'would perhaps produce better novels, plays and magazines.'[131]

Verwoerd was not a man to be deterred by a highly regarded poet lamenting the absence of good novels, any more than by political appeals. Certain developments strengthened his hand. The newspapers were full of dramatic accounts of the flight of whites from the Belgian Congo and of rampaging drunken soldiers after the granting of independence. On 25 June 1960 the 'Dawie' column in *Die Burger* stated: 'For the first time since the "winds of change" began to blow a white minority flees helter-skelter before black

---

130 US Library, Piet Cillié Collection, Laurence Gandar-Nic Olivier, 19 May 1960.
131 D.J. Opperman, 'Uitdyende heelal?', *Die Burger,* 25 May 1960.

terror.' Verwoerd's position was boosted, too, by the steady recovery of the economy, demonstrating that oppression did not deter investors. In October the *South African Mining and Engineering Journal* commented: 'It was certainly remarkable to see how quickly South African politics could be forgotten once the idea of a higher gold price hove over the horizon again.'[132]

In the third quarter of 1960 Afrikaners were caught up in enthusiasm generated by the referendum on a republic that Verwoerd called for October. Verwoerd had taken a huge risk because the NP had not yet secured the majority of votes in any general election, but he never seemed to doubt victory. He sensed that almost all Afrikaners supported a republic, as did quite a substantial minority of English-speakers, who after Macmillan's speech accepted that Britain had withdrawn it support for white rule in Africa. Verwoerd argued that only a republic could bring about white unity, which, in turn, was imperative for an effective response to the racial problem. When republican supporters scored a narrow majority of 74,600 votes, Verwoerd told a victory celebration that the whites were now a united people: 'We have risen above pettiness and selfishness . . . The English-speaking and the Afrikaans-speaking sections have become like the new bride and bridegroom who enter upon the new life in love to create together and to live together as lifemates.'[133]

Verwoerd's clampdown on nationalist dissent

Verwoerd emerged from the referendum with greatly enhanced personal power and status. He realized that if the Afrikaners remained united their position was unassailable. To enforce unity in the movement he turned to the Afrikaner Broederbond, which gave the organization a new lease on life. It had struggled to recover after Hertzog's attack on it in 1935, the divisions of the war years and its failure to produce the apartheid plan. Strijdom, after 1948, had told the Bond to stay out of the political terrain, and, by 1956, the divisions of Potchefstroom, a Broederbond stronghold, were so disheartened that they told the Bond's Executive Council that the Bond no longer had a task or a vision. But Verwoerd saw it as an instrument to promote his goals.[134] By 1960 the Broederbond had about six thousand members in more than four hundred divisions, and most Afrikaans newspaper editors (including Cillié), most church leaders and the vice chancellors of all the Afrikaans universities were Bond members.

Loyalty to Afrikaner nationalism was what held the Bond together, but leading members differed on the best survival strategy. Verwoerd, however, had little time for the 'liberals' in the movement. He was backed by a new Broederbond leadership under Piet Meyer, who became chairman of its Executive Council in November 1960; as chairman also of the Board of Control of the South African Broadcasting Corporation (1959 to 1972), he used the state radio to support the nationalist government.

The first fight within Afrikaner nationalist ranks concerned the position of the col-

---

132 Stanley Greenberg, *Race and State in Capitalist Development* (New Haven; Yale University, 1980), pp. 172-3, 202-5.
133 Pelzer, *Verwoerd Speaks,* p. 427.
134 A.N. Pelzer, *Die Afrikaner-Broederbond* (Cape Town: Tafelberg, 1979), p. 58.

ored people. Verwoerd had failed to fit them into his scheme of a homeland for every nation. When colored people showed no sign of backing blacks in the demonstrations and riots in the aftermath of Sharpeville, nationalists in the western Cape gave a sigh of relief. Two weeks after Sharpeville *Die Burger* noted a marked improvement in the relationship between whites and colored people.

David Botha, a minister in the DRC Mission Church in the Wynberg suburb of Cape Town, wrote to *Die Burger* that the reason for the refusal of the colored people to rise up was simple. They belonged to the white community, culturally, politically and economically. Botha endorsed the idea of a self-governing mission church, but unlike most of his colleagues rejected the nationalist attempt to use it as justification for apartheid. In a book that appeared in October 1960 Botha argued that it was only the discrimination that the state inflicted on colored people that made them seem a different category of people. He advocated the rapid dismantling of all the barriers impeding progress and representation in a common system. In a foreword to the book Van Wyk Louw gave it a rapturous endorsement, writing: 'The colored people are our people. They belong with us.'[135]

A committee of SABRA under the chairmanship of S.P. Cilliers, a Stellenbosch sociologist working in the department where Verwoerd was the first professor, came to a similar conclusion. The Cilliers report, completed early in 1961, concluded that the only viable and just solution was to permit coloreds to become full citizens and to provide for representation in Parliament by colored members elected by colored people. It stressed that it did not propagate 'biological assimilation' but pointed out that the policy of political and economic integration of the previous 150 years had not resulted in any threat to white survival. Colored people belonged to European society in terms of language, culture and religion. Apartheid was not only unjust but also drove colored people into the arms of blacks.[136] The report would never be discussed at a SABRA meeting.

By the final months of 1960 strong support had developed in western Cape circles for the idea that coloreds had to be allowed to elect colored people as their representatives in Parliament. Dawie, *Die Burger*'s columnist, noted: 'My impression is that the NP has been won more than halfway for this principle, and with strong leadership this could be turned into full support.' Verwoerd had set himself against it, because it challenged the powerful image of an all-white Parliament. His political logic also told him that if he granted this, pressure would quickly mount to increase the number of representatives as well as to extend this form of representation to blacks. In the final week of November 1960 he flatly rejected the proposal for direct representation of colored people in Parliament. Colored people, he said, had no intention of helping whites when they stood aside in the riots; they were simply 'pursuing their own interests.' Colored seats in Parliament would lead to increasing integration, 'even biological integration.' The NP leadership must stand as 'walls of granite' on this issue in which the existence of the nation was at stake. *Die Burger* responded by calling Verwoerd's term ' biological integration' an 'abhorrent new euphemism for bastardization.' His response had caused the 'deepest disappointment in twelve years over a particular course a nationalist leader had taken.'[137]

---

135 David Botha, *Die opkoms van ons derde stand* (Cape Town: Human & Rousseau, 1960), p. v.

136 US Library, S.P. Cilliers Collection, 'Verslag van die Komitee insake Kleurlingaangeleenthede', 18 January 1961.

137 Louw, *Dawie*, pp. 195-206; J.J.J. Scholtz, 'In die skemerwereld', in W.D. Beukes (ed.), *Oor grense heen: op pad na 'n Nasionale Pers, 1948-1990* (Cape Town: Nasionale Boekhandel, 1992), pp. 78-9.

In a private letter the hard-nosed Cillié poured out his heart. 'It is to me very hard to suppress my disappointment over what that man has done to our Afrikaner people. You can see in the letters [to the paper] what *Hotnot*-hate, *dominee*-hate [hatred of the clergy], professor-hate and *Burger*-hate he has unleashed. He has summoned up the Neander-thaler in our people against everything that is intelligent and probing. He is using the classic recipe of the tyrant, who makes his power absolute by leading the populace against their recognized leaders in all fields of life.'[138]

M.E. Rothman (M.E.R.), a respected writer, now seventy-seven years old, shared Cillié's disquiet. She wrote to him that she had worked closely with Verwoerd in the 1930s on the poor white issue and knew him and his wife well, but she could see no reason for his harsh policy towards the colored people. She added that what made the 'shock' of his announcement worse was that, unlike other Afrikaner leaders, he himself had an un-known family background. (This was a reference to Verwoerd's parents who were Dutch immigrants.) M.E.R. referred to Van Wyk Louw's essay on 'survival in justice' that had appeared two years earlier in a book *Liberale Nasionalisme*. For her the Afrikaners as a people were marked by two tendencies. 'The one is strong and clear: we want to survive as a people. The second is not always observable but is in my view also there: to harm no other people. The former is necessary, the second indispensable.' She asked Cillié for an assurance that 'you who are youthful and strong, will feel as passionately for survival in justice.'[139]

M.E.R. anticipated grave difficulties in implementing the homelands policy, though she felt there was no alternative but to go through with it – 'out of pure self-preservation which was clearly every nation's duty.' She had persuaded herself, she said, that in pursu-ing this policy Afrikaners were not motivated by self-interest or by wishing to disadvan-tage blacks.[140]

The next battleground was the Afrikaans churches. If church leaders repudiated Ver-woerd he might still be forced to back down. Matters came to a head at an ecumenical conference organized by the World Council of Churches in December 1960 in Cottesloe, Johannesburg. The three affiliated Afrikaans churches, the Cape DRC, the Transvaal DRC and the Hervormde Kerk, had set up study groups of senior church ministers and theo-logical professors to formulate their position. At the end of the Cottesloe conference the DRC delegations accepted the resolutions that drew largely on the memorandum of the Cape DRC, stating that everyone had the right 'to own land where he is domiciled and to participate in the government of his country.' They also stated that the banning of mixed marriages was not grounded in the Scriptures, that migrant labor had 'disintegrating ef-fects' on family life, that job reservation had to be replaced by a more equitable system of la-bor, and that colored people had to be directly represented in Parliament.

In a sympathetic review of Cottesloe, Cillié frankly admitted that the resolutions con-stituted an acute crisis of confidence for the Afrikaner nationalists, who now had to re-solve 'some of the deepest and gravest questions that touched on everyone's existence in

---

138 US Library, Cillié Collection, Cillié-Weber, 13 December 1960.
139 US Library, Cillié Collection, M.E.R.-Cillié, 15 January 1961.
140 Alba Bouwer, et al. (eds.), *M.E.R., 'n kosbare erfenis: briewe, 1916-1975* (Cape Town: Tafelberg, 1975), pp. 156, 168.

South Africa.' But he emphasized that the Afrikaner church leaders involved could not be dismissed as liberals and that the DRC, through its massive involvement in missions, knew more about race relations in a practical sense than the NP did. For him two major tendencies were now battling for predominance in the Afrikaner people – a noble aspiration to move away 'from self-preservation in a narrow sense and from living only for ourselves' and an evil urge 'to grow back into ourselves, back into our own bitterness and sourness, and back to the assumed safety of proven old emotions and attitudes.'[141] He asked: 'Must church leaders interpret the will of God in the way it is expected from an Afrikaner political party or do they have to attempt to interpret God's will as purely as possible?'[142]

Verwoerd wasted little time in urging the Afrikaans churches to distance themselves from the church leaders and the Cottesloe resolutions. His New Year Message for 1961 referred only obliquely to announcements by 'individual church men', but in his speech there was a pointed remark that the churches themselves, in fact, had not yet spoken, as they would at their respective synods of lay members and clergy. The Broederbond, with many church ministers as members, entered the fray with an extraordinary secret circular to all Bond divisions in which it pointed out that the Cottesloe decisions bound no affiliated church until the synod or the assembly of that church endorsed them. It went on to state that while the Bond's Executive itself did not wish to interfere in church matters it supported the racial policies that Cottesloe questioned. Its Executive Council meeting of February 1961 expressed dismay that Bond members at Cottesloe had expressed views in conflict with Bond principles. In its customary delicate phraseology the Executive Council decided to engage in *gesprekke* (conversations) with Cottesloe delegates to bring the 'real facts' to their attention. But the knives were out: the Bond supported Verwoerd.[143]

One Afrikaans Church after the other now condemned the Cottesloe resolutions. In April 1961, for example, the synod of the Transvaal DRC repudiated them and also withdrew from the World Council of Churches. In October of that year the Cape DRC synod followed suit. Apart from a 1963 statement by the Cape church that migrant labor was a 'cancer' in African family life, all of the Afrikaans churches until 1986 refrained from any criticism of apartheid.

At the 1961 meeting of the Transvaal DRC, Beyers Naudé, a Broederbond golden boy of the Transvaal church, offered to retract his support for the Cottesloe resolutions if anyone could offer proof that they were in conflict with the Bible. The synod did not even attempt to do so; its ground for repudiating Cottesloe was that it embarrassed the government at a time when South Africa was under attack. A Bond circular at the time declared: 'True happiness can only come from an *unconditional* commitment to a cause larger than oneself. Such a cause is our national struggle for survival waged for realizing our God-given national calling.' The Bond was employing religious language to urge church, party, and government to stand as one in combating the challenge from without.[144]

---

141 Louw, *Dawie*, pp. 205-6.
142 Louw, *Dawie*, p. 204.
143 E.L.P. Stals, 'Geskiedenis van die Afrikaner-Broederbond, 1918-1994', unpublished manuscript, 1998, p. 504.
144 Willie Jonker, *Selfs die kerk kan verander* (Cape Town: Tafelberg, 1998), p. 72.

Naudé was dismayed to discover that Bond members in the Transvaal DRC had become an all-powerful clique within their church, orchestrating proceedings at synod meetings when anything came up that might embarrass the Bond or Verwoerd. He himself was expelled from the Bond several years later, in 1963, after he had leaked certain Bond documents to a friend who had turned them over to an English newspaper. He then became director of the Christian Institute, an ecumenical body founded to co-ordinate opposition within the existing South African churches to apartheid. By now the Broederbond had completely isolated him and he had lost virtually all support among DRC ministers at large. In 1966 the DRC General Synod described the Christian Institute as based on 'false doctrine' and urged all church members who belonged to withdraw from it.

Verwoerd strengthened his own position even further by his handling of South Africa's membership of the Commonwealth. In March 1961 he went to London for a meeting of Commonwealth heads to apply for South Africa's re-admission on a new status as a republic. Some of the member states expressed such strong criticism of apartheid that Verwoerd withdrew his application altogether. On his return he defended the decision in terms of national honor, and turned defeat into triumph in the eyes of almost all Afrikaners and many English-speaking whites as well. From now on he would invariably cast foreign policy in simple survival terms. He refused to contemplate a return to the Commonwealth since that 'must entail giving up the struggle of the white man to maintain himself in this country.'[145]

SABRA, in which Nic Olivier and A.L. Geyer played the leading roles, was virtually the only nationalist organization left in which the apartheid theorists could express their views. But Olivier and his allies were vulnerable because the Broederbond held the organization's purse strings. Meyer met with 'well-disposed Broeders' to plot a coup at its next annual conference, scheduled for September 1961 in Bloemfontein. It was to discuss the Cilliers report on the colored people, but Meyer's group made sure that it would not happen. At the September conference, the chairman, the widely respected Geyer, called the atmosphere 'unfavorable to an extreme degree' for an objective discussion. Informal Broederbond lobbying had ensured that the large majority of the conference participants were Verwoerd loyalists. In the election for the Executive, Olivier and virtually all his supporters were removed. Geyer, who felt himself closer to Olivier than to Verwoerd, chose not to protect him. As a shrewd observer formulated it, 'his [Geyer's] overriding loyalty belonged to the government, which, more than anything else, had become the living symbol of the unitary concept of the Afrikaner identity and nation he himself had helped to build.'[146]

The purged SABRA, overnight, had become a body unwavering in its support for Verwoerd's uncompromising approach to apartheid. The Broederbond now took over much of the work previously left to SABRA, forming task groups of leading politicians (below cabinet level), civil servants and academics. It understood that the government did not want it to formulate policy but rather to rally support for its policies. Bond suggestions, such as one to restrict new black secondary schools to the reserves, were in line with Verwoerd's own thinking. On the colored issue a western Cape Bond task force issued a re-

145 Pelzer, *Verwoerd Speaks*, p. 516.
146 Hans Holleman, 'The Great Purge', *South African Perspectives*, p. 47.

port that, while reflecting the deadlock in nationalist ranks, stressed the need to preserve Afrikaner unity. Olivier, still a member of the Bond, attended some of the discussions, but was purged from the Bond a few years later.[147]

Before the rise of Verwoerd the strength of the Afrikaner nationalist movement lay in the ability of its constituent parts, ranging from the party through the press, organized business, universities, cultural organizations and the Broederbond to the churches to retain a large degree of autonomy while pursuing a common cause. Verwoerd changed all that. He dominated the party and the cabinet and forced the support organizations of the party to march in lock step. 'Verwoerd was an intellectual giant. He thought for every one of us,' B.J. Vorster, his successor, remarked in the first cabinet meeting he chaired.[148]

Verwoerd considered the apartheid policy an interlocked system that did not brook changes. He projected the image of a 'man of granite' standing firm against any demand for ameliorating the harsher features of apartheid. In 1965 Verwoerd jeopardized South Africa's participation in international sport by announcing that a New Zealand rugby football team would not be welcome to visit South Africa if it included Maori players.

After 1961 Cillié had largely fallen silent. He had made his boldest move in supporting the Cottesloe decisions in *Die Burger*, but found himself isolated when some of the leading churchmen involved took cover or switched sides. He no longer challenged Verwoerd, but became more cynical and gloomier about the possibilities for any reform. In later years he was even prepared to support an elaboration of apartheid, such as the abolition of colored representation in Parliament, which B.J. Vorster, Verwoerd's successor, introduced in 1968.

Cillié wrote one more outstanding essay, entitled 'Back to our belief in freedom' published in 1964. At one level it can be read as a defense of the government's homelands policy as the only realistic policy option. He proposed carving out large, viable territories where blacks could govern themselves and become free, along with the 'incorporation of the non-black [colored and Indian] minorities in our own nationhood in a way that does not mean their permanent subordination.'

At another level, however, Cillié's article is a statement of general principles drawn from Afrikaner history and applied constructively to the contemporary political crisis. 'The Afrikaners', he wrote, 'ought to be the last to oppose in principle the idea of national freedom and the liquidation of colonialism. They inaugurated the century of anti-colonialism with their freedom struggle against British colonialism and set an example to colonized peoples throughout the world . . . Through resisting for many years the mightiest empire in the world they triggered not only a general resistance against colonialism but undermined the self-confidence of imperialists.'

Cillié observed that the Afrikaners' standing in the world had degenerated to a point where they stood accused as the premier colonialists and oppressors. The reason was simple: 'We have rejected domination over us but we did not reject our domination of other peoples as equally despicable.' One reason was 'that Afrikaner people themselves had been born in a colonial era and were not free from certain colonial attitudes . . . We have rejected the domination of ourselves but did not find our domination of other peoples objectionable.' But this had to stop:

---

147 Stals, 'Geskiedenis van die AB', pp. 311-30.
148 B.M. Schoeman, *Vorster se duisend dae* (Cape Town: Human & Rousseau, 1974), p. 14.

We can and should not become the last bastion of a wrong order when the Afrikaners as a people had been forged in resisting a similar order . . . Old-fashioned colonialist [white] supremacy made it impossible for Afrikaners to live with themselves in good conscience because it violated their own best principles. We know from our own history that a people who is worth their salt would, over the long run, not submit to an alien government, and we know that we do not have the stomach to really try it.[149]

The fading of the homelands vision

Few attempts to influence Verwoerd made any impact on him. But one did: an official visit from Dag Hammarskjöld, Secretary General of the United Nations, who arrived in South Africa in January 1961 to investigate charges of the violation of human rights. Verwoerd considered the visit important enough to arrange six off-the-record meetings with him in a visit of six days. Hammerskjöld's memorandum of the meetings noted that he told Verwoerd that the UN favored speedy integration in South Africa, but the prime minister called this totally unacceptable. Hammerskjöld then posed the vital question: was there a chance of apartheid being turned into what he termed a 'competitive alternative' to integration? Verwoerd replied that the homelands policy constituted such a key arrangement, to which UN Secretary General responded that for the homelands policy to be considered a 'competitive alternative' the government must set aside a sufficient and coherent territory for blacks, publish a plan for their economic development, and introduce institutions based on the will of the people that would lead to independence if the people so wished. The government also had to accept the fact that the homelands could not be a complete solution. Africans working outside the homelands had to be entitled to similar rights and protection as those Western countries gave to foreign workers and, in particular, be entitled, after prolonged residence, to citizenship in South Africa with full civic rights.[150]

Verwoerd had a unique opportunity here to develop a plan that could gather sufficient international support for the 'decolonization' of South Africa. But Hammarskjöld tragically was killed a few months later in a plane accident in the Congo, robbing the South African government of a valuable *interlocutor.* Nevertheless, the government, later in 1961, introduced a form of African local government through Urban Bantu Councils, allowing for the election of new bodies that had few powers. The government also introduced partial self-government for the Transkei, the territory that was the flagship of its homelands policy, with a promise of full independence over time, the time unspecified. In 1963 Kaizer Matanzima, in elections for the Transkeian Assembly, came to power; he would soon begin to show a measure of independence of thought and action. A process had been set in train that Verwoerd's government did not completely control.

At first some Western countries watched the experiment with interest. The London *Sunday Times* wrote that the ruling Afrikaner minority seemed intent on an alternative

---

149 Louw *Dawie*, pp. 285-90.
150 Manuscript of Dag Hammarskjöld's memorandum provided to the author by Brian Urquhart, his biographer.

to fighting a multi-racial democracy to the death. If there had to be apartheid, the paper continued, the Transkei represented a courageous step as a visible alternative.[151] *The Guardian* accepted the principle of separate, viable white and black spheres of influence, leading ultimately to full partition. In 1964 the liberal historian C.W. de Kiewiet, now living in the USA, published an article in *Foreign Affairs* after a visit to South Africa. Noting the hopelessness of the situation and the increasing repression, he nevertheless argued that it was unwise to reject out of hand the possibility of the Bantustan experiment offering 'an enlarged political experience' and 'relief' from political subordination in the common area. Verwoerd, De Kiewiet wrote, was addressing the country's grave problems with 'boldness, shrewdness and even imagination.' It was 'by no means absurd to suggest a comparison between Verwoerd and Charles de Gaulle, 'the stern, headstrong but deeply imaginative leader of France.'[152]

Most members of the Third World considered the homelands policy a charade and even among white South Africans doubts started to surface. The economic development of the homelands was moving at a snail's pace. Between 1956 and 1966 fewer than 45,000 jobs were created in the reserves and in the adjacent border areas, a slower rate of progress over ten years than the Tomlinson Commission had required for one year. In 1966 the total product of the homelands was only 1.9 per cent of that of the Republic as a whole. Black family incomes in the larger towns were, on average, three to four times the average homeland income. The average output per head in the homelands was twenty times lower than in the remainder of South Africa.[153] The homelands were not becoming industrialized, nor were they ringed with border area factories that could absorb surplus workers, as had earlier been envisaged.

Political repression

Alongside the homelands policy, which gave the West hope, the government embarked on an intensification of political repression, which steadily cost South Africa international support. In 1961 Verwoerd appointed a tough politician, John Vorster, as Minister of Justice, and Vorster took the view that the security of the state was the highest priority. In the same year a new law gave the government the power to place people under house arrest, and supplemented its power to list or ban or banish individuals or organizations. The police could now detain suspects without a charge under conditions of solitary confinement for successive periods of twelve days, which was soon expanded to ninety, then to 180 and then to an unlimited period. Newspapers could not report on any torturing or third-degree methods since legislation prohibited unauthorized articles on prison conditions. A new Publications Control Board was introduced in 1963 with a team of censors authorized to ban films and books that threatened public morals or security. The press remained relatively free, but subject to constant pressure from the government and curbs on reporting on the ANC and other similar organizations. From 1962 the United Nations

---

151 Cited by *Die Burger*, 29 January 1962 and Steyn, *Van Wyk Louw*, p. 978.
152 C.W. de Kiewiet, 'Loneliness in the Beloved Country', *Foreign Affairs*, 42, 3 (1964), pp. 413-27.
153 Sheila van der Horst, 'The Economic Problems of the Homelands', in N.J. Rhoodie (ed.), *South African Dialogue* (Johannesburg, 1972), p. 186.

General Assembly passed resolutions almost unanimously asking member states to impose diplomatic sanctions on South Africa and to bar South African ships and planes from their territory. The Security Council agreed on an arms embargo.

Despite the international furor and rebukes, the South African government proceeded along the chosen path to suppress all resistance. Under the leadership of Nelson Mandela, an armed wing of the ANC, Umkhonto we Sizwe (Spear of the Nation), was founded at the end of 1961, which embarked on a low-key campaign of sabotage. Umkhonto was effectively destroyed by the capture in 1962 of Mandela, who had gone underground, and by the arrest of several other leaders in the following year in the suburb of Rivonia in Johannesburg. The police alleged that a joint African National Congress-SA Communist plan had been adopted, aimed at launching a foreign military invasion supported by an internal uprising spearheaded by seven thousand local saboteurs and guerrilla fighters.

Bram Fischer, who led the defense team, and who had been in on the planning of the uprising, admitted on behalf of the accused that there had been preparations for guerrilla warfare from as early as 1962, but insisted that no plan had been accepted. In 1964 Mandela and his co-accused were sentenced to life imprisonment on charges of sabotage. In the same year members of a largely white student group, the African Resistance Movement, received sentences of fifteen years, and the police also arrested Bram Fischer, who was sentenced in 1965 to life imprisonment.

Fischer was a man with impeccable Afrikaner family credentials, grandson of Abraham Fischer, Premier of the Orange River Colony, and son of Percy Fischer, Judge-President of the Free State Supreme Court. He had been active in the Communist Party since the 1930s and was listed as a communist in the 1950s but continued his career as an advocate in Johannesburg. He went underground in 1964 and was the most hunted man in South Africa until he was caught.

Throughout his career both as an advocate and as a communist Fischer never denied that he was an Afrikaner. He personally knew some of the leading figures in the nationalist movement. While a student in Oxford in the early 1930s Albert Hertzog had warned him not to lose his Afrikaner identity. In the early 1940s Fischer invited Verwoerd to lunch to persuade him to become a socialist, a suggestion that was turned down. In 1965 he wrote a letter of support to Beyers Naudé noting that while his own backup came mainly from Africans, only an Afrikaner like Naudé could persuade fellow-Afrikaners to turn back from the road they were traveling. This, Fischer stressed, was vital to the survival of the Afrikaner people. His letter ended with the words: 'How strange it might sound today, it is not impossible that one day we may work for the Afrikaner people together.'[154]

At his trial in 1966 Fischer stated: 'I speak as an Afrikaner,' adding that in the previous decade, 'something sinister for the future of my people has happened.' Correctly he observed that the intensification of long-standing segregation, called apartheid, was all laid before the Afrikaner door. 'All this bodes ill for our future. It has bred a deep-rooted hatred for Afrikaners, for our language, for our political and racial outlook . . .' Blacks were losing all belief in future co-operation with Afrikaners. It was important that 'at least one

---

154 Stephen Clingman, *Bram Fischer: Afrikaner Revolutionary* (Cape Town: David Philip, 1998), pp. 134, 375.

Afrikaner' should make his protest against apartheid 'openly and positively.' And in a rousing conclusion he did not cite Karl Marx but Paul Kruger in support of his conviction that apartheid would be overthrown. In 1881, after the Transvaal burghers had risen against the British occupation of their republic, Kruger told the Volksraad of the Orange Free State. '[We] place our case before the entire world. Whether we are victorious or whether we die, freedom will arise in Africa, like the sun from the morning clouds.'[155]

The nationalists acknowledged Fischer's qualities only when he died in 1975. Piet Cillié paid this tribute in *Die Burger*: 'Bram Fischer was made of material that a *volk*, a movement, a party dearly would want on its side . . . We who are of his blood, but despise his politics, cannot escape a great feeling of sorrow about a prodigal son who did not return.'[156]

1966, the heyday of apartheid

By 1966, the final year of Verwoerd's term in office, the scheme for a white South Africa was never more forcefully pursued. All housing construction in the African townships had been frozen since the early 1960s, and in 1964 the government introduced extremely harsh influx controls that expanded the system to peri-urban areas and made possible the eradication of the so-called 'black spots' (black settlements in the white rural areas). In many ways Verwoerd's policies represented a holding action, not a settlement. As a result of influx control in South Africa, the system kept 1 to 1.5 million people in the reserves who otherwise by the end of the 1960s would have become urbanized. But the numerical preponderance of blacks steadily grew. There was now a black population of fourteen million compared to fewer than four million whites. Because of the rapid black population increase, the supposedly white state had to appoint more blacks (as policemen, teachers, nurses, etc.) than whites in the civil service in the 1950s, and large numbers of blacks had been drawn into secondary industry since 1948 despite the apartheid restrictions. In declaring, in 1958, that in twenty years' time the stream of blacks to 'white' South Africa would be reversed, Verwoerd seemed to believe that conviction could prevail over reality.

For the time being a tight ideological defense of apartheid was in place. In a study undertaken in the late 1960s of political, business and bureaucratic elites, between 83 per cent and 96 per cent of Afrikaners agreed with the following statements: that 'Bantu [Africans] should remain Bantu', that a 'doctorate is a veneer' and that they were not inferior but 'different by nature', and that multi-racial democracy was not practicable. Upwards of 80 per cent disagreed with the statement that that there were no differences in abilities between whites and blacks but only a difference in opportunities. Between two-thirds and three-quarters of the English elite agreed with these propositions.[157] What made the ideological commitment stronger in the Afrikaner case was the fusion of apartheid with religion and nationalism. Africans were seen as consisting of various ethnic minorities or nations, each created by God and each with a 'right to survive separately.'

155 Bram Fischer, *What I Did Was Right: Statement from the Dock, 28 March 1966* (London: Mayibuye, n.d.), p. 32.
156 Piet Cillié, *Tydgenote* (Cape Town; Tafelberg, 1980), pp. 81-2.
157 Heribert Adam, 'The South African Power-Elite', in Heribert Adam (ed.) *South Africa: Sociological Perspectives* (London: Oxford University Press, 1971), p. 80.

Verwoerd's attempt to develop apartheid as a form of decolonization fell far short of his earlier promise. He did not put in place any structures in which he could meet with politicians from the Transkei and other homelands to address grievances and discuss common interests. His Urban Bantu Councils failed to attract any significant support. He did not come up with a dynamic plan for economic decentralization and regional development that could reduce the numbers of blacks in the common area. There were two sets of logic that opposed each other. One the one hand there was the 'Verwoerdian logic', rooted in the Afrikaners' own experience, that blacks would not identify with the development of the reserves if they did not have a leading hand in economic projects. On the other hand there was the 'market logic', that only white capital and initiative would produce growth and jobs in the homelands. But even this logic could be questioned. The centripetal forces of the existing centers of economic activity were so strong that even large subsidies for regional development were unlikely to reverse the labor flows.

It was arguably in the interest of white supremacy, faced with a growing preponderance of black numbers, to make some significant concessions to a section of the blacks. Only such a move would split the blacks politically and blunt international hostility. But Verwoerd was not really interested in this either. He embarked on the blanket political exclusion of blacks, which facilitated the mobilization of blacks as a people against the system and the ultimate overthrow of the system.

Muted opposition to Verwoerd in Afrikaner nationalist ranks again began to manifest itself in 1965. Although it was improper to do so, since he was a director of the two northern Afrikaans press companies, he tried to block Nasionale Pers when it announced its plan to publish a Sunday paper to be called *Die Beeld* in Johannesburg.[158] He feared not only competition from the more efficient Nasionale Pers but also a challenge to the Transvaal dominance by a more moderate Cape voice.

Nasionale Pers went ahead and appointed as editor Schalk Pienaar, a brilliant journalist and a quiet, unobtrusive man with an irreverent wit and an irrepressible streak of individualism. Gently Pienaar began mocking the myth of a reverse of the labor flow to the homelands by 1978. He urged the government to accept that the permanently urbanized blacks could not be accommodated by the homelands policy.[159] His newspaper reported that businessmen questioned the viability of most of the reserves.[160] Pienaar and Cillié, longstanding friends and colleagues, no longer saw eye to eye on large issues. While Pienaar entertained serious doubts about Verwoerd, Cillié told a prominent American writer, Alan Drury, that he was the only person who could lead the country in the direction that 'logic, self-preservation . . . simple humanity and decency indicate that it should go.' 'One man, one vote is impossible here,' he said, 'but the development of each race within its own context is something else again.'[161]

It is easy to explain the support for apartheid by rank and file whites by reference to the privileges and security the policy offered. However, endorsement of the system by

---

158 Pienaar, *Getuie van groot tye*, pp. 45-8.
159 Pienaar, *Getuie van groot tye*, p. 63.
160 Steyn, *Van Wyk Louw*, p. 1055.
161 Alan Drury, *'A Very Strange Society': A Journey to the Heart of South Africa* (London: Michael Joseph, 1968), p. 361.

the intelligentsia requires more exploration. Most of the Afrikaner intelligentsia were swayed by the fact that the best and the brightest among them believed in apartheid – Cillié with his powerful and lucid prose and Verwoerd with what De Kiewiet called the 'vigor and resourcefulness' with which he viewed the race issue as the key challenge of South Africa.[162] Van Zyl Slabbert, a student at Stellenbosch in the early 1960s, remembers how exciting his fellow-students found the Tomlinson Commission's vision of economically viable black homelands.[163] Verwoerd's long, mesmerizing speeches spelled out the vision with seemingly inescapable logic. The English-speaking Native Representative Leslie Rubin, strongly opposed to Verwoerd on almost every issue, confessed that occasionally while listening to him even he found himself for a moment wondering 'whether it might all be true, whether in fact under this guiding genius all things might fall readily in place, and all peoples might realize their own destinies, and our country be at peace for evermore.'[164]

In the 1966 general election the NP won 126 of the 166 seats and 58 per cent of the votes cast. The liberal Progressive Party suffered heavy setbacks. At the height of Verwoerd's power, on 6 September 1966, a deranged white messenger assassinated him on the floor of the House of Assembly just before he was to make a speech that was said to have contained important policy announcements.

A few days after Verwoerd's death Schalk Pienaar assessed its significance as follows: 'Man and policy, creator and creation had grown so much together in the crisis of our time that the one cannot be easily seen as separate from the other. And now in the midst of a dynamic growth process the man suddenly is no longer there . . . Verwoerd never sketched the end of the road as he saw it . . . He walked a high and lonely road without people he really trusted. In that sense he left without a will.'[165]

Verwoerd: A complex heritage

In the 25 years after Verwoerd's death a heated debate took place among scholars about the connection between apartheid and economic growth. During the 1970s and 1980s Marxist scholars argued that the high growth rate of the 1960s was due to apartheid and its repression of the black labor force, while liberals believed that apartheid stifled growth. By the beginning of the 1990s, after the collapse of socialism, a new orthodoxy had developed. It was a fusion of a cruder version of the liberal interpretation and the ANC's ideological attack on the apartheid state.

In the popular press apartheid, particularly its systematization under Verwoerd, was now projected as an unmitigated moral, social, economic and political disaster that had set South Africa back by many years. Economic growth and stability were seen as gains made despite apartheid; all shortcomings were blamed on it. In 1994, Howard Preece, an experienced financial journalist, passed a more considered but still negative judgment on apartheid. First, the 'South African economy failed to achieve near its growth poten-

---

162 De Kiewiet, 'Loneliness in the Beloved Country', p. 419.
163 Ivor Wilkins, 'This Man Who Guides the Ordinary People', *Sunday Times,* 19 April 1981.
164 As recounted by Alan Paton, *Journey Continued* (Cape Town: David Philip, 1988), pp. 37, 111.
165 Ton Vosloo (ed.), *Schalk Pienaar: tien jaar politieke kommentaar* (Cape Town: Tafelberg, 1975), p. 9.

tial.'[166] Second, 'the growth and resulting increases accrued almost entirely to the white minority. In other words, the economy did nothing for the great masses of the people even if it was prospering at the macro level.'[167]

To assess apartheid, and Verwoerd's heritage in particular, it is necessary to look more closely at the connection between growth and politics. Just after the Second World War South Africa was positioned exceptionally well for high economic growth. It enjoyed abundant natural resources, good foreign exchange earnings, a relatively sophisticated financial system, a good technological base, a competent civil administration and an established place in the world's trading system. But it had liabilities as well: a deficient system of education for children who were not white, and poor black labor productivity. It also had a manufacturing sector that had failed to build up a substantial export capacity. (The latter, however, was inherited from the segregation era and was as much due to the dependence on gold as to segregation or apartheid.)

In the first twenty-three years of apartheid, between 1948 and 1981, the South African economy grew at a rate of 4.5 per cent.[168] This was about average for a group of twenty comparable middle-size developing countries.[169] Yet liberal scholars tend to believe that apartheid prevented South Africa from growing faster and doing more for the poorest section of the population.

Preece is probably right in believing that South Africa could have grown faster. But it also could also have fared much worse. Between the early 1930s and the late 1990s Argentina, severely handicapped by the lack of a stable, non-corrupt political order, fell from the ranks of the top ten countries in the world, measured by gross domestic product per head, to forty-eighth.[170] The same could have happened to South Africa. In the case of Argentina the system failed to provide continuous political and economic stability.

The idea that South Africa could have done much better derives from the belief, long propounded by liberal scholars, that free markets and democratic politics reinforce each other to produce high growth, political liberty and the easing of ethnic tensions. This model works for developed countries, but, as comparative studies show, it breaks down in those developing countries where ethnic and class cleavages coincide. Here a free market democracy has tended to produce a worsening of racial or ethnic tensions, violence, pervasive instability – together with a downturn of growth – and an erosion or collapse of the democracy.[171] A stable democracy is more likely to be the result of a period of

166 Howard Preece, 'The Economics of Apartheid', in J. Harker (ed.), *The Legacy of Apartheid* (London: Guardian Newspaper, 1994), p. 28.

167 Preece, 'The Economics of Apartheid', p. 28.

168 South African Reserve Bank 1999, *Supplement to the June Quarterly Bulletin*, B-28.

169 In a study Terence Moll took 1960 GDP per caput for his comparison. On a descending scale South Africa was the 8th biggest economy in the group of middle-size developing countries after Austria, Venezuela, Italy, Argentina, Spain, Japan, and Chile. See his, 'Did the Apartheid Economy Fail?' *Journal of South African Studies,* 17, 2 (1991), pp. 271-91.

170 *The Economist Pocket World in Figures* (London: Profile Books, 2001), p. 26.

171 Samuel Huntington and Joan Nelson, *No Easy Choice: Political Participation in Developing Countries* (Cambridge: Harvard University Press, 1976), pp. 19-25; Amy Chua, 'Markets, Democracy and Ethnicity', *The Yale Law Journal*, 1998, pp. 1-97; Donald Horowitz, *Ethnic Groups in Conflict* (Berkeley: University of California Press, 1985).

steady growth over a long period, particularly if it produces a sizeable middle class, prefer-ably based on the private sector, and steadily improving working and living conditions for the proletariat.[172]

By 1948 South Africa was still in the primary stage of industrialization with a heavy emphasis on agriculture and mining. The wages of white workers had risen enough to provide them with a decent living, but blacks and colored workers still had to endure a very harsh working environment. Would a liberal democracy or a socialist system – they were apartheid's main contenders – introduced in 1948 have produced growth, stability and reform? One is here in the realm of counter-factual history where only comparative evidence provides some guidance. The evidence from Latin America suggests that a lib-eral democracy based on universal franchise would almost certainly have generated populist demands, serious strife and flight of capital. In Africa in general democratic in-stitutions were quickly eroded after independence and economic growth was either low or negative. The main reason was a policy of state capitalism that put a misguided faith on the state as an engine of growth and a large expansion of people employed in the pub-lic sector.

When the NP came to power in 1948 liberals were not advocating universal franchise. The leading young liberal historians of the time, Leonard Thompson and Arthur Keppel-Jones, believed, in the words of the latter, that 'government of an undifferentiated public by simple and unrestricted majorities is not workable in a multi-racial society of the South African type.'[173] The liberals' hope was that the introduction of a qualified vote would bring about a moderate multi-racial electorate in which a substantial section would be swayed by their material interests rather than their racial or ethnic identity. But this has not happened in any society and there is no evidence that this was a feasible op-tion in post-war South Africa.[174] Shortly before the 1948 election Jannie Hofmeyr discov-ered that he would be unable to sell to the white electorate the demands that the black urban leadership considered reasonable (see p. 453). And in the unlikely case that he could sell a strictly limited extension of the vote to blacks, it would have almost certain-ly have been rebuffed by them. By 1948 the African National Congress with its com-munist ally was no longer led by a small, conservative elite willing to accept a form of democracy still dominated by whites.

An attempt to introduce a qualified franchise in South Africa in 1948 is unlikely to have ensured stability. The qualification level of the vote would have soon become a strongly contested issue (also within the two white communities with candidates from the English section likely to get much more black and colored support). A feeble white government assailed by both white and black voters would have driven off investors. It is possible to conceive of a scenario of a Hofmeyr government that had come to power in 1948 stumbling from one crisis to another and finally to an election based on universal franchise.

172 Michal O'Dowd, 'The Stages of Economic Growth', Adrian Leftwich (ed.), *South African Economic Growth and Political Change* (London: Allison and Busby, 1974), pp. 29-44.

173 Arthur Keppel-Jones, *Friends or Foes* (Pietermaritzburg: Shuter and Shooter, 1949), p. 8.

174 For a discussion of other comparable countries see Horowitz, *Ethnic Groups in Conflict*; James Jesudason, 'The Resilience of One-Party Dominance in Malaysia and Singapore', in Hermann Giliomee and Charles Simkins (eds.), *The Awkward Embrace: One-Party Domination and Democracy* (Cape Town: Tafelberg, 1999), pp. 127-72.

It is of course also possible that, as in the rest of the continent, the first black government would have been pragmatic, like the one headed by Jomo Kenyatta in Kenya. However, it is much more likely that South Africa might have gone further than state capitalism and drifted into costly experiments in socialism of the kind that the governments in Zambia and Tanzania would soon try. Until the 1970s the planned economies were admired in the developing world, and an ANC government, should it have come to power, would almost certainly have been attracted to this model.

The introduction of the socialist model in South Africa would have brought a precipitous economic decline from which South Africa would have taken many years to recover. Even the implementation of the Freedom Charter, accepted in 1955 as the ANC's main statement of economic and social policy, would have meant major economic disruption. It called for the nationalization of the mines, heavy industry and banks and a redistribution of land. Nelson Mandela acknowledged in his autobiography, published after the ANC had come to power, that the charter was a 'revolutionary document' and that its implementation could not have been achieved 'without radically altering the economic and political structures.'[175] Even a non-communist like Mandela described the writings of Karl Marx and Friedrich Engels in the 1950s as 'a blueprint of the most advanced social order in world history, that [has] led to an unprecedented reconstitution of society and to the removal of all kinds of oppression for a third of mankind.'[176]

It is not difficult to imagine that in the major turmoil following an ANC government coming to power in the 1950s or early 1960s, the strong communist presence within the ANC alliance would have made itself felt. The liberal Alan Paton had a warm affection for the communist leader Bram Fischer and testified in his defense when he stood trial in 1966. However, he had no doubt that communists with their hands on the levers of power would spell great danger.[177] He disagreed with a fellow-liberal who told him that he would be the first to be killed if Bram Fischer's party in alliance with the ANC seized power, but, in his own words, 'was ready to believe that if his friend Bram came to power an emissary would be sent to me with a one-way ticket, and with a message "Get out of here as fast as possible".'[178]

What South Africa did get was apartheid. The NP government's conservative macroeconomic policy during the 1950s laid the foundations for steady growth. Budget surpluses were used to retire debt. By the time Verwoerd came to power the nationalists had already made it clear that they had no plan to nationalize the mines. Excessive wage demands from white workers had been resisted. Although the new educational system for blacks was strongly criticized, it greatly improved basic literacy. The republic that was proclaimed in 1961 represented only a symbolic change that did not affect the ties of trade and investment with Britain. In the mid-1960s, when Verwoerd was at the height of his power, South Africa had a growth rate of six per cent and an inflation rate of only two per cent. In August 1966 *Time* magazine, in an otherwise highly critical assessment, called Verwoerd 'one of the ablest leaders Africa has ever produced.' Attracted by cheap

---

175 Nelson Mandela, *No Easy Walk to Freedom* (London: Little, Brown and Co., 1994), p. 164.
176 Nelson Mandela, 'Whither the Black Consciousness Movement?', in Mac Maharaj (ed.), *Reflections in Prison* (London: Zebra Books, 2001), p. 43.
177 Alexander, *Paton*, p. 291.
178 Paton, *Journey Continued* , p. 69.

labor, a gold-backed currency and high profits, investors from all over the world had ploughed money into the country. 'Production, consumption and the demand for labor [are] soaring.'[179] 'South Africa', *Time* wrote, 'is in the middle of a massive boom.' On 31 July 1966 the *Rand Daily Mail*, the liberal daily most critical of the government, wrote: 'Dr Verwoerd has reached the peak of a remarkable career . . . The nation is suffering from a surfeit of prosperity.' In a subsequent article the paper paid a handsome tribute to Verwoerd as the man who had refined the crude ideology of white supremacy 'into a sophisticated and rationalized philosophy of separate development.'[180] The *Financial Mail*, the premier financial magazine of South Africa at the time, celebrated the period 1961 to 1966 as the 'Fabulous Years' when South Africa's gross national product rose by 30 per cent in real terms. It approvingly quoted a leading London stockbroker who remarked: 'South Africa is one of the last genuinely capitalist countries in the world.'[181]

It was Verwoerd, with his intransigence on racial policy and his tough suppression of black dissent in the early 1960s, who paved the way for the surge of strong growth from 1961. The unproductive labor force and the large turnover of black workers, the result of Verwoerd's intensification of apartheid, had not yet imposed high costs on the South African economy with its small and unsophisticated manufacturing sector. These and other economic costs of apartheid would only become clear a decade or so after his death.

As we have seen, Preece not only believes that South Africa could have grown faster, but also thinks that economic growth under apartheid did nothing for blacks. This is not correct. While it is true that the gap between whites and blacks remained enormous and that a maze of restrictions blocked black progress, the fact is that on average in the two decades after Verwoerd gained power the disposable personal income of all the politically subordinate groups improved (albeit from a very low base) at a rate higher than that of whites.

DISPOSABLE PERSONAL INCOME (AT 1990 PRICES)

	1960 (Rand)	1970 (Rand)	1980 (Rand)
Whites	12,114	17,260	17,878
Asians	2,171	3,674	5,655
Coloreds	2,000	3,033	3,933
Blacks	1,033	1,439	1,903

Source: J.L. Sadie, 'The Economic Demography of South Africa', doctoral diss., US, 2000, p. 310.

These trends were recognized even when Verwoerd was in power. In 1964 Harry Oppenheimer, head of the Anglo American Corporation, by far the largest conglomerate in the country, remarked that in the previous five years the average wages of 'non-white' workers in secondary industry had risen by 5.4 per cent (against those of whites at 3.7 per cent) per year. To him this explained why the country was 'so much more stable than many people are inclined to suppose.'[182] This was of little comfort to those blacks

179 *Time*, 26 August 1966, pp. 20-5.
180 *Rand Daily Mail*, 7 September 1966.
181 *Financial Mail*, 14 July 1967, Supplement, p. 59.
182 Anglo American Corporation, Chairman's Statement in 1964 Annual Report, p. 2.

living on a pittance in the reserves. But for them the glimmer of hope was the prospect of a job, albeit one with a very low wage. In 1965, 73.6 per cent of new entrants to the labor market were absorbed in the formal sector, a rate never achieved before. It would rise to 76.6 per cent in 1970, but would drop to 43.4 per cent in 1998.[183]

Andrew Kenny notes: 'The crucial achievement of apartheid [under Verwoerd] was to ensure white rule in South Africa during the postwar period of communism.'[184] Verwoerd stood as a 'man of granite' against a socialist or populist future. But it was unlikely that he would have been capable of accommodating the demands of a new, more assertive and better skilled black labor force. As his power grew, he himself became much more assertive and ever less willing to tolerate adjustments to apartheid that the high growth rate was beginning to demand.

Schalk Pienaar thought that Verwoerd's dominance in all policy making and of the Afrikaner debate had created a false sense of security, and that nothing could be more dangerous for Afrikaner survival in a hostile world.[185] He would later declare: 'As if it was the most natural thing in the world, Verwoerd considered himself the leader of the Afrikaners and the arbiter of what was good and bad for the Afrikaners.'[186] Verwoerd even ventured into literary criticism. The occasion was the performance of *Die pluimsaad waai ver,* a play by Van Wyk Louw on the Anglo-Boer War performed at the first republican festival in 1966. The play opened with an old woman hesitantly posing the question: '*Wat is 'n volk?*' (What is a nation?) and depicted the complex Afrikaner character and internal divisions during the Anglo-Boer War, with many betraying the cause of freedom and independence.

Verwoerd attacked Louw by expressing a fervent wish that poets and writers would not ask what a nation was but would instead celebrate the nation as the creator of its own glory and destiny. An outraged Pienaar condemned the criticism that Verwoerd's intervention had brought upon Louw's head. 'What is the sin that Van Wyk Louw committed in *Pluimsaad* . . .? That he looked at the heroic time of the freedom struggle and saw more than only heroism? Greatness and pettiness, strength and weakness, wisdom and ignorance . . . If that is the case then Van Wyk Louw's sin is that he dares to express doubts at a time in which there is fear of doubt.'[187] Pienaar later told of the friend's remark which pulled him out of his state of shock on hearing of the Prime Minister's assassination. The friend asked: 'How much longer could the country have suffered Verwoerd?'[188]

183 Personal communication from Jan Sadie, 23 July 2002.
184 Andrew Kenny, 'How Apartheid Saved South Africa', *The Spectator*, 27 November 1999, p. 26.
185 Alex Mouton, ' "Reform from Within": Schalk Pienaar, the Afrikaans Press and Apartheid', *Historia*, 45, 1 (2000), p. 156.
186 Pienaar, *Getuie van groot tye*, p. 50.
187 Steyn, *Van Wyk Louw*, p. 1053.
188 Vosloo, *Pienaar*, p. 65.

Chapter 15

Holding the Fort

The lure of prosperity

A story published in 1952 in *Die Burger's* popular 'Dawie' column tells of the Devil's problem with a small nation placed by his Opponent in South Africa. The Devil had tried in diverse ways to destroy it: he had put it under an alien government, had taken away its republics, had dragged it into two world wars, and sent it into a rebellion (1914-15) and a general strike (1922). 'I am at my wit's end,' the Devil said. 'Only one thing remains: I shall make them prosperous and see if they can survive that.'[1] At the height of an economic boom of the mid-1960s *Die Burger*, under Piet Cillié's editorship, returned to the theme. Incorporating a growing black labor force, an editorial argued, carried its own germ of destruction. 'It would try to break down the white power structure, which whites would resist fiercely in order to retain their political domination. The government and its supporters would have to limit the process as much as possible. 'Otherwise we are still going to see the day when we shall curse our highly praised prosperity.'[2]

By the end of the 1960s the Afrikaners still lagged behind the other white community in some key areas. The percentage of English-speaking children who passed the highest school standard was twice as high as that of Afrikaners, and there were twice the number of English university graduates in the white community. Afrikaners earned only 45 per cent of the total white income although they formed nearly 60 per cent of the white community. Only 4 per cent of Afrikaners earned more than R 8,000 a year, putting them in the highest income stratum, compared to 13 per cent for English-speakers.[3]

But nationalist politicians no longer tried to capitalize on the discrepancy between Afrikaner political power and relative economic backwardness. The country's growing iso-

---

1 Louis Louw (compiler) *Dawie, 1946-1964* (Cape Town: Tafelberg, 1965), p. 98. (Original column published in *Die Burger* on 29 September 1954.)

2 Cited by Ralph Horwitz, *The Political Economy of South Africa* (London: Weidenfeld and Nicolson, 1967), p. 399.

3 Heribert Adam, 'The South African Power Elite', in H. Adam (ed.), *South Africa* (London: Oxford University Press, 1971), p. 79.

lation had drawn the whites together. In the 1966 general election the National Party had for the first time attracted a significant share of the English vote. Afrikaner businessmen were more aware than ever that the color of money was the same regardless of the language one spoke. The largest part of the urban Afrikaner population had established itself as a secure ethnic community.

White farming (more than 80 per cent in Afrikaner hands) now comprised a stable sector, with state aid in the second half of the 1960s averaging 20 per cent of the net farming income.[4] Companies controlled by Afrikaners acquired a growing share of different sectors of the economy. The Afrikaner's aggregate share of the economy, excluding agriculture, rose from 10 to 21 per cent between 1948 and 1975.[5]

The Afrikaner economic share in the entrepreneurial function (selected sectors)

SECTOR	1938-9	1954-5	1975
Agriculture	87	84	82
Mining	1	1	18
Manufacturing and construction	3	6	15
Trade and commerce	8	26	16
Finance	5	10	25

The insurance giant Sanlam, through its subsidiaries Federale Volksbeleggings, Bonuskor and Federale Mynbou, spearheaded the expansion into the mining and industrial sectors. The management of these companies interacted with their English counterparts who embraced a kind of capitalism in which the business of business was profits rather than community commitment. Yet Harry Oppenheimer, heading the Anglo American Corporation agglomerate that towered over the private sector, had come to realize that it was important to break down Afrikaner antipathy to his business empire. In a shrewd move the Anglo American Corporation in 1963 sold a substantial share of General Mining, a mining house it controlled, to Fedmyn. A few years later Fedmyn acquired the majority share and changed the company's name to General Mining. The deal was done at market prices and allowed De Beers, a company in which Oppenheimer also had a majority interest, to keep its diamond monopoly.

With this deal Sanlam had abandoned the old ideal of Afrikaners' capturing a greater share of the economy through companies wholly owned by them. In some nationalist circles there was bitter disappointment about the deal. *Die Vaderland*, a Johannesburg-based Afrikaans daily, noted sadly: 'It is a lethal blow for an old ideal, going back to the Reddingsdaadbond, to acquire for the Afrikaner, however difficult and hard it might be, a place in mining that is very much his own. There will be more opportunities for mak-

---

4 Jill Nattrass, *The South African Economy* (Cape Town: Oxford University Press, 1981), p. 119.
5 The figures in the table are taken from research done by J.L. Sadie. A more detailed table is published in Heribert Adam and Hermann Giliomee, *Ethnic Power Mobilized: Can South Africa Change?* (New Haven: Yale University Press, 1979), pp. 170-71.

ing money and there will be higher positions for Afrikaners in the mining industry. But the original idea is dead and buried . . . in a gold coffin.'[6]

The Sanlam leadership now defined the Afrikaners' economic goals in terms quite different from those of the 1940s. Managing Director Pepler Scholtz said that Afrikaners must co-operate with others, particularly with English-speakers. Instead of speaking of the Afrikaner 'share' of the economy, it was better, he said, to speak of the Afrikaner 'contribution' to it. 'The Afrikaner is not entitled to a share only because he exists. He is only entitled to that share of business that he conquers through his own abilities and hard work.'[7] Yet Afrikaner businessmen were still fully integrated in the nationalist movement. A study found that building successful enterprises was for them a means of gaining prestige and esteem from their fellow Afrikaners, but it also pointed out that as the capitalist system became rooted in a culture, businessmen tended to attach less value to recognition by their fellow ethnics and more to that of their business peers.[8]

The Devil in Dawie's parable cited above had reason to remain hopeful. If Afrikaners were beginning to capture capitalism, capitalism was also capturing more and more Afrikaners. In September 1965 Verwoerd warned that the growth of Afrikaner capitalism might later be used against the Afrikaners themselves.[9] Just before his death, he wrote to the Broederbond's Executive Council that the greater the prosperity and the fewer the political dangers the more difficult it would be to maintain Afrikaner unity.[10] In 1974, Jan Sadie, a Stellenbosch economist, remarked that a new phenomenon had surfaced: 'Afrikaner Hoggenheimers.'[11] This was the old epithet for unscrupulous English-speaking or Jewish businessmen only interested in profits, ignoring the welfare of the Afrikaner or larger white community. In 1975 the Broederbond's Executive Council noted with alarm that Afrikaner businessmen were no longer attaching great value to nationalist goals. It said that Afrikaner businessmen 'considered economic growth and materialist considerations a higher priority than the freedom and sovereignty of the Afrikaner people.'[12]

Whites were less and less willing to pay for solutions, like the Tomlinson Commission proposals, that could give apartheid some moral foundation. In 1973 the Broederbond polled its six hundred branches on the question whether additional 'white' land should be made available for the consolidation of the reserves, over and above the 13 per cent set aside in the 1936 legislation. The divisions overwhelmingly rejected this; agricultural land had to remain in productive hands.[13] The white elite had to give the lead here, but a comfortable middle-class life and a seemingly stable state made it less and less willing to make sacrifices for a political vision. White prosperity steadily undermined white domination.

---

6 Cited by B.M. Schoeman, *Die Geldmag* (Pretoria: Sigma, 1980), p. 82.

7 *Die Volksblad*, 22 August 1969.

8 R.G. Stokes, 'The Afrikaner Industrial Entrepreneur and Afrikaner Nationalism,' *Economic Development and Cultural Change*, 22, 4 (1974), pp. 557-79.

9 J.H.P. Serfontein, *Die verkrampte aanslag* (Cape Town: Human & Rousseau, 1970), p. 55.

10 E.L.P. Stals, 'Geskiedenis van die Afrikaner-Broederbond, 1918-1994', unpublished ms., 1998, p. 405.

11 J.L. Sadie, 'Die ekonomiese faktor in die Afrikaner-gemeenskap', in H.W. van der Merwe (ed.), *Identiteit en verandering* (Cape Town: Tafelberg, 1974), p. 100.

12 Stals, 'Geskiedenis van die AB', p. 374.

13 Stals, 'Geskiedenis van die AB', p. 370.

A secure language?

By 1970 the attempt to establish Afrikaans as a public language had succeeded to a remarkable degree. In 1977 Heinz Kloss, a prominent German language sociologist, observed that outside Europe very few 'new' university languages (as against old ones such as Japanese, Chinese and Arabic) succeeded during the twentieth century in becoming standardized and being employed in all branches of life and learning. Only Hindi and Indonesian, which relied on a great number of speakers, and Hebrew matched the achievement of Afrikaans in becoming employed in Parliament, the civil service, science and technology and as sole medium in both undergraduate and postgraduate teaching.[14]

One of the main reasons for the advance of Afrikaans was Article 137 of the Union Constitution. This clause, which was adopted at the insistence of ex-President Steyn and General J.B.M. Hertzog, provided for the equality of the two official languages. It implied that civil servants had to be bilingual, but this was only strictly enforced after 1948. Van Wyk Louw, poet and essayist, called the Afrikaans language the 'socialism of the poor Afrikaner.' Once the state enforced Afrikaans as an official language, the 'small man' knew that his language would help him to get work.[15] In 1957 Louw wrote that the language movement had triumphed; it had secured more rights than other 'small' languages, like Irish or Welsh, and had built up a respected literature. To Afrikaners, Afrikaans provided a sense of personal worth, as well as jobs and other economic advantages.[16] But Louw warned against complacency; the language could still perish unless it served as a vehicle for the real and vital needs of large groups of people.

Afrikaans mother-tongue schools and universities played a vital role in the rise of Afrikaans. By 1970 the pattern that the two white communities overwhelmingly attended schools that taught only in the mother tongue had been set for more than two decades (see p. 490). Afrikaans-medium schools provided an opportunity to spread the nationalist message to children throughout their school years. Connie Mulder, a cabinet minister in the 1970s, once said: 'I was a teacher of history in an Afrikaans-medium mother-tongue school . . . After a child had been taught history in my classes, there was very little left for the United Party, precious little.'[17] Studies undertaken in the early part of the 1970s showed a strong correspondence between the political views of children and their parents in Afrikaner homes.

At the university level, where there was no compulsion, Afrikaans universities drew almost all the Afrikaner students, and also were better able to attract students from the 'other' white group than their English counterparts were in attracting Afrikaans students.[18] From the early 1930s Afrikaans had made its mark as a language of advanced research in the Arts and Humanities; by the 1970s it had been extended to the natural sciences and medicine. In 1980s it was 32nd in the articles indexed by *Chemical Abstracts*

---

14 Heinz Kloss, *The Unfolding of Afrikaans in its Germanic, African and World Context* (Pietersburg: University of the North, 1977), p. 10.

15 N.P. van Wyk Louw, *Versamelde prosa* (Cape Town: Human & Rousseau, 1986), vol. 2, p. 350.

16 Van Wyk Louw, *Versamelde prosa*, vol. 2, p. 350 (the article was first published in 1957).

17 *HAD,* 23 February 1967, col. 1827.

18 Gerrit Viljoen, 'The Afrikaans Universities and Particularism', in H.W. van der Merwe and David Welsh (eds.), *The Future of the University in South Africa* (Cape Town: David Philip, 1977), p. 176.

(higher than Hindi, Armenian and Arabic) from publications all over the world and 25th in *Index Medicus*.[19]

With the state pursuing a firm policy of bilingualism, a large proportion of Afrikaners found secure jobs in the civil service. By 1968 there were twice as many Afrikaners in the civil service as in 1948. More than a third of the Afrikaner labor force was employed in the public sector, and Afrikaners now dominated the top positions. By 1974 Afrikaners accounted for 80 per cent of the senior staff in government departments.[20]

There were two lethal dangers in this pattern of development. Afrikaners strongly preferred the security of state employment to employment in the private sector, which held a greater risk but offered better opportunities for personal development and financial success. For many of these civil servants the loss of white power could mean becoming unemployable. Secondly, the language of Afrikaans and the Afrikaner-controlled state had become locked in a tight and suffocating embrace. Increasingly the subordinate population saw Afrikaans as the language of the oppressor. Addressing writers, Jakes Gerwel, a black professor of Afrikaans said: 'Afrikaans has become the defining characteristic which the greatest part of the population knows particularly well on account of its arrogance and cruelty.'[21]

Leading Afrikaans writers and poets were becoming estranged from the Afrikaner nationalist movement. Afrikaner dissidents faced a chilly breeze. Beyers Naudé was forced to resign as DRC minister when he took up the directorship of the multi-denominational and multi-racial Christian Institute. The Broederbond purged Nic Olivier, partly because of his opposition to Verwoerd and partly because he divorced his wife, an Afrikaner, and married a Jewish woman. Van Wyk Louw remained a member of the Broederbond and broke with Naudé because he had violated the code of confidentiality.

After the proclamation of the republic in 1961 the nationalist movement lost much of its vitality and creative energy. The Afrikaans newspapers had become conformist. *Die Burger*, the leading paper, no longer issued probing analyses of the ethical dimension of apartheid, and became more concerned with day-to-day politics and attacking the official opposition. The sense of the early 1960s that a political solution was urgently required had disappeared. The Transvaal papers tended to be sensationalist and full of political propaganda; as Van Wyk Louw described it, 'stuffing the readers' ears with what the paper wanted them to believe rather than arguing with them.'[22] The Afrikaans papers did not report on tensions within the party or of the harsh impact of apartheid on the subordinate population. Between 1962 and 1964 the circulation of English language opposition papers grew by ninety thousand copies, that of Afrikaner nationalist papers declined by ten thousand. The chairman of the Transvaal NP estimated that 40 per cent of English-language newspapers readers were Afrikaners.[23]

As an official language, Afrikaans was steadily losing ground to English if the entire population was considered. With rapid black population growth and a declining growth

19 Jean Laponce, *Languages and Territories* (Toronto: University of Toronto Press, 1987), pp. 72-3.

20 Deborah Posel, 'Whiteness and Power in the South African Civil Service', *Journal of Southern African Studies*, 25, 1 (1999), p. 105.

21 G.J. Gerwel, 'Afrikaner, Afrikaans, Afrika', address to Afrikaanse Skrywersgilde, 20 May 1976.

22 J.C. Steyn, *Van Wyk Louw* (Cape Town: Tafelberg, 1998), p. 1016.

23 *Survey of Race Relations, 1964*, pp. 45-7.

rate among white and colored people, the proportion of people who spoke Afrikaans as their mother tongue steadily declined. It was still 18 per cent of the population in 1970, but was projected to decline to 15 per cent by 2000. A considerable proportion of blacks – some estimated it as high as 40 per cent – spoke Afrikaans as their second or third language. But English as the language of commerce and industry was steadily becoming more dominant among urban blacks, with many of them preferring English as the sole medium of instruction in the higher school standards. If Afrikaans became marginalized in black schools it had little prospect of holding its own among Africans as a co-equal official language alongside English.[24]

In the so-called homelands Afrikaans was also retreating. One after the other the homelands chose English and a Bantu language as the official languages, leaving Afrikaans out in the cold. It had become identified among Africans as the language of the oppressor – the medium used, for example, when white policemen arrested pass offenders or when white civil servants issued permits or ordered blacks out of their houses or out of the urban areas.

A far right challenge

The leadership of Afrikaners who were members of nationalist cultural institutions tried to maintain the vitality of the movement through warnings about the dangers facing it. They tended to insist on Afrikaner exclusivity, strict public morality and a rigid application of apartheid. The Afrikaanse Studentebond (a federation of Afrikaner student councils at different universities) in their conferences in the late 1950s and early 1960s debated the threats posed by 'liberalism, Communism, jingoism and Roman Catholicism with their tendency to encourage the fraternization of whites and non-whites.' The scene was described as follows. 'The style was one of defensiveness and an emphasis on Afrikaner survival. Students were warned against the undermining of Christian-National principles and urged to resist alien influences on Afrikaner culture.'[25]

These views developed within the context of an intensification of the Cold War, which had spawned a virulent anti-communist movement among the conservative Afrikaners during the 1960s. They cited anti-communism to dismiss the international criticism of apartheid. They held several major anti-communism conferences that identified an array of threats to white rule and linked up with kindred spirits in the local English community and the United States. They soon displayed a penchant for conspiracy stories in which international financial interests were cunningly working at undermining the established order for the sake of profits.

The principal proponents of anti-communism were the state radio, with Piet Meyer as chairman of the control board; Die Kerkbode, the official journal of the DRC under the editorship of Andries Treurnicht; the South African Observer, a political tract edited by a local English-speaker, S.E.D Brown; and the cabinet minister, Albert Hertzog, son of General Hertzog. As Prime Minister, Verwoerd allowed the anti-communist right free

---

24 Jonathan Hyslop, The Classroom Struggle (Pietermaritzburg: University of Natal Press, 1999), p. 158.
25 C.S. Heymans, 'Die politieke en ideologiese strominge en aktiwiteite in en om die Afrikaanse Studentebond,' master's diss., US, 1981, p. 39-40.

play to set the political tone, while placating reformists through talk of independent black homelands.

Among whites, in general, the warnings about the dangers of communism won strong support. In 1969 a survey revealed that only two per cent of whites saw the rapid growth in numbers of the colored people and blacks as a danger to the political system; the overwhelming majority regarded the greatest threat as stemming from the 'Communist influence, Communist-inspired guerrilla movements and Communism in Black South Africa.' Two years later a survey of the white elite found that only 9 per cent saw the rise of 'black nationalism' as a threat compared to 73 per cent who believed that international communism represented the 'greatest threat to the security of South Africa and the successful realization of the policy of separate development.'[26]

In fact, communist subversion in South Africa had been all but eradicated by 1965 through draconian repressive measures, which included detention without trial. The attention of the anti-communist campaign now shifted elsewhere. As in Europe and the USA, the Afrikaner radical right was haunted not so much by the thought of betrayal by its 'enemies' but by its 'friends.' They tried to target at an early stage 'disloyal' Afrikaners who were propagating a liberalization of the racial order by depicting them as paving the way for communism. An FAK official told a British researcher that 'the struggle against Anglicization from without was over, but the struggle against the enemy from within had begun.'[27]

By 1966 the focus of the anti-communists' wrath was business leaders keen to polish up South Africa's stained international image and also NP reformists, particularly *Die Burger* with Piet Cillié as editor and Schalk Pienaar as deputy editor. Through editorials and the column 'Dawie', they wielded strong influence, particularly during the first half of the year when Parliament sat. Fuelling the anti-*Burger* sentiment was the old animosity of Transvaal nationalists against the Cape 'money power' (Sanlam) and the 'Keerom Street Clique' (Nasionale Pers and the Cape NP), reinforced by rivalry for influence and market share between Nasionale Pers and the northern Afrikaans press groups with which Verwoerd had close ties.

As recounted in the previous chapter, Nasionale Pers in 1965 established a Sunday newspaper, *Die Beeld,* under the editorship of Schalk Pienaar, despite Verwoerd's strong opposition. Its editorial offices were in Johannesburg and the paper was distributed across the country. For Afrikaner conservatives in the north this was a nightmare coming true: a hard-hitting Afrikaans paper in their midst scorning many of the old shibboleths of an inward-looking, often paranoid, nationalism, and exposing the harshness of apartheid and white hypocrisy. One of the first columns Pienaar wrote was headed *Oop Gesprek* ('Open Conversation'), the term coined by Van Wyk Louw, who likened the paper to 'oxygen given to a person submerged in a swamp.' (He was then living in Johannesburg.)[28]

While Cillié had moved much closer to the NP leadership by the mid-1960s, Pienaar

26 Adam, 'The South African Power Elite', p. 91; *Newscheck,* 17 October 1969.

27 Sheila Patterson, *The Last Trek* (London: Routledge and Kegan Paul, 1957), p. 283.

28 Steyn, *Van Wyk Louw*, p. 1017; Alex Mouton, '" Reform from Within": Schalk Pienaar, the Afrikaans Press and Apartheid', *Historia*, 45, 1 (2000), pp. 149-76.

retained his commitment to an independent and critical Afrikaans press. Unlike Cillié, who hardly ever spoke to blacks, Pienaar undertook two extended journeys to African colonies and witnessed the stirring of African nationalism first hand. While Cillié viewed the black challenge abstractly and slightly disparagingly, Pienaar respected the 'black giant' and recognized that blacks craved equality and freedom from white rule. He warned that the time for South African whites to find a satisfactory solution was much shorter than they thought. 'Military bayonets alone would not stop the incoming black gulf.'[29] Pienaar's friendship with John Vorster and P.W. Botha gave him some protection, but these ties also prevented him from writing about the torture of political prisoners, which had become difficult to ignore, or to challenge the fundamentals of apartheid.

Pienaar and Cillié joined forces to expose the anti-communists sniping at reformers, seizing on a speech of October 1967 given by a Potchefstroom academic, Willem de Klerk, to isolate the far right. De Klerk discerned three tendencies in the nationalist movement. There were *verligtes* (enlightened ones), liberals in a new Afrikaans guise, who discarded tradition and favored openness and freedom, also in the field of race relations. There were the *verkramptes* (constricted or narrow reactionaries), who were narrow-minded and insular, clinging to the past and engaged in witch-hunts against everything not traditional. Always seeking a nationalist consensus rather than a clear reform principle, De Klerk rejected both the verligte and verkrampte tendencies in favor of a 'positive Afrikaner-hood' that favored both exclusivity and openness, tradition and progressive thinking.'[30] This third position was quickly forgotten, but his brother, F.W., who became president in 1989, was its embodiment in the years before he rose to the highest position.

Cillié and Pienaar published the full text of the speech in *Die Burger* and *Die Beeld* and began using the term 'verligte' as a badge of honor for those willing to abandon aspects of apartheid, and 'verkrampte' for archconservatives refusing to face reality. These names stuck long after the anti-communists had been discredited. The two camps themselves tended to exaggerate the differences between them on racial policy. Actually, both verkramptes and verligtes subscribed to Afrikaner and general white domination and verligtes only propagated slow and carefully controlled changes that did not affect the foundations of power. There was a class correlation in the split, with the verligtes better educated, wealthier and less dependent on state protection than the verkramptes, but the battle was essentially over the soul of Afrikaner nationalism as the dominant political force.

Verligtes saw themselves as whites, not only as Afrikaners, and the state as one that was increasingly becoming multi-racial. They shared Pienaar's conviction that the government 'cannot, will not and does not want to rule South Africa as if only Afrikaners lived in the country.'[31] Pienaar saw no reason to toe the line of the political leadership slavishly. The Afrikaans press, like the NP as a party, enjoyed what he called 'independence-in-common-commitment' to the Afrikaner cause.[32] He warned against Verwoerd's 'dangerous fiction' that the stream of blacks would start flowing back to the homelands by

29 Schalk Pienaar, *Getuie van groot tye* (Cape Town: Tafelberg, 1979), pp. 35-9.
30 W.J. de Klerk, *Afrikanerdenke* (Potchefstroom: Pro-Rege-pers, 1971), p. 13.
31 Cited by *The Star,* 17 February 1969.
32 Hermann Giliomee, 'Afrikaner Politics' in *Ethnic Power Mobilized*, p. 232-40.

1978, despite an acute shortage of skilled labor that had built up. To him apartheid offered no license to act in a way hurtful to the dignity of people of a different color. He
welcomed racially mixed sport and the establishment of diplomatic relations with other
African states since they provided opportunities for normalizing race relations in South
Africa.

With respect to blacks he remained optimistic that the homelands policy could attain
the goal of 'separate freedoms' for the white and the different black peoples, insisting that
this was 'the means, the way, the goal of NP policy.'[33] He was fundamentally at odds with
Verwoerd's conception of the colored people as a separate nation and believed that they
were 'brown Afrikaners.' He realized that the Afrikaners' exclusion of colored people who
shared their language and culture made a mockery of the attempt to present apartheid
as not based on racism, and also greatly weakened the attempt to get support for Afrikaans
across color lines.[34]

The verkramptes identified the state as an Afrikaner state and apartheid as the up-
holding of a total system that would disintegrate once people started tinkering with it.
Some leading verkramptes felt that the Afrikaner nationalist project would not be complete until the English-speaking section of the white population had been Afrikanerized.
In 1966 Piet Meyer, chairman of the Broederbond's Executive Council, secretly spoke of
the need to get English-speakers to adopt the Afrikaans language, history and world-
view.[35] (Meyer was such a close associate of Verwoerd that it is difficult to believe that
he had not sounded him out.)

'A strong state and weak subjects'

Initially the verkramptes had reason to be confident that Verwoerd's policies would continue. In a state of deep shock after Verwoerd's assassination on 6 September 1966, the
NP caucus elected B.J. (John) Vorster as his successor. He was the candidate of the anti-
communist right, which applauded his attacks on communists and liberals as subversive elements undermining the social order. Vorster had been interned during the Second
World War as an active supporter of the pro-Nazi Ossewa Brandwag, and the liberal
Rand Daily Mail speculated that the rash of bannings, house arrests, and detentions during his term as Minister of Justice between 1961 and 1966 had much to do with his history as a political internee. Vorster once stated in Parliament that an interned communist
had more privileges under the current NP government than an Afrikaner internee under
the United Party during the Second World War.[36] Yet although Vorster represented a
Transvaal constituency, he was in fact a Cape man. He had studied at Stellenbosch, his
father-in-law was a director of Nasionale Pers, and his political mentor was Paul Sauer,
the phlegmatic and cynical Cape politician who had called for a new approach after
Sharpeville.[37]

---

33 *Die Beeld,* 2 January 1966.
34 *Die Beeld,* 3 March 1968. For an extended discussion see Alex Mouton, *Voorloper: die lewe van Schalk Pie-
    naar* (Cape Town: Tafelberg, 2002), pp. 96-146.
35 J.H.P. Serfontein, *Brotherhood of Power* (London: Rex Collings, 1979), p. 323.
36 *HAD,* 1961, column 7687.
37 Dirk en Johanna de Villiers, *Paul Sauer* (Cape Town; Tafelberg, 1977), pp. 147-52.

As a leader Vorster soon attracted warm support from Afrikaners outside the verkrampte ranks. He was less aloof than Dr Verwoerd, played golf regularly, met the press
frequently and made witty after-dinner speeches. The liberal *Rand Daily Mail* soon described him as the most popular prime minister South Africa had ever had. More than his
predecessors, he saw black and colored people as human beings rather than abstractions.
A sport lover, he was much keener than his predecessor to maintain international sport
contacts. They had been jeopardized by Verwoerd's refusal in 1965 to allow a New
Zealand national rugby team that included some Maoris to visit. He started a tortuous
process of the desegregation of sport that took more than fifteen years to complete. When
major strikes erupted in Durban 1973 against abysmally low wages, he told employers
'not only to see in their workers a unit producing for them so many hours of service a
day; they should see them as human beings with souls.'[38] Western diplomats who negotiated with him considered him straightforward, honest and reliable.[39]

Vorster was extremely tough on security issues, often proclaiming his belief that the
security of the state must be priority number one. Security legislation placed in the
hands of the police the kind of powers associated with dictatorships. In terms of a 1967
law the police could detain any person deemed a terrorist until he provided what the
police considered satisfactory answers to questions put to him. No persons other than officials of the state were entitled to have access to him. Allegations of police torture were
frequently made but public investigations were never launched, and the state used all
its power to prevent newspapers from publishing anything about conditions in prison.
The South African Institute of Race Relations estimated that between 1963 and 1983 at
least sixty-eight political prisoners died while in detention.[40]

For a repressive system, apartheid South Africa was a remarkably under-policed state.
In 1984 it was reported that there were only 1.4 policemen per thousand of the population, compared with roughly 2.4 in the United Kingdom, 4.4 in Ulster, 5.7 in Algeria
and 16 in the Soviet Union.[41] So, too, the number of political dissidents suffering persecution was small for a country whose population by 1970 stood at 22,500,000. Almost
a thousand people had been banned since 1950, 350 of these banning orders were still
in force by 1970. In 1970 some eight hundred South Africans were serving prison sentences for contravention of the security laws. Hundreds had left the country on exit permits, while many had had their passports withdrawn or refused.

South Africa's military spending remained low until the early 1980s, when it spent 13
per cent of the total budget on military expenditure, compared to Zimbabwe's 17 per cent,
Israel's 25 per cent and Taiwan's 26 per cent. In 1967 the government passed legislation introducing much stricter military conscription for all white males.

The relatively low numbers of police, soldiers and political prisoners all testified to a
system of domination that was more flexible and subtle than most critics gave it credit
for. The oppressed were confronted not by a monolithic dominant group but two white

---

38 *Survey of Race Relations, 1973*, p. 283.
39 Deon Geldenhuys, *The Diplomacy of Isolation* (Johannesburg: Macmillan, 1983), p. 230.
40 *Survey of Race Relations, 1988-89* (Johannesburg: SA Institute of Race Relations, 1989), p. 553.
41 Brian Pottinger, *The Imperial Presidency: P. W. Botha, the First Ten Years* (Johannesburg: Southern 1988),
   p. 287; *Financial Mail*, 12 April 1985.

communities, with the English-speaking somewhat more liberal than the Afrikaners. English newspaper editors and English clergy, more than their Afrikaner counterparts, together with the main liberal organization, the South African Institute of Race Relations, used the considerable freedom they enjoyed to point out injustices frequently and persistently.

Co-existing uneasily with the authoritarian state was a democracy for whites with civil rights and proper administrative procedures, including regulations for the investigation of all unnatural deaths. In theory people regardless of color had equal standing in the courts. The government pledged itself to respect a free and independent judiciary, and judges on the higher courts prided themselves on their impartiality, although blacks invariably received stiffer sentences. The few newspapers that supported the black struggle were banned and their staff harassed, and the government increasingly clamped down on criticism of the police force and prisons, but the main newspapers were remarkably free. Blacks could criticize apartheid and even mock it; and policing focused on efforts to encourage active resistance and particularly what Vorster called the 'big cancer' in South Africa – 'whites who agitated amongst blacks.'[42]

Officially the government deplored police brutality, although this did not help a black man caught without a pass. Still, repression was not random or unpredictable but properly legalized. In 1971, Fatima Meer, a prominent Asian anti-apartheid activist, wrote: 'The government preserves its structure through a highly sophisticated administrative technique which carefully mixes personal benevolence with the impersonal and hence "impartial" mystique of the law . . . The non-white victim is beginning to believe that he has the sympathy and support of minor and senior officials, including the prime minister, and that both white and black are equally the victims of South African custom and the law of apartheid.'[43] Meer refers to the 'awe-inspiring strength of the state', but adds that this was only possible 'because of the complementary weakness of its subjects.'[44]

Early in the 1970s the most astute analysts pointed out that the country was not on the brink of a political explosion brought about by a closed, race-obsessed group clinging to their privileges. As the most outstanding work of the time argued, the purpose of the system was 'the smooth, frictionless and tolerable domination over cheap labor and political dependents as a prerequisite for the privileges of the minority.'[45] The Afrikaner nationalists in power realized the folly of a ruling class composed only of like-minded individuals with a rigid set of political values and goals. The Prime Minister's Economic Advisory Council included both Afrikaners and English business leaders and they soon developed consensus over the need for a more flexible labor market and the reduction of the state sector in the economy. The Afrikaner Broederbond held endless discussions, only to discover that while there was agreement about the need to retain Afrikaner and general white domination, the differences about the means to ensure this could no longer be reconciled. The Afrikaans press increasingly informed its readers of the dismal conditions under which the subordinate population lived.

---

42 John D'Oliveira, *Vorster: The Man* (Johannesburg: Ernest Stanton, 1977), p. 128
43 Fatima Meer, 'African Nationalism: Some Inhibiting Factors', *South Africa: Sociological Perspectives*, p. 150.
44 Meer, 'African Nationalism', p. 122.
45 Heribert Adam, *Modernizing Racial Domination* (Berkeley: University of California Press, 1971), p. 53.

It was difficult for blacks to organize resistance. The banning of the ANC and the arrests or flight of its leaders left a huge void that, together with an ill-advised emphasis on the armed struggle, kept the organization on the sidelines until the end of the 1970s. The Black Consciousness Movement that sprang up in the late 1960s succeeded in making an inclusive black identity the focus of a black pride and assertion and began to politicize black and colored high school pupils and university students, but failed to establish ties with the black workers. In the adult urban black community, particularly that on the Witwatersrand, ethnic divisions remained salient and the state did its best to reinforce them through housing and educational policies. Overwhelmingly, blacks, feeling that for the time being white power was immutable, focused on wages and salaries. Since these were still quite low, the state and business thought it could buy most of them off.[46]

The police through its elaborate informer system could easily identify those blacks who propagated resistance. What they were not prepared for was a sudden, unplanned revolt by that section of the black population who did not have to dance to the oppressors' tune – school children and students.

As committed as Verwoerd to white supremacy, Vorster was quite a different kind of politician. He would not even try to dominate government as his predecessor did. The result was rampant 'departmentalism', with bureaucrats and politicians responsible for the black population pulling in a verkrampte direction and those wishing to desegregate sport in a verligte one. Vorster's main inclination was, as he often said, 'to hold the fort' by preserving the main props of white power and creating no false expectations.

Keen to break out of South Africa's deteriorating relationship with the world community, Vorster launched his 'Outward Movement.' The first step was to establish diplomatic and economic ties with African states to the north. They formed South Africa's natural market but took only 10 per cent of South Africa's manufacturing exports. He also wished to persuade African states in the region, which were hoping to free South Africa from white rule, to deny bases to the African National Congress and the Pan Africanist Congress. Confident of breaking up the monolithic hostility of the African states, he encouraged dialogue. While the only tangible success was the establishment of diplomatic relationships with Malawi, the African states were careful to limit their support to the liberation organizations to a minimum.

When President Hastings Banda of Malawi paid a state visit to South Africa, Vorster was photographed sitting between two black female guests at a state banquet. In doing so he made a major statement. The Afrikaner elite was still obsessed with the etiquette of race relations and forms of white-black interaction. In 1971 the Executive Council of the Broederbond had discussions with W.M. Eiselen, one of apartheid's architects, on the issue of greeting blacks by handshaking, which was a practice reported to have given rise to 'uncertainty, misconceptions and negative attitudes.' Eiselen dealt with the issue 'very sympathetically', after which the Bond's sent a circular to its divisions giving guidance on the issue.[47] Racial 'incidents' abounded and the government was ill prepared to deal

---

46 Edward Feit, 'Conflict and Cohesion in South Africa', *Economic Development and Cultural Change,* vol. 14 (1968), pp. 490-91; Lawrence Schlemmer, *Black Attitudes: Adaptation and Reaction* (Durban: Institute of Social Research, 1975).

47 Stals, 'Geskiedenis van die Afrikaner-Broederbond', p. 366.

with them. When a black homeland leader, Chief Buthelezi from KwaZulu, and a white woman danced at a press ball in 1972, F.W. de Klerk, a future president, assured voters that the incident was being investigated at the highest level and Connie Mulder, a minister widely backed to succeed Vorster, called it a 'wrong' development that 'repelled' him.[48]

Volkskritiek

During the early 1960s a new literary movement, known as the *Sestigers*, or the Generation of the Sixties, embraced secularization, modernity, racial tolerance and sexual freedom, and used modern literary techniques and subject matter to explore these themes. Historical novels more in the mainstream of Afrikaans literature than the experimental *Sestiger* works also expressed a new mood. In earlier Afrikaans historical novels the leading characters are men of action, firm in their convictions and prepared to use violence to subjugate the world to their will and to root out their enemies. By contrast, the main characters of the novels of Karel Schoeman and Anna M. Louw are introspective and passive fringe figures, often finding themselves marginal to the existing social categories. Struggling to assert themselves, they discover the complexity of social reality and the relativity of values and beliefs. Schoeman's novel *Na die geliefde land* (*Promised Land*), which appeared in 1972, is located in a post-revolutionary South Africa in which a bedraggled and insecure white community finds itself at the mercy of unidentified and unpredictable autocratic rulers. The main characters in Jan Rabie's Bolandia trilogy are mostly of mixed origins, trapped in a painful clash of cultures and conflicting loyalties. Together with the more high-profile work of the more prominent *Sestigers*, which included Etienne le Roux, André Brink and Breyten Breytenbach, this literature helped to change the political imagination of the Afrikaans reading public in subtle yet profound ways. They offered a new conceptualization of the Afrikaners and their history that differed starkly from the image the political leaders and cultural leadership tried to project of the Afrikaners as a people determined to crush all threats to their survival.[49]

Van Wyk Louw had long ago recognized not only the value but also the danger posed by the organization men in Afrikaner society, and he now set himself firmly against their efforts to channel Afrikaans cultural life into the streams the political and cultural leaders wanted it to go. 'A volk', he wrote, 'is not a sect, or clique or association with a fixed program . . . Among the greatest enemies of our volk are those desiring a spiritual one-way traffic and who wish to impose their own narrow vision for this time and eternity.'[50] A few years later his fears of the organization men became real when members of the cultural establishment refused to award the highest award to the main Sestiger novelist, Etienne le Roux, for his brilliant novel *Sewe dae by die Silbersteins* because of what they considered its moral unacceptability.

---

48 *Deurbraak*, February 1973, p. 14
49 Philip John, 'Die Afrikaanse historiese roman en die literêre kritiek', doctoral diss., US, 1998; C.N. van der Merwe, *Breaking Barriers: Stereotypes and the Changing of Values in Afrikaans Writing, 1875-1990* (Amsterdam: Atlanta, 1994).
50 Words, spoken in 1957, quoted by Koos Human, in a speech entitled 'Die verkrampte aanslag', delivered in 1975. A copy of the text is in the US Library, Kannemeyer collection, 242 T, 2 (13).

In 1963 Louw was alarmed when the government introduced a system of censorship. He asked: does this mean that the government wishes to force Afrikaans writers to switch to English to escape censorship? Emblematic of the gulf between the writers and the political leadership was an attack by Verwoerd, at the 1966 republican festival, of Louw's play *Die pluimsaad waai ver* (see p. 541). In the western Cape there was an echo of this in a clash between Opperman, Louw's peer as a poet, and P.W. Botha, who twelve years later would become prime minister. Urged by Botha to sit himself down on a rock and write an ode to the Republic of South Africa, Opperman, who at the time of the 1948 election wrote a poem in which he dreamed of a republic (see p. 486), replied that in Afrikaans the only word that rhymed with rock (*rots*) was vomit (*kots*).[51]

When Louw died in 1970 no member of the government attended the funeral of this, the greatest Afrikaans poet. Hendrik Verwoerd had died in 1966 and after Louw's death the polar opposites in the thinking in the nationalist establishment about survival had disappeared. Towering over the *volksbeweging* structures, Verwoerd tolerated no opposition to his view that undiluted apartheid was essential for survival, while Louw, as the pre-eminent public intellectual, insisted on survival in justice and a commitment to the *oop gesprek*, the open conversation, in order to find an ethical solution for ethnic survival.

Most of the dissenting voices in the Afrikaner community were now outside the party and the Broederbond and the debate had become much more diffuse. No political leader could speak with the intellectual authority and self-confidence of Verwoerd, and none of the Afrikaner critics would achieve quite the same unrivalled stature as Louw. But two individuals, whose styles and suggestions differed greatly, partly filled the void left by Louw as the moral conscience of the Afrikaners. One was Johannes Degenaar, a gentle and humane Stellenbosch philosopher, who posed Socratic questions about apartheid. He attached great value to Louw's concept of the *oop gesprek*, but he rejected his model of white and black nationalists settling the division of the land only after the Afrikaner nationalists had come to an agreement among themselves. He felt strongly that Van Wyk Louw attached too great a value to nationalism. The '*volk*' he considered simply as one of several identifications; nationalism too easily became mired in racism and the search for divine sanction for dominance. Degenaar believed that the Afrikaners had to seek a solution that transcended nationalism.[52]

The other significant figure was Breyten Breytenbach, a poet and essayist whose exceptionally inventive work put him in a class of his own. He grew up in the Little Karoo and the western Cape where he passed through all the Afrikaner nationalist institutions until he left school. Settling in Paris while still in his early twenties, he married a Vietnamese woman (who was considered by the apartheid system as a 'non-white') and became a French citizen. Breytenbach soon rejected apartheid totally as a system without any redeeming features. In a 1965 letter to Van Wyk Louw he stated: 'Our nationalism seems to me to be an absolute ideology tolerating ever less opposition . . . The curbing of the most elementary liberties . . . cannot be justified even if the issue at stake is physi-

51 Steyn, *Van Wyk Louw*, pp. 1034-1065; J.C. Kannemeyer, *D.J. Opperman* (Cape Town: Human & Rousseau, 1986), pp. 311-48.

52 J.J. Degenaar, et al., *Beweging uitwaarts* (Cape Town: John Malherbe, 1969), pp. 7-18, 127-56.

cal survival . . . The Afrikaner is trapped in a labyrinth of laws.'[53] In a letter to *Die Burger* Breytenbach wrote that he hated apartheid. 'If apartheid was representative of Afrikaner- dom', if the two could not be divorced, he saw no hope for the Afrikaners. 'If I could renounce my being an Afrikaner I would do it. I am ashamed of my people.'[54]

In a uniquely compelling way Breytenbach formulated all the ambiguities of his posi- tion. At times over the next thirty years he wrote as if some ideological mafia had cap- tured the Afrikaner soul and had dragged the Afrikaners headlong to disaster. The task of the creative writer was to save them from this elite by helping them to rediscover the humanism of earlier periods of their history and the inhumanity of the present system. He was closer to the mark when he wrote that it was foolish to believe that apartheid was the work of a few bureaucrats and ideologues. 'The Afrikaners are responsible for apart- heid, collectively and individually. Without them it would not exist. It is their way of life . . . Thus we have from the outset insecurity and a correspondingly passionate affir- mation of the nature and the principles of the tribe.'[55]

Breytenbach often wished that he could forget all about the Afrikaners and his own roots in the country. But it was impossible for him just to be an exiled poet. He had be- come involved in revolutionary organizations in Europe that were planning to isolate and ultimately overthrow the apartheid regime. In 1968 the South African government rejected his applications for visas for himself and his wife to visit South Africa to enable him to accept a prestigious prize for his poetry. He always claimed that the reason was that his wife was a Vietnamese woman, but Vorster told his publishers that this posed no problem. However, he considered Breytenbach an enemy of the Afrikaner people and his poetry as 'morally pernicious and politically repulsive.' 'If he put his foot in the coun- try, I should tuck him away so deeply in the prison building that he would never get out.'[56]

Breytenbach's publishers wrote an open letter to him in which they stated that the real reason for the rejection of the visa application was his support for a bloody uprising in South Africa. They added that they were considering contributing a similar amount to an anti-terrorist fund as the royalties they paid to the poet. As a result he cut all ties with his publishers, but the real and lasting antagonism was between Vorster and Breytenbach: a politician who dismissed criticism from the liberal press with disdain but was extraor- dinarily sensitive to attacks from Afrikaners, whether it be from the far right or far left, and a poet in the mould of the prophet Amos, who condemned his people as oppressors by invoking the values that they pretended to share, yet longed to be accepted and even loved. Breytenbach had developed a fatal passion for liberating South Africa, and the Afrikaners in particular, from apartheid. His exile, he wrote in 1972, must force him to maintain a dialogue with the inside. 'He must bark all along the borders.'[57]

53 Steyn, *Van Wyk Louw*, p. 1012.
54 *Die Burger*, 2 June 1965.
55 Breyten Breytenbach, *End Papers* (London: Faber and Faber, 1986), p. 55.
56 J.C. Kannemeyer, *D. J. Opperman: 'n biografie* (Cape Town: Human & Rousseau, 1986).
57 Breytenbach, *End Papers*, p. 76.

An ideological impasse

Vorster's troubles with far-right Afrikaners, those called verkramptes, started soon after he came to power. He privately told a group of conservative MPs of his party that they had got it all wrong in believing that apartheid was an end in itself. The cardinal principle of the NP was 'the retention, maintenance and the immortalization of Afrikaner identity within a white sovereign state.' Apartheid was merely a method to bring this about. 'If there are other better methods of achieving this end we must find those methods and get on with it.'[58] At least one MP, the verkrampte Jaap Marais, soon to be expelled, concluded that Vorster was reneging on fundamental principles.

Vorster made what he called his political confession in a speech on 16 August 1968 in the town of Heilbron in the OFS. The Afrikaners could not go it alone, and survival required 'every white for the struggle ahead.' There was no longer any reason to complain that Afrikaans as a language was going to ruin. The danger now was the 'Super-Afrikaners' – a reference to the far right – who objected to diplomatic relations with other African states and mixed sports teams. He warned against those who predicted that co-operation with the English-speakers would mean the downfall of the Afrikaners.[59]

Vorster's flexibility did not extend to the political structures of apartheid. He declared in his Heilbron speech: 'We [the whites] have our land and we alone will have authority over it. We have our Parliament and in that Parliament we and we alone will be represented.'[60] He stuck to the old apartheid principle that blacks could exercise political rights only in their respective homelands, regardless of where they lived. He opposed the granting of property rights to blacks considered permanent residents in the urban areas. In his view this would only lead to increased pressure for political rights in a common system.

Vorster extended political apartheid to its extreme. In 1968 his government abolished the vestiges of colored representation in the House of Assembly (four whites elected on a separate role by coloreds), the Senate, and the Cape Provincial Council. As a substitute he introduced a Coloured Persons' Representative Council consisting of nominated and elected members with extremely limited powers. Another law passed in the same year made it illegal for parties to be active in the political affairs of another racial group. Also in 1968, the South African Indian Council Act was passed to create an advisory, wholly nominated body to deal with Indian affairs in three provinces (in the fourth, the Orange Free State, Indians were still not allowed to settle). In 1971 all colored voters were removed from municipal voters' rolls and in the next year the terms of office of colored councilors in Cape Town and some other towns in the Cape Province ended. The intention to set up segregated colored municipalities was ill conceived, since none was financially viable.

Even minor changes caused major tensions in the Afrikaner nationalist movement. Albert Hertzog emerged as the verkrampte leader. From his position in the cabinet he attacked the sports policy, the acceptance of black ambassadors and the efforts to bridge the gap between the two white communities. In 1969 he made a speech that sealed his

---

58 Dirk Richard, *Moedswillig die uwe* (Johannesburg: Perskor, 1985), pp. 134-5; J.A du Pisanie, *John Vorster en die Verlig/Verkrampstryd* (Bloemfontein: INEG, 1988), p. 24.

59 B.J. Vorster, *Select Speeches* (Bloemfontein: UOFS, 1977), p. 100.

60 Vorster, *Speeches*, p. 96.

fate. The question, he said, was whether whites 'dare to rule as a minority.' The Afrikaners were, he said, ideal fighters for this because they were Calvinists, loved their freedom and recognized 'racial diversity.' In English-speakers, by contrast, liberalism was so engrained that they were unable to fight against communistic and leftist movements. Hence the survival of European civilization depended on the Afrikaners as Calvinists. The speech was widely considered an insult to the South African English and Vorster dismissed him from the cabinet. Hertzog left the party and founded the Herstigte (Re-established) National Party. It was crushed by the NP in the general election of 1970, when it drew only 4 per cent of the votes polled (but close to 10 per cent of the Afrikaner votes), and failed to win a single seat.

For Vorster all friction had been removed by recognizing 'the right of existence of distinct nations and color groups.' All that was left was removing what he euphemistically called *knelpunte* or bottlenecks in the policy. But *knelpunte* abounded. The main issue at stake between verkramptes and verligtes were the glaring defects of the party policy towards colored people, the group closest to Afrikaners in culture, language and church affiliation. After the steps Vorster had taken they had neither a homeland nor any representation at all in Parliament. From the start, the Coloured Persons' Representative Council, which was supposed to remedy the latter, was doomed to fail. The Labour Party, which won most of the seats, set out to wreck the council, and its alienation increased when the government fabricated a pro-government majority by appointing nominated members who had been defeated in the election.

To stem the unease in its own ranks, the government in 1973 appointed a commission of inquiry into the colored population, headed by Erika Theron, and, for the first time since the NP came to power, a commission included colored members. The report signed by the majority of the Theron Commission did not denounce apartheid and also endorsed some its principal features, like residential segregation. Some of its findings, however, amounted to strong and devastating criticism of government neglect of the colored population. The chapter on economics spoke of 'chronic community poverty' that affected more than 40 per cent of the population. In the cities and towns between 10 and 20 per cent lived in squatter camps and many of the rest in overcrowded houses. A high rate of infant mortality had hardly changed from the 128 deaths per thousand births in the period 1946-51, and 120 in 1965-1970. In the urban labor market coloreds were reported to be suffering from pervasive discrimination since their workers could not join mixed trade unions without government permission. Even in its own terms apartheid had failed because whites, particularly Afrikaners, dominated the senior positions in all state institutions that served them.[61]

The commission recommended a direct say for coloreds at various levels of government. The government accepted the recommendation for a direct colored say in political structures, but also declared that the principle of white self-determination remained paramount. The tone of its response was so churlish that it pushed considerable numbers of colored people into participating in the uprising of 1976 and the public demonstrations of subsequent years.

---

61 J.M.M. Barnard, 'Die Erika Theron Kommissie, 1973-1976', master's diss., US, 1999.

The Afrikaans churches sounded no prophetic warning about the dangers of white power and white privilege. In 1974 the General Synod of the Dutch Reformed Church had accepted a report on race relations that contained an elaborate scriptural justification of apartheid. It still argued that the parable of the tower of Babel was a paradigm of a policy of ethnic diversity. The report declared itself to be as concerned as other churches about social justice, human rights and self-determination, both for groups and individuals. It disagreed, it suggested, only on the best means to achieve those ideals. The report was happy to endorse apartheid as a legitimate policy that promoted a greater degree of social justice.[62]

The report was strongly criticized. Jaap Durand, an Afrikaner theologian, pointed out that there were no hermeneutical grounds to accept ethnic diversity as a God-given principle. John de Gruchy, an English-speaking scholar, observed that the unspoken premise of the DRC report was that Afrikaner survival depended on apartheid. Allan Boesak, a colored, Afrikaans-speaking theologian, expressed his disgust by referring to the 'downward spiral' of DRC thinking on the race issue.[63] The failure of the church to preach its prophetic message made Schalk Pienaar, having come to the end of his career as a journalist, despair. He expressed indignation about the obscenity of white opulence in the midst of a sea of poverty. He wrote that palaces and hovels existing side by side 'made one ask oneself if the vengeance of the eternal God can be kept at bay.' After the DRC 1974 synod he wrote that he found it hard to believe that the church had failed to hear the voices of blacks and saw South Africa simply as 'God's Afrikaner reserve.'[64]

Pienaar's attack on the synod's decision signaled what he called the demise of the Afrikaans *volksbeweging* or popular movement. For more than forty years the constituent parts of party, press and interest-based organizations had sworn a virtually unqualified allegiance to each other and none, within nationalist ranks, had voiced Pienaar's kind of criticism. For Pienaar it was time for the Afrikaans press to assert itself much more forcefully. He deplored the fact that the government failed to realize that a well-disposed but independent Afrikaans press was a better ally than a subservient one.[65]

In 1976, when South Africa came to the end of forty years of high economic growth, the country still seemed remarkably stable. The international isolation of South Africa was not yet serious. The only serious reverses between 1964 and 1974 occurred in the field of sport. South Africa was banned from the Olympic games. South African sports teams could no longer play abroad without major disruption. The United Nations regularly passed motions condemning apartheid and in 1973 the UN General Assembly declared apartheid a crime against humanity (see p. 650).[66] But, although few Afrikaner leaders realized it at the time, only the Cold War and the Soviet threat made the West draw back from punitive steps against South Africa. As the Third World intensified its campaign against both apartheid and Zionism, the West felt more and more uncomfort-

---

62 Dutch Reformed Church, *Human Relations and the South African Scene in the Light of the Scriptures* (Cape Town: NG Kerkuitgewers, 1975), p. 100.

63 John de Gruchy, *The Church Struggle in South Africa* (Cape Town: David Philip, 1979), pp. 69-81.

64 Mouton, 'Reform from Within', p. 173.

65 Ton Vosloo (ed.), *Schalk Pienaar: tien jaar politieke kommentaar* (Cape Town: Tafelberg, 1975), p. 104.

66 Hermann Giliomee, *Liberal and Populist Democracy in South Africa* (Johannesburg: SA Institute of Race Relations, 1996), pp. 8-10.

able with being seen as defenders of the South African state. Unlike Israel, the Afrikaners had no Diaspora lobby that could speak up on its behalf.

A homeland for whites – and for blacks?

Underlying the homelands policy was the fiction that the common area was the white
homeland. Van Wyk Louw was one of the few to raise the issue in a way that seemed to
hint at partition. Addressing his black 'countrymen', he wrote: 'We must make room for
two kinds of peoples in the two halves of this big land of ours. The white and colored
people own a part of this land. It is land that has never been yours. Do not believe it if
someone tells you that all of Africa belongs to you. It is a lie.'[67]

Louw had in mind the pattern of land occupation in the early years of the white settlement. Dispossessing and incorporating the indigenous Khoisan, the whites by 1830
had occupied most of the western half of South Africa, with blacks living in the eastern
half. In 1957 the government proclaimed the area west of the 'Eiselen line' as a colored
'labor preference area.' It ran from Aliwal North in the northeast to a line formed by the
Fish and Kat rivers. It was stipulated that Africans could only be employed there if the
supply of colored labor had been exhausted. By 1962 some thirty thousand Africans
had been endorsed out of the region.

The government did not make any effort to develop the area west of the Eiselen line
as a 'homeland' for those of European descent, coloreds as well as whites. Nor did it see
any reason why it would have to weaken its claim to all of the common area, particularly
the prosperous Witwatersrand region that generated nearly half of the country's gross
domestic product. Afrikaners lived across South Africa, distributed in roughly these proportions: a third on the Witwatersrand, a third in the western Cape and a third scattered
across the rest of the country. Any effort to develop a homeland in the west would soon
be seen by Afrikaners elsewhere as a weakening of the claim to the eastern half. Among
NP politicians a sense of whites and coloreds forming a political and moral community
with a common claim to the land was still weakly developed, and only in the final years of
apartheid were colored people permitted to purchase white farmland. P.W. Botha, leader
of the NP of the Cape Province, in 1977 spoke of the coloreds as 'eventually being assimilated', but quickly retracted it when he became prime minister.[68]

A homeland for whites was only possible if they rapidly lessened their dependence
on black labor. Afrikaners had always been fascinated by the willingness of the Jews in
Israel to create a Jewish state against great obstacles and to rely mainly on themselves
for labor. It required determination and commitment to choose ethnic survival above
the fruits of materialism. The Israelis who visited South Africa were rarely impressed by
the Afrikaner survival strategies. An Israeli visitor remarked to Piet Cillié during the
1960s: 'My people are a dedicated people. Can you say the same of your people?' Cillié
replied that their commitment depended on different things, but the visitor had put
him on the spot, he later confessed. It was indeed doubtful that the Afrikaners, without

---

67 N.P. van Wyk Louw, 'Voorwoord' in D.P. Botha, *Die opkoms van ons derde stand* (Cape Town: Human &
    Rousseau, 1960), p. vii.
68 Anna Starcke, *Survival* (Cape Town: Tafelberg, 1978), p. 59.

facing a strong challenge, would give up their material privileges and be content with a much smaller part of the country.[69]

The apartheid policy as an attempt to create black homelands failed to get off the ground. Verwoerd's ban on private investment in the homelands, which killed almost all hopes for economic development there, was only rescinded in 1974. By 1975 the homelands were still made up of more than a hundred fragments and only then did the government announce consolidation plans to reduce that number substantially. But later that year it declared that land purchases that had been scheduled would be deferred because of the deteriorating economic situation.[70]

By now the lack of development in the homelands had become too stark to ignore. Between 1960 and 1972 only 85,544 jobs were created in the homelands and border areas, well below the number the Tomlinson Commission considered necessary. In 1974 Professor Tomlinson remarked that, until 1970, development of the reserves had been small-scale and fragmentary; a great opportunity had been missed, he said.[71]

The developmental aspect of the homelands policy had largely been replaced by a policy to use the reserves as dumping grounds where the government resettled blacks from 'white' South Africa. The policy saw the removal to the homelands of black rural settlements (called black spots), redundant farm laborers and some of the urban unemployed. Between 1962 and 1982 a total of 1.9 million black people, in the government's own estimate, were relocated to the homelands. When group areas' removals in the towns and cities and evictions of farm laborers were added, 3.5 million people were resettled as a result of apartheid. The conditions in the resettlement camps were bleak, with no or very little hope of getting a job or producing food. Between 1970 and 1980 the population of the homelands increased by 57 per cent, a doubling of the population density since 1950. Agricultural production had, as a result, largely collapsed and the homelands had become overwhelmingly dependent on the earnings of migrant labor.[72]

To curb the flow to the cities, the government froze housing in the urban areas in the 1960s and began building dormitory towns in the homelands from where commuters could travel to work. Even blacks who had a legal right to be in the cities sometimes had to become lodgers or live in bachelor hostels due to a lack of housing. The position of the outsiders was grim. Migrant workers were not free to travel to the cities to look for work, but had to stay in their homeland until recruited.

Citing Albert Geyer, a former *Burger* editor, Piet Cillié explained how the more enlightened elements in the NP embraced the homelands policy. Apartheid was intended to give the nationalist rank and file what they wanted, namely, segregated residential areas, train coaches, public toilets, post office counters and beaches on the assumption that they then would also accept the 'big things', like black national states.[73] The rank and file, however, never really bought the 'big thing' of developing the homelands into viable na-

69 J.C. Steyn, *Penvegter: Piet Cillié van Die Burger* (Cape Town: Tafelberg, 2001); See also Henry Katzew, *Apartheid and Survival* (Cape Town: Simondium, 1965), pp. 78-99.

70 *The Argus*, 16 October 1975.

71 *Die Volksblad*, 24 October 1974, cited by Steyn, *Van Wyk Louw*, p. 1165.

72 Charles Simkins, 'Agricultural Production in the African Reserves of South Africa', *Journal of Southern African Studies*, 7 (1981), pp. 256-83.

73 P. J. Cillié, *Baanbrekers vir vryheid* (Cape Town: Tafelberg, 1990), p. 70.

tional states. On the one hand they relished the security and material rewards for themselves that apartheid seemed to be generating and, on the other hand, were unwilling to make the large sacrifices it would take to make the homelands policy work.

J.P. Bruwer, an NP-supporting anthropologist, pointed out that the homelands had become a dangerous 'dream of theoretical gratification'; what really mattered to Afrikaners was the separateness from blacks they enjoyed in their own daily lives.[74] A 1974 poll, which tested the response to the idea of enlarging the homelands and making them more viable, found that more Afrikaners opposed than accepted it, and that more English-speakers than Afrikaners endorsed it. Read together with other responses in the poll, Afrikaners preferred a well-controlled measure of upper-level integration to making sacrifices for 'separate development.'[75]

The people who were duped, or rather who duped themselves, were the *verligte* intelligentsia. For them the idea of 'separate freedoms' for whites and blacks in their different homelands was the essence of NP policy.[76] As the dismal lack of development became clear, verligte intelligentsia felt that all legs of the policy were under threat. Cillié expressed their dismay: 'Bantu homelands are the essential cornerstone of our [ethnic] relations policy over the longer term. They have fallen by the wayside in our focus of interests and beliefs, which in turn undermines our credibility. We must imbue our policy with idealism and urgency, or else our future will become pitch dark.'[77] Vorster remarked rather feebly that the failure of these territories to produce more jobs was not decisive; the fact was that the government continued with its policy.

Early in 1976 cabinet ministers who belonged to the Broederbond submitted a memorandum to the Executive Council, taking the orthodox line that the retention of political control over 'our white homeland' depended on the degree to which all blacks, including those living in the common territory, could exercise meaningful rights in their homeland as an alternative to 'political co-determination in our white fatherland.'[78] But the document made it clear that these territories could not even absorb their own natural increase. There was little chance of also absorbing blacks living in the common areas.

In the Broederbond Carel Boshoff, who was Verwoerd's son-in-law, and Gerrit Viljoen led the discussions aimed at conceiving a modernized 'master plan for separate development.' But the same divisions in Afrikanerdom at large had begun to paralyze the Bond itself. Conservatives suggested rapid transit for homeland-based laborers, the linking up of townships with homelands, and the consolidation of the territories. But even if the scattered territories of the black homelands were consolidated there would be no improvement in the productive capacity of the economy of these areas. In the mid-1970s Chris Jooste, executive director of SABRA, now a conservative organization, called for efforts to separate the races to ensure that the Afrikaners would keep exclusive control of their country. He mooted the idea of a *volkstaat* or ethnic state for the Afrikaners as a distinct nation, but no one took it up in the discussion.

---

74 *Die Beeld,* 15 May 1966, 3 July 1966 and 19 January 1969.

75 Lawrence Schlemmer, 'Change in South Africa', Robert M. Price and Carl G. Rosberg (eds.), *The Apartheid Regime* (Berkeley: Institute of International Studies, 1980), pp. 260-61.

76 Vosloo, *Pienaar*, p. 2.

77 *Die Burger,* 4 July 1970, editorial.

78 Stals, 'Die geskiedenis van die Afrikaner-Broederbond', p. 375.

Verligte voices argued that these plans were futile at a time when stability and growth depended on jobs for blacks and labor productivity. It was no longer possible to believe that vigorous, job-creating economies could be created in the homelands while the Witwatersrand and other industrial centers exerted such a strong centripetal pressure. In addition to the economic flaws of the policy, the rapid increase in black numbers dashed all hopes of the homelands being able to sustain more than a fraction of their inhabitants. They called for blacks who were permanent residents in the common area to be accommodated politically. The question now was, as Dirk Richard, a columnist in *Die Vaderland*, observed: 'How many and how should we do it without committing suicide?'[79] There was now a growing and fundamental questioning in the Afrikaner intelligentsia of the strategy of clinging to exclusive white power in the face of overwhelming black numbers.

Government attention was increasingly directed to the common area. It asked whites to hold back on their wage demands and to accept reduced social spending in order to reduce the gap between whites and blacks. The assumption was that income gains would moderate black political demands (see pp. 600-01).

New black voices

During the early 1970s there were not many signs that the apartheid system could soon be challenged by blacks. Most of the leaders of the African National Congress and the Pan Africanist Congress were in jail or in exile. The ANC continued to stand for an inclusive democracy and the building of a united and multi-racial nation in South Africa. Weakly funded, it still had not found a way of fusing its attempts to isolate South Africa diplomatically, to build structures in the townships of South Africa or to raise its profile through acts of sabotage. But although the ANC as an organization was weak, the idea for which it stood was strong, being kept alive by thousands of individuals, particularly teachers, students and clergymen.[80]

Trying to fill the void left by the banning of the ANC and PAC were the leaders of the black homelands. Having concluded that white power was immutable, most accepted the system and cautiously tried to win concessions. The exception among them was Chief Gatsha Buthelezi, who became chief minister of the KwaZulu homeland. A shrewd, proud and prickly individual with great staying power, he used his exceptional political skills to put together a platform that formally rejected the homelands system, but also used it as a cover for building a mass movement. He projected himself as both a Zulu nationalist and an African nationalist, and there is reason to believe that Nelson Mandela, in jail in Robben Island, secretly encouraged him to use the Zulu homeland structures in order to promote African nationalism.

To advance Zulu cultural aspirations Buthelezi revived Inkatha, a Zulu cultural movement, which soon had between 150,000 and 200,000 members; to promote a supra-ethnic nationalism he established the Black Unity Front for nationalists both inside and

79 *Die Vaderland*, 8 June 1976.
80 Theo Hanf et al., *South Africa: The Prospects of Peaceful Change* (Bloomington: Indiana University Press, 1981), pp. 244-55.

outside the homelands system. A careful assessment by an American scholar concluded: 'To argue that Buthelezi is a net asset to the regime because he lends credibility to the Bantustans is seriously to undervalue his role as propagandist for nationalism. Buthelezi is in fact the strongest evidence that black initiatives can lead to the backfiring of the best-laid plans of the apartheid strategists.'[81] The new generation of educated blacks viewed Buthelezi with suspicion. It saw him as representing largely the elderly, the traditional, and those in the government's pay. But Buthelezi was a leader for the government to cultivate, not because he could be controlled but because he was his own man with a genuine support base.

During the late 1960s other new black voices were also beginning to be heard. Steve Biko, a mentally tough, highly intelligent and eloquent young black intellectual appeared on the scene as the main spokesman for the Black Consciousness Movement (BCM), which in the first half of the 1970s gathered considerable support on the campuses of black schools and universities and among black journalists and professionals. Its ideal was a non-racial democracy, but it considered the immediate priority to be the organization of blacks, colored people and Asians in a movement that fostered black pride and self-confidence. This implied a rejection of the ANC strategy of relying on whites and other minorities to help blacks fight their liberation struggle. To whites who were sympathetic the BCM assigned the task of educating their own community to prepare for a future democracy. As a medical student in Durban, Steve Biko founded a black students' organization that soon became part of the BCM, whose programs for black community development, were, in turn, strongly supported by journalists, students and high school pupils in the black, colored and Asian communities. Biko impressed Rykie van Reenen, undoubtedly the most outstanding Afrikaans journalist of the century (with Pienaar a close second), as 'the epitome of the new black man who is preparing himself and his people for greater responsibility with everything in his power and with an unwavering commitment.'[82]

In 1972 Steve Biko addressed a conference of student leaders on student activism in the wake of the protests in France and the United States. This was the only occasion when student leaders met across the racial and cultural spectrum in South Africa during the apartheid period. 'Black man,' Biko said, 'you are on your own.' Blacks had only themselves to rely on to develop 'group power' and 'group pride.' Liberals who appeased their own conscience 'hindered the black quest for freedom and fulfillment.' This part of Biko's message pleased the Afrikaners, because it seemed to echo the nationalist call of the 1930s that 'a people saves itself.' But Biko went much further. Blacks were determined to liberate themselves and when this happened they would invite whites to join them – on black terms.

A University of Stellenbosch student leader, Michiel le Roux, representing a new, more moderate generation of Afrikaners, painted a portrait of the way in which *verligte* Afrikaner students saw political realities. They were keen to find out how black and colored people were affected by the apartheid policy, but accepting a black government as envisaged by Biko was unthinkable – their 'identity and interests would be too seriously compromised.' Since a solution demanded sacrifices that were too great, students 'rather

---

81 Gail Gerhart, *Black Power in South Africa* (Berkeley: University of California Press, 1977), p. 307.
82 Rykie van Reenen, *Randakker* (Cape Town: Tafelberg, 1980), p. 87.

refrained from seeking one.' 'This is not simply a cowardly evasion to escape censure: the students believe that they can have significant influence on future developments by remaining acceptable to their community.'

Le Roux's words suggested that it would be difficult for South Africa to avoid a prolonged state of siege, but a conference participant, the noted American sociologist Seymour Martin Lipset, remarked that something else was happening: a system's capacity to act ruthlessly against challengers was undermined once major doubts had arisen about its propriety and morality.[83] For the security police, however, nothing fundamental had changed. It soon began harassing Black Consciousness organizations. Biko was restricted with a banning order to an eastern Cape magisterial district. Abraham Tiro, a black leader who had fled the country, was killed by a letter bomb.

A new voice in the mid-1970s was that of Bishop Desmond Tutu, representing a new generation of black clergy committed to black liberation who had risen to leadership positions in the principal English churches. In May 1976 Tutu wrote to Vorster spelling out the sense of black despair and outrage. Afrikaners knew better than any other people that 'nothing will stop a people from attaining their freedom to be a people who can hold their head high, whose dignity to be human persons is respected.' In the inclusive tradition of the African National Congress he asked for a national convention of white and black leaders to work out an orderly transition to a non-racial and just society. The future choice was stark: whites and blacks 'will survive together or be destroyed together.'[84]

'Give South Africa six months': November 1974

Early in November 1974 John Vorster made an enigmatic comment that briefly stirred the hopes of the subordinate population in South Africa for substantial changes to apartheid: 'Give South Africa six months . . . and you will be surprised where South Africa stands then.'[85] On 23 October 1974 he had declared: 'Southern Africa has come to the crossroads . . .' The alternative to a peaceful settlement 'would be too ghastly to contemplate.'[86] The next day R.F. (Pik) Botha, the South African Minister for Foreign Affairs, addressing the UN Security Council, had stated that South Africa was moving away from discrimination by all the means at its disposal.

It was during this time that the American diplomat George Kennan visited South Africa for a third time. As commentator and diplomat he had become famous for his analysis of the Soviet Union's power. He took what he called a 'historian's view' of South Africa. There were problems, he said, which, at the time they occurred, were insoluble.[87] He implied that the point at which South Africa found itself made it unrealistic to expect far-reaching changes.

It was easy to conclude that the political situation in South Africa would remain dead-

---

83 The contributions of Lipset, Biko and Le Roux are published in H.W. van der Merwe and David Welsh (eds.), *Student Perspectives in South Africa* (Cape Town: David Philip, 1972).
84 *Sunday Times*, 26 November 2000.
85 Vorster, *Speeches*, p. 231
86 Vorster, *Speeches*, p. 221.
87 *Munger's Africana Library*, 1971, p. 3.

locked for a long time. The white electorate jealously guarded against any effort to dilute its own power and privileges. Less than 10 per cent of whites were prepared to accept a black, colored or Indian into their kinship group by marriage, or to tolerate a colored or an African as a friend or neighbor. Only one-fifth of Afrikaners, against one-third of English-speakers, would admit blacks to employment in their own occupation.[88] By the mid-1970s most white voters rejected colored representation in Parliament, more land for the homelands, mixed sport at the local club level and independence for South West Africa.[89] Only a quarter of the NP supporters thought that any drastic changes were necessary.[90]

Leaders of large corporations and the English press called on government to give the black middle class a stake in the system. These calls rested on the assumption that middle-class blacks would see their interests as separate from the great mass of impoverished blacks. But middle-class blacks wanted blacks to be free as a nation, not to enjoy more freedom as a middle class. In the Afrikaner middle class there was increasing support for the qualified franchise, but the black middle class were likely to disrupt the system of white domination until all the excluded blacks were admitted. Among younger, well-educated, urban blacks the idea of separate homelands encountered an almost visceral hostility as representing black inferiority and exclusion. Soweto youths strongly opted for a Western way of life and a multi-racial common government, while rejecting an ethnic identity that would have set them apart in a segregated – and economically unviable – enclave.

Yet at the time that Vorster made his 'Give South Africa six months' speech, a political deadlock combined with periodic black uprisings was not the only possible scenario. Apartheid was changing. During the late 1960s a reformist official had written into the speech of the minister responsible for black education that establishing high schools had to become a policy priority, and the minister had accepted it.[91] Blacks were allowed to perform more skilled jobs (see pp. 598-9).

An even more important development occurred. As the economist Charles Simkins later observed, it was one no one would have predicted. In government circles the idea had taken root that whites were sufficiently well off, and that the state's priority was to meet its obligations to the disenfranchised.[92] Urban blacks were the great beneficiaries. In the 1975-76 budget the personal income of whites was reduced by 7 per cent but that of Asians was raised by 3 per cent, that of coloreds by 19 per cent and that of blacks by 11 per cent.[93] In 1978 Prime Minster Vorster warned whites that the abolition of social and economic inequities would demand significant sacrifices in their living

88 H. Lever, 'Ethnic preferences of white residents in Johannesburg', in S.J. Morse and C. Orpen (eds.), *Contemporary South Africa* (Cape Town: Juta, 1975), pp. 56-8.

89 *The Star*, 16 August 1975.

90 *Rapport*, 6 February 1977.

91 Ken Hartshorne, *Crisis and Challenge: Black Education, 1910-1990* (Cape Town: Oxford University Press, 1992), p. 87.

92 See also Charles Simkins, *Liberalism and the Problem of Power* (Johannesburg: SA Institute of Race Relations, 1986), p. 16.

93 For an extended discussion see J.L. Sadie, 'The Economic Demography of South Africa', doctoral diss., US, 2000, pp. 316-85.

standards and material aspirations. Three years later the Director General of Finance declared that a drastic increase of state spending on blacks at the expense of whites was under way. The government's priority was to satisfy black demands for improved education and public health services. It would do so by keeping the spending on whites constant until a greater equilibrium was reached.

Employers also followed this route. In 1975 it was reported that the wages of a quarter of a million blacks in industry – this was virtually the entire black elite in the common area – had improved on average by 15 to 20 per cent in the previous year.[94]

Internal processes and external events were undermining apartheid.. The subsistence crisis of the homelands sent desperate people streaming to squatter camps in towns and cities, breaking down the system of influx control with their feet and their numbers. Blacks took heart from the collapse of the Portuguese empire in Mozambique and Angola. Black schools and universities sent people out into the world determined to challenge the basic assumptions of the system.

A subtle change had occurred in the Afrikaner leadership. Verwoerd always spoke like a European in Africa. He handed down the homelands policy like a European colonial official would, holding many meetings with black leaders in the reserves to explain it. For him there was never any possibility of a deal between whites and blacks that deviated from this policy. But Vorster had introduced a different note: the Afrikaners craved acceptance by Africa. 'We have a duty towards Africa . . . Africa is our mother . . . You want to do your level best to get your people accepted by Africa, accepted as an African people with every right to be in Africa, as opposed to the here-today-gone-tomorrow idea of the colonialists . . . We are Africans. We are of Africa and to my last day in politics I will strive to have us accepted by the people of Africa.'[95]

The question was whether Vorster had it in him to move away from the homelands policy and offer blacks some form of recognition and representation in a common society, starting with, say, representation in the Senate and the abolition of the pass laws, and hints of further reforms to come. Although only limited, such steps would have represented a major volte-face for the Afrikaner nationalist movement and would have given moderate blacks hope that the system had the potential of reforming itself fundamentally.

When Vorster made his 'six months' speech the political demands of forces inside the country were moderate. In 1974 Buthelezi formulated the fundamental choice before the country as between violence and majority rule. He suggested a national convention where a federal system under a multi-racial government could be negotiated that balanced majority and minority interests. The political rights of all national groups would be protected and majority rule would go hand in hand with 'power-sharing.'[96]

The alternatives to apartheid proposed by whites outside the ruling party's circle still fell well short of untrammeled majority rule. Liberal whites, who had established the Study Project on Christianity in Apartheid Society, produced several reports and press statements in 1972 and 1973. They asked for the restoration of the rule of law, an eco-

---

94 Hermann Giliomee, 'Afrikaner Politics, 1977-1987' in John Brewer (ed.), *Can South Africa Survive?* (London: Macmillan, 1989), pp. 114-16; *South African Digest*, 29 August 1975, p. 7.

95 D'Oliveira, *Vorster*, p. 256.

96 Gatsha Buthelezi, *White and Black Nationalism: Ethnicity and the Future of the Homelands* (Johannesburg: SA Institute of Race Relations, 1974); Hanf, *South Africa*, p. 261.

nomic system in which all could fully share 'in the common responsibility for decisions affecting the common life' and have equal opportunities, and for an educational system which should be compulsory for all at primary level and equally available for all on merit at secondary level (but no compulsory racial integration). The political report, which was written largely by André du Toit, an Afrikaans philosopher from Stellenbosch, called for a move away from the existing Westminster system with its concentration of power in a unitary system. It recommended a first stage in which discrimination was removed and a system introduced in which power was devolved and shared. In the second stage 'a federal multi-racial government' should be introduced.[97]

A biographer of Vorster who wrote in the mid-1970s asked these questions to reach a conclusion on whether his subject had it in him to make a major political leap: Does he have the power? Does he have the skill? Does he really want change? Vorster's abilities were recognized by some of his strongest opponents. Helen Suzman, between 1961 and 1974 a lone, eloquent liberal voice in Parliament, said of Hendrik Verwoerd and his two successors: 'Verwoerd was obviously obsessed, P.W. Botha was a bully who could not argue, but Vorster had a good mind. I liked listening to him in Parliament.'[98] Frederik van Zyl Slabbert, leader of the official opposition between 1979 and 1986, expressed this view: 'He had the intellect, he had the power, but he did not use it.'[99]

Vorster showed what he thought a white minority regime outside South Africa ought to do if it wanted to avoid the catastrophe of a complete loss of power. He told Ian Smith, leader of the embattled Rhodesian regime, to seek a settlement with black nationalist leaders not on the basis of black majority rule but on an agreement to 'promote a society in which merit and not colour determines a man's position and progress.' The corollary of that was that 'at some time in the future merit might not be white but merit might be black. That is the thing you must accept.'[100]

This was a proposition that Afrikaner leaders fifteen years later would try to put on the table in negotiating with the ANC. It was an attempt to purchase a political bargain at yesterday's price – a bargain that was available to white South Africa under Vorster in the mid-1970s, perhaps even in negotiations with Nelson Mandela, who had by then served ten years in prison, and other ANC leaders, but no longer in the 1990s.

Vorster had eliminated the reactionary element in Afrikaner nationalist ranks, led by Albert Hertzog, and was firmly in control of the NP. In Parliament there were few that could match his debating skills and ability to outwit opponents. Verwoerd impressed Afrikaners most with his intellectual abilities and resoluteness, but Vorster was genuinely popular and had the ability to take people with him. It is likely that most Afrikaners would have trusted him if he had declared that the survival of the Afrikaners and the larger white population required a section of blacks to be brought into a common political system. In the mid-1970s a large opinion survey, undertaken on behalf of a German research group, found that 60 per cent of Afrikaners 'would support the leaders even if they acted in ways they did not understand or approve.'[101]

---

97 For a summary of the reports see Peter Randall, *A Taste of Power* (Johannesburg: Sprocas, 1973), particularly pp. 94-6, 214-16.
98 Interview, 24 August 2002.
99 Interview, 25 August 2002.
100 Brand Fourie, *Brandpunte* (Cape Town: Tafelberg, 1991), pp. 136-8.
101 Theo Hanf et al., *Südafrika: Friedlicher Wandel?* (Munich: Kaiser, 1978), pp. 421-2.

Any major move in the direction of what Vorster proposed to Ian Smith would require a partnership with some black leaders. Buthelezi, as the main internal black leader recognized the dangers of attempting to force a rapid transfer to black rule. But he was no moderate willing to do the bidding of the apartheid system. He told a crowd of thirty thousand in Soweto early in 1976: 'History will triumph over apartheid . . . because in the final analysis history is made by majorities and not by minorities . . . Nowhere in the world have minorities prevailed against the majority indefinitely.'[102] In 1977, 44 per cent of a sample of urban blacks named Buthelezi the black leader they most admired. Of those who admired him, 40 per cent were non-Zulus. But Vorster was unable to make up his mind about Buthelezi, who enjoyed majority support among blacks in polls. It was not yet clear whether he was simply a stalking horse for the ANC or whether he was someone with whom a deal could be struck that excluded the black forces pushing for a radical redistribution of power and wealth.

There are only a few straws in the wind that suggest that Vorster pondered an alternative to apartheid and its model of several 'national states' for blacks in their respective reserves. A biographer who interviewed him in the mid-1970s found what he thought was something remarkable: '[H]e consistently evaded serious discussion of the future.' He was, the author noted, like a chess player, determined not to reveal his moves to anybody.[103] Like all politicians Vorster kept a steady eye on his electoral base and professed that he could not move faster than it was prepared to do. Yet when addressing a meeting in Potchefstroom, the heartland of conservatism in the Transvaal, he also said something startlingly different: 'People once said that politics was the art of the possible. I tell you that politics is the art of reconciling conflicting demands and conflicting aspirations.'[104]

The main problem of the Afrikaner leadership was complacency and a tendency to get side-tracked. Inside South Africa the government turned to the short-term advantages to be gained from exploiting intra-black political cleavages. Vorster also had begun to dabble in foreign relations, trying to promote rapprochement with Africa. However, he gained very little that strengthened the chances for a settlement with the majority inside the country. He clung to South West Africa, although the territory was not vital for the defense of South Africa against insurgents. As in the case of Paul Kruger in confronting the Uitlander demand for the franchise in the early 1890s, he preferred to wait rather than deal with the crisis in a way that outflanked or split the opposition. He was soon to give the go-ahead to government officials to promote a better image for the country through some elaborate machinery of lies and other forms of deception.

Faced with Buthelezi's demand for a national convention, Vorster held three meetings with the homeland leaders, but at the last one rejected the idea. When he made his plea for South Africa to be given six months his mind was not focused on internal change but settlements in Rhodesia and other countries on the border that could stabilize the region. But the region would soon be engulfed by violence, and with that the chance of a compromise settlement with South African blacks steadily dwindled.

By the early 1970s Breyten Breytenbach had concluded that the Vorster government

---

102 J. Shepherd Smith, *Buthelezi* (Melville: Hans Strydom Publishers, 1988), p. 144.
103 D'Oliveira, *Vorster*, p. 287.
104 D'Oliveira, *Vorster*, pp. 256, 287.

had no intention of introducing any fundamental reforms. Increasingly he found it obscene to condemn apartheid from the safety of France and to do nothing to advance the liberation struggle. He had helped to form the organization Okhela, that sought to work with both the African National Congress (ANC), black workers and the Black Consciousness Movement.[105]

In a volume called *Skryt*, published in 1972 in the Netherlands (but banned in South Africa), there is a poem entitled 'Brief uit die vreemde' (Letter from a foreign land) to 'Slagter' (Butcher), which is dedicated to 'Balthazar' (Vorster's first name). The context was the death in detention of twenty-one political prisoners between 1963 and 1971 and the widespread suspicion that they had been tortured. There is this passage:

> *Tell me butcher*
> *so that the obstetrics of what you perpetrate*
> *in the name of my survival*
> *could be revealed to me*
> *in my language*

In 1972 Breytenbach and his wife finally received visas to visit South Africa. He used the occasion of the visit to redefine the political conflict: the Afrikaners, he said, 'were a bastard people with a bastard language' who had fallen 'in the trap of the bastard who acquires power.' Apartheid was 'the law of the bastard, fencing off, defending and offending.' For Breytenbach the salvation of the country was almost exclusively in the hands of Africans. Like Albert Camus he saw his people as Africans who were in Africa to stay. Unlike Camus, however, he believed that his people's staying could only be secured by their abdication of power and ensuring their future existence 'within a Black socio-cultural field of reference.' In his other writings he made it clear that the post-apartheid economic system would be socialist, not capitalist.

In 1975 he returned to South Africa on a clandestine visit during which he tried to establish structures for the underground. But some ANC leaders betrayed him. From the moment he landed in South Africa the security police kept him under watch. At the end of his visit he was arrested and brought to trial. In a desperate plea for mitigation, he apologized to the Prime Minister, John Vorster, for calling him a butcher. He appealed to Van Wyk Louw's writings. 'The motivation of my acts was the love for my country. It is perhaps paradoxical but what concerned me was the survival of our *volk*, a survival in justice, like Louw formulated it, and the contents and quality of our civilization.' Unimpressed, the judge remarked that Breytenbach had abused his position as a great figure in South African literature to commit an ugly crime and sentenced him to nine years' imprisonment.[106]

105 Breyten Breytenbach, *A Season in Paradise* (London: Jonathan Cape, 1980), pp. 151-6 and *End Papers* (New York: Farrar, Straus and Giroux, 1986), p. 237. For Breytenbach as political dissident see particularly Francis Galloway, *Breyten Breytenbach as openbare figuur* (Pretoria: HAUM, 1990); Michael Walzer, *The Company of Critics* (New York: Basic Books, 1988) and J.M. Coetzee, 'Resisters', *New York Review of Books*, 2 December 1993. For Degenaar see Andrew Nash, 'The Dialectical Tradition in South Africa' doctoral diss., UCT, 2000, pp. 140-204, and André du Toit (ed.) *In gesprek: opstelle vir Johan Degenaar* (Stellenbosch: Voorbrand, 1986).

106 Jack Viviers, *Breyten* (Cape Town: Tafelberg, 1978), pp. 52-73.

And so John Vorster and Breyten Breytenbach went to their different fates. Vorster would become an impotent figure as a result of a political scandal in which he was embroiled and the violence that engulfed South Africa. Breytenbach would spend eight years in jail. When the NP leadership at the end of the 1980s finally decided to negotiate with the blacks it was in a far weaker position than when Vorster asked the world to give South Africa six months.

A *ligte mistykie* in Angola

In 1974-75 the power balance in southern Africa changed substantially. On the northwestern border South Africa's control over South West Africa/Namibia threatened to bring South Africa into direct confrontation with the world community. South Africa had received a mandate from the League of Nations in 1919 to rule that vast country. (It was more than 50 per cent larger than Spain, and, with a population under a million until the 1950s, had the lowest population density in the world.) South Africa's introduction of apartheid in the territory drew increasing international criticism. The South West African People's Organization (SWAPO), which had established itself in Angola as the main organization for the liberation of Namibia, had been engaged in small-scale guerrilla operations since 1966. In 1967 the UN Security Council made its first move to terminate the mandate and, in 1974, asked South Africa to transfer power to the people of Namibia at the end of 1975. A contact group of major Western powers was established soon after 1974 to negotiate with South Africa on the handing over of power to the indigenous population.

On 25 April 1974 a coup in Lisbon heralded the end of Portuguese rule over its colonies of Angola and Mozambique. South Africa suddenly faced the collapse of the *cordon sanitaire* along its northern border that had shielded it from guerrilla attacks. Within the next eighteen months Portugal would hand over power to the guerrilla movements. Meanwhile an intensifying guerrilla war in Rhodesia threatened the Rhodesian Front regime, headed by Ian Smith, for which South Africa was providing some two thousand 'policemen' to support anti-guerrilla operations.

South African whites were deeply disturbed by the scene of black socialist movements coming to power through military force in states along their northern border. It conjured up images of the nationalization of land and industries, an introduction of contingents of Soviet troops or proxies, and the flight of whites. Even without a worst-case scenario the transfer of power would provide a huge boost to blacks in South Africa. Sensing this, two-thirds of the Afrikaners in polls opposed the withdrawal of South African forces from Rhodesia. Andries Treurnicht, a leading verkrampte in the party, lent his support to a pro-Rhodesia movement with the message: 'We either win together or hang separately.'[107]

Wisely Vorster was wary of extending South Africa's military commitments to beyond the borders. He withdrew South African policemen fighting in Rhodesia and refused to assist a plan for a white-led coup in Mozambique. He pledged that South Africa would leave the new government in Mozambique in peace as long as it was stable and did

---

107 M.A. Tamarkin, *The Making of Zimbabwe* (London: Frank Cass, 1990), pp. 76-7.

not provide bases for South Africa's own guerrilla movements, the African National Congress and the Pan Africanist Congress. But Vorster was under pressure from P.W. Botha, his Minister for Defence, who was aggressive and belligerent. He wished South Africa to act as the regional superpower willing to strike at enemy bases far beyond its own borders to defend its own interests.

Botha would have been thwarted if a crisis had not occurred in the form of a civil war in the Portuguese colony of Angola. Portugal's only preparation for the transfer of power was an agreement with the principal liberation movements to hold elections on 11 November 1975 before granting independence to the victor. By the middle of 1975 Angola faced chaos. The main contenders for power were the Frente Nacional de Libertacão (FNLA), a northern-based nationalist movement led by Holden Roberto, the União Nacional para a Independencia Total de Angola (UNITA), based on a large ethnic group in the central highlands and led by Jonas Savimbi, and the Movimento Popular de Libertacão de Angola (MPLA), a movement of Portuguese leftists and indigenous *mestizos*, based in Luanda, the capital of Angola, which by mid-1975 controlled less than a quarter of the country's territory.[108] Soon there was a rapid escalation of the conflict, which ultimately cost millions of lives.[109]

Whether the trigger was the US assistance to the MPLA's rivals or the MPLA's call for help from Cuba is not yet clear. Neither is it known whether Cuba from the start acted in concert with the Soviet Union. Cuba rushed in combat troops to assist the MPLA, reaching a total of fourteen thousand by early 1976. The Soviet Union flew in advisers and an estimated $200 million of armored cars, rocket launchers and heavy artillery pieces.

South Africa moved into Angola mainly in an attempt to secure non-military regional objectives. Its primary objective was to break out of its diplomatic isolation. It only entered into the fray after the Ford Administration in Washington had asked it to play the role of a US proxy in a remote Cold War hot spot. Secretary of State Henry Kissinger, who considered Soviet and Cuban support for the MPLA a 'serious matter', believed that Washington would not tolerate Moscow's 'hegemonial aspirations' in Angola.[110] The US asked South Africa to provide training for the anti-Marxist movements in Angola (FNLA and UNITA), and it offered financial assistance to that end. The goal was to help the two movements establish *de facto* authority in their respective territories and prevent the MPLA from being recognized as the sole *de jure* government of Angola. The operation would be considered a success if the Organization of African Unity, due to meet at the end of 1975, agreed to recognize a government of national unity in Luanda.

Pretoria believed that intervention in Angola offered South Africa the opportunity to become 'part of Africa instead of the colonial powers', as General Constand Viljoen, a senior general, phrased it.[111] Two African states, Zambia and Zaire, asked South Africa to stem the spread of communism in sub-Saharan Africa by preventing the Cubans and Soviets from installing an MPLA government in Angola.[112] Being asked for assistance

---

108 Chester Crocker, *High Noon in Southern Africa* (New York: W.W. Norton, 1992), p. 49.

109 John Stockwell, *In Search of Enemies: A CIA Story* (New York: W.W. Norton, 1978), p. 68.

110 Deon Geldenhuys, *The Diplomacy of Isolation* (Johannesburg: Macmillan 1984), p. 79.

111 Hilton Hamann, *Days of the Generals* (Cape Town: Zebra, 2001), p. 15.

112 Annette Seegers, *The Military in the Making of Modern South Africa* (London: I.B. Tauris, 1996), pp. 212-13.

by the US and two major African states in the region was extremely heady stuff for the South African government.

Once Cuba and the Soviet Union stepped up their support, both the US and South Africa escalated their assistance to the FNLA and UNITA.[113] In August 1975, after MPLA forces had moved towards hydroelectric projects at Ruacana-Calueque, in the south of Angola, South Africa sent troops to protect them because of their importance to the Namibian economy. South Africa launched Operation Savannah with a mixed force of two thousand soldiers and conscripts. After securing the hydro projects, battle groups moved deep into Angola, and by October were fighting against the MPLA. The intention had been to withdraw before 11 November, but Savimbi persuaded Vorster to keep the troops in Angola until the OAU meeting on 9 December. The South African forces went as far as a town 120 kilometers south of Luanda, and awaited the outcome of a battle between the FNLA, moving in from the north armed with South African artillery, and the MPLA. But the FNLA attack on Luanda on the morning of 9 November failed as a result of poor discipline and co-ordination.[114] On 11 November 1975 an MPLA government was installed in Angola.

The South African attempt to establish a government of national unity in Angola soon went wrong. Never firm, the US commitment began to waver. There had been more than enough warning signals. The US Central Intelligence Agency (CIA) contacts had cautioned that the US might soon terminate its involvement in the wake of increasingly public hostility in the wake of the Vietnamese war and revelations of American covert intervention in Chile and other countries. On 19 December the US Senate cut off all American aid to the FNLA and UNITA, a decision that would soon be endorsed by the House of Representatives. When US officials asked Kissinger whether they should take any further action he only grunted and left the room. Left to decide what the grunt meant, they concluded that it meant that the US should walk away. South Africa had hopelessly miscalculated the consistency of US support for it as a pariah state. The US would do little to assist South Africa when the UN denounced its involvement in Angola.

In South Africa the clandestine nature of the operation caused the government growing problems. For nearly six months the South African public was kept largely in the dark about what had happened. The government manipulated the news, deceived the public and accused critics of being poor patriots. In his memoirs Jannie Geldenhuys, a senior military officer, praised the performance of the South African forces but commented: 'It disturbed me that such an operation was controlled in this manner. One would rather conduct war in the open, with the whole Defence Force involved, and with the public's support.'[115]

The government may well have acted illegally. Some sources claim that legislation prohibited the government from using conscripts outside South Africa (which included Namibia) without their permission, while General Viljoen believes that such permission was unnecessary.[116] Still, even if it was not required, the conscripts could hardly have

---

113 Seegers, *The Military*, pp. 210-13.
114 Interview by author with Constand Viljoen, 30 August 2002.
115 Jannie Geldenhuys, *A General's Story* (Johannesburg: Jonathan Ball, 1995), p. 55.
116 Interview author – Constand Viljoen, 29 August 2002.

known what they gave permission for. The South African propaganda machinery heavily emphasized the communist threat, but the extent of Cuban involvement was only known to a few.

At the end of January 1976, when Parliament opened, the Vorster government failed to inform Parliament. It flew a group of parliamentarians to the operational area where General Viljoen told them that Angola had been invaded four months earlier and that some South African troops were close to Luanda. The parliamentary group was instructed to refrain from using the information for any political or public purpose. Frederik van Zyl Slabbert, a new member representing the Progressive Federal Party, was a member of the group. He commented a few years later that it was 'straight-forward deception at the most elementary level . . . I knew first-hand that governments could get away with murder if the circumstances were right; that people could be misled or deliberately deceived on a massive scale and worse . . . I also learnt how easy it is to find yourself an unwilling co-conspirator in perpetrating the indefensible.'[117]

At the OAU meeting the African states were deadlocked on the issue of recognizing the MPLA as a legitimate government. Finally, Idi Amin of Uganda, the chairman, used his casting vote in favor of the MPLA. South Africa, along with UNITA and the FNLA, had lost. The Angolan adventure was a great humiliation and terminated the effort to win African friends through military intervention. It was a major coup for the Soviet Union, which now claimed that the East-West détente did not apply to remote corners of the Third World. South Africa's military adventure resulted in a massive increase in the number of Cuban soldiers in Angola. Vorster signaled that he had learnt a bitter lesson: 'When it comes to the worst South Africa stands alone.'[118] Schalk Pienaar, now in retirement, commented wryly: 'Angola was a *ligte mistykie*', a slight mistake.

The US volte-face in Angola deeply shocked Vorster and he was now so obsessed by the Soviet threat that he gave little attention to reform. In May 1976 Henry Kissinger informed his government that South Africa could not rely on American assistance if the Soviets organized a military assault on southern Africa.[119] By the early months of 1976 Vorster was for all practical purposes a lame duck politically. In September 1977 the Vorster cabinet was still pre-occupied with the reversal in Angola. Hilgard Muller, Minister of Foreign Affairs, warned cabinet colleagues that, as a result of the failed intervention, the Soviet-backed forces had lost their respect for South Africa and could try their luck elsewhere in Africa. Marais Steyn, another minister, remarked that the balance of power had been disturbed since Angola, and that South Africa was no longer the strongest power.[120]

The collapse of Rhodesia

Along South Africa's northeastern border, Vorster's cautious approach prevailed. In the second half of 1974 he worked with President Kenneth Kaunda of Zambia to bring Ian

---

117 F. Van Zyl Slabbert, *The Last Parliament* (Johannesburg: Jonathan Ball, 1985), p. 41.
118 Geldenhuys, *Diplomacy of Isolation*, pp. 79-81.
119 Fourie, *Brandpunte*, p. 141.
120 *Sunday Times*, 22 October 2000, p. 21.

Smith as head of the Rhodesian government and the leaders of the various black nationalist movements together to reach a political settlement. A meeting failed to achieve anything. Vorster was still reluctant to pressurize Smith, but when he met with Kissinger in July 1976 his hands had been weakened by the outbreak of the Soweto uprising a month earlier (see p. 578). Prior to meeting Vorster, Kissinger had told the House of Representatives that he would explore whether South Africa would be prepared 'to separate its own future from that of Rhodesia and Namibia.' The implication was clear: if South Africa delivered Rhodesia and Namibia the US would not put pressure on it regarding its own vital domestic policies. For Vorster this was an opportunity not to be missed.

South Africa now accepted a solution of the Rhodesian issue on the basis of 'majority rule with adequate protection for minority rights', and began exerting pressure on Rhodesia by delaying supplies, which pulled the plug on white rule.[121] Ian Smith later wrote bitterly of the eagerness of the South Africans 'to throw us to the wolves in their desperate desire to try to buy time and gain credit for solving the Rhodesian problem.'[122]

In 1979 the Rhodesian regime held elections on the basis of universal franchise. Although the election had a 64 per cent poll and was won by a predominantly black party, Western countries refused to recognize it, because the principal liberation movements had refused to participate. A precedent had been set and it would be reaffirmed in South West Africa/Namibia and in South Africa itself. For the West the key question was whether the parties with the capability to wage war and cause major disruption had participated in an election (and had won). The game was all about backing the future winners in the region and re-establishing trade and investment under the successor government it had anointed. Behind this lay the assumption that a liberation government would promptly abandon any socialist convictions once they discovered their dependence on Western trade and investment.

The war in Rhodesia continued until the end of the decade when, all alone, the government capitulated. A socialist movement headed by Robert Mugabe took power there in 1980 after a landslide victory. But South African leaders did not share the benign view of the West of the new government that came to power on its northern border. As Deon Geldenhuys wrote at the time: 'South Africa is far from encouraged by [Zimbabwe]. Mugabe is hardly the personification of a friendly, co-operative neighbor or a leader who offers his white subjects a safe and happy haven.'[123] The question was whether the same pattern would unfold in South Africa. At the end of 1977 Harry Oppenheimer of the agglomerate Anglo American Corporation tried to assure whites that the Western powers would not impose sanctions or 'reject' South Africa. He questioned the government's stand that there was 'nothing between their concept [of apartheid] and one man, one vote. 'It is absolute nonsense to say they wouldn't be satisfied with anything short of one man one vote.'[124]

But a very different message had gone out from the US government. In May 1977 US

---

121 Tamarkin, *The Making of Zimbabwe*, p. 135.
122 Ian Smith, *The Great Betrayal* (London: Blake Publishing, 1997), p. 207
123 Geldenhuys, *Diplomacy of Isolation*, p. 227.
124 Anna Starcke, *Survival* (Cape Town: Tafelberg, 1978), pp. 152-3.

Vice President Walter Mondale told Vorster that the US insisted on a system under which 'every citizen should have the right to vote and every vote should be equally weighted.'[125] Vorster was never prepared to consider the abrupt introduction of universal franchise in a unitary system. He responded to the Mondale demand by observing that the result of such US pressure 'would be exactly the same as if [South Africa] were subverted by Marxists. In the one case it will come about as the result of brute force. In the other case it will be strangulation with finesse.'[126] When Chancellor Helmut Schmidt of Germany urged Vorster to take greater risks to prevent the whites from being crushed by the 'locomotion of history', he replied: 'Afrikaners do not have the luxury to take risks. Once we lose power we shall never get it back.'[127] The specter of communists just beyond the South African border making common cause with a disaffected black majority made him averse to taking a rash step. Besides, South Africa had nuclear arms up its sleeve.

A nuclear capability

In the late 1960s the Vorster government gave the go-ahead for the construction of a uranium-enrichment plant, and in 1974 approved the development of a nuclear explosive capability limited to peaceful applications, such as mining excavations and nuclear energy. In the course of the 1970s the idea of a nuclear deterrent became ever more attractive. There was a build-up of large numbers of Cuban troops in Angola, and the introduction by the Soviets of advanced weapons like the BM-21 multi-rocket system, also called the multi-rocket Stalin Organ, and MIG-23 planes. One scenario in which South Africa could issue a nuclear threat is painted in R.W. Johnson's *How Long Will South Africa Survive?* This scenario is one of large numbers of guerrillas congregating on South Africa's northeastern border, the Soviet Union providing Mozambique with sufficient missile capability to rule out South African strikes, and waves of uprisings by urban blacks in South Africa. In an 'end game' the US could exert great pressure on Pretoria to accept majority rule in order to 'save' South Africa for the West.[128]

Without admitting that South Africa had the bomb, the Vorster government secretly warned the West that it would use extreme measures if pushed into a corner. When the US expressed alarm over the possibility of a nuclear test in the Kalahari desert, Vorster responded in a veiled way in a public speech given in August 1977. He said that if the pressure on South Africa continued 'the time will arrive when South Africa will have no option, small as it is, to say to the world, so far and no further, do your damnedest if you wish.'[129] The implication was clear: South Africa could and might well do its damnedest.

In 1978 an all-South African team produced the first highly enriched uranium and in 1979 the first fully assembled nuclear device. A total of six nuclear devices, which could

125 SAIRR, *Survey of Race Relations, 1977*, p. 573.

126 Geldenhuys, *Diplomacy of Isolation*, p. 243.

127 Interview with author of Marion Dönhoff, Bonn, 23 August 1989; Brand Fourie, *Brandpunte* (Cape Town: Tafelberg, 1991), p. 86.

128 R.W. Johnson, *How Long Will South Africa Survive?* (London: Macmillan, 1977), p. 326; J.E. Spence, 'The Nuclear Option', *African Affairs*, 80, 321 (1981), pp. 441-52.

129 *Die Burger,* 25 August 1977.

be delivered by aircraft or missile, were completed. This was considered to be the minimum for deterrent purposes. They were not stockpiled in assembled form but the nuclear and non-nuclear components were stored separately in concrete steel vaults. Between 1974 and 1993, when F.W. de Klerk announced the existence of the devices prior to abandoning the country's nuclear capability, the total cost of the program came to R750 million, or 0.5 per cent of the military budget.[130]

In 1979 the Botha government accepted the recommendations of a study group which proposed three phases in a program of deterrence. In Phase One there would be strategic ambiguity – the government would neither confirm nor deny that it had a nuclear capability. In Phase Two it would covertly reveal to Western governments, particularly the US, that it had such a capability in the hope of Western intervention to forestall an armed attack from outside South Africa's borders. In Phase Three it would publicly announce the existence of its nuclear arsenal. From the outset, everyone involved in the program knew that the government did not intend or foresee an offensive application of the bomb. In practice the strategy never progressed beyond Phase One, due to the absence of any overt military threat.[131]

Assembling nuclear bombs reveals a can-do mentality and the desire for the white community in South Africa to be taken seriously by the great powers. South Africa was the first country to perform a heart transplant operation and was now running a nuclear power station. It had developed or was in the process of developing the giant G-5 and the G-6 mortar gun with 155-mm shells eagerly sought by Iraq and other countries, a biological and chemical weapons capability, and its own jet fighter.

Within the Afrikaner power elite there were some who thought of using everything in the state's armor to wage an all-out struggle for national existence – a fight to the finish. Foreign politicians and diplomats did not rate this elite's political acumen very highly, but they knew little of the insecurities of a small dominant minority whose very survival as a people depended on some crucial decisions. Chester Crocker, US Assistant Secretary of State for Africa during the 1980s, observed that while the Afrikaner elite behaved as if the country belonged to them, they displayed a strange mix of ethnic insecurity and arrogance. Loyalty and solidarity were the supreme virtues, and outsiders were distrusted. The government had largely cut itself off from the advice of outsiders, but craved Western acceptance.[132] (A Soviet Union insider described the ruling elite in his own country as guided by the same mix.[133])

Police Commissioner Johan Coetzee characterized the struggle as 'a war of attrition [in which there] is no cut-off point. He who lasts the longest wins, because in the final analysis it is about the will of the nation to exist and that of others to wear them down.'[134] Nevertheless, it had already become clear that there were limits to the 'will of the nation.' The government did not contemplate accepting more than a minimum of white casual-

130 J.W. de Villiers, Roger Jardine, et al., 'Why South Africa Gave Up the Bomb', *Foreign Affairs*, 72, 5 (1993), pp. 98-109; *Die Burger*, 25 March 1993.

131 De Villiers, Jardine, et al., 'Why South Africa Gave Up the Bomb', p. 111.

132 Crocker, *High Noon*, pp. 87, 111.

133 George Arbatov, *The System: An Insider's Life in Soviet Politics* (New York: Times Books, 1992), pp. 189-219.

134 Cited by Kurt Campbell, 'The Soldiers of Apartheid', *SAIS Review*, Winter-Spring 1988, p. 43.

ties on battlefields beyond the borders. The war there could not be won by military will alone. Political and diplomatic victories were necessary, and they depended less on will than on skill, particularly in outwitting opponents in the battle to control public perceptions at home and abroad. In this the Afrikaner politicians, with the exception of Foreign Minister Pik Botha, were at a disadvantage from the start, because they had little direct contact with opinion-makers in Western capitals or black South Africans.

One of South Africa's objectives in containing what it considered to be Soviet-backed forces in the region was to win both Western appreciation for its role, and greater sympathy for South Africa's own political dilemmas. But the Western governments were unlikely to back South Africa solely on the ground that it was fighting 'communism.' They backed minorities only when they embodied principles or identities that Western countries would, for their own sake, not allow to go under.[135] Apartheid did not represent political principles worth defending. Fighting apartheid had become one of the great moral causes in the West, and was soon to lead to an intensification of trade and investment boycotts.

In 1979 South Africa announced that in place of its strong pro-Western policy it would now adopt a neutral foreign policy. Western governments recognized this as an empty face-saving gesture from a country that economically, ideologically and psychologically depended on the West. South Africa had nowhere else to turn but the West, which was eager to identify the future winning party in the white-black power struggle.

Soweto 1976

The weakness in Vorster's style of management, which allowed each department to pursue its own ideological ends, finally caught up with itself. It was generally known in the Vorster administration that the education of black, colored and Asian children was a problem area with major resentment building up over apartheid education. Prudence required that no additional irritations be allowed to add to the discontent. The question of the language used as the medium of instruction was a sensitive issue, which the state handled with circumspection in the first fifteen years of 'Bantu education.' The formal policy was that Afrikaans and English must be used on a 50-50 basis as media of instruction in black secondary schools in the white area, but it was not rigorously applied. Vorster did not object when homeland leaders in 1974 requested that the official language in the homelands (in practice, English) also be used in black schools elsewhere.

A combination of Afrikaner political arrogance and cultural insecurity triggered the events that became a watershed moment in the history of apartheid. In 1975 an FAK conference accepted a motion calling on the government to promote Afrikaans in all possible ways to achieve its 'rightful position' in schools for blacks and Asians. Andries Treurnicht, leader of the NP's right wing and deputy minister of Bantu Administration and Development, held the view that the government had the right to decide the medium of instruction in black schools because white taxpayers subsidized the schools.[136]

Any circumspect and properly informed politician or administrator would have real-

---

135 See Heribert Adam, 'Survival Politics' in Adam and Gliomee, *Ethnic Power Mobilized*, pp. 128-44.
136 *Beeld*, 17 June 1976.

ized that a policy that enforced Afrikaans as a language upon Africans would spark protests, particularly in Soweto, the sprawling township outside Johannesburg with a population of well over a million blacks. Most jobs in Johannesburg required a command of English, and, as noted above, Afrikaans had become one of the main symbols of oppression in this most politicized of all black communities. A 1972 survey found that 98 per cent of young Sowetans did not wish to be taught in Afrikaans. One half considered Afrikaners 'the most cruel and least sympathetic people in South Africa.'[137]

It was in this context that the Department of Bantu Administration and Development resolved to enforce the 50-50 rule for Afrikaans and English as media of instruction in black schools. Inspectors in Soweto and other schools in the southern Transvaal area instructed that mathematics and arithmetic had to be taught in Afrikaans alone, despite the fact that most teachers and pupils probably had no command of Afrikaans. Teacher organizations and black parents on school boards in the townships protested strongly, but the government ignored these protests and the dire warnings by the official opposition that a volatile situation was building up in Soweto.

John Kane-Berman, a *Financial Mail* journalist, sketched the scene on the morning of Wednesday 16 June 1976:

> Twenty thousand Soweto schoolchildren marched in protest against a decree by the South African government's Department of Bantu Education that Afrikaans had to be used as one of the languages of instruction in secondary schools . . . Newspaper photographs and several eyewitness accounts suggest that the marching students were good-humored, high-spirited and excited. Some were giving the clenched fist 'Black Power' salute. Others were carrying placards bearing slogans 'Down with Afrikaans', 'We are not Boers', and 'If we must do Afrikaans Vorster must do Zulu.'
>
> Police vehicles rushed to the scene . . . The pupils taunted them and they responded with teargas . . . Apparently no order from the police to the marchers to disperse was heard, and a senior police officer admitted at the time that no warning shots had been fired either. The first child to be killed was evidently a thirteen-year-old schoolboy, Hector Petersen, apparently by a bullet fired at him directly from behind. Several other youngsters were also shot dead. Then, in the words of one newspaper, 'All hell broke loose.'[138]

The issue of Afrikaans was the trigger that brought the Soweto pupils out in protest, but other deep-seated causes were unemployment, poverty, the state of black schools, the pass laws and the insecurity engendered by the homelands policy. Added to this was the role of the Administration Boards, introduced in 1972 to run the townships, and mainly staffed by white officials and absorbing much of the township's revenue. The loss of subsidies from the Johannesburg City Council also exarcerbated black frustration.

General Magnus Malan, a leading figure in the military establishment, later remarked that the police force, to which Vorster felt so close, never really understood how to deal

137 M.L. Edelstein, *What Do Young Africans Think?* (Johannesburg: SA Institute of Race Relations, 1972), pp. 104 -14.
138 John Kane-Berman, *Soweto* (Johannesburg: Ravan Press, 1978), p. 1.

with black protests.[139] Initially led by the Soweto Students' Representative Council, most of whose members were inspired by Black Consciousness, the protestors attacked and burned down Administration Board buildings, beer halls, schools, clinics and libraries and organized several work stoppages. One hundred and seventy-six people died in the first six months, most shot and killed by the police. The uprising spread to townships throughout the southern Transvaal, to the campuses of black universities, and to some towns in other provinces. In Cape Town colored youths clashed with the police in the city center. Black local councilors resigned in numerous towns and there were prolonged school boycotts. By October 1977 between six hundred and seven hundred people had been killed. The uprising, Biko's horrific death and the banning of the black organizations accelerated the international isolation of South Africa. The UN Security Council accepted a mandatory arms embargo of South Africa.

In October 1977 the government banned all the organizations associated with the Black Consciousness Movement; *The World*, the leading black newspaper in Johannesburg, and the Christian Institute, headed by Beyers Naudé. On 12 September 1977, Steve Biko died in horrifying circumstances of head injuries inflicted by security policemen while in custody. Despite the seriousness of his condition, he was given no proper medical treatment and was transported naked five hundred miles on the floor of a van to Pretoria, where he died. On hearing of Biko's death, Jimmy Kruger, Minister of Justice (apparently under the impression that he had died following a hunger strike), declared to a party congress that Biko's death 'left him cold.'

Biko's death in a special way demonstrated to Afrikaners the atrocities that were being committed in the state's defense and in their name. It could not even be proven that he was a revolutionary. Rykie van Reenen wrote in *Beeld* on 18 September 1977, just after his death, that she was deeply impressed when she interviewed him for six hours a month earlier, just before his arrest, and visited the community projects in which he was engaged. 'This young man', she noted, 'was no wrecker, but a builder.' She reacted with a sense of 'trepidation' to the silencing of his voice in the white-black dialogue.

Leadership crisis

By the mid-1970s the Afrikaner people, party and church were still closely aligned, with more than 90 per cent of the Afrikaners supporting the NP; most of them expressed trust in the NP leadership. More than four-fifths of the NP-supporting Afrikaners were 'very religious' and the Afrikaans churches still offered no fundamental criticism of apartheid. The Afrikaner Broederbond tied a large part of the Afrikaner academic, professional and business elite together in its effort to deliberate on the Afrikaners' future options. If the Afrikaners remained united, they could perpetuate white rule for several decades.

The years 1976-1978 were a watershed. Unlike the time of the 1960 Sharpeville uprising, South Africa now had television and the images on the screen left little doubt about black hatred for the white system of rule. Especially disconcerting was the fact that the black youth displayed much greater political disaffection than their parents.

---

139 Hilton Hamann, *Days of the Generals* (Cape Town: Zebra, 2001), p. 49.

A second shock for the nationalist elite was the publication in 1978 of two books on the Afrikaner Broederbond, one of which included an almost complete list of the secret organization's members. It listed 13,262 members in 914 divisions.[140] The organization's influence, always overrated by scholars, was already on the wane, and the publication of members' lists removed the aura of secrecy. All kinds of questions were now being asked about the Bond. In almost every Afrikaner institution, ranging from church councils and synods to university senates and business associations, Bond members were identified as in a minority among members but a majority in leadership positions. Often non-members suspected that some key issues had already been resolved in Bond divisions, making the open discussions a mere formality. The question arose: Did the Bond, as the organization's leaders liked to claim, recruit people because they had leadership potential, or did, as critics argued, people get promoted and become leaders because of their Bond membership? (Piet Cillié privately said that he did not need the Bond when he joined: he was already editor of *Die Burger*.)

In earlier years when South Africa enjoyed stability non-Bond members tended to accept the existence of the organization as simply another bulwark of Afrikaner power. But now that the foundations of white rule had been shaken there were all kinds of questions over a self-recruiting secret organization, whose members filled most of the top positions in Afrikaner communal life. If the Bond spent all its time devising survival plans why was South Africa in such turmoil? Was this elite not simply feathering its own nest?

Because the Bond's deliberations were secret it was difficult to address these questions. A still unpublished study by Ernst Stals shows that the Bond was an important discussion forum where members seriously grappled with the issue of Afrikaner interests and future survival, accommodating divergent views. There was a two-way flow of ideas – circulars and study papers went from the head office to the divisions, which gave feedback or made suggestions of their own. The Bond leadership had an open door to the cabinet, which used the Bond as a valuable source of information and as a sounding board for its own ideas. In the late 1980s a study found that the Bond was the organization that wielded the most influence on the ruling elite with respect to socio-political policy, even edging out the DRC and the Afrikaanse Handelsinstituut and far outstripping Inkatha or ANC-aligned organizations.[141]

But the Bond's ability to give clear direction was limited. Since the early 1970s, when divisions in Afrikaner ranks began to appear, the Bond itself reflected these divisions, and, after the Bond had purged its most conservative members by the early 1980s, it mirrored divisions in NP ranks. Increasingly the cabinet had to lend its ear also to other lobbies and pressure groups beyond Afrikaner ranks, and the Bond became a group that primarily explained government actions to its members.

Yet another blow hit the nationalist leadership in 1978, when the so-called 'information scandal' broke. Like the nuclear bombs that were assembled in the 1970s, a certain governmental mindset was at work here, too. The growing international rejection

---

140 Ivor Wilkins and H. Strydom, *The Super-Afrikaners: Inside the Afrikaner Broederbond* (Johannesburg: Jonathan Ball, 1978). See also J.H.P. Serfontein, *The Brotherhood of Power* (London: Rex Collings, 1979).

141 A.Y. Sadie, 'Regerings- en sake-elite se persepsies oor die invloed van die Suid-Afrikaanse sakesektor op openbare beleidsformulering', doctoral diss., UCT, 1990, p. 214.

of apartheid had created a persecution complex among members of the government, who tended to see the world divided between 'friends of South Africa' and its devious enemies. They had a great yearning for the world to understand the complexities of the situation and, in Vorster's words, to be informed of what white South Africa had 'achieved' for all the people living in it.

South Africa still followed the conventional route to influence opinion, to the increasing irritation of Eschel Rhoodie, a brash and ambitious civil servant in the Department of Information. During the late 1960s, while he was stationed in the US, a CIA agent had made a deep impression on him, telling him that it was futile to go through official channels and customary ways of influencing public opinion, and persuading him of the need for an aggressive, unconventional, proactive approach to turn around the negative image of South Africa.[142]

Rhoodie felt that the greatest threat to Afrikaner survival was the growth of the anti-apartheid lobby in the West. The divestment campaign was rapidly gaining support, especially in universities and churches, and the idea had taken root that since the South African government was inflicting structural violence on the non-white population it was legitimate to support those who were working to overthrow it by violent means. Determined to stem this trend, Rhoodie gained the trust of Connie Mulder, Minister of Information and heir-apparent of Vorster, and of Hendrik van den Bergh, the head of the Bureau for State Security (BOSS), and early in 1974 he made what he called a simple proposal to Vorster and Nic Diederichs, the Minister of Finance. The government was to get rid of all laws and rules based purely on color that affronted the dignity of blacks and were not necessary for survival. To change the negative perceptions of South Africa the country could not rely on diplomats and information officers communicating the official line, but had to wage an unconventional propaganda war with large financial resources. To do this it was necessary to create 'new avenues, instruments, organizations and people that could speak on behalf of South Africa.' Vorster agreed to a war fought on Rhoodie's terms where one 'should not be concerned about rules and regulations.'[143] As Minister of Information, Connie Mulder publicly echoed the approach: 'If we are attacked, no rules apply if we come to the question of our existence. We will use all means at our disposal, whatever they may be.'[144]

Over the next five years, as numerous secret projects were launched, a history of sleaze, corruption, violation of exchange control regulations, lies in Parliament and even murders accumulated. Since one of the thorns in the government's side was its lack of an English newspaper, one of the main projects was to found a new newspaper, *The Citizen*. To do this, the Department of Information employed secret state funds, using Louis Luyt, an Afrikaner fertilizer tycoon, as a front. Its circulation figures were falsified from the start. Luyt, in turn, unsuccessfully tried to buy one of the two English newspaper chains. Through other fronts the Department attempted to buy *The Washington Star*, the French journal *L'Équipe,* and a British investors' journal. A fictitious club of businessmen, called the Club of Ten, placed advertisements in overseas publications. The Department pro-

---

142 Mervyn Rees and Chris Day, *Muldergate* (Johannesburg: Macmillan, 1980), pp. 161-5.
143 Rees and Day, *Muldergate*, p. 171.
144 *International Herald Tribune*, 17 February 1977.

vided funding for an office of the Dutch Reformed Church that tried to counter the work of the World Council of Churches, now playing a prominent role in the anti-apartheid struggle. Through accepting this funding the church itself became part of the government's secret propaganda machine to sell apartheid. A glossy publication detailing the work the DRC had done in the field of missionary work was distributed overseas.

The efforts to manipulate public opinion went far beyond what governments and countries normally do to improve their image. They involved the transfer of large sums of money abroad in violation of exchange control regulations. If it had been revealed political heads would have rolled. In late 1977, Robert Smit, an Afrikaans-speaking NP candidate for the upcoming election, and his wife were murdered in what looked like a deed perpetrated by hired killers. Smit had previously, as a government official, attended meetings of the International Monetary Fund. When the information scandal burst it was widely speculated that Smit had been on the point of revealing the currency control violations. No one was ever arrested for the murders. The affair became even more sinister in the context of testimony given to a subsequent commission of inquiry by Hendrik van den Bergh, head of BOSS, who had aligned himself with Rhoodie and Mulder. Van den Berg boasted that he had men prepared to kill on his instructions.

By early 1978 rumors about the projects of the Department of Information were rife. Vorster seemed distracted, while Mulder, ahead in the race for his succession, was confronted in Parliament with the question of whether the government was funding *The Citizen*. He answered in the negative, which as a commission later found, was a public lie. Vorster, unable to make a clean breast of things, resigned as prime minister to become state president, hoping that his colleagues would stand by him as he so often had done for them. However, the race for Vorster's successor was far too close for Mulder's adversaries to hush up the scandal. On 28 September 1978 P.W. Botha narrowly defeated Mulder to become the next prime minister. Eleven months later Vorster was compelled to resign as state president. A commission of inquiry found that he had known for a long time about the irregular activities of the Department of Information.

Louis Luyt, 'owner' of *The Citizen*, and F.E. O'Brien Geldenhuys, who headed the DRC's foreign 'information office', expressed their feelings in almost identical terms: 'I lived a lie.'[145] Leaders used terms like 'survival' and 'patriotism' to cover up their activities. A Broederbond circular to its divisions after the scandal had broken referred to 'a cynical disillusionment that had taken root among our youth, not to speak about the shock and disillusionment among English-speakers and Non-Whites who always rated the integrity of the Afrikaner leadership highly.' Gerrit Viljoen, Chairman of the Executive, made a plea in a personal letter to the divisions: 'It was now urgently necessary to maintain self-control and discipline, to display unity and loyalty to democratically and properly elected leaders, to avoid gossip and slander and the denigration of leaders.'[146] But the shock had been severe and the rectitude with which the leaders tried to surround themselves had been severely compromised.

---

145 F.E. O'Brien Geldenhuys, *In die stroomversnellings* (Cape Town: Tafelberg, 1982), pp. 72-7.
146 Stals, 'Geskiedenis van die Afrikaner-Broederbond' , pp. 428-9.

The sultan's horse

Among the Afrikaner intelligentsia Van Wyk Louw's phrases of survival in justice and loyal resistance had become common coin during the 1970s. Nationalist editors used (and abused) them to propagate nationalist unity or hail reforms that only marginally altered the apartheid structures. Gerrit Viljoen was one of the few nationalists with the intellectual ability to develop Louw's paradigm of loyal resistance as an argument for incremental reform, which required a stable state. He was a professor of Classics and one of the very few nationalists who defended Louw's play *Die pluimsaad waai ver* when Verwoerd attacked it. He became principal of the Rand Afrikaans University and served as chairman of the Broederbond's Executive Council from 1974 to 1980. In an article on the 'minimal conditions' for Afrikaner survival, he linked up with Van Wyk Louw in warning of the danger that members of a 'small' people could, to use a phrase from ancient Roman history, begin to 'despair of the state.' Like Louw, he stressed that ultimately the Afrikaners' survival would not be justified by political or economic might but 'by the excellence of their intellectual and social life and the ethical values that directed it.'[147]

But Viljoen rejected Louw's view that an ethical crisis, of the kind that clinging to apartheid represented, could be seen as a crisis that threatened the very survival of the volk. For Viljoen this could only be a political crisis for the volk, not a survival crisis. The answer was not to abandon power in a frantic pursuit of justice but to correct injustice from a position of power.[148] But while Viljoen saw the need for a coalition with like-minded blacks, he could not envisage a negotiated solution. The Afrikaner, he wrote, was 'the core of our society, the hub of our politics, the dynamo of our [South Africa's] cultural life. It was he who had to take the lead, take the initiative and anticipate political problems, and it was he who had to tackle and solve these questions creatively.'[149]

But some of the leading Afrikaner writers and academics disagreed profoundly. They rejected the idea that the initiative was still with the Afrikaners, and that the NP, with its obsession with Afrikaner unity, was a suitable vehicle to reform a policy that threatened to lead to a violent struggle. The novelist Jan Rabie, who was above all concerned about the future of Afrikaans as a language, argued that apartheid was alienating the Afrikaner youth and driving the colored people 'into English arms or black nationalism.'[150] Another novelist, André Brink, observed that Afrikaners and Afrikaans as a language would only survive if they became true to their multi-racial history and heritage in a fundamentally transformed political system.[151]

Vorster probably briefly toyed with the idea of a change of course, but after Soweto erupted he dropped all such plans. He did not publicly censure Kruger, because he considered loyalty to his cabinet ministers a higher priority. Nor, for the same reason, did he dismiss the ministers who triggered the Soweto riots by insisting on Afrikaans as a medium

---

147 G. van N. Viljoen, 'Die kwaliteit van ons oorlewing', *Aambeeld*, 6, 1 (1978), pp. 4-5.
148 G. van N. Viljoen, '"Wat is 'n volk?" Die aktualiteit van Van Wyk Louw se riglyne vir die nasionalisme', in F.I.J. van Rensburg (ed.), *Oopgelate kring* (Pretoria: RGN, 1982), p. 140.
149 G. van N. Viljoen, *Ideaal en werklikheid* (Cape Town: Tafelberg, 1978), pp. 31-3.
150 *Die Burger*, 13 July 1978.
151 A.P. Brink, *Literatuur in die strydperk* (Cape Town: Human & Rousseau, 1985), p. 155.

of instruction – truly a massive misjudgment of the Afrikaners' ethnic interests. He understood that reforms introduced by a repressive government did not necessarily enhance stability. Since the racial problem was intractable, it was better to play for time than embark on rash action. Addressing the Broederbond in November 1976, he communicated his conclusion, described as a 'profound analysis' by the Broederbond, that there was no alternative but Hendrik Verwoerd's 'vision of separate homelands.'[152]

On 6 October 1961 *Die Transvaler* reported that T.E. (Eben) Dönges had formulated the stark alternatives before whites: 'Do we prefer a smaller South Africa with political power in the hands of a white man or a bigger South Africa in the hands of a black man?' Described by Allister Sparks, editor of the liberal *Rand Daily Mail*, as 'the De Gaulle of South Africa', Vorster failed to use the ten years of stability between the mid-1960s and the mid-1970s to develop a new strategic approach that offered alternatives to handing over power to blacks over all of South Africa.[153] When he resigned as prime minister in September 1978 he was physically and mentally exhausted.

It was left to Piet Cillié to point out the somber implications of the Soweto uprising for Afrikaner nationalism. If the classic apartheid formula of separate freedoms for whites and blacks was no longer applicable, the alternative of freedom for all in a plural society had to be accepted: 'No common objective for all South Africa's people will suffice unless it includes the prospect of equal citizenship for all the country's children.'[154]

This author interviewed Vorster in 1980 on the day the revolutionary leader Robert Mugabe came to power in Zimbabwe. Had Ian Smith as leader of the white community in Zimbabwe squandered options that could have prevented this fate? He had, Vorster replied, and had rejected Vorster's suggestions. Exasperated, Vorster asked him: 'Do you not know the story of the sultan's horse?' The sultan had sentenced three men to death but promised to set free anyone who could make his horse talk. While two of them were being dragged to the executioner's block the next day they saw the third standing about free. 'What did you tell the sultan? We said it was impossible to make a horse talk.' The free man replied: 'I told the sultan I could make his horse talk, but it would take five years. In that period a lot can happen: The sultan could die, the horse could die or I could die, and, who knows, I may even get the damn horse to talk.'

Vorster noted that when Smith did finally accept majority rule the regime had its back against the wall, unable to set conditions. He had wasted the time when he could have made much better deals. The implications for South Africa of the parable were obvious, but the conversation did not dwell on that. Vorster had held the fort but had not managed to break out and cause disarray in the ranks of those who were beginning to lay siege to it. In 1973 Breyten Breytenbach had given a lecture he called 'A View from the Outside' in which he expressed his contempt of the incessant talk about survival and the agonizing about reform that characterized Afrikaner politics. 'As a group we have had our chance and babbling away we allowed it to pass.'[155]

---

152 Wilkins and Strydom, *The Super-Afrikaners*, p. 214.
153 Rees and Day, *Muldergate*, p. 8.
154 *Die Burger*, 10 and 13 November 1976.
155 B.B. Lasarus [B. Breytenbach], *'n Seisoen in die Paradys* (Johannesburg: Perskor, 1976), p. 121.

Chapter 16

Surrender without defeat

'Adapt or die?'

In 1979 Pieter Willem (P.W.) Botha, the eighth prime minister, was reported to have said: 'We are moving into a changing world, we must adapt otherwise we shall die.'[1] Adapt or die – these striking words seemed to encapsulate Botha's bold approach. But there was a problem with this ringing statement: Botha denied that he ever said 'adapt or die.' He was ambivalent about how much adapting was necessary to avoid death and too confident of the overpowering strength of the state to be morbid about its survival prospects. He was determined, energetic and purposeful, but also brash and impetuous, the kind of leader that was willing to adapt but was also spoiling for a fight.

By the end of the 1970s Afrikaners occupied most of the senior positions in the central government, the security services, three of the four provincial administrations and the public corporations. Yet apartheid South Africa was in some ways not a white state. Even in the 1950s it appointed more blacks than whites. By the early 1980s some two million people, of whom only one-third were white, worked in the public sector, including the homeland governments.

One could almost say that two states co-existed. There was a 'core state' headed by Afrikaner politicians, senior civil servants and generals responding mostly to Afrikaner pressure groups, like the NP caucus, the Afrikaner Broederbond, the Afrikaans churches and the Afrikaanse Handelsinstituut.[2] Beyond this Afrikaner core state there was a multiracial 'outer state' of business leaders, homeland governments with their bureaucracies, and racially mixed security forces. This was a system that was in the process of removing salary and wage disparities and reducing white exclusivity and privilege. All or almost all of those occupying leadership positions in the outer state wanted to avoid sanctions on the grounds that it would slow down this process.

From the early 1970s the NP as the ruling party claimed that the reform of apartheid

---

1 The statement is quoted with sources in Merle Lipton, *Capitalism and Apartheid* (Aldershot: Wildwood House, 1986), p. 51.

2 A.Y. Sadie, 'Regerings- en sake-elite se persepsies oor die invloed van die Suid-Afrikaanse sakesektor op openbare beleidsformulering ', doctoral diss., University of Cape Town, 1990, p. 214.

rather than maintaining apartheid itself was its primary objective. There was something ingenuous in this claim since it was only in the second half of the 1980s that the demolition of the key pillars would come on the agenda. Reform rhetoric was nevertheless the order of the day. Piet Cillié had written at the height of the 1976 Soweto uprising: 'If there is the need to defend the land militarily it must be for what it can become, not what it is.'[3] General Magnus Malan, Chief of the Defence Force during the late 1970s and Minister for Defence during the 1980s, projected the state as the guarantor of values that transcended color lines: 'I must emphasize that the overriding consideration is survival. Survival concerns every citizen in South Africa, directly and indirectly.'[4]

When P.W. Botha succeeded John Vorster in September 1978 as prime minister there was a much greater sense of urgency in the Afrikaner leadership. In his first year in office in 1978 Botha hit South Africa like a storm. He seemed to signal that the idea of reform had triumphed and that far-reaching change was on the way. He called blacks 'fellow South Africans', visited Soweto with 'a message of hope', and toured all the homelands. He urged Afrikaners to study the lessons of their own history. 'The moment you start oppressing people . . . they fight back. We must acknowledge people's rights and . . . set ourselves free by giving to others in a spirit of justice what we demand for ourselves.'[5] There was a hint of great changes being under way. After his first year in office, the *Washington Post* wrote that the changes astonished blacks and kindled hopes of an alternative to violence and despair.[6]

'Total onslaught'

Botha's politics were formed by two quite different influences. He was a career politician who started as a full-time organizer for the National Party, where he learned the importance of organizational efficiency. Identified with the more pragmatic Cape wing of the party, he developed a close relationship with Piet Cillié of *Die Burger*, and with Nasionale Pers, the publishing house on whose Board of Directors he served. As Minister for Community Development he had no compunction about carrying out the highly contentious removal of colored people from District Six, a suburb close to the heart of the Cape Town, which became the symbol of the Afrikaner rejection of a community of fellow-Afrikaans-speakers.

The other influence on Botha was the military. As Minister for Defence between 1966 and 1980, he rapidly built up the South African army, based on a relatively small permanent force and a large annual intake of white conscripts. And, like the security officials and military, the work of counter-revolutionary strategists also influenced him. Highest on his reading list were John J. McCuen's *The Art of Counter-Revolutionary War* and the books of the French strategic thinker André Beaufre, as well as the major French intellectual Raymond Aron. Among French strategists there was a strong tendency to project state interests as the equivalent of the national interest. States had to defend them-

---

3 *Die Burger*, 10 and 13 November 1976, 'Dawie' column.

4 *Sunday Times*, 13 March 1979.

5 Merle Lipton, *Capitalism and Apartheid* (Aldershot: Wildwood House, 1986), pp. 51-2.

6 Dirk and Johanna de Villiers, *PW* (Cape Town: Tafelberg, 1984), p. 152.

selves against communist subversion not only by military means but also by combating political and ideological attacks. There was an emphasis on the amorality of politics and a fear of Soviet expansion. Members of the South African Security Police received training in Taiwan in strategic communication and applied it widely.[7]

Botha and his military strategists concluded that a national security strategy could only be pursued successfully if the state had a central body under the leadership of civilian politicians. This body had to be assisted by senior military officers and civil servants to review security threats, co-ordinate intelligence reports and devise proper responses.[8]

In 1972 legislation had been passed to establish a State Security Council to co-ordinate security operations and the gathering of intelligence, but Vorster failed to make such a council an effective body. The lack of co-ordination had become acute after the debacle of South Africa's invasion of Angola in 1975-76, which was preceded by a series of ad hoc decisions, intense rivalry between security agencies, and disputes between cabinet ministers over the cross-border attack.[9] The prospect of fighting a prolonged war of insurgency on the borders and the unexpected Soweto uprising in 1976 had made the development of a national security plan a matter of even greater urgency.

In 1977 the Department of Defence published a White Paper spelling out the belief of P.W. Botha and the military that South Africa faced a 'total onslaught' on virtually every area of society. Threats could only be countered by a 'total strategy' against subversive elements. A key to this would be an improvement of the socio-economic conditions in the townships, seen as essential for the free-enterprise system to prevail over communism.

The upsurge of guerrilla activity in the southern African region and the introduction of Cuban troops and Soviet advisors in 1975 certainly added up to a formidable threat to the South African state. But Botha and some of his security advisors tended to present the threat in an even more dramatic fashion. Botha was fond of projecting the struggle in the South African region as a vital part of the global conflict between the East and the West, and between free enterprise and communism. Without South Africa, the West would lose the fight against communist tyranny. General Magnus Malan accused Western powers of making themselves available as 'handymen' of the communists, thus indirectly contributing to the destruction of capitalism and the establishment of world communism.[10] In fact, South Africa was a low priority for the Soviet Union during the 1960s and 1970s; it expanded in Africa only when the costs appeared to be low and when it did not interfere with more important foreign policy problems closer at home.[11]

Hand in hand with the thinking about a total onslaught went the idea of 'winning hearts and minds' as an essential part of counter-revolutionary warfare, not only in defending the challenges in Namibia but ultimately also in South Africa itself. General Constand Viljoen, who between 1977 and 1985 was first Chief of the Army and later

7 Interviews by author of Niel Barnard, head of the National Intelligence Agency, 21 April 2002 and with Johan van der Merwe, who between the mid-1980s and mid-1990s headed first the security police and then the police force, 21 November 2002. Both were members of the State Security Council.
8 Annette Seegers, *The Military in the Making of Modern South Africa* (London: I.B. Tauris, 1996), pp. 132-4.
9 Seegers, *The Military*, pp. 133-4.
10 Deon Geldenhuys, *The Diplomacy of Isolation* (Johannesburg: Macmillan, 1984), p. 209.
11 Robert Jaster, *South Africa's Narrowing Security Options* (London: International Institute for Strategic Studies, 1980), pp. 1-2.

Chief of the Defence Force, told the cabinet on several occasions that militarily South Africa could carry on for a long period, but this was of no avail if a political solution were not found. 'We told them [cabinet ministers] that they had to find a formula where all the people living in the country would feel involved and part of the country. We warned the government that as every year passed their strategic options would become fewer.'[12] The military, whose permanent force staff officers were 85 per cent Afrikaners, increasingly became participants in the public debate over survival, and also about the most appropriate means of countering threats. The speeches of senior generals had as their recurring theme that the struggle against revolutionaries was 20 per cent military and 80 per cent socio-economic. 'If South Africa lost the socio-economic struggle we need not bother to fight the military one. The objective is no longer territory but the hearts and mind of men.'[13]

A *grensoorlog* (border war)

When Botha came to power in September 1978 several regional threats were cause for grave concern. There had been a humiliating withdrawal from Angola early in 1976 and the presence of the Cubans, backed by the Soviets, loomed large over the region. Zimbabwe, Mozambique and Angola all had governments leaning towards Afro-Marxism. In 1977, while hosting the Soviet president, Zambia's Kenneth Kaunda had described the Soviets as 'colleagues and comrades' in the struggle.[14] The South West African People's Organization (SWAPO), under the leadership of Sam Nujomo, stood poised to take power in Namibia with United Nations backing, as yet another Afro-Marxist regime in the region. The African National Congress received most of its backing from the Soviet Union and enjoyed close relations with Cuba.

John Vorster and P.W. Botha differed strongly in responding to the threats. While Vorster was determined to limit South Africa's regional commitments to a minimum and defend only the South African border, Botha was willing to project South African power far beyond the borders (see p. 572). For Vorster, South Africa's continued control of Namibia was not decisive for white supremacy. Namibia was less a security issue than a political one; there were nearly 75,000 whites in Namibia, the great majority Afrikaners. The South African government feared a severe voters' backlash if SWAPO came to power in an election marred by large-scale violence and intimidation, all sanctioned by the UN and by poll observers. It could put a damper on all further reform in South Africa.

The government was also very concerned about the proliferation of arms; fighting had intensified in southern Africa from the mid-1970s and explosives, rockets and automatic rifles had poured in. The security establishment in South Africa wanted permission to hit guerrillas as far beyond the border as possible. It also wished to put pressure on neighbor states to refuse sanctuary to ANC guerrillas. Vorster agreed, reluctantly in view of the failed 1975-76 invasion, to cross-border operations. The first target was SWAPO guerrillas operating freely from neighboring states, particularly Angola.

In February 1978 the Vorster government committed itself to independence for Namibia

---

12 Hilton Hamann, *Days of the Generals* (Cape Town: Zebra Press, 2001), p. 56.
13 Speech by General Boshoff, *Cape Times*, 23 August 1975.
14 Chester Crocker, *High Noon in Southern Africa* (New York: Norton, 1992), p. 54.

before the end of 1978, and two months later accepted a plan drawn up by Western powers (USA, Canada, Britain, France and Germany) for a settlement, which would be presented to the UN Assembly after all the parties had agreed. South Africa would remain in control until April 1979 when an election would be held for a government to steer Namibia to independence. As Brand Fourie, a South African diplomat highly regarded by his Western counterparts, formulated it in his memoirs, the majority in the cabinet accepted this position. 'If SWAPO won an open [sic] election under circumstances where we were essentially in control over the territory, it would be clear proof that it enjoys majority support.'[15] Minister of Defence P.W. Botha was a dissenting voice in the cabinet, but he got permission to attack a large SWAPO base in Cassinga, Angola, 250 kilometers north of the Namibian border. In the battle as many as six hundred SWAPO fighters and other followers died.

The cabinet was poised between two quite different roads. The military hawks were confident of their ability to bludgeon the guerrillas into submission and to build up a moderate counter to SWAPO in Namibia through a hearts and minds strategy. The doves on the Namibian issue felt that the cross-border operations might trigger further sanctions and some doubted the possibility of building up a moderate black force. Vorster could have held the line for the doves, but he was worn down by the 'information scandal' that threatened to become public at any moment. He was also angered by the fact that the UN Secretary-General Kurt Waldheim presented the Western Five plan with details going well beyond what South Africa had agreed to. He resigned as prime minister in September 1978 and was succeeded by Botha.

Botha and the military hawks could now set the agenda. South Africa pulled out of the UN plan and announced that it would sponsor internal elections in Namibia in December 1978 with the obvious aim of building an internal counter to SWAPO. As in 1975 with the Angolan invasion, the military hawks believed that moderate African states backed a 'moderate' solution, which meant the exclusion of a SWAPO government in Namibia on account of its presumed communist sympathies.[16]

For the December election in Namibia, 85 per cent of the Namibian potential electorate registered and 78 per cent of those registered voted. The Democratic Turnhalle Alliance, a multi-racial moderate alliance, emerged as the victor. As in the case of the internal election held in Rhodesia in 1979, the international community refused to recognize the election. SWAPO had not participated and South Africa had strongly backed the DTA, which had failed to attract any significant support among the Ovambos, the largest ethnic group.

Botha came to power when world pressure on South Africa on the Namibian issue seemed overwhelmingly strong, but this was an illusion. The threat of intensified international sanctions because of South Africa's stand on Namibia did not materialize. Economically South Africa recovered well after the Soweto uprising. Between 1976 and 1985 the fixed domestic investment from Europe doubled. The dark cloud on the horizon was the Carter administration in Washington, which took a much tougher line on South Africa than its predecessors. But the Soviet invasion of Afghanistan early in 1979 led to

---

15 Brand Fourie, *Brandpunte* (Cape Town: Tafelberg, 1991), p. 169.
16 Geldenhuys, *Diplomacy of Isolation*, p. 227.

increased Western concern over Soviet expansionism, which worked in South Africa's favor. Soon the frigid relationship between South Africa and the Carter administration was replaced with a warmer one with the Reagan administration. It was not hostile to Botha's insistence that no election could be held in Namibia before all foreign troops had withdrawn from neighboring Angola. The number of Cuban troops had increased from 13,000 in 1977 to 25,000 by 1983; in addition there were 5,000 military personnel from the Soviet Union and other East Bloc countries.

A US delegation led by Judge William Clark visited South Africa in 1981, offering a quid pro quo that South Africa quickly seized. In exchange for South Africa working towards an internationally recognized election in Namibia, the US would commit itself to get the Cubans out of the region. 'That will be a new ball game', South African Foreign Minister Pik Botha responded.[17] For the next eight years that was, indeed, the ball game: South African and Cuban troops would withdraw simultaneously and there would be no partisan UN role. Only then would an election be held.

The Botha government continued to attempt to weaken SWAPO so that it would not be a significant factor in a future election. In successive operations in the early 1980s South African troops established a buffer zone in the southern part of Angola and launched military attacks against SWAPO bases. Large-scale aid flowed to UNITA. With South African assistance it had become an efficient force, controlling large parts of the south and putting the MPLA under pressure in the central region. Kept far out by a South Africa-controlled zone in the south of Angola, SWAPO was unable to infiltrate guerrillas in any significant numbers. But there was no indication of a weakening of the will of either Cuba's Fidel Castro or the SWAPO leadership.

Through providing veterinary services, drilling boreholes, building clinics and other 'hearts-and-minds' operations, the South African troops tried to win the support of the population in Ovamboland. Some observers considered it 'one of the most successful counter-insurgency campaigns in history' undertaken by a military force.[18] But this was undercut by the *Koevoet* ('Crowbar'), a special counter-insurgency unit operating as part of the police force, which developed a frightening reputation for cruelty and ruthlessness in capturing and killing SWAPO guerrillas. The northern region of Namibia with its strongly pro-SWAPO Ovambo population remained relatively peaceful throughout the 1980s.

Destabilization

By 1980 South Africa and the black states in the region were not yet on a collision course. Botha had invited them to become part of his Constellation of States, but they rejected the offer and formed the Southern African Development Co-ordinating Council, which aimed at a reduction of their economic dependence on South Africa. There were early signs that their lessened dependence might translate into increased support for ANC guerrillas, at that point infiltrating into South Africa through neighboring countries, particularly Mozambique, Lesotho, Swaziland and Botswana.

---

17 De Villiers, *PW*, p. 358.
18 Brian Pottinger, *The Imperial Presidency* (Johannesburg: Southern, 1988), p. 207; Jannie Geldenhuys, *Dié wat wen: 'n generaal se storie* (Pretoria: Van Schaik, 1993).

From 1981 South Africa embarked on what became known as a campaign of destabilization of the region to achieve its security objectives. In fact the campaign had two objectives: both talk and thump. One was to convince Africans in the region of the folly of Marxist policies. Samora Machel's Mozambican government had embarked on experiments in scientific socialism and nation-building, leading to widespread human rights abuses, serious food shortages and strong resistance in some areas. The other was military intervention to drive ANC guerrillas from the region. In 1982 the National Intelligence Service was instrumental in arranging a visit from CIA head William Casey, who met with Botha and his security advisors. They agreed that it was possible to build a new *cordon sanitaire* by forcing neighboring states to expel guerrillas within their borders in exchange for South Africa's ending its destabilization.[19]

To force its neighbors' hands South Africa bombed ANC facilities in Matola, Maputo and Maseru and supported dissident factions in eastern Zimbabwe, Lesotho and particularly in Mozambique, which had become the main route of ANC guerrillas into South Africa. The FRELIMO government under Samora Machel was an easy target for destabilization by South Africa, using as its instrument the Resistencia Nacional de Mocambique (RENAMO). Unlike UNITA, it was not based on an ethnic group or rival liberation movement; it also lacked a charismatic leader and its system of command and communications was primitive. Its numbers were estimated to have reached fifteen thousand by the mid-1980s, but it was never much more than a band of brigands. It could only operate so successfully because FRELIMO had very tenuous control over large parts of the country. With South African help it cut railway lines, mined roads, blew up fuel depots, destroyed grain stores and disrupted the export and import routes of the border states. More than a million people were displaced.[20] In addition, parcel bombs sent by operatives in the South African security services to Maputo killed Ruth First, a prominent academic and estranged wife of Joe Slovo, one of the ANC's principal military strategists, and seriously injured Albie Sachs, a leading ANC-supporting academic.

By 1984 the pressure on the Machel government in Mozambique was so intense that it signed the Nkomati Accord with South Africa, both sides pledging to deny sanctuary to irregular forces and support for violent actions against the neighboring state. Similar agreements were signed with Zimbabwe, Botswana, Lesotho and Swaziland. The Machel government expelled eight hundred ANC activists, and South Africa returned a thousand RENAMO guerrillas. But on the ground nothing much had changed. Since South Africa had liberally supplied RENAMO with arms before the signing of the accord, it was not seriously weakened. At the same time FRELIMO did not cease its help to ANC guerrillas, although it now occurred in greater secrecy.

The ring of pliant states and the destabilization measures made it difficult for the ANC to wage its armed struggle with any great effect. An ANC insider calculated that approximately half of a total of twelve thousand trained guerrillas were infiltrated into South Africa. Of these six thousand, a third abandoned their mission, and many of the others were turned by the security forces, killed or convicted and sent to jail. In 1987 Zulu Chief Gatsha Buthelezi commented on the lack of any significant success in the armed

---

19 *Sunday Times* (London), 10 October 1982.
20 Joseph Hanlon, *Beggar Your Neighbours* (London: Catholic Institute for International Relations, 1986).

struggle. 'After twenty-five years of endeavor every bridge in the country is still intact and there is not a single factory out of production because of revolutionary activity. The classical circumstances in which the armed struggle wins the day . . . are just not present in South Africa.'[21]

But this success in stemming the armed struggle was not decisive. For blacks engaged in resistance any evidence of ANC-directed armed activity, even if negligible and intermittent, raised the morale. The knowledge that the ANC had a military organization that could retaliate was enough for many young people to fight back, even with stones.[22]

As the conflict in the southern African region escalated, many young white South African males got caught up in it, as regular soldiers, or as conscripts fighting in the war in Angola, doing duty in Namibia or patrolling the townships in South Africa. It was far from a clearly defined struggle to defend the homeland. The government presented the Angolan war as one against a communist threat in the region, but the fact was that the battle zone lay more than three thousand kilometers beyond the South African border and the SWAPO fighters, at least, were fighting for their own land.

Grensliteratuur and other *strydliteratuur* (Border and struggle literature)

From the entanglement in the conflict in Namibia and Angola a new genre developed, called *grensliteratuur* or frontier literature. An early expression was Jaap Steyn's *Op pad na die grens* (1976) (On the Way to the Border) and *Dagboek van 'n verraaier* (1978) (Diary of a Traitor), which highlighted the dilemma of becoming embroiled in a frontier war far beyond the country's borders while South Africa was still trapped in the structural violence of apartheid. Ignoring a blackout that the military authorities had imposed on soldiers in combat, Alexander Strachan, formerly a member of an elite reconnaissance unit fighting behind enemy lines in Angola, wrote of his experiences in *'n Wêreld sonder grense* (A World without Borders), which was published in 1984. This was followed four years later by Gawie Kellerman's *Wie de hel het jou vertel?* (Who the hell told you?). Piet Haasbroek, Etienne van Heerden and Louis Kruger also made powerful contributions.[23]

The stories tell how the violence inflicted by South African soldiers on the indigenous population brutalizes them but also helps them to discover a common humanity with the enemy.[24] A story by Alexander Strachan describes how the main character and a SWAPO fighter suddenly find themselves facing each other. 'I suddenly know at this moment: I do not hate him. I only fear him. And in the whites of his eyes I detect the same fear.'[25] In Strachan's stories the blurring of the traditional boundaries – those between white and black, between friend and enemy, between compassion and fear – induces a trauma, which in turn leads to a quest to understand history anew in order to make sense of the present.[26]

21 *Cape Times,* 17 September 1987.

22 Patti Waldmeir, *Anatomy of a Miracle* (London: Viking, 1997), p. 47.

23 Elsa Joubert, 'Die nuwe oorlogsliteratuur' (*Die Suid-Afrikaan,* August 1985), pp. 46-8.

24 Gawie Kellerman, *Wie de hel het jou vertel?* (Cape Town: Tafelberg, 1988), pp. 26-8.

25 Alexander Strachan, *'n Wêreld sonder grense* (Cape Town: Tafelberg, 1984), p. 29; J.H. Kleynhans, '"'n Wêreld sonder grense" as eksemplaries van die Grensverhaal', master's diss., University of the Orange Free State, 1992.

26 J.C. Cronjé, 'Die grens as meerduidige gegewe in die kontemporêre Afrikaanse poësie', doctoral diss., University of Pretoria, 1989, pp. 135-9.

Ominously, the *grensoorlog* seemed to augur the war white and black South Africans would fight on their home soil if they failed to reach a political accommodation. After the Soweto uprising thousands of young blacks fled the country to be trained as guerrilla fighters.

In 1978 a documentary novel, *Die swerfjare van Poppie Nongena*, by Elsa Joubert was published. An average Afrikaner family could easily relate to the book, because they had someone like Poppie, the main character, working as a servant in their home. Based on oral testimony of a real-life, illiterate Xhosa-speaking woman, the book describes how she tried to keep her family together despite the bureaucratic maze of influx control, but her husband had been driven away, a grandchild had been killed and after the 1976 rebellion she witnessed a much tougher resolve among the children to resist the system at great risk to themselves. A child, Jakkie, who was on the run from the police, might skip the country and come back to kill. In the final page she says: 'Peace will not come . . . Even those who want peace, have been dragged into the troubles. We shall have to get used to it. We can do nothing about it. If the Lord willed Jakkie to go, he had to go. And if my children had to be dragged into it, then they were born for it. And who can take them out of the path for which they were born?'[27] Fourteen years after the book's appearance the managing director of the publishers said: 'I think the book did more than any other Afrikaans book to turn Afrikaners around. It has never stopped selling.'[28]

It was not only the border literature in Afrikaans that undermined apartheid. The work of John Coetzee, writing in English, and André Brink and Breyten Breytenbach, writing in both Afrikaans and English, attacking apartheid as a cruel and inhumane system, were widely read. Jeanne Goosen's short novel *Ons is nie almal so nie* (We are not all like that) brilliantly captured the idea that apartheid also classified and dehumanized whites, even those who opposed it. The main character in her novel, set in the 1950s, is Doris, who is more sensitive to the injuries inflicted on the colored people than her fellow working-class Afrikaners. When her colored neighbors are forced to move out of the 'white area' under the Group Areas Act, she runs after the truck carrying their belongings with a cake as a gift, shouting 'Ons is nie almal so nie' – We are not all like that. The man at the wheel turns up the truck's window. Apartheid has made Doris one of 'them.'[29]

Opinion surveys revealed the alienation of the disenfranchised. A 1981 survey found that fewer than half of the colored people felt proud to be South Africans, only a third were prepared to condemn terrorism outright, and only a quarter (compared to 80 per cent of whites) were willing to fight for their country. Surveys undertaken in early 1980s found that urban blacks overwhelmingly supported Robert Mugabe as leader in Zimbabwe, based on the perception that he was a successful freedom fighter promoting black interests. Half of the urban blacks supported 'terrorism' in some circumstances and three-quarters in another survey expressed sympathy for a band of guerrillas who had attacked a Pretoria bank in 1980. A 1981 poll in KwaZulu and Natal found that nearly half of the blacks were prepared to provide covert aid to the ANC if it infiltrated the

---

27 Elsa Joubert, *Die swerfjare van Poppie Nongena* (Cape Town: Tafelberg, 1978), p. 276.
28 Danie van Niekerk cited by Christopher Wren, 'Apartheid's Children: Afrikaner Writers Today', *New York Times*, book review section, 11 October 1992, p. 29.
29 Jeanne Goosen, *Ons is nie almal so nie* (Pretoria: HAUM, 1990).

country. The older notion that white power was too formidable to confront directly was disintegrating.[30]

But most whites had no intention of giving up all their power, particularly not while the Soviet system offered an alternative to capitalism. They no longer as readily as in the 1960s believed the state propaganda that SWAPO and the ANC were mere communist tools, but the reality was that there were large numbers of Cuban troops in the region. The ANC was closely aligned to the Soviet Union and had an economic policy that presented a dire threat to white interests. Surveys of white students showed a strong willingness to defend the system. Afrikaner students spoke of the government and the Army as *their* government and army. Asked how they would respond to an ANC government, 44 per cent of Afrikaner students (as opposed to 10 per cent of their English-speaking counterparts) said that they would resist physically, while a further 32 per cent said they would emigrate.[31]

'Demography is destiny'

'Demography is destiny', the French philosopher August Comte wrote in the mid-nineteenth century, and this realization had suddenly dawned on Afrikaner nationalists by the end of the 1970s. What Nicolas Eberstadt, an American demographer, called 'the tyranny of numbers' had demolished all the apartheid attempts to preserve the common area as a white area.[32] In 1969 bold headlines in the Afrikaans newspaper *Die Beeld* announced 'a new factor' in South African politics: 'Verwoerd's figures wrong: South Africa will be much blacker.' A black population, growing much faster than anticipated, was expected to reach twenty-eight million by the year 2000. J.H. Coetzee, an influential Potchefstroom anthropologist, noted 'with trepidation' that the fundamental assumptions of the policy had been called into question.[33]

The demographic projections Jan Sadie made in 1951 for the year 2000 had formed the basis for both the Tomlinson Commission report of 1955 and Verwoerd's homelands policy.

SELECTED FIGURES FOR SA POPULATION

	1946 CENSUS	1951 PROJECTIONS FOR 2000 (SADIE)	1974 (ACTUAL)	1991 (ACTUAL)
Whites	2,376,000	5,724,000	4,166,000	5,068,000
Black	8,618,000	18,937,000	17,450,000	28,396,000
Black majority	6,242,000	13,213,000	13,284,000	23,328,000

---

30 Geldenhuys, *Diplomacy of Isolation*, pp. 201-2.
31 See the surveys by Jannie Gagiano published in *Politikon*, 13 (1986), pp. 3-21 and in Gagiano and Hermann Giliomee (eds.), *The Elusive Search for Peace: South Africa, Northern Ireland and Israel* (Cape Town: Oxford University Press, 1990), pp. 191-208.
32 Nicolas Eberstadt, *A Tyranny of Numbers* (Washington: American Enterprise Institute, 1995).
33 *Die Beeld,* 5 and 19 January 1969.

According to Verwoerd's policy, the homelands by 2000 had to accommodate most of the anticipated increase of ten million blacks – from the 8.6 million recorded in the 1946 census to the 18.9 million projected for 2000 by Sadie. But these projections were dramatically wrong, and Sadie would later explain that the demographic tools of the early 1950s were still crude.[34] Already in 1974 the black total was 17.4 million, and by 1991 it stood at 28.3 million, ten million more than Sadie's projection for 2000.

The rapid black population growth reflected the considerable improvements in public health. The black population's rate of natural increase was 50 per cent higher in 1991-96 than in 1941-46. Life expectancy of blacks improved from thirty-eight to sixty-one during this period, from fifty-five to sixty-eight for Asians, from forty-six to sixty-two for colored people, and from sixty-six to seventy-three for whites. Similar major improvements were recorded in infant mortality rates (see table).[35] Eberstadt notes that the rate of infant deaths in the colored community fell by more than two-thirds between 1970 and 1985, mainly as a result of improved government services. He adds: 'Hardly any other population on record has to date enjoyed such a rapid and sustained pace of improvement in child survival.'[36]

INFANT MORTALITY RATES (PER THOUSAND BIRTHS)

	BLACKS	COLOREDS	ASIANS	WHITES
1946-51	162	128	57	36
1985-1991	60	43	15	11

As a result of the black population increase the cities became increasingly black. In 1970 five million blacks lived in the towns and cities in the common area (compared to two million in 1946) against a white population, both urban and rural, of fewer than four million. By 1991 the figures were nearly nine million urban blacks compared to a total white population of five million.[37]

In many ways South Africa was experiencing a quiet revolution far more wide-ranging in its impact that any conventional political revolution.[38] Desperate blacks streamed to the cities in pursuit of sheer survival. As migrants, they changed the racial composition of the urban centers, as consumers transformed the marketing strategies of business and as laborers broke down the color bar in industry. The most successful moved into some previously all-white suburbs although it was against the law; the least successful survived in sprawling squatter camps by scouring the refuse dumps on the perimeters of the cities. No one could still doubt that South Africa was predominantly a black country. More than half the black population was under the age of sixteen and increasingly beyond the control of government or family.

---

34 J.L. Sadie, 'The Political Arithmetic of the SA Population', *Tydskrif vir Rasse-aangeleenthede*, 4, 1 (1951) and an article under same title published in Pierre Hugo (ed.), *South African Perspectives* (Cape Town: Die Suid-Afrikaan, 1989).

35 J.L. Sadie, 'The Economic Demography of South Africa', doctoral diss., US, 2000, pp. 4-9.

36 Eberstadt, *The Tyranny of Numbers*, p. 160. See also SA Institute of Race Relations, *Fast Facts*, 3, 1996.

37 Sadie, 'The Economic Demography', p. 113.

38 John Kane-Berman, *The Silent Revolution* (Johannesburg: SA Institute of Race Relations, 1990).

By 1975 the Broederbond had sounded a somber warning to its divisions: 'The presence of so many blacks together with their ever greater political, economic and social bargaining power, coupled with the perpetual interference from the outside, means that we are approaching a catastrophe, even if we eliminate discrimination.'[39] The weight of black numbers forced a fundamental rethink about apartheid as the solution to Afrikaner survival. In 1982 Piet Cillié, ex-editor of *Die Burger*, expressed the reluctant coming to terms with these facts when speaking at the launch of *Swart verstedeliking* (Black Urbanization) by P. Smit and J. Booysen, a book on black urbanization. The book, he said, contained 'a tough and ominous message' for the Afrikaner. The dream had been shattered 'of a piece of the earth that is irrevocably his own or ought to be his own.' The Afrikaners 'had clung too long, against overwhelming evidence, to the dream of a homelands policy.' They were now being forced to make 'a reassessment so painful that one could pray that this cup would rather pass us by, yet there was no alternative'. He asked: 'What do we substitute for the vision of a promised land for the Afrikaners or the white nation?'[40]

The economic obsolescence of apartheid

Apartheid until the end of the 1960 probably boosted economic growth. The economy of the 1950s and early 1960s was still largely based on agriculture and mining. Employers could use large numbers of unskilled or poorly skilled black and colored labor wastefully and with little concern for productivity. Pass laws and curbs on black political and labor organizations severely restricted the ability of blacks to bargain for higher wages. The government spent little on the development of the homelands or on the rehabilitation of the poorest communities.

By the mid-1970s the period of continued high economic growth since the early 1930s had come to an end. The average annual rate of growth fell from an average of 4.5 per cent in the first thirty years of apartheid to an average of only 1.65 per cent between 1976 and 1994, well below the three per cent annual population increase. In these final eighteen years real per capita income slumped by about 25 per cent, with the poorest people the heaviest hit. The reasons for the economic decline were complex, and some of them were beyond the state's control, such as the sharp rise in energy prices after 1973, the weaker prices for South African gold and other commodity exports, and the slowdown of the growth of South Africa's main trading partners. As a comparative study points out, the economic crisis of the 1980s needs to be seen in perspective, as 'part of a slump which affected middle-income countries worldwide and South Africa has not suffered particularly badly.' The World Bank rated South Africa's performance measured in GDP growth between 1980 and 1985 as twelfth out of twenty comparable developing countries.[41]

---

39 E.L.P. Stals, 'Die geskiedenis van die Afrikaner-Broederbond, 1918-1994', unpublished ms., 1998, p. 374.

40 Piet Cillié, *Baanbrekers vir vryheid* (Cape Town: Tafelberg, 1990), pp. 42-4.

41 Terence Moll, 'From Booster to Brake?: Apartheid and Economic Growth in Comparative Perspective', N. Nattrass and E. Ardington (eds.), *The Political Economy of South Africa* (Cape Town: Oxford University Press, 1990), p. 83. See also Moll's 'Did the Apartheid Economy Fail?', *Journal of Southern African Studies*, 17, 2 (1991), pp. 271-91.

The policy of import substitution behind high tariff walls that had long been in place enabled the manufacturing sector to expand rapidly and boost economic growth. But economic opportunities provided by this policy had been exhausted by the 1970s, and South Africa was quite unprepared for the challenge of renewed growth through exporting manufactured goods. As late as the early 1990s South Africa's manufacturing exports per capita were lower than any upper-middle income country except Brazil.[42] South Africa's competitive advantage in building up a manufacturing sector between the late 1920s and the late 1960s was always its large supplies of cheap labor. The restrictions the government from the 1960s imposed on the employment of black labor on the Witwatersrand and other growth points encouraged employers to mechanize. This in turn helped to create an ever more serious unemployment problem among blacks. This problem was compounded by the extension of trade union rights to all during the 1970s. By the end of the 1970s South Africa's labor costs were outstripping those of its competitors and its competitive advantage in most sectors had dwindled.

Apartheid compounded the problems. At the height of the economic boom of the 1960s the *Financial Mail* warned: 'Race policies precluded the most economic use of the non-white labor force, thus aggravating the inflationary bottlenecks.'[43] Inflation would become a serious economic problem from the early 1970s. The other ways in which apartheid compounded the economic problems included curbs on the training of black and colored workers, the lack of proper funding for black and colored education, the poor productivity of workers, and the large distances the poorest of the workforce had to travel because of the group areas legislation.

Although he never said so in so many words, Hendrik Verwoerd always believed that, confronted with a choice between being rich and integrated and segregated and poor, the Afrikaners would choose the latter. But the strong surge of prosperity over which he presided tilted the scale heavily in favor of the former. Whites had become accustomed to economic growth producing steadily improved social circumstances and a comfortable lifestyle. Very few realized the momentous significance of the demographic shifts that were occurring. Historically, white dominance rested on numbers sufficient to fill not only the top but also the middle-level jobs, particularly in the manufacturing sector. Between 1910 and 1960 the white population formed 20 per cent of the total population, but after 1960 it dropped steadily to 17 per cent in 1976 and 12 per cent in 2000.

Between 1965 and 1980 the white share of middle-level manpower dropped from 82 per cent to 65 per cent. By the early 1970s whites contributed only a quarter of the increase in fully employed, skilled blue-collar workers. Increasingly, the economy had to rely on black and colored people in the manufacturing sectors of the economy and public administration.

Labor in the manufacturing sector had become predominantly black. In 1935, when South Africa had just embarked on its high growth path there were approximately 100,000 white and 100,000 black workers in manufacturing. By 1975 the black figure had trebled to 726,000, and it was now twice that of whites in the sector. It was not the numbers as such but the skill levels that were the crucial factor. Future economic growth

---

42 Gavin Maasdorp, 'Economic Survey, 1970-2000', unpublished paper.
43 *Financial Mail*, 14 July 1967, Supplement, p. 9.

depended on black skills, and those in turn depended on the establishment of institutions where black workers could bargain about working conditions. Even more important, to become a productive workforce they needed a stable living environment, which only industrial and political rights could provide. In short, they had to be allowed to become proper citizens.[44]

The 1970s were marked by numerous strikes by black and colored workers. Because trade union activity was severely restricted, employers were compelled to deal with leaderless striking workers, which the large corporations in particular considered increasingly burdensome. To meet the demand for a stable, skilled black labor force the government made some fundamental shifts. In 1973 it allowed blacks to do skilled work with the permission of the white unions. Soon afterwards that requirement was waived, along with other forms of job reservation and other labor controls. In response, the government in 1979 abolished the curbs on black labor and accepted the inclusion of trade unions with black members in the formal bargaining system.

The government also expanded the provision of high school education for people outside the dominant white group. In 1972, the government approved a new funding formula, allowing the expansion of black education, particularly in secondary schools. Many high schools were now built in the common area.

AFRICAN ENROLMENT IN HIGHER EDUCATION

Year	Secondary School	Highest standard (Std 10)	University students
1960	54,598	717	1,871
1970	122,489	2,938	4,578
1985	1,192,932	34,733	49,164

Source: Race Relations Survey for selected years

A serious problem confronted the government. The economy needed a flexible labor market and wage restraints to enable the formal sector to employ as many people as possible. But for political reasons it was important to increase black wages and narrow the huge gap between whites and blacks. Worker demands were reinforced by an international outcry over 'starvation wages' and racial disparities. After the Durban strikes of 1973 John Vorster urged employers to treat workers 'not as labor units, but human beings with souls.'[45] His government urged employers to narrow the wage gap and undertook to set an example in the civil service. It upset white labor, but it had become so dependent on state protection since the mid-1920s that it lacked the capacity to block these moves. During the 1970s the ratio of white to black wages in mining fell from 21:1 to 6:1 and in manufacturing from 6:1 to 4:1.[46]

Neither government nor employers ever resolved the tension between improved black

44 Moll, 'From Booster to Brake?' pp. 73-87.
45 *House of Assembly Debates*, 1973, col. 346.
46 Stephen Devereaux, *South African Income Distribution, 1900-1980* (Cape Town: University of Cape Town, SALDRU, 1983).

wages and black unemployment. Both employers and the government began giving wage increases higher than the inflation rate. To retain profit levels, employers cut jobs and demanded higher productivity. During the 1960s open black unemployment remained static, but from the mid-1970s there was a large and steadily expanding pool of labor which was 'surplus' to the needs of the modern economy. Black children advanced to school grades their parents could only dream of, but had far less chance of getting a formal job than their parents. In the 1960s, 97 per cent of school-leavers could expect to find employment, but this declined to 72 per cent in the 1970s and then to a mere 7 per cent in the late 1980s.[47] In the Soweto uprising of 1976 the majority who participated were school children and the unemployed – marginal groups who could challenge the system without sacrificing income.

While blacks were becoming industrial citizens the government still tried to prevent them from becoming political citizens. At the heart of the government's policy lay a form of political schizophrenia. On the one hand it wished to create a stable and contented black middle class. In 1977 blacks were allowed to take out a ninety-nine-year leasehold on their houses, implying recognition of their permanence in the common area. The Riekert Commission, which reported in 1979, proposed a two-tier approach towards blacks, dividing them between outsiders (mainly the migrant laborers from the homelands) and insiders. The insiders, qualified to live in the urban areas under Section 10, had the first claim to jobs and housing. A body of approximately two million people, they were relatively privileged, but they were in no enviable position since the other part of policy was to keep all blacks under surveillance. The government stalled when it came to abolishing the hated pass system, imposed on all blacks, with abolition strongly resisted by the police and those civil servants charged with regulating the lives of blacks. They told the government that the laws were necessary to control blacks and limit urbanization.

Despite the steady improvement of the wages of workers since the 1960s, the racial disparities were such that South Africa was near the top of the inequality league of the world. From the early 1970s the government and employers initiated a steady process of redistribution away from whites that changed the position considerably (see pp. 566-7). A significant redistribution of income was the result. By 1994, blacks contributed R23 billion to government revenue, and received R34 billion in cash and in-kind transfers from government, of which the largest part went to social welfare, housing, health and education. This was largely responsible for the budget deficits on the current account, which stood at R890 million in 1982 and reached R28 billion in 1994. Government dissaving (loans to cover current spending) in the previous twelve years amounted to a massive R131 billion.[48]

Whites still received nearly half of the amount the state spent on social services, but they were receiving much less in services than the amount of tax they paid, while blacks were receiving considerably more.[49] Spending on social welfare for colored and Asians

47 J. Hofmeyr, 'The South African Labour Market', unpublished paper, 1996.

48 Jan Sadie, *The Fall and Rise of the Afrikaner in the South African Economy* (Stellenbosch: University of Stellenbosch Annale, 2002), p. 45. Implicit in the computations is the assumption that blacks did not have to pay for the administration, defense, policing and justice.

49 *Cape Times*, 8 March 1996.

rose at an even more rapid rate than that on blacks, and accelerated after 1984 when the government embarked on systematically reducing the disparities that still existed between the three groups that participated in the Tricameral Parliament.

This social spending contributed to the serious fiscal crisis that the state experienced from the mid-1970s. Other major costs were related to the costly war in Namibia and Angola, the huge effort to become self-sufficient in armaments, the expansion of the civil service and the attempt to mollify the white civil servants when the government began experiencing reverses at the polls. There were the large expenses and opportunity costs related to the government's efforts in the 1970s and 1980s to develop decentralized 'growth points' both in the 'border areas' and in the homelands themselves in a futile effort to make the homeland economies viable. By the end of the 1980s it was found that the economic decentralization policy was both flawed and costly.

A severe tax burden now weighed heavily on middle-class whites. In the first half of the 1980s the average proportion of income that middle-income whites paid in taxes trebled. According to an International Monetary Fund study, whites in 1987 paid on average 32 per cent of their incomes in tax, but received only 9 per cent back in benefits.[50] This set the stage for a sharp white political backlash and a vociferous campaign against redistribution by the Afrikaner right wing, with workers and civil servants in the lower ranks in the vanguard.

'If all goes well with the Afrikaner . . .'

In some ways Botha thought quite differently about Afrikaner survival than his predecessors. By the 1970s Afrikaners had shrunk to less than 10 per cent of the population, and neither they nor the larger white community could do without political allies for much longer. But if there was a clearer recognition of political vulnerability on the part of Botha, he still put the Afrikaners and the NP as their instrument at the center of the South African political universe. As he phrased it: 'As long as all goes well with the Afrikaner nation, all will go well with the other language groups and peace will prevail, but if one begins to demolish the Afrikaner nation in its finest form, its splendid history and its splendid traditions, one is chipping away at the cornerstone of the South African structure.'[51]

There was a double-edged quality to the Botha government's acceptance of the need for reforms. There was, on the one hand, a new willingness to agree that income and opportunities would have to be shared more equitably among all the peoples. On the other hand, there was the firm conviction that a strong NP, leading a solid bloc of Afrikaners and retaining power was a prerequisite for successful reform.

To keep his political base Botha insisted on retaining the cornerstones of apartheid like the group areas, segregated education and racially based political participation. His idea of reform was to devolve more functions and funds to the apartheid structures introduced for black, colored and Indian people. Their leaders could ultimately have a say on the executive level where matters of common concern were discussed, but there could

---

50 Cited by F.W. de Klerk in a submission to the Truth and Reconciliation Commission, 21 August 1996.
51 Pottinger, *The Imperial Presidency*, p. 51.

be no mixed legislature for all the different peoples where numbers would be the deciding factor.

Botha saw South Africa's real challenge as providing jobs for the rapidly growing large population by promoting faster economic growth. From the start he emphasized the importance of the private sector as the engine of growth.[52] When he assumed power both Afrikaner and English business leaders had become very concerned about the growth of the public corporations. Their share of the economy nearly doubled between 1948 and 1976 and their share of capital formation increased from 43 per cent in 1960 to an average of 51 per cent in the years 1975-1979.[53] In 1977, *Assault on Private Enterprise* by Andreas Wassenaar, non-executive chairman of Sanlam, accused the government of considering state-owned corporations as Afrikanerdom's answer to the 'somewhat overwhelming non-Afrikaner interests in mining and industry.'[54] Botha eased business anxieties by committing his government to keep a tight rein on the expansion of parastatal corporations. By 1990 their share of capital formation stood at 36 per cent.

In 1979 Botha invited top business leaders to a conference at the Carlton Hotel in Johannesburg to propose a partnership between the state and the private sector for building an economically prosperous South Africa. He proposed forming a Constellation of Southern African states, consisting of South Africa, the homelands and the independent African states in the southern African region, joining together to eradicate poverty by promoting growth and job-creation. Although these proposals failed to materialize, Botha had impressed business leaders with his businesslike approach and his eagerness to solicit their help in addressing the country's most acute problems.

He soon embarked on wide-ranging administrative reforms to improve the capacity of the state. Under Vorster the dominant image of the state had been that of a poorly managed Afrikaner family firm, with a proliferation of unco-ordinated cabinet committees and rampant departmentalism. Botha thoroughly overhauled the machinery of the government; he strengthened the prime minister's office, established a proper cabinet secretariat, reduced the cabinet committees to four, and brought the number of state departments down from thirty-nine to twenty-two.

Botha turned the State Security Council into a key body to discuss and resolve issues in the field of security and foreign policy. He chaired the body on which ministers dealing with security and other strategic interests sat, together with the heads of the various security agencies. The council supervised the working of a National Security Management System, with Joint Management Centers for twelve national regions, sub-JMCs for metropolitan centers and mini-JMCs for each town, where officials and businessmen met under the chairmanship of a military or police officer. The JMCs provided information on local security issues and acted as an early warning system by spotting areas of friction and identifying bureaucratic obstacles to improvements in living conditions in the townships. Behind this lay a managerial approach, which assumed that blacks were primarily interested in having their social needs met.[55]

52 J.J.J. Scholtz, *Vegter en hervormer* (Cape Town: Tafelberg, 1988), pp. 65-7.
53 J.L. Sadie, book review in *Die Burger*, 4 March 1977; USA Senate, Committee on Foreign Relations, *Report on US Corporate Interests, 1978*, p. 25.
54 Andreas Wassenaar, *Assault on Private Enterprise* (Cape Town: Tafelberg, 1977), p. 123.
55 Robert Schrire, *Adapt or Die: The End of White Politics in South Africa* (London: Hurst, 1992), pp. 31-46.

The nettle of constitutional reform

Botha was in a hurry to grasp the nettle of constitutional reform. But for any successful reform some crucial questions had to be addressed properly. The first was whether Botha, as a leader elected by the NP caucus, could introduce reform that would acquire broad legitimacy. There was the suggestion that the envisaged president should be elected by a poll of white voters. With his own electoral base, such a figure would enjoy greater legitimacy. But Botha would have none of this. Personally the least popular of all Afrikaner leaders, he felt the risk of losing was too real. He wanted, in the words of Mangosuthu Buthelezi, Chief Minister of Natal, to be the 'author of change, the arbiter in the conflict about change and the determiner of what can and cannot be done about change.'[56] The deliberations about a new constitution occurred in smoke-filled NP committee rooms with party unity the first consideration and the legitimacy beyond party ranks only a distant second.

The second major question was whether constitutional change should be piecemeal, initially incorporating only the colored and Asian communities, which formed eight and three per cent of the population respectively, or whether it should, from the start, include blacks. The fateful road that the government did take was to bring coloreds and Asians into Parliament, but not blacks. To the more enlightened voters it explained that demolishing the symbolism of white supremacy and exclusivity could not happen in one fell swoop, and that the incorporation of blacks would soon follow. To its more conservative supporters it stressed the need for winning support beyond white ranks. The NP's chief information officer appealed to the right wing's survival instincts. He wrote to Andries Treurnicht, leader of the right-wing faction: ' I would like to know your view on the idea that we at any price have got to associate the coloreds as a bloc of 2.5 million with the whites in order to broaden our own power base, and not surrender them to the "black-power" situation.'[57]

By 1980 acute tensions had developed in the NP between the factions under Botha and Treurnicht. The latter faction could still stomach colored and Indian representation in segregated Parliaments, but Botha insisted that there could be only one government in one country. On 24 February 1982 Treurnicht and twenty-one other NP members of Parliament left the caucus and formed the Conservative Party (CP). Previously the NP had suffered 'splinters', but this was the end of Afrikaner nationalist unity, cultivated over so many decades.

The NP presented the constitution as a form of 'healthy' power-sharing, one in which the NP could not be outvoted by a coalition of the white opposition, coloreds and Indians. There was now a Parliament with a white, a colored and an Indian chamber elected on separate rolls according to a fixed 4:2:1 ratio that corresponded with population size. An electoral college drawn from all three houses elected an executive state president. Each house had its own cabinet and budget to deal with the 'own' affairs of its community, mainly education, housing and social welfare. There were also 'general' affairs (defense, security, and economic policy). Bills were discussed and passed separately by each house.

---

56 Jack Smith, *Buthelezi: The Biography* (Melville: Hans Strydom, 1988), p. 161.
57 Alf Ries and Ebbe Dommisse, *Broedertwis* (Cape Town: Tafelberg, 1982), p. 112.

The power-sharing element was introduced by the requirement that all houses had to approve a bill and that colored and Indian ministers could serve in the general affairs cabinet (Botha appointed the leaders of the colored and Indian chambers to his cabinet). But the lever of white control was retained; the NP as the largest party in the white chamber effectively elected the state president, who could use a President's Council, a multi-racial advisory body of experts mostly supportive of him, to break any deadlocks if a house refused to pass a bill. It was, as the saying of the time went, a form of 'sharing power without losing control.'

In a 1983 referendum the NP presented the constitution as merely a first step in an unspecified 'right direction.' The liberal opposition opposed the constitution as a provocation to blacks by its underlining of their political exclusion, and Buthelezi slammed it. But Chris Heunis, the tough, resourceful and overbearing Minister for Constitutional Development, managed to persuade the Labour Party, the main colored party working within the system, to participate, which set the ball rolling. The NP held a referendum of white voters in which two-thirds of the voters approved the draft constitution. Subsequently elections for the colored and Indian chambers were held, which showed a lack of broad-based legitimacy. Only 30 per cent of the registered colored voters and 24 per cent of the Indians bothered to vote. The system was introduced in September 1984 with Botha as the first elected state president.

Blacks in general saw the partial incorporation of colored people and Indians as a blunt rejection of their demand for common citizenship. Their alienation was aggravated when the government offered the homelands system, together with a new system of segregated black local authorities, as a reason for denying blacks any representation at all in Parliament.

For the government the apartheid model of ten black homelands, each with its own government, held a fatal attraction that blinded it to the need for imaginative responses to escape from a blind alley. The homeland governments, each with its own chief ministers, cabinets, legislatures and fully-fledged civil service, offered channels for black advancement that did not threaten whites. In general these governments concerned themselves with homeland affairs, and did not attempt to extract meaningful concessions from Pretoria.

The exception was Mangosuthu Buthelezi, chief minister of the KwaZulu homeland in Natal. He was also the only internal black leader with any mass following who could act as a counter to the ANC. His tough stand against independence for the Zulu people, forming 20 per cent of the total population, more than any other opposition destroyed the government's hope to construct 'a constellation of black states' out of the homeland system. But in 1979 he fell out with the ANC in exile over the issue of sanctions and the armed struggle. The ANC-Inkatha relationship deteriorated into bitter enmity, with the ANC branding Buthelezi as a counter-revolutionary force. It correctly saw him as much more dangerous than the other homeland leaders, who were, it said, mere puppets. Buthelezi thought that the armed struggle and sanctions were destroying the chance for peaceful change. Yet he also told Botha that violence could not be averted 'by marching to anti-communist drums.' Violence would flow not from Marxist subversion but from white and black leaders' losing control of their constituencies.[58]

---

58 Smith, *Buthelezi*, p. 153.

Buthelezi offered a clear alternative to the NP approach by proposing a multi-racial federation. In 1981 a commission he appointed proposed the integration of the white-controlled province of Natal and the KwaZulu homeland, to be run by an assembly elected by proportional representation and a multi-racial executive making decisions along power-sharing lines. A single body would control education, the local economy and welfare services. These proposals were given flesh by a multi-racial Natal *indaba* in the mid-1980s, and received the backing of the business leadership in the province and the liberal opposition. Here was a last opportunity for the government to avoid losing control over the process of change. If it backed regional integration in KwaZulu-Natal (without trying to control it), it could spark similar initiatives in other regions of the country. From these regions properly elected black leaders could be elevated to the national cabinet. The risks to the NP would be counter-balanced by the advantages of powerful, legitimate black leaders in central government within a federal system. This would stave off some of the internal and international pressures.[59]

Botha's response was in the classic apartheid mode. Buthelezi was welcome to investigate matters that concerned 'his own country', but had no right to deal with matters under the control of central government.[60] Both Vorster and Botha had a poor grasp of modern black politics. Vorster, on the basis of a conversation with a black attorney, believed that black professionals supported radical nationalist organizations only out of narrow self-interest. Botha was deeply suspicious of the ANC, and tended to think it was too subject to communist influence. The Broederbond discussed policy extensively, but only within the framework of apartheid and without hearing the voices of black academics or black professionals. It was only after the Soweto uprising that Gerrit Viljoen proposed meetings of the Afrikaner youth with their militant black counterparts.[61]

By the late 1970s the idea of economically viable homelands had hopelessly faded. Even the Transkei, the best prospect, could meet only 10 per cent of its own food requirements and out of its own resources provided for only 20 per cent of its budgeted expenses. The great majority of people in the homelands were dependent on pensions and the money migrant laborers sent back to their families, most of which flowed back to shops in the common area. Migrant labor thus served as an engine that generated an ever-greater dependency and poverty of blacks in the homelands.[62]

Despite the failure to help the homelands to become economically viable, the government tried to push the policy to its 'logical conclusion.' In the government's scheme of things as many homelands as possible had to become independent, regardless of their viability. The object of the exercise was to reduce the numbers of blacks that could claim South African citizenship. As the homelands became independent, the basis of discrimination, in the government's eyes, would shift from race, which was objectionable to the world, to citizenship of an 'independent country.' Connie Mulder, who became Minister for Plural Relations (previously Bantu Administration and Development) in 1978, open-

59 Lawrence Schlemmer, cited by Roger Southall in 'Buthelezi, Inkatha and the Politics of Compromise', *African Affairs*, 80, 321 (1981), pp. 453-81.

60 Smith, *Buthelezi*, p. 162.

61 Stals, 'Geskiedenis van die AB', pp. 364-89.

62 Hermann Giliomee and Lawrence Schlemmer (eds.), *Up Against the Fences: Poverty, Passes and Privilege in South Africa* (Cape Town: David Philip, 1985).

ly stated that once all the homelands had become independent there would be no black South Africans.

In 1976 the South African government gave 'independence' to the Transkei, although it was the only government in the world that recognized it. The Transkei in 1976 was followed by Bophuthatswana in 1977, Ciskei in 1979 and Venda in 1980. With independence, their citizens, even if they lived in the common area, lost their South African citizenship. In 1981, Xhosa living in squatter camps in Cape Town were deported to their 'independent homeland' under laws covering aliens. The government classified funds supplied to the homelands as 'foreign aid.'

In 1981 Piet Koornhof, the minister who was now responsible for dealing with blacks, bluntly spelled out the political arithmetic of apartheid in its final, surrealistic phase. He observed that already 7.8 million blacks were 'independent citizens', and some 5.6 million blacks were tied to other homelands whose government had expressed an interest in becoming independent. The only homelands that refused to accept independence were likely to be KwaZulu and another tiny homeland. Their combined population was 6.25 million, fewer than the combined 7.8 million whites, coloreds, and Indians living in the common area. His startling conclusion was that 'with so many black people independent, it will be useless for South Africa's enemies to continue pleading for one man one vote.'[63]

A divided Afrikanerdom

The NP split in 1982 was the product of profound socio-economic changes. The NP government never kept only Afrikaner interests in mind, and from the 1960s accelerated the gradual redistribution from whites to the disenfranchised. But by the early 1970s the high growth rate that had made it possible to maintain Afrikaner unity and increase social spending on the subordinate population ended.

The high economic growth between 1933 and 1973 had also profoundly changed the composition of the Afrikaners in terms of jobs, creating conflicts that the NP was unable to contain.

AFRIKANER JOB COMPOSITION

	1936 %	1946 %	1960 %	1980 %	1990 %
Agriculture	41	30	16	7	5
Blue-collar	31	41	40	32	29
White collar	28	29	44	62	66

Source: Jan Sadie, The Fall and Rise of the Afrikaner in the South African Economy, p. 54.

The Conservatives led by Treurnicht included the white workers still insisting on a color bar, the less prosperous farmers opposing the government's cuts of farm subsidies, and civil servants on the lower ranks, whose standard of living was being eroded by high in-

63 Schrire, *Adapt or Die*, p. 52.

flation and taxes.[64] On the reformist side were businessmen who wanted the constraints on black labor to be removed, professional people and academics who increasingly aligned themselves with the universal commitments of their occupation, and journalists, academics, writers and poets, long a mainstay of NP support, who were embarrassed by the inability of apartheid to deal with the black, colored and Asian elites.[65] The Afrikaner Broederbond was no longer able to reconcile intra-Afrikaner differences.

By the mid-1970s virtually the only factor still holding the Afrikaner nationalists together was the belief that Afrikaner political control was a precondition for their existence as a national group. Some in the cultural elite believed that the Afrikaners had a God-given duty to preserve their cultural identity and perhaps also that of other peoples. But among the Afrikaner rank and file the survival of the Afrikaans culture and language ranked low, probably because it was felt that there was little to fear while the NP government made it a special concern.[66] Polls found that fears over the future of the Afrikaans language now ranked in importance only eighth or ninth out of ten indicators, well below the pursuit or defense of material interests.[67] For middle-class Afrikaners survival increasingly meant the maintenance of their lifestyle under a government it could trust.

Botha had considerably more leeway than his predecessors, since large numbers of English-speakers were up for grabs. A new fluidity in white politics had developed after the United Party, led by Sir De Villiers Graaff for more than twenty years, disintegrated in 1977. Between 25 and 40 per cent of English-speakers were sympathetic to the NP's cautious approach to reform. The old Afrikaner-English antipathies had largely dissolved as a result of the common pressure and censure whites faced, both from within and without. This created the opportunity for the NP to project itself as the broadly based coalition that the United Party during the 1930s represented.

Despite English electoral support, the NP leadership made no real effort to incorporate talented English-speakers in decision-making; the NP debate over survival remained a narrow and exclusive Afrikaner one with little or no lateral thinking. Botha and his senior ministers were happy to accept English electoral support, but had little enthusiasm for changing the character of the party, the set pattern of interacting with Afrikaner lobbies and pressure groups, and the camaraderie and mutual trust of an ethnic movement. Botha had risen in the NP as a party organizer, and until he went to Parliament had never known another employer. There was 'an indestructible bond of attachment between him and the party', a friend observed.[68] If Botha, or before him Vorster, did not want to change faster it was not so much because they lacked the base for it, but because they did not want to jeopardize the host of ties that bound the NP as an ethnic party together.

Treurnicht tried to revive the pre-reform Afrikaner nationalist movement by proposing that the clock be turned back to the mid-1960s, when whites under Verwoerd seemed assured of security and boundless progress. Like Verwoerd, he claimed that whites occu-

64 Johann van Rooyen, *Hard Right* (London: I.B. Tauris, 1994), pp. 27-35.

65 Frederik van Zyl Slabbert, *The System and the Struggle* (Johannesburg: Jonathan Ball, 1989), pp. 16-18.

66 Lawrence Schlemmer, *Social Research in a Divided Society* (Pietermaritzburg: University of Natal Press, 1973), p. 15.

67 Lawrence Schlemmer, 'Factors in the Persistence or Decline of Ethnic Group Mobilization: Afrikaners in Post-Apartheid South Africa', doctoral diss., UCT, 1999, pp. 180-93.

68 De Villiers and de Villiers, *PW*, p. 38.

pied the land that was historically theirs and that his party was not racist because it granted to blacks the land that supposedly was theirs.[69] But Afrikaner nationalism had lost its
élan and was without clear goals. It could only be galvanized by the threat of military invasion or the nationalization of the land or industries. The solutions the CP under Treurnicht offered had all been totally discredited. There was no black homeland or black or
colored township that was financially viable.

Yet because the NP government was increasingly distrusted by conservatives Treurnicht
was able to take large numbers of Afrikaners with him. By 1987 the votes of all the right-
wing parties in the general election amounted to almost 30 per cent of all votes, and the
Conservative Party had become the official opposition. By the end of the 1980s nearly
half of the Afrikaners voted for right-wing parties. In general Afrikaner expectations of
black rule were negative. More than four-fifths of Afrikaners in polls taken in 1979, 1984
and 1987 believed that under black majority rule there would be reverse discrimination,
and that the Afrikaans language and culture would be threatened. There was also another
dimension of fear. More than 80 per cent believed that the physical safety of whites would
be threatened, that white possessions would not be safe, and that white women would be
molested. Less than 10 per cent thought that life would continue as before.[70] The extent
of the fears was visible in the ownership of firearms – one firearm per white adult. These
fears translated into growing right-wing support.

Botha himself tried to revive the idea of consolidating the homelands, but it attracted
no support. He spoke incessantly of the Afrikaner being willing to fight for his birthright,
but he gave no indication of how the collapse of influx control and the integration of the
workplace, the main social phenomena of the 1970s and 1980s, could be resisted by arms.

Since the mid-1980s the government's own polling agency had showed that the ANC
would receive more than 60 per cent of the vote in a free election, while the NP could rely
on only 19 to 23 per cent.[71] The ANC strongly insisted on what it called an 'ordinary
democracy.' This meant a liberal democracy on the British model in a unitary state, without checks, such as a second house, to safeguard minority rights.

To Botha and the electorate this was totally unacceptable. A 1988 poll found that only
3 per cent of Afrikaners against 11 per cent of English-speakers accepted a single party
with the majority in control. Only 1 per cent of Afrikaners and 3 percent of English-
speakers wanted Nelson Mandela in power, against 12 per cent and 39 per cent respectively who wanted Buthelezi in power. Whites were worried that the ANC leadership still
subscribed to the Freedom Charter, which called for the nationalization of some strategic
sectors.

On the other hand, whites had come round to accepting the prospect of blacks in government, provided the new, multi-racial order guaranteed security, predictable politicians, competent civil servants, a strong economy and secure property rights. They had
no faith in the ANC with its insistence on simple majority rule; instead they wanted a

---

69 Van Rooyen, *Hard Right*, pp. 35-54.
70 Pierre Hugo, 'Towards Darkness and Death', in P. Hugo (ed.), *South African Perspectives* (Cape Town: *Die
Suid-Afrikaan*, 1989), pp. 254-55; Van Rooyen, *Hard Right*, pp. 54-61.
71 De Klerk, *Die laaste trek*, p. 207.

system with a balance between the new black majority and the other racial minorities. But their expectations of what whites needed to concede were still quite unrealistic.[72]

A liberal or a liberated order?

Back in the early 1930s Albert Geyer, editor of *Die Burger*, correctly predicted that only an alliance of the Afrikaner workers and the intelligentsia could successfully challenge the coalition between Hertzog's NP and Smuts' South African Party (p. 415). By the early 1980s the NP had lost the workers, and the question now was whether the intelligentsia would also defect. Most of the NP-supporting intelligentsia believed that a stable state under NP control remained essential for any reform leading to a freer and more humane society. The Afrikaner intelligentsia who had abandoned the NP agreed that a stable state was essential for a fundamental change to the system, but they increasingly questioned the NP leadership's course of action and its insistence on party unity that made possible only marginal reforms. They also suspected the state of fomenting violence through repressive measures and of waging war against its opponents under cloak of security, triggering a spiral of violence and making any negotiated settlement ever more difficult.

It was in this framework that the Stellenbosch philosopher André du Toit entered the debate with an essay, 'Facing up to the Future', which he expanded into a book, *Die sondes van die vaders* (The Sins of the Fathers). On the cover of his book, Van Wyk Louw's striking words were printed in bold type: 'Can a small people survive for long if it represents something hateful, something evil, in the eyes of the best in – or outside – its fold?' In a somber analysis Du Toit concluded that the moral crisis of Afrikaner power and survival would become ever more acute. The government's insistence that power was essential to ensure Afrikaners' cultural survival would almost inevitably encourage black nationalists to define that culture as its enemy. To survive it was imperative to detach the Afrikaans culture from Afrikaner power.

Du Toit also presented the struggle as one between Afrikaner generations. An older generation was unable to contemplate any future beyond Afrikaner nationalism. A younger generation, however, was facing the prospect of an endless military struggle without a convincing rationale. Uncompromising in its argument, the book offered little comfort. It did not try to persuade the Afrikaners that their language and culture would still thrive under black majority rule. Indeed, one of the implications of the argument was that Afrikaners in future would have to worry about other issues.[73]

Du Toit's essential point was that the moment had arrived that Van Wyk Louw had called 'the dark night of the soul' where a choice had to be made between mere survival and survival in justice. His argument was not meant to influence the ordinary voter, but the people Van Wyk Louw called 'the best', the creative intellectuals. It was their duty to advocate the surrender of power. They were few in number, but Van Wyk Louw had argued that because the Afrikaner people was so small, they would have a profound impact if they declared that they 'despair[ed] of the state.'

---

72 Lawrence Schlemmer, 'South Africa's National Party Government', Peter Berger and Bobby Godsell (eds.), *A Future South Africa* (Cape Town: Human & Rousseau/Tafelberg 1988), pp. 7-28.

73 André du Toit, *Die sondes van die vaders* (Cape Town: Rubicon, 1983), p. 26. An earlier version was published as 'Facing up to the Future', *Social Dynamics*, 7 (1981).

By the end of the 1970s very few of the most outstanding academics, writers and poets still identified with the NP and apartheid. The only one who challenged Du Toit's argument was Jaap Steyn, who pointed out that there was no longer any danger that the Afrikaner intelligentsia would fail to object to injustice. It was rather that merciless criticism of Afrikaner domination could prompt a younger generation to 'write off' the Afrikaners as a people, and their culture. Van Wyk Louw had warned against this as well.[74]

The opposition politician who made the most important contribution to the debate was Frederik van Zyl Slabbert. At Stellenbosch he had studied to become a minister in the DRC, but turned back from the conventional march through the nationalist institutions. He became a lecturer in sociology at the university before moving on to other universities and later entering politics as a member of the liberal Progressive Party. His academic analysis of the nationalist movement, published in 1975, led him to conclude that electorally the government was vulnerable only from the right. At the same time pressure from the extra-parliamentary forces would intensify, which would increasingly put heavy pressure on the economy and would threaten the prospects of both enfranchised and disfranchised.[75]

In 1979 Slabbert became leader of the Progressive Reform Party (PRP), which was now the official opposition in the wake of the United Party's demise in 1977. Slabbert was a fresh breeze in the increasingly stale parliamentary politics, which were attracting ever fewer of the best talents of white society. The nationalists did not quite know how to deal with him, and in the four years they were in Parliament together John Vorster refused to greet Slabbert. Here he was: among the best and brightest in the Afrikaner community, someone passionate about Afrikaans, the writings of Van Wyk Louw and the poetry of Breyten Breytenbach, but repelled by the Afrikaners' political nationalism which he saw as a dire threat to society. He was forceful without being overbearing, highly persuasive, charismatic, a man with a razor-sharp analytical mind. 'His style is so utterly different', a reporter observed. 'It is his unique ability to reduce politics to a series of simple, logical arguments that progress to a single, devastating conclusion.'[76]

That conclusion was that apartheid had irreversibly failed. Time and again he ridiculed the huge gap between the promises of apartheid ideology and the sordid reality. He distinguished between sham and genuine reforms, arguing that sham reforms were very dangerous because they created the illusion of change and a false sense of security.[77] His immediate objective was a political realignment, bringing reformists across party ranks together. Once that had happened the serious task of preparing whites for white-black negotiations for a new constitution could begin.

In 1979 a book that Slabbert co-authored with David Welsh, a political scientist, was published. It provided the intellectual backing for the shift in Progressive policy that Slab-

---

74 J.C. Steyn, 'n Tuiste in eie taal (Cape Town: Tafelberg, 1980), pp. 452-3. For a further discussion see my '"Survival in Justice": An Afrikaner Debate over Apartheid', Comparative Studies in Society and History, 36, 3 (1994), pp. 527-48.

75 It is re-published in Frederik van Zyl Slabbert, The System and the Struggle (Johannesburg: Jonathan Ball, 1989), pp. 21-2.

76 Ivor Wilkins, 'This Man Who Guides the Ordinary People', Sunday Times, 19 April 1981.

77 Hermann Giliomee, The Parting of the Ways: South African Politics (Cape Town: David Philip, 1982), pp. ix-xix.

bert had proposed, from qualified franchise to universal franchise. In the view of Slabbert and Welsh, whites were left with only two options: prolonged siege, leading to a 'near-war situation with full-scale military and paramilitary mobilization', and negotiation by representative leadership, with both sides genuinely seeking compromise through a process of bargaining.[78] The study envisaged a new system that entrenched individual rights, encouraged power-sharing through a grand coalition of black and white parties, and gave a veto right to minorities in crucial issues. In the final paragraph the authors acknowledged that it was almost impossible to persuade the white electorate to give up sole power. It would be an uncertain future since a mass-based black party that received enough votes could avoid having to enter into a coalition and could sweep aside the minority veto. So they appealed to Max Weber who wrote that only by reaching out for the impossible could man attain the possible. 'It may be that politics in South Africa will be the art of the impossible. Is this not a challenge worth accepting?'[79]

The government's proposals for the Tricameral Parliament increased the gulf between Slabbert and Botha. Polls had shown that more than half of the electorate believed that society would be fully integrated in twenty years' time. Slabbert felt that the government ought to have used the referendum held in 1983 to test the waters for incorporating blacks into Parliament. The government's priority, however, was to keep the NP as a party together. Although respecting Slabbert's intellectual abilities, the NP leadership spurned his approach, failing to realize that the estrangement of the white liberal opposition would greatly diminish its prospects of getting credible support from leaders across the color line.

An urban uprising

Credible political institutions for blacks living in the common area had always been the weakest link in the apartheid system. The government tinkered with black local government, stumbling from one disaster to the other. In the wake of the Soweto uprising, a government commission identified black anger over the Administration Boards that ran the townships as a major cause. In the early 1980s the government developed the most disastrous model of all: black local authorities with almost all the powers of their white counterparts, but without a viable revenue base. Few township residents owned property, with the result that the revenue that could be raised by rates was extremely limited. In many townships the beer halls, a main source of revenue, had been destroyed in the Soweto rebellion of 1976 and the subsequent turmoil, and there was no formula for redirecting to the townships the revenue that the neighboring white town or city derived from blacks.

In 1984 black local authorities were elected throughout the country in polls with a low voter turnout. Many residents had stopped paying house rent and the charges for water and electricity. Undeterred, the new councils sharply increased the price of rent and electricity. In September 1984 riots broke out in the Vaal Triangle, southeast of Johannesburg. The local mayor and the deputy mayor were among the first to be killed.

---

78 Slabbert, *The System and the Struggle*, pp. 45-7.
79 Frederik van Zyl Slabbert and David Welsh, *South Africa's Options* (Cape Town: David Philip, 1979), p. 171.

As in the case of the 1976 uprising, the outbreak of violence in the Vaal Triangle in 1984 was not planned or fomented by the African National Congress. But the ANC, with the help of its ally, the South African Communist Party, had established itself as the premier organization challenging the state. In the diplomatic field it had scored major successes in lobbying for diplomatic and economic sanctions. As part of its armed struggle it had carried out 362 violent acts between 1976 and 1983. ANC guerrillas had struck at some high-profile targets, including a SASOL (oil from coal) plant in 1980, the Voortrekkerhoogte military base in Pretoria in 1981, and the Koeberg nuclear reactor near Cape Town in 1982. An ANC car bomb exploded in 1983 at the Air Force headquarters in Church Street, a major street in the city center of Pretoria, killing nineteen people.

In 1979 an ANC delegation had visited Vietnam to learn the tactics the Vietcong had used against the US. It returned convinced of the appropriateness of waging a 'people's war' in the townships with the aim of making them 'ungovernable.' This type of struggle combined high-profile armed attacks by trained units with mass campaigns of civil disobedience. The rebellion that broke out in September 1984 continued with great intensity until the middle of 1986. It was much more broadly based than in 1976, when the Black Consciousness Movement was the main source of inspiration for children and students but lacked the organizational capacity to sustain the protests. The range of protests was also much wider than in 1976. Clergy, students, teachers, lecturers, business people, women's groups and workers mobilized for the dismantling of the apartheid system. There was better strategic thinking and far more successful mobilization of international opinion.

Since the press itself was freer than in 1976, the protests were also much better reported in local and international media, until the state clamped down. The ANC leaders, particularly Oliver Tambo, who had been living in exile for twenty-five years, and Nelson Mandela, Walter Sisulu and Govan Mbeki, who had spent more than twenty years in jail, had acquired almost mythical status in the eyes of the people engaged in the struggle, as well as large sections of the international community.

With the ANC, Pan Africanist Congress and Black Consciousness Movement all banned, radical opponents of the system formed a decentralized umbrella organization consisting of a range of community organizations, trade unions, church bodies and student movements. One of the umbrella bodies was the National Forum, founded in the Black Consciousness tradition. As a result of its radical economic proposals, the forum was starved of funding and largely ineffective despite the presence of talented intellectuals, like Neville Alexander. By far the largest umbrella body was the United Democratic Front (UDF), founded in 1983 as a front for the ANC. As a non-racial organization that welcomed white participation and did not oppose the capitalist system, it received the bulk of foreign funds flowing to organizations in the country.

Two other ANC-aligned organizations were the Congress of South African Trade Unions (COSATU), formed in 1985 out of the previous Federation of South African Trade Unions, which represented the great majority of workers, and the Congress of South African Students (COSAS), which developed out of the youth congresses founded after the Soweto uprising. COSAS members were often called the 'lost generation' – people who after 1976 refused to return to school or attended only intermittently and who now could not find work. Even in Soweto, not noted for high unemployment, almost half of new work-seekers could not get a job in the formal economy.[80]

The protests in the townships of the Vaal Triangle in September 1984 quickly spread to other parts of Transvaal, and to Natal and the eastern Cape. There were numerous symbolic stay-aways and strikes by workers, rent and service charge boycotts, consumer boycotts and marches, often headed by churchmen with mass student participation. In many townships crowds attacked the houses of black town councilors, forcing their resignation and eventually the collapse of the system of local government. They also burned government buildings, shops and liquor outlets. Activists firebombed the houses of black policemen to drive them out of the townships and killed many suspected informers, sometimes by lighting a petrol-soaked rubber tyre placed around the victim's neck. This grisly form of reprisal soon led to the sources of information of the police drying up. The funerals of people who died in clashes with the police became highly charged occasions with the coffins often covered by an ANC flag. Foreign diplomats attended the funerals of prominent activists suspected of being killed by the security forces.

After police opened fire on a peaceful crowd in March 1985 in Uitenhage, the protests spread to Cape Town and other parts of the western Cape. Bombs exploded in Durban and Johannesburg on 16 June, the anniversary of the Soweto uprising. On 20 July 1985 the government declared a state of emergency in some magisterial districts. Two days later the ANC responded by way of a call by its leader Oliver Tambo to make South Africa ungovernable. But severe repressive measures by the state steadily decimated the leadership of the uprising. By November 1985 some eight thousand UDF leaders had been detained. Many leaders of their national and regional executives had been killed, were in jail or had fled the country. In Natal and KwaZulu the competition for turf between Inkatha and the ANC reached the intensity of a low-level civil war.

The government continued with reform in order to regain investor confidence. It kept those pillars of apartheid it considered essential (population registration, segregated education, and the exclusion of blacks from Parliament), while it removed those parts of apartheid deemed to be 'unnecessary.' It granted urban blacks across the country full residential rights and repealed the racial sex laws. In 1986 it scrapped the pass laws and in 1987 allowed blacks full freehold rights to property. It turned a blind eye to inner city areas that were becoming integrated. Public facilities were desegregated on a broad front. All forms of formal job discrimination had been ended. There was still a gap in the spending per capita on pupils. It was widest between white and black children. It stood at 1:7 in 1954 when 'Bantu education' was introduced, rose to an average of 1:10 in the 1960s and after a peak of 1:19 in 1971 steadily dropped to reach 1: 3.5.[81]

But the demands of the leaders of the uprising were much more radical than the reform of apartheid. They wanted the scrapping of apartheid as a system and negotiations for a fully inclusive democracy. The worldwide campaign for the release of Nelson Mandela had built up an irresistible momentum. It was almost universally accepted that negotiations had to be preceded by the release of Mandela and other leaders in jail. Botha

---

80 Pottinger, *Imperial Presidency*, pp. 316-17.
81 Sadie, 'Economic Demography', pp. 322-30.

and his advisors were skeptical that any deal could be struck with the ANC and UDF leaders and were wary of entering into negotiations before the uprising had been suppressed.

In August 1985, when the rebellion was in its eleventh month, Chase Manhattan Bank
suddenly announced that it would not extend its large short-term loan to the South African
government, setting in train a process that would soon lead to South Africa's default on its
international debt. With President Botha scheduled to open the Natal Congress of the
NP on 15 August, there was intense international speculation that he would announce
the release of Mandela among other far-reaching steps. Angered by the unrealistic expectations raised by Pik Botha, Minister of Foreign Affairs, President Botha used the occasion
to display all the defiance of an old-style white supremacist. He was not prepared to lead
white South Africans on 'a road to abdication and suicide.' Without white South Africans
and their influence the country would drift into 'faction strife, chaos and poverty.' He had
no respect for revolutionaries who had turned Africa into a dying continent. Mandela and
'his friends' were in jail, he said, because they had planned a revolution, and would only
be released if they renounced violence.

Hardly noticed was the fact that, in terms of his party's policy, Botha had in fact taken a
major step: he had buried the homelands policy and with it the attempt to deny blacks political rights in the common area. He announced that people in black 'states and communities' that did not want to accept independence were South African citizens and should
be accommodated in a common political system. In the angry disappointment that followed,
scorn was poured on Botha's words that the government had crossed the Rubicon.[82]

Botha's speech fell so far short of expectations that a wave of new sanctions and disinvestment hit South Africa. The Reagan Administration in the US announced a mild
sanctions package, but the US Congress soon went much further by banning all new investments and loans to the South African government. In Britain Margaret Thatcher's
Tory government held out, but the Commonwealth accepted measures that included a
ban on all agricultural and manufacturing imports from South Africa, and on any new
loans and investment. Even Thatcher signaled in 1989 that she could not resist for much
longer if Mandela were not freed. One-fifth of British firms left South Africa, and total
British direct investment had been halved in the course of the 1980s.

Sanctions alone, however, could not bring the state to its knees. Very often disinvestment
led to South African companies acquiring multi-national corporations at bargain base-
ment prices. Trade ties with the West weakened, but those with Asia improved, with the result that the overall volume of foreign trade grew. By the end of 1986 the country had a
trade surplus of R15 billion. But the ban on new foreign loans and investment severely
dented business confidence, and it was estimated that as a result of balance of payment
problems it was impossible for the country now to grow at a rate higher than two per
cent per year.

In March 1986 Botha briefly lifted the partial state of emergency, but on 12 June 1986
he declared a national state of emergency, which would remain in place until 2 February
1990. The state used massive force to crush the revolt. More than twenty thousand people were detained, and the state activated its National Security Management System in

---

82 The speech is in Schrire, *Adapt or Die*, pp. 147-59.

many townships. The State Security Council became the main decision-making body on security issues.

Stability gradually returned. Fatalities had risen from 879 in 1985 to 1,298 in 1986, but declined to 661 in 1987. They would rise again in 1988 to 1,149 and to 1,403 in 1989. The state had suppressed the political challenge, but South Africa had irrevocably changed. Chester Crocker, the US Assistant Secretary of State for Africa, summed up the state of play: '[The] government and its opposition had checkmated each other. Neither could move unilaterally: the black resistance had no hope of forcing the government to capitulate, but the government could no longer hope to regain the legitimacy it lost.'[83]

A frontier war

Between 1985 and 1988 the Afrikaner nightmare of simultaneously suppressing a continuing uprising and fighting a frontier war materialized. There were now more than thirty thousand Cuban troops in Angola, and new Russian aircraft gave South Africa's enemies a degree of air superiority that threatened to make the war for South Africa ever more costly in both lives and equipment. Much was at stake. Confronted by an aggressive right wing accusing it of selling out, the government would be severely hit by a humiliating retreat in Angola. The Soviet Union and Cuba were determined to record a victory in Angola and win a battle in the Cold War. Victory could open the way for a SWAPO incursion in the northern parts of Namibia.

Although heavily outnumbered, South Africa scored a major, largely unheralded military victory in Angola. In a large-scale formal battle at Lomba, the forces of South Africa and UNITA inflicted a crushing defeat on the Cuban and Angolan forces, together with their Russian military advisors. The Cuban-Angolan force retreated to Cuito Cuanavale. The South African/UNITA force laid siege to the town, but did not attempt to take it because its strategic value was limited. A master of revolutionary myth-making, Fidel Castro fabricated the legend that the entire war turned on this battle, and that South Africa had lost it at Cuito Cuanavale. Pouring scorn on this claim, US Assistant Secretary of State, Chester Crocker, pointed out that the SA/UNITA alliance had consolidated their Lomba victory, but decided not to take the town 'when they realized that the price would be too high.' Castro also made exaggerated claims about the final battle just beyond the Namibian border. The battle was inconclusive. South Africa proved that a Cuban attempt to breach the border would exact a toll far higher than it seemed prepared to pay.[84]

Communist penetration in the Third World had been stopped as decisively in Angola as in Afghanistan in the late 1980s. Early in 1988 the Reagan administration received word from the Soviets that they were eager to get out of Africa. Both South Africa and Cuba now prepared to withdraw. For South Africa the financial costs had been high: Between 1985/86 and 1988/89 military expenditures increased by 25 per cent at constant prices to make up 17.7 per cent of the budget.[85] The fruits were ambiguous. South Africa had forced the withdrawal of the Cubans and had thwarted SWAPO attempts to establish a military presence in Namibia. However, SWAPO had managed to survive politically and was sure to win a free election.

---

83 Crocker, *High Noon*, p. 491.
84 Crocker, *High Noon*, pp. 369-71; Seegers, *The SA Military*, p. 259.
85 Sean Archer, 'Defence Expenditure and Arms Procurement', in Jacklyn Cock and Lawrie Nathan (eds.), *War and Society: The Militarisation of South Africa* (Cape Town: David Philip, 1989), pp. 244-59.

The road was now clear for Namibian independence without the South African government's being seen as selling out. P.W. Botha probably thought until near the end that SWAPO could be eliminated as the dominant political force, but most military commanders felt that the objective was to eliminate foreign intervention in the region, not to prevent a one-man-one-vote election in Namibia. They argued that the purpose of the war was to bring about the conditions for a political solution.[86] In 1989, elections for a constituent assembly took place peacefully in Namibia. The demonstration effect on white voters in South Africa was generally positive.

'Serving the cause of democracy'

By November 1985 South Africa had experienced fifteen months of widespread mass violence. There were numerous reports of brutalities committed by the security forces. Yet there was no sign that the government could restore peace. As in his 1975 analysis, Van Zyl Slabbert concluded that any bold reformer giving a new direction would have shrinking electoral support. He had tried to put together a multi-racial coalition that included Buthelezi that could oppose the ANC, but was unsuccessful. He was beginning to consider black majority rule under a liberal constitution as the only viable option. Yet his 1979 study, co-authored with Welsh, had put a huge question mark over the prospects of a deeply divided society remaining peaceful and genuinely democratic without some substantial checks on the majority.[87]

Slabbert's close friend, Breyten Breytenbach, released from jail in 1982, was more adamant than ever in rejecting a compromise solution. The liberal alternative, the poet wrote, was a 'non-starter, a non-adaptable transplant from more clement climes, ill-equipped to do battle with nationalism and extremism.'[88] The intense aversion of Slabbert and Breytenbach to the nationalist leadership and its arrogant ways threatened to spill over in a rejection of their Afrikaner roots. On one occasion Breytenbach declared: 'I don't consider myself an Afrikaner', but he and Slabbert were nothing but full-blooded Afrikaners. It was never more apparent than in their outraged, and sometimes even distraught, reactions to government talk that it was attempting to ensure Afrikaner survival.[89]

Although becoming increasingly despondent about the political deadlock being broken, Slabbert by November 1985 had not yet given up on forming a pact to negotiate a system that differed substantially from an ordinary democracy or simple majority rule. In a private interview with Botha, who later released the tape, he told the president that the idea of an all-powerful ANC was a myth and that he had said to the ANC leadership that it was 'not on' for it to insist that the government must 'negotiate the transfer of power out of [their] own hands to whatever majority.' He also agreed with Botha that whites did not have to give up their 'right to self-determination' if blacks were brought into a common system.[90]

86 Seegers, *The Military*, pp. 262-3.
87 See F. Van Zyl Slabbert and David Welsh, *South Africa's Options* (Cape Town: David Philip, 1983). For a concise statement of this position in a general context see Vernon Bogdanor, 'Forms of Autonomy and the Protection of Minorities', *Daedalus*, 126, 2 (1997), p. 66.
88 Francis Galloway, *Breyten as openbare figuur* (Pretoria: HAUM, 1990), p. 226,
89 Peter Ackroyd, 'Dissident Afrikaner Voice', *The Times* (London), 26 June 1986.
90 *South African Digest*, 28 February 1986, supplement.

Slabbert was obviously available to act as honest broker in future negotiations, perhaps even to work as a partner with the Botha government in dealing with the ANC. But the NP leadership now missed yet another opportunity. Botha spurned the offer, with the result that when the NP government four years later finally did sit and talk to the ANC it was without Slabbert's formidable intellect and skills and without significant support from any other party. All alone, the NP was hardly overflowing with talented negotiators.

The frustrating talk with Botha prompted Slabbert to make an abrupt change of course: from a loyal critic in the system of rule to a critical ally of the liberation movement. Early in 1986 he resigned from Parliament in disgust, calling the institution irrelevant. He seemed to have given up on incremental change, long a mainstay of liberal politics. He no longer saw the racial conflict as a battle between a white-led government and a black-led movement over the control of the state, but between a tyranny and a democratic movement. He wrote: 'I have made no secret of my faith that the cause of democracy is served better by the majority struggling against tyranny than among the minority keeping itself in power.'[91] The protection of the minority's individual rights in a future democracy was to him sufficient.

Slabbert's thinking was influenced by the literature on democratization in the 1970s and 1980s with its emphasis on Latin America. But there was a problem with applying insights from these studies to South Africa. Here huge disparities in wealth and income largely along racial lies existed along with an absence of national cohesion and a lack of institutions where people across the political divide interacted with each other. Hence the need for pluralism, for checks and balances.

What was missing in Slabbert's analysis was the recognition that simple majority rule in a deeply divided society could easily become a liberal veneer for racial domination. Eli Kedourie, noted student of nationalism, wrote after visiting South Africa that the principle of majority decision is 'workable only on condition that majorities are variable, not permanent . . . The worst effects of the tyranny of the majority are seen when the unalloyed Western model is introduced in countries divided by religion or language or race.'[92] Donald Horowitz, an authority on polarized societies, warned South Africans to distinguish between two types of majority rule: one based on racial identity and demography with few floating voters; and another whose outcome was not foreordained by demography.[93]

The latter type would require an electoral system and a constitution that broke up a compact black majority. But this was the last thing the ANC wanted, since it was increasingly assuming an African nationalist guise with occasional bows to the type of non-racialism in which Slabbert as leader of the liberal opposition and also some leaders of the United Democratic Front believed.[94] Slabbert recognized the dangers of the 'unalloyed Western model', but undertook to fight the liberation movement if it became a tyranny.[95]

---

91 *Die Suid-Afrikaan*, October 1988, p. 23.

92 Elie Kedourie, 'One-man-one-vote', *South African International*, 18, 7 (1987), p. 1. For a discussion see Hermann Giliomee and Lawrence Schlemmer, *From Apartheid to Nation-Building* (Cape Town: Oxford University Press, 1990), pp. 206-21.

93 Donald Horowitz, *A Democratic South Africa?* (Cape Town: Oxford University Press, 1991), pp. 98-9.

94 For an analysis see P. Eric Louw, 'Shifting Patterns of Political Discourse in the New South Africa', *Critical Studies in Mass Communication*, 11 (1994), pp. 22-53.

95 See also the exchange of letters between the author and Breyten Breytenbach, *Die Suid-Afrikaan*, February 1988, pp. 22-5 and the comments in Giliomee and Schlemmer, *From Apartheid to Nation-Building*, pp. 206-21.

Many years before, Jan Smuts had warned against the mistake of 'looking upon democracy as a deduction from abstract principles instead of regarding it as the outcome of practical politics.'[96] It was very much in this spirit that Lawrence Schlemmer, a liberal academic and no supporter of the NP, took on Slabbert in an exchange in the journal *Die Suid-Afrikaan*. He felt that simple majority rule was not the answer since it would open the door to the entitlement tendencies of the aspirant black middle class and alienate the minorities. South Africa needed a constitution preventing simple majority rule to hold the ANC in check. Delegitimizing the existing Parliament by calling it irrelevant would seriously impair the prospects for a balanced new political order.

Schlemmer argued that liberal politics was in fact making major breakthroughs. The majority of whites had finally come around to accepting majority rule. Was it not better to work for a settlement in which all groups would enjoy security and in which whites did not have to 'write off their history'? Slabbert replied that liberals who remained neutral in the white-black conflict, pinning their hope on incremental change and innovative white leadership, were fooling themselves. Implicitly he rejected any form of power-sharing in favor of simple majority rule.[97]

Alan Paton, one of the leading liberal voices from the late 1940s to the late 1980s, concluded in the 1950s that the Afrikaners would be able to cling to power and would only give it up when they had concluded that it was in their interests to do so. He firmly believed that if attempts were made to force the Afrikaners to accept majority rule in a unitary state they would rather 'be destroyed than yield.' But he also thought that a voluntary transfer of power was possible. 'When total apartheid is seen to be impossible what will the Afrikaner intellectuals and religious leaders do? Will they choose white domination or the common society? Surely, with their intellectual qualifications and moral views, they must choose the common society.'[98] A biographer formulates it as follows: '[Paton] did not believe that they [the Afrikaners] would be forced from power by blacks, or that Liberals by some electoral jiu-jitsu might take their place. The initiative, he believed, would remain with the Afrikaner until he chose to give it up.'[99]

The implication of Paton's sound insight was that fellow-Afrikaners would be best positioned to influence the Afrikaner nationalists when they had to make the crucial decision. He did not support the ANC's demand for a unitary state, and clung to the conviction that a federation was the best solution. In 1985, just before his death, he warned that an Afrikaner-controlled military dictatorship would be 'the end of Afrikanerdom and the end of any evolutionary process.'[100] As an English liberal, he did not carry much weight with the Afrikaners, but Slabbert retained a strong influence among them, particularly those who read the new, independent political journals, *Die Suid-Afrikaan* and *Vrye Weekblad*, founded in 1984 and 1986 respectively. He would use his influence to start informal talks between 'internal' South Africans and the ANC in other parts of Africa and in Europe.

96 Cited by Arthur Barlow, *That We May Tread Safely* (Cape Town: Tafelberg, 1960), p. 135.
97 *Die Suid-Afrikaan*, October 1988, pp. 20-24.
98 Cited in Leo Marquard, *South Africa and Her People* (London: Lutterworth Press, 1957), p. 136.
99 Peter Alexander, *Alan Paton* (Oxford: Oxford University Press, 1994), p. 300.
100 Alan Paton, *Save the Beloved Country* (Melville: Hans Strydom, 1987), p. 294.

The crumbling pillars of the apartheid state's power: ideological cohesion

By the end of the 1970s, Pik Botha, Minister of Foreign Affairs and the government's star performer on state television, still expressed the traditional determination to cling to power. 'A political system of one-man one-vote within one political entity means our destruction . . . I am not aware of any nation in the history of the world knowingly committed to that sort of suicide.' He was not prepared to accept power-sharing with blacks 'not now, not tomorrow, not in a hundred years.' Whites would fight and die rather than waive the right to govern themselves.'[101]

Almost all analysts agreed that the Afrikaners with their deep attachment to a homeland might take blacks as partners but would not give up all power voluntarily. It was true that rank-and-file Afrikaners, due to the impact of television and the global cultural revolution, were becoming more and more materialistic and individualistic and much better aware of how much apartheid clashed with universal norms.[102] Still, if the Afrikaner leaders stayed together and imbued followers with a sense of both mission and threat, they would be able to persevere in a defense of the status quo.

That status quo rested on three pillars that by 1980 seemed quite firm. They were the ideological cohesion of government, superior state power and black political fragmentation. The idea of a transfer of power would only arise if major changes in each of these three bases occurred.

In fact the pillar of ideological cohesion was beginning to crumble with profound consequences. There was a breakdown of consensus in the Afrikaner leadership about a proper response to the black challenge to the state. The masters of revolution praxis, most notably Lenin and Trotsky, and some major modern theorists, including Samuel Huntington and Theda Skocpol, agreed that revolutionary violence does not have to be successful to be effective. It simply has to create sufficient trouble in the ruling elite over ways to deal with it. Once the leadership is no longer able to apply its instruments of coercion ruthlessly, a crucial pillar in the system of domination disintegrates.[103]

The support the Afrikaans churches gave to apartheid was always indispensable for the NP's ideological cohesion. Polls taken since the early 1970s showed that what counted for Afrikaners was the maintenance of public order and security through a policy sanctioned by the church or in line with privately held moral and religious principles. 'To lead an upright and moral life' was rated first in rank ordering of nine issues in polls taken in 1974 and 1977.[104] This emphasis remained constant. In 2001 nearly 90 per cent of Afrikaners (against 40 per cent of English-speakers) indicated that they considered religion as more important than politics or money.[105]

By the mid-1970s apartheid as an ideology was beginning to collapse in many areas.

---

101 Anna Starcke, *Survival* (Cape Town: Tafelberg, 1978), p. 71; Waldmeir, *Anatomy of a Miracle*, p. 36.

102 Jonathan Hyslop, 'Why Did Apartheid's Supporters Capitulate?' *Society in Transition*, 31, 1, 9 (2001), pp. 36-44.

103 Hermann Giliomee, 'Afrikaner Politics, 1977-87', in John Brewer (ed.), *Can South Africa Survive?* (London: Macmillan, 1989), pp. 108-35.

104 Lawrence Schlemmer, 'Factors in the Persistence or Decline of Ethnic Group Mobilisation: Afrikaners in Post-Apartheid South Africa', doctoral diss., 1999, p. 184. See also his 'South Africa's National Party Government,' in Berger and Godsell, *A Future South Africa*, pp. 27-8.

105 Lawrence Schlemmer, 'Between a Rainbow and a Hard Place', *Fast Facts*, December 2001.

Its historiographical foundations had been swept away by the flood of publications by historians, sociologists and anthropologists which challenged the nationalist interpretation that had found its way into many school texts. It was now quite unfashionable to argue that the land belonged to the whites who had 'planted civilization.'[106] The apartheid view that integration in the workplace or residential areas would trigger major clashes proved to be wrong, although the lack of violence was largely due to the way in which a still reasonably strong state controlled change. Another view that became discredited was that of an incipient inter-tribal war in the African community. Clashes that did take place occurred more along generational or political lines than ethnic lines. The steady Westernization of urban blacks made the call to preserve 'white civilization' look increasingly threadbare.

But the ideology of apartheid would retain its hold on perhaps most Afrikaners if the church continued to endorse the basic idea that God had willed the existence of Afrikaners and indeed all nations. As late as 1974 the Dutch Reformed Church synod reaffirmed the stale story of Babel as a parable of God's creation of distinct peoples. On the basis of this it justified apartheid and rejected non-racial membership for the DRC as an unacceptable erosion of the church's ethnic identity. When the government itself wanted to withdraw from parts of apartheid the DRC was unable to help it. In the early 1980s it refused to support Botha when he wanted to abolish the Immorality Act and the Mixed Marriages Act. But the church was becoming isolated. Very few other peoples had made the happy discovery that God had willed their existence.

Between 1978 and 1982 the church suffered three painful blows. There was the exposure in 1978 of its complicity in the Department of Information's attempts to manipulate public opinion. In 1982 the World Alliance of Reformed Churches, a body whose membership it prized, expelled it. But the blow that hurt most was a step the Dutch Reformed *Sendingkerk* (the 'colored' church) took in 1982. It drafted the Belhar Confession, which spelled out the implications of the Gospel for justice in South Africa, leaving little doubt that apartheid was in conflict with it. The church called on the DRC to confess its guilt for 'providing the moral and theological foundations of apartheid.' This decision was an ironic product of the missions policy, making the church self-governing. When the NP came to power in 1948 there were three colored ministers in the mission church against seventy-nine white ministers; by 1966, when Verwoerd died, there were still three times more white than colored ministers, but in 1978 colored ministers overtook white ministers in the *Sendingkerk* for the first time.[107] Overwhelmingly, the former rejected apartheid.

The DRC finally broke with apartheid at its 1986 and 1990 synods. In 1986 it declared that the church was open to anyone regardless of color. It formally decided to base its view of racial policy on the New Testament, in which 'the idea of race plays no part whatsoever.' The church had made a major about turn, but for some critics of the church this was insufficient: they wanted the church to state that it had acted out of malign and sinful intent in helping to design apartheid in the 1930s and 1940s. The 1986 and 1990 synods refused to make any declaration along such lines, and explicitly stated that some

---

106 J.M. du Preez, *Africana Afrikaner* (Alberton: Liberatius, 1983).
107 Author's interview with David Botha of the Sendingkerk, 31 August 2002.

of those who promoted apartheid also had good intentions. However, it admitted that the church had erred by allowing forced separation to be seen as biblically justified, and by not pointing out this error at a much earlier stage. The great majority of the population, the church declared, had experienced apartheid as a system of oppression and discrimination that violated their human dignity. Such a system clashed with the Bible, and was sinful and a major error.[108]

At a November 1990 conference at Rustenburg to promote national reconciliation, attended by delegates of a wide array of Christian churches, Willie Jonker, one of the leading critical voices in the DRC for more than thirty years, accepted on behalf of himself and the DRC responsibility for the wrongs and sufferings under apartheid. The church leadership present at the meeting endorsed this confession.

One of the most important legitimating props of apartheid had been removed. The church's confession of its errors between 1986 and 1990 was not without ambiguity. Some depicted it as a 'conversion without repentance', but Peter Berger, an American sociologist, pointed out that in the larger history of churches it was rare for a major church to apologize so soon for the error of its ways.[109] So upset were the conservatives that sixty ministers and thirty thousand lay members broke away in 1987 to form the Afrikaanse Protestantse Kerk. In the first half of the 1990s another seventy thousand would break away.

As in the case of the church, the 1984-86 uprising forced the Afrikaner Broederbond into a fundamental reassessment of apartheid as a survival mechanism. In 1986 it sent a memorandum, entitled 'Basic Constitutional Values for the Survival of the Afrikaners', to its divisions for comment. The Bond had given up on negotiating any special deal for Afrikaners and used the terms 'Afrikaner interests' and 'white interests' interchangeably. The document argued the very opposite of long-held core beliefs. It projected the *exclusion* of blacks at the highest level of decision-making as a threat to the survival of whites. Blacks would have to be incorporated and the head of the government did not necessarily have to be white. These steps would entail 'calculated risks', but, as Executive Council chairman Piet de Lange stated: 'The greatest risk we currently run is not to take any risks. Our will to survive as Afrikaners and our energy and faith are the strongest guarantee.'

The Broederbond did not want an Afrikaner abdication, and proposed mechanisms that would check classic majority rule, like special representation of racial groups, group vetoes and a division between 'own' and 'general' affairs. Its proposals reflected a curious amalgam of two quite contradictory models. One was consociationalism or power-sharing, originally proposed by the Dutch scholar Arend Lijphart as a credible democratic alternative to simple majority rule in deeply divided societies. He held up the model of power-sharing by groups based on free association seeking a general consensus through a grand coalition of parties. The other was the apartheid system of legally entrenched racial

---

108 Nederduits Gereformeerde Kerk, *Kerk en samelewing* (October 1986), especially pp. 16, 19, 52-7; *Church and Society* (Pretoria: General Synodical Committee, 1990), paragraphs 280-85; Willie Jonker, *Selfs die kerk kan verander* (Cape Town: Tafelberg, 1998), pp. 192-204.

109 Donald Akenson, *God's Peoples: Covenant and Land in South Africa, Israel and Ulster* (Ithaca: Cornell University Press, 1992), p. 308; *Die Burger,* 22 November 2002, p. 17.

groups, ruling out the principle of freedom of association. The Broederbond and other NP-supporting bodies still proposed the division of 'own' and 'general' affairs based on the key apartheid measure, the Population Registration Act. (The idea of an additional group, based on voluntary identification, had begun to gain ground.)

About a third of the Broeders resigned when the document reached the branches. In the Cape Town division, Piet Cillié, retired editor of *Die Burger*, entered a personal comment: 'Separate freedoms as envisaged in the homelands policy are dead; the present reality dictates that Afrikaners explore the way of shared freedoms', which they had long rejected as 'national suicide.' He was skeptical of building a single nation, but insisted that the order of liberty, freedom and fraternity had to be tried, 'even at the risk of the destruction of our civilization, including the Afrikaner people. We know we must try it because we have no other choice.'[110] Privately he felt that the choice was between 'probable destruction, which was the road of negotiations, and assured destruction.' If the Afrikaner people were to go down 'it must at least be for a worthwhile principle.'[111]

Business leaders felt that the costs of apartheid had become too steep. Anton Rupert, doyen of Afrikaner business, wrote a private letter to President Botha in January 1986 strongly criticizing the government's economic mismanagement. Since the early 1970s central government expenditure had doubled every five years in current prices and inflation was at its highest rate since the 1920s. Low economic growth led to spiraling unemployment. Over the previous nine years there had been no net increase in black employment.[112] He warned: "The biggest source of unrest is unemployment . . . It is a fertile ground for intimidation and subversion.'[113]

Rupert referred to an earlier private comment by the president that he would 'rather be poor than to yield [to blacks]', and that he was not prepared to renounce apartheid. Pointing to the decline of the currency and the country's heavy debt burden, Rupert warned that any attempt to cling to apartheid would lead to a future that would be 'both poor and black.' The belief that apartheid guaranteed the white man's survival was a myth; in fact, 'it threatens his survival.' Apartheid 'is crucifying us; it is destroying our language; it is degrading for a once heroic nation to be the lepers of the world.' He warned Botha that should he fail in the task of removing apartheid 'then one day we shall surely end up with a Nuremburg.'[114]

The disarray extended to the cabinet. At a meeting of a cabinet committee held in March 1986, Botha remarked that he did not favor one-man, one-vote in a unitary or federal state. 'I thought we had clarity, but I do not think we have it any more, because you want me to say we stand for a unitary South Africa. You allow me to say it, you write it in my speeches and I accept it, but what do you mean by that?'[115] Chris Heunis, Minister for Constitutional Development, remarked that the government did not know where it was going. F.W. de Klerk, in charge of white 'own affairs', observed that there were fundamental differences between NP ministers. On the one hand there were those proposing

---

110 Stals, 'Geskiedenis van die AB', pp. 645-48.
111 J.C. Steyn: *Penvegter: Piet Cillié van Die Burger* (Cape Town: Tafelberg, 2002), p. 331.
112 The actual figure was four years. Personal communication, J.L. Sadie, 8 December 2001.
113 Rembrandt Corporation Archives, Stellenbosch, Letter Anton Rupert-P. W. Botha, 24 January 1986.
114 Letter Rupert-Botha, 24 January 1986.
115 *Sunday Times*, 28 August 1994, p. 26.

full power-sharing, like the liberal opposition in Parliament; on the other hand there were those who wanted to build structures in such a way that 'whites will always have enough power to handle themselves in a crisis.' He seemed to prefer the latter.

In its search for a system in which majority rule was balanced, the government asked the South African Law Commission to investigate a non-racial Bill of Rights and the issue of individual and group rights. The cabinet hoped that the committee under the chairmanship of Judge H.J.O. van Heerden, a prominent and respected Afrikaner judge, would come out in favor of group rights. However, it submitted a report which argued that individual rights as entrenched in a Bill of Rights provided sufficient protection for legitimate interests. The committee made no special recommendations about language, incorrectly assuming that the position of Afrikaans as an official language would not be seriously undermined if a new political system were negotiated. Its report did not provide the government with an expert backing for group rights.[116]

On the grass-roots level support for the apartheid system was still strong. A 1984 survey found that upwards of 80 per cent of Afrikaners (and 35-45 per cent of English-speakers also) supported the key pillars of apartheid: the ban on sex between white and non-white; segregated residential areas, schools and public amenities; separate voters' rolls for coloreds and Indians; and homelands for blacks.[117] There was a remarkable degree of identification among Afrikaners, including university students, with the South African state as the custodian of the entire economy and society. A 1989 study found a remarkably high repression potential among Afrikaner university students. They held the security establishment in high regard and valued the state as 'a harbor of white security', but even more because they deemed it as 'good, honest, free and just.' Nearly half of Afrikaner students indicated that they would 'physically resist' an ANC-controlled government (against 10 per cent of English students), while another one-third indicated that they would emigrate.[118]

Yet the new Afrikaner elite also craved the acceptance of both the disenfranchised in South Africa and the Western world. They realized that apartheid as an idea had run its course and that things could not continue as before. A vivid illustration was provided when the Conservative Party, after winning most towns in the Transvaal in the 1988 local government elections, tried to reintroduce forms of social apartheid that had fallen away. Blacks immediately responded by consumer boycotts that crippled local businesses. The central government overruled the local authorities.

Two other crumbling pillars: black fragmentation and disagreements over suppression

The uprising of 1984-86 did much to weaken another major pillar of white power, namely black political fragmentation. It eliminated most of the black councilors, and the ANC succeeded in establishing itself as the dominant and cohesive force in black politics. Buthelezi was no longer considered a national leader, but rather as one commanding

---

116 Interview with members of the committee, 21 December 2001.
117 SA Institute of Race Relations, *Race Relations Survey, 1984* (Johannesburg 1985), pp. 360-61.
118 Jannie Gagiano, 'Ruling Group Cohesion', *The Elusive Search for Peace*, p. 196.

strong support among traditional Zulu in KwaZulu Natal. When the government in 1986 began seeking a model for incorporating blacks into the political structures, it discovered that it had run out of moderate black leaders as negotiating partners. Buthelezi insisted that the government first issue a statement of intent that it was prepared to consider the issue of power-sharing between whites and blacks beyond the limits of the existing constitution, and that it would release Nelson Mandela. Botha refused both demands. Strong enmity remained between the ANC in exile and Buthelezi, but the government was no longer able to play black leaders off against one another.

The lack of consensus about the suppression of the uprising also weakened the state. The government had invested large financial resources in the arms industry and a costly war in Angola, but left the police force under-staffed, under-resourced, and poorly paid. In 1986, General Johan Coetzee, the Police Commissioner, complained that the force was suffering from its ratio of only 1.7 policemen and policewomen per thousand of the population, far below even stable, developed countries (see p. 551).[119] In 1987 the government announced that it would increase the number of policemen from 56,000 to 87,000, or 2.2 per thousand of the population.

While the security forces had showed no sign of any loss of will during the 1984-86 uprising, they could not wipe out black dissent. Police methods to control crowds were often unsophisticated. After the police had shot and killed twenty blacks on 21 March 1985 in Uitenhage in the eastern Cape, a judge found that they had acted provocatively towards the black crowd and were armed solely with lethal weaponry. The judge commented that 'the use of more lethal weapons is not the answer to a lack of members.'[120] During the second half of the 1980s the state employed large numbers of *kitskonstabels*, 'instant constables', who were given limited training and rushed into situations where they sometimes had to control angry crowds.[121]

Top police force officers had come to believe that suppression of dissent offered only a temporary respite in a situation where a rapidly growing black population would offer ever stiffer challenges. It could only buy time for the politicians to find a political solution, not provide a solution through repression. Some operatives on the lower level of the security forces took the law in their own hands. Unit C-10, a secret police unit, used a farm, Vlakplaas, near Pretoria to 'turn' ANC guerrillas and then sent them out to kill state enemies. Another was a military unit, the Citizens Co-operation Bureau, which operated mainly abroad, but also had an internal cell, comprised mainly of ex-policemen, who murdered or severely injured political opponents. The bureau also engaged in research into chemical and biological weapons. Between 1976 and 1994 state agents deliberately killed between two hundred and three hundred people active in the struggle against the state (see pp. 648-55).

Divisions had developed within the National Security Management System between officials in the security branch (military and police) and those in the 'welfare' branch (National Intelligence Service and the Department of Constitutional Development and Planning). The former wanted to detain or ban leaders of the resistance movement before

---

119 Seegers, *The Military*, p. 249.
120 Pottinger, *Imperial Presidency*, p. 287.
121 Pottinger, *Imperial Presidency*, pp. 281-6.

addressing grievances and cultivating more moderate leaders. The welfare arm thought that nothing would be served by removing the leadership of the resistance, since their replacements were often more radical. It was better to leave the existing leaders alone, abolish unenforceable laws, and lift the ban on political organizations.[122]

Senior members of the National Intelligence Service concluded that while the state could survive, it would steadily weaken without a negotiated solution. Mike Louw, second in command of the NIS, remembered the situation in the late 1980s as follows: 'Nowhere was the situation out of hand, but it was clear that politically and morally we were losing our grip. Everywhere in the townships we encountered intimidation and a strong political consciousness. The political system had become obsolete, and a long bloody struggle lay ahead. It had become clear that the sooner we negotiated a new system the better.'[123]

Democracy and its alternatives

Some kind of multi-racial dictatorship ruling through terror and patronage was a possibility often mooted during the 1980s. Senior members of the security forces dabbled in efforts to make this a reality. Allowed a large degree of latitude by the State Security Council, the military received permission to train two hundred blacks as paramilitaries, which Buthelezi could use in Natal and KwaZulu to fight the ANC. In the eastern Cape top military officers were engaged in engineering the formation of a Xhosa resistance movement that could act as a surrogate of the state.[124]

Few cabinet ministers knew of these activities and those who did turned a blind eye. Aware of the severe challenge the state faced, they trusted Botha to give the security forces enough latitude to restore order without resorting to atrocities. For the time being they were prepared to believe state propaganda that the ANC or intra-black violence was responsible for some of the deaths of activists or the explosion of bombs. The ANC's strategy of discrediting the security forces and blaming many of their mistakes on them helped to create a climate where people were prepared to suspend judgment.

Afrikaners strongly questioned whether a stable multi-racial democracy was feasible, but many elements of their political culture pushed them in that direction. Despite the turmoil of the 1980s, respect for the law surprisingly survived. Apartheid showed a gross disrespect for human rights and international law, but it was never lawless. The state had developed a strong tradition of legalism.[125] Afrikaner rule was characterized by an obsession with imposing restrictions through proper legislation and with due process in executing these laws. Opponents of the National Party government were regularly appointed as judges. The government did not attempt to cover up deaths in detention, despite a torrent of unfavorable publicity. Although political opponents were at the mercy of their interrogators in prison, both the policeman and the prisoner knew that neither

---

122 Seegers, *The Military*, p. 248.

123 Author's interview with Mike Louw, 21 November 1994; author's interview with ex-Police Commissioner Johan van der Merwe of the South African Police, 22 November 1996.

124 The volumes of the Truth and Reconciliation Commission report are without an index. A good short cut is the account by Peter Stiff, *Warfare by Other Means* (Alberton: Galago, 2001).

125 For a critical view see John Dugard, 'Foreword', in Richard Abel (ed.), *Politics by Other Means: Law in the Struggle Against Apartheid* (London: Routledge, 1995), p. viii.

was outside the law – as Jews were in Nazi Germany.[126] If there could not be survival in justice, survival at least had to observe properly drafted and promulgated laws and regulations.

Although this Afrikaner obsession with legalism underpinned apartheid, it could also weaken it, most prominently in case of the pass laws, which provided the security forces with one of their most effective ways of policing. When Botha became prime minister in the 1970s offenders were tried in commissioners' courts, which dealt with the accused in batches at a rate of one every thirty seconds. Out of concern about due process, the government in the early 1980s removed these cases to the Department of Justice and the magistrates' courts. With activist groups providing legal assistance to some of the accused, the system began to disintegrate. In Brian Pottinger's words: 'The whole system creaked under the burden of due process and in the last days of the pass laws the public prosecutors were angrily ordering the SA Police members not to bring more offenders before their courts.'[127]

While rank-and-file whites had no real qualm with the state of emergency, Afrikaners in academic, church and professional life balked at living in a semi-permanent state of suspended due process. An analysis of editorials in the DRC's official journal *Die Kerkbode* concluded: 'There is a gradual shift from justification of the state's chosen course of action in the early years of the Emergency toward careful reference to the abnormality of rule through emergency laws, and the possibility of misuse of such power in 1988 and 1989.'[128] NP politicians who did not sit on the State Security Council strongly resented the sidelining of cabinet and the encroachment on their terrain by the National Security Management System. In the cabinet F.W. de Klerk opposed the annual renewal of the state of emergency: 'With respect, the arguments don't impress me. How long will we have a State of Emergency? As long as we live?'[129]

P.W. Botha himself introduced an important barrier to a permanent state of emergency as a way of survival. For nearly twenty-five years he had served first as Minister of Defence and then as head of government with close ties to the military. A military officer described his lasting achievement as that of imbuing the Defence Force with a 'disciplined acceptance of the principle that they serve the political decision-makers.' There was among Afrikaners no glorification of the military leadership, and senior generals did not crave political power. Most generals were disappointed when power was transferred in 1989 from Botha to De Klerk, who distrusted the security establishment, but no one thought of intervening.[130]

Civil society had become much too vibrant for a dictatorship to be imposed with any degree of success. During the 1980s the older liberal organizations began interacting with new, activist ones, enabling whites and blacks to begin define a common destiny. The public debate had shifted to exploring ways of strengthening the economy and its job-

---

126 Heribert Adam, et al., *Comrades in Business* (Cape Town: Tafelberg, 1997), pp. 35-6.
127 Pottinger, *The Imperial Presidency*, p. 189.
128 Christine Anthonissen, 'Critical Discourse Analysis', *Die Kerkbode 1986-1989*', *Scriptorum,* 76, 1 (2001), p. 28.
129 Interview with F.W. de Klerk, 30 May 1990.
130 Bill Sass, 'The Union and SADF', in Jakkie Cilliers and Markus Reichardt (eds.), *About Turn: The Transformation of the SA Military and Intelligence* (Halfway House, 1995), p. 119.

creating capacity and improving the delivery of services. A multitude of think-tanks, seminars and conferences analyzed political and economic trends. Restrictions on the South African press were easily overcome by access to foreign newspapers and radio. Foreign money flooded into the country to finance an 'alternative' press and activists. In all these ways South Africa was different from Israel and Northern Ireland, two other conflict-ridden societies of particular concern to the Western world.[131]

In the 1987 election the NP asked for and received a mandate for a new direction in policy. The party committed itself to put in place a new system based on equal rights for all and to negotiate a settlement for joint decision-making and power-sharing among all population groups. F.W. de Klerk, the fifty-year-old leader of the NP in the Transvaal, the most conservative province, had played a leading role in preventing the Conservatives from routing the NP in the province.

Much of the NP's energy went to assuring whites that it would attempt to secure what it called 'community protection.' With regard to public schools, it promised to seek the 'protection of communities' to enable them to educate their children as they wished. Ideally it wanted to introduce into the new system the Tricameral constitution's distinction between general affairs (mainly public security, defense and the economy) and 'own affairs' of groups (schools and residential areas, coupled with some form of group power to exercise 'self-determination'). Polls showed that between half and two-thirds of the Afrikaner elite, now the main NP support base, desired a form of social apartheid (although not necessarily enforced by law) in schools and residential areas.[132]

NP leaders motivated their demand for the protection of communities on the grounds that it would help to assuage white fears. To this the ANC spokespeople and the liberal opposition replied that to concede white community protection would raise the black fear that whites would retain exclusive access to the much better funded white schools, universities and residential areas. To compound the NP's difficulties, the leaders of the liberal opposition and the main parties in the colored and Indian houses of Parliament rejected 'own affairs' and 'community protection' on the grounds that such demands smacked of apartheid.[133]

In his final years in office Botha explored negotiations with the ANC as an option. He allowed Niel Barnard and Mike Louw, the two most senior officials in the National Intelligence Service (NIS), and other officials to hold secret talks with Mandela in prison. The officials immediately recognized his stature, integrity and lack of bitterness despite having spent twenty-five years in jail. He was no moderate in NP terms, but consistently argued that majority rule, which he considered non-negotiable, had to be balanced by guarantees that ensured that white domination would not be replaced by black domination. In these talks he came across as a pragmatist, who in the early 1960s had been driven by the cruelty of apartheid to resort to armed struggle rather than a doctrinaire revolutionary glorying in violence for its own sake. The intention was not to overthrow the state but to draw attention to the legitimate aspirations of the long-oppressed African people.

131 Hermann Giliomee, 'The Elusive Search for Peace', *The Elusive Search for Peace*, pp. 299-317.
132 F.W. de Klerk, *Die laaste trek – 'n nuwe begin* (Cape Town: Human & Rousseau, 1998), pp. 124-5.
133 Nic Olivier, "'n Opgewarmde nuwe NP-beleid', *Die Suid-Afrikaan*, June 1989, pp. 19-22.

Botha took no action when a large group of Afrikaner academics under the leader-ship of Van Zyl Slabbert in 1987 publicly met with leaders of the ANC in exile in Dakar, Senegal, though he did attack them as 'useful idiots.' In the following year NIS officials met with ANC leaders in exile. Conditions for negotiations with the ANC were much more favorable than they had been six or seven years earlier. The war in Angola was over, the transition to an internationally recognized transfer of power in Namibia was proceed-ing smoothly, the Soviet Union was anxious to withdraw from Africa, and the African states in the region were eager for a settlement that would bring peace to the subconti-nent. In South Africa a semi-stable deadlock existed between the security forces and their challengers.

After suffering a stroke P.W. Botha resigned in August 1989 and has since been univer-sally condemned as a reactionary who failed to cross his Rubicon. In the literature he stands in stark contrast to his successor, F.W. de Klerk, who became NP leader and acting state president in February 1989 and president in September 1989 after a general elec-tion. Yet Botha's period in power was not without major achievements. He broke down the symbolism of a white Parliament and he presided over a dramatic redistribution of in-come to the disenfranchised from the enfranchised, the whites, whose tax rate, according to the International Monetary Fund, was very high for a middle-income country.[134] By the end of the 1989s the state under his command had restored a substantial measure of public order without the spiraling level of bloodshed seen in other multi-ethnic states. As Simon Jenkins, a prominent British journalist, pointed out in 1988 in an assessment of Botha, what he did was 'no mean feat – State of Emergency or no. It demands every ounce of pragmatism in a leader.'[135]

A bridge to democracy

No transition to a democracy would have been possible without both the ANC and the NP forming the bridge over which South Africans could walk. It was above all Mandela and De Klerk who constructed the bridge, using as pillars the NP-ruled state and the ANC as the embodiment of the anti-apartheid struggle. Both showed great skill as leader-conciliators, able to deliver their respective constituencies.[136]

De Klerk was the model nationalist whose family history was interwoven with that of the Afrikaner nationalist movement. One grandfather was a Gereformeerde (Dopper) minister; another was elected to the Transvaal Provincial Council. An uncle was J.G. Strij-dom, prime minister between 1954 and 1958, and his father a cabinet minister. De Klerk belonged to the Gereformeerde (Dopper) Church and studied law at Potchefstroom Uni-versity. His approach was the typical neo-Calvinist one of starting with abstract principles and taking them to their logical conclusion. For much of his political career he consid-ered apartheid as morally and politically sound.

In his parliamentary career, which started in 1972, he carefully avoided becoming part of any NP caucus faction. Intelligent, self-confident and a good debater, he glibly explained

---

134 De Klerk, *Die laaste trek*, p. 173.
135 Simon Jenkins, 'Paradox of Botha's legacy', *Die Suid-Afrikaan*, June 1988, p. 45.
136 I wish to thank Stanley Uys for sharing his thoughts on the two leaders.

away the inconsistencies and injustices of apartheid. He attacked the liberal opposition as short-sighted on survival without offering a plausible alternative. Until the end of the 1980s there was nothing that suggested that he was able to provide transformative leadership.

Soon after De Klerk's election as state president in September 1989 he was faced with some major decisions. In September he overruled the police when he gave permission for a mass march, organized predominantly by the United Democratic Front (UDF), the ANC's internal wing, through the streets of Cape Town to Parliament. 'We cannot have a democracy without protest marches', he said.[137] This was a courageous decision at a time when communist governments in Eastern Europe had become terrified of mass action.

The fall of the Berlin Wall, signaling the beginning of communism's death throes, presented De Klerk with what he saw as a 'God-sent opportunity.' The NP could now tell its constituency that without Soviet backing the ANC, with its ally, the South African Communist Party (SACP), no longer constituted a major threat to stability. He could also argue that communism was so discredited that the ANC would be compelled to accept the free market, property rights and other investment-friendly policies.[138] But the fall of the Wall was a double-edged sword. Anti-communism had long been the main reason why Western governments accepted and even bolstered white rule in South Africa. The disappearance of the communist threat and the ANC's retreat from nationalization made the South African government's anti-communism old fashioned, and deprived it of its strongest argument for Western pressure to force the ANC to accept power-sharing.

By the end of 1989 De Klerk had made a great leap. In April 1987 he had told people in his constituency that it was necessary for whites to take the 'slight risk' of building a system of power-sharing in order to get 'a substantial portion or even a majority of blacks to join them in forging a bastion against the ANC.'[139] Now he decided to invite the ANC into the bastion and work out the power-sharing system with it. In December 1989 he persuaded his cabinet to accept the need to unban the ANC, the Pan Africanist Congress and other liberation movements, and to begin all-party negotiations for a new constitution without preconditions.

When De Klerk, on 2 February 1990, announced this decision in Parliament it was the first time the NP caucus had heard of it. De Klerk still met some residual resistance to negotiating with SACP leaders, but it evaporated after Mandela rejected the exclusion of the ANC 's most loyal ally.

Nelson Mandela was like De Klerk in placing the highest political value on loyalty to his party and people, while willing to act without a mandate to take them to a place he felt they ought to go rather than where they wanted to be. But their career paths had been radically different. Mandela had moved from the Xhosa territory of the Transkei to Johannesburg as a young man and had qualified as a lawyer. He was one of the ANC leaders in the turbulent protest politics. He was almost constantly harassed by the police, but his passionate convictions and an indomitable will enabled him to continue with what seemed a hopeless mission.

---

137 Waldmeir, *Anatomy of a Miracle*, p. 138.
138 Interview with F.W. de Klerk, 30 May 1990.
139 *Pretoria News*, 28 April 1987.

After twenty-seven years in jail Mandela re-entered political life in February 1990 with the unique qualities that the situation required. He had an imposing bearing and a physical presence, together with gravitas and charisma. He also had that rare, intangible quality best described by Seamus Heaney as 'a great transmission of grace.'[140] Even before he was jailed there was an aura around him, and his refusal in prison over the years to barter for his freedom immeasurably enhanced it. He had an autocratic streak, but it was not that of an abrasive modern politician. It was a combination of the style of a tribal chief and that of an instinctive democratic leader, accompanied by old-world courtesy. He knew that there was no need to be strident in presenting the ANC case, since apartheid in the eyes of the world had already been totally discredited.

In his attempt to persuade the Afrikaners to surrender power, he gave them recognition and treated their history with respect. He condemned apartheid as a grave crime against humanity, but considered Afrikaner nationalism a legitimate indigenous movement, which, like African nationalism, had fought British colonialism. In the preceding hundred years both had taken up arms, fighting against impossible odds. When the ANC in 1961 decided to switch from civil disobedience to the armed struggle it was Mandela who founded Umkhonto we Zizwe and became its first commander-in-chief. To demonstrate the symmetry between Afrikaner and African nationalism he decided that the first act of sabotage would take place on 16 December, the day on which Afrikaner nationalists celebrated the Voortrekker victory over Dingane in 1838.[141] When a cabinet minister in the late 1970s offered him freedom provided he would retire to the Transkei, Mandela pointed to the example of the Boer general Christiaan de Wet who had taken up arms against the state in 1914 to protest against South Africa's participation in the First World War, and was soon set free unconditionally. The ANC leaders in jail, he insisted, expected no less.[142] On his prison island he had learned Afrikaans to 'understand the mind of the opposing commander', but also to demonstrate the Freedom Charter's embrace of cultural diversity.

Mandela had started the talks in prison without consulting his imprisoned fellow-leaders or Oliver Tambo, leader of the ANC, living in exile. Some of the ANC leaders in exile still advocated the armed struggle up to the point where the state would be forced to hand over power; others, most notably Thabo Mbeki, had begun talking about abandoning the armed struggle for a negotiated settlement. Inside South Africa, the UDF was reeling under the state's suppressive measures, but its leadership rejected the idea that any leader could negotiate with the government without a proper mandate. Also anathema to the movement was the idea that the discredited institutions of the apartheid state must ratify a settlement.

The ANC into the bastion

NP traditions offered De Klerk considerable leeway in starting on the road of all-party negotiations. While the NP's ethos was egalitarian, its *hoofleier* or chief leader could make

---

140 *Cape Times*, 4 October 2002.
141 Interview by author of Nelson Mandela, 2 February 1992.
142 Waldmeir, *Anatomy of a Miracle*, pp. 16, 90.

major decisions on his own when it came to those fundamentally affecting Afrikaner political survival. General Hertzog decided in 1933 to enter into a coalition with Jan Smuts without informing the cabinet or the caucus. In 1959 Hendrik Verwoerd did not consult anyone before announcing a new homelands policy and the removal of African representation in Parliament. P.W. Botha had a meeting with Mandela in July 1989 without discussing it first with anyone in the cabinet. Now De Klerk announced the lifting of the ban on the ANC and other revolutionary organizations without even informing his party's caucus.

De Klerk, with the assistance especially of Gerrit Viljoen, Minister of Constitutional Development, carried the brunt of the burden to persuade a startled white electorate of the wisdom of the dramatic political about turn. It helped that both came from the NP center and did not have to prove their loyalty to the more conservative NP supporters. Their main argument was that whites as a shrinking proportion of the population would get a much better deal if they negotiated before their backs were against the wall. Viljoen declared: '[We] who want change want it exactly because we realize that our survival depends on orderly change . . . in spite of the risks.'[143] De Klerk said: 'We have not waited until the preponderance of power turned against us before we decided to negotiate a peaceful settlement. We have the means to ensure that the process develops peacefully and in an orderly way.'[144] As part of the process the NP opened its membership to all races in 1992.

From the start the cabinet put all their hopes on the assumption that it had the necessary expertise without which the ANC would find it impossible to govern the country.[145] To the white electorate De Klerk and Viljoen advocated power-sharing as a better system than either white rule or simple majority rule. In May 1990 Viljoen stated: 'The government does not question that the majority has to govern but does ask whether stability and nation-building – especially in a plural society – can be served best by a majority that rules on its own.'[146] The government also promised a labor policy of equal opportunity under which the much better-skilled white workers would still thrive. There was, government speakers seemed to say, not much to fear. Whites might even be better off. Initially the white elite was quite optimistic. A 1989 study found that four-fifths thought that a mutually acceptable settlement between whites and blacks was possible. Although the ANC was then still banned, most of the white elite wanted it to be part of the process.[147]

Initially caught off-guard by De Klerk's announcement, the ANC, in alliance with COSATU, organized mass marches, demonstrations, strikes, stay-aways and consumer boycotts. The ANC was still partly a revolutionary organization with its own army, Umkhonto we Sizwe. Its chief, Chris Hani, boasted at a meeting: 'The ANC will get everything it wants, because all the arms are here.'[148] It was little wonder that some members of the security forces thought that the real fight over South Africa had only just begun. Under the code name Operation Vula, an ANC faction had infiltrated men and weapons into

143 *Sunday Star*, 17 March 1990.
144 *Die Burger*, 31 March 1990.
145 Interview with Johan van der Merwe, 21 November 2002.
146 *Die Burger*, 10 May 1990.
147 E.G. Lombard, 'Elite-houdings oor onderhandelinge in Suid-Afrika', masters diss., US, 1991.
148 De Klerk, *Die laaste trek*, p. 233.

the country and established underground structures. A fierce battle for the political turf erupted between the ANC and Inkatha in KwaZulu and Natal and on the Witwatersrand. Inkatha claimed to have lost several hundred office bearers in Natal through assassinations. In the country as a whole the death toll steadily mounted. Between September 1984 and December 1993, 18,997 people (approximately six hundred whites) died. In a period of eight years the police recorded more than eighty thousand violent incidents.

'A deed that echoed over the world'

De Klerk's best chance for getting a deal that significantly limited the majority's power through group rights or federalism would have been to have spelled out a bottom line when he announced the government's preparedness to negotiate with the ANC and other liberation organizations. But part of the political mantra of the time was that there should be negotiations without preconditions, and De Klerk accepted that.

From the start the ANC and the NP saw themselves as the main players in the negotiations. The ANC wanted the talks to be steered by a 'pact of heavyweights' consisting of members of the NP and ANC that would marginalize all the small parties and give Inkatha only junior status; the NP wanted all the parties included. Both would soon accept the idea of a 'sufficient consensus' to clinch matters, which meant ANC-NP agreement. But there were other serious disagreements. The ANC wanted a popularly elected constituent assembly as soon as possible. The NP attempted to draw the ANC into the task of governing the country, leaving it to a multi-racial government that would have gained experience in running the country to draw up the constitution. Knowing that its hands would be immensely strengthened by an electoral victory, the ANC resisted this offer.

By the end of 1991 the government made a major change of direction. It was sensing that the longer the negotiations were drawn out, the more its base was being eroded. A cabinet minister in De Klerk's small inner circle recounts:

> In the course of 1991 we ran into one crisis after the other in dealing with the turbulent political process and at the same time administering the country. There was an urgent necessity to get the ANC involved in a joint government. We made the crucial shift in November 1991 at a cabinet *bosberaad* (meeting in the bush) where we decided to have an election for an interim constitution-making body and an interim parliament. Our hope was that the NP would do well in the elections and that it would be able to moderate the ANC's positions. In retrospect the big mistake we made was that we did not immediately set up a study commission to develop strong bottom lines with respect to federalism, and a blocking mechanism on cabinet level decision-making and on other central government bodies. The result was that when we came to the actual negotiations we did not have any well-developed federal proposals. We also did not take a hard look at a proper electoral system. One senior minister dismissed it as *sommetjies maak* (making little sums). The consequences of the shift were momentous. Inkatha's alienation from the ruling block had begun and it was soon irreversible. We were losing our allies.[149]

149 Confidential interview, 13 January 1994.

Apart from deciding to have an election for an interim parliament that would also act as an interim constitution-making body, another two crucial decisions were made before the end of 1991. It was decided to pin everything on a power-sharing government instead of demanding group rights or federalism, and the choice was made for a proportional vote electoral system. Given the need this system imposes to establish as broad an electoral platform as possible, the effect would be the acceleration of the disintegration of Afrikaner nationalism. A future black government would deal with the NP as simply yet another party.

De Klerk had one more card to play in his quest for his goal of a power-sharing government: to tell the ANC and Western leaders that he could not lead whites into a system they opposed. In the 1989 election the NP leadership had promised that it would seek the voters' endorsement for any deal that deviated radically from the NP's 1989 election platform. It promised to bring about an inclusive democracy where 'groups' would be recognized as the basic components of the system. There would be power-sharing among them with no group dominating another, and self-determination for each group in its own affairs. De Klerk soon floated the idea of a rotating presidency on the Swiss model.

On two occasions De Klerk promised a referendum. In March 1990 he pledged: 'After the completion of the negotiations the constitutional proposals will be tested in a constitutional manner among the electorate. And only with their support will a constitutional dispensation be introduced.'[150] In January 1992 (before a by-election in Potchefstroom) he declared that any major changeover would require a referendum 'in which every South African will be able to take part and in which the result may be determined globally as well as per parliamentary voters' rolls.'[151] The timing of a white referendum was perhaps the most critical issue confronting De Klerk. If he held it too early it would leave him without any real lever to check ANC demands; if he left it to the very end of the process he would almost certainly enrage his black negotiating partners by allowing whites to exercise a veto. But the fact was that a specific promise had been made.

The Conservative Party (CP) under Andries Treurnicht and other right-wing organizations called De Klerk's speech of 2 February 1990 the start of the Afrikaners' 'Third War of Liberation', following on the Transvaal revolt against the British Annexation (1880-81) and the Anglo-Boer War (1899-1902).[152] Paramilitary groups openly talked of sedition, practiced terrorism and murdered several blacks. The CP used the by-elections to call negotiations into question. It handed the NP a series of reverses. At the beginning of 1992 it scored a stunning victory in a by-election in the safe NP seat of Potchefstroom. This defeat prompted De Klerk to use the referendum for quite a different purpose: to defeat the NP's Afrikaner opponents who rejected negotiations. His justification that the CP stood poised to destroy the negotiations is not very plausible. Poorly led by Treurnicht, the party lacked a coherent political alternative and was rejected by half the Afrikaners and more than 80 per cent of the English-speakers. It had no real chance of winning a general election and halting the negotiations.

In the referendum held in March 1992 the white electorate was asked: 'Do you endorse

---

150 *Die Burger*, 31 March 1990.
151 Rodney Davenport, *The Transfer of Power in South Africa* (Cape Town: David Philip, 1998), p. 11.
152 *Die Burger*, 10 May 1990.

the continuation of the reform process . . . which is aimed at a new constitution through negotiation?' With a turnout of 87 per cent, 69 per cent of the electorate gave its endorsement. The yes vote was, however, ambiguous. Some assumed that it meant the endorsement of the transfer of power to the black majority. Some believed the NP government would not countenance anything but power-sharing. (An election poster put up by the NP read 'Oppose majority rule: Vote yes.') Yet others believed that the NP had a hidden agenda to tie down the ANC and steadily emasculate it as an organization. Nevertheless, almost all the 'yes' voters accepted that it meant the end of apartheid. On the level of the rank and file there were fewer illusions than among the elite. A poll conducted in late 1991 found that only 15 per cent of whites believed that they would be better off in the 'new South Africa.'[153] The referendum result meant, as Mandela observed, that whites understood that the days of white privilege were over.[154]

De Klerk, who had played the major role in securing the 'yes' majority, started his celebration speech by citing a well-known poem by Van Wyk Louw, who had dreamed of the Afrikaners' 'survival in justice.'[155] In haunting words it asks:

> O wide and woeful land, alone
> Under great southern stars,
> will never an intense joy disturb
> Your calm unmoving grief? . . .
> Simple people who perform
> True and singly bitter things
> And singly fall like grains of seed;
> Dumb deeds, small trust, small treachery . . .
> Will never a mighty beauty come . . .
> And never a deed occur in you
> To echo over earth, and taunt
> Time with its impotence? . . .

The 'yes' vote, De Klerk said just after the result was announced, was 'a deed that echoed over the world' and a mighty message of reconciliation of whites with their fellow-South Africans.[156] The world's reaction was overwhelmingly favorable. The Afrikaners were making their exit with some grace. In the referendum of 1992 they surrendered their position of sole rulers before they were defeated. What remained to be seen was whether there was such an animal as a power-sharing government in a racially divided society. On this the government was pinning all its hopes.

---

153 Human Sciences Research Council, *Information Update*, November 1991.
154 *Die Burger*, 19 March 1992.
155 This translation by Guy Butler is published in A.P. Grové and C.J.D. Harvey, *Afrikaans Poems with English Translations* (Cape Town: Oxford University Press, 1962), p. 135.
156 *Die Burger,* 19 March 1992.

Chapter 17

A New South Africa

What kind of democracy?

President de Klerk's decision to lift the state of emergency, tolerate mass action and start negotiations for a democratic government was a great political leap, one that required both vision and courage. Until the referendum of 1992 there were few South Africans outside the ranks of the right wing who refused to give him credit for this. Some liberals or left-wing radicals did try to disparage his achievement by claiming that he had no other option. But this is implausible. Although there was still a high death toll as a result of the political conflict, repression had markedly reduced the level of organized resistance by the end of the 1980s. The momentum of the ANC-led mass action had declined and P.W. Botha had begun to dismantle the National Security Management System that co-ordinated the state response to the challenge. Yet the straitjacket of sanctions was still there. An ex-insider said: 'Sanctions made it vitally important for South Africa to nego-tiate if it wanted to remain part of the Western trade and financial networks, but there was no need to negotiate only about the hand-over of power.'[1] In a television dialogue broadcast in 2001 De Klerk remarked to Van Zyl Slabbert, a previous leader of the liberal opposition and one of the most astute analysts, that he could still have been in office. Both agreed that a form of white domination could have been extended for twenty years. For De Klerk the main objection to clinging to power was that it would be 'devoid of any morality.'[2]

The other assumption that has no real basis was that the only choice in 1990 was be-tween the continuation of an apartheid-style racism, coupled with repression, and a democ-racy based on individual rights and civil liberties. By the end of the 1980s apartheid was crumbling. The Botha government had abolished influx control and the racial sex laws. Blacks and colored people were breaking down group areas. Black and colored students were attending the historically white universities in growing numbers. The government began to rationalize the use of school buildings to provide better facilities for blacks. The

---

1 Interview Chris Heunis, 15 December 2002.
2 The programme *Dwarsklap*, broadcast on kykNet in Johannesburg on 7 August 2001.

gap in white-black per capita spending on education was narrowing, and most of any
deliberate discrimination on the part of the government had been removed. Chris Heunis,
Minister of Constitutional Development, was introducing integrated structures for the
second and third tiers of government. Black representation on the national level was no
longer a contested issue; the question was how to get the negotiations started. Heunis was
prepared to adjust the central pillar of apartheid, population registration, to make provision for people who did not wish to identify with any racial or ethnic group.

Among the whites there was no collapse of political and moral will; that would only
happen if the leadership's will caved in. There was also no naïvety. Democracy had many
forms and some respected foreign scholars were arguing that the introduction of a simple
majoritarianism would be harmful in a deeply divided society since it would replace one
kind of racial or ethnic hegemony with another. Donald Horowitz, for instance, wrote that
'ascriptive majority rule . . . kills democracy by turning elections into censuses and lock-
ing minorities out. If democracy requires the creation of 'shifting temporary alliances',
the pre-formed racial or ethnic majority is not democratic.'[3]

What the whites wanted was something different from such a system – one in which
the interests of the black majority and the white minority were balanced, in which matters were decided by a large degree of consensus, and in which white and black histories
were integrated rather than having a one-sided interpretation imposed from above. De
Klerk knew that he was taking major risks when he set out on his course, but he was as
determined as any of his colleagues to avoid ending up in a situation where the majority
called all the shots, where the civil service shed the white incumbents in large numbers,
and where an ANC-authorized version replaced white history.

To achieve this he needed extraordinary skills and tough-minded colleagues (or people from outside the party ranks) who could help him conduct the negotiations. The party had lost Heunis, the Cape Province leader, the man most equipped in terms of experience and temperament for tough negotiations. He had publicly said that he was no
longer willing to implement apartheid and left in mid-1989. He had clashed earlier with
De Klerk, who as the Transvaal NP leader had a much more conservative base. After the
1987 election De Klerk ran a real risk of being defeated in his seat in the next election.
(His elevation to the office of state president just before that election exempted him from
the obligation to contest a seat.)

De Klerk needed to use his security forces judiciously to convey the impression that
the white-controlled state was no pushover. He also required credible black allies to draw
into the government if the ANC-led alliance refused to make any compromises, and
business leaders to act as intermediaries with Western leaders. A government demand
that the power of a single, undifferentiated majority be broken up by a strong form of
federalism would have encountered strong ANC resistance. But there was a chance that it
could have created the conditions for a more complex form of negotiations, producing a
better system in the end.

When he unbanned the liberation movements De Klerk had not undergone a conversion in a shattering moment of truth. For all his search for principles, he was an adaptable

3 Donald Horowitz, *A Democratic South Africa* (Cape Town: Oxford University Press, 1991), pp. 98-9. See
    also Elaine Spitz, *Majority Rule* (Chatham: Chatham House, 1984).

politician in weighing alternatives in a shifting demographic and political balance. He abandoned apartheid because the homelands policy had failed to achieve 'separate freedoms', not because it was wrong. He told a television interviewer: 'If one believes a policy is unworkable, it becomes immoral to advocate it.' Pragmatic survival instincts preceded morality in his decision to abandon apartheid.[4]

Three factors limited his options. The first was that he had little time to clinch a deal. When he came to power in 1989, half the Afrikaners had already drifted to the right, and the NP was without any direction. Since the party had fought the September 1989 election on the promise that it would be the last time it would exclude blacks, De Klerk set himself only five years to find a solution; he never seemed to consider simply lengthening the term of Parliament.

Then there were economic sanctions. The De Klerk government was very keen to get them lifted to end the severe recession of the early 1990s and turn around the spiraling state debt. Ending sanctions meant meeting the conditions of Western governments, which attached considerable weight to the opinion of the ANC and, in particular, to that of Nelson Mandela. Since progress in the negotiations was the determining factor, De Klerk had to put most of his efforts into keeping the negotiations going rather than waiting for the ANC to make its move.

The third factor was that De Klerk lacked the ruthlessness that characterizes most great leaders in turbulent times. He was not prepared to walk over corpses to retain power. He had no stomach for a show of force. To those who advocated shooting it out, he answered in the stark terms he used in an address to senior police officers just before unbanning the liberation movements: 'For if this Armageddon takes place – and blood flows ankle deep in our streets and four or five million people lie dead – the problem will remain exactly the same as it was before the shooting started.'[5]

From the start De Klerk refused to use as a counterweight the military with its knowledge and experience of counter-revolutionary warfare. In his own terms he was a 'peacemaker.' He and those Afrikaners in control of the security forces did not trust each other.[6] He soon alienated the military by disbanding the National Security Management System and sidelining the State Security Council. He also cut military expenditure and halved conscription.[7]

The NP government prepared to abandon apartheid, but the policy had extracted its revenge. All the main goals of Afrikaner nationalism that had generated enthusiasm had been achieved by 1970 – South Africa's own national symbols, a republican form of government, a secure place for Afrikaans as a public language, single-medium Afrikaans schools and universities and a well-skilled and trained white labor force. But for many of the more idealistic whites the stark contrast between white opulence and black poverty had become obscene. Politics in the apartheid state had less and less appeal for the more gifted Afrikaners, who went into business and the professions. Because apartheid had removed the points of conflict between whites and blacks from the regular political arena

---

4 Interview by David Frost of De Klerk, 14 February 1993, official transcript.
5 Patti Waldmeir, *Anatomy of a Miracle* (London: Viking, 1997), p. 137.
6 *Dwarsklap* program on kykNet, 7 August 2001.
7 Annette Seegers, *The Military in the Making of Modern South Africa* (London: I.B.Tauris, 1996), p. 285.

the NP negotiators had no experience of racial bargaining. The apartheid state's zeal to protect the different cultures had led Afrikaners to relax their vigilance with respect to the Afrikaans language and culture. It had weakened Afrikaner civil society by fostering a paralyzing dependence on the state as the benign patron that co-ordinated the interests of the ethnic group.

Given the history of apartheid oppression, the Afrikaners could not fall back on minority rights. There was, in any event, no longer the self-conscious Afrikaner ethnic group of the 1960s insisting on political self-determination. Only half the Afrikaners still supported the NP, whose leaders had discarded the political definition of the Afrikaners as a white ethnic group and had become a multi-racial party. The Conservative Party and other parties further to the right still embraced the exclusive definition espoused by Afrikaner nationalism in its heyday, but they had no plan, apart from calling for resistance to a black government. The issue of 'morality' was an important factor in the changing power balance. The West's sanctions had hurt the Afrikaners who supported apartheid morally much more than economically. Afrikaners had always considered themselves part of the West, and their ostracism on account of apartheid had seared their leaders' souls. The Conservative Party's position lacked any semblance of morality.

De Klerk knew that his historic destiny as a leader was mainly to concede, and he would manage to do that with what Seamus Heaney, the Irish poet, described as 'a largeness of spirit and a largeness of gesture and generosity.'[8] But that he and his negotiators would manage to retain so little despite a position of relative strength places a serious question mark over his leadership abilities.

This final chapter tells the story of how the ANC managed to prevail and to establish a simple democratic system with a concentrated black majority controlling a highly centralized state. It is not meant as a criticism of De Klerk's decision to negotiate but to explain why the first prize, namely a balanced system, eluded him.

The balance tips

After the referendum of March 1992 on whether the government should continue the negotiations for a democratic government, the close electoral tie that had long existed between the white electorate and the political leadership was severed. There would not be another white election and the prospect of a white referendum to approve the negotiated constitution, as originally promised by President de Klerk, quickly faded. Not only would the ANC leadership not allow it but it had also become clear that the all-party talks at Kempton Park that had started at the end of 1991 would only draw up an interim constitution. The final constitution would be drafted by the first parliament chosen on a universal franchise according to broad guidelines agreed upon at multi-party forum talks at Kempton Park.

The ANC entered the post-referendum round of negotiations with the following objectives in mind: it had to keep together its constituency who were tired of the disruptions; it had to split the NP and its black allies; it had to discredit the security forces, the

8 *Cape Times*, 4 October 2002.

main pillar of the government support, and it had to prevent any structural constraints on majority rule. The latter meant implacable opposition to the two key NP political demands: a federation and white 'self-determination.' At its strongest, self-determination meant a white veto in the government and, at its weakest, white control over the predominantly white schools and universities. Somewhere in between was the proposal of a power-sharing government.

The strong 'yes' vote in the 1992 referendum in response to an open-ended question was not an unmixed blessing for the NP. Both the ANC and Western governments saw it as a sign that whites were not demanding any special protection. In July 1992 Herman Cohen, US Under-Secretary of State for Africa, declared that all sides had to recognize the 'right of the majority to govern.' No side could insist on 'overly complex arrangements intended to guarantee a share of power to particular groups, which will frustrate effective governance. Minorities have the right to safeguards; they cannot expect a veto.'[9] The ANC could not have phrased its key demand better.

When De Klerk met President Bush in Washington in 1990 he informed him that his government was 'in step with your basic value system.'[10] But what were these values? De Klerk demanded a power-sharing government, a concept not tested in the US. He wanted 'equal treatment and opportunities for all', particularly in the labor market, but the USA was moving towards or considering equality of outcomes.[11] The ANC soon projected the demand for equal opportunities as an attempt to exploit the benefits apartheid had provided, for example better education and skills for whites. Without any need to return to its constituency the NP principal negotiators presented themselves to the ANC as people who had renounced all racism, had no hang-ups about culture and ethnicity and could be trusted as partners in a future government.

Roelf Meyer, who in May 1992 replaced Gerrit Viljoen as the government's chief negotiator, would later declare in Belfast, Northern Ireland, that there was no comparison between the conflict situations in the two countries: 'We in South Africa had basically no differences to resolve . . . It was almost as simple a matter as color or race that separated us. We had to remove the problem to reach out to each other, and to discover each other as human beings.'[12] This represented the collapse not only of apartheid ideology but also of any defense of minorities against the claims of a dominant majority. These words opened the door to what Mandela demanded: 'an ordinary democracy.' This is the kind of democracy of a stable, prosperous country without deep racial or ethnic divisions in which individual rights are thought sufficient to assuage minority fears.

The outcome of the negotiations would be decided by the way in which the main contenders read the balance of forces. After the negotiations had ended Meyer declared: 'We, the government] did enormously well because we did not really have any bargaining power.'[13] The ANC itself assessed the situation differently. In a 'strategic perspective paper' on negotiations, issued in November 1992, it pointed out that while the regime had

---

9 Steven Friedman, *The Long Journey* (Johannesburg: Ravan Press, 1993), p. 157.
10 Leon Wessels, *Die einde van 'n era* (Cape Town: Tafelberg, 1994), p. 43.
11 *Cape Times*, 21 October 1991.
12 Padriag O'Malley (ed.), *Ramaphosa and Meyer in Belfast* (Boston: McCormack Institute, 1996). p. 27.
13 *Die Burger*, 15 January 2000.

been weakened, the ANC was unable to overthrow it. 'The regime still commands vast state and other military resources.'[14] On paper the government was strong, but everything turned on the leaders' will and resolve. The fact that De Klerk at an early stage halved the period of military duty for white males signaled that he was reluctant to demonstrate the state's power.

The sheer weight of black numbers affected the power balance. In 1974, when B.J. Vorster made the plea that the world had to give South Africa six months, there were thirteen million more blacks than whites; by the early 1990s the figure was twenty-three million. At the time of Vorster's speech black workers still had few rights and black un-employment was low; now, in the early 1990s, there was a veritable army of black un-employed, available for mobilization in demonstrations. In 1974 the black trade unions were still not a political factor. Now the ANC-aligned trade union federation called COSATU formed a potent instrument that could be deployed at critical moments in the negotiations.

Yet another factor that impinged on the negotiations was the violence that marked the transition. The real nature of the violence is a complex issue, and even the framework in which to judge it is in dispute. South Africa in the early 1990s was neither a rogue state surviving through terrorizing and killing its opponents nor a strong state with a proper-ly manned police force. Unlike Britain and the USA, South Africa was not dealing with a civil rights movement but a liberation movement. The struggle in South Africa was, in fact, a battle for the great prize – the state – with an understaffed and often undisciplined police force on the one side, and embittered, sometimes desperate, freedom fighters on the other. The conflict in Natal between the ANC and Chief Mangosuthu Buthelezi's Inkatha movement was a low-level civil war with massacres by one side followed by retaliation in kind by the other.

Well organized and disciplined on the leadership level, the ANC played its cards right. It deployed a multi-faceted strategy in which negotiations dovetailed with mobilization, propaganda, diplomacy and forms of revolutionary warfare. In the propaganda war over the violence the ANC-aligned forces won hands down in their concerted efforts to dis-credit the security forces. Mandela accused De Klerk either of complicity or of not caring enough about black deaths to stop the violence, and the relationship between them soon turned sour. The ANC continued to state that a 'Third Force', headed by 'men at the highest levels of the security forces', was responsible for most of the intra-black violence. The Truth and Reconciliation Commission would later find that there was 'little evi-dence of a centrally directed, coherent and formally instituted third force.' If there was a problem it was the existence of an informal network with its own command structure, often involving senior security officers who engaged in unlawful activity.[15]

De Klerk felt that violence from any side was to be deplored. He saw the best chance for a settlement in quick and smooth action. He was, however, also compelled to keep the

---

14 SAPA PR Wire Service, 28 November 1992. See also the document published in Peter Stiff, *Warfare by Other Means* (Alberton: Galago, 1992), pp. 431-39. According to a communication to the author on 2 December 2002 by Ronnie Kasrils, a SACP leader, the document is a 'fabrication probably issued by military intelligence.' Johan van der Merwe of the SAP concurs.

15 *Report of the Truth and Reconciliation Commission* (Cape Town: Juta, 1998), vol. 2, pp. 699-702.

security forces on his side. He could not dismiss senior officers at will and could not instruct them to act where no sound evidence existed. As a result his government was unable to change the conviction held by the local English press and the foreign media that the state was mostly to blame for the violence or was doing too little to stamp it out.[16] To deal with this issue, De Klerk appointed Judge Richard Goldstone to investigate any political violence that broke out. He did not interfere with inquests and courts dealing with the deaths of activists.

De Klerk tried to put some distance between himself and his government's security forces. By 1992 he was under strong pressure from both the ANC and foreign governments to show that his hands were clean by firing some of the top army generals. In December 1992 he purged twenty-three military officers, without offering any clear grounds for their dismissal. Subsequently the Attorney General refused to authorize any prosecutions. The episode strengthened the perception that the ANC had gained the upper hand on a key issue.[17]

At this stage the state's security forces became alienated from De Klerk's leadership. The top military officers strongly believed that American pressure had forced De Klerk to embark on the purge. George Meiring, Chief of the Defence Force, states that on the day Nelson Mandela was inaugurated as president he said to De Klerk: 'You never used your strong base to negotiate from, you never used the military as a base for strength, which you had available to you, you never wanted to use it.' [18]

De Klerk still hoped that after the first democratic election his party could exert some power as a gatekeeper for strategic sectors. However, its ability to act as the agent for these sectors was soon questioned. When the ANC renounced nationalization as a policy option, big business quickly accepted it as a future government with which it could do business and scaled down its support for De Klerk and the NP. Most white civil servants decided at an early stage that the negotiations would result in black majority rule and the replacement of many by blacks. They gave up on the NP as the guarantor of their interests, particularly after the ANC promised to pay out pensions and satisfactory retirement packages for those it wished to retrench.[19]

The alienation of the security forces turned to dismay when the chance was missed to negotiate amnesty for the members of all parties. In a visit to South Africa early in 1992 Cyrus Vance, ex-US Secretary of State, urged the different parties to accept a general amnesty to get the issue out of the way. At this point the South African security forces still had no reason to fear that they would be forced to ask for amnesty. Oblivious to the fact that the power balance was turning against the government, Kobie Coetsee, Minister of Justice, delayed amnesty for the ANC leadership, hoping to use it as a bargaining chip against key members of the movement. After the ANC had managed to get amnesty for a large number of its fighters halfway through the negotiations, it insisted that amnesty for

---

16 Adrian Guelke, *South Africa in Transition* (London: I.B. Tauris, 1999), pp. 45-66.

17 H. Hamann, *Days of the Generals* (Cape Town: Zebra, 2001), pp. 195-207.

18 Interview with George Meiring, 11 November 2002; Hamann, *Days of the Generals,* p. 227. De Klerk categorically denies the allegation made in this source that he had said to Meiring that the old state 'need not have given in so easily.' Communication to author by De Klerk, 28 June 2002.

19 J.S. Wessels and A. Viljoen, 'Waarde-oriëntasies en toekomsverwagtinge van die Vereniging van Staatsamptenare', HSRC report, 1992.

the rest and for those members of the security forces who had committed human rights abuses had to be dealt with after the election.

In the perception of the security forces Meyer, eager to have the negotiations succeed, even if substantial concessions had to be made, was as much to blame as Coetsee for the situation in which they suddenly found themselves. In the final round of the negotiations a clause was hurriedly inserted compelling violators of human rights to ask for amnesty to avoid prosecution. The ANC as the future majority party would have the most say on the composition of the commission that would deal with amnesty and on the way in which it would operate.

The NP's black support evaporated when it became clear that it was no longer the sole source of power. Early in 1992 almost nine per cent of blacks backed the NP and a further 14 per cent supported 'a party with De Klerk as leader.'[20] But as the government lost the upper hand in the negotiations, its support among blacks dwindled to between three and four per cent. With the exception of Buthelezi, who had formed the Inkatha Freedom Party, none of the governments in the homelands had built up a strong party. Assured by Nelson Mandela that they would retain their rights and powers, the tradition-al leaders in these areas threw their weight behind the ANC.[21] Homeland blacks became the ANC's strongest support base.

From deadlock to elections

On 15 May 1992 the constitutional negotiations deadlocked on the percentage of sup-port required to make decisions in the constituent assembly. (The NP wanted 75 per cent; the ANC 66 per cent.) The ANC left the negotiating table and announced a campaign of protest marches, demonstrations and strikes to back up its demands. It demanded that the white minority stop frustrating 'the overwhelming majority.'[22] Cyril Ramaphosa, the ANC chief negotiator who had earned his spurs as a trade unionist in the 1980s, under-stood the importance of negotiations in an issue-centered crisis. The issue soon manifested itself in the massacre on 17 July of thirty-eight residents of Boipatong, an ANC-support-ing township 100 miles southeast of Johannesburg, by Inkatha-aligned hostel-dwellers. Claiming police complicity, the ANC suspended its participation in the negotiations in-definitely. Both a court and the Amnesty Committee of the Truth and Reconciliation Com-mission later could find no evidence that the police were involved, as the ANC claimed. However, the ANC managed to control the framing of the event to make it seem that the state, perhaps even De Klerk, was to blame.

The ANC withdrawal from the negotiations and its program of rolling mass action rep-resented a precarious moment, with the unraveling of public order and a meltdown of the economy a real possibility. But if De Klerk wished to secure any balanced settlement he had to sit out the crisis, perhaps mobilizing large contingents of the security forces and

---

20 Poll commissioned by MarkData, February 1992.

21 R.W. Johnson and Lawrence Schlemmer (eds.), 'National Issues and National Opinion', in R.W. Johnson and Lawrence Schlemmer (eds.), *Launching Democracy in South Africa* (New Haven: Yale University Press, 1996), p. 105.

22 Z.B. du Toit, *Die nuwe toekoms* (Pretoria: J.P. van der Walt, 1999), p. 91.

the active citizen force. He had no taste for an extended battle of wills. By now he was pinning his hopes on a government of national unity in which the ANC and NP as the main representatives of the black majority and the white minority would learn to work together through compromises.

To get the negotiations back on track, the government made some key concessions, including granting amnesty to several ANC operatives found guilty of serious crimes, and the fencing of some hostels where Inkatha supporters lived. In the public perception De Klerk had suffered a crucial defeat in the test of wills. The NP-led coalition of white and black parties at the negotiations disintegrated. Outraged, Buthelezi withdrew all support from the government. When the ANC proposed a government of national unity to extend for five years after the first election, De Klerk accepted it as the basic element of the deal.

To give in to the ANC's key demand of all power to the majority had some positive spinn-offs for De Klerk's constituency. Simple majority rule took much of the needle out of white-black political conflict. Perhaps only an ANC government which enjoyed the NP's blessing could adopt a prudent fiscal and monetary policy and could quickly bring political stability to South Africa, while a gracious abdication of power could redeem the Afrikaners in the eyes of many.

But simple majority rule held the risk of massive state intervention in the labor market, pressure to change the ownership of productive assets and the marginalization of Afrikaans as a public language. More importantly, simple majority rule was not what De Klerk had set out to achieve and not what the NP had promised the electorate. In the election of 1989 and the referendum of 1992 the NP undertook to ensure that the majority party did not get all the say in the government. In one of its principal press advertisements before the first democratic election in April 1994 the NP stated boldly: 'We have kept all our promises. We have a Government of National Unity, which means that the political parties will share power.'[23] But the new constitution certainly did not mean that. It decreed that each party that won more than eighty seats in a four-hundred member National Assembly would be able to nominate one of two executive deputy presidents, while each party that won at least twenty seats would be entitled to cabinet posts in proportion to its share of the vote. However, while Mandela assured De Klerk that he needed him and his party, he insisted that this was subordinate to the right of the majority to make the final decision in cabinet. The ANC accepted elected governments for the nine provinces and a limited devolution of power, but it fell well short of federalism. The ANC got what it wanted most: a closed list system of proportional representation, which greatly helped to prevent intra-black ethnic rivalry within the party, a unitary form of government, and no white 'self-determination.'

That the contending parties could agree on a constitution was hailed as a miracle, but the truth is mundane. 'Sufficient consensus' was achieved primarily by incorporating conflicting demands and by deferring their resolution to the post-apartheid regime. There was no clarity about what was meant by negotiations or agreement. The NP thought that it was a mutually beneficial and stable settlement, one that the main parties would change only by mutual agreement. The ANC, by contrast, fought a classic 'war of position' in which each concession it extracted from the government became the platform for the next

---

23 *Die Burger,* 27 April 1994.

challenge in what it called the 'national democratic revolution.' It could amend its position as the balance of forces shifted in its favor.[24] In 1995 Thabo Mbeki, deputy president of South Africa, would tell an ANC conference that the negotiations for an interim constitution were 'contrived elements of a transition' necessary to end white domination. At no time did the ANC consider them 'as elements of permanence.'[25]

The issue of the labor market, for instance, was addressed by incorporating both the principle of merit and the need for affirmative action to redress the 'imbalances' of the past. It is generally agreed that in subsequent years the 'balance' tipped sharply in favor of the latter. The same thing happened in the case of language rights – the key to Afrikaner cultural survival in a future black-ruled state. Back in May 1992, when the second round of negotiations started, De Klerk was as eager as any of his predecessors to secure a future for his constituency and for the Afrikaans language. He would bequeath the money tied to the Nobel Peace Prize, which he and Nelson Mandela jointly won in 1993, to the promotion of Afrikaans. But the government faced an adversary, which, like its counterparts in the rest of Africa, was keen to elevate English, the former colonial language, to the effective public language to secure jobs and status for the black elite and their children.

There had been a time that four official languages – English, Afrikaans and a language from each of the two main Bantu language families – could have been recognized, but the opportunity was allowed to slip away. It was widely predicted that the elevation of eleven languages to the status of official languages would in practice lead to only one, English, becoming the *de facto* official language. Afrikaans still enjoyed a measure of protection through the clause that no language rights might be abridged, but that would be removed by the ANC in the final constitution.

The question of which languages would be used as mediums of instruction in the schools was dealt with by incorporating both the NP's demand for mother-tongue education and the ANC's demand for opening up all schools to all races. The constitution-makers made no attempt to spell out how potential conflicts were to be resolved. This would give a future government the liberty to emphasize what it called the right of black children to have access to all schools and to insist on the language of instruction they preferred. It relegated mother-tongue instruction as a value enshrined in the constitution to a distant third. The new government put pressure on Afrikaans schools to offer English-medium classes parallel to those in Afrikaans where the numbers merited it. Most of the Afrikaans universities voluntarily introduced English streams. Parallel-medium institutions held the real risk that English over the medium term would drive out Afrikaans.

Piet Marais, who was Minister of National Education but not part of the NP's negotiating team, warned De Klerk at a late stage of the negotiations that 'education was not the priority among our negotiators which it should be.' He added that in informal talks he had had with ANC negotiators he had gained the clear impression that they 'displayed an intolerance towards Afrikaans and to the demand that the Afrikaans universities could

---

24 ANC, 'Strategic Perspective on Negotiations'. See also Pierre du Toit, 'Dis tyd vir 'n opvolg-skikking', *Die Burger,* 1 October 2000; for an extended treatment see his inaugural address published by the University of Stellenbosch, 2002.

25 SAPA PR Wire Service, Speech of Thabo Mbeki at ANC National Constitutional Conference, 31 March to 2 April 1995.

continue to imbue their mission with a cultural content.' He urged De Klerk to have a list compiled of bottom lines and undertakings that the NP had given to its voters and indicate which of them it had met. But at that stage all the main issues had already been settled.[26] The issue of the medium of education nearly caused a breakdown in the negotiations for a final constitution that took place in 1995 and 1996. Cyril Ramaphosa, chairperson of the Constitutional Assembly, pointed out that the NP negotiators had left him in the dark over the importance their party attached to education.[27]

A last stand

After the balance of power had tipped against it in mid-1992, the De Klerk government spent much of its energy on avoiding the symbolism of defeat in the transition to a new system. There would be no guerrilla army parading through the streets in a victory march; no toppling of statues and no multi-party control of the security forces in the run-up to the election. The government got its way on constitutional continuity. The product of the all-party negotiations would have no legal force until passed as a law by the Tricameral Parliament. The Chief Justice would swear in the new president, and all the (white) judges would retain their posts. The ANC was ready to indulge the NP in the matter of the symbolism and rituals of power, while it concentrated on the substance.[28]

A right-wing revolt threatened as more details of the deal were made public. About half of the Afrikaners and a million whites in total voted 'no' in the referendum, and they rejected the constitution that was taking shape. But they had no alternative plan and did not even have representatives at the final stage of the negotiations. The other half of the Afrikaners were reform minded and Mandela had won their respect and even affection. Most suspended judgment until the power-sharing government began to tackle the country's problems and resolve conflicting demands.

The military formed a possible source of resistance, but it was small (fewer than seventy thousand full-time soldiers, of whom half were not white) and had a tradition of subservience to the political leadership. The Active Citizens' Force (ACF) had large numbers but was decentralized and reflected the ethnic and political divisions of white society. The major unknown factor was the ex-Chief of the Defence Force, General Constand Viljoen, who was convinced that the ANC was still pursuing a revolutionary agenda and that De Klerk had caved in to their demands.

Called the last of the Boer generals, he was widely respected in the Defence Force for his professionalism and personal integrity. Blunt, determined and committed to the Afrikaner cause, he was the sort of leader to whom many Afrikaners would have flocked in a crisis situation if he had had a credible plan of action. Viljoen joined the Afrikaner Volksfront, a coalition of right-wing parties, organizations and movements, all demanding an Afrikaner volkstaat or ethnic state. De Klerk from the start dismissed the idea and Viljoen later admitted: 'We could never get consensus among our people about where our

---

26 Letter from P.G. Marais to F.W. de Klerk and memo of Marais to author, to be lodged in the US Library Ms. Collection.
27 Interview with Jacko Maree, NP Member of Parliament, 21 April 1998.
28 I wish to thank J.M. Coetzee for some of the points in this paragraph.

volkstaat would be.'[29] Most favored a state with Pretoria as its capital and including parts of the western Transvaal, eastern Transvaal and northern Free State. But while approximately two-thirds of the Afrikaners lived in this area, the great majority of people there were non-Afrikaners. A 1993 poll showed that only one-fifth of the Afrikaners were strong enough in their support for a volkstaat to consider moving there themselves and more than half either opposed it or were uncertain about it.[30]

To further his goal Viljoen planned to disrupt the elections, have De Klerk removed as leader and restart the negotiations. Some believed that he could raise fifty thousand men from the ACF and also some Defence Force units.[31] In a briefing, General George Meiring, Chief of the Defence Force, warned the government and the ANC of the ghastly consequences of Viljoen's opposing the election. To dissuade Viljoen, for whom he had 'the highest regard', he had several meetings with him. At one Viljoen said: 'You and I and our men can take this country in an afternoon,' to which Meiring replied. 'Yes, that is so, but what do we do the morning after the coup?' The white-black demographic balance, the internal and foreign pressures, and all the intractable problems would still be there.[32]

Viljoen's dilemma was compounded by the right-wing fringe elements. In their ranks there was the Afrikaner Weerstandsbeweging (AWB), an ill-disciplined para-military organization under Eugène Terre'Blanche. Viljoen had no wish to join forces with him and his band. In a stand against the constitution-making process the Volksfront entered into a Freedom Alliance with Buthelezi's Inkatha Freedom Party, with Lucas Mangope, who headed the homeland government of Bophuthatswana, and with Oupa Gqozo, leader of the Ciskei government.

The moment of truth arrived when an ANC- instigated rebellion threatened to topple Mangope and take the Bophuthatswana capital of Mafikeng. Mangope called for help from Viljoen, who faced an impossible situation. He had chosen neither the battlefield (to defend a black homeland government in Mafikeng) nor his allies (AWB hotheads yearning to shoot blacks). He withdrew from Mafikeng and was drawn into participating in the election by an ANC promise that the new government would appoint a council of his followers to consider the prospect of an Afrikaner volkstaat. He headed a list of candidates of the Freedom Front, a party he had founded.[33] The Inkatha movement under Buthelezi also decided at the last minute to take part.

The election campaign took place in conditions of turbulence. The ANC and other black-led parties had difficulty canvassing among farm workers, but this was overshadowed by the problems the NP and the liberal Democratic Party encountered in their attempts to campaign in the townships or in dense concentrations of blacks in the homelands. Checking of the vote count showed major discrepancies, and there was a strong suspicion that the final result was determined more by previous opinion polls than the

---

29 *Sunday Independent*, 25 March 2001.
30 Lawrence Schlemmer, 'The Depth and Scope of Support for a Volkstaat', unpublished report of a poll, February 1996.
31 Johann van Rooyen, *Hard Right: The New White Power in South Africa* (London: I.B. Tauris 1994); David Welsh, 'Rightwing terrorism in South Africa', *Terrorism and Political Violence*, 7,1 (1995), pp. 239-64.
32 Interview with George Meiring, 11 November 2002.
33 Pippa Green, 'Divided Hearts and Minds', SA *Leadership*, 13, 19, 1994, p. 1118; *Die Burger,* 23 March 2001.

actual votes counted. But Western monitors and observers afterwards enthusiastically endorsed the election procedure as 'substantially fair and free.' David Welsh, a respected liberal analyst, observed that it was nothing of the kind. 'Hardly any of the sanctimonious foreign observers who fell about themselves to declare it so would for one moment have accepted the validity of an election subject to such flaws in their own countries.'[34] The reality was that it was impossible to call the election fatally flawed and demand a repeat. It might have pushed the country over the precipice.

Election day on 27 April 1994 was peaceful. The ANC won 62.7 per cent of the vote, the NP 20.4 per cent, Buthelezi's IFP 10.5 per cent, Viljoen's Freedom Front 2.2 per cent, the Democratic Party 1.7 per cent and the Pan Africanist Congress 1.2 per cent. The ANC attracted four-fifths of the black vote and was more than 94 per cent dependent on black voters. The NP drew half its votes from people who were not white, emerging as the party with the support of more than 60 per cent of the votes in the white and colored communities. The Afrikaners were split almost right down the middle between the NP reformists and conservatives. The NP won control of the new province of the Western Cape, where 60 per cent of the population was colored, 22 per cent Xhosa, and 24 per cent white, and where 60 percent of the voters spoke Afrikaans as their mother tongue. Colored and Asian support was to an important extent due to anti-black fears and the patronage that the NP had bestowed on these communities during the period of the Tricameral Parliament.[35]

The ethnic support the two parties drew was as follows:

NP AND ANC SHARE OF ETHNIC VOTE IN 1994 (PERCENTAGES)

	AFRICAN	COLORED	ASIAN	WHITE
ANC	81	27	25	3
NP	3	67	50	60

The election was a tribute to both Mandela and De Klerk, the two leaders who had united most South Africans behind the process. But without the last minute support of Buthelezi and Viljoen, and the disciplined supervision of the electoral process by the army and the police under the supervision of General Meiring and General Van der Merwe respectively, the election could easily have ended in disaster.

A commission in pursuit of truth and healing

The new South Africa formally dawned with the inauguration on 10 May 1994 of Nelson Mandela as president of the Republic of South Africa. The ANC dominated the cabinet with eighteen ministers. The NP had six ministers and F.W. de Klerk as one of two deputy presidents in the Government of National Unity. Also in the cabinet were Mangosuthu Buthelezi and two other ministers from the Inkatha Freedom Party (IFP).

A spirit of reconciliation marked the start of the era with Mandela the symbol of the

---

34 David Welsh, 'The Democratic Party', in Andrew Reynolds (ed.), *Election '94: South Africa* (Cape Town: David Philip, 1994), p. 113.
35 For a full analysis see Johnson and Schlemmer, *Launching Democracy*; Reynolds, *Election '94*.

new democracy. He did not spend much time attending cabinet meetings or dealing with the looming crises of spiraling unemployment and the slump in the efficiency of the criminal justice system. He led as a wise statesman, a dignified peacemaker, a consummate politician and an imaginative unifier of people across racial lines, even up to the point of having tea with Mrs Betsie Verwoerd and other widows of NP leaders.[36] He showed no sign of bitterness over the more than twenty-seven years he had spent in jail.

Afrikaners were captivated by Mandela; he cast a spell that produced a state of 'charismatic bewilderment', as Van Zyl Slabbert described it. The culmination was his appearance at the final of the rugby world cup tournament held in Johannesburg, having decided that the national rugby team could retain its green and gold jersey with the springbok emblem despite the fact that for many it symbolized apartheid in sport. Before a crowd of seventy thousand, Mandela appeared on the field donned in the jersey to wish the players well. Fired up, the Springboks went on to win against the odds.

The NP periodically patted itself on the back and told the people that it had abolished apartheid and thus was the co-liberator of the country. This euphoria of self-congratulation could not last. The Afrikaners had lost power, but were behaving like King Lear, who had renounced power but expected everyone to continue treating him as a king. Lear did not see that if he surrendered power – and for this the Fool mocked him – others would take advantage of his weakness. Those who had flattered most grossly – in De Klerk's case the South African liberal press in 1990 and 1991 – had turned against him.[37]

The NP fell from its position of temporary grace when the government in December 1995 established a Truth and Reconciliation Commission to investigate human rights violations that occurred after 1960 when the ANC and other extra-parliamentary organizations were banned. It was to provide a platform where those who had suffered human rights abuses could give testimony. It would also grant amnesty to perpetrators who had made a full confession and make recommendations for the payment of reparations to victims.

Despite its flaws, discussed below, the TRC performed an important therapeutic role in providing victims with the opportunity to tell their story and in acknowledging their suffering. So, too, the hearings exposed the brutality of apartheid and the official web of government lies and deception. The saturation media coverage of the hearings made it impossible for anyone thereafter to deny the atrocities for which the previous regime but also almost all the other parties were responsible. The TRC was not afraid to criticize some of the acts of the liberation movements. The number of public lies was also dramatically reduced with respect to two of the most notorious cases. Steve Biko's fatal injury in detention occurred when he was held by his arms by two security policemen and had his head smashed against a wall. Matthew Goniwe and three friends were murdered by security policemen outside Port Elizabeth. It happened shortly after cabinet ministers with security portfolios visited the city and told the people in command of the security forces that the unrest situation had to be stabilized at all costs.[38]

Both the composition of the TRC and the context in which it would pursue its investi-

36 Pierre du Toit, *South Africa's Brittle Peace* (London: Palgrave, 2001), p. 178.
37 These remarks were stimulated by George Orwell, *Inside the Whale* (Penguin Books, 1984), p. 113.
38 *TRC Report*, vol. 2, pp. 226-8.

gation would determine whether it would achieve its twin objectives of uncovering the truth and promoting reconciliation. The TRC's mandate charged it with the responsibility to be evenhanded, but its composition was hardly balanced. De Klerk wrote in his autobiography that he was 'seriously concerned' when he saw the list of members. The chairman, Archbishop Desmond Tutu, was a patron of the United Democratic Front, the ANC internal front since the early 1980s. Deputy Chairman Alex Boraine had been an opponent in Parliament in the 1970s and 1980s, and was considered by De Klerk as a 'hothead and inquisitor.'[39]

None of the seventeen members was a member of either the NP or the IFP, while most were considered to be tacit or overt ANC supporters. An analysis published by the liberal South African Institute of Race Relations argued that that the commission's staff was overwhelmingly sympathetic to the ANC and that it tended to seek out victims of human rights abuses perpetrated by the government or IFP forces. They were persuaded to tell their story at the public hearings. The study also found that in many cases the level of corroboration of the victims' evidence was not high. Instead of concentrating on the context of a deed the commission focused on the perpetrator or victim, with the result that the context was in most cases only scantily sketched. Cross-examination of victims was not normally allowed in the victim hearings, but hearsay evidence was. The commission did not provide full reasons for its conclusions. It overreached itself in taking on the task of making perpetrator findings.[40]

The context in which the TRC framed the overall conflict was a major source of controversy. In his introduction to the report Archbishop Tutu formally accepted that the Cold War and the struggle between the capitalist and communist systems influenced the conflict in South Africa, but in the end the commission made racism and apartheid virtually the sole causes.[41] Overwhelmingly it framed the political struggle between 1960 and 1994 as one waged against apartheid as a crime against humanity and the South African state's attempt to suppress it. It did not analyze the ANC's judgment in the early 1960s that there was no alternative to an armed struggle.

The charge that apartheid was 'a crime against humanity' had been a central part of the ANC's attack on the government since the early 1970s. The TRC's report pointed out that the UN Security Council in 1976 unanimously accepted that apartheid was a crime against the conscience and dignity of mankind and that on several other occasions similar resolutions were passed by the UN and other international organizations, including the International Law Commission in 1996. The TRC never examined this charge exhaustively. The term 'crimes against humanity' could have a specific content, for instance genocide, but it also could be used in a general sense to refer to 'institutionalized discrimination on racial, ethnic or religious grounds.' It would be inappropriate to describe apartheid as a crime against humanity in the former sense of the word, and accurate in the latter sense. The broad definition of institutionalized discrimination would

---

39 F.W. de Klerk, *Die laaste trek – 'n nuwe begin* (Cape Town: Human & Rousseau, 1998), p. 389.

40 Anthea Jeffery, *The Truth about the Truth Commission* (Johannesburg: SA Institute of Race Relations, 1999), pp. 8-49. See *Report of the Truth and Reconciliation Commission*, particularly the views of the majority and the minority report.

41 *TRC Report*, vol. 1, pp. 13-17.

fit apartheid – and the policies of all the Western colonial powers and of segregation in the American South. But the commission was at pains to depict apartheid as uniquely abhorrent. The charge of genocide that was bandied about by both commission members and cabinet ministers was preposterous since both the black population growth rate and life expectancy increased dramatically during the apartheid years.

The TRC also did not explore the ambiguous history of the UN resolutions and conventions. In 1973 the UN General Assembly declared apartheid a crime against humanity and agreed to the drawing up of an International Convention on the Suppression of the Crime of Apartheid. The main sponsors were the Soviet Union and Guinea and the convention came into operation after twenty countries, all members of the Soviet bloc, ratified it. Approximately seventy countries subsequently signed on. However, all the major Western countries refused to ratify it. At the outset the US stated: 'We cannot accept that apartheid can be made a crime against humanity. Crimes against humanity are so grave in nature that they must be meticulously elaborated and strictly constructed under international law.'[42]

De Klerk implored the commission to take into account dimensions other than the fight against apartheid. There was the long struggle between Afrikaner nationalists wishing to preserve 'national self-determination' and African nationalists wishing to be free, the struggle between various black political movements, and that between the West and an expansionist Soviet Communism. He also argued that apartheid was not only about white privilege but also about development and redistribution of income from whites to blacks. The economy had grown by an average of 3.5 percent per year under apartheid, the black school population grew by 250 per cent in the first twenty-five years of apartheid, and the black share of total personal income had nearly doubled from 20 per cent in the mid-1970s to 37 per cent in 1995, while that of whites had declined from 71 to 49 per cent. [43]

The TRC was not particularly interested in these other dimensions. Tutu wrote elsewhere: '[It] is irrelevant whether racism or apartheid sometimes produced good results. Because the tree was bad the fruit also had to be bad.'[44] The TRC's judgments would all be made from a moral and human rights perspective. There were no historians, political analysts or any other social scientists on the commission, which was made up predominantly of clergymen, human rights lawyers and activists from non-governmental organizations.

In the NP's submission, De Klerk acknowledged the violence generated by apartheid but cited the circumstances, especially the government's counter-insurgency struggle against the ANC and other liberation organizations. But overshadowing everything else in the TRC's agenda were two main questions: Was the white leadership in South Africa prepared to apologize and express remorse for apartheid? Had the government authorized or turned a blind eye to the killings and other human rights violations committed by the security forces?

---

42 *TRC Report*, vol. 1, pp. 94-102; Hermann Giliomee, *Liberal and Populist Democracy in South Africa* (Johannesburg: SA Institute of Race Relations), 1996, pp. 8-9.

43 Text of the submission of F.W. de Klerk to the TRC, 21August 1996, issued by the NP.

44 Desmond Tutu, 'Foreword' to Rodney Davenport and Christopher Saunders, *South Africa: A Modern History* (London: Macmillan, 2000), p. xix.

On 18 February 1998 Tutu called on 'all whites, especially the Afrikaners', to acknowledge that 'dastardly things' had happened in the past. 'You white people – if you reject the
TRC you will carry the burden of guilt to your graves,' he said. *Die Burger* responded that
Tutu had meted out collective guilt, 'one of the most dangerous doctrines in history.'[45] After an outcry Tutu qualified his statement to exempt those Afrikaners who had opposed
apartheid or who had confessed to the TRC.[46]

The members of the old Afrikaner nationalist alliance responded in different ways to
the call for sectors of society to express remorse. The Afrikaanse Handelsinstituut, as the
vehicle of organized Afrikaner business, confessed that apartheid was wrong, morally
and economically. The DRC leadership appeared before the TRC to state that the church
had renounced apartheid at successive synods but found itself divided over the TRC.
Judging that it would not get a fair hearing, Nasionale Pers, the main Afrikaans publishing house, refused to make a submission, and sent a history of the press instead. On behalf of the NP and the previous government De Klerk made a sweeping and eloquent
apology for apartheid:

> Apartheid was wrong. I apologize in my capacity as leader of the National Party to
> the millions of South Africans who suffered the wrenching disruption of forced re-
> movals in respect of their homes, businesses and land. Who over the years suffered
> the shame of being arrested for pass laws offences. Who over the decades and in-
> deed centuries suffered the indignities and humiliation of racial discrimination.
> Who for a long time were prevented from exercising their full democratic rights in
> the land of their birth. Who were unable to achieve their full potential because of
> job reservation. And who in any other way suffered as a result of discriminatory legis-
> lation and policies. This apology is offered in a spirit of true repentance, in full
> knowledge of the tremendous harm that apartheid has done to millions of South
> Africans.[47]

De Klerk's apology failed to satisfy the TRC. What it also wanted to hear was that the
State Security Council, of which De Klerk had been a member, had authorized or condoned the murder and torture of state enemies. De Klerk denied that the SSC had ever
given such instructions and insisted that the terms recorded in the minutes – *verwyder*
or *uitwis* ('eliminate' or 'exterminate' opponents) did not mean that the security forces
were given blanket permission to murder.

At a press conference Tutu rejected De Klerk's claim that he did not know about the
atrocities and other crimes, and maintained that the NP government's policy gave the
security forces 'a license' to commit murder. 'De Klerk knew,' he said, and recounted that
after the Boipatong massacre in June 1992 he had told De Klerk of the allegations that
policemen were involved. Accusing the TRC of bias, the NP sought a court injunction
against Tutu, who retracted his claim.[48]

The truth was murkier than any side publicly acknowledged. The political conflict

---

45 *Cape Times*, 19 February 1998; *Die Burger*, 19 February 1998.
46 Piet Meiring, *Kroniek van die Waarheidskommissie* (Vanderbijlpark: Carpe Diem, 1999), pp. 336-7.
47 Text of testimony of F.W. de Klerk to TRC hearing, 14 May 1997, issued by the NP.
48 Meiring, *Kroniek*, pp. 141-4.

in South Africa was a complex one. The NP government had long demonized the ANC as a mere agent of Soviet expansionism and leaders across white society had urged young people to defend the country against the threat it posed to order and 'civilization.' The ANC itself was responsible for reinforcing these perceptioins. At a conference held in 1985 the ANC had recommitted itself to a 'People's War' whose aim, it said, was 'the seizure of power through a general insurrection.' In broadcasts beamed to South Africa it reinforced the perception that a life and death struggle was being waged. It urged the population to rise up against an illegitimate system and to make the country ungovernable. It sent heavily armed guerrilla fighters into the country, often with instructions to kill policemen. ANC-aligned elements intimidated and on occasion injured or killed members of those organizations making rival claims for black support, particularly the IFP, which opted for change within the apartheid system, at times siding with the white government.

Many white soldiers and policemen were ready to fight in what they assumed to be a showdown over which racial group would rule South Africa, confident that the white public backed them. Some indeed took the injunction to 'eliminate ' and remove state opponents from society literally, and for this the politicians were as much to blame as anyone else.[49]

The South African Communist Party, which played such a key role in the ANC propaganda machine, made it its main objective to discredit the security forces. The propaganda surrounding the Boipatong massacre, which Tutu cited as evidence that De Klerk knew, illustrated this tactic. Immediately after the massacre the ANC disseminated charges of police complicity, offering this as the motive for withdrawing from the constitutional negotiations. Tutu personally, as well as the TRC report, accepted this version of Boipatong. But no grounds existed. De Klerk immediately after the massacre had asked Judge Richard Goldstone's commission to investigate the charges, and a senior British police inspector was called in. Goldstone could find no evidence to support the charges. A criminal court and the TRC's amnesty committee, both of which subsequently dealt with the issue, found no evidence that policemen had played a role in the massacre.

At the same time, however, there was a long history of security policemen having considerable leeway. The fact that there were relatively few prosecutions against policemen in the criminal courts gave policemen the idea that considerable latitude existed. In some cases commanders turned a blind eye, in other cases the supervision was poor and cover-ups often occurred. In the 1977 inquest into Steve Biko's death the officer in charge of the security police in Port Elizabeth was asked where he got the authority to keep an injured man naked and in chains in his cell for 48 hours. He replied: 'We have full authority. It is left to my sound discretion . . . We don't work under statutory authority.'[50] Subsequently the government tightened up the regulations and made better provision for inspection by independent people. During the 1980s the government continued to state publicly that torture, as well as murder, were criminal offences. It gave strict instructions that violators must be brought to book.

---

49 Craig Williamson best portrayed this mindset in his testimony to the TRC. See the interview in *Weekend Argus*, 8/9 July 1995.
50 Donald Woods, *Biko* (New York: Paddington Press, 1978), p. 199.

But particularly in regions like the eastern Cape, where the conflict was intense in the period 1984-86, the security police found themselves locked together with the military in a struggle in which the dictates of making war rather than policing took precedence. Commissioner of Police Johan van der Merwe noted: 'The Police, particularly the Security Branch, were subject to so many influences and involved in so many secret projects that some members later pursued only one goal, and that was the extermination of the enemy.'[51] Torture continued. Leon Wessels, a deputy minister of police in the late 1980s stated: '[It] was foreseen that people would be tortured; everybody in the country knew that people were tortured.'[52]

Policemen understood that if sufficient evidence was produced of torture, assault or murder they were on their own and that if a detainee sustained injuries or died from unnatural causes they would almost certainly have to stand trial. But there was a large gray area and forms of torture that did not result in injuries continued. Supervision was often inadequate and methods of torture like suffocation in a wet bag, which did not result in injuries, went undetected. Much of the state's attempts to crush the insurgency occurred on a decentralized basis, with reporting only on a 'need to know' principle, with the result that people at the top may well not have known. Police chief Van der Merwe notes: 'Members of the Security Branch were accustomed to act independently and most violations heard by the TRC's amnesty committee occurred in secret.'[53]

In testifying to the TRC De Klerk made a distinction between policemen acting in a *bona fide* way in transgressing the law (but to him this did not include murder or serious assault), and those operating in a *male fide* way by flagrantly disregarding instructions and murdering or torturing state opponents. The latter was indeed true of some of the murders committed by Eugene de Kock and other members of the notorious C10 Police Unit at Vlakplaas, which received saturation coverage in the press. But the line between the two cases was often blurred. Was 'mild' torture to extract information about ANC operatives planning to plant bombs *bona fide*? De Klerk acknowledged to the TRC that there were all sorts of blurred distinctions between acceptable and unacceptable methods.[54]

All the fissures in society manifested itself in the TRC. Two of the female African commissioners accused some of the white members of racism. An Asian commissioner pushed hard for Buthelezi to be subpoenaed, which could have had dire consequences for stability. Members of the old security establishment tried to damage the TRC's credibility and the ANC put severe pressure on the body to absolve it from moral criticism. As chairperson, Archbishop Tutu had his flaws but he made his stand on this occasion by declaring that he was prepared to fight a new tyranny with as much commitment as the old one. Even among liberals there was a clear difference between Mary Burton, who took a firm stand on the basis of liberal values and fairness and some of the others, described as slide-away liberals, who sought to advance the liberation struggle rather than the liberal cause.

The old Afrikaner-English cleavage also appeared, particularly in the responses to De Klerk's appearance before the commission. Three of the four English-speaking white

---

51 Interview with Johan van der Merwe, 20 November 2002. For a full statement from the security police see Hermann Stadler, *The Other Side of the Story* (Pretoria: Contact Publishers, 1997) and Submission of Genl Johan van der Merwe to the TRC, 21 October 1996.

52 *TRC Report*, vol. 2, p. 219.

53 Interview with Johan van der Merwe, 20 November 2002.

54 *TRC Report*, vol. 5, p. 267.

members of the commission, Alex Boraine, Richard Lyster and Wendy Orr, figured prominently among those who insisted that De Klerk had not apologized fully for apartheid,
refrained from expressing proper remorse and denied his complicity in the crimes of
apartheid. For them 'expiation and forgiveness by blacks would only come from a full
confession.' Wynand Malan, one of the two Afrikaner members, felt that they had made
a barely concealed attempt to settle old political scores by 'constructing a grand conspiracy theory: the cabinet, the State Security Council, the NP caucus and the Afrikaners
were all collectively guilty.' In his minority report Malan rejected what he termed an attempt to impose a history with a 'single truth' and called for 'a move away from right versus wrong, from black versus white to shades of gray.'[55] But Boraine would have none of
this; Malan, in his view, was simply trying to put a sophisticated spin on apartheid.[56]

The TRC also opened up a major cleavage between NP politicians and the police leadership, who felt that the government had subjected it to unbearable pressure to suppress
the uprising and that the least the NP leaders could do was to accept common responsibility for violations of human rights. Ex-President Botha, who was widely suspected of
having authorized some unlawful acts, refused to co-operate with the TRC and Louis le
Grange, Minister of Police in the first part of the uprising, had died in office.

Having failed to get Botha to accept responsibility, the TRC concentrated all their efforts to get De Klerk to admit that he either took part in decisions that resulted in illegal
acts or did not take part but knew of such decisions. But De Klerk was not involved in
most of the meetings concerning security issues that took place during the 1980s and
was adamant that at those he did attend nothing improper occurred.[57] From start of his
period in office he had used a variety of means to establish the truth and to punish human
rights violations.

Initially De Klerk was sympathetic to the demand that the political and the police
leadership should ask for a form of collective amnesty, although the legislation did not
permit it. (The ANC did put in a request for a collective amnesty.) However, most of his
ex-cabinet colleagues rejected this course. Some, like Kobie Coetsee, were afraid that the
process could end up with a Nuremberg-style court case. In the end only one politician
(Minister of Police Adriaan Vlok) and a few military officers asked for amnesty, but large
numbers of policemen complied.

No political leader pitched up to give moral support. Senior policemen who had to
ask for amnesty felt that they had been left in the lurch. Ex-Police chief Van der Merwe
remarked at the time: 'No policemen will ever vote for the NP again.'[58] Leon Wessels, a
deputy minister of law and order, was more courageous than his colleagues in refusing
to take the line that he was ignorant of the abuses: 'I refuse to condemn them [the soldiers and policemen] because we were on the same side and fought for the same cause,
namely law and order as we saw it, and also to ensure that this country would not be
made ungovernable . . . I do not believe the political defense of "I did not know" is
available to me because in many respects I did not want to know.'[59] General Constand
Viljoen, head first of the Army and then the Defence Force struck a similar note: He

55 *TRC Report, vol. 5*, p. 441; Interview with Wynand Malan, 21 November 2002.
56 Alex Boraine, *A Country Unmasked* , (Oxford: Oxford University Press, 2001), p. 97.
57 De Klerk, *Die laaste trek*, p. 199.
58 Interview with Johan van der Merwe, 21 November 2002.
59 *The Citizen*, 16 October 1997.

had all conflicting parties in mind when he declared: 'Why can't we agree that we all have dirty hands? We fought a war that should have been avoided at the start or stopped at a much earlier stage. We fought a dirty war.'[60]

The TRC satisfied none of the main parties, including the ANC, which tried to stop publication of the interim report that criticized some of the methods it used. The public was split on what the TRC had achieved. A poll taken in late 2000 by the Institute of Justice and Reconciliation, established to continue the TRC's work, found that only 29 per cent of whites felt that the TRC had fostered the building of a united nation, against 77 per cent of blacks and 56 percent of colored people. While three-quarters of both Xhosa and Zulu respondents and half of the English-speakers approved of the activities of the TRC, only a third of the Afrikaners did so. Nearly 80 per cent of Afrikaners (and a slightly lower proportion of English-speakers) agreed with the proposition: 'The TRC will only end badly – therefore South Africans should look to the future and forget the past', but only about 30 per cent of Xhosas and Zulus did so. Most people felt that whites had a real fear of communism at the time of apartheid.[61]

Hovering in the background was the policy of apartheid thought to be dead and discredited. The pollsters received a surprising response when they asked the following question: 'There were certainly some abuses under the old apartheid system, but the ideas behind apartheid were basically good.' Surprisingly large proportions still thought the basic idea was sound, with only a third of Afrikaners who believed it was not true.[62] Below are the responses in full:

RESPONSES TO THE QUESTION WHETHER THE BASIC IDEA OF APARTHEID WAS GOOD

	TRUE	NOT TRUE	DON'T KNOW
All South Africans	39	55	7
Afrikaners	65	29	6
White English	36	60	5
Xhosa-speaking	18	73	9
Zulu-speaking	25	65	10
Colored people	38	55	7

It can be assumed that the non-white respondents did not yearn for undiluted white supremacy, but rather for the version of the 1980s, according to which each population group as designated by apartheid was held responsible for its 'own affairs' with representatives from each group sharing in decision-making about 'general' affairs. Other polls showed that members of apartheid's statutory groups consistently named someone from their own group as the most popular leader.

---

60 Meiring, *Kroniek*, p. 145.

61 *Die Burger,* 12 June 2001.

62 The source of the data was a survey conducted and published by the Cape Town-based Institute for Justice and Reconciliation (www.ijr.org.za). This survey was undertaken at the end of 2000 and the beginning of 2001 and involved 3,727 interviews. The interviews were conducted in the language of choice of the respondent. The responses true/partially true and wrong/partially wrong are combined in the table.

'Giving up on the ideal'

In the new government the NP quickly lost its public profile. De Klerk stated that the ANC ignored the minority parties and refused to share power or seek consensus on critical issues. NP cabinet ministers were expected to work within the ANC's policy framework.[63] No conventions were laid down for the cabinet. The ANC criticized De Klerk when he aired contested issues in public.

In 1996 a new constitution was drafted within the constitutional guidelines that had been drawn up in 1992-93. The ANC refused to accept a power-sharing cabinet as a principle in the final constitution. In protest De Klerk, at the end of 1996, took the NP out of the government. In January 1997, in a speech in London, he declared that no balanced political settlement of the kind the NP had sought had occurred, but rather a surrender of power and with it the loss of 'sovereignty.'

> The decision to surrender the right to national sovereignty is certainly one of the most painful any leader can be asked to take. Most nations are prepared to risk war and catastrophe rather than to surrender this right. Yet this was the decision we had to take. We had to accept the necessity of giving up on the ideal on which we have been nurtured and the dream for which so many generations had struggled for and for which so many of our people had died.[64]

In response, *Die Burger*, under the heading 'Oorgawe' (Surrender), asked whether the leader of a party that had fared so poorly in the negotiations could continue in a leadership position.[65] A spate of critical letters appeared in the Afrikaans press. One such letter stated: 'The NP had received a mandate from us to protect and secure our interests at all times. De Klerk did not get a mandate to lead, like a Judas goat, his unsuspecting people to the political abattoirs.'[66] De Klerk pointed out that he had never promised a white minority veto, but resigned shortly afterwards.

A temporary power-sharing cabinet was the only significant success of the NP negotiators, and the NP's withdrawal from the cabinet vividly underscored the political displacement of the NP and the Afrikaner ruling group. The ensuing disillusionment and dismay among Afrikaners was made worse by a spiraling crime wave and a sharp drop in the rate of arrests and successful prosecutions. South Africa had one of the highest rate of murders per head in the world (sixty-five per hundred thousand compared to ten for the US). During the 1990s more than a thousand farmers, 80 per cent of them Afrikaners, were killed. Although no political motive could be established for these murders, farmers felt that they had to fend for themselves in a world that had been turned upside down. At a protest meeting in the old eastern Transvaal after several murders, a farmer was loudly cheered when he said: 'The country does not belong to Afrikaners any more, it belongs to blacks. We voted it away and we can't get it back.'[67]

---

63 De Klerk, *Die laaste trek*, pp. 374-86, 404-7.
64 Verbatim copy of speech by F.W. de Klerk, 21 January 1997, issued by his office
65 *Die Burger*, 6 February 1997; see also the author's column in *Rapport*, 2 February 1997.
66 *Rapport*, 16 February 1997.
67 *Sunday Independent*, 7 September 1997, p. 3.

The regime change in 1994 was accompanied by a 'purchased revolution' in which large sums were spent to remove staff from posts in the civil service.[68] By the end of 1998, 56,985 early retirement packages had been granted to predominantly white civil servants (these figures exclude members of the Defence Force). The ANC's policy of racial 'representivity' judged the successful transformation of society by the rate of reduction of the number of white civil servants in senior positions. In 1994 whites held 44 per cent of all posts in the civil service; by the beginning of 1999 they held 18 per cent. Of the top management of the civil service (directors general and their deputies), 56 per cent by 1999 were black, colored or Indian, and 42 per cent of the other managerial posts (chief directors and directors) came from these three communities. The government declared that it still considered whites to be over-represented, particularly on the level of senior management.[69]

Medium and large corporations, by 2002, faced heavy fines if they failed to reach the affirmative action targets they had projected in plans submitted to the state. The government had set a medium-term skills development quota for workplace training of 85 per cent black and 54 per cent female. The public corporations were rapidly transformed by the removal of a large proportion of senior white staff. Chris Louw, a radio journalist at the South African Broadcasting Corporation, expressed his dismay when a senior black executive publicly remarked that whites in the corporation had been eliminated from the top management and the senior news management, and that the next target was middle management where white managers, according to the executive, were still 'resisting transformation.' Angrily Louw asked: 'What transformation? Transforming ourselves out of our jobs, rolling over and playing dead?'[70]

A strong demand remained for the scarce skills that mostly white males offered. The new state required more managers than the apartheid state did, since it served far more people as citizens and implemented often complex policies. But, as the top bureaucrat in the Labour Department remarked, young white entrants in the job market 'are feeling the pinch. They are competing in a market increasingly favoring black applicants.'[71] Letters from Afrikaners to the press expressed shock about the little protection the constitution offered against affirmative action.

They were at a loss for an effective response. The country faced staggering problems. It was in the top league of the world for the rate of Aids infection and murder; its unemployment rate was among the highest in the countries with a comparable per capita gross domestic product. There was little hope for a sudden improvement. The country had a very low savings rate. It received less foreign fixed investment and it had the lowest per capita gross domestic product of all comparable economies.[72] With more than a million people, mostly black, who lost their jobs in the 1990s, poverty and income inequality worsened. Between 1996 and 2001 the proportion of the population who lived in acute poverty rose from 41 per cent to 49 per cent. In a survey commissioned in 2000 by the Department of Labour and carried out by a Norwegian institute the proportion

68 Heribert Adam, F. van Zyl Slabbert and Kogila Moodley, *Comrades in Business* (Cape Town: Tafelberg, 1997).
69 Oral Reply, *Parliamentary Debates,* 10 February 1999; *Die Burger,* 24 December 1998.
70 Chris Louw, 'Why we won't roll over and die', *Mail and Guardian,* 2-8 June 2000 and an extended version *Boetman en die swanesang van die verligtes* (Cape Town: Human & Rousseau, 2001).
71 *Financial Mail,* 11 October 2002, p. 27.
72 *Die Burger,* 11 November 2002.

of black unemployed was found to be 45 per cent; for whites it was still in single fig-ures. Few new jobs had been created, mainly because of tough labor laws and strong unions, which guarded against employers taking on the unemployed at lower wages.

Crime and the policy of affirmative action were cited as the main reasons why, for the first time, Afrikaners were emigrating in numbers as large as those of English-speakers.

A decline of Afrikaans and Afrikaner institutions

In 2002 Ton Vosloo, chairman of the board of both Naspers and Sanlam and one of the very few business leaders to champion the cause of Afrikaans, observed: 'It is not to spread panic when one says that Afrikaner people are in a crisis with red lights flashing along their survival path. The examples of marginalization are numerous; the places where space to exist had been conquered, negotiated or established on own initiative are increasingly being questioned. This includes even the self-evident right to be served by the authorities in a language that is officially recognized.'[73]

Superficially the position did not look serious. As of 2002 there were six million speak-ers of Afrikaans as their first language, 15 per cent of the total population, forming the third biggest language community. (Roughly the same proportion of people spoke Afri-kaans as a second language as English.) More blacks and coloreds than whites now spoke Afrikaans as their first language. Together, Afrikaans-speakers made up the largest category of consumers (33 per cent against 28 per cent for English-speakers).

The main underlying cause of the crisis that Vosloo identified was changes in the struc-tures necessary for the reproduction of a language, culture and an ethnic community. Be-tween the 1920s and 1980s single-language Afrikaans schools and universities were the main institutions for socializing youth with a particular set of cultural values into the Afrikaner community. Soon after the transition in 1994 the new government claimed that Afrikaans was used as a language to retain 'apartheid-style racial exclusivity.' It put pres-sure on schools to introduce parallel courses in English to cater for blacks. By the begin-ning of the 1990s there were 1,800 schools which were white and Afrikaans; by 2002 only three hundred single-medium Afrikaans schools remained, of which almost all were racially inclusive.

Three historically Afrikaans universities (Pretoria, Rand Afrikaans and Free State) in-troduced a full set of parallel medium courses; Potchefstroom and Stellenbosch remained predominantly Afrikaans universities. More than half the students at the five institutions by 2000 were not white, almost all following courses in the medium of English. The grow-ing use of English as a language of instruction in schools and universities was a major source of concern. Elsewhere in the world dual-medium education had led inexorably to the displacement of the local language. It also undermines the resolve of the manage-ment of these institutions to take responsibility for the transfer of the language from the present to future generations.[74]

---

73 Ton Vosloo, 'Afrikaans verenig', *Die Burger*, 21 September 2002.
74 Hermann Giliomee, et al., *Kruispad: die toekoms van Afrikaans as openbare taal* (Cape Town: Tafelberg, 2001); J.A. Laponce, *Languages and Their Territories* (Toronto: University of Toronto Press, 1987); E.H. Davies, 'Werklikhede in verband met skoolonderwys', unpublished position paper of the Transvaalse Onderwysunie, Pretoria, 2002.

After 1994 the government appointed large numbers of civil servants who could not speak Afrikaans and failed to introduce appropriate language legislation to give substance to the language clauses in the constitution. In practice both the government and public corporations promoted English as the lingua franca. The Pan South African Language Board, a body set up by the constitution to enforce the language provisions, regularly found that state departments and other public corporations had violated the constitutional provisions, but the government ignored such findings. In the state television service the share of Afrikaans in prime time had dropped precipitously from the pre-1994 situation when it alternated with English on one channel in prime time to less than ten per cent of the channel. This happened despite the fact that a quarter of those who owned television sets were Afrikaans-speakers.[75]

The steady decline of the Afrikaner nationalist movement since the early 1970s accelerated after 1994 and further weakened Afrikaans. The first to defect was Afrikaner business, eager to shed its ethnic character to attract custom across language and racial lines. By the end of the twentieth century big corporations founded by Afrikaners were making rapid strides, but they generally showed little interest in financially supporting the cash-strapped Afrikaans cultural organizations or cultural festivals. Naspers (previously Nasionale Pers) was the only company that regularly funded on a substantial scale the annual Afrikaans arts festivals in Oudtshoorn, Potchefstroom and other towns that channeled considerable Afrikaans cultural and intellectual energy. But even for Naspers, the financial stake in Afrikaans was small. Income from Afrikaans publications, magazines and newspapers made up only 11 per cent of its revenue. Less than half the readers of *Die Burger* were white.

In 1997 the bank Volkskas (now called Absa), founded by the Broederbond sixty years earlier, was reported to have been the biggest corporate sponsor for the ANC conference. During the 1990s Sanlam sold more insurance policies to people who were not white than to whites. It made the first major 'black empowerment' deal, when it sold a profitable subsidiary to a black-owned group. The Afrikaanse Handelsinstituut continued to act as the co-ordinating body of Afrikaner enterprises, but pointed out that it was not in the business of promoting Afrikaans. In 2002 it elected as president Franklin Sonn, a colored man, who declared that the organization was founded on 'reactionary traditions.' He continued: 'I am not an Afrikaner. I have never been one and neither would I like to be one. But I am an Afrikaans person . . .We [Afrikaans-speaking people] contribute most to the national product, we are most loyal to the payment of taxes.'[76]

The NP tried its best to become a catch-all party, which meant that it downplayed its Afrikaans roots. In the 1994 election it had taken its white support for granted and poured virtually all its resources into canvassing other communities, particularly the colored people. Like other parties led by whites it came under increasing pressure from the ANC government to identify with the majority and with 'transformation' as defined by the ANC, which had become a classic dominant party.[77] At its 1997 National Conference Mandela,

---

75 *Financial Mail*, 6 October 2000, p. 24.
76 *Business Day*, 28 October 2002.
77 See Hermann Giliomee and Charles Simkins (eds.), *The Awkward Embrace: One-party Domination and Democracy* (Cape Town: Tafelberg, 1999), pp. 1-46, 137-54.

reading a speech written by the party executive, attacked minority parties as obstacles to transformation. Among Afrikaners and whites in general the priority had become to find a party to stand up to this line. The NP's support slumped both because of its ineffectiveness in the Government of National Unity and its subsequent withdrawal from it. In the 1999 election the share of the vote of the NP (now the New National Party) dropped from the 20 per cent of 1994 to seven per cent.

In the 1999 election 54 per cent of the Afrikaner vote went to the Democratic Party, led by Tony Leon, a Jewish South African, who strongly criticized the failure of the government to deliver services and stamp out corruption. The NNP drew only 20 per cent of the Afrikaner vote in this election and the Freedom Front and other right-wing parties only 13 per cent. Constand Viljoen's idea of an Afrikaner *volkstaat* or ethnic state died after the government disbanded the council it had appointed to investigate the possibility. Only one per cent of Afrikaners (and four per cent of white English-speakers) endorsed the ANC.[78] In the same election the ANC strengthened its control of the black vote and attracted considerably more colored support. The strongest trend in the 1999 election was the dissolution of the ethnic bonds in the white and black communities respectively and the consolidation of two racial blocs.[79]

Faced with extinction, the NNP after the election merged with the DP to form the Democratic Alliance. Discontent with Leon's leadership culminated in the nationalists abandoning the alliance and re-aligning themselves with the ANC. By 2002 the future of the NNP as a coalition partner of the ANC depended on the ANC's building it up as a party with some leverage, putting it in the same situation of dependency as the client parties of the NP government during the 1970s and 1980s.

The Broederbond also redrew its boundaries. Prompted by Member No. 8507 (F.W. de Klerk), who in 1992 addressed the Executive Council of the Broederbond, the organization changed its name to the Afrikanerbond and dropped its aura of racial and male exclusivity and secrecy. For the first time it accepted women and persons who were not white as members.[80] The Bond's membership dropped from a peak of approximately twelve thousand organized into eight hundred branches to between six and eight thousand, of whom five hundred were colored Afrikaans-speakers. The new government identified the Bond as the Afrikaner organization with which it preferred to work.

The Dutch Reformed Church lost nine per cent of its members between 1981 and 1999, but the Anglican Church and other large churches which had opposed apartheid lost members to a similar degree.[81] The DRC adopted a pragmatic rhetoric, arguing that common sense dictated the replacement of apartheid as a system that could not work. Yet it had not accepted, as a principal article of faith, the Belhar Confession adopted by its (colored) church mission in 1982, which called the theological justification of apartheid a heresy. Such acceptance was the condition its colored and black 'sister' churches set for a merger. At its core, therefore, the DRC remained a church for the Afrikaner people, a *volkskerk*. It found it difficult to cope with the processes of secularism and pluralism,

---

78 MarkData poll, communication by L. Schlemmer, 20 November 1999; the other parties that received Afrikaner support were the ACDP (9%), the Federal Alliance (2%) and the UDM (1%).

79 P. Eric Louw, 'South Africa's Second Post-Apartheid Election', *Australian Journal of International Affairs*, 54, 2 (2000), pp. 217-38.

80 E.L.P. Stals, 'Geskiedenis van die Afrikaner-Broederbond, unpublished ms., 1998, pp. 735-41.

81 *Finansies en Tegniek*, 23 October 2002, p. 11.

which, in tandem with the NP government, it had fought to keep at bay.[82] While there was a decline in the support for the main Afrikaans churches, the Afrikaners remained strongly committed to the Christian religion.

An organization that weathered the transformation well was the previously conservative white mineworkers' union, now under the name of MWU-Solidarity. It offered assistance to its membership of 120,000 (87 per cent Afrikaners) in problems they encountered with the policy of affirmative action.[83]

Afrikaners in a new South Africa

In 1998 the most eloquent Afrikaans voice, that of poet, playwright and essayist Breyten Breytenbach, wrote again for the publisher with whom he had cut his links thirty years before. He told Afrikaners that losing power would enable them to terminate the self-abasement of racism and that they could now embrace the reality that most Afrikaner families had bastard origins. The time was ripe, he said, to expand their consciousness and develop a deeper humanism. But he also urged: 'Take your stance to the English,' and asked why the old intra-white tensions had not disappeared: 'Is it because of their pretence at cultural superiority? The fact that they are always on the right side, never responsible for any injustice, never to have to question their assumptions? Is it because they look down on white and brown Afrikaners alike?'[84]

But in the South Africa of the early twenty-first century the Afrikaner-English intra-white tensions and language struggles seemed to be peripheral phenonoma. The two communities had moved much closer together in their political views. Economically there were still differences in the socio-economic profile of the two white communities. The Afrikaners had never caught up with the English-speakers, who had the advantage of entering the urban economy first, but this was no longer an issue. The following data show some of the ethnic differentials in the white population.

ETHNIC DIFFERENTIALS IN THE WHITE GROUP, 1996

	AFRIKANERS	WHITE ENGLISH
Post-school qualific. (%)	21.5	26.7
Semi-professional or high occupational posts (%)	46.2	47.4
Graduates (as % of adults)	9.2	12.2
Monthly household income (in rand)	4,881	5,892

Source: L. Schlemmer, personal communication

Proportionally many more Afrikaners lived in the rural areas and it was in these areas that whites came under the most severe pressure in the final quarter of the twentieth century.

---

82 Dirkie Smit, 'Has There Been Any Change? 'On the role of the DRC, 1974-1990', *Scriptura,* 76,1(2001), p. 123; Jaap Durand, *Ontluisterde Wêreld* (Wellington; Lux Verbi, 2003).
83 A. Mischke, 'Afrikaners maak steeds so', *Rapport,* 19 May 2002.
84 Breyten Breytenbach, *Dog Heart* (Cape Town: Human & Rousseau, 1998), pp. 185-7.

By 2000 two-thirds of the rural towns in the country experienced steady economic decline. Those whites who lived in the midst of large numbers of blacks who were unemployed and desperately poor said that they felt extremely vulnerable. Old-style racist sentiments still resonated in their actions. For some, moving to the large towns and cities with better job prospects was not an option since they would be unable to afford a house there.

In an anonymous letter to *Die Burger* a reader drew a historic parallel. The writer's grandfather, crushed economically in the Anglo-Boer War, had to eke out an existence as a *bywoner* (tenant farmer) for the rest of his life. His father had moved to a town where he practiced a humble craft, but nevertheless had managed to send his children to university. 'I wonder if after five hardworking and honest generations who contributed to the country I shall not become a bywoner, like my grandfather', the melancholy letter writer wrote. In general, however, most whites adapted well financially to the transition.

Below the surface there were still major cultural differences between the two communities. History had happened to the Afrikaners. Their forebears were both colonizers and a colonized people. They had defeated blacks in war but had suffered a shattering defeat at the hands of the British; they had known poverty and contempt for their culture; they had won power and had experienced the corruption of power. With the English-speakers it was different. They were the first nationalists in South Africa who imposed not only their economic but also their cultural values on society – in short how a 'respectable society' should organize itself or more precisely how groups should behave in order to be considered respectable.[85] Both Afrikaners and blacks reacted to this 'first nationalism.' The black intelligentsia embraced it and English as a public language; Afrikaners first accepted it and then embarked on the project of developing a particular culture rooted in the country and Afrikaans as a public language.

After 1994 there was little to distinguish South African English-speakers from their counterparts in the rest of the English-speaking world. At their main cultural showcase, an annual festival in Grahamstown, they tried their best to prevent the festival from becoming culturally unique, downplaying its 'Englishness' and eastern Cape setting in striving for universality. The Afrikaans festival in Oudtshoorn, by contrast, offered a specific cultural experience. Now racially inclusive, it did not shy away from difference, provided that it was celebrated within the broader context of a democratic state. [86]

Afrikaners also defined themselves in terms of what they were not: they were neither 'English South Africans' nor what Afrikaans commentator Dan Roodt called 'Afro-Saxons.'[87] The latter was a reference to the new ruling elite, personified by President Thabo Mbeki, who almost represented a new ruling ethnic group. It divested itself of all ethnic distinctiveness, embraced British-American culture, spoke a kind of English replete with 'progressive' sociological terms, and vigorously promoted the interests of the black middle class under the umbrella of 'liberation' and 'empowerment.'

Leading Afrikaans commentators like radio journalist Chris Louw called for resistance to 'the inevitability of an Anglicized monocultural future.'[88] Roodt argued that South

---

85 Robert Ross, *Status and Respectability in the Cape Colony, 1750-1870* (Cambridge: Cambridge University Press, 1999), pp. 1-5.
86 See Deon Opperman, 'Kulturele neutraliteit sê jy is niks vir niemand', *Rapport*, 3 December 2000; Louise du Toit, 'Distorted Image through the Looking Glass of Identity', *Sunday Independent,* 17 June 2001.
87 See the letter of Dan Roodt, *Business Day*, 10 December 2002.
88 Louw, 'Why we won't roll over'.

Africa faced the same fundamental choice as it had a century earlier between Lord Milner's ideal of unity on the basis of English as public language and cosmopolitanism and General Hertzog's stand between 1910 and 1940 for an indigenous identity and local sovereignty. He denounced Kader Asmal, Minister of National Education, who, as Milner would have done, declared that 'the idea of an Afrikaans university is incompatible with a transformed higher education system.'[89]

In general, Afrikaners felt far more disaffected than English-speakers by the ANC-led cultural revolution which tried to impose British-American notions of respectability and other cultural values. Four-fifths were unhappy at the way their language and culture were being treated, against one-fifth in the case of English-speakers. Support for the proposition that 'people should be part of the new South Africa and forget their differences' was much weaker among Afrikaners than English-speakers (57 per cent versus 81 per cent).[90]

Yet at same time many of the Afrikaner elite were defecting from the language group. About a quarter of (white) Afrikaners – mostly belonging to the upper income categories – indicated in polls that they considered it futile to continue the struggle to maintain Afrikaans as a public language, and the same proportion had decided to educate their own children in English.[91]

A search for new values

Milan Kundera once wrote: 'One cannot judge a nation exclusively by the success of its politics; one must also consider the values that its culture is able to create during the periods of its worst defeat.'[92] With the demise of both apartheid and Afrikaner nationalism, Afrikaners had to discard much of their historic thinking about survival as obsolete. The obsessive attempts to prevent *gelykstelling* or racial leveling, culminating in apartheid, all now smacked of insecurity and bigotry. Van Wyk Louw had suggested that Afrikaners had to choose between 'mere survival' and 'survival in justice.' The white 'yes' vote in the 1992 referendum could be depicted as a choice for the latter. However, Van Wyk Louw thought in terms of the Afrikaners continuing to determine their own political fate, while the collapse of the Government of National Unity in 1996 left the Afrikaners and the larger white community without fomal political power.

Some of the old Afrikaner elite embraced the new ruling elite –'without missing one goose step,' as Breyten Breytenbach put it. In 2000 radio journalist Chris Louw caused a literary sensation when he wrote a furious open letter to Willem de Klerk, a prominent nationalist opinion maker, in which he charged De Klerk and his generation of Afrikaner leaders with paternalism and political cowardice. Without ever having fought a war themselves, they had sent the younger Afrikaners to war on the border and townships and had defended apartheid as a noble cause, but had collapsed when confronted with a tough ANC at the negotiating table.[93]

---

89 Letter to *Business Day*, 11 December 2002.
90 Lawrence Schlemmer, 'Factors in the Persistence or Decline of Ethnic Group Mobilization: Afrikaners in Post-Apartheid South Africa', doctoral diss., UCT, 1999, pp. 259, 271. This and the previous paragraph are based on pp. 240-359 of this work.
91 Lawrence Schlemmer, 'Menings van die publiek', Giliomee, et al. *in* (eds.), *Kruispad*, pp. 94-114.
92 Letter to the *New York Review of Books*, 16 April 1981, p. 43.
93 Louw, *Boetman*, pp. 7-22.

Among the Afrikaners who had made the apartheid state virtually their own, there was a stronger feeling than in the case of others that the tables had been turned. They were a people with a history: they had been the oppressors and were much wealthier as a group than the new ruling majority.[94] In a 1992 poll only four per cent of Afrikaners agreed with the statement 'South Africa is today a land for blacks; whites will have to accept that they will have to take second place'; by 1998 those Afrikaners who agreed had risen to 43 per cent, compared to approximately a quarter of English South Africans and coloreds.[95]

But 1994 also brought with it a sense of relief. Many of the younger generation were delighted to be rid of the stifling cultural conformity of Afrikaner society and the security anxieties of the final decades of apartheid. They were proud to live in a democracy and loved the country's inclusive national symbols. Unlike their parents, they could travel all over the world. National sports teams were welcome in international competitions.

Nevertheless, the close identification that had grown up between the Afrikaans language and white domination, male chauvinism and Afrikaner nationalism, cast a shadow beyond 1994.[96] In reporting on the Truth and Reconciliation Commission, Antjie Krog, a leading poet, asked: 'How can I live with the fact that all the words used to humiliate, all the orders to kill belonged to the language of my heart?'[97] Some of the younger generation rejected the idea of waging a struggle on behalf of Afrikaans as a public language as part of their revolt against patriarchy. A participant in a television program on young Afrikaners said: 'The older people have a tendency to turn everything into an issue. The language issue. The university issue. Everything is issues. The young people must survive, that's our issue.'[98]

But Afrikaans as a language still remained for most the symbol of their sense of place and community. Ton Vosloo called Afrikaans 'the single issue around which all the minority demands of Afrikaans people revolve.' He wanted everything possible to be done to negotiate for it a secure place, and suggested that the best way to do it was to mobilize numbers across color and religion and to be inclusive as possible. He was heartened by what he called the 'astonishing rapport' between white, brown and black Afrikaans-speakers that had grown and concluded: 'We have much to contribute to a united nation.'[99]

Some attempted to reclaim the language, but left open the question whether a new, sole Afrikaner identity would also be claimed. There was a tendency to couple an Afrikaans identity with other identities: people were Afrikaners and South Africans, Afrikaners and Africans, Afrikaners and Afrikaanses, an awkward term used to designate all Afrikaans-speakers regardless of color. The Group of 63, a post-1994 Afrikaans organization, encouraged a search for new myths in the campaign to secure the future of Afrikaans as a public tongue. Its emphasis was not on the unity of Afrikaans-speakers but on their diversity. For the Group of 63, Afrikaans was not simply a standardized, white middle-class language, but a language with many accents, myths and idioms. The group called

---

94 Mads Vestergaard, 'The Negotiation of Afrikaner Identities', *Daedalus,* Winter 2001, p. 39.
95 Communication by Lawrence Schlemmer on Markdata findings, 1 November 2002.
96 Herman Wasserman, 'Postkoloniale kulturele identiteit in Afrikaanse kortverhale na 1994', doctoral diss., US, 2000, pp. 9-50.
97 Antjie Krog, *Country of My Skull* (Johannesburg: Random House, 1998), p. 238.
98 *Rapport* 24 November 2002 on the kykNet program *Jonk en Afrikaans.*
99 Ton Vosloo, 'Afrikaans verenig', *Die Burger,* 21 September 2002.

on those who wished to promote Afrikaans to fight not only for Afrikaans but for all minority languages in South Africa, like Zulu and Xhosa, which were experiencing even more severe marginalization.[100]

By 2000 it appeared as if Afrikaners had become a minority linguistic group rather than an organized ethnic group with myths of origin and kinship, capable of mobilization as a potent force.[101] Leading black intellectuals were prepared to support this non-ethnic linguistic identity in a strategy of avoiding a confrontation with the government on the language issue. They rejected any effort to promote Afrikaans under the banner of a resurgent Afrikaner ethnic group.[102]

Approximately 40 per cent of white Afrikaans-speakers identified with what one can call an ethnic Afrikaner identity. The evidence was that the more unfairly Afrikaans-speakers feel treated the more they identified themselves as Afrikaners.[103] It was from such a group that the more determined efforts of the future to oppose government policies on affirmative action, education and language could be expected to come.

A people with a certain history

Afrikaner history embodies both a fatalistic anticipation of inevitable collective defeat and a mysterious vitality. Afrikaners had been weak before and had known impossible challenges and dismal failures. The first white man who called himself an Afrikaner was banished in 1707, and died a lonely outcast on the west coast of Australia. A sense of utter hopelessness and futility marked the first phases of the Great Trek and the crushing defeat of the Anglo-Boer War of 1899-1902. In 1957, when the apartheid juggernaut seemed headed for full-scale racial war, Dirk Opperman wrote in his poem 'Springbokke': 'Ons is geroep om 'n groot afspraak met die dood te maak' (We are called to make a great appointment with death). 'What does one do,' asked Antjie Krog during the TRC hearings, 'with this load of decrowned skeletons, origins, shame and ash?'[104]

The vitality in Afrikaner history was drawn from a love of the land – the 'wide, melancholy land' in Van Wyk's haunting words – and a conviction that Afrikaners could never be at home elsewhere. It sprang from the early liberation from a dependence on Europe and from the refusal to be mere colonials or second-class Britons, or in today's terms 'Afro-Saxons.' Afrikaners gave themselves and the language they spoke a name derived from the continent of Africa. As late-comers in the cities where English-speakers monopolized the economy they were nevertheless able to carve out a place for themselves, if with great difficulties. With English the sole medium of instruction in most schools in the first years of the twentieth century, they standardized Afrikaans, turned it into a public language used in all walks of life – one of four languages in the world to do so in the twentieth century – and created a national history, literature and press.

Apartheid was a blight on their name and a hidden curse on their future. In a desperate

---

100 www.groep63.org.za, 'Standpunt', 12 October 2002.
101 Schlemmer, 'Factors in the Persistence and Decline of Ethnic Group Mobilization', pp. 316-57.
102 See Neville Alexander's essay in *Kruispad* and one by Jakes Gerwel in *Insig*, October 1999.
103 Elirea Bornman, 'Joseph's Coat: Ethnic Identification in South Africa', *HSRC Information Update*, 4,4 (1994), pp. 29-37.
104 Krog, *Country of My Skull*, p. 128.

attempt to secure their survival through apartheid laws they had brought the country close to civil war. In the end their surrender of power occurred without humiliation. It was because of the magnanimity of a Nelson Mandela but also because the wish expressed in the 1960s by Piet Cillié, editor of *Die Burger*, came true: they surrendered power for a worthwhile principle.[105] The apartheid government was still blamed for the damage it had done to society and the economy. Nothing could ever compensate for the psychological damage it caused, but in terms of impersonal developmental data the performance of the NP government that ruled between 1948 and 1994 was comparatively impressive. It presided over dynamic economic growth that saw the size of the economy increase four and a half times between 1948 and 1994 and a GDP that was among the top thirty in the world. This growth was accompanied by the development of a sophisticated infrastructure and a steady increase in the life expectancy of all population groups.[106]

The Afrikaners had been forced to reconsider many of their assumptions, but most still found it difficult to agree that apartheid in principle was wrong. They had believed that in any negotiated settlement their representatives would drive a very hard bargain, and their hubris convinced them that they alone could rule the country. They had been proven wrong on both counts. Blacks now ruled the country and introduced a widely respected fiscal and monetary policy. Afrikaners still owned most of the farmland and controlled about a third of the listed companies on the Johannesburg Stock Exchange.

They no longer sang the popular song 'Die Lied van Jong Suid-Afrika' (The Song of Young South Africa) about a people's awakening. The people had woken up and had achieved most of their reasonable objectives. Living in an inclusive democracy, they were predominantly a religious, law-abiding and pragmatic people, enjoying freedom of speech and other individual rights. They no longer spoke of themselves as a separate volk with a special calling and destiny, but accepted a common South African identity and the duty to address the challenges that confront the country. Yet they were not attracted to the nation-building creed of one history, one public language, and one 'patriotic' party. They were without strong leaders or organizations, but were rediscovering their own particular identity, one that was forged by their complex and turbulent history and their love for the language they spoke and the harsh but beautiful land in which they lived. Their challenge was to come to terms with this history, to nourish and replenish this love for language and land and to accept the responsibility to hand over their cultural heritage to the next generation. If they were to accept this challenge, they would become part of a new, democratic South Africa in their own special way.

---

105 J.C. Steyn, *Penvegter: Piet Cillié van Die Burger* (Cape Town: Tafelberg, 2002), p. 331.
106 Interview with Jan Sadie, 13 December 2002.

Bibliography

Abedian, I. and Standish, B. 'Poor Whites and the Role of the State', paper presented to the Carnegie inquiry into black poverty, University of Cape Town, 1986.

Abel, R. (ed.) *Politics by Other Means: Law in the Struggle against Apartheid*. London: Routledge, 1995.

Ackroyd, P. 'Dissident Afrikaner Voice', *The Times* (London), 26 June 1986.

Adam, H. et al. *Comrades in Business: Post-Liberation Politics in South Africa*. Cape Town: Tafelberg, 1997.

Adam, H. *Modernizing Racial Domination: South Africa's Political Dominance*. Berkeley: University of California Press, 1971.

Adam, H. 'The South African Power-Elite', in Adam, H. (ed.) *South Africa: Sociological Perspectives*. London: Oxford University Press, 1971.

Adam, H. 'Survival Politics', in Adam, H. and Giliomee, H. *Ethnic Power Mobilized: Can South Africa Change?* New Haven: Yale University Press, 1979.

Adam, H. and Giliomee, H. *Ethnic Power Mobilized: Can South Africa Change?* New Haven: Yale University Press, 1979.

Adhikari, M. (ed.) *Straatpraatjes: Language, Politics and Popular Culture in Cape Town, 1909-1922*. Pretoria: Van Schaik, 1996.

Akenson, D.H. *God's Peoples: Covenant and Land in South Africa, Israel and Ulster*. Ithaca: Cornell University Press, 1992.

Albertyn, J.R. *Die armblanke en die maatskappy: Verslag van die Carnegie-kommissie*. Stellenbosch: Pro Ecclesia, 1932.

Albertyn, J.R., Du Toit, P. and Theron, H.S. *Kerk en stad*. Stellenbosch: Pro Ecclessia, 1947.

Alexander, P. *Alan Paton*. Oxford: Oxford University Press, 1994.

Ally, R. *Gold and Empire*. Johannesburg: Witwatersrand University Press, 1994.

Angas, G.F. The *Kaffirs Illustrated*. London: J. Hogarth, 1849.

Anonymous. *Die bank van oom Bossie*. Issued by Volkskas, 1978.

Anonymous. *Die dagboek van Anna Steenkamp*. Pietermaritzburg: Natalse Pers, 1937.

Anthonissen, C. 'Critical Discourse Analysis, *Die Kerkbode*, 1986-1989', *Scriptorum*, 76, 1, 2001

Appelgryn, M.S. *Thomas François Burgers: Staatspresident 1872-1877*. Pretoria: HAUM, 1979.

Applebaum, A. 'A History of Horror', *New York Review of Books*, 18 October 2001.

Arbatov, G. *The System: An Insider's Life in Soviet Politics*. New York: Times Books, 1992.

Archer, A. 'Defence Expenditure and Arms Procurement', in Cock, J. and Nathan, L. (eds.) *War and Society: The Militarisation of South Africa*. Cape Town: David Philip 1989.

Armstrong, J. and Worden, N. 'The Slaves, 1652-1834', in Elphick, R. and Giliomee, H. (eds.) *The Shaping of South African Society, 1652-1840*. Middletown: Wesleyan University Press, 1988.

Ascherson, N. 'The War that Made South Africa', *New York Review of Books*, 6 December 1979.

Ashforth, A. *The Politics of Official Discourse of Twentieth-Century South Africa*. Oxford: Clarendon Press, 1990.

ATKV. *Monumentaal die bouwerke: ATKV: 1930-1980*. Johannesburg: ATKV, 1980.

Aylward, A. *The Transvaal of Today*. Edinburgh: Blackwood, 1881.

Backman, F.G. 'The Development of Coloured Education with Special Reference to Coloured Education, Teacher Training and School Accommodation', doctoral dissertation, University of Stellenbosch, 1991.

Badenhorst, C.H. 'Die ontwikkeling van die Bantoe op godsdienstige gebied', in *Volkskongres oor die toekoms van die Bantoe*. Stellenbosch: Pro Ecclesia, 1956.

Bank, A. 'Slavery in Cape Town, 1806-1834', masters dissertation, University of Cape Town, 1991.

Bank, A. 'The Great Debate and the Origins of South African Historiography', *Journal of African History*, 38, 1997.

Barlow, A.G. *That We May Tread Safely*. Cape Town: Tafelberg, 1960.

Barnard, F. *Dertien jaar in die skadu van dr. H. F. Verwoerd*. Johannesburg: Voortrekkerpers, 1967.

Barnard, J.M.M. 'Die Erika Theron Kommissie, 1973-1976', masters dissertation, University of Stellenbosch, 1999.

Barnes, L. *Caliban in Africa*. London: Victor Gollancz, 1930.

Barrow, J. *An Account of Travels into the Interior of Southern Africa*. London: Cadell and Davies, 1806.

Becker, G.S. *The Economics of Discrimination*. Chicago: Chicago University Press, 1971.

Beinart, W. *Twentieth-Century South Africa*. Cape Town: Oxford University Press, 1994.

Bell, P. 'Our only sin', *Leadership*, 7, 3, 1988.

Berger, D. 'White Poverty and Government Policy in South Africa, 1890-1934', doctoral dissertation, Temple University, 1982.

Bergh, J.S. and Visagie, J.C. *The Eastern Cape Frontier Zone*. Durban: Butterworths, 1985.

Berlin, I. *Against the Current*. New York: Viking Press, 1979.

Beyers, C. *Die Kaapse Patriotte, 1779-1791*. Cape Town: Juta, 1929.

Beyers, C. *Die Kaapse Patriotte*. Pretoria: Van Schaik, 1967.

Bickford-Smith, V. *Ethnic Pride and Racial Prejudice in Victorian Cape Town*. Johannesburg: Witwatersrand University Press, 1995.

Biewenga, A.W. *De Kaap de Goede Hoop: een Nederlandse vestigingskolonie, 1680-1730*, doctoral dissertation, Vrije Universiteit, Amsterdam, 1998.

Bird, J. *Annals of Natal, Vol. 1*. Cape Town: Maskew Miller, 1920.

[Bird, W.W.] *State of the Cape of Good Hope in 1822*. London: John Murray, 1823.

Bloomberg, C. *Christian-Nationalism and the Rise of the Afrikaner Broederbond*. London: Macmillan, 1990.

Böeseken, A. J. 'Die Kompanjie aan die Kaap, 1652-1795', in Van der Walt, A.J.H., Wiid, J.A. and Geyer, A.L. (eds.) *Geskiedenis van Suid-Afrika*. Cape Town: Nasionale Boekhandel, 1954.

Böeseken, A. J. 'Die koms van die blankes onder Van Riebeeck', in Muller, C.F.J. (ed.) *Vyfhonderd jaar Suid-Afrikaanse geskiedenis*. Pretoria: Academica, 1980.

Böeseken, A.J. (ed.) *Memoriën en instructiën, 1652-1699*. Cape Town: SA Archives Commission, 1966.

Böeseken, A.J. *Simon van der Stel en sy kinders*. Cape Town: Nasou, 1964.

Böeseken, A.J. *Slaves and Free Blacks at the Cape, 1658-1699*. Cape Town: Tafelberg, 1977.

Boeyens, J. '"Black Ivory": The Indenture System and Slavery in Zoutpansberg, 1848-1869', in Eldredge, E. and Morton, F. (eds.) *Slavery in South Africa*. Pietermaritzburg: University of Natal Press, 1994.

Boeyens, J.C.A. 'Die konflik tussen die Venda en die blankes in Transvaal, 1864-1869', *Archives Yearbook of South Africa*, 53, 2, 1990.

Bogdanor, V. 'Forms of Autonomy and the Protection of Minorities', *Daedalus*, 126, 2, 1997.

Bonner, P. *Kings, Commoners and Concessionaires*. Cambridge: Cambridge University Press, 1983.

Bonner, P. et al. (eds.) *Apartheid's Genesis, 1935-1962*. Johannesburg, Ravan Press, 1993.

Booyens, B. '*De Gereformeerde Kerkbode*, 1849-1923', doctoral dissertation, University of Stellenbosch, 1992.

Booyens, B. 'Kerk en staat, 1795-1843', *Archives Yearbook of South Africa*, 1965.

Booyens, B. *Die lewe van D.F. Malan: die eerste 40 jaar*. Cape Town: Tafelberg, 1969.

Boraine, A. *A Country Unmasked*. Oxford: Oxford University Press, 2001.

Borcherds, P.B. *An Autobiographical Memoir*. Cape Town: African Connoisseurs Press, 1861 and 1963.

Bornman, E. 'Joseph's Coat: Ethnic Identification in South Africa, *HSRC Information Update*, 4,4 (1994).

Bosch, D. 'Johannes du Plessis', in Du Preez, J. (ed.) *Sendinggenade*. Bloemfontein: NG Kerk Uitgewers, 1986.

Botha, A.J. *Die evolusie van 'n volksteologie*. Bellville: University of the Western Cape, 1984.

Botha, C.G. *Die Kaapse Hugenote*. Cape Town: Nasionale Pers, 1939.

Botha, C.G. *Social Life and Customs during the Eighteenth Century*. Cape Town: Struik, 1976.

Botha, D.P. 'Historiese agtergrond van die stigting van afsonderlike etniese N.G. Kerkverbande', unpublished paper.

Botha, D.P. *Die opkoms van ons derde stand*. Cape Town: Human & Rousseau, 1960.

Botha, D.P. *Die twee-eeue erfenis van die SA Sendinggestig, 1799-1999*. Cape Town: LUS Uitgewers, 1999.

Botha, F. 'Leier en vriend', in Verwoerd, W.J. (ed.) *Verwoerd: só onthou ons hom*. Pretoria: Protea Boekhuis, 2001.

Botha, H.C. 'Die rol van Christoffel J. Brand in Suid-Afrika', masters dissertation, University of South Africa, 1973.

Botha, H.C. *John Fairbairn in South Africa*. Cape Town: Historical Publication Society, 1984.

Bottomley, J. '"Almost Bled to Death": The Effects of the Anglo-Boer War on Social Transformation in the Orange River Colony', *Historia*, 44, 1, 1999.

Bottomley, J. 'The Orange Free State and the Rebellion of 1914', in Morrell, R. (ed.) *White but Poor: Essays on the History of the Poor Whites in Southern Africa, 1880-1940*. Pretoria: Unisa, 1992.

Bottomley, J. 'Public Policy and White Rural Poverty in South Africa, 1881-1924', doctoral dissertation, Queen's University, 1990.

Bouwer, A. et al. (eds.) *M.E.R.: 'n kosbare erfenis: briewe, 1916-1975*. Cape Town: Tafelberg, 1975.

Bowker, J.M. *Speeches, Letters and Selections from Important Papers*. Grahamstown: Godlonton and Richards, 1864.

Boxer, C. *The Dutch Seaborne Empire*. London: Hutchinson, 1965.

Boxer, C. *Race Relations in the Portuguese Colonial Empire*. Oxford: Oxford University Press, 1963.

Bradford, H. 'Gendering Africander Nationalism, 1899-1902', unpublished paper, 1998.

Bradford, H. *A Taste of Freedom: The ICU in Rural South Africa, 1924-1930*. Johannesburg: Ravan Press, 1988.

Bradlow, E. 'Capitalists and Labourers in the Post-Emancipation Rural Cape', *Historia*, 31, 1, 1986.

Bradlow, F. 'Islam at the Cape of Good Hope', *South African Historical Journal*, 15, 1981.

Bratt, J.D. 'Dutch Calvinism in Modern America: The History of a Conservative Subculture', doctoral dissertation, Yale University, 1978.

Breit, H. *The Writer Observed*. Cleveland: The World Publishing Company, 1956.

Breytenbach, B. *End Papers*. London: Faber and Faber, 1986.

Breytenbach, B. *A Season in Paradise*. London: Jonathan Cape, 1980.

Breytenbach, B. (pseud.: B.B. Lasarus) *'n Seisoen in die Paradys*. Johannesburg: Perskor, 1976.

Brink, A.P. *Literatuur in die strydperk*. Cape Town: Human & Rousseau, 1985.

Brink, A.P. *Mapmakers: Writing in a State of Siege*. London: Faber and Faber, 1983.

Brink, E. '"Maar net 'n klomp factory meide": Afrikaner Family and Community on the Witwatersrand', in Bozzoli, B. (ed.) *Class, Community and Conflict: South African Perspectives*. Johannesburg: Ravan Press, 1987.

Brink, G.W. 'Daniël François Malan, 1874-1959: An Ecclesiological Study of the Influence of his Theology', doctoral dissertation, University of Stellenbosch, 1997.

Brion Davis, D. 'At the Heart of Slavery', *The New York Review of Books*, 17 October 1996.

Brits, J.P. *Op die vooraand van apartheid: die rassevraagstuk en die blanke politiek in Suid-Afrika, 1939-1948*. Pretoria; Unisa, 1994.

Brits, J.P. *Tielman Roos*. Pretoria: University of South Africa, 1987.

Brits, J.P. '"The Voice of the People": Memoranda presented in 1947 to the Sauer Commission', *Kleio*, 32, 2000.

Broodryk, J.J. 'Stellenbosse akademici en die politieke problematiek in Suid-Afrika, 1934-1948', masters dissertation, University of Stellenbosch, 1991.

Brookes, E. et al. *Coming of Age: Studies in South African Citizenship and Politics*. Cape Town: Maskew Millar, 1930.

Broughton, M. *Press and Politics of South Africa*. Cape Town: Purnell, 1961.

Bryce, J. *Impressions of South Africa*. London: Macmilllan, 1899.

Bryce, J. *Impressions of South Africa*. New York: The Century, 1900.

Bryce, J. *Studies in History and Jurisprudence*. Oxford: no publisher given, 1901.

Buchan, J. *Memory-hold-the-door*. London: Hodder and Stoughton, 1940.

Burchell, W.J. *Travels in the Interior of South Africa, Vol. 1*. London: Batchworth Press, 1822.

Burema, I. 'The Joys and Perils of Victimhood', *The New York Review of Books*, 8 April 1999.

Burke, E.E. (ed.) *Journals of Carl Mauch, 1869-1872*. Salisbury, National Archives, 1969.

Burton, D.B. 'The South African Native Affairs Commission SANAC, (1903-1905)', masters dissertation, University of South Africa, 1985.

Buthelzi, G. *White and Black Nationalism: Ethnicty and the Future of the Homelands*. Johannesburg: South African Institute of Race Relations, 1974.

Buxton, E. *General Louis Botha*. London: John Murray, 1924.

Cain, P.J. and Hopkins, A.G. *British Imperialism: Crisis and Deconstruction, 1914-1990*. London: Longman, 1991.

Cain, P.J. and Hopkins, A.G. *British Imperialism: Innovation and Expansion, 1688-1914*. London: Longman, 1993.

Callinicos, L. *A People's History of South Africa*. Johannesburg: Ravan Press, 1982.

Calpin, G.H. *There Are No South Africans*. London: Thomas Nelson, 1940.

Cameron, T. *Jan Smuts: An Illustrated Biography*. Cape Town: Human & Rousseau, 1994.

Campbell, K. 'The Soldiers of Apartheid', *SAIS Review*, Winter-Spring 1988.

Cannadine, D. 'Winston Antagonistes', *New York Review of Books*, 15 June 1989.

Carter, G. *The Politics of Inequality: South Africa since 1948*. London: Thames and Hudson, 1958.

Chua, A. 'Markets, Democracy and Ethnicity', *The Yale Law Journal*, 1998.

Cillié, P.J. *Baanbrekers vir vryheid*. Cape Town: Tafelberg, 1990.

Cillié, P.J. *Hertzog en Malan: die jare van skeuring, 1934-1939*. Potchefstroom: Hertzog-gedenklesing, 1980.

Cillié, P.J. *Tydgenote*. Cape Town: Tafelberg, 1980.

Cilliers, A.C. *Hertzogisme en die handel*. Stellenbosch: Pro Ecclesia, 1941.

Cilliers, S.P. Collection, 'Verslag van die Komitee insake Kleurlingaangeleenthede', 18 January 1961. University of Stellenbosch Library.

Claassen, L.H. 'Die ontstaansgeskiedenis van die Suid-Afrikaanse Akademie vir Taal, Lettere en Kuns', masters dissertation, Rand Afrikaans University, 1977.

Clingman, S. *Bram Fischer: Afrikaner Revolutionary*. Cape Town: David Philip, 1998.

Cloete, B. *Die lewe van F.S. Malan*. Johannesburg: APB, 1946.

Cloete, H. *Five Lectures on the Emigration of the Dutch Farmers*. Pietermaritzburg: Paul Solomon, 1856.

Cloete, H. *The History of the Great Boer Trek*. London: John Murray, 1899.

Coertze, P.J., Language F.J. and Van Eeden, B.I.C. *Die oplossing van die Naturellevraagstuk in Suid-Afrika*. Johannesburg: Publicité, 1943.

Coetser, P.P.J. *Gebeurtenisse uit di Kaffer-oorloge*. 1889, reprinted Cape Town: Struik, 1963.

Coetzee, A. *Die opkoms van die Afrikaanse kultuurgedagte aan die Rand, 1886-1936*. Johannesburg: Afrikaanse Pers, no date.

Coetzee, J.A. *Politieke groepering in die wording van die Afrikanernasie*. Johannesburg: Voortrekkerpers, 1941.

Coetzee, J.C. 'Opvoeding en onderwys van die SA naturel', *Wapenskou*, November 1943.

Coetzee, J.M. *Giving Offense: Essays on Censorship*. Chicago: University of Chicago Press, 1996.

Coetzee, J.M. 'Idleness in South Africa', *Social Dynamics*, 8, 1, 1982.

Coetzee, J.M. 'The Mind of Apartheid', *Social Dynamics*, 17, 1, 1991.

Coetzee, J.M. 'Resisters', *New York Review of Books*, 2 December 1993.

Coetzee, J.M. *White Writing*. New Haven: Yale University Press, 1988.

Coetzer, P.W. and Le Roux, J.H. *Die Nasionale Party, 1V: 1934-1940*. Bloemfontein: INEG, 1986.

Collins, W.W. *Free Statia: Reminiscences of a Lifetime in the Orange Free State*. Bloemfontein: *The Friend*, 1907.

Colquhoun, A.R. *The Africander Land*. London: John Muray, 1906.

Conrad, J. *Heart of Darkness*. Cologne: Könemann, 1999.

Cook, E.T. *Edmund Garrett*. London: Arnold, 1909.

Cory, G. *The Rise of South Africa, Vol. 1*. New York: Longmans Green, 1910.

Craig, G. 'No More Wars', *New York Review of Books*, 20 April 1995.

Crais, C. *The Making of the Colonial Order: White Supremacy and Black Resistance in the Eastern Cape, 1770-1865*. Johannesburg: Witwatersrand University Press, 1997.

Crankshaw, G.B. 'The Diary of C.L. Stretch', masters dissertation, Rhodes University, 1960.

Crocker, C. *High Noon in Southern Africa*. New York: W.W. Norton, 1992.

Cronjé, G. 'Die sosiale ordening van die Afrikaner', in Grobbelaar, P.W. (series ed.) *Die Afrikaner en sy kultuur*. Cape Town: Tafelberg, 1974.

Cronjé, G. *'n Tuiste vir die nageslag*. Johannesburg: Publicité, 1945.

Cronjé, G. 'Werklikheid en ideaal', in Cronjé, G. et al. *Regverdige rasse-apartheid*. Stellenbosch: CSV, 1947.

Cronjé, J.C. 'Die grens as meerduidige gegewe in die kontemporêre Afrikaanse prosa', doctoral dissertation, University of Pretoria, 1989.

Cruse, H.P. *Die geskiedenis van Kleurling-onderwys in die Kaapprovinsie*. Cape Town: Nasionale Pers, no date.

D'Assonville, V.E. *S. J. du Toit van die Paarl, 1847-1911*. Weltevredenpark: Marnix, 1999.

Davenport, T.R.H. *The Afrikaner Bond, 1880-1911*. Cape Town: Oxford University Press, 1966.

Davenport, T.R.H. *The Beginnings of Urban Segregation in South Africa*. Grahamstown: Rhodes University, Institute of Social and Economic Research, 1971.

Davenport, T.R.H. *South Africa: A Modern History*. Johannesburg: Macmillan, 1987.

Davenport, T.R.H. *The Transfer of Power in South Africa*. Cape Town: David Philip, 1998.

Davenport, T.R.H. and Saunders, C. *South Africa: A Modern History*. London: Macmillan, 2000.

Davids, A. 'The Afrikaans of the Cape Muslims from 1815 to 1915: A Socio-Linguistic Study', masters dissertation, University of Natal, 1991.

Davies, R. *Capital, State and White Labour in South Africa*. Brighton: The Harvester Press, 1979.

De Bruyn, G.F.C. 'Die samestelling van die Afrikaner', *Tydskrif vir Geesteswetenskappe*, 15, 1976.

Degenaar, J.J. et al. *Beweging uitwaarts*. Cape Town: John Malherbe, 1969.

Degenaar, J.J. *Moraliteit en politiek*. Cape Town: Tafelberg, 1976.

Degler, C.N. *Neither Black nor White: Slavery and Race Relations in Brazil and the United States*. New York: Macmillan, 1971.

De Grevenbroek, J.G. 'An Account of the Hottentots', in Schapera, I. and Farrington, B. (eds.) *The Early Cape Hottentots*. Cape Town: Van Riebeeck Society, 1933.

De Gruchy, J.W. *The Church Struggle in South Africa*. Cape Town: David Philip, 1979.

De Gruchy, J.W. *The Church Struggle in South Africa*. London: Collins, 1986.

De Jong, C. *Reizen naar de Kaap de Goede Hoop, Ierland en Noorwegen in de jaren 1791 tot 1799*. Haarlem: Bohn, 1802.

De Jongh, P.S. 'Sendingwerk in die Landdrosdistrikte Stellenbosch en Tulbagh, 1799-1830', masters dissertation, University of Stellenbosch, 1968.

De Kiewiet, C.W. *A History of South Africa*. Oxford: Oxford University Press, 1941.

De Kiewiet, C.W. 'Loneliness in the Beloved Country', *Foreign Affairs*, 42, 3, 1964.

De Klerk, F.W. *Die laaste trek: 'n nuwe begin*. Cape Town: Human & Rousseau, 1999.

De Klerk, F.W. Interview with Frost, David, 14 February 1993, official transcript.

De Klerk, W.J. *Afrikanerdenke*. Potchefstroom: Pro-Rege-pers, 1971.

Delius, A. 'The Missing Liberal Policy', *Forum*, 1952.

Delius, P. 'Abel Erasmus: Power and Profit in the Eastern Transvaal', in Beinart, W. et al. (eds.) *Putting a Plough to the Ground*. Johannesburg: Ravan Press, 1986.

Delius, P. *The Land Belongs to Us*. Johannesburg: Ravan Press, 1983.

Delius, P. and Trapido, S. 'Inboekselings and Oorlams', in Bozzoli, B. (ed.) *Town and Countryside in the Transvaal*. Johannesburg: Ravan Press, 1983.

Densch, G. *Minorities in the Open Society*. London: Routledge and Kegan Paul, 1986.

De Nederlandse Ger. Kerk en die Boeren, pamphlet, c. 1900.

Denoon, D. *A Grand Illusion*. London: Longman, 1973.

Denoon, D. *Settler Capitalism*. Oxford: Clarendon Press, 1983.

Devereaux, S. *South African Income Distribution, 1900-1980*. Cape Town: University of Cape Town, SALDRU, 1983.

De Villiers, D. and De Villiers, J.M. *PW*. Cape Town: Tafelberg, 1984.

De Villiers, J.W. and Jardine, R. et al. 'Why South Africa Gave Up the Bomb', *Foreign Affairs*, 72, 5, 1993.

De Villiers, K. 'Die Anglo-Boereoorlog en die mense van Kaapland'. Paper presented at the Klein Karoo National Arts Festival, Oudtshoorn, April 2001.

De Villiers, R. 'Political Parties and Trends', in Calpin, G.H. (ed.) *The South African Way of Life*. Melbourne: William Heineman, 1953.

De Waal, J.H.H. *Die lewe van David Christiaan de Waal*. Cape Town: Nasionale Pers, 1928.

De Waal, J.H.H. *My herinnerings van ons taalstryd*. Cape Town, Nasionale Pers, 1932.

De Wet, C.G. *Die vryliede en vryswartes in die Kaapse nedersetting*. Cape Town: Historiese Publikasie-Vereniging, 1981.

De Wet, C.R. *Three Years' War*. New York: Scribner, 1902.

Dickson, P. 'The Natives Land Act of 1913', masters dissertation, University of Cape Town, 1970.

Diederichs, N. *Nasionalisme as lewensbeskouing en sy verhouding tot internasionalisme*. Bloemfontein: Nasionale Pers, 1936.

Dionne, E.J. *Why Americans Hate Politics*. New York: Simon and Schuster, 1991.

D'Oliveira, J. *Vorster: The Man*. Johannesburg: Ernest Stanton, 1977.

Dooling, W. *Law and Community in a Slave Society: Stellenbosch District, South Africa, c. 1760-1820*. Cape Town: University of Cape Town, 1992.

Drury, A. *'A Very Strange Society': A Journey to the Heart of South Africa*. London: Michael Joseph, 1968.

Dubow, S. 'Afrikaner Nationalism, Apartheid and the Conceptualisation of "Race"', *Journal of African History*, 33, 1992.

Dubow, S. 'Colonial Nationalism, the Milner Kindergarten and the Rise of "South Africanism", 1902-1910', *History Workshop Journal*, 43, 1997.

Dubow, S. 'Race, Civilization and Culture: The Elaboration of Segregationist Discourse in the Inter-War Years', in Marks, S. and Trapido, S. (eds.) *The Politics of Race, Class and Nationalism in Twentieth-Century South Africa*. London: Longman, 1987.

Dubow, S. *Racial Segregation and the Origins of Apartheid in South Africa*, London: Macmillan and Oxford: St Antony's College, 1989.

Dubow, S. *Illicit Union: Scientific Racism in Modern South Africa*. Cambridge: Cambridge University Press, 1995.

Dugard, J. *Human Rights and the South African Legal Order*. Princeton: Princeton University Press, 1978.

Duly, L.C. 'A Revisit with the Cape's Hottentot Ordinance of 1828', in Kooy, M. (ed.) *Studies in Economics and Economic History*. London: Macmillan, 1972.

Duncan, P. *The Road through the Wilderness*. Johannesburg: no publisher given, 1953.

Duncan, P. *South Africa's Rule of Violence*. London: Methuen, 1964.

Du Pisanie, J.A. *John Vorster en die Verlig/Verkrampstryd*. Bloemfontein: INEG, 1988.

Du Plessis, D. *'n Afrikaner vertel: waarom ek 'n Kommunis is*. Cape Town: Communist Party, circa 1940.

Du Plessis, E.P. *'n Volk staan op: die Ekonomiese Volkskongres en daarna*. Cape Town; Human & Rousseau, 1964.

Du Plessis, J. et al. *The Dutch Reformed Church and the Native Problem*. No publisher, no date, ca. 1921.

Du Plessis, J. 'Colonial Progress and Countryside Conservatism: An Essay on the Legacy of Van der Lingen', masters dissertation, University of Stellenbosch, 1988.

Du Plessis, J.C. 'Die ideale van ons kerk in sendingwerk', in *Die NG Kerk in die OVS en die Naturellevraagstuk*. Bloemfontein: Nasionale Pers, 1929.

Du Plessis, J. *The Life of Andrew Murray of South Africa*. London: Marshall Bros., 1919.

Du Plessis, L.J. 'Liberalistiese en Calvinistiese Naturelle-politiek', in Federasie van die Calvinistiese Studenteverenigings van SA (compiler), *Koers in die krisis*. Stellenbosch: Pro Ecclesia, 1940.

Du Plessis, L.J. 'Die Naturellevraagstuk in Suid-Afrika', *Koers*, 8, 1, 1940.

Du Plessis, P.J. 'Die Lewe van Gustav Preller, 1815-1943', doctoral dissertation, University of Pretoria, 1988.

Du Preez, J.M. *Africana Afrikaner*. Alberton: Liberatius, 1983.

Dutch Reformed Church. *Human Relations and the South African Scene in the Light of the Scriptures*. Cape Town: NG Kerkuitgewers, 1975.

Dutch Reformed Church. *Church and Society*. Pretoria: General Synodical Committee, 1990.

Du Toit, A. 'The Cape Afrikaners' Failed Liberal Movement', in Butler, Jeffrey et al. (eds.) *Democratic Liberalism in South Africa*. Middletown: Wesleyan University Press, 1987.

Du Toit, A. 'Confrontation, Accommodation and the Future of Afrikanerdom', *South African Outlook*, October 1977.

Du Toit, A. 'Experiments with Truth: Stockenstrom, Gandhi, and the Truth and Reconciliation Commission', paper presented to the Philosophical Society of Southern Africa, 2002.

Du Toit, A. 'Facing up to the Future', *Social Dynamics*, 7, 1981.

Du Toit, A. (ed.) *In gesprek: opstelle vir Johan Degenaar*. Stellenbosch: Voorbrand, 1986.

Du Toit, A. 'Hendrik Bibault of die raaisel van prof. J.M.L. Franken', in H.C. Bredekamp (ed.) *Afrikaanse geskiedskrywing en letterkunde*. Bellville: University of the Western Cape, 1992.

Du Toit, A. 'Puritans in Africa?' *Comparative Studies in Society and History*, 27, 2, 1985.

Du Toit, A. *Die sondes van die vaders*. Cape Town: Rubicon, 1982.

Du Toit, A. and Giliomee, H. *Afrikaner Political Thought, 1780-1850: Analyses and Documents*. Cape Town: David Philip, 1983.

Du Toit, J.D. *Ds. S.J. du Toit in weg en werk*. Paarl: Paarl Drukpers, 1917.

Du Toit, M. 'A Social History of the Afrikaanse Christelike Vrouevereniging', doctoral dissertation, University of Cape Town, 1992.

Du Toit, P. 'Dis tyd vir 'n opvolg-skikking', *Die Burger* 1 October 2000.

Du Toit, P. *South Africa's Brittle Peace*. London: Palgrave, 2001.

Du Toit, P.S. and Smuts, F. 'Kollege en universiteit', in *Stellenbosch drie eeue*. Stellenbosch: Stellenbosch City Council, 1979.

Du Toit, S. 'Prof. N.J. Hofmeyr, 1827-1909', doctoral dissertation, University of Stellenbosch, 1984.

Du Toit, Z.B. *Die nuwe toekoms*. Pretoria: J.P. van der Walt, 1999.

Duvenage, G.D.J. *Van die Tarka na die Transgariep*. Pretoria: Academica, 1981.

The Economist Pocket World in Figures. London: Profile Books, 2001.

Edelstein, M.L. *What Do Young Africans Think?* Johannesburg: South African Institute of Race Relations, 1972.

Edgar, R. *The Travel Notes of Ralph J. Bunche*. Athens: Ohio State University, 1992.

Ehlers, A. 'The Anglo-Boer War: Stimulus for the Formation of Afrikaans Rural Trust Companies and Boards of Executors', unpublished paper, 1998.

Ehlers, A. 'Die geskiedenis van die trustmaatskappye en eksekuteurskamers van Boland Bank Beperk tot 1971', doctoral dissertation, University of Stellenbosch, 2002.

Ehlers, A. 'Die Helpmekaarbeweging in Suid-Afrika', masters dissertation, University of Stellenbosch, 1986.

Eiselen, W. 'Die aandeel van die blanke ten opsigte van die praktiese uitvoering van die beleid van afsonderlike ontwikkeling', *Journal of Racial Affairs*, 1965.

Eiselen, W. 'Christianity in the Religious Life of the Bantu', in Schapera, I. (ed.) *Western Civilization and the Natives of South Africa*. London: Routledge, 1934.

Eiselen, W. *Die Naturellevraagstuk*. Cape Town: Nasionale Pers, 1929.

Eiselen, W.M. 'Is Separation Possible?', *Journal of Racial Affairs*, 1, 2, 1950.

Elphick, R. *Kraal and Castle: Khoikhoi and the Founding of White South Africa*. New Haven: Yale University Press, 1977.

Elphick, R. 'Evangelical Missions and Racial Equalization in South Africa, 1890-1914', unpublished paper, 1999.

Elphick, R. and Giliomee, H. (eds.) *The Shaping of South African Society, 1652-1820*. Cape Town: Longman Penguin,1979.

Elphick R. and Giliomee, H. (eds.) *The Shaping of South African Society, 1652-1840*. Middletown: Wesleyan University Press, 1988.

Elphick, R. and Giliomee, H. 'The Origins and Entrenchment of European Domination at the Cape, 1652-1840', in Elphick, R. and Giliomee H. (eds.) *The Shaping of South African Society, 1652-1840*. Middletown: Wesleyan University Press, 1988.

Elphick, R. and Giliomee, H. 'The Structure of European Domination at the Cape, 1652-1820', in Elphick, R. and Giliomee, H. (eds.) *The Shaping of South Africa Society*. Cape Town: Longman Penguin,1979.

Elphick, R. and Malherbe, V.C. 'The Khoisan to 1828', in Elphick, R. and Giliomee, H. (eds.) *The Shaping of South Africa Society, 1652-1840*. Middletown: Wesleyan University Press, 1988.

Elphick R. and Shell, R. 'Intergroup Relations', in Elphick, R. and Giliomee, H. (eds.) *The Shaping of South Africa Society, 1658-1840*. Middletown: Wesleyan University Press, 1988.

Engelenburg, F.V. *General Louis Botha*. Pretoria: Van Schaik, 1929.

Engelenburg, F.V. *Louis Botha*. London: George Harrap, 1929.

Erasmus, L.S. 'Die nasionale idee in die onderwys', masters dissertation, University of Stellenbosch, 1954.

Esterhuyse, W.P. *Anton Rupert: Advocate for Hope*. Cape Town: Tafelberg, 1986.

Etherington, N. *The Great Treks: The Transformation of Southern Africa, 1815-1854*. Harlow: Penguin, 2001.

Fagan, H.A. *Our Responsibility*. Stellenbosch: Universiteitsuitgewers, 1960.

Faure, A. *Redevoering by het tweede Eeuw-feest, ter herinnering aan de vestiging der Christelijke Kerk in Zuid-Afrika, gehouden in de Groote Kerk, in de Kaapstad, op Dinsdag en 6 April, 1852*. Cape Town: Van de Sandt de Villiers and Tier, 1852.

Feinberg, H. 'The Natives Land Act in South Africa', *International Journal of African Historical Studies*, 26, 19, 1993.

Feit, E. 'Conflict and Cohesion in South Africa', *Economic Development and Cultural Change*, 14, 1968.

Fischer, B. *What I did was right: Statement from the Dock, 28 March 1966*. London: Mayibuye, no date.

Fischer, M.A. *Tant Miem Fischer se Kampdagboek, Mei 1901-Augustus 1902*. Tafeberg, 1964.

Fisher, J. *Paul Kruger*. London: Secker and Warburg, 1974.

Fisher, R.B. *The Importance of the Cape of Good Hope as a Colony to Great Britain* London: Cadell and Davies, 1816.

Fitzpatrick, J. Percy. *South African Memories*. London: Cassell, 1932.

Forgey, H. 'Die politiek van armoede: 'n vergelyking van die 1932 en 1989 Carnegie-verslag', masters dissertation, Rand Afrikaans University, 1994.

Fouché, L. (ed.) *The Diary of Adam Tas*. Cape Town: Van Riebeeck Society, 1970.

Fourie, B. *Brandpunte*. Cape Town: Tafelberg, 1991.

Fourie, B. 'Buitelandse Sake onder dr. Verwoerd', in Verwoerd, W.J. (ed.) *Verwoerd: só onthou ons hom*. Pretoria: Protea, 2001.

Fourie, J.J. *Afrikaners in die Goudstad, 1924-1961*. Pretoria: HAUM, 1986.

Franken, J.M.L. 'Hendrik Bibault of die opkoms van 'n volk', *Die Huisgenoot*, 21 September 1928.

Franken, J.L.M. *Piet Retief se lewe in die Kolonie*. Pretoria: HAUM, 1949.

Franklin, J.H. *From Slavery to Freedom*. New York: Random House, 1969.

Freyer, A.K. 'The Historical Survey', *Forum*, 5, 2, 1956.

Freyre, G. *The Masters and the Slaves: A Study in the Development of Brazilian Civilization*. New York: Knopf, 1956.

Friedman, B. *Smuts: A Reappraisal*. Johannesburg: Hugh Keartland, 1975.

Friedman, S. *The Long Journey: South Africa's Quest for Negotiated Settlement*. Johannesburg: Ravan Press, 1993.

Fredrickson, G.M. *White Supremacy: A Comparative Study in American and South African History*. New York: Oxford University Press, 1981.

Fukuyama, F. *Trust: The Social Virtues and the Creation of Prosperity*. New York: Free Press, 1995.

Furlong, P.J. *Between Crown and Swastika: The Impact of the Radical Right on the Afrikaner Nationalist Movement in the Fascist Era*. Johannesburg: Witwatersrand University Press, 1991.

Gagiano, J. 'Meanwhile back at the *Boereplaas*', *Politikon*, 13, 1986.

Gagiano, J. 'Ruling Group Cohesion', in Giliomee, H. and Gagiano, J. (eds.) *The Elusive Search for Peace: South Africa, Israel and Northern Ireland*. Cape Town: Oxford University Press, 1990.

Gagiano, J. and Giliomee, H. (eds.) *The Elusive Search for Peace: South Africa, Northern Ireland and Israel*. Cape Town: Oxford University Press, 1990.

Galloway, F. *Breyten Breytenbach as openbare figuur*. Pretoria: HAUM, 1990.

Gann, L.H. *South Africa: War? Revolution? Peace?* Cape Town: Tafelberg, 1979.

Garson, N.G. '"Het Volk", The Botha-Smuts Party in the Transvaal, 1904-1911', *Historical Journal*, 9,1, 1966.

Geldenhuys, D. *The Diplomacy of Isolation*. Johannesburg: Macmillan, 1984.

Geldenhuys, J. *A General's Story*. Johannesburg: Jonathan Ball, 1995.

Geldenhuys, J. *Dié wat wen: 'n generaal se storie uit 'n era van oorlog en vrede*. Pretoria: Van Schaik, 1993.

Gerdener, G.B.A. *Die Afrikaner en die sendingwerk*. Cape Town: NG Kerk Uitgewers, 1959.

Gerdener, G.B.A. 'The DRC and the Racial Situation in South Africa', *Race Relations*, 17, 1-2, 1950.

Gerdener, G.B.A. *Reguit koers gehou*. Cape Town: NG Kerk Uitgewers, 1951.

Gerhart, G. *Black Power in South Africa*. Berkeley: University of California Press, 1977.

Gerstner, J. N. *The Thousand Generation Covenant: Dutch Reformed Covenant Theology and Group Identity in Colonial South Africa*. Leiden: E.J. Brill, 1991.

Gerstner, J. 'A Christian Monopoly: The Reformed Church and Colonial Society under Dutch Rule', in Elphick, R. and Davenport, T.R.H. (eds.) *Christianity in South Africa: A Political, Social and Cultural History*. Cape Town: David Philip, 1997.

Gerwel, G.J. *Literatuur en apartheid*. Kasselsvlei: Kampen, 1983.

Gerwel, J. 'Afrikaner, Afrikaans, Afrika'. Text of speech to Afrikaanse Skrywersgilde, 20 May 1976.

Geyer, A.L. 'Voorsitterrede', *Tydskrif vir Rasse-aangeleenthede*, 11, 4, 1960.

Giliomee, H. 'Die administrasietydperk van Lord Caledon', *Archives Yearbook of South Africa*, 2, 1966.

Giliomee, H. 'The Afrikaners' Economic Advance', forthcoming study.

Giliomee, H. 'Afrikaner Politics', in Adam, H. and Giliomee, H. *Ethnic Power Mobilized: Can South Africa Change?* New Haven: Yale University Press, 1979.

Giliomee, H. 'Afrikaner Politics, 1977-1987', in Brewer, J. (ed.) *Can South Africa Survive?* London: Macmillan, 1989.

Giliomee, H. 'Apartheid, Verligtheid and Liberalism', in Butler, J. et al. (eds.) *Democratic Liberalism in South Africa*. Cape Town: David Philip, 1987.

Giliomee, H. 'Aspects of the Rise of Afrikaner Capital and Afrikaner Nationalism in the Western Cape', in Wilmot J. and Simons, M. (eds.) *The Angry Divide: Social and Economic History of the Western Cape*. Cape Town: David Philip, 1989.

Giliomee, H. 'The Beginnings of Afrikaner Ethnic Consciousness', in Vail, L. (ed.) *The Creation of Tribalism in South Africa*. London: James Currey, 1989.

Giliomee, H. 'The Beginnings of Afrikaner Nationalism, 1870-1915', *South African Historical Journal*, 19, 1987.

Giliomee, H. 'The Burgher Rebellions on the Eastern Frontier, 1795-1815', in Elphick, R. and Giliomee, H. (eds.) *The Shaping of South African Society. 1652-1820*. Cape Town: Longman Penguin, 1979.

Giliomee, H. 'Critical Afrikaner Intellectuals and Apartheid,' *South African Journal of Philosophy*, 19, 4, 2000.

Giliomee, H. 'Democratization in South Africa', *Political Science Quarterly*, 110, 1, 1995.

Giliomee, H. 'The Eastern Frontier, 1770-1812', in Elphick, R. and Giliomee, H. (eds.) *The Shaping of South Africa Society*. Middletown: Wesleyan University Press, 1988.

Giliomee, H. 'The Elusive Search for Peace', in Gagiano, J. and Giliomee, H. (eds.) *The Elusive Search for Peace: South Africa, Northern Ireland and Israel*. Cape Town: Oxford University Press, 1990.

Giliomee, H. *Die Kaap tydens die eerste Britse bewind*. Cape Town: HAUM, 1975.

Giliomee, H. *Liberal and Populist Democracy in South Africa*. Johannesburg: South African Institute of Race Relations, 1996.

Giliomee, H. 'The Non-Racial Franchise and Afrikaner and Coloured Identities, 1910-1994', *African Affairs*, 94, 1995.

Giliomee, H. *The Parting of the Ways: South African Politics*. Cape Town: David Philip, 1982.

Giliomee, H. 'Processes in the Development of the South African Frontier', in Lamar, H. and Thompson, L. (eds.) *The Frontier in History: North America and South Africa Compared*. New Haven: Yale University Press, 1981.

Giliomee, H. and Schlemmer, L. *From Apartheid to Nationbuilding*. Cape Town: Oxford University Press, 1990.

Giliomee, H. and Schlemmer, L. (eds.) *Up against the Fences: Poverty, Passes and Privilege in South Africa*. Cape Town: David Philip, 1985.

Giliomee, H. and Simkins, C. (eds.) *The Awkward Embrace: One-party Domination and Democracy*. Cape Town: Tafelberg, 1999.

Giliomee, H. et al., *Kruispad: die toekoms van Afrikaans as openbare taal*. Cape Town: Tafelberg, 2001.

Gledhill, E. and Gledhill, J. *In the Steps of Piet Retief*. Cape Town: Human & Rousseau, 1980.

Gordon, C.T. 'Aspects of Colour Attitudes and Public Policy in Kruger's Republic', in Kirkwood, K. (ed.) *St Anthony's Papers*. Oxford: Oxford University Press, 1969.

Gordon, C.T. *The Growth of Boer Opposition to Kruger, 1890-1895*. Cape Town: Oxford University Press, 1970.

Graaff, de Villiers *Div looks back*. Cape Town: Human & Rousseau, 1993.

Gray, J.L. 'The Comparative Sociology of South Africa', *South African Journal of Economics*, 5, 1937.

Greenberg, S. *Race and State in Capitalist Development*. New Haven: Yale University Press, 1980.

Green, P. 'Divided Hearts and Minds', *SA Leadership*, 13, 19, 1994.

Grimsley, M. *The Hard Hand of War: Union Military Policy towards Southern Civilians, 1861-1865*. Cambridge: Cambridge University Press, 1995.

Grosskopf, J.F.W. *Rural Impoverishment and Rural Exodus*. Stellenbosch: Pro Ecclesia, 1932.

Grové, A.P. and Harvey, C.D.J. *Afrikaans Poems with English Translations*. Cape Town: Oxford University Press, 1962.

Grundlingh, A.M. et al. *Beyond the Tryline: Rugby and South African Society*. Johannesburg: Ravan Press, 1995.

Grundlingh, A.M. *Die 'Hendsoppers' en 'Joiners': die rasionaal en verskynsel van verraad*. Pretoria: HAUM, 1979.

Grundlingh, A.M. 'The King's Afrikaners: Enlistment and Ethnic Identity in the Union of South Africa's Defence Force in the Second World War', *Journal of African History*, 44, 3, 1999.

Guelke, A. *South Africa in Transition*. London: I.B. Tauris, 1999.

Guelke, L. 'The Anatomy of a Colonial Settler Population, 1657-1750', *The International Journal of African Historical Studies*, 21, 3, 1988.

Guelke, L. 'Freehold Farmers and Frontier Settlers, 1657-1780', in Elphick, R. and Giliomee, H. (eds.) *The Shaping of South Africa Society*. Middletown: Wesleyan University Press, 1988.

Guelke, L. and Shell, R. 'An Early Colonial Landed Gentry: Land and Wealth in the Cape Colony, 1682-1731', *Journal of Historical Geography*, 9, 3, 1983.

Haasbroek, D.J.P. 'Die ontstaan van die nie-blanke stemreg en die verskansing daarvan in die Suid-Afrika Wet van 1909', doctoral dissertation, University of Stellenbosch, 1958.

Haasbroek, D.J.P. 'The Origin of Apartheid in South Africa', *Historia*, 16, l, 1971.

Hamann, H. *Days of the Generals*. Cape Town: Zebra, 2001.

Hancock, W.K. *Smuts*, 2 vols. Cambridge: Cambridge University Press, 1962.

Hancock, W.K. and Van der Poel, J. (eds.) *Selections from the Smuts Papers*, seven vols. Cambridge: Cambridge University Press, 1973.

Hanf, T. et al. *South Africa: The Prospects of Peaceful Change*. Bloomington: Indiana University Press, 1981.

Hanf, T. et al. *Südafrika: Friedlicher Wandel?* Munich: Kaiser, 1978.

Hanlon, J. *Beggar your Neighbours: Apartheid Power in Southern Africa*. London: Catholic Institute for International Relations, 1986.

Harrison, J.F.C. *The Early Victorians*. St Albans: Panther Books, 1971.

Hartshorne, K. *Crisis and Challenge: Black Education, 1910-1990*. Cape Town: Oxford University Press, 1992.

Hartshorne, K. *The Making of Education Policy in South Africa*. Cape Town: Oxford University Press, 1999.

Hatch, J. *The Dilemma of South Africa*. London: Dennis Dobson, 1953.

Hattingh, J.L. 'Die blanke nageslag van Louis van Bengale en Lijsbeth van de Kaap', *Kronos*, 3, 1980.

Headlam, C. (ed.) *The Milner Papers*. London: Cassell and Co., 1933.

Heaton Nicholls, G. *South Africa in My Time*. London: George Allen and Unwin, 1961.

Heese, H. *Reg en onreg: Kaapse regspraak in die agtiende eeu*. Cape Town: University of the Western Cape, 1994.

Heese, H.F. *Groep sonder grense: die rol en status van die gemengde bevolking aan die Kaap, 1652-1795*. Bellville: University of the Western Cape Institute for Historical Research, 1984.

Heese, J.A. *Die herkoms van die Afrikaner*. Cape Town: Balkema, 1971.

Heese, J.A. *Slagtersnek en sy mense*. Cape Town: Tafelberg, 1973.

Heiberg, J.P. 'Dr. A.L. Geyer as Suid-Afrika se hoë kommissaris in die Verenigde Koninkryk, 1950-54', doctoral dissertation, University of Stellenbosch, 2001.

Hertzog-toesprake, 1900-1942, 7 vols. Johannesburg: Perskor, 1977.

Hexham, I. *The Irony of Apartheid: The Struggle for National Independence of Afrikaner Calvinism against British Imperialism*. New York: Edwin Mellen Press, 1981.

Heydenrych, J.J.F.C. 'Die maatskaplike implikasies by die toepassing van Artikel 16 van Wet 23 van 1957', masters dissertation, University of Stellenbosch, 1968.

Heymans, C.S. 'Die politieke en ideologiese strominge en aktiwiteite in en om die Afrikaanse Studentebond', masters dissertation, University of Stellenbosch, 1981.

Hilton, H. *The Age of Atonement: The Influence of Evangelicalism in Social and Economic Thought, 1785-1865*. Oxford: Clarendon, 1988.

Himmelfarb, G. *Poverty and Compassion: The Moral Imagination of the Late Victorians*. New York: Vintage Books, 1991.

Hobson, J.A. *The War in South Africa*. London: Nisbet, 1900.

Hoernlé, R.F.A. *Race and Reason*. Johannesburg: Witwatersrand Univeristy Press, 1945.

Hoernlé, R.F.A. *South African Native Policy and the Liberal Spirit*. Johannesburg: University of Witwatersrand Press, 1939.

Hofmeyr, I. 'Building a Nation from Words: Afrikaans Language, Literature and Ethnic Identity', in Marks, S. and Trapido, S. (eds.) *The Politics of Race, Class and Nationalism in Twentieth-Century South Africa*. London: Longman, 1987.

Hofmeyr, I. 'Popularising History: The Case of Gustav Preller', *Journal of African History*, 29, 3, 1988.

Hofmeyr, J. *Christian Principles and Race Problems*. Johannesburg: South African Institute of Race Relations, 1945.

Hofmeyr, J. 'The South African Labour Market', unpublished paper, 1996.

Hofmeyr, J.H. *Het leven van J.H. Hofmeyr*. Cape Town: Van de Sandt de Villiers, 1913.

Hofmeyr, J.H. *The Life of Jan Hendrik (Onze Jan) Hofmeyr*. Cape Town: Van de Sandt de Villiers, 1913.

Hofmeyr, J.H. 'The Problem of Co-operation, 1886-1895', in Newton, A.P. and Benians, E.A. (eds.) *Cambridge History of the British Empire*, Cambridge: Cambridge University Press, 1936.

Holleman, H. 'The Great Purge', in Adam, H. (ed.) *South Africa: Sociological Perspectives*. London: Oxford University Press, 1971.

Holm, J. *Pidgins and Creole*. Cambridge: Cambridge University Press, 1989.

Horowitz, D. *Ethnic Groups in Conflict*. Berkeley: University of California Press, 1985.

Horwitz, R. *The Political Economy of South Africa*. London: Weidenfeld and Nicolson, 1967.

Huet, P. *Eene kudde en een herder*. Cape Town: N.H. Marais, 1860.

Hughes, R. *The Fatal Shore: The Epic of Australia's Founding*. New York: Vintage Books, 1986.

Hugo, P. 'Towards Darkness and Death: Racial Demonology in South Africa', in Hugo, P. (ed.) *South African Perspectives*. Cape Town: Die Suid-Afrikaan, 1989.

Huntington, S. and Nelson, J. *No Easy Choice: Political Participation in Developing Countries*. Cambridge: Harvard University Press, 1976.

Hyman, H. and Sheatsley, P. 'Attitudes towards Desegregation', *Scientific American*, 211, 1964.

Hyslop, J. *The Classroom Struggle*. Pietermaritzburg: University of Natal Press, 1999.

Hyslop, J. '"Destruction Coming In": Bantu Education as a Response to Social Crisis', in Bonner, P. et al. (eds.) *Apartheid's Genesis, 1935-1962*. Johannesburg: Ravan Press, 1993.

Hyslop, J. 'White Working-class Women and the Invention of Apartheid: "Purified" Afrikaner Nationalist Agitation for Legislation against "Mixed" Marriages', *Journal of African History*, 36, 1, 1995.

Hyslop, J. 'Why Did Apartheid's Supporters Capitulate?', *Society in Transition*, 31, 19, 2001.

James, L. *The Rise and Fall of the British Empire*. London: Abacus, 1998.

Janson, E.J.G. 'Die Burger en die Kleurlingstem, 1943-1948', masters dissertation, University of South Africa, 1987.

Jaster, R. *South Africa's Narrowing Security Options*. London: International Institute for Strategic Studies, 1980.

Jeffery, A. *The Truth about the Truth Commission*. Johannesburg: SA Institute of Race Relations, 1999.

Jenkins, S. 'Paradox of Botha's legacy', *Die Suid-Afrikaan*, June 1988.

Jesudason, J. 'The Resilience of One-Party Dominance in Malaysia and Singapore', in Giliomee, H. and Simkins, C. *The Awkward Embrace: One-Party Domination and Democracy*. Cape Town: Tafelberg, 1999.

John, P. 'Die Afrikaanse historiese roman en die literêre kritiek', doctoral dissertation, University of Stellenbosch, 1998.

Johnson, R.W. *How Long Will South Africa Survive?* London: Macmillan, 1977.

Johnson, R.W. and Schlemmer, L. 'National Issues and National Opinion', in Johnson, R.W. and Schlemmer, L. (eds.) *Launching Democracy in South Africa*. New Haven: Yale University Press, 1996.

Jonker, W. *Selfs die kerk kan verander*. Cape Town: Tafelberg, 1999.

Jooste, L. 'F.C. Erasmus as minister van verdediging, 1948-1959', masters dissertation, University of South Africa, 1995.

Jordaan, J.T. 'Die ontwikkeling van die sendingwerk van die NGK in die Transvaal', doctoral dissertation, University of Pretoria, 1962.

Jordan, W. *White over Black: American Attitudes toward the Negro, 1550-1812*. Baltimore: Penguin Books, 1968.

Joubert, E. 'Die nuwe oorlogsliteratuur', *Die Suid-Afrikaan*, August 1985.

Joubert, E. *Die swerfjare van Poppie Nongena*. Cape Town: Tafelberg, 1978.

Joubert, J.J. 'Die Burger se rol in die Suid-Afrikaanse politiek, 1934-1948', doctoral dissertation, University of South Africa, 1990.

Joubert, J.J. 'Die geskiedskrywing in Die Huisgenoot, 1923-1949', masters dissertation, University of South Africa, 1983.

Judicial Commission of Inquiry into the Recent Rebellion: *Report of the Judicial Commission of Inquiry into the Causes of and Circumstances Relating to the Recent Rebellion in South Africa*. Cape Town: Cape Times, Government Printers, 1916.

Kallaway, P. 'F.S. Malan, the Cape Liberal Tradition and South African politics, 1908-1924', *Journal of African History*, 15, 1, 1974.

Kane-Berman, J. *The Silent Revolution*. Johannesburg: South African Institute of Race Relations, 1990.

Kane-Berman, J. *Soweto*. Johannesburg: Ravan Press, 1978.

Kannemeyer, J.C. *Die Afrikaanse literatuur, 1652-1987*. Pretoria: Academica, 1988.

Kannemeyer, J.C. *D.J. Opperman: 'n biografie*. Cape Town: Human & Rousseau, 1986.

Kannemeyer, J.C. *Langenhoven: 'n lewe*. Cape Town: Tafelberg, 1995.

Kannemeyer, J.C. *Leipoldt: 'n lewensverhaal*. Cape Town: Tafelberg, 1999.

Kannemeyer, J.C. *Ontsyferde stene*. Stellenbosch: Inset, 1996.

Kaplan, D.E. 'The Politics of Industrial Protection', *Journal of South African Studies*, 3, 1, 1977.

Kapp, P.H. 'Dr. John Philip: die grondlegger van Liberalisme in Suid-Afrika', *Archives Yearbook of South Africa*, 1985.

Kapp, P.H. 'Suid-Afrika se eerste waarheidskommissie', *Tydskrif vir Geesteswetenskappe*, 42, 1, 2002.

Karis, T. and Carter, G. (eds.) *From Protest to Challenge*. Stanford: Hoover Institution Press, 1972.

Katz, E. *A Trade Union Aristocracy: A History of White Workers in the Transvaal*. Johannesburg: University of Witwatersrand, 1976.

Katzenellenbogen, S.E. 'Reconstruction in the Transvaal', in Warwick, P. (ed.) *The South African War*. London: Longman, 1980.

Katzew, H. *Apartheid and Survival*. Cape Town: Simondium, 1965.

Kedourie, E. 'One-man-one-vote', *South African International*, 18, 7, 1987.

Keegan, T. *Colonial South Africa and the Origins of the Racial Order*. Cape Town: David Philip, 1996.

Keegan, T. 'Crisis and Catharsis in the Development of Capitalism in South African Agriculture', *African Affairs*, 84, 336, 1985.

Keegan, T. 'The Dynamics of Rural Accumulation in South Africa', *Comparative Studies in Society and History*, 1986.

Keegan, T. 'The Making of the Orange Free State, 1846-1854', *Journal of Imperial and Commonwealth History*, 17, 1, 1988.

Keegan, T. 'The Overthrow of Cape Slavery', *Southern African Review of Books*, July/October 1991.

Keegan, T. *Rural Transformations in Industrializing South Africa*. Johannesburg: Ravan Press, 1986.

Keegan, T. 'The Sharecropping Economy: African Class Formation and the Natives Land Act of 1913 in the Highveld Maize Belt', in Marks, S. and Rathbone, R. (eds.) *Industrialisation and Social Change in South Africa*. London: Longman, 1982.

Keegan, T. 'White Settlement and Black Subjugation on the South African Highveld', in Beinart, W. et al. (eds.) *Putting a Plough to the Ground*. Johannesburg: Ravan Press, 1986.

Keet, B. *Whither South Africa?* Stellenbosch: CSV Publishers, 1956.

Kellerman, G. *Wie de hel het jou vertel?* Cape Town: Tafelberg, 1988.

Kennedy, P. *The Rise and Fall of Great Powers*. New York: Random House, 1987.

Kenney, R.U. *Piet Retief: The Dubious Hero*. Cape Town: Human & Rousseau, 1976.

Kenney, H. *Architect of Apartheid: H.F. Verwoerd – An Appraisal*. Johannesburg: Jonathan Ball, 1980.

Kenny, A. 'How Apartheid Saved South Africa', *The Spectator*, 27 November 1999.

Keppel-Jones. A.M. *Friends or Foes*. Pietermaritzburg: Shuter and Shooter, 1949.

Keppel-Jones, A.M. 'The Political Situation in South Africa', paper presented to the Royal Institute for International Affairs, 27 March 1947.

Keppel-Jones, A.M. *When Smuts Goes*. Cape Town: African Bookman, 1947.

Kestell, J.D. *Het leven van prof. N.J. Hofmeyr*. Cape Town: HAUM, 1911.

Kestell, J.D. and Van Velden, D.E. *Die vredesonderhandelinge*. Cape Town: Human & Rousseau, 1982.

Kinghorn, J. 'Die groei van 'n teologie', in Kinghorn, J. (ed.) *Die NG Kerk en Apartheid*. Johannesburg: Macmillan, 1986.

Kitshoff, M.C. *G.W.A. van der Lingen, 1804-1869*. Groningen: VRB, 1972.

Kitto, H.D.F. *The Greeks*. Harmondsworth: Penguin Books, 1951.

Kleynhans, J.H. '"'n Wêreld sonder grense" as eksemplaries van die Grensverhaal', masters dissertation, University of the Orange Free State, 1992.

Kloss, H. *The Unfolding of Afrikaans in its Germanic, African and World Context*. Pietersburg: University of the North, 1977.

Koen, W.P.G. 'Sanlam tussen twee wêreldoorloë', doctoral dissertation, University of South Africa, 1986.

Kotze, C.R. 'Reaksie van die Afrikaners op die owerheidsbeleid teen hulle, 1806-1824', *Historia*, 14, 1968.

Kotzé, J.G. *Biographical Memories and Reminiscences*. Cape Town, no date.

Kriek, D.J. 'Generaal J.B.M. Hertzog se opvattinge van die verhouding tussen die Afrikaans- en Engelssprekendes na Uniewording', doctoral dissertation, University of Pretoria, 1971.

Kriel, C.J. *Die geskiedenis van die Nederduits Gereformeerde Sendingkerk in Suid-Afrika, 1881-1956*. Paarl: Paarl Drukpers, 1963.

Krikler, J. 'White Working Class Identity and the Rand Revolt', paper presented to the History Workshop, University of Witwatersrand, 5-8 July 2001.

Krikler, J. 'Women, Violence and the Rand Revolt of 1922', *Journal of Southern African Studies*, 22, 3, 1996.

Krog, A. *Country of My Skull*. Johannesburg: Random House, 1999.

Kros, C. 'Economic, Political and Intellectual Origins of Bantu Education, 1926-1951', doctoral dissertation, University of the Witwatersrand University, 1996.

Krüger, B.J. 'Diskussies en wetgewing rondom die landelike arbeidsvraagstuk in die Suid-Afrikaaanse Republiek, 1885-1899,' masters dissertation, University of South Africa, 1965.

Krüger, B.J. *Diskussies en wetgewing rondom die landelike arbeidsvraagstuk in die Suid-Afrikaaanse Republiek, 1885-1899*. Communications of the University of South Africa, C62, 1966.

Krüger, B. *The Pear Tree Blossoms: The History of the Moravian Church in South Africa, 1737-1869*. Genadendal: Moravian Book Depot, 1966.

Krüger, D.W. *Die Kruger-miljoene*. Johannesburg: Perskor, 1979.

Krüger, D.W. *Paul Kruger*, vol. 1. Johannesburg: Dagbreek, 1961.

Kruger, L.-M. 'Gender, Community and Identity: Women and Afrikaner Nationalism in the *Volksmoeder* Discourse of *Die Boerevrou*, 1919-1931', masters dissertation, University of Cape Town, 1991.

Kruger, P. *The Memoirs of Paul Kruger*. New York: The Century, 1902.

Kuper, L. *Passive Resistance in South Africa*. New Haven: Yale University Press, 1957.

Kuyper, A. *The Problem of Poverty*. Grand Rapids: Baker Book House, 1991.

Labour Party. *Die nuwe politiek*. Johannesburg: 1915.

Lacey, M. *Working for Boroko*. Johannesburg: Ravan Press, 1981.

Lambert, J. 'South African British? Or Dominion South Africans?', *South African Historical Journal*, 43, 2000.

Landes, D. *The Wealth and Poverty of Nations*. London: Abacus Books, 1998.

Langenhoven, C.J. *Versamelde werke*. Cape Town: Nasionale Boekhandel, 1958.

Laponce, J. *Languages and Their Territories*. Toronto: University of Toronto Press, 1987.

Lategan, D. 'Die krisis in die sendingkerk', *Gereformeerde Vaandel*, April 1939.

Laubscher, C. 'Die geskiedenis van grondbesit in Distrik Ses tot 1984', doctoral dissertation, University of Stellenbosch, 2001.

Lazar, J. 'Conformity and Conflict: Afrikaner Nationalist Politics in South Africa, 1948-1961', doctoral dissertation, Oxford University, 1987.

Le Cordeur, B. (ed.) *The Journal of Charles Lennox Stretch*. Cape Town: Maskew Miller, 1988.

Le Cordeur, B. and Saunders, C. (eds.) *Kitchingman Papers*. Johannesburg: Brenthurst Press, 1976.

Le Cordeur, B. and Saunders, C. (eds.) *The War of the Axe*. Johannesburg: Brenthurst Press, 1981.

Legassick, M. 'The Frontier Tradition in South African Historiography', in Marks, S. and Atmore, A. (eds.) *Economy and Society in Pre-industrial South Africa*. London: Longman: 1980.

Legassick, M. 'The Making of South African "Native Policy", 1903-1923', seminar paper, Institute of Commonwealth Studies, University of London, 1973.

Legassick, M. 'The Rise of Modern South African Liberalism', seminar paper, Institute of Commonwealth studies, London University, 1973.

Leibbrandt, H.C.V. *The Rebellion of 1815*. Cape Town: Juta, 1902.

Leipoldt, C.L. *Bushveld Doctor*. London: Jonathan Cape, 1937.

Leipoldt, C.L. 'Cultural Development', in Newton, A.P. and Benians, E.A. (eds.) *Cambridge History of the British Empire*. Cambridge: Cambridge University Press, 1936.

Le May, G.H.L. *The Afrikaners: An Historical Interpretation*. Oxford: Blackwell, 1995.

Le May, G.H. *British Supremacy in South Africa, 1899-1907*. Oxford: Clarendon Press, 1965.

Le Roux, J.H. et al. *Generaal J.B.M. Hertzog*. Johannesburg: Perskor, 1987.

Le Roux, J.H. and Coetzer, P.W. *Die Nasionale Party, 1924-1934*. Bloemfontein: INEG, 1980.

Le Roux, N.J. *W.A. Hofmeyr*. Cape Town: Nasionale Boekhandel, 1953.

Lever, H. 'Ethnic Preferences of White Residents in Johannesburg', in Morse, S.J. and Orpen, C. (eds.) *Contemporary South Africa*. Cape Town: Juta, 1975.

Lewin Robinson, A.M. *The Letters of Lady Anne Barnard*. Cape Town: Balkema, 1973.

Lewis, G. *Between the Wire and the Wall: A History of South African 'Coloured' Politics*. Cape Town: David Philip, 1987.

Lewis, J. 'The Germiston By-election of 1932', in Bonner, P. (ed.) *Working Papers in Southern African Studies*. Johannesburg: Ravan Press, 1981.

Lewis, R.A. 'A Study of Some Aspects of the Poor White Problem in South Africa,' masters dissertation, Rhodes University, 1973.

Lewsen, P. 'The Cape Liberal Tradition: Myth or Reality?', *Race*, 13, 1971.

Lewsen, P. *John X. Merriman*. New Haven: Yale University Press, 1982.

Lewsen, P. (ed.) *Selections from the Correspondence of John X. Merriman, 1899-1905*. Cape Town: Van Riebeeck Society, 1966.

Lewsen, P. *Voices of Protest: From Segregation to Apartheid*. Johannesburg: Ad Donker, 1988.

Liebenberg, B.J. *Andries Pretorius in Natal*. Pretoria: Academica, 1977.

Lichtenstein, H. *Travels in South Africa, 1803-1805*, vol. 1. Cape Town: Van Riebeeck Society, 1928.

Lipton, M. *Capitalism and Apartheid*. Aldershot: Wildwood House, 1986.

Liversage, E. 'Die premierskap van generaal Louis Botha tot en met die uitbreek van die Eerste Wêreldoorlog', doctoral dissertation, University of the Orange Free State, 1985.

Lombard, J.A. 'Die sendingbeleid van die NGK van die OVS', doctoral dissertation, University of the North, 1985.

Louw, C. *Boetman en die swanesang van die verligtes*. Cape Town: Human & Rousseau, 2001.

Louw, L. (ed.) *Dawie, 1946-1964*. Cape Town: Tafelberg, 1965.

Louw, M. Interview with author, 21 November 1994.

Louw, N.P. van Wyk. Review of the Carnegie Commission report, *Die Huisgenoot*, 15 September 1933.

Louw, N.P. van Wyk. *Versamelde prosa*, vols. 1 and 2, Cape Town: Tafelberg and Human & Rousseau, 1986.

Louw, P.E. 'South Africa's Second Post-Apartheid Election', *Australian Journal of International Affairs*, 54, 2, 2000.

Maasdorp, G. 'Economic Survey, 1970-2000', unpublished paper, 2002.

MacDonald, J.R. *What I Saw in South Africa*. London: The Echo, 1902.

Maclennan, B. *A Proper Degree of Terror*. Johannesburg: Ravan Press, 1986.

Macmillan, W.M. *Bantu, Boer and Briton*. Oxford: Clarendon Press, 1963.

Macmillan, W.M. *The Cape Colour Question*. London: Faber and Gwyer, 1927.

Macmillan, W.M. *Complex South Africa*. London: Faber and Faber, 1930.

Malan, D.F. *Afrikanervolkseenheid*. Kaapstad: Nasionale Boekhandel, 1959.

Malan, D.F. *Die groot vlug*. Cape Town: Nasionale Pers, 1916.

Malan, D.F. *Die onafhanklikheid van Suid-Afrika*. Cape Town: Nasionale Pers, 1918.

Malan, F.S. 'Autobiography', unpublished manuscript, F.S. Malan papers, Cape Archives.

Malan, F.S. *Die konvensie-dagboek*. Cape Town: Van Riebeeck Society, 1951.

Malan, F.S. *The True Ideal of South African Politics*. Pamphlet, 1904.

Malan, F.S. *The University South Africa Needs*. Cape Town, no publisher given, 1912.

Malan, S.F. *Politieke strominge onder die Afrikaners van die Vrystaatse Republiek*. Durban: Butterworth, 1982.

Malherbe, E.G. *Education and the Poor White: Report of the Carnegie Commission*. Stellenbosch: Pro Ecclesia, 1932.

Malherbe, E.G. *Education in South Africa*. Cape Town: Juta, 1977.

Malherbe, E.G. *Never a Dull Moment*. Cape Town: Timmins Publishers, 1981.

Malherbe, E.G. *Onderwys en die armblanke*. Stellenbosch: Pro Eccelesia. 1932.

Malherbe, V.C. 'The Cape Khoisan in the Eastern Districts of the Colony before and after Ordinance 50 of 1828', doctoral dissertation, University of Cape Town, 1997.

Malherbe, V.C. *The Khoikhoi Rebellion in the Eastern Cape, 1799-1803*. Cape Town: University of Cape Town Press, 1981.

Malherbe, V.C. 'Testing the Burgher Right to the Land', *South African Historical Journal*, 40, 1999.

Mamdani, M. *Citizen and Subject: Contemporary Africa and the Legacy of Late Colonialism*. Princeton: Princeton University Press, 1996.

Mandela, N. *No Easy Walk to Freedom*. London: Little, Brown and Co., 1994.

Mandela, N. 'Whither the Black Consciousness Movement?', in Maharaj, M. (ed.) *Reflections in Prison*. London: Zebra Books, 2001.

Marais, A.H. 'Die Afrikanerdom een en verdeeld', in Geyser, O. and Marais, A.H. (eds.) *Die Nasionale Party*. Pretoria: Academica, 1975.

Marais, B. *Colour: Unsolved Problem of the West*. Cape Town: Howard Timmins, 1952.

Marais, B. ''n Kritiese beoordeling . . .' *Op die Horison*. 9, 1, 1947.

Marais, C. 'Toenadering en samewerking', in Geyser, O. and Marais, A.H. (eds.) *Die Nasionale Party*. Pretoria: Academica, 1975.

Marais, J.S. *The Fall of Kruger's Republic*. Oxford: Clarendon, 1961.

Marais, J.S. *Maynier and the First Boer Republic*. Cape Town: Maskew Miller, 1944.

Markham, V. *The South African Scene*. London: Smith, Elder and Co., 1913.

Marks, S. and Trapido, S. 'Lord Milner and the South African State', *History workshop*, 8, 1979.

Marlowe, J. *Milner*. London: Hamish Hamilton, 1976.

Marquard, L. *South Africa and Her People*. London: Lutterworth Press, 1957.

Marquard, M. *Letters from a Boer Parsonage*. Cape Town: Purnell, 1967.

Marshall, P.J. 'Imperial Britain', *The Journal of Imperial and Commonwealth History*, 23, 3, 1995.

Mason, J.E. '"Fit for Freedom": The Slaves, Slavery and Emancipation in the Cape Colony, South Africa, 1806-1842', doctoral dissertation, Yale University, 1992.

Mason, J. 'Slaveholder Resistance to the Amelioration of Slavery at the Cape', unpublished paper, University of Cape Town Centre of African Studies, 1986.

Matthews, Z.K. 'Future Race Relations in South Africa', *Race Relations*, 5, 4, 1938.

Matthews, Z.K. and M'Timkulu, D.G.S. 'The Future in the Light of the Tomlinson Report', *Race Relations Journal*, 24, 1-2, 1957.

May, H.J. *The South African Constitution*. Cape Town: Juta, 1955.

May, S. *Language and Minority Rights: Ethnicity, Nationalism and the Politics of Language*. London: Longman, 2001.

McCracken, J.L. *The Cape Parliament*. Oxford: Clarendon Press, 1967.

Meer, F. 'African Nationalism: Some Inhibiting Factors', in Adam, H. (ed.) *South Africa: Sociological Perspectives*. London: Oxford University Press, 1971.

Meintjes, J. *General Louis Botha*. London: Cassell, 1970.

Meiring Beck, J.H. *J.H. Meiring Beck*. Cape Town: Maskew Miller, 1921.

Mentzel, O.F. *Description of the Cape of Good Hope, Vol. 3*. Cape Town: Van Riebeeck Society, 1944.

Mentzel, O.F. *Life at the Cape in the Mid-Eighteenth Century*. Cape Town: Van Riebeeck Society, 1919.

Merriman, N.J. *The Kafir, the Hottentot, and the Frontier Farmer: Passages of Missionary Life from the Journals of the Venerable Archdeacon Merriman*. London: George Bell, 1854.

Merrington, P. 'Heritage, Genealogy and the Inventing of Union', paper presented to the University of Cape Town African Studies Seminar, 1997.

Methuen, A.M.S. *Peace or War in South Africa*. London: Methuen, 1901.

Millar, R. 'Science and Society in the Early Career of H.F. Verwoerd', *Journal of Southern African Studies* 19, 4, 1993.

Millar, R. 'Social Science, Philanthropy and Politics: The Carnegie Corporation in South Africa', unpublished paper, 1992.

Millin, S.G. *General Smuts*. London: Faber and Faber, 1936.

Milone, P.D. '*Indische* Culture and Its Relationship to Urban Life', *Comparative Studies in Society and History*, 9, 1967.

Mittner, M.J. '*Die Burger* en die Kleurling-stem', masters dissertation, University of Cape Town, 1986.

Moll, T. 'Did the Apartheid Economy Fail?', *Journal of South African Studies*, 17, 2, 1991.

Moll, T. 'From Booster to Brake: Apartheid and Economic Growth in Comparative Perspective', Nattrass, N. and Ardington, E. (eds.) *The Political Economy of South Africa*. Cape Town: Oxford University Press, 1990.

Molteno, J.T. *The Dominion of Afrikanerdom*. London: Methuen, 1923.

Moodie, D. *The Record*, vols. 1-5. Cape Town: Balkema, 1960.

Moodie, D. 'Class Struggle in the Development of Agrarian Capitalism in South Africa', paper presented to the University of Cape Town Centre for African Studies, 1982.

Moodie, D. *The Rise of Afrikanerdom*. Berkeley: University of California Press, 1975.

Morrell, R. 'The Poor Whites of Middelburg, Transvaal', in Morrell, R. (ed.) *White but Poor: Essays on the History of the Poor White in South Africa, 1880-1940*. Pretoria: Unisa, 1992.

Morris, J. *South African Winter*. London: Faber and Faber, 1957.

Morris, M.L. 'The Development of Capitalism in South African Agriculture', *Economy and Society*, 5, 3, 1976.

Mostert, N. *Frontiers*. New York: Knopf, 1992.

Mouton, A. '"Reform from Within": Schalk Pienaar, the Afrikaans Press and Apartheid', *Historia*, 45, 1, 2000.

Mouton, A. *Voorloper: die lewe van Schalk Pienaar*. Cape Town: Tafelberg, 2002.

Muller, C.F.J. *Die oorsprong van die Groot Trek*. Cape Town: Tafelberg, 1974.

Muller, C.F.J. *Sonop in die Suide: geboorte en groei van die Nasionale Pers, 1915-1948*. Cape Town: Nasionale Boekhandel, 1990.

Muller, T. *'n Inspirasie vir jong Suid-Afrika*. Cape Town: Nasionale Pers, 1925.

Nash, A. 'The Dialectical Tradition in South Africa', doctoral dissertation, University of Cape Town, 2000.

Nash, A. 'Dr Philip, the "Spread of Civilisation" and Liberalism in South Africa', paper presented to the Development Studies Conference on the history of opposition in South Africa, University of the Witwatersrand, Johannesburg, 1978.

Nasson, W. 'Abraham Esau: A Calvinia Martyr in the Boer War', *Social Dynamics*, 11, 1, 1985.

Nattrass, J. *The South African Economy*. Cape Town: Oxford University Press, 1981.

Naude, L. (pseudonym) *Dr. A. Hertzog, die Nasionale Party en die mynwerker*. Pretoria: Nasionale Raad van Trustees, 1969.

Naudé, S.D. 'Willem Cornelius Boers', *Archives Yearbook of South Africa*, 2, 1950.

Neame, L.E. *General Hertzog*. London: Hurst and Blackett, 1930.

Neame, L.E. *The History of Apartheid*. London: Pall Mall Press, 1962.

Neame, L.E. *Some South African Politicians*. Cape Town: Maskew Miller, 1929.

Neame, L.E. 'An important letter', *Tydskrif vir Rasse-aangeleenthede*, 1, 6, 1954.

Nederduits Gereformeerde Kerk. *Kerk en samelewing*, Bloemfontein: Algemene Sinodale Kommissie, 1986.

Neethling, E. *Mag ons vergeet?* Cape Town: Nasionale Pers, 1938.

Nel, M.D.C. 'Generaal Hertzog: beslaggewer van die ban-toebeleid', *Hertzog-annale*, 9, 1962.

Nel, M.D.C. 'Waarom die beleid van apartheid?', *Journal of Racial Affairs*, 11, 4, 1960.

Nepgen, C.C. *Die sosiale gewete van die Afrikaanssprekendes*. Stellenbosch: CSV, 1938.

Newton-King, S. 'Commerce and Material Culture on the Eastern Cape Frontier, 1784-1812', paper presented at the University of the Witwatersrand History Workshop, 1987.

Newton-King, S. 'The Enemy Within: The Struggle for Ascendancy on the Cape Eastern Frontier', doctoral dissertation, University of London, London, 1992.

Newton-King, S. *The Enemy Within: The Struggle for Ascendancy on the Cape Eastern Frontier*. Cambridge: Cambridge University Press, 1999.

Nicol, W. ''n Grootse Roeping', in Cronjé, G. et al. *Regverdige rasse-apartheid*. Stellenbosch: CSV, 1947.

Nicol, W. *Met toga en troffel*. Cape Town: NGK Uitgewers, 1958.

Niebuhr, R. *Moral Man in Immoral Society*. New York: Charles Scribner's Sons, 1932.

Oberholster, A.G. *Die Mynwerkerstaking: Witwatersrand, 1922*. Pretoria: HSRC, 1982.

Oberholster, J.J. (ed.) 'Dagboek van Oskar Hintrager', *Christiaan de Wet-annale*, 1973.

Odendaal, A.A. 'Die Nederduitse Gereformeerde Sending in die Oranje Vrystaat (1842-1910)', doctoral dissertation, University of Stellenbosch, 1970.

O'Brien Geldenhuys, F.E. *In die stroomversnellings*. Cape Town: Tafelberg, 1982.

Odendaal, A. *Vukani Bantu: The Beginnings of Black Protest Politics in South Africa to 1912*. Cape Town: David Philip, 1984.

O'Dowd, M.C. 'An Assessment of English-speaking South Africa's Contribution to the Economy', in De Villiers, A. (ed.) *English-speaking South Africa Today*. Cape Town: Oxford University Press, 1976.

O'Dowd, M.C. 'The General Election of 1924', *South African Historical Journal*, 2, 1970.

O'Dowd, M.C. 'The O'Dowd View', in Schlemmer, L. and Webster, E. (eds.) *Change, Reform and Economic Growth in South Africa*. Johannesburg: Ravan Press, 1978.

O'Dowd, M.C. 'The Stages of Economic Growth', Leftwich, A. (ed.) *South African Economic Growth and Political Change*. London: Allison and Busby, 1974.

Oglethorpe, J. 'Segregasie in die kerk', *Die Stellenbossche Student*, November 1947.

Olivier, G. *N.P. van Wyk Louw*. Cape Town: Human & Rousseau, 1992.

Olivier, N. ''n Opgewarmde nuwe NP-beleid', *Die Suid-Afrikaan*, June 1989.

O'Malley, P. (ed.) *Ramaphosa and Meyer in Belfast*. Boston: McCormack Institute, 1996.

O'Meara, D. *Forty Lost Years: The Apartheid State and the Politics of the National Party*. Johannesburg: Ravan Press, 1996.

O'Meara, D. *Volkskapitalisme: Class, Capital and Ideology in the Development of Afrikaner Nationalism, 1934-1948*. Cambridge: Cambridge University Press, 1983.

Omer-Cooper, J. 'The Mfecane Defended', *Southern African Review of Books*, 4 and 5, July/October 1991.

Omer-Cooper, J. *The Zulu Aftermath*. Evanston: University of Indiana Press, 1966.

O'Neill, J. *Blood-dark Tracks*. London: Granta, 2001.

Opperman, D. J. *Joernaal van Jorik*. Cape Town: Nasionale Pers, 1949.

Opperman, D.J. 'Uitdyende heelal?', *Die Burger*, 25 May 1960.

Orpen, J.M. *Reminiscences of Life in South Africa*. Durban: Davis, 1908.

Orwell, G. *Inside the Whale*. Penguin Books, 1984.

Pakenham, T. *The Boer War*. Weidenfeld and Nicolson, 1979.

Parnell, S. 'Slums, Segregation and the Poor White in Johannesburg, 1920-1934', in Morrell, R. (ed.) *White but Poor: Essays on the History of the Poor White in South Africa, 1880-1940*. Pretoria: Unisa, 1992.

Parry, R. '"In a Sense Citizens, but Not Altogether Citizens": Rhodes, Race and the Ideology of Segregation in the Late Nineteenth Century', *Canadian Journal of African Studies*, 17, 3, 1983.

Paton, A. *Hofmeyr*. Cape Town: Oxford University Press, 1965.

Paton, A. *Journey Continued*. Cape Town: David Philip, 1988.

Paton, A. *Save the Beloved Country*. Melville: Hans Strydom, 1987.

Patterson, O. *Freedom, Vol. 1: Freedom in the Making of Western Culture*. New York: Basic Books, 1991.

Patterson, S. *The Last Trek*. London: Routledge and Kegan Paul, 1957.

Pauw, S. *Beroepsarbeid van die Afrikaners*. Stellenbosch: Pro Ecclesia, 1946.

Peires, J.B. 'The British and the Cape, 1814-1834', in Elphick, R. and Giliomee, H. (eds.) *The Shaping of South African Society, 1652-1840*. Middletown: Wesleyan University Press, 1988.

Peires, J.B. *The Dead Shall Arise*. Johannesburg: Ravan Press, 1989.

Peires, J.B. *The House of Phalo: A History of the Xhosa People in the Days of Their Independence*. Johannesburg: Ravan Press, 1981.

Pelzer, A.N. *Die Afrikaner-Broederbond: eerste vyftig jaar*. Cape Town: Tafelberg, 1979.

Pelzer, A.N. '"Die arm-blanke" in die Suid-Afrikaanse Republiek tussen die jare 1882 en 1899', *Historiese Studies*, 2,4, 1941.

Pelzer, A.N. *Geskiedenis van die Suid-Afrikaanse Republiek*. Cape Town: Balkema, 1950.

Pelzer, A.N. (ed.) *Verwoerd aan die woord*. Johannesburg: Afrikaanse Boekhandel, 1963.

Penn, N. 'The Northern Cape Frontier Zone, 1700-c. 1815', doctoral dissertation, University of Cape Town, 1995.

Philip, J. *Researches in South Africa*. London: Duncan, 1828.

Phillipps, T. *Phillipps, 1820 Settler*. Pietermaritzburg: University of Natal Press, 1960.

Phillips, A. *British Policy in West Africa*. London: James Currey, 1989.

Pienaar, E.C. *Die triomf van Afrikaans*. Cape Town: Nasionale Pers, 1943.

Pienaar, E.C. *Taal en poësie van die Tweede Afrikaanse Taalbeweging*. Cape Town: Nasionale Boekhandel, 1926.

Pienaar, J.J. *Die inspirerende opvoedings- en opheffingsaksie van die Ned. Herv. of Gereformeerde Kerke in die Transvaal gedurende 1902 tot 1910*. Pretoria: NG Boekhandel, 1970.

Pienaar, S. 'Die Afrikaner en sy koerant', *Standpunte*, 108, 1973.

Pienaar, S. *Getuie van groot tye*. Cape Town: Tafelberg, 1979.

Pienaar, S.W. (ed.) *Glo in u volk: dr. D.F. Malan as redenaar*. Cape Town: Tafelberg, 1964.

Pirow, O. *James Barry Munnik Hertzog*. Cape Town: Howard Timmins, 1957.

Plaatje, S.T. *Native Life in South Africa*. London: King, 1916.

Ponelis, F. *The Development of* Afrikaans. Frankfurt: Peter Lang, 1993.

Porter, A. *The Origins of the South African War*. Manchester: Manchester University Press, 1980.

Porter, A. 'The South African War: Context and Motive Reconsidered', *Journal of African History*, 31, 1990.

Posel, D. *The Making of Apartheid, 1948-1961*. Oxford: Clarendon Press, 1991.

Posel, D. 'What's in a Name? Racial Categorisation under Apartheid', paper presented to the History Workshop, Witwatersrand University, 2001.

Posel, D. 'Whiteness and Power in the South African Civil Service: Paradoxes of the Apartheid State', *Journal of Southern African Studies*, 25, 1, 1999.

Potgieter, F.J. 'Die vestiging van die blanke in die Transvaal, 1837-1868', doctoral dissertation, Potchefstroom University, 1955.

Potgieter, M. du T. 'Die Nederduits Gereformeerde Kerk en die blanke onderwys in Kaapland sedert die eerste sinode', doctoral dissertation, University of Stellenbosch, 1961.

Potgieter, P.J.J.S. 'L.J. du Plessis as denker oor staat en politiek', doctoral dissertation, Potchefstroom University, 1976.

Pottinger, B. *The Imperial Presidency: P.W. Botha, the First Ten Years*. Johannesburg: Southern Books, 1988.

Preece, H. 'The Economics of Apartheid', in Harker, J. (ed.) *The Legacy of Apartheid*. London: Guardian Newspaper, 1994.

Preller, J. (ed.) *Konvensie-dagboek van F.S. Malan*. Cape Town: Van Riebeeck Society, 1951.

Preller, G. 'The Union and the Boer', *The State*, 1,6, 1909.

Pretorius, F. *Kommandolewe tydens die Anglo-Boereoorlog, 1899-1902*. Cape Town: Human & Rousseau, 1991.

Pretorius, G. *Bruckner de Villiers*. Cape Town: HAUM, 1959.

Pringle, T. *Narrative of a Residence in South Africa*. 1835, reprinted Cape Town: Struik, 1966.

Prinsloo, D. 'Die Johannesburg-periode in dr. H.F. Verwoerd se loopbaan', doctoral dissertation, Rand Afrikaans University, 1979.

Randall, P. *A Taste of Power*. Johannesburg: Sprocas, 1973.

Rauch, G. van H. 'Die optrede en verantwoording van die NGK in SA met betrekking tot die Tweede Vryheidsoorlog', masters dissertation, University of Stellenbosch, 1979.

Rayner, M. 'Wine and Slaves: The Failure of an Export Economy and the Ending of Slavery in the Cape Colony, South Africa, 1806-1834', doctoral dissertation, Duke University, 1986.

Ries, A. and Dommisse, E. *Broedertwis*. Cape Town: Tafelberg, 1982.

Rees, M. and Day, C. *Muldergate*. Johannesburg: Muldergate, 1980.

Reitz, D. *Commando*. London: Faber and Faber, 1929.

Reitz, F.W. (ed.) *'n Eeu van onreg*, 1899 reprinted Cape Town: Nasionale Pers, 1993.

Reitz, F.W. 'The Native Question,' *Cape Illustrated Magazine*, November 1891.

The Reports of Chavonnes and His Council, and of Van Imhoff on the Cape. Cape Town: Van Riebeeck Society, 1918.

Report of the Economic and Wages Commission, 1926.

Report of the Martial Law Inquiry Judicial Commission. Pretoria: Wallachs, 1922.

Report of the Native Land Commission, U.G. 22. Pretoria: Government Printer, 1916.

Report of the Native Laws Commission, U.G. 28-48.

Report of the Select Committee on Native Affairs, 1917.

Report of the Select Committee on Aborigines, 1836.

Report of the Transvaal Indigency Commission, T.G. 13-08, 1908.

Report of the Transvaal Labour Commission, 1903.

Report on the National Conference on the Poor White Problem, 1934.

Rhoodie, N.J. *Apartheid and Racial Partnership in Southern Africa*. Pretoria: Academica, 1969.

Richard, D. *Moedswillig die uwe*. Johannesburg: Perskor, 1985.

Roberts, M. and Trollope, A.E.G. *The South African Opposition*. London: Longmans, 1947.

Robertson, J. *Liberalism in South Africa, 1948-1963*. Oxford: Oxford University Press, 1971.

Robinson, K. *The Dilemmas of Trusteeship*. London: Oxford University Press, 1965.

Robinson, R. et al. *Africa and the Victorians*. London: Macmillan, 1976.

Robinson, R. 'Non-European Foundations of European Imperialism', in Owen, R. and Sutcliffe, B. (eds.) *Studies in the Theory of Imperialism*. London: Longman, 1972.

Rompel-Koopman, L. *Wat mevrouw generaal Joubert vertelt*. Cape Town: HAUM, 1916.

Ross, A. *John Philip, 1775-1851*. Aberdeen: Aberdeen University Press, 1986.

Ross, J.J. Unpublished report of the Interdenominational African Ministers' Conference, Bloemfontein, 1956. In the possession of SABRA member, Schüler. G.

Ross, R. *Adam Kok's Griquas*. Cambridge: Cambridge University Press, 1976.

Ross, R. *Cape of Torments: Slavery and Resistance in South Africa*. London: Routledge Kegan Paul, 1983.

Ross, R. *A Concise History of South Africa*. Cambridge: Cambridge University Press, 1999.

Ross, R. 'The Fundamentalisation of Afrikaner Calvinism', in Diederiks H. and Quispel, C. (eds.) *Onderscheid en minderheid*. Hilversum: Verloren, 1987.

Ross, R. 'The Rise of the Cape Gentry', *Journal of Southern African Studies*, 9, 2, 1983.

Ross, R. 'The Rule of Law at the Cape of Good Hope in the Eighteenth Century', *Journal of Imperial and Commonwealth History*, 1, 1980.

Ross, R. 'Social and Political Theology of Western Cape Missions', in Bredekamp, H. and Ross, R. (eds.) *Missions and Christianity in South African History*. Johannesburg: Witwatersrand University Press, 1995.

Ross, R. *Status and Respectability in the Cape Colony, 1750-1870*. Cambridge: Cambridge University Press, 1999.

Rousseau, J. 'Iets oor Bantoe-onderwys', in Verwoerd, W.J. (ed.) *Verwoerd: só onthou ons hom*. Pretoria: Protea Boekhuis, 2001.

Rousseau, L. *Die groot verlange: die verhaal van Eugène Marais*. Cape Town: Human & Rousseau, 1974.

Rossouw, H.J. 'Adriaan van Jaarsveld', masters dissertation, University of Stellenbosch, 1935.

R[othman], M.E. *My beskeie deel*. Cape Town: Tafelberg, 1972.

R[othman], M. E. (ed.) *Oorlogsdagboek van 'n Transvaalse burger te velde*. Cape Town: Tafelberg, 1976.

Rotberg, R. *The Founder: Cecil John Rhodes and the Pursuit of Power*. Johannesburg: Southern Books, 1988.

Roux, E. *Time Longer than Rope: A History of the Black Man's Struggle for Freedom in South Africa*. Madison: University of Wisconsin Press, 1966.

Roux, H.A. *De Ethiopische Kerk*. No place, no publisher, 1905.

SABRA. *Integration or Separate Development*. Stellenbosch, 1952.

SABRA. *Die Naturellevraagstuk*. Stellenbosch, 1950.

Sachs, A. *Justice in South Africa*. London: Heinemann, 1973.

Sachs, E.S. *Rebels' Daughters*. London: McGibbon and Kee, 1957.

Sadie, A.Y. 'Regerings- en sake-elite se persepsies oor die invloed van die Suid-Afrikaanse sakesektor op openbare beleidsformulering', doctoral dissertation, University of Cape Town, 1990.

Sadie, J. 'Die demografie van die blanke Afrikanergemeenskap', *Journal for the Study of Economy and Econometrics*, 22, 3, 1998.

Sadie, J. 'Politiek en taal: 'n ontleding', *Die Burger*, 29 August 1958.

Sadie, J.L. 'Assault on Private Enterprise' (Review), *Die Burger*, 4 March 1977.

Sadie, J.L. 'The Economic Demography of South Africa', doctoral dissertation, University of Stellenbosch, 2000.

Sadie, J.L. 'Die ekonomiese faktor in die Afrikaner-gemeenskap', in Van der Merwe, H.W. (ed.) *Identiteit en verandering*. Cape Town: Tafelberg, 1974.

Sadie, J.L. *The Fall and Rise of the Afrikaner in the South African Economy*. Stellenbosch: University of Stellenbosch Annale, 2002.

Sadie, J.L. 'The Political Arithmetic of Apartheid', in Hugo, P. (ed.) *South African Perspectives*. Cape Town: Die Suid-Afrikaan, 1989.

Salomon, L. 'The Economic Background to Afrikaner Nationalism', in Butler, J. (ed.) *Boston University Papers in African History*. Boston: Boston University, 1964.

Salomon, L. 'Socio-Economic Aspects of South African History, 1870-1962', doctoral dissertation, Boston University, 1962.

Sanders, M. 'Complicities: On the Intellectual', doctoral dissertation, Columbia University, 1998.

Sass, B. 'The Union and SADF', in Cilliers, J. and Reichardt, M. (eds.) *About Turn: The Transformation of the SA Military and Intelligence*. Halfway House: Institute for Defence Policy, 1995.

Saunders, C. 'The Annexation of the Transkei', in Saunders, C. and Derricourt, R. (eds.) *Beyond the Cape Frontier*. Cape Town: Longman, 1974.

Scanell, J.P. *Uit die volk gebore: Sanlam se eerste vyftig jaar*. Cape Town: Nasionale Boekhandel, 1968.

Schama, S. *The Embarrassment of Riches: An Interpretation of Dutch Culture in the Golden Age*. London: Fontana Press, 1987.

Schama, S. *Patriots and Liberators: Revolution in the Netherlands, 1780-1813*. New York: Alfred Knopf, 1977.

Scheffler, H. 'Die geskiedenis van die historiese landgoed Muratie'. Private manuscript, 1991. In the possession of Mrs A. Melck, Muratie, Stellenbosch.

Scher, D.M. 'The Disenfranchisement of the Coloured Voters, 1948-1956', unpublished doctoral dissertation, University of South Africa, 1983.

Schlemmer, L. 'Politieke keuses en bebloede sitvlakke', *Die Suid-Afrikaan*, 17 (1988).

Schlemmer, L. 'Between a Rainbow and a Hard Place', *Fast Facts*, December 2001.

Schlemmer, L. *Black Attitudes: Adaptation and Reaction*. Durban: Institute of Social Research, 1975.

Schlemmer, L. 'Change in South Africa', in Price, R.M. and Rosberg, C.G. (eds.) *The Apartheid Regime*. Berkeley: Institute of International Studies, 1980.

Schlemmer, L. 'The Depth and Scope of Support for a Volkstaat', unpublished report of a poll, February 1996.

Schlemmer, L. 'Factors in the Persistence or Decline of Ethnic Group Mobilization: Afrikaners in Post-Apartheid South Africa', doctoral dissertation, University of Cape Town, 1999.

Schlemmer, L. *Social Research in a Divided Society*. Pietermaritzburg: University of Natal Press, 1973.

Schlemmer, L. 'South Africa's National Party Government', in Berger, P. and Godsell, B. (eds.) *A Future South Africa*. Cape Town: Human & Rousseau/Tafelberg, 1988.

Schoeman, B. *My lewe in die politiek*. Johannesburg: Perskor, 1978.

Schoeman, B.M. *Die Broederbond en die Afrikaner-politiek*. Pretoria: Aktuele Publikasies, 1982.

Schoeman, B.M. *Die Geldmag: SA se onsigbare regering*. Pretoria: Sigma, 1980.

Schoeman, B.M. *Van Malan tot Verwoerd*. Cape Town: Human & Rousseau, 1973.

Schoeman, B.M. *Vorster se duisend dae*. Cape Town: Human & Rousseau, 1974.

Schoeman, K. *Armosyn van die Kaap: voorspel tot vestiging, 1415-1651*. Cape Town: Human & Rousseau, 1999.

Schoeman, K. *Armosyn van die Kaap: die wêreld van 'n slavin, 1652-1733*. Cape Town: Human & Rousseau, 2001.

Schoeman, K. *Bloemfontein: die ontstaan van 'n stad, 1846-1946*. Cape Town: Human & Rousseau, 1980.

Schoeman, K. *Dogter van Sion: Machtelt Smit en die 18de-eeuse samelewing aan die Kaap, 1749-1799*. Cape Town: Human & Rousseau, 1997.

Schoeman, K. *In liefde en trou: die lewe van president en mevrou M.T. Steyn*. Cape Town: Human & Rousseau, 1983.

Schoeman, K. *Olive Schreiner: 'n lewe in Suid-Afrika, 1855-1881*. Cape Town: Human & Rousseau, 1989.

Schoeman, K. *Die wêreld van Susanna Smit, 1799-1863*. Cape Town: Human & Rousseau, 1995.

Scholtz, D.A. 'Ds. S.J. du Toit as kerkman en kultuurleier', unpublished doctoral dissertation, University of Stellenbosch, 1975.

Scholtz, G.D. *Dr. Hendrik Frensch Verwoerd*. Johannesburg: Perskor, 1974.

Scholtz, G.D. *Hertzog en Smuts en die Britse Ryk*. Cape Town: Tafelberg, 1975.

Scholtz, G.D. *Het die Afrikaanse volk 'n toekoms?* Johannesburg: Voortrekkerpers, 1954.

Scholtz, G.D. *Die ontwikkeling van die politieke denke van die Afrikaners*, 8 vols, Johannesburg: Voortrekkerpers and Perskor, 1967-1984.

Scholtz, J.J.J. 'In die skemerwêreld', in Beukes, W.D. (ed.) *Oor grense heen: op pad na 'n Nasionale Pers, 1948-1990*. Cape Town: Nasionale Boekhandel, 1992.

Scholtz, J.J.J. *Vegter en hervormer*. Cape Town: Tafelberg, 1988.

Scholtz, J. du P. *Die Afrikaner en sy taal*. Cape Town: Nasou, 1964.

Scholtz, J. du P. *Taalhistoriese opstelle*. Cape Town: Tafelberg, 1981.

Scholtz, L. *Waarom die Boere die oorlog verloor het*. Menlo Park: Protea Boekhuis, 1999.

Schreiner, O.D. *The Nettle*. Johannesburg: South African Institute of Race Relations, 1964.

Schreiner, O. *Thoughts on South Africa*. Johannesburg: Ad Donker, 1992.

Schreuder, D. 'South Africa', in Eddy, J. and Schreuder, D. (eds.) *The Rise of Colonial Nationalism*. Sydney: Allen and Unwin, 1988.

Schreuder, D.M. *Gladstone and Kruger: Liberal Government and Colonial 'Home Rule'*. London: Routledge and Kegan Paul, 1989.

Schreuder, D.M. *The Scramble for Africa, 1877-1895*. Cambridge: Cambridge University Press, 1980.

Schrire, R. *Adapt or Die: The End of White Politics in South Africa*. London: Hurst, 1992.

Schutte, G. 'Between Amsterdam and Batavia: Cape Society and the Calvinist Church under the Dutch East India Company', *Kronos*, 25, 1998-99.

Schutte, G. 'Company and Colonists at the Cape, 1652-1795', in Elphick, R. and Giliomee, H. (eds.) *The Shaping of South Africa Society*. Middletown: Wesleyan University Press, 1988.

Schutte, G.J. 'Abraham Kuyper: vormer van een volksdeel', in Augustijn, C. (ed.) *Abraham Kuyper*. Delft: Meinema, 1987.

Schutte, G.J. 'Arbeid, die geen brood geeft . . .' in Schutte, G.J. (ed.) *Een arbeider is zijn loon waardig*. The Hague: Meinema, 1991.

Schutte, G.J. *Het Calvinistisch Nederland: mythe en werklikheid*. Hilversum: Verloren, 2000.

Schwartz, M.A. *Trends in White Attitudes towards Negroes*. Chicago: University of Chicago Opinion Research Center, 1967.

Scully, P. 'Liberating the Family? Gender, Labour and Sexuality in the Rural Western Cape, South Africa, 1823-1853', doctoral dissertation, University of Wisconsin, 1993.

Seegers, A. *The Military in the Making of Modern South Africa*. London: I.B. Tauris, 1996.

Serfontein, J.H.P. *Die verkrampte aanslag*. Cape Town: Human & Rousseau, 1970.

Serfontein, J.H.P. *Brotherhood of Power*. London: Rex Collings, 1979.

Shain, M. *The Roots of Anti-Semitism in South Africa*. University of Virginia Press, 1994.

Shaw, G. *The Cape Times: An Informal History*. Cape Town: David Philip, 1999.

Shell, R.C.-H. *Children of Bondage: A Social History of the Slave Society at the Cape of Good Hope, 1652-1838*. Johannesburg: Witwatersrand University Press, 1994.

Shell, R.C.-H. 'The Family and Slavery at the Cape, 1680-1808', in James, W. and Simons, M. (eds.) *The Angry Divide: Social and Economic History of the Western Cape*. Cape Town: David Philip, 1989.

Shell, R.C.-H. 'Tender Ties: The Women of the Cape Slave Society', *Societies of Southern Africa*, 17, 1992.

Shepherd Smith, J. *Buthelezi: The Bibliography*. Melville: Hans Strydom Publishers, 1988.

Shifrin, T. '"New Deal for the Coloured People": A Study of NP Policies towards the Coloured People, 1924-1929', honours dissertation, University of Cape Town, 1962.

Shingler, J.D. 'Education and Political Order in South Africa, 1902-1961', doctoral dissertation, Yale University, 1973.

Simkins, C. 'Agricultural Production in the African Reserves of South Africa', *Journal of Southern African Studies*, 7, 1981.

Simons H.J. and Simons, R.E. *Class and Colour in South Africa, 1850-1950*. Harmondsworth: Penguin Books, 1969.

Slabbert, F. van Zyl. 'Hoe ry die boere sit-sit so', *Die Suid-Afrikaan*, August 1988.

Slabbert, F. van Zyl. *The Last White Parliament*. Johannesburg: Jonathan Ball, 1985.

Slabbert, F. van Zyl. *The System and the Struggle*. Johannesburg: Jonathan Ball, 1989.

Slabbert, F. van Zyl and Welsh, D. *South Africa's Options*. Cape Town: David Philip, 1979.

Smit, D. 'Has There Been Any Change? On the Role of the DRC, 1974-1990', *Scriptura*, 76, 1, 2001.

Smit, F.P. *Die staatsopvattinge van Paul Kruger*. Pretoria: Van Schaik, 1951.

Smith, I. 'Capitalism and the South African War', in Thompson, A. and Omissi, D. (eds.) *The Impact of the South African War*. Forthcoming. Basingstoke: Palgrave, 2002.

Smith, I. *The Great Betrayal*. London: Blake Publishing, 1997.

Smith, I. *The Origins of the South African War, 1899-1902*. London: Longman, 1996.

Smuts, J.C. *Africa and Some World Problems*. Oxford: Clarendon Press, 1929.

Smuts, J.C. *Jan Christiaan Smuts*. Cape Town: Cassell and Co., 1952.

Smuts, J.C. *Memoirs of the Boer War*. Johannesburg: Jonathan Ball, 1994.

Southall, R. 'Buthelezi, Inkatha and the Politics of Compromise', *African Affairs*, 80, 321, 1981.

Sparks, A. *The Mind of South Africa*. London: Heinemann, 1990.

Sparrman, A. *A Voyage to the Cape of Good Hope, 1772-1776*, vol. 1. 1785 reprint: New York: Johnson, 1971.

Spence, J.E. 'The Nuclear Option', *African Affairs*, 80, 321, 1981.

Spender, H. *General Louis Botha*. London: Constable and Co., 1916.

Spies, S.B. 'The Oubreak of the First World War and the Botha Government', *South African Historical Journal*, 1, 1969.

Spoelstra, C. (ed.) *Bouwstoffen voor de geschiedenis van de Nederduitsch Gereformeerde Kerk in Zuid-Afrika*. Amsterdam: HAUM, 1906-07.

Spoelstra, B. *Ons volkslewe*. Pretoria: Van Schaik, 1924.

Stals, E.L.P. *Generaal J.B.M. Hertzog en die Afrikaner-Broederbond*. Pretoria: Hertzog Memorial Lecture, 1995.

Stals, E.L.P. 'Die geskiedenis van die Afrikaner-Broederbond, 1918-1994', unpublished manuscript, 1998.

Stapleton, T.J. *Maqoma: Xhosa Resistance to Colonial Advance*. Johannesburg: Jonathan Ball, 1994.

Starcke, A. *Survival*. Cape Town: Tafelberg, 1978.

Stavorinus, J.S. *Voyages to the East-Indies by the Late John Splinter Stavorinus*. London: Robinson, 1798.

Steenekamp, T.J. 'Discrimination and the Economic Position of the Afrikaner', *South African Journal of Economic History*, 5,1, 1990.

Steenekamp, T.J. ''n Ekonomiese ontleding van sosio-politieke groepvorming met spesiale verwysing na die Afrikaner', doctoral dissertation, University of South Africa, 1989.

Steyn, J.C. *Penvegter: Piet Cillié van Die Burger*. Cape Town: Tafelberg, 2002.

Steyn, J.C. *Trouwe Afrikaners*. Cape Town: Tafelberg, 1987.

Steyn, J.C. *Tuiste in eie taal*. Cape Town: Tafelberg, 1980.

Steyn, J.C. *Van Wyk Louw: 'n lewensverhaal*. Cape Town: Tafelberg, 1998.

Stockenstrom, E. *Vrystelling van die slawe*. Stellenbosch: KSV Boekhandel, 1934.

Stockwell, J. *In Search of Enemies: A CIA Story*. New York: W.W. Norton, 1978.

Stokes, R.G. 'The Afrikaner Industrial Entrepreneur and Afrikaner Nationalism', *Economic Development and Cultural Change*, 22, 4, 1974.

Stoler, A. *Comparative Studies in Society and History*, 1989; 1992.

Stone, J. *Colonist or Uitlander?* Oxford: Oxford University Press, 1970s.

Strachan, A. *'n Wêreld sonder grense*. Cape Town: Tafelberg, 1984.

Strydom, J.G. 'Die rasse-vraagstuk in Suid-Afrika', in Federasie van Calvinistiese Studenteverenigings (compiler), *Koers in die krisis*. Stellenbosch: Pro Eccelesia, 1941.

Stultz, N. *Afrikaner Politics in South Africa, 1934-48*. Berkeley: University of California Press, 1974.

Stultz, N. *The nationalists in Opposition, 1934-1948*. Cape Town: Human & Rousseau, 1975.

Streak, M. *The Afrikaner as Viewed by the English, 1795-1854*. Cape Town: Streak, 1974.

Sturgis, J. 'Anglicisation of the Cape of Good Hope in the Early Nineteenth Century', *Journal of Imperial and Commonwealth History*, 11, 1982.

Surridge, K. *Managing the South African War*. Woodbridge: Boydell Press, 1998.

Swanson, M.W. 'The Sanitation Syndrome: Bubonic Plague and Urban Native Policy in the Cape Colony, 1900-1909', *Journal of African History*, 18, 3, 1971.

Swart, J.S.J. 'Die kerklike begeleiding van die Afrikanervolk soos wat 'De Burger' dit in sy aanvangsjare stel', masters dissertation, University of Stellenbosch, 1990.

Swart, R. *Progressive Odyssey*. Cape Town: Human & Rousseau, 1991.

Swart, S. 'Desperate Men: The 1914 Rebellion and the Politics of Poverty', *South African Historical Journal*, 42, 2000.

Swart, S. '"You Were Men in the War Time": The Manipulation of Gender Identity in War and Peace', *Scientia Militaria*, 28, 2, 1998.

Taitz, J. *The War Memoirs of Commandant Ludwig Krause*. Cape Town: Van Riebeeck Society, 1995.

Tamarkin, M.A. *Cecil Rhodes and the Cape Afrikaners*. London: Frank Cass, 1996.

Tamarkin, M.A. *The Making of Zimbabwe*. London: Frank Cass, 1990.

Tamarkin, M.A. 'Volk and Flock: The Cape Sheep Farmers in the Late 19th Century,' forthcoming study.

Taylor, A.J.P. *Essays in English History*. Harmondsworth: Penguin, 1976.

Taylor, A.J.P. *The Troublemakers*. Harmondsworth: Penguin, 1987.

Taylor, J. ' "Our Poor": The Politicisation of the Poor White Problem', *Kleio*, 15, 1992.

Teulié, G. 'A Portrait of the Boer as an Enemy in British Juvenile Literature in the Anglo-Boer War', *South African Journal of Cultural History*, 18, 2, 2001.

Theal, G.M. (ed.) *Belangrijke historische dokumenten over Zuid-Afrika*, vol. 3. Cape Town: Van de Sandt de Villiers, 1911.

Theal, G.M. *Records of the Cape Colony*, vols. 1-36. London: Clowes, 1897-1905.

Theron, Erika. *Sonder hoed of handskoen*. Cape Town: Tafelberg, 1983.

The Truth about the Boer and his Church. Pamphlet issued by the leadership of the Cape Dutch Reformed Church, March 1900.

Thom, H.B. *Dr. D.F. Malan en koalisie*. Cape Town: Tafelberg, 1988.

Thom, H.B. *D.F. Malan*. Cape Town: Nasionale Boekhandel, 1980.

Thom, H.B. (ed.) *Journal of Van Riebeeck*. Cape Town: Van Riebeeck Society, 1954.

Thompson, G. *Travels in Southern Africa*. London: Colburn, 1827.

Thompson, L.M. 'Constitutionalism in the South African Republics', *Butterworths S.A. Law Review*, 1954.

Thompson, L.M. 'The Political Implications of the Tomlinson Report', *Race Relations Journal*, 23, 1956.

Thompson, L.M. *The Political Mythology of Apartheid*. New Haven: Yale University Press, 1985.

Thompson, L.M. *Survival in Two Worlds: Moshoeshoe of Lesotho*. Oxford: Clarendon, 1975.

Thompson, Leonard. *The Unification of South Africa*. Oxford: Clarendon Press, 1960.

Thompson, L.M. *The Unification of South Africa*. Cape Town: Oxford University Press, 1961.

Thunberg, C.P. *Travels in Europe, Africa and Asia, 1770-1779*. London: Richardson, 1793.

Ticktin, D. 'The War Issue and the Collapse of the South African Labour Party, 1914-15', *The South African Historical Journal*, 1, 1969.

Totius. *Versamelde werke*, 11 vols., Cape Town: Tafelberg, 1977.

Transactions of the Missionary Society, 2 vols., London: Bye and Law: 1804.

Transvaalse argiefstukkke, staatsekretaris. Pretoria: Government Printer, 1949.

Trapido, S. 'The Cape in the Atlantic World: Problems of Dutch Colonial Identity', *Societies of Southern Africa*, 18, 1993.

Trapido, S. '"The Friends of the Natives": Merchants, Peasants and the Political and Ideological Structure of Liberalism in the Cape, 1854-1910', in Marks, S. and Atmore, A. (eds.) *Economy and Society in Pre-industrial South Africa*. London: Longman, 1980.

Trapido, S. 'From Paternalism to Liberalism: The Cape Colony, 1820-1834', unpublished paper.

Trapido, S. 'Household Prayers, Paternalism and the Fostering of a Settler Identity', unpublished paper, 2000.

Trapido, S. 'Landlord and Tenant in a Colonial Economy: The Transvaal, 1880-1910', *Journal of Southern African Studies*, 5, 1, 1978.

Trapido, S. 'The Origins of the Cape Franchise Qualifications of 1853', *The Journal of African History*, 5, 1, 1964.

Trapido, S. 'Van Riebeeck Day and the New Jerusalem', unpublished paper, 1993.

Trollope, A. *South Africa*. 1878, reprinted Cape Town: Balkema, 1973.

Truth and Reconciliation Commission of South Africa, *Report*. Cape Town: Juta, 1998.

Van Arkel, P., Quispel G.C. and Ross, R. *De wijngaard des Heren: een onderzoek naar de wortels van de 'blanke baasskap' in Zuid-Afrika*. Leiden: Martinus Nijhoff, 1983.

Van Aswegen, H.J. 'Die verhouding tussen blank en nie-blank in die Oranje Vrystaat, 1854-1902', doctoral dissertation, University of the Orange Free State, 1968.

Van den Boogaart, E. 'Colour Prejudice and the Yardstick of Civility: The Initial Dutch Confrontation with Black Christians, 1590-1635', in Ross, R. (ed.) *Racism and Colonialism: Essays in Ideology and Social Structure*. Leiden: Martinus Nijhoff, 1982.

Van den Heever, C.M. *Generaal J.B.M. Hertzog*. Johannesburg: APB, 1943.

Van der Horst, S. 'The Economic Problems of the Homelands', in Rhoodie, N.J. (ed.) *South African Dialogue*. Johannesburg: McGraw Hill, 1972.

Van der Horst, S. *Native Labour in South Africa*. Cape Town: Oxford University Press, 1942.

Van der Merwe, C.N. *Breaking Barriers: Stereotypes and the Changing of Values in Afrikaans Writing, 1875-1990*. Amsterdam: Atlanta, 1994.

Van der Merwe, C.P. *My naam is Van der Merwe*. Johannesburg: privately published, 1952.

Van der Merwe, H.W. and Welsh, D. (eds.) *Student Perspectives in South Africa*. Cape Town: David Philip, 1972.

Van der Merwe, N.J. *Marthinus Theunis Steyn*, 2 vols. Cape Town: Nasionale Pers, 1921.

Van der Merwe, P.J. 'Die Matabeles en die Voortrekkers', *Archives Yearbook of South Africa*, 1986.

Van der Merwe, P.J. *The Migrant Farmer in the History of the Cape Colony, 1657-1842*. Athens: Ohio University Press, 1995.

Van der Merwe, P.J. *Die noordwaartse beweging van die Boere voor die Groot Trek, 1770-1842*. Den Haag: Van Stockum, 1937.

Van der Merwe, P.J. *Trek*. Cape Town: Nasionale Pers, 1945.

Van der Mescht, A.J.B. 'Bantoe-onderwys sedert die wet op Bantoe-onderwys', masters dissertation, University of Stellenbosch, 1965.

Van der Poel, J. 'The Education of the Native in South Africa', *The Bluestocking*, 1, 3, 1931.

Van der Ross, R.E. *Coloured Viewpoint*. Cape Town: University of the Western Cape, 1984.

Van der Ross, R. *The Rise and Decline of Apartheid*. Cape Town: Tafelberg, 1986.

Van der Watt, G. 'G.B.A. Gerdener: Koersaanwyser in die Nederduitse Gereformeerde Kerk se sending en ekumene', doctoral dissertation, University of the Orange Free State, 1990.

Van Deventer, A. 'Afrikaner Nationalist Politics and Anti-Communism, 1937 to 1945', doctoral dissertation, University of Stellenbosch, 1991.

Van Heerden, P. *Kerssnuitsels*. Cape Town: Tafelberg, 1962.

Van Helten, J.J. and Richardson, P. 'The Development of the South African Gold-mining Industry', *Economic History Review*, 37, 1984.

Van Heyningen, E. 'The Relations between Sir Alfred Milner and W.P. Schreiner's Ministry, 1898-1900', *Archives Yearbook of South Africa*, 1976.

Van Jaarsveld, F.A. *The Afrikaner's Interpretation of South African History*. Cape Town: Simondium, 1964.

Van Jaarsveld, F.A. *The Awakening of Afrikaner Nationalism*. Cape Town: Human and Rousseau, 1961.

Van Jaarsveld, F.A. *Lewende verlede*. Johannesburg: Afrikaanse Pers-Boekhandel, 1961.

Van Jaarsveld, F.A. 'T.F. Burgers', in De Kock, W.J. (ed.) *Suid-Afrikaanse biografiese woordeboek, vol. 1*. Cape Town: Nasionale Raad vir Sosiale Navorsing, 1968.

Van Jaarsveld, F.A. *Wie en wat is die Afrikaner?* Cape Town: Tafelberg, 1981.

Van Meurs, M. *J.C. Smuts*. Amsterdam: Suid-Afrikaanse Instituut, 1990.

Van Niekerk, L.E. *Kruger se regterhand: 'n biografie van W.J. Leyds*. Pretoria: Van Schaik, 1985.

Van Onselen, C. *Studies in the Social and Economic History of the Witwatersrand, Vol. 1: New Babylon*. Harlow: Longman, 1982.

Van Onselen, C. *Studies in the Social and Economic History of the Witwatersrand, 1886-1914, Vol. 2: New Nineveh*. London: Longman, 1982.

Van Onselen, C. *The Seed is Mine: The Life of Kas Maine – A South African Share-cropper, 1894-1985*. Cape Town: David Philip, 1996.

Van Reenen, R. *Randakker*. Cape Town: Tafelberg, 1980.

Van Rooyen, J. *Hard Right: The New White Power in South Africa*. London: I.B. Tauris, 1994.

Van Schoor, M.C.E. and Van Rooyen, J.J. *Republieke en Republikeine*. Cape Town: Nasionale Boekhandel: 1960.

Van Stekelenburg, A.V. 'Een intellektueel in de vroege Kaapkolonie: de nalatenskap van Jan Willem van Grevenbroek, 1644-1726', *Tydskrif vir Nederlands en Afrikaans*, 8, 2001.

Van Wyk, A. *Die Keeromstraatkliek*. Cape Town: Tafelberg, 1983.

Van Wyk, A.H. 'The Power to Dispose of Assets of the Universal Community of Property: A Study in South African Law with Excursions in the Laws of Brazil and the Netherlands', doctoral dissertation, University of Leiden, 1976.

Van Wyk, J.H. 'Geloof, etnisiteit en kontekstualteit', *In die Skriflig*, 35, 3, 2001.

Van Wyk, J.H. 'Homo Dei', *In die Skriflig*, 27, 1, 1993.

Van Wyk, S. 'Die huidige beroepsposisie van die Afrikaner in die stad', doctoral dissertation, University of Pretoria 1967.

Van Zyl, D. *Die retorika en die Afrikaanse historiese roman*. Stellenbosch: US Annale: 1997.

Van Zyl, M.C. *Die protesbeweging van die Transvaalse Afrikaners, 1877-1880*. Pretoria: Academica, 1979.

Vatcher, W.H. *White Laager: The Rise of Afrikaner Nationalism*. New York: Praeger, 1965.

Verhoef, G. 'Nationalism and Free Enterprise in Mining: The Case of Federale Mynbou, 1952-1965', *South African Journal of Economic History*, 10, 1, 1995.

Verslag van die Carnegie-Kommissie. Die armblanke-vraagstuk in Suid-Afrika. Stellenbosch: Pro Ecclesia, 1932.

'Verslag van die Kleurvraagstuk-kommissie van die HNP' (Sauer Commission), 1947.

'Verslag van die sosio-ekonomiese ontwikkeling van die Bantoegebiede binne die Unie van Suid-Afrika' (Tomlinson Commission), 17 vols.. University of Stellenbosch Library, Manuscripts Collection.

Verslag van die Volkskongres oor die Armblankevraagstuk gehou te Kimberley, 2-3 Oktober, 1934. Cape Town: Nasionale Pers, 1934.

Viljoen, C. Interview with author. 29 and 30 August 2002.

Viljoen, G. 'The Afrikaans Universities and Particularism', in Van der Merwe, H.W. and Welsh, D. (eds.) *The Future of the University in South Africa*. Cape Town: David Philip, 1977.

Viljoen, G. van N. *Ideaal en werklikheid*. Cape Town: Tafelberg, 1978.

Viljoen, G. van N. 'Die kwaliteit van ons oorlewing', *Aambeeld*, 6, 1, 1978.

Viljoen, G. van N. ' "Wat is 'n volk?" Die aktualiteit van Van Wyk Louw se riglyne vir die nasionalisme', in Van Rensburg, F.I.J. (ed.) *Oopgelate kring*. Pretoria: RGN, 1982.

Viljoen, J.M.H. *'n Joernalis vertel*. Cape Town: Nasionale Boekhandel, 1953.

Viljoen, S.P. 'The Industrial Achievement of South Africa', *South African Journal of Economics*, 51, 1, 1983.

Visagie, J.C. 'Die Katriviernedersetting, 1829-1839', doctoral dissertation, University of South Africa, 1978.

Visagie, J.C. *Die trek uit Oos-Rietrivier*. Stellenbosch: privately published, 1989.

Visagie, J.C. 'Verset teen die Burgermilisieplan', *Historia*, 38, 2, 1993.

Visagie, J.C. *Voortrekkerstamouers*. Pretoria: Unisa, 2000.

Visagie, J.C. 'Willem Fredrik Hertzog', *Archives Yearbook of South Africa*, 1980.

Visscher, J. *De ondergang van een wereld*. Amsterdam: A.B. Soep, 1903.

Visser, W. 'Die geskiedenis en rol van die persorgane in die politieke en ekonomiese mobilisasie van die georganiseerde Arbeidersbeweging in Suid-Afrika, 1908-1924', doctoral dissertaion, University of Stellenbosch, 2001.

Viviers, J. *Breyten: 'n verslag oor Breyten Breytenbach*. Cape Town: Tafelberg 1978.

Von Meyer, W. *Reisen in Süd-Afrika während der Jahren 1840 und 1841*. Hamburg: J. Erie, 1843.

Vorster, B.J. *Select Speeches*. Bloemfontein: University of the Orange Free State, 1977.

Vos, M.C. *Merkwaardig verhaal*. Amsterdam: Noveker, 1867.

Vosloo, T. (ed.) *Schalk Pienaar: tien jaar politieke kommentaar*. Cape Town: Tafelberg, 1975.

Wagner, R. 'Zoutpansberg: The Dynamics of a Hunting Frontier', in Marks, S. and Atmore, A. (eds.) *Economy and Society in Pre-industrial South Africa*. London: Longman, 1980.

Waldmeir, P. *Anatomy of a Miracle*. London: Viking, 1997.

Walker, A. 'Boer and Boesman: Folk and Fyand: Attitudes to Race in *Ons Klyntji* and *Cape Monthly Magazine*, 1896-1906', honours dissertation, University of Cape Town, 1991.

Walker, E.A. *W.P. Schreiner*. Oxford: Oxford University Press, 1937.

Walker, E.A. *The Great Trek*. London: Adam and Charles Black, 1938.

Walker, E.A. *A History of Southern Africa*. London: Longman, 1957.

Walshe, P. *The Rise of African Nationalism in South Africa*. Berkeley: University of California Press, 1971.

Walzer, M. *The Company of Critics: Social Criticism and Political Commitment in the Twentieth Century*. New York: Basic Books, 1988.

Warwick, P. *Black People and the South African War, 1899-1902*. Cambridge: Cambridge University Press, 1983.

Wassenaar, A. *Assault on Private Enterprise*. Cape Town: Tafelberg, 1977.

Wasserman, H. 'Postkoloniale kulturele identiteit in Afrikaanse kortverhale na 1994', doctoral diss., University of Stellenbosch, 2000.

Watson, G. 'The Westminster Model in Comparative Perspective', Budge, I. and Mackay, D. (eds.) *Developing Democracy*. London: Sage, 1994.

Watson, R.L. *The Slave Question: Liberty and Property in South Africa*. Johannesburg: Witwatersrand University Press, 1991.

Weber, P.A. '*Die Burger* – sy stryd, invloed en tradisie', Scanell, J.P. (ed.) *Keeromstraat 30*. Cape Town: Nasionale Boekhandel, 1965.

Welsh, D. 'The Democratic Party', in Reynolds, A. (ed.) *Election '94: South Africa*. Cape Town: David Philip, 1994.

Welsh, D. 'The Executive and the African Population', in Schrire, R. (ed.) *Leadership in the Apartheid State*. Cape Town: Oxford University Press, 1994.

Welsh, D. 'The Political Economy of Afrikaner Nationalism', in Leftwich, A. (ed.) *South Africa: Economic Growth and Political Change*. London: Allison and Bushby, 1974.

Welsh, D. 'Rightwing Terrorism in South Africa', *Terrorism and Political Violence*, 7, 1, 1995.

Wessels, A. *Albert Wessels: plaasseun en nyweraar*. Johannesburg: Perskor, 1987.

Wessels, E. 'A Cage without Bars', in Pretorius, F. (ed.) *Scorched Earth*. Cape Town: Human & Rousseau, 2001.

Wessels, J.S. and Viljoen, A. 'Waarde-oriëntasies en toekomsverwagtinge van die Vereniging van Staatsamptenare', HSRC report, 1992.

Wessels, L. *Die einde van 'n era*. Cape Town: Tafelberg, 1994.

Western, J. *Outcast Cape Town*. Cape Town: Human & Rousseau, 1982.

Wickens, P.L. 'The Natives Land Act of 1913', *South African Journal of Economics*, 49, 1, 1981.

Wilcocks, R.W. *Die armblanke*. Stellenbosch: Pro Ecclesia, 1932.

Wilkins, I. 'This Man Who Guides the Ordinary People', *Sunday Times*, 19 April 1981.

Wilkins, I. and Strydom, H. *The Super Afrikaners: Inside the Afrikaner Broederbond*. Johannesburg: Jonathan Ball, 1978.

Wilson, F. 'Farming', in Wilson, M. and Thompson, L. (eds.) *Oxford History of South Africa*. Oxford: Clarendon Press, 1971.

Wilson, Francis. *Labour in the South African Gold Mines*. Cambridge: Cambridge University Press, 1972.

Wilson, F. and Ramphele, M. *Uprooting Poverty: The South African Challenge*. Cape Town: David Philip, 1989.

Wilson, M. 'Co-operation and Conflict: The Eastern Cape Frontier', in Wilson, M. and Thompson, L. (eds.) *Oxford History of South Africa*. Oxford: Clarendon Press, 1969.

Winks, R. (ed.) *Slavery*. New York: New York University Press, 1972.

Witz, L. 'The Rise and Fall of the Independent Labour Party', in Bozzoli, B. (ed.) *Class, Community and Conflict: South African Perspectives*, Johannesburg: Ravan Press, 1987.

Woodward, C. Vann. *American Counterpoint: Slavery and Racism in the North-South Dialogue*. Boston: Little, Brown and Company, 1971.

Woodward, C. Vann. *Origins of the New South, 1877-1913*. Baton Rouge: Louisiana State University Press, 1951.

Woodward, C. Vann. *Tom Watson: Agrarian Rebel*. Oxford: Oxford University Press, 1961.

Worden, N. 'Adjusting to Emancipation: Freed Slaves and Farmers in the Mid-Nineteenth-Century South Western Cape', in James, W. and Simons, M. (eds.) *The Angry Divide: Social and Economic History of the Western Cape*. Cape Town: David Philip, 1989.

Worden, N. *Slavery in Dutch South Africa*. Cambridge: Cambridge University Press, 1985.

Worden, N. and Crais, C. (eds.) *Breaking the Chains: Slavery and its Legacy in the Nineteenth-Century Cape Colony*. Johannesburg: Witwatersrand University Press, 1994.

Wren, C. 'Apartheid's Children: Afrikaner Writers Today', *New York Times*, Book Review section, 11 October 1992.

Younghusband, F. *South Africa of Today*. London: Macmillan, 1890.

Yudelman, D. *The Emergence of Modern South Africa*. Westport: Greenwood Press, 1983.

Zaaiman, S.F. *Die Volksblad, 1925-1934*, unpublished manuscript, 1983.

Zietsman, P.H. *Die taal is gans die volk*. Pretoria: University of South Africa, 1992.

Index

'Real historical truth lies concealed in the thickets of contradiction, irony and para-dox. To flush it from where it skulks amidst the shadows of competing interpreta-tions of racially-based nationalisms requires truth-tellers rather than praise-singers; honest historians who tread with the greatest of care, with the sharpest of eyes, the keenest of hearing. For the genuinely curious – those who wish to see the species rather than the spectre – there can be no more experienced or honest guide than Hermann Giliomee.'   CHARLES VAN ONSELEN

'Hermann Giliomee's *The Afrikaners* is all that we have come to expect from him: authoritative, original, well written and full of insights, many of them causing one to ponder not just the might-have-beens of South African history but the difficulties of democratic transition elsewhere in the world too. At a time when much writing about South Africa is either wishful, ideological or both – and when many intellectuals have decided to keep their heads well down, Giliomee is level-headed, independent-minded and wholly unafraid to take on even the most difficult questions.'   R.W. JOHNSON

'It is seldom that a serious academic history has a resonance far beyond the inter-ests of a specialised readership, but here we have a work that has relevance on a number of levels. First, it is the most complete record of the rise, the meaning and the struggle for survival, under dramatic circumstances, of one of a small handful of new languages and language movements in modern history. Second, as the saga unfolds it illuminates and penetrates the equally dramatic texture of a complex, troubled and stirring encounter between world powers and the peoples of one of the world's most interesting emerging economies – South Africa in bondage and libera-tion. Third, for all South Africans and all those interested in the country, it exposes realities largely obscured by the moral and ideological biases of very many other analyses. Finally, for Afrikaans-speakers in all their current stress and confusion, it offers an honest basis for the re-discovery of identity and meaning in the new free-dom for all South Africans.'   LAWRENCE SCHLEMMER

'This is an astute inside account by a savvy analyst whose revisit of Afrikanerdom is also based on solid homework of revealing interviews with the relevant actors. Giliomee combines new insights with balanced judgements of the rise and decline of Afrikaner nationalism and its varied leadership.'   HERIBERT ADAM